PREFACE

The material in this book is intended as an introduction to the field of production and operations management. It is suitable for both undergraduate and graduate students.

The subject matter is somewhat technical in parts. It represents a blend of concepts from industrial engineering, cost accounting, general management, quantitative methods, and statistics. Even so, readers should find the material interesting and informative. Production and operations activities, such as forecasting, choosing a location for an office or plant, allocating resources, designing products and services, scheduling activities, and assuring quality are core activities of most business organizations. Very often, the majority of employees and assets of an organization are controlled by the production/operations function. Some of you are—or will be—employed directly in a production/operations capacity, while others will have jobs that are indirectly related to this area. So whether this is your field of study or not, this field will probably have an impact on your work.

Historically, production and operations management (POM) techniques developed in manufacturing organizations. However, as time went on, it became more and more apparent that nonmanufacturing organizations have to contend with problems similar to those encountered in manufacturing settings. Consequently, the scope of POM has been expanded to cover both manufacturing and service organizations. Moreover, many of the techniques can be directly applied to both areas without modification.

The text contains more material than one could normally hope to cover in a one-semester course. Rather than relying on the author's personal bias, each instructor can choose those topics most suited to his or her own proclivities. Those who prefer quantitative emphasis, for example, will be quite comfortable with the abundance of student problems. Those who prefer a more qualitative approach will welcome the fact that some of the more quantitative material is placed in chapter supplements. Moreover, some of the chapter problems are less quantitative than others, and the cases and readings tend to be qualitative. Obviously, there are many possibilities between these two extremes.

ACKNOWLEDGMENTS

I have gained a great deal in revising this book. I was fortunate again to have an excellent panel of reviewers and focus group who contributed significantly to the final product. The are: Layth Alwan, University of Wisconsin–Milwaukee; Robert T. Amsden, University of Dayton; Donna Bush, Middle Tennessee State University; Charles Dane, Oregon State University; Kiran Desai, Middle Tennessee State University; Edward Gillenwater, University of Mississippi; Marilyn Helms, University of Tennessee–Chattanooga; Shirley Hopkins, University of Denver; Gary Kern, Indiana University–South Bend; Michael Lanier, Murray State University; John Liu, University of Wisconsin–Milwaukee; Murat H. Mercan, Cleveland State University; Joseph Ormsby, Stephen F. Austin State University; Michael Peters, Middle Tennessee State University; Roberta Russell, Virginia Polytech Institute and State University; Bob Schlesinger, San Diego State University; Roger Schoenfeldt, Murray State University; Dwight Smith-Daniels, Arizona State University; Stan Stockton, Emeritus Professor, Indiana University.

Many students offered comments and suggestions, and many others are to be commended for suffering through revisions of problems and solutions and text material. The manuscript went through several stages of proofing and error-checking. Roger Schoenfeldt of Murray State University, Javad Varzandeh of California State University–San Bernardino, W. Rocky Newman of Miami University, and Clyde Brant of Miami University, tirelessly endeavored to ensure the accuracy of the final product and I owe them a great debt of thanks. All four did a terrific job.

Special thanks go to Byron Finch and Rich Luebbe of Miami University of Ohio who developed the *Spreadsheet Applications* text (which may be used with this as well as other POM texts) and Vahid Lotfi of University of Michigan, Flint, and Carl Pegels of SUNY/Buffalo who developed the *Decision Support Systems for Production/Operations Management* software package.

I would also like to thank all the professors who contributed their time by assisting with the supplements. Roger Schoenfeldt assisted me in preparing the Instructor's Manual and Transparency Masters, F. Dean Booth of University of Missouri–Kansas City revised the Test Bank, Lee Tangedahl of University of Montana wrote the Lotus Templates, and Paul Van Ness coauthored the Study Guide.

Finally, I extend my thanks to all the people at Irwin for all of their effort and support. It was a pleasure to be able to work with such a competent and professional group of people. Special thanks go to Dick Hercher, Jim Minatel, and Jean Lou Hess.

William J. Stevenson

PRODUCTION/OPERATIONS MANAGEMENT

Fourth Edition

WILLIAM J. STEVENSON
Rochester Institute of Technology

IRWIN

Homewood, IL 60430
Boston, MA 02116

This Book Is Dedicated to You

Cover Design: Ben Neff

© RICHARD D. IRWIN, INC., 1982, 1986, 1990, and 1993

Senior sponsoring editor: *Richard T. Hercher, Jr.*
Developmental editor: *Jim Minatel*
Marketing manager: *Robb Linsky*
Project editor: *Jean Lou Hess*
Production manager: *Bob Lange*
Designer: *Laurie Entringer*
Art coordinator: *Mark Malloy*
Compositor: *York Graphic Services, Inc.*
Typeface: *10/12 Bembo*
Printer: *Von Hoffmann Press*

Printed in the United States of America
1 2 3 4 5 6 7 8 9 0   VH   9 8 7 6 5 4 3 2

Library of Congress Cataloging-in-Publication Date

Stevenson, William J.
    Production/operations management / William J. Stevenson. — 4th
ed.
        p.   cm.
    Includes index.
    ISBN 0-256-10511-1   ISBN 0-256-11768-3   (Instructor's Edition)
    1. Production management.   I. Title.
TS155.S7824   1993
658.5—dc20   92–28905
    ISBN 0-256-10828-5   (International ed.)

NOTE TO THE STUDENT

The material in this text is part of the core knowledge in your education. Consequently, you will derive considerable benefit from your study of operations management, *regardless of your major*. Practically speaking, production and operations is a course in *management*.

This book describes principles and concepts of production and operations management. You should be aware that many of these principles and concepts are applicable to other aspects of your professional and personal life. Consequently, you should expect the benefits of your study of production and operations management to serve you in those other areas.

After reading each chapter or supplement in the text, attending related classroom lectures, and completing assigned questions and problems, you should be able to do each of the following:

1. *Identify the key features* of that material.
2. *Define and use terminology*.
3. *Solve typical problems*.
4. *Recognize applications* of the concepts and techniques covered.
5. *Discuss the assumptions and limitations* which underlie each model or technique covered.

You will encounter a number of chapter supplements. Check with your instructor to determine whether or not to study them.

This book places an emphasis on problem solving. There are many examples throughout the text illustrating solutions. In addition, at the end of most chapters and supplements you will find a group of solved problems. The examples within the chapter itself serve to illustrate concepts and techniques. Too much detail at those points would be detrimental to learning. However, later on, when you begin to solve the end-of-chapter problems, you will find the *solved problems* quite helpful. Moreover, those solved problems usually illustrate more and different details than the problems within the chapter.

I suggest the following approach for studying and problem solving:

1. Look over the chapter outline and learning objectives.
2. Read the chapter summary, and then skim the chapter.
3. Read the chapter and reread the summary.
4. Look over and try to answer the discussion and review questions.
5. Solve the problems, referring to the solved problems and chapter examples as needed.

Note that the answers to many problems are given at the end of the book. Try to solve each problem before turning to the answer. Remember—tests don't usually come with answers.

A study guide is also available. If your bookstore does not stock it, you can ask them to order it for you.

Good luck!

W. J. S.

CONTENTS IN BRIEF

CONTENTS

I

INTRODUCTION

Introduction to production/operations management involves:

1. Production/operations management   *(Chapter 1)*.
2. Productivity, competitiveness, and strategy   *(Chapter 2)*.
3. Quality management   *(Chapter 3)*.

C hapter 1 introduces you to the field of operations management. It describes the nature and scope of operations management, and how it relates to other parts of the organization. Among the important topics covered are the different types of production systems, a comparison of manufacturing and service operations, a brief history of operations management, and a list of recent trends in operations. After you have read this chapter, you will have a fair understanding of what the operations function of a business organization encompasses.

Chapter 2 discusses operations management in a broader context, and presents the issues of productivity, competition, and strategy. After you have read Chapter 2, you will understand the importance of the operations function relative to the goals of a business organization. Also described in Chapter 2 are time-based strategies, which many organizations are now adopting as they seek to become more competitive, and seek to better serve their customers.

The supplement of Chapter 2 describes *decision theory*.

Chapter 3 focuses on quality management. After you have read the chapter, you will have a good understanding of why quality is being stressed throughout the business community. Of particular interest is the description of *total quality management (TQM)*.

CHAPTER ONE

PRODUCTION AND OPERATIONS MANAGEMENT

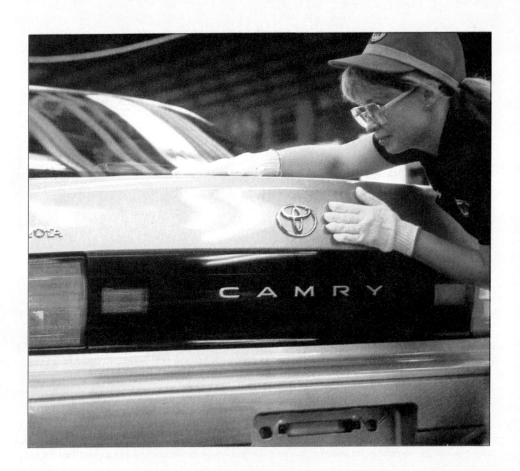

After completing this chapter, you should be able to:

1. Define the term *production/operations management* (P/OM) and give examples.
2. Identify the three major functional areas of organizations and describe how they interrelate.
3. Describe the operations function and the nature of the operations manager's job.
4. Differentiate between design and operation of production systems.
5. Provide a general description of the different types of operations.
6. Compare and contrast service and manufacturing operations.
7. Briefly describe the historical evolution of P/OM.
8. Describe the key aspects of operations management decision making.
9. Identify some of the current trends in operations management.
10. Describe the *Pareto phenomenon* and tell why it is important in problem solving.

This book is about production and operations management (POM), which involves the planning, coordinating, and executing of all activities that create goods or services. The subject matter is fascinating and very timely: productivity, quality, foreign competition, and customer service are very much in the news. These are all a part of production and operations management. This first chapter presents an introduction and overview of POM. Among the issues it addresses are: What is operations management? Why is it important? What does an operations manager do?

The goal of the book is to present a broad conceptual framework for the management of the operations function in organizations. This chapter lays the groundwork for the book. It begins with a brief description of the various functions of business organizations and their relationships to each other. Then the operations function is described in more detail, including a description of methods of classifying production systems and a comparison of manufacturing and service systems. The chapter concludes with a brief description of the historical evolution of POM and a discussion of the major issues that confront POM managers today.

INTRODUCTION

To many people, the term *production* conjures up images of factories, machines, and assembly lines. Interestingly enough, the field of production management in the past focused almost exclusively on manufacturing management. Heavy emphasis was placed on methods and techniques that dealt with operating a factory. In recent years, the scope of production management has broadened considerably. Currently, production concepts and techniques are being applied to a wide range of activities and situations *outside* of manufacturing, that is, in *services* as well as in manufacturing. Among the services are health care, food service, recreation, banking, hotel management, retail sales, education, transportation, and government. Because of this broadened scope, the field has taken on the name *production/operations management (P/OM),* or more simply, **operations management**, a term that more closely reflects the diverse nature of activities to which its concepts and techniques are applied.

Operations management
The management of systems or processes that *create goods* and/or *provide services.*

As an example of an operations management system, consider a luxury cruise ship. Most of the activities performed by the captain and crew during a cruise or in preparation for the cruise fall within the realm of operations management. Among those activities are running the ship, managing food service, providing medical services, training and supervision of the crew, overseeing activities of passengers, and housekeeping. Navigation, maintenance, and general repairs are required to keep the ship on course and in good operating condition. Food and beverages must be ordered, meals must be prepared and served in an appetizing manner, and eating areas must be kept clean. Medical supplies must be on hand and personnel sufficiently prepared to handle a wide range of illnesses and emergencies. Motivation, training, productivity, job assignments, and personal appearance of crew members are important. Passengers must be assigned to cabins, activities must be scheduled, trips ashore at ports of call must be arranged, and other needs must be attended to in order to maintain satisfactory customer relations. Of course, there are other activities involved in operating a luxury ship, but this gives you some idea of the nature and scope of operations management in that regard.

Now consider a bicycle factory. This might be primarily an *assembly* operation: buying components such as frames, tires, wheels, gears, and other items from suppliers, and then assembling bicycles. Or it might also do some of the *fabrication* work itself, forming frames, making the gears and chains, and buy mainly raw materials and a few parts and materials such as paint, nuts and bolts, and tires. Among the key management tasks in either case are scheduling production, deciding which components to make and which to buy, ordering parts and materials, making decisions on which style of bicycle to produce and how many, purchasing new equipment as old equipment wears out or becomes obsolete, maintaining equipment, motivating workers, and insuring that quality standards are met.

   Quite obviously, a cruise ship and a bicycle factory are two completely different types of operations (not many people would mistake a cruise ship for a bicycle factory). One is primarily a service operation, the other a producer of goods. Nonetheless, these two operations have much in common. They both involve scheduling of activities, motivating employees, ordering and managing supplies, selecting and maintaining equipment, satisfying quality standards, and above all, satisfying customers. And in both systems, the success of the business depends on *planning,* both short and long term.

A luxury cruise ship is primarily a service operation. Most of the activities performed by the captain and crew are operations management.

FUNCTIONS WITHIN BUSINESS ORGANIZATIONS

Organizations are formed to pursue goals that are achieved more efficiently by the concerted efforts of a group of people than by individuals working alone. Business organizations are those organizations devoted to producing goods and/or providing services. They may be for-profit or nonprofit organizations. Their goals may be similar or quite different, as may their products and services. Nonetheless, the way they operate, and the functions that exist within business organizations, have much similarity.

   There are three basic functions in a typical business organization: finance, marketing, and production/operations. These are depicted in Figure 1–1. These three functions, and other supporting functions, perform different but *related* activities necessary for the operation of the organization. The interdependency of the major functions is depicted by overlapping circles in Figure 1–2. The functions must interact to achieve the goals and objectives of the organization, and each has an important contribution to make. Often the success of an organization depends not only on how well each area performs but also on how well the areas *interface* with each other. For instance, in manufacturing, it is essential that production and marketing work together. Otherwise, marketing may promote goods that production cannot profitably produce, and production may turn out items for which there is no demand. Similarly, unless finance and production people work closely, funds for expansion or new equipment may not be available when needed.

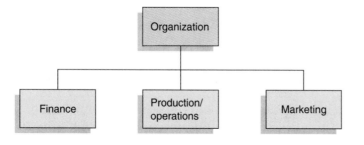

Figure 1–1

The three basic functions of business organizations

Figure 1–2

The three major functions
of business organizations
overlap

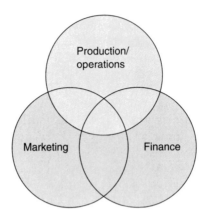

In addition to these three primary functions, there are a number of supporting functions in many organizations, such as personnel, accounting, and engineering. Obviously, the existence of these functions and the emphasis placed on each one depend on the type of business a firm is engaged in.

Let's take a closer look at these functions, beginning with the three primary ones.

OPERATIONS

The operations function consists of all activities that are *directly* related to producing goods or providing services. The production function exists not only in manufacturing and assembly operations, which are *goods-oriented*, but also in such areas as health care, transportation, food handling, and retailing, which are primarily *service-oriented*. Table 1–1 provides some examples that illustrate the diversity of operations management settings.

The operations function is the core of most business organizations; it is responsible for the creation of an organization's goods or services. Inputs are used to obtain finished goods or services using one or more *transformation processes* (e.g., storing, transporting, cutting). To insure that the desired outputs are obtained, measurements are taken at various points in the transformation process *(feedback)* and then

Table 1–1	**Type of operation**	**Examples**
Examples of types of operations	Goods producing	Farming, mining, construction, manufacturing, power generation
	Storage/transportation	Warehousing, trucking, mail service, moving, taxis, buses, hotels, airlines
	Exchange	Retailing, wholesaling, banking, renting or leasing, library loans
	Entertainment	Films, radio and television, plays, concerts, recording
	Communication	Newspapers, radio and TV newscasts, telephone, satellites

compared to previously established standards to determine if corrective action is needed *(control)*. Figure 1–3 shows the conversion process.

Table 1–2 provides some examples of inputs, transformation processes, and outputs.

The essence of the operations function is to *add value* during the transformation process: **value-added** is the term used to describe the difference between the cost

Value-added

The difference between the cost of inputs and the value or price of outputs.

Figure 1–3

The operations function involves the conversion of inputs into outputs

Inputs	Transformation	Outputs
Land	Processes	Goods
Human	Cutting, drilling,	Houses
Physical	grinding, milling	Automobiles
Intellectual	Storing	Clothing
Raw materials	Transporting	Computers
Energy	Teaching	Machines
Water	Farming	Televisions
Chemicals	Extracting	Food
Metals	Mixing	Furniture
Wood	Packing	Textbooks
Fibers	Canning	Magazines
Equipment	Consulting	Shoes
Machines	Advising	CD players
Computers	Copying, faxing	Services
Typewriters		Health care
Trucks		Entertainment
Buses		Car repair
Tools		Car wash
Facilities		Delivery
Hospitals		Gift wrapping
Factories		Legal
Offices		Banking
Retail stores		Education
Warehouses		Fire protection
Schools		Communication
Other		
Information		
Time		

Table 1–2

Examples of inputs, transformation, and outputs

of inputs and the value or price of outputs. In nonprofit organizations, the value of outputs (e.g., highway construction, police and fire protection) is their value to society; the greater the value-added, the greater the effectiveness of these operations. In for-profit organizations, the value of outputs is measured by the prices that customers are willing to pay for those goods or services. Firms use the money generated by value-added for research and development, for investment in new plants and equipment, and as profits. Consequently, the greater the value-added, the greater the amount of funds available for these purposes.

One way that businesses are currently attempting to become more productive is by critically examining the operations performed by their workers in light of whether the operations add value. Those that do not add value are considered wasteful. Eliminating or improving such operations decreases the cost of inputs or of processing, thereby increasing the value-added. For instance, a firm may discover it is producing an item much earlier than the scheduled delivery date to a customer, making it necessary to store the item in a warehouse until delivery. In effect, additional costs are incurred by storing the item without adding to the value of the item. Reducing storage time would reduce the transformation cost and, hence, increase the value-added.

Table 1–3 provides some specific illustrations of the transformation process.

FINANCE

The finance function comprises activities related to securing resources at favorable prices and allocating those resources throughout the organization. Finance and operations management personnel cooperate by exchanging information and expertise in such activities as:

1. *Budgeting.* Budgets must be periodically prepared in order to plan financial requirements. Budgets must sometimes be adjusted, and performance relative to budget must be evaluated.

Table 1–3	**Food processor**		
Illustrations of the transformation process	**Inputs**	**Processing**	**Outputs**
	Raw vegetables	Cleaning	Canned vegetables
	Metal sheets	Making cans	
	Water	Cutting	
	Energy	Cooking	
	Labor	Packing	
	Building	Labeling	
	Equipment		

	Hospital		
	Inputs	**Processing**	**Outputs**
	Doctors, nurses	Examination	Healthy patients
	Hospital	Surgery	
	Medical supplies	Monitoring	
	Equipment	Medication	
	Laboratories	Therapy	

2. *Economic analysis of investment proposals.* Evaluation of alternative investments in plant and equipment requires inputs from both operations and finance people.

3. *Provision of funds.* The necessary funding of operations and the amount and timing of funding can be important and even critical when funds are tight. Careful planning can help avoid cash-flow problems. Note that most for-profit firms obtain the majority of their funds through the revenues generated by sales of goods and services.

MARKETING

Marketing consists of selling and/or promoting the goods or services of an organization. Advertising and pricing decisions are made by marketing people. Marketing is also responsible for assessing customer wants and needs, and for communicating those to operations people (short term) and to design people (long term). That is, operations needs information about demand over the short-to-intermediate term so that it can plan accordingly (e.g., purchase materials or schedule work), while design needs information that would relate to improving current products and services and would suggest new ones. Marketing, design, and production must work closely in order to successfully implement design changes and to develop and produce new products. Marketing can supply information on consumer preferences so that design will know the kinds of products and features needed; operations can supply information about capacities and judge the *manufacturability* of designs. Operations will also have advance warning if new equipment or skills will be needed for new products or services. Finance people should be included in these exchanges in order to provide information on what funds might be available (short term) and to learn what new funds might be needed for new products or services (intermediate to long term). One important piece of information marketing needs from operations is the manufacturing or service **lead time** so that customers can be given realistic estimates of how long it will take to fill their orders.

Lead time
The time necessary to deliver an order or perform a service.

Thus, marketing, operations, and finance must interface on product and process design, forecasting, setting realistic schedules, quality and quantity decisions, and keeping each other informed on the other's strengths and weaknesses.

OTHER FUNCTIONS

There are a host of other supporting functions that interface with operations, finance, and marketing. Among them are accounting and purchasing. Depending on the nature of the organization, there may also be personnel, product design and development, industrial engineering, and maintenance (see Figure 1–4).

Accounting has responsibility for preparing the financial statements, including the income statement and balance sheet. It also supplies information to management on costs of labor, materials, and overhead, and may provide reports on such items as scrap, downtime, and inventories. It must keep track of receivables, payables, and insurance costs, and prepare tax statements for the firm.

Purchasing has responsibility for procurement of materials, supplies, and equipment. Close contact with operations is necessary to ensure correct quantities and timing of purchases. The purchasing department is often called on to evaluate vendors for quality, reliability, service, price, and ability to adjust to changing demand. Purchasing also involves shipping, receiving, and inspecting the purchased goods.

Figure 1–4

Operations interfaces with a number of supporting functions

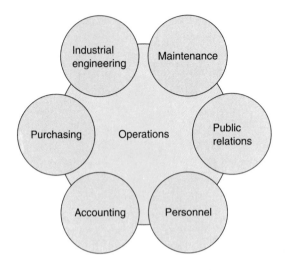

The *personnel* department is concerned with recruitment and training of personnel, labor relations, contract negotiations, wage and salary administration, assisting in manpower projections, and insuring the health and safety of employees.

Public relations has responsibility for building and maintaining a positive public image of the organization. This might involve sponsoring a little league team, donating to cultural events, giving public tours of facilities, sponsoring community affairs (e.g., marathons, bike races), and so on. Donating the use of facilities and providing public service messages and information about the organization, its employees, its products, and its services all fall under the heading of public relations. There are many potential benefits of good public relations. An obvious one is in the marketplace. Other potential benefits include being regarded as a good place to work (labor supply), improving chances of approval for zoning change requests, getting community acceptance of expansion plans, and generating a positive attitude among employees.

Industrial engineering is often concerned with scheduling, performance standards, work methods, quality control, and material handling. This function is typically found in manufacturing plants of medium and large firms.

Maintenance is responsible for general maintenance and repair of equipment, maintenance of buildings and grounds, heating and air conditioning, removing toxic wastes, parking, and perhaps security.

Many of these interfaces are elaborated on in later chapters.

The importance of production/operations management, both for organizations and for society, should be fairly obvious: The consumption of goods and services is an integral aspect of society as we know it. Production/operations management is responsible for creating those goods and services. Organizations exist primarily for the purpose of providing services or creating goods. Hence, production is the *core function* of an organization. Without this core, there would be no need for any of the other functions—the organization would have no purpose. Given the central nature of its function, it is not surprising that more than half of all employed people in this country have jobs within the production/operations area. Furthermore, the operations function controls a major portion of the assets in most organizations.

DESIGNING AND OPERATING PRODUCTION SYSTEMS

We have already noted that the operations manager is responsible for the creation of goods and services. This encompasses acquisition of resources and the conversion of their inputs into outputs using one or more transformation processes. That involves planning, coordinating, and controlling the elements that make up the process, including workers, equipment, facilities, allocation of resources, and work methods. It also includes product and/or service design, a vital, ongoing process that most organizations must do. This is an activity that operations performs in conjunction with marketing. As previously noted, marketing people can be a source of ideas concerning new products and services as well as improvements to existing ones. Operations people can also be a source of new ideas for improvements related to the production aspect of the organization. These can include ideas on new procedures for fabrication and assembly as well as improved designs, handling and storage procedures, and so on. From a practical standpoint, product and service design can be the lifeblood of a competitive organization.

A primary function of an operations manager is to guide the system by decision making. There are various ways of classifying the decisions that an operations manager must make, such as by qualitative versus quantitative aspects; according to the management process (planning, staffing, etc.); and according to whether the decisions relate to system design or system operation. Each of these approaches has its merits. The approach used in this text is the last approach: the material is arranged by topics that relate primarily to *design* and by topics that relate primarily to *operation*.

System design involves decisions that relate to system capacity, the geographic location of facilities, arrangement of departments and placement of equipment within physical structures, product and service planning, and acquisition of equipment. These are usually, but not always, decisions that require long-term commitments. **System operation** involves management of personnel, inventory planning and control, scheduling, project management, and quality assurance. In many instances, the operations manager is more involved in day-to-day operating decisions than with decisions relating to system design. In fact, much of system design lies in the province of top management. However, the operations manager has a vital stake in system design because *system design essentially determines many of the parameters of system operation*. For example, costs, space, capacities, and quality are all directly affected by design decisions. Even though the operations manager is not responsible for making all design decisions, he or she can provide a wide range of information to those decision makers, which will have a bearing on their decisions.

Brief descriptions of design and operating decisions are given in Table 1–4.

System design
Decisions concerning capacity, location, arrangement of departments, product and service planning, and acquisition and placement of equipment.

System operation
Decisions concerning personnel, inventory, scheduling, project management, and quality assurance.

MAJOR CHARACTERISTICS OF PRODUCTION SYSTEMS

There are a number of ways to classify production systems. A brief discussion of some of these ways will help you to develop a better understanding of the nature and scope of operations management. The three ways described here are degree of standardization, type of operation, and manufacturing versus service operations.

DEGREE OF STANDARDIZATION

Production systems produce output that ranges from highly standardized to highly customized. *Standardized output* means that there is a high degree of uniformity in

Table 1–4	Decision area	Basic questions	Chapter
Design and operating decisions	**Design**		
	Product and service design	How can products and services be improved?	5
	Process selection	What processes should the organization use?	5, 6
	Capacity (long range)	How much capacity will be needed? How can the organization best meet capacity requirements?	6
	Layout	What is the best arrangement for departments, equipment, work flow, and storage in terms of cost, productivity?	7
	Design of work systems	What is the best way to motivate employees? How can productivity be improved? How to measure work? How to improve work methods?	8
	Location	What is a satisfactory location for a facility (factory, store, etc.)?	9
	Operation		
	Quality control	How can quality be improved? Are processes performing adequately? What standards should be used? Are standards being met?	10
	Aggregate planning	How much capacity will be needed over the intermediate range? How can capacity needs best be met?	11
	Inventory management	How much to order? When to reorder? Which items should get the most attention?	12
	Materials requirements planning	What materials, parts, and subassemblies will be needed, and when?	13, 14
	Scheduling	How can jobs best be scheduled? Who will do which job? Which equipment to use?	15
	Project management	Which activities are the most critical to the success of a project? What are the goals of a project? What resources will be needed, and when will they be needed?	16
	Waiting lines	What capacity is appropriate?	17

goods or services. Standardized goods include radios, televisions, typewriters, newspapers, canned foods, automobile tires, pens, and pencils. Standardized services include automatic car washes, televised newscasts, taped lectures, and commercial airline service. *Customized output* means that the product or service is designed for a specific case or individual. Customized goods include eyeglasses, custom-fitted clothing, window glass (cut to order), and customized drapery. Customized services include tailoring, taxi rides, and surgery.

Systems with standardized output can generally take advantage of standardized methods, materials, and mechanization, all of which contribute to higher volumes and lower unit costs. With specialized systems, on the other hand, each job is different enough that workers must be more skilled, the work moves slower, and the work is less susceptible to mechanization.

TYPE OF OPERATION

The degree of standardization and the volume of output of a product or service influence the way production is organized. On one end of the scale is a single, large-scale product or service such as the launching of a space shuttle (service) or the construction of a skyscraper (product). On the other end is a continuous process, such as oil refining. In between these extremes are customized individual units of output, such as custom-made furniture, lamps, special-purpose machines, and auto repair; batches, such as paint and food products; and mass production, such as automobiles, typewriters, and appliances.

Let's take a closer look at these different types of operations.

A **project** is a set of activities directed toward a unique goal. Usually, projects are relatively large scale. Examples of situations in which a project approach would be used are development of a new product, installation of a computerized production line, transfer of equipment to a new facility from a current one, and construction of a hospital. Sometimes the situations are of a more personal nature, such as planning for the visit of foreign dignitaries, planning an extended vacation that involves travel, and organizing a walk-for-water or other charitable activity. A key feature of all of these projects is their limited time frame. That is, they do not continue indefinitely; they have specific starting and ending points.

Project

A set of activities directed toward a unique goal, usually large scale, with a limited time frame.

Unit or *batch* production is typically performed by a *job shop*. A **job shop** maintains the ability to render certain types of production but generally is not responsible for specific products. Instead, it performs to customer specifications; jobs tend to vary according to the needs of customers. Examples of job shops are organizations that do repair work (on appliances, televisions, stereos, automobiles), heath care, printing, and so on. Some of these are highly customized; others offer a list of services or products of a more standardized nature from which customers can select. Some systems produce standard batches (e.g., food processors).

Job shop

An organization that renders unit or lot production or service with varying specifications, according to customer needs.

A common method used to produce high volumes of standarized goods is **repetitive production**. Organizations using this type of operation generally confine output to one or a relatively small number of similar products or services and function in such a way as to accomplish production as efficiently as possible. Both the work and the output tend to be highly standardized. These production systems often lend themselves to automation or other use of specialized equipment.

Repetitive production

A production system that renders one or a few highly standardized products or services.

Continuous processing is employed when a highly uniform product or service is produced or rendered. Processing of chemicals, photographic film, newsprint, and oil products are all examples of this type of operation. Machines often provide continuous services, such as air conditioning, heating, continuous cleaning, and monitoring systems.

Continuous processing

A system that produces highly uniform products or continuous services, often performed by machines.

MANUFACTURING OPERATIONS VERSUS SERVICE OPERATIONS

Manufacturing implies production of a *tangible output,* such as an automobile, a clock radio, a golf ball, a refrigerator, or anything else that we can see or touch.

Manufacturing paper is a continuous process that is highly automated and high volume.

Service, on the other hand, generally implies an *act*. A doctor's examination, TV and auto repair, lawn care, and showing a film are examples of services. The majority of service jobs fall into these categories:

Government (federal, state, local).
Wholesale/retail (clothing, food, appliances, stationery, toys, etc.)
Financial services (banking, stock brokerages, insurance, etc.)
Health care (doctors, dentists, hospital care)
Personal services (laundry, dry cleaning, hair/beauty, lawn care, etc.)
Business services (data processing, delivery, employment agencies, etc.)
Education (schools, colleges, etc.)

Manufacturing and service are often similar in terms of *what* is done but different in terms of *how* it is done. For example, both involve design and operating decisions. Manufacturers must decide what size factory is needed, and service organizations (e.g., hospitals) must decide what size building is needed. Both must make location decisions, schedule and control operations, and allocate scarce resources.

Most of the differences between manufacturing and service organizations result because manufacturing is product-oriented and service is act-oriented. The differences involve the following:

1. Customer contact.
2. Uniformity of input.
3. Labor content of jobs.
4. Uniformity of output.
5. Measurement of productivity.

Let us consider each of these differences.

1. By its very nature, service involves a much higher degree of customer contact than manufacturing does. The performance of a service typically occurs at the point of consumption; that is, the two often occur simultaneously. For example, repairing a leaky roof must take place where the roof is, and surgery requires the presence of the surgeon and the patient. On the other hand, manufacturing allows a separation between production and consumption, so that manufacturing often occurs in an isolated environment, away from the consumer. This permits a fair degree of latitude in selecting work methods, assigning jobs, scheduling work, and exercising control over operations. Service operations, because of their contact with customers, can be much more limited in their range of options in these areas. Moreover, customers are sometimes a part of the system (e.g., self-service operations such as gas stations, shopping), so tight control is not possible. Then, too, product-oriented operations can build up inventories of finished goods (e.g., cars, refrigerators), which enables them to absorb some of the shocks caused by varying demand. However, since service operations cannot build up inventories of *time,* service capacity is much more sensitive to demand variability—banks and supermarkets alternate between lines of customers waiting for service and idle tellers or cashiers waiting for customers.

2. Service operations are subject to more variability of inputs than typical manufacturing operations are. Each patient, each lawn, and each TV presents a specific problem that often must be diagnosed before it can be remedied. In manufacturing there is often the ability to carefully control the amount of variability of inputs and thus achieve low variability in outputs. Consequently, job requirements for manufacturing are generally more uniform than for services.

3. Because of the on-site consumption of services and the high degree of variation of inputs, services require a higher labor content, whereas manufacturing can be more capital-intensive (i.e., mechanized), although there are exceptions.

4. Because high mechanization generates products with low variability, manufacturing tends to be smooth and efficient; service activities sometimes appear to be slow and awkward, and output is more variable.

Service operations, such as banks, need to be able to respond immediately to different customer needs. Managing customer contact services, such as this teller station, means matching high variability demand with higher cost labor intensive capacity.

5. Measurement of productivity is more straightforward in manufacturing due to the high degree of uniformity of most manufactured items. In service operations, variations in demand intensity and in requirements from job to job make productivity measurement considerably more difficult. For example, the work load of two doctors might be compared. One may have had a large number of routine cases while the other did not, so their productivity would appear to differ unless a very careful analysis was made.

Table 1–5 gives an overview of manufacturing and service operation differences.

Although it is convenient to think in terms of systems that are devoted exclusively to goods or services, most real systems are a blend of both. For instance, maintenance and repair of equipment are two services performed by virtually every manufacturing firm. Similarly, most so-called service organizations typically sell goods that complement their services. Thus, a lawn care firm usually sells such goods as weed killers, fertilizers, and grass seed. Hospitals dispense medical and surgical supplies along with health services. Restaurants sell food. Movie theaters sell popcorn, candy, and beverages.

Both the service sector and the manufacturing sector are important to the economy. The service sector now accounts for more than 70 percent of jobs in the United States. Moreover, the number of people working in services continues to increase, while the number of people working in manufacturing continues to decrease. Unfortunately, a good portion of the expansion in the service sector is at the lower-skill, lower-wage end, and those jobs tend to have low productivity. Manufacturing is important in that it supplies a large proportion of exports, which are beneficial for international trade. Moreover, many service jobs are *dependent* on manufacturing; that is, they support manufacturing. If the manufacturing sector continues to decline due to its inability to effectively compete with foreign companies, service jobs related to manufacturing (such as maintenance, security, and financial services) will also decline.

IMPLICATIONS FOR DESIGN AND OPERATION OF PRODUCTION SYSTEMS

These different ways of classifying production systems have important implications for designing and operating them. The degree of standardization of output, the type of operation, and whether the system involves mainly goods, mainly services, or some combination of goods and services, all have a bearing on capital requirements, choice of equipment, capacity planning, location planning, layout, inventory management, work force requirements, scheduling, and quality assurance.

Table 1–5	Characteristic	Manufacturing	Service
Differences between manufacturing and service	Output	Tangible	Intangible
	Customer contact	Low	High
	Uniformity of input	Low	High
	Labor content	Low	High
	Uniformity of output	High	Low
	Measurement of productivity	Easy	Difficult

Management of a project is quite different from management of an assembly line, and managing a job shop operation is different than managing a project or a high-volume operation. Forecasting requirements differ for the three types of systems. A high-volume operation requires a steady rate of output. It can be costly as well as difficult to vary that rate; hence, a good forecast is necessary to adequately design the system. Conversely, a job shop has a great deal more flexibility, so forecasting is less crucial at the design stage. Inventory requirements of a job shop differ from those of a system making standard products: Job shops typically make products to order. Thus, they would have little or no finished-goods inventories, but might carry raw materials and supplies for frequently used operations. In repetitive manufacturing systems, an inventory of both raw materials and finished goods generally exists; however, purchasing is standardized, as are most of the activities associated with the operations. Projects tend to be unique, and their requirements vary considerably.

In terms of actual operation, repetitive systems exhibit the highest degree of certainty, job shops the next highest, and projects the lowest. Consequently, repetitive systems involve a more routine set of activities than do job shops, which involve a more routine set of activities than do projects. The differences among the systems and their implications for operations management will be elaborated on throughout the book.

THE OPERATIONS MANAGER
AND THE MANAGEMENT PROCESS

The operations manager is the key figure in the system: he or she has the ultimate responsibility for the creation of goods or services.

As you might imagine, the kinds of jobs that operations managers oversee vary tremendously from organization to organization, largely because of the different products or services involved. Thus, managing a banking operation obviously requires a different kind of expertise than managing a steel-making operation. However, in a very important respect, the jobs are the same: They are both essentially *managerial.* The same thing can be said for the job of any operations manager, regardless of the kinds of goods or services being created. In every case, the operations manager must coordinate the use of resources through the management process, which involves planning, organizing, staffing, directing, and controlling.

Planning involves determining a future course of action. The planning process begins with deciding what is desired; then a method is designed for accomplishing that objective.

Organizing refers to administrative structure. It involves putting the pieces of a system together in such a way that desired results can be achieved. It requires decisions regarding who, what, where, when, and how.

Staffing involves selection and training of the personnel who will operate the system.

Directing refers to issuing commands or orders, making suggestions, or otherwise motivating subordinates to perform their assigned duties in a timely and efficient manner.

Controlling involves measuring the results of operations, deciding if they are acceptable, and instituting corrective action when needed.

Examples of the responsibilities of operations managers according to these classifications are given in Table 1–6.

Table 1–6	Planning	Organizing
	Capacity	Degree of centralization
Responsibilities of operations managers	Location	Subcontracting
	Products and services	Staffing
	Make or buy	Hiring/laying off
	Layout	Use of overtime
	Projects	Directing
	Scheduling	Incentive plans
	Controlling	Issuance of work orders
	Inventory control	Job assignments
	Quality control	

OPERATIONS MANAGERS AND DECISION MAKING

The chief role of an operations manager is that of planner and decision maker. In this capacity, the operations manager exerts considerable influence over the degree to which the goals and objectives of the organization are realized.

Throughout this book you will encounter a broad range of decision areas that involve operations managers, and you will be introduced to the tools necessary to handle those decisions. This section describes general approaches to decision making, including the use of models, quantitative methods, analysis of trade-offs, and the systems approach. We begin with the use of models.

THE USE OF MODELS

Model

An abstraction of reality; a simplified version of a real phenomenon.

A **model** is an abstraction of reality. That is, a model presents a simplified version of something. For example, a child's toy car is a model of a real automobile: It has many of the same visual features (shape, relative proportions, wheels), which makes it quite suitable for the purpose of the child's learning and playing. But it does not have a real engine, it cannot transport people, and it does not weigh 2,000 pounds. Similarly, an instructor commonly uses chalk markings on a blackboard to represent just about anything under the sun. Again, these are models, for although they often communicate a point effectively, they are merely bits of chalk dust arranged on the blackboard.

Other examples of models include wind tunnels, which are designed to model the effects of air turbulence on the outer surfaces of automobiles and airplanes; formulas; graphs and charts; balance sheets and income statements; and financial ratios. Common statistical models include descriptive statistics such as the mean, median, mode, range, and standard deviation, as well as random sampling, normal distribution, and regression equations.

Models are sometimes classified according to whether they are physical, schematic, or mathematical:

Physical models look like their real-life counterparts. Examples include miniature cars, trucks, airplanes, toy animals and trains, and scale-model buildings. The advantage of these models is their visual correspondence with reality.

Schematic models are more abstract than their physical counterparts: that is, they have less resemblance to the physical reality. Examples include graphs and charts, blueprints, pictures, and drawings. The advantage of these models is that they are often relatively simple to construct and to change. Moreover, they have some degree of visual correspondence.

Mathematical models are the most abstract; they do not look at all like their real-life counterparts. Examples include numbers, formulas, and symbols. These models are usually the easiest to manipulate, and are essential forms of inputs for computers and calculators.

The variety of models in use is enormous, ranging from the simple to the exotic; some are very crude, others extremely elegant. Nonetheless, they all have certain common features: They are all decision-making aids, and they are all abstractions (simplifications) of more complex real-life phenomena. Real life involves an overwhelming amount of detail, much of which is irrelevant for any particular problem. Models strip away the unimportant details so that attention can be concentrated on the relatively few important aspects of a situation, thus increasing the opportunity to understand a problem and its solution.

The goal of modeling is to make a model that adequately portrays some real-life phenomenon. Once a model has been developed, a great deal can be learned about it by manipulating its variables and observing the results. If the model is a good one, the knowledge gained will apply to its real-life counterpart.

Since models play a significant role in operations management decision making, they are heavily integrated into the material of this text. As you progress through the text, you will encounter a fair number of these models. For each model, try to learn (1) the purpose of the model, (2) how to use the model to generate results, (3) how results are interpreted and used, and (4) what assumptions and limitations apply.

The last point is particularly important because virtually every model has an associated set of requirements that indicate the conditions under which the model is valid. Failure to satisfy all of the assumptions (i.e., to use a model where it isn't meant to be used) will make the results suspect. Attempts to apply the results to a problem under such circumstances can lead to disastrous consequences. Hence, it is extremely important to be aware of the assumptions and limitations of each model.

Managers use models in a variety of ways and for a variety of reasons. Among them are the following:

1. They are generally easy to use and less expensive than dealing directly with the actual situation.
2. They require users to organize and sometimes quantify information and, in the process, often indicate areas where additional information is needed.
3. They provide a systematic approach to problem solving.
4. They increase understanding of the problem.
5. They enable managers to analyze "what if . . . ?" questions.
6. They require users to be very specific about objectives.
7. They serve as a consistent tool for evaluation.
8. They enable users to bring the power of mathematics to bear on a problem.
9. They provide a standardized format for analyzing a problem.

This impressive list of benefits notwithstanding, there are certain limitations of models that you should also be aware of. Some of the more important limitations are:

1. Quantitative information may be emphasized at the expense of qualitative information.
2. Models may be incorrectly applied, and/or results can be misinterpreted. The widespread use of computerized models adds to this risk because highly sophisticated models may be placed in the hands of users who are not sufficiently grounded in mathematics to appreciate the subtleties of a particular model; they generally cannot fully comprehend the circumstances under which the model can be successfully employed.
3. Model building can become an end in itself.

QUANTITATIVE APPROACHES

Quantitative approaches to problem solving often embody an attempt to obtain mathematically optimum solutions to managerial problems. Although quantitative techniques have traditionally been associated with production and operations management, it was not until World War II that major efforts were made to develop these techniques. In order to handle complex logistics problems associated with military activity, interdisciplinary teams were assembled (e.g., psychologists, mathematicians, economists) that combined efforts in search of workable solutions. These efforts continued and expanded after the war, and many of the resulting techniques found applications in operations management. *Linear programming* and related mathematical techniques are widely used for optimum allocation of scarce resources. *Queuing techniques,* which originated around 1920 in telephone work but remained dormant until work was greatly expanded in the 1950s and 1960s, are useful for analyzing situations in which waiting lines form. *Inventory models,* also popular after some early work, went through a long period of low interest but are now widely used to control inventories. *Project models* such as PERT (program evaluation and review technique) and CPM (critical path method) are useful for planning, coordinating, and controlling large-scale projects. *Forecasting techniques* are widely used as a basis for planning and scheduling. *Statistical models* are currently used in all areas of decision making where elements of risk are present.

In large measure, quantitative approaches to decision making in operations management (as well as in other areas of decision making) have been accepted because of the introduction of calculators and the availability of high-speed computers capable of handling the required calculations. Computers have had an enormous influence on the practice of operations management, particularly in the areas of scheduling and inventory control. Because of their capability for rapid, error-free computations and for keeping track of thousands of bits of information with instantaneous retrieval, computers have made significant inroads in handling some very difficult problem areas. Moreover, the growing availability of software packages covering virtually every quantitative technique in use has greatly enhanced management's use of the computer for problem solving. Many heretofore impractical techniques, such as multiple regression analysis and linear programming, can now be handled with ease, thanks to computer packages and the widespread availability of computers.

Computer software is used to solve complex or large quantitative problems. DSS-POM Version 2.1c by Lotfi and Pegels will be used to show computer solutions to selected examples and solved problems. The main menu is shown here.

Computers have proven invaluable in simulation studies, where analysts explore real-life problems that do not lend themselves to solution using formulas, by varying parameters in repeated computer trials and analyzing the results in order to better understand the problems and to generate alternative solutions.

Because of the emphasis on quantitative approaches in operations management decision making, it is important that you not lose sight of the fact that managers typically use a combination of qualitative and quantitative approaches, and many important decisions are based on qualitative approaches. The reason for the emphasis on quantitative methods is that quantitative analysis is typically more difficult to understand without a fair amount of explanation and demonstration problems.

ANALYSIS OF TRADE-OFFS

The decisions encountered by operations managers can be described as *trade-off* decisions. For example, in deciding on the amount of inventory to stock, the manager must take into account the trade-off between the increased level of customer service that increasing the amount stocked would yield and the increase in costs required to stock that amount. Similarly, in selecting a piece of equipment, a manager must evaluate the merits of extra features relative to the extra cost of those features. Use of overtime to increase output is another example. In that case, the manager must weigh the value of the increased output against the increased costs of overtime (e.g., lower productivity, higher labor costs, lower quality, and increased risk of accidents).

Throughout this book you will be presented with decision models that reflect these kinds of trade-offs. Managers often deal with these decisions by listing the advantages and disadvantages (the "pros and cons") of a course of action in an effort to better understand the consequences of the decisions they must make.

A SYSTEMS APPROACH

A systems viewpoint is almost always beneficial in decision making. A **system** can be defined as a set of interrelated parts that must work together. In the case of a business organization, the organization is viewed as a system composed of subsystems (e.g., marketing subsystem, operations subsystem, finance subsystem), which in turn are composed of lower subsystems. The systems approach emphasizes inter-

System

A set of interrelated parts that must work together.

relationships among subsystems, but its main theme is that *the whole is greater than the sum of its individual parts.* Hence, from a systems viewpoint, the output and objectives of the organization as a whole take precedence over those of any one subsystem and should be optimized even if this requires a less-than-optimum result in one or more subsystems. An alternative approach would be to concentrate on efficiency within subsystems and thereby achieve overall efficiency. That view tends to overlook the fact that organizations must operate in an environment of scarce resources and that subsystems are often in direct competition for those scarce resources, so that an orderly approach to the allocation of resources is called for.

One important result of quantitative techniques is that many of the techniques tend to produce solutions that are optimal in a narrow sense but may not be optimal in a broader sense (e.g., in terms of a department, plant, division, or overall organization). Consequently, managers must evaluate "optimal" solutions produced by quantitative techniques in terms of the larger framework, and perhaps modify decisions accordingly.

An interesting problem that has system connotations involves world hunger. We read in the newspapers about how people in some parts of the world are starving, while in other parts of the world there is an overabundance of food—food that is rotting and being destroyed. The solution seems simple enough: Why not send the surplus food to those who need it? Unfortunately, that "solution" does not deal with certain realities of the situation. There are key aspects of this problem that must be overcome. One is transporting the surplus food from current locations to those areas where it is needed. This is a fairly demanding task. The locations with surplus food must be identified, the food must be temporarily stored, and arrangements for shipping must be made (schedules, timing, available shipping capacity, who will pay for shipping, and so on). An even more formidable task is distributing the food once it reaches the country where it is needed. Not only must the political system of that country be dealt with, as well as possible graft and corruption, but also the transportation system of the region. Often, the region will have poor roads and very limited capacity for moving goods from ports to inland areas. Suitable landing fields are usually nonexistent in these areas. And even if all these problems could be overcome, the "solution" would only be a temporary one; the broader problem that must be addressed is how to permanently solve the hunger problem in the region. Thus, taking a broad, systems perspective enables us to achieve a truer picture of a problem and increases the chances that a meaningful resolution to the overall problem will be realized.

RECOGNITION OF PRIORITIES

In virtually every situation a manager must deal with, certain aspects are more important than others. Recognizing this fact of life will enable the manager to direct his or her efforts to where they will do the most good and to avoid wasting time and energy on insignificant aspects of the situation.

Consider an automobile. It has many parts and systems that can malfunction. Some of these are critical to the operation of the automobile: it would not function without them or would be dangerous to operate without them. Critical items include the engine and drive train, steering, brakes, tires, electrical system, and cooling system. In terms of maintaining and repairing the car, these items should receive the highest priority if the goal is to have reliable transportation.

There are other items that are of much less importance, such as scratches in the paint, minor dents, a missing piece of chrome, and worn seatcovers. In terms of transportation, these should receive attention only after other, more important items have been attended to.

Between these two extremes lies a range of items of intermediate priority. These would be given attention corresponding to their importance to the overall goal. The list might include soft tires, weak battery, wheel alignment, noisy muffler, body rust, inoperative radio, and headlights that need adjustment.

Obviously, certain parts of an automobile are more critical to its operation than others. The same concept applies to management. By recognizing this and setting priorities, a manager will be in a position to more effectively deal with problems as they arise and to prevent many problems from arising at all.

Recognition of priorities in problem solving means solving more important problems first. Also, it is a well-known axiom that a relatively few factors often account for the major share of a problem, so that dealing with those few factors will generally have a disproportionately large impact on the results achieved. This is referred to as the **Pareto phenomenon**. It basically means that all things are not equal; some things (a few) will be very important for achieving an objective or solving a problem, and other things (many) will not. The implication is that a manager should examine the situation, searching for the few factors that will contribute the most to improvement, and then concentrate on those; little or nothing will be gained by focusing efforts on other, less important factors. This is one of the most important and pervasive concepts in operations management. In fact, as you read through this book, try to find a chapter or topic area where this concept does *not* apply. You may come to the conclusion that the concept can be applied at all levels of management and to every aspect of decision making, both professional and personal.

Pareto phenomenon
All things are not equal. A few factors are very important; many factors are less important.

THE HISTORICAL EVOLUTION OF P/OM

Systems for production have existed since ancient times. The Great Wall of China, the Egyptian pyramids, the ships of the Roman and Spanish empires, and the roads and aqueducts of the Romans provide examples of our human ability to organize for production. Even so, most of these examples could be classified as "public works projects." The production of goods for sale, at least in the modern sense, and the modern factory system had their roots in the Industrial Revolution.

THE INDUSTRIAL REVOLUTION

The Industrial Revolution began in the 1770s in England, and spread to the rest of Europe and to the United States in the late eighteenth century and the early nineteenth century. Prior to that time, goods were produced in small shops by craftsmen and their apprentices. Under that system, it was common for one person to be responsible for making a product, such as a horse-drawn wagon or a piece of furniture, from start to finish. Only simple tools were available; the machines that we use today had not been invented. Products were made of parts that were custom fitted to other parts of that product. Because of this, the parts were not interchangeable: a part made for a given wagon, for example, would be slightly different than the same part made for the last wagon produced, or any other wagon, for that matter. Hence, parts could not be made ahead of time because there was no assurance that they would have the exact dimensions needed to fit future wagons. Furthermore, when products broke down in use and needed replacement parts, those parts had to be custom fitted, just as the original parts did. Production was slow and labor-intensive.

Then, a number of inventions changed the face of production forever by substituting machine power for human power. Perhaps the most significant of these was the steam engine invented by James Watt in 1764, because it provided a source of power to operate machines in factories. Hargreave's spinning jenny (1770) and Cartwright's power loom (1885) revolutionized the textile industry. Ample supplies of coal and iron ore provided materials for generating power and making machinery. The new machines, made of iron, were much stronger and more durable than the simple wooden machines they replaced.

About the same time, Adam Smith's book, *The Wealth of Nations* (1776), was published, in which he wrote of the economic benefits of the **division of labor**. This meant breaking up a production process into a series of small tasks, and then assigning different workers to do different tasks. Also known as *specialization of labor,* its benefits included narrowing the scope of work that a worker needed to learn, thereby enabling workers to learn jobs and become proficient at them more quickly; avoiding the delays of workers shifting from one activity to another (as when each worker was responsible for an entire product); and providing an environment that was more conducive to the development of specialized equipment to assist workers.

Another milestone occurred with the introduction of the concepts of **interchangeable parts**, generally attributed to Eli Whitney (1790s), an American inventor who developed a system of making rifles on an assembly line to such tolerances that any part could fit any rifle; the parts did not have to be custom made, they were *standardized*.

Factories began to spring up and grow rapidly, providing jobs for countless people who were attracted in large numbers from rural areas. Working conditions were very poor in those times, and many workers suffered injury or death.

Despite the major changes that were taking place, management theory and practice had not progressed much from early days. What was needed was an enlightened and more systematic approach to management.

SCIENTIFIC MANAGEMENT

The scientific-management era brought widespread changes to the management of factories. The movement was spearheaded by Frederick Winslow Taylor, who is often referred to as the father of scientific management. In 1878, Taylor took a job at the Midvale Steel Works, a company whose president believed in experimentation to improve factory work methods. Taylor began as a laborer, but within six years, he had worked his way up to the position of chief engineer.

Taylor believed in a "science of management" based on observation, measurement, analysis and improvement of work methods, and economic incentives. He studied work methods in great detail to identify the best method for doing each job. Taylor also believed that management should be responsible for planning, carefully selecting and training workers, finding the best way to perform each job, achieving cooperation between management and workers, and separating management activities from work activities.

Division of labor
Breaking up a production process into small tasks, so that each worker performs a small portion of the overall job.

Interchangeable parts
Parts of a product made to such precision that they do not have to be custom fitted.

Taylor's methods emphasized maximizing output. They were not always popular among workers, who sometimes thought the methods were used to unfairly increase output without a corresponding increase in compensation. And, in fact, some companies did abuse workers in their quest for efficiency. Eventually, the public outcry reached the halls of Congress, and hearings were held on the matter. Taylor himself was called to testify in 1911, the same year in which his classic book, *Scientific Management,* was published. The publicity from those hearings actually helped scientific management principles to achieve wide acceptance in industry.

A number of other pioneers also contributed heavily to this movement, including the following:

Frank Gilbreth was an industrial engineer who is often referred to as the father of motion study. He developed principles of motion economy that could be applied to incredibly small parts of a task.

Lillian Gilbreth, a psychologist and the wife of Frank Gilbreth, worked with her husband, and brought emphasis to the human factor in work. Many of her studies focused on worker fatigue. (The Gilbreths were the subject of a classic film of the 1940s, *Cheaper by the Dozen.*)

Henry Gantt recognized the value of nonmonetary rewards to motivate workers, and developed a widely used system for scheduling, called Gantt charts.

Harrington Emerson applied Taylor's ideas to organization structure, and encouraged the use of experts to improve organizational efficiency. He testified in a congressional hearing that railroads could save a million dollars a day by applying principles of scientific management.

Henry Ford, the industrialist, introduced mass production to the automobile industry. Also, with the help of Charles Sorenson, he demonstrated a *moving assembly line* by towing an automobile chassis through a plant while workers added parts.

The T was a brilliantly simple machine; when something went wrong the average owner could get out and fix it. Unimproved dirt tracks built for horses, which made up most of the nation's roads and which defeated fancier cars, posed no problem for it. Its chassis was high, and it could ride right over serious bumps. It was, wrote Keith Sward, a biographer of Ford, all bone and muscle with no fat. Soon the Ford company's biggest difficulty was keeping up with orders. Fortunately for Ford, the teachings of Frederick Winslow Taylor, the first authority on scientific industrial management, had just come into vogue. Taylor, armed always with a watch and an abiding disbelief in the enthusiasm of the average worker for his chores, had brought the new technique of time-and-motion studies to the steel industry and others. Taylor had, for example, measured how much a worker with a shovel could do on a given day; he had found the worker most efficient when instead of scooping up the maximum shovelful, thirty-eight pounds, he scooped up twenty-one pounds, since it allowed him to shovel more loads. Taylor became important because the times demanded it. As machines began to dominate men in factories, allowing one production breakthrough after another, the study of efficiency took on greater meaning. Ford, fascinated by efficiency of production, absorbed Taylor's principles and began to use them in his plant, eventually developing and applying them to an almost mythic degree.

Because the Model T was so successful—it was in such demand that dealers were sometimes commanded to stop taking orders—Ford's attention now turned to manufacturing. The factory and, even more, the process of manufacturing became his real passions. The process, he told everyone, was the fun in his world, for he could see such dramatic changes in production possibilities and accomplishments every day that working in the factory had become like working in the future. Even before the T's success he had been concerned about the production process. In 1908 he had hired an industrial efficiency expert named Walter Flanders and offered him a whopping bonus of $20,000 if he could make the plant produce ten thousand cars in twelve months. Flanders completely reorganized the factory and made the deadline by two days. He also helped convince Ford that they needed a larger space. Flanders understood that the increasing mechanization of the line meant that the days of the garage-shop car maker were over. There was a process now, a *line,* and the process was going to demand more and more money and employees. Flanders understood that every small success on the line, each increment that permitted greater speed of production and cut the cost of the car, mandated as well an inevitable increase in the size of the company. "Henceforth the history of the industry will be the history of the conflict of giants," he told a Detroit reporter.

Ford thereupon bought his Highland Park grounds. Here he intended to employ the most modern ideas about production, particularly those of Frederick Winslow Taylor. These would bring, as Taylor had prophesied, an absolute rationality to the industrial process. The idea was to break each function down into much smaller units so that each could be mechanized and speeded up and eventually flow into a straight-line production of little pieces becoming steadily larger. Continuity above all. What he wanted, and what he soon got, in the words of Keith Sward, was a mechanized process that was "like a river and its tributaries," with the subassembly tributaries merging to produce an ever more assembled car. The process began to change in the spring of 1913. The first piece on the modern assembly line was the magneto coil assembly. In the past a worker—and he had to be a skilled worker—had made a flywheel magneto from start to finish. A good employee could make thirty-five or forty a day. Now, however, there was an assembly line for magnetos. It was divided into twenty-nine different operations performed by twenty-nine different men. In the old system it took twenty minutes to make a magneto; now it took thirteen.

Ford and his men soon moved to bring the same rationality to the rest of the factory. Quickly they imposed a comparable system for the assembly of motors and transmissions. Then, in the summer of 1913, they took on the final assembly, which, as the rest of the process had speeded up, had become the great bottleneck. The workers moved as quickly as they could around a stationary metal object, the car they were putting together. If the men could remain stationary as the semifinished car moved up the line through them, less of the workers' time—Ford's time—would be wasted.

Charles Sorensen, who had become one of Ford's top production people, had a Model T chassis pulled slowly by a windlass across 250 feet of factory floor, timing the process all the while. Behind him walked six workers, picking up parts from carefully spaced piles on the floor and fitting them to the chassis. That was the birth of the assembly line, the very essence of what would become America's industrial revolution. Before, it had taken some thirteen hours to make a car; now they had cut the time of assembly in half, to five hours and fifty minutes. Not satisfied, they pushed even harder, lengthening the line and bringing in more specialized workers for the final assembly. Within weeks they could complete a car in only two hours and thirty-eight minutes. Now the breakthroughs came even more rapidly. In January 1914, Ford installed the first automatic conveyor belt. It was, he said, the first moving line ever used in an industrial plant, and it was fashioned after the overhead trolley that the Chicago meatpackers employed to move beef. Within two months of that innovation, Ford could assemble a car in an hour and a half. It was a stunning accomplishment, but it merely whetted their zeal. Everything now had to be timed, rationalized, broken down into smaller pieces, and speeded up. Just a few years before, in the days of stationary chassis assembly, the best record for putting a car together had been 728 hours of one man's work; with the new moving line it required only ninety-three minutes. Ford's top executives celebrated their victory with a dinner at Detroit's Pontchartrain

Hotel. Fittingly, they rigged a simple conveyor belt to a five-horsepower engine with a bicycle chain and used the conveyor to serve the food around the table. It typified the spirit, camaraderie, and confidence of the early days.   —*Source: David Halberstam,* The Reckoning *(New York: Morrow 1986), pp. 79–81.*

Ford not only perfected the interchangeable part, he perfected the interchangeable worker. By 1915, when the assembly lines at Highland Park were fully installed and output reached capacity, assembly workers numbered more than 7,000. Most were recent arrivals to Detroit, often coming directly from the farm. Many more were new to the United States.

A 1915 survey revealed that Highland Park workers spoke more than fifty languages and that many of them could barely speak English. . . . How could this army of strangers cooperate to produce a greater volume of a complex product (the Model T) than any company had previously imagined—and do it with consistent accuracy?

The answer lay in taking the idea of the division of labor to its ultimate extreme. The skilled fitter in Ford's craft-production plant of 1908 had gathered all the necessary parts, obtained tools from the tool room, repaired them if necessary, performed the complex fitting and assembly job for the entire vehicle, then checked over his work before sending the completed vehicle to the shipping department.

In stark contrast, the assembler on Ford's mass-production line had only one task—to put two nuts on two bolts or perhaps to attach one wheel to each car. He didn't order parts, procure his tools, repair his equipment, inspect for quality, or even understand what the workers on either side of him were doing. Rather, he kept his head down and thought about other things. The fact that he might not even speak the same language as his fellow assemblers or the foreman was irrelevant to the success of Ford's system. (The use of "he," "him," and "his" is deliberate; until World War II, workers in auto factories in the United States and Europe were exclusively male.)

Someone, of course, did have to think about how all the parts came together and just what each assembler should do. This was the task for a newly created professional, the industrial engineer. Similarly, someone had to arrange for the delivery of parts to the line, usually a production engineer who designed conveyor belts or chutes to do the job. Housecleaning workers were sent around periodically to clean up work areas, and skilled repairmen circulated to refurbish the assemblers' tools. Yet another specialist checked quality. Work that was not done properly was not discovered until the end of the assembly line, where another group of workers was called into play—the rework men, who retained many of the fitters' skills.

With this separation of labor, the assembler required only a few minutes of training. Moreover, he was relentlessly disciplined by the pace of the line, which speeded up the slow and slowed down the speedy. The foreman—formerly the head of a whole area of the factory with wide-ranging duties and responsibilities, but now reduced to a semiskilled checker—could spot immediately any slacking off or failure to perform the assigned task. As a result, the workers on the line were as replaceable as the parts on the car.   —*Source: James P. Womack, Daniel T. Jones, and Daniel Roos,* The Machine That Changed the World *(New York: Harper Pernial, 1990), pp. 30–32*

THE HUMAN RELATIONS MOVEMENT

Whereas the scientific-management movement heavily emphasized the technical aspects of work design, the human relations movement emphasized the importance of the human element in job design. The focal point of this movement was the work of Elton Mayo at the Hawthorne division of Western Electric in the 1930s. His studies revealed that worker motivation, in addition to the physical and technical aspects of work, is critical for improving productivity.

DECISION MODELS AND MANAGEMENT SCIENCE

Decision models are quantitative methods used to guide decision making. One of the first models was developed in 1915 by F. W. Harris. It was a mathematical model for inventory management. Then, in the 1930s, three coworkers at Bell Telephone Labs, H. F. Dodge, H. G. Romig, and W. Shewhart, developed statistical procedures for sampling and quality control. In 1935, L. H. C. Tippett conducted studies that provided the groundwork for statistical-sampling theory.

These quantitative models were not widely used at once in industry. However, the onset of World War II changed all that. The war generated tremendous pressures on manufacturing output, and specialists from many different disciplines combined efforts to achieve advancements in the military and in manufacturing. After the war, efforts to develop and refine quantitative tools for decision making continued, resulting in decision models for forecasting, inventory management, project management, and other areas of P/OM.

During the 1960s and 1970s, management science techniques were highly regarded; in the 1980s, they lost some favor. However, the widespread use of personal computers and user-friendly software in the workplace may cause a resurgence in the popularity of these techniques.

THE GROWTH OF TECHNOLOGY

Prior to the Industrial Revolution, production relied on physical power, primarily from humans, but also from animals such as horses and oxen. The Industrial Revolution saw a sudden shift toward machines. For the next 150 years or so, there were gradual improvements in technology. With the widespread use of automation in the 1950s and 1960s, there was another burst in technological advancement.

This was followed by rapid advancements in computer technology over the next few decades, which led to much greater use of computers and computerized

Toyota is one of several Japanese manufacturers that have led the way in developing new manufacturing and management practices. Such Japanese successes in quality and efficiency have influenced companies in the United States and worldwide.

Table 1–7

Historical summary of operations management

Approximate date	Contribution/concept	Originator
1776	Division of labor	Adam Smith
1790	Interchangeable parts	Eli Whitney
1911	Principle of scientific management	Frederick W. Taylor
1911	Motion study; use of industrial psychology	Frank and Lillian Gilbreth
1912	Chart for scheduling activities	Henry Gantt
1913	Moving assembly line	Henry Ford
1915	Mathematical model for inventory management	F. W. Harris
1930	Hawthorne studies on worker motivation	Elton Mayo
1935	Statistical procedures for sampling and quality control	H.F. Dodge, H. G. Romig, W. Shewhart, L. H. C. Tippett
1940	Operations research applications in warfare	Operations research groups
1947	Linear programming	George Dantzig
1951	Commercial digital computers	Sperry Univac
1960	Extensive development of quantitative tools	Numerous
1975	Emphasis on manufacturing strategy	W. Skinner
1980s	Emphasis on quality, flexibility, time-based competition	Japanese manufacturers

equipment in the workplace. Today, computers are used in office automation, product design, industrial-process control, robots, scheduling, and other applications. In effect, computers are an integral part of modern P/OM systems.

THE INFLUENCE OF JAPANESE MANUFACTURERS

A number of Japanese manufacturers have developed or refined management practices that have increased the productivity of their operations and the quality of their products. This has made them very competitive, and has caused other companies to become interested in these new approaches, which emphasize problem solving, worker involvement, emphasis on quality and on continual improvement, and in achieving customer satisfaction in their products. The Japanese can be credited with spawning the "quality revolution" that is occurring in industrialized countries, and with generating widespread interest in time-based management.

The influence of the Japanese on U.S. companies, both manufacturing and services, has been enormous, and promises to continue for the foreseeable future. Because of that influence, this book will provide considerable information about Japanese methods and successes.

Table 1–7 provides a chronological summary of some of the key developments in the evolution of operations management.

RECENT TRENDS

A number of trends currently command considerable attention in business, as they heavily influence planning and decision making. Many of the trends relate to competition, particularly foreign competition and the impact it has on manufacturing companies.

1. **Global competition.** In manufacturing, competition—and companies—are becoming increasingly global in nature. The restructuring of the Soviet Union, the reunification of Germany, and the European Economic Community have created a European market that represents a major market for goods, possibly exceeding that of the United States. Numerous foreign manufacturing companies have operations in Europe, or plan to. Moreover, many foreign companies have established manufacturing plants in the United States. Other markets, such as China, loom on the horizon. The result has been a marked increase in the level of competition throughout the world, and manufacturing companies have little choice but to join in or be overwhelmed by this trend.

2. **Operations strategy.** Operations strategy is being given an increasingly important role as businesses recognize that failure to include it can reduce competitive abilities.

3. **Total quality management (TQM).** Many firms are now adopting a total quality management approach to their businesses. Under this approach, the entire organization, from the president down, becomes committed to, and involved in, a never-ending quest to improve the quality of goods and services. Key features often include a team approach, finding and eliminating problems, emphasis on serving the customer, and continuously working to improve the system.

4. **Flexibility.** The ability to quickly adapt to changes in volume of demand, in the mix of products demanded, and in product design, has become a major competitive factor.

5. **Time reduction.** Many companies are focusing efforts on reducing the time needed to accomplish various tasks in order to gain a competitive edge. For instance, if two companies can provide the same product at the same price and quality, but one can deliver it four weeks earlier than the other, the quicker company will invariably get the sale. Areas for potential time reduction include processing time, equipment preparation time, information retrieval time, paperwork time, product design time, and the time needed to respond to a customer complaint.

6. **Technology.** Technological changes in products and processes can have major implications for production systems, effecting competitiveness and quality, but unless technology is carefully integrated into an existing system, it can do more harm than good, raising costs, reducing flexibility, and actually reducing productivity.

7. **Worker involvement.** More and more companies are pushing the responsibility for decision making and problem solving to lower levels in the organization.

Flexibility
The ability to adapt quickly to changes.

Recent advances in computing technology have led to shortened product design time and increased productivity and quality. Here is an example of IBM CAEDS software that is used for engineering and product design.

Increased government regulations and public awareness of the problems of environmental neglect have led to new technologies, such as this Cilcorp clean smokestack.

The reasons for this trend include recognition of the knowledge workers possess about the production process and the contributions they can make to improving the production system. A key to worker involvement is the use of *teams* of workers who solve problems and make decisions on a consensus basis.

8. **Environmental issues.** Pollution control and waste disposal are key issues managers must contend with. Regulations are increasing in number and complexity, and penalties for pollution and inadequate control of wastes can be severe. While this has placed an added burden on some industries, society on the whole should reap tremendous benefits of cleaner air and water, and less damage to the environment in general. Some of the consequences of *not* paying attention to environmental issues can be seen in the industrialized cities of former iron curtain countries and the former Soviet Union, where years of neglect have resulted in catastrophic damage to the environment that will require years and enormous amounts of money to recover from. Waste disposal regulation has led to the creation of opportunity for businesses that specialize in waste management and recycling.

SUMMARY

Operations management is that part of a business organization that is responsible for planning and coordinating the use of the organization's resources to convert inputs into outputs. The operations function is one of three primary functions of business organizations; the other two are marketing and finance.

The operations function is present in service-oriented organizations as well as in product-oriented organizations. Operations decisions involve both design decisions and operating decisions. Design decisions relate to capacity planning, product design, process design, layout of facilities, and selecting locations for facilities. Operating decisions relate to quality assurance, scheduling, inventory management, and project management.

The chapter provides a brief discussion of the historical evolution of production/operations management and a listing of recent trends in the field. Among those recent trends are global competition, increasing emphasis on quality, integrating technology into production systems, increasing worker involvement in problem solving and decision making, particularly through the use of teams, increasing emphasis on flexibility and time reduction, and increasing attention to environmental issues.

KEY TERMS

continuous processing, 13
division of labor, 24
flexibility, 30
interchangeable parts, 24
job shop, 13
lead time, 9
model, 18
operations management, 4

Pareto phenomenon, 23
project, 13
repetitive production, 13
system, 21
system design, 11
system operation, 11
value-added, 7

DISCUSSION AND REVIEW QUESTIONS

1. Briefly describe the term *production/operations management*.
2. Identify the three major functional areas of business organizations and briefly describe how they interrelate.
3. Describe the operations function and the nature of the operations manager's job.
4. Contrast system design and system operations. Give four examples of topics for each.
5. Give five important differences between manufacturing and service operations.
6. Briefly discuss each of these terms related to the historical evolution of production/operations management:
    a. The Industrial Revolution
    b. Scientific management
    c. Interchangeable parts
    d. Division of labor
7. Why are services important? Why is manufacturing important?
8. Identify some of the current trends in operations management.
9. Contrast the terms *mass production* and *job shop*. What kinds of products does each system produce?
10. Describe the *Pareto phenomenon* and tell why it is important in problem solving.
11. List the tradeoffs you would consider for each of these decisions:
    a. Driving your own car versus public transportation.
    b. Buying a computer now versus waiting for an improved model.
    c. Buying a new car versus buying a used car.
    d. Speaking up in class versus waiting to get called on by the instructor.

SELECTED BIBLIOGRAPHY

Chase, Richard, and Nicholas Aquilano. *Production and Operations Management.* 6th ed. Homewood, Ill.: Richard D. Irwin, 1992.

Hendrick, Thomas, and Franklin Moore. *Production/Operations Management.* 9th ed. Homewood, Ill.: Richard D. Irwin, 1985.

Womack, James P.; Daniel Jones; and Daniel Roos. *The Machine that Changed the World.* New York: Harper Perennial, 1991.

Wren, Daniel A. *The Evolution of Management Thought.* New York: Ronald Press, 1972.

CASE   BRUEGGER'S BAGEL BAKERY

Bruegger's Bagel Bakery headquarters is located in Albany, New York. The company has over 50 retail outlets in the northeast, some of which are located more than 200 miles from Albany.

Bruegger's produces a variety of bagels, including plain, onion, poppyseed, sesame, and cinnamon raisin, as well as assorted flavors of cream cheese. Bagels are the major source of revenue for the company.

Production of bagels is done in batches, according to flavor, with each flavor being produced on a daily basis. Production of bagels at Bruegger's is divided into three phases. The first phase occurs at the main plant in Albany, where the main ingredients of flour, water, yeast, and flavorings are combined in a special mixing machine. After the dough has been thoroughly mixed, it is transferred to another machine that shapes the dough into individual bagels. Once the bagels have been formed, they are loaded onto refrigerated trucks for shipping to individual stores. The second phase of production occurs in the trucks. The dough rises during shipping, and by the time the bagels reach a store, they are ready for the third and final phase of production. The bagels are unloaded from the trucks and temporarily stored until the final two steps of processing. These steps involve boiling the bagels in a kettle of water and malt for one minute, and then baking the bagels in an oven for approximately 15 minutes.

The process is depicted in Figure 1.

Quality is an important feature of a successful business. Customers judge the quality of bagels by their appearance (size, shape, and shine), taste, and consistency. Customers are also sensitive to the service they receive (fast, courteous, and helpful) when they make their purchases. Bruegger's devotes careful attention to quality at every stage of operation, from choosing suppliers of ingredients, careful monitoring of ingredients, and keeping equipment in good operating condition to monitoring output at each step in the process. At the stores, employees are instructed to watch for deformed bagels and to remove them when they find them. (Deformed bagels are returned to the main plant where they are sliced into bagel chips, packaged, and then returned to the stores for sale, thereby reducing the scrap rate.) Employees who work in the stores are carefully chosen and then trained so that they are competent to operate the necessary equipment in the stores and to provide the desired level of service to customers.

The company operates with minimal inventories of raw materials and inventories of partially completed bagels at the main plant and very little inventory of bagels at the stores. One reason for this is to maintain a high degree of freshness in the final product by continually supplying fresh product to the stores. A second reason is to keep costs down; minimal inventories mean less space is needed for storage. Storage space is also saved because the dough rises during shipment, which means the company does not need to have storage space at the main plant for the rising step.

Questions

1. Name two other food items, and two nonfood items, that would lend themselves to batch production.

2. Quality is very important to Bruegger's.
   a. What features of bagels do customers look at to judge their quality of bagels?
   b. At what points in the production process do workers check bagel quality?
   c. List the steps in the production process, beginning with purchasing ingredients, and ending with the sale, and state how quality can be positively affected at each step.

3. Bruegger's maintains relatively little inventory at either its main plant or its retail stores. List the benefits and the risks of this policy.

4. Bruegger's has a single bagel-making machine that is located at the main plant. Another possibility would be to have a bagel-making machine at each store. What advantages does each alternative have?

CHAPTER TWO

PRODUCTIVITY, COMPETITIVENESS, AND STRATEGY

After completing this chapter, you should be able to:

1. Define the term *productivity* and explain why it is important to organizations, and to countries.

2. List some of the reasons for poor productivity and some ways of improving it.

3. List and briefly discuss the primary ways that business organizations compete.

4. List five reasons for the poor competitiveness of some U.S. companies.

5. Define the term *strategy* and tell why strategy is important for competitiveness.

6. Contrast *strategy* and *tactics*.

7. Compare organization strategy and operations strategy, and explain why it is important to link them.

8. Describe and give examples of *time-based* strategies.

LEARNING
OBJECTIVES

☐

CHAPTER
OUTLINE

☐

This chapter discusses productivity, competitiveness, and strategy: three separate but related topics that are vitally important to business organizations. *Productivity* relates to how effective an organization is in the use of its resources; *competitiveness* relates to how effective an organization is in the marketplace compared with other organizations that offer similar products or services; and *strategy* shapes the plans that determine the direction an organization takes in pursuing its goals.

Slumping productivity gains and the impressive successes of foreign competitors in the U.S. marketplace have caused many U.S. companies not only to rethink their strategies, but to place increased emphasis on *operations strategy*.

INTRODUCTION

In this chapter you will learn what productivity is, why it is important, and some ways organizations can improve productivity. You will learn about the different ways companies compete, and why some firms do a very poor job of competing. And you will learn how effective strategies can lead to productive, competitive organizations. Of special note are time-based strategies and lean production, which are described at the end of the chapter.

PRODUCTIVITY

One of the primary responsibilities of an operations manager is to achieve *productive use* of an organization's resources. The term *productivity* is used to describe this. **Productivity** is an index that measures output (goods and services) relative to the input (labor, materials, energy, and other resources) used to produce them. It is usually expressed as the ratio of output to input:

Productivity

A measure of the effective use of resources, usually expressed as the ratio of output to input.

$$\text{Productivity} = \frac{\text{Output}}{\text{Input}} \qquad (2-1)$$

A productivity ratio can be computed for a single operation, a department, an organization, or even an entire country.

Companies often employ two types of productivity measurements: labor productivity and multifactor productivity. *Labor productivity* reflects output relative to labor hours worked, and *multifactor productivity* reflects a combination of some or all of the resources used to obtain a given output.

Examples of labor productivity include:

$$\frac{\text{Yards of carpet installed}}{\text{Labor hours}} = \text{Yards of carpet installed per labor hour}$$

$$\frac{\text{Number of offices cleaned}}{\text{Number of shifts}} = \text{Number of offices cleaned per shift}$$

$$\frac{\text{Board feet of lumber cut}}{\text{Number of weeks}} = \text{Board feet of lumber cut per week}$$

Similar examples can be listed for *machine productivity* (e.g., the number of pieces per hour turned out by a machine).

Example 1

Determine the productivity for these cases:

a.   Four workers installed 720 square yards of carpeting in eight hours.

b.   A machine produced 68 usable pieces in two hours.

Solution:

a. $\text{Productivity} = \dfrac{\text{Yards of carpet installed}}{\text{Labor hours worked}}$

$= \dfrac{720 \text{ square yards}}{4 \text{ workers} \times 8 \text{ hours/worker}}$

$= \dfrac{720}{32}$

$= 22.5 \text{ yards/hour}$

b. $\text{Productivity} = \dfrac{\text{Usable pieces}}{\text{Production time}}$

$= \dfrac{68 \text{ pieces}}{2 \text{ hours}}$

$= 34 \text{ pieces/hour}$

Calculations of multifactor productivity measure inputs and outputs using a common unit of measurement, such as cost or value. For instance, the measure might use cost of inputs and price of the output:

$$\dfrac{\text{Quantity of production at standard price}}{\text{Labor cost} + \text{Materials cost} + \text{Overhead}} \qquad (2\text{--}2)$$

Example 2

Determine the multifactor productivity for a situation in which 250 pieces have been produced at a standard price of $30 each, with a labor cost of $80, $30 of material, and overhead of $155.

Solution:

$\text{Productivity} = \dfrac{\text{Quantity at standard price}}{\text{Labor cost} + \text{Materials cost} + \text{Overhead}}$

$= \dfrac{250 \text{ pieces} \times \$30/\text{piece}}{\$80 + \$30 + \$155}$

$= \dfrac{\$7,500}{\$265}$

$= 28.30$

Productivity measures are useful on a number of levels. For an individual department or organization, productivity measures can be used to track performance *over time*. This allows managers to judge performance, and to decide where improvements are needed.

Productivity measures can also be used to judge the performance of an entire industry, or the (national) productivity of a country as a whole. These productivity measures are *aggregate* measures determined by combining productivity measures of various companies or industries.

In essence, productivity measurements serve as scorecards of the effective use of resources. Business leaders are concerned with productivity as it relates to *competitiveness:* If two firms both have the same level of output, but one, because of higher productivity, requires less input, that one will be able to charge a lower price, and consequently increase its share of the market. Or that firm might elect to charge the same price, thereby reaping a greater profit. Government leaders are concerned with national productivity because there is a close relationship between productivity and a nation's *standard of living.* High levels of productivity are largely responsible for the relatively high standards of living enjoyed by people in industrial nations. Furthermore, wage and price increases that are not accompanied by productivity increases tend to create inflationary pressures on a nation's economy.

Productivity growth in the U.S. in recent years has lagged behind that of other leading industrial countries, most notably Japan, Korea, the U.K., and West Germany. This has been a cause of concern for government officials and business leaders. Although U.S. productivity is still among the highest in the world, it is losing ground to other nations. Moreover, a significant portion of U.S. productivity can be attributed to high *agricultural* productivity; *manufacturing* productivity tends to be lower.

Consider the following: In the 1960s, annual productivity growth in the United States averaged about 2.5 percent; in the 1970s, it averaged only 1.3 percent; and in the 1980s, it averaged less than 1 percent a year. In fact, productivity growth was *negative* in both 1989 and 1990 (i.e., productivity decreased), and in 1991, productivity growth was a meager 0.2 percent. (See Figure 2–1.)

The obvious question is: How are certain nations, industries, or companies able to achieve productivity gains while others are not? Actually, there are many reasons cited by theorists and researchers. Among the most prominent are:

1. A lower propensity to save and a higher propensity to consume in a country, which slows capital formation and attracts foreign goods.

2. Increasing government regulations add to the administrative (and nonproductive) burden of many companies.

Figure 2–1

U.S. productivity growth rates in recent decades

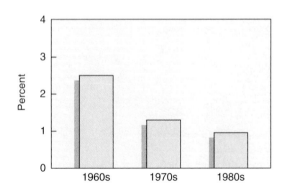

3. In the United States, there is an increasing demand for services, but services are generally less productive than manufacturing operations.

4. An emphasis on *short-run* performance (e.g., annual profits and sales) reduces the incentive to develop long-term solutions to problems. In addition, in periods of inflation and increased costs of borrowed money, managers are, perhaps understandably, hesitant to commit funds for long periods of time because it reduces their flexibility to take advantage of other opportunities that might arise in the meantime.

Many authorities place much of the responsibility for lagging productivity gains in the United States on management. They point out that foreign competitors have had to deal with similar (or worse) conditions than their U.S. counterparts and yet have come out ahead on productivity improvements. It should be noted that some argue that most foreign competitors started out with productivity so low that the improvements merely reflect catching up to U.S. manufacturers. To a certain extent, that is true. Moreover, foreign competitors were able to learn much about quality and productivity improvements by studying Western methods. However, many of those companies have achieved productivity levels that equal or surpass those of their U.S. counterparts. It seems that they are using the lessons learned to go beyond their teachers. Some cite the inability of U.S. managers to successfully integrate technological improvements into the production process; a common complaint is that U.S. managers seem to be "throwing technology at the problem" rather than wisely analyzing their processes to see if and how technology can be used to gain competitive advantage.

Another point at issue is the difficulty of accurately *measuring* productivity. For example, it can be difficult to measure white-collar productivity, particularly if jobs involve thinking or creative efforts. Also, if job content is variable, as it often is in services, this can distort productivity measurements. For example, suppose a restaurant employs four waitresses, who serve 80 meals on Wednesday and 90 meals on Thursday during the same two-hour interval. It would appear the waitresses were more productive on Thursday; but perhaps the lower output on Wednesday reflected the fact that fewer people came into the restaurant. Or consider the case of two emergency room doctors, one of whom attended to six patients with minor injuries while the other spent an equal amount of time with one seriously injured patient. To say that the one who attended six patients had the higher productivity distorts the reality of the situation. Quality differences may also distort productivity measurements. One way this can happen is when comparisons are made over time, such as comparing the productivity of a factory in the 1990s with one in the 1960s. Few would disagree that quality is now much higher than it was then, but there is no simple way to incorporate quality into productivity measurements.

All in all, productivity measurements must be viewed with an awareness of related factors, and of a certain amount of distortion in the figures. Consequently, it is best to treat productivities as approximate indicators rather than precise measurements.

FACTORS THAT AFFECT PRODUCTIVITY

Numerous factors affect productivity. Among them are methods, capital, quality, technology, and management.

Consider a student who plans to type a lengthy term paper. The student is an average typist and can turn out about three pages per hour. How could the student increase productivity (i.e., turn out more pages per hour)? One way would be to enroll in a short course offered by the college to improve typing skills (method). Another way might be to replace a typewriter with a more expensive computer and word-processing package (capital) to gain the speed of automatic features such as spell checking and error correction (quality). Still other productivity improvements might be achieved through improving organization and preparation for the actual typing (management). The incentive of receiving a good grade and the pride of doing a good job might also be important. The point is that all of these factors are potential sources of productivity, not only for typing papers but for any kind of work, and it is generally up to the manager to see that they are fully exploited.

A commonly held misconception is that workers are the main determinant of productivity. According to that theory, the route to productivity gains involves getting employees to work harder. However, the fact is that many productivity gains in the past have come from *technological* improvements. Familiar examples include:

Paint rollers

Power lawn mowers

Electronic typewriters

Copying machines

Microwave ovens

Automatic washers, dryers, dishwashers, electric blenders

Long-distance direct dialing, pay-
  by-phone, cellular phones

Computerized billing and inventories

Automation

Calculators

Computers, personal computers

However, as noted in the previous section, technology alone won't give productivity gains; it must be used wisely and thoughtfully. In fact, without careful planning, technology can actually *reduce* productivity, especially if it leads to inflexibility, high costs, or mismatched operations.

IMPROVING PRODUCTIVITY

There are a number of key steps that a company or a department can take toward improving productivity:

1. Develop productivity measures for all operations; measurement is the first step in managing and controlling an operation.
2. Look at the system as a whole in deciding which operations to concentrate on; it is overall productivity that is important. This concept is illustrated in Figure 2–2, which shows several operations feeding their output into a *bottleneck* operation. The capacity of the bottleneck operation is less than the combined capacities of the operations that provide input, so units queue up waiting to be processed; hence the term bottleneck. Productivity improvements to any *non*bottleneck operation will not affect the productivity of the system. Improvements in the bottleneck operation *will* lead to increased productivity, up to the point where the output rate of the bottleneck equals the output rate of the operations feeding it.
3. Develop methods for achieving productivity improvements, such as soliciting ideas from workers (perhaps organizing teams of workers, engineers, and managers to work on this), studying how other firms have increased productivity, and reexamining the way work is done.

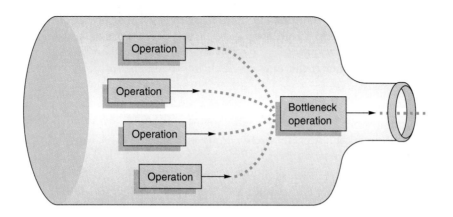

Figure 2–2

Bottleneck operation

4. Establish reasonable goals for improvement.

5. Make it clear that management supports and encourages productivity improvement. Consider incentives to reward workers for contributions.

6. Measure improvements, and publicize them.

7. Don't confuse productivity with *efficiency;* efficiency is a narrower concept that pertains to getting the most out of a given set of resources, whereas productivity is a broader concept that pertains to effective use of overall resources. For example, an efficiency perspective on mowing a lawn given a hand mower would focus on the best way to use the hand mower; a productivity perspective would include the possibility of using a power mower.

COMPETITIVENESS

Companies must be **competitive** to sell their goods and services in the marketplace. Competitiveness is an important factor in determining whether a company prospers, barely gets by, or fails. Business organizations compete with one another in a variety of ways. Key among them are price, quality, product or service differentiation, flexibility, and time to perform certain activities.

Competitiveness

How effective an organization is in the marketplace compared with others that offer similar goods or services.

1. **Price** is the amount a customer must pay for the product or service. If all other factors are equal, consumers will choose the product or service that has the lower price. Organizations that compete on price may settle for lower profit margins, but most focus on lowering production costs.

2. **Quality** refers to materials and workmanship as well as design. Generally, it relates to the buyer's perceptions of how well the product or service will serve its purpose.

3. **Product differentiation** refers to any special features (design, cost, quality, ease of use, convenient location, warranty, etc.) that cause a product or service to be perceived by the buyer as more suitable than a competitor's product or service.

4. **Flexibility** is the ability to respond to changes. The better a company or department is able to respond to changes, the greater its competitive advantage over another company that is not as able to respond. The changes might relate to increases or decreases in volume demanded, or to changes in product mix.

Japanese companies, including SONY, established themselves as the leading producers of consumer electronics, replacing U.S. companies in global markets.

5. **Time** refers to a number of different aspects of an organization's operations. One is how quickly a product or service is delivered to a customer. Another is how quickly new products or services are developed and brought to the market. And another is the rate at which improvements in products or processes are made.

In the past, U.S. firms were among the most competitive in the entire world. Some still are today. But in the years since the 1950s, many U.S. firms have lost their roles as market leaders to foreign competitors, often the Japanese, but others as well. Products such as cameras, televisions, VCRs, tape decks, and automobiles were once the domain of U.S. companies—but no more. Consider that in 1960, Japan accounted for only about one percent of the free world's output of automobiles, while the United States accounted for over 50 percent. Over the next twenty years, Japan's share grew to about 24 percent while the U.S. share fell to 22 percent by 1980. Then during the 1980s, both shares slipped a few percentage points as other foreign producers gained a share of the market. The Japanese continued to make inroads into the U.S. market, establishing automobile plants in the United States.

How did this happen? Basically, many U.S. companies lost their competitive edge: they were less competitive than their rivals. Some key reasons for this failure were detailed in a recent study conducted by MIT, which is our next subject.

READING   THE CAUSES OF POOR U.S. COMPETITIVENESS AND ITS POTENTIAL CURES[1]

According to the report of the MIT Commission, there are five basic causes of poor U.S. global competitiveness.

The first is decision making based on short-term horizons. Overemphasis on short-term financial results has led to underinvestment in research and development (R&D) and to favoring opportunities that promised short-term profits over those with perhaps much greater long-term potential.

The second is certain strategic weaknesses that failed to recognize the threats posed by foreign competitors, neglected the manufacturing function relative to other functional areas of companies, and underinvested in physical and human capital.

The third is a lack of cooperation among departments within firms that led to too little communication among marketing, product design, process design, engineering, and manufacturing. Consequently, firms have ended up with products unsuitable to customer needs or wants, products that needed redesigning, products unsuitable to the manufacturing capa-

bilities of an organization, and products lacking sufficient quality to be competitive in the marketplace.

Fourth is the tendency to view labor as a cost factor to be minimized instead of a valuable resource, underestimating the importance of training, motivation, and adaptability.

Fifth, weaknesses in technological practice, often characterized by emphasizing *product* development at the expense of *process* development, have led to a failure to bring new products rapidly to the market, and subsequently, to a loss of market position.

According to the Commission, the cures to poor competitiveness follow directly from the causes:

1. Put less emphasis on short-term financial results and invest more in R&D.

2. Include responses to foreign competition in strategies, pay more attention to the operations function, and invest more in humans and equipment.

3. Remove communication barriers within organizations; encourage different functions to cooperate. Recognize the value of communication with other organizations.

[1] Lester Thurow, et al., "Interim Results of the MIT Commission on Industrial Productivity," AAAS Annual Meeting, Boston, February 15, 1988.

4. Recognize that labor can be a valuable asset, and act accordingly to develop that asset.

5. Place greater emphasis on process design and less on product design. Emphasize quality at the design stage.

STRATEGY

An organization's *strategy* has a long-term impact on the nature and characteristics of the organization. In large measure, strategies affect the ability of an organization to compete, or, in the case of a nonprofit organization, the ability to serve its intended purpose.

In this section, you will learn about both organization strategies and operations strategies, and how they influence an organization. The nature of an organization's strategies depends on its mission.

MISSION

An organization's **mission** is the basis of the organization—the reason for its existence. Missions vary from organization to organization, depending on the nature of their business. A hospital's mission would be to provide health care; a construction firm's mission might be to construct new, single-family homes; and an insurance firm's mission might be to provide life insurance only, or perhaps a full range of insurance (home, auto, life, accident). Part of the mission of nonprofit organizations is to provide services to clients, while in for-profit organizations, part of the mission is to provide profits for owners (stockholders, partners).

It is important that an organization have a clear and simple **mission statement**, one which answers the question "What business are we in?" The mission statement should serve to guide formulation of strategies for the organization as well as decision making at all levels. Not all organizations have mission statements; perhaps there is a lack of awareness of how important such a statement is, or perhaps its leaders are unclear themselves about what the mission should be. But without a clear mission, it is unlikely that an organization will achieve its true potential, as there is little direction for formulating strategies.

Mission
The reason for existence of an organization.

Mission statement
A clear statement of purpose that serves as a guide for strategy and decision making.

European companies such as Saab have also remained competitive as producers of high quality products for narrower markets. Euro 92 and ISO 9000 are expected to provide the impetus to reelevate the global competitiveness of European manufacturers. At this Saab Scania chassis factory in Södertälji, a work group assembles an entire truck. This new approach is also used for assembling special trucks in limited production runs.

STRATEGIES AND TACTICS

A mission statement provides a general direction for an organization and gives rise to organizational *goals,* which provide substance to the overall mission. For example, one goal of an organization may be to capture a certain percent of market share for a product; another goal may be to achieve a certain level of profitability. Taken together, the goals and the mission establish a destination for the organization.

Strategies are plans for achieving goals. If you think of goals as destinations, then strategies are the road maps for reaching the destinations. Strategies provide *focus* for decision making. Generally speaking, organizations have overall strategies called *organization strategies,* which relate to the entire organization, and they also have *functional strategies,* which relate to each of the functional areas of the organization. The functional strategies should support the overall strategies of the organization, just as the organizational strategies should support the goals and mission of the organization.

Tactics are the methods and actions that are intended to accomplish strategies. They are more specific in nature than strategies, and they provide guidance and direction for carrying out actual *operations,* which need the most specific and detailed plans and decision making in an organization. You might think of tactics as the "how to" part of the process (e.g., how to reach the destination, following the strategy roadmap) and operations as the actual "doing" part of the process.

It should be apparent that the overall relationship that exists from the mission down to actual operations is *hierarchical* in nature. This is illustrated in Figure 2–3.

A simple example may help to put this hierarchy into perspective.

Strategy

A plan for achieving organizational goals.

Tactics

The methods and actions taken to accomplish strategies.

Figure 2–3

Planning and decision making is hierarchical in organizations

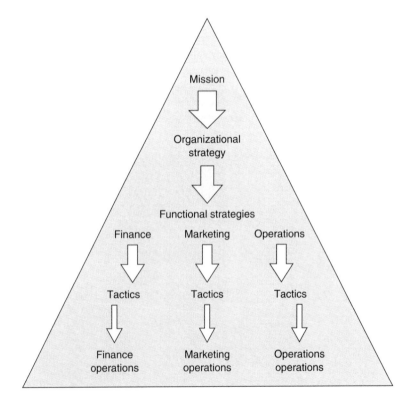

Rita is a high school student in Southern California. She would like to have a career in business, have a good job, and earn enough income to live comfortably.

A possible scenario for achieving her goals might look something like this:

Mission: Live a good life

Goal: Successful career; good income

Strategy: Obtain a college education

Tactics: Select a college and a major; decide how to finance college

Operations: Register, buy books, take courses, study

Example 3

OPERATIONS STRATEGY

The organization strategy provides the overall direction for the organization. It is broad in scope, covering the entire organization. **Operations strategy** is narrower in scope, dealing primarily with the operations aspect of the organization. Operations strategy relates to products, processes, methods, operating resources, quality, costs, lead times, and scheduling. Table 2–1 provides a comparison of an organization's mission, its overall strategy, and its operations strategy, tactics, and operations.

In order for operations strategy to be truly effective, it is important to link it with the organization strategy. That is, the two should not be formulated independently. Rather, formulation of organization strategy should take into account the realities of operations' strengths and weaknesses, capitalizing on strengths and deal-

Operations strategy

The approach, consistent with the organization strategy, that is used to guide the operations function.

Table 2–1

Comparison of mission, organization strategy, and operations strategy

	Management level	Time horizon	Scope	Level of detail	Relates to
The Overall organization					
Mission	Top	Long	Broad	Low	Survival, profitability
Strategy	Senior	Long	Broad	Low	Growth rate, market share
Production/ Operations					
Strategic	Senior	Moderate to long	Broad	Low	Product selection, choice of location, choice of technology, new facilities
Tactical	Middle	Moderate	Moderate	Moderate	Employment levels, output levels, equipment selection, facility layout
Operational	Low	Short	Narrow	High	Scheduling personnel, adjusting output rates, inventory management, purchasing

ing with weaknesses. Similarly, operations strategy must be consistent with the overall strategy of the organization, and must be formulated to support the goals of the organization. This requires that senior managers work with the functional areas to formulate strategies that will support, rather than conflict with, each other and the overall strategy of the organization. As simple and as obvious as this may seem, it doesn't always happen in practice. Instead, we may find power struggles between various functional units. Such struggles are detrimental to the organization because they pit functional units against each other, rather than focusing energy on becoming more competitive and better serving the customer. Some of the latest approaches in organizations, involving teams of managers and workers, may reflect a growing awareness of the synergistic effects of working together rather than competing internally.

Operations strategy can have a major influence on the competitiveness of an organization. If it is well designed and well executed, there is a good chance that the organization will be successful; if it is not well designed or executed, the chances are much less that the organization will be successful.

In the 1970s and early 1980s, operations strategy was often neglected in favor of marketing and financial strategies. That may have been due to the fact that many chief executive officers (CEOs) had backgrounds in areas other than operations, so perhaps did not fully appreciate the importance of the operations function. Mergers and acquisitions were common; leveraged buyouts were used, and conglomerates were formed that joined dissimilar operations. These did little to add value; they were purely financial in nature. Decisions were made by individuals who were unfamiliar with a particular business, often to the detriment of that business. Meanwhile, foreign competitors began to fill the vacuum that resulted with a careful focus on operations strategy.

In the late 1980s and early 1990s, many companies began to realize this approach was not working. They recognized that they were less competitive than other companies. This caused them to focus attention on operations strategy. (Recall the cures for lack of competitiveness suggested a few pages earlier by the MIT study.) Toward that end, many firms are developing strategies that have *quality* or *time* as their central concern.

STRATEGY FORMULATION

In order to formulate an effective strategy, senior management must take into account the *distinctive competencies* of the organizations, and they must *scan the environment*.

Distinctive competencies are those special attributes or abilities possessed by an organization that give it a *competitive edge*. In effect, distinctive competencies relate to the ways that organizations compete. As noted previously, these can include price (based on some combination of low costs of resources such as labor and materials, low operating costs, and low production costs); quality (high performance or consistent quality); time (rapid delivery or on-time delivery); flexibility (variety or volume); customer service; and location. Table 2–2 lists the major distinctive competencies and examples of services and companies that exhibit those competencies.

The most effective organizations seem to use an approach that develops distinctive competencies based on customer needs as well as on what the competition is doing. Marketing and operations work closely to match customer needs with oper-

Distinctive competencies
The special attributes or abilities that give an organization a competitive edge.

Table 2–2

Examples of distinctive competencies

Competency	Examples of companies or services	Competency	Examples of companies or services
Price		**Flexibility**	
Low cost	U.S. Mail first-class postage Motel-6, Red Roof Inns Mail-order computers	Variety	Burger King ("Have it your way") Job shop Hospital emergency room
Quality			
High-performance design and/or high quality	Sony TV Lexus, Cadillac Disneyland Five-star restaurants or hotels	Volume	MacDonald's ("Buses welcome") Toyota Supermarkets (additional checkouts)
Consistent quality	MacDonald's restaurants Kodak, Xerox, Motorola Electrical power	**Service**	
		Superior customer service	Disneyland Hewlett-Packard IBM
Time			
Rapid delivery	MacDonald's restaurants Express Mail UPS Domino's Pizza	**Location**	
		Convenience	Supermarkets, dry cleaners Mall stores Service stations Banks, ATMs
On-time delivery	One-hour photo Domino's Pizza Federal Express Express Mail		

Cadillac has long represented high quality in U.S. auto making. Recognizing recent challenges by Japanese competitors, Cadillac has redoubled efforts and was recognized for success in receiving the 1990 Baldridge Award.

By offering on-time overnight delivery, Federal Express set U.S. time standards in delivering urgent packages. They are now in the process of competing globally as well.

Automatic teller machines (ATMs) are numerous, conveniently located, and available 24 hours. Networks are expanding to serve international customers.

ations capabilities. Competitor competencies are important for several reasons. For example, if a competitor is able to supply high-quality products, it may be necessary to meet that high quality as a baseline. However, by itself, merely *matching* a competitor is usually not sufficient to gain market share. It may be necessary to exceed that dimension (e.g., exceed the quality level of the competitor), or else gain an edge by excelling in one or more other dimensions, such as rapid delivery, or service after the sale.

Environmental scanning is the considering of events and trends that present either threats or opportunities for the organization. Generally these include competitors' activities; changing consumer needs; legal, economic, political, and environmental issues; the potential for new markets; and the like. Depending on the nature of an organization and the locations of its customers, these issues may be global, national, regional, or local. Thus, the disintegration of the former Soviet Union in 1991–92, the reunification of Germany, and the formation of the European Economic Community would have major input into the strategic planning of such global companies as the Ford Motor Company, GM, Toyota, Kodak, Coca-Cola, PepsiCo, and IBM, but would have little direct impact on local businesses such as supermarkets or landscaping firms. Note, however, that companies that are *local suppliers* for global companies may be affected even though they, themselves, are not global.

Another key factor to consider when developing strategies is technological change, as this can present real opportunities and threats to an organization. Technological changes occur in products (high-definition TV, improved computer chips, improved cellular telephone systems, and improved designs for earthquake-proof structures); in services (faster order processing, faster delivery); and in processes (robotics, automation, computer-assisted processing, point-of-sale scanners, and flexible manufacturing systems). The obvious benefit is a competitive edge; the risk is that incorrect choices, poor execution, and higher-than-expected operating costs will create competitive *disadvantages*.

All of these factors can be thought of as *external factors*. The key external factors can be summarized as the following:

1. *Economic conditions*. These include the general health and direction of the economy, inflation and deflation, interest rates, tax laws, and tariffs.
2. *Political conditions*. These include favorable or unfavorable attitudes toward business, political stability or instability, and wars.
3. *Legal environment*. This includes antitrust laws, government regulations, trade restrictions, minimum wage laws, product liability laws and recent court experience, labor laws, and patents.
4. *Technology*. This can include the rate at which product innovations are occurring, current and future process technology (equipment, materials handling), and design technology.
5. *Competition*. This includes the number and strength of competitors, the basis of competition (price, quality, special features), and the ease of market entry.
6. *Markets*. This includes size, location, brand loyalties, ease of entry, potential for growth, long-term stability, and demographics.

The organization must also take into account various *internal factors* that relate to possible strengths or weaknesses. Among the key internal factors are the following:

Environmental scanning

The considering of events and trends that present threats or opportunities for a company.

1. *Human resources.* This includes the skills and abilities of managers, workers, and staff personnel; special talents (creativity, designing, problem solving); loyalty to the organization; expertise; dedication; and experience.

2. *Facilities and equipment.* Capacities, location, age, and cost to maintain or replace can have significant impact on operations.

3. *Financial resources.* Cash flow, access to additional funding, existing debt burden, and cost of capital are important considerations.

4. *Customers.* Loyalty, existing relationships, and understanding of wants and needs are important.

5. *Products and services.* This includes existing products and services as well as the potential for new products and services.

6. *Technology.* This includes existing technology, the ability to integrate new technology, and the probable impact of technology on current and future operations.

7. *Suppliers.* Supplier relationships, dependability of suppliers, quality, flexibility, and service are typical considerations.

8. *Other.* Other factors include patents, labor relations, company or product image, distribution channels, relationships with distributors, maintenance of facilities and equipment, access to resources, and access to markets.

NEW STRATEGIES

Traditional strategies of business organizations have tended to emphasise cost minimization or product differentiation. While not abandoning those strategies, many organizations are adopting new strategies that are based on *quality* and/or *time*.

Quality-based strategies focus on satisfying the customer by integrating quality into all phases of the organization. This includes not only the final product or service that is provided to the customer, but also the *processes* related to that (such as design, production, or service after the sale).

Time-based strategies focus on reducing the time required to accomplish various activities (such as the time taken to develop new products or services and to market them, the time needed to respond to a change in customer demand, or the time needed to deliver a product or perform a service). By doing so, organizations seek to improve service to the customer, and to gain a competitive advantage over rivals who take more time to accomplish the same tasks.

These new approaches are rapidly gaining favor throughout the business world. They are exciting and challenging, for they promise to significantly change the way business organizations operate. Time-based strategies are described in the following section, and quality-based strategies are described in the next chapter.

Quality-based strategy
Strategy that focuses on quality in all phases of an organization.

Time-based strategy
Strategy that focuses on reduction of time needed to accomplish tasks.

TIME-BASED STRATEGIES

Time-based approaches focus on reducing the time needed to conduct the various activities in a process. The rationale is that by reducing time, costs are generally less, productivity is higher, quality tends to be higher, product innovations appear on the market earlier, and customer service is improved.

Some of the areas in which organizations have achieved time reduction are:

Planning time: The time needed to react to a competitive threat, to develop strategies and select tactics, to approve proposed changes to facilities, to adopt new technologies, and so on.

Product/service design time: The time needed to develop and market new or re-designed products or services.

Processing time: The time needed to produce goods or provide services. This can involve scheduling, repairing equipment, wasted efforts, inventories, quality, training, and the like.

Changeover time: The time needed to change from producing one type of product or service to another one. May involve new equipment settings and at-tachments, different methods, equipment, schedules, or materials.

Delivery time: The time needed to fill orders.

Response time for complaints: These might be complaints from customers regard-ing quality, timing of deliveries, incorrect shipments, and so on. These might also be complaints from employees regarding working conditions (safety, lighting, heat or cold), equipment problems, quality problems, and similar matters.

The following reading from *The Harvard Business Review* provides two examples of how companies have improved their competitiveness through the use of time-based changes in the way they operate.

READING   TIME-BASED INNOVATION   *George Stalk, Jr.*

A company that can bring out new products three times faster than its competitors enjoys a huge advan-tage. Today, in one industry after another, Japanese manufacturers are doing just that to their Western competition:

· In projection television, Japanese producers can develop a new television in one-third the time re-quired by U.S. manufacturers.

· In custom plastic injection molds, Japanese compa-nies can develop the molds in one-third the time of U.S. competitors and at one-third the cost.

· In autos, Japanese companies can develop new products in half the time—and with half as many people—as the U.S. and German competition.

To accomplish their fast-paced innovations, leading Japanese manufacturers have introduced a se-ries of organizational techniques that precisely parallel their approach to flexible manufacturing:

· In manufacturing, the Japanese stress short produc-tion runs and small lot sizes. In innovation, they favor smaller increments of improvement in new products, but introduce them more often—versus the Western approach of more significant improvements made less often.

· In the organization of product development work, the Japanese use factory cells that are cross-functional teams. Most Western new product development ac-tivity is carried out by functional centers.

· In the scheduling of work, Japanese factories stress local responsibility, just as product development scheduling is decentralized. The Western approach to both requires plodding centralized scheduling, plot-ting, and tracking.

The effects of this time-based advantage are dev-astating; quite simply, American companies are losing leadership of technology and innovation—suppos-edly this country's source of long-term advantage. Unless U.S. companies reduce their new product development and introduction cycles from 36–48 months to 12–18 months, Japanese manufacturers will easily out-innovate and outperform them. Taking the initiative in innovation will require even faster cycle times.

Residential air conditioners illustrate the Japanese ability to introduce more technological innovation in smaller increments—and how in just a few years these improvements add up to remarkably superior products. The Japanese introduce innovations in air conditioners four times faster than their American competitors; in technological sophistication the Japanese products are seven to 10 years ahead of U.S. products.

Look at the changes in Mitsubishi Electric's three-horsepower heat pump between 1975 and 1985. From 1975 to 1979, the company did nothing to the product except change the sheet metal work, partly to improve efficiency but mostly to reduce materials costs. In 1979, the technological sophistication of the product was roughly equal to that of the U.S. competition. From this point on, the Japanese first established, and then widened the lead.

In 1980, Mitsubishi introduced its first major improvement: a new product that used integrated circuits to control the air-conditioning cycle. One year later, the company replaced the integrated circuits with microprocessors and added two important innovations to increase consumer demand. The first was "quick connect" freon lines. On the old product (and on the U.S. product), freon lines were made from copper tubing and cut to length, bent, soldered together, purged, and filled with freon—an operation requiring great skill to produce a reliable air conditioner. The Japanese substituted quick-connect freon lines—precharged hoses that simply clicked together. The second innovation was simplified wiring. On the old product (and still today on the U.S. product) the unit had six color-coded wires to connect. The advent of microprocessors made possible a two-wire connection with neutral polarity.

These two changes did not improve the energy-efficiency ratio of the product; nor were they intended to. Rather, the point was to fabricate a unit that would be simpler to install and more reliable, thereby broadening distribution and increasing demand. Because of these innovations, white-goods outlets could sell the new product, and local contractors could easily install it.

In 1982, Mitsubishi introduced a new version of the air conditioner featuring technological advances related to performance. A high-efficiency rotary compressor replaced the outdated reciprocating compressor. The condensing unit had louvered fins and inner fin tubes for better heat transfer. Because the balance of the system changed, all the electronics had to change. As a result, the energy-efficiency ratio improved markedly.

In 1983, Mitsubishi added sensors to the unit and more computing power, expanding the electronic control of the cycle and again improving the energy-efficiency ratio.

In 1984, Mitsubishi came out with another version of the product, this time with an inverter that made possible an even higher energy-efficiency ratio. The inverter, which requires additional electronics for the unit, allows unparalleled control over the speed of the electric motor, dramatically boosting the appliance's efficiency.

Using time-based innovation, Mitsubishi transformed its air conditioner. The changes came incrementally and steadily. Overall they gave Mitsubishi—and other Japanese companies on the same track—the position of technological leadership in the global residential air-conditioning industry.

In 1985, a U.S. air-conditioner manufacturer was just debating whether to use integrated circuits in its residential heat pump. In view of its four- to five-year product development cycle, it could not have introduced the innovation until 1989 or 1990—putting the American company ten years behind the Japanese. Faced with this situation, the U.S. air-conditioner company followed the example of many U.S. manufacturers that have lost the lead in technology and innovation: it decided to source its air conditioners and components from its Japanese competition.

Consider the remarkable example of Atlas Door, a 10-year-old U.S. company. It has grown at an average annual rate of 15 percent in an industry with an overall annual growth rate of less than 5 percent. In recent years, its pretax earnings were 20 percent of sales, about five times the industry average. Atlas is debt free. In its tenth year the company achieved the number one competitive position in its industry.

The company's product: industrial doors. It is a product with almost infinite variety, involving limitless choices of width and height and material. Because of the importance of variety, inventory is almost useless in meeting customer orders; most doors can be manufactured only after the order has been placed.

Historically, the industry had needed almost four months to respond to an order for a door that was out of stock or customized. Atlas's strategic advantage was time: it could respond in weeks to any order. It had

(continued)

structured its order-entry, engineering, manufacturing, and logistics systems to move information and products quickly and reliably.

First, Atlas built just-in-time factories. These are fairly simple in concept. They require extra tooling and machinery to reduce changeover times and a fabrication process organized by product and scheduled to start and complete all of the parts at the same time. But even the performance of the factory—critical to the company's overall responsiveness—still only accounted for 2½ weeks of the completed product delivery cycle.

Second, Atlas compressed time at the front end of the system, where the order first entered and was processed. Traditionally, when customers, distributors, or salespeople called a door manufacturer with a request for price and delivery, they would have to wait more than one week for a response. If the desired door was not in stock, not in the schedule, or not engineered, the supplier's organization would waste even more time, pushing the search for an answer around the system.

Recognizing the opportunity to cut deeply into the time expenditure in this part of the system, Atlas first streamlined, then automated its entire order-entry, engineering, pricing, and scheduling processes. Today Atlas can price and schedule 95 percent of its incoming orders while the callers are still on the telephone. It can quickly engineer new special orders because it has preserved on computer the design and production data of all previous special orders—which drastically reduces the amount of re-engineering necessary.

Third, Atlas tightly controlled logistics so that it always shipped only fully complete orders to construction sites. Orders require many components. Gathering all of them at the factory and making sure that they are with the correct order can be a time-consuming task. It is even more time-consuming, however, to get the correct parts to the job site *after* they have missed the initial shipment. Atlas developed a system to track the parts in production and the purchased parts for each order, ensuring arrival of all necessary parts at the shipping dock in time—a just-in-time logistics operation.

When Atlas started operations, distributors were uninterested in its product. The established distributors already carried the door line of a larger competitor; they saw no reason to switch suppliers except, perhaps, for a major price concession. But as a start-up, Atlas was too small to compete on price alone. Instead, it positioned itself as the door supplier of last resort, the company people came to if the established supplier could not deliver or missed a key date.

Of course, with industry lead times of almost four months, some calls inevitably came to Atlas. And when it did get a call, Atlas commanded a higher price because of its faster delivery. Atlas not only got a higher price but its time-based processes also yielded lower costs: it thus enjoyed the best of both worlds.

In 10 short years, the company replaced the leading door suppliers in 80 percent of the distributors in the country. With its strategic advantage the company could be selective, becoming the house supplier for only the strongest distributors.

In the wake of this indirect attack, the established competitors have not responded effectively. The conventional view is that Atlas is a "garage shop operator" that cannot sustain its growth: competitors expect the company's performance to degrade to the industry average as it grows larger. But this response—or nonresponse—only reflects a fundamental lack of understanding of time as the source of competitive advantage. The extra delay in responding only adds to the insurmountable lead the indirect time-based attack has created. While the traditional companies track costs and size, the new competitor derives advantage from time, staying on the cutting edge, leaving its rivals behind.

Source: Reprinted by permission of *Harvard Business Review*. "Time—The Next Source of Competitive Advantage," by George Stalk, Jr., July–August 1988.

LEAN PRODUCTION[2]

Lean production is a new, time-based approach to the production of manufactured goods. In the earliest days of manufacturing, goods were produced using **craft production**: highly skilled workers using simple, flexible tools produced in small quantities according to customer specifications.

Craft production
The early approach to manufacturing; highly skilled workers using simple, flexible tools to produce small quantities of customized goods.

In 1894, the Honorable Evelyn Henry Ellis, a wealthy member of the English Parliament, set out to buy a car. . . . He didn't go to a car dealer—there weren't any. Nor did he contact an English automobile manufacturer—there weren't any of those either.

Instead, he visited the noted Paris machine-tool company of Panhard et Levassor and commissioned an automobile. Today, P&L, as it was known, is remembered only by classic-car collectors and auto history buffs, but, in 1894, it was the world's leading car company. . . .

It got its start—and a jump on other potential competitors—when in 1887 Emile Levassor, the "L" of P&L, met Gottlieb Daimler, the founder of the company that today builds the Mercedes-Benz. Levassor negotiated a license to manufacture Daimler's new "high-speed" gasoline engine.

By the early 1890s, P&L was building several hundred automobiles a year. The cars were designed according to the *Système Panhard*—meaning the engine was in the front, with passengers seated in rows behind, and the motor drove the rear wheels.

When Ellis arrived at P&L, which was still primarily a manufacturer of metal-cutting saws rather than automobiles, he found in place the classic craft-production system. P&L's work force was overwhelmingly composed of skilled craftspeople who carefully hand-built cars in small numbers.

These workers thoroughly understood mechanical design principles and the materials with which they worked. What's more, many were their own bosses, often serving as independent contractors within the P&L plant or, more frequently, as independent machine-shop owners with whom the company contracted for specific parts or components.

The two company founders, Panhard and Levassor, and their immediate associates were responsible for talking to customers to determine the vehicle's exact specifications, ordering the necessary parts, and assembling the final product. Much of the work, though, including design and engineering, took place in individual craft shops scattered throughout Paris.

One of our most basic assumptions in the age of mass production—that cost per unit falls dramatically as production volume increases—was simply not true for craft-based P&L. If the company had tried to make 200,000 identical cars each year, the cost per car probably wouldn't have dipped much below the cost per car of making ten.

What's more, P&L could never have made two—much less 200,000—identical cars, even if these were built to the same blueprints. The reasons? P&L contractors didn't use a standard gauging system, and the machine tools of the 1890s couldn't cut hardened steel.

Instead, different contractors, using slightly different gauges, made the parts. They then ran the parts through an oven to harden their surfaces enough to withstand heavy use. However, the parts freqently warped in the oven and needed further machining to regain their original shape.

---

[2] The primary source for this section was the excellent presentation of research in the book *The Machine that Changed the World,* by James P. Womack, Daniel T. Jones, and Daniel Roos, published by Harper Perennial, 1991.

When these parts eventually arrived at P&L's final assembly hall, their specifications could best be described as approximate. The job of the skilled fitters in the hall was to take the first two parts and file them down until they fit together perfectly.

Then they filed the third part until it fit the first two, and so on until the whole vehicle—with its hundreds of parts—was complete.

This sequential fitting produced what we today call "dimensional creep." So, by the time the fitters reached the last part, the total vehicle could differ significantly in dimensions from the car on the next stand that was being built to the same blueprints.

Because P&L couldn't mass-produce identical cars, it didn't try. Instead, it concentrated on tailoring each product to the precise desires of individual buyers.

It also emphasized its cars' performance and their hand-fitted craftsmanship in which the gaps between individual parts were nearly invisible.

To the consumers Panhard was trying to woo, this pitch made perfect sense. These wealthy customers employed chauffeurs and mechanics on their personal staffs. Cost, driving ease, and simple maintenance weren't their primary concerns. Speed and customization were.

Evelyn Ellis was no doubt typical of P&L's clients. He didn't want just any car; he wanted a car built to suit his precise needs and tastes. He was willing to accept P&L's basic chassis and engine, he told the firm's owners, but he wanted a special body constructed by a Paris coachbuilder.

He also made a request to Levassor that would strike today's auto manufacturer as preposterous: He asked that the transmission, brake, and engine controls be transferred from the right to the left side of the car. (His reason wasn't that the English drove on the left—in that case, moving the controls to the left side of the vehicle was precisely the wrong thing to do. Besides, the steering tiller remained in the middle. Rather, he presumably thought the controls were more comfortable to use in that position.)

For P&L, Ellis's request probably seemed simple and reasonable. Since each part was made one at a time, it was a simple matter to bend control rods to the left rather than the right and to reverse the linkages. For today's mass-producer, this modification would require years—and millions or hundreds of millions of dollars—to engineer. (American companies still offer no right-side-drive option on cars they sell in drive-on-the-left Japan, since they believe the cost of engineering the option would be prohibitive.)

Once his automobile was finished, Ellis, accompanied by a mechanic engaged for the purpose, tested it extensively on the Paris streets. For, unlike today's cars, the vehicle he had just bought was in every sense a prototype. When he was satisfied that his new car operated properly—quite likely after many trips back to the P&L factory for adjustment—Ellis set off for England.   —*Source: James P. Womack, Daniel T. Jones, and Daniel Roos. The Machine that Changed the World (New York: Harper Perennial, 1991), pp. 21–23.*

Mass production

Lower-skilled workers using complex machinery to produce high volumes of standardized goods.

Customized goods were relatively expensive to produce and did not lend themselves to high-volume production. Over time, those methods were replaced by **mass production**: high volumes of standardized goods produced by low-skilled or semiskilled workers tending expensive, dedicated machinery. Such systems are intolerant to disruption, which greatly increases the cost of operation. Consequently, buffers are built into these systems to offset such disruptions. Extra workers, extra inventories, and extra space are provided to achieve smooth production. As these systems are costly and time-consuming to change, there is a great resistance to frequent changes. Moreover, the variety possible using mass production tends to be limited. Consequently, such systems can be thought of as fairly rigid; once in place, there is a great incentive to keep them running: Avoid disruption, and avoid frequent changes (e.g., in product or process design).

Mass production techniques can rightly be credited with making manufactured goods available in large quantities at affordable prices. It is because of mass production that the standard of living in industrialized countries is as high as it is. But mass production systems have some inherent weaknesses that cannot be easily overcome. And they were designed to function in an era that was much different than today's world.

Competitive pressures and consumer demands now require an increasing variety of output and frequent changes due to innovations in product design. Mass production systems are fairly intolerant of such changes; costs rise dramatically in the face of such changes. Furthermore, quality is increasingly important, and mass production systems do not lend themselves to high quality. Because the emphasis is on maintaining a constant rate of output, when mistakes occur during the production process, the defective units are allowed to continue being processed. Then, at the end of the line, massive inspection and rework is undertaken to uncover and correct defects. Not only is this costly and time consuming, but it is also unlikely that all, or even most, defects will be found. As a result, some defective goods are shipped to customers. And as inefficient and ineffective as this system is, stopping the line to correct defects as they occur would not only be too disruptive and costly, the skill level of the workers is generally too low to accomplish desired results.

The rationale for using low-skilled workers in mass production systems can be traced to the origins of these systems. When mass production was first introduced in the United States, the workforce was composed of rural workers, who often had little formal education, and non-English-speaking immigrants with a variety of native tongues. Those conditions favored dividing jobs into relatively simple tasks that required very little training or skill to perform. Given that scenario, workers were expected merely to perform their narrow tasks. They were not expected to know anything about the equipment they used, nor were they expected to maintain or repair it. Everything was handled by specialists.

Lean production systems are so named because they use much less of certain resources than mass production systems use—less space, less inventory, and fewer workers—to produce a comparable amount of output. Lean production systems use a highly skilled work force and flexible equipment. In effect, they incorporate advantages of both mass production (high volume, low unit cost) and craft production (variety and flexibility). And quality is higher than in mass production.

Lean production
Fewer, highly skilled workers using flexible equipment and fewer resources to produce high-volume, high-quality goods.

Lean production systems use a more highly skilled workforce than do mass production systems, enabling them to accomplish more with their workers. Workers are more involved in maintaining and improving the system than their mass production counterparts. They are taught to stop production if they discover a defect, and to work with other employees to find and correct the cause of the defect so that it won't reoccur. This results in an increasing level of quality over time, and eliminates the need to inspect and rework at the end of the line.

Lean production systems use small production batch sizes. This makes it less likely that a large number of defectives will be produced before they are discovered and the cause corrected, and it results in a lower amount of rework to correct defects.

And because lean production systems operate with lower amounts of inventory, additional emphasis is placed on anticipating when problems might occur *before* they arise, and avoiding those problems through careful planning. Even so, problems still occur at times, and quick resolution is important. Workers participate in both the planning and correction stages. Technical experts are still used, but more in the capacity of consultants rather than in place of workers. The focus is on designing a system (products and process) so that workers will be able to achieve high levels of quality and quantity.

Compared to workers in more traditional systems, much more is expected of workers in lean production systems. They must be able to function in teams, playing active roles in operating and improving the system. Individual creativity is much less important than team success. And responsibilities are much greater, which can lead to pressure and anxiety not present in traditional systems. Moreover, a flatter organizational structure means career paths are not as steep in lean production organizations. And workers tend to become generalists rather than specialists, another contrast to more traditional organizations.

Unions often oppose conversion from a traditional system to a lean system because they view the added responsibility and multiple tasks involved as expansion of job requirements without comparable increases in pay. In addition, workers sometimes complain that the company is the primary beneficiary of employee-generated improvements.

SUMMARY

Productivity is one measure of an organization's effective use of its resources. Productivity comparisons help managers judge an organization's ability to compete and/or to serve its customers. Organizations or countries that have relatively high productivity have a competitive edge.

Companies compete in a number of ways, including price, quality, special features or services, and time. Some companies suffer from poor competitiveness, often due to strategic weaknesses.

Strategies are the basic approaches used by an organization's to achieve its goals. Strategies provide focus for planning and decision making. Organizations typically have overall strategies which pertain to the entire organization, and strategies for each of the functional areas. Functional strategies are narrower in scope and should be linked to the overall strategy. Many organizations have adopted either time-based strategies or quality-based strategies as they seek to become more competitive and/or they attempt to become more productive and better serve their customers. Time-based approaches are described in this chapter; quality-based approaches are described in the next chapter.

KEY TERMS

competitiveness,
craft production,
distinctive competencies,
environmental scanning,
lean production,
mass production,
mission,

mission statement,
operations strategy,
productivity, 36
quality-based strategy,
strategy, 44
tactics, 44
time-based strategy,

Problem

1. A company that processes fruits and vegetables is able to produce 400 cases of canned peaches in one half hour with two workers. What is labor productivity?

Solution:

$$\text{Labor productivity} = \frac{\text{Quantity produced}}{\text{Labor hours}}$$

$$= \frac{400 \text{ cases}}{2 \text{ workers} \times \frac{1}{2} \text{ hour/worker}}$$

$$= 400 \text{ cases per hour}$$

Problem

2. A wrapping paper company produced 2,000 rolls of paper one day at a standard price of $1 per roll. Labor cost was $160, material cost was $50, and overhead was $320. Determine the multifactor productivity.

Solution:

$$\text{Multifactor productivity} = \frac{\text{Quantity produced @ standard price}}{\text{Labor cost} + \text{Material cost} + \text{Overhead}}$$

$$= \frac{2,000 \text{ rolls} \times \$1/\text{roll}}{\$160 + \$50 + \$320}$$

$$= 3.77$$

1. What is productivity and why is it important? Who in an organization is primarily responsible for productivity?
2. List some of the factors that can affect productivity and some of the ways that it can be improved.
3. It has been said that a typical Japanese automobile manufacturer produces more cars with fewer workers than their U.S. counterpart. What are some possible explanations for this, assuming that U.S. workers are as hardworking as Japanese workers?
4. From time to time, various groups clamor for import restrictions or tariffs on foreign-produced goods, particularly automobiles. In what way might these be helpful? In what ways might these be harmful?
5. List the key ways that organizations compete.
6. What are the key reasons for the poor competitiveness of some companies?
7. The United States has the highest agricultural productivity of any country in the world. What do you suppose are the primary reasons for this high productivity?
8. Most experts seem to agree that workers are not primarily responsible for poor productivity. Who is?

"If only people would
work a little harder, we
could increase
productivity."

9. What are distinctive competencies, and how do they relate to strategy formulation?

10. Contrast the terms *strategies* and *tactics*.

11. Contrast *organization strategy* and *operations strategy*.

12. Explain what is meant by the term *time-based strategies* and give three examples.

13. Describe and contrast these forms of production: craft, mass production, and lean production.

14. What is the implication of the cartoon in terms of increasing productivity?

PROBLEMS

1. Suppose that a company produced 300 standard bookcases last week using eight workers, and that it produced 240 standard bookcases the week before using six workers. In which period was productivity higher? Explain.

2. The manager of a crew that installs carpeting has tracked the crew's output over the past several weeks, obtaining these figures:

Week	Crew size	Yards installed
1	4	960
2	3	702
3	4	968
4	2	500
5	3	696
6	2	500

Compute the labor productivity for each of the weeks. On the basis of your calculations, what can you conclude about crew size and productivity?

3. Compute the multifactor productivity measure for each of the weeks shown. What do the productivity figures suggest? The standard price is $140 per unit. Assume 40-hour weeks and an hourly wage of $12. Overhead is 1.5 times weekly labor cost. Material cost is $6 per pound.

Week	Output (units)	Workers	Material (lbs)
1	300	6	45
2	338	7	46
3	322	7	46
4	354	8	48
5	222	5	40
6	265	6	42
7	310	7	46

4. A company that makes shopping carts for supermarkets and other stores recently purchased some new equipment that reduces the labor content of the jobs involved in producing the shopping carts. Prior to buying the new equipment, 5 workers were used, and they produced an average of 80 carts per hour. Labor cost was $10 per hour and machine cost was $40 per hour. With the new equipment, it was possible to transfer one of the workers to another department, and equipment cost increased by $10 per hour while output increased by 4 carts per hour.

   a. Compute labor productivity under each system. Use carts per worker per hour as the measure of labor productivity.

   b. Compute the multifactor productivity under each system. Use carts per dollar cost (labor plus equipment) as the measure.

   c. Comment on the changes in productivity according to the two different measures, and which one you feel is the more pertinent for this situation.

SELECTED BIBLIOGRAPHY

Blackburn, Joseph D., ed. *Time-Based Competition.* Homewood, Ill.: Business One Irwin, 1991.

Buffa, E. S. *Meeting the Competitive Challenge: Manufacturing Strategies for U.S. Companies.* Homewood, Ill.: Richard D. Irwin, 1984.

Hall, Robert. *Attaining Manufacturing Excellence.* Homewood, Ill.: Dow-Jones Irwin, 1987.

Hayes, Robert H., and Steven C. Wheelwright. *Restoring Our Competitive Edge: Competing through Manufacturing.* New York: John Wiley & Sons, 1984.

Hill, Terry. *Manufacturing Strategy.* Homewood, Ill.: Richard D. Irwin, 1989.

NBC White Paper: *"If Japan Can . . . Why Can't We?"* (Film available from Films, Inc.)

Peterson, Ronald S. "The Critical Issues for Manufacturing Management." *Operations Management Review* 2, no. 4, 1984, pp. 15–20.

Porter, Michael E. *Competitive Advantage: Creating and Sustaining Superior Performance.* New York: The Free Press, 1984.

Skinner, Wickham. "Manufacturing—Missing Link in Corporate Strategy." *Harvard Business Review,* May–June 1969, pp. 136–45.

Stalk, George, Jr. "Time—The Next Source of Competitive Advantage." *Harvard Business Review,* July–August 1988, pp. 41–51.

Wheelwright, Steven C. "Japan—Where Operations Really Are Strategic." *Harvard Business Review,* July–August 1981, pp. 67–74.

Womack, James P.; Daniel T. Jones; and Daniel Roos. *The Machine that Changed the World.* New York: Harper Perennial, 1991.

READING   A WHIRLPOOL FACTORY RAISES PRODUCTIVITY—AND PAY OF
WORKERS: BENTON HARBOR, MICH., PLANT RELIES ON TEACHING
PEOPLE HOW TO IMPROVE QUALITY   *Rick Wartzman*

For Ed Mileski, a maintenance mechanic at Whirlpool Corp.'s riverfront factory here, enhanced productivity with oil and steel has meant new irons and woods.

Thanks to improved efficiency at this aging tooling and plating operation, Mr. Mileski was able to afford a new $300 set of golf clubs. For George Perkins, meanwhile, soaring productivity has provided a $1,000 video camera, among other luxuries. And for machine operator Jerry Robinson, it has meant help in sending two sons to college.

To each of the plant's 265 employees, in fact, improved productivity meant an extra $2,700 of pay last year. A special gain-sharing program lifted average blue-collar compensation to more than $26,400. And that has changed the workers' attitudes.

A New Understanding

"Productivity used to be a dirty word around here," says Lloyd Spoonholtz, president of Machinists Local 1918, which put aside years of contention with management to devise the gain-sharing formula. "People thought they'd have to work harder without getting anything for it. Now they're starting to understand that productivity pays."

The gain in productivity—output per hour of work—has also reduced Whirlpool's costs and bolstered its profit. And it has benefited Whirlpool's customers. Aided by productivity advances throughout its operations, the company has been able to hold down prices of its washing machines while improving their quality.

Unfortunately, Benton Harbor is the exception in the U.S., where productivity growth has faltered since 1973. Partly through downsizing, manufacturers have made progress, but their performance still isn't "fully satisfactory" compared with that of some other nations, says Carl Thor, vice chairman of the American Productivity and Quality Center in Houston. In the non-manufacturing sector, where four out of five Americans are employed, productivity stagnated in the 1980s.

Dwindling Lead

The upshot: Although America still has the highest level of productivity in the world, its rate of increase trails that of other countries, and Germany and Japan are now doing better in some important industries. The implications of that dwindling lead are critical.

The cost of the nation's productivity slowdown already has been immense. Had productivity continued to grow as fast after 1973 as it did in earlier postwar decades, calculates Isabel Sawhill, an economist at the Urban Institute, median family income in 1990 would have been about $47,000 rather than $35,000.

The connection between gains in productivity and how comfortably we live is illuminated by a look at the Benton Harbor factory, which turns metal rods into parts for washers and dryers. It also points a possible way out of the mess in which many U.S. businesses are still mired.

Increased Earnings

Since 1988, Benton Harbor's productivity has surged more than 19%, to 110.6 parts manufactured per man hour from 92.8. Moreover, the number of parts rejected has sunk to a world-class 10 per million from 837 per million.

The result is that, despite a labor contract offering no regular wage or cost-of-living increases over that span, the average worker's pay at the factory has risen nearly 12%. Adjusted for inflation, it fell 2.6%. But that's still better than the fate of the average U.S. manufacturing worker, whose real wage declined 4.6% over the same period. And if the Benton Harbor workers maintain their pace, their pay gains soon will outstrip inflation.

The pickup in productivity here hasn't been achieved by spending millions of dollars on fancy machines. Although not as bad as in the 1950s, when rats and snakes roamed the shop floor, the Benton Harbor factory still isn't a high-tech plant. The air is filled with the pungent smell of cutting oil, the floor is grimy, and the equipment is mostly old and very noisy. Instead of building a state-of-the-art plant, Whirlpool overhauled the manufacturing process and taught its workers to improve quality.

It wasn't easy. Productivity used to be lousy at the plant, which seemed destined for the oblivion that befell many factories in this depressed town of 13,000 on the southeastern shore of Lake Michigan. Its workers' attitude was that "if a machine broke, you just sat down" until someone came along sooner or later and fixed it, says Bill Bonfoey, a 31-year Whirlpool veteran. Workers hid inferior parts, he adds, so "an inspector wouldn't see them."

By the mid-1980s, it became apparent that such behavior could spell ruin. In an adjacent Whirlpool plant, it did.

Six years ago, Whirlpool said it would end virtually all its manufacturing here. The company had redesigned its automatic washer, reducing the amount of labor involved, and no longer needed two final-assembly operations. So, it had to choose between the one here and one in Clyde, Ohio. The less-productive Benton Harbor plant was condemned, and more than 1,000 jobs vanished. The only part of the operation here to survive was the small tooling and plating shop, which was set apart from the main plant by a narrow waterway.

"It was a real awakening" when demolition began on the 750,000-square-foot factory in late 1987, says John Mack, the supervisor in charge of manufacturing at Benton Harbor. Some workers still gaze into the barren tract of dune grass where the big sister plant once stood.

At first, many of them doubted the tooling and plating facility would remain open much longer, either. But the company assured them they had one hope: Improve output. "Productivity has become job security for an awful lot of us," says Ed Barton, who works at the plant's shipping docks.

Although the company won more flexible work rules in its last two labor contracts, the main ingredient to success has been the gain-sharing agreement, which was hammered out in 1988. Reaching that agreement, however, was difficult.

The Contentious Past

Chain-smoking Winstons behind a beat-up metal desk at the Machinists union hall, Mr. Spoonholtz recalls the bitter strikes and lockouts in previous years and says that, heading into the 1980s, the company and its workers "were adversaries." His first inclination when he heard about the proposed gain-sharing program, he says, was to tell Whirlpool "to go to hell."

But both sides, feeling the heat of intensifying industry competition, knew they had to compromise, or the Benton Harbor plant would die. Meeting on neutral turf in Chicago, a private consultant helped them come up with a system tailored to rev up productivity as well as reward it.

The concept is straightforward: The bigger the gain in output, the larger the pool of money the workers share with the company. The precise percentage of the pool going to the workers is determined by the quality of their output, as measured by the number of rejected parts. The workers divide their share of the pool evenly. The company's share ends up being divided between shareholders and consumers—that is, by balancing profits and prices.

In some respects, every company, in paying workers, does what the Benton Harbor plant does,

(continued)

though not so explicitly. A company raising workers' pay, after all, must meet the cost by increasing prices or productivity. The Whirlpool workers here, though, assume all the risk up front: If they don't produce more, they don't get more.

Declining Costs

As productivity has gone up at Benton Harbor, labor costs have fallen, because workers' earnings haven't risen as fast as their productivity. As a result, from 1989 to 1991, the cost of a washing-machine agitator shaft decreased 13% to $1.95, and a spin pinion fell 24% to $1.65.

The parts made at Benton Harbor account for only about 5% of a Whirlpool washer—not enough to change its cost. But other Whirlpool factories and some outside suppliers also have raised their productivity and thus lowered costs. For example, Whirlpool's Columbia, S.C., division has raised its productivity nearly 20% since 1990 while cutting costs about 9%.

"The appliance industry as a whole has done an exceptionally good job of becoming more productive," says Jonathan Goldfarb, an analyst at Merrill Lynch & Co. General Electric Co. has speeded up order-to-delivery time to five weeks from 18 at its Louisville, Ky., appliance plant, and Maytag Corp. cited "enhanced manufacturing efficiencies" in reporting that first-quarter net income jumped 90% from dismal year-earlier levels. Whirlpool, Mr. Goldfarb says, has "been in the forefront" of the appliance industry's productivity drive. For the past two years, he says, the company has gained market share while outpacing its rivals on the bottom line.

Whirlpool has been able to funnel its productivity gains into initiatives ranging from research to more effective distribution. But what especially matters to consumers is Whirlpool's ability to keep a lid on prices. Following a decades-old appliance-industry pattern of defying inflation, the retail price of a mid-line Whirlpool washer today is about $399, roughly the same as several years ago. In some markets, it's even lower. By comparison, consumer prices rose 19.5% in the past four years.

Changed Attitudes

The turnaround here at Benton Harbor began with changes in the attitudes of both labor and management. For the company, that shift has brought, among other things, a new willingness to try to teach its workers how to improve quality.

Raising quality is important. With less time wasted on making bad parts, productivity increases. The cost of scrapping bad parts drops. And if more parts are made correctly, less inventory has to be kept on hand. Then, with output increasing, the company can gradually pare the payroll through attrition.

One key to quality is awareness. Benton Harbor workers now go to the Clyde plant to see how their products are put into the final product. With this understanding, they can make subtle adjustments that help the line flow more smoothly.

Upstairs from the factory floor, a new training center offers interactive computer lessons on everything from sharpening general math skills to learning how to handle gauges and other tools. "Whirlpool in the past has been very good at getting people to use their hands," says Al Voorhis, the division manager. "Now we're getting them to use their heads."

Mr. Mileski, the mechanic, is trying to do just that. He and some fellow workers are seeking ways to recapture more of the oil used to cool and lubricate the machines. They estimate that if their recycling plan works, it will add another $41,000 to the gain-sharing pool. "That's straight into our pockets," Mr. Mileski says.

A Whirlpool Plant's Gains

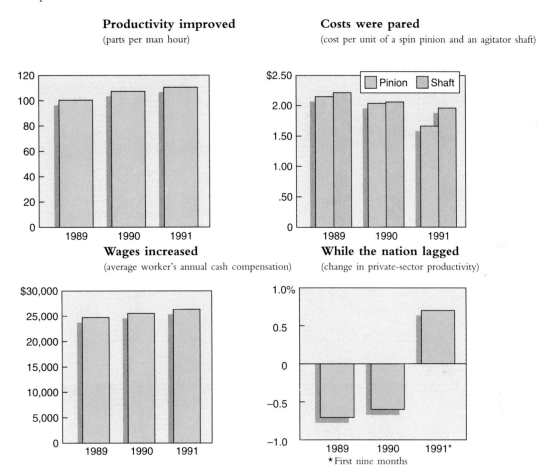

Productivity improved
(parts per man hour)

Costs were pared
(cost per unit of a spin pinion and an agitator shaft)

Wages increased
(average worker's annual cash compensation)

While the nation lagged
(change in private-sector productivity)

*First nine months

Sources: Whirlpool Corp.; American Productivity and Quality Center

But perhaps most important is that the foremen are, at long last, telling workers to stress quality over quantity. Managers have "talked quality for nearly 30 years," says Mr. Spoonholtz, the local union chief. "Now, they're finally living it."

Some Work Harder

Besides working a little smarter, some are working a little harder. Charles Whorton, a plant janitor, says he's inclined to give the floor an extra scrub each day.

(continued)

READING   *(concluded)*

That not only bespeaks an attitudinal change but also can directly affect productivity: A clean plant is safer and more productive. Cecil Joe Martin, who converts 5,000-pound steel coils into bars, says he doesn't "sit on his duff" as much as he once did.

But not everyone likes all the changes. Charles Bevelhymer, who runs a drilling machine, says that with everyone receiving the same amount of gain-sharing, unproductive workers leech off the more productive. He also denounces as "socialistic" a company move to set up teams in which a variety of tasks will be shared.

Occasionally, distrust between labor and management resurfaces. Rumors have flown through the plant that Whirlpool sabotaged parts or clandestinely shipped them out at night so the workers will get a smaller gain-sharing payout—a charge that Whirlpool has emphatically denied. Still, the Machinists' Mr. Spoonholtz likes to double-check the company's calculations on his home computer.

All in all, most workers here seem to have come to see a firm link between their productivity and their pay. "We all still like to gripe," says Mr. Robinson, the machine operator. "But if you're griping on the way to the bank, that's OK."

Questions

1. Who has benefited from Whirlpool's productivity gains?

2. How did Whirlpool achieve the productivity gains?

3. What was the main ingredient to success? What are its key features?

4. What benefits have employees received from the productivity gains? What benefits has the company received?

Source: Reprinted with permission from *THE WALL STREET JOURNAL,* © 1992 Don Jones & Company, Inc. All Rights Reserved Worldwide.

READING   AN AMERICAN TRAGEDY: HOW A GOOD COMPANY DIED   *Zachary Schiller*

The Rust Belt is back. So say bullish observers as U.S. exports surge, long-moribund industries glow with newfound profits, and unemployment dips to lows not seen in a decade. But in the smokestack citadels, there's disquiet. Too many machine-tool and auto-parts factories are silent; too many U.S. industries still can't hold their own.

What went wrong since the heyday of the 1960s? That's the issue Max Holland, a contributing editor of *The Nation,* takes up in his nutsy-boltsy but fascinating study *When the Machine Stopped.*★

The focus of the story is Burgmaster Corp., a Los Angeles-area machine-tool maker founded in 1944 by Czechoslovakian immigrant Fred Burg. Holland's

---

★Max Holland, *When the Machine Stopped: A Cautionary Tale from Industrial America* (Boston, Mass.: Harvard Business School Press, 1988).

father worked there for 29 years, and the author interviewed 22 former employees. His shop-floor view of this small company is a refreshing change from academic treatises on why America can't compete.

The discussions of spindles and numerical control can be tough going. But Holland compensates by conveying the excitement and innovation of the company's early days and the disgust and cynicism accompanying its decline. Moreover, the fate of Burgmaster and its brethren is crucial to the U.S. industrial economy: Any manufactured item is either made by a machine tool or by a machine made by a machine tool.

Producing innovative turret drills used in a wide variety of metalworking tasks, Burgmaster was a thriving enterprise by 1965, when annual sales amounted to about $8 million. The company needed backing to expand, however, so it sold out to Buffalo-based conglomerate Houdaille Industries Inc.

Houdaille was in turn purchased in a 1979 leveraged buyout led by Kohlberg Kravis Roberts & Co. By 1982, when debt, competition, and a sickly machine-tool market had battered Burgmaster badly, Houdaille went to Washington with a petition to withhold the investment tax credit for certain Japanese-made machine tools.

Thanks to deft lobbying, the Senate passed a resolution supporting Houdaille's position, but President Reagan refused to go along. Houdaille's subsequent attempt to link Burgmaster up with a Japanese rival also failed, and Burgmaster was closed.

Holland uses Bergmaster's demise to explore some key issues of economic and trade policy. Houdaille's charge that a cartel led by the Japanese government had injured U.S. toolmakers, for example, became a rallying point for those who would blame a fearsome Japan Inc. for the problems of U.S. industry.

Holland describes the Washington wrangling over Houdaille in painful detail. But he does show that such government decisions are often made without much knowledge of what's going on in industry. He shows, too, that Japanese producers succeeded less because of government help than because they made better, cheaper machines.

For those who see LBOs as a symptom of what ails the U.S. economy, Holland offers plenty of ammunition. He argues persuasively that the LBO crippled Burgmaster by creating enormous pressure to generate cash. As Burgmaster pushed its products out as fast as possible, he writes, it routinely shipped defective machines. It promised customers features that engineers hadn't yet designed. And although KKR disputes the claim, Holland concludes that the LBO choked off Burgmaster's investment funds just when foreign competition made them most necessary. As for Houdaille, it was recapitalized and sold to Britain's Tube Investments Group.

But Burgmaster's problems had started even before the LBO. Holland's history of the company under Houdaille is a veritable catalog of modern management techniques that flopped. One of the most disastrous was a system for computerizing production scheduling that was too crude for complex machine-tool manufacturing. Holland gives a dramatic depiction of supply snafus that resulted in delays and cost increases.

As an independent company, "Burgmaster thrived because the Burgs knew their business," Holland writes. Their departure under Houdaille was followed by an "endless and ultimately futile search for a better formula." But, he concludes: "No formula was a substitute for management involvement on the shop floor."

In the end, however, Holland puts most of the blame for the industry's decline on government policy. He targets tax laws and macroeconomic policies that encourage LBOs and speculation instead of productive investment. He also criticizes Pentagon procurement policies for favoring exotic, custom machines over standard, low-cost models. This adds up to an industrial policy, Holland writes—a bad one.

The point is well taken, but Holland gives it excessive weight. Like their brethren in Detroit and Pittsburgh, domestic tool-makers in the 1970s were too complacent when imports seized the lower end of the product line. The conservatism that had for years served them in their cyclical industry left them ill-prepared for change. Even now some of the largest U.S. tool-makers are struggling to restructure. Blame the government, yes. But blame the industry, too.

Questions

1. How important are machine tools to manufacturing? Why?

2. How did the leveraged buyout affect Burgmaster?

3. What external factors contributed to the firm's demise? What internal factors contributed?

4. Did P/OM play a significant role in the downfall of the company? Explain.

CASE   HOME-STYLE COOKIES

The Company

The Lew-Mark Baking Company is located in a small town in western New York State. The bakery is run by two brothers, Lew and Mark, who formed the company after they purchased an Archway® Cookie franchise. It is the largest Archway franchise with exclusive rights to New York and New Jersey. The company employs fewer than 200 people. The work force is mainly blue collar, and the atmosphere is informal.

The Product

The company's only product is soft cookies. It makes over 50 varieties of soft cookies. Larger companies, such as Nabisco, Sunshine, and Keebler, have traditionally produced biscuit cookies, in which most of the water has been baked out, resulting in crisp cookies. Also, Archway cookies do not have any additives or preservatives. The high quality of the cookies has enabled the company to develop a strong niche market for their product.

The Customers

The cookies are sold in convenience stores and supermarkets throughout New York and New Jersey. Archway® markets its cookies as "good food" because no additives or preservatives are used. This appeals to a segment of the market that is health conscious. Many customers are over 45 years of age, and prefer a cookie that is soft and not too sweet. Parents with young children also buy the cookies.

The Production Process

Cookies are made using a batch processing system. The company has two continuous band ovens that it uses to bake the cookies. The production process begins once management determines which cookies are to be baked. Cookies are baked based on orders from distributors. At the start of each shift, a list of the cookies that are to be made that day is delivered to the person in charge of mixing. That person checks a master list that indicates the ingredients needed for each type of cookie, and then enters that information into the computer. The computer then determines the amount of each ingredient needed, according to the quantity of cookies ordered, and relays that information to storage silos located just outside the plant where the main ingredients (flour, sugar, and cake flour) are stored. The ingredients are automatically sent to giant mixing machines, where the ingredients are combined with proper amounts of eggs, water, and flavorings. After the ingredients have been mixed, the batter is poured into a cutting machine where it is cut into individual cookies. The cookies are then dropped onto a continuous band (conveyor belt) and transported through one of two ovens. Filled cookies, such as apple, date, and raspberry, require an additional step for filling and folding.

The nonfilled cookies are cut on a diagonal rather than straight. The diagonal-cut cookies require less space than straight-cut cookies would, and the result is a higher level of productivity. In addition, the company recently increased the length of each oven by 25 feet, which also increased the rate of production.

As the cookies emerge from the ovens, they are fed onto spiral cooling racks that are 20 feet high and 3 feet wide. As the cookies come off the cooling racks, workers manually place the cookies into boxes, removing any broken or deformed cookies in the process. Then, the boxes are wrapped, sealed, and labeled automatically.

Inventory

Most cookies are immediately loaded onto trucks and shipped to distributors. A small percentage are stored temporarily in the company's warehouse, but they must be shipped shortly because of their limited shelf life. Other inventory includes individual cookie boxes, shipping boxes, labels, and cellophane for wrapping. Labels are reordered frequently, in small batches, because FDA label requirements are subject to change, and the company does not want to get stuck with labels it can't use. The bulk silos are refilled two or three times a week, depending on how quickly supplies are used.

Cookies are baked in a sequence that minimizes downtime for cleaning. For instance, light-colored cookies (e.g., chocolate chip) are baked before dark-colored cookies (e.g., fudge), and oatmeal cookies are baked before oatmeal raisin cookies. This permits the company to avoid having to clean the processing equipment between every time a different type of cookie is produced.

Quality

The bakery prides itself on the quality of its cookies. Cookies are sampled randomly by a quality control inspector as they come off the line to assure that their taste and consistency are satisfactory, and that they have been baked to the proper degree. Also, workers on the line are responsible for removing defective cookies when they spot them. The company has also installed an X-ray machine on the line that can detect any small bits of metal filings that may have gotten into cookies during the production process. Also, the use of automatic equipment for transporting raw materials and mixing batter has made it easier to maintain a sterile process.

Scrap

The bakery is run very efficiently and has minimal amounts of scrap. For example, if a batch is mixed improperly, it is sold for dog food. Broken cookies are used in the oatmeal meal cookies. These practices reduce the use of ingredients and save on waste disposal costs. The company also uses heat reclamation: The heat that escapes from the two ovens is captured and used to boil the water that supplies heat to the building. Also, the use of automation in the mixing process resulted in a reduction in waste over manual methods that were used previously.

New Products

Ideas for new products come from customers, employees, and observations of competitors' products. New ideas are first examined to determine if the cookies can be made using existing equipment. If they can, a sample run is made to determine the cost and time requirements. If the results are satisfactory, marketing tests are conducted to see if there is a demand for the product.

Potential Improvements

There are a number of areas of potential improvement at the bakery. One possibility would be to automate packing the cookies into boxes. Although labor costs are not high, automating the process might save some money and increase efficiency. So far, the owners have resisted this move because they feel an obligation to the community to employ the 30 women who now do the boxing manually. Another possible improvement would be to use suppliers who are located closer to the plant. That would reduce delivery lead times and transportation costs, but the owners are not convinced that the quality would be as good with local suppliers. Several other opportunities have been proposed in recent years, but the owners rejected them because they felt that there was a potential that quality of the product would suffer.

Questions

1. Briefly describe the cookie-production process.
2. What are two ways that the company has increased productivity? Why did increasing the length of the ovens result in a faster output rate?
3. Do you think that the company is making the right decision by not automating the packing of cookies? Explain your reasoning. What obligation does a company have to its employees in a situation such as this? What obligation does it have to the community? Is the size of the town a factor? Would it make a difference if the company was located in a large city? Is the size of the company a factor? What if it was a much larger company?
4. What factors cause Lew-Mark to carry minimal amounts of certain inventories? What benefits result from this policy?
5. As a consumer, what things would you look at in judging the quality of a cookie you bought in a supermarket?
6. What advantages, and what limitations, stem from not using preservatives in their cookies?
7. Briefly describe the company's strategy.

DECISION MAKING

After completing this supplement, you should be able to:

1. State what the chief role of an operations manager is.

2. Outline the steps in the decision-making process.

3. List some causes of poor decisions.

4. Describe the different environments under which operations decisions are made.

5. Describe and use techniques that apply to decision making under uncertainty.

6. Describe and use the expected–value approach.

7. Construct a decision tree and use it to solve a problem.

8. Compute the expected value of perfect information.

9. Conduct sensitivity analysis on a simple decision problem.

T he chief role of the operations manager is that of decision maker. In this capacity, the operations manager has considerable influence over the degree to which the goals and objectives of the organization are achieved.

Throughout this book you will be exposed to a broad range of decision areas that are encountered in operations management and to the tools necessary to handle those decisions. In this supplement the process of decision making is examined, as are typical causes of poor decisions, and the classification of decision problems according to degree of certainty. The major portion of the supplement is devoted to decision theory, which is a general approach to decision making that has applications in many areas of operations management.

THE DECISION PROCESS

Decision making is a fundamental process of management, and most of the efforts of managers are related to this process. Unfortunately, decisions do not always turn out as planned. Most successful decision making follows a process that consists of these steps:

1. Identify the problem.
2. Specify objectives and the decision criteria for choosing a solution.
3. Develop alternatives.
4. Analyze and compare alternatives.
5. Select the best alternative.
6. Implement the chosen alternative.
7. Monitor the results to ensure that desired results are achieved.

Success or failure in decision making often depends on how well each of these steps is handled.

Identifying the problem is the focal point of the process. Unless it is done carefully, the remaining steps can be misdirected. One danger is that problem-solving efforts will be directed toward removing the *symptoms* of the problem rather than the actual problem itself, leaving the problem to resurface at a later time. For instance, athletic injuries are sometimes treated with painkilling drugs that can effectively mask the symptoms but do not heal the actual injury. Even worse, the person may feel so much better that he or she returns to action and risks aggravating the injury. Or consider the young driver who became so annoyed at the strange noises coming from his car's engine that he was forced to turn up the volume on the car's radio to drown them out! *Solutions must address the basic problem, not the symptoms.*

The decision maker must *identify the criteria* by which proposed solutions will be judged. Common criteria often relate to costs, profits, return on investment, increased productivity, risk, company image, impact on demand, and similar variables.

The ability to satisfactorily handle problems often depends on the degree of success one has in *developing suitable alternatives*. In the search for alternatives, there is always the danger that one or more potentially superior alternatives will be overlooked. Consequently, the optimal alternative may turn out to be less than optimum. Obviously, there is a limit to the number of possible alternatives that can be identified. Much depends on the experience and creativity of the decision maker as well as on the nature of the situation. However, as a general rule, efforts expended in carefully identifying alternatives can yield substantial dividends in terms of the overall decision. One alternative that is frequently overlooked, possibly because it seems too simple, is to do nothing. The beauty of doing nothing lies not only in the fact that no time or effort is needed, but also in that it may cost nothing and requires no implementation.

Analyzing and comparing alternatives is often enhanced by the use of mathematical or statistical techniques. Many of these are described and demonstrated throughout this book.

Selection of the best alternative will depend on the objectives of the decision maker and the criteria that are being used to evaluate alternatives.

Implementing a solution simply means carrying out the actions indicated by the chosen alternative. Examples include buying the machine, refusing the loan application, beginning development of a new product, and authorizing the use of overtime. Of course, if the alternative selected is to do nothing, no action will be required to implement it. Note that many decision makers use this approach by default: By the time they get around to making a decision, it's too late!

Effective decision making requires that the results of the decision be *monitored* to make certain that the desired consequences have been achieved. If they have not, the decision maker may have to repeat the entire process; or perhaps a review of the situation may reveal an error in the actual implementation, an error in calculations, a wrong assumption, or some similar point that will allow the situation to be remedied quickly.

The decision process is not always completed in a sequential manner. Instead, there is usually a certain amount of backtracking and feedback involved, especially in terms of developing and analyzing alternatives. For example, if none of the alternatives analyzed can achieve the desired results, additional alternatives must be developed. Or perhaps the problem has not been clearly identified, and so additional work must be done there as well as on the other steps in the process.

CAUSES OF POOR DECISIONS

Occasionally, despite the best efforts of a manager, a decision turns out rather poorly due to unforeseeable circumstances. Luckily, such occurrences are not all that common. More often, failures can be traced to some combination of the following reasons: mistakes in the decision process, bounded rationality, or suboptimization.

In many cases, managers fail to appreciate the importance of each step in the decision process that was just outlined. They may skip a step or not devote enough effort to completing it before jumping to the next step. Sometimes this is due to a manager's style of making quick decisions or to failure to recognize the consequences of a poor decision. The manager's ego can be a factor. This sometimes happens after a period in which the manager has experienced a series of successes—important decisions that all turned out right. Under these circumstances, some managers get the impression that they can do no wrong, but soon run into trouble. This is enough to bring some managers back down to earth, but others seem oblivious to the negative results and continue the process they associate with their previous successes, not recognizing that some of that success was due more to luck than to any special abilities of their own. A part of the problem may be the manager's unwillingness to admit a mistake. Then, too, some managers demonstrate an inability to make a decision: they hem and haw, stalling long past the time when the decision should have been rendered.

Of course, not all managers fall into these traps—it seems safe to say that the majority do not. Even so, this does not necessarily mean that every decision works out as expected. Another factor with which managers must contend is **bounded rationality**, a term that refers to the limits imposed on decision making because of costs, human abilities, time, technology, and the availability of information. Because of these limitations, managers cannot always expect to reach decisions that are optimal in the sense of providing the best possible outcome (e.g., highest profit, least cost). Instead, they must often resort to achieving a *satisfactory* solution.

Still another cause of poor decisions is that organizations typically departmentalize decisions. Naturally, there is a great deal of justification for the use of departments in terms of overcoming span-of-control problems and human limitations. However, one problem that can arise is **suboptimization**. This occurs as a result of different departments each attempting to reach a solution that is optimum for that department. Unfortunately, what is optimal for a specific department may not be optimal for the organization as a whole. For example, the quality control department of a nail manufacturer may want to introduce a program that will guarantee that every nail produced is perfect. However, to cover costs, the price charged might be so ridiculously high that no one would be likely to buy the product!

DECISION ENVIRONMENTS

The environments in which operations management decisions are made can be classified according to the degree of certainty present. There are three basic categories: certainty, risk, and uncertainty.

> **Certainty** means that relevant parameters such as costs, capacity, and demand have known values.
>
> **Risk** means that certain parameters have probabilistic outcomes.
>
> **Uncertainty** means that it is impossible to assess the likelihood of various possible future events.

Consider these situations:

1. Profit per unit is $5. We have an order for 200 units. How much profit will we make? (This is an example of *certainty* since unit profits and total demand are known.)
2. Profit is $5 per unit. Based on previous experience, there is a 50 percent chance of an order for 100 units and a 50 percent chance of an order for 200 units. What is expected profit? (This is an example of *risk* since demand outcomes are probabilistic.)
3. Profit per unit is $5. The probabilities of potential demands are unknown. (This is an example of *uncertainty*.)

The importance of these three decision environments is that they require different techniques of analysis. Some techniques are better suited for one category than for others. You should make note of the environment for which each technique is appropriate.

DECISION THEORY

Decision theory represents a general approach to decision making. It is suitable for a wide range of operations management decisions. Among them are capacity planning, product and service design, equipment selection, and location planning. Decisions that lend themselves to a decision theory approach tend to be characterized by these elements:

1. A set of possible future conditions exists that will have a bearing on the results of the decision.
2. The manager has a list of alternatives to choose from.
3. There is a known payoff for each alternative under each possible future condition.

In order to use this approach, a decision maker would employ this process:

1. Identify the possible future conditions (e.g., demand will be low, medium, or high; the number of contracts awarded will be one, two, or three; the competitor will introduce a new product, or the competitor will not introduce a new product). These are called *states of nature.*
2. Develop a list of possible *alternatives,* one of which may be to do nothing.
3. Determine or estimate the *payoff* associated with each alternative for every possible future condition.
4. If possible, estimate the *likelihood* of each possible future condition.
5. Evaluate alternatives according to some *decision criterion* (e.g., maximize expected profit), and select the best alternative.

The information for a decision is often summarized in a **payoff table**, which shows the expected payoffs for each alternative under the various possible states of nature. These tables are helpful in choosing among alternatives because they facilitate comparison of alternatives. Consider the payoff table below, which illustrates a capacity planning problem.

Payoff table

Table showing the expected payoffs for each alternative in every possible state of nature.

	Possible future demand		
Alternatives	**Low**	**Moderate**	**High**
Small facility	$10★	$10	$10
Medium facility	7	12	12
Large facility	(4)	2	16

★Present value in $ millions.

The payoffs are shown in the body of the table. In this instance, the payoffs are in terms of present values, which represent equivalent current dollar values of expected future income minus costs. This is a convenient measure because it places all alternatives on a comparable basis. We see in the table that if a small facility is built, the payoff will be the same for all three possible states of nature. For a medium facility, low demand will have a present value of $7 million, whereas both moderate and high demand will have present values of $12 million. A large facility will have a loss of $4 million if demand is low, a present value of $2 million if demand is moderate, and a present value of $16 million if demand is high.

The problem for the decision maker is to select one of the alternatives, taking the present values into account.

Evaluation of the alternatives differs depending on the degree of certainty associated with the possible future conditions. Again, there are three possibilities to consider: complete certainty, risk, and uncertainty.

Decision Making under Certainty

When it is known for certain which one of the possible future conditions will actually happen, the decision is usually relatively straightforward: Simply choose the alternative that has the best payoff under that state of nature. This is illustrated in Example 1.

Example 1

Determine the best alternative in the preceding payoff table, if it is known with certainty that demand will be: (*a*) low, (*b*) moderate, (*c*) high.

Solution

Choose the alternative with the highest payoff. Thus, if we know demand will be low, we would elect to build the small facility and realize a payoff of $10 million. If we know demand will be moderate, a medium factory would yield the highest payoff ($12 million versus either $10 or $2 million). For high demand, a large facility would provide the highest payoff.

Although complete certainty is rare in such situations, exercises such as the preceding one do provide some perspective on the analysis. Moreover, in some instances, there may be an opportunity to consider allocation of funds to research efforts, which may reduce or remove some of the uncertainty surrounding the states of nature.

Decision Making under Uncertainty

At the opposite extreme is complete uncertainty: no information is available on how likely the various states of nature are. Under those conditions, four possible decision criteria are *maximin, maximax, Laplace,* and *minimax regret.* These approaches can be defined as follows:

> **Maximin**
>
> The best of the worst possible payoffs for each alternative.

> **Maximax**
>
> The alternative with the best possible payoff.

> **Laplace**
>
> The best average payoff of any of the alternatives.

> **Minimax regret**
>
> The best of the worst regrets for each alternative.

Maximin—Determine the worst possible *payoff* for each alternative, and then choose the alternative that has the "best worst."

Maximax—Determine the best possible payoff, and choose the alternative with that payoff.

Laplace—Determine the average payoff for each alternative, and choose the alternative with the best average.

Minimax regret—Determine the worst *regret* for each alternative, and choose the alternative with the "best worst."

The next two examples illustrate these decision criteria.

Example 2

Referring to the preceding payoff table, determine which alternative would be chosen under each of these strategies:

a.   Maximin

b.   Maximax

c.   Laplace

Solution

a.   The worst payoffs for the alternatives are:

Small facility: $10 million
Medium facility: $7 million
Large facility: −$4 million

Hence, since $10 million is the best, choose to build the small facility using the maximin strategy.

b.   The best payoffs are:

Small facility: $10
Medium facility: 12
Large facility: 16

The best overall payoff is the $16 million in the third row. Hence, the maximax criterion leads to building a large facility.

c.   For the Laplace criterion, first find the row totals, and then divide each of those amounts by the number of states of nature (three in this case). Thus, we have:

	Row total	Row average
Small facility	30	10.00
Medium facility	31	10.33
Large facility	14	4.67

Since the medium facility has the highest average, it would be chosen under the Laplace criterion.

The maximin approach is essentially a pessimistic one in that it takes into account only the worst possible outcome for each alternative. The actual outcome may not be as bad as that, but this approach establishes a "guaranteed minimum."

The maximax approach is an optimistic, "go for it" strategy; it does not take into account any payoff other than the best.

The Laplace approach treats the states of nature as equally likely.

Determine which alternative would be chosen using a minimax regret approach to the capacity planning program.

Example 3

Solution

The first step in this approach is to prepare a table of **opportunity losses,** or **regrets**. To do this, subtract every payoff *in each column* from the largest positive payoff in that column. For instance, in the first column, the largest positive payoff is 10, so each of the three numbers in that column must be subtracted from 10. Going down the column, the regrets will be 10 − 10 = 0, 10 − 7 = 3, and 10 − (−4) = 14. In the second column, the largest positive payoff is 12. Subtracting each payoff from 12 yields 2,

(continued)

Regret

The difference between a given payoff and the best payoff in the same column.

Example 3

(concluded)

0, and 10. In the third column, 16 is the largest payoff. The regrets are 6, 4, and 0. These results are summarized in a regret table:

	Regrets			
Alternatives	**Low**	**Moderate**	**High**	**Worst**
Small facility	0	2	6	6
Medium facility	3	0	4	4
Large facility	14	10	0	14

The second step is to identify the worst regret for each alternative. For the first alternative, the worst is 6; for the second, the worst is 4; and for the third, the worst is 14.

The best of these "worsts" would be chosen using minimax regret. The lowest regret is 4, which is for a medium facility. Hence, that alternative would be chosen.

Solved Problem 6 at the end of the chapter illustrates decision making under uncertainty when the payoffs represent costs.

The main weakness of these approaches (except for Laplace) is that they do not take into account *all* of the payoffs. Instead, they focus on the worst or best, and so they lose some information. The weakness of Laplace is that it treats all states of nature as equally likely. Still, for a given set of circumstances, each has certain merits that can be helpful to a decision maker.

Decision Making under Risk

Between the two extremes of certainty and uncertainty lies the case of risk: the probability of occurrence for each state of nature can be estimated. (Note that because the states are mutually exclusive and collectively exhaustive, these probabilities must add to 1.00.) A widely used approach under such circumstances is the *expected monetary value criterion*. The expected value is computed for each alternative, and the one with the highest expected value is selected. The expected value is the sum of the payoffs for an alternative where each payoff is *weighted* by the probability for the relevant state of nature. Thus, the approach is:

Expected monetary value (EMV)

The best expected value among the alternatives.

Expected monetary value criterion (EMV)—Determine the expected payoff of each alternative, and choose the alternative that has the best expected payoff.

Example 4

▌

Using the expected monetary value criterion, identify the best alternative for the previous payoff table for these probabilities: low = .30, moderate = .50, and high = .20.

Solution

Find the expected value of each alternative by multiplying the probability of occurrence for each state of nature by the payoff for that state of nature and summing them:

$$EV_{small} = .30(\$10) + .50(\$10) + .20(\$10) = \$10$$
$$EV_{medium} = .30(\$7) + .50(\$12) + .20(\$12) = \$10.5$$
$$EV_{large} = .30(-\$4) + .50(\$2) + .20(\$16) = \$ 3$$

Hence, choose the medium facility because it has the highest expected value.

The expected monetary value approach is most appropriate when a decision maker is neither risk-averse nor risk-seeking, but instead is risk-neutral. Typically, well-established organizations with numerous decisions of this nature tend to use expected value since it provides an indication of the long-run, average payoff. That is, the expected-value amount (e.g., $10.5 million in the last example) is not an actual payoff but an expected or average amount that would be approximated if a large number of identical decisions were to be made. Hence, if a decision maker applies this criterion to a large number of similar decisions, the expected payoff for the total will equal the sum of the individual expected payoffs.

DECISION TREES

A **decision tree** is a schematic representation of the alternatives available to a decision maker and their possible consequences. The term gets its name from the treelike appearance of the diagram (see Figure 2S–1). Although tree diagrams can be used in place of a payoff table, they are particularly useful for analyzing situations that involve *sequential* decisions. For instance, a manager may initially decide to build a small facility only to discover that demand is much higher than anticipated. In this case, the manager may then be called upon to make a second decision on whether to expand or build an additional facility.

A decision tree is composed of a number of *nodes* that have *branches* emanating from them (see Figure 2S–1). Square nodes are used to denote decision points, and circular nodes are used to denote chance events. The tree is read from left to right. Branches leaving square nodes represent alternatives; branches leaving circular nodes represent chance events (i.e., the possible states of nature).

After the tree has been drawn, it is analyzed from *right to left;* that is, starting with the last decision that might be made. For each decision, choose the alternative that will yield the greatest return. If chance events follow a decision, choose the alternative that has the highest expected monetary value (or lowest expected loss).

> **Decision tree**
> A schematic representation of the available alternatives and their possible consequences.

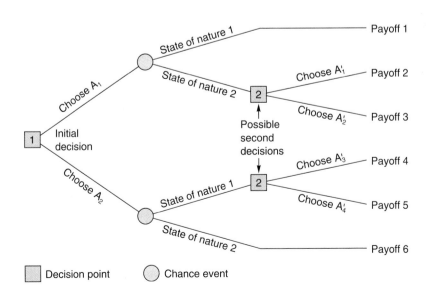

Figure 2S–1

Format of a decision tree

Example 5

Analyze the decision tree below and determine which initial alternative (build small or build large) should be chosen in order to maximize expected monetary value.

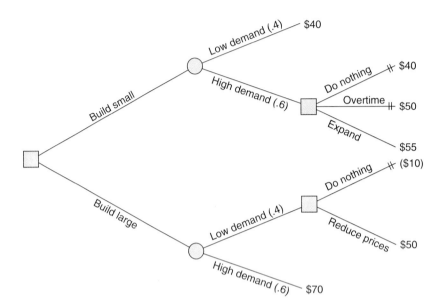

Solution

The dollar amounts at the branch ends indicate the estimated payoffs (usually in terms of present value) if the sequence of chance events and decisions that is traced back to the initial decision occurs. For example, if the initial decision is to build a small facility and it turns out that demand is low, the expected value will be $40 (thousand). Similarly, if a small facility is built, demand turns out high, and a later decision is made to expand, the expected value will be $55. The figures in parentheses on branches leaving the chance nodes indicate the probabilities of those states of nature. Hence, the probability of low demand is .4, and the probability of high demand is .6.

   Analyze the decisions from right to left:

1. Determine which alternative would be selected for each possible second decision. For a small facility with high demand, there are three choices: *do nothing, work overtime,* and *expand.* Since *expand* has the highest payoff, it would be chosen. Indicate this by placing a double slash through each of the other alternatives. Similarly, for a large facility with low demand, there would be two choices: *do nothing* and *reduce prices. Reduce prices* would be chosen because it has the higher expected value, so a double slash is placed on the other branch.

2. Determine the product of the chance probabilities and their respective payoffs for the remaining branches:

Build small		
Low demand	.4($40) =	$16
High demand	.6($55) =	33
Build large		
Low demand	.4($50) =	20
High demand	.6($70) =	42

3. Determine the expected value of each initial alternative:

Build small: $16 + $33 = $49
Build large: $20 + $42 = $62

Hence, the choice should be to build the large facility because it has a larger expected value than the small facility.

EXPECTED VALUE OF PERFECT INFORMATION

In certain situations it is possible to ascertain which state of nature will actually occur in the future. For instance, the choice of location for a restaurant may weigh heavily on whether a new highway will be constructed or whether a zoning permit will be issued. A decision maker may have probabilities for these states of nature; however, it may be possible to delay a decision until it is clear which state of nature will occur. This might involve taking an option to buy the land. If the state of nature is favorable, the option can be exercised; if the state is unfavorable, the option can be allowed to expire. The question to consider is whether the cost of the option will be less than the expected gain due to delaying the decision (i.e., the expected payoff *above* the expected value). The expected gain is the *expected value of perfect information,* or EVPI.

> **Expected value of perfect information**—the difference between the expected payoff under certainty and the expected payoff under conditions of risk.

Expected value of perfect information

The difference between the expected payoff under certainty and the expected payoff under risk.

Other possible ways of obtaining perfect information depend somewhat on the nature of the decision being made. For example, information about consumer preferences might come from market research; additional information about a product could come from product testing; legal experts might be called on; and so on.

There are two ways to determine the EVPI. One is to compute the expected payoff under certainty and subtract the expected payoff under risk. That is,

$$\begin{array}{l} \text{Expected value of} \\ \text{perfect information} \end{array} = \begin{array}{l} \text{Expected payoff} \\ \text{under certainty} \end{array} - \begin{array}{l} \text{Expected payoff} \\ \text{under risk.} \end{array} \qquad \textbf{(2S–1)}$$

Using the information from Example 4, determine the expected value of perfect information using Formula 2S–1.

Example 6

▮

Solution

First, compute the expected payoff under certainty. To do this, identify the best payoff under each state of nature. Then combine these by weighting each payoff by the probability of that state of nature and adding the amounts. Thus, the best payoff under low demand is $10, the best under moderate demand is $12, and the best under high demand is $16. The expected payoff under certainty is, then:

.30($10) + .50($12) + .20($16) = $12.2

(continued)

Example 6

(concluded)

The expected payoff under risk, as computed in Example 4, is $10.5. The EVPI is the difference between these:

EVPI = $12.2 − $10.5 = $1.7

This figure indicates the upper limit on the amount the decision maker should be willing to spend to obtain perfect information in this case. Thus, if the cost equals or exceeds this amount, the decision maker would be better off not spending additional money and simply going with the alternative that has the highest expected payoff.

A second approach is to use the regret table to compute the EVPI. To do this, find the expected regret for each alternative. The minimum expected regret is equal to the EVPI.

Example 7

▮

Determine the expected value of perfect information for the capacity-planning problem using the expected regret approach.

Solution

Using information from Examples 2, 3, and 4, we can compute the expected regret for each alternative. Thus:

Small facility	.30(0) + .50(2) + .20(6) = 2.2
Medium facility	.30(3) + .50(0) + .20(4) = 1.7[minimum]
Large facility	.30(14) + .50(10) + .20(0) = 9.2

The lowest expected regret is 1.7, which is associated with the second alternative. Hence, the EVPI is $1.7 million, which agrees with the previous example using the other approach.

SENSITIVITY ANALYSIS

Generally speaking, in a decision problem such as the kind being discussed here, both the payoffs and the probabilities are estimated values. Consequently, it can be useful for the decision maker to have some indication of how sensitive the choice of an alternative is to changes in one or more of these values. Unfortunately, it is impossible to consider all possible combinations of every variable in a typical problem. Nevertheless, there are certain things a decision maker can do to judge the sensitivity of probability estimates.

Sensitivity analysis

Determining the range of probability for which an alternative has the best expected payoff.

Sensitivity analysis provides a range of probability over which the choice of alternative would remain the same. The approach illustrated here is useful when there are two states of nature and involves constructing a graph and then using algebra to determine a range of probabilities for which a given solution is best. In effect, the graph provides a visual indication of the range of probability over which the various alternatives are optimal, and the algebra provides exact values of the endpoints of the ranges. The following example illustrates the procedure.

Given the following table, determine the range of probability for state of nature #2, that is, $P(2)$, for which each alternative is optimal under the expected-value approach.

Example 8

		State of nature	
		#1	#2
	A	4	12
Alternative	B	16	2
	C	12	8

Solution

First, plot each alternative relative to $P(2)$. To do this, plot the #1 value on the left side of the graph and the #2 value on the right side. For instance, for alternative A, plot 4 on the left side of the graph and 12 on the right side. Then connect these two points with a straight line. The three alternatives are plotted on the graph as shown below.

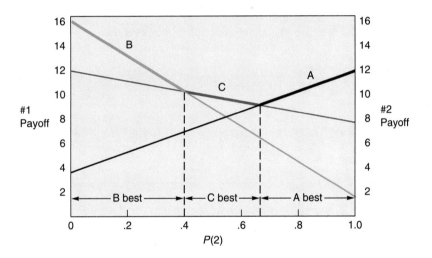

The graph shows the range of values of $P(2)$ over which each alternative is optimal. Thus, we see that for low values of $P(2)$ [and thus high values of $P(1)$, since $P(1) + P(2) = 1.0$], alternative B will have the highest expected value; for intermediate values of $P(2)$, alternative C is best; and for higher values of $P(2)$, alternative A is best.

For exact values of the ranges, we need to determine where the upper parts of the lines intersect. Note that at the intersections, the two alternatives represented by the lines would be equivalent in terms of expected value. Hence, the decision maker would be indifferent between the two at that point. To determine the intersections, we must obtain the equation of each line. This is relatively simple to do. Since these are straight lines, they have the form $y = a + bx$, where a is the y-intercept value at the left axis, b is the slope of the line, and x is $P(2)$. Slope is defined as the change in y for a one-unit change in x. In this type of problem, the distance between the two vertical

(continued)

Example 8

(concluded)

axes is 1.0. Consequently, the slope of each line is equal to the right-hand value minus the left-hand value. The slopes and equations are:

	#1	#2	Slope	Equation
A	4	12	$12 - 4 = +8$	$4 + 8P(2)$
B	16	2	$2 - 16 = -14$	$16 - 14P(2)$
C	12	8	$8 - 12 = -4$	$12 - 4P(2)$

From the graph, we can see that alternative B is best from $P(2) = 0$ to the point where that straight line intersects the straight line of alternative C, and that begins the region where C is better. To find that point, we can solve for the value of $P(2)$ at their intersection. This requires setting the two equations equal to each other and solving for $P(2)$. Thus,

$$16 - 14P(2) = 12 - 4P(2)$$

Rearranging terms gives us

$$4 = 10P(2)$$

Solving, we obtain $P(2) = .40$. Thus, alternative B is best from $P(2) = 0$ up to $P(2) = .40$. B and C are equivalent at $P(2) = .40$.

Alternative C is best from that point until its line intersects alternative A's line. To find that intersection, we set those two equations equal and solve for $P(2)$. Thus,

$$4 + 8P(2) = 12 - 4P(2)$$

Rearranging terms, we have

$$12P(2) = 8$$

Solving, we obtain $P(2) = .67$. Thus, alternative C is best from $P(2) > .40$ up to $P(2) = .67$, where A and C are equivalent. For values of $P(2)$ greater than .67 up to $P(2) = 1.0$, A is best.

Note: If a problem calls for ranges with respect to $P(1)$, find the $P(2)$ ranges as above, and then subtract each $P(2)$ from 1.00 (e.g., .40 becomes .60, and .67 becomes .33).

SUMMARY

Decision making is an integral part of operations management. Successful decision making comprises a number of steps, the first of which is to carefully define the problem.

Decision theory is a general approach to decision making that is useful in many different aspects of operations management. Decision theory provides a framework for analysis of decisions. It includes a number of different techniques that can be classified according to the degree of uncertainty associated with a particular decision problem. Two visual tools useful for analyzing some decision problems are decision trees and graphical sensitivity analysis.

KEY TERMS

bounded rationality, 72
certainty, 72
decision tree, 77

expected monetary value
(EMV), 76

The solved problems in this chapter refer to the following payoff table:

SOLVED PROBLEMS

		New bridge built	No new bridge
Alternative locations	A	1	14
for new	B	2	10
warehouse	C	4	6

Problem

1. Assume the payoffs represent profits. Determine the alternative that would be chosen under each of these decision criteria:
   a. Maximin.
   b. Maximax.
   c. Laplace.

Solution

	New bridge	No new bridge	Maximin (worst)	Maximax (best)	Laplace (average)
A	1	14	1	14[best]	15 ÷ 2 = 7.5[best]
B	2	10	2	10	12 ÷ 2 = 6
C	4	6	4[best]	6	10 ÷ 2 = 5

Thus, the alternatives chosen would be C under maximin, A under maximax, and A under Laplace.

Problem

2. Using graphical sensitivity analysis, determine the range of probability for no new bridge for which each alternative would be optimal.

Solution

Plot a straight line for each alternative. Do this by plotting the payoff for new bridge on the left axis and the payoff for no new bridge on the right axis and then connecting the two points. Each line represents the expected profit for

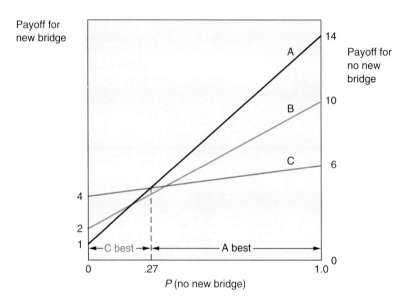

an alternative for the entire range of probability of no new bridge. Because the lines represent expected profit, the line that is highest for a given value of P(no new bridge) is optimal. Thus, from the graph, we can see that for low values of this probability, alternative C is best, and for high values, alternative A is best (B is never the highest line, so it is never optimal).

The dividing line between the ranges where C is optimal and where A is optimal occurs where the two lines intersect. To find that probability, we must first formulate the equation for each line. To do this, let the intersection with the left axis be the y-intercept; the slope equals the right-side payoff minus the left-side payoff. Thus, for C we have $4 + (6 − 4)P$, which is $4 + 2P$. For A we have $1 + (14 − 1)P$, which is $1 + 13P$. Setting these two equal to each other, we can solve for P:

$$4 + 2P = 1 + 13P$$

Solving, $P = .27$. Therefore, the ranges for P(no new bridge) are:

A: $.27 < P ≤ 1.00$
B: never optimal
C: $0 ≤ P < .27$

Problem

3. Using the information in the payoff table, develop a table of regrets, and then:
   a. Determine the alternative that would be chosen under minimax regret.
   b. Determine the expected value of perfect information using the regret table, assuming that the probability of a new bridge being built is .60.

Solution

To obtain the regrets, subtract all payoffs in each column from the best payoff in the column. The regrets are:

	New bridge	No new bridge
A	3	0
B	2	4
C	0	8

a. Minimax regret involves finding the worst regret for each alternative and then choosing the alternative that has the "best" worst. Thus, A would be chosen:

	Worst
A	3[best]
B	4
C	8

b. Once the regret table has been developed, the EVPI can be computed as the smallest expected regret. Since the probability of a new bridge is given as .60, we can deduce that the probability of no new bridge is $1.00 - .60 = .40$. The expected regrets are:

A: $.60(3) + .40(0) = 1.80$
B: $.60(2) + .40(4) = 2.80$
C: $.60(0) + .40(8) = 3.20$

Hence, the EVPI is 1.80.

Problem

4. Using the probabilities of .60 for a new bridge and .40 for no new bridge, compute the expected value of each alternative in the payoff table, and identify the alternative that would be selected under the expected-value approach.

Solution

A: $.60(1) + .40(14) = 6.20$[best]
B: $.60(2) + .40(10) = 5.20$
C: $.60(4) + .40(6) = 4.80$

Problem

5. Compute the EVPI using the information from the previous problem.

Solution

Using Formula 2–1, the EVPI is the expected payoff under certainty minus the maximum expected value. The expected payoff under certainty involves multiplying the best payoff in each column by the column probability and then summing those amounts. The best payoff in the first column is 4, and the best in the second is 14. Thus,

$$\text{Expected payoff under certainty} = .60(4) + .40(14) = 8.00$$

The expected value of perfect information is then

$$\text{EVPI} = 8.00 - 6.20 = 1.80$$

(Note that this agrees with the result obtained in Solved Problem 3b.)

Problem

6. Suppose now that the values in the payoff table represent *costs* instead of profits.
    a. Determine the choice that would be made under each of these strategies: maximin, *minimin,* and Laplace.
    b. Develop the regret table, and identify the alternative that would be chosen using minimax regret. Then find the EVPI if P(new bridge) = .60.
    c. Using sensitivity analysis, determine the range of P(no new bridge) for which each alternative would be optimal.
    d. If P(new bridge) = .60 and P(no new bridge) = .40, find the alternative that would be chosen to minimize expected cost.

Solution

a. Note: *Minimin* is the reverse of maximax; for costs minimin identifies the lowest (best) cost.

	New bridge	No new bridge	Maximin (worst)	Minimin (best)	Laplace (average)
A	1	14	14	1[best]	15 ÷ 2 = 7.5
B	2	10	10	2	12 ÷ 2 = 6
C	4	6	6[best]	4	10 ÷ 2 = 5[best]

b. Develop the regret table by subtracting the *lowest cost* in each column from each of the values in the column. (Note that none of the values are negative.)

	New bridge	No new bridge	Worst
A	0	8	8
B	1	4	4
C	3	0	3[best]

$$\text{EVPI} = .60(3) + .40(0) = 1.80$$

c. The graph is identical to that shown in Solved Problem 2. However, because the lines now represent expected *costs,* the best alternative for a given value of P(no new bridge) is the *lowest* line. Hence, for very low values of P(no new bridge), A is best; for intermediate values, B is best; and for high values, C is best. We can set the equations of A and B, and B and C, equal to each other in order to determine the values of P(no new bridge) at their intersections. Thus,

A–B: $1 + 13P = 2 + 8P$; solving, $P = .20$
B–C: $2 + 8P = 4 + 2P$; solving, $P = .33$

Hence, the ranges are:

A best: $0 \leq P < .20$
B best: $.20 < P < .33$
C best: $.33 < P \leq 1.00$

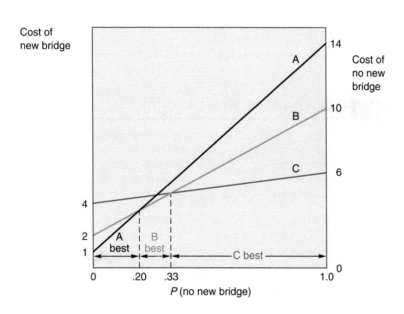

d. Expected-value computations are the same whether the values represent costs or profits. Hence, the expected payoffs for costs are the same as the expected payoffs for profits that were computed in Solved Problem 4. However, now we want the alternative that has the *lowest* expected payoff rather than the one with the highest payoff. Consequently, alternative C is the best because its expected payoff is the lowest of the three.

---

1. What is the chief role of the operations manager?
2. Outline the steps in the decision-making process.
3. Explain the term *bounded rationality.*
4. Explain the term *suboptimization.*

DISCUSSION AND REVIEW QUESTIONS

5. What are some of the reasons that poor decisions are made?
6. What information is contained in a payoff table?
7. What is sensitivity analysis, and how can it be useful to a decision maker?
8. Contrast maximax and maximin decision strategies. Under what circumstances would one rather than the other be appropriate?
9. Under what circumstances is expected monetary value appropriate as a decision criterion? When isn't it appropriate?
10. What is a systems approach, and how can failure to use this approach lead to poor decisions?
11. Explain or define each of these terms:
    a. Laplace criterion.
    b. Minimax regret.
    c. Expected value.
    d. Expected value of perfect information.
12. What information does a decision maker need to do an expected-value analysis of a problem? What options are available to the decision maker if the probabilities of the states of nature are unknown? Can you think of a way sensitivity analysis might be used in such a case?
13. Explain why a systems approach to productivity improvements would be beneficial and why, without that perspective, actual improvements might end up being less than anticipated.

PROBLEMS

1. A small building contractor has recently experienced two successive years in which work opportunities exceeded the firm's capacity. The contractor must now make a decision on capacity for next year. He has estimated profits under each of the two states of nature he believes might occur, as shown in the table below. Which alternative should be selected if the decision criterion is:
    a. Maximax?
    b. Maximin?
    c. Laplace?
    d. Minimax regret?

| | Next year's demand | |
Alternative	Low	High
Do nothing	$50★	$60
Expand	20	80
Subcontract	40	70

★Profit in $ thousands.

2. (Refer to the previous problem.) Suppose after a certain amount of discussion, the contractor finds he is able to subjectively assess the probabilities of low and high demand: $P(low) = .3$ and $P(high) = .7$.
    a. Determine the expected profit of each alternative. Which alternative is best? Why?
    b. Analyze the problem using a decision tree. Show the expected profit of each alternative on the tree.
    c. Compute the expected value of perfect information. How could the contractor use this knowledge?

3. (Refer to the previous two problems.) Construct a graph that will enable you to perform sensitivity analysis on the problem. Over what range of P(high) would the alternative of doing nothing be best? Expand? Subcontract?

4. A firm that plans to expand its product line must decide whether to build a small or a large facility to produce the new products. If it builds a small facility and demand turns out to be low, the net present value after deducting for building costs will be $400,000. If demand turns out to be high, the firm can either maintain the small facility or expand it. Expansion would have a net present value of $450,000, and maintaining the small facility would have a net present value of $50,000.

   If a large facility is built and demand is high, the estimated net present value is $800,000. If demand turns out to be low, the net present value will be −$10,000.

   The probability that demand will be high is estimated to be .60, and the probability of low demand is estimated to be .40.
   a. Analyze using a tree diagram.
   b. Compute the EVPI. How could this information be used?

5. (Refer to the previous problem.) Determine the range over which each alternative would be best in terms of the value of P(demand low).

6. The lease of Theme Park, Inc., is about to expire, and management must decide whether to renew the lease for another 10 years or to relocate near the site of a proposed motel. The town planning board is currently debating the merits of granting approval to the motel. A consultant has estimated the net present values of Theme Park's two alternatives under each state of nature as shown below. What course of action would you recommend using:
   a. Maximax?
   b. Maximin?
   c. Laplace?
   d. Minimax regret?

Options	Motel approved	Motel rejected
Renew	$ 500,000	$4,000,000
Relocate	5,000,000	100,000

7. (Refer to the previous problem.) Suppose that, after some thought, the manager has decided that there is a .35 probability that the motel's application will be approved.
   a. If the manager uses maximum expected monetary value as the decision criterion, which alternative should be chosen?
   b. Represent this problem in the form of a decision tree.
   c. If the manager has been offered the option of a temporary lease while the town planning board considers the motel's application, would you advise the manager to sign the lease? The lease will cost $24,000.

8. Construct a graph that can be used for sensitivity analysis for the preceding problem.
   a. How sensitive is the solution to the problem in terms of the probability estimate of .35?
   b. Suppose that, after consulting with a member of the town planning board, management decides that an estimate of approval is approximately .45. How sensitive is the solution to this revised estimate? Explain.
   c. Suppose the manager is confident of all the estimated payoffs except the $4 million. If the probability of approval is .35, for what range of payoff for Renew/rejected will the alternative selected using maximum expected value remain the same?

9. A firm must decide whether to construct a small, medium, or large stamping plant. A consultant's report indicates a .20 probability that demand will be low and an .80 probability that demand will be high.

   If the firm builds a small facility and demand turns out to be low, the net present value will be $42 million. If demand turns out to be high, the firm can either subcontract and realize the net present value of $42 million or expand greatly for a net present value of $48 million.

   A medium-size facility could be built as a hedge: if demand turns out to be low, its net present value is estimated at $22 million; if demand turns out to be high, the firm could do nothing and realize a net present value of $46 million, or it could expand and realize a net present value of $50 million.

   If the firm builds a large facility and demand is low, the net present value will be −$20 million, whereas high demand will result in a net present value of $72 million.

   a.   Analyze this problem using a decision tree.
   b.   What would the maximin alternative be?
   c.   Compute the EVPI and interpret it.
   d.   Perform sensitivity analysis on $P(high)$.

10. A manager must decide how many machines of a certain type to buy. The machines will be used to fill demand for a new gear. The manager has narrowed the decision down to two alternatives: buy one machine or buy two. If only one machine is purchased and demand is more than it can handle, a second machine can be purchased at a later time. However, the cost per machine would be lower if the two machines were to be purchased at the same time.

   The estimated probability of low demand is .30, and the estimated probability of high demand is .70.

   The net present value associated with the purchase of two machines initially is $75,000 if demand is low and $130,000 if demand is high.

   The net present value for one machine and low demand is $90,000. If demand is high, there are three options. One option would be to do nothing, and it would have a net present value of $90,000. A second option would be to subcontract; it would have a net present value of $110,000. The third option would be to purchase a second machine. This option would have a net present value of $100,000.

   How many machines should the manager purchase initially? Use a decision tree to analyze this problem.

11. Determine the course of action that has the highest EMV for the accompanying tree diagram. (See diagram on the following page.)

12. Space engineers have three alternative designs from which to choose the configuration of a component for an unmanned space shot. The space vehicle is likely to encounter one of four different conditions, which have probabilities of occurrence as listed in the following payoff table along with the payoffs for each combination of design and state of nature. Additional data from previous flights are available but will require additional expenditure to analyze. However, the project director is quite confident that analysis of the data will clearly indicate which state of nature will be encountered. What amount would be justified for the data analysis?

	States of nature			
	A	**B**	**C**	**D**
Probability:	.3	.4	.2	.1
Design				
001	20★	10	10	0
002	15	10	0	40
003	10	20	30	30

★ ($100).

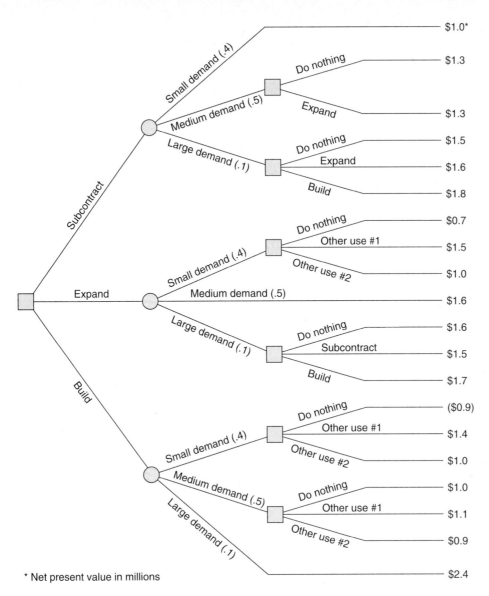

(Diagram is used for Problem 11 on page 90.)

* Net present value in millions

13. The director of social services of a certain county has just learned of additional infor-mation requirements mandated by the state. This will place an additional burden on the agency. The director has identified three acceptable alternatives to handle the in-creased work load. One is to reassign present staff members, another is to hire and train two new workers, and the third is to redesign current practice so that workers can readily collect the information with little additional effort. An unknown factor is the caseload for the coming year, during which time the new data will be collected on a trial basis. The estimated costs for various options and caseloads are shown in the table that follows:

	Caseload		
	Moderate	High	Very high
Reassign staff	$50★	60	85
New staff	60	60	60
Redesign collection	40	50	90

★Cost in thousands

Assuming that probabilities of various caseloads are unreliable, based on past experience, what decision would be appropriate using each of the following criteria?
a.   Maximin.
b.   Maximax.
c.   Minimax regret.
d.   Laplace.

14. After contemplating the caseload question, the director mentioned in the previous problem has decided that reasonable caseload probabilities are .10 for moderate, .30 for high, and .60 for very high.
a.   Which alternative will yield the minimum expected cost?
b.   Construct a decision tree for this problem. Indicate the expected costs for the three decision branches.
c.   Determine the expected value of perfect information using an opportunity loss table.

15. Suppose the director of social services will have the option of hiring an additional staff member if one staff member is hired initially and the caseload turns out to be high or very high. Under that plan, the first entry in row 2 of the cost table (see Problem 13) will be 40 instead of 60, the second entry will be 75, and the last entry will be 80. Assume the caseload probabilities are as noted in Problem 14. Construct a decision tree that shows the sequential nature of this decision, and determine which alternative will minimize expected cost.

16. A manager has compiled estimated profits for various alternative courses of action but is reluctant to assign probabilities to the states of nature. The payoff table is:

		State of nature	
		#1	#2
	A	20	140
Alternative	B	120	80
	C	100	40

a.   Plot the expected-value lines on a graph.
b.   Is there any alternative that would never be appropriate in terms of maximizing expected profit? Explain on the basis of your graph.
c.   For what range of $P(2)$ would alternative A be the best choice if the goal is to maximize expected profit?
d.   For what range of $P(1)$ would alternative A be the best choice if the goal is to maximize expected profit?

17. Repeat all parts of the preceding question assuming the values in the payoff table are estimated *costs* and the goal is to minimize expected costs.

18. The research staff of a marketing agency has assembled the following payoff table of estimated profits:

		Receive contract	Not receive contract
	#1	10	−2
	#2	8	3
Proposal	#3	5	5
	#4	0	7

Relative to the probability of not receiving the contract, determine the range of probability for which each of the proposals would maximize expected profit.

19. Given this payoff table:

State of nature

		#1	#2
	A	120	20
Alternative	B	60	40
	C	10	110
	D	90	90

a. Determine the range of $P(1)$ for which each alternative would be best, treating the payoffs as profits.

b. Answer part *a* treating the payoffs as costs.

SELECTED BIBLIOGRAPHY

Bierman, Harold; Charles P. Bonini; and Warren H. Hausman. *Quantitative Analysis for Business Decisions*. 8th ed. Homewood, Ill.: Richard D. Irwin, 1991.

Eppen, G. D.; F. J. Gould; and C. P. Schmidt. *Introductory Management Science*. 2nd ed. Englewood Cliffs, N.J.: Prentice Hall, 1987.

Levin, Richard I.; Charles A. Kirkpatrick; and David S. Rubin. *Quantitative Approaches to Management*. 5th ed. New York: McGraw-Hill, 1982.

Stevenson, William J. *Introduction to Management Science*. 2nd ed. Homewood, Ill.: Richard D. Irwin, 1992.

Taylor, Bernard W. *Introduction to Management Science*. 2nd ed. Dubuque, Iowa: Wm. C. Brown, 1986.

Ulvila, J. W., and R. V. Brown. "Decision Analysis Comes of Age." *Harvard Business Review*, September–October 1982, p. 130.

CHAPTER THREE

QUALITY MANAGEMENT

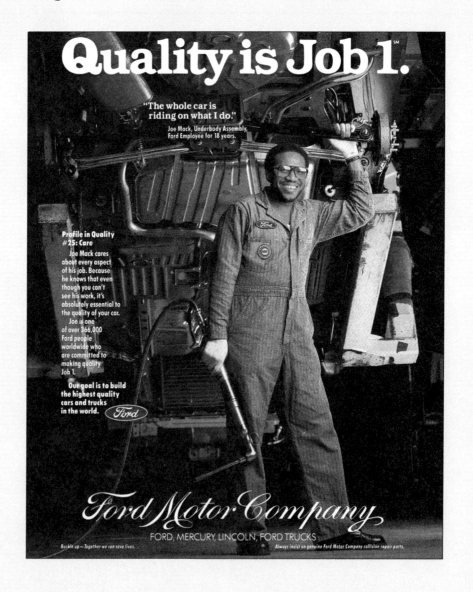

After completing this chapter, you should be able to:

1. Define the term *quality*.

2. Explain why quality is important, and consequences of poor quality.

3. Discuss the determinants of quality.

4. List various costs associated with quality.

5. Contrast the modern approach to quality with the "inspection" approach.

6. Discuss the philosophies of four quality gurus.

7. Discuss total quality management and explain the widespread interest in it.

As the 20th century nears its end, business organizations are involved in what is becoming a "quality revolution." It began in Japan, and has now spread to North America and other parts of the world. It involves an entirely new way of thinking about—and dealing with—quality that encompasses the entire organization. This new approach has been given a variety of names, but the one we shall use is *total quality management,* or TQM.

This chapter is devoted to quality management. It presents a definition of quality, discusses the importance of quality and the determinations of quality, highlights the views of leading experts on modern quality management, and describes the total quality management approach. A later chapter is devoted to quality control procedures and quality improvement.

INTRODUCTION

Quality

The ability of a product or service to consistently meet or exceed customer expectations.

Broadly defined, **quality** refers to the ability of a product or service to consistently meet or exceed customer expectations. Quality means getting what you pay for. Prior to the increased level of competition that Japanese manufacturers injected into the U.S. marketplace in the 1970s and 1980s, customers often got less than they paid for—quality was not uppermost in the minds of U.S. business organizations. Instead, they tended to focus on cost and productivity rather than on quality. It wasn't that quality was *un*important, it's just that it wasn't *very* important.

Partly because of this thinking, foreign companies, many of them Japanese, captured a significant share of the U.S. market. For instance, in the automotive sector, two leading Japanese manufacturers, Honda and Toyota, now account for around 20 percent of the auto sales in the United States. Both Honda and Toyota have built a reputation for quality and reliability in their cars.

This is not to say that all foreign manufacturers, or even all Japanese manufacturers, produce high-quality products, or that no U.S. companies produce high-quality products. However, on the average, there does appear to be a gap between the quality of the typical Japanese product and the typical U.S. product. For example, while many U.S. companies measure poor quality in terms of defectives per *hundred,* many Japanese firms have achieved such a high level of quality that they measure poor quality in terms of defectives per *million* units produced.

Many U.S. companies have changed their views about quality in the last decade, and changed them drastically. Stung by the successes of foreign competitors, they have embraced quality in a big way. They are hiring consultants, sending their people (including top executives) to seminars, and initiating a vast array of quality improvement programs. It is clear that these companies have recognized the importance of quality. They are realizing that quality isn't something that is tacked on as a special feature, but something that is an *integral part* of a product or service.

We begin our study of quality with the basics: the dimensions of quality, the determinants of quality, the costs of quality, and the consequences of poor quality.

QUALITY: THE BASICS

Any serious effort to improve quality must begin with a clear understanding of the meaning of the word *quality.*

THE DIMENSIONS OF QUALITY

The term *quality* is used in a variety of ways. Sometimes it is used to refer to the *grade* of a product, such as "USDA Choice, or "grade A" eggs. At other times, it is used to refer to materials, workmanship, or special features, such as "waterproof," or "subtle aroma." And sometimes it is related to price, as in "cheap" or "expensive."

The implication in these various connotations of quality is that customers value certain aspects of a product or service, and therefore associate those aspects with the quality that they perceive a product or service has. In fact, it may be obvious that from a customer perspective, quality does not pertain to a single aspect of a product or service, but to a number of different *dimensions* of the product or service.

Although they may vary somewhat from product to product, or between a product and a service, generally speaking, the **dimensions of quality** include:

Dimensions of quality

Performance, special features, conformance, reliability, durability, and service after sale.

Performance, which refers to the main characteristics of the product or service.

Special features, which refers to extra characteristics.

Conformance, which refers to how well a product or service corresponds to the customer's expectations.

Reliability, which refers to consistency of performance.

Durability, which refers to the useful life of the product or service.

Service after sale, which refers to handling of complaints, or checking on customer satisfaction.

These dimensions are further described by the examples presented in Table 3–1. When referring to a product, the first four dimensions are sometimes used to judge its *fitness for use* by a customer.

Dimension	(product) Automobile	(service) Automobile repair
1. Performance	everything works, fit and finish ride, handling, grade of materials used	all work done, at agreed price friendliness, courtesy competency, quickness

2. Special features
  safety
  aesthetics
  convenience
 	
  high tech
	
	antilock brakes, airbags
	interior design, soft touch
	placement of gauges and controls
	cellular phone,
	CD player
		
		separate waiting area
		clean work/waiting areas
		location, call when ready
		
		computer diagnostics

3. Reliability	infrequency of breakdowns	work done correctly, ready when promised
4. Durability	useful life in miles, resistance to rust and corrosion	work holds up over time
5. Service after sale	handling of complaints and/or requests for information	handling of complaints

Table 3–1

Examples of quality dimensions for a product and a service

THE DETERMINANTS OF QUALITY

The degree to which a product or a service successfully satisfies its intended purpose has four primary determinants. They are:

1. The design.
2. How well it conforms to the design.
3. Ease of use.
4. Service after delivery.

The design phase is the starting point for the level of quality that is eventually achieved. Design involves decisions regarding specific characteristics of a product or service such as size, shape, location, and so on. **Quality of design** refers to the intention of designers to include or exclude certain features in a product or service. For example, there are many different models of automobiles on the market today. They differ in terms of size, appearance, roominess, fuel economy, comfort, and materials used. These differences reflect choices made by designers that determine the quality of design. Design decisions must take into account customer wants, production or service capabilities, safety and liability (both during production and after delivery), costs, and other similar considerations.

Customer wants may be determined from information provided by marketing, perhaps through the use of consumer surveys or other market research, such as the use of **focus groups**, which consist of consumers brought together to express their views on a product or service (what they like, what they don't like, what they would like to have).

Designers must work closely with representatives of operations to ascertain that designs are manufacturable; that is, that production or service has the equipment, capacity, and skills necessary to produce or provide a particular design.

A poor design can result in difficulties in production or service. For example, materials might be difficult to obtain, specifications difficult to meet, or procedures difficult to follow. Moreover, if a design is inadequate or inappropriate for the circumstances, the best workmanship in the world may not be enough to achieve the desired quality. Thus, we cannot expect a worker to achieve good results if the given tools or procedures are inadequate. Similarly, a superior design usually cannot offset poor workmanship.

Quality of conformance refers to the degree to which goods and services conform to (i.e., *achieve*) the intent of the designers. This is affected by such factors as the capability of equipment used; the skills, training, and motivation of workers; the extent to which the design lends itself to production; the monitoring process to assess conformance; and corrective action-taking (e.g., through problem solving) when necessary.

The determination of quality does not stop once the product or service has been sold or delivered. *Ease of use* and user instructions are important. They increase the chances (but do not guarantee) that a product will be used for its intended purposes and in such a way that it will continue to function properly and safely. (Companies involved in liability litigation often argue that injuries and damages occurred because the user misused the product.) Much the same reasoning can be applied to services. Customers, patients, clients, or other users must be clearly informed on what they should or should not do; otherwise, there is the danger that they will take some action that will adversely affect quality. Some examples include the doctor who fails to specify that a medication should be taken *before* meals and *not*

Quality of design

Intention of designers to include or exclude features in a product or service.

Focus group

In market research, a group of consumers who express their opinions of a product or service.

Quality of conformance

The degree to which goods or services conform to the intent of the designers.

with orange juice, the TV installer who doesn't take the time to show the owner how to properly adjust the color, and the attorney who neglects to inform a client of a deadline for filing a claim.

Much consumer education takes the form of printed instructions and labeling. Thus, it is important for manufacturers to ensure that directions for unpacking, assembling, using, maintaining, and adjusting the product—and what to do if something goes wrong (e.g., flush eyes with water, call a physician, induce vomiting, do not induce vomiting, disconnect set immediately)—are *clearly visible* and *easily understood.*

Products do not always perform as expected, and services do not always yield the desired results, for a variety of reasons. Whatever the reason, it is important from a quality standpoint to remedy the situation—either through recall and repair of the product, adjustment, replacement or buyback, or reevaluation of a service—and then do whatever is necessary to bring the product or service up to standard.

The Consequences of Poor Quality

It is important for management to recognize the different ways in which the quality of a firm's products or services can affect the organization and to take this into account in developing and maintaining a quality assurance program. Some of the major ways that quality affects an organization are:

1. Loss of business.
2. Liability.
3. Productivity.
4. Costs.

A poor design, or defective products or services, can result in *loss of business:* Failure to devote adequate attention to quality can damage the organization's image and lead to a decreased share of the market, in the case of a profit-oriented firm, or increased criticism and/or controls, in the case of a government agency or other nonprofit organization.

> A potentially . . . devastating consequence to the bottom line is the reaction of the consumer who receives a defective or otherwise unsatisfactory product or service. A recent study showed that, while a satisfied customer will tell a few people about his or her experience, a dissatisfied person will tell an average of 19 others.
>
> Unfortunately, the company is usually the last to know of dissatisfaction. People rarely complain directly to the provider of poor quality goods and services. In fact, studies suggest that people usually complain, if at all, to their most immediate contact (e.g., a salesperson or service mangager) and that these complaints are rarely transmitted further. A more common response is simply to switch to a competing product or service. Typically, formal complaints are received from less than 5 percent of dissatisfied customers.   —*Source: The Ernst & Young Quality Improvement Consulting Group,* Total Quality: An Executive's Guide for the 1990s *(Homewood, Ill.: Business One Irwin, 1990), pp. 6–7.*

Organizations must pay special attention to their potential *liability* due to damages or injuries resulting from either faulty design or poor workmanship. This applies to both products and services. Thus, a poorly designed steering arm on a car might cause the driver to lose control of the car, but so could improper assembly of the steering arm. However, the net result is the same. Similarly, a tree surgeon might be called to cable a tree limb. If the limb later falls and causes damage to a neighbor's car, the accident might be traced to a poorly designed procedure for cabling or to improper workmanship. Liability for poor quality has been well established in the courts. An organization's liability costs can often be substantial, especially if large numbers of items are involved, as is the case in the automobile industry, or if potentially widespread injury or damage (e.g., an accident at a nuclear power plant) is involved. Express written warranties as well as implied warranties generally guarantee the product as safe when used as intended. The courts have tended to extend this to uses that are *foreseeable,* even if the use was not the one intended by the producer. In the health care field, medical malpractice claims and insurance costs are contributing to skyrocketing costs and have drawn the attention of both doctors and legislators.

Productivity and quality are often closely related. Poor quality can adversely affect productivity during the manufacturing process if parts are defective and have to be reworked or if an assembler has to try a number of parts before finding one that fits properly. Similarly, poor quality in tools and equipment can lead to injuries and defective output, which must be reworked or scrapped, thereby reducing the amount of usable output for a given amount of input. Conversely, improving and maintaining good quality can have a positive effect on productivity.

Poor quality increases certain *costs* incurred by the organization. These include scrap and rework costs, warranty costs, replacement and repair costs after purchase, and any other costs expended in transportation, inspection in the field, and payments to customers or discounts used to offset the inferior quality. In some instances, the costs can be substantial. Liability claims and legal expenses are perhaps obvious. Other costs can also be substantial. For instance, rework costs involve the salaries of workers and the additional resources needed to perform the rework (e.g., equipment, energy, raw materials). Beyond those costs are such items as inspection of reworked parts, disruption of schedules, the added costs of parts and materials in inventory waiting for reworked parts, and the paperwork needed to keep track of the items until they can be reintegrated into the process. Aside from these out-of-pocket costs are opportunity costs related to lost sales due to dissatisfied customers who switch their business to competitors.

The following section provides further detail on costs associated with quality.

THE COSTS OF QUALITY

Any serious attempt to deal with quality issues must take into account the costs associated with quality. Those costs can be classified into three categories:

> *Failure* costs (internal or external failures).
> *Appraisal* costs.
> *Prevention* costs.

Failure costs

Costs caused by defective parts or products, or faulty services.

Failure costs are incurred by defective parts or products, or faulty services. *Internal failures* are those that are discovered during the production process; *external failures* are those that are discovered after delivery to the customer. Internal failures occur for a variety of reasons, including defective material from vendors, incorrect machine settings, faulty equipment, incorrect methods, incorrect processing, carelessness, and faulty or improper material handling procedures. The costs of internal failures include lost production time, scrap and rework, investigation costs, possible equipment damage, and possible employee injury. External failure causes are defectives or poor service that go undetected by the producer. Resulting costs include warranty work, handling of complaints, replacements, liability/litigation, and loss of customer goodwill. A common rule of thumb about loss of goodwill is this: A satisfied customer tells three or four others, but a dissatisfied customer tells eight or nine others.

Appraisal costs relate to inspection, testing, and other activities intended to uncover defective products or services, or to assure that there are no defectives. Included are the cost of inspectors, testing, test equipment, labs, quality audits, field testing, and the like.

Prevention costs relate to attempts to prevent defects from occurring. They include such costs as planning and administration systems, working with vendors, training, quality control procedures, and extra attention in both the design and production phases to decrease the probability of defective workmanship.

Appraisal costs
Costs of activities designed to ensure quality or uncover defects.

Prevention costs
Costs of preventing defects from occurring.

MODERN QUALITY MANAGEMENT

For a long time, the responsibility for quality in an organization rested with its quality control department. In manufacturing companies, there was heavy reliance on inspection to weed out defectives or to catch mistakes before they got to the customer. In mass production systems, where the high cost of system disruption is to be avoided, emphasis shifted to finding and correcting defectives at the end of the line. Unfortunately, by that time, many defects cannot be found—they are hidden from view, embedded deeply in the product. Not surprisingly, many companies resigned themselves to the fact that a certain percentage of output would be defective in some way. They uncovered what they could, but perfection was a long way off.

During the 1950s and 1960s, efforts in many companies shifted to detecting defects *during* the production process, which helped to eliminate some causes of defects in the production process. Nonetheless, this still focused only on the production part of the process. It usually did not extend to the *design* of either products or processes, nor did it extend to suppliers. Suppliers, for example, were generally regarded as adversaries. Companies often used multiple suppliers, playing one off against another, and there was heavy emphasis on price. Workers under this system were regarded in the same vein as equipment: there to perform a specific job. Decision making was the province of management. The system was autocratic, and top-down, with workers having little, if any, input.

Modern quality management is now evolving to the point where emphasis is on *preventing* mistakes rather than on *finding* and *correcting* them. Moreover, quality is no longer the exclusive domain of the quality control department. Instead, it is the responsibility of everybody in the organization. And suppliers are being treated less as adversaries, and more as partners. In this more enlightened approach, price is only one of several considerations that are taken into account when dealing with suppliers.

These and other aspects of modern quality management have been strongly influenced by several well-known quality "gurus."

QUALITY GURUS

Many individuals have contributed to the current theory and practice of modern quality management. Among the most influential and widely known of these individuals are W. Edwards Deming, J. M. Juran, Philip Crosby, and Kaoru Ishikawa, all of whom have reached a wide range of people through their writing, teaching,

W. Edwards Deming

Joseph Juran

Phillip B. Crosby

and consulting. And because of this, they have been accorded a "guru-like" status by business.

W. Edwards Deming is, perhaps, the senior guru. A statistics professor at New York University in the 1940s, he went to Japan after World War II to assist the Japanese in improving quality and productivity. The Japanese were so impressed that in 1951, after a series of lectures presented by Deming, they established the **Deming Prize**, which is awarded annually to firms that distinguish themselves with quality management programs.

Deming Prize

Prize established by the Japanese and awarded annually to firms that distinguish themselves with quality management programs.

Although Deming was regarded with reverance by the Japanese, he was largely unknown to business leaders in the United States. In fact, he worked with the Japanese for almost 30 years before he gained recognition in his own country. In recent years, U.S. companies have turned their attention to Deming, embraced his philosophy, and requested his assistance in setting up quality improvement programs. By the late 1980s, he was the featured speaker at heavily attended seminars on quality in the United States.

Deming compiled a now-famous list of 14 points he believes are the prescription needed to achieve quality in an organization. They are listed in Table 3–2. His basic message is that the cause of inefficiency and poor quality is the *system,* not the employees, and that it is *management's responsibility* to correct the system in order to achieve desired results. In addition to the 14 points, he stresses the need to reduce variation in output (deviation from a standard). In order to accomplish this, Deming emphasizes the importance of distinguishing between *special causes* of variation (i.e., correctable), and *common causes* of variation (i.e., random).

Joseph Juran, like Deming, taught Japanese manufacturers how to improve on quality, and could be considered a major force in the Japanese success in quality.

Juran views quality as fitness-for-use. He also believes that roughly 80 percent of quality defects are management controllable and, hence, that it is management's responsibility to correct this deficiency. He describes quality management in terms of a *trilogy* that consists of quality planning, quality control, and quality improvement.[1] According to Juran, quality planning is necessary to establish processes *capable* of meeting quality standards; that quality control is necessary in order to know when corrective action is needed; and that quality improvement will help to find

---

[1] J. M. Juran, "The Quality Trilogy," *Quality Progress* 19, no. 8 (August 1986), pp. 19–24.

1. Create constancy of purpose toward improvement of product and service with a plan to become competitive and to stay in business. Decide whom top management is responsible to.

2. Adopt the new philosophy. We are in a new economic age. We can no longer live with commonly accepted levels of delays, mistakes, defective materials, and defective workmanship.

3. Cease dependence on mass inspection. Require, instead, statistical evidence that quality is built in. (*Prevent* defects rather than *detect* defects.)

4. End the practice of awarding business on the basis of price tag. Instead, depend on meaningful measures of quality, along with price. Eliminate suppliers that cannot qualify with statistical evidence of quality.

5. Find problems. It is management's job to work continually on the system (design, incoming materials, composition of material, maintenance, improvement of machine, training, supervision, retraining).

6. Institute modern methods of training on the job.

7. The responsibility of foremen must be changed from sheer numbers to quality . . . [which] will automatically improve productivity. Management must prepare to take immediate action on reports from foremen concerning barriers such as inherent defects, machines not maintained, poor tools, fuzzy operational definitions.

8. Drive out fear, so that everyone may work effectively for the company.

9. Break down barriers between departments. People in research, design, sales, and production must work as a team, to foresee problems of production that may be encountered with various materials and specifications.

10. Eliminate numerical goals, posters, and slogans for the work force, asking for new levels of productivity without providing methods.

11. Eliminate work standards that prescribe numerical quotas.

12. Remove barriers that stand between the hourly worker and his right to pride of workmanship.

13. Institute a vigorous program of education and retraining.

14. Create a structure in top management that will push every day on the above 13 points.

Table 3–2

Deming's 14 points

W. Edwards Deming, *Quality Productivity, and Competitive Position* (Cambridge, Mass.: MIT, Center for Advanced Engineering Study, 1982), pp. 16–17.

better ways of doing things. The essence of Juran's message is the commitment of management to continual improvement.

Philip Crosby, the author of *Quality Is Free,* developed the concept of *zero defects.* He believes that any level of defects is too high, and that management must install programs that help the organization move toward that goal. Among some of his key points are:[2]

1. Top management must demonstrate its commitment to quality and its willingness to give support to achieve good quality.

[2] Philip Crosby, *Quality without Tears: The Art of Hassle-Free Management* (New York: McGraw-Hill, 1984).

Table 3–3	Contributor	Known for
A summary of key contributors to quality management.	Deming	14 points; special and common causes of variation
	Juran	Quality is fitness for use; quality trilogy
	Crosby	Quality is free; zero defects
	Ishikawa	Cause-and-effect diagrams; quality circles

2. Management must be persistent in efforts to achieve good quality.
3. Management must spell out very clearly what it wants in the way of quality and what workers must do to achieve that.
4. Make it (or do it) right the first time.

The idea behind his quality-is-free concept is that the costs of poor quality are much greater than traditionally defined; in fact, they are so great that, rather than costing money, quality improvement saves money—the improvements more than pay for themselves.

Kaoru Ishikawa, the late Japanese quality expert, was strongly influenced by Deming and Juran, although he made significant contributions of his own to quality management. Among his key contributions were the development of cause-and-effect diagrams for quality improvement (described in Chapter 10) and the use of quality circles that involve workers in quality improvement (also described in Chapter 10).

Table 3–3 provides a summary of these important contributors to modern quality management.

The prescriptions offered by these quality gurus form the basis of total quality management.

TOTAL QUALITY MANAGEMENT

Total quality management

A philosophy that involves everyone in an organization in the quest for quality, with customer satisfaction as the driving force.

The term **total quality management (TQM)** refers to an organization-wide effort to achieve quality. It can accurately be described as a *philosophy* about quality that is intended to involve everyone in the organization in a quest for quality. It extends to suppliers as well as to customers. In fact, in TQM, the *customer* is the focal point, and customer satisfaction is the driving force. And total involvement is important. Everyone, from the chief executive officer on down, must be involved and committed.

The TQM approach can be described as follows:

1. Find out what customers want. This might involve the use of surveys, focus groups, interviews, or some other technique that integrates the customer's voice in the decision-making process.
2. Design a product or service that will meet (or exceed) what customers want. Make it easy to use, and easy to produce.
3. Design a production process that facilitates doing the job right the first time. Determine where mistakes are likely to occur and try to prevent them. When mistakes do occur, find out why so that they are less likely to occur again. Strive to "mistake-proof" the process.

4. Keep track of results, and use those to guide improvement in the system. Never stop trying to improve.

5. Extend these concepts to suppliers and to distribution.

Successful TQM programs are built through the dedication and combined efforts of everyone in the organization. As noted, top management must be committed and involved. If they aren't, TQM will become just another fad that quickly dies and fades away.

The preceding description provides a good idea of what TQM is all about, but it doesn't tell the whole story. There are a number of other elements of TQM that are important, including:

1. *Continual improvement.*   The quest for quality and better service to the customer should be a continual, never-ending one. Competitors will seek to provide better service, and customers will come to expect better service. Hence, to cease improvement efforts will very likely lead to loss of competitive advantage and a decreased level of customer satisfaction.

2. *Competitive benchmarking.*   This means identifying companies or other organizations that are the best at something and then modeling your own organization after them. The company need not be in the same line of business as yours. For example, Xerox used the mail order company L. L. Bean to benchmark order filling.

3. *Employee empowerment.*   Giving workers the responsibility for improvements, and the authority to make changes to accomplish them, provides strong motivation for employees, and puts decision making into the hands of those who are closest to the job and have considerable insight into problems and solutions.

4. *Team approach.*   The use of teams for problem solving, and to achieve consensus, takes advantage of group thinking, gets people involved, and promotes a spirit of cooperation and shared values among employees.

5. *Knowledge of tools.*   Everyone in the organization is trained in the use of quality control and improvement tools.

The entire organization must be subject to the search for improved ways of performing; nothing should be regarded as sacred or untouchable. A view that is sometimes helpful is to consider the *internal customers,* and strive to satisfy them. That is, every activity in an organization has one or more "customers" who receive their output. By thinking in terms of what is needed to satisfy these customers, it is very often possible to improve the system, and in doing so, increase the satisfaction of the ultimate customer.

The term **quality at the source** refers to the philosophy of making each worker responsible for the quality of his or her work. This incorporates the notion of "Do it right" as well as the notion of "If it isn't right, fix it." Workers are expected to provide goods or services that meet specifications and to find and correct mistakes that occur. In effect, each worker becomes a quality inspector for his or her work. When the work is passed on to the next operation in the process (the internal cutomer), or, if that step is the last step in the process, to the ultimate customer, the worker is "certifying" that it meets quality standards.

This accomplishes a number of things. One is that it places direct responsibility for quality on the person(s) who directly affect it. Another, it removes the adversarial relationship that often exists between quality control inspectors and production

Quality at the source

The philosophy of making each worker responsible for the quality of his or her work.

READING   SIX-SIGMA QUALITY

Motorola refers to its quality program as **six-sigma quality**, where *sigma* is the standard deviation of a normal distribution, and *six-sigma* quality is an error rate of about 3 defectives per million units. This means that the percentage of the distribution that is more than six standard deviations from the mean of the distribution is 0.0003 percent. In some organizations, an error-free rate of 99 percent is regarded as very good; only one defective in every hundred units. However, consider that at that rate, a high-volume operation such as the U.S. Postal Service would lose or mishandle five million pieces of mail every day. Or suppose that the 99 percent error-free referred to health care. That would mean that one out of every 100 patients was misdiagnosed, or offered the wrong treatment or the wrong prescription. In Motorola's case, the six sigma is a goal the company is striving for; actual defective rates are currently higher. But it serves as a reminder that no matter how good quality is, there is always room for improvement.

Motorola's "six-sigma" quality program is one of the best in the world. Motorola works closely with and trains its suppliers to improve the quality of parts as shown here.

workers. And it motivates workers by giving them control over their work as well as pride in their work.

Suppliers are regarded as partners in the process, and long-term relationships are encouraged. This gives suppliers a vital stake in providing quality goods and services. Suppliers, too, are expected to provide quality at the source, thereby reducing or eliminating the need to inspect deliveries from suppliers.

Quality function deployment is a term used to refer to involving customers in the design stage of new or redesigned products. The idea is to try to match customer requirements with engineering characteristics of a product. To facilitate communication and cooperation among departments, teams that include representatives from manufacturing, marketing, and engineering collaborate on the design. Quality function deployment is described in Chapter 5.

It would be incorrect to think of TQM as merely a collection of techniques. Rather, TQM reflects a different way of viewing the entire way of life of the people in the organization. It is about the *culture* of an organization. To truly reap the benefits of TQM, the culture of an organization must change.

Table 3–3 illustrates the differences in culture of a TQM organization compared to a more traditional organization.

TQM programs are touted as a way for U.S. companies to regain their competitiveness, which is a very worthwhile objective. Nonetheless, TQM programs are not without criticism. Here are some of the major ones:

1. Blind pursuit of TQM programs: overzealous advocates may focus attention on quality even though other priorities may be more important (e.g., responding quickly to a competitor's advances).

Quality function deployment

The process of involving customers in the design stage of new or redesigned products.

Table 3–3

Comparing the cultures of TQM and traditional organizations

Aspect	Traditional	TQM
Overall mission	Maximize return on investment	Meet or exceed customer satisfaction
Objectives	Emphasis on short term	Balance of long term and short term
Management	Not always open; sometimes inconsistent objectives	Open; encourages employee input; consistent objectives
Role of manager	Issue orders; enforce	Coach, remove barriers, build trust
Customer requirements	Not highest priority; may be unclear	Highest priority; important to identify and understand
Problems	Assign blame; punish	Identify and resolve
Problem solving	Not systematic; individuals	Systematic; teams
Improvement	Erratic	Continual
Suppliers	Adversarial	Partners
Jobs	Narrow, specialized; much individual effort	Broad, more general; much team effort
Focus	Product oriented	Process oriented

2. Programs may not be linked to the strategies of the organization in a meaningful way.

3. Quality-related decisions may not be tied to market performance. For instance, customer satisfaction may be carried so far that the cost of satisfying a customer far exceeds any direct or indirect benefit of doing so.

4. Failure to carefully plan a program before embarking on it can lead to false starts, employee confusion, and meaningless results.

QUALITY AWARDS

The Malcolm Baldrige Award and the Deming Prize are awarded annually to firms that have integrated quality management in their operations.

THE BALDRIGE AWARD

In 1987, Congress passed the Malcolm Baldrige National Quality Improvement Act. This legislation was designed to inspire increased efforts on the part of U.S. business organizations to improve the quality of their products and services. Named after the late Malcolm Baldrige, an industrialist and former Secretary of Commerce, the annual **Baldrige Award** is administered by the National Institute of Standards and Technology. It is limited to businesses located in the United States.

The purpose of the award competition is to stimulate efforts to improve quality, to recognize quality achievements of U.S. companies, and to publicize successful programs. A maximum of two awards are given annually in each of three categories: large manufacturer, large service organization, and small business (500 or fewer employees).

Baldrige Award

Annual award given by the U.S. government to recognize quality achievements of U.S. companies.

*Cadillac won the 1990
Baldrige Award in the
manufacturing category.
Here, the award
announcement is presented
at the Cadillac Assembly
line to the employees who
helped earn it.*

Businesses that apply for the award are required to submit an application of no more than 75 pages documenting their quality systems. Those who pass an initial screening must undergo a more intense evaluation by a group of examiners from government and industry, and consultants. The examination includes an on-site visit by the evaluating team. Applicants are evaluated in seven main areas: leadership, information and analysis, strategic planning, human resource management, quality assurance of products and services, quality results, and customer satisfaction. Table 3–4 contains a detailed listing of the items included in each area and the maximum number of points that evaluators can assign. Note that the category with the greatest number of points is customer satisfaction.

Examiners look for such things as the extent to which top management incorporates quality values in daily management; if products or services are at least as good as those of competitors; if employees are being trained in quality techniques; if the business works with suppliers to improve quality; and if customers are satisfied. All applicants receive a written summary of the strengths and weaknesses of their quality management and suggestions for improvement.

Among the winners of the Baldrige Award are Motorola (1988), Westinghouse (1988), Globe Metallurgical (1988), Xerox (1989), Milliken (1989), Cadillac (1990), IBM (1990), Federal Express (1990), Solectron (1991), and Zytec (1991).

The Baldrige Award has been both praised and criticized.[3] Among the praises of the Baldrige Award are these: It has raised the quality-consciousness of U.S. businesses, those who compete often find the process very motivating, and some of these contenders have made giant strides in quality and competitiveness. Among the criticisms: The award process can involve tremendous amounts of time and effort of

---

[3] See, for example, "Is the Baldrige Overblown?" *Fortune*, July 1, 1991, pp. 61–65; and "Does the Baldrige Award Really Work?" *Harvard Business Review*, January–February 1992, pp. 126–47.

Categories/Items	Maximum points
1.0 Leadership	**100**
1.1 Senior executive leadership	40
1.2 Quality values	15
1.3 Management for quality	25
1.4 Public responsibility	20
2.0 Information and analysis	**70**
2.1 Scope and management of quality data and information	20
2.2 Competitive comparisons and benchmarks	30
2.3 Analysis of quality data and information	20
3.0 Strategic quality planning	**60**
3.1 Strategic quality planning process	35
3.2 Quality goals and plans	25
4.0 Human resource utilization	**150**
4.1 Human resource management	20
4.2 Employee involvement	40
4.3 Quality education and training	40
4.4 Employee recognition and performance management	25
4.5 Employee well-being and morale	25
5.0 Quality assurance of products and services	**140**
5.1 Design and introduction of quality products and services	35
5.2 Process quality control	20
5.3 Continuous improvement of process	20
5.4 Quality assessment	15
5.5 Documentation	10
5.6 Business process and support service quality	20
5.7 Supplier quality	20
6.0 Quality results	**180**
6.1 Product and service quality results	90
6.2 Business process, operational, and support service quality results	50
6.3 Supplier quality results	40
7.0 Customer satisfaction	**300**
7.1 Determining customer requirement and expectations	30
7.2 Customer relationship management	50
7.3 Customer service standards	20
7.4 Commitment to customers	15
7.5 Complaint resolution for quality improvement	25
7.6 Determining customer satisfaction	20
7.7 Customer satisfaction results	70
7.8 Customer satisfaction comparison	70
Total points	**1,000**

Table 3–4

Malcolm Baldrige Award evaluation categories and points

both employees and top management at substantial cost (sometimes millions of dollars); executives may falsely believe that the award is a cure-all; applicants nominate themselves (as opposed to, say, being nominated by satisfied customers); winning does not mean that a business has top quality products or has solved all of its quality problems; and winning may be followed by relaxation under the belief that "we have it made." And some say that the number of awards (a maximum of six per year) is too few, considering the large number of organizations that are potential candidates.

The Deming Prize

The Deming Prize, named in honor of American statistician Dr. W. Edwards Deming, is Japan's highly coveted award that recognizes successful quality efforts. It is given annually to any company that meets the award's standards. Although typically given to Japanese firms, Florida Power and Light became the first U.S. company to win the award, in 1989. Other well-known companies that have received this prestigious award include Toyota and NEC.

The major focus of the judging is on statistical quality control, making it much narrower in scope than the Baldrige award, which focuses more on customer satisfaction. Companies that win the Deming Prize tend to have quality programs that are detailed and well-communicated throughout the company. In addition, their quality improvement programs reflect involvement of senior management, involvement of employees, customer satisfaction, and training.

ISO 9000

The International Organization for Standardization (ISO) is an international organization whose purpose is to promote worldwide standards that will improve operating efficiency, improve productivity, and reduce costs. The ISO is comprised of the national standards bodies of 91 countries. The U.S. representative body is the American National Standards Institute (ANSI). The work of the ISO is conducted by some 180 technical committees. ISO 9000 is the work of the Quality Management and Quality Assurance Committee.

ISO 9000 is a series of standards that outline the requirements for Quality Management Systems (QMS). There are essentially five standards associated with the ISO 9000 Series:

ISO 9000

ISO 9001

ISO 9002

ISO 9003

ISO 9004

The first standard, ISO 9000, is a set of guidelines for the selection and use of standards ISO 9001, 9002, and 9003, which relate to quality assurance.

ISO 9001 pertains to companies involved in the design, development, production, installation, and servicing of products or services.

ISO 9002 has coverage similar to ISO 9001, but excludes companies involved in design and development (i.e., it pertains to companies involved in the production, installation, and servicing of products or services).

ISO 9003 pertains to companies involved in final inspection and test, such as distributors or value-added contractors.

ISO 9004 is employed as a guideline for the application of the elements of the Quality Management System.

In the United States, the ISO 9000 Series has been reissued as the ANSI/ASQC Q90 Series. The two series are technically equivalent, but the Q90 Series adopts customary American language and spelling. This eases the use of the ISO 9000 Series for U.S. companies.

The ISO 9000 Series is an essential factor for companies that want to deal with the European Community (EC). They must go through a process that involves documenting quality procedures and on-site assessment. The purpose of this is to achieve *certification* as a company that meets ISO 9000 standards. The process often takes one to one and a half years. With certification comes *registration* in an ISO directory that companies seeking suppliers can refer to for a list of certified companies.

In addition to the obvious benefits of certification for companies who want to deal with the EC, the ISO 9000 certification and registration process is particularly helpful for companies that do not currently have a quality management system; it provides guidelines for establishing the system and making it effective.

SUMMARY

The success of foreign companies in North American markets has shown that they are formidable competitors. They have built reputations for quality products. Moreover, they have achieved their success using management techniques quite different than those traditionally practiced in the United States. This has caused American managers to reexamine their own approaches, and to adopt some of those different approaches in order to improve quality and to become more competitive.

Quality is defined according to various dimensions that pertain to customer satisfaction. The consequences of poor quality include loss of market share, liability claims, a decrease in productivity, and an increase in costs. Determinants of quality are design, conformance to design, ease of use, and service after delivery.

Modern quality management is directed at preventing mistakes rather than finding them after they occur. Currently, there is widespread interest within the business community in improving quality and competitiveness.

Total quality management (TQM) is a broad program intended to pervade an entire organization. The driving force is customer satisfaction. Involvement and commitment at all levels of the organization, training programs, and continuous improvement are hallmarks of this approach.

Two awards of distinction, the Baldrige Award and the Deming Prize, are given annually to organizations that have shown great achievement in quality management.

KEY TERMS

appraisal costs, 101
Baldrige Award, 107
Deming Prize, 102
dimensions of quality, 97
failure costs, 100
focus groups, 98
prevention costs, 101
quality, 96

quality at the source, 105
quality function deployment, 106
quality of conformance, 98
quality of design, 98
six-sigma quality, 106
total quality management (TQM), 104

DISCUSSION AND REVIEW QUESTIONS

1. List and briefly explain the six dimensions of quality.
2. Explain the terms *quality of design* and *quality of conformance*.
3. What are some possible consequences of poor quality?
4. Use the dimensions of quality to describe typical characteristics of these products and services:
   a. A television set
   b. A restaurant meal (product)
   c. A restaurant meal (service)
   d. Painting a house
5. List the four determinants of quality.
6. How does modern quality management differ from the "inspection" approach?
7. Describe the major elements of total quality management (TQM) programs.
8. What are some of the criticisms of the Baldrige Award?
9. What are some of the criticisms of TQM programs?

SELECTED BIBLIOGRAPHY

Crosby, Philip B. *Quality without Tears: The Art of Hassle Free Management.* New York: McGraw-Hill, 1984.

Deming, W. E. *Out of Crises.* Cambridge, Mass.: MIT Center for Advanced Engineering Study, 1982.

Garvin, David A. *Managing Quality.* New York: Free Press, 1988.

Gitlow, Howard S., and Shelly J. Gitlow. *The Deming Guide to Quality and Competitive Position.* Englewood Cliffs, N.J.: Prentice Hall, 1987.

Hall, Robert. *Attaining Manufacturing Excellence.* Homewood, Ill.: Dow-Jones Irwin, 1987.

Hunt, V. Daniel. *Quality in America.* Homewood, Ill.: Business One Irwin, 1992.

Juran, J. M. "The Quality Trilogy." *Quality Progress* 19, no. 8 (August 1986), pp. 19–24.

Schonberger, R. J. *World Class Manufacturing.* New York: Free Press, 1986.

READING   CALCOMP: DISASTER BECOMES SUCCESS   *Michelle Vranizan*

Flash back to the early 1980s. The only thing world-class about CalComp was the mess it was in.

The company that practically invented the computer plotter—a device engineers and architects use to print intricate, oversized schematics—had become arrogant, inattentive and lazy.

Every last plotter that rolled off the assembly line didn't work well enough to ship without some rejiggering. A legion of field technicians was needed to make house calls on installed machines that malfunctioned every few weeks. Competitors such as Hewlett-Packard jumped into the breach, stealing dissatisfied customers.

Flash forward to the CalComp of 1992, recognized locally as a leader in world-class manufacturing. No more mass assembly lines. No more bugs. No more field technicians.

Hewlett-Packard still sells more pen plotters. But CalComp is a strong No. 2 and has a tight grip on other segments of the plotter and digitizer business. Now bursting with confidence, the $525 million subsidiary of Lockheed Corp. is plowing into other areas of the multi-billion dollar computer graphics industry.

The difference between 1982 and 1992?

Quality.

Specifically, a quality program spearheaded six years ago by CalComp President William Conlin that permeates every square inch of the company's grassy Anaheim headquarters and the attitudes of its 2,800 employees.

At CalComp, quality boils down to pleasing customers with gracefully built, innovative products that work from the start, rarely break down, are competitively priced and are upgraded faster than the other guy's.

"We built a manufacturing system that improves every day," said Bernard Masson, senior vice president of the plotter division, which accounts for about 60 percent of CalComp's revenue. "The product we build tomorrow will be better than the ones we build today."

In the early 1970s and 1980s, CalComp's manufacturing process was fractured. Product design and manufacturing weren't coordinated. The company stockpiled parts and the plotter division alone had more than 650 suppliers. A plotter was only tested for imperfections after it was made.

The system worked as long as CalComp only sold 1,000 or so plotters a year to customers who used mainframes or mini-computers, also very temperamental machines prone to breakdowns.

Then along came personal computers, which worked straight out of the box. When personal computers became the preferred tools for engineering and graphics, CalComp managers realized the old way of doing things had to go.

Conlin signed on in late 1983 and CalComp took its first steps toward world-class manufacturing soon after.

CalComp embraced the teachings of quality gurus such as W. Edwards Deming and Richard J. Schonberger, focusing first on the factory.

In the beginning, changes were simple, such as writing down the steps it took to assemble a plotter—something CalComp had never done before, Masson said.

Next, assembly workers were taught quality principles, given a say in how things were done and encouraged to catch mistakes on the line.

Managers instituted "statistical process controls," a fancy title for using quantifiable measures to zero in on a problem, fix it and move on to the next problem.

One example of how this works: At one time, printed circuit boards built into the plotters were mysteriously developing bad spots. Through process of elimination, workers discovered that built-up static electricity from their own hands was zapping the circuits. Now everyone in the factory wears a grounding wire around one shoe to discharge electricity.

Also as part of its quality program, CalComp decentralized divisions and product lines to give groups more control over their destiny.

Other steps CalComp took:

1. When a new product is conceived, a team of more than a dozen people representing virtually every department shepherds it from development to delivery. With this kind of teamwork engineers don't end up designing parts that factory workers can't put together, said Linda Gronski, an operating unit manager in the plotter division.

2. Instead of stockpiling parts, CalComp cut inventories to the bare minimum and now takes delivery of just enough parts for the next week's work. Some suppliers even deliver parts on a daily basis.

3. CalComp put strict quality controls on suppliers and reduced its vendors in the plotter division to about 180. CalComp started a three-tier preferred-supplier program, dubbed "a mini-Malcolm Baldridge award" contest by one supplier. Parts from suppliers on the highest tier are expected to be so perfect CalComp doesn't even inspect them before building them into products.

By keeping inventories down, CalComp cut its overhead costs. It also can avoid writing off obsolete parts should demand shift suddenly and can direct energies to new products more quickly, company executives said.

For example, in most years, CalComp sells about 300 electrostatic plotters, a sort of giant laser printer that sells for about $50,000. But demand for electrostatic plotters rose substantially in 1991 and CalComp was able to ship 300 in the last quarter alone—"and that was a new model," Conlin said.

Readjusting attitudes toward work was the most important part of the jump to quality, CalComp managers said.

Today, front-line workers are treated with as much respect as executives. Assembly workers are never reprimanded for stopping the line if they can't solve a problem. Gronski and other production managers wear beepers and are expected to attend to problems immediately.

Pete Loya, a four-year employee who helps assemble the company's Pacesetter plotter, talks proudly of the time CalComp sent him to Boston to check out a supplier. For Loya, such perks plus a competitive salary make him happy he's at CalComp during a shaky economy.

"I plan on retiring here," he said. "It makes you feel like shooting for the top."

CalComp's nimbleness paid off in 1991, when the recession hurt orders for some products while demand for others increased.

(continued)

READING   *(concluded)*

Several competitors lost revenue and trimmed employees during the year, but CalComp maintained both, Conlin said. After heavy investments in research and development, CalComp may even have made a small profit, analysts said. Lockheed does not disclose CalComp's exact revenue or earnings.

It is difficult to find anyone who finds fault with CalComp's quality quest.

"They are the best," said Terry Wells, co-owner of Everest Electronic Equipment, an Anaheim company that supplies CalComp with sheet metal. "They practice what they preach. Everyone else knows the language, but very few participate."

Suppliers said they benefited from classes at CalComp on quality processes: They use the information to transform their businesses and attract other customers.

"When Xerox found out where we were with CalComp, they decided to send a team of people out to visit us," said Harry Esayian, owner of Zac Precision in Anaheim, which makes machine parts for dozens of CalComp products.

Draftsmen and engineers who use CalComp plotters and digitizers might be unfamiliar with the company's quality programs. But they appreciate the results.

"I'm always talking up the plotter because it's a good deal," said customer David Terry, who has a Santa Ana engineering firm that designs waste water-treatment plants. "They're low-cost and no-maintenance. We're real happy."

CalComp hopes to use what it has learned over the past seven years to enter a bigger chunk of the computer-graphics market.

Already this year, the company's digitizer division has begun supplying Pi, a manufacturer of pen computers, with touch-sensitive surfaces and electronic styluses. Negotiations are continuing to sell the same supplies to Japanese computer companies, Conlin said.

Other divisions are working on products such as photographic- and poster-quality printers and digitizing surfaces for graphic artists.

"Now we have a handle on not just making products but introducing them," Conlin said. "We've shrunk the time between spending our first dollar and making our first dollar."

Questions

1. In general terms, what was wrong in the early 1980s at Calcomp?
2. Specifically, what was wrong with:
   a. design and manufacturing?
   b. inventory?
   c. suppliers?
3. In general terms, what change helped to turn things around at Calcomp?
4. What steps were taken to improve the situation?
5. What benefits have resulted from the changes?

Source: *The Orange County Register,* March 1, 1992.

NEWSCLIP   WHERE DID THEY GO WRONG?

Why some quality programs never get off the ground

Fifty times a year, at one factory or office after another, Corning Inc. Chairman James R. Houghton gives pretty much the same spiel. Quality, quality, quality. World-class. Customer focus. Worker participation. At each site, a sermon for the employee ranks, then a no-nonsense performance review with local managers.

Tiresome? Just a bit. Houghton has been preaching this gospel since 1983. But he keeps at it. "After eight years, if I stop talking about quality now, it would be a disaster," he says. The effort has paid off: Operating profits are up 111 percent in five years.

In most companies, it doesn't work that way. There are quality efforts, but something's missing. Pronouncements from the executive suite fall flat. Skeptical workers pay little heed. Managers re-

sist, caught up in deadlines and turf battles. Or a program does catch on—then dies in a few years. "The majority of quality efforts fizzle out early, or give some improvements but never fulfill their initial promise," says Boston Consulting Group Vice-President Thomas M. Hout.

Managing for quality isn't easy. It requires active, unwavering leadership from the CEO, organizational change of the largest order—and time. "I'm not very patient," says CEO I. MacAllister Booth, whose Polaroid Corp. is shooting for a tenfold gain in customer satisfaction over the next five years and a halving of the time it takes new products to break even. "You talk about five years, seven years, and I get very frustrated with the pace."

Still there's too much at stake not to keep at it. Like most American executives, Booth faces an unforgiving global marketplace. And the battles lost to Japanese competition prove that

keeping up, much less winning, requires more than speeches.

Done right, quality becomes a competitive weapon. Companies that embrace quality have an edge of up to 10¢ on every sales dollar over rivals, says quality pioneer Armand V. Feigenbaum of General Systems Co. in Pittsfield, Mass. That's because fewer defects mean less rework and wasted management time, lower costs, and higher customer-retention

CEO I. MacAllister Booth, whose Polaroid Corp. is shooting for a tenfold gain in customer satisfaction over the next five years.

(continued)

rates. Cabot Corp. saved $1 million a year and freed new production capacity by cutting defects 90 percent at its Franklin (La.) carbon-black plant over a period of two years.

Yet sometimes, resistance to change is so stubborn as to require a cultural wake-up call. Polaroid was, for decades, one of the nation's most innovative and successful companies. But without breakthrough products to replace the maturing instant-photography franchise, its revenues have stagnated. "I've spent a good part of my life thinking about quality," Booth says. "Now, there's an implication that we've been asleep at the switch for 20 years. That's not easy for me or the rest of the folks in the company" to accept.

Polaroid's overhaul raised wrenching questions. Should it embrace the incremental change that total quality programs tend to produce—or aim for the dramatic innovation that can make or break a technology company? Polaroid's scientists argue that the structure imposed by continuous improvement could inhibit revolutionary change. Booth's manufacturing lieutenants countered that the same structure would provide needed discipline. Even now, the debate isn't resolved.

That's not surprising. The people who must implement quality programs often have conflicting goals and priorities. More-

over, there's a wide range of quality strategies, from benchmarking against competitors to self-managed work teams. Nearly every one can upset the traditional corporate ways and power structures.

After his arrival in 1987, Cabot CEO Samuel Bodman forced out executives who were used to simply giving orders and were uneasy with the quasi-democracy of many quality programs. "I didn't foresee the degree of difficulty people had in changing the way they worked," he says. Employees, too, may react cynically if they've endured rounds of layoffs, or if this is the latest of many programs long on rhetoric but short on substance.

Resistance materializes from all fronts. The American Quality Foundation, a New York think tank studying management issues and quality, has found that Americans react poorly to programs geared to perfection. "We also found that 70 percent of American workers are afraid to speak up with suggestions or to ask for clarification," says AQF President Joshua Hammond. Moreover, he says, Americans prefer to jump into a project without heavy planning—the opposite of the way the Japanese work. And in the U.S., teams must be structured so that the individual has a chance to shine.

How then to break down these barriers—and get an effec-

tive quality program rolling? "If all you have is symbolism, nothing happens," says David Garvin, a professor at the Harvard business school. That's why Allen-Bradley Co., Corning, and other manufacturers put quality objectives into the bonus plans of top brass, why Corning has incentives for factory workers as well, and why CEO Alexander V. d'Arbeloff at instrument maker Teradyne named a fast-track product manager the company's first quality director. "That tends to get their attention," says Garvin.

John A. Young put Hewlett-Packard Co.'s quality effort in motion in 1979 by setting a firm companywide goal: a tenfold reduction of warranty expenses. As HP neared that goal, he set another, equally concrete: reducing software defects by 90 percent.

The reason many initiatives fail, argues BCG's Hout, is that top managers too often have other priorities. Three years ago, the general manager of a division at a large defense electronics contractor unveiled a big program, then plunged into dealing with the unit's plummeting revenues and layoffs. Quality went nowhere.

As CEO of Florida Power & Light Co., John J. Hudiburg drove hard in the other direction. In 1989, FPL became the first to win Japan's prestigious Deming prize for quality in a category for

NEWSCLIP *(concluded)*

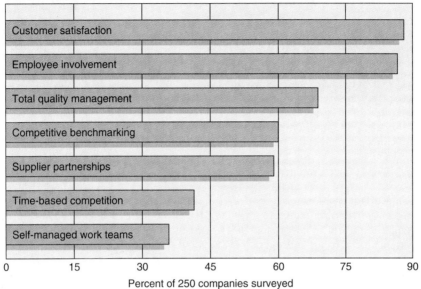

Share of companies using:

How Quality Strategies Stack Up

non-Japanese businesses. But workers and their managers had to compile hundreds of pages of analysis required by the contest judges. The result: instant bureaucracy. Morale plummeted as workdays lengthened. By the time the Deming prize arrived, Hudiburg had been sidelined (he since has retired and did not return calls for comment).

James L. Broadhead, CEO of FPL Group, Florida Power & Light's parent, dismantled the quality-improvement department, which had swelled to 75 employees. "It was becoming a bureaucratic organization that was out-

living its usefulness," says Michael T. Fraga, an FPL vice-president who today heads a quality staff of just six. Now, FPL urges employees to use the training within their departments. And some of the staff were spun off into Qualtec, now one of the larger quality consulting firms.

The prospect of becoming another FPL worries some CEOs. When Stephen V. Ardia, chief executive of Goulds Pumps Inc., found his executives bogged down in quality-related administrative tasks, he ordered shorter meetings and less paperwork. And Alcoa Corp.'s CEO Paul H.

O'Neill just scrapped the company's decade-long continuous improvement strategy, calling it a "major mistake." Alcoa, he decided, needed "quantum" quality improvements instead to meet world standards.

Indeed, companies have to implement quality strategies that make sense for them. It may take years to figure out exactly what works, and even more time to get it right. But one thing is clear: If it means no more than a few speeches and a lapel pin, quality won't work at all.

Source: *Business Week/Quality* 1991.

U.S. industry has plowed several million dollars into quality programs over the past decade. So much so, that many U.S. managers are convinced they make quality products. Unfortunately, customers don't always think so. IBM's CEO John Akers probably put it best, when he was quoted in this newspaper as saying, "I am sick and tired of visiting plants to hear nothing but great things about quality and cycle time—and then to visit customers who tell me of problems."

Mr. Akers isn't alone. Our experience suggests that as many as two out of every three quality management programs in place for more than a couple of years are stalled; they no longer meet the CEO's expectations for tangible improvement in product or service quality, customer satisfaction, and operating performance.

What is to be done with these "stalled" programs? We at McKinsey have found the following to be useful:

■ *Shut down programs in businesses where dramatic change in economic performance is needed.* Quality management programs yield incremental, not dramatic, improvements. Sagging profits and depressed sales call for tougher measures, such as radical downsizing, restructuring, or surging of superfluous management layers. If you have a gradual improvement program in place to sap losses, bite the bullet and shut it down.

After taking over as CEO of Alcoa, one of Paul O'Neill's first initiatives was to shut down Alcoa's decade-long quality effort because, he told *Business Week* last October, "the business needed restructuring and dramatic change, not gradual improvement over several years." To close the gap in competitiveness and productivity between Alcoa and some of the leading aluminum companies, such as Kobe Steel, he opted for a "quantum improvement" program like benchmarking.

■ *Link programs to strategic planning processes.* If incremental improvement is what you need, make sure you evaluate programs as part of your strategic planning processes; set specific goals for your senior managers and make these goals part of their performance reviews. Some companies like Allen-Bradley and Corning are already doing this. They incorporate quality improvement objectives in the bonus plans of senior executives.

But while you set priorities and objectives for your managers, do not let them, in turn, set goals for lower-level employees. It is demotivating and ineffective. Over and over we find that, given some guiding principles or areas for improvement, they set much higher goals for themselves. Reward them for reaching their goals. John Cleghorn, president of Royal Bank of Canada, was recently quoted in the *Toronto Globe & Mail* as saying that "quality companies put faith in their people. . . . When employees see their opinions are valued, they see themselves making a difference to the success of the company. And they do."

■ *Focus programs outward on market "break points."* It is one thing to stress the importance of customer satisfaction; it is quite another to actually achieve measurable improvements. For a computer company, achieving on-time delivery rates below 90 percent may be judged by customers as unacceptable, while about 98 percent is judged clearly outstanding; anything in between is just satisfactory. On-time delivery improvement programs should be geared toward reaching either 90 percent or 98 percent—the market "break points" where improved performance will change customer behavior, resulting in higher prices or sales volume. Forget the improvement program that targets between 96 percent and 98 percent. You are wasting money.

MBNA Corp., the fourth-largest credit-card issuer in the U.S., keeps its customers twice as long as the industry average because it religiously focuses on 14 items that it believes are break-point issues to its customers, including answering every phone within two rings and processing every credit-line increase request within an hour. Emphasizing the notion of break points pushes improvement efforts to understand customer behavior, focuses on what is deemed by customers as most important, and measures impact.

■ *Choose a single theme.* Nothing is more counterproductive than tens or sometimes hundreds of teams chasing wildly different "quality" priorities. Team A slashes cycle time in a components warehouse while Team B reduces defects in circuit-board assembly, and so on. At year end, despite these small wins, neither cycle time nor defects, measured at the business or company level, demonstrates any tangible improvement.

Contrast this with Hewlett Packard, where CEO John Young focused the entire company by, in 1979, setting a goal of a tenfold reduction in warranty expenses and following it up, as Hewlett Packard neared that, with a goal of a 90 percent reduction in software defects. However, focusing on a single goal carries a risk: It may be inappropriate for the company at that time or may be viewed as an end in itself, rather than as the means to achieve a much higher and broader goal.

■ *Emphasize results, not process.* It is remarkable how often the focus with process diverts attention from results and creates excess staff and bureaucracy. (Before it was rolled back, the TQM effort at Florida Power & Light included a staff and a group of "quality consultants" that had swelled to 75.)

The Baldrige Award criteria are useful for an assessment of the completeness of a TQM effort, but making the prize the goal puts too much emphasis on process, and arguably yields mainly PR, not sustainable competitive wins. Motorola won the Baldrige Award in its inaugural year (1988). But its chairman, George Fisher, remarked then: "Yes we won the Baldrige Award. But all that means is that we are on our way with an effective process aimed at achieving total customer satisfaction. We still have a long way to go."

A result that Motorola wants out of its investments is a reduction of defects to within "six sigma" (no more than 3.4 defects per million—or 99.9997% perfect). Mr. Fisher is even trying to set exacting standards on such areas as basic research and meetings, where standards are not easily set. Alcoa's use of benchmarks was also driven by a need to set exacting standards, because, as Mr. O'Neill says, "world standards are measurable, and they are practiced somewhere."

A combination of these suggestions can help restart a stalled program by tying it to measurable achievements that make a real difference.

Questions

1. List the four approaches McKinsey suggests.
2. For each approach, state the rationale for that approach.

II

FORECASTING

T his part deals solely with forecasting (Chapter 4). It is presented early in the book because forecasts are the basis for a wide range of design and operating decisions. Consequently, this chapter serves as a basis for many of the remaining chapters.

Although forecasts are frequently developed as part of the marketing function, operations people are often called upon to assist in forecast development. More important, though, is the fact that *operations makes major use of forecasts*. Hence, the subject of forecasting is exceedingly important for operations management.

CHAPTER FOUR

FORECASTING

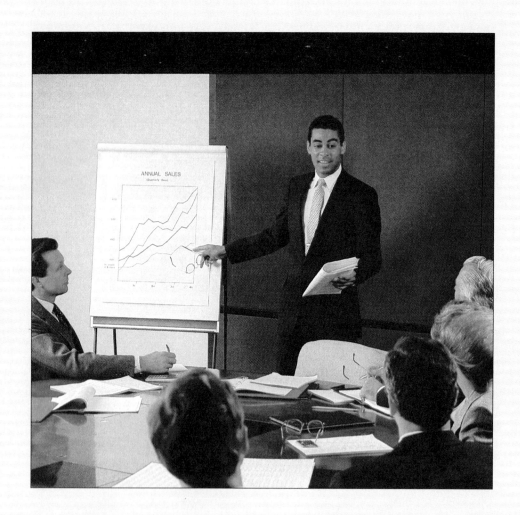

After completing this chapter, you should be able to:

1. Describe at least four qualitative forecasting techniques and the advantages and disadvantages of each.
2. Compare and contrast qualitative and quantitative approaches to forecasting.
3. Briefly describe averaging techniques, trend and seasonal techniques, and regression analysis, and solve typical problems.
4. Describe two measures of forecast accuracy.
5. Describe two ways of evaluating and controlling forecasts.
6. Identify the major factors to consider when choosing a forecasting technique.
7. List the elements of a good forecast.
8. Outline the steps in the forecasting process.

LEARNING
OBJECTIVES

CHAPTER
OUTLINE

4

Planning is an integral part of a manager's job. If uncertainties cloud the planning horizon, it can be quite difficult for a manager to plan effectively. Forecasts can help managers by reducing some of the uncertainty, thereby enabling them to develop more meaningful plans than they might otherwise. A **forecast** is a statement about the future.

This chapter deals with business forecasting. Its purpose is to provide a survey of business forecasting. It covers basic forecasting techniques, how to monitor a forecast, the necessary steps in preparing a forecast, and elements that are common to forecasts.

INTRODUCTION

At one time or another, we have all witnessed weather forecasts that were flops, even though most of the time the forecasters are close in predicting what the weather will be. Forecasting demand is a lot like forecasting the weather. In both instances, there is no such thing as a sure bet: predictions usually turn out to be in the ballpark, but occasionally they miss the mark completely. Moreover, in both instances, the forecasts serve as a *basis for planning*. Weather forecasts influence travel and recreation plans, choice of clothing each day, and whether to walk or ride to work. Farmers rely on weather forecasts to determine when to plant and harvest and when to take precautionary steps (e.g., protect against frost). In business, forecasts are the basis for capacity planning, budgeting, sales planning, production and inventory planning, manpower planning, purchasing planning, and more. Forecasts play such an important role in the planning process because they enable managers to *anticipate the future* and to *plan* accordingly.

In a sense, there are two uses for forecasts. One is to help managers *plan the system*, and the other is to help them *plan the use of the system*. Planning the system generally involves long-range plans concerning the types of products and services to offer, what facilities and equipment to have, where to locate, and so on. Planning the use of the system refers to short-range and intermediate-range planning, which involve such tasks as planning inventory and work force levels, planning purchasing and production, budgeting, and scheduling.

Business forecasting pertains to more than predicting demand. Forecasts are also used to predict profits, revenues, costs, productivity changes, prices and availability of energy and raw materials, interest rates, movements of key economic indicators (e.g., GNP, inflation, government borrowing), and prices of stocks and bonds, as well as other variables. For the sake of simplicity, the focus of the chapter will be on the forecasting of demand. But keep in mind that the concepts and techniques apply equally well to these other variables.

In spite of the use of computers and sophisticated mathematical models in forecasting, it is not an exact science. Instead, successful forecasting often requires a skillful blending of art and science. Experience, judgment, and technical expertise all play a role in developing useful forecasts. Along with these, a certain amount of luck and a dash of humility can be helpful, since the worst forecasters occasionally produce a very good forecast, and even the best forecasters sometimes miss completely. Forecasting techniques currently in use range from the mundane to the exotic. Some work better than others, but no one technique works all of the time.

Generally speaking, the responsibility for preparing demand forecasts lies with marketing or sales rather than operations. Nonetheless, operations people are called on to make certain forecasts as well as to help others to prepare forecasts. In addition, since forecasts are major inputs for many operations decisions, it is essential for operations managers and staff to be knowledgeable about the kinds of forecasting techniques that are available, the assumptions that underlie their use, and their limitations. It is also important for managers to consider *how* forecasts affect operations. In other words, forecasting is an integral part of operations management.

FEATURES COMMON TO ALL FORECASTS

There are a wide variety of forecasting techniques in use. In many respects, they are quite different from each other, as you shall soon discover. Nonetheless, there are certain features that are common to all, and it is important to recognize them.

1. Forecasting techniques generally assume that the same underlying causal system that existed in the past will continue to exist in the future.

2. Forecasts are rarely perfect; actual results usually differ from predicted values. We are unable to predict *precisely* how an often large number of related factors will impinge upon the variable in question; this, and the presence of randomness, preclude a perfect forecast. Allowances should be made for inaccuracies.

3. Forecasts for groups of items tend to be more accurate than forecasts for individual items because forecasting errors among items in a group usually have a canceling effect. Opportunities for grouping may arise if parts or raw materials are used for multiple products or if a service is demanded by a number of independent sources.

4. Forecast accuracy decreases as the time period covered by the forecast—the time *horizon*—increases. Generally speaking, short-range forecasts must contend with fewer uncertainties than longer-range forecasts, so they tend to be more accurate.

An important consequence of this last point is that flexible business organizations, that is, those that can respond quickly to changes in demand, require a shorter forecasting horizon and, hence, benefit from more accurate short-range forecasts than competitors who are less flexible, and who must therefore use longer forecast horizons.

STEPS IN THE FORECASTING PROCESS

There are five basic steps in the forecasting process:

1. *Determine the purpose* of the forecast and when it will be needed. This will provide an indication of the level of detail required in the forecast, the amount of resources (manpower, computer time, dollars) that can be justified, and the level of accuracy necessary.

2. *Establish a time horizon* that the forecast must cover, keeping in mind that accuracy decreases as the time horizon increases.

3. *Select a forecasting technique.*

4. *Gather and analyze the appropriate data*, and then *prepare the forecast. Identify any assumptions* that are made in conjunction with preparing and using the forecast.

5. *Monitor the forecast* to see if it is performing in a satisfactory manner. If it is not, reexamine the method, assumptions, validity of data, and so on; modify as needed; and prepare a revised forecast.

APPROACHES TO FORECASTING

There are two general approaches to forecasting: qualitative and quantitative. Qualitative methods consist mainly of subjective inputs, which often defy precise numerical description. Quantitative methods involve either the extension of historical data or development of associative models that attempt to utilize *causal (explanatory) variables* to make a forecast.

Qualitative techniques permit inclusion of *soft* information (human factors, personal opinions, hunches) in the forecasting process. Those factors are often omitted or downplayed when quantitative techniques are used because they are difficult or impossible to quantify. Quantitative techniques consist mainly of analyzing objective, or *hard,* data. They usually avoid personal biases that sometimes contaminate qualitative methods. In practice, either or both approaches might be used to develop a given forecast.

FORECASTS BASED ON JUDGMENT AND OPINION

Judgmental forecasts rely on analysis of subjective inputs obtained from various sources, such as consumer surveys, the sales staff, managers and executives, and panels of experts. Quite frequently, these sources provide insights that are not otherwise available.

FORECASTS BASED ON TIME SERIES (HISTORICAL) DATA

Some forecasting techniques depend on uncovering relationships between variables that can be used to predict future values of one of them; others simply attempt to project past experience into the future. The second of these approaches exemplifies forecasts that use historical, or time series, data. The theme of that approach is that the future will be like the past. Some of the models merely attempt to smooth out random variations in historical data, and others attempt to identify specific patterns in the data. In effect, approaches based on historical data treat the data as a mirror that reflects the combination of all forces influencing the variable in question (e.g., demand), without trying to identify or measure those forces directly.

ASSOCIATIVE FORECASTS

Associative models identify one or more *explanatory* variables that can be used to predict future demand. For example, demand for paint might be related to such variables as the price per gallon and the amount spent on advertising, as well as specific characteristics of the paint (e.g., drying time, ease of cleanup). The analysis in such cases yields a mathematical equation that enables the manager to predict volume of sales, for example, on the basis of given values of the "explaining" variable(s).

FORECASTS BASED ON JUDGMENT AND OPINION

When a forecast must be prepared quickly, there is usually not enough time to gather and analyze quantitative data. At other times, especially when political and economic conditions are changing, available data may be obsolete, and more up-to-date information might not yet be available. Similarly, the introduction of new

Judgmental forecasts

Forecasts that use subjective inputs such as opinions from consumer surveys, sales staff, managers, executives, and experts.

Associative model

Forecasting technique that uses explanatory variables to predict future demand.

products, as well as the redesign of existing products or packaging, all suffer from the absence of historical data that would be useful in forecasting. In such instances, forecasts based on judgment and experience are commonly used. Among those are forecasts that use executive opinions, consumer surveys, opinions of the sales staff, and opinions of experts.

EXECUTIVE OPINIONS

A small group of upper-level managers (e.g., marketing, product, engineering, manufacturing, and financial managers) may meet and collectively develop a forecast. This approach is often used as a part of long-range planning and new product development. It has the advantage of bringing together the considerable knowledge and talents of these management people. However, there is the risk that the view of one person will prevail, as well as the possibility that diffusing responsibility for the forecast over the entire group may result in less pressure to produce a good forecast.

SALES FORCE COMPOSITE

The sales staff is often a good source of information because of its direct contact with consumers. Thus, these people are often aware of any plans the customers may be considering for the future. There are, however, several drawbacks to this approach. One is that salespeople may be unable to distinguish between what customers would *like* to do and what they actually *will* do. Another is that salespeople are sometimes overly influenced by recent experiences. Thus, after several periods of low sales, their estimates may tend to become pessimistic, and after several periods of good sales, they may tend to be too optimistic. In addition, if forecasts are to be used to establish sales quotas, there will be a conflict of interest because it would be to the salesperson's advantage to provide low sales estimates.

CONSUMER SURVEYS

Since the consumer is the one who will ultimately determine demand, it seems natural to solicit input from consumers. In some instances, every customer or potential customer can be contacted. In most cases, however, there are too many customers or there is no way to identify all potential customers. Because of these and similar factors, organizations that seek consumer input usually resort to the use of consumer surveys, which enable them to *sample* consumer opinions. The obvious advantage of such surveys is that they can tap information that might not be available elsewhere. On the other hand, surveys require a considerable amount of knowledge and skill to handle correctly. A great deal of care is necessary to construct a survey, administer it, and correctly interpret the results in order to obtain valid information. They can be expensive and time-consuming. In addition, even under the best of conditions, surveys involving the general public must contend with the possibility of irrational behavior patterns. For example, much thoughtful information-gathering done by a consumer before purchasing a new car is often undermined by the glitter of a new car showroom or a high-pressure sales pitch. Along the same lines, low response rates to a mail survey should (but often don't) make the results suspect.

If these and similar pitfalls can be avoided, surveys can produce useful information both for forecasting and for product design and promotion.

OUTSIDE OPINION

Occasionally, outside opinions are needed to make a forecast. These may include advice on political or economic conditions in the United States or in a foreign country, or some other aspect of importance with which an organization lacks familiarity.

OPINIONS OF MANAGERS AND STAFF

Delphi method

Managers and staff complete a series of questionnaires, each developed from the previous one, to achieve a consensus forecast.

A manager may use staff to generate a forecast or to provide several forecasting alternatives from which to choose. At other times, a manager may solicit opinions from a number of other managers and/or staff people. The **Delphi method** is sometimes useful in this regard. It involves circulating a series of questionnaires among those individuals who possess the knowledge and ability to contribute meaningfully. Responses are kept anonymous, which tends to encourage honest responses. Each new questionnaire is developed using the information extracted from the previous one, thus enlarging the scope of information on which participants can base their judgments. The goal is to achieve a consensus forecast.

The Delphi technique originated in the Rand Corporation in 1948, where it was used to assess the potential impact of an atomic bomb attack on the United States. Since that time, it has been applied to a variety of situations, not all of which involve forecasting. The discussion here will be limited to its use as a forecasting tool.

As a forecasting tool, the Delphi technique is useful for *technological* forecasting. That is, the technique is a method for assessing changes in technology and their impact on an organization. Often the goal is to predict *when* a certain event will occur. For instance, the goal of a Delphi forecast might be to predict when video telephones might be installed in at least 50 percent of residential homes or when a vaccine for a disease might be developed and ready for mass distribution. For the most part, these are long-term, single-time forecasts. In these situations, there is usually very little hard information to go by, or data are costly to obtain, so the problem does not lend itself to analytical techniques. Rather, judgments of experts or others who possess sufficient knowledge to make predictions are used.

The main reasons for using a Delphi approach are the following:

1. A group of experts can provide needed judgmental input.
2. More individuals may be needed than can effectively interact in a face-to-face situation, and/or the individuals cannot be conveniently assembled in one place. Time and cost can also be factors.
3. It is important to avoid a "bandwagon effect."
4. It is desirable to preserve the anonymity of the participants.

There are also a number of weaknesses in the Delphi approach, some of them fairly serious. Among them are the following:

1. The questions may contain ambiguous phrasing so that panel members reach a false consensus.
2. Panel membership may change, especially if the process requires a long time (some may take a year or more).
3. The "experts" may not be experts.

4. Studies have failed to prove that Delphi forecasts generally achieve a high degree of accuracy.

5. Preserving anonymity removes accountability and responsibility.

FORECASTS BASED ON TIME SERIES DATA

A **time series** is a time-ordered sequence of observations taken at regular intervals over a period of time (hourly, daily, weekly, monthly, quarterly, annually, and so on). The data may be measurements of demand, earnings, profits, shipments, accidents, output, precipitation, productivity, and the consumer price index. Forecasting techniques that are based on time series data are made on the assumption that future values of the series can be estimated from past values of the series. In spite of the fact that no attempt is made to identify variables that influence the series, these methods are widely used, often with very satisfactory results.

Analysis of time series data requires the analyst to identify the underlying behavior of the series. This can often be accomplished by merely *plotting* the data and visually examining the plot. One or more patterns might appear: trends, seasonal variations, cycles, and constant variations (variations around an average). In addition, there can be random and irregular variations. These behaviors can be described as follows:

1. **Trend** refers to a gradual, long-term movement in the data. Population shifts, changing incomes, and cultural changes often account for such movements.

2. **Seasonality** refers to short-term, fairly regular variations generally related to weather factors or to factors such as holidays and vacations. Restaurants, supermarkets, and theaters experience weekly and even daily "seasonal" variations.

3. **Cycles** are wavelike variations of more than one year's duration. These are often related to a variety of economic and political factors and even agricultural conditions.

4. **Irregular variations** are due to unusual circumstances such as severe weather conditions, strikes, or a major change in a product or service. They do not reflect typical behavior, and inclusion in the series can distort the overall picture. Whenever possible, these should be identified and removed from the data.

Time series

A time-ordered sequence of observations taken at regular intervals over a period of time.

Trend

Gradual, long-term movement in data.

Seasonality

Short-term regular variations related to weather or season.

Cycles

Wavelike variations lasting more than one year.

Irregular variations

Those due to unusual circumstances, not reflective of typical behavior.

Demand for products such as lawnmowers and snowthrowers are subject to seasonal fluctuations. Toro matches these fluctuations by adjusting its manufacturing capacity for both products.

Random variations

Residual variations after all
other behaviors are
accounted for.

5. **Random variations** are the residual variations that remain after all of the
    other behaviors have been accounted for. These behaviors are illustrated in
    Figure 4–1. The small "bumps" in the plots represent random variability.

In the remainder of this section, various approaches to the analysis of time series
data are described. Before turning to those discussions, one point should be emphasized: A demand forecast should be based on a time series of past *demand* rather than
sales. Sales would not truly reflect demand unless demand was less than the amount
of a good or service available for sale. Similarly, shipments would not truly reflect
demand if there are backlogs of orders; the timing of shipments would not correspond to the timing of demand.

TECHNIQUES FOR AVERAGING

Historical data typically contain a certain amount of random variation, or *noise,* that
tends to obscure systematic movements in the data. This randomness arises from the

Figure 4–1

Trend, seasonal, cyclical,
random, and irregular
variations

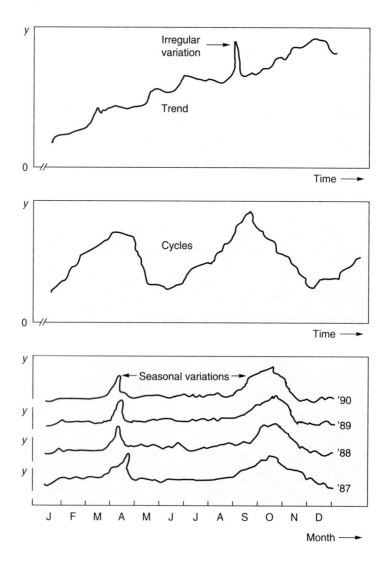

combined influence of many—perhaps a great many—relatively unimportant factors, and it cannot be reliably predicted. Ideally, it would be desirable to completely remove any randomness from the data and leave only "real" variations, such as changes in the *level* of demand (e.g., a step change). However, as a practical matter, it is usually impossible to distinguish these two kinds of variations, so the best one can hope for is to smooth out the randomness but leave the nonrandom variations intact. In effect, small variations are treated as random—they are smoothed out. Averaging techniques are often used for this purpose.

Averaging techniques smooth out some of the fluctuations in a time series because the individual highs and lows in the data offset each other when they are combined into an average. A forecast based on an average thus tends to exhibit less variability than the original data (see Figure 4–2). This can be advantageous because many of these movements merely reflect random variability rather than a true change in level, or trend, in the series. Moreover, because responding to changes in expected demand often entails considerable cost (e.g., changes in production rate, changes in the size of a work force, inventory changes), it is desirable to avoid reacting to minor variations. Thus, minor variations are treated as random variations, whereas larger variations are viewed as more likely to reflect "real" changes, although these, too, are smoothed to a certain degree.

Averaging techniques generate a forecast that reflects recent values of a time series (e.g., the average value over the last several periods). These techniques work best when a series tends to vary around an average, although they can also handle step changes or gradual changes in the level of the series. Three techniques for averaging are described in this section:

1. Naive forecasts.
2. Moving averages.
3. Exponential smoothing.

Naive Forecasts

The simplest forecasting technique is the naive method. A **naive forecast** for any period equals the previous period's actual value. For example, if demand last week was 50 units, the naive forecast for the upcoming week is 50 units. Similarly, if demand in the upcoming week turns out to be 54 units, the forecast for the following week would be 54 units.

Although at first glance the naive approach may appear *too* simplistic, it is nonetheless a legitimate forecasting tool. Consider the advantages: It has virtually no cost, it is quick and easy to prepare because data analysis is nonexistent, and it is easy for users to understand. The main objection to this method is its inability to provide highly accurate forecasts. However, if resulting accuracy is acceptable, this approach

Naive forecast

The forecast for any period equals the previous period's actual value.

Data 〰〰〰
Forecast – – – – –

Figure 4–2

Averaging applied to three possible patterns

Ideal   Step change   Gradual change

deserves serious consideration. Moreover, even if other forecasting techniques offer better accuracy, they will almost always involve a greater cost. The accuracy of a naive forecast can serve as a standard of comparison against which to judge the cost and accuracy of other techniques. Hence, managers must answer the question: Is the increased accuracy of another method worth the additional resources required to achieve that accuracy?

The naive concept can also be applied to a series that exhibits seasonality or trend. For example, if monthly sales exhibit a seasonal pattern, demand for the current December can be based on demand for the preceding December, demand for January can be based on demand from the preceding January, and so on. Similarly, if trend is present, the increase (or decrease) from this period's actual demand to the next period's demand can be estimated as the same change observed between the last two periods. For instance, if June's demand is 90 units higher than May's, a naive forecast for July that allowed for trend would be June's actual demand plus an additional 90 units. Then, if July's demand was only 85 units greater than June's, August's forecast would be July's actual plus 85 units.

Naive forecasts are sometimes used as starting points for more sophisticated techniques.

Moving Averages

Moving average

Technique that averages a number of recent actual values, updated as new values become available.

One weakness of the naive method is that the forecast must *trace* the actual data, with a lag of one period; it does not smooth at all. But by expanding the amount of historical data a forecast is based on, this difficulty can be overcome. A **moving average** forecast uses a *number* of the most recent actual data values in generating a forecast. The moving average forecast can be computed using the following equation:

$$\text{MA}_n = \frac{\sum_{i=1}^{n} A_i}{n} \tag{4-1}$$

where

i = "Age" of the data (i = 1,2,3 . . .)
n = Number of periods in the moving average
A_i = Actual value with age i

For example, MA_3 would refer to a three-period moving average, and MA_5 would refer to a five-period moving average.

Example 1

∎

Compute a three-period moving average forecast given demand for shopping carts for the last five periods:

Period	Age	Demand
1	5	42
2	4	40
3	3	43
4	2	40
5	1	41

Solution

$$MA_3 = \frac{43 + 40 + 41}{3} = 41.33$$

If actual demand in period 6 turns out to be 39, the moving average forecast for period 7 would be:

$$MA_3 = \frac{40 + 41 + 39}{3} = 40.00$$

Note that in a moving average, as each new actual value becomes available, the forecast is updated by adding the newest value and dropping the oldest and then recomputing the average. Consequently, the forecast "moves" by reflecting only the most recent values.

In computing a moving average, the "age" column in the preceding example would not be included; it is shown merely to illustrate the concept. Instead, it would simplify computation to include a *moving total* column, which gives the sum of the *n* most current values from which the average will be computed. It is relatively simple to update the moving total: Subtract the oldest value from the newest value, and add that amount to the moving total for each update.

Figure 4–3 illustrates a three-period moving average forecast plotted against actual demand over 31 periods. Note how the moving average forecast *lags* the actual values and how smooth the forecasted values are compared to the actual values.

The moving average can incorporate as many data points as desired, beginning with the latest value and working backward. Hence, a 10-period moving average forecast would be the average of the latest 10 actual values. In selecting the number of periods to include, the decision maker must take into account that the number of data points in the average determines its sensitivity to each new data point: The fewer the data points in an average, the more responsive the average tends to be, as

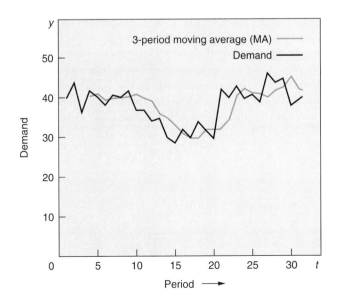

Figure 4–3

A moving average forecast tends to smooth and lag changes in the data

Figure 4–4

The more periods in a
moving average, the
greater the forecast will lag
changes in the data

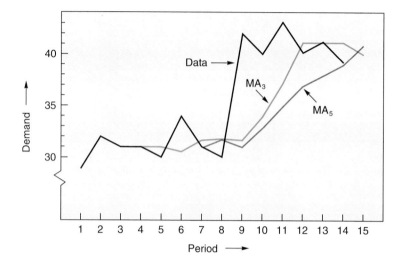

depicted in Figure 4–4. Hence, if responsiveness is important, a moving average
with relatively few data points should be used. This will permit quick adjustment to,
say, a step change in the data, but it will also cause the forecast to be somewhat
responsive even to random variations. Conversely, moving averages based on more
data points will smooth more but be less responsive to "real" changes. Hence, the
decision maker must weigh the cost of responding more slowly to changes in the
data against the cost of responding to what might simply be random variations.

The advantages of a moving average forecast are that it is easy to compute and
easy to understand. A disadvantage is that data storage requirements can be significant, especially if large numbers of moving average forecasts are being made. This is
because individual values that make up the average must be separately identified so
that with each new forecast, the oldest value can be discarded. A more serious
consideration is that all values in the average are weighted equally. Hence, in a
10-period moving average, each value is given a weight of ⅒: the oldest value is
given the *same weight* as the most recent value. Decreasing the number of values in
the average will increase the weight of more recent values, but this will be at the
expense of losing potential information from less recent values.

A *weighted average* is similar to a moving average, except that it assigns more
weight to the most recent values in a time series. For instance, the most recent value
might be assigned a weight of .40, the next most recent value a weight of .30, the
next after that a weight of .20, and the next after that a weight of .10. Note that the
weights sum to 1.00, and that the heaviest weights are assigned to the most recent
values.

Example 2

Given the following demand data,

a. Compute a weighted average forecast using a weight of .40 for the most recent
period, .30 for the next most recent, .20 for the next, and .10 for the next.
b. If the actual demand for period 6 is 39, forecast demand for period 7 using the
same weights as in *a.*

Period	Demand
1	42
2	40
3	43
4	40
5	41

Solution

a. Forecast $= .40(41) + .30(40) + .20(43) + .10(40) = 41.0$

b. Forecast $= .40(39) + .30(41) + .20(40) + .10(43) = 40.2$

Note that if four weights are used, only the *four most recent* demands are used to prepare the forecast.

The advantage of a weighted average over a (simple) moving average is that the weighted average is more reflective of the most recent occurrences. However, the choice of weights is somewhat arbitrary, and generally involves the use of trial and error to find a suitable weighting scheme.

Exponential Smoothing

Exponential smoothing is a sophisticated weighted averaging method that is still relatively easy to use and understand. Each new forecast is based on the previous forecast plus a percentage of the difference between that forecast and the actual value of the series at that point. That is:

New forecast = Old forecast + α(Actual − Old forecast)

Exponential smoothing
Weighted averaging method based on previous forecast plus a percentage of the forecast error.

where α is a percentage and (Actual − Old forecast) represents the forecast error. More concisely,

$$F_t = F_{t-1} + \alpha(A_{t-1} - F_{t-1}) \tag{4–2}$$

where

$\quad\quad F_t$ = Forecast for period t
$\quad F_{t-1}$ = Forecast for period $t - 1$
$\quad\quad \alpha$ = Smoothing constant
$\quad A_{t-1}$ = Actual demand or sales for period $t - 1$

The smoothing constant α represents a percentage of the forecast error. Each new forecast is equal to the previous forecast plus a percentage of the previous error. For example, suppose the previous forecast was 42 units, actual demand was 40 units, and $\alpha = .10$. The new forecast would be computed as follows:

$$F_t = 42 + .10(40 - 42) = 41.8$$

Then, if the actual demand turns out to be 43, the next forecast would be:

$$F_t = 41.8 + .10(43 - 41.8) = 41.92$$

The sensitivity of forecast adjustment to error is determined by the smoothing constant, α. The closer its value is to zero, the slower the forecast will be to adjust to forecast errors (i.e., the greater the smoothing). Conversely, the closer the value of α is to 1.00, the greater the sensitivity and the less the smoothing. This is illustrated in the continuation of this series in Example 3.

Example 3

Use exponential smoothing to develop a series of forecasts for the following data, and compute (Actual − Forecast) = Error, for each period.

a.   Use a smoothing factor of .10.
b.   Use a smoothing factor of .40.
c.   Plot the actual data and both sets of forecasts on a single graph.

Period (t)	Actual demand
1	42
2	40
3	43
4	40
5	41
6	39
7	46
8	44
9	45
10	38
11	40
12	

Solution

		$\alpha = .10$		$\alpha = .40$	
Period (t)	Actual demand	Forecast	Error	Forecast	Error
1	42	—	—	—	—
2	40	42	−2	42	−2
3	43	41.8	1.2	41.2	1.8
4	40	41.92	−1.92	41.92	−1.92
5	41	41.73	−0.73	41.15	−0.15
6	39	41.66	−2.66	41.09	−2.09
7	46	41.39	4.61	40.25	5.75
8	44	41.85	2.15	42.55	1.45
9	45	42.07	2.93	43.13	1.87
10	38	42.35	−4.35	43.88	−5.88
11	40	41.92	−1.91	41.53	−1.53
12		41.73		40.92	

The forecasting module of DSS-POM (2.1c) is used here to solve Example 3. The first two screens show the actual data, the forecast, error, and tracking signal. The final screen shows a scatter plot of both the actual data and the forecast.

Selecting a smoothing constant is basically a matter of judgment or trial and error. The goal is to select a smoothing constant that will balance the benefits of smoothing random variations with the benefits of responding to real changes if and when they occur. Commonly used values of α range from .05 to .50.

Some computer packages include a feature that permits automatic modification of the smoothing constant if the forecast errors become unacceptably large.

Exponential smoothing is one of the most widely used techniques in forecasting, partly because of its minimal data storage requirements and ease of calculation, and partly because of the ease with which the weighting scheme can be altered—simply by changing the value of α.

A number of different approaches can be used to obtain a starting forecast, such as the average of the first several periods; a subjective estimate; or the first actual value as the forecast for period 2 (i.e., the naive approach). For simplicity, the naive approach is used in this book.

The effect of the smoothing constant α on the forecasts can be seen more easily by rewriting the equation

$$F_t = F_{t-1} + \alpha(A_{t-1} - F_{t-1})$$

with the F_{t-1} terms grouped:

$$F_t = \alpha A_{t-1} + (1 - \alpha)F_{t-1} \tag{4-3}$$

A large value of alpha will put more weight on the most recent value of the series (i.e., A_{t-1}) and less weight on older data (i.e., reflected by F_{t-1}) than would a smaller value of alpha. For example, consider $\alpha = .5$ and $\alpha = .2$. For $\alpha = .5$, the equation is

$$F_t = .5A_{t-1} + .5F_{t-1}$$

For $\alpha = .2$, the equation is

$$F_t = .2A_{t-1} + .8F_{t-1}$$

If you are interested, the overall weighting pattern for past data is demonstrated in the footnote below.[1]

TECHNIQUES FOR TREND

The trend component of a time series reflects the effects of any long-term factors on the series. Analysis of trend involves searching for an equation that will suitably describe trend (assuming that trend is, in fact, present in the data). The trend component may be linear, or it may not. Some commonly encountered nonlinear trend functions are illustrated in Figure 4–5. A simple plot of the data can often reveal the nature of the trend component. The discussion here will focus exclusively on linear trend because linear trends are fairly common and because they are the easiest to work with.

There are two important techniques that can be used to develop forecasts when trend is present. One involves use of a trend equation, and the other is an extension of exponential smoothing.

---

[1] Expanding equation 4–3 yields

$$F_t = \alpha A_{t-1} + (1 - \alpha)[\alpha A_{t-2} + (1 - \alpha)F_{t-2}]$$

We can continue to expand, to produce an equation of the form:

$$F_t = \alpha A_{t-1} + \alpha(1 - \alpha)A_{t-2} + \alpha(1 - \alpha)^2 A_{t-3} + \alpha(1 - \alpha)^3 A_{t-4} + \cdots$$

For $\alpha = .2$, this becomes

$$F_t = .2A_{t-1} + .16A_{t-2} + .128A_{t-3} + .1024A_{t-4} + \cdots$$

and for $\alpha = .5$ this becomes:

$$F_t = .5A_{t-1} + .25A_{t-2} + .125A_{t-3} + .0625A_{t-4} + \cdots$$

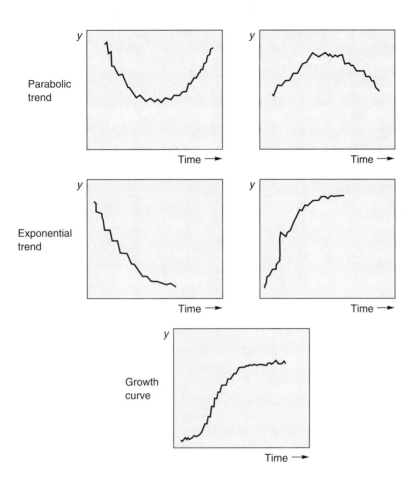

Figure 4–5

Graphs of some common nonlinear trends

Parabolic trend

Exponential trend

Growth curve

Trend Equation

A **linear trend equation** has the form

$$y_t = a + bt \qquad (4-4)$$

where

Linear trend equation
$y_t = a + bt$, used to develop forecasts when trend is present.

t = Specified number of time periods from $t = 0$

y_t = Forecast for period t

a = Value of y_t at $t = 0$

b = Slope of the line

For example, consider the trend equation $y_t = 45 + 5t$. The value of y_t when $t = 0$ is 45, and the slope of the line is 5, which means that, on the average, the value of y_t will increase by 5 units for each 1-unit increase in t. If $t = 10$, the forecast, y_t, is $45 + 5(10) = 95$ units. The equation can be plotted by finding two points on the line. One can be found by substituting some value of t into the equation (e.g., $t = 10$) and then solving for y_t. The other point is a (i.e., y_t at $t = 0$). Plotting those two points and drawing a line through them will yield a graph of the linear trend line.

The coefficients of the line, *a* and *b,* can be computed from historical data using these two equations:

$$b = \frac{n\Sigma ty - \Sigma t\Sigma y}{n\Sigma t^2 - (\Sigma t)^2} \tag{4-5}$$

$$a = \frac{\Sigma y - b\Sigma t}{n} \tag{4-6}$$

where

n = Number of periods
y = Value of the time series

These equations are identical to those used for computing a linear regression line, except that t replaces x in the equations. Manual computation of the coefficients of a trend line can be simplified by use of Table 4–1, which lists values of Σt and Σt^2 for up to 20 ($n = 20$) periods.

Trend-Adjusted Exponential Smoothing

A variation of simple exponential smoothing can be used when a time series exhibits trend. It is called **trend-adjusted exponential smoothing** or, sometimes, *double smoothing,* to differentiate it from simple exponential smoothing, which is appropriate only when data vary around an average or have step or gradual changes. If a series exhibits trend, and simple smoothing is used on it, the forecasts will all *lag* the trend. For example, if the data are increasing, each forecast will be too low. Conversely, decreasing data will result in forecasts that are too high. Again, plotting the data can indicate when trend-adjusted smoothing would be preferable to simple smoothing.

Trend-adjusted exponential smoothing

Variation of exponential smoothing used when a time series exhibits trend.

Table 4–1	n	Σt	Σt^2
Values of Σt and Σt^2	1	1	1
	2	3	5
	3	6	14
	4	10	30
	5	15	55
	6	21	91
	7	28	140
	8	36	204
	9	45	285
	10	55	385
	11	66	506
	12	78	650
	13	91	819
	14	105	1,015
	15	120	1,240
	16	136	1,496
	17	153	1,785
	18	171	2,109
	19	190	2,470
	20	210	2,870

The trend-adjusted forecast (TAF) is composed of two elements: a smoothed error and a trend factor:

$$\text{TAF}_{t+1} = S_t + T_t \tag{4–7}$$

where

S_t = Smoothed forecast
T_t = Current trend estimate

Calculator sales for a California-based firm over the last 10 weeks are shown in the following table. Plot the data, and visually check to see if a linear trend line would be appropriate. Then determine the equation of the trend line, and predict sales for weeks 11 and 12.

Example 4

Week	Unit sales
1	700
2	724
3	720
4	728
5	740
6	742
7	758
8	750
9	770
10	775

Solution

a. A plot suggests that a linear trend would be appropriate:

(continued)

Example 4

(concluded)

b.

Week (t)	y	ty
1	700	700
2	724	1,448
3	720	2,160
4	728	2,912
5	740	3,700
6	742	4,452
7	758	5,306
8	750	6,000
9	770	6,930
10	775	7,750
	7,407	41,358

From Table 4–1, for $n = 10$, $\Sigma t = 55$ and $\Sigma t^2 = 385$. Using Formulas 4–5 and 4–6, we can compute the coefficients of the trend line:

$$b = \frac{10(41{,}358) - 55(7{,}407)}{10(385) - 55(55)} = \frac{6{,}195}{825} = 7.51$$

$$a = \frac{7{,}407 - 7.51(55)}{10} = 699.40$$

Thus, the trend line is $y_t = 699.40 + 7.51t$, where $t = 0$ for period 0.

c. By substituting values of t into this equation, we can obtain forecasts for future periods. For the next two periods ($t = 11$ and $t = 12$), the forecasts are:

$$y_{11} = 699.40 + 7.51(11) = 782.01$$
$$y_{12} = 699.40 + 7.51(12) = 789.51$$

d. For purposes of illustration, the original data, the trend line, and the two projections (forecasts) are shown on the following graph:

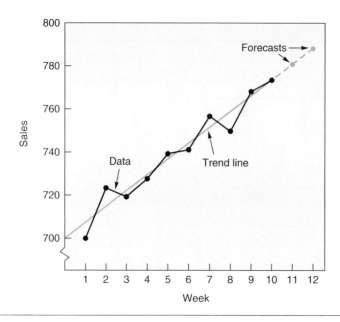

and

$$S_t = \text{TAF}_t + \alpha_1(A_t - \text{TAF}_t)$$
$$T_t = T_{t-1} + \alpha_2(\text{TAF}_t - \text{TAF}_{t-1} - T_{t-1})$$

where α_1 and α_2 are smoothing constants. In order to use this method, one must select values of α_1 and α_2 (usually through trial and error) and make a starting forecast and an estimate of trend.

Example calculations are illustrated in Table 4–2. Notice that an initial estimate of trend is estimated from the first four values, and that the starting forecast (period 5) is developed using the previous (period 4) value of 728 plus the initial trend estimate:

$$\text{Starting forecast} = 728 + 9.30 = 737.30$$

Although manual computations are somewhat more involved for trend-adjusted smoothing than for a linear trend line, trend-adusted smoothing has the ability to adjust to *changes* in trend. Of course, trend projections are much simpler with a trend line than with trend-adjusted forecasts, so a manager must decide which benefits are most important when choosing between these two techniques for trend.

TECHNIQUES FOR SEASONALITY

Seasonal variations in time series data are regularly repeating upward or downward movements in series values that can be tied to recurring events. *Seasonality* may refer to regular annual variations. Familiar examples of seasonality relate to weather variations (e.g., sales of winter and summer sports equipment) and vacations or holidays (e.g., airline travel, greeting card sales, visitors at tourist and resort centers). The term *seasonal variation* is also applied to daily, weekly, monthly, and other regularly recurring patterns in data. For example, rush hour traffic occurs twice a day: incoming in the morning and outgoing in the late afternoon. Theaters and restaurants often experience weekly demand patterns, with demand higher later in the week than earlier. Banks may experience daily seasonal variations (heavier

Seasonal variations
Regularly repeating movements in series values that can be tied to recurring events.

Table 4–2

	t (Period)	A_t (Actual)	
Model development	1	700	Trend estimate $= \dfrac{728 - 700}{3} = \dfrac{28}{3} = 9.3$
	2	724	
	3	720	Starting forecast $= 728 + 9.3 = 737.3$
	4	728	
			$\text{TAF}_t + \alpha_1(A_t - \text{TAF}_t) = S_t \quad\quad T_{t-1} + \alpha_2(\text{TAF}_t - \text{TAF}_{t-1} - T_{t-1}) = T_t$
	5	740	$737.3 + .4(740 - 737.3) = 738.38 \quad\quad 9.3 + .3(0) = 9.30$
	6	742	$747.68 + .4(742 - 747.68) = 745.41 \quad\quad 9.30 + .3(747.68 - 737.30 - 9.30) = 9.62$
Model test	7	758	$755.03 + .4(758 - 755.03) = 756.22 \quad\quad 9.62 + .3(755.03 - 747.68 - 9.62) = 8.94$
	8	750	$765.16 + .4(750 - 765.16) = 759.10 \quad\quad 8.94 + .3(765.16 - 755.03 - 8.94) = 9.30$
	9	770	$768.40 + .4(770 - 768.40) = 769.04 \quad\quad 9.30 + .3(768.40 - 765.16 - 9.30) = 7.48$
	10	775	$776.52 + .4(775 - 776.52) = 775.91 \quad\quad 7.48 + .3(776.52 - 768.40 - 7.48) = 7.67$
Forecast	11		$783.58 = 775.91 + 7.67$

Example 5

Using the calculator data from the previous example (where it was concluded that the data exhibited a linear trend), use trend-adjusted exponential smoothing to prepare forecasts for periods 5 through 11, with $\alpha_1 = .4$ and $\alpha_2 = .3$.

Solution

The initial estimate of trend is based on the net change of 28 for the *three* changes from period 1 to period 4, for an average of 9.30. The data and calculations are shown in Table 4–2.

A plot of the actual data and predicted values is shown below.

traffic during the noon hour and just before closing), weekly variations (heavier toward the end of the week), and monthly variations (heaviest around the end of the month because of social security checks, payrolls, and welfare checks being cashed or deposited). Mail volume; sales of toys, beer, automobiles, and turkeys; highway usage; hotel registrations; and gardening are common examples of seasonal variations.

Seasonality in a time series is expressed in terms of the amount that actual values deviate from the *average* value of a series. If the series tends to vary around an average value, then seasonality would be expressed in terms of that average (or a moving average); if trend is present, seasonality would be expressed in terms of the trend value.

There are two different models of seasonality, additive and multiplicative. In the *additive* model, seasonality is expressed as a *quantity* (e.g., 20 units) that is added or subtracted from the series average in order to incorporate seasonality. In the *multiplicative* model, seasonality is expressed as a *percentage* of the average (or trend) amount (e.g., 1.10) that is then multiplied by the value of a series to incorporate seasonality. Figure 4–6 illustrates the two models for a linear trend line. In practice, the multiplicative model is used much more widely than the additive model. Therefore, we focus exclusively on the multiplicative model.

Figure 4–6

Seasonality: the additive and multiplicative models compared using a linear trend

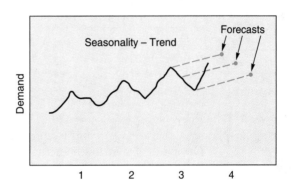

The seasonal percentages in the multiplicative model are referred to as *seasonal relatives* or *seasonal indexes*. For example, suppose that the seasonal relative for the quantity of toys sold in May at a store is 1.20. This indicates that toy sales for that month are 20 percent above the monthly average. If the seasonal relative for July is .90, this indicates that July sales are 90 percent of the monthly average.

Figure 4–7

Naive approaches with seasonality

Knowledge of seasonal variations is an important factor in planning and scheduling in many retail businesses. Moreover, seasonality can be an important factor in capacity planning for systems that must be designed to handle peak loads (e.g., public transportation, electric power plants, highways, and bridges). Knowledge of the extent of seasonality in a time series can enable one to *remove* seasonality from the data (i.e., to seasonally adjust data) in order to discern other patterns, or lack of patterns, in the series. Thus, we frequently read or hear about "seasonally adjusted unemployment" and "seasonally adjusted personal income."

The simplest seasonal model is a variation of the naive technique described for averages. Instead of using the last *period's* actual demand as the forecast amount, the seasonal naive model uses last *season's* actual amount for the forecast. Hence, our forecast of theater attendance this Friday evening would equal last Friday's attendance using the seasonal naive model, and November toy sales in one year might be estimated based on toy sales in the preceding November. If trend and seasonal variations are present, the naive model might be the last seasonal's demand plus 10 percent, or whatever increase or decrease is appropriate. (See Figure 4–7.)

Again, the naive approach can either be used alone or serve as a standard of comparison against which other, more refined techniques can be judged.

The next section describes the computation of seasonal relatives. That is followed by an example that illustrates how seasonal relatives can be combined with a trend equation to make forecasts when seasonality and trend are both present.

Centered Moving Average

Centered moving average

A moving average positioned at the center of the data that were used to compute it.

A commonly used method for representing the trend portion of a time series involves a **centered moving average.** Computations are the same as for a moving average forecast, as are the resulting values. However, the values are not projected as in a forecast; instead, they are *positioned in the middle* of the periods used to compute the moving average. The implication is that the average is most representative of that point in the series. For example, suppose we have the following time series data:

Period	Demand	Three-period centered average	
1	40		
2	46	42.67	Average $= \dfrac{40 + 46 + 42}{3} = 42.67$
3	42		

The three-period average is 42.67. As a centered average, it would be positioned at period 2; the average is most representative of the series at that point.

The ratio of demand at period 2 to this centered average at period 2 is an estimate of the seasonal relative at that point. Because the ratio is 46/42.67 = 1.08, the series is about 8 percent above average at this point. In order to achieve a reasonable estimate of seasonality for any season (e.g., Friday attendance at a theater), it is usually necessary to compute seasonal ratios for a number of seasons and then average these ratios. For instance, in the case of theater attendance, average the relatives of five or six Fridays for the Friday relative, average five or six Saturdays for the Saturday relative, and so on.

Example 6

The manager of a parking lot has computed daily relatives for the number of cars per day in the lot. The computations are repeated here (about three weeks are shown for illustration). A seven-period centered moving average is used because there are seven days (seasons) per week.

Day	Volume	Moving total	Centered MA$_7$	Volume/MA
Tues	67			
Wed	75			
Thur	82			
Fri	98		71.86	98/71.86 = 1.36 (Friday)
Sat	90		70.86	90/70.86 = 1.27
Sun	36		70.57	36/70.57 = 0.51
Mon	55	503 ÷ 7 =	71.00	55/71.00 = 0.77
Tues	60	496 ÷ 7 =	71.14	60/71.14 = 0.84 (Tuesday)

Day	Volume	Moving total	Centered MA$_7$	Volume/MA
Wed	73	494 etc.	70.57	$73/70.57 = 1.03$
Thur	85	497 .	71.14	$85/71.14 = 1.19$
Fri	99	498 .	70.71	$99/70.71 = 1.40$ (Friday)
Sat	86	494 .	71.29	$86/71.29 = 1.21$
Sun	40	498	71.71	$40/71.71 = 0.56$
Mon	52	495	72.00	$52/72.00 = 0.72$
Tues	64	499	71.57	$64/71.57 = 0.89$ (Tuesday)
Wed	76	502	71.86	$76/71.86 = 1.06$
Thur	87	504	72.43	$87/72.43 = 1.20$
Fri	96	501	72.14	$96/72.14 = 1.33$ (Friday)
Sat	88	503	73.00	$88/73.00 = 1.21$
Sun	44	507	73.57	$44/73.57 = 0.60$
Mon	50	505	72.71	$50/72.71 = 0.69$
Tues	70	511		
Wed	80	515		
Thurs	81	509		

The estimated Friday relative is $(1.36 + 1.40 + 1.33)/3 = 1.36$. Relatives for other days can be computed in a similar manner. For example, the estimated Tuesday relative is: $(0.84 + 0.89)/2 = 0.87$.

The number of periods needed in a centered moving average is equal to the number of data points within a season. Hence, with monthly data, a 12-period moving average would be needed. When the number of periods is even, one additional step is needed because the middle of an even set falls between two periods. The additional step involves taking a centered two-period moving average of the even-numbered centered moving average, which results in averages that "line up" with data points and, hence, permit determination of seasonal ratios. (See Solved Problem 4 at the end of this chapter for an example of this.)

The reason a centered moving average is used to obtain representative values is that, because it "looks forward" and "looks backward" by virtue of its centered position, it is able to closely follow data movements, regardless of whether they involve trends, cycles, or random variability alone. Figure 4–8 illustrates how a three-period centered moving average closely tracks the data originally shown in Figure 4–3.

If both trend and seasonality appear in a series, each component can be determined separately, and they can then be combined to obtain a forecast.

Seasonal relatives are used in two different ways in forecasting. One way is to *deseasonalize* data; the other way is to *incorporate seasonality* in a forecast.

To deseasonalize data is to remove the seasonal component from the data in order to get a clearer picture of the nonseasonal (e.g., trend) aspects. Deseasonalizing data can be accomplished by *dividing* each data point by its corresponding seasonal relative (e.g., divide November demand by the November relative, divide December demand by the December relative, and so on). The result is data with seasonality removed.

Figure 4–8

A centered moving average closely tracks the data

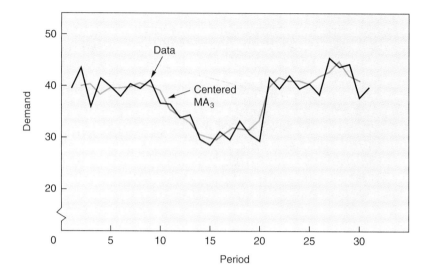

Incorporating seasonality in a forecast is useful when demand has both trend (or average) and seasonal components. Incorporating seasonality can be accomplished in this way:

1. Obtain trend estimates for desired periods using a trend equation.
2. Add seasonality to the trend estimates by *multiplying* (assuming a multiplicative model is appropriate) these trend estimates by the corresponding seasonal relative (e.g., multiply the November trend estimate by the November seasonal relative, multiply the December trend estimate by the December seasonal relative, and so on).

This is illustrated in the following example.

Example 7

A furniture manufacturer wants to predict quarterly demand for a certain loveseat for periods 15 and 16, which happen to be the second and third quarters of a particular year. The series consists of both trend and seasonality. The trend portion of demand can be projected using the equation $y_t = 124 + 7.5t$. Quarter relatives are $Q_1 = 1.20$, $Q_2 = 1.10$, $Q_3 = 0.75$, and $Q_4 = 0.95$. Use this information to predict demand for periods 15 and 16.

Solution

The trend values at $t = 15$ and $t = 16$ are:

$$y_{15} = 124 + 7.5(15) = 236.5$$
$$y_{16} = 124 + 7.5(16) = 244.0$$

Multiplying the trend value by the appropriate quarter relative will yield a forecast that includes both trend and seasonality. Since we are told that $t = 15$ is a second quarter and $t = 16$ is a third quarter, the forecasts are:

Period 15: $236.5(1.10) = 260.15$

Period 16: $244.0(0.75) = 183.00$

TECHNIQUES FOR CYCLES

When cycles (up and down movement similar to seasonal variations, but of longer duration—say, two to six years between peaks) occur in time series data, they often are so irregular that it is difficult or impossible to project them from past data because turning points are difficult to identify. A short moving average or a naive approach may be of some value, although both will produce forecasts that lag cyclical movements by one or several periods.

The most commonly used approach is explanatory: Search for another variable that relates to, and *leads,* the variable of interest. For example, the number of housing starts (permits to build houses) in a given month often is an indicator of demand a few months later for products and services that are directly tied to construction of new homes (landscaping, sales of washers and dryers, sales of carpeting and furniture, new demands for shopping, transportation, schools, etc.). Thus, if an organization is able to establish a high correlation with such a *leading variable* (i.e., changes in the variable precede changes in the variable of interest), an equation that describes the relationship can be developed, enabling forecasts to be made. It is important that there be a persistent relationship between the two variables. Moreover, the higher the correlation, the better the chances that the forecast will be on target.

OTHER TECHNIQUES FOR TIME SERIES

A number of other techniques that can be used to analyze time series data are beyond the scope of this text. However, one of these, the *Box-Jenkins technique,* is worthy of note because of its increasing popularity and its ability to provide accurate forecasts.

The main advantage of the Box-Jenkins method is that it is better able to handle data that include complex patterns than are the techniques described previously. Also, the resulting forecasts often possess a high degree of accuracy compared to other methods. The main disadvantages of the technique are its processing costs and complexity. The computations are fairly long and involved, and a computer program is essential. Furthermore, it is virtually impossible to communicate the assumptions that must be satisfied in order to obtain valid results to users who do not possess considerable mathematical sophistication.

ASSOCIATIVE FORECASTING TECHNIQUES

Associative techniques rely on identification of related variables that can be used to predict values of the variable of interest. For example, sales of beef may be related to the price per pound charged for beef as well as the prices of substitutes such as chicken, pork, and lamb; real estate prices are usually related to property location; and crop yields are related to soil conditions, as well as to amounts and timing of water and fertilizer applications.

The essence of associative techniques is the development of an equation that summarizes the effects of **predictor variables**. The primary method of analysis is known as **regression**. Although a detailed explanation of regression analysis is beyond the scope of this text, a brief overview of regression is given. This should suffice to place this approach into perspective relative to the other forecasting approaches described in the chapter.

Predictor variables

Variables that can be used to predict values of the variable of interest.

Regression

Technique for fitting a line to a set of points.

SIMPLE LINEAR REGRESSION

The simplest and most widely used form of regression involves a linear relationship between two variables. A plot of the values might appear like that in Figure 4–9. The object in linear regression is to obtain an equation of a straight line that minimizes the sum of squared vertical deviations of data points from the line. This **least squares line** has the equation

Least squares line

Minimizes the sum of the squared deviations around the line.

$$y_c = a + bx \tag{4–8}$$

where

y_c = Predicted (dependent) variable
x = Predictor (independent) variable
b = Slope of the line
a = Value of y_c when $x = 0$ (i.e., the height of the line at the y intercept)

(Note that it is conventional to represent values of the predicted variable on the y axis and values of the predictor variable on the x axis.) A graph of a linear regression line is illustrated in Figure 4–10.

The coefficients a and b of the line are computed using these two equations:

$$b = \frac{n(\Sigma xy) - (\Sigma x)(\Sigma y)}{n(\Sigma x^2) - (\Sigma x)^2} \tag{4–9}$$

$$a = \frac{\Sigma y - b\Sigma x}{n} \text{ or } \bar{y} - b\bar{x} \tag{4–10}$$

where

n = Number of paired observations

The accuracy of regression estimates depends on the extent to which sample data scatter around the line: the greater the scatter, the less accurate estimates will be. Scatter can be summarized using the standard error of estimate, s_e, where

$$s_e = \sqrt{\frac{\Sigma y^2 - a\Sigma y - b\Sigma xy}{n - 2}} \tag{4–11}$$

Figure 4–9

A straight line is fitted to a set of sample points

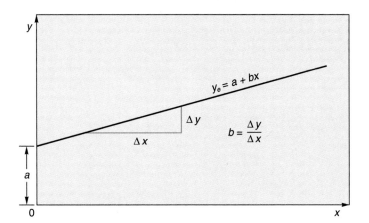

Figure 4–10

Equation of a straight line

The line intersects the *y* axis where *y* = *a*. The slope of the line = *b*.

Healthy Hamburgers has a chain of 12 stores in northern Illinois. Sales figures and profits for the stores are given in the following table. Obtain a regression line for the data, and predict profit for a store assuming sales of $10 million.

Example 8

Sales, *x* (millions)	Profits, *y* (millions)
$ 7	$0.15
2	0.10
6	0.13
4	0.15
14	0.25
15	0.27
16	0.24
12	0.20
14	0.27
20	0.44
15	0.34
7	0.17

Solution

First, plot the data and decide if a linear model is reasonable (i.e., do the points seem to scatter around a straight line? Figure 4-11 suggests they do). Next, compute the quantities Σx, Σy, Σxy, and Σx^2. Calculations are shown for these quantities in Table 4–3. One additional calculation, Σy^2, is included for later reference.

Substituting into the equations, we find:

$$b = \frac{n(\Sigma xy) - (\Sigma x)(\Sigma y)}{n(\Sigma x^2) - (\Sigma x)^2} = \frac{12(35.29) - 132(2.71)}{12(1,796) - 132(132)} = 0.01593$$

$$a = \frac{\Sigma y - b(\Sigma x)}{n} = \frac{2.71 - 0.01593(132)}{12} = 0.0506$$

(continued)

Example 8

(concluded)

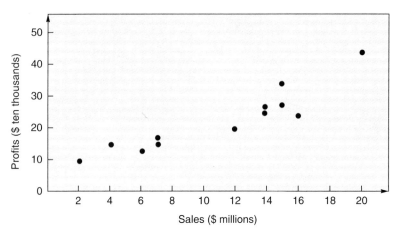

Figure 4–11

A linear model seems
reasonable

Thus, the regression equation is: $y_c = 0.0506 + 0.01593x$. For sales of $x = 10$ (i.e.,
$10 million), estimated profit is: $y_c = 0.0506 + 0.01593(10) = 0.2099$, or $209,900.
(It may appear strange to you that substituting $x = 0$ into the equation produces a predicted profit of $50,600 because it seems to suggest that amount of profit will occur
with no sales. However, the value of $x = 0$ is *outside of the range of observed values*. The
regression line should only be used for the range of values it was developed from; the
relationship may be nonlinear outside that range. The purpose of the a value is simply
to establish the height of the line where it crosses the y axis.)

Table 4–3

Calculations for regression coefficients for Healthy Hamburgers

x	y	xy	x^2	y^2
7	0.15	1.05	49	0.0225
2	0.10	0.20	4	0.0100
6	0.13	0.78	36	0.0169
4	0.15	0.60	16	0.0225
14	0.25	3.50	196	0.0625
15	0.27	4.05	225	0.0729
16	0.24	3.84	256	0.0576
12	0.20	2.40	144	0.0400
14	0.27	3.78	196	0.0729
20	0.44	8.80	400	0.1936
15	0.34	5.10	225	0.1156
7	0.17	1.19	49	0.0289
132	2.71	35.29	1,796	0.7159

For the Healthy Hamburgers example, the standard error of estimate is

$$s_e = \sqrt{\frac{0.7159 - 0.0506(2.71) - 0.01593(35.29)}{12 - 2}} = 0.04075 \text{ or } \$40,750$$

A confidence interval for the predicted value of y (i.e., y_c) for a given value of x (i.e., x_g) can be obtained using the equation

$$\text{Confidence interval} = y_c \pm ts_{\text{reg}} \qquad (4\text{--}12)$$

where

$$s_{\text{reg}} = s_e \sqrt{1 + \frac{1}{n} + \frac{(x_g - \bar{x})^2}{\Sigma x^2 - [(\Sigma x)^2/n]}}$$

and

$\bar{x}$ = Mean of x values
x_g = Some given value of x
t = Standardized value obtained from a t table

For convenience, some selected values of t are listed in Table 4–4.

For the Healthy Hamburgers data, s_{reg} for $x_g = 10$ is

$$s_{\text{reg}} = 0.04075 \sqrt{1 + \frac{1}{12} + \frac{(10 - 11)^2}{1,796 - (132)^2/12}} = 0.04247$$

A 95 percent confidence interval for the predicted value of y is:

$$y_c \pm t(s_{\text{reg}}) = (0.0506 + 0.01593(10)) \pm 2.23 \ (0.04247)$$
$$= 0.2099 \pm 0.0947, \text{ or } 0.1152 \text{ to } 0.3046$$

That is, estimated profit on sales of $10 million is $209,900, and on the basis of the sample data we are 95 percent confident that actual profits will be in the range of $115,200 to $304,600.

Table 4–4

Selected values of t for 95 percent confidence intervals

Degrees of freedom	t
5	2.57
6	2.45
7	2.37
8	2.31
9	2.25
10	2.23
11	2.20
12	2.18

Degrees of freedom = $n - 2$.

It is interesting to note how wide the confidence interval is in this case, because after a certain point an interval can be so wide that it is meaningless. Although the interval here is somewhat wider than we would like, it does give an indication of the extent to which profits could vary on sales of $10 million.

Because the regression equation is developed from sample data that include random variability, there is always the risk that no real relationship exists between the variables. In that case, the average y would produce comparable predictions, so the added cost and effort of regression could be avoided. A simple test can be used to determine if a *significant* relationship exists, that is, if the slope is nonzero:

$$t_{\text{test}} = b/s_b \qquad\qquad (4\text{--}13)$$

where

$b =$ Slope of line

$$s_b = s_e \sqrt{\frac{1}{\Sigma x^2 - [(\Sigma x)^2/n]}}$$

For Healthy Hamburgers, the standard error of the slope s_b is:

$$s_b = 0.04075 \sqrt{\frac{1}{1{,}796 - (132)(132)/12}} = 0.0022$$

$$t_{\text{test}} = b/s_b = 0.01593/0.0022 = 7.24$$

This value must be compared to one found in a t table (see Table 4–4) using the appropriate degrees of freedom. Conclude the relationship is significant if $t_{\text{test}} > t$. (If $n > 30$, a z value obtained from the normal table can be used in place of t.) Since $t_{\text{test}} = 7.24$ and $t = 2.23$ from Table 4–4, we conclude that there is a relationship between the two variables.

One application of regression in forecasting relates to the use of indicators. These are uncontrollable variables that tend to lead or precede changes in a variable of interest. For example, changes in the federal reserve's discount rate may influence certain business activities. Similarly, an increase in housing starts during the spring and summer months may lead to increased demand for appliances, carpets, furniture, and similar items in the fall and winter months. Careful identification and analysis of indicators may yield insight into possible future demand in some situations. There are numerous published indexes from which to choose.[2] Among them are the following:

Net change in inventories on hand and on order
Interest rates for commercial loans
Industrial output
Consumer price index
The wholesale price index
Stock market prices

Other potential indicators are population shifts, local political climates, and activities of other firms (e.g., the opening of a shopping center may result in increased sales for nearby businesses).

___

[2] See, for example, *The National Bureau of Economic Research, The Survey of Current Business, The Monthly Labor Review,* and *Business Conditions Digest.*

In order for an indicator to be valid, three conditions are required:

1. There should be a logical explanation for the relationship between movements of an indicator and movements of the variable of interest.
2. Movements of the indicator must precede movements of the dependent variable by enough time so that the forecast isn't outdated before it can be acted upon.
3. There should be a fairly high correlation between the two variables.

Correlation measures the strength and direction of relationship between two variables. Correlation can range from -1.00 to $+1.00$. A correlation of $+1.00$ indicates that changes in one variable are always matched by changes in the other; a correlation of -1.00 indicates that increases in one variable are matched by decreases in the other; and a correlation close to zero indicates little *linear* relationship between two variables. The correlation between two variables can be computed using the equation

Correlation

A measure of the strength and direction of relationship between two variables.

$$r = \frac{n(\Sigma xy) - (\Sigma x)(\Sigma y)}{\sqrt{n(\Sigma x^2) - (\Sigma x)^2} \cdot \sqrt{n(\Sigma y^2) - (\Sigma y)^2}} \qquad (4-14)$$

Sales of 19-inch color television sets and three-month lagged unemployment are shown in the following table. Determine if unemployment levels can be used to predict demand for 19-inch color TVs and, if so, derive a predictive equation.

Example 9

Period	1	2	3	4	5	6	7	8	9	10	11
Units sold	20	41	17	35	25	31	38	50	15	19	14
Unemployment (three-month lag)	7.2	4.0	7.3	5.5	6.8	6.0	5.4	3.6	8.4	7.0	9.0

Solution

1. Plot the data to see if a linear model seems reasonable. In this case, a linear model seems appropriate *for the range of the data.*

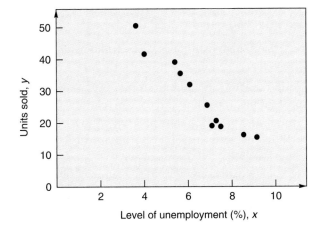

(continued)

Example 9

(concluded)

2. Compute the correlation coefficient to confirm that it is not close to zero.

x	y	xy	x^2	y^2
7.2	20	144.0	51.8	400
4.0	41	164.0	16.0	1,681
7.3	17	124.1	53.3	289
5.5	35	192.5	30.3	1,225
6.8	25	170.0	46.2	625
6.0	31	186.0	36.0	961
5.4	38	205.2	29.2	1,444
3.6	50	180.0	13.0	2,500
8.4	15	126.0	70.6	225
7.0	19	133.0	49.0	361
9.0	14	126.0	81.0	196
70.2	305	1,750.8	476.3	9,907

$$r = \frac{11(1{,}750.8) - 70.2(305)}{\sqrt{11(476.3) - (70.2)^2} \cdot \sqrt{11(9{,}907) - (305)^2}} = -.966$$

This is a fairly high negative correlation.

3. Compute the regression line:

$$b = \frac{11(1{,}750.8) - 70.2(305)}{11(476.4) - 70.2(70.2)} = -6.89$$

$$a = \frac{305 - (-6.9145)(70.2)}{11} = 71.85$$

$$y = 71.85 - 6.89x$$

Note that the equation pertains only to unemployment levels that are in the range 3.6 to 9.0, since sample observations covered only that range. In addition, if you suspect that r is close to zero, test the slope, b, for significance; r is significant when b is.

COMMENTS ON THE USE OF LINEAR REGRESSION ANALYSIS

Use of simple regression analysis implies that certain assumptions have been satisfied. Basically, these are:

1. Variations around the line are random. If they are, no patterns such as cycles should be apparent when the line and data are plotted.
2. Deviations around the line should be normally distributed. A concentration of values close to the line with a small proportion of larger deviations supports the assumption of normality.
3. Predictions are being made only within the range of observed values.

If the assumptions are satisfied, regression analysis can be a powerful tool. Particularly useful are the confidence intervals for predicted values. To obtain the best results, observe the following:

1. Always plot the data to verify that a linear relationship is appropriate.
2. Always test the relationship (slope) for significance.

3. The data may be time-dependent. Check this by plotting the dependent variable versus time; if patterns appear, use analysis of time series instead of regression, or use time as an independent variable as part of a *multiple regression analysis*.

4. A small correlation may imply that other variables are important.

In addition, note these weaknesses of regression:

1. Simple linear regression applies only to linear relationships with *one* independent variable.

2. A considerable amount of data is needed to establish the relationship—in practice, say, 20 or more observations.

3. All observations are weighted equally.

4. The cost and complexity involved make this technique unattractive for situations that require forecasts for many individual items.

CURVILINEAR AND MULTIPLE REGRESSION ANALYSIS

Simple linear regression may prove inadequate to handle certain problems because a linear model is inappropriate or because more than one predictor variable is involved. When nonlinear relationships are present, curvilinear regression is called for; models that involve more than one predictor require the use of multiple regression analysis. Both of these techniques are beyond the scope of this text; however, you should be aware that such models are being used. For the most part, the computations lend themselves more to computers than to hand calculation. This usually adds to the cost of the forecast, as does the acquisition of additional data called for by the use of multiple predictor variables. In each case, it is necessary to weigh the additional cost and effort required against potential improvements in accuracy of predictions.

ACCURACY AND CONTROL OF FORECASTS

Accuracy and control of forecasts is a vital aspect of forecasting. To begin with, the complex nature of most real-world variables makes it almost impossible to correctly predict future values of those variables on a regular basis. Consequently, it is essential to include an indication of the extent to which the forecast might deviate from the value of the variable that actually occurs. This will provide the forecast user with a better perspective on how far off a forecast might be.

Moreover, because some techniques will provide more accuracy than others in a given situation, in choosing among different techniques, the decision maker needs a measure of accuracy that can be used as a basis for comparison.

Finally, some forecasting applications involve a series of forecasts (e.g., weekly revenues), whereas others involve a single forecast that will be used for a one-time decision (e.g., deciding on the size of a power plant). When periodic forecasts are made, it is important to monitor forecast errors to determine if the errors are within reasonable bounds. If they are not, it is necessary to take corrective action. This is called *controlling* the forecast.

Forecast **error** is the difference between the value that occurs and the value that was predicted for a given time period. Hence, Error = Actual − Forecast:

$$e_t = A_t - F_t \tag{4-15}$$

Error

Difference between the actual value and the value that was predicted for a given period.

Positive errors result when the forecast is too low, and negative errors result when the forecast is too high. For example, if actual demand for a week is 100 units and forecast demand was 90 units, the forecast was too low; the error is $100 - 90 = +10$.

There are two somewhat different ways in which forecast errors influence decisions. One is in making a choice between various forecasting alternatives, and the other is in evaluating the success or failure of a technique in use. We shall begin by examining ways to summarize forecast error over time, and discover how that information can be applied to a choice among forecasting alternatives. Then we shall consider methods for controlling forecasts (i.e., evaluating the performance of a given forecasting method in use).

MEASURING THE ACCURACY OF FORECASTS

There are two aspects of forecast accuracy that have potential significance when deciding among forecasting alternatives. One is the historical error performance of a forecast, and the other is the ability of a forecast to respond to changes.

Mean absolute deviation

The average absolute error.

Mean squared error

The average of squared errors.

Two commonly used measures for summarizing historical errors are the **mean absolute deviation (MAD)** and the **mean squared error (MSE)**. MAD is the average absolute error, and MSE is the average of squared errors. The formulas used to compute MAD[3] and MSE are:

$$MAD = \frac{\Sigma|Actual - forecast|}{n} \qquad (4\text{--}16)$$

$$MSE = \frac{\Sigma(Actual - forecast)^2}{n - 1} \qquad (4\text{--}17)$$

The sample standard deviation, s, equals the square root of MSE.

The following example illustrates the computation of MAD and MSE.

Example 10

∎

Compute MAD and MSE for the following data.

Period	Actual	Forecast	$(A - F)$ error	|Error|	Error^2
1	217	215	2	2	4
2	213	216	−3	3	9
3	216	215	1	1	1
4	210	214	−4	4	16
5	213	211	2	2	4
6	219	214	5	5	25
7	216	217	−1	1	1
8	212	216	−4	4	16
			−2	22	76

---

[3] The absolute value, represented by the two vertical lines in Formula 4–16, ignores minus signs; all data are treated as positive values. For example, −2 becomes +2.

Solution

Using the figures shown in the table,

$$\text{MAD} = \frac{\Sigma|e|}{n} = \frac{22}{8} = 2.75$$

$$\text{MSE} = \frac{\Sigma e^2}{n-1} = \frac{76}{8-1} = 10.86$$

From a computational standpoint, the difference between these two measures is that one weights all errors evenly (MAD) and the other weights errors according to their *squared* values (MSE).

One use for these measures is to compare alternative forecasting methods. For instance, using either MAD or MSE, a manager could compare the results of exponential smoothing with values of .1, .2, and .3, and select the one that yielded the *lowest* MAD or MSE for a given set of data.

In some instances, historical error performance is secondary to the ability of a forecast to respond to changes in data patterns. Choice among alternative methods would then focus on the cost of not responding quickly to a change relative to the cost of responding to changes that are not really there (i.e., random fluctuations).

Overall, the operations manager must settle on the relative importance of historical performance versus responsiveness as well as on whether to use MAD or MSE to measure historical performance.

CONTROLLING THE FORECAST

It is necessary to monitor forecast errors to insure that the forecast is performing adequately. This can be accomplished by comparing forecast errors to predetermined values, or *action limits,* as illustrated in Figure 4–12. Errors that fall within the limits would be judged acceptable, and errors outside of either limit would signal that corrective action is needed.

There are a variety of possible sources of forecast errors, including the following:

1. The model may be inadequate due to (*a*) the omission of an important variable, (*b*) a change or shift in the variable that the model cannot deal with (e.g., sudden appearance of a trend or cycle), or (*c*) the appearance of a new variable (e.g., new competitor).

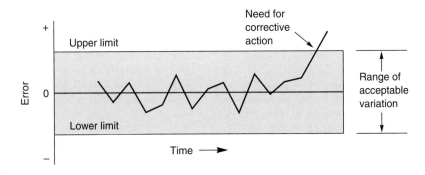

Figure 4–12

Monitoring forecast errors

2. Irregular variations may occur due to severe weather or other natural phenomena, temporary shortages or breakdowns, catastrophes, or similar events.

3. The forecasting technique may be used incorrectly, or the results may be misinterpreted.

4. There may be random variations in the data. Randomness is the inherent variation that remains in the data after all causes of variation have been accounted for.

A forecast is generally deemed to perform adequately when the errors exhibit only random variations. Hence, the key to judging when to reexamine the validity of a particular forecasting technique is whether forecast errors are random. If they are not random, investigate to determine which of the other sources is present and how to correct the problem.

Forecasts can be monitored using either *tracking signals* or *control charts*. A **tracking signal** focuses on the ratio of *cumulative* forecast error to the corresponding value of MAD:

Tracking signal

The ratio of cumulative forecast error to the corresponding value of MAD, used to monitor a forecast.

$$\text{Tracking signal} = \frac{\Sigma(\text{Actual} - \text{Forecast})}{\text{MAD}} \qquad (4\text{–}18)$$

The resulting values are compared to predetermined limits. These are based on judgment and experience and often range from ± 3 to ± 8. We shall use limits of ± 4 for the most part. These are roughly comparable to three standard deviation limits. Values within the limits suggest—but do not guarantee—that the forecast is performing adequately. After an initial value of MAD has been computed, MAD can be updated using exponential smoothing:

$$\text{MAD}_t = \text{MAD}_{t-1} + \alpha(|\text{Actual} - \text{Forecast}|_t - \text{MAD}_{t-1}) \qquad (4\text{–}19)$$

Control chart

Monitoring approach that sets limits for individual forecast errors; the limits are multiples of the square root of MSE.

The **control chart** approach involves setting upper and lower limits for *individual* forecast errors (instead of cumulative errors, as is the case with a tracking signal). The limits are multiples of the square root of MSE. This method assumes the following:

1. Forecast errors are randomly distributed around a mean of zero.
2. The distribution of errors is normal.

In effect, the square root of MSE is an estimate of the standard deviation of the distribution of errors. That is,

$$s = \sqrt{\text{MSE}} \qquad (4\text{–}20)$$

Recall that for a normal distribution, approximately 95 percent of the values (errors in this case) can be expected to fall within limits of $0 \pm 2s$, and approximately 99 percent of the values can be expected to fall within $\pm 3s$ of zero. Hence, if the forecast is "in control," 99 percent or 95 percent of the errors should fall within the limits, depending on whether $3s$ or $2s$ limits are being used. Points that fall outside these limits should be regarded as evidence that corrective action is needed (i.e., that the forecast is not performing adequately). Figure 4–12 illustrates this concept.

Using a control chart, it can be very informative to plot the errors. A plot helps you to visualize the process and enables you to check for possible patterns *within the limits* that suggest an improved forecast is possible.[4]

---

[4] The theory and application of control charts, as well as various methods for detecting patterns in the data, are covered in more detail in Chapter 10, on quality assurance.

Monthly sales of leather jackets at the Lucky Leather Shoppe for the past 24 months are shown in the following table, as are the forecasts and errors for those months. Determine if the forecast is working using these approaches:

Example 11

1. A tracking signal, beginning with month 10, updating MAD with exponential smoothing. Use limits of ± 4 and $\alpha = .2$.
2. A control chart with $2s$ limits. Use data from the first eight months to develop the control chart, then evaluate the remaining data with the control chart.

Month	A (sales)	F (forecast)	A − F (error)	$\lvert e \rvert$	Cumulative $\lvert e \rvert$
1	47	43	4	4	4
2	51	44	7	7	11
3	54	50	4	4	15
4	55	51	4	4	19
5	49	54	−5	5	24
6	46	48	−2	2	26
7	38	46	−8	8	34
8	32	44	−12	12	46
9	25	35	−10	10	56
10	24	26	−2	2	58
11	30	25	5	5	
12	35	32	3	3	
13	44	34	10	10	
14	57	50	7	7	
15	60	51	9	9	
16	55	54	1	1	
17	51	55	−4	4	
18	48	51	−3	3	
19	42	50	−8	8	
20	30	43	−13	13	
21	28	38	−10	10	
22	25	27	−2	2	
23	35	27	8	8	
24	38	32	6	6	
			−11		

Solution

a. The sum of absolute errors through the 10th month is 58. Hence, the initial MAD is $58/10 = 5.8$. The subsequent MADs are updated using the formula $\text{MAD}_{\text{new}} = \text{MAD}_{\text{old}} + .2(\lvert e \rvert - \text{MAD}_{\text{old}})$. The results are shown in the following table.

The tracking signal for any month is:

$$\frac{\text{Cumulative error at that month}}{\text{Updated MAD at that month}}$$

(continued)

Example 11

(continued)

t (month)	$\lvert e \rvert$	$MAD_t = MAD_{t-1} + .2(\lvert e \rvert - MAD_{t-1})$	Cumulative error	Tracking signal = Cumulative error$_t \div MAD_t$
10 ..			−20	−20/5.800 = −3.45
11 ..	5	5.640 = 5.8 + .2(5 − 5.8)	−15	−15/5.640 = −2.66
12 ..	3	5.112 = 5.640 + .2(3 − 5.64)	−12	−12/5.112 = −2.35
13 ..	10	6.090 = 5.112 + .2(10 − 5.112)	−2	−2/6.090 = −0.33
14 ..	7	6.272 = 6.090 + .2(7 − 6.090)	5	5/6.272 = 0.80
15 ..	9	6.818 = 6.272 + .2(9 − 6.272)	14	14/6.818 = 2.05
16 ..	1	5.654 = 6.818 + .2(1 − 6.818)	15	15/5.654 = 2.65
17 ..	4	5.323 = 5.654 + .2(4 − 5.654)	11	11/5.323 = 2.07
18 ..	3	4.858 = 5.323 + .2(3 − 5.323)	8	8/4.858 = 1.65
19 ..	8	5.486 = 4.858 + .2(8 − 4.858)	0	0/5.486 = 0.00
20 ..	13	6.989 = 5.486 + .2(13 − 5.486)	−13	−13/6.989 = −1.86
21 ..	10	7.591 = 6.989 + .2(10 − 6.989)	−23	−23/7.591 = −3.03
22 ..	2	6.473 = 7.591 + .2(2 − 7.591)	−25	−25/6.473 = −3.86
23 ..	8	6.778 = 6.473 + .2(8 − 6.473)	−17	−17/6.778 = −2.51
24 ..	6	6.622 = 6.778 + .2(6 − 6.778)	−11	−11/6.622 = −1.66

Because the tracking signal is within ±4 of zero, there is no evidence of a problem.

b. (1) Check to make sure that the average error is approximately zero, because a large average would suggest a biased forecast.

$$\text{Average error} = \frac{\Sigma \text{ errors}}{n} = \frac{-11}{24} = -0.46 \text{ [OK]}$$

(2) Compute the standard deviation:

$$s = \sqrt{\frac{\Sigma e^2}{n - 1}}$$

$$= \sqrt{\frac{4^2 + 7^2 + 4^2 + 4^2 + (-5)^2 + (-2)^2 + (-8)^2 + (-12)^2}{8 - 1}} = 6.91$$

(3) Determine 2s control limits:

$$0 \pm 2s = 0 \pm 2(6.91) = -13.82 \text{ to } +13.82$$

(4) (a) Check to see if all errors are within the limits. (They are.)
(b) Plot the data (see the following graph), and check for nonrandom patterns. Note the strings of positive and negative errors. This suggests nonrandomness (and that an improved forecast is possible). The tracking signal did not reveal this.

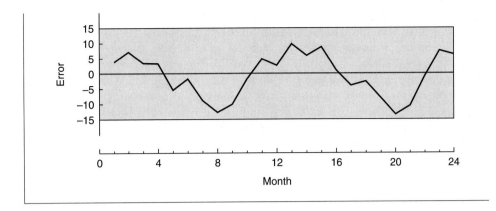

Example 11

(concluded)

Like the tracking signal, a control chart focuses attention on deviations that lie outside predetermined limits. However, with either approach, it is desirable to check for possible patterns in the errors, even if all errors are within the limits. Some of the most common patterns are illustrated in Figure 4–13. Checking is usually done by visual inspection, although statistical tests are sometimes used. If a pattern is discovered, this means that errors are *predictable* and, thus, nonrandom. The implication is that the forecast can be improved. For example, trend in the errors means the errors are getting progressively worse. In time series data, adding or increasing a trend response may be needed. In an explanatory model, recomputing the slope or other adjustment may be called for.

Comment   The control chart approach is generally superior to the tracking signal approach. A major weakness of the tracking signal approach is its use of cumulative errors: Individual errors can be obscured so that large positive and negative values can cancel each other. Conversely, with control charts, every error is judged in-

Figure 4–13

Examples of possible patterns

Bias (too many observations on one side of the zero line)

Cycling (periodic upward and downward movement)

Trend (a persistent upward or downward movement)

dividually. Hence, it can be misleading to rely on a tracking-signal approach to monitor errors. In fact, the historical roots of the tracking-signal approach date from a time when the use of computers in business was just beginning. At that time, it was much more difficult to compute standard deviations than it was to compute average deviations; *for that reason,* the concept of a tracking signal was developed. Now, of course, modern computers and calculators can easily provide standard deviations. Nonetheless, the use of tracking signals has persisted, probably because users are unaware of its inferiority relative to the control chart approach.

CHOOSING A FORECASTING TECHNIQUE

There are many different kinds of forecasting techniques available, and no one technique works best in every situation. When selecting a technique for a given situation, the manager or analyst must take a number of factors into consideration.

Perhaps the two most important factors are *cost* and *accuracy.* How much money is budgeted for generating the forecast? What are the possible costs of error, and what are the possible benefits that might accrue from an accurate forecast? Generally speaking, the higher the accuracy, the higher the cost, so it is important to weigh cost-accuracy trade-offs carefully. The best forecast is not necessarily the most accurate or the least costly; rather, it is some combination of accuracy and cost deemed best by management.

Other factors include the availability of historical data; the availability of computers; the ability of decision makers to utilize certain techniques; the time needed to gather data, analyze them, and prepare the forecast; and any prior experience with a technique. The forecast horizon is important because some techniques are more suited to long-range forecasts and others work best for the short range. For example, moving averages and exponential smoothing are essentially short-range techniques, since they produce forecasts for the *next* period, whereas trend equations can be used to project over much longer time periods. Several of the qualitative techniques are well suited to long-range forecasts because they do not require historical data. The Delphi technique and executive opinion methods are often used for long-range planning. Since new products and services lack historical data, forecasts for these must be made on the basis of subjective estimates. In many cases, experience with similar items can be relevant. Table 4–5 provides some additional perspectives on forecasts in terms of the forecast horizon.

Table 4–5 Forecast factors, by range of forecast	Factor	Short range	Intermediate range	Long range
	1. Frequency	Often	Occasional	Infrequent
	2. Level of aggregation	Item	Product family	Total output Type of product/ service
	3. Type of model	Smoothing Projection Regression	Projection Seasonal Regression	Managerial Judgment
	4. Degree of management involvement	Low	Moderate	High
	5. Cost per forecast	Low	Moderate	High

In some instances, a manager may decide to use more than one forecasting technique. The purpose would be to obtain independent forecasts. If the different methods produced approximately the same predictions, that would lend confidence to the results; disagreement among the forecasts would indicate that additional analysis may be needed.

The following section outlines some additional considerations that pertain both to choosing a forecasting methodology and to preparing a forecast.

ELEMENTS OF A GOOD FORECAST

A properly prepared forecast should fulfill certain requirements:

1. The forecast should be *timely*. Usually, a certain amount of time is needed to respond to the information contained in a forecast. For example, capacity cannot be expanded overnight, nor can inventory levels be changed immediately. Hence, the forecasting horizon must cover the time necessary to implement possible changes.

2. The forecast should be *accurate,* and the degree of accuracy should be stated. This will enable users to plan for possible errors and will provide a basis for comparing alternative forecasts.

3. The forecast should be *reliable;* it should work consistently. A technique that sometimes provides a good forecast and sometimes a poor one will leave users with the uneasy feeling that they are liable to get burned every time a new forecast is issued.

4. The forecast should be in *meaningful units*. Financial planners need to know how many *dollars* will be needed, production planners need to know how many *units* will be needed, and schedulers need to know what *machines* and *skills* will be required. Hence, choice of units will depend on user needs.

5. The forecast should be *in writing*. Although this will not guarantee that all concerned are using the same information, it will at least increase the likelihood of it. In addition, a written forecast will permit an objective basis for evaluating the forecast once actual results are in.

6. The forecasting technique should be *simple to understand and use*. Users often lack confidence in forecasts based on sophisticated techniques because they do not understand the circumstances in which the techniques are appropriate or the limitations of the techniques; misuse of techniques is an obvious consequence. Not surprisingly, fairly crude forecasting techniques enjoy widespread popularity because users are more comfortable using them.

USING FORECAST INFORMATION

A manager can take a *reactive* or a *proactive* approach to a forecast. A reactive approach views forecasts as probable descriptions of future demand, and a manager reacts to meet that demand (e.g., adjusts production rates, adjusts inventories, adjusts the work force). Conversely, a proactive approach seeks to actively influence demand (e.g., via advertising, pricing, or product/service changes).

Generally speaking, a proactive approach would require either an explanatory model (e.g., regression) or a subjective assessment of the influence on demand. It is possible, then, that a manager might use two forecasts: one to predict what will happen under the status quo and a second one based on a "what if. . ." approach, if the results of the status quo forecast are unacceptable.

OPERATIONS STRATEGY

Forecasts are the basis for planning. Clearly, the more accurate an organization's forecasts, the better prepared it will be to take advantage of future opportunities and to reduce potential risks. Maintaining accurate, up-to-date information on prices, demand, and other variables can have a significant impact on forecast accuracy.

There are other things an organization can do to improve forecasts. These do not involve searching for improved techniques. Rather, they relate to the fact that accuracy tends to be inversely related to the forecast horizon; forecasts that cover shorter time frames tend to be more accurate than longer-term forecasts. Recognizing this, management might choose to devote efforts to *shortening the time horizon that forecasts must cover.* Essentially, this means shortening the *lead time* needed to respond to a forecast. This might involve building *flexibility* into operations to permit rapid response to changing demands for products and services, as well as changing volumes in quantities demanded. It might also mean shortening the lead time required to obtain supplies, equipment, and raw materials or the time needed to train or retrain employees. It can also mean shortening the time needed to *develop* new products and services.

SUMMARY

Forecasts are vital inputs for both the design and the operation of the productive systems because they help managers to anticipate the future.

Forecasting techniques can be classified as either qualitative or quantitative. Qualitative techniques rely on judgment, experience, and expertise to formulate forecasts, and quantitative techniques rely on the use of historical data or associations among variables to develop forecasts. Some of the techniques are quite simple, and others are quite complex. Some work better than others, but no technique works all the time. Moreover, all forecasts include a certain degree of inaccuracy, and some allowance should be made for this. All techniques assume that the same underlying causal system that existed in the past will continue to exist in the future.

The qualitative techniques described in this chapter include consumer surveys, sales force estimates, executive opinions, and manager and staff opinions. Two major quantitative approaches are described: analysis of time series data and associative techniques. The time series techniques rely strictly on the examination of historical data; predictions are made by projecting past movements of a variable into the future without considering specific factors that might influence the variable. Associative techniques attempt to explicitly identify influencing factors and to incorporate that information into equations that can be used for predictive purposes.

Because all forecasts tend to be inaccurate, it is important to provide a measure of accuracy for each forecast. Several measures of forecast accuracy can be computed. These are often used to help managers evaluate the performance of a given technique as well as choose among alternative forecasting techniques. Control of forecasts involves deciding whether or not a forecast is performing adequately, using either a control chart or a tracking signal.

Selection of a forecasting technique involves choosing a technique that will serve the intended purpose at an acceptable level of cost and accuracy.

The various forecasting techniques are summarized in Table 4–6. Table 4–7 lists the formulas used in the forecasting techniques and in the methods for measuring their accuracy.

Approaches	Brief description	Table 4–6

Forecasting approaches

Qualitative:

Judgmental methods:

    Consumer surveys . . . . Questioning consumers on future plans

    Sales force composites . . . . . Joint estimates obtained from salespeople

    Executive opinion . . . . Finance, marketing, and manufacturing managers join to prepare forecast

    Delphi technique . . . . Series of questionaires answered anonymously by managers and staff; successive questionnaires are based on information obtained from previous surveys

    Outside opinion . . . . Consultants or other outside experts prepare the forecast

Quantitative:

Time series:

    Naive . . . . Next value in a series will equal the previous value

    Moving averages . . . . Forecast is based on an average of recent values

    Exponential smoothing . . . . Sophisticated form of averaging

Associative models:

    Simple regression . . . . Values of one variable are used to predict values of another variable

    Multiple regression . . . . Two or more variables are used to predict values of another variable

---

KEY TERMS

    b. Select the one with the smaller mean absolute error:

Table 4–7

Summary of formulas

Technique	Formula	Definitions
Naive forecast	$F_t = A_{t-1}$	F = forecast A = actual data
Moving average forecast	$F = \dfrac{\sum\limits_{i=1}^{n} A_i}{n}$	t = period n = number of periods
Exponential smoothing forecast	$F_t = F_{t-1} + \alpha(A_{t-1} - F_{t-1})$	α = smoothing factor
Linear trend forecast	$y_t = a + bt$ where $b = \dfrac{n\Sigma ty - \Sigma t \Sigma y}{n\Sigma t^2 - (\Sigma t)^2}$ $a = \dfrac{\Sigma y - b\Sigma t}{n}$	a = y intercept b = slope
MAD	$MAD = \dfrac{\sum\limits^{n}\|e\|}{n}$	MAD = mean absolute deviation e = error, $A - F$
MSE	$MSE = \dfrac{\sum\limits^{n} e^2}{n - 1}$	MSE = mean squared error
Tracking signal	$TS = \dfrac{\sum\limits^{n} e}{MAD}$	
Control limits	$UCL = 0 + 2s$ $LCL = 0 - 2s$	$s = \sqrt{MSE}$

SOLVED PROBLEMS

Problem

1. *Forecasts based on averages.* Given the following data:

Period	Number of complaints
1	60
2	65
3	55
4	58
5	64

Prepare a forecast using each of these approaches:
a. The naive approach.
b. A 3-period moving average.
c. A weighted average using weights of .50 (most recent), .30, and .20.
d. Exponential smoothing with a smoothing constant of .40.

Solution

a. The most recent value of the series becomes the next forecast: 64.

b. $MA_3 = \dfrac{55 + 58 + 64}{3} = 59.$

c. $F = .50(64) + .30(58) + .20(55) = 60.4.$

d.

Period	Number of complaints	Forecast	Calculations
1	60		
2	65	60	[Use previous value of series]
3	55	62	60 + .40(65 − 60) = 62
4	58	59.2	62 + .40(55 − 62) = 59.2
5	64	58.72	59.2 + .40(58 − 59.2) = 58.72
6		60.83	58.72 + .40(64 − 58.72) = 60.83

Problem

2. *Time series analysis.* Apple's Citrus Fruit Farm ships boxed fruit anywhere in the continental United States. Using the following information, forecast shipments for the first four months of next year.

Month	Seasonal relative	Month	Seasonal relative
Jan.	1.2	Jul.	0.8
Feb.	1.3	Aug.	0.6
Mar.	1.3	Sep.	0.7
Apr.	1.1	Oct.	1.0
May	0.8	Nov.	1.1
Jun.	0.7	Dec.	1.4

The monthly forecast equation being used is:

$y_t = 402 + 3t$

where

$t_0 =$ January of *last* year
$y_t =$ Number of shipments

Solution

a. Determine trend amounts for the first four months of next year: January, $t = 24$; February, $t = 25$; etc. Thus,

$Y_{Jan} = 402 + 3(24) = 474$
$Y_{Feb} = 402 + 3(25) = 477$

$$Y_{Mar} = 402 + 3(26) = 480$$
$$Y_{Apr} = 402 + 3(27) = 483$$

b. Multiply each monthly trend by the corresponding seasonal relative for that month.

Month	Seasonal relative	Forecast
Jan...........	1.2	474(1.2) = 568.8
Feb.	1.3	477(1.3) = 620.1
Mar..........	1.3	480(1.3) = 624.0
Apr.	1.1	483(1.1) = 531.3

Problem

3. *Linear trend line.* Develop a linear trend line for the following data. Plot the line and the data on a graph, and visually verify that a linear trend line is appropriate. Then use the equation to predict the next two values of the series.

Period	Demand
1	44
2	52
3	50
4	54
5	55
6	55
7	60
8	56
9	62

Solution

Period, t	Demand, y	ty	
1	44	44	From Table 4–1, with $n = 9$,
2	52	104	
3	50	150	$\Sigma t = 45$ and $\Sigma t^2 = 285$
4	54	216	
5	55	275	
6	55	330	
7	60	420	
8	56	448	
9	62	558	
	488	2,545	

$$b = \frac{n\Sigma ty - \Sigma t\Sigma y}{n\Sigma t^2 - (\Sigma t)^2} = \frac{9(2,545) - 45(488)}{9(285) - 45(45)} = 1.75$$

$$a = \frac{\Sigma y - b\Sigma t}{n} = \frac{488 - 1.75(45)}{9} = 45.47$$

Thus, the trend equation is $y_t = 45.47 + 1.75t$. The next two forecasts are:

$$y_{10} = 45.47 + 1.75(10) = 62.97$$
$$y_{11} = 45.47 + 1.75(11) = 64.72$$

A plot of the data indicates that a linear trend line is appropriate:

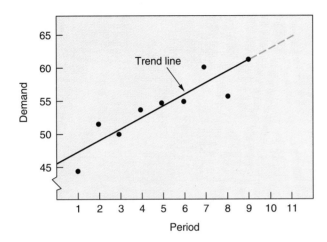

Problem

4. *Seasonal relatives.* Obtain estimates of quarter relatives for these data:

Year:		1				2				3			4
Quarter:	1	2	3	4	1	2	3	4	1	2	3	4	1
Demand:	14	18	35	46	28	36	60	71	45	54	84	88	58

Note that each season has an *even* number of data points. When an even-numbered moving average is used (in this case, a 4-period moving average), the "centered value" will not correspond to an actual data point; the center of 4 is *between* the second and third data points. To correct for this, a *second* set of moving averages must be computed using the MA_4 values. The MA_2 values are centered between the MA_4 values and, hence, they "line up" with actual data points. For example, the first MA_4 value is 28.25. It is centered between 18 and 35 (i.e., between quarter 2 and quarter 3). When the average of the first two MA_4 values is taken (i.e., MA_2) and centered, it lines with the 35 and, hence, with quarter 3.

So, whenever an even-numbered moving average is used as a centered moving average (e.g., MA_4, MA_{12}), a second moving average, a 2-period moving average, is used to achieve correspondence with periods.

This procedure is not needed when the number of periods in the centered moving average is odd. See Example 6 in this chapter for an example with an odd number of periods.

Year	Quarter	Demand	MA$_4$	MA$_2$	Demand/MA$_2$
1 1		14			
	2	18			
			28.25		
	3	35		30.00	1.17
			31.75		
	4	46		34.00	1.35
			36.25		
2 1		28		39.38	0.71
			42.50		
	2	36		45.63	0.79
			48.75		
	3	60		50.88	1.18
			53.00		
	4	71		55.25	1.29
			57.50		
3 1		45		60.50	0.74
			63.50		
	2	54		65.63	0.82
			67.75		
	3	84		69.38	1.21
			71.00		
	4	88			
4 1		58			

	Quarter			
	1	**2**	**3**	**4**
	0.71	0.79	1.17	1.35
	0.74	0.82	1.18	1.29
	1.45	1.61	1.21	2.64
			3.56	
Average for the quarter:	0.725	0.805	1.187	1.320

The sum of these relatives is 4.037. Multiplying each by 4.00/4.037 will make the total 4.00. The resulting relatives are: quarter 1, 0.718; quarter 2, 0.798; quarter 3, 1.176; quarter 4, 1.308.

Problem

5. *Regression analysis.* A large midwestern retailer has developed a linear relationship that summarizes the effect of advertising expenditures on sales volume, as shown in the following graph. Using the graph, determine an equation of the form $y = a + bx$ that describes this relationship.

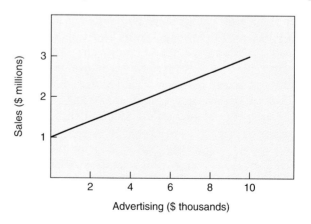

Solution

The linear equation has the form $y = a + bx$, where a is the value of y when $x = 0$ (i.e., where the line intersects the y axis) and b is the slope of the line (the amount by which y changes for a one-unit change in x).

Accordingly, $a = 1$ and $b = (3 - 1)/(10 - 0) = 0.2$, so $y = a + bx$ becomes $y = 1 + 0.2x$. [*Note:* $(3 - 1)$ is the change in y.]

Problem

6. *Regression analysis.* The owner of a small hardware store has noted a sales pattern for window locks that seems to parallel the number of break-ins reported each week in the newspaper. The data are:

Sales:	46	18	20	22	27	34	14	37	30
Break-ins:	9	3	3	5	4	7	2	6	4

a. Plot the data to determine which type of equation, linear or nonlinear, is appropriate.
b. Obtain a regression equation for the data.
c. Test for significance.
d. Estimate sales if the number of break-ins is 5.
e. Place a 95 percent confidence interval around the estimate of sales for five break-ins.

Solution

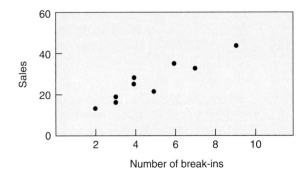

b. The computations for a straight line are:

x	y	xy	x^2	y^2
9........	46	414	81	2,116
3........	18	54	9	324
3........	20	60	9	400
5........	22	110	25	484
4........	27	108	16	729
7........	34	238	49	1,156
2........	14	28	4	196
6........	37	222	36	1,369
4........	30	120	16	900
43	248	1,354	245	7,674

$$b = \frac{n(\Sigma xy) - (\Sigma x)(\Sigma y)}{n(\Sigma x^2) - (\Sigma x)^2} = \frac{9(1,354) - 43(248)}{9(245) - 43(43)} = 4.275$$

$$a = \frac{\Sigma y - b(\Sigma x)}{n} = \frac{248 - 4.275(43)}{9} = 7.129$$

Hence, the equation is: $y_c = 7.129 + 4.275x$.

c.   To test for significance, first compute s_e and then s_b:

$$s_e = \sqrt{\frac{\Sigma y^2 - a\Sigma y - b\Sigma xy}{n - 2}} = \sqrt{\frac{7,674 - 7.129(248) - 4.275(1,354)}{9 - 2}} = 4.10$$

$$s_b = s_e \sqrt{\frac{1}{\Sigma x^2 - [(\Sigma x)^2/n]}} = 4.10 \sqrt{\frac{1}{245 - [(43)^2/9]}} = 0.652$$

Then compute:

$$t = b/s_b = 4.275/0.652 = 6.56$$

Because this greatly exceeds 2.0, conclude the slope is nonzero.

d.   For $x = 5$, $y_c = 7.129 + 4.275(5) = 28.50$.

e.   From Table 4–4 for $df = n - 2 = 7$, $t = 2.37$. The confidence interval for 95 percent is:

$$y_c \pm ts_{\text{reg}} = 28.50 \pm 2.37 \left[4.10 \sqrt{1 + \frac{1}{9} + \frac{(5 - 43/9)^2}{245 - (43)^2/9}} \right]$$

$$= 28.50 \pm 10.25, \text{ or } 18.25 \text{ to } 38.75$$

Problem

7.   *Accuracy and control of forecasts.* The marketing manager of a large manufacturer of industrial pumps must choose between two alternative forecasting
techniques. Both techniques have been used to prepare forecasts for a six-
month period. Using MAD as a criterion, which technique has the better
performance record?

		Forecast	
Month	Demand	Technique 1	Technique 2
1	492	488	495
2	470	484	482
3	485	480	478
4	493	490	488
5	498	497	492
6	492	493	493

Solution

a.   Check to see that each forecast has an average error of approximately
zero. (See computations that follow.)

b. Select the one with the smaller mean absolute error:

Month Demand	Technique 1	e	$\|e\|$	Technique 2	e	$\|e\|$
1 492	488	4	4	495	−3	3
2 470	484	−14	14	482	−12	12
3 485	480	5	5	478	7	7
4 493	490	3	3	488	5	5
5 498	497	1	1	492	6	6
6 492	493	−1	1	493	−1	1
		−2	28		+2	34

$$\text{MAD}_1 = \frac{\Sigma|e|}{n} = \frac{28}{6} = 4.67$$

$$\text{MAD}_2 = \frac{\Sigma|e|}{n} = \frac{34}{6} = 5.67$$

Technique 1 is superior in this comparison, although six observations would generally be too few on which to base a realistic comparison.

Problem

8. *Control chart.* Given the demand data that follow, prepare a naive forecast for periods 2 through 10. Then determine each forecast error, and use those values to obtain $2s$ control limits. If the next two periods' demands turn out to be 125 and 130, can you conclude that the forecasts are in control?

Period:	1	2	3	4	5	6	7	8	9	10
Demand:	118	117	120	119	126	122	117	123	121	124

Solution

For a naive forecast, each period's demand becomes the forecast for the next period. Hence, the forecasts and errors are:

Period	Demand	Forecast	Error	Error^2
1	118	—	—	—
2	117	118	−1	1
3	120	117	3	9
4	119	120	−1	1
5	126	119	7	49
6	122	126	−4	16
7	117	122	−5	25
8	123	117	6	36
9	121	123	−2	4
10	124	121	3	9
			+6	150

$$s = \sqrt{\frac{\Sigma \; \text{error}^2}{n-1}} \qquad (n = \text{Number of errors})$$

$$= \sqrt{\frac{150}{9-1}} = 4.33$$

The control limits are $2(4.33) = \pm 8.66$

The forecast for period 11 was 124. Demand turned out to be 125, for an error of $125 - 124 = +1$. This is within the limits of ± 8.66. If the next demand is 130 and the naive forecast is 125 (based on the period 11 demand of 125), the error is $+5$. Again, this is within the limits, so we cannot conclude the forecast is not working properly. If we had more values—at least five or six—we could plot the errors to see if we could detect any patterns (which would suggest nonrandomness was present).

DISCUSSION AND REVIEW QUESTIONS

1. Is one approach to forecasting, either quantitative or qualitative, superior? Explain.
2. What are the main advantages that quantitative techniques for forecasting have over qualitative techniques? What limitations do quantitative techniques have?
3. List the specific weaknesses of each of these approaches to developing a forecast:
   a. Consumer surveys.
   b. Sales force composite.
   c. Committee of managers or executives.
4. Briefly describe the Delphi technique. What are some of its main benefits and weaknesses?
5. What is the purpose of establishing control limits for forecasts?
6. What factors would you consider in deciding whether to use wide or narrow control limits for a forecast?
7. Contrast the use of MAD and MSE in evaluating forecasts.
8. What advantages does exponential smoothing have over moving averages as a forecasting tool?
9. How does the number of periods in a moving average affect the responsiveness of the forecast?
10. What factors enter into the choice of a value for the smoothing constant in exponential smoothing?
11. How accurate is your local five-day weather forecast? Explain.
12. Explain how using a centered moving average with a length equal to length of a season eliminates seasonality from a time series.
13. Contrast the terms *sales* and *demand*.
14. Contrast the reactive and proactive approaches to forecasting. Give several examples of types of organizations or situations in which each type is used.
15. Explain how flexibility in production systems relates to the forecast horizon and forecast accuracy.

PROBLEMS

1. National Mixer, Inc., carries a line of electric blenders. Given the following monthly sales data:
   a. Compute three-month and five-month moving average forecasts. Begin at January.

b. Plot the original data and the two moving averages on the same graph.
c. What effect does the number of periods in a moving average have on the extent of smoothing?

Month	Demand (000 units)	Month	Demand (000 units)
Jan............	20	Jul.	18
Feb.	24	Aug.	21
Mar.	18	Sept.	24
Apr.	14	Oct............	22
May	25	Nov.	28
Jun.	20	Dec.	32

2. National Mixer, Inc., also sells can openers. Monthly sales for a seven-month period were as follows:

Month	Sales (000 units)
Feb.	19
Mar.	18
Apr.	15
May	20
Jun.	18
Jul.	22
Aug.	20

a. Plot the monthly data on a sheet of graph paper.
b. Forecast September sales volume using each of the following:
    (1) A linear trend equation.
    (2) A five-month moving average.
    (3) Exponential smoothing with a smoothing constant equal to .20, assuming a March forecast of 19,000.
    (4) The naive approach.
    (5) A weighted average using .60 for August, .30 for July, and .10 for June.
c. Which method seems least appropriate? Why?
d. What does use of the term *sales* rather than *demand* presume?

3. Monthly sales of snowmobiles for a suburban Toronto dealer for the past year are:

Month	Units sold	Month	Units sold
Jan............	92	Jul.	4
Feb.	88	Aug.	3
Mar............	80	Sept.	6
Apr.	60	Oct.	12
May	10	Nov............	25
Jun.	1	Dec.	82

a. Smooth this data using a three-month *centered* moving average.
b. Plot the original sales data and the centered moving average on the same graph.

    c.   Would it make sense to use a three-month moving average to *predict* sales for the following January? Explain.

4. A dry cleaner uses exponential smoothing to forecast usage of equipment at its main plant. August usage was forecast to be 88 percent of capacity; actual usage was 89.6 percent of capacity. Forecasts use a smoothing constant of .1.
    a.   Prepare a forecast for September.
    b.   Assuming actual September usage of 92 percent, prepare a forecast for October usage.

5. The owner of Wine Sales & Service wants to forecast wine demand. Demand for the preceding four years is shown in the following table. Forecast demand for next year using:
    a.   Exponential smoothing with $\alpha = .40$.
    b.   A three-year moving average.
    c.   A weighted average using .50 for year 4, .30 for year 3, and .20 for year 2.
    d.   The naive approach.

Year	Demand (000 cases)
1	809
2	810
3	808
4	812

6. An electrical contractor's records during the last five weeks indicate the number of job requests:

Week:	1	2	3	4	5
Requests:	20	22	18	21	22

Predict the number of requests for week 6 using each of these methods:
    a.   Naive.
    b.   A four-period moving average.
    c.   Exponential smoothing with $\alpha = .30$.

7. Tread-On-Us Carpet & Tile Company sold 700,000 square feet of carpet last year, 800,000 square feet the year before, and 600,000 square feet the year before that. Using a three-year moving average, predict carpet sales for this year. Then, assuming actual sales for this year turn out to be 780,000 square feet, predict sales for next year.

8. A cosmetics manufacturer's marketing department has developed a linear trend equation that can be used to predict annual sales of its popular Hand & Foot Cream:

$$y_t = 80 + 15t$$

where

y_t = Annual sales (000 bottles)
t_0 = 1982

    a.   Are annual sales increasing or decreasing? By how much?
    b.   Predict annual sales for 1995 using the equation.

9. A management consultant, using historical sales data, has developed a predictive equation for sales of white pine trees for a tree farm:

$$y_t = 480 - 50t + 10t^2$$

where

y_t = Number of trees sold in year t
t = 0 at 1983

   a.   Plot the equation for years 1986 to 1993.
   b.   Forecast sales of white pine trees for 1995.

10. From the following graph, determine the linear equation of the trend line using 1981 as the base year for Glib Sales, Inc.

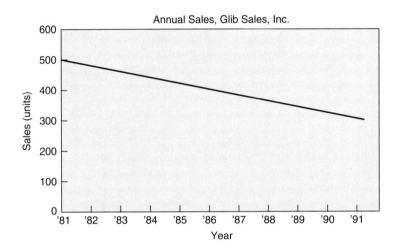

11. Freight car loadings over a 12-year period at a busy port are:

Year	Number (00)	Year	Number (00)
1	220	7	350
2	245	8	360
3	280	9	400
4	275	10	380
5	300	11	420
6	310	12	450

   a.   Compute a linear trend line for freight car loadings.
   b.   Plot the trend line and the original data on the same graph.
   c.   Use the trend equation to predict loadings for year 15.

12. The following equation summarizes the trend portion of quarterly sales of automatic dishwashers over a long cycle. Sales also exhibit seasonal variations. Using the information given, prepare a forecast of sales for each quarter of 1995.

$$y_t = 40 - 6.5t + 2t^2$$

where

y_t = Unit sales
t = 0 at the fourth quarter of 1992

Quarter	Relative
1................	1.1
2................	1.0
3................	.6
4................	1.3

13. Develop a linear trend equation for the following data on bread deliveries, and use it to predict deliveries for periods 11 through 14.

Period	Dozen deliveries	Period	Dozen deliveries
1...............	200	6	222
2...............	214	7	248
3...............	211	8	241
4...............	228	9	253
5...............	235	10	267

14. Use trend-adjusted smoothing with $\alpha_1 = .3$ and $\alpha_2 = .2$ to smooth the bread delivery data in the preceding problem.

15. Refer to the freight car loading data in Problem 11. Because of the apparent trend in those data, the manager has decided to use trend-adjusted exponential smoothing to predict future loading demand.

   a. Assume an initial forecast of 380 loadings. Use trend-adjusted smoothing with these constants: (1) $\alpha_1 = .2$, $\alpha_2 = .2$; (2) $\alpha_1 = .4$, $\alpha_2 = .2$; and (3) $\alpha_1 = .4$, $\alpha_2 = .40$. Use an initial trend estimate of 20. Start at period 9.
   b. Which of the combinations in part a is the most accurate? Explain.
   c. If there were more data, control charts could be constructed. How might those control charts be useful in comparing these forecasting alternatives?

16. Sales of waterbeds at a specialty store during the past seven weeks were:

Week:	1	2	3	4	5	6	7
Number sold:	26	24	29	33	32	37	36

   a. Use two different appropriate methods to predict the number of units that will be sold during week 8. Explain why these methods are appropriate.
   b. If actual sales during the next five weeks turn out to be 40, 45, 44, 50, and 53, which of the two methods would have provided a better forecast? Explain what probably occurred, based on a comparison of the new data with the original data.

17. A gift shop in a tourist center is open on weekends (Friday, Saturday, and Sunday). The owner-manager hopes to improve scheduling of part-time employees by determining seasonal relatives for each of these days. Data on recent activity at the store (sales transactions per day) have been tabulated, and they are shown below. Develop seasonal relatives for the shop.

	Week					
	#1	#2	#3	#4	#5	#6
Friday	149	154	152	150	159	163
Saturday	250	255	260	268	273	276
Sunday	166	162	171	173	176	183

18. Use a naive trend approach to predict sales transactions for the gift shop in the previous problem for the following week.

19. An analyst must decide between two different forecasting techniques: a linear trend equation and the naive approach. The linear trend equation is $y_t = 124 + 2t$, and it was developed using data from periods 1 through 10. Based on data for periods 11 through 20 as shown, which of these two methods has the greater accuracy? (The data are for daily sales of trail bikes.)

t	Units Sold	t	Units Sold
11	147	16	152
12	148	17	155
13	151	18	157
14	145	19	160
15	155	20	165

20. The manager of a fashionable restaurant that is open Wednesday through Saturday has commented that the restaurant does about 35 percent of its business on Friday night, 30 percent on Saturday night, and 20 percent on Thursday night. What seasonal relatives would describe this situation?

21. Coal shipments from Mountain Coal Company's no. 4 mine for the past seven years are:

Year	Tons shipped (000)
1	405
2	410
3	420
4	415
5	412
6	420
7	424

  a. Explain why simple exponential smoothing would not be an appropriate forecasting method.

  b. Use an appropriate technique to develop a forecast for the next three years.

22. Obtain estimates of daily relatives for the number of customers at a restaurant for the evening meal, given the following data. (*Hint:* Use a seven-day moving average.)

Day	Number served	Day	Number served
1	80	15	84
2	75	16	77
3	78	17	83
4	95	18	96
5	130	19	135
6	136	20	140
7	40	21	37
8	82	22	87
9	77	23	82
10	80	24	98
11	94	25	103
12	125	26	144
13	135	27	144
14	42	28	48

23. A pharmacist has been monitoring sales of a certain over-the-counter pain reliever. Daily sales during the last 15 days were:

Day:	1	2	3	4	5	6	7	8	9
Number sold:	36	38	42	44	48	49	50	49	52
Day:	10	11	12	13	14	15			
Number sold:	48	52	55	54	56	57			

   a. Without doing any calculations, which method would you suggest using to predict future sales—a linear trend equation or trend-adjusted exponential smoothing? Why?
   b. If you now learn that on some of the days the store ran out of the pain reliever in question, would that knowledge cause you any concern? Explain.
   c. Assume that the data refer to demand rather than sales. Using trend-adjusted smoothing with an initial forecast of 50 for week 8, an initial trend estimate of 2, and $\alpha_1 = \alpha_2 = .3$, develop forecasts for days 9 through 16. What is the MSE for the eight forecasts for which there are actual data?

24. Lawn mower sales for a dealer in Orange County, California, for the past year are shown in the following table, along with monthly (seasonal) relatives, which are supplied to the dealer by the regional distributor.

Month	Units sold	Index	Month	Units sold	Index
Jan.	640	0.80	Jul.	765	0.90
Feb.	648	0.80	Aug.	1,000	1.17
Mar.	600	0.80	Sept.	1,038	1.20
Apr.	761	0.94	Oct.	1,026	1.14
May	735	0.89	Nov.	967	1.20
Jun.	850	1.00	Dec.	1,107	1.23

   a. Plot the data.
   b. Deseasonalize lawn mower sales.
   c. Plot the deseasonalized data on the same graph as the original data. Comment on the two graphs.

25. A quality control analyst has kept a record of the defective rate of a process she has been working to improve during a period of about four weeks. The following data (percentages) were recorded:

	Week			
	1	2	3	4
Monday	10.2	9.4	8.4	7.8
Tuesday	8.2	7.3	7.0	6.5
Wednesday	7.2	6.8	6.3	5.0
Thursday	6.8	6.0	5.4	4.8
Friday	9.4	9.0	8.2	7.1

   a. Determine daily relatives for the defective rate. Then use the relatives to remove seasonality from the data. (*Hint:* See Problem 24.)
   b. Compute a linear trend equation for the deseasonalized data.
   c. Using the trend equation and seasonal relatives, predict the defective rate for each day of week 5.

26. A farming cooperative manager wants to estimate quarterly relatives for grain ship-ments, based on the data shown (quantities are in metric tons):

Year	Quarter			
	1	2	3	4
1	200	250	210	340
2	210	252	212	360
3	215	260	220	358
4	225	272	233	372
5	232	284	240	381

Determine quarter relatives. (*Hint:* Use a centered four-period moving average ini-tially, and then use a centered two-period moving average of the four-period moving average.)

27. Long-Life Insurance has developed a linear model that it uses to determine the amount of straight life insurance a family of four should have, based on the current age of the head of the household. The equation is:

$$y = 32 - .1x$$

where

y = Insurance needed ($000)

x = Current age of head of household

a. Plot the relationship on a piece of graph paper.
b. Use the equation to determine the amount of straight life insurance to recom-mend for a family of four if the head of the household is 30 years old.

28. Timely Transport provides local delivery service for a number of downtown and sub-urban businesses. Delivery charges are based on distance and weight involved for each delivery: 10 cents per pound and 15 cents per mile. In addition, there is a $10 storage and handling fee per parcel.
a. Develop an expression that summarizes delivery charges.
b. Determine the delivery charge for transporting a 40-pound parcel 26 miles.

29. The following values represent summary information produced by a regression analysis of cash flow relative to sales.

$n = 14, \Sigma x = 50, \Sigma x^2 = 1,700$
$\Sigma xy = 1,540, \Sigma y = 200, \Sigma y^2 = 4,400$

a. Determine the least squares equation.
b. Compute the correlation coefficient.
c. Is the slope of the line significantly different from zero? Is the correlation signifi-cantly different from zero? Explain briefly.

30. The manager of a seafood restaurant was asked to establish a pricing policy on lobster dinners. Experimenting with prices produced the following data:

Average number sold per day, y	Price, x
200	$6.00
190	6.50
188	6.75

(continued)

Average number sold per day, y	Price, x
180..................	7.00
170..................	7.25
162..................	7.50
160..................	8.00

a. Plot the data and a regression line on the same graph.
b. Using the regression equation, obtain a 95 percent confidence interval for estimated demand for a price of $7.00.
c. Compute the correlation coefficient and interpret it.

31. The following data were collected during a study of consumer buying patterns.

Observation	x	y	Observation	x	y
1	15	74	8	18	78
2	25	80	9	14	70
3	40	84	10	15	72
4	32	81	11	22	85
5	51	96	12	24	88
6	47	95	13	33	90
7	30	83			

a. Plot the data.
b. Fit a linear regression line to the data using the least squares method.
c. Is the slope of the line significantly different from zero?
d. Use the equation determined in part b to predict the value of y for $x = 41$.
e. Determine a 95 percent confidence interval for the predicted value of y for $x = 41$.

32. Lovely Lawns, Inc., intends to use sales of lawn fertilizer to predict lawn mower sales. The store manager feels that there is probably a six-week lag between fertilizer sales and mower sales. The pertinent data are:

Period	Fertilizer sales (tons)	Number of mowers sold (six-week lag)
1	1.6	10
2	1.3	8
3	1.8	11
4	2.0	12
5	2.2	12
6	1.6	9
7	1.5	8

a. Compute the correlation between the two variables. Does it appear that there is a relationship between these variables that will yield good predictions?
b. Use the least squares method to obtain a linear regression line for the data.
c. Predict lawn mower sales for the first week in August, given fertilizer sales six weeks earlier of 2 tons.

33. A financial planner wants to develop a linear regression model that he can use to evaluate clients' portfolios. He has collected relevant data on 20 clients, and he has used his microcomputer to analyze the data. The computer output included the following information:

$$y = 470.4 + 25.1x$$

where

$x =$ Beginning portfolio value

$y =$ Portfolio value two years later

$s_e = 4.30$

$s_b = 6.21$

$r = +.924$

a. Is the relationship significant? Explain.
b. How well does the regression equation fit the data? Explain.
c. If the planner determines that s_{reg} for a certain new client's portfolio of 98 is 3.70, develop a 95 percent confidence interval for the dependent variable, and interpret your answer.

34. Two different forecasting techniques (F1 and F2) were each used to forecast demand for cases of bottled water. Actual demand and the two sets of forecasts are as follows:

Period	Demand	Predicted Demand	
		F1	F2
1	68	66	66
2	75	68	68
3	70	72	70
4	74	71	72
5	69	72	74
6	72	70	76
7	80	71	78
8	78	74	80

a. Compute MAD for each set of forecasts. Given your results, which forecast appears to be the most accurate? Explain.
b. Compute the MSE for each set of forecasts. Given your results, which forecast appears to be the most accurate?
c. In practice, *either* MAD *or* MSE would be employed to compare forecast errors. What factors might lead a manager to choose MSE rather than MAD? What factors might lead to choosing MAD?

35. The manager of a travel agency has been using a seasonally adjusted forecast to predict demand for packaged tours. The actual and predicted values are:

Period	Demand	Predicted
1	129	124
2	194	200
3	156	150
4	91	94

(continued)

Period	Demand	Predicted
5	85	80
6	132	140
7	126	128
8	126	124
9	95	100
10	149	150
11	98	94
12	85	80
13	137	140
14	134	128

    a.   Compute MAD for the fifth period, then update it period by period using exponential smoothing with $\alpha = .3$.

    b.   Compute a tracking signal for periods 5 through 14 using the initial and updated MADs. If limits of ± 3 are used, what can you conclude?

36. Two independent methods of forecasting based on judgment and experience have been prepared each month for the past 10 months. The forecasts and actual sales are as follows.

Month	Sales	Forecast 1	Forecast 2
1	770	771	769
2	789	785	787
3	794	790	792
4	780	784	798
5	768	770	774
6	772	768	770
7	760	761	759
8	775	771	775
9	786	784	788
10	790	788	788

    a.   Compute the MSE and MAD for each forecast. Does either method seem superior? Explain.

    b.   Compute a tracking signal for the 10th month for each forecast. What does it show? (Use action limits of ± 4.)

    c.   Compute $2s$ control limits for each forecast.

    d.   Prepare a naive forecast for periods 2 through 11 using the given sales data. Compute each of the following: (1) MSE, (2) MAD, (3) tracking signal at month 10, and (4) $2s$ control limits. How do the naive results compare with the other two forecasts?

37. The classified department of a monthly magazine has used a combination of quantitative and qualitative methods to forecast sales of advertising space. Results over a 20-month period are as follows:

Month	Error	Month	Error
1	−8	11	1
2	−2	12	6
3	4	13	8

(continued)

Month	Error	Month	Error
4	7	14	4
5	9	15	1
6	5	16	−2
7	0	17	−4
8	−3	18	−8
9	−9	19	−5
10	−4	20	−1

a. Compute a tracking signal for months 11 through 20. Compute an initial value of MAD for month 11, and then update it for each month using exponential smoothing with $\alpha = .1$. What can you conclude? Assume limits of ± 4.

b. Using the first half of the data, construct a control chart with $2s$ limits. What can you conclude?

c. Plot the last 10 errors on the control chart. Are the errors random? What is the implication of this?

38. A textbook publishing company has compiled data on total annual sales of its business texts for the preceding nine years:

Year:	1	2	3	4	5
Sales (000):	40.2	44.5	48.0	52.3	55.8
Year:	6	7	8	9	
Sales (000):	57.1	62.4	69.0	73.7	

a. Using an appropriate model, forecast textbook sales for each of the next five years.

b. Prepare a control chart for the forecast using the original data. Use $2s$ limits.

c. Suppose actual sales for the next five years turn out as follows:

Year:	10	11	12	13	14
Sales (000):	77.2	82.1	87.8	90.6	98.9

Is the forecast performing adequately? Explain.

39. The owner of a catering company wants to use exponential smoothing to forecast demand for the catering service. These historical values reflect recent experience:

Week:	1	2	3	4	5	6	7	8	9
Demand:	9	12	11	8	10	7	12	7	9
Week:	10	11	12	13	14				
Demand:	10	13	12	11	10				

a. Use the first half of the data to develop a model. Choose between a smoothing constant of .10 and one of .30.

b. Test your choice of a smoothing constant on the remainder of the data, using a control chart with two standard deviation limits.

c. Forecast the expected demand for week 15.

d. If actual demand turns out to be 8, is the forecast in control? Forecast the demand for the following week. If actual demand turns out to be 13, is the forecast in control? Explain.

Chambers, John C.; S. K. Mullick; and Donald D. Smith. "How to Choose the Right Forecasting Technique." *Harvard Business Review,* July–August 1971, pp. 45–74.

Hanke, John E., and Arthur G. Reitsch. *Business Forecasting.* 4th ed. Boston: Allyn & Bacon, 1992.

SELECTED BIBLIOGRAPHY

Levenbach, Hans, and James P. Cleary. *The Modern Forecaster: The Forecasting Process through Data Analysis.* Belmont, Calif.: Lifetime Learning Publications, 1984.

Riggs, James L. *Production Systems: Planning, Analysis, and Control.* 3rd ed. New York: John Wiley & Sons, 1981.

Stevenson, William J. *Business Statistics: Concepts and Applications.* 2nd ed. New York: Harper & Row, 1985.

Tersine, R. J., and W. Riggs. "The Delphi Technique: A Long-Range Planning Tool." *Business Horizons* 19, no. 2, 1976.

Wheelwright, Steven C.; Spyros Madridakis; and Victor McGee. *Forecasting Methods and Applications.* 2nd ed. New York: John Wiley & Sons, 1983.

PART THREE

III

DESIGN OF PRODUCTION SYSTEMS

Production system design encompasses decisions involving:

1. Product and service design   (*Chapter 5*).
2. Process selection and capacity planning   (*Chapter 6*).
3. Facilities layout   (*Chapter 7*).
4. Design of work systems   (*Chapter 8*).
5. Location planning   (*Chapter 9*).

S atisfying the customer begins with product and service design. Moreover, decisions made in this area tend to have a major impact on operations as well as on the overall success of the organization.

Similarly, process selection and capacity planning have a major impact on the ability of the production system to perform, and to satisfy customers. Flexibility, production time, and cost are key considerations in process design.

Process selection and layout are closely related. Layout decisions involve the arrangement of departments and equipment within departments, which affects the flow of work through a system, and impacts productivity, cost, and flexibility. Layout decisions are influenced by decisions made in product and service design.

Capacity and location decisions both influence operating costs and the ability to respond to customer demand. Location decisions also have an impact on transportation costs, labor availability, material costs, and access to markets.

Work design focuses on the human element in production systems. Increasingly, managers are coming to the view that workers are a valuable asset and can contribute greatly to the success of the organization. Strategic planning is beginning to incorporate employee participation as a means of improving production systems.

Design decisions have strategic significance for business organizations. Many of these decisions are not made by the operations manager. Nonetheless, because of the important links between operations and each of the strategic areas mentioned here, it is essential to the success of the organization to involve all of the functional areas of the organization in design decisions.

CHAPTER FIVE

PRODUCT AND SERVICE DESIGN

After completing this chapter, you should be able to:

1. Discuss the importance of product and service design.
2. Describe the design process.
3. Explain the concept of standardization and discuss its advantages and disadvantages.
4. Discuss the concept of modular design, including its advantages and disadvantages.
5. Describe the contributions of R&D to product and service design.
6. Define reliability, perform simple reliability computations, and suggest possible ways of improving reliability.

T he essence of any organization is the products or services it offers. There is an obvious link between the *design* of those products or services and the success of the organization: Organizations that have well-designed products or services are more likely to realize their goals than those with poorly designed products or services. Hence, organizations have a vital stake in achieving good product and service design.

This chapter presents the major aspects of product and service design: the objectives of product and service design, the design process, Taguchi methods for product design, research and development, design of services, and reliability.

INTRODUCTION

Product and service design plays a strategic role in the degree to which an organization is able to achieve its goals. It is a major factor in customer satisfaction, product and service quality, and production costs. The customer connection is obvious: The product or service is the main concern of the customer, and becomes the ultimate basis for judging the organization. The quality connection is twofold. Quality is obviously affected by design, but also, during production, by the degree to which production conforms to the intent of design. A key factor there is *manufacturability,* which refers to the ease with which design features can be achieved by production. Similarly, design affects cost, both the cost of materials specified by design and the cost required to achieve the intent of design (e.g., labor and equipment costs).

OBJECTIVES OF PRODUCT AND SERVICE DESIGN

The objectives of product and service design may vary somewhat from situation to situation. Generally, however, the objectives are:

1. To bring new or revised products or services to the market as quickly as possible.
2. To design products and/or services that have customer appeal.
3. To increase the level of customer satisfaction.
4. To increase quality.
5. To reduce costs.

In a competitive environment, getting new or improved products or services to the market ahead of competitors gives an organization a competitive advantage that can lead to increased profits as well as increased market share, and can create an image of the organization as a leader. In the not-for-profit sector, getting new or improved products or services to the market as quickly as possible enables organizations to increase their level of customer service. For example, the approval by the FDA of new drugs to combat cancer and AIDS as quickly as possible results in a major benefit to society. Similarly, the quick approval and marketing of nonfat food products provides another health benefit to society. Improvements in processing of transactions at post offices can mean lower postal rates and less waiting time for customers.

Design must take into account customer wants and needs. And design should take into account who the customers are (i.e., the target market). Consider Ford's Model T:

> To appeal to his target market of average consumers, Ford had also designed unprecedented ease of operation and maintainability into his car. He assumed that his buyer

would be a farmer with a modest tool kit and the kinds of mechanical skills needed for fixing farm machinery. So the Model T's owner's manual, which was written in question-and-answer form, explained in sixty-four pages how owners could use simple tools to solve any of the 140 problems likely to crop up with the car.

For example, owners could remove cylinder-head carbon, which causes knocking and power loss, from chamber roofs and piston crowns by loosening the fifteen cap screws that held the cylinder head and using a putty knife as a scraper. Similarly, a single paragraph and one diagram told customers how to remove carbon deposits from their car's valves with the Ford Valve Grinding Tool, which came with the auto. . . . And, if a part needed replacement, owners could buy a spare at a Ford dealer and simply screw or bolt it on. With the Ford Model T, there was no fitting required.— Source: James Womack, Daniel Jones, and Daniel Roos, *The Machine that Changed the World* (New York: Harper Perennial, 1990), p. 30.

THE DESIGN PROCESS

The design process begins with the *motivation* for design. For a new business or a new product, the motivation may be obvious: to achieve the goals of the organization. For an existing business, in addition to that general motivation, there are more specific factors to consider, such as government regulations, the appearance of new technologies that have product or process applications, competitive pressures, and customer needs.

Ultimately, the *customer* is the driving force for product and service design. Failure to satisfy customers can result in customer complaints, returns, warranty claims, and so on. Loss of market share becomes a potential problem if customer satisfaction is not achieved.

In order for the design process to occur, there must be *ideas* for new or improved designs. These can come from a variety of sources. The most obvious source is the customer. *Marketing* can tap this source of ideas in a number of ways, such as the use of focus groups, surveys, and the analyses of buying patterns.

Some organizations have *research and development departments* (described later in the chapter) that also generate ideas for new or improved products and services.

Competitors are another important source of ideas. By studying a competitor's products or services, and how it operates (e.g., pricing policies, return policies, warranties, and so on), an organization can learn a great deal that can help to achieve design improvements. Beyond that, some companies buy a competitor's newly designed product the moment it appears on the market. Using a procedure called **reverse engineering**, they then carefully dismantle and inspect the product.

Reverse engineering
Dismantling and inspecting a competitor's product to discover product improvements.

CAEDS software from IBM may be used at several stages of engineering design, such as testing new models, creating original designs, or documenting operations.

This may uncover product improvements that can be incorporated in their own product. The Ford Motor Company used this approach in developing its highly successful Taurus model; it examined competitors' automobiles, searching for the *best-in-class* products (e.g., the best hood release, the best dashboard, the best window handle). Sometimes reverse engineering can lead to a product that is *superior* to the one being examined. That is, designers are able to conceive an improved design, enabling them to "leap frog" the competition by introducing an improved version of a competitor's product within a short time. This may deny the competitor some of the rewards that usually result from being the first to introduce a new product, or one with new features.

Ideas for new or improved products and services cannot be entertained in a vacuum; production *capabilities* must be a basic consideration. In order to assure this, design and production must work together; design needs to clearly understand the capabilities of production (e.g., equipment, skills, types of materials, schedules, technologies, special abilities). This will help in choosing designs that match capabilities. On the other hand, when opportunities and capabilities do not match, management must consider the potential for expanding or changing capabilities in order to take advantage of those opportunities.

Forecasts of future demand can be very useful, supplying information on the timing and volume of demand as well as information on demands for new products and services.

The design of a product or service must take into account its cost, its target market, and its function. **Manufacturability** is a key concern for manufactured goods: Ease of fabrication and/or assembly is important for cost, productivity, and quality. Similarly, with services, ease of providing the service, cost, productivity, and quality are of great concern.

In general, design, production, and marketing must work closely together, keeping each other informed and taking into account the wants and needs of the customer. In addition, there can be legal or regulatory considerations as well as *life cycle* factors that influence the design function.

Manufacturability

The ease of fabrication and/or assembly.

REGULATIONS AND LEGAL CONSIDERATIONS

Organizations are faced with an increasing array of government agencies established to regulate their activities. Among the more familiar ones are the Food and Drug Administration, the Environmental Protection Agency, the National Highway Safety Commission, and the Consumer Products Safety Commission. Bans on cyclamates, red food dye, phosphates, and asbestos in recent years have sent designers scurrying back to their drawing boards to find alternative designs that will prove acceptable to both the government regulators and their customers. Similarly, pollution standards for automobiles and safety features such as seat belts, safety glass, and energy-absorbing bumpers and frames have had a substantial impact on automotive design. And much attention has been directed toward the design of toys with the idea of removing sharp edges, small pieces that can cause choking, and toxic materials. In the construction field, government regulations require the use of lead-free paint, safety glass in entranceways, access to public buildings for handicapped persons, and standards for insulation, electrical wiring, plumbing, and so on.

Product liability can be a strong incentive for design improvement. **Product liability** means that a manufacturer is liable for any injuries or damages caused by a

Product liability

A manufacturer is liable for any injuries or damages caused by a faulty product.

KEEP IT SIMPLE—
AND SAVE
What Cadillac gained
from redesigning the
Seville's rear bumper

- Number of parts cut in half— to 63
- Assembly time chopped 57%—to less than 8 minutes
- Estimated annual labor savings: $462,000*

* FOR SEVILLE AND ELDORADO MODELS

DATA: CADILLAC MOTOR CAR DIV. OF GENERAL MOTORS CORP.

By redesigning the Seville's rear bumper, Cadillac cut the number of parts, thus reducing assembly time and labor costs. The new design also leads to higher quality as there are fewer parts and steps that might be defective. Art reprinted from October 25, 1991, issue of Business Week *by special permission, copyright © 91 by McGraw-Hill, Inc.*

faulty product because of either poor workmanship or poor design. In recent years, many business firms have been involved in lawsuits related to their products, including the Firestone Tire & Rubber Co. (which underwent a major recall of its tires), the Ford Motor Co. (concerning, among other problems, the gas tank of its Pinto), General Motors Corp. (steering problems with its Corvair), manufacturers of hairdryers (asbestos particles), toy manufacturers, and countless others. Also, manufacturers are faced with the implied warranties created by state laws under the **Uniform Commercial Code**, which says, in effect, that products carry an implication of *merchantability* and *fitness;* that is, a product must be usable for its intended purposes.

> **Uniform Commercial Code**
> Products carry an implication of merchantability and fitness.

The suits and potential suits have resulted in increases in legal and insurance costs, expensive settlements with injured parties, and costly recalls. Moreover, increasing customer awareness of product safety can adversely affect product image and subsequent demand for a product.

Because of these factors, it is extremely important to design products that are reasonably free of hazards. When hazards do exist, it is necessary to install safety guards or other devices for reducing accident potential. Adequate warning notices of risks must also be provided. Consumer groups, business firms, and various government agencies often work together to develop industrywide standards that help avoid some of the hazards. Major advances have been made in the area of toy manufacturing in terms of safety standards.

It is interesting to reflect on the role of operations management people in product and service design since operations will have the ultimate responsibility for *converting* the design into reality. During the conversion process, design errors and deficiencies are frequently detected, and ideas for improvements are generated. Many of the mistakes can be avoided by involving operations personnel in the design stages. In fact, it often happens that when operations people are not consulted during product or service design, they become involved by initiating redesign efforts.

Finally, a humorous look at some of the different ways various individuals and departments in the design process can interpret a "design" is illustrated in Figure 5–1. The point is, there must be sufficient information to determine the customer's

Figure 5–1

Differing views of design created through lack of information

Source: *Educational Center Newsletter,* Minneapolis, Minnesota.

As proposed by the marketing department.

As specified in the product request.

As designed by the senior designer.

As produced by manufacturing.

As used by the customer.

What the customer wanted.

wants, as well as communication and agreement among those responsible for designing, producing, and marketing the product or service.

PRODUCT LIFE CYCLES

Many new products exhibit a **product life cycle** in terms of demand. When an item is first introduced, it may be treated as a curiosity. Demand is generally low because potential buyers are not yet familiar with the item. Many potential buyers recognize that all of the bugs have probably not been worked out and that the price may drop after the introductory period. With the passage of time, production and design improvements usually create a more reliable and less costly product. Demand then grows for these reasons and because of increasing awareness of the product or service. At the next stage in the life cycle, the product reaches maturity: there are few, if any, design changes, and demand levels off. Eventually, the market becomes saturated, which leads to a decline in demand. These stages in the cycle are illustrated in Figure 5–2.

In the last stage of a life cycle, some firms adopt a defensive research posture whereby they attempt to prolong the useful life of a product or service by one or more of the following: improving the reliability of the item, reducing costs of producing the item (and, hence, the price), redesigning it, or changing the packaging.

As an example of products in various stages of the life cycle, consider the music industry: Digital audio tapes are in the introductory stage, compact disks are in the growth stage, cassettes are in the maturity-saturation stage, and eight-track tapes are in the decline stage.

Some products do not seem to go through such a life cycle. Wooden pencils, paper clips, nails, knives, forks and spoons, drinking glasses, and similar items don't seem to exhibit life cycles, but most new products do. It is easy to identify the various stages for such items as slide rules, black-and-white televisions, textbook editions, computers, calculator models, and TV series.

Wide variations exist in the amount of time a particular product takes to pass through a given phase of its life cycle; some products pass through various stages in a relatively short period; others take considerably longer. Often it is a matter of the basic *need* for the item and the *rate of technological change*. For instance, some toys,

Product life cycle
Incubation, growth, maturity, saturation, and decline.

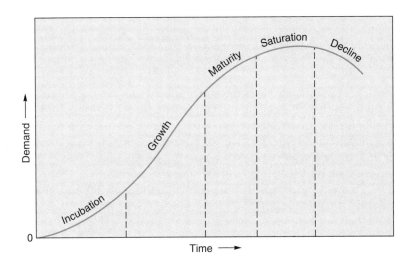

Figure 5–2

Products or services may exhibit life cycles over time

novelty items, and style items have a life cycle of less than one year, whereas other, more crucial items, such as slide rules, may last for 50 years or more before yielding to technological change.

ROBUST DESIGN

Some products will perform as designed only within a narrow range of conditions, while other products will perform as designed over a much broader range of conditions. The latter case describes a product that has *robust design*. Consider a pair of fine leather boots—obviously not made for trekking through mud or snow. Now consider a pair of heavy rubber boots—just the thing for mud or snow. The rubber boots have a design that is more *robust* than the fine leather boots.

The more robust a product (or service) is, the less likely that it will fail due to a change in the environment in which it is used or in which it performed (in the case of a service). Hence, the extent to which designers can build robustness into the product or service, the better it should hold up, and the higher the level of customer satisfaction.

A similar argument can be made for robust design as it pertains to the *production process*. Environmental factors can have a negative effect on the quality of a product or service. The more resistant a design is to those influences, the less likely is the negative effect. For example, many products go through a heating process: food products, ceramics, steel, petroleum products, and pharmaceutical products. Furnaces often do not heat uniformly; heat may vary either by position in an oven, or over an extended period of production. One approach to this problem might be to develop a superior oven; another might be to design a system that moves the product during heating to achieve uniformity. A robust-design approach would be to develop a product that is unaffected by minor variations in temperature during processing.

Taguchi's Approach

Japanese engineer Genichi Taguchi's approach is based on the robust design. Its premise is that it is often easier to design a product that is insensitive to environmental factors, either in manufacturing or in use, than it is to control the environmental factors.

The central feature of Taguchi's approach—and the feature used most often by U.S. companies—is *parameter design*. This involves determining the specification settings for both the product and the process that will result in robust design in terms of manufacturing variations, product deterioration, and conditions during use.

The Taguchi approach modifies the conventional statistical methods of experimental design. It involves determining which factors are controllable, and which are not controllable (or are too expensive to control), and then determining the optimal levels of the controllable factors relative to product performance. The value of this approach is its ability to achieve major advances in design of a product or a process fairly quickly, using a relatively small number of experiments.

Critics of Taguchi's methods charge that the methods are inefficient and incorrect, and often lead to nonoptimal solutions. Nonetheless, his methods are widely used, and have been credited with helping to achieve major improvements in U.S. products and manufacturing processes.

THE DESIGN OF SERVICES

Because of the differences between services and products, the design of services must take into account different elements than the design of products.

Consider these differences:

1. Products are generally tangible; services are generally intangible. Consequently, service design often focuses more on intangible factors (e.g., peace of mind, ambiance) than does product design.

2. Services are often produced and received at the same time (e.g., a haircut, a car wash). Because of this, there is less latitude in finding and correcting errors *before* the customer has a chance to discover them. Consequently, training, process design, and customer relations are particularly important.

3. Services cannot be inventoried. This poses restrictions on flexibility, and makes capacity design very important.

4. Services are highly visible to consumers, and must be designed with that in mind; this adds an extra dimension to process design usually not present in product design.

5. Some services have low barriers to entry and exit. This places additional burden on service design to continually be aware of what competitors are offering.

6. Location is often important in service design, with convenience as a major factor. Hence, design of services and choice of location are often closely linked.

STANDARDIZATION

An important question that often arises in both product/service design and process design concerns the degree of standardization. **Standardization** refers to the extent to which there is absence of variety in a product, service, or process. Standardized products are made in large quantities of identical items; calculators, computers, and 2 percent milk are examples. Standardized service implies that every customer or item served receives essentially the same service. An automatic car wash is an example of this; each car, regardless of how clean or dirty it is, receives the same service. Standardized processes are processes used to deliver standardized service or produce standardized goods.

Standardization carries with it a number of important benefits as well as certain disadvantages. Among the benefits are *interchangeable* parts, which greatly lower the cost of production while increasing productivity and making replacement or repair relativity easy compared with what it would be with customized parts. Design costs are generally lower. For example, General Motors recently announced a plan to standardize key components of its automobiles across product lines; such components as brakes, electrical systems, and other "under the skin" parts would be the same instead of having different units for different cars. By reducing variety, GM expects to save time and money, and increase quality and reliability in its products.

Another benefit of standardization is reduced time and cost to train employees, and reduced time to design jobs. Similarly, scheduling of work and inventory handling become much more routine, as do purchasing and accounting activities.

Lack of standardization can at times lead to serious difficulties as well as competitive struggles, particularly when systems run under different conditions are incompatible. Consider a few examples: When VCRs were first introduced, there were two formats for tapes: VHS and Beta. Machines could play one or the other, but not

Standardization

Extent to which there is absence of variety in a product, service, or process.

both. This meant that producers needed to make two sets of tapes. High-definition television, now being introduced in the United States, might have been introduced much earlier, but three competing—and incompatible—systems were proposed, which led to prolonged debate and study before one system could be agreed upon. The lack of standardization in computer software and operating systems (Macintosh versus IBM) has presented users with hard choices because of the difficulty in switching from one system to the other. And the fact that U.S. manufacturers use the English system of measurement, while most of the rest of the world's manufacturers use the metric system, has led to problems in selling U.S. goods in foreign countries and in buying foreign machines for use in the United States. Competing in the European Community may be a bit more difficult because of this. Similarly, for years U.S. auto manufacturers have complained about inability to freely enter the Japanese market, but only recently have they begun to offer cars with steering wheels on the right side—the universal standard in Japan.

Standardization also has some disadvantages. A major one relates to the reduction in variety. This can limit the range of customers to whom a product or service appeals. But that creates a risk that a competitor will introduce a better product or greater variety (a feature of lean production), and realize a competitive advantage. Customers may only reluctantly accept a product because nothing else suits their needs. Another disadvantage is that a design may be frozen (standardized) prematurely, but once frozen, there may be compelling reasons for resisting modification. A familiar example of this is the keyboard arrangement of a typewriter. Studies have demonstrated that another arrangement of keys would be more efficient, but the cost of replacing all of the equipment in existence, plus the need to retrain typists, would not be worth the benefit. Similarly, U.S.-made color TV sets have a lower scanning rate (lines per inch) than foreign-made sets, resulting in poorer resolution. Early freezing of design was partly to blame for this.

Obviously, there are important issues related to standardization that designers must consider when making choices. The major advantages and disadvantages of standardization are summarized in Table 5–1.

MODULAR DESIGN

Modular design is another form of standardization. Modules represent groupings of component parts into subassemblies, usually to the point where the individual parts lose their separate identity. One familiar example of modular design is a television set with easily removed control panels. Computers, too, have modular parts that can be replaced if they become defective. By arranging modules in different configurations, different computer capabilities can be obtained. Modular design is also found in the construction industry. One firm in Rochester, New York, makes prefabricated motel rooms complete with wiring, plumbing, and even room decorations in its factory and then moves the complete rooms via rail to the construction site, where they are integrated into the structure.

One advantage of modular design of equipment is that failures are often easier to diagnose and remedy because there are fewer pieces to investigate compared with a nonmodular design. Similar advantages are found in ease of repair and replacement; the faulty module is conveniently removed and replaced with a good one. The manufacture and assembly of modules generally involves simplifications: fewer parts are involved, so purchasing and inventory control become more rou-

Modular design

A form of standardization in which component parts are subdivided into modules that are easily replaced or interchanged.

Advantages	Table 5–1

Advantages

1. Fewer parts to deal with in inventory and in manufacturing.
2. Reduced training costs and time.
3. More routine purchasing, handling, and inspection procedures.
4. Orders can be filled from inventory.
5. Opportunities for long production runs and automation.
6. Need for fewer parts justifies increased expenditures on perfecting designs and improving quality control procedures.

Disadvantages

1. Designs may be frozen with too many imperfections remaining.
2. High cost of design changes increases resistance to improvements.
3. Decreased variety results in less consumer appeal.

Advantages and disadvantages of standardization

tine, fabrication and assembly operations become more standardized, and training costs often are less.

The main disadvantages of modular design stem from the decrease in variety: the number of possible configurations of modules is much less than the number of possible configurations based on individual components. Another disadvantage that is sometimes encountered is the inability to disassemble a module in order to replace a faulty part; the entire module must be scrapped—usually a more costly procedure.

RESEARCH AND DEVELOPMENT

Research and development (R&D) refers to organized efforts that are directed toward increasing scientific knowledge or product (and process) innovation. Most of the advances in semiconductors, medicine, communications, and space technology can be attributed to R&D efforts at colleges and universities, research foundations, government agencies, and private enterprises.

Research and development

Organized efforts to increase scientific knowledge or product innovation.

Some R&D efforts involve *basic research,* others *applied research,* and others still, *development.*

Basic research has the object of advancing the state of knowledge about a subject, without any near-term expectation of commercial applications.

Applied research has the object of achieving commercial applications.

Development converts the results of applied research into useful commercial applications.

Basic research, because it does not lead to near-term commercial applications, is generally underwritten by the government and large corporations. Conversely, applied research and development, because of the potential for commercial applications, appeals to a wide spectrum of business organizations.

The benefits of successful R&D can be tremendous. Some research leads to patents, with the potential of licensing and royalties. However, many discoveries are not patentable, or companies don't wish to divulge details of their ideas and so do not follow the patent route. Even so, the first organization to bring a new product or service to the market generally stands to profit from it before the others

Sophisticated software such as CADAM from IBM is often used in R&D. CADAM can easily show the cutaway view of the internal workings as well as the exterior features of products such as this pump.

can catch up. (Recall the earlier discussion of life cycles; early products may be priced higher because a temporary monopoly exists until competitors bring their versions out.)

The costs of R&D can be considerable. Kodak, for example, spends an average of $2 million *a day* on R&D. And other large companies spend even more in the automotive, computer, communications, and pharmaceutical industries. Even so, U.S. companies in general have been criticized for spending too little on R&D—insufficient R&D efforts are often cited as a factor in loss of competitive advantage.

The following reading presents an interesting comparison of differing R&D strategies, with respect to the products to which R&D is applied, and with respect to seeking small versus "home run" innovations.

READING   TOYING WITH HIGH TECH   *Andrew Pollack*

What do you do with an exotic metal alloy that has the ability to "remember" its original shape and return to that shape when heated?

In the United States, the answer is: Use it to make pipe joints in fighter planes and think about using it for satellites that could be launched in compact form and would unfold automatically in space.

But in Japan, the answer is: Use the alloy to make eyeglass frames, air-conditioner louvers, and a toy in which a boy's head and a girl's head are separated by a wire made of the alloy. When the toy is dunked in hot water, the wire returns to a ring shape, bringing the heads together in a kiss.

The example illustrates a major difference between the two nations, which are now vying for world supremacy in high technology.

In the United States, technological emphasis is often on a big military or space project, with little regard for immediate commercial applications.

In Japan, which has no big military or space programs, the emphasis is overwhelmingly on commercial uses, particularly for consumers. Technology advances bit by bit, tested at each step in a variety of applications, some of them exceedingly trivial. Indeed, the Japanese have a penchant for finding low-tech applications for high-tech products.

"We are now in the age of popularization of advanced technology," said Masanori Moritani, senior researcher at the Nomura Research Institute, a division of the Nomura Securities Co. "Especially in Japan, companies are very eager to apply advanced technology."

James C. Abegglen, a Japan watcher associated with the Boston Consulting Group, agreed: "The Americans go for the home run. The Japanese get singles and steal bases."

Other examples of the difference in approach abound:

In the United States, one of the first feasible uses of solar electricity generation was to provide power to satellites. Japan came up with a more down-to-earth application—the solar-powered calculator. Now companies here are coming out with the solar-powered radio, the solar-powered watch, and the solar-powered rechargeable battery recharger.

In the United States, more than half the market for graphite composite materials—lightweight but strong materials being used as substitutes for metal—is for aerospace and aircraft uses. In Japan, 80 percent of the market is for tennis racquets, golf clubs, and other sports equipment, which account for but a small part of its American use.

In the United States, laser development has facilitated everything from surgery to fusion energy, and now lasers may be used for weapons to destroy enemy missiles. Japan produces the only existing consumer products using lasers—the laser videodisk system and the digital audiodisk system.

In new ceramics, the United States has emphasized military uses and the space shuttle heat shield. Japanese companies have come up with ceramic scissors, ballpoint pen tips, and sake warmers.

Which approach, the home run or the barrage of singles, will win the game is hotly debated, with each nation wishing it had some of the attributes of the other.

Some American electronics executives question the value of devoting so much technological research to military and space efforts with little commercial value. Many Japanese executives, however, are envious of the American system's ability to make great advances and are worried that their consumer-based technology is too limited.

Aside from Japan's lack of big military or space programs, another reason for the emphasis on consumer applications is that technology development programs run by the Ministry of International Trade and Industry do not always provide much money, despite the publicity they receive. So companies must find other ways to pay for technological development quickly.

"Whether we like it or not, our research efforts must be directed at smaller versions, to find a way to earn some profit," said Kazuo Iga, director of the corporate products development division of the Matsushita Electric Industrial Co. His company uses the shape memory alloy to make air-conditioner louvers that change direction depending on the temperature, directing hot air down to warm a room and cool air up to cool it.

The Sanyo Electric Company produces a variety of solar cells for many different uses. The cost of manufacturing the family of cells has fallen to the point that they are beginning to be used in quantities in homes, cars, and other applications.

Moreover, the intensely competitive nature of the Japanese consumer electronics industry leads each company to employ new technologies, no matter how frivolously, to make its product stand out. This practice is abetted by the Japanese love of novelty. One product, for example, is a voice-activated cradle, which starts rocking when the baby cries.

Such experimentation often produces benefits in allowing companies to hone their technology and reduce costs by mass production. "You can develop a high-technology base by developing low-technology products with high volume," said Bruce F. Rubinger, director of studies for the Global Competitiveness Council, a research organization in Boston.

Solar energy is an example. The Sanyo Electric Co. is producing four million solar batteries for calculators each month. Now it thinks it has forced the cost down enough to introduce a solar roof tile to provide electricity for homes.

In ceramics, as well, some experts think small consumer applications can help develop more serious ones.

The Japanese are even starting to apply their civilian technology to military systems, spurred in part by an agreement last year with the United States calling for more cooperation in defense technology.

Devices used to record images in video cameras have potential uses for missile guidance systems. Mitsubishi Heavy Industries has been approached by General Motors for help in designing tank transmissions.

Source: "High Tech: Japan's Approach," *New York Times,* June 12, 1984. Copyright © 1984 by The New York Times Company. Reprinted by permission.

QUALITY FUNCTION DEPLOYMENT

Quality function deployment (QFD) is a structured approach for integrating the "voice of the customer" into the product development process. The purpose is to insure that customer requirements are factored into every aspect of the process, from product planning to the production floor. Listening to, and understanding, the customer is the central feature of QFD. Requirements are often in the form of a general statement, such as, "It should be easy to adjust the cutting height of the lawn mower." Once the requirements are known, they must be translated into technical terms related to production of the product. For example a statement about changing the height of the lawn mower may relate to the mechanism used to accomplish that, its position, instructions for use, tightness of the spring that controls the mechanism, materials needed, and so on. For manufacturing purposes, these must be stated in terms of actual materials, dimensions, and machinery used for processing.

The structure of QFD is based on a set of matrices. The main matrix relates customer requirements (what) and their corresponding technical requirements (how). This concept is illustrated in Figure 5–3.

Additional features are usually added to the basic matrix to broaden the scope of analysis. Typical additional features include importance weightings and competitive evaluations. And a correlational matrix is usually constructed for technical requirements; this can reveal if there are conflicting technical requirements. When these additional features are added, the resulting set of matrices has the form illustrated in Figure 5–4. It is often referred to as the "house of quality," because of its houselike appearance.

An example of an analysis using this format is illustrated in Figure 5–5. The data relate to a commercial printer (customer) and the company who supplies their paper for printing (us). At first glance, the display appears fairly complex. It contains a considerable amount of information for product and process planning. The key is to break it up into separate parts, and consider them one at a time. For example, a key part is the list of customer requirements down the left side of the figure. Next, note the technical requirements, listed vertically near the top. The important relation-

Figure 5–3

The main QFD Matrix

ships, and their degree of importance, are shown in the center of the figure. The circle with a dot inside indicates the strongest positive relationship. In other words, it denotes the most important technical requirements for satisfying customer requirements. Now look at the "importance to customer" numbers that are shown next to each customer requirement (1 is the most important). Designers will take into account the importance values and the strength of correlation in determining where to focus the greatest effort.

Next, consider the correlation matrix at the top of the "house." Of special interest is the strong negative correlation between "paper thickness" and "roll roundness." Designers will have to either find some way to overcome that, or make a trade-off decision.

On the right side of the figure is a competitive evaluation comparing the supplier's performance on the customer requirements with each of the two key competitors (A and B). For example, the supplier (X) is worst on the first customer requirement and best on the third customer requirement. The line connects the X performances. Ideally, design will cause all of the Xs to be in the highest positions.

Across the bottom are importance weightings, target values, and technical evaluations. The technical evaluations can be interpreted in a manner similar to the competitive evaluations (note the line connecting the Xs). The target values typically contain technical specifications, so we don't discuss those. The importance weightings are the sums of values assigned to the relationships (see the lower right-hand key for relationship weights). The 3 in the first column is the product of the importance to the customer = 3 and the small ($\triangle$) weight = 1. The importance weightings and target evaluations help designers focus on desired results. In this example, we can see that the first technical requirement has the lowest importance weighting, while the next four technical requirements all have relatively high importance weightings.

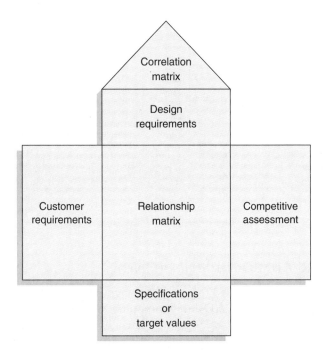

Figure 5–4

The house of quality

Source: V. Daniel Hunt, *Quality in America* (Homewood, Ill.: Business One Irwin, 1992), p. 270. Reprinted by permission.

Figure 5–5

Source: Ernst and Young Consulting Group, *Total Quality* (Homewood, Ill.: Dow-Jones Irwin, 1991), p. 121. Reprinted by permission.

COMPUTER-AIDED DESIGN (CAD)

Computers are increasingly used for product design, particularly for manufacturing. **Computer-aided design (CAD)** uses computer graphics for product design. The designer can modify an existing design or create a new one on a CRT by means of a light pen, a keyboard, a joystick, or a similar device. Once the design is entered into the computer, the designer can maneuver it on the screen: it can be rotated to

Computer-aided design

Product design using computer graphics.

provide the designer with different perspectives, it can be split apart to give the designer a view of the inside, and a portion of it can be enlarged for closer examination. When the design has been completed, the designer can obtain a printed version. In addition, the design can be filed electronically, making it accessible to manufacturing personnel and others in the firm who have need for this information (e.g., marketing).

A growing number of products are being designed in this way. Some of the products include transformers, automobile parts, aircraft parts, integrated circuits, and electric motors.

A major benefit of CAD is the increased productivity of designers. No longer is it necessary to laboriously prepare mechanical drawings of products or parts and revise them repeatedly to correct errors or incorporate revisions. A rough estimate is

NEWSCLIP   A QFD SNAPSHOT

How a pencilmaker sharpened up its product by listening to "the voice of the customer" through quality function deployment

Devised by Japan's Professor Yoji Akao (right), QFD has been winning adherents since being transplanted to the U.S. in the late 1980s. In this example of how it works, Writesharp Inc. is imaginary, but the technique in the accompanying diagram is real.

First, Writesharp's customers were surveyed to determine what they value in a pencil and how they rate the leading brands. Each wish list item was correlated with a pencil's functional characteristics (see FUNCTIONAL CHARACTERISTICS matrix). "Reverse engineering"—tearing down a competitor's product to see what makes it tick—produced the competitive benchmark measurements for the various functions.

An analysis of the plots quickly revealed that the improvement with the biggest potential was a better-quality lead (see CUSTOMER SATISFACTION/ CUSTOMER DEMANDS matrix). An interdepartmental team was as-

signed the task of evaluating new lead formulations that would last longer and generate less dust. Another team ran tests to determine whether substituting cedar for oak in the wood casing would improve shape quality, or hexagonality, and thus reduce the pencil's tendency to roll down slanted desktops.

The lead-formulation team organized its work with a similar matrix chart, segmented to show the functional contributions of the ingredients in pencil lead. This revealed that the binder, or glue, used in forming the lead was the key variable. Tests found a polymer that dramatically reduced dusting by retaining more moisture and also wore down more slowly. While this binder was more expensive, better production controls—going slightly beyond the performance of Competitor Y—promised to reduce waste enough to trim total per-pencil manufacturing costs by 1¢.

Changing the wood, meanwhile, yielded only marginal enhancements. So the company decided to upgrade the process

Japanese Professor Yoji devised the system and created the term "quality function deployment." This QFD matrix combines benchmarking, customer demands, a product's characteristics, and customer satisfaction to measure and improve product quality.

controls used for cutting the wood and match the quality of Competitor X (see BENCHMARKS matrix).

Source: *Business Week/Quality,* 1991, pp. 22–23.

(continued)

		Functional characteristics △ Strong correlation ○ Some correlation □ Possible correlation				Customer satisfaction Scale: 1 to 5 (5 = best)				
		Pencil length (inches)	Time between sharpenings (written lines)	Lead dust (particles per line)	Hexagonality	Importance rating (5 = highest)	Writesharp (now)	Competitor X (now)	Competitor Y (now)	Writesharp (target)
Customer demands	Easy to hold	○			○	3	4	3	3	4
	Does not smear		○	△		4	5	4	5	5
	Point lasts	□	△	○		5	4	5	3	5
	Does not roll	□			△	2	3	3	3	4
Benchmarks	Writesharp (now)	5	56	10	70%		Writesharp (now)	Competitor X (now)	Competitor Y (now)	Writesharp (target)
	Competitor X (now)	5	84	12	80%					
	Competitor Y (now)	4	41	10	60%					
	Writesharp (target)	5.5	100	6	80%					
	Market price						15¢	18¢	14¢	16¢
	Market share						16%	12%	32%	20%
	Profit						2¢	3¢	2¢	4¢

that CAD increases the productivity of designers from 3 to 10 times. A second major benefit of CAD is the creation of a data base for manufacturing that can supply needed information on product geometry and dimensions, tolerances, material specifications, and so on. It should be noted, however, that such a data base is necessary for CAD to function and that this entails a considerable amount of effort.

Some CAD systems allow the designer to perform engineering and cost analyses on proposed designs. For instance, the computer can determine the weight and volume of a part and do stress analysis as well. When there are a number of alternative designs, the computer can quickly go through the possibilities and identify the best one, given the designer's criteria.

The following reprint gives some indication of the breadth of use of computer-aided design. This article refers to CAD–CAM (CAM stands for computer-aided manufacturing).

READING   COMPUTERS SPEED THE DESIGN OF MORE WORKADAY PRODUCTS

The same computer technology used to design cars and missiles now is being used to design sneakers and spoons. The reason: Computer-aided design and manufacturing systems have become cheaper and easier to use, encouraging even decidedly low-tech companies to trade their drafting tables for computer terminals.

"CAD–CAM companies have been beating down our doors for years," says Alfred Zeien, vice chairman of Gillette Co., whose Braun subsidiary in Germany uses computers to design hair dryers and electric shavers. "We were finally convinced they could deliver."

Other makers of workaday products also have been convinced. Hasbro Bradley Inc. uses computers to design parts for GI Joe aircraft carriers; Craft Patterns does the same for dog houses. ITT Corp.'s computers draw the fire hydrants; Oneida Ltd.'s make spoons and forks.

Computers take the drudgery out of design. Instead of laboriously drawing and redrawing blueprints, engineers create designs electronically and alter them at the push of a few buttons. Some computer programs also analyze the designs to see how well they handle stress or changes in temperature. Manufacturers say that encourages experimentation, yields better-quality goods, and helps them introduce products more quickly.

"It allows us to try blue-sky projects," says W. David Lee, who heads a product development group at the Arthur D. Little Inc. consulting firm. Using computerized design techniques, Mr. Lee's group produced a U.S. Army canteen that keeps coffee warm for eight hours in arctic temperatures and a gas stove that needs less insulation for Maytag Co.'s Hardwick Stove division.

Walter Stewart, a senior vice president at Oneida, says that adding CAD–CAM is "a matter of survival." Oneida estimates that it takes 70 weeks to design and produce a flatware set using conventional methods—nearly twice the time of Asian competitors who work longer hours and, Oneida contends, produce lower-quality goods. To compete better, Oneida began in 1983 to use computers to design flatware and to make dies that punch out stainless steel forks and knives.

IBM Professional CADAM and CAITA were used to design this seat, which is also shown at the beginning of this chapter. In this version, the shape of the seat, particularly the headrest and side cushions, have been altered. Such changes are easier and faster to test using a computer than traditional methods.

As a result, Oneida says it now can match the turnaround time of its Asian competitors on some items. It also can bid on rush jobs that it might otherwise lose. Last summer, for instance, it produced spoon designs using the hot-selling Care Bear characters for General Mills Inc. in only two days. Oneida also says that more precise tooling reduces the number of imperfections in the flatware which must be laboriously ground or polished out.

Manufacturers also use CAD–CAM to customize products. The Kennedy Valve unit of ITT designs fire hydrants by piecing together computer drawings of different size nozzles and pipes. "It's like working with building blocks," says Bruce Platusich, manager of product engineering.

In a more sophisticated application, privately owned Techmedica Inc., Camarillo, Calif., produces artificial bones by computer. Techmedia uses cross-sections of a patient's bone produced by a CT scan, or computer tomography, as a basis for the bone design. The computer then directs a machine that cuts

(continued)

READING   *(concluded)*

the replacement bone out of a block of titanium alloy.

Anthony Hedley, director of surgical research at the Huntington Arthritis Center in Phoenix, says Techmedica can deliver an artificial bone in two weeks—a fraction of the time of suppliers that aren't computerized. As a result of the speeded up delivery and precision design, he says, some bone cancer patients are spared amputations.

Manufacturers also say CAD–CAM fattens their profit margins. By reducing product development time with computers, Gillette says it can quickly "abort" a project that doesn't meet cost goals. Hasbro Bradley says it can gear up faster for mass production by using computers to design molds.

"With some toys you can sell all you can make by Thanksgiving," says Hugh Maxwell, Hasbro Bradley's senior vice president for operations. If the company can produce a mold just one week faster, he estimates, it can sell another $300,000 worth of some toys.

But CAD–CAM has some shortcomings. Longtime employees sometimes resist learning the technology. And because the systems are so complex, they can be out of commission as much as 30 percent of the time, says Harley Shaiken, a Massachusetts Institute of Technology researcher. Among reasons for the downtime, he says, are computer breakdowns,

inexperienced workers, and management failure to devise schedules that take advantage of the technology. (Confirms Henry Eichfeld, an official at Computervision Corp., a large CAD–CAM maker: "Thirty percent downtime isn't atypical for the world of data processing.")

What's more, whatever cost savings result from the use of CAD–CAM don't necessarily translate into lower prices for consumers. Converse Inc., for instance, uses computers to design sneakers. But John O'Neil, president, says the company's large investment in CAD–CAM "means the cost of speeding up the process won't be reflected in the cost of the shoe."

Brian Smith, president of privately owned Craft Patterns, St. Charles, Illinois, has another problem with CAD–CAM. He says that he can only use his company's $165,000 design system at night because it saps too much power from the main computer. But he isn't complaining. He says the alternative—using pen and ink to design woodworking patterns for dog houses, high chairs, and other furniture—"is a total mess."

Source: Bob Davis, "Computers Speed the Design of More Workaday Products," *The Wall Street Journal,* January 18, 1985, p. 25. Reprinted by permission of *THE WALL STREET JOURNAL.* © 1985 Dow Jones & Company, Inc. All Rights Reserved Worldwide.

Reliability

The ability of a product, part, or system to perform its intended function under a prescribed set of conditions.

Reliability is a measure of the ability of a product, part, or system to perform its intended function under a prescribed set of conditions. The importance of reliability is underscored by the fact that prospective buyers use it when comparing alternatives and sellers use it as one determinant of price. Also, it can have an impact on repeat sales, it can reflect on the product's image, and if it is too low, there may be legal implications.

There are three important aspects of reliability:

1. Reliability as a probability.
2. Definition of failure.
3. Prescribed operating conditions.

If an item has a reliability of, say, .90, this means that the probability it will function as intended is 90 percent and that the probability it will fail is $1 - .90 = 10$ percent. Hence, it is expected that, on the average, 1 of every 10 such items will fail or, equivalently, that the item will fail, on the average, once in every 10 trials. Similarly, a reliability of .985 implies 15 failures per 1,000 parts or trials.

The term **failure** is used to describe a situation in which an item does not perform as intended. This includes not only those instances in which the item does not function at all, but also instances in which performance is substandard and instances in which the item functions in a way not intended. For example, a smoke alarm might fail to respond to the presence of smoke (not operate at all), or it might sound an alarm that is too faint to provide an adequate warning (substandard performance), or it might sound an alarm even though no smoke is present (an unintended response).

Reliabilities are always specified with respect to some set of conditions, called **normal operating conditions**. These can include load, temperature, and humidity ranges, as well as operating procedures and maintenance schedules. Failure of users to heed such conditions often results in premature failure of parts or complete systems. For example, using a passenger car to tow heavy loads causes excess wear and tear on the drive train; driving over potholes or curbs often results in untimely tire failure; and using a calculator to drive nails usually has a marked impact on its usefulness for performing mathematical operations.

Failure

Situation in which a product, part, or system does not perform as intended.

Normal operating conditions

The set of conditions under which an item's reliability is specified.

MEASURING RELIABILITY

Engineers and designers have a number of techniques at their disposal for assessing the reliability of parts, products, and systems. However, a discussion of those techniques is not within the scope of this text. Instead, let us turn our attention to the issue of quantifying overall product or system reliability. Probability is used in two ways.

1. The probability that the product or system will function on any given trial.
2. The probability that the product or system will function for a given length of time.

The first of these focuses on *one point in time* and is often used when a system must operate for one time or a relatively few numbers of times. The second of these focuses on the *length of service*. The distinction will become more evident as we examine each of these approaches in more detail.

The probability that a product or system will perform on a given trial is a function of the reliabilities of its component parts and how they are interrelated. Suppose a system is composed of two components and that both must operate in order for the system to function. The system reliability is the *product* of the reliabilities of the components. Thus, if one component has a probability of .9 and the other component has a probability of .8, the system has a probability of .72.

$$\boxed{.9} - \boxed{.8} = \boxed{.9 \times .8 = .72}$$

Similarly, if three components with reliabilities of .9, .8, and .9 must all work, the system reliability is .648:

$$\boxed{.9} - \boxed{.8} - \boxed{.9} = \boxed{.9 \times .8 \times .9 = .648}$$

Note that even though the individual components of a system might have high reliabilities, the system as a whole can have considerably less reliability because all components that are in series (as the ones in the preceding examples are) must function. As the number of series components increases, the system reliability decreases. For example, a system comprising eight components in series, each with a reliability of .99, has a reliability of only $.99^8 = .923$.

Obviously, many products and systems have a large number of component parts that must all operate, and some way to increase overall reliability is needed. One approach is to use **redundancy** in the design. This involves providing backup parts for some items. Consider the case of a component with a reliability of .9 and a backup with a reliability of .8 that automatically switches on if the original fails. The probability that the original part functions is .9. Of the 10 percent of the parts that fail (i.e., $1 - .9$), 80 percent will be "saved" by the backup. Hence, the resulting probability for this pair is $.9 + .8(.1) = .98$.

Redundancy

The use of backup components to increase reliability.

| Example 1 | Determine the reliability of the system shown below. |

Solution

The system can be reduced to a series of three components:

| .98 | $.90 + .90(1 - .90)$ | $.95 + .92(1 - .95)$ |

The system reliability is, then, the product of these:

$.98 \times .99 \times .996 = .966$

The second way of looking at reliability involves the incorporation of a time dimension: probabilities are determined relative to a specified length of time. This approach is commonly used in product warranties, which pertain to a given period of time after purchase of a product.

A typical profile of product failure rate over time is illustrated in Figure 5–6. Because of its shape, it is sometimes referred to as a "bathtub curve." It often happens that a number of items fail shortly after they are put into service, not because they wear out, but simply because they are defective to begin with. The rate of such failures decreases rapidly once the truly defective items are weeded out. During the second phase, there are few failures because most of the defective items have been eliminated, and it is too soon to encounter items that fail because they have worn out. In some cases, this phase can cover a relatively long period of time. In the third phase, failures due to wear-out occur, and the failure rate increases.

Information on the distribution and length of each phase requires the collection of historical data and analysis of those data. It often turns out that the **mean time between failures (MTBF)** can be modeled by a negative exponential distribution, such as that depicted in Figure 5–7. Equipment failures as well as product failures may occur in this pattern. In such cases, the exponential distribution can be used to determine various probabilities of interest. The probability that equipment or a product put into service at time 0 will fail *before* some specified time, *T*, is equal to the area under the curve between 0 and *T*. Reliability is concerned with the probability that a product will last *at least until* time *T*; reliability is equal to the area under the curve *beyond T*. (Note that the total area under the curve in each phase is treated as 100 percent for computational purposes.) Observe that as the specified length of service increases, the area under the curve to the right of that point (i.e., the reliability) decreases.

Determining values for the area under a curve to the right of a given point, *T*, is a relatively simple matter using a table of exponential values. An exponential distribution is completely described using a single parameter, the distribution mean, which reliability engineers often refer to as the mean time between failures. Using the symbol *T* to represent length of service, we can easily determine the probability that failure will not occur before time *T* (i.e., the area in the right tail):

$$P(\text{no failure before } T) = e^{-T/\text{MTBF}}$$

Mean time between failures

The average length of time between failures of a product or component.

Figure 5–6

Failure rate is a function of time

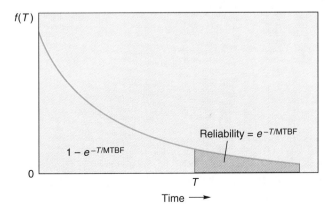

Figure 5–7

An exponential distribution

where

$$e = \text{Natural logarithm, } 2.7183\ldots$$
$$T = \text{Length of service before failure}$$
$$\text{MTBF} = \text{Mean time between failures}$$

The probability that failure will occur before time T is 1.00 minus that amount:

$$P(\text{failure before } T) = 1 - e^{-T/\text{MTBF}}$$

Selected values of $e^{-T/\text{MTBF}}$ are listed in Table 5–2.

Product life can sometimes be modeled by a normal distribution. Obtaining probabilities involves the use of a table (refer to Table B in Appendix B). The table provides areas under a normal curve from (essentially) the left end of the curve to a specified point z, where z is a *standardized* value computed using the formula

$$z = \frac{T - \text{Mean wear-out time}}{\text{Standard deviation of wear-out time}}$$

Thus, in order to work with the normal distribution, it is necessary to know the mean of the distribution and its standard deviation. A normal distribution is illustrated in Figure 5–8. Table B in Appendix B contains normal probabilities (i.e., the

Table 5–2	T/MTBF	$e^{-T/\text{MTBF}}$	T/MTBF	$e^{-T/\text{MTBF}}$	T/MTBF	$e^{-T/\text{MTBF}}$
Values of $e^{-T/\text{MTBF}}$	0.10	9048	2.60	0743	5.10	0061
	0.20	8187	2.70	0672	5.20	0055
	0.30	7408	2.80	0608	5.30	0050
	0.40	6703	2.90	0550	5.40	0045
	0.50	6065	3.00	0498	5.50	0041
	0.60	5488	3.10	0450	5.60	0037
	0.70	4966	3.20	0408	5.70	0033
	0.80	4493	3.30	0369	5.80	0030
	0.90	4066	3.40	0334	5.90	0027
	1.00	3679	3.50	0302	6.00	0025
	1.10	3329	3.60	0273	6.10	0022
	1.20	3012	3.70	0247	6.20	0020
	1.30	2725	3.80	0224	6.30	0018
	1.40	2466	3.90	0202	6.40	0017
	1.50	2231	4.00	0183	6.50	0015
	1.60	2019	4.10	0166	6.60	0014
	1.70	1827	4.20	0150	6.70	0012
	1.80	1653	4.30	0136	6.80	0011
	1.90	1496	4.40	0123	6.90	0010
	2.00	1353	4.50	0111	7.00	0009
	2.10	1255	4.60	0101		
	2.20	1108	4.70	0091		
	2.30	1003	4.80	0082		
	2.40	0907	4.90	0074		
	2.50	0821	5.00	0067		

Figure 5–8

A normal curve

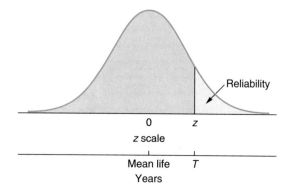

By means of extensive testing, a manufacturer has determined that its Super Sucker Vacuum Cleaner models have an expected life that is exponential with a mean of four years. Find the probability that one of these cleaners will have a life that ends:

Example 2

a.   After the initial four years of service.
b.   Before four years of service are completed.
c.   Not before six years of service.

Solution

MTBF = 4 years

a. T = 4 years:

$$T/\text{MTBF} = \frac{4 \text{ years}}{4 \text{ years}} = 1.0$$

From Table 5–2, $e^{-1.0} = .3679$.

b.   The probability of failure before T = 4 years is $1 - e^{-1}$, or $1 - .3679 = .6321$.

c. T = 6 years:

$$T/\text{MTBF} = \frac{6 \text{ years}}{4 \text{ years}} = 1.50$$

From Table 5–2, $e^{-1.5} = .2231$.

---

area that lies to the left of z). To obtain a probability that service life will not exceed some value T, compute z and refer to the table. To find the reliability for time T, compute z, obtain the probability from Table B for the area to the left of z, and subtract this probability from 100 percent. To obtain the value of T that will provide a given probability, locate the nearest probability under the curve *to the left* in Table B. Then use the corresponding z in the preceding formula and solve for T.

IMPROVING RELIABILITY

Reliability can be improved in a number of ways, some of which are listed in Table 5–3.

    Because overall system reliability is a function of the reliability of individual components, improvements in their reliability can increase system reliability. Un–

fortunately, inadequate production or assembly procedures can negate even the best of designs, and this is often a source of failures. As we have just seen, system reliability can be increased by the use of backup components. Failures in actual use can often be reduced by upgrading user education and refining maintenance recommendations or procedures. Finally, it may be possible to increase the overall reliability of the system by simplifying the system (and thereby reducing the number of components that could cause the system to fail) or altering component relationships (e.g., increasing the reliability of interfaces).

A fundamental issue in improving reliability is: How much reliability is needed? The answer depends on the potential benefits of improvements and on the cost of

Table 5–3 Potential ways to improve reliability	1. Improve component design.
	2. Improve production and/or assembly techniques.
	3. Improve testing.
	4. Use redundancy.
	5. Improve preventive maintenance procedures.
	6. Improve user education.
	7. Improve system design.

Example 3
∎

The mean life of a certain ball bearing can be modeled using a normal distribution with a mean of six years and a standard deviation of one year. Determine each of the following:

a. The probability that a ball bearing will wear out *before* seven years of service.
b. The probability that a ball bearing will wear out *after* seven years of service (i.e., find its reliability).
c. The service life that will provide a wear-out probability of 10 percent.

Solution

Wear-out mean = 6 years
Wear-out standard deviation = 1 year
Wear-out life is normally distributed

a. Compute z and use it to obtain the probability directly from Appendix B, Table B (see diagram).

$$z = \frac{7 - 6}{1} = +1.00$$

.8413

0   +1.00
z scale

6   7
Years

Thus, $P(T < 7) = .8413$.

b. Subtract the probability determined in part *a* from 100 percent (see diagram).

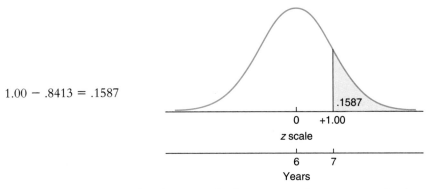

$$1.00 - .8413 = .1587$$

c. Use the normal table and find the value of *z* that corresponds to an area under the curve of 10% (see diagram).

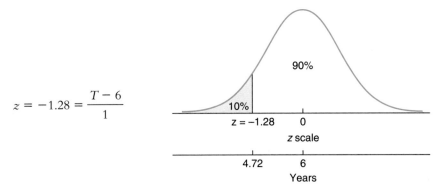

$$z = -1.28 = \frac{T - 6}{1}$$

Solving for *T*, we find $T = 4.72$ years.

those improvements. Generally speaking, reliability improvements become increasingly costly. Thus, although initially benefits may increase at a much faster rate than costs, eventually the opposite becomes true. The optimal level of reliability is the point where the incremental benefit received equals the incremental cost of obtaining it. In the short term, this tradeoff is made in the context of relatively fixed parameters (e.g., costs). However, in the longer term, efforts to improve reliability and reduce costs will lead to higher optimal levels of reliability (continuous improvement).

OPERATIONS STRATEGY

There are four major recommendations on operations strategy in the area of product and service design that can improve competitiveness:

1. Invest more in R&D.
2. Shift some emphasis away from short-term performance to long-term performance.
3. Work toward continual (albeit gradual) improvements instead of using a "big bang" attitude.
4. Work to shorten the product development cycle.

Dollars invested in research and development can have a tremendous impact on a company's *future* competitiveness, affecting quality and reliability, technological innovation, and product improvement. The average Japanese company invests a far more in R&D than the typical Western company. Western managers must be willing to initially sacrifice some short-term performance in favor of R&D that will eventually lead to *both* long-term and (later) short-term performance. However, accomplishing this will require a different attitude than the one that now prevails in many companies.

One of the hallmarks of Japanese success is the emphasis on *continual* improvement in products and process. In contrast, many Western managers appear bent on making a big splash (the tortoise and the hare?). "Little" things such as product reliability improvements can have long-lasting effects on consumer attitudes and buying patterns.

Getting new products to the market before competitors do usually results in substantial profits. Over the last decade, Japanese producers of automobiles and major appliances have introduced new products and product innovations an average of one year earlier than their Western counterparts. The implication is clear: Western managers must devote efforts to shortening their product development cycles to be competitive.

SUMMARY

Product and service design is a key factor in satisfying the customer. Organizations must be continually aware of what customers want, what the competition is doing, what government regulations are, and what new technologies are available in order to be successful in product and service design.

The design process involves motivation, ideas for improvement, organizational capabilities, and forecasting. Legal and regulatory considerations, as well as product life cycles, influence design choices. What degree of standardization to incorporate in designs is also an important consideration for designers.

Research and development efforts can sometimes play a significant role in product and process innovations, although these are sometimes so costly that only large companies or the government can afford to underwrite them.

Reliability of a product or service is often a key dimension in the eyes of the customer. Measuring and improving reliability are important aspects of product and service design.

KEY TERMS

computer-aided design
  (CAD), 206
failure, 211
manufacturability, 194
mean time between failures
  (MTBF), 213
modular design, 200
normal operating conditions, 211
product liability, 194

product life cycle, 197
redundancy, 212
reliability, 210
research and development
  (R&D), 201
reverse engineering, 193
standardization, 199
Uniform Commercial Code, 195

Problem

1. A product design engineer must decide if a redundant component is cost-justified in a certain system. The system in question has a critical component with a probability of .98 of operating. System failure would involve a cost of $20,000. A switch could be added that would automatically transfer the system to the backup component in the event of a failure, for a cost of $100. Should the backup be added if the backup probability is also .98?

Solution

Since no probability is given for the switch, we must assume its probability of operating when needed is 100 percent. The expected cost of failure (i.e., without the backup) is $20,000(1 − .98) = $400.

With the backup, the probability of *not* failing would be:

$$.98 + .02(.98) = .9996$$

Hence, the probability of failure would be 1 − .9996 = .0004. The expected cost of failure with the backup would be the added cost of the backup plus the failure cost:

$$\$100 + \$20,000(.0004) = \$108$$

Since this is less than the cost without the backup, it appears that adding the backup is definitely cost-justifiable.

Problem

2. Due to the extreme cost of interrupting production, a firm has two standby machines available in case a particular machine suffers a breakdown. The machine in use has a reliability of .94, and the backups have reliabilities of .90 and .80. In the event of a failure, either backup can be pressed into service, and if it fails, the other backup can be used. Compute the system reliability.

Solution

$R_1 = .94$, $R_2 = .90$, and $R_3 = .80$

The system can be depicted in this way:

```
        ┌─────┐
        │ .80 │
        └─────┘
        ┌─────┐
        │ .90 │
        └─────┘
      ┌─┤ .94 ├─┐
        └─────┘
```

$$
\begin{aligned}
R_{\text{system}} &= R_1 + R_2(1 - R_1) + R_3(1 - R_2)(1 - R_1) \\
&= .94 + .90(1 - .94) + .80(1 - .90)(1 - .94) = .9988
\end{aligned}
$$

Problem

3. A hospital has three *independent* fire alarm systems, with reliabilities of .95, .97, and .99. In the event of a fire, what is the probability that a warning would be given?

Solution

A warning would *not* be given if all three alarms failed. The probability that at least one alarm would operate is $1 - P$(none operate):

$$P(\text{none operate}) = (1 - .95)(1 - .97)(1 - .99) = .000015$$
$$P(\text{warning}) = 1 - .000015 = .999985$$

Problem

4. A weather satellite has an expected life of 10 years from the time it is placed into earth orbit. Determine its probability of no wear-out before each of the following lengths of service. (Assume the exponential distribution is appropriate.)

   a. 5 years.   *b.* 12 years.   *c.* 20 years.   *d.* 30 years.

Solution

   MTBF = 10 years

Compute the ratio T/MTBF for $T = 5, 12, 20,$ and 30, and obtain the values of $e^{-T/\text{MTBF}}$ from Table 5–2. The solution is summarized in the following table.

T	MTBF	T/MTBF	$e^{-T/\text{MTBF}}$
a. 5	10	0.50	.6065
b. 12	10	1.20	.3012
c. 20	10	2.00	.1353
d. 30	10	3.00	.0498

Problem

5. What is the probability that the satellite described in Solved Problem 4 will fail between 5 and 12 years after being placed into earth orbit?

Solution

$$P(5 \text{ years} < \text{Failure} < 12 \text{ years}) = P \text{ (failure after 5 years)}$$
$$- P(\text{failure after 12 years})$$

Using the probabilities shown in the previous solution, we find:

$$P(\text{failure after 5 years}) = .6065$$
$$-P(\text{failure after 12 years}) = \underline{.3012}$$
$$.3053$$

The corresponding area under the curve is illustrated as follows:

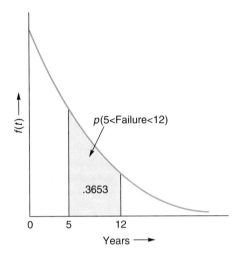

Problem

6. One line of radial tires produced by a large company has a wear-out life that can be modeled using a normal distribution with a mean of 25,000 miles and a standard deviation of 2,000 miles. Determine each of the following:

   a. The percentage of tires that can be expected to wear out within ±2,000 miles of the average (i.e., between 23,000 miles and 27,000 miles).

   b. The percentage of tires that can be expected to fail between 26,000 miles and 29,000 miles.

Solution

Notes: (1) Miles are analogous to time and are handled in exactly the same way time is; (2) the term *percentage* refers to a *probability*.

a. The phrase "within ±2,000 miles of the average" translates to within one standard deviation of the mean" since the standard deviation equals 2,000 miles. Therefore, the range of z is $z = -1.00$ to $z = +1.00$, and the area under the curve between those points is found as the difference between $P(z < +1.00)$ and $P(z < -1.00)$, using values obtained from Appendix B, Table B:

$$\begin{array}{r} P(z < +1.00) = .8413 \\ -P(z) < -1.00) = .1587 \\ \hline P(-1.00 < z < +1.00) = .6826 \end{array}$$

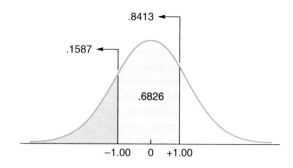

b.   Wear-out mean = 25,000 miles
Wear-out standard deviation = 2,000 miles

$$P(26,000 < \text{Wear-out} < 29,000) = P(z < z_{29,000}) - P(z < z_{26,000})$$

$$z_{29,000} = \frac{29,000 - 25,000}{2,000} = +2.00 \rightarrow .9772$$

$$z_{26,000} = \frac{26,000 - 25,000}{2,000} = +0.50 \rightarrow .6915$$

The difference is .9772 − .6915 = .2857, which is the expected percentage of tires that will wear out between 26,000 miles and 29,000 miles.

DISCUSSION AND REVIEW QUESTIONS

1. What are some of the factors that cause organizations to redesign their products and services?
2. Contrast applied research and basic research.
3. What is CAD? Describe some of the ways it can be used by a product designer.
4. What are some of the main advantages and disadvantages of standardization?
5. What is modular design, and what are its main advantages and disadvantages?
6. Define the term *reliability*.
7. Explain why a product or system might have an overall reliability that is low even though it is made up of components that have fairly high reliabilities.
8. What are some of the ways that reliability can be improved?
9. What is meant by the term *product life cycle*? Why would this be a consideration in product design?

10. Why is R&D a key factor in productivity improvement? What are some of the ways R&D contributes to productivity improvements?

11. What is redundancy and how can it improve product design?

---

1. Consider the following system:

   Determine the probability that the system will operate under each of these conditions:
   a. The system as shown.
   b. Each system component has a backup with a probability of .90 and a switch that is 100 percent reliable.
   c. Backups with .90 probability and a switch that is 99 percent reliable.

2. A product is composed of four parts. In order for the product to function properly in a given situation, each of the parts must function. Two of the parts each have a probability of .96 of functioning, and two have a probability of .99. What is the overall probability that the product will function properly?

3. A system consists of three identical components. In order for the system to perform as intended, all of the components must perform. Each has the same probability of performance. If the system is to have a .92 probability of performing, what is the minimum probability of performing needed by each of the individual components?

4. A product engineer has developed the following equation for the cost of a system component: $C = (10P)^2$, where C is the cost in dollars and P is the probability that the component will operate as expected. The system is composed of two identical components, which must both operate in order for the system to operate. The engineer can spend $173 for the two components. To the nearest two decimal places, what is the largest component probability that can be achieved?

5. The guidance system of a ship is controlled by a computer that has three major modules. In order for the computer to function properly, all three modules must function. Two of the modules have reliabilities of .97, and the other has a reliability of .99.
   a. What is the reliability of the computer?
   b. A backup computer identical to the one being used will be installed to improve overall reliability. Assuming the new computer automatically functions if the main one fails, determine the resulting reliability.
   c. If the backup computer must be activated by a switch in the event that the first computer fails, and the switch has a reliability of .98, what is the overall reliability of the system? (*Both* the switch and the backup computer must function in order for the backup to take over.)

6. One of the industrial robots designed by a leading producer of servomechanisms has four major components. Component reliabilities are .98, .95, .94, and .90. All of the components must function in order for the robot to operate effectively.
   a. Compute the reliability of the robot.
   b. Designers want to improve the reliability by adding a backup component. Due to space limitations, only one backup can be added. The backup for any component will have the same reliability as the unit it is a backup for. Which component should get the backup in order to achieve the highest reliability?
   c. If one backup that has a reliability of .92 can be added to any one of the main components, which one should get it to obtain the highest overall reliability?

7. A production line comprises three machines A, B, and C, with reliabilities of .99, .96, and .93, respectively. The machines are arranged in such a way that if one breaks

down, the others must also shut down. Engineers are weighing two alternative designs for increasing the line's reliability. Plan 1 involves adding an identical backup *line,* and plan 2 involves providing a backup for each *machine.* In either case, three machines (A, B, and C) would be used with reliabilities equal to the original three.

    a.   Which plan will provide the higher reliability?

    b.   Explain why the two reliabilities are not the same.

    c.   What other factors might enter into the decision of which plan to adopt?

8. A water treatment plant has five major components that must all function in order for the plant to operate as intended. Assuming that each component of the system has the same reliability, what is the minimum reliability each one must have in order for the overall system to have a reliability of .98?

9. Repeat the previous problem under the condition that one of the components will have a backup with a reliability equal to that of any one of the other components.

10. Hoping to increase the chances of reaching a performance goal, the director of a research project has assigned three separate research teams the same task. The director estimates that the team reliabilities are .9, .8, and .7 for successfully completing the task in the allotted time. Assuming that the teams work independently, what is the probability that the task will not be completed in time?

11. An electronic chess game has a useful life that is exponential with a mean of 30 months. Determine each of the following:

    a.   The probability that any given unit will operate for at least: (1) 39 months, (2) 48 months, (3) 60 months.

    b.   The probability that any given unit will fail sooner than: (1) 33 months, (2) 15 months, (3) one-half year.

    c.   The length of service after which the percentage of units that have failed will approximately equal: (1) 50 percent, (2) 85 percent, (3) 95 percent, (4) 99 percent.

12. A manufacturer of programmable calculators is attempting to determine a reasonable free-service period for a model it will introduce shortly. The manager of product testing has indicated that the calculators have an expected life of 30 months. Assume product life can be described by an exponential distribution.

    a.   If service contracts are offered for the expected life of the calculator, what percentage of those sold would be expected to fail during the service period?

    b.   What service period would result in a failure rate of approximately 10 percent?

13. Lucky Lumen light bulbs have an expected life that is exponentially distributed with a mean of 5,000 hours. Determine the probability that one of these light bulbs will last:

    a.   At least 6,000 hours.

    b.   No longer than 1,000 hours

    c.   Between 1,000 hours and 6,000 hours.

14. Planetary Communications, Inc., intends to launch a satellite that will enhance reception of television programs in Alaska. According to its designers, the satellite will have an expected life of six years. Assume the exponential distribution applies. Determine the probability that it will function for each of these time periods:

    a.   More than 9 years.

    b.   Less than 12 years.

    c.   More than 9 years but less than 12 years.

    d.   At least 21 years.

15. An office manager has received a report from a consultant that includes a section on equipment replacement. The report indicates that typewriters have a service life that is normally distributed with a mean of 41 months and a standard deviation of 4 months. On the basis of this information, determine the percentage of typewriters that can be expected to fail in these time periods:

    a.   Before 38 months of service.

    b.   Between 40 and 45 months of service.

    c.   Within ± 2 months of the mean life.

16. According to a study underwritten by a major television manufacturer, its 19-inch color TV picture tubes have a mean service life that can be modeled by a normal distribution that has a mean of six years and a standard deviation of one-half year.

   a. What probability can you assign to these service lives: (1) Five years? (2) Six years? (3) Seven and one-half years?

   b. If the manufacturer offers service contracts of four years on these picture tubes, what percentage can be expected to fail from wear-out during the service period?

17. In the previous problem, what service period would achieve an expected wear-out rate of:

   a. 2 percent?

   b. 5 percent?

SELECTED BIBLIOGRAPHY

Bierman, Harold, Jr.; Charles P. Bonini; and Warren H. Hausman. *Quantitative Analysis for Business Decisions.* 8th ed. Homewood, Ill.: Richard D. Irwin, 1991.

Groover, Mikell P. *Automation, Production Systems, and Computer-Aided Manufacturing.* Englewood Cliffs, N.J.: Prentice Hall, 1980.

————, and E. W. Zimmers, Jr. *CAD/CAM: Computer-Aided Design and Manufacturing.* Englewood Cliffs, N.J.: Prentice Hall, 1984.

Hare, Van Court, Jr. *Systems Analysis: A Diagnostic Approach.* New York: Harcourt Brace Jovanovich, 1967.

Hopeman, Richard J. *Production and Operations Management.* 4th ed. Columbus, Ohio: Charles E. Merrill Publishing, 1980.

Kushner, Lawrence M. "Product Safety Standards and Product Innovation, Too," *Harvard Business Review,* July–August 1980, p. 36.

Malott, Robert H. "Let's Restore Balance to Product Liability Law." *Harvard Business Review,* May–June 1983, p. 66.

Moore, Franklin G., and Thomas E. Hendrick. *Production/Operations Management.* 9th ed. Homewood, Ill.: Richard D. Irwin, 1984.

READING   MANAGING COMPLEXITY AND THE FLOW OF DOLLARS   *John Hagel III*

Product complexity is not necessarily undesirable. It is often a concomitant of innovation and can play an important role in building, or maintaining, advantages over competing products. Managing complexity is, therefore, a matter of business judgment—of weighing its costs against its value to customers and, from that, its potential returns.

Why Design Matters

Intricacy of product design usually does not get the attention it deserves as a driver of product development expense. Although managers understand that such complexity boosts development expense to some degree, few realize how extraordinarily sensitive that expense can be to variations in complexity.

In fact, intricacy of product design often has a far greater impact on expense than how product development is organized or managed—even though efforts to trim development spending have usually focused more on these latter choices than on complexity.

The pioneering research of software development expert Lawrence Putnam, on the relationship between complexity in product design and development expense, suggests that this relationship is not linear, but exponential. He found that increasing the number of lines of code in a software product would not just double the development expense—it would raise it by a power of three, holding other variables constant.

(continued)

McKinsey's work on product development has turned up similar results. For example, we conducted a detailed comparison of the development projects of two companies that were introducing similar data networking products. Our analysis showed that one company had spent 13 times as much as the other. When we explored what factors were responsible for this enormous discrepancy, we discovered that product complexity accounted for about 74 percent of the differential.

The effect of design complexity on development expense does not end when a product is introduced; it creates a permanent burden that lives on in subsequent generations of the same product. In the case of the data networking products discussed above, we found that 25 percent of the ongoing development budget for product enhancement at the high-cost company could be traced directly to the choices it had made regarding product complexity when the product was first introduced.

This 25 percent complexity burden was not a result of efforts to make the product still more complex. It represented the incremental expense of implementing enhancements in a product that was already highly complex. To put the point another way, the high-cost company spent one-third more on continuing development activities than it would have if it had chosen to introduce the less complex product offered by its competitor. It had unintentionally built into its development budget a cost weight it would carry into the future.

If customers had valued the additional complexity highly enough—if it had led enough of them to buy the high-cost company's product instead of its competitor's—the firm's choice, of more complexity and more cost, might have made good business sense. As it turned out, they did not.

Cross-Functional Implications

Although the complexity of product design tends to have its most significant cost impact on development expense, it has other less direct effects as well. For example, manufacturing expense may increase with the complexity of product design. In some cases, complexity will increase the number of components used in a product, leading both to higher manufacturing costs and higher inventory investment. More complex designs may also require a tightening of per-

formance standards for the manufacturing process and an expansion of quality testing procedures. These outcomes, in turn, lead to higher first-pass expense and raise reject rates.

Customer service expense can also rise with increases in the complexity of product design. Some product categories are typically accompanied by customer training programs. For example, factory equipment or advanced medical diagnostic instrumentation may undergo jumps in training program expense as customers require more handholding to learn how to use more complex products. Training expense may increase, at the same time and for the same reason, for the technical service organization. Field service expense may rise as well if more complex product designs increase either the need for preventive maintenance or the likelihood of product failure.

Even marketing and sales can be affected by the complexity of product design—as, for instance, when a company seeks to market a high-cost product to a customer segment that does not attach a high value to the complexity embedded in the product.

Why are so few companies aware of the full impact of product complexity? The main reason seems to be that managers' radar screens—the systems that define and shape the reality perceived by managers—are rarely designed to track and highlight complexity. Complexity tends to remain in the shadows, hidden.

Complexity is so hard to see, in part, because the relevant dimensions of complexity vary so much from product to product. For each type of product, some dimensions of complexity will have disproportionate effects on development expense. In software products, for example, the key dimension of complexity is the number of lines of code; in printed circuit boards, it is the number of components and the density with which they are packed on the board.

Identifying the primary dimensions of product complexity and quantifying their impact on development spending can be a substantial, and difficult, undertaking. Existing financial or operations reports offer little help—not least because development programs are rarely organized in a way that directly corresponds to the primary dimensions of complexity.

Not surprisingly, it is rarely possible to quantify with confidence the impact of design complexity by comparing the numbers for actual projects. It is usually more productive to generate a series of detailed "what if" scenarios around a single development effort and, in this way, to explore the resource implications of stepping down the complexity of a product, feature by feature.

Although there are substantial difficulties in quantifying the impact of complexity on development expense, management can use some relatively quick tests to determine if complexity is likely to be an issue. First, a detailed feature/performance comparison between a company's products and those of its competitors may uncover a feature/performance surplus. This surplus could represent unnecessary increments of complexity—or, if a customer values additional features highly enough, a source of competitive advantage.

Second, a comparison of development expense/revenue ratios could reveal that the yield from a firm's development spending is below that of its competition. Alternatively, management could analyze relative margin yields—how many dollars of gross margin a product line generates as compared with the percentage of the dollars spent on development.

To ascertain whether and to what extent potential customers value additional features, firms can employ conjoint analysis—in which respondents are presented with a series of choices between two packages of attributes. This methodology, which has been used for years to test options for consumer packaged goods, can help electronics companies pinpoint which increments of complexity are worth their costs.

Costs of complexity

Product complexity can affect a wide range of costs:

1. Prototype development
2. Manufacturing
3. Inventory
4. Quality testing
5. First-pass manufacturing
6. Eliminating rejects
7. Customer training
8. Field service

Questions

1. How can complexity be a source of competitive advantage? How can it be a source of competitive disadvantage?

2. Why aren't managers more aware of the full impact of complexity? Why is complexity so hard to see?

3. List four areas of an organization (e.g., design) that are affected by high complexity in a product.

Source: *Electronic Business,* January 9, 1989, pp. 38–40.

CHAPTER SIX

PROCESS SELECTION AND CAPACITY PLANNING

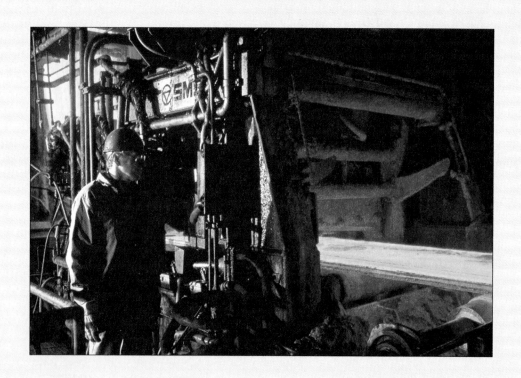

After completing this chapter, you should be able to:

1. Explain the importance of process selection and how process selection relates to product and service design and capacity planning.

2. Describe the different types of processing.

3. Describe automated approaches to processing.

4. Explain the need for management of technology.

5. Explain the importance of capacity planning.

6. Discuss ways of defining and measuring capacity.

7. Describe some of the factors that determine effective capacity alternatives.

8. Discuss the major considerations related to developing capacity alternatives.

9. Briefly describe approaches that are useful for evaluating process selection and capacity alternatives.

Product and service choices, process selection, capacity planning, and choices about location and layout are among the most basic decisions managers must make, because those decisions have long-term consequences for the organization.

In this chapter, process selection and capacity planning are examined. Process selection is both exciting and challenging; technological advances in processing provide many new options for competitive advantage, but they also pose numerous risks for the unwary decision maker. The first half of the chapter is devoted to process planning. The remainder of the chapter focuses on capacity planning.

PROCESS SELECTION

Process selection refers to the way an organization chooses to produce or provide its goods or services. Essentially it involves choice of technology and related issues, and it has major implications for capacity planning, layout of facilities, equipment, and design of work systems. Figure 6–1 provides an overview of where process selection fits into system design.

Process selection occurs as a matter of course when new products or services are being planned. However, it also occurs periodically due to technological changes in equipment as well as changes in existing products or services.

Make or Buy

The very first step in process planning is to consider the issue of whether to make or buy some or all of a product or to subcontract some or all of a service. A manufacturer might decide to purchase certain parts rather than make them; in some instances, all parts are purchased, with the manufacturer simply doing assembly operations. Many firms contract out janitorial service, and some contract for repair services. If a decision is made to buy or contract, this lessens or eliminates the need for process selection.

In make or buy decisions, a number of factors are usually considered, such as:

1. *Available capacity.* If an organization has available capacity, it often makes sense for the organization to produce an item or perform a service itself. The additional costs would be relatively small compared with those required to buy items or subcontract services.

Figure 6–1

Process selection and system design

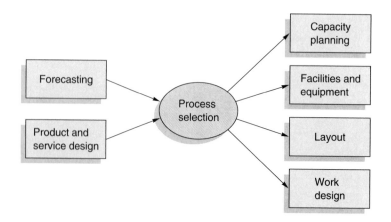

2. *Expertise.* If a firm lacks the expertise to do a satisfactory job, buying might be a more reasonable alternative.

3. *Quality considerations.* Firms that specialize can usually offer higher quality than an organization can obtain itself. Conversely, special quality requirements or the ability to closely monitor quality may cause a firm to perform the work itself.

4. *The nature of demand.* When demand for an item is high and steady, the organization is often better off doing the work itself. However, wide fluctuations in demand or small orders are usually better handled by others who are able to combine orders from multiple sources, which results in higher volume and tends to offset individual buyer fluctuations.

5. *Cost.* Any cost savings achieved from buying or making must be weighed against the preceding factors. Cost savings might come from the item itself or from transportation cost savings realized by making the item rather than buying it.

In some cases, a firm might choose to perform part of the work itself and let others handle the rest in order to maintain flexibility and to hedge against loss of a subcontractor. Moreover, this provides a bargaining tool in negotiations with contractors, or a head start if the firm decides later to take over the operation entirely.

If the organization decides to perform some or all of the processing, then the issue of process selection becomes important.

TYPES OF PROCESSING

There are basically three types of processing systems: continuous systems, intermittent systems, and projects. Continuous systems are highly specialized systems de-

SIMFACTORY II.5 is a simulation program that can be used in designing a process. This continuous flow example was created by graphically entering the factory description. The software then generates an animated picture.

signed to provide large volumes of one or a few standardized items. Intermittent systems are more generalized, making them more suited to handle lower volumes of items that present a variety of processing requirements. Projects have limited life spans and are best suited to complex, special-purpose jobs. Each of these systems is briefly described in the following sections.

Continuous Processing

Continuous processing Highly specialized system producing large volumes of one or a few standardized items.

Continuous processing systems produce high volumes of standardized output. The ultimate continuous processing systems produce a single product such as flour or sugar. Generally, these products are measured on a continuous basis rather than counted as discrete units. Other examples include liquid and powder detergents, gasoline and oil, and water treatment. Note that the output of these systems is highly uniform (standardized). Other continuous processing systems produce output that allows for some variety; products are highly similar, but not identical. Examples include automobiles, televisions, computers, calculators, cameras, and video equipment. Typically, these products are produced in discrete units. This form of processing is often referred to as *repetitive manufacturing.*

The highly standardized output of continuous processing lends itself to highly standardized methods and equipment. Because of division of labor, skill requirements of workers are usually fairly low. Equipment tends to be highly specialized, which tends to make it expensive relative to more general-purpose equipment, but the high volumes of output result in a low cost per unit. As a general rule, such products are made for inventory rather than for customer order. Examples in the service area include programs for mass inoculations, automatic car washes, mechanical harvesters, mail service, and fast-food operations. Applications in services are less plentiful because services tend to be more customized on a per-unit basis.

Intermittent Processing

Intermittent processing System that produces lower volumes of items or services with a greater variety of processing requirements.

Intermittent processing is used when systems handle a variety of processing requirements. Volume is much lower than in flow systems. Intermittent systems are characterized by general-purpose equipment that can satisfy a variety of processing requirements, semiskilled or skilled workers who operate the equipment, and a narrower span of supervision than for most continuous systems.

One form of intermittent processing occurs when *batches,* or *lots,* of similar items are processed in the same manner. An example would be food processing. A canning factory might process a variety of vegetables; one run may involve sliced carrots, the next green beans, and the next corn or beets. All might follow an identical process of washing, sorting, slicing, cooking, and packing, although the equipment would need to be cleaned and adjusted between runs. Another form of intermittent processing is done by a *job shop,* which is designed to handle a greater variety of job requirements than batch processing. Lot sizes may be large, or as small as a single unit. What distinguishes that kind of operation from batch processing is that the job requirements often vary considerably from job to job, so that the sequence of processing steps, and the job content of the steps, varies considerably. An auto repair shop is an example of a job shop. Each car is handled on an individual basis. Large repair shops may have specialists who deal in one kind of repair (e.g., brake jobs), but cars are still handled one at a time. As another example, a machine shop might handle jobs for many customers, processing lots of one or a few items up to several hundred or more items. Even for large jobs, there is usually so much variety among successive jobs that the batch processing described for the canning factory would be too restrictive to handle the variety. Differences in job processing requirements present routing and scheduling challenges, as well as a frequent need to adjust equipment settings or make other alterations for successive jobs. Processing cost per unit is generally higher than it would be under continuous processing.

Further examples of intermittent processing are textbook publication, bakeries, health care systems, and educational systems. In some cases, the outputs are made for inventory (clothing, automobile tires), and in others, they are designed to meet customer needs (health care) or specifications (special tools, parts, or equipment). Marketing efforts in such systems are often directed toward promoting system capabilities or customized services.

Projects

Projects are set up to handle complex jobs consisting of unique sets of activities that must be completed in a limited time span. Examples of application include large or unusual construction projects, new product development or promotion, planning and coordinating space missions, and organizing and handling the logistics of disaster relief efforts. Because of their limited life spans and the nonrepetitive nature of activities, these systems differ considerably from continuous and intermittent processing systems. Projects are covered in Chapter 16.

> **Projects**
> Complex jobs consisting of unique, nonrepetitive sets of activities with limited life spans.

MATCH THE PROCESS AND THE PRODUCT

A key concept in process selection is the need to match market requirements with process capabilities. The difference between success and failure in production can sometimes be traced to choice of process. Products range from highly customized to highly standardized. Generally, volume requirements tend to increase as standardization increases; customized products tend to be low volume, and standardized products tend to be high volume. These factors should be considered in determining the process to be used.

Certain processes are more amenable to low-volume, customized products, while others are more suited to moderate-variety products, and still others to higher volume, highly standardized products. By matching product requirements with process choices, producers can achieve the greatest degree of efficiency in their operations. Table 6–1 illustrates this important concept. Examples of products are placed in their ideal positions.

Notice that the examples all line up along the diagonal of the table. This is the most efficient alignment. If a producer should choose some other combination (e.g., assembly line for a customized product or service), he would find that the highly customized requirements of the various products were in direct conflict with the more uniform requirements needed to effectively operate in the assembly-line mode. Similarly, a job shop arrangement (machines and personnel are capable of handling a wide variety of processing requirements) would be wasted on a highly standardized product; equipment and personnel need to be highly specialized.

The table can provide insights to those making process selections as well as to those managing existing operations. For new products, decision makers should make every attempt to achieve a matching of product and process requirements. For an ongoing operation, a manager should examine existing processes in light of the table in order to see how well processes and products are matched. Poor matches

Table 6–1

Product-process matrix

Process	Product			
	Customized (low volume)	High variety (low-moderate volume)	Moderate variety (moderate volume)	Standardized (high volume)
Job shop	Advertising Dental work Equipment repair			
Batch		Magazines Food processing		
Repetitive			Autos TVs	
Continuous flow				Sugar Flour

Sources: Adapted from Robert H. Hayes and Stephen C. Wheelwright, "Link Manufacturing Product and Process Life Cycles," *Harvard Business Review,* Jan-Feb 1979, pp. 133–40; and Irwin Business Insights video tape series, 1988.

would suggest the potential for improvement, perhaps with a substantial increase in efficiency and lowering of cost.

Another consideration is that products and services often go through *life cycles* that begin with low volume that increases as products or services become more well known. When that happens, a manager must know when to shift from one type of process (e.g., job shop) to the next (e.g., batch), and perhaps to the next (e.g., assembly line). Of course, some operations remain at a certain level (e.g., magazine publishing), while others increase (or decrease as markets become saturated) over time. Again, it is important for a manager to assess his or her products and services and make a judgment on whether to plan for changes in processing over time.

AUTOMATION

Automation

The substitution of machinery for human labor.

Automation is the substitution of machinery for human labor. The machinery includes sensing and control devices that enable it to operate automatically. A key question in process planning is whether to automate or not. And if the decision is made to automate, the question becomes how much to automate. Automation can range from factories that are completely automated to a single automated operation.

Automation offers a number of advantages over human labor. One is that automation has low variability; it is difficult for a human to perform a task in exactly the same way, and in the same amount of time, on a repetitive basis. In a production setting, variability is detrimental to quality and to meeting schedules. Moreover, machines do not get bored or distracted, nor do they go out on strike, ask for higher wages, or file labor grievances.

Automation is frequently touted as a necessary strategy for competitiveness. However, automation also has certain disadvantages and limitations as compared to human labor. To begin with, automation can be costly; technology can be expensive. Usually it requires high volumes of output to offset high costs. And automation is much less flexible than humans are. And once a process has been automated, there is substantial reason for not changing it. Moreover, automation often becomes an emotional issue with workers because of the fear of job loss.

The issue of whether to automate or the degree to which automation should be used must be carefully examined so that all the ramifications are clearly understood by decision makers. Also, much thought and careful planning are necessary to successfully *integrate* automation into a production system. Otherwise, it can lead to major problems. GM invested heavily in automation in the 1980s only to find its costs increasing while flexibility and productivity took a nosedive. Its market had shrunk while GM was increasing its capacity!

COMPUTER-AIDED MANUFACTURING (CAM)

Computer-aided manufacturing (CAM) refers to the use of computers in process control, ranging from numerically controlled machines to robots to automated assembly systems. These systems replace human functions with machine functions. They have the advantage of reducing labor; handling dangerous, dirty, or boring tasks; and yielding high, consistent quality. As you might suppose, such equipment can be very expensive.

Computer-aided manufacturing
The use of computers in process control, replacing human functions with machine functions.

Numerically controlled (N/C) machines are programmed to follow a set of processing instructions based on mathematical relationships that tell the machine the details of the operations to be performed. The instructions are stored on a device such as a floppy disk, magnetic tape, or microprocessor. Although N/C machines have been used for many years, they are an important part of new approaches to manufacturing. Individual machines may have their own computer; this is referred to as *computerized numerical control (CNC)*. Or one computer may control a number of N/C machines, which is referred to as *direct numerical control (DNC)*.

Numerically controlled machines
Machines that perform operations by following mathematical processing instructions.

The use of robots in manufacturing is sometimes an option to consider. A **robot** consists of three parts: a mechanical arm, a power supply, and a controller. Unlike film versions of robots, which vaguely resemble human beings, industrial robots are much less glamorous in appearance and much less mobile: most robots are stationary except for their movable "arms."

Robot
A machine consisting of a mechanical arm, a power supply, and a controller.

Computer aided manufacturing is widely used in many aspects of heavy industry. Republic Engineered Steels uses CAM here in their nondestructive evaluation facility to program testing equipment and to gather and evaluate results.

Robots are used to handle a wide variety of tasks, including welding, assembly, loading and unloading machines, painting, and testing. They relieve humans from heavy or dirty work and are often used to eliminate drudgery tasks.

Some uses of robots are fairly simple, whereas others are much more complex. At the lowest level are robots that follow a fixed set of instructions. Next are programmable robots, which can repeat a set of movements after being led through the sequence. In effect, these robots "play back" a mechanical sequence much as a video recorder plays back a visual sequence. At the next level up are robots that follow instructions from a computer. At the top end are robots that can recognize objects and make certain decisions.

Robots move in one of two ways. Point-to-point robots move to predetermined points and perform a specified operation; they then move on to the next point and perform another operation; and so on. Continuous-path robots follow a continuous (moving) path while performing an operation.

Robots can be powered in one of three ways: pneumatically (air-driven), hydraulically (fluids under pressure), or electronically.

Figures 6–2 through 6–5 illustrate robots. Table 6–2 describes in more detail some of the various kinds of robots currently being used.

Japanese manufacturing firms are major users of robots. Note, however, that a key reason for this is the acute labor shortage that exists in Japan.

A **flexible manufacturing system (FMS)** is a group of machines including supervisory computer control, automatic material handling, and possibly robots or other automated processing equipment. Reprogrammable controllers enable these systems to produce a variety of *similar* products. Systems may range from three or four machines to more than a dozen. They are designed to handle intermittent processing requirements with some of the benefits of automation and with some of the flexibility of individual, or stand-alone, machines (e.g., N/C machines). Flexible manufacturing systems offer reduced labor costs compared with more traditional manufacturing methods, lower capital investment and higher flexibility than "hard" automation, relatively quick changeover time, and more consistent quality than traditional manufacturing methods.

Flexible manufacturing system (FMS)

A group of machines designed to handle intermittent processing requirements and produce a variety of similar products.

A robot assembles and tests a hard drive unit in a clean room at IBM. Using a robot reduces the chance that contaminants will damage the assembly by reducing the number of people in the clean room.

Although these are important benefits, there are also certain limitations to FMS. One is that these systems can handle a relatively narrow range of part variety, so they must be used for a family of similar parts that all require similar machining. Also, FMS involves longer planning and development times than more conventional processing equipment because of the increased complexity and cost. Further-

Special hand with one movable jaw
   A hand with single-acting jaw should be considered when there is any access underneath a part, as when it is on a rack. Where this hand can be applied, it will scoop up a part quite quickly. Simplicity of the design makes this one of the most economical hands.

Special hand for cartons
   The dual-jaw hand will open wide to grasp inexactly located objects of light weight. Lifting and placement of carboard cartons is an application. Actuators and jaws can be remounted in any of several positions on the fixed back plate, making it practical for the same dual-jaw hand to move large cartons on one day and smaller cartons the next.

Special hand with modular gripper
   This special hand, with pair of pneumatic actuators, is one of the many special hand designs for industrial robots. It would be suitable for parts of light weight. Lifting capacity is dependent upon friction developed by the fingers, but heavier parts could be handled if the fingers could secure a more positive purchase—as under a flange or lip.

Source: Reprinted with permission of the publisher, from *Robotics In Practice* © 1980 Joseph F. Engelberger. Published by AMACOM, a division of the American Management Association.

Figure 6–2

Examples of robot "hands"

Figure 6–3

Work comes to robot: Here cars move down the line to two IRB 2000 robots that are invert mounted. They dispense urethane on the windshield and backlite opening.

Figure 6–4

Robots on an assembly line: Auto bodies on this assembly line at Ford are spot welded by an IRB 6000 robot.

Figure 6–5

Typical articulations of a playback robot with point-to-point control

Source: Reprinted, with permission of the publisher, from *Robotics In Practice* © 1980 Joseph F. Engelberger. Published by AMACOM, a division of the American Management Association. All rights reserved.

a) Extend and retract arm (Out - in = O)

b) Elevate and depress arm (Down - up = D)

c) Rotate left or right (Rotate = R)

d) Turn on hand assembly axis (Swivel = S)

e) Pivot hand assembly (Bend = B)

Table 6–2

Industrial robots all have armlike projections and grippers that perform factory work customarily done by humans. The term is usually reserved for machines with some form of built-in control system and capable of stand-alone operation. But in Japan, it also includes manipulators operated by humans, either directly or remotely.

A *pick-and-place robot* is the simplest version, accounting for about one third of all U.S. installations. The name comes from its usual application in materials handling: picking something from one spot and placing it at another. Freedom of movement is usually limited to two or three directions—in and out, left and right, and up and down. The control system is electromechanical.

A *servo robot* is the most common industrial robot because it can include all robots described below. The name stems from one or more servomechanisms that enable the arm and gripper to alter direction in midair, without having to trip a mechanical switch. Five to seven directional movements are common, depending on the number of "joints," or articulations, in the robot's arm.

A *programmable robot* is a servo robot directed by a programmable controller that memorizes a sequence of arm-and-gripper movements; this routine can be repeated perpetually. The robot is reprogrammable by leading its gripper through the new task.

A *computerized robot* is a servo model run by a computer. The computer controller does not have to be taught by leading the arm and gripper through a routine; new instructions can be transmitted electronically. The programming for such "smart" robots may include the ability to optimize work routine instructions.

A *sensory robot* is a computerized robot with one or more artificial senses, usually sight or touch.

An *assembly robot* is a computerized robot, probably a sensory model, designed specifically for assembly line jobs. For light, batch-manufacturing applications, the arm's design may be fairly anthropomorphic.

Here, an IBM robot assembles a PC keyboard.

Source: Reprinted from the June 9, 1980, issue of *Business Week* by special permission, © 1980 by McGraw-Hill, Inc., New York, NY 10020. All rights reserved.

more, companies sometimes prefer a gradual approach to automation, and FMS represents a sizable chunk of technology.

Computer-integrated manufacturing (CIM) is a system for linking a broad range of manufacturing activities through an integrating computer system, including engineering design, flexible manufacturing systems, and production planning and control, although not all elements are absolutely necessary. For instance, CIM might be as simple as linking two or more FMSs by a host computer. More encompassing systems can link scheduling, purchasing, inventory control, shop control, and distribution. In effect a CIM system integrates information from other areas of an organization with manufacturing.

The overall goal of using CIM is to link various areas of an organization to achieve rapid response to customer orders and/or product changes, to allow rapid production, and to reduce *indirect* labor costs.

Computer-integrated manufacturing (CIM)

A system for linking a broad range of manufacturing activities through an integrating computer sytem.

OPERATIONS STRATEGY

Process selection often requires engineering expertise. Many U.S. managers in this position have little technical knowledge; their education and experience lie in the fields of marketing, finance, and the like. In contrast, many Japanese managers faced with the same decisions do have engineering backgrounds. Consequently, there seems to be a tendency in Western firms to delegate technical decisions to engineers. Engineering white elephants are not uncommon, and neither are systems based on narrow viewpoints of problems and solutions. In the long run, the solution may be to hire and promote managers who have both managerial and technical skills and expertise. In the short run, managers must work with technical experts, asking questions and increasing their understanding of the benefits and limitations of sophisticated processing equipment and technology, and ultimately making decisions themselves. Thus, there is a real need for *management of technology*.

Throughout this book, the importance of *flexibility* as a competitive strategy is stressed. However, flexibility does not always offer the best choice in processing decisions. Flexible systems or equipment are often more expensive and less efficient than less flexible alternatives. And, in certain instances, flexibility is not needed because products are in mature stages, requiring few design changes, and there is a steady volume of output. Ordinarily, this type of situation calls for specialized processing equipment, with no need for flexibility. The implication is clear: Flexibility should be adopted with great care; applications should be matched with situations in which a *need* for flexibility clearly exists.

In practice, flexible systems are chosen for either of two reasons: because demands are varied, or because of uncertainty about what demand will be. The second reason can be overcome through improved forecasting.

CAPACITY PLANNING

In this section, we examine the importance of capacity decisions, the measurement of capacity, how capacity requirements are determined, and the development and evaluation of capacity alternatives.

The term **capacity** refers to an upper limit or ceiling on the load that an operating unit can handle. The operating unit might be a plant, a department, a machine, a store, or a worker. The load can be specified in terms of either *inputs* or *outputs*. For instance, a machine may be able to process 45 pounds of raw material

Capacity

The upper limit or ceiling on the load that an operating unit can handle.

per hour. Hence, its input capacity is 45 pounds per hour. Another machine might produce 18 castings per hour; its capacity in terms of the castings output is 18 pieces per hour. Whether to use input or output capacity is sometimes a matter of choice, and sometimes it is dictated by the situation, as we shall see.

The capacity of an operating unit is an important piece of information for planning purposes: It enables managers to quantify production capability, in terms of either inputs or outputs, and thereby make other decisions or plans related to those quantities. The basic questions in capacity planning of any sort are the following:

1. What kind of capacity is needed?
2. How much is needed?
3. When is it needed?

The question of what kind of capacity is needed relates to the products and services that management intends to produce or provide. Hence, in a very real sense, capacity planning is governed by those choices.

The most fundamental decisions in any organization relate to the products and/or services it will offer. Virtually all other decisions relative to capacity, facilities, location, and the like are governed by product and service choices. Thus, a decision to produce high-quality steel will necessitate certain types of processing equipment and certain kinds of labor skills, and it will suggest certain types of arrangement of facilities. It will influence the size and type of building as well as the plant location. Notice how different each of these factors would be if the choice were to operate a family restaurant, and how still different they would be if the choice were to operate a hospital.

In some instances, capacity choices are made very infrequently, and in others, they are made much more regularly, as part of an ongoing process. Generally speaking, the factors that influence this frequency are the stability of demand, the rate of technological change in both equipment and product design, and competitive factors. Other factors relate to the type of product or service and whether style changes are important, as for automobiles and clothing. In any case, it is important for management to periodically review product and service choices in order to ensure that changes will be made when they are needed for cost, competitive effectiveness, or other reasons.

IMPORTANCE OF CAPACITY DECISIONS

Capacity decisions are among the most fundamental of all the design decisions managers are called on to make. One reason for the importance of capacity decisions relates to their potential impact on the ability of the organization to meet future demands for products and services; capacity essentially limits the rate of output possible. A second reason for the importance of capacity stems from the relationship between capacity and operating costs. Ideally, capacity and demand requirements will be matched, which will tend to minimize operating costs. In practice, this is not always achieved, either because actual demand differs from expected demand or because demand tends to vary (e.g., cyclically). In such cases, a decision might be made to attempt to balance the costs of over- and undercapacity. A third reason for the importance of capacity decisions is the initial cost involved, of which capacity is usually a major determinant. Typically, the greater the capacity of a productive unit, the greater its cost. This does not necessarily imply a one-for-one relationship; larger units tend to cost *proportionately* less than smaller units. A fourth reason for the importance of capacity decisions stems from the long-term commitment of resources that is often required and the fact that, once they are implemented, it may be difficult or impossible to modify those decisions without incurring major costs.

DEFINING AND MEASURING CAPACITY

Capacity often refers to an upper limit on the *rate* of output. Even though this seems simple enough, there are subtle difficulties in actually measuring capacity in certain cases. These difficulties arise because of different interpretations of the term *capacity* and problems with identifying suitable measures for a specific situation.

In selecting a measure of capacity, it is important to choose one that does not require updating. For example, dollar amounts are often a poor measure of capacity (e.g., capacity of $30 million a year) because price changes necessitate continual updating of that measure.

In situations where only one product or service is involved, the capacity of the productive unit may be expressed in terms of that item. However, when multiple products or services are involved, as is often the case, using a simple measure of capacity based on units of output can be misleading. For example, an appliance manufacturer may produce both refrigerators and freezers. If the output rates for these two products are different, it would not make sense to simply state capacity in units without reference to either refrigerators or freezers. The problem is compounded if the firm in question has other products. One possible solution is to state capacities in terms of each product. Thus, the firm may be able to produce 100 refrigerators per day *or* 80 freezers per day. In some cases this approach is helpful, but in others it is not. For instance, in a situation where an organization has many different products or services, it may not be practical to list all of the relevant capacities. This is especially true if there are frequent changes in the mix of output, because this would necessitate a continually changing composite index of capacity. The preferred alternative in such cases is to use a measure of capacity that refers to *availability of inputs.* Thus, a hospital has a certain number of beds, a factory has a certain number of machine hours available, and a bus has a certain number of seats and a certain amount of standing room.

No single measure of capacity will be appropriate in every situation. Rather, the measure of capacity must be somewhat tailored to the situation at hand. Table 6–3 provides some examples of commonly used measures of capacity.

Up to this point, we have been using a working definition of capacity. Although it is functional, it could stand some refinement. There are, in fact, three different definitions of capacity that are useful:

1. *Design capacity:* the maximum output that can possibly be attained.
2. *Effective capacity:* the maximum possible output given a product mix, scheduling difficulties, machine maintenance, quality factors, and so on.
3. *Actual output:* the rate of output actually achieved. It cannot exceed effective capacity and is often less than effective capacity due to breakdowns, defective output, shortages of materials, and similar factors.

Design capacity is the maximum rate of output achieved under ideal conditions. Effective capacity is usually less than design capacity (it cannot exceed design capacity) owing to realities of changing product mix, the need for periodic maintenance

	Measure of capacity		Table 6–3
Type of business	**Resources available**	**Output**	
Automobile manufacturing	Labor hours, machine hours	Number of cars or trucks per shift	Examples of commonly used measures of capacity
Steel mill	Size of furnace	Tons of steel per week	
Oil refinery	Size of refinery	Gallons of fuel oil per day	
Farm	Number of acres, cows	Tons of grain per year, gallons of milk per week	
Restaurant	Number of tables	Number of meals served per day	
Theater	Number of seats........	Number of performances per week	
Retail sales........	Size of display area, number of cashiers	Units sold per day	

of equipment, lunch breaks, coffee breaks, problems in scheduling and balancing operations, and similar circumstances. Actual output cannot exceed effective capacity and is often less than effective capacity because of machine breakdowns, absenteeism, and other problems outside the control of the operations managers.

These different measures of capacity are useful in defining two measures of system effectiveness: efficiency and utilization. *Efficiency* is the ratio of actual output to effective capacity. *Utilization* is the ratio of actual output to design capacity.

$$\text{Efficiency} = \frac{\text{Actual output}}{\text{Effective capacity}} \qquad\qquad (6\text{–}1)$$

$$\text{Utilization} = \frac{\text{Actual output}}{\text{Design capacity}} \qquad\qquad (6\text{–}2)$$

It is quite common for managers to focus exclusively on efficiency, but in many instances, such emphasis can be misleading. This happens when effective capacity is low compared to design capacity. In those cases, high efficiency would seem to indicate effective use of resources when that is not the case. The following example illustrates this point.

Given the information below, compute the efficiency and the utilization of the vehicle repair department:

Example 1

Design capacity = 80 trucks per day
Effective capacity = 40 trucks per day
Actual output = 36 units per day

Solution

$$\text{Efficiency} = \frac{\text{Actual output}}{\text{Effective capacity}} = \frac{36 \text{ units per day}}{40 \text{ units per day}} = 90\%$$

(continued)

Example 1

(concluded)

$$\text{Utilization} = \frac{\text{Actual output}}{\text{Design capacity}} = \frac{36 \text{ units per day}}{80 \text{ units per day}} = 45\%$$

Thus, compared to the effective capacity of 40 units per day, 36 units per day looks pretty good. However, compared to the design capacity of 80 units per day, 36 units per day is much less impressive although probably more meaningful.

Because effective capacity acts as a lid on actual output, the real key to improving capacity utilization is to increase effective capacity. Consider the following example. George H. wants to travel from his home in Washington, D.C., to his sister's home in Baltimore, which is 60 miles away. He could borrow his son's bike or borrow his son's car. Instead of using the bike and concerning himself with pedaling as *efficiently* as possible, he could make the trip in less time (same output in a shorter time) by using the car.

Hence, increasing utilization depends on being able to increase effective capacity, and this requires a knowledge of what is constraining effective capacity. The following section explores some of the main determinants of effective capacity.

DETERMINANTS OF EFFECTIVE CAPACITY

Many decisions made with respect to system design have an impact on capacity. The same is true for many operating decisions. Some of these factors are briefly described in this section and then elaborated on at other points in the book. The main factors relate to the following:

1. Facilities.
2. Products or services.
3. Processes.
4. Human considerations.
5. Operations.
6. External forces.

Facilities Factors   The design of facilities, including size and provision for expansion, is very important. Locational factors, such as transportation costs, distance to market, labor supply, energy sources, and room for expansion, are also important. Likewise, layout of the work area often determines how smoothly work can be performed, and environmental factors such a heating, lighting, and ventilation also play an important role in determining whether personnel can perform effectively or whether they must struggle to overcome poor design characteristics.

Product/Service Factors   Product or service design can have a tremendous influence on capacity. For example, when items are highly similar, the ability of the system to produce those items is generally much greater than when successive items tend to differ. For example, a restaurant that offers a limited menu can usually prepare and serve meals at a faster rate than a restaurant with a very extensive menu. Generally speaking, the more uniform the output, the more opportunities there are for standardization of methods and materials, which leads to greater capacity. The particular mix of products or services rendered must also be considered since different items will have different rates of output.

Process Factors   The quantity capability of a process is an obvious determinant of capacity. A more subtle determinant is the influence of output *quality*. For instance, if quality of output does not meet standards, the rate of output will be slowed by the need for inspection and rework activities.

Human Factors   The tasks that make up a job, the variety of activities involved, and the training, skill, and experience required to perform a job all have an impact on the potential and actual output. In addition, employee motivation has a very basic relationship to capacity, as do absenteeism and labor turnover.

Operation Factors   If there are any differences in equipment capabilities for alternative pieces of equipment and/or for differences in job requirements, there can be scheduling problems. Inventory stocking decisions, late deliveries, and acceptability of purchased materials and parts can all influence effective capacity. Quality inspection and control procedures also have an impact on effective capacity.

As an example, inventory problems had a negative impact on capacity when General Motors first introduced its front-wheel-drive cars. Unexpected high demand, created by shortages and rapid price increases of gasoline, exceeded the supply of cars. Company officials lamented the fact that they could not take advantage of the opportunity to increase sales because of a shortage of component parts, which the company could not quickly overcome. Thus, insufficient capacity in one area affected overall capacity.

External Factors   Product standards, especially minimum quality and performance standards, can restrict management's options in increasing and using capacity. Thus, pollution standards on either products or equipment often reduce effective capacity. So, too, does paperwork required by government regulatory agencies by engaging employees in nonproductive activities. A similar effect occurs when a union contract limits the number of hours and type of work an employee may do.

A summary of all these factors is presented in Table 6-4. In general, *inadequate planning* is a major limiting determinant of effective capacity.

Table 6–4

Factors that determine effective capacity

A. Facilities
   1. Design
   2. Location
   3. Layout
   4. Environment
B. Product/service
   1. Design
   2. Product or service mix
C. Process
   1. Quantity capabilities
   2. Quality capabilities
D. Human factors
   1. Job content
   2. Job design
   3. Training and experience

   4. Motivation
   5. Compensation
   6. Learning rates
   7. Absenteeism and labor turnover
E. Operational
   1. Scheduling
   2. Materials management
   3. Quality assurance
   4. Maintenance policies
   5. Equipment breakdowns
F. External factors
   1. Product standards
   2. Safety regulations
   3. Unions
   4. Pollution control standards

Determining Capacity Requirements

Capacity planning decisions involve both long-term and short-term considerations. Long-term considerations relate to overall *level* of capacity, such as facility size; short-term considerations relate to probable *variations* in capacity requirements created by such things as seasonal, random, and irregular fluctuations in demand. Because the time intervals covered by each of these categories can vary significantly from industry to industry, it would be misleading to attempt a precise definition for these terms. Nevertheless, the distinction will serve as a framework within which to discuss capacity planning.

The link between marketing and operations is crucial to realistic determination of capacity requirements. Through customer contacts, demographic analyses, and forecasts, marketing can supply vital information to operations for ascertaining capacity needs for both the long term and the short term.

We determine *long-term* capacity needs by forecasting demand over a time horizon and then converting those forecasts into capacity requirements. Some of the basic demand patterns that might be identified by a forecast are illustrated in Figure 6–6. In addition to these basic patterns are more complex patterns, such as a combination of cycles and trends.

When trends are identified, the fundamental issues are (1) how long the trend might persist, since few things last forever, and (2) the slope of the trend. If cycles are identified, interest focuses on (1) the approximate length of the cycles, since cycles are rarely uniform in duration, and (2) the amplitude of the cycles (i.e., deviation from average).

Short-term capacity needs are less concerned with cycles or trends than with seasonal variations and other variations from average. These deviations are particularly important because they can place a severe strain on a system's ability to satisfy demand at some times and yet result in idle capacity at other times.

Seasonal patterns can be identified using standard forecasting techniques. Although commonly thought of as annual fluctuations, seasonal variations are often reflected in monthly, weekly, and even daily capacity requirements. Table 6–5 provides some examples of items that tend to exhibit seasonal demand patterns.

Figure 6–6

Some possible demand patterns

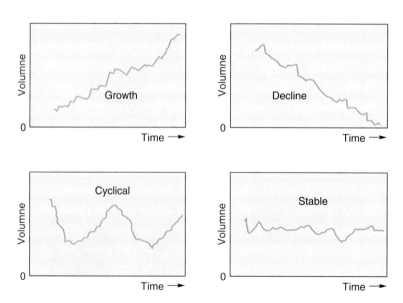

Period	Items	Table 6–5
Year	Beer sales, toy sales, airline traffic, clothing, vactions, tourism, power usage, gasoline consumption, sports and recreation, education	Examples of seasonal demand patterns
Month	Welfare and social security checks, bank transactions	
Week	Retail sales, restaurant meals, automobile traffic, automotive rentals, hotel registrations	
Day	Telephone calls, power usage, automobile traffic, public transportation, classroom utilization, retail sales, restaurant meals	

When we analyze time intervals that are too short to have seasonal variations, we may often describe variations in demand by probability distributions such as the normal, uniform, or Poisson distribution. For example, we might describe the amount of coffee served during the midday meal at a luncheonette by a normal distribution with a certain mean and standard deviation. The number of customers that enter a branch of a bank on Monday mornings might be described by a Poisson distribution with a certain mean. It does not follow, however, that *every* instance of random variability will lend itself to description by a standard statistical distribution. Service systems in particular may experience a considerable amount of variability in capacity requirements unless requests for service can be scheduled. Manufacturing systems, because of their typical isolation from customers, and the more uniform nature of production, are less likely to experience them. Waiting line models are sometimes useful when analyzing service systems.

Perhaps the most troublesome variations are the irregular ones: they are virtually impossible to predict. They are created by such diverse forces as major equipment breakdowns, freak storms that disrupt normal routines, foreign political turmoil that causes oil shortages, discovery of health hazards (nuclear accidents, unsafe chemical dumping grounds, carcinogens in food and drink), and so on.

DEVELOPING CAPACITY ALTERNATIVES

Aside from the general considerations regarding the development of alternatives (i.e., conduct a reasonable search for possible alternatives, consider doing nothing, take care not to overlook nonquantitative factors), there are some specific considerations relevant to developing capacity alternatives. Among the considerations to be discussed in this section are the following:

1. Design flexibility into systems.
2. Take a "big picture" approach to capacity changes.
3. Prepare to deal with capacity "chunks."
4. Attempt to smooth out capacity requirements.
5. Identify the optimal operating level.

The long-term nature of many capacity decisions and the risks inherent in long-term forecasts suggest potential benefits from designing flexible systems. For example, in many instances, provision for future expansion in the original design of a structure can be obtained at a small price compared to what it would cost to remodel an existing structure that did not have such a provision. Hence, if future expansion of a restaurant seems likely, water lines, power hookups, and waste disposal lines can be put in place initially so that if expansion becomes a reality, modification to the existing structure can be minimized. Similarly, a new golf course may start as a 9-hole operation, but if provision is made for future expansion by obtaining options on adjacent land, it may progress to a larger (18-hole) course. Other considerations in flexible design involve layout of equipment, location, equipment selection, production planning, scheduling, and inventory policies. These are discussed in later chapters.

When developing capacity alternatives, it is important to consider how parts of the system interrelate. For example, when making a decision to increase the number of rooms in a motel, one should also take into account probable increased demands for parking, entertainment and food, and housekeeping. This is a "big picture" approach.

Capacity increases are often acquired in fairly large chunks rather than smooth increments, making it difficult to achieve a match between desired capacity and feasible capacity. For instance, the desired capacity of a certain operation may be 55 units per hour, but suppose that machines used for this operation are able to produce 40 units per hour each. One machine by itself would cause capacity to be 15 units per hour short of what is needed, but two machines would result in an excess capacity of 25 units per hour. The illustration becomes even more extreme if we shift the topic, to open-hearth furnaces or to the number of airplanes needed to provide a desired level of capacity.

Unevenness in capacity requirements can create certain problems as well. For instance, during periods of inclement weather, public transportation ridership tends to increase substantially relative to periods of pleasant weather. Consequently, the system tends to alternate between underutilization and overutilization. Increasing the number of buses or subway cars will reduce the burden during periods of heavy demand, but this will aggravate the problem of overcapacity at other times and most certainly add to the cost of operating the system. Unfortunately, there do not seem to be any simple solutions to such problems.

The unevenness in demand for products and services can be traced to a variety of sources. The bus ridership problem is weather-related to a certain extent, but demand could be considered to be partly random (i.e., varying because of chance factors). Still another source of varying demand is seasonality. Seasonal variations are generally easier to cope with than random variations because they are *predictable*. Consequently, allowances can be made in planning and scheduling activities and inventories. However, seasonal variations can still pose problems because of their uneven demands on the system: at certain times the system will tend to be overloaded, and at certain other times it will tend to be underloaded. One possible approach to this problem is to try to identify products or services that have complementing demand patterns, that is, patterns that tend to offset each other. For instance, demand for snow skis and demand for water skis might complement each other: demand for water skis is greater in the spring and summer months, and demand for snow skis is greater in the fall and winter months. The same might apply to heating and air-conditioning equipment. The ideal case is one in which products or services with complementing demand patterns involve the use of the same resources but at different times, so that overall capacity requirements remain fairly stable. Figure 6–7 illustrates complementing demand patterns.

Possible strategies for handling variations in a narrower time frame include subcontracting, working overtime, and using inventories to absorb demand fluctuations. These and other strategies are discussed in more detail in later chapters.

Production units typically have an ideal or optimal level of operation in terms of unit cost of output. At the ideal level, cost per unit is the lowest for that production unit; larger or smaller rates of output will result in a higher unit cost. This concept is illustrated in Figure 6–8. Notice how unit costs rise as the rate of output varies from the optimal level.

The explanation for the shape of the cost curve is this: At low levels of output, the costs of facilities and equipment must be absorbed (paid for) by very few units. Hence, the cost per unit is high. As output is increased, there are more units to absorb the "fixed" cost of facilities and equipment, so unit costs decrease. However, beyond a certain point, unit costs will start to rise. To be sure, the fixed costs are being spread over even more units, so that does not account for the increase. But other factors now become important, such as worker fatigue; equipment breakdowns; the loss of flexibility, which leaves less of a margin for error; and, generally, more difficulty in coordinating operations.

The optimal operating rate and the amount of the minimum cost both tend to be a function of the general capacity of the operating unit. As the general capacity, say, of a plant increases, the optimal output rate increases, and the minimum cost for

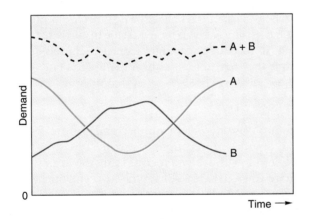

Figure 6–7

A and B have complementing demand patterns

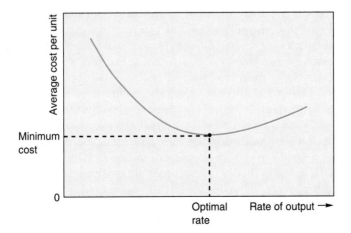

Figure 6–8

Production units have an optimal rate of output for minimum cost

Figure 6–9

Minimum cost and
optimal operating rate are
functions of size of a
production unit

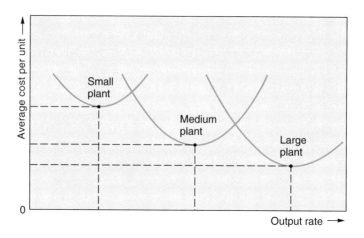

the optimal rate decreases. Thus, larger plants tend to have higher optimal output rates and lower minimum costs than lower plants. These points are illustrated in Figure 6–9.

In choosing the capacity of an operating unit, management must take these relationships into account along with the availability of financial and other resources and forecasts of expected demand. In order to do this, it is necessary to determine enough points for each size facility to be able to make a comparison among different sizes. In some instances, facility sizes are givens, whereas in others, facility size is a continuous variable (i.e., any size can be selected). In the latter case, an ideal facility size can be selected. In most cases, though, management must make a choice from given sizes, and none may have a minimum at the desired rate of output.

EVALUATING ALTERNATIVES

Alternatives for future capacity need to be examined from a number of different perspectives. Most obvious are economic considerations: Will an alternative be economically feasible? How much will it cost? How soon can we have it? What will operating and maintenance costs be? What will the useful life be? Will it be compatible with present personnel and present operations?

Less obvious, but nonetheless important, are possible negative public opinions. For instance, the decision to build a new power plant is almost sure to stir up reaction, whether it is to be coal-fired, hydroelectric, or nuclear. Any option that has the possibility of disrupting lives and property is bound to generate hostile reactions. Construction of new facilities may necessitate moving personnel to a new location. Embracing a new technology may mean retraining some people and even terminating some. Relocation can cause unfavorable reactions, particularly if a town is about to lose a major employer. Conversely, community pressure in a new location may arise if the presence of the company is viewed unfavorably (noise, traffic, pollution).

A number of techniques are useful for evaluating capacity alternatives from an economic standpoint. Some of the more common ones are cost-volume analysis, financial analysis, decision theory, and waiting line analysis. Cost-volume analysis is described in this chapter. Financial analysis is mentioned briefly and described in more detail in the chapter supplement, and decision analysis and waiting line analysis are described in other chapters.

Calculating Processing Requirements

When evaluating capacity alternatives, a necessary piece of information is the capacity requirements of products that will be processed with a given alternative. To get this information, one must have reasonably accurate demand forecasts for each product, and know the standard processing time per unit for each product on each alternative machine, the number of work days per year, and the number of shifts that will be used.

A department works one shift, 250 days a year, and has these figures for a machine that is currently being considered:

Example 2

Product	Annual demand	Standard processing time per unit (hr.)	Processing time needed (hr.)
#1	400	5.0	2,000
#2	300	8.0	2,400
#3	700	2.0	1,400
			5,800

Working one 8-hour shift, 250 days a year provides an annual capacity of $8 \times 250 = 2,000$ hours a year. We can see that three machines would be needed to handle the required volume:

$$\frac{5,800 \text{ hours}}{2,000 \text{ hours/machine}} = 2.90 \text{ machines}$$

Comparing alternatives, a different machine might have lower processing times, so that fewer machines would be needed (e.g., two). Suppose the first alternative cost $10,000 per machine, for a total of $30,000, while the second alternative cost $12,000 per machine, for a total of $24,000 for two machines. Hence, the second alternative, although more expensive on a per-machine basis, would require a smaller total cost.

Cost–Volume Analysis

Cost-volume analysis, or **break-even analysis**, as it is commonly referred to, focuses on relationships between cost, revenue, and volume of output. The purpose of cost-volume analysis is to estimate the income of an organization under different operating conditions. It can be particularly useful as a tool for comparing capacity alternatives.

Break-even analysis
Estimates of income based on relationships between cost, revenue, and volume of output.

Use of the technique requires identification of all costs related to the production of a given product. These costs are then assigned to one of two categories: fixed costs or variable costs. *Fixed costs* are those that tend to remain constant regardless of volume of output. Examples include rental costs, property taxes, equipment costs, heating and cooling expenses, and certain administrative costs. *Variable costs* vary directly with volume of output. The major components of variable costs are generally materials and labor costs. We will assume that variable cost per unit remains the same regardless of volume of output.

The total cost associated with a given volume of output is equal to the sum of the fixed cost and the variable cost per unit times volume:

A. Fixed, variable, and total costs.

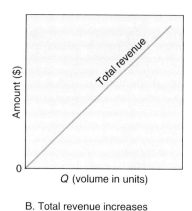

B. Total revenue increases
linearly with output.

C. Profit = TR - TC.

Figure 6–10

$$\text{Total cost} = \text{Fixed cost} + \text{Variable cost per unit} \times Q \text{ units} \qquad (6\text{–}3)$$

Figure 6–10a shows the relationship between volume of output and fixed costs, total variable costs, and total (fixed plus variable) costs.

Revenue per unit, like variable cost per unit, is assumed to be the same regardless of quantity of output. Thus, it too will have a linear relationship to output, as illustrated in Figure 6–10b. We will assume that all of the output can be sold. The total revenue associated with a given quantity of output, Q, is:

$$\text{Total revenue} = \text{Revenue per unit} \times Q \text{ units} \qquad (6\text{–}4)$$

Figure 6–10c describes the relationship betwen profit—which is the difference between total revenue and total (i.e., fixed plus variable) cost—and volume of output. The volume at which total costs and total revenue are equal is referred to as the **break-even point (BEP)**. When volume is less than the break-even point, there is a loss rather than a profit; when volume is greater than the break-even point, there is a profit. The greater the deviation from this point, the greater the profit or loss. Total profit can be computed using the formula:

$$\begin{aligned} \text{Profit} &= \text{Total revenue} - \text{Total cost} \\ &= \text{Revenue per unit} \times Q - (\text{Fixed cost} \\ &\quad + \text{Variable cost per unit} \times Q) \end{aligned} \qquad (6\text{–}5)$$

The required volume needed to generate a specified profit is:

$$\text{Volume} = \frac{\text{Specified profit} + \text{Fixed cost}}{\text{Revenue per unit} - \text{Variable cost per unit}} \qquad (6\text{–}6)$$

A special case of this is the volume of output needed for total revenue to equal total cost. This is the break-even point, computed using the formula:

$$Q_{\text{BEP}} = \frac{\text{Fixed cost}}{\text{Revenue per unit} - \text{Variable cost per unit}} \qquad (6\text{–}7)$$

The break-even symbols and formulas are summarized in Table 6–6. The use of these formulas is illustrated in the following example.

Example 3

The owner of Old-Fashioned Berry Pies, S. Simon, is contemplating adding a new line of pies that will require leasing new equipment for a monthly payment of $6,000. Variable costs would be $2.00 per pie, and pies would retail for $7.00 each.

a. How many pies must be sold in order to break even?

b. What would the profit (loss) be if 1,000 pies are sold in a month?

c. How many pies must be sold to realize a profit of $4,000?

Solution

FC = $6,000, VC = $2 per pie, Rev = $7 per pie

a. $Q_{BEP} = \dfrac{FC}{Rev - VC} = \dfrac{\$6,000}{\$7 - \$2} = 1,200$ pies/month

b. For $Q = 1,000$, $P = Rev \times Q - (FC + VC \times Q)$
$$= \$7 \times 1,000 - (\$6,000 + \$2 \times 1,000) = -1,000$$

c. $P = \$4,000$; solve for Q in the preceding equation:

$\$4,000 = \$7Q - (\$6,000 + \$2Q)$

Rearranging terms, we obtain

$\$5Q = \$10,000 \qquad Q = 2,000$ pies

Before the break-even model is used, it is necessary to make certain that the assumptions of the model are reasonably satisfied. The assumptions are:

1. One product is involved.
2. Everything that is produced can be sold.
3. The variable cost per unit is the same regardless of the volume.
4. Fixed costs do not change with volume changes.
5. The revenue per unit is the same regardless of volume.

Table 6–6

Summary of break-even formulas

FC = Fixed costs
VC = Variable cost per unit
TC = Total cost
Rev = Revenue per unit
Q = Quantity of output

Q_{BEP} = Break-even quantity
TR = Total revenue
P = Profit
SP = Specified profit

1. TC = FC + VC × Q
2. TR = Rev × Q
3. P = TR − TC = Rev × Q − (FC + VC × Q) = Q(Rev − VC) − FC

4. $Q_{BEP} = \dfrac{FC}{Rev - VC}$

5. Volume needed to generate a specified profit:

$$Q = \dfrac{SP + FC}{Rev - VC}$$

Cost-volume analysis can be a valuable tool for comparing capacity alternatives. As with any quantitative tool, it is important to verify that the assumptions on which the technique is based are reasonably satisfied for a particular situation. For example, revenue per unit or variable cost per unit are not always constant. In addition, fixed costs may not be constant over the range of possible output. If demand is subject to random variations, one must take that into account in the analysis. Cost-volume analysis requires that fixed and variable costs can be separated, and this is sometimes exceedingly difficult to accomplish.

Cost-volume analysis works best with one product or a few products that have the same cost characteristics. Otherwise, the analysis can become fairly complex, although not impossible.

In any case, an important benefit of cost-volume considerations is the conceptual framework it provides for integrating cost, revenue, and profit estimates into capacity decisions.

Financial Analysis

A problem that is universally encountered by managers is how to allocate scarce funds. A common approach is to use *financial analysis* to rank investment proposals. At this point, it is unnecessary to go into much detail about these methods.

Two important terms in financial analysis are *cash flow* and *present value*.

> **Cash flow** refers to the difference between the cash received from sales (of goods or services) and other sources (e.g., sale of old equipment) and the cash outflow for labor, materials, overhead, and taxes.
>
> **Present value** expresses in current value the sum of all future cash flows of an investment proposal.

Cash flow

Difference between cash received from sales and other sources, and cash outflow for labor, material, overhead, and taxes.

Present value

The sum, in current value, of all future cash flows of an investment proposal.

The three most commonly used methods of financial analysis are payback, present value, and internal rate of return.

Payback is a crude but widely used method that focuses on the length of time it will take for an investment to return its original cost. For example, an investment with an original cost of $6,000 and a monthly net cash flow of $1,000 has a payback period of six months. Payback ignores the *time value of money*. Its use is easier to rationalize for short-term projects than for long-term ones. However, some now feel that use of this method is one of the contributing factors in the failure of U.S. firms to match productivity increases achieved by other nations.

The *present value (PV)* method summarizes the initial cost of an investment, its estimated annual cash flows, and any expected salvage value in a single value called the *equivalent current value*, taking into account the time value of money (i.e., interest rates).

The *internal rate of return (IRR)* summarizes the initial cost, expected annual cash flows, and estimated future salvage value of an investment proposal in an *equivalent interest rate*. In other words, this method identifies the rate of return that equates the estimated future returns and the initial cost.

These techniques are appropriate when there is a high degree of *certainty* associated with estimates of future cash flows. In many instances, operations managers and other managers must deal with situations that can be better described by risk or uncertainty. Methods for dealing with financial analysis under conditions of risk or uncertainty are often handled using decision theory.

Decision Theory

Decision theory is a helpful tool for financial comparison of alternatives under conditions of either risk or uncertainty. It is suited to capacity decisions as well as to a wide range of other decisions managers are called on to make. Decision theory was described in the supplement to Chapter 2, but the same approaches can be applied to capacity decisions. There would be little benefit in repeating the discussion that appears in the Chapter 2 supplement. Suffice it to say that decision theory is an important managerial tool for capacity decisions.

Waiting Line Analysis

Analysis of waiting lines is often useful for designing service systems. Waiting lines have a tendency to form in a wide variety of service systems (e.g., airport ticket counters, telephone calls to a cable television company, and hospital emergency rooms). The lines are symptoms of bottleneck operations. Analysis is useful in helping managers choose a capacity level that will be cost-effective through balancing the cost of having customers wait with the cost of providing additional capacity. It can aid in the determination of expected costs for various levels of service capacity.

This topic is described in detail in Chapter 17.

SUMMARY

Process selection is an important aspect in planning the design of a production system, and it can have major implications on productivity, cost, competitiveness, and flexibility. New products and services, changes in products or services, and technological changes are some of the reasons organizations become involved in process selection.

Basic issues in process selection include the type of processing to use (e.g., steady, high-volume; intermittent, lower-volume; or one-of-a-kind, large-scale projects), the level of automation or computer-assisted processing to use, the amount of flexibility to build in, and costs of processing.

Capacity refers to a system's potential for producing goods or delivering services over a specified time interval. Capacity decisions are important because capacity is a ceiling on output, and capacity is a major determinant of operating costs.

As a general rule, a variety of factors interfere with capacity utilization, so that effective capacity is somewhat less than design capacity. These factors include such things as facilities design and layout, human factors, product/service design, equipment failures, scheduling problems, and quality considerations.

Capacity planning involves long-term and short-term considerations. Long-term concern relates to the overall level of capacity, and short-term concern relates to variations in capacity requirements due to seasonal, random, and irregular fluctuations in demand. Ideally, capacity will match demand, since it is typically most efficient to operate at or close to full capacity. For this reason, there is a close link between forecasting and capacity planning, particularly in the long term. In the short term, emphasis shifts to describing and coping with variations in demand.

Development of capacity alternatives is enhanced by taking a systems approach to planning, by recognizing that capacity increments are often acquired in chunks, by designing flexible systems, and by considering product/service complements as a way of dealing with various patterns of demand.

In evaluating capacity alternatives, a manager must consider both quantitative and qualitative aspects. Quantitative analysis usually reflects economic factors, and qualitative considerations include such intangibles as public opinion and personal preferences of managers. Cost-volume analysis, financial analysis, decision theory, and waiting line analysis are available tools for analyzing alternatives.

KEY TERMS

automation, 234
break-even analysis, 251
break-even point (BEP), 252
capacity, 240
cash flow, 254
computer-aided manufacturing
  (CAM), 235
computer-integrated
  manufacturing (CIM), 240

continuous processing, 232
flexible manufacturing systems
  (FMS), 236
intermittent processing, 232
numerically controlled (N/C)
  machines, 235
present value, 254
projects, 233
robot, 235

**SOLVED
PROBLEMS**

Problem

1. *Make or buy.* A firm's manager must decide whether to make or buy a certain item used in the production of vending machines. Cost and volume estimates are as follows:

	Make	Buy
Annual fixed cost	$150,000	None
Variable cost/unit	$60	$80
Annual volume (units)	12,000	12,000

  a. Given these figures, should the firm buy or make this item?
  b. There is a possibility that volume could change in the future. At what volume would the manager be indifferent between making and buying?

Solution

  a. Determine the annual cost of each alternative:

  Total cost = Fixed cost + Volume × Variable cost

  Make: $150,000 + 12,000($60) = $870,000
  Buy: 0   + 12,000($80) = $960,000

Because the annual cost of making is less than the annual cost of buying, it would seem reasonable for the manager to choose to make the item.

  b. To determine the volume at which the two choices would be equivalent, set the two total costs equal to each other, and solve for volume: $TC_{make} = TC_{buy}$. Thus, $150,000 + Q($60) = 0 + Q($80). Solving, $Q = 7,500$ units. Therefore, at a volume of 7,500 units a year, the manager would be indifferent between making and buying. For lower volumes, the choice would be to buy, and for higher volumes, the choice would be to make.

Problem

2. A small firm produces and sells novelty items in a five-state area. The firm expects to consolidate assembly of its electric turtle line at a single location instead of the current situation, which consists of three widely scattered operations. The leading candidate for location will have a monthly fixed cost of $42,000 and variable costs of $3 per turtle. Turtles sell for $7 each. Prepare a table that shows total profits, fixed costs, variable costs, and revenues for monthly volumes of 10,000, 12,000, and 15,000 units.

Solution

Revenue = $7 per unit
Variable cost = $3 per unit
Fixed cost = $42,000 per month

Profit = Revenue × Volume − (FC + VC × Volume)
Total cost = FC + VC × Volume

Volume	Total revenue	Total VC	Fixed cost	Total cost	Total profit
10,000	$ 70,000	$30,000	$42,000	$72,000	$(2,000)
12,000	84,000	36,000	42,000	78,000	6,000
15,000	105,000	45,000	42,000	87,000	18,000

Problem

3. (Refer to the previous problem.) Develop an equation that can be used to compute profit for any volume using the information in the previous problem, and use that equation to determine profit for the case where volume equals 22,000 units.

Solution

Profit = $7/unit × Q − ($42,000 + $3/unit × Q)

where Q = volume. For Q = 22,000, profit is

$7(22,000) − ($42,000 + $3 × 22,000) = $46,000

DISCUSSION AND REVIEW QUESTIONS

1. Explain the importance of process selection in system design.
2. Briefly describe continuous processing, intermittent processing, and projects, and indicate the kinds of situations in which each would be used.
3. Briefly discuss the advantages and disadvantages of automation.
4. Briefly describe computer-assisted approaches to production.
5. What is a flexible manufacturing system, and why is it important?
6. Why is *management of technology* important?

7. Why might the choice of equipment that provides flexibility sometimes be viewed as a management cop-out?

8. Contrast *design* and *effective* capacity.

9. List and briefly explain three factors that may inhibit capacity utilization.

10. How do long-term and short-term capacity considerations differ?

11. Give two examples of items that exhibit these seasonal demand patterns:
    a. Annual.
    b. Monthly.
    c. Weekly.
    d. Daily.

12. Give some examples of ways that flexibility can be built into system design.

13. Why is it important to adopt a "big picture" approach to capacity planning?

14. What is meant by "capacity in chunks," and why is that a factor in capacity planning?

15. What kinds of capacity problems are currently being experienced by many elementary and secondary schools? What are some of the alternatives being used to deal with those problems?

16. How can a systems approach to capacity planning be useful?

17. How do capacity decisions influence productivity?

18. Identify some additional examples of companies that have continuous, intermittent, or project processing.

19. Describe the product-process matrix, and give an additional example of a product and a service for each category.

20. Why is it important to achieve a position on the diagonal of the product-process matrix?

21. How could the product-process matrix be used to audit existing processes? What benefits might this lead to?

22. Briefly discuss how uncertainty affects process selection and capacity decisions.

23. How do volume and flexibility affect process selection? How does volume affect the degree of automation?

PROBLEMS

1. A producer of pottery is considering the addition of a new plant to absorb the backlog of demand that now exists. The primary location being considered will have fixed costs of $9,200 per month and variable costs of 70 cents per unit produced. Each item is sold to retailers at a price that averages 90 cents.
   a. What volume per month is required in order to break even?
   b. What profit would be realized on a monthly volume of (1) 61,000 units? (2) 87,000 units?
   c. What volume would be needed to obtain a profit of $16,000 per month?
   d. What volume is required to provide a revenue of $23,000 per month?
   e. Plot the total cost and total revenue lines.

2. A small firm intends to increase the capacity of a bottleneck operation by adding a new machine. Two alternatives, A and B, have been identified, and the associated costs and revenues have been estimated: Annual fixed costs would be $40,000 for A and $30,000 for B; variable costs per unit would be $10 for A and $12 for B; and revenue per unit would be $15 for A and $16 for B.
   a. Determine each alternative's break-even point in units.
   b. At what volume of output would the two alternatives yield the same profit?

   c.   If expected annual demand is 12,000 units, which alternative would yield the higher profit?

3. A producer of felt-tip pens has received a forecast of a demand of 30,000 pens for the coming month from its marketing department. Fixed costs of $25,000 per month are allocated to the felt-tip operation, and variable costs are 37 cents per pen.
   a.   Find the break-even quantity if pens sell for $1 each.
   b.   What price must pens be sold for to obtain a monthly profit of $15,000, assuming that estimated demand materializes?

4. A real estate agent is considering installing a cellular telephone in her car. There are three billing plans to choose from, all of which involve a weekly charge of $20. Plan A has a cost of $0.45 a minute for daytime calls and $0.20 a minute for evening calls. Plan B has a charge of $0.55 a minute for daytime calls and a charge of $0.15 a minute for evening calls. Plan C has a flat rate of $80 with 200 minutes of calls allowed per week and a cost of $0.40 per minute beyond that, day or evening.
   a.   Determine the total charge under each plan for this case: 120 minutes of day calls and 40 minutes of evening calls in a week.
   b.   Prepare a graph that shows total weekly cost for each plan versus daytime call minutes.
   c.   If the agent will use the service for daytime calls, over what range of call minutes will each plan be optimal?

5. (Refer to the previous problem.) Suppose that the agent expects both day and evening calls. At what point (i.e., proportion of call minutes for daytime calls) would she be indifferent between plans A and B?

6. A firm plans to begin production of a new small appliance soon. The manager must decide whether to purchase the motors for the appliance from a vendor at $7 each or to produce them in-house. Either of two processes could be used for in-house production; one would have an annual fixed cost of $160,000 and a variable cost of $5 per unit, and the other would have an annual fixed cost of $190,000 and a variable cost of $4 per unit. Determine the range of annual volume for which each of the alternatives would be best.

7. A manager is trying to decide whether to purchase a certain part or to have it produced internally. Internal production could use either of two processes. One would entail a variable cost of $17 per unit and an annual fixed cost of $200,000; the other would entail a variable cost of $14 per unit and an annual fixed cost of $240,000. Three vendors are willing to provide the part. Vendor A has a price of $20 per unit for any volume up to 30,000 units. Vendor B has a price of $22 per unit for demand of 1,000 units or less, and $18 per unit for larger quantities. Vendor C offers a price of $21 per unit for the first 1,000 units, and $19 per unit for additional units.
   a.   If the manager anticipates an annual volume of 10,000 units, which alternative would be best from a cost standpoint? For 20,000 units, which alternative would be best?
   b.   Determine the range for which each alternative is best. Are there any alternatives that are never best? Which?

8. A company manufactures a product using three machine cells. Each cell has a design capacity of 250 units per day and an effective capacity of 230 units per day. At present, actual output averages 200 units per cell, but the manager estimates that productivity improvements soon will increase that to 225 units per day. Annual demand is currently 50,000 units. It is forecasted that within two years, annual demand will triple. The company could produce at the rate of 400 per day using available capacity. How many cells should the company plan for in order to satisfy predicted demand under these conditions? Assume 240 workdays per year.

9. A manager must decide between these alternatives:

Machine	Cost
A	$40,000
B	$30,000
C	$80,000

Product forecasts and processing times on the machines are as follows:

Product	Annual demand	Processing time per unit (minutes) A	B	C
#1	16,000	3	4	2
#2	12,000	4	4	3
#3	6,000	5	6	4
#4	30,000	2	2	1

Which machine would have the lowest total cost, and how many of that machine would be needed? Machines operate 10 hours a day, 250 days a year.

10. (Refer to the previous problem.) Consider this additional information: The machines differ in terms of hourly operating costs: The A machines have an hourly operating cost of $10 *each,* B machines have an hourly operating cost of $11 each, and C machines have an hourly operating cost of $12 each. Which alternative would be selected, and how many machines, in order to minimize total cost while satisfying capacity processing requirements?

SELECTED BIBLIOGRAPHY

Adam, Everette E., Jr., and Ronald J. Ebert. *Production and Operations Management: Concepts, Models and Behavior.* 4th ed. Englewood Cliffs, N.J.: Prentice Hall, 1989.

Hill, Terry. *Manufacturing Strategy.* Homewood, Ill.: Richard D. Irwin, 1989.

Moore, Franklin, and Thomas E. Hendrick. *Production/Operations Management.* 9th ed. Homewood, Ill.: Richard D. Irwin, 1985.

Toward a New Era in U.S. Manufacturing: The Need for a National Vision. Washington, D.C.: National Academy Press, 1986.

LINEAR PROGRAMMING

After completing this supplement, you should be able to:

1. Describe the type of problem that would lend itself to solution using linear programming.

2. Formulate a linear programming model from a description of a problem.

3. Solve a simple linear programming problem using the graphical method.

4. Use the simplex technique to solve linear programming problems.

5. Interpret computer solutions of linear programming problems.

6. Do sensitivity analysis on the solution of a linear programming problem.

LEARNING OBJECTIVES

SUPPLEMENT OUTLINE

In 1947, George Dantzig developed the use of linear algebra for determining optimal solutions to problems that involved restrictions, or *constraints*. For example, a problem might relate to determining the optimal quantities of several products to produce given each product's profit per unit, as well as such constraints as labor hours, machine time, and raw materials needed. The result was a class of techniques generally known as *linear programming*. These techniques are now widely used to solve constrained optimization problems.

INTRODUCTION

Linear programming (LP) techniques involve a sequence of steps that will lead to an optimal solution to a class of problems, in cases where an optimum exists. There are a number of different linear-programming techniques; some are special-purpose (i.e., used to find solutions for specific types of problems) and others are more general in scope. This supplement describes the two general-purpose solution techniques: graphical linear programming and the simplex method. Grapical linear programming is presented because it provides a visual portrayal of many of the important concepts of linear programming. However, it is limited to problems that involve only two variables. Simplex is a mathematical approach that lacks the visual features of the graphical approach, but it can handle more than two variables, making it much more useful for solving real problems, which often involve a large number of variables.

Linear programming models are used to help operations managers make decisions in many different areas. These include allocation of scarce resources, assignment problems (assigning workers to jobs, jobs to machines, and so on), transportation problems (determining distribution plans for shipping goods from multiple origins to multiple destinations, such as from 4 warehouses to 10 retail outlets), blending problems (petroleum products, diets), and other problems. As you can see, linear programming has a broad range of application. Moreover, in all applications, the use of linear programming guarantees an optimal solution to the mathematical model.

LINEAR PROGRAMMING MODELS

Linear programming models are mathematical representations of linear programming problems. These models have certain characteristics in common. Knowledge of these characteristics enables us to recognize problems that can be solved using linear programming. In addition, it also can help us formulate LP models. The characteristics can be grouped into two categories: components and assumptions. First, let's consider the components.

There are four components that provide the structure of a linear programming model:

1. *Objective.*
2. *Decision variables.*
3. *Constraints.*
4. *Parameters.*

Objective

The goal of an LP model: maximization or minimization.

Linear programming algorithms require that a single goal or **objective**, such as the maximization of profits, be specified. There are two general types of objectives:

maximization and minimization. A maximization objective might involve profits, revenues, efficiency, or rate of return. Conversely, a minimization objective might involve cost, time, distance traveled, or scrap. The profit, cost, etc., per unit of output or input is specified in an **objective function**.

    Decision variables represent choices available to the decision maker in terms of amounts of either inputs or outputs. For example, some problems involve choosing a combination of inputs that will minimize total costs, while others involve selecting a combination of outputs that will maximize profits or revenues.

    Constraints are limitations that restrict the alternatives available to decision makers. There are three types of constraints: less than or equal to ($\leq$), greater than or equal to ($\geq$), and simply equal to ($=$). A $\leq$ constraint implies an upper limit on the amount of some scarce resource (e.g., machine hours, labor hours, materials) available for use. A $\geq$ constraint specifies a lower bound that must be achieved in the final solution (e.g., must contain at least 10 percent real fruit juice, must get at least 30 MPG on the highway). The $=$ constraint is more restrictive in the sense that it specifies *exactly* what a decision variable should equal (e.g., make 200 units of product A). A linear-programming model can consist of one or more constraints.[1] In cases where there are multiple constraints, they may all be of the same type (e.g., all $\leq$ constraints), or they might be a mixture of types (e.g., three $\leq$ constraints and one $\geq$ constraint). Many possibilities exist. Taken as a whole, the constraints of a given problem define the set of all feasible combinations of decision variables: this set is referred to as the **feasible solution space**. Linear-programming algorithms are designed to search the feasible solution space for the combination of decision variables that will yield an optimum in terms of the objective function.

    An LP model consists of a mathematical statement of the objective and a mathematical statement of each constraint. These statements consist of symbols (e.g., x_1, x_2) that represent the decision variables and numerical values, called **parameters**. The parameters are fixed values; the model is solved *given* those values.

    In order for linear programming models to be used effectively, certain *assumptions* must be satisfied. These are:

1. *Linearity:* the impact of decision variables is linear in constraints and the objective function.
2. *Divisibility:* noninteger values of decision variables are acceptable.
3. *Certainty:* values of parameters are known and constant.
4. *Nonnegativity:* negative values of decision variables are unacceptable.

    Example S–1 illustrates the components of an LP model.

MODEL FORMULATION

An understanding of the components of linear-programming models is necessary for model formulation. This helps provide organization to the process of assembling information about a problem into a model.

    Naturally, it is important to obtain valid information on what constraints are appropriate, as well as on what values of the parameters are appropriate. If this is not

Objective function

Mathematical statement of profit, cost, etc., per unit of output or input.

Decision variables

Amounts of either inputs or outputs.

Constraints

Limitations that restrict the available alternatives.

Feasible solution space

The set of all feasible combinations of decision variables as defined by the constraints.

Parameters

Numerical values.

---

[1]The number of constraints is unrestricted; large problems can easily have hundreds of constraints.

Example S–1

$$\text{Decision variables} \begin{cases} x_1 = \text{Quantity of product 1 to produce} \\ x_2 = \text{Quantity of product 2 to produce} \\ x_3 = \text{Quantity of product 3 to produce} \end{cases}$$

Maximize	$5x_1 + 8x_2 + 4x_3$ (profit)	(Objective function)
Subject to		
Labor	$2x_1 + 4x_2 + 3x_3 \le 250$ hours	
Material	$7x_1 + 6x_2 + 5x_3 \le 100$ pounds	(Constraints)
Product 1	$x_1 \qquad\qquad \ge 10$ units	
	$x_1, x_2, x_3 \ge 0$	(Nonnegativity constraints)

First, the decision variables are listed and defined. These typically represent *quantities*. In this case, they are quantities of three different products that might be produced.

Next, the objective function is stated. It includes every decision variable in the model and the contribution (profit per unit) of each decision variable. Thus, product x_1 has a profit of $5 per unit. The profit from product x_1 for a given solution will be 5 times the value of x_1 specified by the solution; the total profit from all products will be the sum of the individual product profits. Thus, if $x_1 = 10$, $x_2 = 0$, and $x_3 = 12$, the value of the objective function would be:

$$5(10) + 8(0) + 4(12) = 98$$

The objective function is followed by a list (in no particular order) of three constraints. Each constraint has a right-side numerical value (e.g., the labor constraint has a right-side value of 250) that indicates the amount of the constraint and an algebraic sign that indicates whether that amount is a maximum ($\le$), a minimum ($\ge$), or an equality ($=$). The left side of each constraint consists of the variables that are subject to that particular constraint and a coefficient for each variable that indicates how much of the right-side quantity *one unit* of the decision variable represents. For instance, for the labor constraint, one unit of x_1 will require two hours of labor. The sum of the values on the left side of each constraint represents the amount of that constraint used by a solution. Thus, if $x_1 = 10$, $x_2 = 0$, and $x_3 = 12$, the amount of labor used would be:

$$2(10) + 4(0) + 3(12) = 56 \text{ hours}$$

Because this amount does not exceed the quantity on the right-hand side of the constraint, it is feasible.

Note that the third constraint refers to only a single variable; x_1 must be at least 10 units. Its coefficient is, in effect, 1, although it is not shown.

Finally, there are the nonnegativity constraints. These are listed on a single line; they reflect the condition that no decision variable is allowed to have a negative value.

Lotfi and Pegels DSS-POM (2.1c) initial data entry screen for Example S–1.

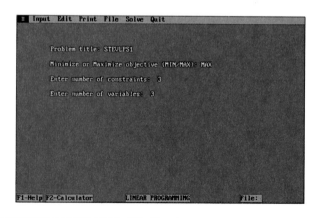

done, the usefulness of the model will be questionable. Consequently, in some instances, considerable effort must be expended to obtain that information.

Once all the information has been obtained, the next step is to construct a model. There are a number of different procedures that might be employed. One approach is to identify the decision variables, then write out the objective function, and then formulate each of the constraints. This approach follows a logical sequence from beginning to end. Another approach is to let the problem guide you in formulating a model. With this approach, pieces of the model are identified in the order in which they occur in the problem statement. For instance, if the first words of a problem are "A manager wants to maximize profits," this would lead to:

Maximize   (profits)

But if the first words are "A department has 2,000 pounds of raw material with which to prepare its products," this would lead to:

Subject to
Raw material $\leq$ 2,000 pounds

Or the first words may be "A supervisor would like to know how much of each of two products to make." This would lead to:

x_1 = Quantity of product 1
x_2 = Quantity of product 2

Following this approach will cause you to skip around the model according to the sequence of the problem statement; following the first approach will cause you to skip around the problem statement. Try both approaches, and decide which works best for you.

Once a model has been formulated, the next task is to solve it. In the following sections, three approaches to problem solution are described: graphical solutions, simplex solutions, and computer solutions.

GRAPHICAL LINEAR PROGRAMMING

Grapical linear programming is a method for finding optimal solutions to two-variable problems. This section describes that approach.

Graphical linear programming
Graphical method for finding optimal solutions to two-variable problems.

OUTLINE OF GRAPHICAL PROCEDURE

The graphical method of linear programming involves plotting the constraints on a graph and identifying an area that satisfies all of the constraints. The area is referred to as the *feasible solution space*. Next, the objective function is plotted and used to identify the optimal point in the feasible solution space. The coordinates of the point can sometimes be read directly from the graph, although generally an algebraic determination of the coordinates of the point is necessary.

The general procedure followed in the graphical approach is:

1. Set up the objective function and the constraints in mathematical format.
2. Plot the constraints.
3. Identify the feasible solution space.
4. Plot the objective function.
5. Determine the optimum solution.

The technique can best be illustrated through solution of a typical problem. Consider the following:

> Two products can be produced on a certain machine. There are 12 hours of machine time available to produce these products. Product 1 requires 1 hour per unit, and product 2 requires 3 hours per unit. Both products require one raw material: product 1 uses 4 pounds of raw material per unit, and product 2 uses 3 pounds. There are 24 pounds of this raw material available for these two products. If the goal is to maximize the profit from these two products, and product 1 contributes $4 per unit to profit and product 2 contributes $5 per unit, what quantity of each should be produced?

To solve this problem, we must first set it up in mathematical format. This involves the following:

1. Identify the decision variables. In this case, they are x_1 = quantity of product 1 and x_2 = quantity of product 2.
2. Formulate the objective function. It is

    Maximize $Z = 4x_1 + 5x_2$

3. Identify and formulate the constraints. There are two constraints: machine time and raw material. The constraints are

    Machine time $x_1 + 3x_2 \le 12$
    Raw material $4x_1 + 3x_2 \le 24$

4. Add the nonnegativity constraints. They are $x_1, x_2, \ge 0$.

Thus, the model is

   Maximize $Z = 4x_1 + 5x_2$
   Subject to
      Machine time $x_1 + 3x_2 \le 12$
      Raw material $4x_1 + 3x_2 \le 24$
                          $x_1, x_2 \ge 0$

The next step is to plot the constraints.

PLOTTING CONSTRAINTS

The procedure for plotting constraints is quite simple:

1. Replace the inequality sign with an equal sign. This transforms the constraint into an equation of a *straight line*.
2. Determine where the line intersects each axis.
    a.   To find where it crosses the x_2 axis, set x_1 equal to zero and solve the equation for the value of x_2.
    b.   To find where it crosses the x_1 axis, set x_2 equal to zero and solve the equation for the value of x_1.
3. Mark these intersections on the axes, and connect them with a straight line.
4. Indicate by shading (or by arrows at the ends of the constraint line) whether the inequality is greater than or less than. (A general rule to determine which side of the line satisfies the inequality is to pick the point (0,0) and see whether it is greater than or less than the constraint amount.)
5. Repeat steps 1–4 for each constraint.

First, let's plot the machine hours constraint, which is $x_1 + 3x_2 \leq 12$.

1. Make it an equality: $x_1 + 3x_2 = 12$.
2. Set $x_1 = 0$ and solve for x_2: $(0) + 3x_2 = 12$, so $x_2 = 4$.
   Set $x_2 = 0$ and solve for x_1: $x_1 + 3(0) = 12$, so $x_1 = 12$.
3. Mark the points on the graph, and connect them with a straight line.
4. Shade the area that satisfies the constraint. (Inserting $x_1 = 0$, $x_2 = 0$ into the equation yields a value of 0, which is less than 12. Hence, all points on that side of the line are less than 12.) See Figure 6S–1. Note that only the area in the first quadrant is shaded due to the nonnegativity constraints.

The second constraint can be plotted similarly.

1. Make it an equality: $4x_1 + 3x_2 = 24$.
2. Set $x_1 = 0$ and solve for x_2: $4(0) + 3x_2 = 24$, so $x_2 = 8$.
   Set $x_2 = 0$ and solve for x_1: $4x_1 + 3(0) = 24$, so $x_1 = 6$.
3. Mark the points on the graph, and connect them with a straight line.
4. Shade in the area that satisfies this constraint (see Figure 6S–2). Note that some of the points satisfy only one of the constraints, and other points satisfy both.

IDENTIFYING THE FEASIBLE SOLUTION SPACE

The feasible solution space is the set of all points (i.e., the *area*) that satisfies all constraints. (Recall that the x_1 and x_2 axes form nonnegativity constraints). The heavily shaded area shown in Figure 6S–2 is the feasible solution space for our problem.

PLOTTING THE OBJECTIVE FUNCTION LINE

The objective function is actually a *family* of lines; the lines are parallel, but each represents a different amount. For example, one line could be $4x_1 + 5x_2 = 20$, another $4x_1 + 5x_2 = 40$, and another $4x_1 + 5x_2 = 60$. These lines are illustrated in

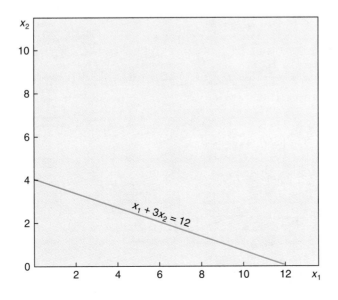

Figure 6S–1

The machine constraint

Figure 6S–3. Note that the lines are *parallel* and that the farther away from the origin the line is, the greater the value of the objective function. In addition, each line is an *isoprofit* line: every combination of x_1 and x_2 on the line will yield the same profit (e.g., \$40).

These are but a few of the many different lines that could be drawn. Some of these lines would cross the feasible solution space, and some would not. This is important since points that do not lie within the feasible solution space cannot possibly be feasible solutions. Given the three lines in Figure 6S–3, only the line $4x_1 + 5x_2 = 20$ has points within the feasible solution space. However, it is not difficult to see that other lines parallel to this, but farther from the origin, could be

Figure 6S–2

The raw material constraint is added to the graph

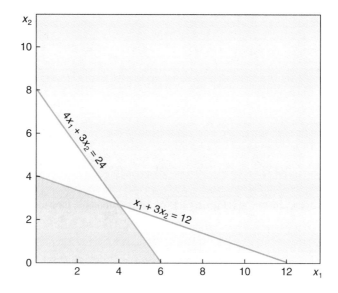

Figure 6S–3

Three isoprofit lines

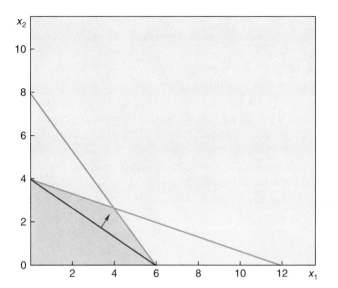

drawn. What we want is the last line that just touches the feasible solution space because it will yield the greatest *feasible* value for the objective function.

Instead of using trial and error, we can easily identify the line that will yield the maximum profit for an x_1, x_2 combination in the feasible solution space. All we need is an isoprofit line that crosses the feasible solution space.[2]

To plot the objective function, select a value to set it equal to. One easy-to-use value is the product of the x_1 and x_2 coefficients (in this case, 4 and 5: $4 \times 5 = 20$). This is one of the lines plotted in Figure 6S–3. Note that it does cross the feasible solution space. However, that will not always happen. When a line is outside of the feasible solution space, divide the selected value of the objective function (e.g., 60) by a constant so that it does cross the feasible solution space (e.g., $60/3 = 20$, and 20 crosses the space). Conversely, if the line crosses the feasible solution space but is too close to the origin to be useful, multiply the value by a constant—1.5, 2, 10, 100, or some other number—to obtain a more useful line.

Plot the line as you would a constraint line: set $x_1 = 0$ and solve for x_2, and then set $x_2 = 0$ and solve for x_1.

Since the profit increases as the line moves away from the origin, "slide" the line parallel to itself, away from the origin (imagine a series of parallel lines being drawn). The objective is to identify the farthest point in the feasible solution space touched by one of the parallel lines. The x_1 and x_2 coordinates of that point indicate the quantities of x_1 and x_2 that will maximize the objective function. (See Figure 6S–4.) In this example, the point is where the two constraints intersect. Although we can read this directly from the graph in some cases, it is usually best to use algebra to determine the exact coordinates of the intersection. We can do this by solving the equations of the two lines simultaneously (i.e., find the one value of x_1 and one value of x_2 that will satisfy both equations). To do this, we make both constraints equalities:

$$x_1 + 3x_2 = 12$$
$$4x_1 + 3x_2 = 24$$

---

[2] Strictly speaking, the line need not cross the feasible solution space. However, it is convenient to work with such a line.

We have two equations and two unknowns. What we want is one equation with one unknown since this would enable us to readily determine the value of one of the two variables. Then by substituting that value into one of the two constraints, we can determine the value of the other variable.

When solving equations simultaneously, we usually have to modify one or both of the equations to obtain one set of coefficients that are equal. Following such modification, when we subtract one equation from the other, one of the terms will drop out, leaving the one variable in a single equation. In this instance, the x_2 coefficients are equal, so modifying is not necessary. (The first solved problem at the end of this section illustrates the more general case.) Hence, merely subtracting one from the other will produce the desired result:

$$\begin{array}{r} 4x_1 + 3x_2 = 24 \\ -(\ x_1 + 3x_2 = 12) \\ \hline 3x_1 \qquad\ = 12 \end{array}$$

Solving, we find that $x_1 = 4$. Next, we substitute this value into one of the equations to find the value of x_2. Either equation will do. For example, the second equation yields:

$$4 + 3x_2 = 12$$

Solving, we find $x_2 = 8/3$, or 2.67.

Thus, the solution to the problem that will maximize profit is to produce 4 units of product 1 and 2.67 units of product 2. Substituting these values into the objective function will indicate the optimal profit:

$$4(4) + 5(2.67) = 29.35$$

SOLUTIONS AND CORNER POINTS

The feasible solution space in graphical linear programming is a polygon. Moreover, the solution to any problem will be at one of the corner points of the polygon. In rare instances, the objective function will be parallel to one of the constraint lines. In such a case, *every* combination of x_1 and x_2 on the segment of the constraint that touches the feasible solution space represents an optimal solution. Hence, there are multiple optimal solutions to the problem. Even in such a case, the solution will also be a corner point. In fact, the solution will be at *two* corner points: those at the ends of the segment that touches the feasible solution space. Figures 6S–5 and 6S–6 illustrate solutions at corner points and an objective function line that is parallel to a constraint line, respectively. Figure 6S–5 shows the same problem that was solved in this section with a different objective function: $Z = 2x_1 + 14x_2$.

MINIMIZATION

Graphical minimization problems are quite similar to maximization problems. There are, however, two important differences. One is that the constraints are usually "greater than or equal to" instead of "less than or equal to." This causes the feasible solution space to be outside of the polygon instead of inside. The other difference is that the optimal point is the one closest to the origin. The optimal corner point is found by sliding the objective function (which is an *isocost* line) *toward* the origin instead of away from it.

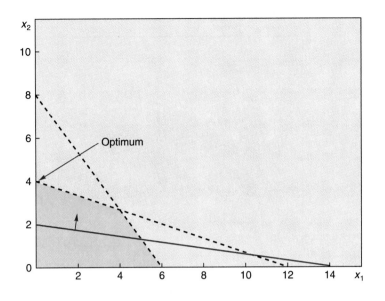

Figure 6S–5

The solution is always at a corner point

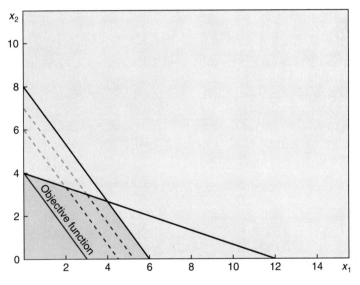

Figure 6S–6

The objective function is parallel to one of the constraint lines

---

Solve the following problem using graphical linear programming.

Example S–2

█

Minimize $Z = 8x_1 + 12x_2$
Subject to $5x_1 + 2x_2 \geq 20$
                        $4x_1 + 3x_2 \geq 24$
                                   $x_2 \geq 2$
                        $x_1, x_2 \geq 0$

Solution

1. Plot the constraints (shown in Figure 6S–7).
    a. Change constraints to equalities.

(continued)

Example S–2

(concluded)

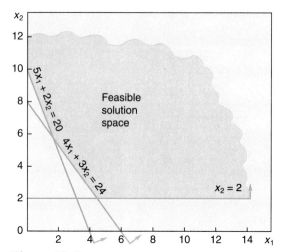

Figure 6S–7

The constraints define the feasible solution space

    b.   For each constraint, set $x_1 = 0$ and solve for x_2; then set $x_2 = 0$ and solve for x_1.

    c.   Graph each constraint. Note that $x_2 = 2$ is a horizontal line parallel to the x_1 axis and 2 units above it.

2.   Shade the feasible solution space (see Figure 6S–7).

3.   Plot the objective function.

    a.   Select a value for the objective function that causes it to cross the feasible solution space. Try $8 \times 12 = 96$; $8x_1 + 12x_2 = 96$ (acceptable).

    b.   Graph the line (see Figure 6S–8).

Figure 6S–8

The optimum is the last point the objective function touches as it is moved toward the origin

4.   Slide the objective function toward the origin, being careful to keep it parallel to the original line.

Example S–2

(concluded)

5. The optimum (last feasible point) is shown in Figure 6S–8. The x_2 coordinate ($x_2 = 2$) can be determined by inspection of the graph. Note that the optimum point is at the intersection of the line $x_2 = 2$ and the line $4x_1 + 3x_2 = 24$. Substituting the value of x_2 into the latter equation will yield the value of x_1 at the intersection:

$$4x_1 + 3(2) = 24 \qquad x_1 = 4.5$$

Thus, the optimum is $x_1 = 4.5$ units and $x_2 = 2$.

6. Compute the minimum cost:

$$8x_1 + 12x_2 = 8(4.5) + 12(2) = 60$$

SLACK AND SURPLUS

If a constraint forms the optimal corner point of the feasible solution space, it is called a **binding constraint**. In effect, it limits the value of the objective function; if the constraint could be relaxed (less restrictive), an improved solution would be possible. For constraints that are not binding, making them less restrictive will have no impact on the solution.

> **Binding constraint**
>
> A constraint that forms the optimal corner point of the feasible solution space.

If the optimal values of the decision variables are substituted into the left side of a binding constraint, the resulting value will exactly equal the right-hand value of the constraint. However, for a nonbinding constraint, there will be a difference. If the left side is greater than the right side, we say that there is **surplus**; if the left side is less than the right side, we say that there is **slack**. Slack can only occur in a ≤ constraint; it is the amount by which the left side is less than the right side when the optimal values of the decision variables are substituted into the left side. And surplus can only occur in a ≥ constraint; it is the amount by which the left side exceeds the right side of the constraint when the optimal values of the decision variables are substituted into the left side.

> **Surplus**
>
> When the optimal values of decision variables are substituted into a ≥ constraint and the resulting value exceeds the right side value.

> **Slack**
>
> When the optimal values of decision variables are substituted into a ≤ constraint, and the resulting value is less than the right side value.

For example, suppose the optimal values for a model are $x_1 = 10$ and $x_2 = 20$. If one of the constraints is

$$3x_1 + 2x_2 \leq 100$$

substituting the optimal values into the left side yields

$$3(10) + 2(20) = 70$$

Because the constraint is ≤, the difference between the values of 100 and 70 (i.e., 30) is slack. Suppose the optimal values had been $x_1 = 20$ and $x_2 = 20$. Substituting these values into the left side of the constraint would yield $3(20) + 2(20) = 100$. Because the left side equals the right side, this is a binding constraint; slack is equal to zero.

Now consider the constraint.

$$4x_1 + x_2 \geq 50$$

If the optimal values are $x_1 = 10$ and $x_2 = 15$, substituting into the left side yields

$$4(10) + 15 = 55$$

Because this is a ≥ constraint, the difference between the left and right side values is *surplus*. If the optimal values had been $x_1 = 12$ and $x_2 = 2$, substitution would result in the left side being equal to 50. Hence, the constraint would be a binding constraint, and there would be no surplus (or surplus would be zero).

THE SIMPLEX METHOD

The **simplex** method is a general-purpose linear-programming algorithm that is widely used to solve large-scale problems. Although it lacks the intuitive appeal of the graphical approach, its ability to handle problems with more than two decision variables makes it extremely valuable for solving problems often encountered in operations management.

The simplex technique involves a series of iterations; successive improvements are made until an optimal solution is achieved. The technique requires simple mathematical operations (addition, subtraction, multiplication, and division), but the computations are lengthy as well as tedious, and the slightest error can lead to a good deal of frustration. For these reasons, most users of the technique rely on computers to handle the computations while they concentrate on the solutions. Still, some familiarity with manual computations is helpful in understanding the simplex process. You will discover that it is better *not* to use your calculator in working through these problems because rounding can easily distort the results. Instead, it is best to work with numbers in fractional form.

Even though simplex can readily handle three or more decision variables, you will gain considerable insight on the technique if we use a two-variable problem to illustrate it because you will be able to compare what is happening in the simplex calculations with a graphical solution to the problem.

Let's consider the simplex solution to the same problem that we used to illustrate a graphical solution. That problem is repeated here:

$$
\begin{aligned}
\text{Maximize} \quad & Z = 4x_1 + 5x_2 \\
\text{Subject to} \quad & x_1 + 3x_2 \leq 12 \\
& 4x_1 + 3x_2 \leq 24 \\
& x_1, x_2 \geq 0
\end{aligned}
$$

The solution is shown graphically in Figure 6S–9. Now let's see how the simplex technique can be used to obtain the solution.

The simplex technique involves generating a series of solutions in tabular form, called **tableaus**. By inspecting the bottom row of each tableau, one can immediately tell if it represents the optimal solution. Each tableau corresponds to a corner point of the feasible solution space. The first tableau corresponds to the origin. Subsequent tableaus are developed by shifting to an adjacent corner point in the

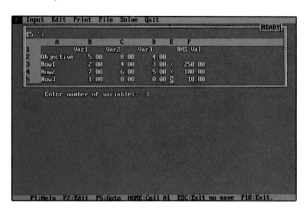

Example S–1 objective function and constraints in Lotfi and Pegels DSS- POM (2.1c).

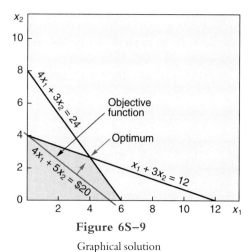

Figure 6S–9

Graphical solution

direction that yields the highest rate of profit. This process continues as long as a positive rate of profit exists. Thus, the process involves the following steps:

1. Set up the initial tableau.
2. Develop a revised tableau using the information contained in the first tableau.
3. Inspect to see if it is optimum.
4. Repeat steps 2 and 3 until no further improvement is possible.

SETTING UP THE INITIAL TABLEAU

Obtaining the initial tableau is a two-step process. First, we must rewrite the constraints to make them equalities, and also modify the objective function slightly. Then we put this information into a table and supply a few computations that are needed to complete the table.

Rewriting the objective function and constraints involves the addition of *slack variables,* one for each constraint. These variables represent the amount of each resource that will not be used if the solution is implemented. In the initial solution, with each of the real variables equal to zero, the solution consists solely of slack. The constraints with slack added become equalities:

$$(1) \quad x_1 + 3x_2 + 1s_1 \qquad = 12$$
$$(2) \quad 4x_1 + 3x_2 \qquad + 1s_2 = 24$$

It is useful in setting up the table to represent each slack variable in every equation. Hence, we can write these equations in an equivalent form:

$$(1) \quad x_1 + 3x_2 + 1s_1 + 0s_2 = 12$$
$$(2) \quad 4x_1 + 3x_2 + 0s_1 + 1s_2 = 24$$

The objective function can be written in similar form:

$$Z = 4x_1 + 5x_2 + 0s_1 + 0s_2$$

The slack variables are given coefficients of zero in the objective function because they do not produce any contributions to profits. Thus, the information above can be summarized as:

Maximize $\quad Z = 4x_1 + 5x_2 + 0s_1 + 0s_2$
Subject to

$$(1) \quad x_1 + 3x_2 + 1s_1 + 0s_2 = 12$$
$$(2) \quad 4x_1 + 3x_2 + 0s_1 + 1s_2 = 24$$

This forms the basis of our initial tableau, which is shown in Table 6S–1.

Table 6S–1

Partial initial tableau

Profit per unit for variables in solution		Decision variables				Objective row
C		4	5	0	0	
	Variables in solution	x_1	x_2	s_1	s_2	Solution quantity
0	s_1	1	3	1	0	12
0	s_2	4	3	0	1	24

To complete the first tableau, we will need two additional rows, a Z row and a $C - Z$ row. The Z row values indicate the reduction in profits that would occur if one unit of the variable in that column were added to the solution. The $C - Z$ row shows the potential for increasing profits if one unit of the variable in that column were added to the solution.

To compute the Z values, multiply the coefficients in each column by their respective row profit per unit amounts, and sum within columns. To begin with, all values are zero:

C	x_1	x_2	s_1	s_2	Quantity
0	(1)0	(3)0	(1)0	(0)0	(12)0
0	(4)0	(3)0	(0)0	(1)0	(24)0
Z	0	0	0	0	0

The last value in the Z row indicates the total profit associated with a given solution (tableau). Since the initial solution has $x_1 = 0$ and $x_2 = 0$, it is not surprising that profit is 0.

Values in the $C - Z$ row are computed by subtracting the Z value in each column from the value of the objective row for that column. Thus,

Variable row:	x_1	x_2	s_1	s_2
Objective row (C):	4	5	0	0
Z	0	0	0	0
$C - Z$	4	5	0	0

The completed tableau is shown in Table 6S–2.

THE TEST FOR OPTIMALITY

If all the values in the $C - Z$ row of any tableau are zero or negative, the optimal solution has been obtained. In this case, the $C - Z$ row contains two positive values, 4 and 5, indicating that improvement is possible.

Table 6S–2

The initial tableau

$C \rightarrow$		4	5	0	0	
$\downarrow$	Variables in solution	x_1	x_2	s_1	s_2	Solution quantity
0	s_1	1	3	1	0	12
0	s_2	4	3	0	1	24
	Z	0	0	0	0	0
	$C - Z$	4	5	0	0	

DEVELOPING THE SECOND TABLEAU

Values in the $C - Z$ row reflect the profit potential for each unit of the variable in a given column. For instance, the 4 indicates that each unit of variable x_1 added to the solution will increase profits by \$4. Similarly, the 5 indicates that each unit of x_2 will contribute \$5 to profits. Given a choice between \$4 per unit and \$5 per unit, we select the larger and focus on that column, which means that x_2 will come into the solution. Now we must determine which variable will leave the solution. (At each tableau, one variable will come into the solution, and one will go out of solution, keeping the number of variables in the solution constant. Note that the number of variables in the solution must always equal the number of constraints. Thus, since in this problem there are two constraints, all solutions will have two variables.)

To determine which variable will leave the solution, we use the numbers in the body of the table in the column of the entering variable (i.e., 3 and 3). These are called **row pivot values**. Divide each one into the corresponding solution quantity amount, as shown in Table 6S–3. The smaller of these two ratios indicates the variable that will leave the solution. Thus, variable s_1 will leave and be replaced with x_2. In graphical terms, we have moved up the x_2 axis to the next corner point. By determining the smallest ratio, we have found which constraint is the most limiting. Turn back to Figure 6S–2. Note that the two constraints intersect the x_2 axis at 4 and 8, the two row ratios we have just computed. The second tableau will describe this corner point; it will indicate the profits and quantities associated with that corner point. It will also reveal if the corner point is an optimum, or if we must develop another tableau.

Row pivot values

The numbers in the *column* of the entering variable in the initial tableau, used to determine which variable will leave the solution.

At this point we can begin to develop the second tableau. The row of the leaving variable will be transformed into the **new pivot row** of the second tableau. This will serve as a foundation on which to develop the other rows. To obtain this new pivot row, we simply divide each element in the s_1 row by the row pivot value (intersection of the entering column and leaving row), which is 3. The resulting numbers are:

New pivot row

The row of the leaving variable in the second tableau; the foundation on which to develop the other rows.

	x_1	x_2	s_1	s_2	Solution quantity
Pivot-row value	1/3	1	1/3	0	4

C		4	5	0	0	Solution quantity	
	Variables in solution	x_1	x_2	s_1	s_2		
0	s_1	1	3	1	0	12/3 = 4	← Smallest positive ratio
0	s_2	4	3	0	1	24/3 = 8	
	Z	0	0	0	0	0	
	$C - Z$	4	5	0	0		

↑
Largest positive

Table 6S–3

The leaving and entering variables

These numbers become the new x_2 row of the second tableau.

The pivot-row numbers are used to compute the values for the other constraint rows (in this instance, the only other constraint row is the s_2 row). The procedure is:

1. Find the value that is at the intersection of the constraint row (i.e., the s_2 row) and the entering variable column. It is 3.
2. Multiply each value in the new pivot row by this value.
3. Subtract the resulting values, column by column, from the current row values.

	x_1	x_2	s_1	s_2	Quantity
Current value:	4	3	0	1	24
$-3 \times$ (main row)	$-3(1/3)$	$-3(1)$	$-3(1/3)$	$-3(0)$	$-3(4)$
New row value	3	0	-1	1	12

The two new rows are shown in Table 6S–4. The new Z row can now be computed. Multiply the row unit profits and the coefficients in each column for each row. Sum the results within each column. Thus,

Row	Profit	x_1	x_2	s_1	s_2	Quantity
x_2	5	5(1/3)	5(1)	5(1/3)	5(0)	5(4)
s_1	0	0(3)	0(0)	0(−1)	0(1)	0(12)
New Z row		5/3	5	5/3	0	20

Next, we compute the $C - Z$ row:

	x_1	x_2	s_1	s_2
C	4	5	0	0
Z	5/3	5	5/3	0
$C - Z$	7/3	0	$-5/3$	0

The completed second tableau is shown in Table 6S–5. It tells us that, at this point, 4 units of variable x_2 are the most we can make (see column *Solution quantity*, row x_2) and that the profit associated with $x_2 = 4$, $x_1 = 0$ is $20 (see row Z, column *Solution quantity*).

The fact that there is a positive value in the $C - Z$ row tells us that this is not the optimal solution. Consequently, we must develop another tableau.

Table 6S–4	**C**		4	5	0	0		
Partially completed second tableau		**Variables in solution**	x_1	x_2	s_1	s_2		**Solution quantity**
	5	x_2	1/3	1	1/3	0		4
	0	s_2	3	0	−1	1		12

DEVELOPING THE THIRD TABLEAU

The third tableau will be developed in the same manner as the previous one.

1. Determine the entering variable: Find the column with the largest positive value in the $C - Z$ row (7/3, in the x_1 column).

2. Determine the leaving variable: Divide the solution quantity in each row by the row pivot. Hence,

$$\frac{4}{1/3} = 12 \qquad 12/3 = 4$$

The smaller ratio indicates the leaving variable, s_2. See Table 6S–6.

3. Divide each value in the row of the leaving variable by the row pivot value (3) to obtain the new pivot-row values:

	x_1	x_2	s_1	s_2	Quantity
Current value	3	0	−1	1	12
New pivot-row value	1	0/3	−1/3	1/3	12/3 = 4

$C \rightarrow$		4	5	0	0	
Variables in solution		x_1	x_2	s_1	s_2	**Solution quantity**
5	x_2	1/3	1	1/3	0	4
0	s_2	3	0	−1	1	12
	Z	5/3	5	5/3	0	20
	$C - Z$	7/3	0	−5/3	0	

Table 6S–5

Completed second tableau

C		4	5	0	0	
Variables in solution		x_1	x_2	s_1	s_2	**Solution quantity**
5	x_2	1/3	1	1/3	0	$\dfrac{4}{1/3} = 12$
0	s_2	3	0	−1	1	12/3 = 4 ←Leaving variable is s_2
	Z	5/3	5	5/3	0	20
	$C - Z$	7/3	0	−5/3	0	

↑
Entering variable
is x_1

Table 6S–6

The leaving and entering variables

Figure 6S–10

Graphical analogies to simplex tableaus

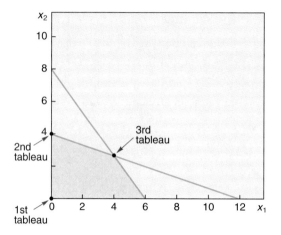

4. Compute values for the x_2 row: Multiply each new pivot-row value by the x_2 row pivot value (i.e., 1/3) and subtract the product from corresponding current values. Thus,

	x_1	x_2	s_1	s_2	Quantity
Current value:	1/3	1	1/3	0	4
$-1/3 \times$ (main row)	$-1/3(1)$	$-1/3(0)$	$-1/3(-1/3)$	$-1/3(1/3)$	$-1/3(4)$
New row value	0	1	4/9	$-1/9$	8/3

At this point, it will be useful to consider the tableaus in relation to a graph of the feasible solution space. This is shown in Figure 6S–10.

5. Compute new Z row values. Note that now variable x_1 has been added to the solution mix; that row's unit profit is $4.

Row	Profit	x_1	x_2	s_1	s_2	Quantity
x_2	$5	5(0)	5(1)	5(4/9)	5(-1/9)	5(8/3)
x_1	$4	4(1)	4(0)	4(-1/3)	4(1/3)	4(4)
New Z row		4	5	8/9	7/9	88/3

6. Compute the $C - Z$ row values:

	x_1	x_2	s_1	s_2
C	4	5	0	0
Z	4	5	8/9	7/9
$C - Z$	0	0	$-8/9$	$-7/9$

The resulting values of the third tableau are shown in Table 6S–7. Note that each of the $C - Z$ values is either 0 or negative, indicating that this is the final solution. The optimal values of x_1 and x_2 are indicated in the quantity column: $x_2 = 8/3$, or 2⅔, and $x_1 = 4$. (The x_2 quantity is in the x_2 row and the x_1 quantity in the x_1 row.) Total profit is 88/3, or 29.33 (quantity column, Z row).

Optimal solution for Example S–1. (DSS-POM [2.1c] will also show intermediate solutions.)

C		4	5	0	0			Table 6S–7
	Variables in solution	x_1	x_2	s_1	s_2	**Solution quantity**		The third tableau contains the optimal solution
5	x_2	0	1	4/9	−1/9	8/3		
4	x_1	1	0	−1/3	1/3	4		
	Z	4	5	8/9	7/9	88/3		
	C − Z	0	0	−8/9	−7/9			

HANDLING ≥ AND = CONSTRAINTS

Up to this point, we have experienced ≤ constraints. Constraints that involve equalities and ≥ constraints are handled in a slightly different way.

When an equality constraint is present, use of the simplex method requires addition of an **artificial variable**. The purpose of such variables is merely to permit development of an initial solution. For example, the equalities

Artificial variable

Variable added when an equality constraint is present, to permit development of an initial solution.

(1) $7x_1 + 4x_2 = 65$
(2) $5x_1 + 3x_2 = 40$

would be rewritten in the following manner using artificial variables a_1 and a_2:

(1) $7x_1 + 4x_2 + 1a_1 + 0a_2 = 65$
(2) $5x_1 + 3x_2 + 0a_1 + 1a_2 = 40$

Slack variables would not be added. The objective function, say, $Z = 2x_1 + 3x_2$, would be rewritten as:

$$Z = 2x_1 + 3x_2 + Ma_1 + Ma_2$$

where

M = A large number (e.g., 999)

Since the artificial variables are not desired in the final solution, selecting a large value of M (much larger than the other objective coefficients) will insure their deletion during the solution process.

For $\geq$ constraints, surplus variables must be *subtracted* instead of added to each constraint. For example, the constraints

(1) $3x_1 + 2x_2 + 4x_3 \geq 80$
(2) $5x_1 + 4x_2 +\ \ x_3 \geq 70$
(3) $2x_1 + 8x_2 + 2x_3 \geq 68$

would be rewritten as equalities:

(1) $3x_1 + 2x_2 + 4x_3 - 1s_1 - 0s_2 - 0s_3 = 80$
(2) $5x_1 + 4x_2 +\ \ x_3 - 0s_1 - 1s_2 - 0s_3 = 70$
(3) $2x_1 + 8x_2 + 2x_3 - 0s_1 - 0s_2 - 1s_3 = 68$

As equalities, each constraint must then be adjusted by inclusion of an artificial variable. The final result looks like this:

(1) $3x_1 + 2x_2 + 4x_3 - 1s_1 - 0s_2 - 0s_3 + 1a_1 + 0a_2 + 0a_3 = 80$
(2) $5x_1 + 4x_2 +\ \ x_3 - 0s_1 - 1s_2 - 0s_3 + 0a_1 + 1a_2 + 0a_3 = 70$
(3) $2x_1 + 8x_2 + 2x_3 - 0s_1 - 0s_2 - 1s_3 + 0a_1 + 0a_2 + 1a_3 = 68$

If the objective function happened to be

$5x_1 + 2x_2 + 7x_3$

it would become

$5x_1 + 2x_2 + 7x_3 + 0s_1 + 0s_2 + 0s_3 + Ma_1 + Ma_2 + Ma_3$

SUMMARY OF MAXIMIZATION PROCEDURE

The main steps in solving a maximization problem with only $\leq$ constraints using the simplex algorithm are these:

1. Set up the initial tableau.
   a. Rewrite the constraints so that they become equalities; add a slack variable to each constraint.
   b. Rewrite the objective function to include the slack variables. Give slack variables coefficients of 0.
   c. Put the objective coefficients and constraint coefficients into tableau form.
   d. Compute values for the Z row; multiply the values in each constraint row by the row's C value. Add the results within each column.
   e. Compute values for the $C - Z$ row.
2. Set up subsequent tableaus.
   a. Determine the entering variable (the largest positive value in the $C - Z$ row). If a tie exists, choose one column arbitrarily.
   b. Determine the leaving variable: Divide each constraint row's solution quantity by the row's pivot value; the smallest positive ratio indicates the leaving variable. If a tie occurs, divide the values in each row by the row pivot value, beginning with slack columns and then other columns, moving from left to right. The leaving variable is indicated by the lowest ratio in the first column with unequal ratios.
   c. Form the new pivot row of the next tableau: Divide each number in the leaving row by the row's pivot value. Enter these values in the next tableau in the same row positions.
   d. Compute new values for remaining constraint rows: For each row, multiply the values in the new pivot row by the constraint row's pivot value,

and subtract the resulting values, column by column, from the original row values. Enter these in the new tableau in the same positions as the original row.

e. Compute values for Z and $C - Z$ rows.

f. Check to see if any values in the $C - Z$ row are positive; if they are, repeat 2a–2f. Otherwise, the optimal solution has been obtained.

MINIMIZATION PROBLEMS

The simplex method handles minimization problems in essentially the same way it handles maximization problems. However, there are a few differences. One is the need to adjust for $\geq$ constraints, which requires both artificial variables and surplus variables. This tends to make manual solution more involved. A second major difference is the test for the optimum: A solution is optimal if there are no *negative* values in the $C - Z$ row.

Solve the following problem for the quantities of x_1 and x_2 that will minimize cost.

Example S–3

$$\begin{aligned} \text{Minimize} \quad & Z = 12x_1 + 10x_2 \\ \text{Subject to} \quad & x_1 + 4x_2 \geq 8 \\ & 3x_1 + 2x_2 \geq 6 \\ & x_1, x_2 \geq 0 \end{aligned}$$

Solution

1. Rewrite the constraints so that they are in the proper form:

   $x_1 + 4x_2 \geq 8$ becomes $x_1 + 4x_2 - 1s_1 - 0s_2 + 1a_1 + 0a_2 = 8$
   $3x_1 + 2x_2 \geq 6$ becomes $3x_1 + 2x_2 - 0s_1 - 1s_2 + 0a_1 + 1a_2 = 6$

2. Rewrite the objective function (coefficients of C row):

   $12x_1 + 10x_2 + 0s_1 + 0s_2 + 999a_1 + 999a_2$

3. Compute values for rows Z and $C - Z$:

C	x_1	x_2	s_1	s_2	a_1	a_2	Quantity
999	1(999)	4(999)	−1(999)	0(999)	1(999)	0(999)	8(999)
999	3(999)	2(999)	0(999)	−1(999)	0(999)	1(999)	6(999)
Z	3,996	5,994	−999	−999	999	999	13,986
$C - Z$	−3,984	−5,984	999	999	0	0	

4. Set up the initial tableau:

C		12	10	0	0	999	999	
	Variables in solution	x_1	x_2	s_1	s_2	a_1	a_2	**Solution quantity**
999	a_1	1	4	−1	0	1	0	8
999	a_2	3	2	0	−1	0	1	6
	Z	3,996	5,994	−999	−999	999	999	13,986
	$C - Z$	−3,984	−5,984	999	999	0	0	

(continued)

5. Find the entering variable (largest negative $C - Z$ value: x_2 column) and leaving variable (smaller of $8/4 = 2$ and $6/2 = 3$; hence, row a_1).

6. Divide each number in the leaving row by the pivot value (4, in this case) to obtain values for the new pivot row of the second tableau:

$$1/4 \quad 4/4 = 1 \quad -1/4 \quad 0/4 \quad 1/4 \quad 0/4 \quad 8/4 = 2$$

7. Compute values for other rows; a_2 is:

	x_1	x_2	s_1	s_2	a_1	a_2	Quantity
Current value	3	2	0	−1	0	1	6
−2 × (new main row)	−2/4	−2	2/4	−0/4	−2/4	−0/4	−4
New row	10/4	0	+2/4	−1	−2/4	1	2

8. Compute a new Z row:

Row	Cost	x_1	x_2	s_1	s_2	a_1	a_2	Quantity
x_2	10	10(1/4)	10(1)	10(−1/4)	10(0)	10(1/4)	10(0)	10(2)
a_2	999	999(10/4)	999(0)	999(2/4)	999(−1)	999(−2/4)	999(1)	999(2)
Z		2,500	10	497	−999	−497	999	2,018

9. Compute the $C - Z$ row:

	x_1	x_2	s_1	s_2	a_1	a_2
C	12	10	0	0	999	999
Z	2,500	10	497	−999	−497	999
$C - Z$	−2,488	0	−497	999	1,496	0

10. Set up the second tableau:

C		12	10	0	0	999	999	
	Variables in solution	x_1	x_2	s_1	s_2	a_1	a_2	Quantity
10	x_2	1/4	1	−1/4	0	1/4	0	2
999	a_2	10/4	0	2/4	−1	−2/4	1	2
	Z	2,500	10	497	−999	−497	999	2,018
	$C - Z$	−2,488	0	−497	999	1,496	0	

11. Repeat the process.
    a. Check for optimality: It is not optimum because of negatives in $C - Z$ row.
    b. Determine the entering variable: The largest negative is in column x_1.
    c. Determine the leaving variable: $2/(1/4) = 8$, $2/(10/4) = 0.8$. Therefore, it is row a_2.
    d. Find new pivot-row value using the pivot value of $10/4$:

    $$1 \quad 0 \quad 0.2 \quad -0.4 \quad -0.2 \quad 0.4 \quad 0.8$$

    e. Determine values for new x_2 row:

    $$0 \quad 1 \quad -0.3 \quad 0.1 \quad 0.3 \quad -0.1 \quad 1.8$$

f. Determine new values for row Z:

Row	Cost	x_1	x_2	s_1	s_2	a_1	a_2	Quantity
x_2	10	10(0)	10(1)	10(−0.3)	10(0.1)	10(0.3)	10(−0.1)	10(1.8)
x_1	12	12(1)	12(0)	12(0.2)	12(−0.4)	12(−0.2)	12(0.4)	12(0.8)
Z		12	10	−0.6	−3.8	0.6	3.8	27.6

g. Determine values for the $C - Z$ row:

	x_1	x_2	s_1	s_2	a_1	a_2
C	12	10	0	0	999	999
Z	12	10	−0.6	−3.8	0.6	3.8
$C - Z$	0	0	0.6	3.8	998.4	995.2

h. Set up the next tableau. Since no $C - Z$ values are negative, the solution is optimal. Hence, $x_1 = 0.8$, $x_2 = 1.8$, and the minimum cost is 27.60.

C		12	10	0	0	999	999	
	Variables in solution	x_1	x_2	s_1	s_2	a_1	a_2	**Quantity**
10	x_2	0	1	−0.3	0.1	0.3	−0.1	1.8
12	x_1	1	0	0.2	−0.4	−0.2	0.4	0.8
	Z	12	10	−0.6	−3.8	0.6	3.8	27.6
	$C - Z$	0	0	0.6	3.8	998.4	995.2	

SENSITIVITY ANALYSIS

A decision maker is often interested in more than the immediate solution to a problem. He or she can benefit from sensitivity analysis of the solution in several ways. In preparing the problem for a linear-programming solution, the decision maker may have used subjective estimates for certain parameters (e.g., the coefficients of the constraints, the coefficients of the objective function, and the right-hand-side values of the constraints). Understandably, the decision maker would want to know how sensitive the optimal solution is to changes in the value of one or more of those parameters. If the solution is relatively insensitive to reasonable changes, the decision maker can feel more confident in implementing the solution. Conversely, if the solution is sensitive to such changes, he or she will undoubtedly want to obtain more precise estimates of the suspect parameters.

A related issue involves a specific change in a parameter. For instance, there may be a price change that would alter a coefficient in the objective function. Similarly, a change in a production process could require a change in a coefficient of one of the constraints. Again, sensitivity analysis could provide the decision maker with the necessary insight.

A third possibility is the question of whether it might be beneficial to obtain larger amounts of certain resources. This question often arises when large amounts of some resources are unused by the optimal solution; by adding more of the other resources, it may be possible to realize a disproportionate increase in the value of the objective function.

Thus, we see that there are a number of reasons that a decision maker might want to pursue sensitivity analysis. We will explore two of these possibilities: a change in an objective function coefficient and a change in the right-hand-side value of a constraint. We will not consider a change in a coefficient of a constraint. Also, the following discussion pertains to *one* change, with all other parameters remaining unchanged. For the procedure where more than one change is of interest, see the last source in the Bibliography at the end of this supplement.

Much of the information needed for sensitivity analysis is contained in the final simplex tableau. That plus the original problem statement will suffice to perform the analysis. Let's see how sensitivity analysis could be applied to the maximization problem that was solved using simplex earlier in this section. That problem and its final tableau are reproduced in Table 6S–8 for easy reference.

First, consider changes to one of the objective function coefficients. Sensitivity analysis will answer this question for a variable in the solution: For what range of values will the solution quantities of all the decision variables remain the same? This is known as the **range of optimality**. Of course, if one of the coefficients of the objective function is changed, the total profit (e.g., 88/3) will change even if the optimal quantities of x_1 and x_2 do not change.

Range of optimality

The range of values for which the solution quantities of all the decision variables remains the same.

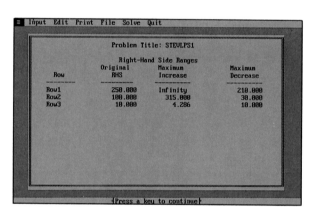

These are the final two DSS-POM (2.1c) screens for Example S–1. Screen 1, the ranges for objective function coefficients. Screen 2, the right-hand-side ranges.

Table 6S–8

Maximize $Z = 4x_1 + 5x_2$
Subject to $x_1 + 3x_2 \leq 12$
             $4x_1 + 3x_2 \leq 24$

C		**4**	**5**	**0**	**0**	
	Variables in solution	x_1	x_2	s_1	s_2	**Solution quantity**
5	x_2	0	1	4/9	−1/9	8/3
4	x_1	1	0	−1/3	1/3	4
	Z	4	5	8/9	7/9	88/3
	$C − Z$	0	0	−8/9	−7/9	

The analysis involves computing a series of ratios using the $C - Z$ row of the final tableau and the row corresponding to the variable whose range of optimality is to be determined. The elements of the bottom row are divided by the corresponding elements of the variable's row. For instance, for variable x_1, the ratios are:

$$\frac{C - Z:}{x_1:} \qquad \frac{0}{1} = 0 \qquad \frac{0}{0} = \text{(undefined)} \qquad \frac{-8/9}{-1/3} = 8/3 \qquad \frac{-7/9}{1/3} = -7/3$$

The positive ratio closest to zero indicates the amount by which the original coefficient of x_1 in the objective function could be increased without changing the optimal solution quantities. Thus, the 4 could be increased by $8/3 = 2.67$ (i.e., to 6.67) and not change the solution. Similarly, the 4 could be decreased by the negative amount closest to zero (i.e., $-7/3 = 2.33$) and not change the solution quantities. Hence, the range of optimality for the x_1 coefficient is:

$$4 - 2.33 \le c_1 \le 4 + 2.67$$

If c_1 remains at 4, the range of optimality for x_2 is determined as follows:

$$\frac{C - Z:}{x_2} \qquad \frac{0}{0} = \text{(undefined)} \qquad \frac{0}{1} = 0 \qquad -\frac{-8/9}{4/9} = -2 \qquad \frac{-7/9}{-1/9} = 7$$

The smallest positive ratio is 7; hence, the original coefficient of 5 can be increased by 7, or up to $5 + 7 = 12$. The negative ratio closest to zero is -2. Hence, the original x_2 coefficient can be decreased by that amount. Therefore, its lower bound is $5 - 2 = 3$. Thus, the range of optimality for c_2 is 3 to 12.

In this example, there are two decision variables, and both are in the solution. In some cases one or more of the decision variables will not be in the solution. In those situations, we talk about the *range of insignificance,* which refers to the range over which that variable will remain out of the solution. In order for that variable to come into the solution, its objective function coefficient would have to increase by an amount greater than the value that appears in row $C - Z$ in this variable's column. For instance, if -4 appeared, the variable's objective function coefficient would have to increase by more than 4 for it to come into the solution. Its range of insignificance would be 0 to 4.

Now let's consider changes to the right-hand side of a constraint. Again, remember that only one constraint is assumed to change; all others remain fixed at their original amounts. First, it should be noted that some constraints are not candidates for change; nothing beneficial would be accomplished by increasing their amounts (assuming a $\le$ constraint). This is the case for constraints that are slack in the final solution, since such constraints are not limiting factors on the problem. Hence, the **range of feasibility** for a slack constraint on the *down* side is equal to its value in the final solution. Thus, if $s_1 = 250$ in the final solution of a problem, the first constraint's right-side original amount can be decreased by that amount and not change the solution. On the *up* side, the right-side value can be increased by any amount and not change the solution; increasing it will merely increase the amount of slack. Note that a constraint that is slack will have a 0 in the $C - Z$ row for the column that corresponds to that slack variable.

If a constraint is a limiting factor, its slack variable will not appear in the final solution. (In some rare instances, a slack variable will appear but have a solution quantity equal to zero. In effect, there is no slack for that constraint even though it appears in the solution.) For slack variables not in the solution, there will be a

Range of feasibility

The range of values for the right-hand side of a constraint over which the shadow price remains the same.

negative value under its column in the $C - Z$ row. These negative amounts are
known as **shadow prices**. They indicate how much a one-unit decrease in the
original amount of a constraint would decrease the final value of the objective
function. Thus, we can see in Table 6S-8 that a one-unit decrease in the first
constraint of that problem would lead to a decrease in the final value of the objective function of $8/9 = 0.89$. Similarly, a decrease of one unit in the second constraint would lead to a decrease in the objective function of $7/9 = 0.78$. Conversely, a one-unit *increase* in one of these values would have the opposite effect: a
one-unit increase in the first constraint would increase the optimal value of the
objective function by 0.89, and a one-unit increase in the second constraint would
lead to an increase of 0.78. The question that can be answered by sensitivity analysis
is this: Over what range of right-side values of a constraint will these shadow prices
remain valid?

To determine the range of feasibility for a constraint, first identify the values in
the body of the final tableau under the column for that constraint's slack variable.
For instance, for s_1 in Table 6S-8, the values are $4/9$ and $-1/3$. Next, divide these
values into the corresponding values in the quantity column. For s_1, the results are:

$$\frac{8/3}{4/9} = +6 \qquad \frac{4}{-1/3} = -12$$

The positive ratio closest to zero indicates the amount by which the original constraint can be *decreased,* and the negative ratio closest to zero indicates the amount by
which the original value of the constraint can be *increased.* In this instance, the first
constraint's original right-side value was 12. It could be decreased by as much as
6 units or increased by as much as 12 units and have an impact of $8/9 = 0.89$ per
unit on the optimal value of the objective function. Similarly, the ratios for s_2 are:

$$\frac{8/3}{-1/9} = -24 \qquad \frac{4}{1/3} = +12$$

Hence, if the first constraint remained unchanged, the second could be increased by
as much as 24 units or decreased by as much as 12 units and have an impact of
$7/9 = 0.79$ per unit on the optimal value of the objective function.

COMPUTER SOLUTIONS

The simplex procedure provides an all-purpose method for solving linear-programming problems. Unfortunately, for all but the smallest problems, the computational
burden imposed by the simplex procedure is considerable. This is true even for
problems that are moderate in size; for larger problems, manual computations
would require a herculean effort for solution. Fortunately, standard computer
packages for solving linear programming problems using simplex are widely available. In practice, they are used almost exclusively in lieu of manual computations.
Therefore, computer solutions represent the most realistic avenue for handling LP
problems.

One of the most widely used linear-programming packages is **LINDO**. Developed by Linus Schrage of the University of Chicago, it is available in both main-
frame and personal computer versions. Also, there are many other packages available for mainframes and personal computers. Although these packages have a high
degree of similarity in terms of input and output, they do have minor differences.
Therefore, rather than describe a particular package, the discussion here will present

a generic overview of how computers are used to obtain solutions to linear programming models.

Consider this LP model:

Maximize $60x_1 + 50x_2$
Subject to $4x_1 + 10x_2 \leq 100$
             $2x_1 + x_2 \leq 22$
             $3x_1 + 3x_2 \leq 39$
             $x_1, x_2 \geq 0$

The problem, as input into the computer, would look something like this:

```
MAX 60X1 + 50X2
ST
        4X1 + 10X2 < = 100
        2X1 + X2 < = 22
        3X1 + 3X2 < = 39
```

(Caps for letters may or may not be required. If not, the first constraint would look like this: $4x1 + 10x2 < =100$.) Note the key differences between this input and our basic model:

1. Two keystrokes are used for the $\leq$ constraints. (Some programs treat $<$ as equivalent of $\leq$ and require only a single keystroke.)
2. The nonnegative constraints are not needed; they are automatically assumed by the computer code (program).
3. Slack and surplus variables are not used; the computer uses them automatically, as needed.
4. Although this particular model does not involve any coefficients expressed as fractions (e.g., $\frac{1}{2}x_1, \frac{1}{4}x_2$), fractions are not allowed. Instead, all coefficients must be integers or decimals (e.g., $.5x_1, 2.5x_2$).

Often, users have the option of choosing the type of output they want. One option is to be given all of the tableaus; another is to be given only the final tableau; and still another is to be given only the final solution. Beyond that, most programs provide additional information on sensitivity analysis.

Table 6S-9 presents an example of how the computer output might appear for the preceding LP model. The output shows the optimal values of the variables and

---

Table 6S-9

Sample computer output

```
AFTER 2 ITERATIONS
THIS SOLUTION IS OPTIMAL:

VARIABLE        QUANTITY
   S1              24
   X1               9
   X2               4

OPTIMAL Z    =     740

VARIABLE      REDUCED COST
   X1              0
   X2              0

              DUAL PRICE
   S1              0
   S2            −10
   S3            −13.33
```

Table 6S–10

A second sample of
computer output

LP OPTIMUM FOUND AT STEP 3

OBJECTIVE FUNCTION VALUE

1)   740.000

VARIABLE	VALUE	REDUCED COST
X1	9.00000	0.00000
X2	4.00000	0.00000

ROW	SLACK OR SURPLUS	DUAL PRICES
2)	24.00000	0.00000
3)	0.00000	10.00000
4)	0.00000	13.33334

the optimal value of the objective function. The terms *reduced cost* and *dual price* will be explained later in this section.

However, the numbers are those that appear in the $C - Z$ row of the final tableau.

A slightly different version of computer output is shown in Table 6S-10. Aside from a slightly different format, the main difference between the two sets of output is that one program reports the dual prices as negative amounts, and the other reports them as positives.

Computer packages generally have the capability of providing individual tableaus in addition to providing the optimal solution. For instance, a LINDO printout of the tableaus would appear as follows:

```
MAX       60 X1 + 50 X2
SUBJECT TO
    2)    4 X1 + 10 X2 <= 100
    3)    2 X1 +  X2 <= 22
    4)    3 X1 + 3 X2 <= 39
END

THE TABLEAU

ROW  (BASIS)       X1        X2   SLK   2   SLK     3  SLK     4
  1 ART         -60.000   -50.000   0.000     0.000     0.000     0.000
  2 SLK    2      4.000    10.000   1.000     0.000     0.000   100.000
  3 SLK    3      2.000     1.000   0.000     1.000     0.000    22.000
  4 SLK    4      3.000     3.000   0.000     0.000     1.000    39.000

        X1 ENTERS AT VALUE   11.000     IN ROW   3 OBJ. VALUE =  660.00

THE TABLEAU
ROW (BASIS)        X1        X2   SLK   2   SLK     3  SLK     4
  1 ART           0.000   -20.000   0.000    30.000     0.000   660.000
  2 SLK    2      0.000     8.000   1.000    -2.000     0.000    56.000
  3        X1     1.000     0.500   0.000     0.500     0.000    11.000
  4 SLK    4      0.000     1.500   0.000    -1.500     1.000     6.000

        X2 ENTERS AT VALUE   4.0000     IN ROW   4 OBJ. VALUE =  740.00
```

```
THE TABLEAU
ROW   (BASIS)        X1        X2   SLK   2   SLK    3   SLK    4
  1 ART            0.000     0.000   0.000   10.000    13.333   740.000
  2 SLK     2      0.000     0.000   1.000    6.000    -5.333    24.000
  3         X1     1.000     0.000   0.000    1.000    -0.333     9.000
  4         X2     0.000     1.000   0.000   -1.000     0.667     4.000

      LP OPTIMUM FOUND AT STEP        2
          OBJECTIVE FUNCTION VALUE
  1)          740.000000

  VARIABLE          VALUE        REDUCED COST
        X1        9.000000         0.000000
        X2        4.000000         0.000000

  ROW          SLACK OR SURPLUS     DUALPRICES
      2)          24.000000          0.000000
      3)           0.000000         10.000000
      4)           0.000000         13.333333

  NO. INTERATIONS =  2
```

The output is somewhat self-explanatory, with the addition of a few comments. The top row of each tableau has the label ART. This stands for *artificial,* and the values in the row are the negative of what ordinarily appears in the bottom row of a tableau. Thus, in the last tableau 10.000 and 13.333 appear in the top row, and in Table 6S–9 these appear as negatives. Hence, the top row is $Z - C$ rather than $C - Z$. Note, too, that row Z does not appear at all. Finally, SLK refers to a slack variable. However, LINDO begins numbering with the top row, so s_1 is labeled SLK 2, s_2 is SLK 3, and so on. Also, the spacing along the top labels is such that the number of each slack variable appears directly over the appropriate column, but its label is shifted a bit to the left. Thus, the third column is SLK 2.

Computers handle linear programming problems with such ease, speed, and accuracy that you may wonder why you should even learn how to solve problems manually. Actually, there are several good reasons for learning the manual approach. One is to gain insight into how solutions are generated. Without this knowledge, the computer becomes a black box that mysteriously comes up with solutions. People who use computers under those circumstances rarely fare as well as those who possess a basic understanding of the underlying process, both in formulating problems and in understanding the results. Solving a small number of manageable problems manually can provide valuable insight that is not easily obtained another way. In addition, the opportunity to sharpen quantitative skills is important; the world of information is becoming increasingly quantitative, and those who have the ability to deal with it in a confident manner are less likely to be intimidated either by quantitative information or by computers. Still another reason to learn manual solution is that other techniques for solving linear programming problems use procedures that are very similar to some of those used in simplex. Consequently, learning and understanding those techniques is easier after exposure to the simplex procedure.

Manual calculations for sensitivity analysis problems yield a tremendous amount of insight into sensitivity analysis. Nonetheless, as a practical matter, the speed and accuracy delivered by a computer solution makes that the preferred approach for solving real problems. Moreover, most computer packages either automatically include sensitivity analysis or provide the option of obtaining that information in addition to the optimal solution. Although various software packages differ in how they present the results, these differences usually are minor; all packages present much the same general information.

With that in mind, let us consider a sample of computer output. Table 6S–11 repeats the final tableau of the preceding LP solution for reference, and Table 6S–12 illustrates a computer printout of sensitivity analysis of the microcomputer problem.

Table 6S–11

Final tableau

C			60	50	0	0	0	
Variables in solution			x_1	x_2	s_1	s_2	s_3	**Solution quantity**
0	s_1		0	0	1	6	$-40/3$	24
60	x_1		1	0	0	1	$-1/3$	9
50	x_2		0	1	0	-1	$2/3$	4
	Z		60	50	0	10	$40/3$	740
	$C - Z$		0	0	0	-10	$-40/3$	

Table 6S–12

Computer printout of sensitivity analysis

```
MAX 60X1 + 50X2

SUBJECT TO
2)   4X1 + 10X2 ≤ 100
3)   2X1 + X2 ≤ 22
4)   3X1 + 3X2 ≤ 39
END

    LP OPTIMUM FOUND AT STEP   3
         OBJECTIVE FUNCTION VALUE
             740.00

    VARIABLE          VALUE         REDUCED COSTS
          X1          9.00              0.00
          X2          4.00              0.00

    ROW         SLACK OR SURPLUS    DUAL PRICES
          2          24.00              0.00
          3           0.00             10.00
          4           0.00             13.33
         SENSITIVITY ANALYSIS
             OBJECTIVE COEFFICIENT RANGES
    VARIABLE    CURRENT    ALLOWABLE    ALLOWABLE
                VALUE      INCREASE     DECREASE
    X1          60.00       40.00        10.00
    X2          50.00       10.00        20.00

             RIGHT-HAND SIDE RANGES
    ROW         CURRENT    ALLOWABLE    ALLOWABLE
                VALUE      INCREASE     DECREASE
    2          100.000     INFINITY      24.00
    3           22.00        4.00         4.00
    4           39.00        4.50         6.00
```

The printout begins with the original problem and the optimal values of the variables. The optimal values of the decision variables are given first, under the VARIABLE heading, followed by the optimal values of the slack variables, which are listed under the ROW heading. Just to the right of the optimal values of the decision variables are reduced costs, and to the right of the optimal slack values are dual prices. Here, row 2 refers to s_1, row 3 refers to s_2, and row 4 refers to s_3. The dual prices are equal to the values in row $C - Z$ of the final tableau (see Table 6S–11). Recall that for variables that are in the solution, the $C - Z$ values will be equal to zero. A nonzero reduced cost, then, would appear if a decision variable was not in the solution; that nonzero reduced cost would indicate the amount by which the variable's objective function coefficient could be increased without it coming into the solution. Thus, if a reduced cost was 2.00, that variable's objective function would have to be increased by more than 2.00 in order for it to be in the solution if the problem were to be reworked with that one change.

The dual prices are the shadow prices for the slack or surplus variables (slack variables in this case).

In the remaining portion of the printout, sensitivity analysis results are shown. First, the objective coefficient ranges (ranges of optimality) are shown, followed by the right-hand-side ranges (ranges of feasibility). For each decision variable, CURRENT VALUE refers to its objective function coefficient; the next column indicates the amount of possible increase and the next column the amount of possible decrease that will result in the same optimal values of the variables that are in the solution. For the right-side ranges, the slack variables are listed (actually, row 2 refers here to s_1, row 3 to s_2, and row 4 to s_3). CURRENT VALUE refers to the original right-side values of the constraints. The next two columns show the amount by which the right side of a constraint can be changed and still be within the range of feasibility.

SOLVED PROBLEMS

Problem

1. A small construction firm specializes in building and selling single-family homes. The firm offers two basic types of houses, model A and model B. Model A houses require 4,000 labor hours, 2 tons of stone, and 2,000 board feet of lumber. Model B houses require 10,000 labor hours, 3 tons of stone, and 2,000 board feet of lumber. Due to long lead times for order-

ing supplies and the scarcity of skilled and semiskilled workers in the area, the firm will be forced to rely on its present resources for the upcoming building season. It has 400,000 hours of labor, 150 tons of stone, and 200,000 board feet of lumber. What mix of model A and B houses should the firm construct if model As yield a profit of $1,000 per unit and model Bs yield $2,000 per unit? Assume that the firm will be able to sell all the units it builds.

Solution

a.   Formulate the objective function and constraints.[3]

Maximize $Z = 1,000A + 2,000B$
Subject to
Labor $4,000A + 10,000B \le 400,000$ labor hours
Stone $2A + 3B \le 150$ tons
Lumber $2,000A + 2,000B \le 200,000$ board feet
                                $A, B \ge 0$

b.   Graph the constraints and objective function, and identify the optimum corner point (see graph). Note that the lumber constraint is *redundant:* it does not form a boundary of the feasible solution space.

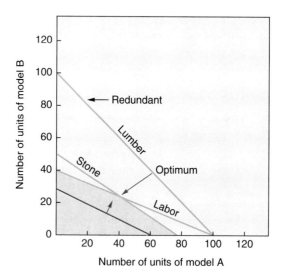

c.   Determine the optimal quantities of models A and B, and compute the resulting profit. Since the optimum point is at the intersection of the stone and labor constraints, we solve those two equations for their common point.

---

[3] For the sake of consistency, we will assign to the horizontal axis the first decision variable mentioned in the problem. Hence, in this case, variable A will be represented on the horizontal axis and variable B on the vertical axis.

$$\text{Labor} \quad 4{,}000A + 10{,}000B = 400{,}000$$
$$\underline{-2{,}000 \times (\text{Stone} \quad 2A + \quad 3B = \quad 150)}$$
$$4{,}000B = 100{,}000$$
$$B = \quad 25$$

Substitute $B = 25$ in one of the equations, and solve for A:

$$2A + 3(25) = 150 \qquad A = 37.5$$

Problem

2. Solve the following problem using graphical linear programming:

$$\begin{aligned}
\text{Maximize} \quad & Z = 12x_1 + 6x_2 \\
\text{Subject to} \quad & (1) \ \ 2x_1 + 4x_2 \le 16 \\
& (2) \ \ 5x_1 + 3x_2 \ge 15 \\
& (3) \ \ x_1 \qquad\quad \le 5 \\
& \qquad x_1, \, x_2 \ge 0
\end{aligned}$$

Solution

a. Plot constraints, shade in the feasible solution space, and plot the objective function (see graph).

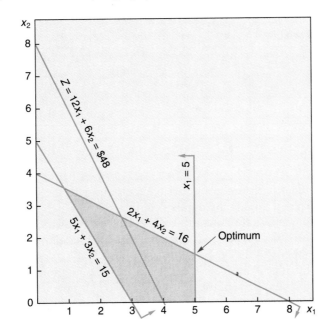

b. It is apparent from the graph that $x_1 = 5$ at the optimum. To determine the value of x_2, substitute $x_1 = 5$ in the equation $2x_1 + 4x_2 = 16$, and solve for x_2:

$$2(5) + 4x_2 = 16 \qquad x_2 = 1.5$$

c. Compute the value of the objective function at $x_1 = 5$, $x_2 = 1.5$:

$$Z_{\text{max}} = \$12(5) + \$6(1.5) = \$69$$

Problem

3. Solve the following problem for the quantities of x, y, and w that will maximize the objective function.

Maximize $Z = 20x + 16y + 10w$
Subject to   (1) $4x + 2y + 3w \leq 120$
             (2) $5x + 4y + 2w \leq 100$
             (3) $2x + 3y + 3w \leq 90$
                        $x, y, w \geq 0$

Solution

a. Start by rewriting the constraints as equalities using slack variables:

   (1) $4x + 2y + 3w + 1s_1 + 0s_2 + 0s_3 = 120$
   (2) $5x + 4y + 2w + 0s_1 + 1s_2 + 0s_3 = 100$
   (3) $2x + 3y + 3w + 0s_1 + 0s_2 + 1s_3 = 90$

b. Next, develop the initial tableau:

Tableau 1

C		20	16	10	0	0	0	
	Variable	x	y	w	s_1	s_2	s_3	Quantity
0	s_1	4	2	3	1	0	0	120
0	s_2	5	4	2	0	1	0	100
0	s_3	2	3	3	0	0	1	90
	Z	0	0	0	0	0	0	0
	C − Z	20	16	10	0	0	0	

c. Identify the entering variable (column with the largest *positive C − Z* value). Divide the numbers in that column (i.e., 4, 5, and 2) into their respective row quantities. The smallest resultant indicates the leaving variable. Hence, x is the entering variable, and s_2 is the leaving variable.

d. Divide all numbers in the s_2 row by the pivot number (i.e., 5) to obtain the pivot row of the next tableau. To compute new s_1 and s_3 rows, use the pivot number for each row (e.g., 4 for s_1 row) to multiply each pivot-row value, and subtract the resulting values from the corresponding values of the previous tableau.

e. Compute values for the Z and $C − Z$ rows.

f. If the $C − Z$ row values are all negative or zero, the optimal solution has been found. If any positive values appear, repeat steps *c–e*.

g. The second and third tableaus are as follows. The optimal quantities are $x = 10.91$, $y = 0$, and $w = 22.73$. The corresponding value of the objective function with those quantities is 445.46. In addition, note that constraints 2 and 3 have been fully used, but 8.18 of constraint 1 remains.

Tableau 2

C		20	16	10	0	0	0	
	Variable	x	y	w	s_1	s_2	s_3	Quantity
0	s_1	0.0	−1.2	1.4	1.0	−0.8	0.0	40.0
20	x	1.0	0.8	0.4	0.0	0.2	0.0	20.0
0	s_3	0.0	1.4	2.2	0.0	−0.4	1.0	50.0
	Z	20.0	16.0	8.0	0.0	4.0	0.0	400.0
	$C − Z$	0.0	0.0	2.0	0.0	−4.0	0.0	

Tableau 3

C		20	16	10	0	0	0	
	Variable	x	y	w	s_1	s_2	s_3	Quantity
0	s_1	0.0	−2.09	0.0	1.0	−0.55	−0.64	8.18
20	x	1.0	0.55	0.0	0.0	0.27	−0.18	10.91
10	w	0.0	0.64	1.0	0.0	−0.18	0.45	22.73
	Z	20.0	17.27	10.0	0.0	3.64	0.91	445.46
	$C − Z$	0.0	−1.27	0.0	0.0	−3.64	−0.91	

Problem

4. Given the third tableau of the preceding problem, perform sensitivity analysis. Specifically, do the following:
   a. Determine the range of insignificance of variable y.
   b. Determine the range of optimality for the coefficient of variable x.
   c. Determine the range of feasibility for the third constraint.
   d. If the third constraint can be increased at a cost of $.20 per unit and 200 units are available, how many should the firm purchase?

Solution

a. The value of −1.27 for the y column in row $C − Z$ indicates that the unit contribution of y in the objective function would have to increase by more than $1.27 in order for it to come into solution. Its range of insignificance is $0 to $17.27.

b. Dividing the values in row $C − Z$ by the values in row x produces these ratios:

$$\frac{x}{1.0} = 0 \qquad \frac{y}{0.55} = -2.31 \qquad \frac{w}{0.0} = \text{und.} \qquad \frac{s_1}{0.0} = \text{und.}$$
$$\frac{0.0}{1.0} = 0 \qquad \frac{-1.27}{0.55} = -2.31 \qquad \frac{0.0}{0.0} = \text{und.} \qquad \frac{0.0}{0.0} = \text{und.}$$

$$\frac{s_2}{0.27} = -13.5 \qquad \frac{s_3}{-0.18} = +5.06$$
$$\frac{-3.64}{0.27} = -13.5 \qquad \frac{-0.91}{-0.18} = +5.06$$

The smallest positive ratio is 5.06, and the negative ratio closest to zero is -2.31. Hence, the coefficient of x of \$20 can be decreased by as much as \$2.31 and increased by as much as \$5.06 and not affect the optimal solution quantities; its range of optimality is \$17.69 to \$25.06.

c. First, divide the values in the quantity column by the corresponding values in the s_3 column since we are interested in the third constraint. The ratios are:

$$\frac{8.18}{-0.64} = -12.78$$

$$\frac{10.91}{-0.18} = -60.61$$

$$\frac{22.73}{0.45} = 50.51$$

The smallest positive ratio indicates the amount by which the right-hand side can be decreased, and the negative ratio closest to zero (i.e., -12.78) indicates the maximum amount of increase. Hence, the range of feasibility for the third constraint is (using the original right-hand-side value of 90):

$$90 - 50.51 = 39.49 \text{ to } 90 + 12.78 = 102.78$$

d. The shadow price of the third slack variable is -0.91, which means an increase of \$.91 in the value of the objective function for each unit of increase in the third constraint's right-side value *up to the upper end of the range of feasibility*. Since the cost to acquire additional units is \$.20 each, the net increase will be $+\$.71$ per unit. Thus, acquire as many units as possible. In part *c* we found that an increase of 12.78 units was possible. Thus, acquire that amount. Note that beyond that point, the shadow price will change, so additional units of this constraint might just add to slack; another constraint would become binding (limiting) on the solution.

DISCUSSION AND REVIEW QUESTIONS

1. For which decision environment is linear programming most suited?
2. What is meant by the term *feasible solution space?* What determines this region?
3. In graphical linear programming problems, what is the upper limit on the number of:
    a. Variables in a problem?
    b. Constraints in a problem?
4. What is an isocost line? An isoprofit line?
5. What does sliding an objective function line toward the origin represent? Away?
6. In the simplex technique, how is the entering variable determined for a maximization problem? How is the leaving variable determined?
7. With what aspect of a graphical solution does a simplex tableau correspond? To what does the initial tableau correspond?
8. In what direction does the second solution move away from the initial solution in a two-variable problem?

9. After the optimal solution has been obtained, it is possible to consider acquisition of additional scarce resources in a maximization problem. How does one determine:
    a. If it is worthwhile to add a given resource?
    b. The change in the value of the objective function for a change within the feasible range?

10. Explain what is meant by the terms *slack variable* and *artificial variable*.

11. What mix of surplus, slack, and artificial variables is used in each of the following constraints?
    a. $\leq$ b. $=$ c. $\geq$

12. Is there any theoretical limit to the number of decision variables that can be handled by the simplex method?

13. How are the numbers in the $C - Z$ row in slack columns interpreted?

14. At what point does it become apparent that a tableau contains the optimal solution in a maximization problem?

PROBLEMS

1. Solve for the optimal quantities using graphical linear programming:
    a. Maximize $Z = 10x_1 + 20x_2$ (profit)
        Subject to
        Cutting $5x_1 + 2x_2 \leq 40$ labor hours
        Sewing $4x_1 + 4x_2 \leq 48$ labor hours
                    $x_1, x_2 \geq 0$
    b. Maximize $Z = 6A + 3B$ (revenue)
        Subject to
        Material $20A + 5B \leq 600$ lb.
        Machinery $25A + 20B \leq 1,000$ hr.
        Labor $20A + 30B \leq 1,200$ hr.
                        $A, B \geq 0$

2. Use graphical linear programming to determine the quantities that will minimize cost:

    a. Minimize $Z = 1.80S + 2.20T$
        Subject to
        Potassium $5S + 8T \geq 200$ gr.
        Carbohydrate $15S + 6T \geq 240$ gr.
        Protein $4S + 12T \geq 180$ gr.
        T $T \geq 10$ gr.
                            $S, T \geq 0$
    b. Minimize $Z = 1.50C + 1.20D$
        Subject to   (1) $-8C + 4D \leq 104$
                        (2) $30C + 5D \geq 210$
                        (3) $7C + 7D \geq 133$
                             $C, D \geq 0$

3. An appliance manufacturer produces two models of microwave ovens: H and W. Both models require fabrication and assembly work; each H uses four hours of fabrication and two hours of assembly, and each W uses two hours of fabrication and six hours of assembly. There are 600 fabrication hours available this week and 480 hours of assembly. Each H contributes $40 to profits, and each W contributes $30 to profits. What mix of H and W will maximize profits?

4. A small candy shop is preparing for the holiday season. The owner must decide how many bags of deluxe mix and how many bags of standard mix of Peanut/Raisin Delite to put up. The deluxe mix has ⅔ pound raisins and ⅓ pound peanuts, and the standard

mix has ½ pound raisins and ½ pound peanuts per bag. The shop has 90 pounds of raisins and 60 pounds of peanuts to work with.

Peanuts cost $.60 per pound and raisins cost $1.50 per pound. The deluxe mix will sell for $2.90 per pound, and the standard mix will sell for $2.55 per pound. The owner estimates that no more than 110 bags of one type can be sold.

If the goal is to maximize *profits,* how many bags of each type should be prepared? What is the expected profit?

5. A firm produces cast-iron parts that require three basic operations: casting, grinding, and drilling. Available time for casting is 36,000 minutes; for grinding, 2,250 minutes; and for drilling, 3,600 minutes per week. Two products, x and y, require these operations. Product x requires 80 minutes for casting, 2.5 minutes for grinding, and 9 minutes for drilling per unit. Product y requires 60 minutes for casting, 4.5 minutes for grinding, and 4 minutes for drilling per unit. Each unit of x contributes $4 to profits, and each unit of y contributes $2. What combination of x and y will maximize profits on a weekly basis?

6. A retired couple supplement their income by making fruit pies, which they sell to a local grocery store. During the month of September they produce apple and grape pies. The apple pies are sold for $1.50 to the grocer, and the grape pies are sold for $1.20. The couple is able to sell all of the pies they produce due to the high quality they maintain. They follow a policy, for instance, of always using fresh ingredients. Flour and sugar are purchased once each month. For the month of September, they have 1,200 cups of sugar and 2,100 cups of flour. Each apple pie requires 1½ cups of sugar and 3 cups of flour, and each grape pie requires 2 cups of sugar and 3 cups of flour. Determine the number of grape and number of apple pies that will maximize revenues if the couple working together can make an apple pie in six minutes and a grape pie in three minutes. They plan to work no more than 60 hours. In addition, determine the amounts of sugar and/or flour that will be unused.

7. Solve Problem 1*a* using simplex.

8. Solve Problem 1*b* using simplex, and then determine the following:
   a. The range of feasibility for each constraint.
   b. The range of optimality or insignificance, whichever is appropriate, for the coefficients of the objective function.

9. Solve Problem 3 using simplex, and interpret your answer. Then:
   a. Find the range of feasibility for each constraint, and interpret your answers.
   b. Determine the range of insignificance or optimality, whichever is appropriate, for each coefficient of the objective function. Interpret your results.

10. Repeat the preceding procedure for Problem 5.

11. Given this information:

Maximize	$Z = 10.50x + 11.75y + 10.80z$
Subject to	
Cutting	$5x + 12y + 8z \leq 1,400$ minutes
Stapling	$7x + 9y + 9z \leq 1,250$ minutes
Wrapping	$4x + 3y + 6z \leq 720$ minutes
	$x, y, z \geq 0$

   a. Solve for the quantities of products x, y, and z that will maximize revenue.
   b. Follow the instructions in parts *a* and *b* of Problem 9 for this problem.

12. A small firm makes three similar products, which all follow the same three-step process, consisting of milling, inspection, and drilling. Product a requires 12 minutes of milling, 5 minutes for inspection, and 10 minutes of drilling per unit; product b requires 10 minutes of milling, 4 minutes for inspection, and 8 minutes of drilling per unit; and product c requires 8 minutes of milling, 4 minutes for inspection, and 16 minutes of drilling. The department has 20 hours available during the next period for milling, 15 hours for inspection, and 24 hours for drilling. Product a contributes $2.40

per unit to profit, b contributes \$2.50 per unit, and c contributes \$3.00 per unit. Use the simplex method to determine the optimal mix of products in terms of maximizing contribution to profits for the period. Then, find the range of optimality or insignificance, whichever is appropriate, for the profit coefficient of each variable.

13. Use the simplex method to solve these problems:

    a.   Minimize $Z = 21x_1 + 18x_2$
          Subject to

$$(1)\ 5x_1 + 10x_2 \geq 100$$
$$(2)\ 2x_1 + \ \ 1x_2 \geq 10$$
$$x_1, x_2 \geq 0$$

    b.   Minimize $Z = 2x + 5y + 3z$
          Subject to

$$(1)\ 16x + 10y + 18z \geq 340$$
$$(2)\ 11x + 12y + 13z \geq 300$$
$$(3)\ \ \ 2x + \ \ 6y + \ \ 5z \geq 120$$
$$x, y, z \geq 0$$

14. Determine the combination of variables x_1, x_2, x_3, and x_4 that will maximize profits given this LP model:

Maximize $Z = 34x_1 + 18x_2 + 27x_3 + 40x_4$
Subject to

Labor	$x_1 + \ x_2 + \ x_3 + \ x_4 \leq 4{,}000$	
Product 4	$x_4 \geq \ \ 500$	
Machine	$2x_1 + \ x_2 + 3x_3 \ \ \leq 4{,}200$	
Material A	$4x_2 \ + 3x_4 \leq 2{,}000$	
Material B	$x_1 + \ x_2 \ + 2x_4 \leq 2{,}300$	
	$x_1, x_2, x_3, x_4 \geq 0$	

15. Find the combination of A, B, C, D, and E that will maximize revenues given the following information:

Maximize $Z = 1.50A + 2.10B + 3.00C$
                      $+ 1.40D + 1.80E$

Subject to
$$(1)\ \ \ 2A + 8B \ \ \ \ \ \ \ + \ \ D \ \ \ \ \ \ \ \ \leq 220$$
$$(2)\ \ \ \ \ A \ \ \ \ \ \ + 3C \ \ \ \ \ \ \ + \ \ E \leq 140$$
$$(3)\ \ \ \ \ \ \ \ \ \ \ 4B \ \ \ \ \ \ + 3D + 2E \leq 150$$
$$(4)\ \ \ 5A + 2B + \ \ C \ \ \ \ \ \ \ + 3E \leq 185$$
$$(5)\ \ \ \ \ A + \ \ B + \ \ C + \ \ D + \ \ E \leq \ \ 50$$
$$(6)\ C \ \ \ \ \ \ \ \ \ \ \ \ \ \ \ \ \leq \ \ 10$$
$$A, B, C, D, E \geq 0$$

16. A wood products firm uses leftover time at the end of each week to make goods for stock. Currently, there are two products on the list of items that are produced for stock: a chopping board and a knife holder. Both items require three operations: cutting, gluing, and finishing. The manager of the firm has collected the following data on these products:

		Time per unit (minutes)		
Item	**Profit/unit**	**Cutting**	**Gluing**	**Finishing**
Chopping board	\$2	1.4	5	12
Knife holder	\$6	0.8	13	3

The manager has also determined that, during each week, 56 minutes are available for cutting, 650 minutes are available for gluing, and 360 minutes are available for finishing.

a. Determine the optimal quantities of the decision variables.

b. Which resources are not completely used by your solution? How much of each resource is unused?

17. A dietitian has been asked by the athletic director of a university to develop a snack that athletes can use in their training programs. The dietitian intends to mix two separate products together to make the snack. The following information has been obtained by the dietitian:

Nutrient	Minimum amount required (gr.)	Contribution per ounce (gr.)	
		Product A	Product B
Carbohydrates	20	2	5
Protein	12	6	1
Calories	450	90	50

Product A costs $.20 per ounce, and product B costs $.10 per ounce.

a. Determine the optimal quantities of the two products for cost minimization. What is the cost per snack?

b. Are any requirements exceeded? If so, which ones, and by how much?

18. The manager of the deli section of a grocery superstore has just learned that the department has 112 pounds of mayonnaise, of which 70 pounds is approaching its expiration date and must be used. In order to use up the mayonnaise, the manager has decided to prepare two items: a ham spread and a deli spread. Each pan of the ham spread will require 1.4 pounds of the mayonnaise, and each pan of the deli spread will require 1.0 pound. The manager has received an order for 10 pans of ham spread and 8 pans of the deli spread. In addition, the manager has decided to have at least 10 pans of each spread available for sale. Both spreads will cost $3 per pan to make, but ham spread sells for $5 per pan and deli spread sells for $7 per pan.

a. Determine the solution that will minimize cost.

b. Determine the solution that will maximize profit.

19. An advertising firm often uses linear programming to determine an optimal allocation of advertising budgets. Recently, a client asked for a plan that would allocate a $12,000 budget among radio, TV, and newspaper advertisements with the stipulation that no more than 40 percent of the budget be allocated to any one medium. The client wanted a plan that would maximize the effectiveness of advertisements.

The advertising firm did some research that yielded an effectiveness index for each medium and also determined the cost for an ad for each medium, as shown:

Medium	Effectiveness	Cost per ad
Radio	2.4	$200
TV	3.2	400
Newspaper	1.6	300

Determine the number of ads in each medium in order to maximize effectiveness.

20. The owner of a business that makes and sells wood products intends to expand the work schedule by one-half day each week and wants to optimize the use of that additional time. The firm makes five different items: a chair, a table, a desk, a bookcase, and

a food serving cart. The respective profits per units are $16, $30, $40, $42, and $32. The products require essentially the same basic operations: cutting, sanding and finishing, and assembly. The times for these operations differ for the various items. However, the times are fairly standard. They are shown in the following table:

	Time (minutes) per operation		
Item	Cutting	Sanding and finishing	Assembly
Chair	8	12	4
Table	6	10	3
Desk	9	15	5
Bookcase	9	12	4
Food cart	12	8	6

There are 320 minutes available for cutting, 400 for sanding and finishing, and 270 for assembling. What combination of products should be produced in the additional period each week in order to maximize profits? What will the total profit be?

21. A chocolate maker has contracted to operate a small candy counter in a fashionable store. To start with, the selection of offerings will be intentionally limited. The counter will offer a regular mix of candy made up of equal parts of cashews, raisins, caramels, and chocolates, and a deluxe mix that is one-half cashews and one-half chocolates. These will be sold in one-pound boxes. In addition, the candy counter will offer individual one-pound boxes of cashews, raisins, caramels, and chocolates.

A major attraction of the candy counter is that all candies are made fresh right at the counter. However, there is limited storage space for supplies and ingredients. Bins are available that can hold the amounts shown in the table:

Ingredient	Capacity (pounds per day)
Cashews	120
Raisins	200
Caramels	100
Chocolates	160

In order to present a good image and to encourage purchases, the counter will make at least 20 boxes of each type of product each day. Any leftover boxes at the end of the day will be removed and given to a nearby nursing home for goodwill.

The profit per box for the various items has been determined as follows:

Item	Profit per box
Regular	$.80
Deluxe	.90
Cashews	.70
Raisins	.60
Caramels	.50
Chocolates	.75

a. Formulate the LP model.
b. Solve for the optimal values of the decision variables and the maximum profit.

22. Given the following model:

x_1 = Quantity of Regular Blend
x_2 = Quantity of Extra Blend
x_3 = Quantity of Puppy Delite

Maximize $0.20x_1 + 0.18x_2 + 0.25x_3$
Subject to
  K9 $\frac{1}{3}x_1 + \frac{1}{2}x_2 \le 1,500$ lbs.
  K8 $\frac{1}{3}x_1 + \frac{1}{4}x_2 + \frac{1}{10}x_3 \le 1,000$ lbs.
  K1 $\frac{1}{3}x_1 + \frac{1}{4}x_2 + \frac{9}{10}x_3 \le 1,000$ lbs.
      $x_1, x_2, x_3 \ge 0$

Final Tableau

C		0.20	0.18	0.25	0	0	0	
	Variables	x_1	x_2	x_3	s_1	s_2	s_3	**Quantity**
0.18	x_2	0	1	−3.6	4	0	−4	2,000
0	s_2	0	0	−0.8	0	1	−1	0
0.20	x_1	1	0	5.4	−3	0	6	1,500
	Z	0.2	0.18	0.432	0.12	0	0.48	660
	$C - Z$	0	0	−0.182	−0.12	0	−0.48	

The final tableau is shown above.
a. What is the marginal value of a pound of K9? Over what range is the value valid?
b. By how much would profit decrease if there was one less pound of K1 available?
c. The manager believes it is possible to increase the profit per pound of Puppy Delite to $.40. Would that alter the optimal solution? Explain.
d. If the profit per unit of the Extra Blend dropped to $.16 a pound, would the optimal quantities of the variables in solution change? Would the optimal value of the objective function change? If so, what would its new value be?

23. A garden store prepares various grades of pine bark for mulch: nuggets (x_1), mini-nuggets (x_2), and chips (x_3). The process requires pine bark, machine time, labor time, and storage space. The following model has been developed.

Maximize $9x_1 + 9x_2 + 6x_3$ (profit)
Subject to
  Bark $5x_1 + 6x_2 + 3x_3 \le 600$ pounds
  Machine $2x_1 + 4x_2 + 5x_3 \le 660$ minutes
  Labor $2x_1 + 4x_2 + 3x_3 \le 480$ hours
  Storage $1x_1 + 1x_2 + 1x_3 \le 150$ bags
      $x_1, x_2, x_3 \ge 0$

In addition, the optimal tableau shown below was obtained:
a. What is the marginal value of a pound of pine bark? Over what range is this price value appropriate?
b. What is the maximum price the store would be justified in paying for additional pine bark?

Optimal Tableau

C		9	9	6	0	0	0	0	
	Variables	x_1	x_2	x_3	s_1	s_2	s_3	s_4	Quantity
9	x_1	1	1.5	0	0.5	0	0	1.5	75
0	s_2	0	3.5	0	1.5	1	0	−9.5	135
0	s_3	0	2.5	0	0.5	0	1	−4.5	105
6	x_3	0	−0.5	1	−0.5	0	0	2.5	75
	Z	9	10.5	6	1.5	0	0	1.5	1,125
	C − Z	0	−1.5	0	−1.5	0	0	−1.5	

c. What is the marginal value of labor? Over what range is this value in effect?

d. The manager obtained additional machine time through better scheduling. How much additional machine time can be effectively used for this operation? Why?

e. If the manager can obtain *either* additional pine bark *or* additional storage space, which one should be chosen, and how much should be obtained (assuming additional quantities cost the same as usual)?

f. If a change in the chip operation would increase the profit on chips from $6 per bag to $7 per bag, would the optimal quantities change? Would the value of the objective function change? If so, what would the new value(s) be?

SELECTED BIBLIOGRAPHY

Anderson, David R.; Dennis J. Sweeney; and Thomas A. Williams. *An Introduction to Management Science: Quantitative Approaches to Decision Making.* 5th ed. St. Paul, Minn.: West Publishing, 1988.

Bierman, Harold; Charles P. Bonini; and Warren H. Hausman. *Quantitative Analysis for Business Decisions.* 7th ed. Homewood, Ill.: Richard D. Irwin, 1986.

Cook, Thomas M., and Robert A. Russell. *Introduction to Management Science.* 3rd ed. Englewood Cliffs, N.J.: Prentice Hall, 1985.

Eppen, G. D.; F. J. Gould; and C. P. Schmidt. *Introductory Management Science.* 2nd ed. Englewood Cliffs, N.J.: Prentice Hall, 1987.

Levin, Richard; Charles A. Kirkpatrick; and David S. Rubin. *Quantitative Approaches to Management.* 5th ed. New York: McGraw-Hill, 1982.

Stevenson, W. J. *Introduction to Management Science.* 2nd ed. Homewood, Ill.: Richard D. Irwin, 1992.

CASE: CLEARMOUNT SOUTHERN INCORPORATED

A forecast of expected business volume and prices for the coming fall season, and a review of production standards, had produced the information in Table 1 for the production of fabric.

The profits are based on expected costs and prices. More specifically they represent so-called operating profit, also known as *variable margin, contribution to profit and overhead,* and *gross profit* and were determined from the difference between expected selling price and expected variable costs.

In order to effectively direct sales efforts, keeping in mind the expected profits per yard, the anticipated sales volume on certain styles for which demand was considered limited, as well as productive requirements and capacity, it was desired to ascertain:

1. Optimal yardage to be sold (as a goal or target) for each style.
2. Resultant profit, per style and overall.
3. Resultant utilization of productive facilities, cards through looms.

Source: Professor Norbert L. Enrick, Ph.D., Administrative Sciences, Kent State University, Ohio. Reprinted by permission.

Table 1

Marketable fabric styles, demand limits on sales, productive requirement, and productive capacity

Market-able styles	Sales limit 1,000s of yards per week	Profit[a] per 100,000 yards (in dollars)	Production time needed per 100,000 yards of fabric per production process in 100's of delivery hours[b]						
			Cards	Drawing	Roving	Spinning	Loom 40"	Loom 46"	Loom 60"
A	3.0	9,020	3.3	2.0	35.2	1,348	28.4		
B	6.0	6,420	3.7	2.2	34.5	794	22.6		
C	10.0	5,480	3.5	2.1	37.7	1,128	31.0		
D		4,790	4.4	2.7	47.8	1,162	33.4		
E		2,690	3.1	1.8	34.3	1,050		28.4	
F		5,620	3.8	2.3	41.4	1,228		28.7	
G	10.0	5,130	4.5	2.7	42.3	1,071		23.7	
H	30.0	6,890	5.1	3.1	55.6	1,354		34.7	
I	7.5	9,080	3.9	2.4	42.9	1,468			34.1
J	5.0	7,290	2.9	1.7	31.2	1,064			25.6
K	4.0	10,530	3.6	2.1	38.9	1,334			30.8
L	3.0	12,040	3.8	2.3	41.8	1,436			30.8
M		6,900	3.3	2.0	30.9	794			20.5
Normal capacity per 120-hour week in 1,000s of delivery hours			27.0	14.4	257	7,204	155	21.7	16.3

[a] Estimated from expected selling price less expected variable costs.
[b] Successive processing through carding, drawing, roving, spinning, and the loom group shown (40-inch, 46-inch, or 60-inch). Fabric styles cannot be switched from wider to narrower looms or vice versa. A "delivery" is an output position. For example, a roving frame has some 100 spindles or "deliveries."

CHAPTER SEVEN

FACILITIES LAYOUT

7

After completing this chapter, you should be able to:

LEARNING OBJECTIVES

☐

CHAPTER OUTLINE

☐

T his is the third in a series of chapters on design of production systems. The previous chapters dealt with products, and process and capacity planning; this chapter deals with layout design. Layout refers to the configuration of departments, work centers, and equipment, with particular emphasis on movement of work (customers or materials) through the system. Decisions in any one of these four design areas usually have impacts on the others. Thus, both layout and location decisions affect capacity. Conversely, efforts to increase capacity may involve modifications in layout and changes in location. Moreover, any time a new location is established, or products or services are introduced or changed, there are layout implications.

This chapter describes the main types of layout designs along with models used to evaluate design alternatives.

INTRODUCTION

As in other areas of system design, layout decisions are important for three basic reasons: (1) they require substantial investments of both money and effort, (2) they involve long-term commitments, which make mistakes difficult to overcome, and (3) they have a significant impact on the cost and efficiency of short-term operations. In addition, personnel may resist changes to an existing layout because such changes often require them to alter daily routines or to undergo retraining.

THE NEED FOR LAYOUT DECISIONS

The need for layout planning arises in the process of designing new facilities as well as in redesigning existing facilities. In the latter instance, the most common reasons for redesign of layouts include:

1. Inefficient operations (e.g., high cost, bottlenecks).
2. Accidents or safety hazards.
3. Changes in the design of products or services.
4. The introduction of new products or services.
5. Changes in the volume of output or mix of outputs.
6. Changes in methods or equipment.
7. Changes in environmental or other legal requirements.
8. Morale problems (e.g., lack of face-to-face contact).

Naturally, the reasons for layout redesign influence the objectives being sought. For instance, if morale or safety problems exist, the objectives of a new layout plan would include remedying those problems. Even so, the main objectives in the majority of layout analyses relate to minimizing either the cost of materials handling or the movement of customers within a system and improving quality and productivity.

BASIC LAYOUT TYPES

There are three basic types of layouts: product, process, and fixed-position. *Product layouts* are most conducive to repetitive processing, *process layouts* are used for intermittent processing, and *fixed-position layouts* are used when projects require layouts, although not all projects do. The characteristics of each layout type will be described in this section, along with the advantages and disadvantages associated with each. Hybrid layouts, which are combinations of these pure types, are also briefly described.

PRODUCT LAYOUTS

Product layouts are used to achieve a smooth and rapid flow of large volumes of products or customers through a system. This is made possible by highly standardized products or services that require highly standardized (repetitive) processing operations. A job is divided into a series of standardized tasks, permitting specialization of both labor and equipment. The large volumes handled by these systems usually make it economical to invest substantial sums of money in equipment and job design. Because only one or a few very similar items are involved, it is feasible to arrange an entire layout to correspond to the technological processing requirements of the product or service involved. For instance, if a portion of a manufacturing operation required the sequence cutting, sanding, and painting the appropriate pieces of equipment would be arranged in that same sequence. Moreover, because each item follows the same sequence of operations, it is often possible to utilize fixed-path material-handling equipment such as conveyors to transport items between operations. The resulting arrangement forms a line like the one depicted in Figure 7–1. In manufacturing environments, the lines are referred to as **production lines** or **assembly lines**, depending on the type of activity involved. In nonmanufacturing processes, the term *line* may or may not be used. For instance, it is common to refer to a cafeteria line as such but not a car wash, although, from a conceptual standpoint, the two are nearly identical. Figure 7–2 illustrates a typical cafeteria serving-line layout. Examples of this type of layout are less plentiful in nonmanufacturing environments because processing requirements usually exhibit too much variability to make standardization feasible. Without high standardization, many of the benefits of continuous processing are lost. When lines are used, certain compromises may be made. For instance, an automatic car wash provides equal treatment to all cars—the same amount of soap, water, and scrubbing—even though cars may differ considerably in cleaning needs. As a result, some very dirty

Figure 7–1

A flow line for production or service

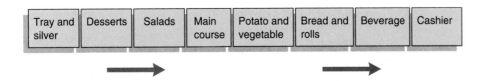

Figure 7–2

Cafeteria line

cars do not come out completely clean, and some relatively clean cars go through the same system with some waste of soap, water, and energy.

Product layouts achieve a high degree of both labor and equipment utilization, and that tends to offset the high equipment costs usually associated with this type of layout. Because items move quickly from operation to operation, investment in work-in-process is often minimal. However, operations are so closely tied to each other that the entire system has a high vulnerability to being shut down due to either mechanical failure or high absenteeism. Maintenance procedures are geared to this. Preventive maintenance—periodic inspection and replacement of worn parts or those with high failure rates—is used to reduce the probability of break-downs during the operations. Of course, no amount of preventive activity can completely eliminate failures, so measures designed to provide quick repair must also be taken, which include maintaining an inventory of spare parts and having repair personnel available to quickly restore equipment to normal operation. These procedures are fairly expensive; because of the specialized nature of equipment, problems become more difficult to diagnose and resolve, and spare-part inventories can be extensive.

The main advantages of product layouts are:

1. There is a high rate of output.
2. Unit cost is low due to high volume; the high cost of specialized equipment is spread over many units.
3. Labor specialization reduces training costs and time, and results in a wide span of supervision.
4. Material-handling cost is low per unit, and material handling is simplified because units follow the same sequence of operations.
5. There is a high utilization of labor and equipment.
6. Routing and scheduling are encompassed in the initial design of the system and do not require much attention once the system is operating.
7. Accounting, purchasing, and inventory control are fairly routine.

The primary disadvantages of product layouts include:

1. The intensive division of labor usually creates dull, repetitive jobs that do not provide much opportunity for advancement and may lead to morale problems.
2. Poorly skilled workers may exhibit little interest in maintaining equipment or in quality of output.
3. The system is fairly inflexible in response to either changes in the volume of output or changes in product or process design.
4. The system is highly susceptible to shutdowns caused by equipment break-downs or excessive absenteeism.
5. Preventive maintenance, the capacity for quick repairs, and spare-parts inventories are necessary expenses.
6. Incentive plans tied to individual output are impractical since they would tend to cause variations among outputs of individual workers that would adversely affect high utilization of labor and equipment.

U-Shaped Layouts

Although a straight production line may have intuitive appeal, a U-shaped line (see Figure 7–3) has a number of advantages that make it worthy of consideration. One

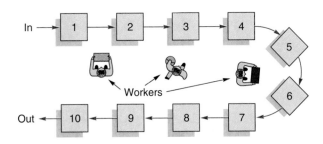

Figure 7–3
A U-shaped production line

A printed circuit board manufacturing layout is simulated here using SIMFACTORY. Notice that the line is U-shaped and also has a U-shaped component.

disadvantage of a long, straight line is that it interferes with cross travel of workers and vehicles. A U-shaped line is more compact; it often requires a little more than half the length of a straight production line. In addition, a U-shaped line permits increased communication among workers on the line because workers are clustered, and it also facilitates teamwork. And flexibility in work assignments is increased because workers can handle not only adjacent stations, but also stations on opposite sides of the line. Moreover, if materials enter the plant at the same point that finished products leave it, a U-shaped line will minimize material handling.

Of course, not all situations lend themselves to U-shaped layouts: Highly automated lines reduce the teamwork and communication benefits. And entry and exit points may be on opposite sides of a building. Also, operations may need to be separated due to noise or contamination factors.

PROCESS LAYOUTS

Process layouts are designed to facilitate processing items or providing services that present a variety of processing requirements. The layouts feature departments or other functional groupings in which similar kinds of activities are performed. A manufacturing example of a process layout can be found in a *machine shop,* which has separate departments for milling, grinding, drilling, and so on. Items that require those operations are frequently moved in lots to the departments in a sequence dictated by technical considerations. Different products may present quite different processing requirements and sequences of operations. Consequently, variable-path material-handling equipment (forklift trucks, jeeps, tote boxes) is needed to handle the variety of routes and items. The use of general-purpose machines provides the flexibility necessary to handle a wide range of processing requirements. Workers

Process layout
Layout that can handle varied processing requirements.

Figure 7–4

A process layout is typified by departmental work centers

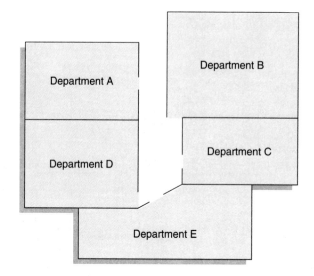

who operate the equipment are usually skilled or semiskilled. Figure 7–4 illustrates the departmental arrangement typical of a process layout.

Process layouts are quite common in nonmanufacturing environments. Examples include hospitals, colleges and universities, banks, auto repair shops, airlines, and public libraries. For instance, hospitals have departments or other units that specifically handle surgery, maternity, pediatrics, psychiatric, emergency, and geriatric care. Similarly, universities have separate schools or departments that concentrate on one area of study such as business, engineering, science, or math. And most business organizations have administrative departments such as accounting and payroll.

Because a process layout arranges equipment by type rather than by processing sequence, the system is much less vulnerable to shutdown caused by either mechanical failure or absenteeism. In manufacturing systems especially, idle equipment is usually available to replace machines that are temporarily out of service. Moreover, since items are often processed in lots, there is considerably less dependence between successive operations than with a product layout. Maintenance costs tend to be lower because the equipment is less specialized than with product layouts, and grouping of machinery permits repair personnel to become somewhat specialized in handling repairs. And machine similarity reduces the necessary investment in spare parts. On the negative side, routing and scheduling must be done on a continual basis in order to accommodate the variety of processing demands typically imposed on these systems. Material handling is inefficient, and unit handling costs are generally much higher than in product layouts. In-process inventories can be substantial due to batch processing. Furthermore, it is not uncommon for such systems to have equipment utilization rates under 50 percent because of routing and scheduling complexities related to the variety of processing demands being handled.

In sum, process layouts have advantages as well as disadvantages. The advantages of process layouts include:

1. Systems can handle a variety of processing requirements.
2. The system is not particularly vulnerable to equipment failures.
3. General-purpose equipment is often less costly than the specialized equipment used in product layouts and is easier and less costly to maintain.
4. It is possible to use individual incentive systems.

The disadvantages of process layouts include:

1. In-process inventory costs can be high if batch processing is used in manufacturing systems.
2. Routing and scheduling pose continual challenges.
3. Equipment utilization rates are low.
4. Material handling is slow and inefficient, and more costly per unit than under product layouts.
5. Job complexities often reduce the span of supervision and result in higher supervisory costs than with product layouts.
6. Special attention necessary for each product or customer (routing, scheduling, machine setups, and so on) and low volumes result in higher unit costs than with product layouts.
7. Accounting, inventory control, and purchasing are much more involved than under product layouts.

FIXED-POSITION LAYOUTS

In **fixed-position layouts**, the item being worked on remains stationary, and workers, materials, and equipment are moved about as needed. This is in marked contrast to product and process layouts. Almost always, the nature of the product dictates this kind of arrangement: weight, size, bulk, or some other factor makes it undesirable or extremely difficult to move the product. Fixed-position layouts are used in large construction projects (buildings, power plants, dams), shipbuilding, and production of large aircraft and space mission rockets. In those instances, attention is focused on timing of material and equipment deliveries so as not to clog up the work site and to avoid having to relocate materials and equipment around the work site. Lack of storage space can present significant problems, for example, at construction sites in crowded urban locations. Because of the many diverse activities carried out on large projects and because of the wide range of skills required, special efforts are needed to coordinate the activities, and the span of control can be quite narrow. For these reasons, the administrative burden is often much higher than it would be under either of the other layout types. Material handling may or may not be a factor: in many cases, there is no tangible product involved (e.g., designing a computerized inventory system). When goods and materials are involved, material handling often resembles process-type, variable-path, general-purpose equipment, even though the actual equipment used might differ somewhat depending on the nature of the work. Projects might require use of earth-moving equipment and trucks to haul materials to, from, and around the work site, for example.

> **Fixed-position layout**
> Layout in which the product or project remains stationary, and workers, materials, and equipment are moved as needed.

Fixed-position layouts are widely used for farming, firefighting, road building, home building, remodeling and repair, and drilling for oil. In each case, there are compelling reasons for bringing workers, materials, and equipment to the "product's" location instead of the other way around.

COMBINATION LAYOUTS

The three basic layout types are ideal models that may be altered to satisfy the needs of a particular situation. In fact, it is not hard to discover layouts that represent some combination of these pure types. For instance, supermarket layouts are essentially of a process nature, and yet we find most use fixed-path material-handling devices such as roller-type conveyors both in the stockroom and at checkouts and belt-type conveyors at the cash registers. Hospitals also use the basic process arrangement, although frequently patient care involves more of a fixed-position approach, in which nurses, doctors, medicines, and special equipment are brought to the patient. By the same token, faulty parts made in a product layout may require off-line reworking, which involves customized processing. And one frequently observes the use of conveyors in both farming and construction activities.

Process layouts and product layouts represent two ends of a continuum from small batches to continuous production. Process layouts are conducive to the production of a wider range of products or services than product layouts, which is desirable from a customer standpoint where customized products are often in demand. However, process layouts tend to be less efficient than product layouts, and they involve higher unit production costs than product layouts, and sometimes lower quality. Some manufacturers are attempting to move away from process layouts in an effort to capture some of the benefits of product layouts. Ideally, a system would be flexible and yet efficient, with low unit production costs. Cellular manufacturing, group technology, and flexible manufacturing systems represent efforts to move toward this ideal.

CELLULAR LAYOUTS

CELLULAR MANUFACTURING

Cellular manufacturing

Layout in which machines are grouped into a cell that can process items that have similar processing requirements.

Cellular manufacturing is a type of layout in which machines are grouped into what is referred to as a *cell.* Groupings are determined by the operations needed to perform work for a set of similar items, or *part families,* that require similar processing. In effect, the cells become miniature versions of product layouts. The cells may have no conveyorized movement of parts between machines, or a flow line connected by a conveyor (automatic transfer). A comparison of a typical functional (process) layout and a cellular manufacturing layout is given in Figure 7-5. Observe that in the cellular layout, machines are arranged to handle all of the operations necessary for a group (family) of similar parts. Thus, all of the parts follow the same route, although minor variations (e.g., skipping an operation) are possible. In contrast, the functional layout involves multiple paths for parts. Moreover, there is little effort or need to identify part families; the distinction in the figure is merely for purposes of comparison.

There are numerous benefits of cellular manufacturing. These relate to the grouping of equipment. They include faster throughput time, less material handling, less work-in-process inventory, and reduced setup time.

GROUP TECHNOLOGY

Group technology

The grouping into part families of items with similar design or manufacturing characteristics.

For cellular manufacturing to be effective, there must be groups of items that have similar processing characteristics. Moreover, these items must be identified. The grouping process is known as **group technology** and involves identifying items with similarities in either *design characteristics* or *manufacturing characteristics,* and grouping them into part families. Design characteristics include size, shape, and function; manufacturing or processing characteristics involve the type and sequence of operations required. In many cases, design and processing characteristics are

Figure 7–5

Comparison of functional and cellular manufacturing layouts

Source: Adapted from D. Fogarty and T. Hoffman, *Production and Inventory Management* (Cincinnati: South-Western Publishing, 1983), p. 472.

correlated, although this is not always the case. Thus, design families may be different from processing families. Figure 7-6 illustrates a group of parts with similar processing characteristics but different design characteristics.

Once similar items have been identified, items can be classified according to their families, and a coding system can be developed. The coding system facilitates retrieval from a data base for purposes of design and manufacturing. For instance, a designer can readily determine if there is an existing part similar or identical to one that needs to be designed. It may happen that an existing part, with some modification, would be satisfactory. This greatly enhances the productivity of design. Similarly, planning the manufacturing of a new part would involve matching it with one of the part families in existence, thereby alleviating much of the burden of specific processing details.

The conversion to group technology and cellular manufacturing requires a systematic analysis of parts to identify the part families. This is often a major undertaking; it is a time-consuming job that involves the analysis of a considerable

Figure 7–6

A group of parts with similar manufacturing process requirements but different design attributes

Source: Mikell P. Groover, *Automation, Production Systems, and Computer-Aided Manufacturing* © 1980, p. 540. Reprinted by permission of Prentice Hall, Inc., Englewood Cliffs, New Jersey.

amount of data. Three primary methods for accomplishing this are visual inspection, examination of design and production data, and production flow analysis.

Visual inspection is the least accurate of the three but also the least costly and the simplest to perform. Examination of design and production data is more accurate but much more time-consuming; it is perhaps the most commonly used method of analysis. Production flow analysis involves examination of operations sequences and machine routings to uncover similarities; hence, the analysis has a manufacturing perspective and not a design perspective. Moreover, the operation sequences and routings are taken as givens; in reality the existing procedures may be far from optimal.

Conversion to cellular manufacturing can involve costly realignment of equipment. Consequently, a manager must weigh the benefits of a switch from a process layout to a cellular one against the cost of moving equipment as well as the cost and time needed for grouping parts.

FLEXIBLE MANUFACTURING SYSTEMS

As discussed in Chapter 6, flexible manufacturing systems (FMSs) are more fully automated versions of cellular manufacturing: A computer controls the transfer of parts from machine to machine as well as the start of work at each machine. As you might suspect, these systems are quite expensive. However, they enable manufacturers to achieve some of the benefits of product layouts with small batch sizes and much greater flexibility in a system that is capable of operating with little or no human intervention.

Caterpillar employs flexible manufacturing cells at their KK plant in East Peoria, Illinois. A rough gear forging arrives where it is processed by automated tools that mill, drill, deburr, and ream the metal. The teeth are cut and the gear is heat treated before it is assembled on an axle. Such flexible cells allow Caterpillar to quickly accommodate different projects.

DESIGNING PRODUCT LAYOUTS: LINE BALANCING

Many of the benefits of a product layout relate to the ability to divide required work into a series of elemental tasks (e.g., "assemble parts *C* and *D*") that can be performed quickly and routinely by low-skilled workers or by specialized equipment. The durations of these elemental tasks typically range from as little as a few seconds to 15 minutes or more. Most of the time requirements are so brief that it would be impractical to assign only one task to each worker. For one thing, most workers would quickly become bored by the limited job scope. For another, the number of workers required to complete even a simple product or service would be enormous. Instead, tasks are usually grouped into manageable bundles that are assigned to workstations manned by one or two operations.

Line balancing

The process of assigning groups of tasks that have approximately equal time requirements to different workstations.

The process of deciding how to assign tasks to workstations is referred to as **line balancing**. The goal of line balancing is to obtain task groupings that represent approximately equal time requirements. This minimizes the idle time along the line and results in a high utilization of labor and equipment. Idle time occurs if task times are not equal among workstations; some stations will have the capability to produce at higher rates than others. These "fast" stations will experience periodic waits for the output from slower stations or else be forced into idleness to avoid buildups of work between stations. Unbalanced lines are undesirable both in terms of inefficient utilization of labor and equipment and because they may create morale problems for workers at the slower stations who must work continuously.

Lines that are perfectly balanced will have a smooth flow of work as activities along the line are synchronized to achieve maximum utilization of labor and equipment. The major obstacle to attaining a perfectly balanced line is the difficulty in forming task bundles that have the same duration. One cause of this is that it may not be feasible to combine certain activities into the same bundle, either because of differences in equipment requirements or because the activities are not compatible (e.g., risk of contamination of paint from sanding). Another cause of difficulty is that differences among elemental task lengths cannot always be overcome by grouping tasks. A third cause of an inability to perfectly balance a line is that a required technological sequence may prohibit otherwise desirable task combinations. For instance, consider a series of three operations that have durations of two minutes, four minutes, and two minutes, as shown in the following diagram. Ideally, the first and third operations could be combined at one workstation and have a total time equal to that of the second operation. However, it may not be possible to combine the first and third operations. In the case of an automatic car wash, scrubbing and drying operations could not realistically be combined at the same workstation due to the need to rinse cars between these two operations:

Cycle time

The maximum time allowed at each workstation to complete its set of tasks on a unit.

A key aspect of an assembly line, or a production line, is its **cycle time**, which is the time allowed at each workstation to perform its set of tasks. An easy way to think about cycle time is as the time between successive units coming off the line. Thus, if a new unit comes off the end of the line every two minutes, then the cycle time is two minutes. That means that each workstation on the line has a *maximum* of two minutes from the time it begins work on a new unit until it sends the unit on to the next station.

We can gain some insight into task groupings and cycle time by considering a simple example.

Suppose that the work required to fabricate a certain product can be divided up into five elemental tasks, with the task times and precedence relationships as shown on the next page.

$$\rightarrow \boxed{0.1 \text{ min.}} \rightarrow \boxed{0.7 \text{ min.}} \rightarrow \boxed{1.0 \text{ min.}} \rightarrow \boxed{0.5 \text{ min.}} \rightarrow \boxed{0.2 \text{ min.}} \rightarrow$$

Two important pieces of information in any listing of elemental task times are the sum of the task times and the length of the longest elemental task. The longest task (one minute in this case) indicates the *minimum* possible cycle time (the time interval between units coming off the line), and the sum of the times (2.5 minutes) indicates the *maximum* cycle time that would make sense. Thus, combining the tasks at a single workstation would require a cycle time of two and one-half minutes. At the other extreme, even by assigning each task to a different workstation, the cycle time could not be less than one minute, since the third task requires that length of time. The maximum and minimum cycle times are important because they can be used to determine upper and lower bounds on a line's output potential. Once the cycle time has been decided on, daily capacity of the line can be found by dividing operating time per day by a line's cycle time:

$$\text{Output capacity} = \frac{\text{OT}}{\text{CT}} \tag{7-1}$$

where

$\text{OT} = \text{Operating time per day}$

$\text{CT} = \text{Cycle time}$

Let's assume that the line will operate for eight hours per day (480 minutes). With a cycle time of 1.0 minute, output would be:

$$\frac{480 \text{ minutes per day}}{1.0 \text{ minute per unit}} = 480 \text{ units per day}$$

With a cycle time of 2.5 minutes, the output would be:

$$\frac{480 \text{ minutes per day}}{2.5 \text{ minutes per unit}} = 192 \text{ units per day}$$

Assuming that no parallel activities are to be employed (e.g., two lines), the output selected for the line must fall in the range of 192 units per day to 480 units per day.

As a general rule, the cycle time is determined by the desired output. That is, a desired output level is selected, and the cycle time is computed. If the cycle time does not fall between the maximum and minimum bounds, the desired output rate must be revised. The cycle time can be computed using this formula:

$$\text{CT} = \frac{\text{OT}}{D} \tag{7-2}$$

where D = Desired output rate

For example, suppose that the desired output rate is 480 units. Using Formula 7-2, we can compute the necessary cycle time:

$$\frac{480 \text{ minutes per day}}{480 \text{ units per day}} = 1.0 \text{ minute per unit}$$

The number of workstations that will be needed is a function of both the desired output rate and our ability to combine elemental tasks into workstations. The *theoretical minimum* number of stations necessary to provide a specified rate of output can be determined as follows:

$$N_{\min} = \frac{D \times \Sigma t}{\mathrm{OT}}$$

(7–3)

where

$N_{\min}$ = Theoretical minimum number of stations
D = Desired output rate
Σt = Sum of task times
OT = Operating time

Suppose the desired rate of output is the maximum of 480 units per day.[1] (This will require a cycle time of 1.0 minute.) The minimum number of stations required to achieve this goal is:

$$N_{\min} = \frac{480 \text{ units per day} \times 2.5 \text{ minutes per unit}}{480 \text{ minutes per day per station}} = 2.5 \text{ stations}$$

Because 2.5 stations is not feasible, it is necessary to *round up* (because 2.5 is the minimum) to three stations. Thus, the actual number of stations used will equal or exceed three, depending on how successfully the tasks can be grouped into work bundles.

Example 1

∎

Combine the five elemental tasks described in the preceding illustration into three workstations. Assign tasks to workstations according to precedence, beginning with the first task. Use a cycle time of 1.0 minute.

Solution

The cycle time of 1.0 minute represents an *upper limit* on the sum of task times assigned to any workstation. With this in mind, we assign the first two tasks to the first workstation since their times sum to 0.8 minute. Obviously, the next task must be assigned to a separate workstation because its length equals the cycle time. The remaining two tasks can be assigned to the third workstation, for a station time of 0.7 minute. The resulting assignments are illustrated below.

---

[1] At first glance, it might seem that the desired output would logically be the maximum possible output. However, you will see why that is not always the best alternative.

Because the goal of line balancing is to minimize idle time, the percentage of idle time associated with a given assignment of tasks to workstations is of particular interest. The idle time per cycle for each station is:

Idle time per station = Cycle time − Station time

The idle times for the above assignments and a cycle time of 1.0 minute are shown in the table below:

Station	Station time	Station idle time
1	0.8	0.2
2	1.0	0.0
3	0.7	0.3
		0.5

The percentage of idle time is the ratio of idle time per cycle to total time available per cycle:

$$\text{Percentage of idle time} = \frac{\text{Idle time per cycle}}{N_{\text{actual}} \times \text{CT}} = \frac{0.5}{3(1.0)} = .167 \text{ or } 16.7\%$$

Efficiency can also be computed. It equals 100% − percentage of idle time. Note that an idle time percentage of zero means the line is perfectly balanced.

The extent to which workstations can be *packed* influences both the number of stations needed and the percentage of idle time.

Example 2

Assign the given tasks to workstations in a way that minimizes idle time, and compute the resulting percentage of idle time and the efficiency. (Note that the total task times and the longest task time are the same as in the preceding example.) Assume $D = 480$ units per day.

→ | 0.3 minute | → | 1.0 minute | → | 0.3 minute | → | 0.4 minute | → | 0.5 minute | →

Solution

An output of 480 units per day will require a cycle time of 1.0 minute:

$$\text{CT} = \frac{\text{Operating time per day}}{\text{Desired output rate}} = \frac{480 \text{ minutes per day}}{480 \text{ units per day}} = 1.0$$

Assign tasks, beginning with the first task. The first station will consist solely of the first task because the second task's time equals the cycle time. The second station will consist of the second task; the third station will consist of the third and fourth tasks; and a fourth station will be required to handle the last task. These assignments are as follows:

(continued)

Example 2

(concluded)

$\rightarrow$ | Station 1 0.3 minute | $\rightarrow$ | Station 2 1.0 minute | $\rightarrow$ | Station 3 0.3 minute + 0.4 minute | $\rightarrow$ | Station 4 0.5 minute | $\rightarrow$

The resulting idle times for this assignment are:

Station	Station time	Station idle time
1	0.3	0.7
2	1.0	0.0
3	0.7	0.3
4	0.5	0.5
		1.5

The percentage of idle time is:

$$\text{Percentage of idle time} = \frac{\text{Idle time per cycle}}{N \times \text{CT}} = \frac{1.5}{4(1.0)} = 37.5\%$$

Efficiency is $1 - .375 = .625$, or 62.5%.

Note that the overall efficiency is lower in Example 2 than it was in Example 1 (the percentage of idle time is greater), even though the sum of the task times and the cycle time are identical. The reason for the decrease in efficiency can be attributed to the use of a fourth workstation in the second example. Of course, that station was unavoidable because of the inability to obtain as high a degree of packing of the first three stations as was possible in Example 1.

This brings us back to the question of whether the selected level of output should equal the maximum output possible. The minimum number of workstations needed is a function of the desired output rate:

$$N = \frac{D \times \Sigma t}{\text{OT}}$$

Therefore, a lower rate of output may produce a need for fewer stations. Hence, the manager must consider whether the potential savings realized by having fewer workstations would be greater than the decrease in contribution resulting from producing fewer units.

The preceding examples serve to illustrate some of the fundamental concepts of line balancing. But compared to most real-life situations, they are rather simple; the number of branches and tasks involved are often much greater than in these examples. Consequently, the job of line balancing can be a good deal more complex than you might suspect. In many instances, the number of alternatives for grouping tasks is so great that it would be virtually impossible to conduct an exhaustive review of all possibilities. For this reason, many real-life problems of any magnitude are solved using *heuristic* (intuitive) approaches. The purpose of a heuristic approach is to reduce the number of alternatives that must be considered, but it does not guarantee an optimal solution.

Some of the heuristic rules used in practice are:

1. Assign tasks to workstations, longest tasks first, and continue until all tasks have been assigned.
2. Assign tasks in order of most number of following tasks.
3. Assign tasks according to *positional weight,* which is the sum of a task's time and the times of all following tasks.

Unfortunately, none of these rules works all the time, so it is usually necessary to try several rules in the hopes of discovering a good solution to a problem. Although heuristic rules do not guarantee an optimal solution to line balancing problems, they often provide reasonably good solutions with a limited amount of effort. Moreover, they are intuitively appealing: The rules offer rational, step-by-step handling of fairly complex problems.

Computerized approaches to the line balancing problem may incorporate heuristic rules such as those listed above, or they may use dynamic programming.[2]

All tasks have precedence relationships, which govern the sequence in which they must be performed (i.e., certain tasks must be completed before others can begin). The next section provides some guidelines for line balancing.

SOME GUIDELINES FOR LINE BALANCING

In balancing an assembly line, tasks are assigned *one at a time* to the line, starting at the first workstation. At each step, the unassigned tasks are checked to determine which of them are eligible for assignment. Next, the eligible tasks are checked to see which of them will fit in the workstation being loaded. Then a heuristic is used to select one of the tasks that will fit, and the task is assigned. This process is repeated until there are no eligible tasks that will fit. Then we start loading the next workstation. This continues until all tasks are assigned. The objective is to minimize the idle time for the line subject to technological and output constraints.

Technological constraints tell us which elemental tasks are *eligible* to be assigned at a particular position on the line. Technological constraints can result from the precedence or ordering relationships among the tasks. The precedence relationships require that certain tasks must be performed before others (and so, must be assigned to workstations before others). Thus, in a car wash, the rinsing operation must be performed before the drying operation. The drying operation, then, is not eligible for assignment until the rinsing operation is assigned. Technological constraints may also result from two tasks being "incompatible" (e.g., because of space restrictions or the nature of the operations, they cannot be placed in the same work center). For example, sanding and painting operations would not be assigned to the same work center because of the dust from the sanding operation.

Output constraints, on the other hand, determine the maximum amount of work that can be assigned to each workstation, and this determines whether an eligible task *will fit* at a workstation. The desired output rate determines the cycle time, and the sum of the task times assigned to any workstation must not exceed the

---

[2] See, for example, M. Held, R. M. Karp, and R. Sharesian, "Assembly-Line Balancing: Dynamic Programming with Precedence Constraints," *Operations Research* 11, no. 3 (May–June 1963).

cycle time. If a task can be assigned to a workstation without exceeding the cycle time, then the task will fit.

Once we know which tasks are *eligible* and *will fit,* we still need to select the task to be assigned (if there is more than one to choose from). This is where the heuristic rules come in. They help us decide which task to assign from among those that are eligible and will fit.

Just to clarify the terminology a bit, *following tasks* are all tasks that you would encounter by following all paths from the task in question through the precedence diagram. Similarly, *preceding tasks* are all tasks you would encounter by tracing all paths *backward* from the task in question. In the precedence diagram below, tasks b, d, e, and f are followers of task a. Tasks a, b, and c are preceding tasks for e.

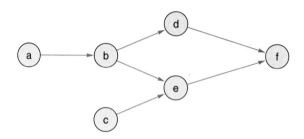

The *positional weight* for a task is the sum of the task times for itself and all its following tasks.

None of the heuristics described above *guarantees* the *best* solution, or even a good solution to the line-balancing problem, but they do provide guidelines for developing a solution. It may be useful to apply several different heuristics to the same problem and pick the best (least idle time) solution out of those developed.

A **precedence diagram**, which shows the sequence of operations, can be helpful to work with in line balancing. This diagram can easily be constructed from a list of sequential activities. Example 3 illustrates the use of such a diagram and the use of the heuristic rules for task assignments.

precedence diagram

Diagram showing the sequence of tasks.

OTHER FACTORS

The preceding discussion on line balancing presents a relatively straightforward approach to approximating a balanced line. In practice, the ability to do this usually involves additional considerations, some of which are technical and some of which are not.

Example 3

Using the information contained in the table shown, do each of the following:

1. Draw a precedence diagram.
2. Assuming an eight-hour workday, compute the cycle time needed to obtain an output of 400 units per day.
3. Determine the minimum number of workstations required.
4. Assign tasks to workstations using this rule: Assign tasks according to greatest number of following tasks. In case of a tie, use the tiebreaker of assigning the task with the longest processing time first.

Example 3

(continued)

Task	Immediate predecessor	Task time
a	—	0.2
b	a	0.2
c	—	0.8
d	c	0.6
e	b	0.3
f	d,e	1.0
g	f	0.4
h	g	0.3
	$\Sigma t =$	3.8

Solution

1. Drawing a precedence diagram is a relatively straightforward task. Begin with ac-
    tivities with no predecessors. We see from the list that a and c have no immediate
    predecessors. We build from here.

Task b follows a, and d follows c.

Task e follows b.

Task f follows e and d.

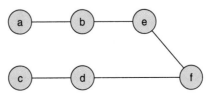

(continued)

Example 3

(continued)

Task g follows f, and h follows g.

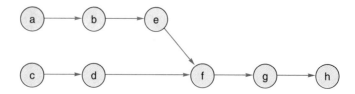

2. $CT = \dfrac{OT}{D} = \dfrac{480 \text{ minutes per day}}{400 \text{ units per day}} = 1.2 \text{ minutes per cycle}$

3. $N = \dfrac{D \times \Sigma t}{OT} = \dfrac{400 \text{ units per day} \times 3.8 \text{ minutes per unit}}{480 \text{ minutes per day per station}}$

    $= 3.17$ stations (round to 4)

4. Beginning with station 1, make assignments following this procedure: Determine from the precedence diagram which tasks are eligible for assignment. Then determine which of the eligible tasks will fit the time remaining for the station. Use the tiebreaker if necessary. Once a task has been assigned, remove it from consideration. When a station cannot take any more assignments, go on to the next station. Continue until all tasks have been assigned.

Station	Time remaining	Eligible	Will fit	Assign (task time)	Idle
1	1.2 min.	a,c★	a,c★	a (0.2)	
	1.0	c,b★★	c,b★★	c (0.8)	
	0.2	b,d	b	b (0.2)	
	0	e,d	None	—	0.0
2	1.2	e,d	c,d	d (0.6)	
	0.6	e	e	e (0.3)	
	0.3★★★	f	None	—	0.3
3	1.2	f	f	f (1.0)	
	0.2	g	None	—	0.2
4	1.2	g	g	g (0.4)	
	0.8	h	h	h (0.3)	
	0.5	—	—	—	0.5
					1.0 min.

★ Neither a nor c have any predecessors, so both are eligible. Task a was assigned since it has more followers.
★★ Once a is assigned, b and c are now eligible. Both will fit in the time remaining of 1.0 minute. The tie cannot be broken by the "most followers" rule, so the longer task is assigned.
★★★ Although f is eligible, this task will not fit, so station 2 is left with 0.3 minute of idle time per 1.2-minute cycle.

These assignments are shown in the following diagram. If you look carefully at this solution, you may discover that it can be improved upon. Thus, this solution is not necessarily optimal. One should not expect that heuristic approaches will produce optimal solutions; they merely provide a practical way to deal with what can be highly complex problems that do not lend themselves to optimizing techniques.

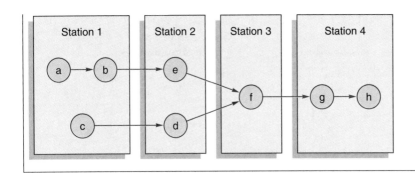

Example 3

(concluded)

Technical considerations include skill requirements of different tasks. If skill requirements of tasks are quite different, it may not be feasible to place the tasks in the same workstation. Similarly, if the tasks themselves are incompatible, such as sanding and painting or use of fire and use of volatile liquids, it may not be feasible even to place them in stations that are near to each other.

Although it is convenient to treat assembly operations as if they occur at the same rate time after time, it is more realistic to assume that whenever humans are involved, variability in task completion times will occur. The reasons for the variations are numerous, including fatigue, boredom, and non-work-related thoughts. Hence, even in a "perfectly balanced line," the actual performance may not reflect a perfect balance. Likewise, absenteeism can affect line balance.

Thus, developing a workable plan for balancing a line requires consideration of other factors besides precedence relationships, such as human factors, equipment and space limitations, and incompatible operations.

DESIGNING PROCESS LAYOUTS

The main issue in design of process layouts concerns the relative positioning of the departments involved. As illustrated in Figure 7–7, a list of departments must be assigned to a list of locations. The problem is to develop a reasonably good layout; some combinations will be more desirable than others. For example, some departments may benefit from adjacent locations, and others should be separated. Painting and sanding departments that are too close to each other could cause painting to be contaminated by particles from the sanding operations. Conversely, two departments that share some of the same equipment would benefit from being close together.

Layouts can also be influenced by such external factors as the locations of entrances, loading docks, elevators, windows, and areas of reinforced flooring. Also important are noise levels, safety, and the size and locations of restrooms.

In a few instances, such as the layouts of supermarkets, gas stations, and fast-food chains, there are sufficient numbers of installations with similar characteristics to justify development of standardized layouts. A good example of a standardized layout is provided by McDonald's hamburger outlets. The use of the same basic pattern in all outlets facilitates construction of new structures and employee training. Food preparation, order taking, and customer service follow the same pattern throughout the chain. Installation and service of equipment are also standardized. Supermarket chains often benefit from standardized layouts, although in a different respect: Customers acquainted with the layout of any store in the chain can readily locate desired items in other stores in the chain. In addition, most supermarkets

Figure 7-7

Work centers must be
assigned to locations

Locations

A	B	C
D	E	F

**Work centers to
be assigned**

1
2
3
4
5
6

locate departments such as meat, produce, and bakery around the perimeter of the store and provide wide aisles to permit customers to ponder choices and to achieve customer circulation throughout the store. Bread and milk are often placed away from the entrance in order to expose customers who stop in just to pick up those items to additional merchandise.

The majority of layout problems involve single locations rather than multiple locations, and they present unique combinations of factors that do not lend themselves to a standardized approach. Consequently, these layouts require customized designs.

The major obstacle to finding the most efficient layout of departments is the large number of assignments that are possible. For example, there are over 300,000 different ways that nine departments can be assigned to nine locations if the locations form a single line. Different location configurations (e.g., nine departments in a 3 × 3 grid) often reduce the number of possibilities, as do any special requirements (e.g., the stamping department may have to be assigned to a location with reinforced flooring). Still, the remaining number of layout possibilities usually is too large to allow each one to be examined, even with computer assistance. Unfortunately, no algorithms (solution procedures) exist that can identify the best layout arrangement under all circumstances. Often planners must rely on heuristic rules to guide trial-and-error efforts for a satisfactory solution to each problem.

MEASURES OF EFFECTIVENESS

One advantage of process layouts is their ability to satisfy a variety of processing requirements. Customers or materials in these systems require different operations and different sequences of operations, which causes them to follow different paths through the system. Material-oriented systems necessitate the use of variable-path material-handling equipment to move materials from work center to work center, and in customer-oriented systems, people must travel or be transported from work center to work center. In both cases, transportation costs or time can be significant. Because of this factor, one of the major objectives in process layout is to minimize transportation cost, distance, or time. This is usually accomplished by locating departments with relatively high interdepartmental work flow as close together as possible.

Other concerns in choosing among alternative layouts include initial costs in setting up the layout, expected operating costs, the amount of effective capacity created, and the ease of modifying the system if the need arose.

In situations that involve efforts to improve an existing layout, costs of relocating any work center must be weighed against the potential benefits of such a move.

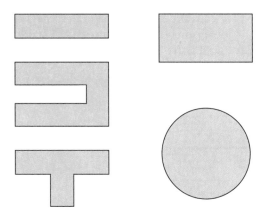

Figure 7–8

Buildings can have a
variety of shapes

INFORMATION REQUIREMENTS

The design of process layouts requires the following information:

1. A list of departments or work centers to be arranged, their approximate dimensions, and the dimensions of the building or buildings that will house the departments.
2. A projection of future work flows between the various work centers.
3. The distance between locations and the cost per unit of distance to move loads between locations.
4. The amount of money to be invested in the layout.
5. A list of any special considerations (e.g., heavy equipment will require reinforced flooring; sanding and painting operations should be separated).

The ideal situation is to first develop a layout and then design the physical structure around the layout, which permits maximum flexibility in design. In fact, this procedure is commonly followed when new facilities are being constructed. Nonetheless, many layouts must be developed in situations where there is an existing structure. In those instances, floor space, the dimensions of the building, location of entrances and elevators, and other similar factors must be carefully weighed in designing the layout. Some of the building shapes resulting from layout development are illustrated in Figure 7–8. Multilevel structures pose special problems for layout planners.

MINIMIZING TRANSPORTATION COSTS OR DISTANCES

The most common goals in designing process layouts are minimization of transportation costs or distances traveled. In such cases, it can be very helpful to summarize the necessary data in *from-to charts* like those illustrated in Tables 7–1 and 7–2. Table 7–1 indicates the distance between each of the locations, and Table 7–2 indicates actual or projected work flow between each pair. For instance, the distance chart reveals that a trip from location A to location B will involve a distance of 20 meters. (Distances are often measured between department centers.) Oddly enough, the length of a trip between locations A and B may differ depending on the *direction* of the trip, due to one-way routes, elevators, or other factors. To simplify the discussion, we shall assume a constant distance between any two locations regardless of direction. However, it would not be realistic to assume that interdepartmental work flows are equal; there is no reason to suspect that department 1 will send as much work to department 2 as department 2 sends to 1. For example, several departments may send goods to packaging, but packaging may send only to the shipping department.

Transportation costs can also be summarized in from-to charts, but to avoid the added complexity that would entail, we shall assume that costs are a direct, linear function of distance.

Table 7–1

Distance between locations (meters)

		Location		
From	To	A	B	C
A		—	20	40
B		20	—	30
C		40	30	—

Table 7–2

Interdepartmental work flow (loads per day)

		Department		
From	To	1	2	3
1		—	10	80
2		20	—	30
3		90	70	—

Example 4

∎

Assign the three departments shown in Table 7–2 to locations A, B, and C, which are separated by the distances shown in Table 7–1, in such a way that transportation cost is minimized. Use this heuristic: Assign departments with the greatest interdepartmental work flow first.

Solution

Ranking departments according to highest work flow and locations according to highest interlocation distances helps in making assignments. If interlocation distances are independent of direction of flow, work flow between departments can be summed to achieve a clearer picture of the need for closeness. Thus:

Trip	Distance (meters)	Department pair	Work flow
A–B 20		3–1 .... 90 } 170	
B–A 20		1–3 80	
B–C 30		3–2 .... 70 } 100	
C–B 30		2–3 30	
A–C 40		2–1 .... 20 } 30	
C–A 40		1–2 10	

From these listings, we can see that departments 1 and 3 have the highest interdepartmental work flow and that locations A and B are the closest. Thus, it would seem reasonable to consider assigning 1 and 3 to locations A and B, although it is not yet obvious which department should be assigned to which location. Further inspection of the work flow list reveals that 2 and 3 have higher work flow than 1 and 2, so 2 and 3 should probably be located more closely than 1 and 2. Hence, it would seem reasonable to place 3 between 1 and 2, or at least centralize that department with respect to the other two. The resulting assignments might appear as illustrated in Figure 7–9.

Note that work flows between departments in the diagram are the sum of the flow each way (e.g., the 170 between 1 and 3 is the combined flow of 90 loads from 3 to 1 and 80 loads from 1 to 3).

If we know that the cost per meter to move any load is $1, we can compute the total daily transportation cost for this assignment by multiplying each department's number of loads by the trip distance, and summing those quantities:

Example 4

(continued)

Depart-ment	Number of loads to:	Location	Distance to:	Loads × Distance
1	2: 10	A.........	C: 40	10 × 40 = 400
	3: 80		B: 20	80 × 20 = 1,600
2	1: 20	C	A: 40	20 × 40 = 800
	3: 30		B: 30	30 × 30 = 900
3	1: 90	B.........	A: 20	90 × 20 = 1,800
	2: 70		C: 30	70 × 30 = 2,100
				7,600

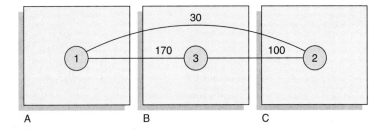

A   B   C

Figure 7–9

Interdepartmental work flows for assigned departments

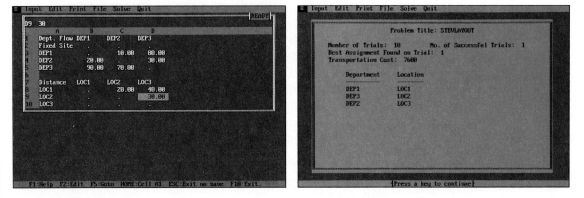

DSS-POM (2.1c) input screen for Example 4 (left). Completed solution (after 10 iterations) is shown at the right.

(continued)

Example 4

(concluded)

At $1 per load-meter, the cost for this plan would be $7,600 per day. Even though it might appear that this arrangement yields the lowest transportation cost, we cannot be absolutely positive of that without actually computing the total cost for every alternative and comparing it to this one. Although we could do so in this case, where the number of alternatives is quite small (i.e., there are 3! = 6 possible arrangements), in problems with more departments, the number is likely to be too large to even consider examining every alternative. Instead, we must rely on the choice of reasonable heuristic rules such as those demonstrated above to guide us to a solution that will be satisfactory, if not optimal.

Figure 7–10

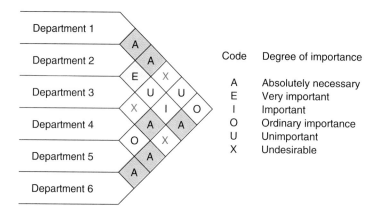

CLOSENESS RATINGS

Although the preceding approach is widely used, it suffers from the limitation of being able to focus on only one objective, and many situations involve multiple criteria. Richard Muther developed a more general approach to the problem, which allows for subjective input from analysts or managers to indicate the relative importance of each combination of department pairs.[3] That information is then summarized in a grid like the one shown in Figure 7–10. The grid is read in the same way as the mileage chart on a road map, except that letters rather than distances appear at the intersections. The letters represent the importance of closeness for each department pair, with A being the most important and X being an undesirable pairing. Thus, in the grid we can see that it is "absolutely necessary" to locate 1 and 2 close to each other because there is an A at the intersection of those departments on the grid. On the other hand, we also can see that 1 and 4 should not be close together because their intersection has an X. In practice, the letters on the grid are often accompanied by numbers that indicate the reason for each assignment; they are omitted here to simplify the illustration. Muther suggests the following list:

1. Use same equipment or facilities.
2. Share the same personnel or records.
3. Sequence of work flow.
4. Ease of communication.

---

[3] R. Muther, *Systematic Layout Planning* (Boston: Industrial Education Institute, 1961).

5. Unsafe or unpleasant conditions.

6. Similar work performed.

As with the previous examples, no optimizing algorithm exists, so trial-and-error alternatives must be developed and compared using heuristic rules.

Assign the six departments in Figure 7–10 to a 2 × 3 set of locations using the heuristic rule: Assign critical departments first.

Example 5

Solution

Critical pairs of departments are those with A or X ratings. We can prepare a list of those by referring to the grid:

As	Xs
1–2	1–4
1–3	3–6
2–6	3–4
3–5	
4–6	
5–6	

Next, form a cluster of A links, beginning with the department that appears most frequently in the A list (in this case, 6). For instance:

Take the remaining As in order, and add them on to this main cluster where possible, rearranging the cluster as necessary. Form separate clusters for departments that do not link with the main cluster. In this case, they all link with the main cluster:

Next, graphically portray the Xs:

Observe that, as it stands, the cluster of As also satisfies the X separations, and it is a fairly simple exercise to fit the cluster into a 2 × 3 arrangement:

1	2	6
3	5	4

(continued)

Example 5

(concluded)

It is interesting to note that the lower-level ratings have also been satisfied with this arrangement, even though no attempt was made to explicitly consider these E and I ratings. Naturally, not every problem will yield the same results, so it may be necessary to do some additional adjusting to see if improvements can be made, keeping in mind that the A and X assignments deserve the greatest consideration.

Note that departments are considered close not only when they touch side to side, but also if they touch corner to corner.

The value of this rating approach is that it permits the use of multiple objectives and subjective inputs. Its limitations relate to the use of subjective inputs in general: they are imprecise and unreliable.

COMPUTER ANALYSIS

The size and complexity of process layout problems have led to the development of a number of computerized packages. Three of the most well-known packages are ALDEP, CORELAP, and CRAFT.

ALDEP (automated layout design program) and CORELAP (computerized relationship layout planning) both use preference ratings (A-E-I-O-U-X format) and either building or space requirements. ALDEP uses an initial random selection of a department and location and then a search of remaining departments' closeness ratings with the chosen department in order to assign locations. That procedure is continued until all departments have been assigned. The completed layout is evaluated and scored according to how well the preferences have been satisfied. The program is rerun a number of times, and the best layout is identified. CORELAP processes location assignments using the preference ratings to order the choice of departments. Hence, the program begins with a department pair that has an A rating, then another A pair, and so on until all A relationships have been assigned. Next, the E relationship pairs are assigned, and so on down the line until all departments have been assigned to locations.

CRAFT (computerized relative allocation of facilities technique) seeks to minimize material flow cost. The program requires information on material flow rates between departments, unit-distance transportation costs, and an initial layout. The program exchanges department pairs until no further improvement can be achieved. The output is a printout of a rectangular layout that may or may not be optimal.

The obvious advantage of computerized analyses of layout problems is the ability to handle large problems and to consider many different layout alternatives. Even so, in most instances, the results of computer analysis require additional manual adjustments before they can be used. In some cases, this is due to irregularly shaped layouts produced by the program, and in others there is the need to check the logic of certain assignments. In the case of the CRAFT program, where the analyst must submit an initial feasible layout, different initial layouts will sometimes lead to different final solutions, so the experience and judgment of the analyst in preparing the initial layout can be an important factor.

Other computer programs exist to handle layout assignments, and it is highly likely that additional packages will be developed in the future. Although current programs cannot guarantee optimal solutions to problems, it is impossible to predict what course new program developments will take. For the present, it appears that knowledge and experience are valuable resources for dealing with process layout problems.

SUMMARY

Layout decisions are an important aspect of the design of productive systems, affecting operating costs and efficiency. Layout decisions are related to decisions involving location, products and service design, process selection, and capacity.

A major determinant of layout design is the type of processing required of a system. The three basic types are continuous, intermittent, and project. Continuous processing is characterized by a high volume of one or a few similar products or services. Intermittent processing provides the processing capability needed to deal with a broader range of products or services than continuous processing allows. Projects are the form of processing used to plan and coordinate complex jobs with relatively brief life spans. Product layouts are typically used for continuous processing, process layouts for intermittent processing, and fixed-position layouts for projects, although some projects do not require layouts.

Product layouts are geared to high-volume output of standardized items. Workers and equipment are arranged according to the technological sequence required by the product or service involved. Emphasis in design is on work flow through the system. Very often, specialized processing and handling equipment is used. Although costly, such equipment contributes to rapid processing, and the resulting high volume of output means cost per unit is relatively low. Product layouts are highly vulnerable to breakdowns, and preventive maintenance is often used to reduce the occurrence of breakdowns.

Process layouts group similar activities into departments or other work centers. Such systems can handle a wide range of processing requirements and are less susceptible to breakdowns. However, the variety of processing requirements necessitates continual routing and scheduling and the use of variable-path material-handling equipment. Also, the rate of output of such systems is generally much lower than that of product layouts.

Fixed-position layouts are used when size, fragility, cost, or other factors make it undesirable or impractical to move a product through a system. Instead, workers, equipment, and materials are brought to the product.

Other layout types include U-shaped lines, combination layouts, and cellular layouts.

The main design efforts in product layout development focus on dividing up the work required to produce a product or service into a series of tasks that are as nearly equal as possible, in an effort to achieve a high degree of utilization of labor and equipment. In process layout, design efforts often focus on the relative positioning of departments to minimize transportation costs or to meet other requirements concerning nearness of certain department pairs.

Many layout problems possess such a large number of possible alternatives that it is virtually impossible to examine each one. Instead, heuristic rules are used to guide discovery of alternatives. The solutions thus obtained are usually satisfactory although not necessarily optimal. Computer packages are available to reduce the effort required to obtain solutions to layout problems. For the most part, these too rely on heuristic methods.

KEY TERMS

**SOLVED
PROBLEMS**

Problem

1. The tasks shown in the following precedence diagram are to be assigned to workstations with the intent of minimizing idle time. Management has designed an output rate of 275 units per day. Assume 440 minutes are available per day.

   a. Determine the appropriate cycle time.
   b. What is the minimum number of stations possible?
   c. Assign tasks using the "positional weight" rule: Assign tasks with highest following times (including a task's own time) first. Break ties using greatest number of following tasks.

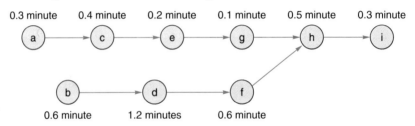

0.3 minute   0.4 minute   0.2 minute   0.1 minute   0.5 minute   0.3 minute

  (a) → (c) → (e) → (g) → (h) → (i)

     (b) → (d) → (f)

  0.6 minute   1.2 minutes   0.6 minute

Solution

a. $\text{CT} = \dfrac{\text{Operating time}}{\text{Desired output}} = \dfrac{440 \text{ minutes per day}}{275 \text{ units per day}} = 1.6 \text{ minutes}$

b. $N = \dfrac{\text{Desired output} \times \Sigma t}{\text{Operating time}} = \dfrac{275 \text{ per day} \times 4.2}{440 \text{ minutes per day}} = 2.6 \text{ (round to 3)}$

c. Add positional weights (following time including task time) to the diagram:

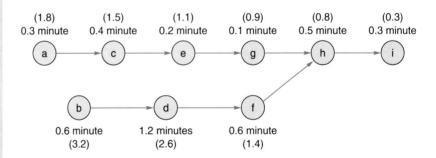

  (1.8)   (1.5)   (1.1)   (0.9)   (0.8)   (0.3)
0.3 minute   0.4 minute   0.2 minute   0.1 minute   0.5 minute   0.3 minute

  (a) → (c) → (e) → (g) → (h) → (i)

     (b) → (d) → (f)

  0.6 minute   1.2 minutes   0.6 minute
   (3.2)   (2.6)   (1.4)

Station	Time remaining★	Eligible	Will fit	Assign task/time	Station idle time
1 . . . . 1.6		a, b	a, b	b / 0.6	
	1.0	a, d	a	a / 0.3	
	0.7	c, d	c	c / 0.4	
	0.3	e, d	e	e / 0.2	
	0.1	g, d	g	g / 0.1	
	0	—	—	—	0
2 . . . . 1.6		d	d	d / 1.2	
	0.4	f	none	none	0.4
3 . . . . 1.6		f	f	f / 0.6	
	1.0	h	h	h / 0.5	
	0.5	i	i	i / 0.3	
	0.2	—	—	—	0.2
					0.6

★ The initial time for each station is the cycle time computed in part *a*.

The resulting assignments are shown below.

(Note that the time needed to produce 275 units will be 275 × 1.6 minutes = 440.0 minutes. With 440 minutes per day available, this leaves 0 minutes of "slack.")

Problem

2. Assign nine departments to locations in 3 × 3 grid so that the closeness ratings in the following matrix are satisfied. (The unimportant and ordinary-importance pair ratings have been omitted to simplify the example.) The location of department 4 must be in the upper right-hand corner of the grid to satisfy a town ordinance.

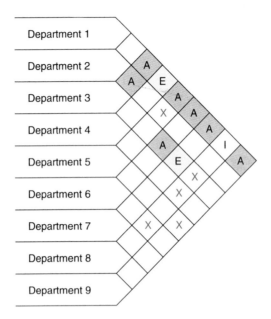

Solution

Note that department 1 has many A ratings, making it a strong candidate for the center position in the grid. We can form a cluster of departments that should be close together:

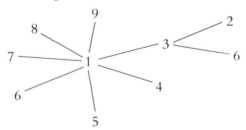

Next, we can identify departmental pairings that should be avoided:

These departments should be spaced around the perimeter of the grid. After a bit of trial and error, the final grid shown below emerged. Check it against the rating matrix to see if it satisfies the ratings.

2	3	4
9	1	6
8	7	5

Problem

3. For the set of tasks given below, do the following:

   a. Develop the precedence diagram. This describes the technological constraints.

   b. Determine the maximum cycle time for a desired output of 500 units in a 7-hour day.

   c. Determine the minimum number of work stations for output of 500 units per day.

   d. Balance the line using the *largest positional weight* heuristic. Break ties with the *most following tasks* heuristic.

   e. Calculate the percentage idle time for the line.

Task	Task time	Immediate predecessors
A	45 sec.	—
B	11	A
C	9	B
D	50	—
E	26	D
F	11	E
G	12	C
H	10	C
I	9	F, G, H
J	10	I
	193 sec.	

Solution

a.

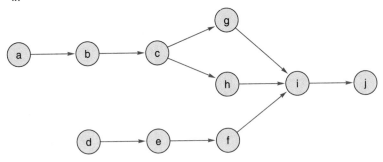

b. $\quad CT = \dfrac{OT}{D} = \dfrac{7(60)}{500} = .84 \text{ minutes} = 50.4 \text{ seconds}$

c. $\quad N = \dfrac{(D)(\Sigma t)}{OT} = \dfrac{(500)(193)}{(420)(60)} = 3.83 \text{ or } 4 \text{ stations}$

d.

Task	Followers	Positional weight
A	B, C, G, H, I, J	106
B	C, G, H, I, J	61
C	G, H, I, J	50
D	E, F, I, J	106
E	F, I, J	56
F	I, J	30
G	I, J	31
H	I, J	29
I	J	19
J	—	10

Worksheet

Station	Time remaining	Eligible	Will fit	Assign	Idle
I	50.4	A, D	A, D	A (tie)	
	5.4	B, D	—	—	5.4
II	50.4	B, D	B, D	D	
	.4	B, E	—	—	.4
III	50.4	B, E	B, E	B	
	39.4	C, E	C, E	E	
	13.4	C, F	C, F	C	
	4.4	F, G, H	—	—	4.4
IV	50.4	F, G, H	F, G, H	G	
	38.4	F, H	F, H	F	
	27.4	H	H	H	
	17.4	I	I	I	
	8.4	J	—	—	8.4
V	50.4	J	J	J	
	40.4	—	—	—	40.4
					59.0

I	II	III	IV	V
A	D	B, E, C	G, F, H, I	J

e. $\dfrac{\text{Percentage of}}{\text{idle time}} = \dfrac{\text{Total idle time}}{(\text{Number of stations})(\text{CT})} = \dfrac{59.0}{5(50.4)} = .234 \text{ or } 23.4\%$

DISCUSSION AND REVIEW QUESTIONS

1. List some common reasons for redesigning layouts.
2. Briefly describe each of the three basic layout types.
3. What are the main advantages of a product layout? The main disadvantages?
4. What are the main advantages of a process layout? The main disadvantages?

5. What is the goal of line balancing? What happens if a line is unbalanced?

6. Why are routing and scheduling continual problems in a process layout?

7. Compare equipment maintenance strategies in product and process layouts.

8. Briefly outline the impact that job sequence has on each of the layout types.

9. The City Transportation Planning Committee must make a decision on whether to begin a long-term project to build a subway system or to upgrade bus service. Since you are an expert in fixed-path and variable-path material-handling equipment, your counsel has been sought on this matter. How would you compare the advantages and limitations of subway versus bus?

10. Identify the fixed-path and variable-path material-handling equipment commonly found in supermarkets.

11. What are heuristic approaches, and why are they used in designing layouts?

12. Why are product layouts atypical in nonmanufacturing environments?

13. According to a recent study by the Alliance of American Insurers, it would cost more than three times the original purchase price in parts and labor to replace a totally wrecked Chevrolet. Explain some of the reasons for this large discrepancy in terms of the processes used to assemble the original car versus those required to reconstruct the wrecked car.

14. What are some of the ways that layout can help or hinder productivity?

15. What is cellular manufacturing? What are its main benefits and limitations?

16. What is group technology?

17. What is a flexible manufacturing system?

PROBLEMS

1. An assembly line with 17 tasks is to be balanced. The longest task is 2.4 minutes, and the sum of task times is 18 minutes. The line will operate for 450 minutes per day.
   a. Determine the minimum and maximum cycle times.
   b. What range of output is theoretically possible for the line?
   c. What is the minimum number of stations needed if the maximum output rate is to be sought?
   d. What cycle time will provide an output rate of 125 units per day?
   e. What output potential will result if the cycle time is (1) 9 minutes? (2) 15 minutes?

2. A large manufacturer of plastic saddles is planning to add a new line of multicolored saddles, and you have been asked to balance the process, given the following task times and precedence relationships. Assume that cycle time is to be the minimum length possible.

Task	Length (minutes)	Immediate predecessor
a	0.2	—
b	0.4	a
c	0.3	—
d	1.3	b, c
e	0.1	—
f	0.8	e
g	0.3	d, f
h	1.2	g

Do each of the following:

a. Draw the precedence diagram.
b. Assign tasks to stations in order of greatest number of following tasks.
c. Determine the percentage of idle time.
d. Compute the rate of output that could be expected for this line assuming a 420-minute working day.

3. In the previous problem:
a. What is the shortest cycle time that will permit use of only two workstations? Is this cycle time feasible? Identify the tasks you would assign to each station.
b. Determine the percentage of idle time that would result if two stations were to be used.
c. What would the daily output be under this arrangement?
d. Determine the output rate that would be associated with the maximum cycle time.

4. As part of a major plant renovation project, the industrial engineering department has been asked to balance a revised assembly operation to achieve an output of 480 units per eight-hour day. Task times and precedence relationships are as follows:

Task	Duration (minutes)	Follows task
a	0.1	—
b	0.2	a
c	0.1	b
d	0.2	—
e	0.6	d
f	0.6	c
g	0.5	e, f

Do each of the following:

a. Draw the precedence diagram.
b. Determine the maximum cycle time.
c. Determine the minimum number of stations needed.
d. Assign tasks to stations on the basis of greatest number of following tasks; use longest processing time as a tiebreaker. If ties still exist, assume indifference in choice.
e. Compute the percentage of idle time for the assignment in part d.
f. Assign tasks to workstations in order of greatest number of preceding tasks, using the same tiebreaker as in d.
g. Compute the percentage of idle time for the assignment in part f.

5. Twelve tasks, with times and precedence requirements as shown in the following table, are to be assigned to workstations using a cycle time of 1.5 minutes. Three heuristic rules will be tried: (1) greatest positional weight, (2) greatest number of following tasks, and (3) longest task first.

In each case, the tiebreaker will be shortest task time.

Task	Length (minutes)	Follows task
a	0.1	—
b	0.2	a
c	0.9	b
d	0.6	c
e	0.1	—
f	0.2	d, e
g	0.4	f
h	0.1	g
i	0.2	h
j	0.7	i
k	0.3	j
l	0.2	k

   a.   Draw the precedence diagram for this line.
   b.   Assign tasks to stations under each of the three rules.
   c.   Compute the percentage of idle time for each rule.

6.   Arrange six departments into a 2 × 3 grid so that these conditions are satisfied: 1 close to 2, 5 close to 6, 2 close to 5, and 3 not close to 1.

7.   Using the information given in the preceding problem, develop a Muther-type grid using the letters A, O, and X. Assume any pair combinations not mentioned have an O rating.

8.   Using the information in the following grid, determine if the department locations shown are appropriate. If they are not, modify the assignments so that the conditions are satisfied.

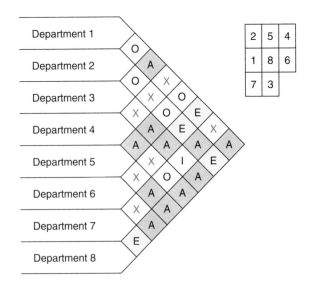

9. Arrange the eight departments shown in the accompanying Muther grid into a 2 × 4 format. *Note:* Department 1 must be in the location shown.

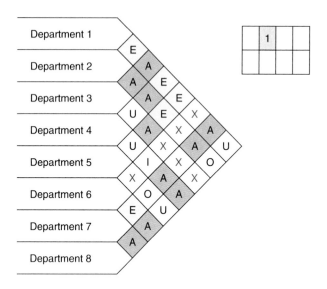

10. Arrange the departments so they satisfy the conditions shown in the following rating grid into a 3 × 3 format. Place department 5 in the lower left corner of the 3 × 3 grid.

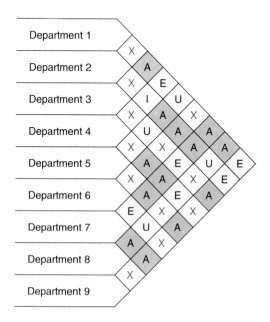

11. Assign six work centers to locations A–F, given the following information, so that the total distance traveled is minimized. Assume work center 6 must be in location A. Compute the total cost of your plan if the transportation cost is $2 per load per foot. Assume the reverse distances are equal (e.g., B to A = 50 feet = A to B).

		Distance between locations (feet)					
From	**To**	**A**	**B**	**C**	**D**	**E**	**F**
A		—	50	100	50	80	130
B			—	50	90	40	70
C				—	140	60	50
D					—	50	120
E						—	50
F							—

		Number of trips per day between centers					
From	**To**	**1**	**2**	**3**	**4**	**5**	**6**
1		—	90	25	23	11	18
2		35	—	8	5	10	16
3		37	2	—	1	0	7
4		41	12	1	—	4	0
5		14	16	0	9	—	3
6		32	38	13	2	2	—

A	B	C
D	E	F

12. Eight work centers must be arranged in an L-shaped building. The locations of centers 1 and 3 are designated as shown in the accompanying diagram. Assuming transportation costs are $1 per load per meter, develop a suitable layout that minimizes transportation costs using the given information. Compute the total cost. (Assume the reverse distances are the same.)

		Distances (meters)							
From	**To**	**A**	**B**	**C**	**D**	**E**	**F**	**G**	**H**
A		—	40	40	60	120	80	100	110
B			—	60	40	60	140	120	130
C				—	45	85	40	70	90
D					—	40	50	40	45
E						—	90	50	40
F							—	40	60
G								—	40
H									—

From	To	1	2	3	4	5	6	7	8
					Loads per day				
1		—	10	5	90	365	135	125	0
2		0	—	140	10	0	35	0	120
3		0	220	—	110	10	0	0	200
4		0	110	240	—	10	0	0	170
5		5	40	100	180	—	10	40	10
6		0	80	40	70	0	—	10	20
7		0	45	20	50	0	40	—	20
8		0	0	0	20	0	0	0	—

13. Develop a process layout that will minimize the total distance traveled by patients at a medical clinic, using the following information on projected departmental visits by patients and distance between locations. Assume a distance of 35 feet between the reception area and each potential location. Use the format shown.

From	To	A	B	C	D	E	F
			Distance between locations (feet)				
A		—	40	80	100	120	160
B			—	40	60	80	120
C				—	20	40	80
D					—	20	40
E						—	40
F							—

From	To	1	2	3	4	5	6	Reception
				Trips between departments (per day)				
Reception		10	10	200	20	0	100	—
1		—	0	0	80	20	40	10
2		0	—	0	0	0	20	40
3		40	0	—	10	190	10	10
4		30	50	0	—	10	70	0
5		60	40	60	30	—	20	10
6		10	100	0	20	0	—	30

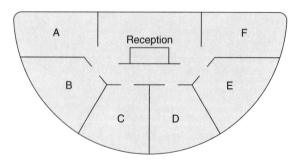

14. Ten labs will be assigned to the circular layout shown. Recalling a similar layout's congestion in the halls, the new lab manager has requested an assignment that will mini-

mize traffic between offices. In addition, movement in the halls is restricted to a counterclockwise route. Develop a suitable layout using the following information.

Number of trips per day between departments

From \ To	1	2	3	4	5	6	7	8	9	10
1	—	40	1	20	20	4	0	2	6	5
2	0	—	2	15	25	10	2	12	13	6
3	50	35	—	10	13	4	0	4	7	1
4	6	1	8	—	0	14	10	20	22	11
5	3	2	7	35	—	22	5	9	19	10
6	5	5	10	0	2	—	15	0	1	20
7	20	16	50	4	9	2	—	1	3	0
8	10	6	14	2	4	44	13	—	1	25
9	5	5	18	1	2	40	30	42	—	32
10	30	30	35	20	15	5	40	10	15	—

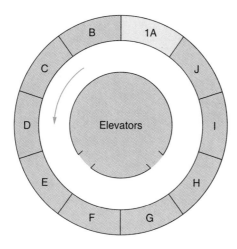

15. Rebalance the assembly line in Solved Problem 3. This time, use the *longest operation time* heuristic. Break ties with the *most following tasks* heuristic. What is the percent idle time for your line?

SELECTED BIBLIOGRAPHY

Fogarty, Donald W., and Thomas R. Hoffman. *Production and Inventory Management.* Cincinnati: South-Western Publishing, 1983.

Foulkes, Fred K., and J. L. Hirsch. "People Make Robots Work." *Harvard Business Review,* January–February 1984, p. 94.

Francis, R. L., and J. A. White. *Facility Layout and Location: An Analytical Approach.* Englewood Cliffs, N.J.: Prentice Hall, 1974.

Gerwin, D. "Do's and Don'ts of Computerized Manufacturing." *Harvard Business Review,* March–April 1982, pp. 107–16.

Gold, B. "CAM Sets New Rules for Production." *Harvard Business Review,* November–December 1982, pp. 88–94.

Groover, Mikell P. *Automation, Production Systems, and Computer-Aided Manufacturing*. Englewood Cliffs, N.J.: Prentice Hall, 1980.

Hendrick, T. E., and F. G. Moore. *Production/Operations Management*. 9th ed. Homewood, Ill.: Richard D. Irwin, 1985.

Hicks, P. E., and T. E. Cowan. "CRAFT-M for Layout Rearrangement." *Industrial Engineering* 8 (May 1976), pp. 30–35.

Kilbridge, M. D., and L. Wester. "A Heuristic Method of Assembly Line Balancing." *Journal of Industrial Engineering* 12 (July–August 1961).

Lee, R. C., and J. M. Moore. "CORELAP—Computerized Relationship Layout Planning." *Journal of Industrial Engineering* 18 (March 1967), pp. 195–200.

Muther, R., and K. McPherson. "Four Approaches to Computerized Layout Planning." *Industrial Engineering* 2 (1970), pp. 39–42.

Reed, R. *Plant Location, Layout and Maintenance*. Homewood, Ill.: Richard D. Irwin, 1967.

CHAPTER EIGHT

DESIGN OF
WORK SYSTEMS

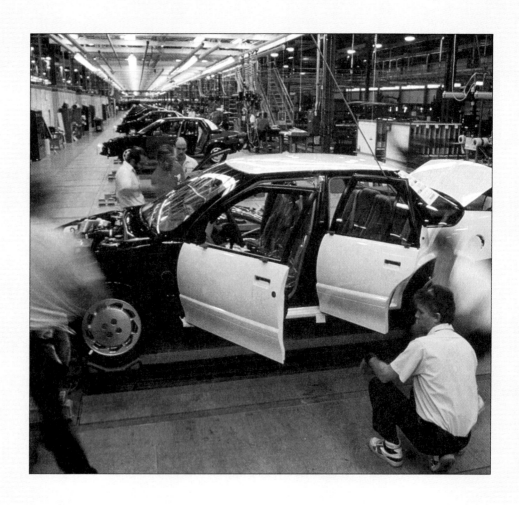

After completing this chapter, you should be able to:

1. Explain the importance of work design.
2. Briefly describe the two basic approaches to job design.
3. Discuss the advantages and disadvantages of specialization and automation.
4. Explain the term *sociotechnical system*.
5. Explain the purpose of methods analysis and describe how methods studies are done.
6. Describe four commonly used techniques for motion study.
7. Discuss the impact of working conditions on job design.
8. Define a standard time.
9. Discuss and compare time study methods.
10. Describe work sampling and perform calculations.
11. Compare stopwatch time study and work sampling.
12. Contrast time and output pay systems.

This chapter is devoted to design of work systems. Work design involves *job design, work measurement* and the establishment of time standards, and worker *compensation.*

As you read this chapter, note how decisions in the other design areas have an impact on work systems, and how decisions on work design have an impact on the other areas. For example, product or service design decisions (e.g., operate a coal mine, offer computer dating service, sell sports equipment) in large measure determine the kinds of activities workers will be involved with. Similarly, layout decisions often influence work design. Process layouts tend to necessitate broader job content than product layouts. The implication of these interrelationships is that it is essential to adopt a systems approach to design; decisions in one area must be related to the overall system.

INTRODUCTION

The importance of work system design is underscored by the fact that the organization depends on human efforts (i.e., work) to accomplish its goals. Work design is one of the oldest areas of operations management. In the past, it has often been deemphasized in operations management courses in favor of other topics. In recent years, however, there has been renewed interest in this area, which has come from somewhat different directions: Some of the interest has resulted from studies that reveal a general dissatisfaction felt by many workers with their jobs. And some of the interest has been sparked by increasing concerns over productivity. It is perhaps ironic that one of the oldest areas of operations management is now an important key to productivity improvement and to continuous improvement.

OPERATIONS STRATEGY

It is important for management to make design of work systems a key element of its operations strategy. In spite of the major advances in computers and manufacturing technology, people are still the heart of a business; they can make or break it, regardless of the technology used. That is not to say that technology is unimportant, but that technology alone is not enough.

The topics described in this chapter—job design, methods analysis, motion study, work standards, and incentives—all have an impact on productivity. They lack the glamour of high tech; they are closer to the back-to-the-basics fundamentals of work improvement.

Workers can be a valuable source of insight and creativity since they actually perform the jobs and are closest to the problems that arise. All too often, managers have overlooked contributions and potential contributions of employees, sometimes because of ignorance and sometimes because of a false sense of pride. Union-management differences also contribute to this. More and more, though, companies are attempting to develop a spirit of cooperation between employees and managers, based in part on the success of Japanese companies.

In the same vein, more and more companies are focusing some of their attention on improving the quality of work life and on instilling pride and respect among workers. Many organizations are reaping surprising gains through worker *empowerment,* giving workers more say over their jobs.

People work for a variety of reasons. Economic necessity is among the most important, but beyond that, people work for socialization, to give meaning and purpose to their lives, for status, for personal growth, and for other reasons. These can play an important role in the lives of workers, and should be accorded serious consideration in the design of work systems.

JOB DESIGN

Job design is concerned with specifying the contents and methods of jobs. In general, the goal of job design is to create a work system that is productive and efficient, taking into consideration the costs and benefits of various alternatives for the organization and for the workers. Practically speaking, job designers are concerned with *who* will do a job, *how* the job will be done, and *where* the job will be done.

> **Job design**
> The act of specifying the contents and methods of jobs.

In order for job design to be successful, it must be:

1. Carried out by experienced personnel who have the necessary training and background.
2. Consistent with the goals of the organization.
3. In written form.
4. Understood and agreed to by both management and employees.

The factors that affect job design and the implications of various alternatives are often so complex that a person without a good background in job design is likely to overlook important aspects of it. Workers and managers alike should be consulted in order to take advantage of their knowledge as well as to keep them informed. Because they are intimately involved with the work, employees are the source of valuable ideas for job improvements. Managerial support for job design depends on the commitment and involvement of managers. It is usually easier to sell a design to these two groups if they have been included in the process. Finally, establishing a written record of the job design can serve as a basis for referral if questions arise about it.

Current practice in job design contains elements of two basic schools of thought. One might be called the *efficiency* school because it emphasizes a systematic, logical approach to job design; the other is called the *behavioral* school because it emphasizes satisfaction of wants and needs.

The efficiency approach, a refinement of Frederick Winslow Taylor's scientific management concepts, has received considerable emphasis in the past. The behavioral approach emerged during the 1950s and has continued to make inroads into many aspects of job design. One of the main contributions of the behavioral approach is that it has reminded managers of the fact that humans are complex beings, and the efficiency approach may not be appropriate in every instance.

The behavioral view received a shot in the arm in the 1970s, when the report *Work in America* was released, detailing some of the problems that currently exist in our work systems.[1] The report revealed an apparently widespread dissatisfaction on the part of workers across the spectrum of jobs. Two points were of special interest to job designers. One was that many workers felt that their jobs were not interesting; the other was that workers wanted more control over their jobs. The central

---

[1] Upjohn Institute for Employment Research, *Work in America* (Cambridge, Mass.: MIT Press, 1973).

An employee at Ford, a specialist, paints trucks without a mask. For safety, a forced-air downdraft system pulls the paint down through the floor grates where it is trapped in water.

issue seemed to be the degree of specialization associated with jobs: high specialization appeared to generate the most dissatisfaction. It is noteworthy that the issue of specialization is a primary source of disagreement between the efficiency and behavioral approaches.

SPECIALIZATION

Specialization

Concentration on some aspect of a product or service.

Specialization is a term used to describe jobs that have a very narrow scope. Examples range from assembly lines to medical specialties. College professors often specialize in teaching certain courses, some auto mechanics specialize in transmission repair, and some bakeries specialize in wedding cakes. The main rationale for specialization is the ability to concentrate one's efforts and thereby become proficient in some aspect of a product of service.

Sometimes the amount of knowledge or training required of a specialist and the complexity of the work suggest that individuals who choose such work are not unhappy with their jobs. This seems to be especially true in the "professions" (doctors, lawyers, professors, etc.). However, at the other end of the scale are assembly line workers, who are also specialists, although much less glamourous. The advantage of these highly specialized jobs is that they yield high productivity and low unit costs. In fact, such specialization is largely responsible for the high standard of living that exists today in industrial nations.

Unfortunately, many of these jobs can be described as monotonous or downright boring, and they are apparently the source of much of the dissatisfaction that exists in industry today. Even so, it would be wrong to conclude that all workers oppose this type of work. Some workers undoubtedly prefer a job with limited requirements and responsibility for making decisions. Others are not capable of handling jobs with larger scopes. Nonetheless, many workers are frustrated in such jobs, and this manifests itself in a number of ways. Turnover and absenteeism are often high in these jobs. For example, in the automotive industry, absenteeism runs

Advantages

For management:
1. Simplifies training
2. High productivity
3. Low wage costs

For labor:
1. Low education and skill requirements
2. Minimum responsibilities
3. Little mental effort needed

Disadvantages

For management:
1. Difficult to motivate quality
2. Worker dissatisfaction, possibly resulting in absenteeism, high turnover, disruptive tactics, poor attention to quality

For labor:
1. Monotonous boring work
2. Limited opportunities for advancement
3. Little control over work
4. Little opportunity for self-fulfillment

as high as 20 percent, although not every absentee is a frustrated worker on an assembly line. Workers may also take out their frustrations through disruptive tactics, deliberate slowdowns, or poor attention to product quality.

The seriousness of these problems has caused job designers and others to seek ways of alleviating them. Some of those approaches are discussed in the following sections. Before we turn to them, it will be helpful to reflect on the advantages and disadvantages of specialization, which are summarized in Table 8–1.

BEHAVIORAL APPROACHES TO JOB DESIGN

In an effort to make jobs more interesting and meaningful, job designers frequently consider job enlargement, job rotation, job enrichment, and increased use of mechanization.

Job enlargement means giving a worker a larger portion of the total task. This constitutes horizontal loading—the additional work is on the same level of skill and responsibility as the original job. Schematically, this can be depicted as:

Job enlargement
Giving a worker a larger portion of the total task, by horizontal loading.

⟵ Present job ⟶

The goal is to make the job more interesting by increasing the variety of skills required and by providing the worker with a more recognizable contribution to the overall output. For example, in a supermarket setting, instead of having employees work exclusively in the produce or meat department, they might be given assignments in two or more of these departments. Similarly, a production worker's job might be expanded so that he or she is responsible for a *sequence* of activities instead of only one activity.

Job rotation means periodically having workers exchange jobs. This approach can be used to avoid having one or a few employees stuck in boring or monotonous jobs. It works best when workers can be transferred to more interesting jobs; there is little advantage in merely having workers exchange one boring job for another. Job rotation allows workers to broaden their learning experience and enables workers to fill in for others in the event of sickness or absenteeism.

Job rotation
Workers periodically exchange jobs.

Job enrichment

Increasing responsibility for planning and coordination tasks, by vertical loading.

Job enrichment involves an increase in the level of responsibility for planning and coordination tasks. In effect, it represents a vertical loading:

Present job

An example of this is to have stock clerks in supermarkets handle reordering of goods, thus increasing their responsibilities. The job enrichment approach focuses on the motivating potential of worker satisfaction. Among the proponents of this approach is Frederick Herzberg, who published a study indicating that factors such as achievement, recognition, and responsibility have the potential for generating satisfaction but not dissatisfaction, while factors such as supervision, pay, and working conditions have the opposite potential of leading to dissatisfaction but not satisfaction.[2] According to this view, job enrichment can be a source of satisfaction by adding more of the factors that have satisfaction potential.

In a later study, Richard Hackman and G. R. Oldham proposed that job enrichment can lead to improved worker performance if the worker perceives that the work is meaningful, accepts responsibility for the outcome, and receives knowledge of the results.[3] However, they point out that job enrichment should not be used without a careful investigation of the need for changes and of what changes are most apt to succeed. In effect, they warn that not all jobs or workers are amenable to job enrichment, nor would they necessarily benefit from enrichment. Toward that end, they have developed a questionnaire that can be used to diagnose the motivating potential of job enrichment.[4] The diagnosis focuses on four dimensions:

1. Is there a problem with motivation and job satisfaction?
2. What is the motivating potential of the job?
3. What aspects of the job are causing difficulty?
4. Will employees accept the necessary changes?

Increased use of mechanization often enables designers to free workers from repetitious work, which tends to be monotonous and boring. This mechanization may take the form of automation, which is discussed more fully in the following section.

The essence of these approaches to job design is that they attempt to increase the motivational power of jobs by increasing worker satisfaction through improvement in the *quality of work life*. Many firms are currently involved in or seriously considering programs related to quality of work life. In addition to the aforementioned approaches, organizations are also experimenting with choice of locations (e.g., medium-sized cities or campus-like settings, when feasible), flexible work hours, and quality circles, which are described in the chapter on quality assurance.

[2] F. Herzberg, B. Mausner, and B. Snyderman, *The Motivation to Work* (New York: John Wiley & Sons, 1959).

[3] J. Richard Hackman, G. R. Oldham, Jane L. Pearce, and Jane Caminis, "A New Strategy for Job Enrichment," *California Management Review,* Summer 1975, pp. 57–77.

[4] Richard Hackman and G. R. Oldham, "Development of the Job Diagnostic Survey," *Journal of Applied Psychology* 60 (1975), pp. 159–70.

AUTOMATION

The use of mechanical and/or electronic devices in place of human effort is referred to as **automation**. Under this heading come automatic processing equipment, computers, industrial robots, and similar devices. A key feature of these devices is their ability to exert control over a process without human intervention. There are numerous benefits, as well as potential drawbacks, associated with automation.

Among the benefits of automation are the following:

1. The jobs most susceptible to automation are those that are repetitive, boring, and monotonous. Hence, the jobs that are least desirable from a human standpoint often lend themselves to automation.
2. Automation yields a highly uniform output and generally results in higher quality compared with human-generated output.
3. The rate of output generally exceeds human capabilities.
4. Human conflicts are avoided.

Among the potential drawbacks of automation are the following:

1. The traditional argument against automation is that it displaces humans. Although automation has been shown to result in more jobs rather than fewer, and the jobs created are more interesting than those lost, the workers must be retrained, which adds to the cost. Moreover, workers often tend to resist change, and fear loss of jobs.
2. Automated systems often involve substantial costs, and this necessitates a high volume of output to make the system economical.
3. Automated systems can be inflexible because they are often restricted by design to a narrow range of tasks.
4. Automated systems do no problem solving or continuous improvement; workers are needed for those jobs.

Compared with American firms, the Japanese are much greater users of automated processing in the automotive and steel industries, but they are considerably less automated in agriculture. The successes of the Japanese in the areas of quality and productivity in industrial applications of automation, and the U.S. successes in agriculture, have caused managers in many U.S. firms to give more attention to the possible benefits of automation. There has not yet been a wholesale rush toward it. One possible reason is the resistance of labor unions. Another is the enormous cost, coupled with a long period of time before payoffs can be realized. Still another reason is the costs and difficulties of retraining employees and the problems associated with integrating automated systems into current operations.

SOCIOTECHNICAL SYSTEMS

The **sociotechnical systems** approach is concerned with the human-technology interface. Specifically, it recognizes that choice of technology can and often does have an impact on the social structure within an organization, and that technological changes (redesign of layout, automation, introduction of new techniques) can and often do have detrimental effects on worker performance. Proponents of this approach argue that there are often technological alternatives that would produce

Automation

The use of mechanical and/or electronic devices in place of human effort.

Sociotechnical systems

Approach that focuses on both technological efficiency and sociological benefits.

desired results and still be consistent with sociological considerations. Hence, the focus is on finding a design that is consistent with both technological efficiency and the existing sociological system. This approach is very similar to job enrichment in that it seeks task variety, skill variety, task autonomy, and feedback. It goes beyond that approach by giving workers more say in how work is actually done and by allowing workers to self-organize. Because of this, a certain amount of controversy surrounds the sociotechnical approach, and there has not been widespread acceptance of this approach, although some foreign firms are using it. It may be that such an approach is more suited to Japan's work environment, where staff personnel such as industrial engineers and quality control experts are viewed as consultants, available to assist workers but not to specify work procedures. A major obstacle to greater use of the sociotechnical approach appears to be the reluctance of managers to entrust more of their authority to their workers. Although in some cases such fears are unfounded, in other cases they are not. Consequently, much additional work remains to be done before we can say how, and to what extent, sociotechnical systems should be used in job design.

METHODS ANALYSIS

Job design often begins with a methods analysis of an overall operation. You might call it a macro view of the job. It then moves from the general to specific details of the job, concentrating on arrangement of the workplace and movements of the worker. Methods analysis can be a good source of productivity improvements.

The need for methods analysis can come from a number of different sources, such as:

1. Changes in tools and equipment.
2. Changes in product design, or new products.
3. Changes in materials or procedures.
4. Government regulations or contractual agreements.
5. Other factors (e.g., accidents, quality problems).

The analysis and design of jobs and job flows can also be automated with tools such as the SAS software shown here.

Methods analysis is done both for existing jobs and for jobs that have not yet been performed. At first glance, it might seem strange to analyze methods of a nonexisting job. However, someone has to establish a method for a new job, and it is usually wise to have a person who is trained to handle this do it at the start rather than allow the job to begin and then try to improve it later. For an existing job, the procedure is generally to have the analyst first observe the job as it is currently being done and then devise improvements. For a brand new job, the analyst must rely on a description of the job and an ability to visualize the operation in advance.

The basic procedure in methods analysis is:

1. Identify the operation to be studied, and gather all pertinent facts regarding tools, equipment, materials, and so on.
2. If the job is currently being done, discuss the job with the operator and supervisor to get their input.
3. Study and document the present method of an existing job using process charts. For new jobs, develop charts based on information about the activities involved.
4. Analyze the job.
5. Propose new methods.
6. Install the new methods.
7. Follow up installation to assure that improvements have been achieved.

Selecting an Operation to Study   Sometimes a foreman or supervisor will request that a certain operation be studied. At other times, methods analysis will be part of an overall program to increase productivity and reduce costs. Some general guidelines for selecting a job to study are to consider jobs that:

1. Have a high labor content.
2. Are done frequently.
3. Are unsafe, tiring, unpleasant, and/or noisy.
4. Are designated as problems (e.g., quality problems, scheduling bottlenecks).

Documenting the Present Method   Use charts, graphs, and verbal descriptions of the way the job is now being done. This will provide a good understanding of the job and serve as a basis of comparison against which revisions can be judged.

Analyzing the Job and Proposing New Methods   Analyzing the job requires that the analyst carefully consider the what, why, when, where, and who of the job. Often, simply going through these questions will clarify the review process by encouraging the analyst to take a "devil's advocate" attitude toward both the present and the proposed methods.

Analyzing and improving methods is facilitated by the use of various charts such as *flow process charts* and *worker-machine charts*. Another chart that is sometimes useful is a *gang process chart*.

Using time and motion study will often lead to more efficient manufacturing processes. Here, a Ford Explorer body, which has been welded, painted, and trimmed, is carefully lowered onto the chassis with the drivetrain components already in place. This operation, which is performed 84 times per hour, eliminates the need to install the engine through the hood.

Flow process chart

Chart used to examine the overall sequence of an operation by focusing on movements of the operator or flow of materials.

Flow process charts are used to review and critically examine the overall sequence of an operation by focusing on either the movements of the operator or the flow of materials. These charts can be very helpful in identifying nonproductive parts of the process (e.g., delays, temporary storages, distances traveled).

Figure 8–1 describes the symbols used in constructing a flow process chart, and Figure 8–2 illustrates a flow process chart.

The uses for flow process charts include studying the flow of material through a department, studying the sequence that documents or forms take, analyzing movement and care of surgical patients, layout of department and grocery stores, and mail handling.

Experienced analysts usually develop a checklist of questions they ask themselves to generate ideas for improvements. Some representative questions are:

1. Why is there a delay or storage at this point?
2. How can travel distances be shortened or avoided?
3. Can materials handling be reduced?
4. Would a rearrangement of the workplace result in greater efficiency?
5. Can similar activities be grouped?
6. Would the use of additional or improved equipment be helpful?
7. Does the worker have any ideas for improvements?

Worker-machine chart

Chart used to determine portions of a work cycle during which an operator and equipment are busy or idle.

A **worker-machine chart** is helpful for visualizing the portions of a work cycle during which an operator and equipment are busy or idle. The analyst can easily see when the operator and machine are working independently as well as when their work overlaps or is interdependent. One use of this type of chart is to determine how many machines or how much equipment the operator can manage.

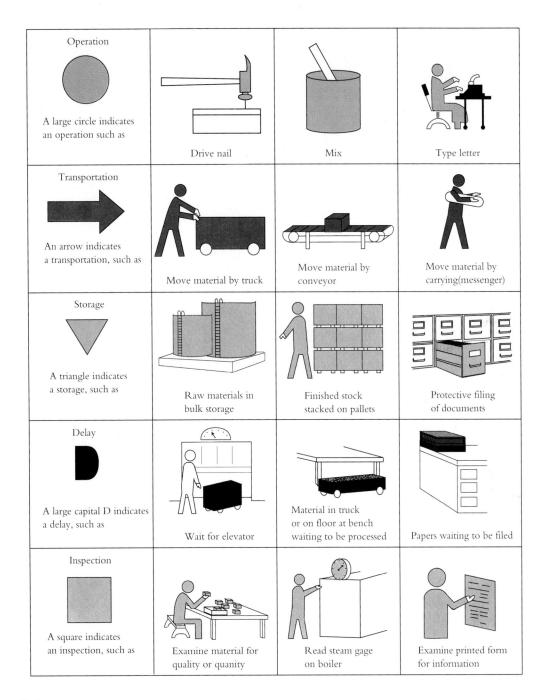

Figure 8–1

Process chart symbols

Source: Benjamin W. Niebel, *Motion and Time Study,* 8th ed. (Homewood, Ill.: Richard D. Irwin, 1988), p. 33. © 1988 by Richard D. Irwin, Inc. Reprinted by permission.

Figure 8–2

Format of a flow process chart

FLOW PROCESS CHART	ANALYST	PAGE					
Job Requisition of petty cash	D. Kolb	1 of 2	Operation	Movement	Inspection	Delay	Storage
Details of method							
Requisition made out by department head			◯	⇨	☐	D	▽
Put in "pick-up" basket			◯	⇨	☐	D	▽
To accounting department			◯	⇨	☐	D	▽
Account and signature verified			◯	⇨	☐	D	▽
Amount approved by treasurer			◯	⇨	☐	D	▽
Amount counted by cashier			◯	⇨	☐	D	▽
Amount recorded by bookkeeper			◯	⇨	☐	D	▽
Petty cash sealed in envelope			◯	⇨	☐	D	▽
Petty cash carried to department			◯	⇨	☐	D	▽
Petty cash checked against requisition			◯	⇨	☐	D	▽
Receipt signed			◯	⇨	☐	D	▽
Petty cash stored in safety box			◯	⇨	☐	D	▽
			◯	⇨	☐	D	▽
			◯	⇨	☐	D	▽
			◯	⇨	☐	D	▽
			◯	⇨	☐	D	▽

Source: Elias M. Awad, *Systems Analysis and Design,* 4th ed. (Homewood, Ill.: Richard D. Irwin, 1985, p. 113. © 1985 by Richard D. Irwin, Inc. Reprinted by permission.

An example of a worker-machine chart is presented in Figure 8–3. Among other things, the chart highlights worker and machine utilization.

Another multiactivity chart is the **gang process chart**. It is useful in coordinating and analyzing a *team* of workers because it provides a cross-sectional view of the work at any point. The chart also reveals individual utilizations. An example of this kind of chart is shown in Figure 8–4.

Gang process chart

Multiactivity chart showing both individual operations and work being done by the team at any point.

Installing the Improved Method   Successful implementation of proposed method changes requires convincing management of the desirability of the new method and obtaining the cooperation of the worker. If the worker has been consulted throughout the process and has made suggestions that are incorporated in the proposed changes, this part of the task will be considerably easier than if the analyst has assumed sole responsibility for the development of the proposal.

Figure 8–3

Worker-machine chart

| Product: Produce | Operator: L.W. |
| Process: | Charted by: R.G. |

Step	Employee	Time (seconds)	Machine
1	Accepts produce from customer and places on scale	0 1	
2	Punches in price/lb	2	
3		3	Calculates and displays total price
4	Removes produce	4	
5	Notes price and marks on produce	5 6	
6	Hands produce to customer	7 8	

Summary

	Employee		Machine	
	Time (seconds)	%	Time (seconds)	%
Work	7	87.5	1	12.5
Idle	1	12.5	7	87.5

If the proposed method constitutes a major change from the way the job has been performed in the past, workers may have to undergo a certain amount of training, and full implementation may take some time to achieve.

The Follow-Up In order to insure that changes have been made and that the proposed method is functioning as expected, the analyst should review the operation after a reasonable period and consult again with the operator.

MOTION STUDY

Motion study is the systematic study of the human motions used to perform an operation. The purpose is to eliminate unnecessary motions and to identify the best sequence of motions for maximum efficiency. Hence, motion study can be an important avenue for productivity improvements. Present practice evolved from the work of Frank Gilbreth, who originated the concepts in the bricklaying trade in the early part of this century. Through the use of motion study techniques, Gilbreth is generally credited with increasing the average number of bricks laid per hour by

Motion study

Systematic study of the human motions used to perform an operation.

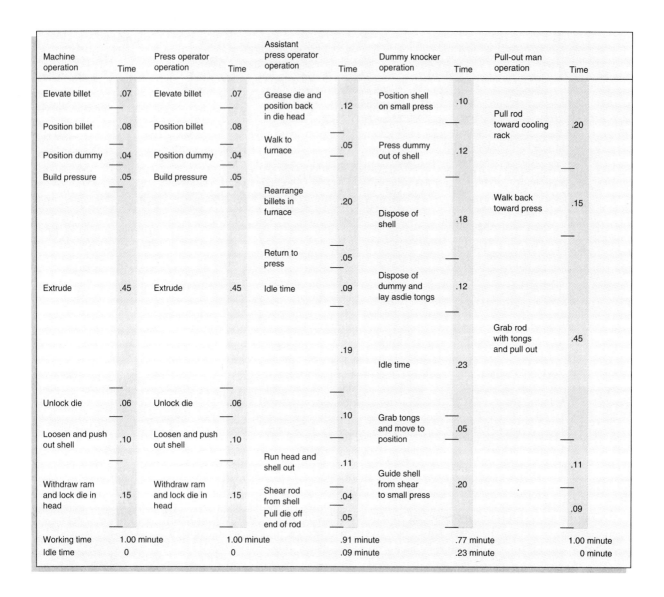

Machine operation	Time	Press operator operation	Time	Assistant press operator operation	Time	Dummy knocker operation	Time	Pull-out man operation	Time
Elevate billet	.07	Elevate billet	.07	Grease die and position back in die head	.12	Position shell on small press	.10	Pull rod toward cooling rack	.20
Position billet	.08	Position billet	.08	Walk to furnace	.05	Press dummy out of shell	.12		
Position dummy	.04	Position dummy	.04						
Build pressure	.05	Build pressure	.05	Rearrange billets in furnace	.20	Dispose of shell	.18	Walk back toward press	.15
				Return to press	.05				
Extrude	.45	Extrude	.45	Idle time	.09	Dispose of dummy and lay asdie tongs	.12		
					.19			Grab rod with tongs and pull out	.45
						Idle time	.23		
Unlock die	.06	Unlock die	.06		.10	Grab tongs and move to position	.05		
Loosen and push out shell	.10	Loosen and push out shell	.10	Run head and shell out	.11	Guide shell from shear to small press	.20		.11
Withdraw ram and lock die in head	.15	Withdraw ram and lock die in head	.15	Shear rod from shell	.04				.09
				Pull die off end of rod	.05				
Working time	1.00 minute		1.00 minute		.91 minute		.77 minute		1.00 minute
Idle time	0		0		.09 minute		.23 minute		0 minute

Figure 8–4

Multiactivity chart (gang process): Hydraulic extrusion process, proposed method

Source: Benjamin W. Niebel, *Motion and Time Study*, 8th ed. (Homewood, Ill.: Richard D. Irwin, 1988), p. 157. © 1988 by Richard D. Irwin, Inc. Reprinted by permission.

a factor of 3, even though he was not a bricklayer by trade. When you stop to realize that bricklaying had been carried on for centuries, Gilbreth's accomplishment is even more remarkable.

There are a number of different techniques that motion study analysts can use to develop efficient procedures. The most-used techniques are:

1. Motion study principles.
2. Analysis of therbligs.

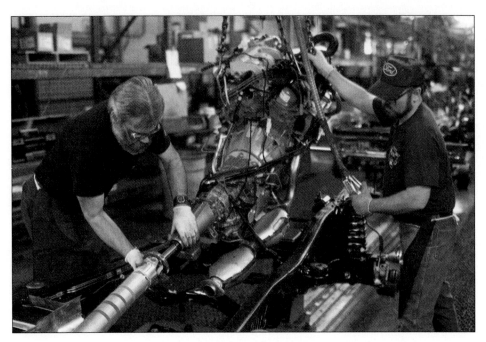

Two workers at the Ford plant in Louisville, Kentucky, work together to lower the transmission and engine assembly onto a Ford Ranger pickup truck chassis. The plant produces three different models including the Ford Ranger and Mazda Navajo.

3. Micromotion study.
4. Charts.

The work of Gilbreth laid the foundation for development of **motion study principles**, which are guidelines for designing motion-efficient work procedures. The guidelines are divided into three categories: principles for use of the body, principles for arrangement of the workplace, and principles for the design of tools and equipment. The principles are listed in Table 8–2.

Motion study principles
Guidelines for designing motion-efficient work procedures.

In developing work methods that are motion-efficient, the analyst tries to:

1. Eliminate unnecessary motions.
2. Combine activities.
3. Reduce fatigue.
4. Improve the arrangement of the workplace.
5. Improve the design of tools and equipment.

Therbligs are basic elemental motions. The name *therblig* is Gilbreth spelled backwards (except for the *th*). The idea behind the development of therbligs is to break jobs down into minute elements and base improvements on an analysis of these basic elements by eliminating, combining, or rearranging them.

Therblig
The basic elemental motions that a job can be broken down into.

Although a complete description of therbligs is outside the scope of this text, a list of some common ones will illustrate the nature of these basic elemental motions:

Search implies hunting for an item with the hands and/or the eyes.
Select means to choose from a group of objects.
Grasp means to take hold of an object.
Hold refers to retention of an object after it has been grasped.

Table 8–2

——

Motion study principles

A. The use of the human body.
    1. Both hands should begin and end their basic divisions of accomplishment simultaneously and should not be idle at the same instant, except during rest periods.
    2. The motions made by the hands should be made symmetrically and simultaneously away from and toward the center of the body.
    3. Momentum should assist workers wherever possible, and should be minimized if it must be overcome by muscular effort.
    4. Continuous curved motions are preferable to straight-line motions involving sudden and sharp changes in direction.
    5. The least number of basic divisions should be used; these should be confined to the lowest practicable classifications. These classifications, summarized in ascending order of the time and fatigue expended in their performance, are:
        a. Finger motions.
        b. Finger and wrist motions.
        c. Finger, wrist, and lower arm motions.
        d. Finger, wrist, lower arm, and upper arm motions.
        e. Finger, wrist, lower arm, upper arm, and body motions.
    6. Work done by the feet should be done simultaneously with work done by the hands. However, it is difficult to move the hand and foot simultaneously.
    7. The middle finger and the thumb are the strongest working fingers. The index finger, fourth finger, and little finger are not capable of handling heavy loads over extended periods.
    8. The feet are not capable of efficiently operating pedals when the operator is in a standing position.
    9. Twisting motions should be performed with the elbows bent.
    10. To grip tools, workers should use the segments of the fingers closest to the palm of the hand.
B. The arrangement and conditions of the workplace.
    1. Fixed locations for all tools and material should be provided to permit the best sequence and to eliminate or reduce the therbligs search and select.
    2. Gravity bins and drop delivery should reduce reach and move times; also, wherever possible, ejectors should remove finished parts automatically.
    3. All materials and tools should be located within the normal working area in both the vertical and the horizontal planes.
    4. A comfortable chair for the operator and the workstation's height should be so arranged that the work can be efficiently performed by the operator alternately standing or sitting.
    5. Proper illumination, ventilation, and temperature should be provided.
    6. The visual requirements of the workplace should be considered so that eye fixation demands are minimized.
    7. Rhythm is essential to the smooth and automatic performance of an operation, and the work should be arranged to permit an easy and natural rhythm wherever possible.
C. The design of tools and equipment.
    1. Multiple cuts should be taken whenever possible by combining two or more tools in one, or by arranging simultaneous cuts from both feeding devices, if available (cross slide and hex turret).

(continued)

2. All levers, handles, wheels, and other control devices should be readily accessible to the operator and designed to give the best possible mechanical advantage and to utilize the strongest available muscle group.

3. Parts should be held in position by fixtures.

4. The use of powered or semiautomatic tools, such as power nut- and screwdrivers and speed wrenches, should always be investigated.

Table 8–2

—

Motion study principles

(concluded)

Adapted from Benjamin W. Niebel, *Motion and Time Study* (Homewood, Ill.: Richard D. Irwin, Inc., 1993), pp. 206–207.

Transport load means movement of an object after hold.

Release load means to deposit the object.

Some other therbligs are *inspect, position, plan, rest,* and *delay*.

Describing a job using therbligs often takes a substantial amount of work. However, for short, repetitive jobs, therbligs analysis may be justified.

Frank Gilbreth and his scientist wife, Lillian, were also responsible for introducing motion pictures for studying motions, called **micromotion study**. This approach is used not only in industry but in many other areas of human endeavor, such as sports and health care. Use of the camera and slow-motion replays enables analysts to study motions that would otherwise be too rapid to see. In addition, the resulting films provide a permanent record that can be referred to for training workers and analysts as well as for settling job disputes involving work methods.

Micromotion study
Use of motion pictures and slow motion to study motions that otherwise would be too rapid to analyze.

The cost of micromotion study limits its use to repetitive activities, where even minor improvements can yield substantial savings owing to the number of times an operation is repeated, or where other considerations justify its use (e.g., surgical procedures).

Motion study analysts often use charts as a tool for analyzing and recording motion studies. Activity charts and process charts such as those described earlier can be quite helpful. In addition, a *simo chart* like the one shown in Figure 8–5 can be used to study simultaneous motions of the hands. These charts are invaluable in studying operations such as typing, sewing, surgical and dental procedures, and certain assembly operations.

WORKING CONDITIONS

Working conditions are an important aspect of job design. Physical factors such as temperature, humidity, ventilation, illumination, color, and noise can have a significant impact on worker performance in terms of productivity, quality of output, and accidents.

1. **Temperature and humidity.** Although human beings can function under a fairly wide range of temperatures, work performance tends to be adversely affected if temperatures are outside a very narrow *comfort band*. Although individuals tend to differ in terms of what they consider comfortable ranges, it is generally agreed that office workers and others who exert little physical effort on the job function best when temperatures are between 65°F and 72°F. For moderately strenuous activi-

Figure 8–5

A simultaneous motion chart

SIMO CHART

OPERATOR: Ken Reisch
DATE: May 21,
OPERATION: Assembly
PART: Lace Finger
METHOD: Proposed
CHART BY: Joseph Riley

TIME SCALE (winks)	ELEMENT TIME	LEFT-HAND DESCRIPTION	SYMBOL	MOTION CLASS 1 2 3 4 5 5 4 3 2 1	SYMBOL	RIGHT-HAND DESCRIPTION	ELEMENT TIME	TIME SCALE (winks)
4548	12	Reach for finger	RE		RE	Reach for finger	12	4548
4560	19	Grasp finger	G		G	Grasp finger	19	4560
4579	31	Move finger	M		M	Move finger	31	4579
4610	75	Position and release finger	P RL		P RL	Position and release finger	75	4610
4685	15	Reach for clamp	RE		RE	Reach for clamp	15	4685
4700	15	Grasp clamp	G		G	Grasp clamp	15	4700
4715								4715
7541	12	Grasp assembly	G		G	Grasp assembly	12	7541
	18	Move and release assembly	M RL		M RL	Move and release assembly	18	
7559								7559

SUMMARY

%	TIME	LEFT-HAND SUMMARY	SYM.	RIGHT-HAND SUMMARY	TIME	%
8.56	249	Reach	RE	Reach	245	8.4
7.49	218	Grasp	G	Grasp	221	7.6
12.16	354	Move	M	Move	413	14.2
30.47	887	Position	P	Position	1124	38.6
39.33	1145	Use	U	Use	876	30.1
1.03	30	Idle	I	Idle	0	0.0
.96	28	Release	RL	Release	32	1.1
100.0	2911	TOTALS			2911	100.0

Source: Benjamin W. Niebel, *Motion and Time Study,* 8th ed. (Homewood, Ill.: Richard D. Irwin, 1988), p. 229. © 1988 by Richard D. Irwin, Inc. Reprinted by permission.

ties, temperatures in the range of 60°F to 70°F are preferable, and for very strenuous activities, temperatures in the range of 55°F to 65°F are best.

Heating and cooling are less of a problem in offices than in factories and other work environments where high ceilings allow heat to rise and where there is often a constant flow of trucks and other moving and handling equipment through large doors. These conditions make it difficult to maintain a constant temperature. Solutions range from selection of suitable clothing to space heaters and other localized heating or cooling devices.

Humidity is generally an important variable in maintaining a comfortable working environment. Humidities in the range of 30 percent to 50 percent are most conducive to comfort, although, as a general rule, choice of temperature level depends on humidity level because humans tend to be more sensitive to variations in temperature at high humidities. Thus, high humidity will require more cooling on a warm day, and more heating on a cold day, than low humidity.

2. **Ventilation.**   Unpleasant and noxious odors can be distracting as well as dangerous to workers. Moreover, unless smoke and dust are periodically removed, the air can quickly become stale and unpleasant. Large fans and air-conditioning equipment are commonly used to exchange and recondition the air.

3. **Illumination.**   The amount of illumination required depends largely on the type of work being performed; the more detailed the work, the higher the level of illumination needed for adequate performance. Other important considerations are the amount of glare and contrast. From a safety standpoint, good lighting in halls, stairways, and other dangerous points is important. However, because illumination is expensive, high illumination in all areas is not generally desirable.

Sometimes natural daylight can be used as a source of illumination. Not only is it free, but it also provides some psychological benefits. Workers in windowless rooms may feel "cut off" from the outside world and experience various psychological problems. On the down side, the inability to control natural light (e.g., cloudy days) can result in dramatic changes in light intensity.

4. **Color.**   There are two features of color that are important in job design. One is the effect of colors on moods and feelings, and the other is the visual discriminations the use of color permits.

Color produces emotional and psychological effects in many situations. Some of the known effects of various colors are these:

Red conveys warmth, action, and stimulation. It is a high-visibility color.

Yellow is also a high-visibility color. It can give the impression of cheerfulness and freshness.

Blue is a low-visibility color. It may convey coolness and may promote thoughtfulness or depression.

Green is another low-visibility color. It is often associated with calm and restfulness.

Brown is a natural color. Earth tones impart a natural, peaceful feeling. It is a low-visibility color.

Orange is a high-visibility color that attracts attention more than any other color. It imparts feelings of warmth and stimulation.

The implications for job designers relate to the type of atmosphere and emotions that are best suited for the job. Red is generally taboo in hospitals, whereas green is widely used. Bright colors lend themselves to coloring the surroundings in jobs that involve a high degree of creativity; browns are used to convey peaceful surroundings, and blues are more appropriate where quiet deliberations are involved. Of course, these are broad generalizations, but the point is that consideration of colors should be a part of job design.

Colors are also used to designate safe or hazardous areas or conditions. Here are some common uses:

Red is frequently used for fire protection equipment, gasoline storage containers, danger signs, emergency warning lights, and hot pipes.

Yellow indicates caution. It is frequently used to designate walkways, edges of stairs, corners, and ends of loading docks. Heavy equipment, school buses, and forklifts are usually yellow because of its high visibility.

Blue is sometimes used to mark control devices, water pipes, and valves.

Green is used to designate safety areas or equipment.

Purple is used for radiation hazards.

Orange is frequently used to indicate dangerous parts of equipment and safety starting buttons and switches.

Color coding is also a means of identifying electrical wiring, especially where a number of different wires might need to be traced through partitions or equipment.

5. **Noise and vibration.**   Noise is unwanted sound. It is caused by the vibrations of machines or equipment as well as by humans. Noise can be annoying or distracting, leading to errors and accidents. It can also damage or impair hearing if it is loud enough. Figure 8–6 illustrates loudness levels of some typical sounds.

Successful sound control begins with measurement of the offending sounds. In a new operation, selection and placement of equipment can eliminate or reduce many potential problems. In the case of existing equipment, it may be possible to redesign the equipment or substitute other equipment. In some instances, the source of noise can be isolated from other work areas. If that isn't feasible, acoustical

Figure 8–6

Decibel values of typical sounds (db)

Source: Benjamin W. Niebel, *Motion and Time Study*, 8th ed. (Homewood, Ill.: Richard D. Irwin, 1988), p. 248. © 1988 by Richard D. Irwin, Inc. Reprinted by permission.

walls and ceilings or baffles that deflect sound waves may prove useful. Sometimes the only solution is to provide protective devices for those in the immediate vicinity (e.g., personnel who guide jet aircraft into landing gates wear protective devices over their ears).

Vibrations can be a factor in job design even without a noise component, so merely eliminating sound may not be sufficient in every case. Vibrations can come from tools, machines, vehicles, human activity, air conditioning systems, pumps, and other sources. Corrective measures include padding, stabilizers, shock absorbers, cushioning, and rubber mountings.

6. **Work breaks.** The frequency, length, and timing of work breaks can have a significant impact on both productivity and quality of output. One indication of the relationship between worker efficiency and work breaks is illustrated in Figure 8–7. It reveals that efficiency generally declines as the day wears on, but it also shows how breaks for lunch and rest can cause an upward shift in efficiency.

An important variable in the rate of decline of efficiency and potential effects of work breaks is the amount of physical and/or mental requirements of the job. Steelworkers, for instance, may need rest breaks of 15 minutes per hour due to the strenuous nature of their jobs. Physical effort is not the only condition that indicates the need for work breaks. People working at CRTs also need periodic breaks; moreover, you as a student have undoubtedly experienced the benefits of study breaks.

7. **Safety.** Worker safety is one of the most basic issues in job design. This is an area that needs constant attention from management, employees, and designers. Workers cannot be effectively motivated if they feel they are in physical danger.

From an employer standpoint, accidents are undesirable because they are expensive (insurance and compensation); they usually involve damage to equipment and/or products; they require hiring, training, and makeup work; and they gener-

Figure 8–7

A typical relationship between worker efficiency and time of day

Source: Benjamin W. Niebel, *Motion and Time Study,* 8th ed. (Homewood, Ill.: Richard D. Irwin, 1988), p. 270. © 1988 by Richard D. Irwin, Inc. Reprinted by permission.

ally interrupt work. From a worker standpoint, accidents mean physical suffering, mental anguish, potential loss of earnings, and disruption of the work routine.

It is generally agreed that the two basic causes of accidents are worker *carelessness* and accident *hazards*. Under the heading of carelessness come unsafe acts. Examples include driving at high speeds, drinking and driving, failure to use protective equipment, overriding safety controls (e.g., taping control buttons down), disregarding safety procedures (e.g., running, throwing objects, cutting through, failing to observe one-way signs), improper use of tools and equipment, and failure to use reasonable caution in danger zones. Unsafe conditions include unprotected pulleys, chains, material-handling equipment, machinery, and so on. Also, poorly lit walkways, stairs, and loading docks constitute hazards. Toxic wastes, gases and vapors, and radiation hazards must be contained. In many instances, these cannot be detected without special equipment, so they would not be obvious to workers or emergency personnel. Protection against hazards involves use of proper lighting, clearly marking danger zones, use of protective equipment (hardhats, goggles, earmuffs, gloves, heavy shoes and clothing), safety devices (machine guards, dual control switches that require an operator to use both hands), emergency equipment (emergency showers, fire extinguishers, fire escapes), and thorough instruction in safety procedures and use of regular and emergency equipment. Housekeeping (clean floors, open aisles, waste removal, etc.) is another important safety factor.

An effective program of safety and accident control requires the cooperation of both workers and management. Workers must be trained in proper procedures and attitudes, and they can contribute to a reduction in hazards by pointing out hazards to management. Management must enforce safety procedures and use of safety equipment. If supervisors allow workers to ignore safety procedures or look the other way when they see violations, workers will be less likely to take proper precautions. Some firms use contests that compare departmental safety records. However, accidents cannot be completely eliminated, and a freak accident may seriously affect worker morale and might even contribute to additional accidents. Posters can be very effective, particularly if they communicate in specific terms *how* to avoid accidents. For example, the admonition to "be careful" is not nearly as effective as "wear hardhats," "walk, don't run," "hold on to rail," and so on.

Effective accident control begins with measurement of accident experience. Commonly used measures include frequency of accidents, severity, and average seriousness. Accidents that cause serious injury and loss of work time beyond the day of the injury are called **lost-time accidents**, and these cases are the ones generally used to quantify experience, although minor accidents can serve as a warning of impending major accidents. Frequency, severity, and seriousness are defined as follows:

Lost-time accidents

Accidents that cause serious injury and loss of work time beyond the day of the injury.

$$Frequency = \text{Number of lost-time accidents} \\ \text{per million labor hours worked}$$
$$Severity = \text{Number of days lost per million} \\ \text{labor hours worked}$$
$$Average\ seriousness = \text{Number of days lost} \div \text{Number of lost-time accidents}$$

Use of hours worked is standard practice because it allows for meaningful comparisons based on *exposure*. However, the last measure, average seriousness, avoids the need to determine the number of hours worked. The frequency of accidents is useful as a measure of how often accidents are occurring; severity can be high because of numerous accidents with little time lost per accident or because of one or two very serious accidents. The lost-time figure is based on the number of days a worker is actually absent from his regular job plus possible standard changes based on the nature of the injury. For instance, loss of a portion of a finger or toe results in a specified charge of lost-time in addition to time actually lost.

Accident measures are necessary to assess a department's or company's experience over time, as well as to judge the experience of a company against that of the industry as a whole. In other words, frequency and severity of accidents vary by type of work; the nature and seriousness of accident hazards in electrical work, office work, logging, steel work, and so on are quite different. In order to get a clear picture of any firm's accident experience, it is necessary to compare its record with other firms engaged in the same type of business, since jobs in these firms will have the same hazards. In addition, accident records can be used to help management pinpoint areas where corrective action is needed. Although it is infinitely better to *prevent* accidents rather than take corrective action, hazards are not always obvious, and corrective action can prevent *future* accidents.

The importance of safety considerations in systems design was emphasized by the enactment of the Occupational Safety and Health Act (**OSHA**) in 1970 and the creation of the Occupational Safety and Health Administration. The law was intended to insure that workers in all organizations have healthy and safe working conditions. It provides specific safety regulations as well as inspectors to see that they are adhered to. Inspections are carried out both randomly and to investigate complaints of unsafe conditions. OSHA officials are empowered to issue warnings, to impose fines, and even to invoke court-ordered shutdowns for unsafe conditions.

> **OSHA**
> Occupational Safety and Health Act of 1970; Occupational Safety and Health Administration.

Early experience with OSHA was mixed. Although OSHA caused a general improvement in working conditions and safety records, sometimes overzealous inspectors demanded strict compliance with certain regulations that many employers felt were too detailed and unrealistic in terms of costs and benefits. Congress subsequently ordered OSHA to eliminate nuisance regulations and to try to be more realistic in administering federal regulations.

OSHA must be regarded as a major influence on operations management decisions in all areas relating to worker safety. OSHA has promoted the welfare and safety of workers in its role as a catalyst, spurring companies to make changes that they knew were needed but "hadn't gotten around to making yet."

WORK MEASUREMENT

Job design and methods analysis concentrate on *how* a job is done. Work measurement is concerned with determining the *length of time* it should take to complete the job. Job times are vital inputs for manpower planning, estimating labor costs, scheduling, budgeting, and designing incentive systems. Moreover, from the workers' standpoint, time standards provide an indication of expected output. Time standards reflect the amount of time it should take an average worker to do a given job working under typical conditions. The standards include expected activity time plus allowances for probable delays.

> **Standard time**
> The amount of time it should take a qualified worker to complete a specified task, working at a sustainable rate, using given methods, tools and equipment, raw materials, and workplace arrangements.

More formally, a **standard time** is the amount of time it should take a qualified worker to complete a specified task, working at a sustainable rate, using given methods, tools and equipment, raw material inputs, and workplace arrangement. Whenever a time standard is developed for a job, it is essential to provide a complete description of the parameters of the job because the actual time to do the job is sensitive to all of these factors; changes in any one of the factors can materially affect time requirements. For instance, changes in product design or changes in job performance brought about by a methods study should trigger a new time study to update the standard time. As a practical matter, though, minor changes are occasionally made that do not justify the expense of restudying the job. Consequently, the standards for many jobs may be slightly inaccurate. Periodic time studies may be used to update the standards.

Organizations develop time standards in a number of different ways. Although some small manufacturers and service organizations rely on subjective estimates of job times, the most commonly used methods of work measurement are:

1. Stopwatch time study.
2. Historical times.
3. Predetermined data.
4. Work sampling.

Each of these techniques is described in some detail on the following pages.

STOPWATCH TIME STUDY

Stopwatch time study was formally introduced by Frederick Winslow Taylor in the late nineteenth century. Today it is the most widely used method of work measurement. It is especially appropriate for short, repetitive tasks.

Stopwatch time study involves developing a time standard based on observations of one worker taken over a number of cycles. Once established, it is then applied to the work of all others in the organization who perform the same task. The basic steps in a time study are these:

Stopwatch time study
Development of a time standard based on observations of one worker taken over a number of cycles.

1. Define the task to be studied, and inform the worker who will be studied.
2. Determine the number of cycles to observe.
3. Time the job, and rate the worker's performance.
4. Compute the standard time.

The analyst who will study the job should be thoroughly familiar with it since it is not unusual for workers to attempt to include extra motions during the study in hope of gaining a standard that allows more time per piece (i.e., the worker will be able to work at a slower pace and still meet the standard). Furthermore, the analyst will need to check that the job is being performed efficiently before setting the time standard.

In most instances, an analyst will want to break all but very short jobs down into basic elemental motions (e.g., reach, grasp) and obtain times for each element. There are several reasons for this: One is that some elements are not done in every cycle, and the breakdown enables the analyst to get a better perspective on them. Another is that the worker's proficiency may not be the same for all elements of the job. A third reason is to build a file of elemental times that can be used to set times for other jobs. This use will be described a bit later.

It is important to inform the worker who will be observed about the study in order to avoid suspicion or misunderstandings. Workers sometimes feel uneasy about being studied, and they may fear changes that might result. The analyst should make an attempt to discuss these things with the worker prior to studying the operations to allay such fears and to enlist the cooperation of the worker.

The number of cycles that must be timed is a function of three things: (1) the variability of observed times, (2) the desired accuracy, and (3) the desired level of confidence for the estimated job time. Very often the desired accuracy is expressed as a percentage of the mean of the observed times. For example, the goal of a time study may be to achieve an estimate that is within 10 percent of the actual mean. The sample size needed to achieve that goal can be determined using this formula:

$$n = \left(\frac{zs}{a\overline{x}}\right)^2 \qquad\qquad (8\text{--}1)$$

where

z = Number of normal standard deviations needed for desired confidence

s = Sample standard deviation

a = Desired accuracy percentage

$\overline{x}$ = Sample mean

Typical values of z used in this computation are:[5]

Desired confidence percent	z value
90	1.65
95	1.96
95.5	2.00
98	2.33
99	2.58

Of course, the value of z for any desired confidence can be obtained from the normal table in Appendix B (Table A or Table B).

An alternate formula that is used when the desired accuracy is stated as an *amount* (e.g., within one minute of the true mean) instead of a percentage is:

$$n = \left(\frac{zs}{e}\right)^2 \qquad\qquad (8\text{--}2)$$

where

e = Accuracy or maximum acceptable error

To make a preliminary estimate of sample size, it is typical to take a small number of observations (say, 10 to 20) and then compute values of $\overline{x}$ and s to use in the formula for n. Toward the end of the study, the analyst may want to recompute n using revised estimates of $\overline{x}$ and s based on the increased data available.

---

[5] Theoretically, a t value rather than a z should be used because the population standard deviation is unknown. However, the use of z is simpler and provides reasonable results when the number of observations is 30 or more, as it generally is. In practice, z is used almost exclusively.

Example 1

A time study analyst wants to estimate the time required to perform a certain job. A preliminary study yielded a mean of 6.4 minutes and a standard deviation of 2.1 minutes. The desired confidence is 95 percent. How many observations will be needed (including those already taken) if the desired maximum error is:

a. ± 10 percent of the sample mean?

b.   One-half minute?

Solution

a. $s = 2.1$ minutes $z = 1.96$
     $\bar{x} = 6.4$ minutes $a = 10\%$

$$n = \left(\frac{zs}{a\bar{x}}\right)^2 = \left(\frac{1.96(2.1)}{.10(6.4)}\right)^2 = 41.36 \text{ (round up to 42)}$$

b. $e = .5$ $n = \left(\frac{zs}{e}\right)^2 = \left(\frac{1.96(2.1)}{.5}\right)^2 = 67.77 \text{ (round up to 68)}$

In an actual situation, the analyst would not be "given" the value of s but would compute it from sample data. This can be done using either of two formulas:

$$s = \sqrt{\frac{\Sigma(x_i - \bar{x})^2}{n - 1}} \quad \text{or} \quad s = \sqrt{\frac{\Sigma x_i^2 - (\Sigma x_i)^2/n}{n - 1}} \tag{8-3}$$

An example of this computation is provided as a solved problem at the end of this chapter.

Development of a time standard involves computation of three times: the *observed time* (OT), the *normal time* (NT), and the *standard time* (ST).

Observed Time   The observed time is simply the average of the observed times. Thus,

$$OT = \frac{\Sigma x_i}{n} \tag{8-4}$$

where

OT = Observed time
Σx_i = Sum of observed times
n = Number of observations

Normal Time   The normal time is the observed time adjusted for worker performance. It is computed by multiplying the observed time by a *performance rating*. That is,

$$NT = OT \times PR \tag{8-5}$$

where

NT = Normal time
PR = Performance rating

This assumes that a single performance rating has been made for the entire job. If ratings are made on an element-by-element basis, the normal time is obtained by multiplying each element's average time by its performance rating and summing those values:

$$NT = \Sigma(\bar{x}_j \times PR_j) \qquad\qquad (8\text{--}6)$$

where

$\bar{x}_j$ = Average time for element j

PR_j = Performance rating for element j

The reason for including this adjustment factor is that the worker being observed may be working at a rate different from a "normal" rate, either because of an attempt to deliberately slow the pace or because the worker's natural abilities differ from the norm. For this reason, an efficiency factor, or performance rating, is made by the observer to adjust the observed times to an "average" pace. For instance, a performance rating of 0.9 indicates a pace that is 90 percent of normal, whereas a rating of 1.05 indicates a pace that is slightly faster than normal; a normal rating is 1.00. For long jobs, each element may be rated; for short jobs, a single rating may be made for an entire cycle.

When assessing performance, the analyst must compare the observed performance to his or her concept of normal. Obviously, there is room for debate about what constitutes normal performance, and performance ratings are sometimes the source of considerable conflict between labor and management. Although no one has been able to suggest a way around these subjective evaluations, sufficient training and periodic *recalibration* by analysts using training films can provide a high degree of consistency in the ratings of different analysts.

Standard Time   Normal time is the length of time a worker should take to perform a job if there are no delays or interruptions. It does not take into account such factors as personal delays (getting a drink of water or going to the restroom), unavoidable delays (machine adjustments and repairs, talking to a supervisor, waiting for materials), or rest breaks. The standard time for a job is the normal time adjusted for these delays using an allowance factor:

$$ST = NT \times AF \qquad\qquad (8\text{--}7)$$

where

ST = Standard time

AF = Allowance factor

The allowance factor can be computed in one of two ways, depending on how allowances are specified. If allowances are based on the *job time*, the allowance factor must be computed using the formula

$$AF_{job} = 1 + A \qquad\qquad (8\text{--}8)$$

where

A = Allowance percentage based on job time

If allowances are based on a percentage of the time worked (i.e., the *workday*), the appropriate formula is

$$AF_{day} = \frac{1}{1 - A} \qquad\qquad (8\text{–}9)$$

where

A = Allowance percentage based on workday

Some typical allowance percentages (A) are listed in Table 8–3.

Example 2

Compute the allowance factor for these two cases:

a. The allowance is 20 percent of *job* time.
b. The allowance is 20 percent of *work* time.

Solution

$A = .20$

a. AF = $1 + A$ = 1.20, or 120%.

b. AF = $\dfrac{1}{1 - A} = \dfrac{1}{1 - .20}$ = 1.25, or 125%.

Example 3

A time study of an assembly operation yielded the following observed times, for which the analyst gave a performance rating of 1.10. Using an allowance of 15 percent of *job* time, determine the appropriate standard time for this operation.

Observation	Time (minutes)	Observation	Time (minutes)
1	4.20	6	4.18
2	4.15	7	4.14
3	4.08	8	4.14
4	4.12	9	4.19
5	4.15		37.35

Solution

$n = 9$ PR = 1.10 $A = .15$

a. OT = $\dfrac{\Sigma x_i}{n} = \dfrac{37.35}{9}$ = 4.15 minutes.

b. NT = OT $\times$ PR = 4.15(1.10) = 4.565 minutes.

c. ST = NT $\times$ (1 + A) = 4.565(1.15) = 5.25 minutes.

	Percent	**Table 8–3**

Typical allowance percentages for working conditions

A. Constant allowances:
  1. Personal allowance 5
  2. Basic fatigue allowances 4
B. Variable allowances:
  1. Standing allowance 2
  2. Abnormal position allowance:
    a. Slightly awkward 0
    b. Awkward (bending) 2
    c. Very awkward (lying, stretching) 7
  3. Use of force or muscular energy (lifting, pulling, or pushing):
    Weight lifted, pounds:
      5 0
      10 1
      15 2
      20 3
      25 4
      30 5
      35 7
      40 9
      45 11
      50 13
      60 17
      70 22
  4. Bad light:
    a. Slightly below recommended 0
    b. Well below.. 2
    c. Quite inadequate 5
  5. Atmospheric conditions (heat and humidity)—variable 0–10
  6. Close attention:
    a. Fairly fine work 0
    b. Fine or exacting................................. 2
    c. Very fine or very exacting........................ 5
  7. Noise level:
    a. Continuous 0
    b. Intermittent–loud................................ 2
    c. Intermittent–very loud 5
    d. High-pitched–loud 5
  8. Mental strain:
    a. Fairly complex process........................... 1
    b. Complex or wide span of attention 4
    c. Very complex................................... 8
  9. Monotony:
    a. Low 0
    b. Medium 1
    c. High.. 4
  10. Tediousness:
    a. Rather tedious 0
    b. Tedious... 2
    c. Very tedious 5

Source: Benjamin W. Niebel, *Motion and Time Study,* 8th ed. (Homewood, Ill.: Richard D. Irwin, 1988), p. 416. © 1988 by Richard D. Irwin, Inc. Reprinted by permission.

Table 8–4

Summary of time study computations

A. Sample size

$$n = \left(\frac{zs}{a\bar{x}}\right)^2 \tag{8–1}$$

$$n = \left(\frac{zs}{e}\right)^2 \tag{8–2}$$

B. Observed time

$$OT = \frac{\Sigma x_i}{n} \tag{8–4}$$

C. Normal time

$$NT = OT \times PR \tag{8–5}$$

D. Standard time

$$ST = NT \times AF \tag{8–7}$$

where

$$AF_{job} = 1 + A \tag{8–8}$$

$$AF_{day} = \frac{1}{1 - A} \tag{8–9}$$

Symbols:

a = Allowable error as percentage of average time
A = Allowance percentage
AF = Allowance factor
AF_{job} = Allowance expressed as percentage of job time
AF_{day} = Allowance expressed as percentage of working day
e = Maximum acceptable error
n = Number of observations needed
NT = Normal time
OT = Observed, or average, time
s = Standard deviation of observed times
ST = Standard time
x_i = Time for ith observation (i = 1,2,3, . . . , n)

The formulas and symbols used for time study computations are summarized in Table 8–4.

In spite of the obvious benefits that can be derived from work measurement using time study, there are also some limitations that must be mentioned. One limitation relates to the subjective nature of performance rating. This has created innumerable conflicts between labor and management and in some companies is a continual sore spot. Another limitation is the fact that only those jobs that can be observed can be studied. This eliminates most managerial and creative jobs, as these involve mental as well as physical aspects. In addition, the cost of the study rules out its use for irregular operations and infrequently occurring jobs. Finally, it disrupts the normal work routine, and workers resent it in many cases.

STANDARD ELEMENTAL TIMES

Standard elemental times are derived from a firm's own historical time study data. Over the years, a time study department can accumulate a file of elemental times that are common to many jobs. After a certain point, many such times can be taken from the file, instead of the analysts having to go through a complete time study to get them, although others may require actual timing.

Standard elemental times

Time standards derived from a firm's historical time data.

The procedure for using standard elemental times consists of the following steps:

1. Analyze the job to identify the standard elements.
2. Check the file to see which elements have historical times, and record them. Use time study to obtain others, if necessary.
3. Modify the file times if necessary (explained below).
4. Sum the elemental times to obtain the normal time, and factor in allowances to obtain the standard time.

In some cases, the file times may not pertain exactly to a specific task. For instance, standard elemental times might be on file for "move the tool 3 centimeters" and "move the tool 9 centimeters," when the task in question involves a move of 6 centimeters. However, it is often possible to interpolate between values on file to obtain the desired time estimate.

One obvious advantage of this approach is the potential savings in cost and effort created by not having to conduct a complete time study for each job. A second advantage is that there is less disruption of work, again because the analyst does not have to time the worker. A third advantage is that performance ratings do not have to be done; they are generally *averaged* in the file times. The main disadvantage of this approach is that times may not exist for enough standard elements to make it worthwhile, and the file times may be biased or inaccurate.

The method described in the following section is a variation of this that helps avoid some of these problems.

PREDETERMINED TIME STANDARDS

Predetermined time standards involve the use of published data on standard elemental times. A commonly used system is *methods-time measurement* (MTM), which was developed in the late 1940s by the Methods Engineering Council. The MTM tables are based on extensive research of basic elemental motions and times. In order to use this approach, the analyst is required to divide the job into its basic elements (reach, move, turn, disengage), measure the distances involved (if applicable), rate the difficulty of the element, and then refer to the appropriate table of data to obtain the time for that element. The standard time for the job is obtained by adding the times for all of the basic elements. Times of the basic elements are measured in time measurement units (TMUs); one TMU equals 0.0006 minutes. One minute of work may involve 100 or more basic elements, and a typical job may involve several hundred or more of these basic elements. The analyst requires a considerable amount of skill to adequately describe the operation and develop realistic time estimates. A few of the MTM tables are presented in Table 8–5 to give you an idea of the kind of information they provide.

Predetermined time standards

Published data based on extensive research to determine standard elemental times.

A high level of skill is required to generate a predetermined time standard. Analysts generally take training or certification courses to develop the necessary skills to do this kind of work.

Table 8–5

A portion of the MTM tables

Table II—Move—M

Distance moved (inches)	Time (TMU)				Weight Allowance			Case and description
	A	B	C	Hand in motion B	Weight (pounds) up to:	Dy-namic factor	Static con-stant TMU	
¾ or less	2.0	2.0	2.0	1.7				
1	2.5	2.9	3.4	2.3	2.5	1.00	0	A. Move object to other hand or against stop.
2	3.6	4.6	5.2	2.9				
3	4.9	5.7	6.7	3.6	7.5	1.06	2.2	
4	6.1	6.9	8.0	4.3				
5	7.3	8.0	9.2	5.0	12.5	1.11	3.9	
6	8.1	8.9	10.3	5.7				
7	8.9	9.7	11.1	6.5	17.5	1.17	5.6	B. Move object to approxi-mate or indefinite location.
8	9.7	10.6	11.8	7.2				
9	10.5	11.5	12.7	7.9	22.5	1.22	7.4	
10	11.3	12.2	13.5	8.6				
12	12.9	13.4	15.2	10.0	27.5	1.28	9.1	
14	14.4	14.6	16.9	11.4				
16	16.0	15.8	18.7	12.8	32.5	1.33	10.8	
18	17.6	17.0	20.4	14.2				
20	19.2	18.2	22.1	15.6	37.5	1.39	12.5	C. Move object to exact location.
22	20.8	19.4	23.8	17.0				
24	22.4	20.6	25.5	18.4	42.5	1.44	14.3	
26	24.0	21.8	27.3	19.8				
28	25.5	23.1	29.0	21.2	47.5	1.50	16.0	
30	27.1	24.3	30.7	22.7				
Addi-tional	0.8	0.6	0.85		TMU per inch over 30 inches			

(continued)

TABLE III A—Turn—T

Table 8–5

A portion of the MTM tables

(concluded)

Weight	Time (TMU) for degrees turned										
	30°	45°	60°	75°	90°	105°	120°	135°	150°	165°	180°
Small—0 to 2 pounds	2.8	3.5	4.1	4.8	5.4	6.1	6.8	7.4	8.1	8.7	9.4
Medium—2.1 to 10 pounds	4.4	5.5	6.5	7.5	8.5	9.6	10.6	11.6	12.7	13.7	14.8
Large—10.1 to 35 pounds	8.4	10.5	12.3	14.4	16.2	18.3	20.4	22.2	24.3	26.1	28.2

Source: MTM Association for Standards and Research. Copyrighted by the MTM Association for Standards and Research. No reprint permission without written consent from MTM Association, 16–01 Broadway, Fair Lawn, New Jersey 07410.

Among the advantages of predetermined time standards are the following:

1. They are based on large numbers of workers under controlled conditions.
2. The analyst is not required to rate performance in developing the standard.
3. There is no disruption of the operation.
4. Standards can be established even before a job is done.

Although proponents of predetermined standards claim that the approach provides much better accuracy than stopwatch studies, not everyone agrees with that claim. Some argue that many activity times are too specific to a given operation for them to be generalized from published data. Others argue that different analysts perceive elemental activity breakdowns in different ways, and that this adversely affects the development of times and produces varying time estimates among analysts. Still others claim that analysts differ on the degree of difficulty they assign a given task and thereby obtain different time standards.

WORK SAMPLING

Work sampling is a technique for estimating the proportion of time that a worker or machine spends on various activities. Introduced by L. H. C. Tippett in 1934 in the textile industry, it is now widely used to study work activities.

Unlike time study, work sampling does not require timing an activity. In fact, it does not even involve continuous observation of the activity. Instead, an observer is required to make brief observations of a worker or machine at random intervals over a period of time and simply note the nature of the activity. For example, a machine may be busy or idle; a secretary may be typing, filing, talking on the telephone, and so on; and a carpenter may be carrying supplies, taking measurements, cutting wood, and so on. The resulting data are *counts* of the number of times each category of activity or nonactivity was observed.

Although work sampling is occasionally used to set time standards, its two primary uses are in (1) ratio-delay studies, which concern the percentage of a worker's time that involves unavoidable delays or the proportion of time a machine is idle, and (2) analysis of nonrepetitive jobs. In a ratio-delay study, a hospital administrator, for example, might want to estimate the percentage of time that a certain piece of X-ray equipment is not in use. In a nonrepetitive job, such as secretarial

Work sampling

Technique for estimating the proportion of time that a worker or machine spends on various activities.

work or maintenance, it can be important to establish the percentage of time an employee spends doing various tasks.

Nonrepetitive jobs typically involve a broader range of skills than repetitive jobs, and workers in these jobs are often paid on the basis of the highest skill involved. Therefore, it is important to determine the proportion of time spent on the high-skill level. For example, a secretary may take dictation, type, file, answer the telephone, schedule appointments, and do other routine office work. If the secretary spends a high percentage of time filing instead of typing or taking shorthand, the compensation will be lower than for a secretary who spends a high percentage of time typing and taking shorthand. Work sampling can be used to verify those percentages and can therefore be an important tool in developing the job description. In addition, work sampling can be part of a program for validation of job content that is needed for "bona fide occupational qualifications"—that is, advertised jobs requiring the skills that are specified.

Work sampling estimates include some degree of error; the same number of observations taken at different times during the week will probably produce slightly different estimates, and all estimates will usually differ from the actual (but unknown) values. Hence, it is important to treat work sampling estimates as *approximations* of the actual proportion of time devoted to a given activity. The goal of work sampling is to obtain an estimate that provides a specified confidence not differing from the true value by more than a specified error. For example, a hospital administrator might request an estimate of X-ray idle time that will provide a 95 percent confidence of being within 4 percent of the actual percentage. Hence, work sampling is designed to produce a value, $\hat{p}$, which estimates the true proportion, p, within some allowable error, e: $\hat{p} \pm e$. The variability associated with sample estimates of p tends to be approximately normal for large sample sizes. Consequently, the normal distribution can be used to construct a confidence interval and to determine required sample sizes. One (nonclassical) way to view the sampling distribution is to imagine all of the *possible* true proportions that could produce a given sample value of $\hat{p}$. The result is a distribution of possible true proportions that is (1) normal and (2) centered around the sample proportion. The most likely values of the actual proportion are quite close to the sample proportion; a true value close to the center of the distribution is much more likely than a value in one of the tails. This concept is illustrated in Figure 8–8. The degree to which this distribution is narrow or spread out is a function of the sample size and p. The amount of maximum probable error is a function of both the sample size and the desired level of confidence.

For large samples, the maximum error e can be computed using the formula

$$e = z\sqrt{\frac{\hat{p}(1 - \hat{p})}{n}} \tag{8-10}$$

where

z = Number of standard deviations needed to achieve desired confidence
$\hat{p}$ = Sample proportion (the number of occurrences divided by the sample size)
n = Sample size

In most instances, management will be required to specify the desired confidence level and the amount of allowable error, and the analyst will be required to determine a sample size sufficient to obtain these results. The appropriate value for n can be determined by solving Formula 8–10 for n, which yields

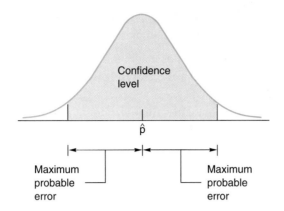

Figure 8–8

A confidence interval for
the estimate of the true
proportion is based on a
normal distribution

$$n = \left(\frac{z}{e}\right)^2 \hat{p}(1 - \hat{p}) \qquad\qquad\qquad (8\text{–}11)$$

Note: If the resulting value of *n* is noninteger, round *up*.

The manager of a small supermarket chain wants to estimate the proportion of time stock clerks spend making price changes to previously marked merchandise. The manager wants a 98 percent confidence that the resulting estimate will be within 5 percent of the true value. What sample size should be used?

Example 4

Solution

$e = .05 \qquad z = 2.33$ (see p. 377) $\qquad \hat{p}$ is unknown

When no sample estimate of *p* is available, a preliminary estimate of sample size can be obtained using $\hat{p} = .50$. Then, after 20 or so observations, a new estimate of $\hat{p}$ can be obtained from those observations and a revised value of *n* computed using the new $\hat{p}$. In fact, it would be prudent to recompute the value of *n* at two or three points during the study to obtain a better indication of the necessary sample size. Thus, the initial estimate of *n* is

$$n = \left(\frac{2.33}{.05}\right)^2 .50(1 - .5) = 542.89, \text{ or } 543 \text{ observations}$$

Suppose that, in the first 20 observations, stock clerks were found to be changing prices twice, making $p = 2/20 = .10$. The revised estimate of *n* at that point would be

$$n = \left(\frac{2.33}{.05}\right)^2 .1(1 - .1) = 195.44, \text{ or } 196$$

Suppose a second check is made after a total of 100 observations, and assume $\hat{p} = .11$ at this point (including the initial 20 observations). Recomputing *n* yields

$$n = \left(\frac{2.33}{.05}\right)^2 .11(.89) = 212.60, \text{ or } 213$$

Perhaps one more check might be made to settle on a final value for *n*. If the computed value of *n* is less than the number of observations already taken, sampling would be terminated at that point.

Determining the sample size is only one part of work sampling. The overall procedure consists of the following steps:

1. Clearly identify the worker(s) or machine(s) to be studied.
2. Notify the workers and supervisors of the purpose of the study to avoid arousing suspicions.
3. Compute an initial estimate of sample size using a preliminary estimate of p, if available (say, from analyst experience or past data). Otherwise, use $\hat{p} = .50$.
4. Develop a random observation schedule.
5. Begin taking observations. Recompute the required sample size several times during the study.
6. Determine the estimated proportion of time spent on the specified activity.

As always, careful problem definition can prevent mistakes such as studying the wrong worker or wrong activity. Similarly, it is important to inform related parties of the purpose and scope of the study in order to reduce unnecessary fears that might be generated by unannounced data collection. It is also important to obtain random observations in order to achieve valid results.

Observations must be spread out over a period of time so that a true indication of variability is obtained. If observations are bunched too closely in time, there is some risk that the behaviors observed during that time will not genuinely reflect typical performance. The degree to which observations should be spread out will depend in part on the nature of the activity being studied, and a decision on this is usually best left to the analyst. Determination of a random observation schedule involves the use of a **random number table** (see Table 8–6), which consists of *unordered sequences* of numbers (i.e., random). Use of such tables enables the analyst to incorporate randomness into the observation schedule. Numbers obtained from the table can be used to identify observation times for a study. Any size number (i.e., any number of digits read as one number) can be obtained from the table. The digits are in groups of four for convenience only. The basic idea is to obtain numbers from the table and to convert each one so that it corresponds to an observation time. There are a number of ways to accomplish this. The approach we will use is

Random number table

Table consisting of unordered sequences of numbers, used to determine random observation schedules.

Table 8–6		**1**	**2**	**3**	**4**	**5**	**6**
Portion of a random number table	1	6912	7264	2801	8901	4627	8387
	2	3491	1192	0575	7547	2093	4617
	3	4715	2486	2776	2664	3856	0064
	4	1632	1546	1950	1844	1123	1908
	5	8510	7209	0938	2376	0120	4237
	6	3950	1328	7343	6083	2108	2044
	7	7871	7752	0521	8511	3956	3957
	8	2716	1396	7354	0249	7728	8818
	9	2935	8259	9912	3761	4028	9207
	10	8533	9957	9585	1039	2159	2438
	11	0508	1640	2768	4666	9530	3352
	12	2951	0131	4359	3095	4421	3018

as follows. We will obtain three sets of numbers from the table for each observation: the first set will correspond to the *day,* the second to the *hour,* and the third to the *minute* when the observation is to be made. The number of digits necessary for any set will equal the number of days in the study, the number of hours per day, and minutes per hour. For instance, if the study will cover 47 days, a two-digit number will be needed; and if the activity is performed for eight hours per day, a one-digit number will be needed for hours. Of course, since each hour has 60 minutes, a two-digit number will be needed for minutes. Thus, we would need a two-digit number for the day, a one-digit number for the hour, and a two-digit number for minutes. For a study that requires observations over a seven-day period in an office that works nine hours per day, one-digit numbers would be needed for days, one-digit numbers for hours, and two-digit numbers for minutes.

Suppose we want three observations in this last case (i.e., 7 days, 9 hours, 60 minutes). We might begin by determining the days on which observations will be made, then the hours, and finally the minutes. Let's begin at the upper left-hand corner of Table 8–6 and read across: The first number is 6, which indicates day 6. The second number is 9. Since it exceeds the number of days in the study, it is simply ignored. The third number is 1, indicating day 1, and the next is 2, indicating day 2. Hence, observations will be made on days 6, 1, and 2. Next we determine the hours. Suppose we read the second row of column 1, again obtaining one-digit numbers. We find:

3 (=3rd hour), 4 (=4th hour), 9 (=9th hour)

Moving to the next row and reading two-digit numbers, we find:

47 (=47th minute), 15 (=15th minute), 24 (=24th minute)

Combining these results yields

Day	Hour	Minute
6	3	47
1	4	15
2	9	24

This means that on day 6 of the study, an observation is to be made during the 47th minute of the 3rd hour; on day 1, during the 15th minute of the 4th hour; and on day 2, during the 24th minute of the 9th hour. For simplicity, these times can be put in chronological order by day. Thus,

Day	Hour	Minute
1	4	15
2	9	24
6	3	47

A complete schedule of observations might appear as follows, after all numbers have been arranged in chronological order.

	Day 1				**Day 2**		
Observa-tion	Time	Busy (✔)	Idle (✔)	Observa-tion	Time	Busy (✔)	Idle (✔)
1	4:15			24	8:04		
2	8:42			25	9:15		
3	9:02			26	9:24		
4	9:31			27	9:35		
5	9:48			28	10:12		
6	9:57			29	10:27		
7	10:20			30	10:38		
8	11:02			31	10:58		
9	11:13			32	11:50		
10	11:55			33	1:14		
11	1:29			34	1:43		
12	1:41			35	1:57		
13	2:00			36	3:10		
14	2:33						

The general procedure for using a random number table is to read the numbers in some sequence (across rows, down or up columns), discarding any that lack correspondence. It is important to vary the starting point from one study to the next in order to avoid taking observations at the same times, since the times would quickly become known to workers and the random element would be lost. There are various ways to choose a starting point. One is to use the serial number on a dollar bill to select a starting point. However, so that everyone ends up with the same results, you will be instructed in the problems in this chapter as to the starting point and the direction to read in.

In sum, the procedure for identifying random times at which to make work sampling observations involves the following steps:

1. Determine the number of days in the study and the number of hours per day. This will indicate the required number of digits for days and hours.
2. Obtain the necessary number of sets for *days,* ignoring any sets that exceed the number of days.
3. Repeat step 2 for *hours.*
4. Repeat step 2 for *minutes.*
5. Link the days, hours, and minutes in the order that they were obtained.
6. Place the observation times in chronological order.

Advantages

1. Observations are spread out over a period of time, making results less susceptible to short-term fluctuations.
2. There is little or no disruption of work.
3. Workers are less resentful.
4. Studies are less costly and less time-consuming, and the skill requirements of the analyst are much less.
5. The study can be interrupted without affecting the results.
6. Many different studies can be conducted simultaneously.
7. No timing device is required.
8. Lends itself to nonrepetitive tasks.

Disadvantages

1. There is much less detail on the elements of a job.
2. Workers may alter their work patterns when they spot the observer, thereby invalidating the results.
3. In many cases, there is no record of the method used by the worker.
4. Observers may fail to adhere to a random schedule of observations.
5. It is not well suited for short, repetitive tasks.
6. Much time may be required to move from one workplace to another and back to satisfy the randomness requirement.

Table 8–7

Advantages and disadvantages of work sampling compared with stopwatch time study

A comparison of work sampling and time study is presented in Table 8–7. It suggests that work sampling is a less formal, less detailed approach to determining job times that is best suited to nonrepetitive jobs.

COMPENSATION

A significant issue that relates to the design of work systems is compensation. It is important for organizations to develop suitable compensation plans for their employees, especially since the success or failure of a firm depends in large measure on the efforts of its employees. If wages are set too low, organizations may find it difficult to attract and hold competent workers and managers. Conversely, if wages are set too high, the increased costs may result in lower profits or force the organization to increase its prices, which might adversely affect demand for the organization's products or services.

Organizations use two basic systems for compensating employees: *time-based systems* and *output-based systems*. **Time-based systems**, also known as *hourly* and *measured daywork* systems, compensate employees for the time the employee has worked during a pay period. Salaried workers also represent a form of time-based compensation. **Output-based (incentive) systems** compensate employees according to the amount of output they produce during a pay period, thereby tying pay directly to performance.

Time-based systems are more widely used than incentive systems, particularly for office, administrative, and managerial employees, but also for blue-collar workers. One of the reasons for this is that computation of wages is straightforward and

Time-based system

Compensation based on time the employee has worked during a pay period.

Output-based system

Compensation based on amount of output produced during a pay period.

managers can readily estimate labor costs for a given manpower level. Employees often prefer time-based systems because the pay is steady and they know how much they will receive for each pay period. In addition, employees may resent the pressures associated with an output-based system.

Another reason for using time-based systems is that many jobs do not lend themselves to the use of incentives. In some cases it may be difficult or impossible to measure output. For example, jobs that require creative or mental work cannot be easily measured on an output basis. Other jobs may include irregular activities or have so many different forms of output that measuring output and determining pay are fairly complex. Also, in the case of assembly lines, the use of *individual* incentives would disrupt the even flow of work. However, *group* incentives are sometimes used successfully in such cases. Finally, *quality* considerations may be more important than *quantity*. For example, in health care, greater emphasis is generally placed on the quality of patient care than on the number of patients processed.

On the other hand, there are situations in which the use of incentives is desirable. Incentives reward workers for their output, presumably causing some workers to produce more than they might under a time-based system. The advantage is that certain (fixed) costs do not vary with increases in output, so the overall cost per unit decreases if output increases. Workers may prefer incentive systems because they see a relationship between their efforts and their pay and because it presents the opportunity for them to earn more than they might under a time-based system.

On the negative side, incentive systems involve a considerable amount of paperwork, computation of wages is more difficult than under time-based systems, output has to be measured and standards set, cost-of-living increases are difficult to integrate into incentive plans, and contingency arrangements for unavoidable delays have to be developed.

The main advantages and disadvantages of time-based and output-based plans are outlined in Table 8–8.

In order to obtain the maximum benefit from an incentive plan, the plan should be:

1. Accurate.
2. Easy to apply.
3. Consistent.
4. Easy to understand.
5. Fair.

In addition, there should be an obvious relationship between effort and reward, and there should not be a limit on earnings.

Incentive systems may focus on the output of each individual or on the output of a group. Each of these approaches is briefly described below.

Individual Incentive Plans

Individual incentive plans take a variety of forms. The simplest plan is *straight piecework*. Under this plan, a worker's pay is a direct linear function of his or her output. In the past, piecework plans were fairly popular. Now minimum wage legislation makes them somewhat impractical. Even so, many of the plans currently in use represent variations of the straight piecework plan. They typically incorporate a

	Management	Worker	Table 8–8
Time-based			Comparison of time-based and output-based pay systems
Advantages	1. Stable labor costs 2. Easy to administer 3. Simple to compute pay 4. Stable output	1. Stable pay 2. Less pressure to produce than under output system	
Disadvantages	1. No incentive for workers to increase output	1. Extra efforts not rewarded	
Output-based			
Advantages	1. Lower cost per unit 2. Greater output	1. Pay related to efforts 2. Opportunity to earn more	
Disadvantages	1. Wage computation more difficult 2. Need to measure output 3. Quality may suffer 4. Difficult to incorporate wage increases 5. Increased problems with scheduling	1. Pay fluctuates 2. Worker may be penalized because of factors beyond their control (e.g., machine breakdowns)	

base rate that serves as a floor: workers are guaranteed that amount as a minimum, regardless of output. The base rate is tied to an output standard: if the worker produces less than the standard, that worker will be paid at the base rate. This protects workers from pay loss due to delays, breakdowns, and similar problems. In most cases, incentives are paid for output above standard, and the pay is referred to as a *bonus*.

GROUP INCENTIVE PLANS

Group incentive plans stress sharing of productivity gains with employees. There are a variety of plans in use. Some focus exclusively on output, and others reward employees for output and for reductions in material and other costs. The following four well-known plans reflect the main features of most of the plans currently in operation.

The *Scanlon plan* was developed by the late Joseph Scanlon during the 1930s in cooperation with the management of a machine tool company that was on the brink of bankruptcy. The main feature of the plan was to encourage reductions in labor costs by allowing workers to share in any reductions achieved. The plan involved formation of worker committees to actively seek out areas for improvement.

The *Kaiser plan* was introduced during the 1960s. Like the Scanlon plan, it involved the use of committees to suggest ways of reducing costs, with savings shared by employees. However, in addition to reductions in labor costs, it also provided for workers to share in reductions in material and supply costs.

The *Lincoln plan* was developed over a period of about 20 years (1914 to 1934) at the Lincoln Electric Company in Cleveland, Ohio. It includes profit sharing, job enlargement, and participative management. Like the other plans, it involves the use of evaluation committees to generate suggestions. The three main components of the plan are a piecework system, an annual bonus, and a stock purchase provision. Lincoln officials credit the plan with enabling the company to increase its market share and profitability, and with reducing the unit cost of its basic product while competitors have experienced substantial increases in their costs.

The *Kodak plan* uses a combination of premium wage levels and an annual bonus related to company profits instead of more traditional incentives. Workers are encouraged to help set goals and to decide on reasonable performance levels with the idea that because of their involvement, they will be more apt to produce at a premium rate.

One form of group incentive is related to the *team approach* that many companies are now using for problem solving and continuous improvement. The emphasis is on *team* performance rather than *individual* performance. Consequently, rewards are given on a team basis instead of on the more traditional individual basis.

MANAGEMENT COMPENSATION

Many organizations that traditionally rewarded managers and senior executives on the basis of *output* are now seriously reconsidering that approach. With the new emphasis on customer service and quality, reward systems are being restructured to reflect those new dimensions of performance. In addition, executive pay in many companies is being more closely tied to the success of the company or division that executive is responsible for. This is quite different than the policy in recent years that increased the compensation of top executives even as workers were being laid off and the company was losing large amounts of money!

SUMMARY

The design of work systems involves job design, work measurement, and compensation.

Job design is concerned with the content of jobs and work methods. In the past, job design tended to focus on efficiency. However, there now seems to be an increasing awareness and consideration of the behavioral aspects of work and worker satisfaction. Current concern about productivity has thrust job design into the limelight. However, the jobs usually associated with high productivity are often the same jobs that are the greatest source of worker dissatisfaction, creating somewhat of a paradox for job designers.

Methods analysis and motion study techniques are often used to develop the "efficiency" aspects of jobs, but do not directly address their behavioral aspects. Nonetheless, they are an important part of job design. Working conditions are also an important aspect of job design, not only because of the behavioral and efficiency factors, but also because of concern for the health and safety of workers.

Work measurement is concerned with specifying the length of time needed to complete a job. Such information is vital for personnel planning, cost estimating, budgeting, scheduling, and worker compensation. Commonly used approaches include stopwatch time study and predetermined times. A related technique is work sampling, which can also be used to obtain data on activity times. More commonly, work sampling is used to estimate the proportion of time a worker spends on a certain aspect of the job.

Organizations can choose from a variety of compensation plans. It is important to do so carefully, for compensation is important to both the worker and the organization, and, once adopted, it is usually difficult to substantially change a compensation plan.

SOLVED PROBLEMS

Problem

1. Compute the mean and standard deviation of these observed times:

Observation	Time (minutes)
1	3.6
2	4.1
3	4.4
4	3.7
5	4.2

Solution

$$\bar{x} = \text{Average time} = \frac{3.6 + 4.1 + 4.4 + 3.7 + 4.2}{5} = \frac{20.0}{5} = 4.0$$

Using $s = \sqrt{\dfrac{\Sigma(x_i - \bar{x})^2}{n-1}}$:

x_i	$\bar{x}$	$(x_i - \bar{x})$	$x_i - \bar{x})^2$
3.6	4.0	−0.4	0.16
4.1	4.0	0.1	0.01
4.4	4.0	0.4	0.16
3.7	4.0	−0.3	0.09
4.2	4.0	0.2	0.04
		0.0	0.46

$$s = \sqrt{\frac{0.46}{5-1}} = 0.34 \text{ minutes}$$

Using $s = \sqrt{\dfrac{\Sigma x_i^2 - (\Sigma x_i)^2/n}{n-1}}$:

x_i	x_i^2
3.6	12.96
4.1	16.81
4.4	19.36
3.7	13.69
4.2	17.64
20.0	80.46

$$s = \sqrt{\frac{80.46 - 20^2/5}{5-1}} = 0.34 \text{ minutes}$$

Problem

2. *Work sampling.* An analyst has been asked to prepare an estimate of the proportion of time that a turret lathe operator spends adjusting the machine, with a 90 percent confidence level. Based on previous experience, the analyst believes the proportion will be approximately 30 percent.

   a. If the analyst uses a sample size of 400 observations, what is the maximum possible error that will be associated with the estimate?

   b. What sample size would the analyst need in order to have the maximum error be no more than ± 5 percent?

Solution

$\hat{p} = .30$ $z = 1.65$ (for 90 percent confidence)

a. $\quad e = z\sqrt{\dfrac{\hat{p}(1-\hat{p})}{n}} = 1.65\sqrt{\dfrac{.3(.7)}{400}} = .038$

b. $n = \left(\dfrac{z}{e}\right)^2 \hat{p}(1 - \hat{p}) = \left(\dfrac{1.65}{.05}\right)^2 (.3)(.7) = 228.69$, or 229

Problem

3. *Work sampling.* The owner of a large gift shop wants to estimate the proportion of time shoppers spend in a certain part of the store. The shop is open nine hours a day, six days a week. Twelve observations will be taken over a 30-day period. Determine the random observation times using Table 8–6 and these instructions:

   a. For days, read the first two digits of column 2, going down, and then the first two digits of column 3, going down.

   b. For hours, read one-digit numbers in row 4 from left to right.

   c. For minutes, read two-digit numbers using the first two digits in column 1, going down, and then the second two digits in column 1, going down.

Solution

a. Days: Random number	b. Hours: Random number	c. Minutes: Random number
72★	1	69†
11	6	34
24	3	47
15	2	16
72★	1	85†
13	5	39
77★	4	78†
13	6	27
82★	1	29
99★	9	85†
16	5	05
01	0‡	29
28	1	12
05		91†
27		15
19		32
09		10

★Since there will be 30 days in the study, random numbers larger than 30 are not relevant.
†There are 60 minutes per hour. Larger number do not correspond, so they are discarded.
‡The store is open nine hours per day. The numbers 1–9 correspond to the hours 1–9; 0 is not applicable.

Combining these results, in the order they appeared, produces the following results:

Day	Hour	Minute
11 1		34
24 6		47
15 3		16
13 2		39
13 1		27
16 5		29
01 4		05
28 6		29
05 1		12
27 9		15
19 5		32
09 1		10

Arranging the results chronologically by day, hour, and minute (but maintaining the same *combinations*) produces this list of observation times:

Observations	Day	Hour	Minute
1	01	4	05
2	05	1	12
3	09	1	10
4	11	1	34
5	13	1	27
6	13	2	39
7	15	3	16
8	16	5	29
9	19	5	32
10	24	6	47
11	27	9	15
12	28	6	29

DISCUSSION AND REVIEW QUESTIONS

1. What is job design, and why is it important?
2. What are some of the main advantages and disadvantages of specialization from a management perspective? From a worker's perspective?
3. Contrast the meanings of the terms *job enlargement* and *job enrichment*.
4. What is the purpose of job enlargement and job enrichment?
5. Explain what is meant by the term *sociotechnical approach*.
6. What are some of the ways in which automation can improve production operations? What are some of the potential problems that a manager should be aware of when considering automation?

7. Some Japanese firms have a policy of rotating their managers among the different managerial jobs. In contrast, American managers are more likely to specialize in a certain area (e.g., finance or operations). Discuss the advantages and disadvantages of each of these approaches. Which do you prefer? Why?

8. What are motion study principles? How are they classified?

9. What are some of the reasons that methods analyses are needed? How is methods analysis linked to productivity improvements?

10. How are devices such as flow process charts and worker-machine charts useful?

11. What is a time standard? What factors must be taken into account when developing standards?

12. What are some of the main uses of time study information?

13. Could performance rating be avoided by studying a group of workers and averaging their times? Explain briefly.

14. If an average worker could be identified, what advantage would there be in using that person for a time study? What are some of the reasons that an average worker might not be studied?

15. What are some of the main limitations of time study?

16. Comment on the following: "At any given instant, the standard times for many jobs will not be strictly correct."
    a. Why is this so?
    b. Does this mean that those standards are useless? Explain.

17. Why do workers sometimes resent time studies?

18. List advantages and disadvantages of:
    a. Time-based pay plans?
    b. Incentive plans?

PROBLEMS

1. An analyst has timed a metal-cutting operation for 50 cycles. The average time per cycle was 10.40 minutes, and the standard deviation was 1.20 minutes for a worker with a performance rating of 125 percent. Assume an allowance of 16 percent of job time. Find the standard time for this operation.

2. A job was timed for 60 cycles and had an average of 1.2 minutes per piece. The performance rating was 95 percent, and allowances are 10 percent, based on an eight-hour day. Determine each of the following:
    a. Observed time.
    b. Normal time.
    c. Standard time.

3. A time study was conducted on a job that contains four elements. The observed times and performance ratings for six cycles are shown in the following table.

Element	Performance rating	Observations (minutes per cycle)					
		1	2	3	4	5	6
1	90%	0.44	0.50	0.43	0.45	0.48	0.46
2	85	1.50	1.54	1.47	1.51	1.49	1.52
3	110	0.84	0.89	0.77	0.83	0.85	0.80
4	100	1.10	1.14	1.08	1.20	1.16	1.26

      a.   Determine the average cycle time for each element.

      b.   Find the normal time for each element.

      c.   Assuming an allowance factor of 15 percent of job time, compute the standard time for this job.

4. A worker-machine operation was found to involve 3.3 minutes of machine time per cycle in the course of 40 cycles of stopwatch study. The worker's time averaged 1.9 minutes per cycle, and he was given a rating of 120 percent (machine rating is 100 percent). Midway through the study, the worker took a 10-minute rest break. Assuming an allowance factor of 12 percent of labor time, determine the standard time for this job.

5. A recently negotiated union contract allows workers in a grinding department 48 minutes for rest, 20 minutes for personal time, and 28 minutes for delays for an eight-hour shift. A time study analyst observed a job that is performed continuously and found an average time of 6.0 minutes per cycle for a worker she rated at 95 percent. What standard time is applicable for that operation?

6. The data in the table below represent time study observations for a woodworking operation.

      a.   Based on the observations, determine the standard time for the operation, assuming an allowance of 15 percent based on job time.

      b.   How many observations would be needed to estimate the mean time for element 2 within 1 percent of its true value with a 95.5 percent confidence?

      c.   How many observations would be needed to estimate the mean time for element 2 to within .01 minute of its true value with a 95.5 percent confidence?

| | Performance | Observation (minutes per cycle) | | | | | |
Element	rating	1	2	3	4	5	6
1	110%	1.20	1.17	1.16	1.22	1.24	1.15
2	115	0.83	0.87	0.78	0.82	0.85	1.32★
3	105	0.58	0.53	0.52	0.59	0.60	0.54

★Unusual delay; disregard time.

7. How many observations should a time study analyst plan for in the case of an operation that has a standard deviation of 1.5 minutes per piece if the goal is to estimate the mean time per piece to within 0.4 minutes and obtain a confidence of 95.5 percent?

8. About how many work cycles should be timed in order to estimate the average cycle time to within 2 percent of the sample mean with a confidence of 99 percent if a pilot study yielded these times (minutes): 5.2, 5.5, 5.8, 5.3, 5.5, and 5.1?

9. In an initial survey designed to estimate the percentage of time air-express cargo loaders are idle, an analyst found that loaders were idle in 6 of the 50 observations.

      a.   Estimate the percentage of idle time.

      b.   Based on the initial results, approximately how many observations would you require in order to estimate the actual percentage of idle time to within 5 percent with a confidence of 95 percent?

10. A certain job in an insurance office involves telephone conversations with policyholders. The office manager estimates that about half of this person's time is spent on the telephone. How many observations would be needed in a work sampling study to estimate that time percentage to within 6 percent and have a confidence of 98 percent?

11. Design a schedule of work sampling observations in which there are eight observations made during one eight-hour day. Using Table 8–6, read the *last digit* going down column 4 for hour (e.g., 1 7 4 4 6 . . .), and then read across row 3 from left to right in sets of two for minutes (e.g., 47 15 24 86 . . .). Arrange the times chronologically.

12. The manager of a large office intends to conduct a work sampling of the time the staff spends on the telephone. The observations will be taken over a period of 50 workdays. The office is open five days a week for eight hours a day. Although the study will consist of 200 random observations, in this problem you will be asked to determine times for 11 observations. Use random numbers from Table 8–6.

   a. Determine times for 11 observations. For days, read sets of two-digit numbers going across row 4 from left to right (e.g., 16 32 15 46 . . .), and do the same in row 5.

   b. For hours, read one-digit numbers going *down,* using the first digit of column 1 (e.g., 6 4 3 1 . . .).

   c. For minutes, read two-digit numbers going *up* column 4 using the first two digits (e.g., 30 46 10 . . .), and then repeat for the second two digits going *up* column 4 (e.g., 95 66 39 . . .).

   d. Arrange the combinations chronologically by day, hour, and minute.

   e. Assume March 1 is a Monday and that there are no holidays in March, April, or May. Convert your observation days to dates in March, April, and May.

13. A work sampling study is to be conducted on rush-hour traffic (4 to 7 P.M.) 5 days per week. The study will encompass 40 days. Determine the day, hour, and minute for 10 observations using the following procedure:

   a. Read two-digit numbers going *down* the first two digits of column 5 (e.g., 46 20 38 . . .), and then down the second two digits of that column (e.g., 27 93 56 . . .) for days.

   b. For hours, read one-digit numbers going from left to right across row 1 and then across row 2. (Read only 4s, 5s, and 6s.)

   c. For minutes, read two-digit numbers going *down* column 6, first using the *last* two digits (e.g., 87 17 64 . . .), and then, after exhausting those numbers, repeat using the first two digits of that column (e.g., 83 46 00 19 . . .).

   Arrange your times chronologically by day, then hour, and then minute.

SELECTED BIBLIOGRAPHY

Barnes, Ralph M. *Motion and Time Study: Design and Measurement of Work.* 8th ed. New York: John Wiley & Sons, 1980.

Buffa, Elwood Spencer. *Operations Management: The Management of Productive Systems.* 2d ed. New York: John Wiley & Sons, 1980.

Chase, Richard B., and Nicholas J. Aquilano. *Production and Operations Management.* 6th ed. Homewood, Ill.: Richard D. Irwin, 1992

Davis L. E. "Job Satisfaction Research: The Post-Industrial View." *Industrial Relations* 10 (1971), pp. 176–93.

————, and A. B. Cherns, eds. *Quality of Working Life; Cases.* Vol. 2. New York: Free Press, 1975.

————, and J. C. Taylor, eds. *Design of Jobs.* Middlesex, England: Penguin Books, 1972.

Dickson, Paul. *The Future of the Workplace.* New York: Weybright and Talley, 1975.

Fory, N., and H. Gordon. "Worker Participation: Contrasts in Three Countries." *Harvard Business Review* 54, no. 3 (May–June 1976), pp. 71–83.

Herbst, P. G. *Socio-technical Design: Strategies in Multidisciplinary Research.* London: Tavistock, 1974.

Herzberg, Frederick. "One More Time: How Do You Motivate Employees?" *Harvard Business Review,* January–February 1968.

Hopeman, Richard J. *Production and Operations Management.* 4th ed. Columbus, Ohio: Charles E. Merrill Publishing, 1980.

Huchinson, R. D. *New Horizons for Human Factors in Job Design.* New York: McGraw-Hill, 1981.

Konz, S. *Work Design: Industrial Ergonomics.* 2nd ed. New York: John Wiley & Sons, 1981.

Monks, Joseph G. *Operations Management: Theory and Problems.* New York: McGraw-Hill, 1977.

Moore, Franklin, and Thomas Hendrick. *Production/Operations Management.* 8th ed. Homewood, Ill.: Richard D. Irwin, 1980.

Mundel, Marvin E. *Motion and Time Study.* 5th ed. Englewood Cliffs, N.J.: Prentice Hall, 1978.

Nadler, G. *Work Design.* Rev. ed. Homewood, Ill.: Richard D. Irwin, 1970.

Niebel, Benjamin W. *Motion and Time Study.* 8th ed. Homewood, Ill.: Richard D. Irwin, 1988.

Smith, George L., Jr. *Work Measurement: A Systems Approach.* Columbus, Ohio: Grid Publishing, 1978.

Van Der Zwaan, A. H. "The Sociotechnical Systems Approach: A Critical Evaluation." *International Journal of Production Research* 13, no. 2 (1975), pp. 149–63.

READING   MAKING HOTPLATES   *Edgar F. Huse*

A group of 10 workers were responsible for assembling hotplates (instruments for heating solutions to a given temperature) for hospital and medical laboratory use. A number of different models of hotplates were being manufactured. Some had a vibrating device so that the solution could be mixed while being heated. Others heated only test tubes. Still others could heat solutions in a variety of different containers.

With the appropriate small tools, each worker assembled part of a hotplate. The partially completed hotplate was placed on a moving belt, to be carried from one assembly station to the next. When the hotplate was completed, an inspector would check it over to insure that it was working properly. Then the last worker would place it in a specially prepared cardboard box for shipping.

The assembly line had been carefully balanced by industrial engineers, who had used a time and motion study to break the job down into subassembly tasks, each requiring about three minutes to accomplish. The amount of time calculated for each subassembly had also been "balanced" so that the task performed by each worker was supposed to take almost exactly the same amount of time. The workers were paid a straight hourly rate.

However, there were some problems. Morale seemed to be low, and the inspector was finding a relatively high percentage of badly assembled hotplates. Controllable rejects—those "caused" by the operator rather than by faulty materials—were running about 23 percent

After discussing the situation, management decided to try something new. The workers were called together and asked if they would like to build the hotplates individually. The workers decided they would like to try this approach, provided they could go back to the old program if the new one did not work well. After several days of training, each worker began to assemble the entire hotplate.

The change was made at about the middle of the year. Productivity climbed quickly. By the end of the year, it had leveled off at about 84 percent higher than during the first half of the year, although no other changes had been made in the department or its personnel. Controllable rejects had dropped from 23 percent to 1 percent during the same period. Absenteeism had dropped from 8 percent to less than 1 percent. The workers had responded positively to the change, and their morale was higher. As one person put it, "Now, it is *my* hotplate." Eventually, the reject rate dropped so low that all routine final inspection was done by the assembly workers themselves. The full-time inspector was transferred to another job in the organization.

Questions

1. What changes in the work situation might account for the increase in productivity and the decrease in controllable rejects?

2. What might account for the drop in absenteeism and the increase in morale?

3. What were the major changes in the situation? Which changes were under the control of the manager? Which were controlled by the workers?

4. What might happen if the workers were to go back to the old assembly line method?

Source: Reproduced by permission from *The Modern Manager* by Edgar F. Huse, copyright © 1979 by West Publishing Company. All rights reserved. Based on the following articles: E. Huse and M. Beer, "An Eclectic Approach to Organizational Development," *Harvard Business Review* 49 (September–October 1971), pp. 103–12; M. Beer and E. Huse, "A Systems Approach to Organization Development," *Journal of Applied Behavioral Science* 8 (January–February 1972), pp. 79–101; and "The Drive to Make Dull Jobs Interesting," *U.S. News & World Report,* July 17, 1972, p. 50.

LEARNING CURVES

After completing this supplement, you should be able to:

1. Explain the concept of a learning curve.
2. Use the learning curve table to make activity time projections.
3. List and briefly describe some of the main applications of learning curves.
4. Outline some of the cautions and criticisms of learning curves.

LEARNING OBJECTIVES

SUPPLEMENT OUTLINE

A basic consideration in the design of work systems relates to the fact that learning is usually present when humans are involved. Consequently, it can be highly desirable to be able to predict how learning will affect task times and costs. This supplement addresses those issues.

THE CONCEPT OF LEARNING CURVES

Human performance of activities typically shows improvement when the activities are done on a repetitive basis: the time required to perform a task decreases with increasing repetitions. *Learning curves* summarize this phenomenon. The degree of improvement and the number of tasks needed to realize the major portion of the improvement is a function of the task being done. If the task is short and somewhat routine, only a modest amount of improvement is apt to occur, and it generally occurs during the first few repetitions. If the task is fairly complex and has a longer duration, improvements will occur over a longer interval (i.e., a larger number of repetitions). Because of this, learning factors have little relevance for planning or scheduling routine activities, but they do have relevance for complex repetitive activities.

Figure 8S–1 illustrates the basic relationship between increasing repetitions and a decreasing time per repetition. It should be noted that the curve will never touch the *x* axis; that is, the time per unit will never be zero.

T. P. Wright drew attention to learning curves in a 1936 article in which he described how the direct labor cost of producing a certain airframe decreased with experience.[1] Since that time, a number of other studies have confirmed the general relationship that Wright described, which is now alternately referred to as an experience curve, a progress function, or an improvement function. Experts now widely agree that the learning effect is the result of other factors in addition to actual worker learning. Some of the improvement can be traced to preproduction factors, such as selection of tooling and equipment, product design, methods analysis, and, in general, the amount of effort expended prior to the start of the work. Other contributing factors may involve changes once production has begun, such as changes in methods, tooling, and design. In addition, management input can be an important factor through improvements in planning, scheduling, motivation, and control.

It is interesting to note that changes made once production is under way can cause a temporary *decrease* in output rate until workers adjust to the change, even though they eventually lead to an increased output rate. If a number of changes are made during production, the learning curve would be more realistically described by a series of scallops instead of a smooth curve, as illustrated in Figure 8S–2. Nonetheless, it is convenient to work with a smooth curve, which can be interpreted as the *average* effect.

From an organizational standpoint, the thing that makes the learning effect more than an interesting curiosity is its *predictability,* which becomes readily apparent if the relationship is plotted on a log-log scale (see Figure 8S–3). The straight line that results reflects a constant learning percentage, which is the basis of learning curve estimates: every *doubling* of repetitions results in a *constant percentage* decrease

---

[1] T. P. Wright, "Factors Affecting the Cost of Airplanes," *Journal of the Aeronautical Sciences* 3 (February 1936).

Figure 8S–1

The learning effect: Time per repetition decreases as the number of repetitions increases

Figure 8S–2

Improvements may create a scallop effect in the curve

Figure 8S–3

On a log-log graph, learning curves are straight lines

in the time per repetition. This applies both to the *average* time and to the *unit* time. Typical decreases range from 10 percent to 20 percent. By convention, learning curves are referred to in terms of the *complements* of their improvement rates. For example, an 80 percent learning curve denotes a 20 percent decrease in unit (or average) time with each doubling of repetitions, and a 90 percent curve denotes a 10 percent improvement rate. Thus, a 100 percent curve would imply no improvement at all.

| Example S–1 | An activity is known to have an 80 percent learning curve. It has just taken a worker 10 hours to produce the first unit. Determine expected completion times for these units: the 2nd, 4th, 8th, and 16th (note successive doubling of units). |

Solution

Each time the cumulative output doubles, the time per unit for that amount should be approximately equal to the previous time multiplied by the learning percentage (80 percent in this case). Thus:

Unit	Unit time (hours)
1	10
2 .... 0.8(10)	= 8
4 .... 0.8(8)	= 6.4
8 .... 0.8(6.4)	= 5.12
16 .... 0.8(5.12)	= 4.096

Example S–1 illustrates an important point, and also raises an interesting question. The point it makes is that the time reduction *per unit* becomes less and less as the number of repetitions increase. For example, the second unit required two hours less time than the first, and the improvement from the 8th to the 16th unit was only a bit more than one hour. The question the example raises is: How do we compute times for values such as three, five, six, seven, and other units that don't fall into this pattern?

The unit time (i.e., the number of direct labor hours required) for the *n*th unit can be computed using the relationship:

$$T_n = T_1 \times n^b \tag{8S–1}$$

where

T_n = Time for *n*th unit
T_1 = Time for first unit
b = ln (learning percent)/ln 2

For example, for an 80 percent curve with $T_1 = 10$ hours, the time for the third unit would be computed as:

$$T_3 = 10(3^{\ln .8/\ln 2}) = 7.02$$

Generally, it is not necessary to use the formula; values can be determined using Table 8S–1.

Table 8S–1

Learning curve coefficients

Unit number	70% Unit time	70% Total time	75% Unit time	75% Total time	80% Unit time	80% Total time	85% Unit time	85% Total time	90% Unit time	90% Total time
1	1.000	1.000	1.000	1.000	1.000	1.000	1.000	1.000	1.000	1.000
2	.700	1.700	.750	1.750	.800	1.800	.850	1.850	.900	1.900
3	.568	2.268	.634	2.384	.702	2.502	.773	2.623	.846	2.746
4	.490	2.758	.562	2.946	.640	3.142	.723	3.345	.810	3.556
5	.437	3.195	.513	3.459	.596	3.738	.686	4.031	.783	4.339
6	.398	3.593	.475	3.934	.562	4.299	.657	4.688	.762	5.101
7	.367	3.960	.446	4.380	.534	4.834	.634	5.322	.744	5.845
8	.343	4.303	.422	4.802	.512	5.346	.614	5.936	.729	6.574
9	.323	4.626	.402	5.204	.493	5.839	.597	6.533	.716	7.290
10	.306	4.932	.385	5.589	.477	6.315	.583	7.116	.705	7.994
11	.291	5.223	.370	5.958	.462	6.777	.570	7.686	.695	8.689
12	.278	5.501	.357	6.315	.449	7.227	.558	8.244	.685	9.374
13	.267	5.769	.345	6.660	.438	7.665	.548	8.792	.677	10.052
14	.257	6.026	.334	6.994	.428	8.092	.539	9.331	.670	10.721
15	.248	6.274	.325	7.319	.418	8.511	.530	9.861	.663	11.384
16	.240	6.514	.316	7.635	.410	8.920	.522	10.383	.656	12.040
17	.233	6.747	.309	7.944	.402	9.322	.515	10.898	.650	12.690
18	.226	6.973	.301	8.245	.394	9.716	.508	11.405	.644	13.334
19	.220	7.192	.295	8.540	.388	10.104	.501	11.907	.639	13.974
20	.214	7.407	.288	8.828	.381	10.485	.495	12.402	.634	14.608
21	.209	7.615	.283	9.111	.375	10.860	.490	12.892	.630	15.237
22	.204	7.819	.277	9.388	.370	11.230	.484	13.376	.625	15.862
23	.199	8.018	.272	9.660	.364	11.594	.479	13.856	.621	16.483
24	.195	8.213	.267	9.928	.359	11.954	.475	14.331	.617	17.100
25	.191	8.404	.263	10.191	.355	12.309	.470	14.801	.613	17.713
26	.187	8.591	.259	10.449	.350	12.659	.466	15.267	.609	18.323
27	.183	8.774	.255	10.704	.346	13.005	.462	15.728	.606	18.929
28	.180	8.954	.251	10.955	.342	13.347	.458	16.186	.603	19.531
29	.177	9.131	.247	11.202	.338	13.685	.454	16.640	.599	20.131
30	.174	9.305	.244	11.446	.335	14.020	.450	17.091	.596	20.727
31	.171	9.476	.240	11.686	.331	14.351	.447	17.538	.593	21.320
32	.168	9.644	.237	11.924	.328	14.679	.444	17.981	.590	21.911
33	.165	9.809	.234	12.158	.324	15.003	.441	18.422	.588	22.498
34	.163	9.972	.231	12.389	.321	15.324	.437	18.859	.585	23.084
35	.160	10.133	.229	12.618	.318	15.643	.434	19.294	.583	23.666
36	.158	10.291	.226	12.844	.315	15.958	.432	19.725	.580	24.246
37	.156	10.447	.223	13.067	.313	16.271	.429	20.154	.578	24.824
38	.154	10.601	.221	13.288	.310	16.581	.426	20.580	.575	25.399
39	.152	10.753	.219	13.507	.307	16.888	.424	21.004	.573	25.972
40	.150	10.902	.216	13.723	.305	17.193	.421	21.425	.571	26.543

The table shows two things for some selected learning percentages. One is a unit value for each of the outputs listed. This enables us to easily determine how long any unit will take to produce. The second is a cumulative value, which enables us to compute the total number of hours needed to complete any given number of repetitions. The computation for both of these is a relatively simple operation: Multiply the table value by the time required for the first unit.

Example S–2

Production Airlines is negotiating a contract involving production of 20 small jets. The initial jet required the equivalent of 400 days of direct labor. Estimate the expected number of labor days of direct labor for:

a.   The 20th jet.
b.   All 20 jets.

Assume an 80 percent learning curve is appropriate.

Solution

Using Table 8S–1 with $n = 20$ and an 80 percent learning percentage, we find these factors: Unit = .381, Cumulative = 10.485.

a.   Expected time for 20th jet: 400(.381) = 152.4 labor days.
b.   Expected total time for all 20: 400(10.485) = 4,194 labor days.

Use of the table requires a time for the first unit. If it happens that, for some reason, the completion time of the first unit is not available, or if the manager believes the completion time for some later unit is more reliable, it can be used to obtain a revised estimate of the initial time, and that value can be used in conjunction with the table.

Example S–3

The manager in the previous problem feels there were some unusual problems encountered in producing the first jet and would like to revise that estimate based on a completion time of 276 labor days for the third jet.

Solution

The unit value for $n = 3$ and an 80 percent curve is .702 (Table 8S–1). Divide the actual time for unit 3 by the table value to obtain the revised estimate for unit 1's time: 276 labor days ÷ .702 = 393.2 labor days.

APPLICATIONS OF LEARNING CURVES

Learning curve theory has found useful applications in a number of areas, including:

1.   Manpower planning and scheduling.
2.   Negotiated purchasing.
3.   Pricing new products.
4.   Budgeting, purchasing, and inventory planning.

Knowledge of output projections in learning situations can help managers make better decisions on how many workers they will need than they could from basing decisions on initial output rates. Of course, managers obviously recognize that improvement will occur; what the learning curve contributes is a method for quantifying expected future improvements.

Negotiated purchasing often involves contracting for specialized items that may have a high degree of complexity. Examples include aircraft, computers, and special-purpose equipment. The direct labor cost per unit of such items can be expected to decrease as the size of the order increases. Hence, negotiators first settle on the number of units and then negotiate price on that basis. The government requires learning curve data on contracts that involve large, complex items. For contracts that are terminated before delivery of all units, suppliers can use learning curve data to argue for an increase in the unit price for the smaller number of units. Conversely, the government can use that information to negotiate a lower price per unit on follow-on orders on the basis of projected additional learning gains.

Organizations must establish prices for their new products and services, often well in advance of production on a sufficiently large scale to make a firm determination of costs. Generalizing from the cost of the first few units would result in a much higher price than can be expected after a number of units have been produced. However, the manager needs to use the learning curve to avoid underpricing as well as overpricing. The manager may project initial costs by using the learning progression known to represent an organization's past experience, or else do a regression analysis of the initial results.

The learning curve projections help managers to plan costs and labor, purchasing, and inventory needs. For example, initial cost per unit will be high, and output will be fairly low, so purchasing and inventory decisions can reflect this. As productivity increases, purchasing and/or inventory actions must allow for increased usage of raw materials and purchased parts to keep pace with output. Because of learning effects, the usage rate will increase over time. Hence, failure to refer to a learning curve would lead to substantial *overestimates* of labor needs and *underestimates* of the rate of material usage.

The learning principles can sometimes be used to evaluate new workers during training periods. This is done by measuring each worker's performance, graphing the results, and then comparing them to an expected rate of learning. The comparison can reveal which workers are underqualified, average, and overqualified for a given type of work (see Figure 8S–4). Moreover, measuring a worker's progress can help predict whether the worker will make a quota within a required period of time.

CAUTIONS AND CRITICISMS

Managers using the learning curves should be aware of its limitations and pitfalls. This section briefly outlines some of the major cautions and criticisms of learning curves.

1. Learning rates may differ from organization to organization and by type of work. Therefore, it is best to base learning rates on empirical studies rather than on assumed rates.
2. Projections based on learning curves should be regarded as *approximations* of actual times and treated accordingly.

Figure 8S–4

Worker learning curves can help guide personnel job placement

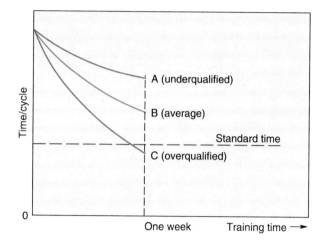

Figure 8S–5

Learning curves are useful for production start-up, but not usually for mass production

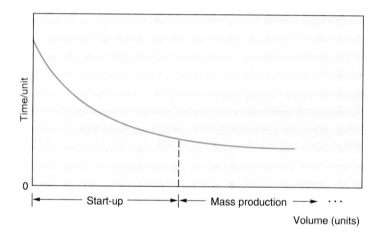

3. Because time estimates are based on the time for the first unit, considerable care should be taken to insure that the time is valid. It may be desirable to revise the base time as later times become available. Since it is often necessary to estimate the time for the first unit prior to production, this caution is quite important.

4. It is entirely possible that at some point the curve might level off or even tip upward, especially near the end of a job. The potential for savings at that point is so slight that most jobs do not command the attention or interest to sustain improvements. Then, too, some of the better workers or other resources may be shifted into new jobs that are starting up.

5. Some of the improvements may be more apparent than real: improvements in times may be caused in part by *increases* in *indirect* labor costs.

6. In situations that involve mass production, learning curves may be of initial use in predicting how long it will take before the process stabilizes. However, for the most part, the concept does not apply to mass production because the decrease in time per unit is imperceptible for all practical purposes (see Figure 8S–5).

7. Users of learning curves sometimes fail to include carryover effects; previous experience with similar activities can reduce initial activity times, although it should be noted that the *learning rate* remains the same.

8. Shorter product life cycles, flexible manufacturing, and cross-functional workers can affect the ways in which learning curves may be applied.

SOLVED PROBLEMS

Problem

1. An assembly operation has a 90 percent learning curve. The line has just begun work on a new item, and the initial unit required 28 hours. Estimate the time that will be needed to complete:
   a. The first five units.
   b. Units 20 through 25.

Solution

Use the cumulative portion of the 90 percent column of Table 8S–1.

a. Table value: 4.339.
   Estimated time for five units: 28(4.339) = 121.49 hours.

b. The total time for units 20 through 25 can be determined by subtraction:

	Hours
Total time for 25 units:	28(17.713) = 495.96
−Total time for 19 units:	28(13.974) = 391.27
Total time for 20 through 25	104.69

Problem

2. A manager wants to determine an appropriate learning rate for a new type of work his firm will undertake. He has obtained completion times for the initial six repetitions of a job of this type. What learning rate is appropriate?

Unit	Completion time (hours)
1	15.9
2	12.0
3	10.1
4	9.1
5	8.4
6	7.5

Solution

According to theory, the time per unit decreases at a constant rate each time the output *doubles* (e.g., unit 1 to 2, 2 to 4, and 3 to 6). The ratios of these observed times will give us an approximate rate. Thus,

$$\frac{Unit\ 2}{Unit\ 1} = \frac{12.0}{15.9} = .755 \qquad \frac{Unit\ 4}{Unit\ 2} = \frac{9.1}{12.0} = .758 \qquad \frac{Unit\ 6}{Unit\ 3} = \frac{7.5}{10.1} = .743$$

Not surprisingly, there is some variability; the rate is usually a smoothed approximation. Even so, the ratios are fairly close—a rate of 75 percent seems reasonable in this case.

DISCUSSION AND REVIEW QUESTIONS

1. If the learning phenomenon applies to all human activity, why isn't the effect noticeable in mass production or high-volume assembly work?
2. Under what circumstances might a manager prefer a learning rate of approximately 100 percent?
3. What would a learning percentage of 120 percent imply?
4. Explain how an increase in indirect labor cost can contribute to a decrease in direct labor cost per unit.
5. List the kinds of factors that create the learning effect.
6. Explain how changes in a process, once it is underway, can cause scallops in a learning curve.
7. What are some of the areas in which learning curves are useful?
8. What factors might cause a learning curve to "tip up" toward the end of a job?
9. What is the implication of item 7 in the list of cautions and criticisms in this supplement?

PROBLEMS

1. An aircraft company has an order to refurbish the interiors of 18 jet aircraft. The work has a learning curve percentage of 80. On the basis of previous experience with similar jobs, the industrial engineering department estimates that the first plane will require 300 hours to refurbish. Estimate the amount of time that will be needed to complete:
   a. The 5th plane.
   b. The first 5 planes.
   c. All 18 planes.
2. Estimate the time it will take to complete the 4th unit of a 12-unit job involving a large assembly if the initial unit required approximately 80 hours for each of these learning percentages:
   a. 72 percent.
   b. 87 percent.
   c. 95 percent.
3. A small contractor intends to bid on a job that will involve installation of 30 in-ground swimming pools. Because this will be a new line of work for the contractor, he believes there will be a learning effect for the job. After reviewing time records from a similar type of activity with his daughter, who is majoring in operations management at a nearby university, the contractor is convinced that an 85 percent curve is appropriate. He estimates that the first pool will take his crew eight days to install. How many days should the contractor budget for:
   a. The first 10 pools?
   b. The second 10 pools?
   c. The final 10 pools?

4. A manager wants to determine an appropriate learning percentage for a certain activity. Toward that end, times have been recorded for completion of each of the first six repetitions. They are:

Repetition	Time (minutes)
1	46
2	39
3	35
4	33
5	32
6	30

    a. Determine the approximate learning percentage.
    b. Using your answer from part *a,* estimate the average completion time per repetition assuming a total of 40 repetitions are planned.

5. Students in an operations management class have been assigned four transportation problems by their instructor. One student noted that it took her 50 minutes to complete the first problem. Assume that the four problems are quite similar and that a 70 percent learning curve is appropriate. How much time can this student plan to spend solving the remaining problems?

6. A subcontractor is responsible for outfitting six satellites that will be used for solar research. Four of the six have been completed in a total of 600 hours. If the crew has a 75 percent learning curve, how long should it take them to finish the last two units?

7. The 5th unit of a 40-unit job took 14.5 hours to complete. Answer the following questions, assuming a 90 percent learning curve is appropriate:
    a. About how long should the last unit take to complete?
    b. How much time should it take to complete the 10th unit?
    c. Estimate the average time per unit for the 40 units.

8. The labor cost to produce a certain item is $8.50 per hour. Job setup costs $50, and material costs are $20 per unit. Overhead is charged at a rate of 50 percent of labor, materials, and setup costs.

    The job has a 90 percent learning rate, and the foreman estimates that the initial unit will require five hours. The item can be purchased for $88.50 per unit.
    a. Determine the unit cost for 20 units.
    b. What is the minimum production quantity that would make production cost less than purchase cost?

9. The government agency for which a contractor has been working has notified the contractor of a desire to extend the original contract to include three additional units. The initial contract called for four units to be built and delivered. The contractor must now estimate the total time required to complete the next three units.

    Upon reviewing records for the original contract, it was discovered that data for the second unit are inaccurate and cannot be used. It is known that the first unit required 16 days, the third 12.5 days, and the fourth 11.5 days.
    Determine an estimated time for the next three units.

10. A firm has a training program for a certain operation. The progress of trainees is carefully monitored. A standard has been established that requires a trainee to be able to complete the sixth repetition of the operation in six hours or less. Those who are unable to do this are assigned to other jobs.

    Currently, three trainees have each completed two repetitions. Trainee A had times of 9 hours for the first and 8 hours for the second repetition; trainee B had times of 10 hours and 8 hours for the first and second repetitions; and trainee C had times of 12 and 9 hours.

Which trainee(s) do you think will make the standard? Explain your reasoning.

SELECTED BIBLIOGRAPHY

Abernathy, W. J. "The Limits of the Learning Curve." *Harvard Business Review,* September–October 1974, pp. 109–19.

Andress, Frank J. "The Learning Curve as a Production Tool." *Harvard Business Review,* January–February 1954, pp. 87–95.

Fabrycky, W. J.; P. M. Ghare; and P. E. Torgersen. *Industrial Operations Research.* Englewood Cliffs, N.J.: Prentice Hall, 1972.

Holdham, J. H. "Learning Curves—Their Applications in Industry." *Production and Inventory Management* (fourth quarter 1970), pp. 40–55.

Yelle, Y. E. "The Learning Curve: Historical Review and Comprehensive Survey." *Decision Sciences* 10 (1979), pp. 302–28.

CASE   PRODUCT RECALL

An automobile manufacturer is conducting a product recall after it was discovered that a possible defect in the steering mechanism could cause loss of control in certain cars. The recall covers a span of three model years. The company has sent out letters to car owners promising to repair the defect at no cost at any dealership.

The company's policy is to pay the dealer a fixed amount for each repair. The repair is somewhat complicated, and the company expected learning to be a factor. In order to set a reasonable rate for repairs, company engineers conducted a number of repairs themselves. It was then decided that a rate of $88 per repair would be appropriate, based on a flat hourly rate of $22 per hour and a 90 percent learning rate.

Shortly after dealers began making repairs, the company received word that several dealers were encountering resistance from workers who felt the flat rate was much too low and who were threatening to refuse to work on those jobs. One of the dealers has collected data on job times and has sent that information to the company: Three mechanics each completed two repairs. Average time for the first unit was 9.6 hours, and average time for the second unit was 7.2 hours. The dealer has suggested a rate of $110 per repair.

You have been asked to investigate the situation and to prepare a report.

Questions

1. Prepare a list of questions that you will need to have answered in order to analyze this situation.

2. Prepare a list of observations regarding the information provided in the case.

3. What preliminary thoughts do you have on solutions/partial solutions to points you have raised?

LOCATION PLANNING

9

After completing this chapter, you should be able to:

LEARNING OBJECTIVES

□

CHAPTER OUTLINE

□

419

When a well-known real estate broker was asked what the three most important determinants of value of a property are, he said, "That's easy. Location, location, and location."

Evidently, in the residential market, location is a rather important factor. Although factors such as style of house, number of bedrooms and bathrooms, how well it has been maintained, and how modern the kitchen is undoubtedly enter into the picture, some locations will be more desirable than others.

In many respects, the choice of location for a business organization is every bit as important as it is for a house, although for different reasons.

Location decisions represent an integral part of the strategic planning process of virtually every organization. Although it might appear that location decisions are mostly one-time problems pertaining to new organizations, the fact is that existing organizations often have a bigger stake in these kinds of decisions than new organizations have.

This chapter examines the issue of location analysis. It begins with a brief overview of the reasons firms must make location decisions, the nature of these decisions, and a general procedure for developing and evaluating location alternatives.

THE NEED FOR LOCATION DECISIONS

Existing organizations become involved in location decisions for a variety of reasons. Firms such as banks, fast-food chains, supermarkets, and retail stores view locations as part of marketing strategy, and they look for locations that will help them to expand their markets. Basically, the location decisions in those cases reflect *addition* of new locations to an existing system.

A similar situation occurs when an organization experiences a growth in demand for its products or services that cannot be satisfied by expansion at an existing location. The addition of a new location to complement an existing system is often a realistic alternative.

Some firms become presented with location decisions through depletion of basic inputs. For example, fishing and logging operations are often forced to relocate due to the temporary exhaustion of fish or forests at a given location. Mining and petroleum operations face the same sort of situation, although usually over a longer-time horizon.

For other firms, a shift in their markets causes them to consider relocation, or the costs of doing business at a particular location reach a point where other locations begin to look more attractive.

THE NATURE OF LOCATION DECISIONS

Location decisions for many types of businesses are made rather infrequently, but they tend to have a significant impact on the organization. In this section we shall look at the importance of location decisions, the usual objectives managers have when making location choices, and some of the options that are open to them.

IMPORTANCE OF LOCATION DECISIONS

There are two primary reasons that location decisions are a highly important part of production systems design. One is that they entail a long-term commitment, which makes mistakes difficult to overcome. The other is that location decisions often have an impact on operating costs (both fixed and variable) and revenues as well as on operations. For instance, a poor choice of location might result in excessive transportation costs, a shortage of qualified labor, loss of competitive advantage, inadequate supplies of raw materials, or some similar condition that would be detrimental to operations. For services, a poor location could result in loss of customers.

OBJECTIVES OF LOCATION DECISIONS

As a general rule, profit-oriented organizations base their decisions on profit potential, whereas nonprofit organizations strive to achieve a balance between cost and the level of customer service they provide. It might seem to follow, then, that these organizations would attempt to identify the "best" location available. However, this is not necessarily the case.

In many instances, there may be no one location that is significantly better than the others. There may be numerous acceptable locations from which to choose, as evidenced by the fact that successful organizations can be found in a wide variety of locations. Furthermore, the number of possible locations that would have to be examined in order to find the best location may be too large to make an exhaustive search practical. Consequently, most organizations do not set out with the intention of identifying the *one best* location; rather, they hope to find a number of *acceptable* locations from which to choose—and to avoid choosing a location that will create future problems.

LOCATION OPTIONS

There are essentially four options that managers can consider in location planning. One is to expand an existing facility. This option can be attractive if there is adequate room for expansion, especially if the location has desirable features that are not readily available elsewhere. Expansion costs are often less than those of other alternatives.

Another option is to add new locations while retaining existing ones, as is done in many retail operations. In such cases, it is essential to take into account what the impact will be on the total system. For instance, opening a new store in a shopping mall may simply draw customers who already patronize an existing store in the same chain rather than expand the market. On the other hand, adding locations can be a defensive strategy designed to maintain a market share or to prevent competitors from entering a market.

A third option is to shut down at one location and move to another. An organization must weigh the costs of a move and the resulting benefits against the costs and benefits of remaining in an existing location. As mentioned, a shift in markets, exhaustion of raw materials, and the cost of operations often cause firms to seriously consider this option.

Finally, organizations have the option of doing nothing. If a detailed analysis of potential locations fails to uncover benefits that make one of the previous three alternatives attractive, a firm may decide to maintain the status quo, at least for the time being.

GENERAL PROCEDURE FOR MAKING LOCATION DECISIONS

The way an organization approaches location decisions often depends on its size and the nature or scope of its operations. New or small organizations tend to adopt a rather informal approach to location decisions. New firms typically locate in a certain area simply because that is where the owner lives. Similarly, managers of small firms often want to keep operations in their own backyard, so they tend to focus almost exclusively on local alternatives. Large established companies, particularly ones that already operate in more than one location, tend to take a more formal approach. Moreover, they generally consider a wider range of geographic locations. The discussion here pertains mainly to a formal approach to location decisions.

The general procedure for making location decisions usually consists of the following steps:

1. Decide on the criteria that will be used to evaluate location alternatives, such as increased revenues or community service.
2. Identify factors that are important, such as location of markets or raw materials.
3. Develop location alternatives:
    a. Identify the general region for a location.
    b. Identify a small number of community-site alternatives.
4. Evaluate the alternatives and make a selection.

Step 1 is simply a matter of managerial preference. Steps 2 through 4 may need some elaboration.

FACTORS THAT AFFECT LOCATION DECISIONS

Many factors can influence location decisions. However, it often happens that one or a few factors are so important that they tend to dominate the decision. For example, in manufacturing, the potentially dominating factors usually include availability of an abundant energy and water supply and proximity to raw materials. Thus, nuclear reactors require large amounts of water for cooling, heavy industries such as steel and aluminum production need large amounts of electricity, and so on. Transportation costs can also be a major factor in location decisions. In service organizations, possible dominating factors are market-related and include traffic patterns, convenience, and competitors' locations, as well as proximity to the market. For example, car rental agencies locate near airports and midcity, since that is where their business comes from.

Once the most important factors have been determined, an organization will try to narrow the search for suitable alternatives to one geographic region. Then a small number of community-site alternatives are identified and subjected to detailed analysis. Community and site factors are often so intertwined that it makes more sense to consider them jointly than to attempt to first decide on a community and then try to find an acceptable site.

REGIONAL FACTORS

The primary regional factors involve raw materials, markets, and labor considerations.

Location of Raw Materials   There are three primary reasons firms locate near or at the source of raw materials: necessity, perishability, and transportation costs. In the *necessity* category are mining operations, farming, forestry, and fishing. Obviously, such operations must locate where the raw materials are. In the *perishability* category are firms involved in canning or freezing of fresh fruit and vegetables, processing of dairy products, baking, and so on. *Transportation costs* are important in industries where processing eliminates much of the bulk connected with a raw material, making it much less expensive to transport the product or material after processing. Examples include aluminum reduction, cheese making, and paper production. In situations where inputs come from different locations, some firms choose to locate near the geographic center of the sources. For instance, steel producers use large quantities of both coal and iron ore, and many are located somewhere between the Appalachian coal fields and places where the iron ore is mined. Transportation costs are often the reason that vendors locate near their major customers. Moreover, regional warehouses are used by supermarkets and other retail operations to supply multiple outlets. Often the choice of new locations and additional warehouses reflects the locations of existing warehouses or retail outlets.

In many instances it is desirable to process raw materials, such as oil, close to their source or the market.

Location of Markets   Profit-oriented firms often locate near the markets they intend to serve as part of their competitive strategy, whereas nonprofit organizations choose locations relative to the needs of the users of their services. Other factors include distribution costs or the perishability of a finished product.

Retail sales and services are usually found near the center of the markets they serve. Examples include fast-food restaurants, service stations, dry cleaners, and supermarkets. Quite often their products and those of their competitors are so similar that they rely on convenience to attract customers. Hence, these businesses seek locations with high population densities or high traffic. The competition/convenience factor is also important in locating banks, hotels and motels, auto repair shops, drugstores, newspaper boxes, and shopping centers. Similarly, doctors, dentists, and lawyers typically serve clients who reside within a limited area, as do barbers and beauticians.

Competitive pressures for retail operations can be extremely important factors. In some cases, a market served by a particular location may be too small to justify two or more competitors (e.g., one hamburger stand per block), so that a search for potential locations would tend to concentrate on locations without competitors. In other cases, the opposite might be true: it could be desirable to locate near competitors. Large department stores often locate near each other, and small stores like to locate in shopping centers with large "anchor" stores. The large stores are able to attract large numbers of shoppers who become potential purchasers in the smaller stores or in the other large stores.

Some firms must locate close to their markets because of the perishability of their products. Examples include bakeries, flower shops, and stores that sell fresh seafood. For other types of firms, distribution costs are the main factor in closeness to market. For example, sand and gravel dealers usually serve a limited area because of the high distribution costs associated with their products. Still other firms require close customer contact, so they too tend to locate within the area they expect to serve. Typical examples are tailor shops, home remodelers, home repair services, cabinetmakers, rug cleaners, and lawn and garden services.

Locations of many government services are near the markets they are designed to serve. Hence, post offices are typically scattered throughout large metropolitan areas. Police, fire, and emergency health care locations are frequently selected on the basis of client needs. For instance, fire stations would tend to locate in areas of high hazards, police patrols often concentrate on high crime areas, and emergency health care facilities are usually found in central locations because they provide ready access from all directions.

This General Motors Corp. auto and engine factory is located in Arizpe, Mexico. Mexico's surplus of qualified workers, low wages, and proximity to the U.S. markets have led Ford and Volkswagen to build plants in Mexico. Mercedes-Benz and Nissan are constructing new plants in Mexico also. J. D. Power & Associates ranked the GM Arizpe plant number one among GM's North American plants for fewest defects per car in 1991.

Labor Factors   The primary labor considerations relate to the cost and availability of labor, wage rates in an area, labor productivity and attitudes toward work, and whether there is a serious potential for problems with unions.

Labor costs are very important for organizations that are labor-intensive. The shift of the textile industry from the New England states to southern states was partly due to labor costs.

Skills of potential employees may be a factor, although some companies prefer to train their new employees rather than rely on previous experience alone. Increasing specialization in many industries makes this possibility even more likely than in the past. Although most companies concentrate on the supply of blue-collar workers, some firms are more interested in scientific and technical people as potential employees, and they look for areas with high concentrations of those types of workers.

Worker attitudes toward turnover, absenteeism, and similar factors may differ among potential locations—workers in large urban centers may exhibit different attitudes than workers who reside in small towns or in rural areas. Furthermore, attitudes in different parts of the country, or in different countries, may be markedly different in this respect.

Some companies offer their current employees jobs if they move to a new location. However, in many instances, employees are reluctant to move, especially when it means leaving families and friends. Furthermore, in families with two wage earners, relocation would require that one wage earner give up a job and then attempt to find another job in the new location.

Other Factors   Climate and taxes sometimes play a role in location decisions. For example, a string of unusually severe winters may cause some firms to seriously consider moving to a milder climate, especially if delayed deliveries and work disruptions caused by inability of employees to get to work have been frequent occurrences. Similarly, the business and personal income taxes in some northern states reduce their attractiveness to companies seeking new locations. Many companies have been attracted to the Sun Belt states by ample supplies of low-cost energy or labor, by the climate, and by tax considerations.

The growth in multinational operations over the past several decades is evidence of the importance of foreign locations. Some firms are attracted to foreign locations because of nearby deposits of aluminum, copper, timber, oil, or other natural resources. Other firms view foreign locations as a way to expand their markets, and still others are attracted by ample supplies of labor. Some countries may offer financial incentives to companies in order to create jobs for their people. Developing countries may establish tariffs to protect their young industries from outside competition, which may also reduce the amount of "foreign" competition a firm must face if it located in such a country. (However, until recently, the Fisher-Price Toy Company factory in Atamoros, Mexico, was not allowed to sell the Muppet toys it makes in Mexico. U.S. companies were encouraged to locate factories in Mexico and were allowed to import raw materials duty-free, but they were required to export all of their output.) The new free-trade agreement with Mexico eliminates such restrictions.

Many developing countries offer an abundant supply of cheap labor. For example, a considerable amount of the clothes sold in the United States carry labels indicating that they were made in Korea, China, or Taiwan. In some instances, it can be less expensive to ship raw materials or semifinished goods to foreign countries for fabrication and assembly and then ship them to their final destinations than it is to produce them in the United States. However, it is essential to recognize that the final cost per unit is the most important factor. In some cases, the low cost of labor in a foreign country can be negated by low productivity.

A firm contemplating a foreign location must carefully weigh the potential benefits against the potential problems. A major factor is the effectiveness of a country's government and its attitude toward American firms. Import restrictions can pose problems in terms of bringing in equipment and spare parts.

Some of the problems of a foreign location can be caused by language and cultural differences between the United States and the host country. U.S. firms often find it necessary to use U.S. technical personnel but find it difficult at times to convince workers to move to a foreign country; workers may have to leave their families behind or else subject them to substandard housing or educational systems. Companies are now exerting additional efforts to reduce these obstacles. They are also improving their efforts to see to it that the people they send abroad are familiar with local customs and have a reasonable facility with the language of the host country.

COMMUNITY CONSIDERATIONS

Many communities actively try to attract new businesses because they are viewed as potential sources of future tax revenues and as sources of new job opportunities. However, communities do not, as a rule, want firms that will create pollution problems or otherwise lessen the quality of life in the community. Local groups may actively seek to exclude certain companies on such grounds, and a considerable amount of effort may be required on the part of the company to convince local officials that the company will be a "responsible citizen." Furthermore, some organizations discover that even though overall community attitude is favorable, there may still be considerable opposition to specific sites from nearby residents who object to possible increases in levels of noise, traffic, or pollution. Examples of this include resistance to airport expansion, changes in zoning, construction of nuclear facilities, and highway construction.

From a company standpoint, a number of factors determine the desirability of a community as a place for its workers and managers to live. They include facilities for education; shopping; recreation; transportation; religious worship; entertainment; the quality of police, fire, and medical services; local attitudes toward the company; and the size of the community. Community size can be particularly important if a firm will be a major employer in the community; a future decision to terminate or reduce operations in that location could have a serious impact on the economy of a small community.

Other community-related factors involve the cost and availability of utilities, environmental regulations, taxes (state and local, direct and indirect), and existence of development support (bond issues, tax abatement, low-cost loans, and grants).

SITE-RELATED FACTORS

The primary considerations related to sites involve land, transportation, and zoning or other restrictions.

Evaluation of potential sites may require consulting with engineers or architects, especially in the case of heavy manufacturing or when large buildings or facilities with special requirements are to be erected. Soil conditions, load factors, and drainage rates can be critical and often necessitate certain kinds of expertise in evaluation.

Because of the long-term commitment usually required, land costs may be secondary to other site-related factors, such as room for future expansion, current utility and sewer capacities and any limitations on these that could hinder future growth, and sufficient parking space for employees and customers. In addition, many firms find access roads for trucks or rail spurs important.

Industrial parks may be worthy alternatives for firms involved in light manufacturing or assembly work, as well as for warehouse operations and customer service facilities. Typically, the land is already developed—power, water, and sewer hookups have been attended to, and zoning restrictions do not require special attention.

Saturn considered many factors such as geography, labor, climate, and access to markets when deciding to locate its new plant in Tennessee. This overhead view shows the transportation network that allows workers, parts, and finished cars to move easily in and out of the area.

On the negative side, industrial parks may place restrictions on the kinds of activities that can be conducted, and that can limit options for future development of a firm's products and services as well as the processes it may consider. In some cases there are rather stringent regulations governing the size, shape, and architectural features of buildings, which limits managerial choice in these matters. Also, there may not be an adequate allowance for possible future expansion.

For firms with executives who travel frequently, the size and proximity of the airport or train station as well as travel connections can be important, although schedules and connections are subject to change.

A summary of the factors that affect location decisions is provided in Table 9–1.

TRENDS IN LOCATIONS AND POSSIBLE FUTURE STRATEGIES

Recent trends in locating facilities, particularly manufacturing facilities, reflect a combination of competitive factors and technological factors. One such trend is for foreign producers, especially Japanese automotive firms, to locate plants in the United States. One reason for this is the fact that the United States represents a tremendous market for Japanese cars, trucks, and recreational vehicles. By locating in the United States, these firms can shorten delivery times and reduce delivery

Level	Factors	Considerations	Table 9–1
Region/country	Location of raw materials or supplies	Proximity, modes and costs of transportation, quantity available	Factors that affect location decisions
	Location of markets	Proximity, distribution costs, target market, trade practices/restrictions	
	Labor	Availability (general and for specific skills), age distribution of work force, attitudes toward work, union or nonunion, productivity, wage scales, unemployment compensation laws	
Community	Facilities	Schools, churches, shopping, housing, transportation, entertainment, etc.	
	Services	Medical, fire, and police	
	Attitudes	Pro/con	
	Taxes	State/local, direct and indirect	
	Environmental regulations	State/local	
	Utilities	Cost and availability	
	Development support	Bond issues, tax abatement, low-cost loans, grants	
Site	Land	Cost, degree of development required, soil characteristics, room for expansion, drainage, parking	
	Transportation	Type (access roads, rail spurs, air freight)	
	Environmental/legal	Zoning restrictions	

costs. Furthermore, they can avoid any future tariffs or quotas that might be applied to imports.

Another trend is just-in-time manufacturing techniques (see Chapter 14 for details), which encourage suppliers and customers to locate near each other in order to reduce supplier lead times. For this reason, some U.S. firms are reconsidering decisions to locate offshore. Moreover, in light manufacturing (e.g., electronics), low-cost labor is becoming less important than nearness to markets; users of electronics components want suppliers that are close to their manufacturing facilities. One offshoot of this is the possibility that the future will see a trend toward smaller factories located close to markets. In some industries, small, automated **microfactories** with narrow product focuses will be located near major markets to reduce response time.

Advances in information technology will enhance the ability of manufacturing firms to gather, track, and distribute information that links purchasing, marketing, and distribution with design, engineering, and manufacturing. This will reduce the need for these functions to be located close together, thereby permitting a strategy of locating production facilities near major markets.

Two other factors are causing companies to locate manufacturing facilities in countries that contain their markets (e.g., Japanese auto companies establishing factories in the United States). One is to counter negative sentiments such as "not made in this country." Thus, Japanese factories in the United States produce cars using United States workers. A second factor relates to currency fluctuations and devaluations. These changes can have a significant impact on demand and, hence, on profits. Changes in currency value alter the price of foreign goods, but not the price of goods produced within a country. For instance, if a country devalues its currency, prices within the country don't change, but foreign-produced goods become more expensive. If demand is elastic, then demand for those foreign goods will fall. Furthermore, currency changes may result in increased costs of parts supplied by foreign producers. By locating and selling within a country, and buying from suppliers in that country, manufacturers can avoid the impact of currency changes.

Microfactory

Small factory with a narrow product focus, located near major markets.

Many Japanese auto makers have located plants in the United States such as this Toyota plant located in Georgetown, Kentucky. Producing in the United States reduces transportation costs, allows manufacturers to avoid high import tariffs, eliminates the effects of currency fluctuations, and can improve sales. Many U.S. buyers are more receptive to a "foreign" product when it is "Made in the USA."

EVALUATING LOCATION ALTERNATIVES

This section contains descriptions of several techniques that are used to help managers evaluate location alternatives: locational cost-volume analysis, factor rating, and the center of gravity method.

LOCATIONAL COST-VOLUME ANALYSIS

The economic comparison of location alternatives is facilitated by the use of cost-volume-profit analysis. The analysis can be done numerically or graphically. We will demonstrate the graphical approach here because it enhances understanding of the concept and because it indicates the ranges over which one of the alternatives is superior to the others.

The procedure for **locational cost-volume analysis** involves these steps:

1. Determine the fixed costs and the variable costs associated with each location alternative.
2. Plot the total-cost lines for all location alternatives on the same graph.
3. Determine which location has the lowest total cost for the expected level of output.

This method assumes the following:

1. Fixed costs are constant for the range of probable output.
2. Variable costs are linear for the range of probable output.
3. The required level of output can be closely estimated.
4. Only one product is involved.

Locational cost-volume analysis
Numerical or graphical technique for evaluating location choices in economic terms.

Fixed and variable costs for four potential plant locations are shown below:

Example 1

Location	Fixed cost per year	Variable cost per unit
A	$250,000	$11
B	100,000	30
C	150,000	20
D	200,000	35

a. Plot the total-cost lines for these locations on a single graph.
b. Identify the range of output for which each alternative is superior (i.e., has the lowest total cost).
c. If expected output at the selected location is to be 8,000 units per year, which location would provide the lowest total cost?

Solution

a. To plot the total-cost lines, select an output that is approximately equal to the expected output level (e.g., 10,000 units per year). Compute the total cost for each location at that level:

(continued)

Example 1

(concluded)

	Fixed cost	+	Variable cost	=	Total cost
A	$250,000	+	$11(10,000)	=	$360,000
B	100,000	+	30(10,000)	=	400,000
C	150,000	+	20(10,000)	=	350,000
D	200,000	+	35(10,000)	=	550,000

Plot each location's fixed cost (at Output = 0) and the total cost at 10,000 units; and connect the two points with a straight line. (See the accompanying graph.)

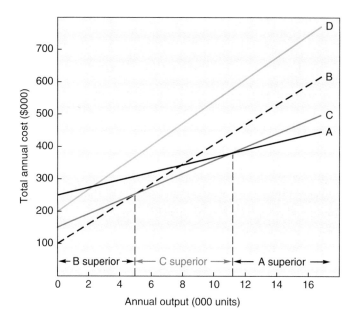

b. The *approximate* ranges for which the various alternatives will yield the lowest costs are shown on the graph. Note that location D is never superior. The *exact* ranges can be determined by finding the output level at which lines B and C and lines C and A cross. To do this, set their total cost equations equal and solve for Q, the break-even output level. Thus, for B and C we have:

$$\underset{\text{(B)}}{\$100,000 + \$30Q} = \underset{\text{(C)}}{\$150,000 + \$20Q}$$

Solving, we find $Q = 5,000$ units per year.
For C and A we have:

$$\underset{\text{(C)}}{\$150,000 + \$20Q} = \underset{\text{(A)}}{\$250,000 + \$11Q}$$

Solving, we find $Q = 11,111$ units per year.

c. From the graph we can see that for 8,000 units per year, location C would provide the lowest total cost.

In a situation where the expected level of output is close to the middle of the range over which one alternative is superior, the choice is readily apparent. If the expected level of output is very close to the edge of a range, it simply means that the two alternatives will yield comparable annual costs, so management would be indifferent in choosing between the two *in terms of total cost.* However, it is important to recognize that in most situations, other factors besides costs must also be considered. A general scheme for including a broad range of factors is presented later in this section. Before turning to that, let's consider another kind of cost that is often considered in location decisions: transportation costs.

THE TRANSPORTATION MODEL

Transportation costs sometimes play an important role in location decisions. These can stem from either the movement of raw materials or the movement of finished goods. If a facility will be the sole source or destination of shipments, then the transportation costs can be included in a locational cost-volume analysis by incorporating the transportation cost per unit being shipped into the variable cost per unit. (If raw materials are involved, the transportation cost must be converted into cost per unit of *output* in order to correspond to other variable costs.)

When a problem involves shipment of goods from multiple sending points to multiple receiving points, and a new location (sending or receiving point) is to be added to the system, a separate analysis of transportation should be undertaken. In such instances the *transportation model* of linear programming can be very helpful. It is a special-purpose algorithm used to determine the minimum transportation cost that would result if a potential new location were to be added to an existing system. It can also be used if a *number* of new facilities are to be added or if an entire new system is being developed. The model is used to analyze each of the configurations being considered, and it reveals the minimum costs each would entail. This information can then be included in the evaluation of location alternatives.

A description of the procedure for the transportation model and examples of its use in location decisions are the subject of the supplement to this chapter. A solved problem at the end of this chapter illustrates how results of a transportation analysis can be combined with the results of a locational cost-volume analysis.

FACTOR RATING

A typical location decision involves both qualitative and quantitative inputs, and these tend to vary from situation to situation depending on the needs of each particular organization. **Factor rating** is a general approach that is useful both for evaluating a given alternative and for comparing alternatives. The value of factor rating is that it provides a rational basis for evaluation and facilitates comparison among alternatives by establishing a *composite* value for each alternative that summarizes all related factors. Factor rating enables decision makers to incorporate their personal opinions as well as quantitative information into the decision process.

The following procedure is used to develop a factor rating:

1. Determine the factors that are relevant (e.g., location of market, water supply, parking facilities, revenue potential).

2. Assign a weight to each factor that indicates its relative importance compared to all other factors. Typically, weights sum to 1.00.

Factor rating

General approach to evaluating locations that includes quantitative and qualitative inputs.

3. Decide on a common scale for all factors (e.g., 0 to 100).
4. Score each location alternative.
5. Multiply the factor weight by the score for each factor, and sum the results for each location alternative.
6. Choose the alternative that has the highest composite score.

This procedure is illustrated in the next example.

Example 2

A small manufacturing firm has recently decided to expand its operations to include several new lines, which it hopes to produce in a separate location because of space limitations in its existing plant. The following rating sheet illustrates relevant factors, factor weightings, and actual ratings for two alternative locations, along with the necessary computations to obtain composite scores for each alternative.

Factor	Weight	Scores (out of 100) Alt. 1	Alt. 2	Weighted scores Alternative 1	Alternative 2
Proximity to raw material	.10	100	60	.10(100) = 10.0	.10(60) = 6.0
Labor costs	.05	80	80	.05(80) = 4.0	.05(80) = 4.0
Water supply	.40	70	90	.40(70) = 28.0	.40(90) = 36.0
Transportation costs	.10	86	92	.10(86) = 8.6	.10(92) = 9.2
Climate	.20	40	70	.20(40) = 8.0	.20(70) = 14.0
Taxes	.15	80	90	.15(80) = 12.0	.15(90) = 13.5
	1.00			70.6	82.7

Thus, alternative 2 is better because it has the higher composite score.

In some cases, managers may prefer to establish minimum *thresholds* for composite scores. If an alternative fails to meet that minimum, it can be rejected without further consideration. If none of the alternatives meets the minimum, this means that either additional alternatives must be identified and evaluated or the minimum threshold must be reevaluated.

THE CENTER OF GRAVITY METHOD

Center of gravity method

Technique for locating a distribution center that minimizes distribution cost.

The **center of gravity method** is a technique that can be used to determine the location of a distribution center that will minimize distribution costs. The method treats distribution cost as a linear function of the distance and the quantity shipped. The quantity to be shipped to each destination is assumed to be fixed (i.e., will not change over time). An acceptable variation is that quantities are allowed to change, as long as their relative amounts remain the same (e.g., seasonal variations).

The method includes the use of a map that shows the locations of destinations. It is important that the map be accurate and drawn to scale. The method involves overlaying a coordinate system on the map so that relative locations can be determined. The location of the 0,0 point of the coordinate system, and its scale, is unimportant. Once the coordinate system is in place, the coordinates of each destination can be determined. (See Figure 9-1, parts a and b.)

If the quantities to be shipped to every location are *equal*, the coordinates of the center of gravity (i.e., the location of the distribution center) can be obtained by finding the average of the x coordinates and the average of the y coordinates (see Figure 9-1). These averages can be easily determined using the following formulas:

$$\bar{x} = \frac{\Sigma x_i}{n}$$

$$\bar{y} = \frac{\Sigma y_i}{n}$$

where $x_i = x$ coordinate of destination i
$y_i = y$ coordinate of destination i **(9–1)**
n = number of destinations

Determine the coordinates of the center of gravity for the problem that is depicted in Figure 9–1c. Assume that the shipments from the center of gravity to each of the four destinations will be equal quantities.

Example 3

Solution

The coordinates of the destinations can be obtained from Figure 9–1b:

Destination	x, y
D1	2, 2
D2	3, 5
D3	5, 4
D4	8, 5
	18 16

$$\bar{x} = \frac{\Sigma x_i}{n} = \frac{18}{4} \qquad \bar{y} = \frac{\Sigma x_i}{n} = \frac{16}{4}$$

$$= 4.5 \qquad\qquad = 4$$

Hence, the center of gravity is at (4.5, 4), which places it just west of destination D3 (see Figure 9–1).

When the number of units to be shipped are not the same for all destinations (usually the case), a *weighted average* must be used to determine the center of gravity, with the weights being the *quantities* to be shipped.

The appropriate formulas are:

$$\bar{x} = \frac{\Sigma x_i Q_i}{\Sigma Q_i}$$

$$\bar{y} = \frac{\Sigma y_i Q_i}{\Sigma Q_i}$$

where Q_i = Quantity to be shipped to destination i
$x_i = x$ coordinate of destination i   **(9–2)**
$y_i = y$ coordinate of destination i

Figure 9-1

Center of gravity method

a. Map showing destination.

b. Add a coordinate system.

c. Center of gravity.

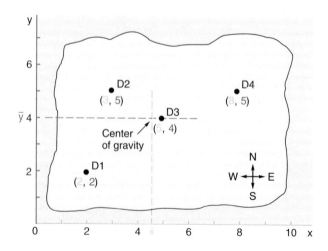

Suppose that the shipments for the problem depicted in Figure 9-1a are not all equal, but instead are the following:

Example 4

Destination	x,y	Weekly quantity
D1		800
D2		900
D3		200
D4		100
		2,000

Determine the center of gravity.

Solution

Because the quantities to be shipped differ among destinations, the weighted average formulas must be used.

$$\bar{x} = \frac{\Sigma x_i Q_i}{\Sigma Q_i} = \frac{(800) + (900) + (200) + (100)}{2,000} = \frac{6,100}{2,000} = 3.05 \text{ [round to 3]}$$

$$\bar{y} = \frac{\Sigma y_i Q_i}{\Sigma Q_i} = \frac{(800) + (900) + (200) + (100)}{2,000} = \frac{7,400}{2,000} =$$

Hence, the coordinates of the center of gravity are approximately (3,3.7). This would place it south of destination D2, which has coordinates of (3,5) (see Figure 9–2).

SUMMARY

Location decisions confront both new and existing organizations. Factors such as growth, market shifts, depletion of raw materials, and the introduction of new products and services are among the reasons organizations become concerned with location decisions. The importance of these decisions is underscored by the long-

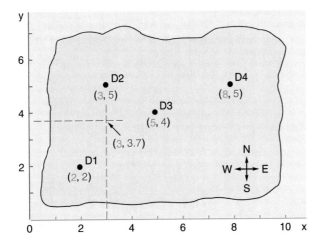

Figure 9-2

Center of gravity for Example 2

term commitment they typically involve and by their potential impact on the operating system.

The primary options available to existing organizations in terms of location are to expand an existing location, move to a new location, maintain existing facilities while adding another facility in a new location, or do nothing.

Among the major factors that influence location decisions in practice are location of raw materials and sources of supply, labor supply, market considerations, community-related factors, site-related factors, and climate. Foreign locations may be attractive in terms of labor costs, abundance of raw materials, or as potential markets for a firm's products or services. Problems sometimes encountered in foreign countries involve language differences, cultural differences, anti-foreigner sentiments, and political instability.

A common approach to narrowing the range of location alternatives is to first identify a country or region that seems to satisfy overall needs and then identify a number of community-site alternatives for more in-depth analysis. There are a variety of methods used to evaluate location alternatives. The ones described in the chapter include locational cost-volume analysis, factor rating, and the center of gravity method. The transportation model is briefly mentioned; a more complete description of that subject is contained in the chapter supplement.

KEY TERMS	**center of gravity method,** 432	**locational cost-volume**
	factor rating, 431	**analysis,** 429
		microfactories, 428

SOLVED PROBLEMS

Problem

1. A farm implements dealer is seeking a fourth warehouse location to complement three existing warehouses. There are three potential locations: Charlotte, Atlanta, and Columbia, S.C. Charlotte would involve a fixed cost of $4,000 per month and a variable cost of $4 per unit; Atlanta would involve fixed costs of $3,500 per month and a variable cost of $5 per unit; and Columbia would involve a fixed cost of $5,000 per month and a variable cost of $6 per unit. Use of the Charlotte location would increase system transportation costs by $19,000 per month, Atlanta would add $22,000 per month, and Columbia would add $18,000 per month to transportation costs. Which location would result in the lowest total cost to handle 800 units per month?

Solution

Given: Volume = 800 units per month

	FC per month	VC per unit	Transportation cost per month
Charlotte	$4,000	$4	$19,000
Atlanta	3,500	5	22,000
Columbia	5,000	6	18,000

Monthly total cost = FC + VC + Transportation cost

Charlotte: $4,000 + $4 per unit × 800 units + $19,000 = $26,200
Atlanta: 3,500 + 5 per unit × 800 units + 22,000 = 29,500
Columbia: 5,000 + 6 per unit × 800 units + 18,000 = 27,800

Hence, Charlotte would result in the lowest total cost for this monthly volume.

Problem

2. A small printing firm is about to lose its lease, so it must move to another location. Two sites are currently under consideration. Site A would have fixed costs of $8,000 per month, and site B would have fixed costs of $9,400 per month. Variable costs are expected to be $5 per unit at site A and $4 per unit at site B. Monthly demand has been steady at 8,800 units for the last several years and is not expected to deviate from that amount in the foreseeable future. Assume units sell for $6 per unit. Determine which location would yield the higher profit under these conditions.

Solution

Profit = (Revenue per unit) × Q − [FC + (VC per unit) × Q]

Site	Revenue	FC	VC	Monthly profit
A	$52,800	$8,000	$44,000	$ 800
B	$52,800	$9,400	$35,200	$8,200

Hence, site B is expected to yield the higher monthly profit.

---

1. In what ways can the location decision have an impact on the production system?
2. How would you respond to this statement: "The importance of the location decision is often vastly overrated; the fact that virtually every type of business is located in every section of the country means there should be no problem in finding a suitable location"?
3. What are the community factors that influence location decisions?
4. In what ways are manufacturing and nonmanufacturing location decisions similar? Different?
5. What are some of the potential benefits of locating in foreign countries? What are some of the possible drawbacks?
6. What is factor rating, and how does it work?
7. Outline the general approach for developing location alternatives.
8. What are the basic assumptions in locational cost–volume analysis?
9. Discuss recent trends in location and possible future strategies.

---

1. A newly formed firm must decide on a plant location. There are two alternatives under consideration: locate near the major raw materials or locate near the major customers. Locating near the raw materials will result in lower fixed and variable costs than locat-

ing near the market, but the owners feel there would be a loss in sales volume because of the tendency of customers to favor local suppliers. Revenue per unit will be $185 in either case. Using the following information, determine which location would produce the greater profit.

	Omaha	Kansas City
Annual fixed costs ($ millions)	$1.2	$1.4
Variable cost per unit	$36	$47
Expected annual demand (units)	8,000	12,000

2. The owner of Genuine Subs, Inc., hopes to expand her present operation by adding one new outlet. Three locations have been studied. Each would have the same labor and materials costs (food, serving containers, napkins, etc.) of $0.76 cents per sandwich. Sandwiches sell for $1.65 each in all locations. Rent and equipment costs would be $5,000 per month for location A, $5,500 per month for location B, and $5,800 per month for location C.

   a. Determine the volume necessary at each location to realize a monthly profit of $10,000.

   b. If expected sales at A, B, and C are 21,000 per month, 22,000 per month, and 23,000 per month, respectively, which location would yield the greatest profits?

3. A small producer of machine tools wants to move to a larger building. Two alternatives have been identified. Location A would have fixed costs of $800,000 per year and variable costs of $14,000 per unit; location B would have annual fixed costs of $920,000 and variable costs of $13,000 per unit. The finished items sell for $17,000 each.

   a. At what volume of output would the two locations have the same total cost?

   b. For what range of output would location A be superior? For what range would B be superior?

4. A company that produces pleasure boats has recently decided to expand one of its lines. Current facilities are insufficient to handle the increased workload, so the company is considering three alternatives, A (new location), B (subcontract), and C (expand existing facilities).

   Alternative A would involve substantial fixed costs but relatively low variable costs: fixed costs would be $250,000 per year, and variable costs would be $500 per boat. Subcontracting would involve a cost per boat of $2,500, and expansion would require an annual fixed cost of $50,000 and a variable cost of $1,000 per boat.

   a. For what range of output would each alternative yield the lowest total cost?

   b. Which alternative would yield the lowest total cost for an expected annual volume of 150 boats?

   c. What other factors might be considered in choosing between expansion and subcontracting?

5. Rework part b of the previous problem using this additional information: Expansion would result in an increase of $70,000 per year in transportation costs, subcontracting would result in an increase of $25,000 per year, and adding a new location would result in an increase of $4,000 per year.

6. A firm that has recently experienced an enormous growth rate is seeking to lease a small plant in either Memphis, Biloxi, or Birmingham. Prepare an economic analysis of the three locations given the following information: Annual costs for building, equipment, and administration would be $40,000 for Memphis, $60,000 for Biloxi, and

$100,000 for Birmingham. Labor and materials are expected to be $8 per unit in Memphis, $4 per unit in Biloxi, and $5 per unit in Birmingham. The Memphis location would increase system transportation costs by $50,000 per year, the Biloxi location would increase them by $60,000 per year, and the Birmingham location would increase those costs by $25,000 per year. Expected annual volume is 10,000 units.

7. A retired auto mechanic hopes to open his own rustproofing shop. Customers would be area new-car dealers. Two locations are being considered, one in the center of the city and one on the outskirts of the city. The in-city location would involve fixed monthly costs of $7,000 and labor, materials, and transportation costs of $30 per car. The outside location would have fixed monthly costs of $4,700 and labor, materials, and transportation costs of $40 per car. Dealer price at either location will be $90 per car.

   a. Which location will yield the greatest profit if monthly demand is (1) 200 cars? (2) 300 cars?

   b. At what volume of output will the two sites yield the same monthly profit?

8. For each of the four types of organizations shown, rate the importance of each of the factors listed, using L = Low importance, M = Moderate importance, and H = High importance, in terms of making location decisions.

Factor	Local bank	Steel mill	Food warehouse	Public school
Convenience for customers	———	———	———	———
Attractiveness of building	———	———	———	———
Nearness to raw materials	———	———	———	———
Large amounts of power	———	———	———	———
Pollution controls	———	———	———	———
Labor cost and availability	———	———	———	———
Transportation costs	———	———	———	———
Construction costs	———	———	———	———

9. Using the following factor ratings, determine which location alternative should be chosen on the basis of maximum composite score, A, B, or C.

Factor (100 points each)	Weight	Location A	B	C
Convenient	.15	80	70	60
Parking facilities	.20	72	76	92
Display area	.18	88	90	90
Shopper traffic	.27	94	86	80
Operating costs	.10	98	90	82
Neighborhood	.10	96	85	75
	1.00			

10. A manager has received an analysis of several cities being considered for a new office complex. The data (10 points maximum) are:

| | Location | | |
Factor	A	B	C
Business services	9	5	5
Community services	7	6	7
Real estate cost	3	8	7
Construction costs	5	6	5
Cost of living	4	7	8
Taxes	5	5	4
Transportation	6	7	8

   a. If the manager weights the factors equally, how would the locations stack up?
   b. If business services and construction costs are given weights that are double the weights of the other factors, how would the locations stack up?

11. A toy manufacturer produces toys in five locations throughout the country. Raw materials (primarily barrels of powdered plastic) will be shipped from a new, centralized warehouse whose location is to be determined. The monthly quantities to be shipped to each location are the same. A coordinate system has been established, and the coordinates of each location have been determined as shown. Determine the coordinates of the centralized warehouse.

Location	(x,y)
A	3,7
B	8,2
C	4,6
D	4,1
E	6,4

12. A clothing manufacturer produces women's clothes at four locations in southern California. Relative locations have been determined, as shown in the table below. The location of a central shipping point for bolts of cloth must now be determined. Weekly quantities to be shipped to each location are shown below. Determine the coordinates of the location that will minimize distribution costs.

Location	(x,y)	Weekly quantity
A	5,7	15
B	6,9	20
C	3,9	25
D	9,4	30

13. A company that handles hazardous waste wants to minimize the shipping cost for shipments to a disposal center from five receiving stations it operates. Given the locations of the receiving stations and the volumes to be shipped daily, determine the location of the disposal center.

Location of processing station, (x,y)	Volume, tons per day
10,5	26
4,1	9
4,7	25
2,6	30
8,7	40

14. Determine the center of gravity for the destinations shown on the following map. Monthly shipments will be the quantities listed in the table.

Destination	Quantity
D1	900
D2	300
D3	700
D4	600
D5	800

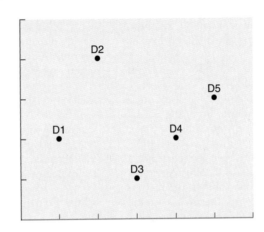

Adam, Everette E., Jr., and Ronald J. Ebert. *Production and Operations Management: Concepts, Models and Behavior.* 4th ed. Englewood Cliffs, N.J.: Prentice Hall, 1989.

Buffa, E. S. *Operations Management: Problems and Models.* 3rd ed. New York: John Wiley & Sons, 1972.

Hayes, Robert H., and Stephen Wheelright. *Restoring Our Competitive Edge: Competing through Manufacturing.* New York: John Wiley & Sons, 1984.

Reed, R., Jr. *Plant Location, Layout, and Maintenance.* Homewood, Ill.: Richard D. Irwin, 1967.

Schmenner, R. W. "Look Beyond the Obvious in Plant Location." *Harvard Business Review,* January–February 1979, pp. 126–32.

Schollhammer, H. *Locational Strategies of Multinational Firms.* Los Angeles: Center for International Business, Los Angeles World Trade Center, 1974.

Toward a New Era in U.S. Manufacturing: The Need for a National Vision. Washington: National Academy Press, 1986.

"What Management Needs to Know before Picking a Plant Site." *Dun's Review,* October 1979, p. 14ff.

SELECTED BIBLIOGRAPHY

READING   U.S. Semiconductor Makers Automate, Cut Chip Production in Southeast Asia   *Steven P. Galante*

PORTLAND, Maine—This New England city has lost jobs to Southeast Asia time and again over the past 15 years, in industries ranging from shoemaking to shipbuilding. Now Portland is striking back.

In a one-story factory owned by Schlumberger Ltd.'s Fairchild Camera & Instrument Corp. subsidiary, automated machines are doing the work once performed almost exclusively by hand in Southeast Asia. The machines are welding semiconductor chips, each smaller than an infant's fingernail, onto matchbook-sized metal frames.

"We think we can make more money doing it here than we can 10,000 miles away," says Kirk P. Pond, general manager of Fairchild's digital products division, explaining the decision to bring the assembly operation back to the U.S. from Singapore and Indonesia.

Such thinking would have been scoffed at just a few years ago. For more than a decade, American semiconductor makers have divided their production into onshore and offshore operations. Domestic plants have done the highly skilled tasks, and overseas facilities, where wages are low, have done the final work that requires a lot of labor but less skill.

Boon of Automation

Automation is changing that. Machines can now mount circuits onto their metal frames, wire the circuits in place and test the finished product for flaws— all far more rapidly than humans.

A Southeast Asia worker using manual equipment can wire as many as 120 integrated circuits to their frames in an hour. But the 34 automated machines here in Portland each can wire 640 circuits in an hour. And since one person can monitor eight machines at a time, the output per person is a stunning 5,120 circuits an hour.

Labor, obviously, becomes a smaller portion of the overall manufacturing cost. When transportation and inventory costs are considered, it becomes more economical to assemble chips at a U.S. plant than at an Asian plant—even if the Asian plant is equally automated, according to some analysts.

"The rise in the use of automated equipment is rapidly dispelling the advantages that used to exist for assembly in Asia," says Robert M. Clary, an electronics consultant at Rose Associates in Los Altos, Calif.

And that has major implications for countries such as Malaysia, the Philippines and Singapore, which have relied heavily on electronics for jobs and exports. A drift of assembly operations back to the U.S. could slow the industry's growth in Asia, and make it more difficult for Asian countries to acquire technological skills.

Plans Dropped

Advanced Micro Devices Inc., Sunnyvale, Calif., has dropped plans to enlarge its Singapore assembly plant and is slowing work on a facility in Bangkok. And Motorola Inc. of Schaumburg, Ill., has put plans to expand in Malaysia and Thailand on hold.

U.S. manufacturers aren't likely to scrap their existing Asian facilities just to replace them with automated U.S. plants, according to G. Dan Hutcheson, a vice president at VLSI Research Corp. in San Jose, Calif. "But as companies build new lines in the future," he says, "they're going to build them onshore."

Automation isn't the only factor prompting the chip makers to bring assembly back home. Economic changes sweeping through the marketplace are making it more important for producers to have assembly operations close to customers. Automation, however, is making that economically possible.

The "most profound thing" taking place in the industry is a move toward closer cooperation between chip makers and their customers, says Mr. Pond, the head of Fairchild's Portland plant.

Staying on Target

"I've got many, many customers to whom I can ship zero days late and no more than one day early," he says. Without onshore assembly, such timely deliveries would be difficult, unless Fairchild itself stocked a large and expensive inventory.

Southeast Asian governments are watching the trend towards onshore manufacturing with dismay. Singapore is considering more generous tax incentives and possibly even low-interest loans to lure U.S. semiconductor makers, says a spokesman for that country's Economic Development Board. Malaysian officials say they are reviewing their investment incentives, too.

Source: *The Wall Street Journal,* August 21, 1985, p. 28. Reprinted by permission of the *The Wall Street Journal,* © 1985 by Dow Jones & Company, Inc. All Rights Reserved Worldwide.

Update: Cypress Semiconductor Moves Assembly Out of United States

The following news item reflects the most current change in the semiconductor industry. The decision many companies made in the mid 1980s to settle their assembly operations in the United States is being reconsidered as offshore sites have become fully automated.

A day after announcing its Hyper-Sparc chip set, Cypress Semiconductor announced that it is moving its U.S. assembly operation offshore to streamline its manufacturing operations. The company also said it will lay off about 200 workers. Cypress president T. J. Rodgers attributed the workforce reduction largely to the wide gap in labor costs between U.S. manufacturing and assembly operations that are based elsewhere. He noted that when the company originally set up its U.S. assembly in 1984, it incorporated a high degree of automation to offset the difference between the U.S.'s $10-per-hour labor cost and the 50 cent-per-hour overseas cost. Since then, he said, competitors' offshore plants have become fully automated yet still pay low wages. Rodgers said the company can no longer afford the extra $8 million required per year to keep its assembly operation in Silicon Valley.

Source: *Byte,* August 1992, p. 18. Reprinted by permission of McGraw-Hill.

Questions

1. How is the semiconductor industry changing? What impact is this having on location decisions? Why?

2. Why aren't U.S. manufacturers likely to scrap their existing Asian facilities?

3. Why are timely deliveries difficult without onshore assembly?

4. What major factors influenced the Cypress decision to move offshore? What difficulties might this decision cause?

THE TRANSPORTATION MODEL

After completing this supplement, you should be able to:

1. Describe the nature of a transportation problem.

2. Solve transportation problems manually and interpret the results.

3. Set up transportation problems in the general linear-programming format.

4. Interpret computer solutions.

**LEARNING
OBJECTIVES**

**SUPPLEMENT
OUTLINE**

445

The transportation problem involves finding the lowest-cost plan for distributing stocks of goods or *supplies* from multiple origins to multiple destinations that *demand* the goods. For instance, a firm might have three factories that are all capable of producing identical units of the same product, and four warehouses that stock or demand those products, as depicted in Figure 9S–1. The *transportation model* can be used to determine how to allocate the supplies available from the various factories to the warehouses that stock or demand those goods, in such a way that total shipping cost (time, distance, etc.) is minimized. Usually, analysis of the problem will produce a shipping plan that pertains to a certain period of time (day, week), although once the plan is established, it will generally not change unless one or more of the parameters of the problem (supply, demand, unit shipping cost) changes.

INTRODUCTION

Although the diagram in Figure 9S–1 illustrates the nature of the transportation problem, in real life managers must often deal with allocation problems that are considerably larger in scope. Consider that a beer maker may have four or five breweries and hundreds or even thousands of distributors. Similarly, an automobile manufacturer may have eight assembly plants scattered throughout the United States and Canada and thousands of dealers that must be supplied with those cars. In such cases, the ability to identify the optimal solution makes the transportation model quite important.

The shipping (supply) points can be factories, warehouses, departments, or any other place from which goods are sent. Destinations can be factories, warehouses, departments, or other points that receive goods. The information needed to use the model consists of the following:

Figure 9S–1

The transportation problem involves determining a minimum-cost plan for shipping from multiple sources to multiple destinations

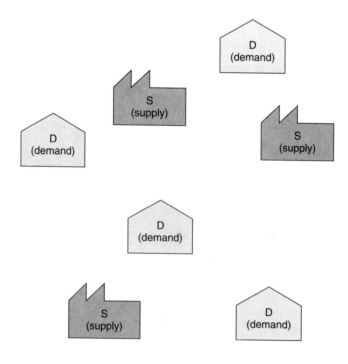

1. A list of the origins and each one's capacity or supply quantity per period.
2. A list of the destinations and each one's demand per period.
3. The unit cost of shipping items from each origin to each destination.

This information is arranged into a *transportation table* such as the one shown in Table 9S–1.

The transportation model is one of a class of linear-programming models, so named because of the linear relationships among variables. In the transportation model, transportation costs are treated as a direct linear function of the number of units shipped. For instance, if the unit cost to ship is $7 and 10 units are shipped, the cost would be 10($7) = $70. If 20 units are shipped, the cost would be 20($7) = $140. Hence, transportation cost is a linear function of the amount shipped.

Use of the transportation model implies that certain assumptions are satisfied. The major ones are:

1. The items to be shipped are homogeneous (i.e., they are the same regardless of their source or destination).
2. Shipping cost per unit is the same regardless of the number of units shipped.
3. There is only one route or mode of transportation being used between each source and each destination.

The transportation model starts with the development of a feasible solution, which is then sequentially tested and improved until an optimal solution is obtained. The description of the technique on the following pages focuses on each of the major steps in the process in this order:

1. Obtaining an initial solution.
2. Testing the solution for optimality.
3. Improving suboptimal solutions.

Table 9S–1

A transportation table

OBTAINING AN INITIAL SOLUTION

In order to begin the process, it is necessary to develop a feasible distribution plan. There are a number of different methods for obtaining such a plan. The discussion here will focus on two widely used approaches: the **northwest-corner method** and the **intuitive approach**. The latter is a heuristic approach that yields an initial solution that is often optimal or near optimal. The northwest-corner method is much less efficient; it merely provides a convenient starting point. Even so, it is an easy-to-understand approach that merits consideration. Each method will be demonstrated using Table 9S–1.

These methods require that total supply equal total demand. If you refer to Table 9S–1, you will see that they are equal. Later you will learn what to do if they are not equal.

Northwest-corner method

Method of obtaining an initial solution to the transportation model by beginning with the upper left-hand corner of the table.

Intuitive approach

Heuristic approach to obtaining an initial solution.

THE NORTHWEST-CORNER METHOD

1. The northwest-corner method begins with the cell that is in the upper left-hand (northwest) corner of the table, allocating (assigning) as many units as possible to that cell. Factory 1 can supply 100 units, but warehouse A needs only 80 units. Hence, assign 80 units to cell 1–A, completely exhausting A's demand and leaving factory 1 with a supply of 20 units (see Table 9S–2).

2. Staying in row 1 and moving to column B, we see that warehouse B has a demand for 90 units, 20 of which can be supplied by factory 1. Assigning 20 units to cell 1–B exhausts factory 1's supply and leaves warehouse B with a demand for 70 additional units.

3. Staying in column B and dropping down to row 2, we observe that factory 2 has a supply of 200 units. Assigning 70 units to cell 2–B satisfies B's demand and leaves factory 2 with 130 units.

4. Staying in row 2 and moving to column C, we observe that warehouse C has a demand for 120 units, which can be filled by factory 2. Assigning 120 units to cell 2–C satisfies C's demand and still leaves factory 2 with 10 units.

5. Staying in row 2 and moving to column D, we find that warehouse D has a demand of 160 units. Assigning 10 units to cell 2–D exhausts factory 2's supply and leaves D with a need for an additional 150 units.

6. The remaining demand of warehouse D for 150 units can be just satisfied by factory 3's supply. This is a consequence of starting with equal supply and demand. Hence, assign 150 units to be shipped from factory 3 to warehouse D.

Table 9S–2

Northwest-corner solution

Is this distribution plan optimal (i.e., does it minimize transportation costs)? In a moment, we shall see how to test it to determine if further improvements are possible. In the meantime, it will be instructive to compute the transportation costs associated with this initial solution. The cost for each cell is the product of units assigned to that cell and the unit transportation cost for the cell. (Empty cells have no cost.) Thus:

		Total cost
1–A	80($4) =	$ 320
1–B	20($7) =	140
2–B	70($3) =	210
2–C	120($8) =	960
2–D	10($8) =	80
3–D	150($5) =	750
		$2,460

As previously mentioned, the northwest-corner method is merely a convenient way to obtain a feasible solution. Because it does not take costs into account, it frequently does not yield the optimal solution. Note that with the given supplies and demands, the same solution would be generated even if the costs were quite different. It will be interesting, then, to see how well the intuitive method does, since it explicitly takes costs into account in obtaining an initial solution.

THE INTUITIVE APPROACH

With the intuitive approach, cell allocations are made according to cell cost, beginning with the lowest cost. The procedure involves these steps:

1. Identify the cell with the lowest cost.
2. Allocate as many units as possible to that cell, and cross out the row or column (or both) that is exhausted by this.
3. Find the cells with the next lowest cost from among the *feasible* cells.
4. Repeat steps 2 and 3 until all units have been allocated.

Cell 1–D has the lowest cost ($1) (see Table 9S–3). The factory 1 supply is 100, and the warehouse D demand is 160. Therefore, the most we can allocate to this

Table 9S–3

Table 9S–5

Table 9S–4

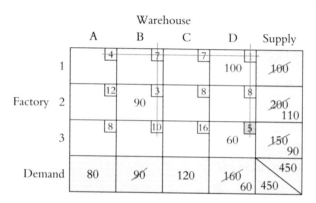

cell is 100 units. Since the supply of 100 is exhausted, we cross out the costs in the first row as well as the supply of 100. In addition, we must adjust the column total to reflect the allocation, which leaves 60 units of unallocated demand in column D.

The next lowest cost is $3 in cell 2–B. Allocating 90 units to this cell exhausts the column total and leaves 110 units for the supply of factory 2 (see Table 9S–4). Next, we cross out the costs for column B.

The next lowest cost (that is not crossed out) is the $5 in cell 3–D. Allocating 60 units to this cell exhausts the column total and leaves 90 units for row 3. We now cross out the costs in column D (see Table 9S–5).

At this point, there is a *tie* for the next lowest cell cost: cell 3–A and cell 2–C each has a cost of $8. Break such a tie arbitrarily. Suppose we choose cell 3–A. There is a demand of 80 units, and there is a remaining supply of 90 units in the row. The smaller of these is 80, so that amount is placed in cell 3–A (see Table 9S–6). This exhausts the column, so we cross out the cell costs in column A. Also, the remaining supply in factory 3 is now 10.

The other cell in the tie, cell 2–C, still remains. There is a supply of 110 remaining in the row and a demand of 120 in the column. The smaller of these two amounts, 110, is assigned to the cell, and the row costs are crossed out. The row total is changed to zero, and the column total is changed to 10 units. The only remaining cell with a cost that has not been crossed out is cell 3–C. Both supply and demand are 10 units, so 10 units are assigned to the cell. This completes the initial allocation. (See Table 9S–7.)

Table 9S–6

Table 9S–7

Initial allocation using intuitive approach

Warehouse	A	B	C	D	Supply
Factory 1	[4]	[7]	[7]	[1] 100	100
Factory 2	[12]	[3] 90	[8] 110	[8]	200
Factory 3	[8] 80	[10]	[16] 10	[5] 60	150
Demand	80	90	120	160	450 / 450

Now let's determine if this initial solution obtained using the intuitive method is optimum.

TESTING FOR OPTIMALITY

Testing for optimality and revising suboptimal solutions are the same regardless of how the initial solution was developed (e.g., northwest-corner method or intuitive). The process involves analysis of each unused (empty) cell to determine if there is a potential for reducing the total cost of the solution. This is accomplished by transferring one unit into an empty cell and noting the impact this has on costs. If costs are increased, then that implies that using the cell would increase total costs. If costs remain the same, that would imply that an alternative option with the same total cost as the current plan exists. However, if analysis reveals a cost decrease, that implies that an improved solution is possible. The test for optimality requires that *every* unused cell be evaluated for potential improvement. Either of two methods can be used: stepping-stone or MODI.

EVALUATING EMPTY CELLS: THE STEPPING-STONE METHOD

Stepping-stone method
Cell evaluation by borrowing one unit from a full cell to assess the impact of shifting units into the empty cell.

In the **stepping-stone method**, cell evaluation proceeds by borrowing one unit from a full cell and using it to assess the impact of shifting units into the empty cell. For instance, if a shift of one unit causes an increase of $5, we can assume that total costs would be increased by $5 times the number of units shifted into the cell. Obviously, such a move would be unwise since the objective is to decrease costs.

The name *stepping-stone* derives from early descriptions of the method that likened the procedures to crossing a shallow pond by stepping from stone to stone. Here, the occupied cells are the "stones"; shifting units into empty cells requires borrowing units from occupied cells. In order to maintain the balance of supply and demand for every row and column, a shift of one unit into an empty cell requires a series of shifts from other occupied cells.

The best way to understand the evaluation process is to consider a simple example. Suppose we want to evaluate cell 1–A (see Table 9S–8). We must shift one unit into that cell, which would imply that one unit will be shipped from factory 1 to warehouse A. However, factory 1 has only 100 units it can ship, and all are allocated to warehouse D. Therefore, in order to ship one unit to A, we borrow a unit from cell 1–D. This creates two problems: Column A now has one extra unit, and column D is short one unit (i.e., A has $1 + 80 = 81$ units but needs only 80 units, and D has $99 + 60 = 159$ but needs 160 units). We remedy these problems by subtracting one unit from cell 3–A and adding it to cell 3–D; this gives column A a total of $1 + 79 = 80$ and column D a total of $99 + 61 = 160$. (Note that instead of actually making each addition or subtraction of the single unit, a $+$ or $-$ sign is simply inserted in the appropriate cell to signify the operation.)

Let's see what effect such a shift would have on costs. For each cell to which a unit is added, the cost will increase by the transportation cost for that cell; for cells that gave up a unit, costs will decrease by the cell's transportation cost. We can summarize this with a *T account* as follows.

Cell 1–A

+		**–**	
(1–A)	+4	(1–D)	−1
(3–D)	+5	(3–A)	−8
	+9		−9

0

Thus, shifting units around this path would have no impact whatsoever on transportation costs: use of cell 1–A would be an equivalent-cost alternative. Manage-

Table 9S–8

Evaluation path for cell 1–A

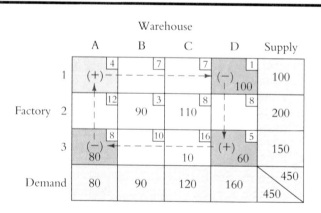

ment may prefer to use it for other reasons, or management may prefer to stay with the original solution. In any case, knowledge of such alternatives adds a certain degree of flexibility to decision making.

So far, we have not discovered any improvement potential—but there are still five unused cells that must be analyzed. Before we evaluate the remaining empty cells, it is important to mention that constructing paths using the stepping-stone method requires a minimum number of occupied cells and unless that number exists, it will be impossible to evaluate all the empty cells in this manner. The number of occupied cells must equal the sum of the number of rows and columns minus 1, or $R + C - 1$, where R = Number of rows and C = Number of columns. In this example, $R = 3$ and $C = 4$, so we must have $3 + 4 - 1 = 6$ used or completed cells (which we do have). If there are too few occupied cells, the matrix is said to be *degenerate*. A method for overcoming this problem is explained later in this supplement.

For now, let's continue evaluating the unused cells. Suppose we now consider cell 2–A. Begin by adding a unit to the empty cell. Moving to the right in row 2, we have what seems to be a choice: borrow a unit from 90 or from 110. However, borrowing from 90 will leave column B one unit short, and since adding and borrowing must involve occupied cells and there are no others in the B column, the 90 cannot be used. Instead, we must borrow from the 110 and add one unit to the 10 in cell 3–C. We can complete our path back to the original cell by subtracting a unit from the 80 units in cell 3–A. The $+/-$ path is shown in Table 9S–9. The impact on total cost for the path associated with cell 2–A would be:

Cell 2–A

+		−	
(2–A)	+12	(2–C)	−8
(3–C)	+16	(3–A)	−8
	+28		−16

$$+12$$

This means that for every unit shifted into cell 2–A, the total cost would *increase* by \$12. Hence, we should avoid shipping units from factory 2 to warehouse A.

At this point, let's consider some helpful rules for obtaining evaluation paths, since you may still be a little unsure of how to actually do it.

Table 9S–9

Evaluation path for cell 2–A

1. Start by placing a + sign in the cell you wish to evaluate.
2. Move horizontally (or vertically) to a completed cell. (It is okay to pass *through* an empty cell or a completed cell without stopping.) Choose a cell that will permit your next move to another completed cell. Assign a − sign to the cell.
3. Change direction and move to another completed cell. Again, choose one that will permit your next move. Assign a + sign to the cell.
4. Continue this process of moving to completed cells and alternating + and − signs until you can complete a closed path back to the original cell. Make only horizontal and vertical moves.
5. You may find it helpful to place a small dot or checkmark in cells that have been evaluated to keep track of them.

Let's try another one, say, 3–B. Start by placing a + sign in cell 3–B. Move to the 90 in cell 2–B, and place a − sign there. Move to the 110 in cell 2–C, and place a + sign there. Move to cell 3–C, and give it a − sign. The path is shown in Table 9S–10. This one was fairly easy. Let's see what the impact on cost would be:

Cell 3–B

	+		−
(3–B)	+10	(2–B)	−3
(2–C)	+8	(3–C)	−16
	+18		−19

$$\boxed{-1}$$

The −1 indicates that for each unit we can shift into cell 3–B, our cost will decrease by $1. Hence, if we could shift 100 units, we could save $100 over the present solution. However, at this point we are not ready to make any changes since there may be some other empty cell that would yield even greater savings, and we can only make one shift at a time.

Evaluation of cell 2–D is quite similar to the evaluation of cell 3–B. The evaluation path is shown in Table 9S–11. The cost impact would be:

Table 9S–10

Evaluation path for cell 3–B

Warehouse

Factory		A	B	C	D	Supply
	1	ₒ [4]	[7]	[7]	[1] 100	100
	2	ₒ [12]	[3] (−) → 90	[8] (+) ↓ 110	[8]	200
	3	[8] 80	[10] (+) ←	[16] (−) 10	[5] 60	150
Demand		80	90	120	160	450 / 450

ₒ Previously evaluated

Cell 2–D

+		–	
(2–D)	+8	(3–D)	–5
(3–C)	+16	(2–C)	–8
	+24		–13

+11

Thus, no improvement is possible.

There are two cells remaining to be evaluated: 1–B and 1–C. Let's consider 1–B first. It is a little more involved than the previous paths. Begin by placing a + in cell 1–B. Move to cell 1–D (100 units) and give it a –. Move vertically to 3–D (60 units) and give it a +. Move to the left and put a – in cell 3–C (10 units). Move up to 110 and put a + in that cell. Move to the left to 90 units (cell 2–B) and give it a – sign, completing the path. The path is shown in Table 9S–12. The cost impact of the path would be zero.

Warehouse

● Previously evaluated

Table 9S–11

Evaluation path for cell 2–D

Warehouse

Previously evaluated

Table 9S–12

Evaluation path for cell 1–B

Cell 1–B

+		–	
(1–B)	+7	(1–D)	–1
(3–D)	+5	(3–C)	–16
(2–C)	+8	(2–B)	–3
	+20		–20

0

Thus, no improvement is possible using this cell path.

The last empty cell is 1–C. Its evaluation path is shown in Table 9S–13. Begin with 1–C as +, 1–D as –, 3–D as +, and 3–C as –. The cost impact would be:

Cell 1–C

+		–	
(1–C)	+7	(3–D)	–1
(3–D)	+5	(3–C)	–16
	+12		–17

$\boxed{-5}$

Hence, for each unit we can transfer into this empty cell, we improve the cost by $5.

At this point, each of the unused cells has been evaluated. The resulting costs are summarized below.

Cell	1–A	2–A	3–B	2–D	1–B	1–C
Cost	0	+12	$\boxed{-1}$	+11	0	$\boxed{-5}$

Cells with a positive total do not present opportunities for improvement. The fact that 1–A and 1–B are both zero indicates that at least one other equivalent alternative exists. The interesting fact here is that two cells have negative evaluations, indicating that the present solution is not an optimum. In a later section, you will learn how to develop an improved solution.

Table 9S–13

Evaluation path for cell 1–C

● Previously evaluated

EVALUATING EMPTY CELLS: THE MODI METHOD

Another method for evaluating empty cells is the **modified distribution method (MODI)**. It involves computing row and column index numbers that can be used for cell evaluation. In many respects, it is simpler than the stepping-stone method because it avoids having to trace cell evaluation paths. However, the cell evaluations it produces are identical to those obtained using the stepping-stone method. Note, though, that if a solution is not optimal, *one* stepping-stone path must be traced to obtain an improved solution. This is explained in detail in the next section.

The MODI procedure consists of these steps:

1. Make an initial allocation using the northwest-corner or intuitive method. Check for degeneracy, and adjust if necessary.
2. Obtain an index number for each row and column. Do this using only *completed* cells. Note that there will always be at least one completed cell in each row and in each column.
   a. Begin by assigning a zero to the first row.
   b. Determine the column index for any completed cells in row 1 using the relationship: Column index = Cell cost − Row index. For example, if a cell cost is $8 per unit, the column index will be 8 − 0 = 8.
   c. Each new column value will permit the calculation of *at least* one new row value, and vice versa. Continue until all rows and columns have index numbers, using only completed cells.
3. Obtain cell evaluations for *empty* cells using the relationship:

   Cell evaluation = Cell cost − (Row index + Column index)

   Obtain these in any order.

Comments:

1. Row or column values may be positive, negative, or zero.
2. A reallocation requires that new row and column cost values be calculated.

Let's see how the MODI method can be used for cell evaluations.

We begin by assigning a zero to row 1 (see Table 9S–14). Since we can only work with occupied cells and since cell 1–D is the only such cell in row 1, we focus

Modified distribution method (MODI)

Evaluating empty cells by computing row and column index numbers.

Table 9S–14

MODI index numbers

Table 9S–15	Cell	Evaluation
MODI cell evaluation	1–A	$4 - (0 + 4) = 0$
	1–B	$7 - (0 + 7) = 0$
	1–C	$7 - (0 + 12) = -5$
	2–A	$12 - (-4 + 4) = 12$
	2–D	$8 - (-4 + 1) = 11$
	3–B	$10 - (4 + 7) = -1$

on it. Since the sum of the row and column index numbers must add to the cell cost (which is 1), we can see that the index number for column D must be 1. There are no other occupied cells in row 1, so we shift to column D, cell 3–D. Again, the sum of the row and column index numbers must add to the cell cost (which is 5). Since the column index for D is 1, the index number for row 3 must be 4, as $4 + 1 = 5$.

We can use this row 3 index number and the other two occupied cells in row 3 to obtain index numbers for columns A and C. For column A, the A index number plus 4 must equal the 3–A cell cost of 8. Hence, the index for A is 4: $4 + 4 = 8$. For C, the index plus 4 must equal 16; hence, the index number is 12.

Next, for row 2, using cell 2–C and a C index of 12, the row index is -4. Then, using cell 2–B, the column index is 7: $7 + (-4) = 3$. This completes the row and column index numbers.

The cell evaluation for each empty cell is determined by subtracting from the cost of the empty cell the sum of the row and column index numbers:

$$\text{Cell evaluation} = \text{Cell cost} - (\text{Row index} + \text{Column index})$$

All of the evaluations are shown in Table 9S–15. Note that these agree with the evaluations obtained using the stepping-stone method. Again, because some evaluations are negative, the solution is not optimal.

OBTAINING AN IMPROVED SOLUTION

The presence of negative cell evaluations is evidence that an improved solution is possible. By the same token, if no negatives appear, an optimum has been achieved.

In this case, there are two cells with negative evaluations: 3–B, with a value of -1, and 1–C, with a value of -5. Select the value that implies more improvement (i.e., -5), and ignore the other.

The implication of the -5 is that a savings of $5 per unit will be realized for every unit that can be shifted into cell 1–C. Recall the path used to evaluate the cell; it is reproduced in Table 9S–16A. In the course of the evaluation, a single unit was added or subtracted to certain cells, as denoted by the $+$ and $-$ signs. We want to repeat that procedure, but instead of shifting *one* unit, we want to shift *as many as possible*. The *quantities* in the cells that have $-$ signs (i.e., 10 in cell 3–C and 100 in cell 1–D) are potential candidates for shifting, since the $-$ implies units are subtracted from those cells. It is the *smaller* of these quantities that is the limiting factor. That is, we can subtract 10 from both numbers (10 and 100), but if we try to subtract 100 from both, we end up with 0 and -90. The negative value would imply shipping from the warehouse back to the factory! Hence, 10 units can be shifted. In general, shift the minimum quantity that occupies a negative position in the $\pm$ path.

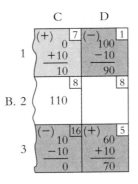

Table 9S–16

Evaluation path for cell 1–C (see A) and reallocation of 10 units around the path (see B)

Table 9S–17

Revised solution

	Warehouse				
	A	B	C	D	Supply
1	4	7	7 10	1 90	100
Factory 2	12	3 90	8 110	8	200
3	8 80	10	16	5 70	150
Demand	80	90	120	160	450 / 450

To accomplish the shift, add 10 units to each cell that has a + sign and subtract 10 units from each cell with a − sign. (Because the signs alternate, the row and column totals will still be satisfied.) This is shown in Table 9S–16.

The improved solution is shown in Table 9S–17. The total costs are:

			Total cost
1–C	10($7)	=	$ 70
1–D	90($1)	=	90
2–B	90($3)	=	270
2–C	110($8)	=	880
3–A	80($8)	=	640
3–D	70($5)	=	350
			$2,300

Note that the revised solution has a total cost that is $50 less than the previous solution ($2,300 versus $2,350), which is exactly equal to the cell evaluation value times the number of units shifted: -5×10 units = $-\$50$.

Is this the optimum? Once again, we must evaluate each empty cell to determine if further improvements are possible. Recall that we must check to see if there are enough completed cells to allow all empty cells to have evaluation paths. Thus,

$$R + C - 1 = 3 + 4 - 1 = 6$$

Since there are six completed cells, the second round of cell evaluations can proceed. The cell paths and their values are shown in Tables 9S–18 to 9S–23. Since all are either zero or positive, this solution is the optimum. (*Note:* MODI could have been used instead of stepping-stone.)

Table 9S–18

Evaluation of cell 1–A

Table 9S–19

Evaluation of cell 1–B

Previously evaluated

Table 9S–20

Evaluation of cell 2–A

Evaluation of cell 2–D

Table 9S–22

Evaluation of cell 3–B

Table 9S–23

Evaluation of cell 3–C

SPECIAL PROBLEMS

Not all transportation problems are as straightforward as the one just presented. Various irregularities often crop up, which require certain adjustments before a solution can be obtained. Two of the most common irregularities are unequal supply and demand, and degeneracy, a term that refers to an insufficient number of completed cells to allow evaluation of every empty cell.

A frequently encountered situation is one in which supply and demand are not equal. Table 9S–24 illustrates such a case. Total supply (capacity) of the two sources is 200 units, but total demand of the destinations is only 170. Hence, there is a deficiency in demand of 30 units. This condition can be remedied by adding a **dummy** destination with a demand equal to the difference between supply and demand. Since there is no such destination, no units will actually be shipped, and unit shipping costs for each dummy cell are $0. This is illustrated in Table 9S–25.

Once the dummy has been added, the transportation method can then be applied in the usual manner. The final solution will have a total number of units assigned to the dummy that equals the original difference between supply and demand (see Table 9S–26). These numbers indicate which source(s) (e.g., factories) will hold the extra units or will have excess capacity. In the example shown, factory 1 will ship only 70 units even though it has the capacity to ship 100 units.

Dummy

Imaginary number added equal to the difference between supply and demand when these are unequal.

Table 9S–24

Supply exceeds demand by 30 units

A dummy column with a demand of 30 units is added to the matrix; dummy cell costs are zero

---

Table 9S–26

Units in the dummy column are not shipped; factory 1 will ship only 70 units

A similar situation exists when demand exceeds supply (see Table 9S–27). In those cases a dummy *row* (e.g., factory) with a supply equal to the difference between supply and demand must be added (see Table 9S–28). Again, units will not actually be shipped, so transportation costs are $0 for each cell in the dummy row. Units in the dummy row in the final solution indicate the destinations that will not receive all the units they desire and the amount of the shortage for each. For example, Table 9S–29 indicates that destination A will be 20 units short and destination B, 30 units short.

Table 9S–27

Demand exceeds supply by 50 units

Table 9S–28

A dummy row with a supply of 50 units is added to the matrix so supply will equal demand

Table 9S–29

Units in the dummy row will not be shipped; destination A will receive 100 − 20 = 80 units and B will receive 200 − 30 = 170 units

The total transportation cost for this distribution plan is:

		Total cost
1–B .... 80($1)	=	$ 80
2–A .... 80($4)	=	320
3–B .... 90($4)	=	360
Dummy–A .... 20($0)	=	0
Dummy–B .... 30($0)	=	0
		$760

Note: When using the intuitive approach, if a dummy row or column exists, make assignments to dummy cell(s) *last*.

DEGENERACY

We have seen that the transportation method involves evaluation of empty cells using completed cells as "stepping stones." **Degeneracy** exists if there are two few completed cells to allow all necessary paths to be constructed. The condition occurs if an allocation (other than the final one) exhausts *both* the row (supply) and the column (demand) quantities. It can occur in an initial solution or in subsequent solutions, so it is necessary to test for degeneracy after each iteration using $R + C - 1$.

An example of a matrix with too few completed cells is shown in Table 9S–30. Note that there are only four completed cells, although the necessary number is five: $3 + 3 - 1 = 5$. Because of this, it is impossible to develop an evaluation path for cells 1–B, 1–C, 2–A, or 3–A. The situation can be remedied by placing a very small quantity, represented by the symbol ϵ, into one of the empty cells and then treating it as a completed cell. The quantity is so small that it is negligible; it will be ignored in the final solution.

The idea is to select a position for ϵ that will permit evaluation of all remaining empty cells. For example, putting it in cell 3–A will permit evaluation of all empty cells (see Table 9S–31). Some experimentation may be needed to find the best spot for ϵ, since not every cell will enable construction of evaluation paths for the remaining cells. Moreover, avoid placing ϵ in a minus position of a cell path that turns out to be negative because reallocation requires shifting the smallest quantity

Degeneracy

The condition of too few completed cells to allow all necessary paths to be constructed.

Table 9S–30

There are two few completed cells; some empty cells cannot be evaluated

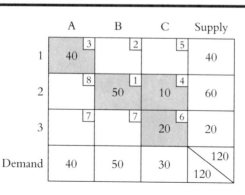

	A	B	C	Supply
1	[3] 40	[2]	[5]	40
2	[8]	[1] 50	[4] 10	60
3	[7] ϵ	[7]	[6] 20	20
Demand	40	50	30	120 / 120

Table 9S–31

Cell 3–A becomes a completed cell with the addition of a very small quantity, represented by the symbol ϵ

in a minus position. Since the smallest quantity is ϵ, which is essentially zero, no reallocation will be possible.

The cell evaluations (not shown) are all positive, so this solution is optimal. (Note that cell 3–A is considered to be a completed cell and is therefore *not* evaluated.)

SUMMARY OF PROCEDURE

1. Make certain that supply and demand are equal. If they are not, determine the difference between the two amounts. Create a dummy source or destination with a supply (or demand) equal to the difference so that demand and supply are equal.
2. Develop an initial solution using either the northwest-corner method or the intuitive approach.
3. Check to see that the number of completed cells is equal to $R + C - 1$. If it isn't, the solution is degenerate and will require insertion of a minute quantity, ϵ, in one of the empty cells, making it a completed cell.
4. Evaluate each of the empty cells. If any evaluations turn out to be negative, an improved solution is possible. Identify the cell that has the largest negative evaluation. Reallocate units around its evaluation path.
5. Repeat steps 3 and 4 until all cells have zero or positive values. When that occurs, the optimal solution has been achieved.

LOCATION DECISIONS

The transportation model can be used to compare location alternatives in terms of their impact on the total distribution costs for a system. The procedure involves working through a separate problem for each location being considered and then comparing the resulting total costs. Let's consider a simple example of this.

A previous example dealt with unequal supply and demand. The original table is reproduced in Table 9S–32. Suppose the firm has recently decided to open a third distribution center that will have an expected demand of 30 units, which will result in equality of supply and demand. The question is whether to locate in a suburb of Boston or in Albany, New York. The transportation costs for each location are shown in Table 9S–33. In order to determine which will yield the lower transportation costs for the system, we must work the problem twice—once using the

Table 9S–32
———
Supply exceeds demand
by 30 units

	To: A	B	Supply
From: 1	[5]	[9]	100
2	[4]	[2]	100
Demand	80	90	200 / 170

Table 9S–33
———
Transportation costs for
Boston and Albany

Cost per unit to Boston	Cost per unit to Albany
From:	From:
1............ $3	1............ $4
2............ $6	2............ $1

Boston costs and once using the Albany costs. The resulting optimal solution for each location and its total cost are shown in Tables 9S–34 and 9S–35. The total cost with the Boston location is $10 less than with the Albany location, making Boston the better location *on the basis of transportation cost*. Of course, we have already seen that there are many aspects of location decisions, and transportation cost is only one of them. There may be other, more important factors that favor one location over the other.

You may also be wondering how important a difference of $10 is. Remember that this is simply an example designed to demonstrate use of the method in location decisions. Of course, if an actual situation produced such a small difference, for practical purposes the locations would undoubtedly be rated even in terms of transportation costs. However, suppose the units of supply and demand are in hundreds. Then the cost difference would be 100($10) = $1,000. In addition, the supply and demand quantities are generally for a short period of time (e.g., week, month, or quarter). Consequently, the difference on an annual basis would be much larger. For instance, if the amounts are in hundreds of units per week, the annual difference would be $1,000(52) = $52,000, which would undoubtedly be regarded as significant.

If other costs differ among locations, such as production costs, these can easily be included in the analysis, provided they can be determined on a per-unit basis. In this regard, note that merely adding or subtracting a constant to all cost values in any row or column will not affect the optimum solution, so any additional costs should only be included if they have a varying effect within a row or column.

OTHER APPLICATIONS

We have seen how the transportation model can be used to minimize the costs associated with distributing goods, and we have seen how the model can be used for comparing location alternatives. The model is also used in a number of other ways. For example, in a slight variation of the model, profits can be used in place of costs.

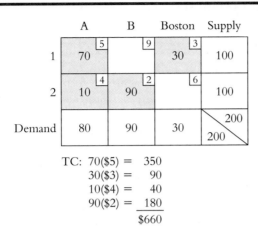

Table 9S–34

Optimal plan using
Boston warehouse

	A	B	Boston	Supply
1	[5] 70	[9]	[3] 30	100
2	[4] 10	[2] 90	[6]	100
Demand	80	90	30	200 / 200

TC: 70($5) = 350
    30($3) = 90
    10($4) = 40
    90($2) = 180
             $660

Table 9S–35

Optimal plan using
Albany warehouse

	A	B	Albany	Supply
1	[5] 80	[9]	[4] 20	100
2	[4]	[2] 90	[1] 10	100
Demand	80	90	30	200 / 200

TC: 80($5) = 400
    20($4) = 80
    90($2) = 180
    10($1) = 10
             $670

In such cases, each of the cell profits can be subtracted from the largest profit, and the remaining values (opportunity costs) can be treated in the same manner as shipping costs.

Some of the other uses of the model include production planning and scheduling (see Chapter 11), problems involving assignment of personnel or jobs to certain departments or machines (see Chapter 15), capacity planning, and transshipment problems.[1]

The use of the transportation model for capacity planning parallels its use for location decisions. Proposed capacity alternatives can be subjected to transportation analysis to determine which one would generate the lowest total shipping cost. For example, it is perhaps intuitively obvious that a factory or warehouse that is close to its market—or has low transportation costs for some other reason—should probably have a larger capacity than other locations. Of course, many problems are not so simple, and they require actual use of the model.

---

[1] Transshipment relates to problems with major distribution centers that in turn redistribute to smaller market destinations. See, for example, W. J. Stevenson, *Introduction to Management Science,* 2nd ed. (Homewood, Ill.: Richard D. Irwin, 1992).

COMPUTER SOLUTIONS

Although manual solution of transportation problems is fairly straightforward, computer solutions are generally preferred, particularly for moderate or large problems. Many software packages call for data input in the same tabular form used throughout this chapter. A more general approach is to format the problem as a standard linear-programming model (i.e., specify the objective function and a set of constraints). That approach enables one to use the more general version of an LP package (such as LINDO) to solve a transportation problem. Let's consider this general approach.

Table 9S–36 repeats the transportation model presented earlier in this supplement. The decision variables for a transportation model are the quantities to be shipped. Because each cell represents a potential transportation route, each must have a decision variable. We can use the symbol x_{1A} to represent the decision variable for cell 1–A, x_{1B} for cell 1–B, and so on. The objective function consists of the cell costs and these cell symbols:

$$\text{Minimize} \quad 4x_{1A} + 7x_{1B} + 7x_{1C} + 1x_{1D} + 12x_{2A} + 3x_{2B} + 8x_{2C} \\ + 8x_{2D} + 8x_{3A} + 10x_{3B} + 16x_{3C} + 5x_{3D}$$

Because the amounts allocated in any row or column must add to the row or column total, each row and column must have a constraint. Thus, we have

$$\begin{aligned}
\text{Supply (rows)} \quad & x_{1A} + x_{1B} + x_{1C} + x_{1D} = 100 \\
& x_{2A} + x_{2B} + x_{2C} + x_{2D} = 200 \\
& x_{3A} + x_{3B} + x_{3C} + x_{3D} = 150 \\
\text{Demand (columns)} \quad & x_{1A} + x_{2A} + x_{3A} = 80 \\
& x_{1B} + x_{2B} + x_{3B} = 90 \\
& x_{1C} + x_{2C} + x_{3C} = 120 \\
& x_{1D} + x_{2D} + x_{3D} = 160
\end{aligned}$$

We do not need a constraint for the total; the row and column constraints take care of this.

If supply and demand are not equal, add the appropriate dummy row or column to the table before writing the constraints.

Table 9S–36

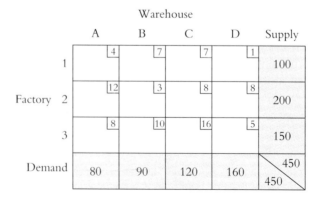

Problem

1. Use the intuitive technique to develop an initial solution to the following problem, and then determine if the solution is optimal. If it is not, develop the optimal solution.

SOLVED PROBLEMS

To:	A	B	Supply
From: 1	9	6	75
2	5	3	75
Demand	80	90	

Solution

a. First check to see if supply and demand are equal. Total demand = 170 and total supply = 150; therefore, it will be necessary to create a dummy origin (supply) with zero transportation costs in each of its cells (see following table).

To:	A	B	Supply
From: 1	9	6	75
2	5	3	75
Dummy	0	0	20
Demand	80	90	170 / 170

b. Find the cell that has the lowest unit transportation cost. When a dummy is present and the intuitive method is being used, leave the dummy allocation until last. Thus, aside from the $0 costs in the dummy row, the lowest cost is $3 for cell 2–B. Assign as many units as possible to this cell. The column total is 90, and the row total is 75. Because 75 is the smaller of the two, assign 75 to cell 2–B. This exhausts the row total, so cross out the 75, and cross out the cell costs for the second row. Revise the column total to 15.

To:	A	B	Supply
From: 1	[9]	[6]	75
2	[5]	[3] 75	7̶5̶
Dummy	[0]	[0]	20
Demand	80	9̶0̶ 15	170 170

The next smallest cell cost is \$6 in cell 1–B. We want to assign as many units as possible to this route (cell). The remaining demand for column B is 15, and the row total is 75. We assign the smaller of these, 15, to cell 1–B, thereby exhausting the column and reducing the row supply to 60. Next we draw a line through the cell costs of column B.

To:	A	B	Supply
From: 1	[9]	[6] 15	7̶5̶ 60
2	[5]	[3] 75	7̶5̶
Dummy	[0]	[0]	20
Demand	80	9̶0̶ 1̶5̶	170 170

Still ignoring the dummy row, the next lowest cell cost is \$9 in 1–A, where a supply of 60 and a demand of 80 exist. We assign the smaller of these, 60 units, to cell 1–A, so row 1 costs must be crossed out. Also, the revised column A total becomes 20.

To:	A	B	Supply
From: 1	[9] 60	[6] 15	7̶5̶ 6̶0̶
2	[5]	[3] 75	7̶5̶
Dummy	[0]	[0]	20
Demand	8̶0̶ 20	9̶0̶ 1̶5̶	170 170

At this point, only the dummy row remains. Cell dummy–A has a supply and a demand of 20; assigning this amount to the cell exhausts both the supply and the demand, finishing the initial allocation.

To:	A	B	Supply
From: 1	[9] 60	[6] 15	7̶5̶ 60
2	[5]	[3] 75	7̶5̶
Dummy	[0] 20	[0]	2̶0̶
Demand	8̶0̶ 20	9̶0̶ 15	170 / 170

c. The next step is to evaluate this solution to determine if it is the optimal solution. First we must check for degeneracy: $R + C - 1 = 3$ (rows) + 2 (columns) − 1 = 4, the required number of filled or completed cells. Because there are four completed cells, the solution is not degenerate.

The evaluation can use either the stepping-stone method or MODI. Suppose we use MODI. We always begin by placing a zero at the left edge of row 1. This is the row 1 index number. We can use it to find the column index number for any cell in row 1 that is a completed cell. Because both cell 1–A and cell 1–B are completed, we can obtain both of their column index numbers. For completed cells, the sum of the row and the column index numbers must equal the cell cost. For cell 1–A, 0 + Column index = 9, so the column A index must be 9. Similarly, for cell 1–B, 0 + Column index = 6, so the column index must be 6. Next, these index numbers are used to find values of row index numbers for completed cells in their respective columns. Thus, for cell 2–B, 6 + Row index = 3, so the row index must be −3. For dummy–A, 9 + Row index = 0, so the row index must be −9.

To:	A 9	B 6	Supply
From: 0 / 1	[9] 60	[6] 15	75
−3 / 2	[5]	[3] 75	75
−9 / Dummy	[0] 20	[0]	20
Demand	80	90	170 / 170

Next, we use these index numbers to evaluate the empty cells. A cell evaluation is determined by subtracting from the cell cost the sum of its row and column index numbers. Thus, for cell 2–A, we have $5 - (-3 + 9) = -1$, and for cell dummy–B, we have $0 - (-9 + 6) = 3$.

To:	A 9	B 6	Supply
From: 0 1	[9] 60	[6] 15	75
−3 2	[5] (−1)	[3] 75	75
−9 Dummy	[0] 20	[0] (+3)	20
Demand	80	90	170 / 170

The appearance of a negative cell evaluation tells us this solution can be improved on. When negatives appear, we select the cell with the largest negative as the focal point of our effort to improve the solution. Because there is only one such cell, it is the one we select.

d. The −1 in cell 2–A tells us that for every unit we can move into this cell, we can reduce the total cost of the solution by $1. Obviously, we would like to put as many units as possible into this cell. Naturally, we are limited by the row and column totals (row 2 and column A), but we are also constrained by the need for all row and column totals to be maintained. In order to put units into cell 2–A, we must take them from some other cell, which will be in another row or column. Fortunately, this matter is simple to resolve: Determine the stepping-stone path for cell 2–A, and use it to guide the reallocation. That path is illustrated in the following table:

To:	A	B	Supply
From: 1	[9] 60 (−)--(+)	[6] 15	75
2	[5] (+)--(+)	[3] 75 (−)	75
Dummy	[0] 20	[0]	20
Demand	80	90	170 / 170

The amount that can be shifted into cell 2–A is the *smallest* quantity that appears in a *negative position* of the path. Note that there are two such quantities, 60 and 75. Because 60 is the smaller of these, it is shifted around the entire path (i.e., added where there is a + sign and subtracted where there is a − sign). The result is our revised solution:

To:	A	B	Supply
From: 1	[9]	[6] 75	75
2	[5] 60	[3] 15	75
Dummy	[0] 20	[0]	20
Demand	80	90	170 / 170

e. This improved solution may be optimal, or it may need further revision. To find out, we must evaluate it.

First, we check for degeneracy: $R + C - 1 = 3 + 2 - 1 = 4$. Because there are four completed cells, the solution is not degenerate.

Next, we develop MODI index numbers using the completed cells. We always begin by assigning an index of 0 to the first row. Then, for any completed cell in the first row, the column index number is the same as the cell cost. Thus, because cell 1−B has a cell cost of 6, the column B index number is 6. Using this value and the cell cost for completed cell 2−B enables us to find the index number for row 2: Cell cost − Column index = Row index. Thus, $3 - 6 = -3$. This row 2 index number can be used with the cell cost of completed cell 2−A to find the column A index number, $5 - (-3) = 8$, and the index of 8 can be used with the cell cost of dummy−A to find the dummy index number: $0 - 8 = -8$. These index numbers are shown in the following table.

To:	A 8	B 6	Supply
From: 0 / 1	[9]	[6] 75	75
−3 / 2	[5] 60	[3] 15	75
−8 / Dummy	[0] 20	[0]	20
Demand	80	90	170 / 170

Evaluations for the empty cells can now be determined.

Cell 1−A: $9 - (0 + 8) = 1$
Cell dummy−B: $0 - (-8 + 6) = 2$

Because there are no negative evaluations, the current solution is optimal: Ship 75 units from 1 to B, 60 units from 2 to A, and 15 units from 2 to B. The 20 units in dummy−A means that destination A will be 20 units short of satisfying its demand of 80 units.

The total cost of the optimal solution is $795:

$$75(6) = 450$$
$$60(5) = 300$$
$$15(3) = 45$$
$$20(0) = 0$$
$$\overline{795}$$

Problem

2. A firm that specializes in nonferrous casting must decide between locating a new foundry in Chicago or Detroit. Transportation costs from each proposed location to existing warehouses are shown in the following table, along with transportation costs for existing locations for a certain type of casting. Each will be able to supply 2,500 units per month. Explain how to determine which location should be chosen on a transportation cost basis.

From Detroit to:	Cost per unit	From Chicago to:	Cost per unit
A	$10	A	$12
B	8	B	13
C	15	C	5

Solution

This decision requires solving two transportation problems, one using Detroit costs and the other using Chicago costs.

a. Set up the two transportation matrices.

	Warehouse			
	A	B	C	Supply
1	17	10	6	30
2	7	12	14	20
Chicago	12	13	5	25
Demand	25	10	40	

b. Solve each problem.

c. The problem that yields the lowest total cost will indicate the preferred location.

1. What information is needed to use the transportation model?
2. What check must you make before proceeding to develop an initial solution? What corrective action might need to be taken?
3. Would it ever make sense to have a situation that required both a dummy row and a dummy column? Explain briefly.
4. What is linear about the objective function in a transportation problem?
5. Why do the + and − signs alternate in cell evaluation paths?
6. How do you know if a solution is optimal?
7. What does a zero value for an evaluation path indicate?
8. If a solution is not optimal:
   a. How do you decide which empty cell to shift units into?
   b. How do you know which cells to include in the shifting operation?
   c. How do you decide how many units to shift?
9. What is meant by the term *degeneracy?* How is it overcome?
10. How is the transportation model useful in location decisions? How does use of the transportation model in location decisions differ from its use as a tool to develop an optimal distribution plan for a given set of sources and destinations?
11. How are total costs determined for a given distribution plan?
12. What interpretation is given to quantities allocated to dummy destinations? Dummy sources?
13. What is the MODI method? How does it differ from the stepping-stone method?

PROBLEMS

1. Obtain the optimal distribution plan for the following transportation problem. Develop the initial solution using:
   a. The northwest-corner method.
   b. The intuitive approach.
   Use the stepping-stone method for cell evaluations.

From: \ To:	A	B	C	Supply
1	[3]	[4]	[2]	40
2	[5]	[1]	[7]	60
3	[8]	[7]	[4]	50
Demand	30	45	75	150 / 150

2. A given shipping combination may be undesirable for a reason other than shipping cost. Use of that combination can be avoided by replacing that cell's unit cost with a larger cost. Assume cell 3–C in the previous problem represents such a case. Assign a unit cost of $100 to that cell, and find the minimum cost solution using the intuitive method for the initial allocation.

3. Given the following transportation problem, do each of the following:
   a. Develop an initial feasible solution using each of the two methods described in this supplement.
   b. Use the stepping-stone method to evaluate the northwest-corner solution.
   c. Repeat part b using MODI.
   d. Find the optimal solution.

From: \ To:	A	B	C	D	Supply
1	[18]	[12]	[14]	[16]	40
2	[23]	[24]	[27]	[33]	80
3	[42]	[34]	[31]	[26]	130
Demand	90	80	30	50	

4. Using the intuitive method to generate an initial solution, determine the optimal distribution plan for the following problem, and compute the total cost for that plan. Use the MODI method for cell evaluation.

From: \ To:	A	B	C	D	Supply
1	[14]	[24]	[18]	[28]	48
2	[17]	[18]	[25]	[16]	56
3	[30]	[16]	[22]	[30]	32
Demand	41	34	35	20	

5. Refer to problem 3. Due to a temporary condition, origin 3 has experienced a capacity reduction of 20 units per period. Using the intuitive method to develop an initial solution, determine a temporary distribution plan that will minimize transportation costs.

6. Refer to problem 4. The market supplied by destination D is experiencing a period of rapid growth. Projected demand is for 60 units per period. A new factory with a capacity of 50 units is planned for one of two locations, Baltimore or Philadelphia. Transportation costs are as follows. Which location would result in the lower total cost? Use the MODI method for cell evaluation.

From Baltimore to:	Cost per unit	From Philadelphia to:	Cost per unit
A	$18	A	$31
B	16	B	25
C	22	C	19
D	27	D	20

7. Determine the optimal shipping plan for the following transportation matrix. Use the intuitive method to develop the initial solution. What is the total cost for your plan?

To: From:	Dallas	Buffalo	Miami	Supply
Chicago	4	9	6	25
Milwaukee	12	10	7	55
Cleveland	11	5	8	40
Demand	35	40	45	

8. A toy manufacturer wants to open a third warehouse that will be used to supply three retail outlets. The new warehouse will have a capacity to supply 500 units of backyard playsets per week. Two locations are being studied, N1 and N2. Transportation costs for location N1 to stores A, B, and C would be $6, $8, and $7, respectively; for location N2, the costs would be $10, $6, and $4, respectively. The existing system is shown in the following table. Use the intuitive method to develop an initial solution. Which location would result in the lower transportation costs for the system?

To: From:	Store A	B	C	Capacity (Units/week)
Warehouse 1	8	3	7	500
Warehouse 2	5	10	9	400
Demand (Units/week)	400	600	350	

9. A large firm is contemplating construction of a new manufacturing facility. The two leading locations are Toledo and Cincinnati. The new factory would have a supply capacity of 160 units per week. Transportation costs from each potential location are shown in the following table. Also shown are transportation costs for existing locations. Using the intuitive method to develop an initial solution, determine which location would provide the lower transportation costs.

From Toledo to:	Cost per unit	From Cincinnati to:	Cost per unit
A	$18	A	$ 7
B	8	B	17
C	13	C	13

	A	B	C	Supply (Units/week)
1	10	14	10	210
2	12	17	20	140
3	11	11	12	150
Demand (Units/week)	220	220	220	

10. A large retailer is planning to open a new store. Three locations are currently under consideration: South Coast Plaza, Fashion Island, and Laguna Hills. Transportation costs for the locations are shown below. Also shown are costs, demands, and supplies for existing locations and warehouses (origins). Each of the locations has a demand potential of 300 units per week. Use the intuitive method to develop the initial solution. Which location would yield the lowest transportation costs for the system?

From	To:		
warehouse:	SCP	FI	LH
1	$ 4	$7	$5
2	11	6	5
3	5	5	6

	A	B	Supply (Units/week)
1	15	9	660
2	10	7	340
3	14	18	200
Demand (Units/week)	400	500	

11. Set up problem 1 in a general linear programming format using an objective function and a set of constraints.

12. Set up problem 3 in a general linear programming format using an objective function and a set of constraints.

13. A soft drink manufacturer has recently begun negotiations with brokers in areas where it intends to distribute new products. Before finalizing agreements, however, the firm wants to determine shipping routes and costs. The firm has three plants with capacities as follows:

Plant	Capacity (cases per week)
Metro	40,000
Ridge	30,000
Colby	25,000

Estimated demands in each of the warehouse localities are:

Warehouse	Demand (cases per week)
SR1	24,000
SR2	22,000
SR3	23,000
SR4	16,000
SR5	10,000

The estimated shipping costs per case for the various routes are:

From:	To: RS1	RS2	RS3	RS4	RS5
Metro	.80	.75	.60	.70	.90
Ridge	.75	.80	.85	.70	.85
Colby	.70	.75	.70	.80	.80

Determine the optimal shipping plan that will minimize total shipping cost under these conditions:
a. Route Ridge–RS4 is unacceptable.
b. All routes are acceptable.
c. What is the additional cost of the Ridge–RS4 route not being acceptable?

14. Solve this LP problem using the transportation method. Find the optimal transportation plan and the minimum cost. Also, decide if there is an alternate solution. If there is one, identify it.

Minimize $8x_{11} + 2x_{12} + 5x_{13} + 2x_{21} + x_{22} + 3x_{23} + 7x_{31} + 2x_{32} + 6x_{33}$

Subject to
$$x_{11} + x_{12} + x_{13} = 90$$
$$x_{21} + x_{22} + x_{23} = 105$$
$$x_{31} + x_{32} + x_{33} = 105$$

$$x_{11} + x_{21} + x_{31} = 150$$
$$x_{12} + x_{22} + x_{32} = 75$$
$$x_{13} + x_{23} + x_{33} = 75$$
$$\text{All variables} \geq 0$$

15. Write an objective function and a set of constraints for problem 1.

16. Write an objective function and a set of constraints for problem 2.

SELECTED BIBLIOGRAPHY

Bierman, Harold; Charles P. Bonini; and Warren H. Hausman. *Quantitative Analysis for Business Decisions.* 8th ed. Homewood, Ill.: Richard D. Irwin, 1991.

Eppen, G. D.; F. J. Gould; and C. P. Schmidt. *Introductory Management Science.* 2nd ed. Englewood Cliffs, N.J.: Prentice Hall, 1987.

Levin, Richard I.; Charles A. Kirkpatrick; and David Rubin. *Quantitative Approaches to Management.* 5th ed. New York: McGraw-Hill, 1982.

Stevenson, William J. *Introduction to Management Science.* 2nd ed. Homewood, Ill.: Richard D. Irwin, 1992.

PART FOUR

OPERATING AND CONTROLLING THE SYSTEM

The chapters in this section cover the following general topics:

1. Quality control and continuous improvement *(Chapter 10)*.
2. Aggregate planning *(Chapter 11)*.
3. Inventory management *(Chapter 12)*.
4. Material requirements planning *(Chapter 13)*.
5. Just-in-time systems *(Chapter 14)*.
6. Scheduling *(Chapter 15)*.
7. Project management *(Chapter 16)*.
8. Waiting lines *(Chapter 17)*.

The topics in this part relate to operating and controlling the production of goods and services. Chapters 10 and 11 serve as a link between the design decisions discussed in Part III, and the operating decisions described in the remaining chapters. Chapter 10 deals with conformance to design, and Chapter 11 deals with intermediate-range planning.

Chapters 12 and 13 deal with various aspects of inventories. The first of these two chapters deals with general inventory management decisions, particularly as they relate to finished goods inventories. Chapter 13 deals with inventories in a manufacturing/assembly operation.

Chapter 14 describes just-in-time production systems.

Chapter 15 deals with scheduling decisions involving fairly routine types of activities. Chapter 16 deals with planning and scheduling of projects.

Chapter 17 is concerned with the analysis of waiting lines, which are commonly found in service systems when arrivals are random.

QUALITY CONTROL AND
CONTINUOUS IMPROVEMENT

10

After completing this chapter, you should be able to:

1. List and briefly explain the elements of the control process.

2. Explain how control charts are used to monitor a process, and the concepts that underlie their use.

3. Use and interpret control charts.

4. Use run tests to check for nonrandomness in process output.

5. Discuss the concept of continuous improvement, why it is important, and management requirements.

6. Explain the plan-do-check-act cycle.

7. Describe the continuous improvement process.

8. Describe the methods and tools used in continuous improvement.

T his chapter covers two topics that are increasingly important in business organizations: quality control and continuous improvement. The first portion of the chapter is devoted to quality control and the latter portion to continuous improvement.

Quality control focuses on the conversion of inputs into outputs. The purpose of quality control is to assure that processes are performing in an acceptable manner. This is accomplished by monitoring process output using statistical techniques. If the results are acceptable, no further action is required; unacceptable results call for corrective action.

In the best companies, the emphasis is on designing quality *into the process,* thereby greatly reducing the need for inspection or control efforts. As you might expect, different business organizations are in difference stages of this evolutionary process: The least progressive rely heavily on inspection. Many occupy a middle ground that involves some inspection and a great deal of process control. And the most progressive have achieved an inherent level of quality that is high enough that they are able to avoid wholesale inspection activities as well as process control activities. That is the ultimate goal. Figure 10–1 illustrates these phases of quality assurance.

Quality assurance that relies primarily on inspection after production is referred to as *acceptance sampling.* It is described in the chapter supplement. Quality assurance efforts that occur during production are referred to as *process control;* this is described in the following sections. Designing quality into the system derives from several

Figure 10–1

Phases of quality assurance

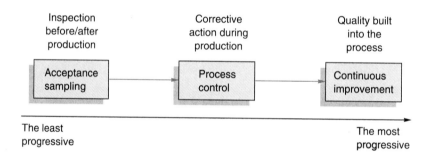

Continuous improvement means having everyone involved in a production process contribute to the quality of the finished product, including suppliers. American manufacturers are beginning to see the advantages of this philosophy. Here at John Deere's combine factory in East Moline, Illinois, workers have suppliers fix faulty parts.

sources, one of which is improvement efforts. The term *continuous improvement* refers to ongoing improvement efforts.

Continuous improvement is an approach that views quality improvement as a never-ending quest. Efforts are directed toward making continual changes—sometimes very small changes—in the conversion process in order to raise the level of customer satisfaction. Continuous improvement differs from the more traditional approach of making improvements sporadically, on a "when necessary" basis (often due to the occurrence of a crisis), or attempting to make *major* improvements.

INTRODUCTION

Prior to the Industrial Revolution, production was carried out by skilled craftsmen. Pride of workmanship and reputation often provided the necessary motivation to see that a job was done right. Lengthy apprenticeships required by guilds caused this attitude to carry over to new workers. Moreover, one person or a small group of people were responsible for an entire product.

The Industrial Revolution was accompanied by a division of labor; each worker was responsible for only a small portion of each product. Pride of workmanship became less meaningful since workers could not readily identify with the final product. The responsibility for quality control shifted to the foremen. Inspection was either nonexistent or haphazard, although in some instances 100 percent inspection was used.

In 1924, W. Shewhart of Bell Telephone Laboratories introduced statistical control charts that could be used to monitor production. Then, around 1930, H. F. Dodge and H. G. Romig, also of Bell Labs, introduced tables for acceptance sampling. Nevertheless, statistical quality control procedures were not widely used until World War II, when the U.S. government began to require vendors to use them.

Just after the war, the American Society for Quality Control was founded. Over the years, the society has promoted quality control with its publications, conferences, and training programs.

Armand Feigenbaum's book *Total Quality Control* was published in 1961. Up to that time, quality efforts were directed toward correction. Feigenbaum's book expanded the concept of quality control to encompass the entire range of production, from design to sale, and to include *prevention* as well as corrective action.

During the 1950s and 1960s, W. Edwards Deming is credited with introducing statistical quality control methods to Japanese manufacturers. Prior to that time, much of the output by the Japanese was of inferior quality. However, by the late 1970s, the Japanese began to acquire a reputation for high quality in automobiles, appliances, steel, and electronics, some of which can be attributed to quality control efforts. Now, Japanese manufacturers are formidable competitors in the world marketplace. One consequence is that manufacturers in other industrialized countries have intensified their efforts to improve the quality of their products.

During the 1970s and 1980s, quality assurance methods spread to service organizations such as banks, government agencies, health care, and hotels.

STATISTICAL PROCESS CONTROL

Quality control is concerned with the **quality of conformance** of a process: Does the output of a process conform to the intent of design? Toward that end, **statistical process control** is used to evaluate the output of a process to determine its

Quality of conformance
A product or service conforms to the intent of its design.

Statistical process control
Statistical evaluation of the output of a process during production.

acceptability. To do this, periodic samples are taken from the process and compared to a predetermined standard. If the sample results are not acceptable, the process is stopped and corrective action is taken. If the sample results are acceptable, the process is allowed to continue.

Two different statistical tools are used for quality control: *control charts* and *run tests*. Typically, they are used together. Both are described in this chapter.

THE CONTROL PROCESS

Sampling and corrective action are just a part of the control process. Effective control requires the following steps:

1. Define.
2. Measure.
3. Compare to a standard.
4. Evaluate.
5. Take corrective action if necessary.
6. Evaluate corrective action.

The first step means to define in as much detail as possible what it is that is to be controlled. It is not sufficient, for example, to simply refer to a painted surface. The paint can have a number of characteristics that might be of interest, such as its thickness, hardness, and resistance to fading or chipping. Different characteristics may require different approaches for control purposes.

Only those characteristics that can be counted or measured are candidates for control. Thus, it is important to consider how measurement will be accomplished.

There must be a standard of comparison that can be used to evaluate the measurements. This will relate to the level of quality being sought.

A definition of *out of control* must be established. Even a process that is functioning as it should will not yield output that conforms exactly to a standard, simply because of the natural (i.e., random) variations inherent in all processes, whether they are manual or mechanical. In other words, a certain amount of variation is inevitable. The main task of quality control is to distinguish random from nonrandom variability, because nonrandom variability means that a process is out of control.

In the event that a process is judged to be out of control, corrective action must be taken. This involves uncovering the cause of nonrandom variability (e.g., worn equipment, incorrect methods, failure to follow specified procedures).

To insure that corrective action is effective, it is necessary to closely monitor the output of a process for a sufficient period of time to verify that the problem has been eliminated.

In a nutshell, control is achieved by inspecting a portion of the goods or services, comparing the results to a predetermined standard, evaluating departures from the standard, taking corrective action when necessary, and following up to insure that problems have been corrected.

VARIATIONS AND CONTROL

All processes that provide a good or a service exhibit a certain amount of "natural" variation in their output. The variations are created by the combined influences of countless minor factors, each one so unimportant that even if it could be identified and eliminated, the decrease in process variability would be negligible. In effect, this variability is inherent in the process. It is often referred to as *chance* or **random variation**, although it sometimes is referred to as *common variablilty*. The amount of inherent variability differs from process to process. For instance, older machines generally exhibit a higher degree of natural variability than newer machines, partly because of worn parts and partly because newer machines may incorporate design improvements, which lessen variability.

A second kind of variability that may occur in process output is called **assignable variation**. Sometimes this is called *special variation*. Unlike natural variation, the main sources of assignable variation can usually be identified (assigned to a specific cause) and eliminated. Such factors as tool wear, equipment that needs adjustment, defective materials, and human factors (carelessness, fatigue, failure to follow correct procedures, and so on) are typical sources of assignable variation.

When samples of process output are taken, and sample *statistics* such as the sample mean or range are computed, they, too, exhibit these same variations. That is, there is variation in the values of sample means, and variation in the values of sample ranges. The variability of a sample statistic can be described by its *sampling distribution,* which is a theoretical distribution that describes the *random* variability of sample statistics.

The goal of sampling is to determine if there are nonrandom—and thus, correctible—sources of variation present in the output of a process. The sampling distribution provides the theoretical basis for accomplishing this. Let's see how this is done.

Suppose we have a process that fills bottles with soft drink. If we accurately measured the amount of soft drink in a large number of bottles, we would discover slight differences among the bottles. And if we were to arrange these amounts on a graph, we would obtain a frequency distribution that reflected the *process variability*.

While there will be some random variation in the filling of these soft drink bottles, good quality management will keep the fill level within acceptable levels. Continuous improvement efforts are aimed at reducing underfills and overfills.

We would find that the values were clustered close to the process average (e.g., 16 ounces), but that some of the values would vary somewhat from the mean.

If we now went back to the process and took many *samples,* say, of 10 bottles each, and computed the *mean* amount of soft drink in each sample, we would discover that these values also vary, just as the *individual* values varied. And they, too, would have a distribution of values.

If the process contained *only* random variability, the distribution of process values would represent the inherent process variability, and the distribution of sample means would represent the random variability of the sample means.

The two distributions are illustrated in Figure 10–2. Notice that the sampling distribution exhibits much less variability (i.e., it is less spread out) than the process distribution. This reflects the *averaging* that occurs in computing the sample means: high and low values in samples tend to offset each other, resulting in less variability among sample means than among individual values. Note too, that both distributions have the same mean; the mean of the sampling distribution is the same as the mean of the process. Finally, note the shape of the sampling distribution. It is a *normal* distribution. The fact that it is a normal distribution does *not* depend on the process distribution; it is a general result related to random sampling. The *central limit theorem* provides the basis for the assumption that sampling distributions will be normal or at least approximately normal, even if the population (i.e., the process) is not normal.

The fact that sampling distributions tend to be normal yields certain advantages, as they are easy to work with, and it is not necessary to determine what type of distribution to use every time the issue of control is dealt with.

The normal distribution can be used to help judge if a process is performing adequately. If the output reflects only random variability, one would conclude that the process is *stable* (i.e., in control). But if there is evidence of nonrandom variability, one would conclude that the process is not stable (i.e., out of control). To understand how the normal distribution is used, consider the following: approximately 95.5 percent of the area under a normal curve (and, hence, 95.5 percent of the sample means, for example) will have values that are within ±2 standard deviations of the distribution mean, and approximately 99.7 percent of the sample means will have values that are within ±3 standard deviations of the distribution mean. (See Figure 10–3.) These values are typically used for control limits.

It is important to recognize that because any limits will leave some area in the *tails* of the distribution, there is a small probability that a value will fall outside of the limits *even though only random variations are present.* For example, if ±2 sigma (standard deviation) limits are used, they would include 95.5 percent of the values. Consequently, the complement of that number (100 percent − 95.5 percent = 4.5 percent) would not be included. That percentage (or *probability*) is sometimes re-

Figure 10–2

The sampling distribution of means is normal, and it has less variability than the process

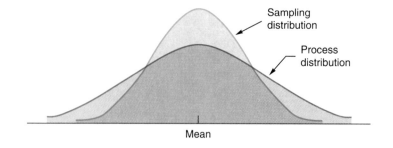

Mean

ferred to as the probability of a **Type I error**, where the "error" is concluding that nonrandomness is present when only randomness is present. It is also referred to as an *alpha* risk, where alpha (α) is the sum of the probabilities in the two tails. This concept is illustrated in Figure 10–4.

Using wider limits (e.g., ±3 sigma limits) would reduce the probability of a Type I error because it would decrease the area in the tails. However, wider limits make it more difficult to detect nonrandom variations if they *are* present. For example, the mean of the process might shift (an assignable source of variation) enough to be detected by two-sigma limits, but not enough to be readily apparent if three-sigma limits were being used. That could lead to another kind of error, known as a **Type II error**, which is concluding that a process is in control when it is actually out of control (i.e., that nonrandom variations are not present, when they are). In theory, the *costs* of making each error should be balanced by their probabilities. However, in practice, two-sigma limits and three-sigma limits are commonly used without specifically referring to the probability of a Type II error.

Type I error

Concluding that nonrandomness is present when only randomness is present.

Type II error

Concluding that nonrandomness is not present, when it actually is.

CONTROL CHARTS

A **control chart** is a time-ordered plot of sample statistics. It is used to distinguish between random variability and nonrandom variability. The basis for the control chart is the sampling distribution, because a sampling distribution essentially describes random variability. There is, however, one minor difficulty that relates to the use of a sampling distribution that is normal: The theoretical distribution ex-

Control chart

A time-ordered plot of sample statistics, used to distinguish between random and nonrandom variability.

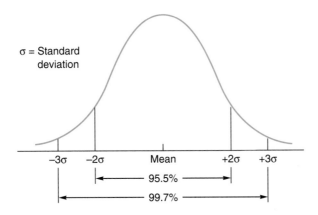

Figure 10–3

Percentage of values within given ranges in a normal distribution

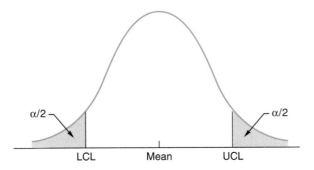

Figure 10–4

The probability of a Type I error

tends in either direction to *infinity*. Therefore, *any* value is theoretically possible, even one that is a considerable distance from the mean of the distribution. However, as a practical matter, we know that, say, 95.5 percent of the values will be within ±2 standard deviations of the mean of the distribution. Therefore, we could decide to draw the line, so to speak, at values that represent ±2 standard deviations from the mean, and conclude that any value that was farther away than these limits would be judged as a nonrandom variation. In effect, then, these limits are **control limits**: the dividing lines between random deviations from the mean of the distribution and nonrandom deviations from the mean of the distribution. Figure 10–5 illustrates how control limits are based on the sampling distribution.

Control charts have two limits that separate what will be regarded as random variation and nonrandom variation. The larger value is the *upper control limit* (UCL), and the smaller value is the *lower control limit* (LCL). A sample statistic that falls between these two limits would suggest (but not prove) randomness, while a value outside, or on, either limit would suggest (but not prove) nonrandomness.

Figure 10–6 illustrates the components of a control chart. In effect, each sample is represented by a single value (e.g., the sample mean) on the chart. Moreover, each value is compared to the extremes of the sampling distribution (the control limits) to judge if it is within the acceptable (random) range. This concept is illustrated in Figure 10–7.

There are a number of different types of control charts to choose from, depending on the type of data involved. These fall into one of two categories: control charts for **variables** or control charts for **attributes**. Attribute data are *counted* (e.g.,

Control limits

The dividing lines between random and nonrandom deviations from the mean of the distribution.

Variables

Generate data that are *measured*.

Attributes

Generate data that are *counted*.

Figure 10–5

Control limits are based on the sampling distribution

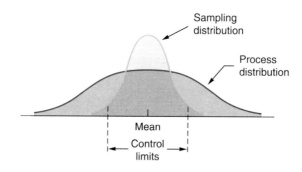

Figure 10–6

Example of a control chart

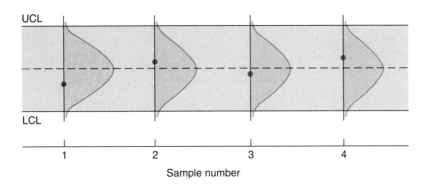

the number of defective parts in a sample, or the number of complaints); variables data are *measured,* usually on a continuous scale (e.g., amount of time needed to complete a task, length or width of a part).

Two control charts for variables data are described in the next section, and two control charts for attribute data are described in the section following that.

CONTROL CHARTS FOR VARIABLES

Mean and range charts are used to monitor variables. Control charts for means monitor the *central tendency* of a process, and range charts monitor the *dispersion* of a process.

Mean charts

A **mean control chart**, sometimes referred to as $\bar{x}$ ("*x*-bar") charts, can be constructed in one of two ways. The choice depends on what information is available. If a reasonable estimate of the process standard deviation, σ, is available, control limits can be computed using these formulas:

> **Mean control chart**
> Control chart used to monitor the central tendency of a process.

$$\text{Upper control limit (UCL):} = \bar{\bar{x}} + z\sigma_{\bar{x}} \qquad \textbf{(10–1)}$$
$$\text{Lower control limit (LCL):} = \bar{\bar{x}} - z\sigma_{\bar{x}}$$

where $\sigma_{\bar{x}} = \sigma/\sqrt{n}$

$\sigma_{\bar{x}}$ = Standard deviation of distribution of sample means

σ = Process standard deviation

n = Sample size

z = Standard normal deviate

$\bar{\bar{x}}$ = Average of sample means

The following example illustrates the use of these formulas.

Means of samples taken from a process for making aluminum rods have a mean of 2 centimeters. The process variability is approximately normal and has a standard deviation of 0.1 centimeter. Determine control limits that will include 99.74 percent of sample means if the process is generating random output for these sample sizes:

Example 1

1. $n = 16$.
2. $n = 25$.

(continued)

Example 1

(concluded)

Solution

$$\bar{\bar{x}} = 2 \text{ cm}, \quad \sigma = 0.1 \text{ cm}, \quad z = 3 \text{ (from Appendix B, Table A)}$$
$$\text{UCL} = \bar{\bar{x}} + z(\sigma/\sqrt{n})$$
$$\text{LCL} = \bar{\bar{x}} - z(\sigma/\sqrt{n})$$

1. $n = 16$: UCL $= 2 + 3(0.1/\sqrt{16}) = 2 + 0.075 = 2.075$
    LCL $= 2 - 3(0.1/\sqrt{16}) = 2 - 0.075 = 1.925$
2. $n = 25$: UCL $= 2 + 3(0.1/\sqrt{25}) = 2 + 0.06 = 2.06$
    LCL $= 2 - 3(0.1/\sqrt{25}) = 2 - 0.06 = 1.94$

Note that increasing the sample size results in control limits that are closer to the process mean.

A second approach is to use the sample *range* as a measure of process variability. The appropriate formulas for control limits are

$$\text{UCL} = \bar{\bar{x}} + A_2\bar{R} \qquad\qquad (10\text{--}2)$$
$$\text{LCL} = \bar{\bar{x}} - A_2\bar{R}$$

Values of A_2 can be obtained from Table 10–1.

Table 10–1

Factors for three-sigma control limits for $\bar{x}$ and R charts

Number of observations in subgroup, n	Factor for $\bar{x}$ chart, A_2	Factors for R chart	
		Lower control limit, D_3	Upper control limit, D_4
2	1.88	0	3.27
3	1.02	0	2.57
4	0.73	0	2.28
5	0.58	0	2.11
6	0.48	0	2.00
7	0.42	0.08	1.92
8	0.37	0.14	1.86
9	0.34	0.18	1.82
10	0.31	0.22	1.78
11	0.29	0.26	1.74
12	0.27	0.28	1.72
13	0.25	0.31	1.69
14	0.24	0.33	1.67
15	0.22	0.35	1.65
16	0.21	0.36	1.64
17	0.20	0.38	1.62
18	0.19	0.39	1.61
19	0.19	0.40	1.60
20	0.18	0.41	1.59

Source: Adapted from Eugene Grant and Richard Leavenworth, *Statistical Quality Control,* 5th ed. (New York: McGraw-Hill, 1980).

Twenty samples of $n = 8$ have been taken from a milling process. The average sample range for the 20 samples was 0.016 centimeters, and the average mean was 3 centimeters. Determine three-sigma control limits for this process.

Example 2

Solution

$\bar{\bar{x}} = 3$ cm, $\quad \bar{R} = 0.016$, $\quad A_2 = 0.37$ for $n = 8$ (from Table 10–1)

$\text{UCL} = \bar{\bar{x}} + A_2\bar{R} = 3 + 0.37(0.016) = 3.006$ cm
$\text{LCL} = \bar{\bar{x}} - A_2\bar{R} = 3 - 0.37(0.016) = 2.994$ cm

Note that this approach assumes that the range is in control.

Range charts

Range control charts are used to monitor process variability; they are sensitive to changes in process dispersion. Although the underlying sampling distribution is not normal, the concepts for use of range charts are much the same as those for use of mean charts. Control limits for range charts are found using the average sample range in conjunction with these formulas:

$$\text{UCL}_R = D_4\bar{R}$$
$$\text{LCL}_R = D_3\bar{R}$$

(10–3)

Range control charts
Control charts used to monitor process dispersion.

where values of D_3 and D_4 are obtained from Table 10–1.

Twenty-five samples of $n = 10$ observations have been taken from a milling process. The average sample range was 0.01 centimeter. Determine upper and lower control limits for sample ranges.

Example 3

Solution

$\bar{R} = 0.01$ cm, $\quad n = 10$

From Table 10–1, for $n = 10$, $D_4 = 1.78$ and $D_3 = 0.22$.

$\text{UCL}_R = 1.78(0.01) = 0.0178$ or 0.018
$\text{LCL}_R = 0.22(0.01) = 0.0022$ or 0.002

In the preceding example, a sample range of 0.018 centimeters or more would suggest that the process variability had increased. A sample range of 0.002 or less would imply that the process variability had decreased. In the former case, this would mean that the process was producing too much variation; we would want to investigate this in order to remove the cause of variation. In the latter instance, even though decreased variability is desirable, we would want to determine what was causing it: Perhaps an improved method has been used, in which case we would want to identify it. Possibly the improved quality has come at the expense of productivity. Or this may only be a random occurrence; we would expect these about 1 percent of the time. Hence, it can be beneficial to investigate points beyond the lower limit as well as points beyond the upper limit in a range chart.

Using Mean and Range Charts

Mean control charts and range control charts provide different perspectives on a process. As we saw, mean charts are sensitive to shifts in the process mean, whereas range charts are sensitive to changes in process dispersion. Because of this difference in perspective, both types of charts might be used to monitor the same process. The logic of using both is readily apparent in Figure 10–8. In diagram A, the mean chart picks up the shift in the process mean, but because the dispersion is not changing, the range chart fails to indicate a problem. Conversely, in diagram B, a change in process dispersion is less apt to be detected by the mean chart than by the range chart. Hence, use of both charts provides more complete information than either chart alone. Even so, in some cases, a single chart may suffice. For example, a process may be more susceptible to changes in the process mean than it is to changes in dispersion, so it might be unnecessary to monitor dispersion. Because of the time and cost involved in constructing control charts, gathering the necessary data, and evaluating the results, only those aspects of a process with a tendency to cause problems should be monitored.

Figure 10–8

Mean and range charts used together complement each other

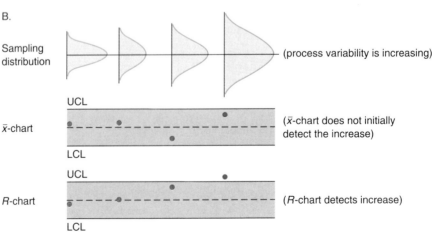

Once control charts have been set up, they can serve as a basis for deciding when to interrupt a process and search for assignable causes of variation. To determine initial control limits, the following procedure can be used:

1. Obtain 20 to 25 samples. Compute the appropriate sample statistic(s) for each sample (e.g., mean).
2. Establish preliminary control limits using the formulas, and graph them.
3. Plot the sample statistics on the control chart(s), and note if any points fall outside of the control limits.
4. If all points are within limits, assume that the process is in control. If not, investigate and correct assignable causes of variation. Then resume the process and collect another set of observations upon which control limits can be based.

CONTROL CHARTS FOR ATTRIBUTES

Control charts for attributes are used when the process characteristic is *counted* rather than measured. For example, the number of defective items in a sample would be counted, whereas the length of each item would be measured. There are two types of attribute control charts, one for the percentage of defective items in a sample (a *p*-chart) and one for the number of defects (called a *c*-chart). A *p*-chart is appropriate when both the defectives and nondefectives can be counted. For instance, if glass bottles are inspected for chipping and cracking, both the good bottles and the defective ones can be counted. However, one can count the number of accidents that occur during a given period of time but *not* the number of accidents that did not occur. Similarly, one can count the number of scratches on a polished surface, the number of bacteria present in a water sample, and the number of crimes committed during the month of August, but one cannot count the number of nonoccurences. In such cases, a *c*-chart is appropriate.

p-Chart

A **_p_-chart** is used to monitor the proportion of defectives generated by a process. The theoretical basis for a *p*-chart is the binomial distribution, although for large sample sizes, the normal distribution provides a good approximation to it. Conceptually, a *p*-chart is constructed and used in much the same way as a mean chart.

> *p*-chart
>
> Control chart for attributes, used to monitor the proportion of defectives in a process.

The center line on a *p*-chart is the average fraction defective in the population, *p*. The standard deviation of the sampling distribution when *p* is known is

$$\sigma_p = \sqrt{\frac{p(1-p)}{n}}$$

Control limits are computed using the formulas

$$\text{UCL}_p = p + z\sigma_p$$
$$\text{LCL}_p = p - z\sigma_p$$

(10–4)

If *p* is unknown, it can be estimated from samples. That estimate, $\bar{p}$, replaces *p* in the preceding formulas, as illustrated in the following example.

Example 4

∎

Using the following information, construct a control chart that will describe 95.5 percent of the chance variation in the process when the process is in control. Each sample contains 100 items.

Sample	Number of defectives	Sample	Number of defectives
1	14	11	8
2	10	12	12
3	12	13	9
4	13	14	10
5	9	15	11
6	11	16	10
7	10	17	8
8	12	18	12
9	13	19	10
10	10	20	16
			220

Solution

z for 95.5 percent is 2.00 (from Appendix B, Table A).

$$\bar{p} = \frac{\text{Total number of defectives}}{\text{Total number of observations}} = \frac{220}{20(100)} = .11$$

$$\hat{\sigma}_p = \sqrt{\frac{\bar{p}(1 - \bar{p})}{n}} = \sqrt{\frac{.11(1 - .11)}{100}} = .03$$

Control limits are

$$\text{UCL}_p = \bar{p} + z(\hat{\sigma}_p) = .11 + 2.00(.03) = .17$$
$$\text{LCL}_p = \bar{p} - z(\hat{\sigma}_p) = .11 - 2.00(.03) = .05$$

Plotting the control limits and the sample percentages, we can see that the process is initially in control, although the last point is close to the upper limit.

Note: If the computed LCL is negative, use zero as the lower limit.

c-Chart

When the goal is to control the number of defects per unit, a **c-chart** is used. Units might be automobiles, hotel rooms, typed pages, or rolls of carpet. The underlying sampling distribution is the Poisson distribution. Use of the Poisson distribution assumes that defects occur over some *continuous* region and that the probability of more than one defect at any particular spot is negligible. The mean number of defects per unit is c, and the standard deviation is $\sqrt{c}$. For practical reasons, the normal approximation to the Poisson is used. The control limits are

$$UCL_c = c + z\sqrt{c}$$
$$LCL_c = c - z\sqrt{c}$$

(10–5)

If the process average is unknown, it can be estimated from sample data, using
$\bar{c}$ = Number of defects/Number of samples.

c-chart

Control chart for attributes, used to monitor the number of defects per unit.

Rolls of coiled wire are monitored using a c-chart. Eighteen rolls have been examined, and the number of defects per roll has been recorded in the following table. Is the process in control? Plot the values on a control chart that uses $z = 2$.

Example 5

Sample	Number of defects	Sample	Number of defects
1	3	10	1
2	2	11	3
3	4	12	4
4	5	13	2
5	1	14	4
6	2	15	2
7	4	16	1
8	1	17	3
9	2	18	1
			45

Solution

$$\bar{c} = 45/18 = 2.5$$
$$UCL_c = \bar{c} + 2\sqrt{\bar{c}} = 2.5 + 2\sqrt{2.5} = 5.66$$
$$LCL_c = \bar{c} - 2\sqrt{\bar{c}} = 2.5 - 2\sqrt{2.5} = -0.66 \rightarrow 0$$

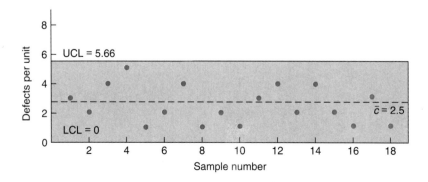

When the computed lower control limit is negative, the effective lower limit is zero, since negative observations cannot occur. (The calculation sometimes produces a negative lower limit due to the use of the normal distribution to approximate the Poisson distribution: the normal is symmetrical whereas the Poisson is not symmetrical when c is close to zero.)

TOLERANCES, CONTROL LIMITS, AND PROCESS VARIABILITY

Three commonly used terms refer to the variability of process output. Each term relates to a slightly different aspect of that variability, so it is important to differentiate these terms.

Tolerances
Specifications for range of acceptable values established by engineering design or customer requirements.

Process variability
Natural or inherent variability in a process.

> **Tolerances** are specifications established by engineering design or customer requirements. They indicate a range of values in which individual units of output must fall in order to be acceptable.
>
> **Control limits** are statistical limits that reflect the extent to which *sample statistics* such as means and ranges can vary due to randomness alone.
>
> **Process variability** reflects the natural or inherent variability in a process. It is also referred to as *process capability*.

Control limits and process variability are directly related: control limits are based on sampling variability, and sampling variability is a function of process variability. This relationship can be seen in the way control limits are calculated. For example, control limits for an $\bar{x}$-chart are computed using the formula:

$$\text{Control limits} = \frac{\text{Process}}{\text{mean}} \pm z\frac{\text{Process variability}}{\sqrt{n}}$$

On the other hand, there is no direct link between tolerances and either control limits or process variability. Tolerances are specified in terms of a product or service, not in terms of the *process* by which the product of service is generated. Hence, in a given instance, the output of a process may or may not conform to specifications, even though the process may be statistically in control. Consider the three cases illustrated in Figure 10–9. In the first case, process capability and output specifications are well matched, so that nearly all of the process output can be expected to meet the specifications. In the second case, the process variability is much less than what is called for, so that virtually 100 percent of the output should be within tolerance. However, in the third case, the specifications are tighter than what the process is capable of, so that even when the process is functioning as it should, a sizable percentage of the output will fail to meet the specifications. In other words,

Figure 10–9
Process capability and specifications may or may not match

in the third case, the process could be in control and still be generating unacceptable output. Thus, we cannot automatically assume that a stable process will provide desired output. Instead, we must specifically check to see if a process is *capable* of meeting specifications, and not simply set up a control chart to monitor it. A process should be in control and within specifications *before* production begins—in essence, "Set the toaster correctly at the start. Don't burn the toast and then scrape it!"

RUN TESTS

When a process is stable, or in statistical control, the output it generates will exhibit natural variability over a period of time. The presence of patterns, such as trends, cycles, or bias in the output, indicates that assignable, or nonrandom, causes of variation exist. Hence, a process that produces output with such patterns is not in a state of statistical control. This is true even though all of the points on a control chart may be within the control limits. For this reason, it is usually prudent to subject control chart data to run tests to determine if patterns can be detected.

A **run** is defined as a sequence of observations with a certain characteristic, followed by one or more observations with a different characteristic. The characteristic can be anything that is observable. For example, in the series A A A B, there are two runs: a run of three As followed by a run of one B. Underlining each run helps in counting them. In the series <u>A A</u> <u>B B B</u> <u>A</u>, there are three runs, as indicated by the underlining.

Run
Sequence of observations with a certain characteristic.

Two useful run tests involve examination of the number of runs *up and down* and the number of runs with respect to the *median*.[1] In order to count these runs, first transform the data into a series of Us and Ds (for *up* and *down*) and into a series of As and Bs (for *above* and *below* the median). Consider the following sequence, which has a median of 36.5. With respect to the median, the first two values are below it, the next two are above it, the next to last is below, and the last is above. Thus, there are four runs:

$$\begin{array}{cccccc} 25 & 29 & 42 & 40 & 35 & 38 \\ \underline{B} & \underline{B} & \underline{A} & \underline{A} & \underline{B} & \underline{A} \end{array}$$

In terms of up and down, there are three runs in the same data. The second value is up from the first value, the third is up from the second, the fourth value is down from the third, and so on:

$$\begin{array}{cccccc} 25 & 29 & 42 & 40 & 35 & 38 \\ - & \underline{U} & \underline{U} & \underline{D} & \underline{D} & \underline{U} \end{array}$$

(The first value does not receive either a U or a D, since nothing precedes it.)

To determine if any patterns are present in control chart data, one must transform the data into both As and Bs and Us and Ds and then count the number of runs in each case. These numbers must then be compared to the number of runs that would be expected in a completely random series. For both the median and the

---

[1] The median and mean are approximately equal for control charts. The use of the median depends on its ease of determination; use the mean instead of the median if it is given.

up/down run tests, the expected number of runs is a function of the number of observations in the series. The formulas are

$$E(r)_{\text{med}} = \frac{N}{2} + 1 \tag{10-6a}$$

$$E(r)_{\text{u/d}} = \frac{2N - 1}{3} \tag{10-7a}$$

where N is the number of observations.

The actual number of runs in any given set of observations will vary from the expected number, due to chance and to any patterns that might be present. Chance variability is measured by the standard deviation of runs. The formulas are

$$\sigma_{\text{med}} = \sqrt{\frac{N - 1}{4}} \tag{10-6b}$$

$$\sigma_{\text{u/d}} = \sqrt{\frac{16N - 29}{90}} \tag{10-7b}$$

Distinguishing chance variability from patterns requires use of the sampling distributions for median runs and for up/down runs. Both distributions are approximately normal. Consequently, we know, for instance, that 95.5 percent of the time a process that is random will produce an observed number of runs that is within two standard deviations of the expected number. If the observed number of runs falls in that range, we can conclude that there are probably no nonrandom patterns; for observed numbers of runs beyond such limits, we begin to suspect that patterns are present. Hence, either too few or too many runs can be an indication of nonrandomness.

In practice, it is often easiest to compute the number of standard deviations, z, by which an observed number of runs differs from the expected number. This z value would then be compared to the value ± 2 (z for 95.5 percent) or some other desired value (e.g., ± 1.96 for 95 percent, ± 2.33 for 98 percent). A test z that exceeds these limits indicates patterns are present. (See Figure 10–10.) The computation of z takes the form

$$z_{\text{test}} = \frac{\text{Observed number of runs} - \text{Expected number of runs}}{\text{Standard deviation of number of runs}}$$

Figure 10–10

A sampling distribution for runs is used to distinguish chance variation from patterns

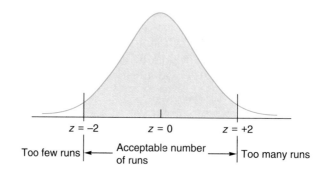

For the median and up/down tests, z is found using these formulas:

Median:
$$z = \frac{r - [(N/2) + 1]}{\sqrt{(N-1)/4}} \qquad \textbf{(10–8)}$$

Up and down:
$$z = \frac{r - [(2N - 1)/3]}{\sqrt{(16N - 29)/90}} \qquad \textbf{(10–9)}$$

where

N = Total number of observations

r = Observed number of runs of either As and Bs or Us and Ds, depending on which test is involved.

It is desirable to apply both run tests to any given set of observations because each test is different in terms of the types of patterns it can detect. Sometimes both will pick up a certain pattern, but sometimes only one will detect nonrandomness. If either does, the implication is that some sort of nonrandomness is present in the data.

Example 6

Twenty sample means have been taken from a process. The means are shown in the following table. Use median and up/down run tests with $z = 2$ to determine if assignable causes of variation are present. Assume the median is 11.0.

Solution

The means are marked according to above/below the median and up/down. The solid lines represent the runs.

Sample	A/B	Mean	U/D	Sample	A/B	Mean	U/D
1	B	10.0	—	11	B	10.7	D
2	B	10.4	U	12	A	11.3	U
3	B	10.2	D	13	B	10.8	D
4	A	11.5	U	14	A	11.8	U
5	B	10.8	D	15	A	11.2	D
6	A	11.6	U	16	A	11.6	U
7	A	11.1	D	17	A	11.2	D
8	A	11.2	U	18	B	10.6	D
9	B	10.6	D	19	B	10.7	U
10	B	10.9	U	20	A	11.9	U

A/B: 10 runs   U/D: 17 runs

The expected number of runs for each test is:

$$E(r)_{\text{med}} = \frac{N}{2} + 1 = \frac{20}{2} + 1 = 11$$

$$E(r)_{\text{u/d}} = \frac{2N - 1}{3} = \frac{2(20) - 1}{3} = 13$$

(continued)

Example 6	The standard deviations are
(concluded)	

$$\sigma_{\text{med}} = \sqrt{\frac{N-1}{4}} = \sqrt{\frac{20-1}{4}} = 2.18$$

$$\sigma_{\text{u/d}} = \sqrt{\frac{16N-29}{90}} = \sqrt{\frac{16(20)-29}{90}} = 1.80$$

The z_{test} values are

$$z_{\text{med}} = \frac{10-11}{2.18} = -0.46$$

$$z_{\text{u/d}} = \frac{17-13}{1.80} = +2.22$$

Although the median test does not reveal any pattern, since its z_{test} value is less than ± 2, the up/down test does; its value exceeds $+2$. Consequently, we conclude that nonrandom variations are present in the data and, hence, that the process is not in control.

If ties occur in either test (e.g., a value equals the median, or two values in a row are the same), assign A/B or U/D in such a manner that z_{test} is as large as possible. If z_{test} still does not exceed ± 2 (± 1.96, etc.) then you can be reasonably confident that a conclusion of randomness is justified.

OPERATIONS STRATEGY

It is neither necessary nor desirable to use control charts on every production process. The key to deciding is not necessarily the cost or effort required to maintain the control charts, but the fact that some processes tend to stay in control. Some processes are highly stable; and some processes that previously produced unacceptable output may have been subjected to improvements that resulted in quality being *designed into* the process or product, making continual monitoring unnecessary. Hence, to use a "shotgun" approach that puts control charts on many processes would be wasteful.

Managers should use control charts on processes that tend to go out of control, and even then, only on a temporary basis until the causative problems have been permanently corrected. Similarly, when a process is changed significantly, or a new process is introduced, it makes sense to monitor the output until it becomes apparent that the process is stable. After that, unless there is some compelling reason to believe that the process is apt to become unstable, there is no reason to continue with a control chart.

CONTINUOUS IMPROVEMENT

Continuous improvement

Philosophy that seeks to make never-ending improvements to the process of converting inputs into outputs.

Continuous improvement is a *philosophy* that seeks to improve any and all factors that are related to the process of converting inputs into outputs. It covers equipment, methods, materials, and people. A key part of the continuous improvement philosophy is belief that improvement efforts should never cease. Under continuous improvement, the old adage "If it ain't broke, don't fix it" gets transformed into "Just because it isn't broke doesn't mean it can't be improved."

The concept of continuous improvement is not new, but until recently did not receive much interest in the United States, even though it originated here. However, many Japanese companies have used it for years, and it has become a cornerstone of the Japanese approach to production. The Japanese use the term **kaizen** to refer to continuous improvement. The successes of Japanese companies have caused other companies to reexamine many of their approaches. One result has been a strong interest in the continuous improvement approach.

Kaizen

Japanese term for continuous improvement.

A successful continuous improvement process can only occur if the environment is conducive to such an approach. This places certain requirements on management.

MANAGEMENT REQUIREMENTS

Successful continuous improvement systems must have both the support and involvement of management at all levels of the organization. First and foremost, continuous improvement requires a fundamental change in organizational *culture* in order to sustain long-term efforts for improvement. Management's responsibility is to encourage and foster what for most organizations is a major change in their culture. This requires a number of management behaviors, including:

1. Developing a vision statement, strategies, and tactics with the help of subordinates.
2. Developing a management style that encourages openness, trust, and cooperation.
3. Maintaining constancy of purpose, especially during difficult times.
4. Making decisions that adhere to the stated philosophy.
5. Developing a reward system that promotes cooperation.
6. Adopting a balanced view between the short term and the long term.

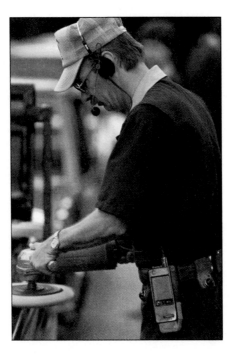

An advanced voice recognition system at this Ford Motor Company plant in Louisville, Kentucky, allows a paint department inspector to use tools while making a record of his inspection, which improves quality and efficiency. The small, red objects on the inspector's belt are infrared sensors that carry data between the transmitter/receiver on his belt and the computer, eliminating the need for wires.

7. Instituting continuous training programs.
8. Recognizing accomplishments in a way that supports group efforts as well as individual efforts.

Management's role in continuous improvement, particularly top management, is crucial to success. Without the leadership of top management playing an active role in satisfying these requirements, no continuous improvement effort will succeed, regardless of the desires and efforts of subordinates.

THE CONTINUOUS IMPROVEMENT PROCESS

Process improvement activities are often conducted by *teams*. The improvement process typically involves these steps:

1. Select a process for improvement, and set goals for improvement.
2. Study and document the current process.
3. Seek ways to improve the process.
4. Design an improved process.
5. Implement the improved system.
6. Evaluate it.
7. Document the improved solution, communicate it to all concerned, and establish appropriate training in the new system.

Steps 4–6 may be repeated as necessary until satisfactory results have been obtained. The process is summarized in Figure 10–11.

A number of key elements in the improvement cycle further illustrate the nature of the activities involved. These include:

1. Standardization (documentation).
2. The plan-do-check-act cycle.
3. Methods and tools used.

These are described briefly in the following sections.

Figure 10–11

The continuous improvement process

STANDARDIZATION

Standardization is the process of carefully documenting the best way to perform an operation. It applies in two ways. One is before attempting to improve the process. This involves determining the best *current* method of performing the operation under consideration, and *documenting* it. This not only provides insight into the process, but also a basis of comparison for any improvements that are made.

The second application of standardization occurs after the process has been improved: Document the new method so that it becomes the new standard for the operation. It is then a reference for training workers, a reference for other, related processes, and for *further* improvement, perhaps at a later time.

Standardization illustrates the *disciplined* approach frequently used in continuous improvement activities. It is important to carefully document improvements; this can be difficult to adhere to, particularly in the excitement of frequent achievements.

Standardization

Process of documenting the method of performing an operation, both before and after improvements.

THE PLAN-DO-CHECK-ACT CYCLE

The plan-do-check-act (PDCA) cycle, also referred to as either the Shewhart cycle or the Deming Wheel, is the conceptual basis for continuous improvement

Plan-do-check-act cycle

A framework for improvement activities.

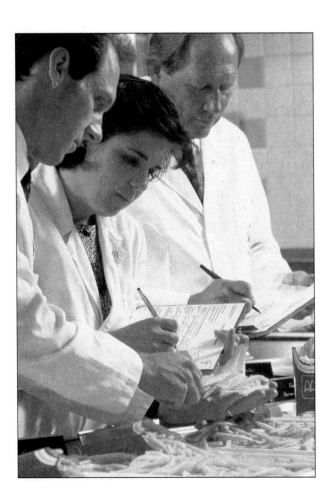

Standardization is the key component of McDonald's strategy and all foods are prepared according to a strict reference manual. Farmers even have special guidelines to follow in raising potatoes for french fries. Here, quality assurance staff checks all aspects of french fries, from the sweetness of the ketchup to the length of the fries.

Figure 10–12

The PDCA cycle

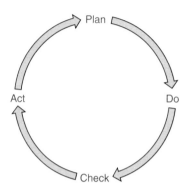

activities. The cycle is illustrated in Figure 10–12. Representing the process with a circle underscores its continuing nature.

There are four basic steps in the cycle:

Plan. Begin by studying the current process. Standardize that process. Then collect data in order to identify problems. Next, analyze data, and develop a plan for improvement. Specify measures to be used for evaluating the plan.

Do. Implement the plan, on a small scale if possible. Document any changes that are made during this phase. Collect data systematically for evaluation.

Check. Evaluate the data collection during the *do* phase. Check to see how closely the results match the original goals of the *plan* phase.

Act. If the results are successful, *standardize* the new method and communicate the new method to all people associated with the process. Implement training for the new method. Consider opportunities for replicating the same changes in other, similar processes. If the results are not successful, either revise the plan and repeat the process, or cease this project.

In replicating successful results elsewhere in the organization, the cycle is repeated. Similarly, if the plan was not successful and further modifications are to be attempted, this cycle is repeated.

Employing this sequence of steps provides a systematic approach to continuous improvement.

METHODS AND TOOLS

The improvement process has a number of phases in which various methods and tools are used. They include:

1. Identifying the problem.
2. Describing the current and revised processes.
3. Generating ideas for process improvement.
4. Achieving consensus among team members.
5. Evaluating and monitoring results.

Flow chart

Visual representation of the key steps in a process.

Word descriptions of the current process and of proposed revisions are essential. However, in terms of visualizing the process, a graphical depiction can be very useful. A **flow chart** is a visual representation of the key steps in a process. The process might be a physical process, such as the movement of material through a

Figure 10–13

A flow chart

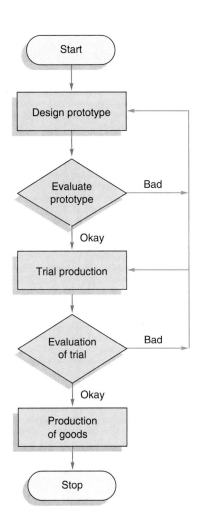

production operation, or it might be a decision process, portraying the decisions that are made with respect to a certain activity. Figure 10–13 illustrates a flow chart.

Problems should be attacked according to their importance to the organization. Ideally, the most important or pressing problem will be solved first. This necessitates establishing a measure of importance and using it to rank problems. A good key measure is often the extent to which a problem interferes with meeting customer requirements (both internal and external customers). Problems may relate to defective products, complaints about service, equipment breakdown, missed delivery dates, and so on.

A **check sheet** is a simple tool that is frequently used for problem identification. Check sheets provide a format that enables users to record and organize data in a way that facilitates collection and analysis. Check sheets are designed on the basis of what the users are attempting to learn by collecting data. They facilitate data collection by providing a format in which data can be recorded by means of checkmarks or other simple symbols.

Many different formats can be used for a check sheet and there are many different types of sheets. One frequently used form of check sheet deals with type of defect, another with location of defects. Both are illustrated in Figure 10–14.

Check sheet

A tool for recording and organizing data to identify a problem.

Figure 10–14

Two examples of check sheets

Day	Time	Type of Defect					Total
		Missing label	Off center	Smeared print	Loose or folded	Other	
M	8-9	||||	||				6
	9-10		|||				3
	10-11	|	|||	|			5
	11-12		|		|	| (Torn)	3
	1-2		|				1
	2-3		||	|||	|		6
	3-4		||	卌 |			8
Total		5	14	10	2	1	32

A. Label defects on packages

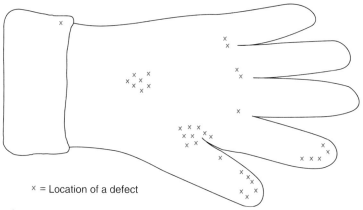

× = Location of a defect

**B. Defect location on work gloves
(results of tests performed on 1,000 gloves)**

The first check sheet shows tallies that denote the type of defect and the time of day each occurred. It appears that problems with missing labels tend to occur early in the day and that smeared print tends to occur late in the day, whereas off-center labels are found throughout the day. Identifying types of defects and when they occur can help in pinpointing causes of the defects.

The second check sheet makes it very easy to see where on the product defects are occurring. In this case, defects seem to be occurring on the tips of the thumb and first finger, in the finger valleys (especially between the thumb and first finger), and in the center of the gloves. Again, this may help determine why the defects occur and help correct the problems.

Pareto analysis is a technique for focusing attention on the most important problem areas. The Pareto concept, named after the 19th-century Italian economist Vilfredo Pareto, is that a relatively few factors generally account for a large percentage of the total cases (e.g., complaints, defects, problems). The idea is to classify the cases according to degree of importance and then focus on resolving the most important, leaving the less important ("trivial many"). Often referred to as the 80–20 rule, it states that approximately 80 percent of the problems (or value, cost,

Pareto analysis

Technique for classifying problem areas according to degree of importance, and focusing on the most important.

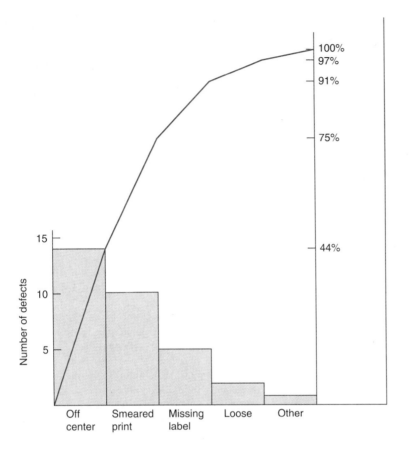

Figure 10–15

A Pareto diagram based on data in Figure 10–14

etc.) come from 20 percent of the items (or other factors). For instance, 80 percent of machine breakdowns come from 20 percent of the machines, and 80 percent of the product defects come from 20 percent of the causes of defects.

Often, it is useful to prepare a chart that shows the number of occurrences by category, arranged in order of frequency. Figure 10–15 illustrates such a chart corresponding to the first check sheet shown in Figure 10–14. The dominance of the problem with off-center labels becomes apparent. Presumably, efforts would be focused on trying to resolve this problem. Once that is accomplished, the remaining defects would be addressed in similar fashion; "smeared print" would be the next major category to be resolved, and so on. Additional check sheets would be used to collect data to verify that the defects in these categories have been eliminated or greatly reduced. Hence, in later Pareto diagrams, categories such as "off center" may still appear but would be much less prominent.

Brainstorming is a technique in which a group of people share thoughts and ideas on problems in a way that encourages unrestrained collective thinking. The idea is to achieve a relaxed atmosphere that will generate a free flow of ideas on identifying problems, and finding causes, solutions, and ways to implement solutions. In successful brainstorming, criticism is absent, one or a few members are not allowed to dominate sessions, and all ideas are welcomed.

Brainstorming
Technique for generating a free flow of ideas in a group of people.

Control charts can also be used to identify problems in a process by signaling the probable existence of assignable (special) causes of variation.

READING   PUTTING DEMING'S PRINCIPLES TO WORK   *By Robert Williams*

Before I joined Savin Corp., I spent 10 years working with W. Edwards Deming while he was consulting with my previous employer. Mr. Deming's statistical analysis approach to quality helped get Japanese industry back on its feet after World War II and, to borrow a phrase, the rest is history. In the 1990s, this total quality approach will make history again. Not in Japan, and not in manufacturing, but in the service industry.

The service sector in the United States in 1991 bears an eerie resemblance to American manufacturing 10 or 15 years ago. Costs are high. Profit margins are narrowing. Quality standards are inconsistent at best, and competitive pressures are mounting each year.

A Deming-style "total quality management" approach to improving service quality is rooted in the unglamorous and never fashionable discipline of statistics. I speak from Savin's experience in the copier industry, where a company's fortunes ride on the quality of its services. Using Mr. Deming's statistical approach to total quality management, we have reduced service expenses 35 percent over the past 12 months while improving service quality. Here are some examples of how it was done:

· "Callbacks" are anathema to every business that sends technicians on service calls. A customer callback means the job wasn't completed right the first time, and the service provider has to eat the cost of a second visit. Early last year, a careful study by Savin found that the callbacks were related to deficiencies in our training process. One of our branch managers suggested stripping our dealer training centers of their instructors so we could run marathon training programs for all of our branch technicians.

While this approach could have corrected our callback problem, the time and expense involved had the potential to outrun the cost of making the callbacks, in addition to disrupting dealer support. To find an affordable solution that would reduce callbacks sharply at an affordable cost, we turned to the tools of statistical analysis.

I asked our branch service managers to prepare a Pareto diagram of callbacks for each field engineer. The Pareto principle states that cause and effect are not linearly related. There usually will be a few causes—20 percent or fewer by volume—that will account for 80 percent or more of the effect.

Using the Pareto principle against our callback problem in one branch showed that if we retrained only five field engineers—those with the record number of callbacks—we could drop the branch average for callbacks by 19 percent. Retraining five engineers was a lot less daunting than retraining 45, many of whom didn't really need to be retrained. Of course, this was a process that could be repeated whenever the callback situation got out of control again. This was a case where using a statistical tool focused our corrective action to where it was needed, and helped us reduce waste at an affordable cost.

· In a technical service business, small details gone awry can collectively kill productivity and drain the profitability from a service call. We found, for instance, that significant time was being wasted on service calls when our engineers had to go back to their vehicles for spare parts. It is physically unrealistic and impractical to expect a field engineer to carry every conceivable part that might be needed. Considering, however, the salaries paid to skilled technicians, the time they spent shuttling back and forth for parts represented some of the most expensive travel in corporate America.

By using statistical analysis, we were able to determine those parts that the engineers were most likely to use on a call. We were able to assemble a call kit containing those parts with the highest probability for use, and this is what our field engineers began carrying onto customers' premises. The result was a significant decrease in the time spent retrieving extra parts. Service calls are now finished much faster, which pleases customers. And we are able to make more service calls, which delights Savin.

· Even a problem as small as tiny screws being occasionally dropped into machines during service calls can be helped by statistical analysis. When we studied the variation found in the service call process, we were able to quantify the time being wasted retrieving those little screws. As a result, we equipped each technician with a magnetic screwdriver and the problem of wayward screws was virtually eliminated.

Interviewing is another technique that can be used to identify problems and/ or collect information about a problem. Internal problems may require interviewing employees; external problems may require interviewing external customers.

Ideas for improvement can come from a number of sources. One source may be *research and development*. Another may be *customers,* and another may be *competitors*. *Employees* can be valuable sources of information for improvements. Customer satisfaction is the ultimate goal of improvement activities, and customers can offer many valuable suggestions about products and the service process, although they are less apt to have suggestions for *manufacturing* processes.

One way companies have tapped employees for ideas concerning quality improvement is through the use of **quality circles**. These are groups of workers who get together periodically to discuss ways of improving products and processes. Not only is this a valuable source of worker input, it can help to motivate workers if handled properly, by demonstrating management interest in worker ideas. Quality circles are usually less structured and more informal than teams that are involved in continuous improvement, but in some organizations, quality circles have evolved into continuous improvement teams. Perhaps a major distinction between the two groups is the amount of authority given to the group. Typically, quality circles have had very little authority to implement any but minor changes; continuous improvement teams are sometimes given a great deal of authority. Consequently, continuous improvement teams have the added motivation generated by *empowerment*.

The team approach works best when it reaches decisions based on consensus. This may involve one or more of the following methods. *List reduction* is applied to a list of possible problems or solutions. Its purpose is to clarify items, and in the process, reduce the list of items by posing questions about affordability, feasibility, and likelihood of solving the problem for each item. A *balance sheet* approach lists the pros and cons of each item, and focuses discussion on important issues. *Paired comparisons* is a process that involves comparing each item of a list with every other item, two at a time. For each pair, team members select the preferred item. This approach can help by forcing a choice between items. It works best when the list of items is fairly small, say, five or less.

An approach that can inject new energy into improvement efforts is called *benchmarking*. Summarized in Table 10–2, **benchmarking** is the process of measuring an organization's performance on a key customer requirement against the best in the industry, or against the best in any industry. The purpose of benchmarking is to establish a standard against which performance can be judged, and to identify a model for learning how to improve. A benchmark demonstrates the degree to which customers of other organizations are satisfied. Once a benchmark has been identified, the goal is to meet or exceed that standard through improvements in appropriate processes.

The benchmarking process usually involves these steps:

1. Identify a critical process that needs improvement (e.g., order entry, distribution, service after sale).

---

1. What organization does it the best?	**Table 10–2**
2. How do they do it?	
3. How do we do it now?	The benchmarking
4. How can we change to match or exceed the best?	approach

Interviewing

Technique for identifying problems and collecting information.

Quality circles

Groups of workers who meet to discuss ways of improving products or processes.

Benchmarking

Process of measuring performance against the best in the same or any other industry.

2. Identify an organization that excels in the process, preferably the best.
3. Contact the benchmark organization, visit it, and study the benchmark activity.
4. Analyze the data.
5. Improve the critical process at your own organization.

Selecting an industry leader provides insight into what competitors are doing; but competitors may be reluctant to share this information. Several organizations are responding to this difficulty by conducting benchmarking studies and providing that information to other organizations without revealing the sources of the data.

Selecting an organization that is a world leader in a different industry is another alternative. (Xerox, for example, benchmarked the order entry system of L. L. Bean.) Aside from the obvious advantage of easier access to the benchmark activity, there is the added advantage of acquiring insights that exceed those of competitors. Moreover, in the public sector, there may not be a competitor.

A number of tools are used for analyzing data and problem solving. Among the most useful, **cause-and-effect diagrams** offer a structured approach to problem solving. They are also referred to as **fishbone diagrams,** because of their shape, or *Ishikawa diagrams,* after Japanese professor Kaoru Ishikawa, who developed the approach to help workers who were overwhelmed in problem solving by the number of factors that needed to be examined. The diagrams help organize problem-solving efforts by providing several layers of *categories* that may be factors in causing problems. Often, cause-and-effect diagrams are used after brainstorming sessions to organize the ideas generated. One form of a cause-and-effect diagram is illustrated in Figure 10–16.

An example of an application of such a cause-and-effect diagram is shown in Figure 10–17. Each of the factors listed in the diagram is a potential source of ticket errors. Some are more likely causes than others, depending on the nature of the errors. If the cause is still not obvious at this point, additional investigation into the *root cause* may be necessary, involving a more in-depth analysis. Often, more de-

Cause-and-effect diagram

Tool for analyzing data by organizing causative factors into layers of categories; also called *fishbone diagram.*

Figure 10–16

One format of a cause-and-effect diagram

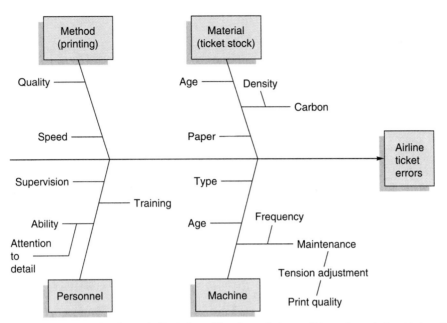

Figure 10–17

Cause-and-effect diagram for airline ticket errors

Reprinted from Howard Gitlow, Shelly Gitlow, Alan Oppenheim, and Rosa Oppenheim, *Tools and Methods for the Improvement of Quality* (Homewood, Ill.: Richard D. Irwin, 1989), p. 384, by permission.

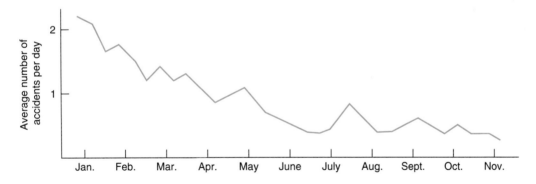

Figure 10–18

A run chart shows performance over time

tailed information can be obtained by asking *who, what, where, when, why,* and *how* questions about factors that appear to be the most likely sources of problems.

When improvement occurs over a period of time, a **run chart** can be useful in displaying the progress. Figure 10–18 illustrates the results of continuous improvement efforts to decrease the accident frequency at an assembly plant.

A method that is sometimes employed as the result of an improvement study is designed to "mistake proof" a process. It is referred to as *fail safe*. **Fail-safe methods** can improve both design quality and quality during production. Fail-safe meth-

Run chart

Tool for charting improvements that occur over a period of time.

Fail-safe methods

Provide warnings or additional guidance to increase the probability of correct operations.

Figure 10–19

Employing graphical tools in problem solving

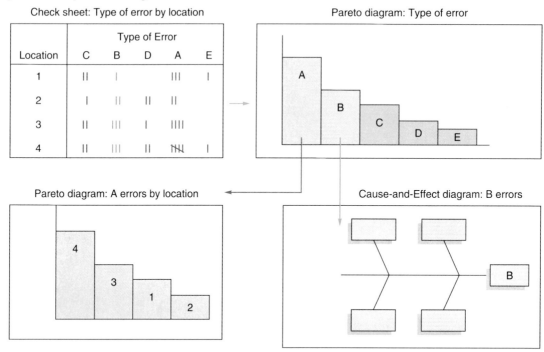

ods are like a combination lock, which will not open unless the correct sequence of numbers is used, or like the warning light for a seatbelt. Fail-safe methods provide additional warnings or guidance that increase the probability that output will possess intended quality levels. They can also be applied to automatic inspection during production: all items are inspected, and defective work or items are caught before additional work is performed.

Simple fail-safe methods can have a major impact on reduction of human error in work and on reduction of costs. However, many operations probably do not need fail-safe methods. Those that do are ones that have high costs associated with failure.

ILLUSTRATIONS OF THE USE OF GRAPHICAL TOOLS

This section present some illustrations of the use of graphical tools in process or product improvement. The first example, in Figure 10–19, begins with a check sheet that can be used to develop a Pareto chart of the types of errors found. That then leads to a more focused Pareto diagram of the most frequently occurring type of error, and a cause-and-effect diagram of the second most frequently occurring error. Additional cause-and-effect diagrams might also be used.

Figure 10–20 illustrates the use of Pareto charts to measure the amount of improvement achieved in a before-and-after depiction of errors.

Figure 10–21 illustrates the use of control charts in tracking a process that is initially out of control through two phases of improvement.

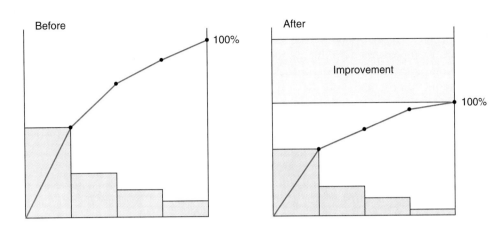

Figure 10–20

Comparison of before and after using Pareto charts

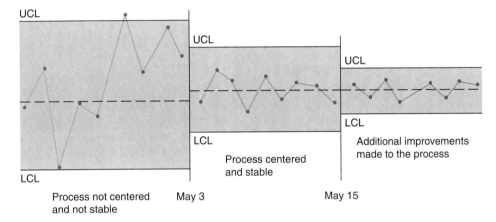

Figure 10–21

Using a control chart to track improvements

Continuous improvement is important because its underlying theme is that the quest for quality is never finished—it is always possible to improve. Furthermore, improvements do not need to be major breakthroughs; small, steady improvements are more certain and may serve to reinforce efforts. But continuous improvement is not a panacea. If an organization's products and processes are in fairly good shape, then continuous improvement efforts can be beneficial. However, if an organization is not in good shape, if its products or processes have major defects, continuous improvement is probably not the appropriate approach. In such instances, major breakthroughs are actually needed. Consider this analogy. If a car is in fairly good condition, periodic maintenance and an occasional washing would be appropriate, but if the car is in need of major repairs, more than periodic maintenance and washings will be needed to get the car into shape.

Thus, it is necessary to differentiate between situations in which continuous improvement is appropriate and situations in which much more is needed.

OPERATIONS STRATEGY

SUMMARY

This chapter described two perspectives relating to quality: Quality control and continuous improvement. Quality control focuses on detecting departures from randomness in a process, in order to know when to implement corrective action. Continuous improvement focuses on improving the process of producing goods and services.

Quality control is based largely on statistical procedures. Two key tools are control charts and run tests. We considered four types of control charts and two types of run tests. A summary of quality control formulas is provided in Table 10–3.

Continuous improvement is based on the philosophy that the quest for improvement must be never ending—the organization should strive to achieve ever increasing levels of customer satisfaction. Typically, teams of workers identify and solve problems using a variety of problem-solving tools, including statistical and graphical tools, in a structured approach.

Table 10–3

Summary of formulas

Control charts

Name	Symbol	Control limits
Mean	$\bar{x}$	$\bar{\bar{x}} \pm z\dfrac{\sigma}{\sqrt{n}}$ or $\bar{\bar{x}} \pm A_2\bar{R}$
Range	R	$UCL = D_4\bar{R}, \; LCL = D_3\bar{R}$
Percent defective	p	$\bar{p} \pm z\sqrt{\dfrac{\bar{p}(1-\bar{p})}{n}}$
Number of defects	c	$\bar{c} \pm z\sqrt{\bar{c}}$

Run tests

Name	Number of runs Observed	Number of runs Expected	Standard deviation	z
Median	r	$\dfrac{N}{2} + 1$	$\sqrt{\dfrac{N-1}{4}}$	$\dfrac{r - [(N/2) + 1]}{\sqrt{(N-1)/4}}$
Up/down	r	$\dfrac{2N-1}{3}$	$\sqrt{\dfrac{16N-29}{90}}$	$\dfrac{r - [2N-1)/3]}{\sqrt{(16N-29)/90}}$

KEY TERMS

SOLVED PROBLEMS

Problem

1. *Process distribution and sampling distribution.* An industrial process that makes 3-foot sections of plastic pipe produces pipe with an average inside diameter of 1 inch and a standard deviation of 0.05 inches.

    a. If one piece of pipe is randomly selected, what is the probability that its inside diameter will exceed 1.02 inches (assuming the population is normal)?

    b. If a random sample of 25 pieces of pipe is selected, what is the probability that the sample *mean* will exceed 1.02 inches?

Solution

$$\mu = 1.00, \quad \sigma = 0.05$$

a. $z = \dfrac{x - \mu}{\sigma} = \dfrac{1.02 - 1.00}{0.05} = 0.4$

Using Appendix B, Table A, $P(x > z) = .5000 - .1554 = .3446$.

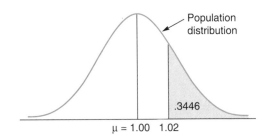

b. $z = \dfrac{\bar{x} - \mu}{\sigma/\sqrt{n}} = \dfrac{1.02 - 1.00}{0.05/\sqrt{25}} = 2.00$

Using Appendix B, Table A,

$P(\bar{x} > z) = .5000 - .4772 = .0228$

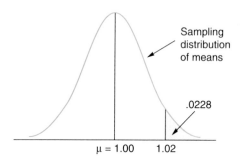

Problem

2. *Control charts for means and ranges.* Drop-forged steel handles have a designed weight of 10 ounces. Five samples of four observations each have been taken. Use the sample data in conjunction with Table 10–1 to construct upper and lower control limits for both a mean chart and a range chart. Is the process in control?

	Sample 1	Sample 2	Sample 3	Sample 4	Sample 5
	10.2	10.3	9.7	9.9	9.8
	9.9	9.8	9.9	10.3	10.2
	9.8	9.9	9.9	10.1	10.3
	10.1	10.4	10.1	10.5	9.7
Totals . . .	40.0	40.4	39.6	40.8	40.0

Solution

a. Determine the mean and range of each sample.

$\bar{x} = \dfrac{\Sigma x}{n}$, Range = Largest − Smallest

Sample	Mean	Range
1	40.0/4 = 10.0	10.2 − 9.8 = 0.4
2	40.4/4 = 10.1	10.4 − 9.8 = 0.6
3	39.6/4 = 9.9	10.1 − 9.7 = 0.4
4	40.8/4 = 10.2	10.5 − 9.9 = 0.6
5	40.0/4 = 10.0	10.3 − 9.7 = 0.6

b. Compute the average mean and average range:

$\bar{\bar{x}} = \dfrac{10.0 + 10.1 + 9.9 + 10.2 + 10.0}{5} = \dfrac{50.2}{5} = 10.04$

$$\bar{R} = \frac{0.4 + 0.6 + 0.4 + 0.6 + 0.6}{5} = \frac{2.6}{5} = 0.52$$

c. Obtain factors A_2, D_4, and D_3 from Table 10–1 for $n = 4$:

$$A_2 = 0.73, \ D_4 = 2.28, \ D_3 = 0$$

d. Compute upper and lower limits:

$$\text{UCL}_{\bar{x}} = \bar{\bar{x}} + A_2\bar{R} = 10.04 + 0.73(0.52) = 10.42$$
$$\text{LCL}_{\bar{x}} = \bar{\bar{x}} - A_2\bar{R} = 10.04 - 0.73(0.52) = 9.66$$
$$\text{UCL}_R = D_4\bar{R} = 2.28(0.52) = 1.19$$
$$\text{LCL}_R = D_3\bar{R} = 0(0.52) = 0$$

e. Plot sample means and ranges on their respective control charts, or otherwise verify that points are within limits.

The smallest sample mean is 9.9, and the largest is 10.2. Both are well within the control limits. Similarly, the largest sample range is 0.6, which is also within the control limits. Hence, we conclude the process is in control. Note, however, that for illustrative purposes, the number of samples was deliberately small; 20 or more samples would give a clearer indication of control limits and whether the process was in control.

Problem

3. *Type I error (alpha risk).* After several investigations of points outside control limits revealed nothing, a manager began to wonder about the probability of a Type I error for the control limits being used ($z = 1.90$).
   a. Determine the alpha risk for this value of z.
   b. What z would provide an alpha risk of about 2 percent?

Solution

a. Using Appendix B, Table A, we find that the area under the curve between $z = 0$ and $z = +1.90$ is .4713. Therefore, the area (probability) of values *within* -1.90 to $+1.90$ is $2(.4713) = .9426$, and the area *beyond* these values is $1 - .9426 = .0574$.

b. The alpha risk (Type I error probability) is always specified as an *area* in the tail(s) of a distribution. With control charts, we are involved with two-sided control limits. Consequently, half of the risk lies in each tail. Hence, the area in the right tail is 1 percent, or .0100. This means that .4900 should be the area under the curve between $z = 0$ and the value of z we are looking for. The closest value is .4901 for $z = +2.33$. Thus, control limits based on $z = \pm2.33$ would provide an alpha risk of about 2 percent.

Problem

4. p-*chart and* c-*chart.* Using the appropriate control chart, determine two-sigma control limits for each case:
   a. An inspector found an average of 3.9 scratches in the exterior paint of each of the automobiles being prepared for shipment to dealers.
   b. Before shipping lawnmowers to dealers, an inspector attempts to start each mower and notes any that do not start on the first try. The lot size is 100 mowers, and an average of 4 did not start (4 percent).

Solution

The choice between these two types of control chart relates to whether *two* types of results can be counted (*p*-chart) or whether *only occurrences* can be counted (*c*-chart).

a. The inspector can only count the scratches that occurred, not the ones that did not occur. Consequently, a *c*-chart is appropriate. The sample average is 3.9 scratches per car. Two–sigma control limits are found using the formula

$$\text{UCL} = \bar{c} + z\sqrt{\bar{c}}$$
$$\text{LCL} = \bar{c} - z\sqrt{\bar{c}}$$

where $\bar{c} = 3.9$ and $z = 2$. Thus,

$$\text{UCL} = 3.9 + 2\sqrt{3.9} = 7.85 \text{ scratches}$$
$$\text{LCL} = 3.9 - 2\sqrt{3.9} = -0.05 \ (0 \text{ scratches})$$

(Note: Only round to zero if the lower limit is *negative*.)

b. The inspector can count both the lawnmowers that started and those that did not start. Consequently, a *p*-chart is appropriate. Two–sigma control limits can be computed using the following:

$$\text{UCL} = \bar{p} + z\sqrt{\frac{\bar{p}(1 - \bar{p})}{n}}$$

$$\text{LCL} = \bar{p} - z\sqrt{\frac{\bar{p}(1 - \bar{p})}{n}}$$

where

$\bar{p} = .04$
$n = 100$
$z = 2$

Thus,

$$\text{UCL} = .04 + 2\sqrt{\frac{.04(.96)}{100}} = 0.079$$

$$\text{LCL} = .04 - 2\sqrt{\frac{.04(.96)}{100}} = 0.001$$

Problem

5. *Run tests.* The number of defectives per sample for 11 samples is shown below. Determine if nonrandom patterns are present in the sequence.

	Sample										
	1	2	3	4	5	6	7	8	9	10	11
Number of defectives	22	17	19	25	18	20	21	17	23	23	24

Solution

Since the median isn't given, it must be estimated from the sample data. To do this, array the data from low to high; the median is the middle value. (In this case, there are an odd number of values. For an even number of values, average the middle two to obtain the median.) Thus,

17   17   18   19   20   21   22   23   23   24   25
         (5 below)   ↑   (5 above)
                        median

The median is 21.

Next, code the observations using A/B and U/D:

Sample	A/B	Number of defectives	U/D
1	|A	22	—
2	|B	17	|D
3	|B	19	|U
4	|A	25	|U
5	|B	18	|D
6	|B	20	|U
7	tie	21	|U
8	|B	17	|D
9	|A	23	|U
10	|A	23	tie
11	|A	24	|U

Note that with each test there are tied values. How these are resolved can affect the number of observed runs. Suppose we adhere to this rule: Assign a letter (A or B, U or D) in such a way that the resulting difference between the observed and expected number of runs is as large as possible. To accomplish this, it will be necessary to initially ignore ties and count the runs to see whether there are too many or too few. Then return to the ties and make the assignments. The rationale for this rule is that it is a conservative method for retaining data; if we can conclude the data are random using this approach, we can be reasonably confident that the data are random and that our method has not "created" randomness. With this in mind, assign a B to sample 7 since the expected number of runs is

$$E(r)_{\text{med}} = N/2 + 1 = 11/2 + 1 = 6.5$$

and the difference between the resulting number of runs, 5, and 6.5 is greater than between 6.5 and 7 (which occurs if A is used instead of B). Similarly, in the up/down test, a U for sample 10 produces 6 runs, whereas a D produces 8 runs. Since the expected number of runs is

$$E(r)_{\text{u/d}} = (2N - 1)/3 = (22 - 1)/3 = 7$$

it makes no difference which one we use: they both yield a difference of 1. For the sake of illustration, suppose we assign a D.

The computations for the two tests are summarized below. Since neither test reveals nonrandomness, we conclude the data are random.

	Runs observed	E(r)	σ_r	z	Conclude
Median	5	6.5	1.58	−0.95	Random
Up/down.........	8	7.0	1.28	0.78	Random

DISCUSSION AND REVIEW QUESTIONS

1. List the elements in the control process.
2. What are the key concepts that underlie the construction and interpretation of control charts?
3. What is the purpose of a control chart?
4. Why is order of observation important in process control?
5. Briefly explain the purpose of each of these control charts:
   a. x-bar   b. Range   c. p-chart   d. c-chart
6. What is a run? How are run charts useful in process control?
7. If all observations are within control limits, does that guarantee that the process is random? Explain.
8. Why is it usually desirable to use both a median run test and an up/down run test on the same data?
9. If both run tests are used, and neither reveals nonrandomness, does that prove that the process is random? Explain.
10. Define and contrast control limits, tolerances, and process variability.
11. A customer has recently tightened the specs for a part your company supplies. The specs are now much tighter than the machine being used for the job is capable of. Briefly identify alternatives you might consider to resolve this problem. (See Figure 10–9C.)
12. A new order has come into your department. The capability of the machine used for this type of work is such that virtually all of the output can be expected to be well within the specs. (See Figure 10–9B.)
    a.   What benefits might be derived from this situation?
    b.   What alternatives might be considered by the manager?
14. List the management requirements of continuous improvement.
15. Describe the PDCA cycle.
16. Explain the meaning and importance of standardization in continuous improvement.
17. Briefly describe each of these graphical tools for process improvement:
    a. Pareto chart   b. Check sheet   c. Flow chart   d. Run chart
    e. Cause-and-effect diagram
18. Briefly describe these process improvement tools:
    a. Brainstorming   b. Benchmarking

PROBLEMS

1. Manufacturing specifications call for motor housings that weigh between 24 and 25 pounds. The housings are cast using a process that produces castings with a mean of 24.5 pounds and a standard deviation of 0.2 pounds. The distribution of output is normal.

   a.   What percentage of housings will not meet the weight specs?

   b.   Within what values will 99.7 percent of sample means of this process fall, if samples of $n = 16$ are taken and the process is in control (random)?

2. An automatic filling machine is used to fill 1-liter bottles of cola. The machine's output is approximately normal with a mean of 1.0 liter and a standard deviation of 0.01 liter. Output is monitored using means of samples of 25 observations.

   a.   Determine upper and lower control limits that will include roughly 95.5 percent of the sample means when the process is in control.

   b.   Graph the control chart and plot these sample means: 1.005, 1.001, 0.998, 1.002, 0.995, and 0.999. Is the process in control?

3. A grinding and deburring operation is monitored using a mean and a range chart. Six samples of $n = 20$ observations have been obtained and the sample means and ranges computed:

Sample	Mean	Range
1	3.06	0.42
2	3.15	0.50
3	3.11	0.41
4	3.13	0.46
5	3.06	0.46
6	3.09	0.45

   a.   Using the factors in Table 10–1, determine upper and lower limits for mean and range charts.

   b.   Is the process in control?

4. Using samples of 200 observations each, a quality inspector found the following:

Sample	1	2	3	4
Number of defectives	4	2	5	9

   a.   Determine the fraction defective in each sample.

   b.   If the true fraction defective for this process is unknown, what is your estimate of it?

   c.   What is your estimate of the mean and standard deviation of the sampling distribution of fractions defective for samples of this size?

   d.   What control limits would give an alpha risk of .03 for this process?

   e.   What alpha risk would control limits of 0.047 and 0.003 provide?

   f.   Using control limits of 0.047 and 0.003, are any of the sample fractions defective beyond the control limits? If so, which one(s)?

   g.   Suppose now that the long-term fraction defective of the process is known to be 2 percent. What are the values of the mean and standard deviation of the sampling distribution?

   h.   Construct a control chart for the process, assuming a fraction defective of 2 percent, using two-sigma control limits. Are any of the samples beyond the control limits? If so, which one(s)?

5. A continuous process cuts plastic tubing into nominal lengths of 80 centimeters. Samples of five observations each have been taken, and the results are as listed. Using factors from Table 10–1, determine upper and lower control limits for mean and range charts, and decide if the process is in control.

			Sample		
1	**2**	**3**	**4**	**5**	**6**
79.2	80.5	79.6	78.9	80.5	79.7
78.8	78.7	79.6	79.4	79.6	80.6
80.0	81.0	80.4	79.7	80.4	80.5
78.4	80.4	80.3	79.4	80.8	80.0
81.0	80.1	80.8	80.6	78.8	81.1

6. An automatic screw machine produces 2-inch hex nuts. Using the following sample data and $n = 200$, construct a control chart for the fraction defective using two-sigma limits. Is the process in control? If not, eliminate any values that are outside of the limits, and compute revised limits.

						Sample						
1	**2**	**3**	**4**	**5**	**6**	**7**	**8**	**9**	**10**	**11**	**12**	**13**
Number of defectives ... 1	2	2	0	2	1	2	0	2	7	3	2	1

7. The postmaster of a small western city receives a certain number of complaints about mail delivery each day. Assume that the distribution of daily complaints is Poisson. Construct a control chart with three-sigma limits using the following data. Is the process in control?

							Day						
1	**2**	**3**	**4**	**5**	**6**	**7**	**8**	**9**	**10**	**11**	**12**	**13**	**14**
Number of complaints .. 4	10	14	8	9	6	5	12	13	7	6	4	2	10

8. Construct a control chart with three-sigma limits for the number of defects per spool of cable, given the following data. Is the process in control?

Observation	Number of defects	Observation	Number of defects
1	2	8	0
2	3	9	2
3	1	10	1
4	0	11	3
5	1	12	1
6	3	13	2
7	2	14	0

9. During long runs of canned vegetables through a labeling machine, a few labels invariably fail to adhere properly and eventually fall off. Using the following sample data, which are based on samples of 100 observations each, construct a control chart for the

fraction defective using 95 percent control limits, and determine if the process is in control.

Sample	Number of defectives	Sample	Number of defectives
1	5	9	5
2	3	10	8
3	6	11	3
4	7	12	4
5	4	13	5
6	6	14	6
7	8	15	6
8	4	16	7

10. Tolerances for a metal shaft are much wider than the process used to machine the shafts is capable of. Consequently, the decision has been made to allow the cutting tool to wear a certain amount before replacement. The tool wears at the rate of 0.004 centimeters per piece. The process has a natural variation, σ, of 0.01 centimeters and is normally distributed. Tolerances are 15 to 17 centimeters, and $n = 1$. For two-sigma limits, how many shifts can the process turn out before tool replacement becomes necessary? (See diagram.)

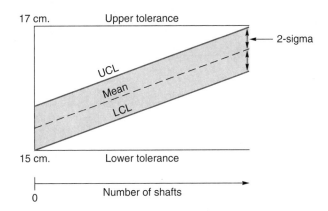

11. Tolerances for the plastic tubing mentioned in Problem 5 are 78 centimeters and 81 centimeters. Based on the data given in the problem, are the tolerances being met? Estimate the percentage of process output that can be expected to fall within the tolerances.

12. A process that produces bars of soap is to be investigated. Historically, the process has had a standard deviation equal to 0.146. The means of 39 samples of $n = 14$ are:

Sample	Mean	Sample	Mean	Sample	Mean
1	3.86	6	3.83	11	3.88
2	3.90	7	3.87	12	3.86
3	3.83	8	3.88	13	3.88
4	3.81	9	3.84	14	3.81
5	3.84	10	3.80	15	3.83

(continued)

Sample	Mean	Sample	Mean	Sample	Mean
16	3.86	24	3.86	32	3.76
17	3.82	25	3.88	33	3.83
18	3.86	26	3.90	34	3.77
19	3.84	27	3.81	35	3.86
20	3.87	28	3.86	36	3.80
21	3.84	29	3.98	37	3.84
22	3.82	30	3.96	38	3.79
23	3.89	31	3.88	39	3.85

a. Construct an $\bar{x}$-chart for this process with three-sigma limits. Is the process in control?

b. Analyze the data using a median run test and an up/down run test. What can you conclude?

13. For each of the accompanying control charts, analyze the data using both median and up/down run tests with $z = \pm 1.96$ limits. Are nonrandom variations present? Assume the center line is the long-term median.

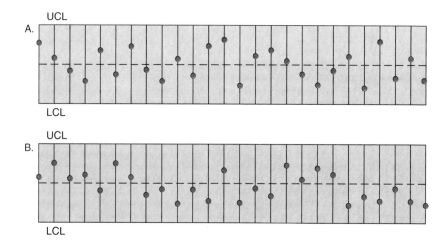

14. Analyze the data in the problems listed below using median and up/down run tests with $z = \pm 2$.

a. Problem 9.

b. Problem 7.

15. Use both types of run test to analyze the daily expense voucher listed. Assume a median of $31.

Day	Amount	Day	Amount	Day	Amount
1	$27.69	7	34.73	13	33.98
2	28.13	8	35.09	14	25.56
3	33.02	9	33.39	15	24.46
4	30.31	10	32.51	16	29.65
5	31.59	11	27.98	17	31.08
6	33.64	12	31.25	18	33.03

(continued)

Day	Amount	Day	Amount	Day	Amount
19	29.10	33	27.14	47	26.11
20	25.19	34	30.38	48	29.84
21	28.60	35	31.96	49	31.75
22	20.02	36	32.03	50	29.14
23	26.67	37	34.40	51	37.78
24	36.40	38	25.67	52	34.16
25	32.07	39	35.80	53	38.28
26	44.10	40	32.23	54	29.49
27	41.44	41	26.76	55	30.81
28	29.62	42	30.51	56	30.60
29	30.12	43	29.35	57	34.46
30	26.39	44	24.09	58	35.10
31	40.54	45	22.45	59	31.76
32	36.31	46	25.16	60	34.90

16. A company has just negotiated a contract to produce a part for another firm. In the process of manufacturing the part, as the cutting tool wears, the inside diameter of successive parts becomes smaller and smaller. However, the specs are so wide relative to machine capabilities that it is possible to initially set the diameter at a large value and let the process run for a while before replacing the cutting tool. (This situation is somewhat similar to the one described in Problem 10.)

    The inside diameter decreases at an average rate of 0.001 cm per part, and the process has a standard deviation of 0.01 cm. The variability is approximately normal. Assuming three-sigma control limits, how frequently must the tool be replaced if the process specs are 3 cm and 3.5 cm, and the initial setting of the UCL is at the upper spec? Use $n = 1$.

17. (Refer to Solved Problem 2.) Suppose the process specs are 9.65 and 10.35. Based on the data given, does it appear that the specs are being met? If not, what should one look for?

18. A production process consists of a three-step operation. The scrap rate of the first step is 10 percent, and the rate is 6 percent for the other two steps.
    a. If the desired daily output is 450 units, how many units must be started to allow for loss due to scrap?
    b. If the scrap rate for each step could be cut in half, how many units would this save in terms of the scrap allowance?
    c. If the scrap represents a cost of $10 per unit, how much is it costing the company per day for the original scrap rate?

19. (Refer to the data in Example 5.) Two additional observations have been taken. The first resulted in three defects, and the second had four defects. Using the set of 20 observations, perform run tests on the data. What can you conclude about the data?

20. A machine operator has obtained the following measurements:

Sample			
1	2	3	4
4.5	4.6	4.5	4.7
4.2	4.5	4.6	4.6
4.2	4.4	4.4	4.8
4.3	4.7	4.4	4.5
4.3	4.3	4.6	4.9

    a. Determine the mean of each sample.

    b. If the process parameters are unknown, estimate its mean and standard deviation.

    c. Estimate the mean and standard deviation of the sampling distribution.

    d. What would three-sigma control limits for the process be? What alpha risk would they provide?

    e. What alpha risk would control limits of 4.14 and 4.86 provide?

    f. Using limits of 4.14 and 4.86, are any sample means beyond the control limits? If so, which one(s)?

    g. Construct control charts for means and ranges using Table 10–1. Are any samples beyond the control limits? If so, which one(s)?

    h. Explain why the control limits are different for means in parts *d* and *g*.

    i. If the process had a known mean of 4.4 and a known standard deviation of 0.18, what would three-sigma control limits be for a mean chart? Are any sample means beyond the control limits? If so, which one(s)?

21. Suppose that a table lamp fails to light when it is turned on. Prepare a simple cause-and-effect diagram to analyze possible causes.

22. Prepare a cause-and-effect diagram to analyze possible causes of the frequent late delivery of parts ordered from a supplier.

SELECTED BIBLIOGRAPHY

Baker, Thomas R. "Quality Engineering by Design." *Quality Progress,* December 1986, pp. 32–42.

Duncan, A. J. *Quality Control and Industrial Statistics.* 5th ed. Homewood, Ill.: Richard D. Irwin, 1986.

Enrick, Norbert L. *Quality, Reliability, and Process Improvement.* 8th ed. New York: Industrial Press, 1985.

Ernst & Young Consulting Group. *Total Quality.* Homewood, Ill.: Dow-Jones Irwin, 1990.

Garvin, David A. "Quality on the Line." *Harvard Business Review,* September–October 1983, p. 64.

Gitlow, Howard S.; Shelly Gitlow; Alan Oppenheim; and Rosa Oppenheim. *Tools and Methods for the Improvement of Quality.* Homewood, Ill.: Richard D. Irwin, 1989.

Gitlow, Howard S., and Paul T. Hertz. "Product Defects and Productivity." *Harvard Business Review,* September–October 1983, p. 131.

Grant, Eugene L., and Richard S. Leavenworth. *Statistical Quality Control.* 5th ed. New York: McGraw-Hill, 1980.

Hall, Robert W. *Attaining Manufacturing Excellence.* Homewood, Ill.: Dow Jones-Irwin, 1987.

Hunt, V. Daniel. *Quality in America.* Homewood, Ill.: Business One Irwin, 1992.

Juran, J. M. "The Quality Trilogy." *Quality Progress* 19, no. 8 (August 1986), pp. 19–24.

Juran, J. M., and F. M. Gryma, Jr. *Quality Planning and Analysis.* 2nd ed. New York: McGraw-Hill, 1980.

Kume, Hitoshi. *Statistical Methods for Quality Improvement.* Tokyo: AOTS Chosakai, 1985.

Leonard, Frank S., and Earl Sasser. "The Incline of Quality." *Harvard Business Review,* September–October 1982, pp. 163–71.

Reddy, Jack, and Abe Berger. "Three Essentials of Product Quality." *Harvard Business Review,* July–August 1983, pp. 153–59.

Schein, Lawrence, and Melissa A. Berman, eds. *Total Quality Performance.* Research Report No. 909. New York Conference Board, 1988.

CASE   FRIENDLY MARKETS

Jean Marsh, the manager of a supermarket, was perturbed by the large number of complaints from customers, particularly on Tuesdays, so over the last eight weeks she obtained Tuesday's complaint records from the store's service desk. These are listed below.

Analyze these data using a check sheet, a Pareto diagram, and run charts. Then construct a cause-and-effect diagram for each of the two leading categories on the Pareto diagram. What do the run charts reveal? What does the Pareto diagram reveal?

June 4	June 11	June 18	June 25
out of butter	couldn't find item	overcharged	wanted smaller size
out of eggs	fish smelled	meat bad	restroom not clean
checkout lines too long	light out in parking lot	overcharged	couldn't find item
overcharged	out of bread	couldn't find item	overcharged
lines too long	undercharged	overcharged	out of frozen peas
overcharged	out of bread	couldn't find item	lines too long
meat not fresh	fish bad	lines too long	restroom not clean
out of giant bread	slippery floor	lines too long	couldn't locate rice
broken shopping cart	out of bread	overcharged	meat smelled funny
out of 42 oz. Tide	wrong price	wrong price	too cold in store
slippery floor	broken cart	cart won't steer	couldn't find aspirin
cashier rude	empty boxes in aisles	windows dirty	telephone not working
store too warm	store too warm	broken shopping cart	no Bounty paper towels
	store messy	store cold	out of Life cereal
	no lights in dairy case		double charged
	out of Dove soap		noisy air conditioner
			too warm in store

July 2	July 9	July 16	July 23
overcharged	restroom dirty	lines too long	meat past sale date
lines too long	overcharged	couldn't find rice	noisy air conditioner
out of bread	out of doughnuts	lines too long	fish have "fishy smell"
wrong price	broken shopping cart	out of bread	meat past sale date
noisy shopping cart	lines too long	undercharged	lines too long
out of bananas	meat old	out of Hershey syrup	overcharged
out of sugar	out of bread	out of Life cereal	lines too long
too cold in store	bad fish	out of vanilla sauce	out of Ragu pizza
out of bread	wrong price	overcharged	double charged
out of Mighty Dog dog food	torn package	out of bread	didn't like music
			restroom not clean

CASE   ANYONE FOR SUSHI?

The operations manager of a firm that produces frozen dinners had received numerous complaints about the firm's Chick-n-Gravy dinners from supermarkets that sell this item. The manager then asked her assistant, Ann, to investigate the matter and to report her recommendations.

Ann's first task was to sift through the list of complaints to determine what problems were gener-

ating the complaints. The majority of complaints centered on five defects: underfilled packages, a missing item, spills/mixed items, unacceptable taste, and packages improperly sealed.

Next, she took samples of dinners from the two production lines and examined each sample, making note of any defects that she found. A summary of those results is shown in the accompanying table.

| | | | Defect Observed | | | | |
Date	Time	Line	Underfilled	Missing item	Spill/ mixed	Unacceptable taste	Improperly sealed
5/12	0900	1		√√	√	√√√	
5/12	1330	2			√√		√√
5/13	1000	2				√	√√√
5/13	1345	1	√√		√√		
5/13	1530	2		√√	√√√		√
5/14	0830	1		√√√		√√√	
5/14	1100	2	√		√	√√	
5/14	1400	1			√		√
5/15	1030	1		√√√		√√√√√	
5/15	1145	2			√	√√	
5/15	1500	1	√		√		
5/16	0845	2				√√	√√
5/16	1030	1		√√√	√	√√√	
5/16	1400	1					
5/16	1545	2	√	√√√√√	√	√	√√

The data resulted from inspecting approximately 800 frozen dinners. What should Ann recommend to the manager?

INSPECTION AND ACCEPTANCE SAMPLING

After completing this supplement, you should be able to:

1. Explain the purpose of acceptance sampling.
2. Contrast acceptance sampling and process control.
3. Discuss the key issues related to inspection.
4. Compare and contrast single and multiple sampling plans.
5. Determine the average outgoing quality of inspected lots.

There are three points in the production process where monitoring takes place: before production, during production, and after production. The logic of checking conformance before production is to make sure that inputs are acceptable. The logic of checking conformance during production is to make sure that the conversion of inputs into outputs is proceeding in an acceptable manner. The logic of checking conformance of output is to make a final verification of conformance before passing goods on to customers.

Monitoring before and after production involves *acceptance sampling* procedures; monitoring during the production process is referred to as *process control*. Figure 10S–1 gives an overview of where these two procedures are applied in the production process.

For both acceptance sampling and process control, inspection provides key data for decision making.

INSPECTION

To determine if a process is functioning as intended, or to verify that a shipment of raw materials or final products does not contain more than a specified percentage of defectives, it is necessary to physically examine at least some of the items in question. The purpose of inspection is to provide information on the degree to which items conform to a standard. The basic issues here are:

1. How much to inspect and how often.
2. At what points in the process inspection should occur.
3. Whether to inspect in a centralized location or on site.
4. Whether to inspect attributes or variables.

Consider, for example, inspection at an intermediate step in the manufacture of personal computers. Because inspection costs are often significant, the question naturally arises of whether it is necessary to inspect every computer, or whether a small sample of computers will suffice. Moreover, although there are numerous points in the production process where inspections could be made, it is not generally cost-effective to inspect at every point. Hence, the question comes up of which points to inspect at. Once these have been identified, a decision must be made on whether to remove the computers from the line and take them to a lab, where specialized equipment might be available to run certain tests, or whether to test them where they are being made. We will examine these points in the following sections.

How Much to Inspect and How Often

The amount of inspection can range from no inspection whatsoever to inspecting each item numerous times. Low-cost, high-volume items such as paper clips, roof-

Figure 10S–1

Acceptance sampling and process control

ing nails, and wooden pencils often require little inspection because (1) the cost associated with passing defectives is quite low and (2) the processes that produce these items are usually highly reliable, so that defectives are rare. Conversely, high-cost, low-volume items that have large costs associated with passing defectives often require more intensive inspections. Thus, critical components of a manned-flight space vehicle are closely scrutinized because of the risk to human safety and the high cost of mission failure. In high-volume systems, one option that may be employed is *automated* inspection.

The majority of quality control applications lies somewhere between the two extremes. Most require some inspection, but it is neither possible nor economically feasible to critically examine every part or activity for control purposes. The cost of inspection, resulting interruptions of a process or delays caused by inspection, and the manner of testing typically outweigh the benefits of 100 percent inspection. However, the cost of letting undetected defectives slip through is high enough that inspection cannot be completely ignored. The amount of inspection needed is governed by the costs of inspection and the expected costs of passing defective items. As illustrated in Figure 10S–2, if inspection activities increase, inspection costs increase, but the costs of undetected defectives decrease. The goal, of course, is to minimize the sum of these two costs. In other words, it may not pay to attempt to catch every defective, particularly if the cost of inspection exceeds the penalties associated with letting some defectives get through.

As a rule, operations that have a high proportion of human involvement necessitate more inspection effort than mechanical operations because the latter tend to be more reliable.

The frequency of inspection depends largely on the rate at which a process may go out of control or the number of lots being inspected. A stable process will necessitate only infrequent checks, whereas an unstable one, or one that has recently given trouble, will require more frequent checks. Likewise, many small lots will require more samples than a few large lots because it is important to obtain sample data from each lot.

Figure 10S–2

The amount of inspection is optimal when the sum of the costs of inspection and passing defectives is minimized

WHERE IN THE PROCESS TO INSPECT

In many operations, there are many possible inspection points. Because each inspection adds to the cost of the product or service, it is important to restrict inspection efforts to the points where they can do the most good. In manufacturing, some of the typical inspection points are:

1. *Raw materials and purchased parts.* There is little sense in paying for goods that do not meet quality standards and little sense in expending time and effort on material that is bad to begin with.

2. *Finished products.* Customer satisfaction and the firm's image are at stake here, and repairing or replacing products in the field is usually quite a bit more costly than when it is done at the factory. Likewise, the seller is usually responsible for shipping costs on returns, and payments may be held up pending delivery of satisfactory goods.

3. *Before a costly operation.* The point is to not waste costly labor or machine time on items that are already defective.

4. *Before an irreversible process.* In many cases, items can be reworked up to a certain point, but beyond that they cannot. For example, pottery can be reworked prior to firing. After that, defectives must be discarded or sold as seconds at a lower price.

5. *Before a covering process.* Painting, plating, and assemblies often mask defects.

In the service area, inspection points are incoming purchased materials and supplies, personnel, service interfaces (e.g., service counter), and outgoing completed work (e.g., repaired appliances, automobiles). Table 10S–1 illustrates a number of examples.

Each situation is different. A manager must weigh the costs and benefits of inspections at each potential point in a process when deciding to assign inspections.

CENTRALIZED VERSUS ON-SITE INSPECTION

Some situations require that inspections be done *on site.* For example, inspecting the hull of a ship for cracks requires inspectors to visit the ship. At other times, specialized tests can best be performed in a lab. This is the case with many medical tests, and it also applies to various tests in business and industry (analyzing food samples, testing metals for hardness, running viscosity tests on lubricants, and so on).

The central issue in the decision of whether to inspect on site or in the lab is whether the advantages of specialized lab tests are worth the time and interruption needed to obtain the results. Reasons favoring on-site inspection include quicker decisions and avoidance of introduction of extraneous factors (e.g., damage or other alteration of samples during transportation to the lab). On the other hand, specialized equipment and a more favorable testing environment (less noise and confusion, lack of vibrations, absence of dust, and workers "helping" with inspections) offer strong arguments for using a lab.

In unit (one-by-one) production, some companies rely on self-inspections by operators if errors can be traced back to specific operators. This places responsibility for errors at their source.

Type of business	Inspection points	Characteristics	Table 10S–1
Fast food	Cashier	Accuracy	Examples of inspection points in service organizations
	Counter area	Appearance, productivity	
	Eating area	Cleanliness, no loitering	
	Building and grounds	Appearance, safety hazards	
	Kitchen	Cleanliness, purity of food, food storage, health regulations	
	Parking lot	Safe, well-lighted	
Hotel/motel	Accounting/billing	Accuracy, timeliness	
	Building and grounds	Appearance and safety	
	Main desk	Appearance, waiting times, accuracy of bills	
	Maid service	Completeness, productivity	
	Personnel	Appearance, manners, productivity	
	Reservations/occupancy	Over/underbooking, percent occupancy	
	Restaurants	Kitchen, menus, meals, bills	
	Room service	Waiting time, quality of food	
	Supplies	Ordering, receiving, inventories	
Supermarket	Cashiers	Accuracy, courtesy, productivity	
	Deliveries	Quality, quantity	
	Produce	Freshness, well-stocked	
	Aisles and stockrooms	Uncluttered	
	Inventory control	Stock-outs	
	Shelf stock	Ample supply, rotation of perishables	
	Shelf displays	Appearance	
	Checkouts	Waiting time	
	Shopping carts	Good working condition, ample supply, theft/vandalism	
	Parking lot	Safe, well-lighted	
	Personnel	Appearance	

ACCEPTANCE SAMPLING

Acceptance sampling is a form of inspection that is applied to lots or batches of items either before or after a process instead of during the process. In the majority of cases, the lots represent incoming purchased items or final products awaiting shipment to warehouses or customers. The purpose of acceptance sampling is to decide if a lot satisfies predetermined standards. Lots that are judged to satisfy standards are passed or *accepted;* those that do not are *rejected.* Rejected lots may be subjected to 100 percent inspection, or purchased goods may be returned to the supplier for credit or replacement (especially if destructive testing is involved).

Acceptance sampling
Form of inspection applied to lots or batches of items before or after a process, to judge conformance with predetermined standards.

Acceptance sampling procedures are most useful when one or more of the following conditions exist:

1. A large number of items must be processed in a short time.
2. The cost consequences of passing defectives are low.
3. Destructive testing is required.
4. Fatigue or boredom caused by inspecting large numbers of items leads to inspection errors.

Acceptance sampling procedures can be applied to both attribute and variable inspection. However, inspection of attributes is perhaps more widely used, so for purposes of illustration, the discussion here will focus exclusively on attribute sampling plans.

SAMPLING PLANS

Sampling plans

Plans that specify lot size, sample size, number of samples, and acceptance/rejection criteria.

Sampling plans specify the lot size, N; the sample size, n; the number of samples to be taken; and the acceptance/rejection criteria. There are a variety of sampling plans in use. Some plans call for selection of a single sample, and others call for two or more samples, depending on the nature of the plan. Some of the different kinds of plans are briefly described in the following paragraphs.

Single-Sampling Plan   In this plan, one random sample is drawn from each lot, and every item in the sample is examined and classified as either "good" or "defective." If any sample contains more than a specified number of defectives, c, that lot is rejected.

Double-Sampling Plan   A double-sampling plan allows for the opportunity to take a second sample if the results of the initial sample are inconclusive. For example, if the quality of the initial sample is high, the lot can be accepted without need for a second sample. If the quality in the initial sample is poor, sampling can also be terminated and the lot rejected. For results between those two cases, a second sample is then taken and the items inspected, after which the lot is either accepted or rejected on the basis of the evidence obtained from both samples. A double-sampling plan specifies the lot size, the size of the initial sample, accept/reject criteria for the initial sample (e.g., $c_1 = 2$, $c_2 = 5$: if two or fewer defectives are found, accept the lot; if more than five defectives are found, reject the lot; and if three, four, or five defectives are found, take a second sample), the size of the second sample, and a single acceptance number (e.g., $c_3 = 6$: accept the lot if the total number of defectives found in both samples is six or fewer; otherwise, reject the lot).

Multiple-Sampling Plan   A multiple-sampling plan is very similar to a double-sampling plan, except that more than two samples may be required. A sampling plan will specify each sample size and two limits for each sample. The values increase with the number of samples. If, for any sample, the cumulative number of defectives found (i.e., those in the present sample plus those found in all previous samples) exceeds the upper limit specified for that sample, sampling is terminated and the lot is rejected. If the cumulative number of defectives is less than or equal to the lower limit, sampling is terminated and the lot is passed. If the number is between the two limits, another sample is taken. The process continues until the lot is either accepted or rejected.

Choosing a Plan   The cost and time required for inspection often dictate the kind of sampling plan used. The two primary considerations are the number of samples needed and the total number of observations required. Single-sampling plans involve only a single sample, but the sample size is large relative to the total number of observations taken under double- or multiple-sampling plans. In a situation where the cost to obtain a sample is relatively high compared to the cost to analyze the observations, a single-sampling plan would be more desirable. For instance, if a sample of moon soil is needed, clearly the cost of returning for a second or third sample would far outweigh the cost of analyzing a single large sample. Conversely, in situations where item inspection costs are relatively high, such as destructive testing, it may be better to use double or multiple sampling, because the average number of items inspected per lot will be lower. This stems from the fact that if the lot quality is either very good or very poor, this will often show up initially, and sampling can be terminated.

OPERATING CHARACTERISTIC CURVE

An important feature of a sampling plan is how well it discriminates between lots of high quality and lots of low quality. The ability of a sampling plan to discriminate is described by its **operating characteristic (OC) curve**. A typical curve for a single-sampling plan is shown in Figure 10S–3. The curve shows the probability that use of the sampling plan will result in lots with various *fractions defective* being accepted. For example, we can see from the graph that a lot with 3 percent of

Operating characteristic curve

Probability curve that shows the probabilities of accepting lots with various fractions defective.

Figure 10S–3

A typical OC curve for proportions

Figure 10S–4

The steeper the OC curve, the more discriminating the sampling plan

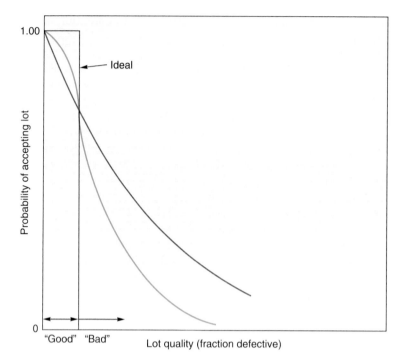

defectives (a fraction defective of .03) would have a probability of about .90 of being accepted (and, hence, a probability of 1.00 − .90 = .10 of being rejected). Note that there is a downward relationship: as lot quality decreases, the probability of acceptance decreases, although the relationship is not linear. For instance, if a lot contains 20 percent defectives, the probability of acceptance drops to about .04.

It is interesting to note that even lots containing more than 20 percent defectives still have some probability of being accepted, whereas lots with as few as 3 percent defectives stand some chance of being rejected. Clearly, a sampling plan does not provide perfect discrimination between good and bad lots; some low-quality lots will invariably be accepted, and some lots with very good quality will invariably be rejected.

The degree to which a sampling plan discriminates between good and bad lots is a function of the steepness of the graph's OC curve: the steeper the curve, the more discriminating the sampling plan. This is illustrated in Figure 10S–4. Note the curve for an ideal plan (i.e., one that can discriminate perfectly between good and bad lots). In order to achieve that, it would be necessary to inspect 100 percent of each lot. Obviously, if you are going to do that, theoretically *all* of the defectives can be eliminated (although errors and boredom might result in a few defectives remaining). However, the point is that 100 percent inspection provides a perspective from which to view the OC curves of other sampling plans.

It should be noted that the cost and the time that would be needed to conduct 100 percent inspection often rule out 100 percent inspection, as does destructive testing, leaving acceptance sampling as the only viable alternative.

Acceptable quality level

The percentage level of defects at which consumers are willing to accept lots as "good."

For these reasons, consumers are generally willing to accept lots that contain small percentages of defective items as "good," especially if the cost related to a few defectives is low. Often this percentage is in the neighborhood of 2 percent to 4 percent defective. This figure is known as the **acceptable quality level (AQL).**

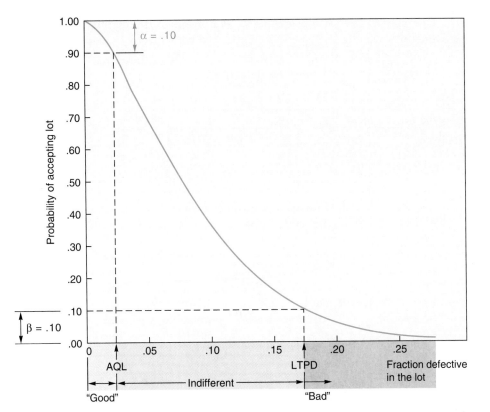

Because of the inability of random sampling to clearly identify lots that contain more than this specified percentage of defectives, consumers recognize that some lots that actually contain more will be accepted. However, there is usually an upper limit on the percentage of defectives that a consumer is willing to tolerate in accepted lots. This is known as the **lot tolerance percent defective (LTPD)**. Thus, the consumer would like quality equal to or better than the AQL, and is willing to live with some lots with quality as poor as the LTPD, but would prefer not to accept any lots that have a defective percentage that exceeds the LTPD. The probability that a lot containing defectives exceeding the LTPD will be accepted is known as the **consumer's risk**, or beta (β), or the probability of making a *Type II error;* the probability that a lot containing the acceptable quality level will be rejected is known as the **producer's risk**, alpha (α), or the probability of making a *Type I error*. Many sampling plans are designed so that they have a producer's risk of 5 percent and a consumer's risk of 10 percent, although other combinations are also used. It is possible to use trial and error to design a plan that will provide selected values for alpha and beta given the AQL and the LTPD. However, standard references such as the government MIL-STD tables are widely used to obtain sample sizes and acceptance criteria for sampling plans. Figure 10S–5 illustrates an OC curve with the AQL, LTPD, producer's risk, and consumer's risk.

A certain amount of insight can be gained by actually constructing an OC curve. Suppose we want the curve for a situation in which a sample of $n = 10$ items is drawn from lots containing $N = 2,000$ items, and a lot is accepted if no more than $c = 1$ defective is found. Because the sample size is small relative to the lot size, it is reasonable to use the binomial distribution to obtain the probabilities that a lot

Lot tolerance percent defective

The upper limit on the percentage of defects that a consumer is willing to accept.

Consumer's risk

The probability that a lot containing defectives exceeding the LTPD will be accepted.

Producer's risk

The probability that a lot containing the acceptable quality level will be rejected.

will be accepted for various lot qualities.[1] A portion of the cumulative binomial table found in Appendix B, Table D is reproduced below to facilitate the discussion.

							Fraction defective, p						
n	x	.05	.10	.15	.20	.25	.30	.35	.40	.45	.50	.55	.60
10 … 0		.5987	.3487	.1969	.1074	.0563	.0282	.0135	.0060	.0025	.0010	.0003	.0001
$c = 1 \rightarrow$ 1		.9139	.7361	.5443	.3758	.2440	.1493	.0860	.0464	.0233	.0107	.0045	.0017
2		.9885	.9298	.8202	.6778	.5256	.3828	.2616	.1673	.0996	.0547	.0274	.0123
3		.9990	.9872	.9500	.8791	.7759	.6496	.5138	.3823	.2660	.1719	.1020	.0548

To use the table, select various lot qualities (values of p listed across the top of the table), beginning with .05, and find the probability that a lot with that percentage of defectives would be accepted (i.e., the probability of finding zero or one defective in this case). Hence, for $p = .05$, the probability of one or no defectives is .9139. For a lot with 10 percent defectives (i.e., a fraction defective of .10), the probability of one or fewer defectives drops to .7361, and for 15 percent defectives, the probability of acceptance is .5443. In effect, we simply read the probabilities across the row for $c = 1$. By plotting these points (e.g., .05 and .9139, .10 and .7361) on a graph and connecting them, we obtain the OC curve illustrated in Figure 10S–6.

---

[1] Since sampling is generally done "without replacement," if the ratio n/N is 5 percent or more, the hypergeometric distribution would be more appropriate since the probability of finding a defective would vary from observation to observation. We shall only consider the more general case of the binomial distribution (i.e., $n/N < 5$ percent).

Figure 10S–6

OC curve for $n = 10$, $c = 1$

When $n > 20$ and $p < .05$, the Poisson distribution is useful in constructing operating characteristic curves for proportions. In effect, the Poisson distribution is used to approximate the binomial distribution. The Poisson approximation involves treating the mean of the binomial distribution (i.e., np) as the mean of the Poisson (i.e., μ):

$$\mu = np \qquad\qquad (10S-1)$$

As with the binomial distribution, various values of lot quality, p, are selected, and the probability of accepting a lot (i.e., finding two or fewer defectives) is determined by referring to the cumulative Poisson table. Values of p in increments of .01 are often used in this regard. The following example illustrates this use of the Poisson table.

Use the cumulative Poisson table to construct an OC curve for this sampling plan:

Example 1

$$N = 5{,}000, \qquad n = 80, \qquad c = 2$$

Solution

Selected values of p	$\mu = np$	$P_{ac}[P(x \le 2)$ from Appendix B, Table C]
.01	80(.01) = 0.8	.953
.02	80(.02) = 1.6	.783
.03	80(.03) = 2.4	.570
.04	80(.04) = 3.2	.380
.05	80(.05) = 4.0	.238
.06	80(.06) = 4.8	.143
.07	80(.07) = 5.6	.082
.08	80(.08) = 6.4	.046

Operating characteristic curves can be constructed for variables sampling plans as well as for attributes sampling plans. It is beyond the scope of this presentation to go into detail on this. The purpose here is merely to illustrate the concept of an OC curve and to show how its construction is based on an underlying *sampling distribution*.

AVERAGE QUALITY OF INSPECTED LOTS

An interesting feature of acceptance sampling is that the level of inspection automatically adjusts to the quality of lots being inspected, assuming rejected lots are subjected to 100 percent inspection. The OC curve reveals that the greater the percentage of defectives in a lot, the less likely the lot is to be accepted. Generally speaking, good lots have a high probability of being accepted, and bad lots have a low probability of being accepted. If the lots being inspected are mostly good, few will end up going through 100 percent inspection. But the poorer the quality of the lots, the greater the number of lots that will come under closer scrutiny. This tends to improve overall quality of lots by weeding out defectives. In this way, the level of inspection is affected by lot quality.

Average outgoing quality

Average of inspected lots (100 percent) and uninspected lots (p).

If all lots have some given percentage of defectives, p, the **average outgoing quality** (AOQ) of the lots can be computed using the following formula, assuming defectives are replaced with good items.

$$AOQ = P_{ac} \times p\left(\frac{N - n}{N}\right) \qquad\qquad (10S{-}2)$$

where

$$P_{ac} = \text{Probability of accepting the lot}$$
$$p = \text{Fraction defective}$$
$$N = \text{Lot size}$$
$$n = \text{Sample size}$$

In practice, the last term is often omitted since it is usually close to 1.0 and therefore has little effect on the resulting values. The formula becomes

$$AOQ = P_{ac} \times p \qquad\qquad (10S{-}3)$$

Use this formula instead of the preceding one for computing AOQ values.

By allowing the percentage, p, to vary, a curve such as the one in the following example can be constructed in the same way that an OC curve is constructed. The curve illustrates the point that if lots are very good or very bad, the average outgoing quality will be high. The maximum point on the curve becomes apparent in the process of calculating values for the curve.

Example 2

∎

Construct the AOQ curve for this situation:

$$N = 500, \qquad n = 10, \qquad c = 1$$

Solution

Let values of p vary from .05 to .40 in steps of .05. The probabilities of acceptance, P_{ac}, can be read from Appendix B, Table D.

$$AOQ = P_{ac} \times p$$

p	P_{ac}	AOQ
.05	.9139	.046
.10	.7361	.074
.15	.5443	.082
.20	.3758	.075
.25	.2440	.061
.30	.1493	.045
.35	.0860	.030
.40	.0464	.019

The average outgoing quality limit (AOQL) appears to be just above 8 percent.

Problem

1. *Inspection.* A process for manufacturing shock absorbers for light trucks produces 5 percent defectives. Inspection cost per shock is $0.40, and 100 percent inspection generally catches all defectives, due to the nature of the inspection and the small volume produced. Any defectives installed on trucks must eventually be replaced at a cost of $12 per shock. Is 100 percent inspection justified?

**SOLVED
PROBLEMS**

Solution

Five percent of the output is defective. The expected cost per shock for replacement is thus $0.05(\$12) = 60$ cents. Since this is greater than the inspection cost per shock of 40 cents, 100 percent inspection is justified.

Problem

2. *Acceptance sampling.* Shipments of 300 boxes of glassware are received at a warehouse of a large department store. Random samples of five boxes are checked, and the lot is rejected if more than one box reveals breakage. Construct the OC curve for this plan.

Solution

When the sample size is less than five percent of the lot size, the binomial distribution can be used to obtain P_{ac} for various lot percentages defective. Here, $n/N = 5/300 = .017$, so the binomial can be used. A portion of the cumulative binomial table is shown below. Note that $c = 1$.

Cumulative binomial probabilities

	n	x	.05	.10	.15	.20	.25	.30
	5 ...	0	.7738	.5905	.4437	.3277	.2373	.1681
$c = 1$ →		1	.9974	.9185	.8352	.7373	.6328	.5282
		2	.9988	.9914	.9734	.9421	.8965	.8369
		3	1.0000	.9995	.9978	.9933	.9844	.9692
		4	1.0000	1.0000	.9999	.9997	.9990	.9976
		5	1.0000	1.0000	1.0000	1.0000	1.0000	1.0000

.35	.40	.45	.50	.55	.60	.65	.70	.75	.80
.1160	.0778	.0503	.0313	.0185	.0102	.0053	.0024	.0010	.0003
.4284	.3370	.2562	.1875	.1312	.0870	.0540	.0308	.0156	.0067
.7648	.6826	.5931	.5000	.4069	.3174	.2352	.1631	.1035	.0579
.9460	.9130	.8688	.8125	.7438	.6630	.5716	.4718	.3672	.2627
.9947	.9898	.9815	.9688	.9497	.9222	.8840	.8319	.7627	.6723
1.0000	1.0000	1.0000	1.0000	1.0000	1.0000	1.0000	1.0000	1.0000	1.0000

The table indicates that $P_{ac} = .9974$ when lot quality is 5 percent defective, .9185 for 10 percent defective, .8352 for 15 percent, and so on. The resulting curve is:

Problem

3. Develop the AOQ curve for the previous problem.

Solution

$$AOQ = P_{ac} \times p$$

(Values of lot quality, p, are taken from the portion of the binomial table shown.)

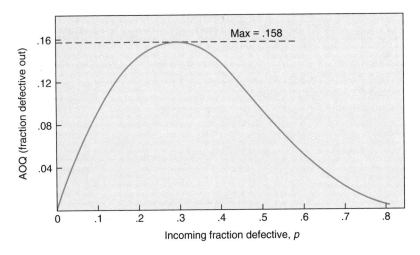

p	P_{ac}	AOQ	p	P_{ac}	AOQ
.05	.9974	.050	.45	.2562	.115
.10	.9185	.092	.50	.1875	.094
.15	.8352	.125	.55	.1312	.072
.20	.7373	.147	.60	.0870	.052
.25	.6328	.158	.65	.0540	.035
.30	.5258	.158	.70	.0380	.027
.35	.4284	.150	.75	.0156	.012
.40	.3370	.135	.80	.0067	.005

**DISCUSSION
AND REVIEW
QUESTIONS**

1. Answer these questions with respect to inspection:
   a. What level of inspection is optimal?
   b. What factors guide the decision of how much to inspect?
   c. What are the main considerations in choosing between centralized inspection and on-site inspection?
   d. What points are potential candidates for inspection?
2. What is the purpose of acceptance sampling?
3. How does acceptance sampling differ from process control?
4. What is an operating characteristic curve, and how is it useful in acceptance sampling?
5. What general factors govern the choice between single-sampling plans and multiple-sampling plans?
6. Briefly explain or define each of these terms:
   a. AOQ.   b. AOQL.   c. LTPD.   d. Alpha risk.   e. Beta risk.

PROBLEMS

1. An assembly operation for trigger mechanisms of a semiautomatic spray gun produces a small percentage of defective mechanisms. Management must decide whether to continue the current practice of 100 percent inspection or whether to replace defective mechanisms after final assembly, when all guns are inspected. Replacement at final assembly costs $30 each; inspection during trigger assembly costs $12 per hour for labor and overhead. The inspection rate is one trigger per minute.
   a. Would 100 percent inspection during trigger assembly be justified if there are (1) 4 percent defective? (2) 1 percent defective?
   b. At what point would management be indifferent between 100 percent inspection of triggers and only final inspection?
2. Random samples of $n = 20$ circuit breakers are tested for damage caused by shipment in each lot of 4,000 received. Lots with more than one defective are pulled and subjected to 100 percent inspection.
   a. Construct the OC curve for this sampling plan.
   b. Construct the AOQ curve for this plan, assuming defectives found during 100 percent inspection are replaced with good parts. What is the approximate AOQL?
3. Auditors use a technique called *discovery sampling* in which a random sample of items is inspected, and if any defectives are found, the entire lot of items being sampled is subjected to 100 percent inspection.
   a. Draw an OC curve for the case where a sample of 15 credit accounts will be inspected out of a total of 8,000 accounts.
   b. Draw an OC curve for the case where 150 accounts out of 8,000 accounts will be examined. (*Hint:* Use $p = .001, .002, .003, . . .$)
   c. Draw the AOQ curve for the preceding case, and estimate the AOQL.
4. Random samples of lots of textbooks are inspected for defectives just prior to shipment to the warehouse. Each lot contains 3,000 books.
   a. On a single sheet of graph paper, construct OC curves for $n = 100$ and (1) $c = 0$, (2) $c = 1$, and (3) $c = 2$. (*Hint:* Use $p = .001, .002, .003, . . .$)
   b. On a single sheet of graph paper, construct OC curves for $c = 2$ and (1) $n = 5$, (2) $n = 20$, and (3) $n = 120$.
   c. Construct AOQ curves for the first two cases in part *b*.
5. A manufacturer receives shipments of several thousand parts from a supplier every week. The manufacturer has the option of conducting a 100 percent inspection before accepting the parts or not. The decision is based on a random sample of 15 parts. If parts are not inspected, defectives become apparent during a later assembly operation,

at which time replacement cost is $6.25 per unit. Inspection cost for 100 percent inspection is $1 per unit.

a. At what fraction defective would the manufacturer be indifferent between 100 percent inspection and leaving discovery of defectives until the later assembly operation?

b. For the sample size being used, what is the maximum number of sample defectives that would cause the lot to be passed without 100 percent inspection (based on your answer to part a)?

c. If the shipment actually contains 5 percent defectives:
   (1) What is the probability that it would be accepted without 100 percent inspection?
   (2) What is the probability it would be rejected in favor of 100 percent inspection?
   (3) What would the correct decision be?
   (4) What is the probability of a Type I error? Type II error?

d. Answer the questions in part c for a shipment that contains 20 percent defectives.

6. (Refer to the preceding problem, part c). Suppose there are two defectives in the sample.

a. If the acceptance number is $c = 1$, what decision should be made? What type of error is possible?

b. If the acceptance number is $c = 3$, what decision should be made? What type of error is possible?

c. Determine the average outgoing quality for each of these percent defectives if $c = 1$.
   (1) 5 percent.
   (2) 10 percent.
   (3) 15 percent.
   (4) 20 percent.

AGGREGATE PLANNING

11

After completing this chapter, you should be able to:

1. Explain what aggregate planning is and how it is useful.

2. Identify the variables that decision makers have to work with in aggregate planning and some of the possible strategies they can use.

3. Describe some of the graphical and quantitative techniques planners use.

4. Prepare aggregate plans and compute their costs.

Aggregate planning

Medium-range capacity planning, usually covering 2 to 12 months.

In the spectrum of production planning, **aggregate planning** is medium-range capacity planning that typically covers a time horizon of anywhere from 2 to 12 months. It is particularly useful for organizations that experience seasonal or other fluctuations in either demand or capacity. The goal of aggregate planning is to achieve a production plan that will effectively utilize the organization's resources to satisfy expected demand. Planners must make decisions on output rates, employment levels and changes, inventory levels and changes, back orders, and subcontracting.

The purpose of this chapter is to introduce the concept of aggregate planning, discuss the pertinent costs and possible strategies, and illustrate some of the different approaches used in aggregate planning.

INTRODUCTION

THE CONCEPT OF AGGREGATION

Aggregate planning is essentially a "big picture" approach to planning. Planners generally try to avoid focusing on individual products or services—unless, of course, the organization has only one major product or service. Instead, they focus on overall, or aggregate, capacity.

For purposes of aggregate planning, it is often convenient to think of capacity in terms of labor hours or machine hours per period, or output rates (barrels per period, units per period), without worrying about how much of this item or how much of that item will actually be involved. This approach frees planners to make decisions about the use of resources in a general way without having to get into the complexities of individual product or service requirements. Often aggregation is done by product groupings, where products (or services) with similar requirements are lumped together for planning purposes. This makes the problem of obtaining an acceptable unit of aggregation easier since different product groupings may lend themselves to different aggregate measures.

It is useful to think of aggregate planning as a *macro approach* to developing a production plan. For instance, consider the task of planning a vegetable garden. Aggregate planning would consist of deciding on the overall size (capacity) of the garden; taking into account how much time and effort the gardener is willing to commit to the garden for preparing the soil, planting, weeding, watering, and fertilizing; and calculating the amount of funds available for plants, seeds, and supplies. In addition, the gardener must consider how much output is desired (e.g., enough to feed a family of four). This can be done without getting into the details of precisely how many tomato plants or cucumber plants there will be. Decisions of that nature are best left until the broad plans have been worked out.

Now consider how aggregate planning might work in a manufacturing setting. Think of an automobile manufacturer that makes a variety of cars and trucks. For purposes of aggregate planning, a decision on the number of cars and number of trucks to be produced will be made without specifying the breakdown of two-door versus four-door cars, options, etc. Similarly, a decision on four-cylinder and six-cylinder engines will be made without concern for which engines will go with which cars or trucks. Planners will generally take into account the expected demand for cars, trucks, and engine blocks and the available capacity for making those items. If expected demand and capacity are approximately equal, planners will devote their efforts to meeting demand as efficiently as possible. If capacity exceeds demand, advertising and promotion might be realistic options. If capacity is less than demand, contracting some of the work to outside firms may be an option. In any event, planners will be looking at aggregate measures of capacity in making their decisions.

Finally, consider how aggregate planning might work in a large department store. Space allocation is often an aggregate decision. That is, a manager might decide to allocate 20 percent of the available space in the clothing section to women's sportswear, 30 percent to juniors, and so on, without regard to what brand names will be offered, how much of juniors will be slacks, and so on. The aggregate measure might be square feet of space or racks of clothing.

In each of these examples, we see that an aggregate approach permits planners to make general decisions about intermediate-range capacity without having to deal with highly specific details. They can instead concern themselves with overall decisions on levels of output, employment, and inventories. They do this by lumping demand for all products into one or a few categories, and planning on that level.

AGGREGATE PLANNING IN PERSPECTIVE

Organizations become involved with capacity decisions on three levels: long term, intermediate term, and short term. Long-term decisions relate to product and service selection (i.e., determining which products or services to offer), facility size and location, equipment decisions, and layout of facilities. These long-term decisions essentially define the capacity constraints within which intermediate, or aggregate, planning must function. Intermediate decisions, as we have said, relate to general levels of employment, output, and inventories. These, in turn, define the boundaries within which short-range capacity decisions must be made. Thus, short-term decisions essentially relate to deciding on the best way to achieve desired results within the constraints resulting from long-term and intermediate-term decisions. These involve scheduling jobs, machine loading, job sequencing, and the like. The three levels of capacity decisions are highlighted in Table 11–1.

Long-term capacity decisions were covered in Chapter 6, and scheduling and related matters are covered in a later chapter. This chapter covers the intermediate capacity decisions.

AN OVERVIEW OF AGGREGATE PLANNING

Aggregate planning begins with a forecast of expected demand for the intermediate range. This is followed by a general plan to meet demand requirements by setting output, employment, and finished-goods inventory levels. A number of plans might be considered. Each plan must be examined in light of feasibility and cost. If a plan is reasonably good but has minor difficulties, it may be reworked. Conversely, a poor plan should be discarded and alternative plans considered until an acceptable one is uncovered. The production plan is essentially the output of aggregate planning.

THE PURPOSE AND SCOPE OF AGGREGATE PLANNING

In this section, we examine the basic problem that aggregate planning addresses— namely, the balancing of supply and demand—along with the purpose of aggregate planning, and the primary decision variable available to planners, and associated costs.

Table 11–1
———

Overview of
planning levels

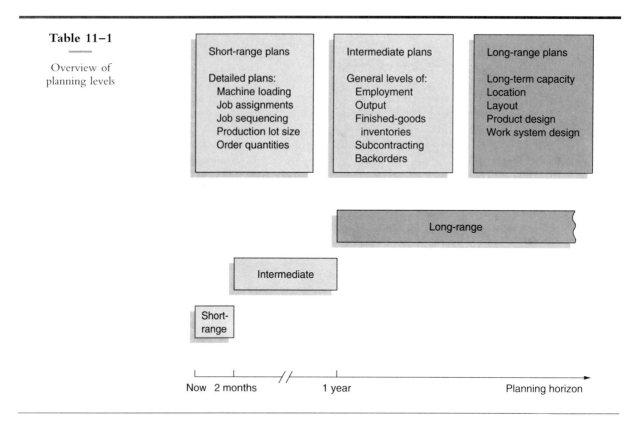

DEMAND AND CAPACITY

Aggregate planners are concerned with the *quantity* and the *timing* of expected demand. If total expected demand for the planning period is much different from available capacity over that same period, the major approach of planners will be either to increase demand (if demand is less than capacity) or increase capacity (if demand exceeds capacity). On the other hand, even if capacity and demand are approximately equal for the planning horizon as a whole, planners may still be faced with the problem of dealing with *uneven* demand within the planning interval. The problem of uneven demand is illustrated in Figure 11–1. Note that in some periods, expected demand exceeds projected capacity, in others expected demand is less than projected capacity, and in some periods the two are roughly equal. The task of aggregate planners is to achieve rough equality of demand and capacity over the entire planning horizon.

THE PURPOSE OF AGGREGATE PLANNING

The purpose of aggregate planning is to develop a feasible production plan on an aggregate level that achieves a balance of expected demand and supply. Moreover, planners are usually concerned with minimizing the cost of the production plan, although cost is not the only consideration.

INPUTS TO AGGREGATE PLANNING

There are a number of important informational needs for effective aggregate planning. First, the available resources over the planning period must be known, includ-

Figure 11–1

Projected demand for a 12-period planning horizon

Part of Cincinnati Milacron's aggregate plan for competing with Japanese imports was a new team approach and reduced development time. The team and the new Vista plastic injection molding machine are shown here. Cincinnati Milacron CEO Harold Faig is featured on the first page of the chapter.

ing facilities. Then, a forecast of expected demand must be available. Finally, planners must take into account any policies regarding changes in employment levels (e.g., some organizations view layoffs as very undesirable, so they would exclude that option from consideration or perhaps use it only as a last resort).

Table 11–2 lists the major inputs to aggregate planning.

DEMAND AND CAPACITY OPTIONS

Management has a wide range of decision options at its disposal for purposes of aggregate planning. These include pricing changes, promotion, backlogging orders, using overtime, using part-time workers, subcontracting, adding or deleting extra shifts, and stockpiling inventories. Some of these, such as pricing and promotion,

Table 11–2	Resources	Costs
Aggregate planning inputs	Workforce/production rates	Inventory carrying cost
	Facilities and equipment	Back orders
	Demand forecast	Hiring/firing
		Overtime
	Policy statements on workforce changes	Inventory changes
	Subcontracting	Subcontracting
	Overtime	
	Inventory levels/changes	
	Back orders	

represent options that are intended to alter the pattern of demand. Others, such as using part-time workers, overtime, and subcontracting, represent options that are intended to alter capacity or supply. We can examine these options in more detail.

Demand Options   The basic demand options are the following:

1. *Pricing.*   Pricing differentials are commonly used to shift demand from peak periods to off-peak periods. Some airlines, for example, offer lower fares for mid-week travel and charge higher fares other times. Many airlines also offer lower fares for night travel. Similarly, movie theaters may offer reduced rates for matinees, and some restaurants offer "early bird specials" in an attempt to shift some of the heavier dinner demand to an earlier time that traditionally has less traffic. Some restaurants may also offer smaller portions at reduced rates, and most have smaller portions and prices for children. The smaller portions act to decrease demand. To the extent that pricing is effective, demand will be shifted so that it more closely corresponds to capacity, albeit for an *opportunity cost* that represents the lost profit stemming from capacity insufficient to meet demand during certain periods.

An important factor to consider is the *degree* of price elasticity for the product or service; the more the elasticity, the more effective pricing will be in influencing demand patterns.

2. *Promotion.*   Advertising and other forms of promotion, such as displays and direct marketing, can sometimes be very effective in shifting demand so that it conforms more closely to capacity. Obviously, timing of these efforts and knowledge of response rates and response patterns will be needed to achieve the desired results. Unlike pricing policy, there is much less control over the timing of demand here; there is always the risk that promotion can worsen the condition it was intended to improve.

3. *Backorders.*   An organization can shift demand to other periods by allowing back orders. Hence, orders are taken in one period and deliveries promised for a later period. The success of this approach depends on how willing customers are to wait for delivery. Moreover, the cost associated with back orders can be difficult to pin down since it would include lost sales, annoyed or disappointed customers, and perhaps additional paperwork.

4. *New demand.*   Many organizations are faced with the problem of having to provide products or services for peak demand in situations where demand is very uneven. For instance, demand for public transportation tends to be very intense during the morning and late afternoon rush hours but much lighter at other times. Creating new demand for the buses at other times (e.g., trips by schools, clubs, and

senior citizen groups) would make use of the excess capacity during those slack times. Similarly, many fast-food restaurants are open for breakfast in order to use their capacities more fully, and some landscaping firms in northern climates use their equipment during the winter months for snow plowing. Manufacturing firms that experience seasonal demands for certain products (e.g., snowblowers) are sometimes able to develop a demand for a complementary product (e.g., lawn mowers, garden equipment) that makes use of the same production processes. They thereby achieve a more consistent use of labor, equipment, and facilities.

Capacity Options   The basic options for altering the availability of capacity (supply) are the following:

1. *Hire and fire workers.*   The extent to which operations are labor intensive determines the impact that changes in the level of a work force will have on capacity. The resource requirements of each worker can also be a factor. For instance, if a supermarket with 14 checkout lines generally has 10 operating, an additional four checkout workers could be added. Hence, the ability to add workers is constrained at some point by other resources needed to support the workers. Conversely, there may be a lower limit on the number of workers needed to maintain a viable operation (e.g., a skeleton crew).

Union contracts may restrict the amount of hiring and firing a company can do. Moreover, because firing and laying off can present serious problems for workers, some firms have policies that either prohibit or limit downward adjustments to a work force. On the other hand, hiring presumes an available supply of workers. This may change from time to time and, at certain times of low supply, have an impact on the ability of an organization to pursue this approach.

Use of hiring and firing entails certain costs. Hiring costs include recruitment, screening, and training to bring new workers "up to speed." And quality may suffer. Some savings may occur if workers who have recently been laid off are rehired. Firing costs include severance pay, the cost of realigning the remaining work force, and potential bad feelings toward the firm on the part of fired workers, as well as some loss of morale for workers who are retained (i.e., in spite of company assurances, some workers will nevertheless believe that they may also be laid off in time).

An increasing number of organizations view workers as assets rather than as variable costs, and would not consider this approach. Similarly, companies that have life-time employment security would not use this approach. Instead, they might use slack time for maintenance, problem solving, or education of workers.

2. *Overtime/slack time.*   Use of overtime or slack time is a less severe method for changing capacity than hiring and firing workers, and it can be used across the board or selectively as needed. It can also be implemented more quickly than hiring and firing and allows the firm to maintain a steady base of employees. The use of overtime can be especially attractive in dealing with seasonal demand peaks by reducing the need to hire and train people who will have to be laid off during the off season. It also maintains a skilled work force and allows employees a chance to increase earnings. Moreover, in situations that involve crews, it is often necessary to use a full crew rather than to hire one or two additional people. Thus, having the entire crew work overtime would be preferable to hiring some extra people.

It should be noted that some union contracts allow workers to refuse overtime. In those cases, it may be difficult to muster a full crew to work overtime or to get an entire production line into operation after regular hours. And although workers often like the additional income overtime can generate, they may not appreciate having to work on short notice or the fluctuations in income that result. Still other considerations relate to the fact that overtime often results in lower productivity, poorer quality, more accidents, and increased payroll costs, whereas idle time results in less efficient use of machines and other fixed assets.

3. *Part-time workers.*   In certain instances, the use of part-time workers is a viable option—much depends on the nature of the work, training and skills needed, and union agreements. Seasonal work requiring low-to-moderate job skills lends itself to part-time workers, who generally cost less than regular workers in both hourly wages and fringe benefits. However, unions may regard such workers unfavorably because they typically do not pay union dues and may lessen the power of unions. Department stores, restaurants, and supermarkets make use of part-time workers. So do parks and recreation departments, resorts, travel agencies, hotels, and other service organizations with seasonal demands. In order to be successful, these organizations must be able to hire part-time employees when they are needed.

4. *Inventories.*   The use of finished-goods inventories allows firms to produce goods in one period and sell or ship them in another period, albeit at a cost of holding or carrying those goods as inventory until they are needed. The cost includes not only storage costs and the cost of money tied up that could be invested elsewhere, but also the cost of insurance, obsolescence, deterioration, spoilage, breakage, and so on. In essence, inventories can be built up during periods when production capacity exceeds demand and drawn down in periods when demand exceeds production capacity.

This method is more amenable to manufacturing than services since manufactured goods can be stored whereas services generally cannot. However, an analogous approach used by services is to make efforts to streamline services (e.g., standard forms) or otherwise do a portion of the service during slack periods (e.g., organize the workplace). In spite of these possibilities, services tend to be unable to make much use of inventories to alter capacity requirements.

5. *Subcontracting.*   Subcontracting enables planners to acquire temporary capacity, although it affords less control over the output and may lead to higher costs as well as quality problems. The question of whether to make or buy (in a case that involves manufacturing) or whether to perform a service or hire someone else to do the work generally depends on such factors as available capacity, relative expertise, quality considerations, cost, and the amount and stability of demand.

In some cases, a firm might choose to perform part of the work itself and let others handle the rest in order to maintain flexibility and as a hedge against loss of a subcontractor. Moreover, this gives the organization a bargaining tool in negotiations with contractors and a head start if it decides at a later date to take over the operation entirely.

BASIC STRATEGIES FOR MEETING UNEVEN DEMAND

As we see, managers have a wide range of decision options they can consider for achieving a balance of demand and capacity in aggregate planning. Since the options that are most suited to influencing demand generally fall more in the realm of marketing than in operations (with the exception of backlogging), we shall concentrate on the capacity options, which are in the realm of operations but include the use of back orders.

There are a number of strategies aggregate planners might adopt. Some of the more prominent ones are:

1. Maintain a level work force.
2. Maintain a steady output rate.
3. Match demand period by period.
4. Use a combination of decision variables.

There are other possible strategies that we might consider, but these will suffice to give you a sense of how aggregate planning operates in a vast number of organizations. The first three strategies are "pure" strategies in that each has a single focal point; the last strategy is "mixed" in that it lacks the single focus. Under the **level capacity strategy**, variations in demand are met by using some combination of inventories, overtime, part-time workers, subcontracting, and back ordering. The essence is to maintain a steady rate of *regular-time* output, although *total* output could vary. Maintaining a steady rate of output implies absorbing demand variations with inventories, subcontracting, or backlogging. Matching capacity to demand implies a **chase demand strategy**; the planned output for any period would be the expected demand for that period.

Many organizations find a level work force strategy very appealing. Since work force changes through hiring and firing can have a major impact on the lives and morale of employees and can be disruptive for managers, organizations often prefer to handle uneven demand in other ways. Moreover, changes in work force size can be very costly, and there is always the risk that there will not be a sufficient pool of workers with the appropriate skills when needed. Aside from these considerations, such changes can involve a significant amount of paperwork. Unions tend to favor a level work force because the freedom to hire and fire workers diminishes union strengths.

In order to maintain a constant level of output and still meet demand requirements, an organization must resort to some combination of subcontracting, backlogging, and use of inventories to absorb fluctuations. Subcontracting requires an investment in evaluating sources of supply as well as possible increased costs, less control over output, and perhaps quality considerations. Backlogs can lead to lost sales, increased record keeping, and lower levels of customer service. Allowing inventories to absorb fluctuations can entail substantial costs by having money tied up in inventories, having to maintain relatively large storage facilities, and incurring other costs related to inventories. Furthermore, inventories are not usually an alternative for service-oriented organizations. However, there are certain advantages, such as minimum costs of recruitment and training, minimum overtime and idle-time costs, fewer morale problems, and stable use of equipment and facilities.

A chase strategy presupposes a great deal of ability and willingness on the part of managers to be flexible in adjusting to demand. A major advantage of this approach is that inventories can be kept relatively low, which can yield substantial savings for an organization. A major disadvantage is the lack of stability in operations—the atmosphere is one of dancing to demand's tune. When forecast and reality differ, morale can suffer since it quickly becomes obvious to all that efforts have been wasted.

Organizations may opt for a strategy that involves some combination of decision variables without a single guiding focus. This allows managers greater flexibility in dealing with uneven demand and perhaps in experimenting with a wide variety

Level capacity strategy

Maintaining a steady rate of regular-time output while meeting variations in demand by a combination of options.

Chase demand strategy

Matching capacity to demand; the planned output for a period would be the expected demand for that period.

IBM planners need to balance large product lines. Many of these computers use some of the same parts, labor, and assembly facilities so good aggregate planning is necessary to avoid scheduling conflicts or parts shortages and match demand.

of approaches. However, the absence of a clear focus may lead to an erratic approach and confusion on the part of employees.

CHOOSING A STRATEGY

Whatever strategy an organization is considering, two important factors are *company policy* and *costs*. Company policy may set constraints on the available options or the extent to which they can be used. For instance, company policy may discourage firing and layoffs except under extreme conditions. Similarly, subcontracting may not be a viable alternative due to the desire to maintain secrecy about some aspect of the manufacturing of a product (e.g., a secret formula or blending process). Often, union agreements impose restrictions. For example, a union contract may specify both minimum and maximum numbers of hours part-time workers can be used.

As a general rule, aggregate planners seek to match supply and demand within the constraints imposed on them by policies or agreements and at minimum cost. In fact, alternatives are usually evaluated in terms of their overall costs. In the next section, a number of different techniques for aggregate planning are described along with some examples of cost evaluation of alternative plans.

TECHNIQUES FOR AGGREGATE PLANNING

Numerous techniques can be used to help decision makers with the task of aggregate planning. Generally, they fall into one of two categories: informal trial-and-error techniques and mathematical techniques. In practice, the informal techniques are more commonly used. However, a considerable amount of research has been devoted to mathematical techniques, and even though they are not widely used, they often serve as a basis for comparing the effectiveness of alternative techniques for aggregate planning. Thus, it will be instructive to briefly examine them as well as the informal techniques.

A general procedure for aggregate planning consists of the following steps:

1. Determine demand for each period.

2. Determine capacities (regular time, overtime, subcontracting) for each period.

3. Determine company or departmental policies that are pertinent (e.g., maintain a safety stock of 5 percent of demand, maintain a reasonably stable work force).

4. Determine unit costs for regular time, overtime, subcontracting, holding inventories, back orders, and other relevant costs.

5. Develop alternative plans and compute the cost for each.

6. If satisfactory plans emerge, select the one that best satisfies objectives. Otherwise, return to step 5.

It can be helpful to use a worksheet that summarizes demand, capacity, and cost for each plan, such as the one illustrated in Table 11–3. In addition, graphs can be used to guide development of alternatives.

Table 11–3

Worksheet

Period	1	2	3	4	5	Total
Forecast						
Output						
Regular						
Overtime						
Subcontract						
Output − Forecast						
Inventory						
Beginning						
Ending						
Average						
Backlog						
Costs:						
Output						
Regular						
Overtime						
Subcontract						
Hire/Fire						
Inventory						
Back orders						
Total						

INFORMAL TECHNIQUES

Informal approaches consist of developing simple tables or graphs that enable planners to visually compare projected demand requirements with existing capacity, and this provides them with a basis for developing alternative plans for achieving intermediate-range goals. Alternatives are usually evaluated in terms of their overall costs. The chief disadvantage of such techniques is that they do not necessarily result in the optimal aggregate plan.

Very often, graphs can be used to guide the development of alternatives. Some planners prefer cumulative graphs, and others prefer to see a period-by-period breakdown of a plan. For instance, Figure 11–2 shows a cumulative graph for a plan with steady output (the slope of the dashed line represents the production rate) and inventory absorption of demand variations. Figure 11–3 shows a period-by-period breakdown of the same plan. The obvious advantage of a graph is that it provides a visual portrayal of a plan. The choice between these two types of graphs depends on the preference of the planner.

Figure 11–2

A cumulative graph and inventory profile

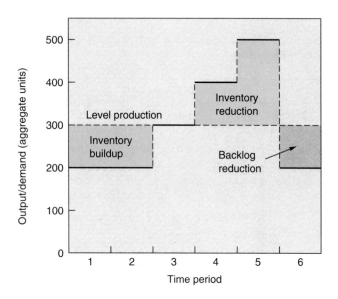

Figure 11–3

Level production and fluctuations in demand absorbed by inventory

Two examples will be used to illustrate the development and comparison of aggregate plans. In the first example, regular output is held steady, with inventory absorbing demand variations. This plan is portrayed in Figures 11–2 and 11–3. In the second example, a lower rate of regular output is used, supplemented by use of overtime. In both examples, some backlogs are allowed to build up.

These examples and other examples and problems in this chapter are based on the following assumptions:

1. The regular output capacity is the same in all periods. No allowance is made for holidays, different numbers of workdays in different months, and so on. This has been done for simplicity and ease of computation.

2. Cost (backlog, inventory, subcontracting, etc.) is a linear function composed of unit cost and number of units. This is often a reasonable approximation to reality, although there may only be narrow ranges over which this is true. Cost is sometimes more of a step function.

3. Plans are feasible. That is, sufficient inventory capacity exists to accommodate a plan, subcontractors with appropriate quality and capacity are standing by, and changes in output can be made as needed.

4. All costs associated with a decision option can be represented by a lump sum or by unit costs that are independent of the quantity involved. Again, a step function may be more realistic; but for purposes of illustration as well as simplicity, this assumption is appropriate.

5. Cost figures can be reasonably estimated and are constant for the planning horizon.

6. Inventories are built up and drawn down at a uniform rate throughout each period, and output occurs at a uniform rate throughout each period. However, backlogs are treated as if they exist for an entire period, even though in periods where they initially appear, they would tend to build up toward the end of the period. Hence, this assumption is a bit unrealistic for some periods, but it simplifies computations.

Example 1

∎

Planners for a company are about to prepare the aggregate plan that will cover six periods. They have assembled the following information:

Period	1	2	3	4	5	6	Total
Forecast	200	200	300	400	500	200	1,800

Costs:
　Output
　　Regular time　=　$2 per unit
　　Overtime　=　$3 per unit
　　Subcontract　=　$6 per unit
　Inventory　=　$1 per unit per period on average inventory
　Back orders　=　$5 per unit per period

They now want to evaluate a plan that calls for a steady rate of regular-time output, mainly using inventory to absorb the uneven demand but allowing some backlog. They intend to start with zero inventory on hand in the first period. Prepare an aggregate plan and determine its cost using the preceding information. Assume a level output rate of 300 units per period with regular time (i.e., 1,800/6 = 300). Note that the planned ending inventory is zero. There are 15 workers.

Solution

Period	1	2	3	4	5	6	Total
Forecast	200	200	300	400	500	200	1,800
Output							
Regular	300	300	300	300	300	300	1,800
Overtime	—	—	—	—	—	—	
Subcontract	—	—	—	—	—	—	
Output − Forecast	100	100	0	(100)	(200)	100	0
Inventory							
Beginning	0	100	200	200	100	0	
Ending	100	200	200	100	0	0	
Average	50	150	200	150	50	0	600
Backlog	0	0	0	0	100	0	100
Costs:							
Output							
Regular	$600	600	600	600	600	600	$3,600
Overtime	—	—	—	—	—	—	
Subcontract	—	—	—	—	—	—	
Hire/Fire	—	—	—	—	—	—	
Inventory	$ 50	150	200	150	50	0	$ 600
Back orders	$ 0	0	0	0	500	0	$ 500
Total	$650	750	800	750	1,150	600	$4,700

Note that the total regular-time output of 1,800 units equals the total expected demand. Ending inventory equals beginning inventory plus or minus the quantity

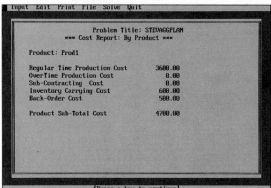

The first two screens show input for Example 1 using Lotfi and Pegels DSS-POM (2.1c). The third screen shows the production schedule solution and the fourth shows cost reports for six periods.

Output − Forecast. Average inventory equals one half the sum of beginning and ending inventories. If Output − Forecast is negative, inventory is decreased in that period by that amount. If insufficient inventory exists, a backlog equal to the shortage amount appears, as in period 5. This is taken care of using the excess output in period 6.

The costs were computed as follows. Regular cost in each period equals 300 units × $2 per unit or $600. Inventory cost equals average inventory × $1 per unit. Back order cost is $5 per unit. The total cost for this plan is $4,700.

Note that the first two quantities in each column are givens. The remaining quantities in the upper portion of the table were determined working down each column, beginning with the first column. The costs were then computed based on the quantities in the upper part of the table.

After reviewing the plan developed in the preceding example, planners have decided to develop an alternative plan. They have learned that one person is about to retire from the company. Rather than replace him, they would like to stay with the smaller work force and use overtime to make up for the lost output. The reduced regular-time output is 280 units per period. The maximum amount of overtime output per period is 40 units. Develop a plan and compare it to the previous one.

Example 2

(continued)

Example 2

(concluded)

Solution

Period	1	2	3	4	5	6	Total
Forecast	200	200	300	400	500	200	1,800
Output							
Regular	280	280	280	280	280	280	1,680
Overtime	0	0	40	40	40	0	120
Subcontract	—	—	—	—	—	—	
Output − Forecast	80	80	20	(80)	(180)	80	0
Inventory							
Beginning	0	80	160	180	100	0	
Ending	80	160	180	100	0	0	
Average	40	120	170	140	50	0	520
Backlog	0	0	0	0	80	0	80
Costs:							
Output							
Regular	$560	560	560	560	560	560	$3,360
Overtime	0	0	120	120	120	0	$ 360
Subcontract	—	—	—	—	—	—	
Hire/Fire	—	—	—	—	—	—	
Inventory	$ 40	120	170	140	50	0	$ 520
Back orders	$ 0	0	0	0	400	0	$ 400
Total	$600	680	850	820	1,130	560	$4,640

The amount of overtime that must be scheduled has to make up for lost output of 20 units per period for six periods, which is 120. This is scheduled toward the center of the planning horizon since that is where the bulk of demand occurs. Scheduling it earlier would increase inventory carrying costs; scheduling it later would increase the backlog.

Overall, the total cost for this plan is $4,640, which is $60 less than for the previous plan. Regular-time production cost and inventory cost are down, but there is overtime cost. However, this plan achieves savings in back order cost, making it somewhat less costly overall than the other plan.

Example 3

A third option is to use temporary workers to fill in during months of high demand. Suppose that it costs an additional $100 to hire and train a temporary worker, and that a temporary worker can produce at the rate of 15 units per period (compared to the rate of 20 units per period for regular workers).

Dividing the number of units needed (120) by the output rate of 15 per temporary worker, we find that 8 worker-periods are needed (e.g., 2 workers for 4 months each, 4 workers for 2 months each, etc.).

Noting that Periods 4 and 5 have the heaviest demand, we might suggest to try using 4 temporary workers for 2 months each (i.e., Periods 4 and 5). The results are summarized in the following plan.

Period	1	2	3	4	5	6	Total
Forecast	200	200	300	400	500	200	1,800
Output							
Regular	280	280	280	340	340	280	1,800
Overtime	—	—	—	—	—	—	
Subcontract	—	—	—	—	—	—	
Output − Forecast	80	80	(20)	(60)	(160)	80	0
Inventory							
Beginning	0	80	160	140	80	0	
Ending	80	160	140	80	0	0	
Average	40	120	150	110	40	0	460
Backlog	0	0	0	0	80	0	80
Costs:							
Output							
Regular	$560	$560	$560	$680	$680	$560	$3,600
Overtime	—	—	—	—	—	—	
Subcontract	—	—	—	—	—	—	
Hire/Fire	$0	0	0	400	400	0	$ 800
Inventory	$40	$120	$150	$110	$ 40	0	$ 460
Back orders	$0	0	0	0	400	0	$ 400
Total	$600	680	710	1,190	1,520	560	$5,260

Overall, the total cost for this plan is $5,260, making it the most expensive of the three alternatives examined.

These are only three of many possible options that could be tried. Perhaps some of the others would result in a lower cost. With trial and error, you can never be completely sure you have identified the lowest-cost alternative unless every possible alternative is evaluated. Of course, the purpose of these examples is to illustrate the process of developing and evaluating an aggregate plan, rather than to find the lowest-cost plan. Some of the problems at the end of the chapter involve still other alternatives for this situation.

In practice, successful achievement of a good plan depends on the resourcefulness and the persistence of the planner. And a good computer package can eliminate the computational burden of trial-and-error techniques.

MATHEMATICAL TECHNIQUES

A number of mathematical techniques have been proposed over the last two decades to handle aggregate planning. They range from mathematical programming models to heuristic and computer search models. This section briefly describes some of the better-known techniques.

Linear Programming   Linear-programming models are methods for obtaining optimal solutions to problems involving the allocation of scarce resources in terms of cost minimization or profit maximization. With aggregate planning, the goal is

Table 11–4
———
Transportation notation for aggregate planning

r = Regular production cost per unit
t = Overtime cost per unit
s = Subcontracting cost per unit
h = Holding cost per unit per period
b = Backorder cost per unit per period
n = Number of periods in planning horizon

		Period 1	Period 2	Period 3	. . .	Ending inventory period n	Unused capacity	Capacity
Period	Beginning inventory	0	h	$2h$	. . .	nh	0	I_0
1	Regular time	r	$r + h$	$r + 2h$	. . .	$r + nh$	0	R_1
	Overtime	t	$t + h$	$t + 2h$	. . .	$t + nh$	0	O_1
	Subcontract	s	$s + h$	$s + 2h$	. . .	$s + nh$	0	S_1
2	Regular time	$r + b$	r	$r + h$	. . .	$r + (n - 1)h$	0	R_2
	Overtime	$t + b$	t	$t + h$	. . .	$t + (n - 1)h$	0	O_2
	Subcontract	$s + b$	s	$s + h$	. . .	$s + (n - 1)h$	0	S_2
3	Regular time	$r + 2b$	$r + b$	r	. . .	$r + (n - 2)h$	0	R_3
	Overtime	$t + 2b$	$t + b$	t	. . .	$t + (n - 2)h$	0	O_3
	Subcontract	$s + 2b$	$s + b$	s	. . .	$s + (n - 2)h$	0	S_3
	Demand				. . .			Total

usually to minimize the sum of costs related to regular labor time, overtime, subcontracting, inventory holding costs, and costs associated with changing the size of the work force. Constraints involve capacities of work force, inventories, and subcontracting.

E. H. Bowman proposed formulating the problem in terms of a transportation-type programming model (described in detail in the supplement to Chapter 9) as a way to obtain aggregate plans that would match capacities with demand requirements and minimize costs.[1] In order to use this approach, planners must identify capacity (supply) of regular time, overtime, subcontracting, and inventory on a period-by-period basis, as well as related costs of each variable.

The notation and setup of a transportation table are shown in Table 11–4. Note the systematic way that costs change as you move across a row from left to right.

———
[1] E. H. Bowman, "Production Planning by the Transportation Method of Linear Programming," *Journal of Operations Research Society* 4 (February 1956), pp. 100–103.

Note that regular cost, overtime cost, and subcontracting cost are at their lowest when the output is consumed (delivered, etc.) in the same period it is produced (at the intersection of period 1 row and column for regular cost, at the intersection of period 2 row and column for regular cost, and so on). If goods are made available in one period but carried over to later periods (i.e., moving across a row), holding costs are incurred at the rate of h per period. Thus, holding goods for two periods results in a unit cost of $2h$, irrespective of whether the goods came from regular production, overtime, or subcontracting. Conversely, in the case of back orders, the unit cost increases as you move across a row from right to left, beginning at the intersection of a row and column for the same period (e.g., period 3). For instance, if some goods are produced in period 3 to satisfy back orders from period 2, a unit back order cost of b is incurred. And if goods in period 3 are used to satisfy back orders two periods back (e.g., from period 1), a unit cost of $2b$ is incurred. Unused capacity is generally given a unit cost of 0, although it is certainly possible to insert an actual cost if that seems relevant. Finally, beginning inventory is given a unit cost of 0 if it is used to satisfy demand in period 1. However, if it is held over for use in later periods, a holding cost of h per unit is added for each period. If the inventory is to be held for the entire planning horizon, a total unit cost of h times the number of periods, n, will be incurred.

Example 4 illustrates the setup and final solution of a transportation model of an aggregate planning problem.

Given the following information, set up the problem in a transportation table and solve for the minimum-cost plan:

Example 4

| | **Period** | | |
	1	2	3
Demand	550	700	750
Capacity			
Regular	500	500	500
Overtime	50	50	50
Subcontract	120	120	100
Beginning inventory	100		

Costs
Regular time .... $60 per unit
Overtime .... 80 per unit
Subcontract .... 90 per unit
Inventory carrying cost .... $1 per unit per month
Backorder cost .... $3 per unit per month

Solution

The transportation table and solution (see the supplement to Chapter 9) are shown in Table 11–5. Some of the entries require additional explanation:

(continued)

Example 4

(concluded)

a. In this example, inventory carrying costs are $1 per unit per period (costs are shown in the upper right-hand corner of each cell in the table). Hence, units produced in one period and carried over to a later period will incur a holding cost that is a linear function of the length of time held.

Table 11–5

Transportation solution

	Supply from	Demand for — Period 1	Demand for — Period 2	Demand for — Period 3	Unused capacity (dummy)	Total capacity available (supply)
Period	Beginning inventory	[0] 100	[1]	[2]	[0]	100
1	Regular time	[60] 450	[61] 50	[62]	[0]	500
	Overtime	[80]	[81] 50	[82]	[0]	50
	Subcontract	[90]	[91] 30	[92]	[0] 90	120
2	Regular time	[63]	[60] 500	[61]	[0]	500
	Overtime	[83]	[80] 50	[81]	[0]	50
	Subcontract	[93]	[90] 20	[91] 100	[0]	120
3	Regular time	[66]	[63]	[60] 500	[0]	500
	Overtime	[86]	[83]	[80] 50	[0]	50
	Subcontract	[96]	[93]	[90] 100	[0]	100
	Demand	550	700	750	90	2,090

b. Linear-programming models of this type require that supply (capacity) and demand be equal. A dummy column has been added (unused capacity) to satisfy that requirement. Since it does not "cost" anything extra to not use capacity in this case, cell costs of $0 have been assigned.

c. No backlogs were needed in this example.

d. The quantities (e.g., 100 and 450 in column 1) are the amounts of output or inventory that will be used to meet demand requirements. Thus, the demand of 550 units in period 1 will be met using 100 units from inventory and 450 obtained from regular-time output.

In a case where backlogs are not permitted, the cell costs for the backlog positions can be made prohibitively high so that no backlogs will appear in the solution.

The main limitations of LP models are the assumptions of linear relationships among variables, the inability to continuously adjust output rates, and the need to specify a single objective (e.g., minimize costs) instead of using multiple objectives (e.g., minimize cost while stabilizing the work force.)

Goal Programming **Goal programming** is a variation of linear programming that permits the user to specify multiple goals. One version involves the use of priority-based goals. The solution represents an attempt to optimize the goals according to priorities. Several applications of goal programming to aggregate planning have been reported in the literature.[2]

> **Goal programming**
> Variation of linear programming that specifies multiple goals according to priorities.

Linear Decision Rule Another optimizing technique, the **linear decision rule**, was developed during the 1950s by Charles Holt, Franco Modigliani, John Muth, and Herbert Simon.[3] It seeks to minimize the combined costs of regular payroll, hiring and layoffs, overtime, and inventory using a set of cost-approximating functions, three of which are *quadratic* (contain squared terms), to obtain a single quadratic equation. Using calculus, two linear equations (hence the name *linear decision rule*) can be derived from the quadratic equation. One of the equations can be used to plan the output for each period in the planning horizon, and the other can be used to plan the work force for each period.

> **Linear decision rule**
> Optimizing technique that seeks to minimize combined costs, using a set of cost-approximating functions to obtain a single quadratic equation.

Although the model has found some applications, its chief function seems to be as a benchmark against which proposed techniques can be evaluated. In practice, the model suffers from three limitations: (1) a specific type of cost function is assumed, (2) considerable effort must usually be expended in obtaining relevant cost data and developing cost functions for each organization, and (3) the method can produce solutions that are unfeasible or impractical.

Management Coefficients A heuristic model proposed by E. H. Bowman, **management coefficients**, attempts to incorporate previous managerial planning performance into a decision model.[4] The rationale for the model is based on improving performance rather than on trying to develop a "new" optimizing method. The procedure involves the use of multiple regression analysis to build a decision model.

> **Management coefficients**
> Heuristic technique that uses multiple regression analysis to build a decision model based on past managerial performance.

Parametric Production Planning A heuristic technique known as **parametric production planning** was proposed by C. H. Jones in the late 1960s.[5] The model uses a search routine to develop two decision rules for output and workforce size. In

> **Parametric production planning**
> Heuristic technique that uses a search routine to develop two decision rules for output and workforce size.

---

[2] See, for example, D. A. Goodman, "A New Approach to Scheduling Aggregate Production and Work Force," *AIIE Transactions* 5 (June 1973), pp. 153–41; and S. M. Lee and L. J. Moore, "A Practical Approach to Production Scheduling," *Production and Inventory Management* (1st quarter 1974), pp. 79–92.

[3] Charles C. Holt, Franco Modigliani, John F. Muth, and Herbert A. Simon, *Planning Production, Inventories and Work Force* (Englewood Cliffs, N.J.: Prentice Hall, 1960).

[4] E. H. Bowman, "Consistence and Optimality in Managerial Decision Making," *Management Science* 4 (January 1963), pp. 100–103.

[5] C. H. Jones, "Parametric Production Planning," *Mangement Science* 13, no. 11 (July 1967), pp. 843–66.

some respects, it is similar to the linear decision rule: It uses quadratic cost-approximating functions and provides two decision rules. Unlike the linear decision model, it can be used with essentially any cost function.

Simulation models

Computerized models that can be tested under many conditions to identify acceptable solutions to problems.

Simulation Models   A number of **simulation models** have been developed for aggregate planning. (Simulation is described in detail in the supplement to Chapter 17.) The essence of the models is the development of computerized models that can be tested under a variety of conditions in an attempt to identify reasonably acceptable (although not always optimal) solutions to problems.

All of the above models are summarized in Table 11–6.

Aggregate planning techniques other than trial and error do not appear to be widely used. Instead, in the majority of organizations, aggregate planning seems to be done more on the basis of experience, along with trial-and-error methods. It is difficult to say exactly why some of the mathematical techniques mentioned are not

Table 11–6	**Technique**	**Solution approach**	**Characteristics**
Summary of planning techniques	Graphical/ charting	Trial and error	Intuitively appealing, easy to understand; solution not necessarily optimal
	Linear programming	Optimizing	Computerized; linear assumptions not always valid
	Goal programming	Optimizing	Allows use of multiple goals
	Linear decision rule	Optimizing	Complex, requires considerable effort to obtain pertinent cost information and to construct model; cost assumptions not always valid
	Management coefficients	Heuristic	Uses multiple regression to incorporate past managerial performance into a model; attempts to use that as a base to improve performance
	Parametric planning	Heuristic	Uses a search routine to develop two decision rules
	Simulation	Trial and error	Computerized models allow managers to examine models under a variety of conditions

used to any great extent. We can only speculate. Perhaps the level of mathematical sophistication discourages greater use; or the assumptions required in certain models may appear unrealistic; or the models may be too narrow in scope. Whatever the reasons, none of the techniques to date have captured the attention of aggregate planners on a broad scale. Goal programming and simulation are two techniques that seem to be gaining in favor. Suffice it to say that research on improved approaches to aggregate planning is continuing.

DISAGGREGATING THE AGGREGATE PLAN

For the production plan to be translated into meaningful terms for production, it is necessary to *disaggregate* the aggregate plan. This involves breaking down the aggregate plan into specific product requirements in order to determine labor requirements (skills, size of work force), materials, and inventory requirements. This process is discussed in some depth in Chapter 13, Material Requirements Planning. At this stage, however, it will be helpful for you to have some understanding of the need for disaggregation, as well as what the term implies.

Working with aggregate units facilitates intermediate planning. However, for the production plan to be operationalized, those aggregate units must be converted, or decomposed, into units of actual products or services that are to be produced or offered. For example, a lawn mower manufacturer may have an aggregate plan that calls for 200 lawn mowers in January, 300 in February, and 400 in March. That company may produce push mowers, self-propelled mowers, and riding mowers. Although the mowers probably contain some of the same parts and involve some similar or identical operations for fabrication and assembly, we expect certain basic differences in the materials, parts, and operations that each type requires. Hence, the 200, 300, and 400 aggregate lawn mowers that are to be produced during those three months must be translated into specific numbers of mowers of each type prior to actually purchasing the appropriate materials and parts, scheduling operations, and planning inventory requirements.

Master schedule

The result of disaggregating an aggregate plan to show quantity and timing of specific end items for a schedule horizon.

The result of disaggregating the aggregate plan is a **master schedule**, showing the quantity and timing of *specific* end items for a schedule horizon, which often covers about six to eight weeks ahead. A master schedule shows demand for individual products rather than an entire product group, along with the timing of production. The master schedule contains important information for marketing as well as for production. It reveals when orders are scheduled for production and when completed orders are to be shipped.

Rought-cut capacity planning

Approximate balancing of capacity and demand to test the feasibility of the master schedule.

Once a tentative master schedule has been developed, **rough–cut capacity planning** is done to test the feasibility of the master schedule relative to available capacities, to assure that no obvious capacity constraints exist. This means checking capacities of production and warehouse facilities, labor, and vendors to assure that no gross deficiencies exist that will render the master schedule unworkable. The master schedule then serves as the basis for *short-range* planning. It should be noted that whereas the aggregate plan covers an interval of, say, 12 months, the master schedule covers only a portion of this. In other words, the aggregate plan is disaggregated in stages, or phases, that may cover a few weeks to two or three months. Moreover, the master schedule may be updated monthly, even though it covers two or three months. For instance, the lawn mower master schedule would probably be updated at the end of January to include any revisions in planned output for February and March as well as new information on planned output for April.

The concept of disaggregating the aggregate plan is illustrated in Figure 11–4. The illustration makes a simple assumption in order to clearly show the concept of disaggregation: The totals of the aggregate and the disaggregated units are equal. In reality, that is not always true—as a consequence, it can require considerable effort to disaggregate the aggregate plan.

MASTER SCHEDULING

A master schedule indicates the quantity and timing (i.e., delivery times) for a product, or a group of products, but it does not show planned *production*. For instance, a master schedule may call for delivery of 50 cases of cranberry-apple juice to be delivered on May 1. But this may not require any production; there may be 200 cases in inventory. Or it may require *some* production: If there were 40 cases in inventory, an additional 10 cases would be needed to achieve the specified delivery amount. Or it may involve production of 50 or more cases: In some instances, it is more economical to produce large amounts rather than small amounts, with the excess temporarily placed in inventory until it is needed. Thus, the *production lot size* might be 70 cases, so if additional cases were needed (e.g., 50 cases), a run of 70 cases would be made.

Master production schedule (MPS)

This schedule indicates the quality and timing of planned production.

The **master production schedule (MPS)** indicates the quantity and timing of planned production, taking into account desired delivery quantity and timing as well as on-hand inventory. The master production schedule is one of the primary outputs of the master scheduling process, as illustrated in Figure 11–5.

INPUTS

The master schedule has three inputs: the beginning inventory, which is the actual quantity on-hand from the preceding period; forecasts for each period of the schedule; and customer orders, which are quantities already *committed* to customers.

Figure 11–4

Disaggregating the aggregate plan

Aggregate plan	Month Planned output*	Jan.	Feb.	Mar.	Apr.	May
		200	300	400	400	350

*Aggregate units

Master schedule	Month Planned output*	Jan.	Feb.	Mar.
	Push	100	100	100
	Self-propelled	75	150	200
	Riding	25	50	100
	Total	200	300	400

*Actual units

Figure 11–5

The master scheduling process

Inputs

Beginning inventory
Forecast
Customer orders

Master scheduling

Outputs

Projected inventory
Master production schedule
Uncommitted inventory

OUTPUTS

The master scheduling process uses this information on a period-by-period basis in order to determine the projected inventory, production requirements, and the resulting uncommitted inventory, which is referred to as **available-to-promise (ATP) inventory**. Knowledge of the uncommitted inventory can enable marketing to make realistic promises to customers about deliveries of new orders.

Available-to-promise (ATP) inventory
Uncommitted inventory.

The master scheduling process begins with a preliminary calculation of projected on-hand inventory. This reveals when additional inventory (i.e., production) will be needed. Consider this example. A company that makes industrial pumps wants to prepare a master production schedule for June and July. Marketing has forecasted demand of 120 pumps for June and 160 pumps for July. These have been evenly distributed over the four weeks in each month: 30 per week in June and 40 per week in July, as illustrated in Figure 11–6.

Now, suppose that there are currently 64 pumps in inventory (i.e., beginning inventory is 64 pumps), and that there are customer orders that have been committed (booked) and must be filled. This additional information is shown in Figure 11–7.

Figure 11–7 contains the three primary inputs to the master scheduling process: The beginning inventory, the forecast, and the customer orders that have been booked or committed. This information is necessary to determine three quantities: the projected on-hand inventory, the master production schedule, and the uncommitted (available-to-promise) inventory. The first step is to calculate the projected on-hand inventory, one week at a time, until it falls below a specified limit. In this example, the specified limit will be zero. Hence, we will continue until the projected on-hand inventory becomes negative.

The projected on-hand inventory is calculated as follows:

$$\text{Projected on-hand inventory} = \text{Inventory from previous week} - \text{Current week's requirements} \quad (11–1)$$

where the current week's requirements is the *larger* of Forecast and Customer orders (committed).

For the first week, projected on-hand inventory equals Beginning inventory minus the larger of Forecast and Customer orders. Because Customer orders (33) is larger than the Forecast (30), the Customer orders amount is used. Thus, for the first week, we obtain:

$$\text{Projected on-hand inventory} = 64 - 33 = 31$$

Projected on-hand inventories are shown in Figure 11–8 for the first three weeks (i.e., until the projected on-hand amount becomes negative).

When the projected on-hand inventory becomes negative, this is a signal that production will be needed to replenish inventory. Hence, a negative projected

| | June | | | | July | | | |
	1	2	3	4	5	6	7	8
Forecast	30	30	30	30	40	40	40	40

Figure 11–6

Weekly forecast requirements for industrial pumps

Figure 11–7

Eight-week schedule showing forecasts, customer orders, and beginning inventory

Beginning inventory	June				July			
64	1	2	3	4	5	6	7	8
Forecast	30	30	30	30	40	40	40	40
Customer orders (committed)	33	20	10	4	2			

Figure 11–8

Projected on-hand inventory is computed week by week until it becomes negative

Beginning inventory	June				July			
64	1	2	3	4	5	6	7	8
Forecast	30	30	30	30	40	40	40	40
Customer orders (committed)	33	20	10	4	2			
Projected on-hand inventory	31	1	−29					

Customer orders are larger than Forecast in week 1; projected on-hand inventory is 64 − 33 = 31

Forecast is larger than customer orders in week 2; projected on-hand inventory is 31 − 30 = 1

Forecast is larger than customer orders in week 3; projected on-hand inventory is 1 − 30 = −29

on-hand inventory will require planned production. Suppose that a production lot size of 70 pumps is used, so that whenever production is called for, 70 pumps will be produced. (Determination of lot size is discussed in the following two chapters.) Hence, the negative projected on-hand inventory in the third week will require production of 70 pumps, which will meet the projected shortfall of 29 pumps, and leave 41 (i.e., 70 − 29 = 41) pumps for future demand.

These calculations continue for the entire schedule, and every time projected inventory becomes negative, another production lot of 70 pumps is added to the schedule. The calculations are illustrated in Figure 11–9. The result is the master schedule and projected on-hand inventory for each week of the schedule. These can now be added to the master schedule (see Figure 11–10).

It is now possible to determine the amount of inventory that is uncommitted, and hence, available-to-promise (ATP). Several methods are used in practice. The one we shall employ involves a "look ahead" procedure: Sum booked customer orders week by week until (but not including) a week in which there is an MPS amount. For example, in the first week, this procedure will result in summing Customer orders of 33 (week 1) and 20 (week 2) to obtain 53. In the first week, this amount is subtracted from the Beginning inventory of 64 pumps plus the MPS (zero in this example) to obtain the amount that is available-to-promise. Thus,

Figure 11–9

Determining the MPS and projected on-hand inventory

Week	Inventory from previous week	Require-ments*	Net inventory before MPS	(70) MPS	Projected inventory
1	64	33	31		31
2	31	30	1		1
3	1	30	−29	+ 70 =	41
4	41	30	11		11
5	11	40	−29	+ 70 =	41
6	41	40	1		1
7	1	40	−39	+ 70 =	31
8	31	40	−9	+ 70 =	61

*Requirements equals the larger of Forecast and Customer orders in each week.

Figure 11–10

Projected on-hand inventory and MPS are added to the master schedule

		June				July			
64		1	2	3	4	5	6	7	8
Forecast		30	30	30	30	40	40	40	40
Customer orders (committed)		33	20	10	4	2			
Projected on-hand inventory		31	1	41	11	41	1	31	61
MPS				70		70		70	70

$$64 + 0 − (33 + 20) = 11$$

This inventory is uncommitted, and can be delivered in either week 1 or 2, or part can be delivered in week 1 and part in week 2. (Note that the ATP quantity is only calculated for the first week, and for other weeks in which there is an MPS quantity. Hence, it is calculated for weeks 1, 3, 5, 7, 8.) See Figure 11–11.

For weeks other than the first week, the Beginning inventory drops out of the computation, and ATP is the look ahead quantity subtracted from the MPS quantity.

Thus, for week 3, the promised amounts are 10 + 4 = 14, and the ATP is 70 − 14 = 56.

For week 5, Customer orders are 2 (future orders have not yet been booked). The ATP is 70 − 2 = 68.

For weeks 7 and 8, there are no Customer orders, so for the present, all of the MPS amount is available to promise.

As additional orders are booked, these would be entered in the schedule, and the ATP amounts would be updated to reflect those orders. Marketing can use the ATP amounts to provide realistic delivery dates to customers.

Figure 11–11

The available-to-promise inventory quantities have been added to the master schedule

	June				July			
64	1	2	3	4	5	6	7	8
Forecast	30	30	30	30	40	40	40	40
Customer orders (committed)	33	20	10	4	2			
Projected on-hand inventory	31	1	41	11	41	1	31	61
MPS			70		70		70	70
Available-to-promise inventory (uncommitted)	11		56		68		70	70

SUMMARY

Aggregate planning establishes general levels of employment, output, and inventories for periods of two to eighteen months. In the spectrum of planning, it falls between the broad design decisions of long-range planning and the very specific and detailed short-range planning decisions. It begins with an overall forecast for the planning horizon and ends with preparations for applying the plans to specific products and services.

The essence of aggregate planning is the aggregation of products or services into one "product" or "service." This permits planners to consider overall levels of employment and inventories without having to become involved with specific details that are better left to short-range planning. Planners often use informal graphical and charting techniques to develop plans, although various mathematical techniques have been suggested. It appears that the complexity and the restrictive assumptions of these techniques limit their widespread acceptance in practice.

KEY TERMS

aggregate planning, 550
available-to-promise (ATP) inventory, 573
chase demand strategy, 557
goal programming, 569
level capacity strategy, 557
linear decision rule, 569
management coefficients, 569

master production schedule, (MPS), 572
master schedule, 571
parametric production planning, 569
rough-cut capacity planning, 571
stimulation models, 570

SOLVED PROBLEM

Problem

A manager is attempting to put together an aggregate plan for the coming year. She has obtained a forecast of expected demand for the planning horizon. Basically, the plan must deal with demand that is highly seasonal; demand is relatively high in periods 3 and 4 and again in periods 10 and 11, as can be seen from the following forecasts:

Period	1	2	3	4	5	6	7	8	9	10	11	12	Total
Forecast	190	230	260	280	210	170	160	160	220	250	260	180	2,570

The department now has 20 full-time people, each of whom can produce 10 units of output per period at a cost of $6 per unit. Inventory carrying cost is $5 per unit per period, and backlog cost is $10 per unit per period. The manager is considering a plan that would involve hiring two people to start working in period 1, one on a temporary basis who would work only through period 5. This would cost $500 in addition to unit production costs.

a. What is the rationale for this plan?
b. Determine the total cost of the plan, including production, inventory, and back order costs.

Solution

a. With the current work force of 20 people each producing 10 units per period, regular capacity is 2,400 units. That is 170 units less than expected demand. Adding one worker would increase regular capacity to 2,400 + 120 = 2,520 units. That would still be 50 units short, or just the amount one temporary worker could produce in five periods. Since one of the two seasonal peaks is quite early, it would make sense to start the temporary worker right away to avoid some of the backorder cost.

b. The production plan for this strategy is as follows:

Period	1	2	3	4	5	6	7	8	9	10	11	12	Total
Forecast	190	230	260	280	210	170	160	160	220	250	260	180	2,570
Output													
Regular	220	220	220	220	220	210	210	210	210	210	210	210	2,570
Overtime	—	—	—	—	—	—	—	—	—	—	—	—	—
Subcontract	—	—	—	—	—	—	—	—	—	—	—	—	—
Output − Forecast	30	(10)	(40)	(60)	10	40	50	50	(10)	(40)	(50)	30	0
Inventory													
Beginning	0	30	20	0	0	0	0	20	70	60	20	0	
Ending	30	20	0	0	0	0	20	70	60	20	0	0	
Average	15	25	10	0	0	0	10	45	65	40	10	0	220
Backlog	0	0	20	80	70	30	0	0	0	0	30	0	230
Costs:													
Output													
Regular @ $6	$1,320	1,320	1,320	1,320	1,320	1,260	1,260	1,260	1,260	1,260	1,260	1,260	$15,420
Overtime													
Subcontract													
Inventory @ $5	$ 75	125	50	0	0	0	50	225	325	200	50	0	$ 1,100
Backorder @ $10	0	0	200	800	700	300	0	0	0	0	300	0	$ 2,300
Total	$1,395	1,445	1,570	2,120	2,020	1,560	1,310	1,485	1,585	1,460	1,610	1,260	$18,820

The total cost for this plan is $18,820, plus the $500 cost for hiring and for the layoff, giving a total of $19,320. This plan may or may not be good. We would need information on other costs and options before settling on one plan.

Although the calculations are relatively straightforward, the backlogs can sometimes seem difficult to obtain. Consider these rules for computing the backlog:

1. Start with the Output − Forecast value. If it is positive and there was a backlog in the preceding period, reduce the backlog by this amount. If the amount exceeds the backlog, the difference becomes the ending inventory for the period. If they are exactly equal, the backlog and the ending inventory will both be equal to zero.

2. If Output − Forecast is negative, subtract it from the beginning inventory. If this produces a negative value, that value becomes the backlog for that period.

DISCUSSION AND REVIEW QUESTIONS

1. What three levels of planning involve operations managers? What kinds of decisions are made at the various levels?
2. What are the three phases of intermediate planning?
3. What is aggregate planning? What is its purpose?
4. Why is there a need for aggregate planning?
5. What are the most common decision variables for aggregate planning in a manufacturing setting? In a service setting?
6. What difficulty may an organization that offers a variety of products and/or services have to deal with in aggregate planning that an organization with one or a few similar products or services would not?
7. Briefly discuss the advantages and disadvantages of each of these planning strategies:
   a. Maintain a level rate of output, and let inventories absorb fluctuations in demand.
   b. Vary the size of the work force to correspond to predicted changes in demand requirements.
   c. Maintain a constant workforce size, but vary hours worked to correspond to predicted demand requirements.
8. What are the primary advantages and limitations of informal graphical and charting techniques for aggregate planning?
9. Briefly describe the planning techniques listed below, and give an advantage and disadvantage for each one:
   a. Linear programming.
   b. Linear decision rule.
   c. Management coefficients.
   d. Simulation.
10. What are the inputs to master scheduling? What are the outputs?

PROBLEMS

1. (Refer to Example 1.) The president of the firm has decided to shut down the plant for vacation and installation of new equipment in period 4. After installation, the cost per unit will remain the same, but the output rate for regular time will be 450.
   a. Prepare graphs like those in Figures 11−2 and 11−3 for this revised case.
   b. Regular output is the same as in Example 1 for periods 1, 2, and 3; 0 for period 4; and 450 for each of the remaining periods. Note, though, that the forecast of 200

units in period 4 must be dealt with. Prepare the aggregate plan, and compute its total cost.

2. (Refer to Example 1.) Suppose that the regular output rate will drop to 290 units per period due to an expected change in production requirements. Costs will not change. Prepare an aggregate plan and compute its total cost for each of these alternatives:

   a. Use overtime at a fixed rate of 20 units per period as needed. Plan for an ending inventory of zero for period 6. Backlogs cannot exceed 90 units per period.

   b. Use subcontracting at a *maximum* rate of 50 units per period; the usage need not be the same in every period. Have an ending inventory of zero in the last period. Again, backlogs cannot exceed 90 units in any period. Compare these two plans.

3. (Refer to Example 2.) Do each of the following:

   a. Prepare graphs like those in Figures 11−2 and 11−3 for the data given in Example 2. Combine regular time and overtime, and use those amounts for output in the graphs.

   b. Suppose you can use a combination of overtime and subcontracting, but you cannot use subcontracting in more than two periods. Up to 50 units of subcontracting and either 0 or 40 units of overtime are allowed per period. Subcontracting is $6 per unit, and overtime is $3 per unit. (*Hint:* Use subcontracting only when overtime units are not sufficient to decrease backlogs to 80 units or fewer.) Plan for an ending inventory balance of 0 for period 6. Prepare a plan that will minimize total cost.

4. (Refer to Example 2.) Determine if a plan to use subcontracting at a maximum rate of 50 units per period as needed with no overtime would achieve a lower total cost than the plan shown in Example 2. Again, plan for a zero inventory balance at the end of period 6.

5. The solved problem illustrated an aggregate plan that involved use of hiring and a layoff as well as inventory absorption of demand variations and some buildup of backlogs. As noted, for the merits of that plan to be assessed, certain other information would be needed. If you were the manager, what information would you want? Be specific.

6. Prepare two graphs like those in Figure 11−2 for the solved problem at the end of this chapter. Also, prepare a graph like the one in Figure 11−3.

7. (Refer to the solved problem.) Prepare two additional aggregate plans. Call the one in the solved problem plan A. For plan B, hire one more worker at a cost of $200 in that period. Make up any shortfall using subcontracting at $8 per unit, with a maximum of 20 units per period (i.e., use subcontracting to reduce backorders when the forecast exceeds regular output). Note that the ending inventory in period 12 should be zero. Therefore, Total forecast = Total output + Quantity subcontracted. An additional constraint is that backorders cannot exceed 80 units in any period. For plan C, assume no workers are hired (so regular output is 200 units per period instead of 210 as in plan B). Use subcontracting as needed, and try to minimize backorders. The constraints of 20 units of subcontracting per period and 70 units of backorders still apply. Compute the total cost of each plan. Which plan has the lowest cost?

8. (Refer to the solved problem.) Suppose another option is to use part-time workers to assist during seasonal peaks. The cost per unit, including hiring and training, is $11. The output rate is 10 units per worker per period for all workers. A maximum of 10 workers can be used, and the same number of part-time workers must be used in all periods that have part-time workers. The ending inventory in period 12 should be 30 units. The limit on backlogs is 20 units per period. Try to make up backlogs as soon as possible. Compute the total cost for this plan, and compare it to the cost of the plan used in the solved problem.

9. (Refer to the solved problem.) Prepare an aggregate plan that uses overtime ($9 per unit, maximum output 25 units per period) and inventory variation. Try to minimize backlogs. The ending inventory in period 12 should be zero, and the limit on backlogs

is 60 units per period. Note that Total forecast = Total regular output + Quantity overtime. Compute the total cost of your plan, and compare it to the total cost of the plan used in the solved problem.

10. (Refer to the solved problem.) Prepare an aggregate plan that uses some combination of hiring ($200 per worker), layoff ($100 per worker), subcontracting ($8 per unit, maximum of 20 units per period, must use for a minimum of three consecutive periods), and overtime ($9 per unit, maximum of 25 per period, maximum of 100 for the planning horizon). Compute the total cost, and compare it to any of the other plans you have developed. Which plan has the lowest total cost?

11. Verify the transportation solution shown in Example 4.

12. (Refer to Example 4.) Suppose that, due to an increase in warehousing costs and other costs, inventory carrying costs are now $2 per unit per month. All other costs and quantities remain the same. Determine a revised solution to this transportation problem.

13. (Refer to Example 4.) Suppose that regular-time capacity will be reduced to 440 units in Period 3 to accommodate a companywide safety inspection of equipment. What will the additional cost of the optimal plan be as compared to the one shown in Example 4? Assume all costs and quantities are the same as given in Example 4 except for period 3's regular-time output.

14. Solve the preceding problem using an inventory carrying cost of $2 per unit per period.

15. Dundas Bike Components Inc. of Wheelville, Illinois, manufactures bicycle wheels in two different sizes for the Big Bike Co. assembly plant located across town. David Dundas, the firm's owner-manager, has just received Big Bike's order for the next six months.

	20-inch wheels	24-inch wheels
Nov.	1,000 units	500 units
Dec.	900	500
Jan.	500	300
Feb.	700	500
Mar.	1,100	400
Apr.	1,100	600

a. Under what circumstances will it be possible for David to develop just one aggregate plan rather than two (one for each size wheel)? Explain in two to three sentences—no calculations.

b. Currently David employs 30 full-time, highly skilled employees, each of whom can produce 50 wheels per month. Because skilled labor is in short supply in the Wheelville area, David would like to develop a pure level output plan. There is no inventory of finished wheels on hand at present, but David would like to have 300 on hand at the end of April. Big Bike will tolerate backorders of up to 200 units per month. Show your level plan in tabular form.

c. Calculate the total annual cost of your plan using these costs:

Regular	$5.00	Hiring	$300
Overtime	$7.50	Layoff	$400
Part-time	NA	Inventory	$1.00
Subcontract	NA	Backorder	$6.00

16. Prepare a master schedule for industrial pumps in the manner of Figure 11–12 in the chapter. Use the same inputs as the example, but change the MPS rule from "schedule production when the projected on-hand inventory would be negative without pro-

duction" to "schedule production when the projected on-hand inventory would be less than 10 without production."

17. Update the master schedule shown in Figure 11–12 given these updated inputs: It is now the end of week 1; customer orders are 25 for week 2, 16 for week 3, 11 for week 4, 8 for week 5, and 3 for week 6. Use the MPS rule of ordering production when projected on-hand inventory would be negative without production.

18. Prepare a master schedule like the one shown in Figure 11–12 given this information: The forecast for each week of an eight-week schedule is 50 units. The MPS rule is to schedule production if the projected on-hand inventory would be negative without it. Customer orders (committed) are:

Week	Customer orders
1	52
2	35
3	20
4	12

Use a production lot size of 75 units.

19. (Refer to the previous problem.) Prepare a master schedule like the one shown in Figure 11–12 if the MPS rule is to schedule production if the projected on-hand inventory would be 5 units or less without production, and the production lot size is 70 units. The beginning inventory is 18 units.

SELECTED BIBLIOGRAPHY

Buffa, Elwood S., and Jeffery G. Miller. *Production-Inventory Systems: Planning and Control.* 3rd ed. Homewood, Ill.: Richard D. Irwin, 1974.

Fogarty, Donald W., and Thomas R. Hoffmann. *Production and Inventory Management.* Cincinnati: South-Western Publishing, 1983.

Krajewski, L., and L. Ritzman. "Disaggregation in Manufacturing and Service Organizations." *Decision Sciences* 8, no. 1 (1977), pp. 1–18.

———. *Operations Management.* 2nd ed. Reading, Mass.: Addison-Wesley, 1990, Chapter 14.

Leone, Robert A., and John R. Meyer. "Capacity Strategies for the 1980s." *Harvard Business Review,* November–December 1980, p. 133.

McLain, J. O., and L. J. Thomas. "Horizon Effects in Aggregate Production Planning with Seasonal Demand." *Management Science* 23, no. 7 (March 1977), pp. 728–36.

Posner, M. E., and W. Szwarc. "A Transportation Type Aggregate Production Model with Backordering." *Management Science* 29, no. 2 (February 1983), pp. 188–99.

Vollmann, Thomas E.; William L. Berry; and D. Clay Whybark. *Manufacturing Planning and Control Systems.* 3rd ed. Homewood, Ill.: Richard D. Irwin, 1992.

Ware, Norman, and Donald Fogarty. "Master Schedule/Master Production Schedule: The Same or Different?" *Production and Inventory Management Journal,* First Quarter, 1990, pp. 34–37.

CHAPTER TWELVE

INVENTORY MANAGEMENT

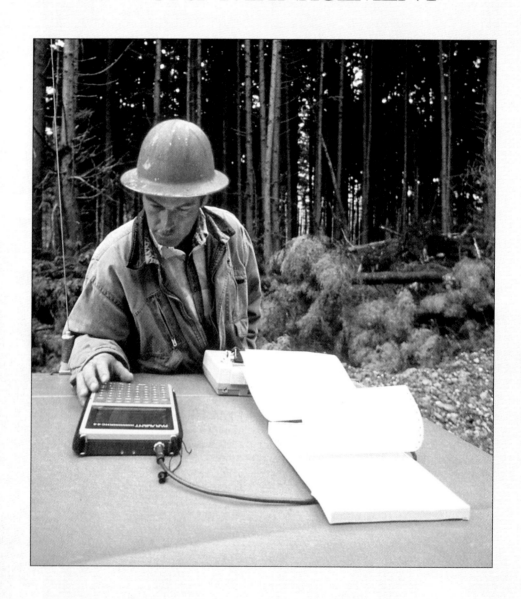

12

After completing this chapter, you should be able to:

1. Define the term *inventory*.
2. Contrast independent and dependent demand.
3. List the major reasons for holding inventories.
4. List the main requirements for effective inventory management.
5. Discuss periodic and perpetual review systems.
6. Describe the A–B–C approach and explain how it is useful.
7. Discuss the objectives of inventory management.
8. Describe the basic EOQ model and its assumptions and solve typical problems.
9. Describe the economic run size model and solve typical problems.
10. Describe the quantity discount model and solve typical problems.
11. Describe reorder point models and solve typical problems.

LEARNING OBJECTIVES

☐

CHAPTER OUTLINE

☐

583

Good inventory management is essential to the successful operation of most organizations. There are a number of reasons for this. One is the amount of money inventory represents; another is the impact that inventories have on the daily operations of an organization. Some organizations have excellent inventory management, and many have satisfactory inventory management. But too many have unsatisfactory inventory management. In some instances, that is a sign that management does not recognize the importance of inventories. More often than not, though, the recognition is there—what is lacking is an understanding of what needs to be done and how to do it. In this chapter, the concepts that underlie good inventory management are explored.

The preceding chapter described *aggregate* inventory planning. This chapter and the next one narrow the focus to *individual items*. The next chapter deals with inventory methods that are best suited for managing inventories of component parts and subassemblies, while this chapter describes methods that are best suited for finished goods, raw materials, purchased parts, and retail items.

The chapter discusses the different functions of inventories, the requirements for effective inventory management, the objectives of inventory control, and techniques for determining *how much* to order and *when* to order.

INTRODUCTION

Inventory

A stock or store of goods.

An **inventory** is a stock or store of goods. Many firms stock hundreds or even thousands of items, ranging from small things such as pencils, paper clips, screws, nuts, and bolts to large items such as machines, trucks, construction equipment, and airplanes. Naturally, many of the items a firm carries in inventory relate to the kind of business it engages in. Thus, manufacturing firms carry supplies of raw materials, purchased parts, partially completed items, and finished goods, as well as spare parts for machines, tools, and other supplies. Department stores carry clothing, furniture, carpeting, stationery, appliances, gifts, cards, and toys. Some also stock sporting goods, paints, and tools. Hospitals stock drugs, surgical supplies, life-monitoring

---

We proceed as follows. First look for a five-by-five-by-three-foot bin of gears or parts that looks like it has been there awhile. Pick up a gear and ask, casually, "How much is this worth?" You then ask, "How many of these are in the bin?" followed by, "How long has this bin been here?" and, "What's your cost of money for this company?" I recall one case in a nameless South American country where the unit cost times the number of parts times the time it had been there times the interest rate resulted in a cost-per-day figure that would insure comfortable retirement for the plant manager on the bank of the Rio de la Plata at one of the better resorts to be found there. The plant manager suddenly realized that what he was holding was not just a chunk of high-test steel, but was *real money*. He then pointed out that *he* now understood the value of the inventory but could I suggest a way to drive the point home to upper management? I suggested that he go to the accounting department and borrow enough money to be equal to the bin's value for as long as it had been sitting there, and pile it on the top of the bin. I further suggested that he do that for every bin on the production line. We rapidly figured out that by the time we had the money piled up on the bin, you would not even be able to *see* the bin. My opinion was that if the upper managers were given a tour of the line with the money piled up, they would *never forget it*.

Gene Woolsey, "On Doing Good Things and Dumb Things in Production and Inventory Control," *Interfaces* 5, no. 3 (May 1975). Copyright 1975, The Institute of Management Science. Reprinted by permission.

equipment, sheets and pillow cases, and more. Supermarkets stock fresh and canned foods, packaged and frozen foods, household supplies, magazines, baked goods, dairy products, and miscellaneous items.

INDEPENDENT AND DEPENDENT DEMAND

A major distinction in the way inventory planning and control are managed is whether demand for items in inventory is *independent* or *dependent*. **Dependent demand** items are typically subassemblies or component parts that will be used in the production of a final or finished product. Demand (i.e., usage) of subassemblies and component parts is *derived* from the number of finished units that will be produced. A classic example of this is demand for wheels for new cars. If each car is to have five wheels, then the total number of wheels required for a production run is simply a function of the number of cars that are to be produced in that run. For example, 200 cars would require $200 \times 5 = 1,000$ wheels. **Independent demand** items, on the other hand, are the finished goods or other *end items*. Generally speaking, these items are sold, or at least shipped out, rather than used in making another product. In such cases, there is usually no way to precisely determine how many of these items will be demanded during any given time period because demand typically includes elements of randomness. Therefore, forecasting plays an important role in stocking decisions, whereas for dependent demand items, stock requirements are determined by reference to the production plan. This chapter focuses on management of independent demand items, and the next chapter focuses on dependent demand.

Dependent demand

Demand for items in inventory that are subassemblies or component parts to be used in the production of finished goods.

Independent demand

Demand for items that are finished items.

TYPES OF INVENTORIES

Some of the key types of inventories carried by business firms are:

> Raw materials and purchased parts.
> Partially completed goods (work in process) or goods in transit.
> Finished-goods inventories (manufacturing firms) or merchandise (retail stores).
> Replacement parts, tools, and supplies.

FUNCTIONS OF INVENTORY

Inventories serve a number of important functions. Among the most salient reasons for holding inventories are the following:

1. To meet anticipated demand.
2. To smooth production requirements.
3. To decouple components of the production-distribution system.
4. To protect against stock-outs.
5. To take advantage of order cycles.
6. To hedge against price increases, or to take advantage of quantity discounts.
7. To permit operations.

Let's take a look at each of these.

This tree-cutting operation at Weyerhaeuser balances the need for an inventory of lumber with cost considerations and the future supply of raw material, trees.

1. *To meet anticipated customer demand.*   A customer can be a person who walks in off the street to buy a new stereo system, a mechanic who requests a tool at a tool crib, or a manufacturing operation. These inventories are referred to as *anticipation stocks* because they are held to satisfy planned or expected demand.

2. *To smooth production requirements.*   Firms that experience seasonal patterns in demand often build up inventories during off-season periods in order to meet overly high requirements that exist during certain seasonal periods. These inventories are aptly named *seasonal inventories*. Companies that process fresh fruits and vegetables must deal with seasonal inventories. So do stores that sell greeting cards, or skis, or snowmobiles, or Christmas trees.

3. *To decouple operations.*   Unless successive steps in a production or distribution system have a buffer of inventories between them, they are so interdependent that an interruption at one point will quickly cause the entire system to grind to a halt, as individual steps in the operations have to cease and operations shut down one after the other in domino fashion. Thus, an inventory of raw materials offers a manufacturer some protection from disruption in deliveries caused by the weather or problems with a supplier. Similarly, inventories between successive manufacturing steps act as a buffer that allows other operations to continue temporarily if some operations suffer breakdowns or other problems. Also, finished-goods inventories separate manufacturing and selling operations, so that income may be generated when a disruption in manufacturing occurs.

4. *To protect against stock-outs.*   Delayed deliveries and unexpected increases in demand increase the risk of shortages. Delays can be due to weather conditions, supplier stock-outs, deliveries of wrong materials, quality problems, and so on. The risk of shortages can be reduced by holding *safety stocks,* which are stocks in excess of anticipated demand.

5. *To take advantage of order cycles.*   To minimize purchasing and inventory costs, it is often necessary to buy quantities that exceed immediate usage requirements. This

necessitates storing some or all of the purchased amount for later use. Similarly, it is usually economical to produce in large rather than small quantities. Again, the excess output must be stored for later use. Hence, inventory storage enables a firm to buy and produce in *economic lot sizes* without having to try to match purchases or production with demand requirements in the short run. This results in *periodic* orders, or order *cycles*. The resulting stock is known as *cycle stock*. Order cycles are not always due to economic order sizes. In some instances, it is practical or economical to group orders and/or to order at fixed intervals.

6. *To hedge against price increases.*   Occasionally a firm will suspect that a substantial price increase is about to be made and purchase larger-than-normal amounts to avoid the increase. The ability to store extra goods also allows a firm to take advantage of price discounts for large orders.

7. *To permit operations.*   The fact that production operations take a certain amount of time (i.e., they are not instantaneous) means that there will generally be some *work-in-process* inventory. In addition, intermediate stocking of goods—including raw materials, semifinished items, and finished goods at production sites, as well as goods stored in warehouses—leads to *pipeline* inventories throughout a production-distribution system.

OBJECTIVES OF INVENTORY CONTROL

Inadequate control of inventories can result in both understocking and overstocking of items. Understocking results in missed deliveries, lost sales, dissatisfied customers, and production bottlenecks; overstocking unnecessarily ties up funds that might be more productive elsewhere. Although overstocking may appear to be the lesser of the two evils, the price tag for excessive overstocking can be staggering when inventory holding costs are high, as illustrated by the little story about the bin of gears at the beginning of the chapter. Moreover, matters can easily get out of hand. For example, it is not unheard of for a manager to discover that his or her firm has more than a 100-year supply of some item. (No doubt the firm got a good buy on it!)

There are two main concerns in inventory management. One relates to the *level of customer service* (i.e., have the right goods, in sufficient quantities, in the right place, and at the right time.) The other relates to the costs of ordering and carrying inventories.

The overall objective of inventory management is to achieve satisfactory levels of customer service while keeping inventory costs within reasonable bounds. Toward this end, the decision maker's problem is to achieve a balance in stocking, avoiding both overstocking and understocking. The two fundamental decisions that must be made relate to the *timing* and *size* of orders (i.e., when to order and how much to order). The majority of material in this chapter is devoted to models that can be applied to assist in making those decisions.

REQUIREMENTS FOR EFFECTIVE INVENTORY MANAGEMENT

Management has two basic functions with respect to inventory. One is to establish a system of accounting for items in inventory, and the other is to make decisions regarding how much to order and when to order. To be effective, management must have the following:

1. A system to *keep track of the inventory* on hand and on order.
2. A reliable *forecast of demand* that includes an indication of possible *forecast error.*
3. Knowledge of *lead times* and *lead time variability.*
4. Reasonable estimates of inventory *holding costs, ordering costs,* and *shortage costs.*
5. A *classification system* for inventory items.

Let's take a closer look at each of these requirements.

INVENTORY ACCOUNTING SYSTEMS

Periodic system

Physical count of items in inventory made at periodic intervals (weekly, monthly).

Inventory accounting systems can be periodic or perpetual. Under a **periodic system,** a physical count of items in inventory is made at periodic intervals (weekly, monthly) in order to decide how much to order of each item. Many small grocers use this approach; a manager periodically checks the shelves and stockroom to determine the quantity on hand. Then the manager estimates how much will be demanded prior to the next period's delivery and bases the order quantity on that information. An advantage of this type of system is that orders for many items occur at the same time, and there can be economies in processing and shipping orders. There are also several disadvantages of periodic reviews. One is the lack of control between reviews. Another is the need to protect against shortages between review periods by carrying extra stock. A third disadvantage is the need to make a decision on order quantities at each review.

Perpetual inventory system

System that keeps track of removals from inventory continuously, thus monitoring current levels of each item.

A **perpetual inventory system** (also known as a *continual* system) keeps track of removals from inventory on a continuous basis, so the system can provide information on the current level of inventory for each item. When the amount on hand reaches a predetermined minimum, a fixed quantity, *Q*, is ordered. An obvious advantage of this system is the control provided by the continuous monitoring of inventory withdrawals. Another advantage is the fixed-order quantity; management can identify an *economic order size* (this concept is discussed in detail later in the chapter). One disadvantage of this approach is the added costs of record keeping. Moreover, a physical count of inventories must still be performed periodically (e.g., annually) to verify records because of errors, pilferage, spoilage, and other factors that can reduce the effective amount of inventory. Bank transactions such as customer deposits and withdrawals are examples of continuous recording of inventory changes.

Two-bin system

Two containers of inventory; reorder when the first is empty.

Perpetual systems range from very simple to very sophisticated. A **two-bin system** is an example of a very elementary system. It involves the use of two containers for inventory. Items are withdrawn from the first bin. When its contents are exhausted, it is time to reorder. Sometimes an order card is placed at the bottom of the first bin. The second bin contains enough stock to satisfy expected demand until the order is filled, plus an extra cushion of stock that will reduce the chance of a stock-out if the order is late or if usage is greater than expected. The advantage of this system is that there is no need to record each withdrawal from inventory; the disadvantage is that the reorder card may not be turned in for a variety of reasons (it is misplaced, the person responsible forgets to, etc.).

Perpetual systems can be either *batch* or *on-line.* In batch systems, inventory records are collected periodically and entered into the system. In on-line systems, the transactions are recorded instantaneously. The advantage of on-line systems is that the system is always up-to-date; with a batch system, a sudden surge in demand could result in reducing the amount of inventory below the reorder point between the periodic read-ins, although frequent batch collections can minimize that problem.

Supermarkets, discount stores, and department stores have always been major users of periodic accounting systems. However, in the last few years many have switched to computerized checkout systems using a laser scanning device that reads a **universal product code** (UPC), or bar code, printed on an item tag or on product packaging. A typical grocery product code is illustrated below.

Universal product code
Bar code printed on a label that has information about the item to which it is attached.

0 14800 23208

The zero on the left identifies this as a grocery item, the first five numbers (14800) indicate the manufacturer (Mott's), and the last five numbers (23208) indicate the specific item (natural-style applesauce). Items in small packages, such as candy and gum, use a six-digit number.

UPC scanners represent a major change in the inventory systems of stores that use them. In addition to the increase in speed and accuracy these systems provide, they give managers continuous information on inventories, they reduce the need for periodic inventories and order-size determinations, and they improve the level of customer service by indicating the price and quantity of each item on the customer's receipt, as illustrated below.

```
          BRAVO CAPELLINI           .79
          BUB YUM DBL LIME          .30 T
          2/ LO FAT MILK H G       1.03
          LACTAID MILK              .91
          WEGMAN 2/ MILK QT         .55
          NEWSPAPER                 .35
          KR CAS BRICK CHEES       1.59
          GRAPES-GREEN
   .91 LB @ .89 PER LB              .81

          TAX DUE                   .02
          TOTAL                    6.35

          CASH                     20.00*
          CHANGE                   13.65

     10/07/92 18:01 21  16   23100   2570
```

Bar coding represents an important development for other sectors besides retailing. Manufacturing and service industries also benefit from the simplified production and inventory control it provides. In manufacturing, bar codes attached to parts, subassemblies, and finished goods greatly facilitate counting and monitoring activities. Automatic routing and scheduling are also possible with bar codes, as are automatic sorting and packaging. Outside of retailing, a system known as Code 39 is used rather than UPC for bar coding.

Bar codes are used not only in retail trade but also in manufacturing operations and distribution to track inventory.

DEMAND FORECASTS AND LEAD TIME INFORMATION

Since inventories will be used to satisfy demand requirements, it is essential to have reliable estimates of the amount and timing of demand. Similarly, it is essential to know how long it will take for orders to be delivered. In addition, it is necessary to know the extent to which demand and lead times might vary; the more potential variability, the greater the need for additional stock to insure against a shortage between deliveries. Thus, there is a crucial link between forecasting and inventory management.

COST INFORMATION

Three basic costs are associated with inventories: holding, transaction (ordering), and shortage costs.

Holding or **carrying costs** relate to physically holding items in storage. They include interest, insurance, taxes,[1] depreciation, obsolescence, deterioration, spoilage, pilferage, breakage, and warehousing costs (heat, light, rent, security). Holding costs also include opportunity costs associated with having funds tied up in inventory that could be used elsewhere.

The significance of the various components of holding cost depends on the type of item involved, although taxes, interest, and insurance are generally based on the dollar value of an inventory. Items that are easily concealed (such as pocket cameras, transistor radios, and calculators) or fairly expensive (cars, TVs) are prone to theft. Fresh seafood, meats and poultry, produce, and baked goods are subject to rapid deterioration and spoilage. Other items, such as dairy products, salad dressings, medicines, batteries, and film, also have limited shelf lives.

Holding costs are stated in either of two ways. One way is to specify cost as a percentage of unit price, and the other is to specify a dollar amount per unit. In any

Holding (carrying) costs
Costs of physically holding items in storage.

---

[1] In some states.

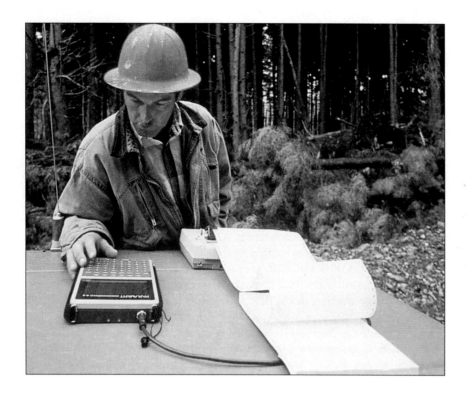

Weyerhaeuser employees use a computer to gauge timber cutting costs at the cut site. This helps keep more accurate, up-to-date records of costs and cut-tree inventory.

case, typical annual holding costs range from 20 percent to 40 percent of the value of an item. Thus, to hold a $1 item for one year could cost from 20 cents to 40 cents.

Ordering costs are the costs associated with ordering and receiving inventory. These include determining how much is needed, typing up invoices, inspecting goods upon arrival for quality and quantity, and moving the goods to temporary storage. Ordering costs are generally expressed as a fixed dollar amount per order, regardless of order size.

Ordering costs
Costs of ordering and receiving inventory.

When a firm produces its own inventory instead of ordering it from a supplier, the costs of machine setup (preparing equipment for the job by adjusting the machine, changing cutting tools, and so on) are analogous to ordering costs (i.e., they are expressed as a fixed charge per run, regardless of the size of the run).

Shortage costs result when demand exceeds the supply of inventory on hand. These costs can include the opportunity cost of not making a sale, loss of customer goodwill, lateness charges, and similar costs. Furthermore, if the shortage occurs in an item carried for internal use (e.g., to supply an assembly line), the cost of lost production or downtime is considered a shortage cost. Such costs can easily run into hundreds of dollars a minute or more.

Shortage costs
Costs resulting when demand exceeds the supply of inventory on hand.

Shortage costs are usually difficult to measure, and they are often subjectively estimated. In the chapter supplement there is an example that shows how to evaluate the sensitivity of decisions to these estimates.

CLASSIFICATION SYSTEM

An important aspect of inventory management is the fact that items kept in inventory are not of equal importance in terms of dollars invested, profit potential, sales or usage volume, and stock-out penalties. For instance, a producer of electrical equipment might have electric generators, coils of wire, and miscellaneous nuts and bolts among the items carried in inventory. It would be unrealistic to devote equal attention to each of these items. Instead, a more reasonable approach would be to allocate control efforts according to the *relative importance* of various items in inventory.

A-B-C approach

Classifying inventory according to some measure of importance, and allocating control efforts accordingly.

The **A-B-C approach** involves classifying inventory items according to some measure of importance—usually annual dollar usage (i.e., dollar value per unit multiplied by annual usage rate)—and then allocating control efforts accordingly. Typically, three classes of items are used: A (very important), B (moderately important), and C (least important). However, the actual number of categories may vary from organization to organization, depending on the extent to which a firm wants to differentiate control efforts. Generally speaking, with three classes of items, A items often account for about 5 percent to 10 percent of the *number* of items in inventory but about 60 percent to 70 percent of the *dollar usage*. At the other end of the scale, C items might account for about 60 percent of the number of items but only about 15 percent of the dollar usage of an inventory. These percentages vary from firm to firm, but the point is that, in most instances, a relatively small number of items will account for a large share of the value or cost associated with an inventory, and these items should receive a relatively greater share of control efforts. For instance, A items should receive close attention to make sure the customer service levels are attained, through frequent reviews of amounts on hand and control over withdrawals, where possible. The C items should receive only loose control (two-bin system, bulk orders), and the B items should have a control effort that lies between these two extremes.

The A-B-C concept is illustrated in Figure 12–1.

Figure 12–1

A typical A-B-C breakdown in percentage of dollar value and percentage of items by category

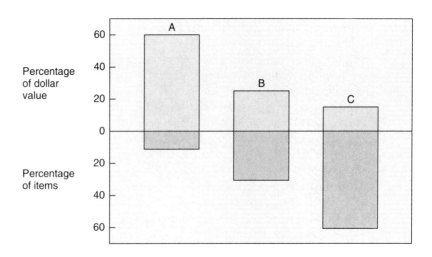

Classify the inventory items as A, B, or C based on annual dollar value, given the following information:

Example 1

∎

Item	Annual demand	× Unit cost	= Annual dollar value
1	1,000	$4,300	$4,300,000
2	5,000	720	3,600,000
3	1,900	500	950,000
4	1,000	710	710,000
5	2,500	250	625,000
6	2,500	192	480,000
7	400	200	80,000
8	500	100	50,000
9	200	210	42,000
10	1,000	35	35,000
11	3,000	10	30,000
12	9,000	3	27,000

Solution

One can easily see that the first two items have a relatively high annual dollar value. Hence, it seems reasonable to classify them as A items. The next four items appear to have moderate annual dollar values and should be B items. The remainder should be C items, based on their relatively low dollar values.

HOW MUCH TO ORDER: ECONOMIC ORDER QUANTITY MODELS

The question of how much to order is frequently determined by using an **economic order quantity (EOQ)** model. EOQ models identify the optimal order quantity in terms of minimizing the sum of certain annual costs that vary with order size.

Economic order quantity
The order size that minimizes total cost.

Three order size models are described in the following sections:

1. The economic order quantity model.
2. The economic order quantity model with noninstantaneous delivery.
3. The quantity discount model.

BASIC ECONOMIC ORDER QUANTITY (EOQ) MODEL

The basic EOQ model is the simplest of the three models. It is used to identify the order size that will minimize the sum of the annual costs of holding inventory and the annual costs of ordering inventory. The unit purchase price of items in inventory is not generally included in the total cost because the unit cost is unaffected by the order size unless quantity discounts are a factor. If holding costs are specified as

Table 12–1

Assumptions of the basic
EOQ model

1. There is only one product involved.
2. Annual usage (demand) requirements are known.
3. Usage is spread evenly throughout the year so that the usage rate is rea-
    sonably constant.
4. Lead time does not vary.
5. Each order is received in a single delivery.
6. There are no quantity discounts.

Figure 12–2

The inventory cycle:
Profile of inventory level
over time

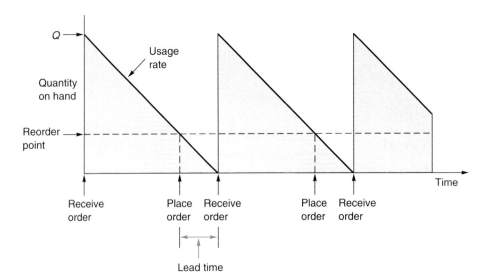

a percentage of unit cost, then unit cost is indirectly included in the total cost as a
part of holding costs.

The basic model involves a number of assumptions, some of which may appear
to be idealistic. They are listed in Table 12–1. The implications of some of the
assumptions can be seen in the diagram of an inventory cycle in Figure 12–2.

The cycle begins with receipt of an order of Q units. These are withdrawn at
a constant rate over time. When the quantity on hand is just sufficient to satisfy
demand during lead time (the time between submitting an order and receiving that
order), an order for Q units is submitted to the supplier. Because it is assumed that
both the usage rate and the lead time do not vary, the order will be received at the
precise instant that the inventory on hand falls to zero. Thus, orders are timed to
avoid both excess stock and stock-outs.

The optimal order quantity reflects a trade-off between carrying costs and ordering costs: as order size is varied, one type of cost will increase while the other
one decreases. For example, if the order size is relatively small, the average inventory will be low, which will result in low carrying costs. However, a small order size
will necessitate frequent orders, and that will drive up annual ordering costs. Conversely, annual ordering costs can be held down by ordering large quantities at
infrequent intervals, but that would result in higher average inventory levels and

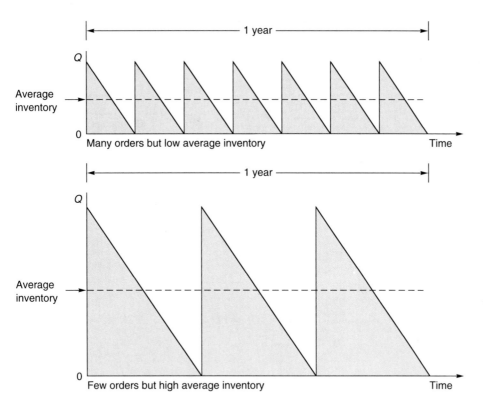

Figure 12–3

Average inventory level and number of orders per year are inversely related: As one increases, the other decreases

therefore increased carrying costs. These two extremes are illustrated in Figure 12–3.

Thus, the ideal solution will typically be an order size that causes neither a few very large orders nor many small orders, but one that lies somewhere between those two extremes. The exact amount to order will depend on the relative magnitudes of carrying and ordering costs.

Annual carrying cost is computed by multiplying the average amount of inventory on hand by the cost to carry one unit for a year, even though any given unit would not be held for a year. (Note, however, that 12 units each held for one month is equivalent to holding 1 unit for an entire year.) The average inventory is simply one half of the order quantity: the amount on hand decreases steadily from Q units to 0, for an average of $(Q + 0)/2$, or $Q/2$. Using the symbol H to represent the average annual carrying cost per unit, the *total annual carrying cost* is

$$\text{Annual carrying cost} = \frac{Q}{2}H$$

Carrying costs are thus a linear function of Q: carrying costs increase or decrease in direct proportion to changes in the order quantity Q, as illustrated in Figure 12–4A.

On the other hand, annual ordering costs will decrease as order size increases, since for a given annual demand, the larger the order size, the fewer the number of orders needed. For instance, if annual demand is 12,000 units and the order size is 1,000 units per order, there must be 12 orders over the year. But if $Q = 2,000$ units, only 6 orders will be needed; and if $Q = 3,000$ units, only 4 orders will be needed. In general, the number of orders per year will be D/Q, where $D =$ Annual

Figure 12–4

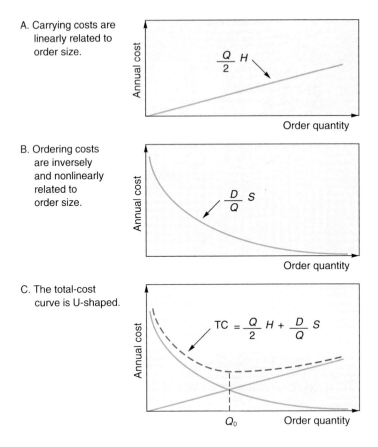

A. Carrying costs are linearly related to order size.

B. Ordering costs are inversely and nonlinearly related to order size.

C. The total-cost curve is U-shaped.

demand and Q = Order size. Unlike carrying costs, ordering costs are relatively insensitive to order size; regardless of the amount of an order, there are certain activities that must be done, such as determine how much is needed, periodically evaluate sources of supply, and prepare the invoice. Even inspection of the shipment to verify quality and quantity characteristics is not strongly influenced by order size since large shipments are sampled rather than completely inspected. Hence, there is a fixed ordering cost. *Annual ordering cost* is a function of the number of orders per year and the ordering cost per order:

$$\text{Annual ordering cost} = \frac{D}{Q}S$$

where S = Ordering cost.

Because the number of orders per year, D/Q, decreases as Q increases, annual ordering cost is inversely related to order size, as illustrated in Figure 12–4B.

The total annual cost associated with carrying and ordering inventory when Q units are ordered each time is:

$$\text{TC} = \begin{matrix} \text{Annual} \\ \text{carrying} \\ \text{cost} \end{matrix} + \begin{matrix} \text{Annual} \\ \text{ordering} \\ \text{cost} \end{matrix} = \frac{Q}{2}H + \frac{D}{Q}S \qquad (12\text{–}1)$$

where

D = Demand, usually in units per year

Q = Order quantity, in units

S = Ordering cost, in dollars

H = Carrying cost, usually in dollars per unit per year

(Note that D and H must be in the same units, e.g., months, years.) Figure 12–4C reveals that the total-cost curve is U-shaped and that *it reaches its minimum at the quantity where carrying and ordering costs are equal.* An expression for the optimal order quantity, Q_0, can be obtained using calculus.[2] The result is the formula

$$Q_0 = \sqrt{\frac{2DS}{H}} \qquad (12\text{–}2)$$

Thus, given annual demand, the ordering cost per order, and the annual carrying cost per unit, the optimal (economic) order quantity can be computed. The minimum total cost is then found by substituting Q_0 for Q in Formula 12–1.

The length of an order cycle is

$$\text{Length of order cycle} = \frac{Q_0}{D} \qquad (12\text{–}3)$$

A local distributor for a national tire company expects to sell approximately 9,600 steel-belted radial tires of a certain size and tread design next year. Annual carrying costs are $16 per tire, and ordering costs are $75. The distributor operates 288 days a year.

Example 2

∎

a. Determine the EOQ.

b. How many times per year does the store reorder?

c. Determine the length of an order cycle.

Solution

D = 9,600 tires per year

H = $16 per unit per year

S = $75

a. $Q_0 = \sqrt{\dfrac{2DS}{H}} = \sqrt{\dfrac{2(9,600)75}{16}} = 300$ tires.

(continued)

---

[2] The minimum point of the total-cost curve can be found by differentiating TC with respect to Q, setting the result equal to zero, and solving for Q. Thus,

1. $\dfrac{d\,TC}{dQ} = \dfrac{dQ}{2}H + d(D/Q)S = H/2 - DS/Q^2$

2. $0 = H/2 - DS/Q^2$, so $Q^2 = \dfrac{2DS}{H}$ or $Q_0 = \sqrt{\dfrac{2DS}{H}}$

Note, too, that the second derivative is positive, which indicates a minimum has been obtained.

Example 2

(concluded)

b.   Number of orders per year: $D/Q_0 = \dfrac{9{,}600 \text{ tires}}{300 \text{ tires}} = 32.$

c.   Length of order cycle: $Q_0/D = \dfrac{300 \text{ tires}}{9{,}600 \text{ tires}} = \tfrac{1}{32}$ of a year, which is $\tfrac{1}{32} \times 288$, or nine workdays.

Carrying costs are sometimes stated as a percentage of the purchase price of an item rather than as a dollar amount per unit. However, as long as the percentage is converted into a dollar amount, the EOQ formula is still appropriate.

Example 3

▮

Piddling Manufacturing assembles television sets. It purchases 3,600 black-and-white picture tubes a year at $65 each. Ordering costs are $31, and annual carrying costs are 20 percent of the purchase price. Compute the optimal quantity and the total annual cost of ordering and carrying the inventory.

Solution

$D = 3{,}600$ picture tubes per year

$S = \$31$

$H = .20(\$65) = \$13$

$Q_0 = \sqrt{\dfrac{2DS}{H}} = \sqrt{\dfrac{2(3{,}600)(31)}{13}} = 131$ picture tubes

$$
\begin{aligned}
TC &= \text{Carrying costs} + \text{Ordering costs} \\
&= \quad (Q_0/2)H \quad + \quad (D/Q_0)S \\
&= \quad (131/2)13 \quad + (3{,}600/131)31 \\
&= \quad\ \ \$852 \quad\ \ + \quad\ \ \$852 \quad = \$1{,}704
\end{aligned}
$$

Note that the ordering and carrying costs are equal at the EOQ, as illustrated in Figure 12–4C.

Comment   Holding and ordering costs are typically estimated values rather than values that can be precisely determined, say, from accounting records. In fact, holding costs are sometimes *designated* by managers instead of computed. Consequently, the EOQ should be regarded as an approximate quantity rather than an exact quantity. Thus, rounding the calculated value is perfectly acceptable; stating a value to several decimal places would tend to give an unrealistic impression of the precision involved. An obvious question, then, is this: How good is this "approximate" EOQ in terms of minimizing cost? The answer is that the EOQ is fairly robust; even if it is off by a large margin, the total cost suffers relatively little. An EOQ that varies by less than −20 percent to +30 percent from the true value will yield a total cost that is within ±5 percent of the minimum. This is due to the way the EOQ is calculated: Errors may cancel each other out, and taking the square root reduces the effect of errors. Hence, there is actually a range or "zone" of workable values for the EOQ, as depicted in Figure 12–5.

Figure 12–5

The total-cost curve is relatively flat near the EOQ

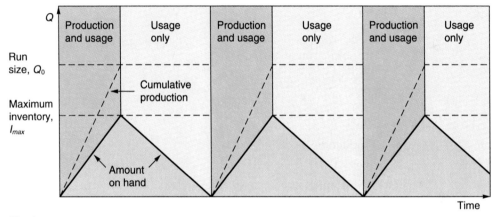

Figure 12–6

EOQ with noninstantaneous replenishment

EOQ with Noninstantaneous Replenishment

The basic EOQ model assumes that orders are delivered as whole units at a single point in time (instantaneous replenishment). However, in some instances such as when a firm is both a producer and user, or when deliveries are spread over time, inventories tend to build up gradually instead of instantaneously.

If usage and production (or delivery) rates are equal, there will not be an inventory buildup since all output will be used immediately, and the question of lot size doesn't come up. In the more typical case, the production or delivery rate *exceeds* the usage rate, creating the situation depicted in Figure 12–6. In the production case, because the production rate is greater than the usage rate, production occurs over only a portion of each cycle, and usage occurs over the entire cycle. During the production phase of the cycle, inventory builds up at a rate equal to the difference between production and usage rates. For example, if the daily production rate is 20 units and the daily usage rate is 5 units, inventory will build up at the rate of $20 - 5 = 15$ units per day. As long as production occurs, the inventory level will continue to build; when production ceases, the inventory level will begin to decrease. Hence, the inventory level will be maximum at the point where production ceases. When the amount of inventory on hand is exhausted, production is resumed, and the cycle repeats itself.

When a company makes the product itself, there are no ordering costs as such. Nonetheless, with every run there are setup costs—costs required to prepare the equipment for the job, such as cleaning, adjusting, and changing tools and fixtures. These are analogous to ordering costs. Like ordering costs, setup costs are also independent of the lot (run) size, and they are treated in the formula in exactly the same way as ordering costs. Hence, the larger the run size, the fewer the number of runs needed and, hence, the lower the annual setup cost. The number of runs is D/Q, and the annual setup cost is equal to the number of runs per year times the setup cost per run: $(D/Q)S$.

Total cost is

$$TC_{min} = \text{Carrying cost} + \text{Setup cost}$$

$$= \left(\frac{I_{max}}{2}\right)H + (D/Q_0)S \tag{12–4}$$

where I_{max} = Maximum inventory.

The economic run quantity is

$$Q_0 = \sqrt{\frac{2DS}{H}} \sqrt{\frac{p}{p - u}} \tag{12–5}$$

where

p = Production or delivery rate

u = Usage rate

The maximum and average inventory levels are

$$I_{max} = \frac{Q_0}{p}(p - u) \qquad \text{and} \qquad I_{average} = \frac{I_{max}}{2} \tag{12–6}$$

The cycle time (the time between orders, or between the beginnings of runs) for the economic run size is a function of the run size and usage (demand) rate:

$$\text{Cycle time} = \frac{Q_0}{u} \tag{12–7}$$

Similarly, the run time (the production time) is a function of the run size and the production rate:

$$\text{Run time} = \frac{Q_0}{p} \tag{12–8}$$

Example 4

▌

A toy manufacturer uses 48,000 rubber wheels per year for its popular dump truck series. The firm makes its own wheels, which it can produce at a rate of 800 per day. The toy trucks are assembled uniformly over the entire year. Carrying cost is $1 per wheel a year. Setup cost for a production run of wheels is $45. The firm operates 240 days per year. Determine each of the following:

a.   The optimal run size.
b.   The minimum total annual cost for carrying and setup.
c.   The cycle time for the optimal run size.
d.   The run time.

Solution

$D = 48,000$ wheels per year

$S = \$45$

$H = \$1$ per wheel per year

$p = 800$ wheels per day

$u = 48,000$ wheels per 240 days, or 200 wheels per day

a. $Q_0 = \sqrt{\dfrac{2DS}{H}} \sqrt{\dfrac{p}{p-u}} = \sqrt{\dfrac{2(48,000)45}{1}} \sqrt{\dfrac{800}{800-200}}$

$= 2,400$ wheels

b. $TC_{min} = $ Carrying cost $+$ Setup cost $= \left(\dfrac{I_{max}}{2}\right)H + (D/Q_0)S$

Thus, we must first compute I_{max}:

$I_{max} = \dfrac{Q_0}{p}(p-u) = \dfrac{2,400}{800}(800-200) = 1,800$ wheels

$TC = \dfrac{1,800}{2} \times \$1 + \dfrac{48,000}{2,400} \times \$45 = \$900 + \$900 = \$1,800$

Note again the equality of cost (in this instance, setup and carrying costs) at the EOQ.

c. Cycle time $= \dfrac{Q_0}{u} = \dfrac{2,400 \text{ wheels}}{200 \text{ wheels per day}} = 12$ days. Thus, a run of wheels will be made every 12 days.

d. Run time $= \dfrac{Q_0}{p} = \dfrac{2,400 \text{ wheels}}{800 \text{ wheels per day}} = 3$ days. Thus, each run will require 3 days to complete.

QUANTITY DISCOUNTS

Quantity discounts are price reductions for large orders offered to customers to induce them to buy in large quantities. For example, a Chicago surgical supply company publishes the price list shown in Table 12–2 for boxes of gauze strips. Note that the price per box decreases as order quantity increases.

Quantity discounts
Price reductions for large orders.

If quantity discounts are offered, the customer must weigh the potential benefits of reduced purchase price and fewer orders that will result from buying in large quantities against the increase in carrying costs caused by higher average inventories.

Order quantity	Price per box
1 to 44	$2.00
45 to 69	1.70
70 or more	1.40

Table 12–2

Price list for extra-wide gauze strips

Hence, the buyer's goal in the case of quantity discounts is to select the order quantity that will minimize total cost, where total cost is the sum of carrying cost, ordering cost, *and* purchasing cost:

TC = Carrying cost + Ordering cost + Purchasing cost

$$= \left(\frac{Q}{2}\right)H \quad + \quad \left(\frac{D}{Q}\right)S \quad + \quad PD \tag{12–9}$$

where P = Unit price.

Recall that in the basic EOQ model, determination of order size does not involve the purchasing cost. The rationale for not including unit price is that under the assumption of no quantity discounts, price per unit is the same for all order sizes. Inclusion of unit price in the total-cost computation in that case would merely increase the total cost by the amount P times D. A graph of total annual purchase cost versus quantity would be a horizontal line. Hence, including purchasing costs would merely raise the total-cost curve by the same amount (PD) at every point. That would not change the EOQ. This is illustrated in Figure 12–7.

When quantity discounts are offered, there is a separate U-shaped total-cost curve for each unit price. Again, including unit prices merely raises each curve by a constant amount. However, because the unit prices are all different, each curve is raised by a different amount: Smaller unit prices will raise a total-cost curve less than larger unit prices. In addition, no one curve applies to the entire range of quantities; each curve applies to only a *portion* of the range. This is illustrated in Figure 12–8. Hence, the applicable or *feasible* total cost is initially on the curve with the highest unit price and then drops down, curve by curve, at the *price breaks,* which are the minimum quantities needed to obtain the discounts. Thus, in Table 12–2, the price breaks for gauze strips are at 45 and 70 boxes. The result is a total-cost curve with *steps* at the price breaks.

Figure 12–7

Adding *PD* doesn't change the EOQ

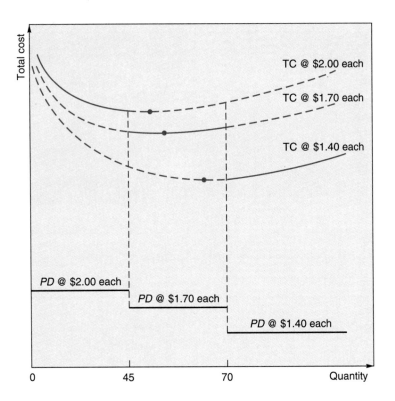

Figure 12–8

The total-cost curve with quantity discounts is composed of a portion of the total-cost curve for each price

Note that even though each curve has a minimum, those points are not necessarily feasible. For example, the minimum point for the $1.40 curve in Figure 12–8 appears to be about 65 units. However, the price list shown in Table 12–2 indicates that an order size of 65 boxes will involve a unit price of $1.70. The actual total-cost curve is denoted by the solid lines; only those price-quantity combinations are feasible. The objective of the quantity discount model is to identify an order quantity that will represent the lowest total cost for the entire set of curves.

There are two general cases of the model: in one, carrying costs are constant (e.g., $2 per unit), and in the other, carrying costs are stated as a percentage of purchase price (e.g., 20 percent of unit price). When carrying costs are constant, there will be a single EOQ that is the same for all of the cost curves. Consequently, the total-cost curves line up vertically, the only differing feature among the curves being that lower unit prices are reflected by lower total-cost curves. This is illustrated in Figure 12–9A. For purposes of illustration, the horizontal purchasing cost lines have been omitted.

When carrying costs are specified as a percentage of unit price, each curve will have a different EOQ. Since carrying costs are a percentage of price, lower prices will mean lower carrying costs and larger EOQs. Thus, as price decreases, each curve's EOQ will be to the right of the next higher curve's EOQ, as illustrated in Figure 12–9B.

The procedure for determining the overall EOQ differs slightly, depending on which of these two cases is relevant. For carrying costs that are constant, the procedure is:

1. Compute the common EOQ.

Figure 12–9

A. When carrying costs are constant, all curves have the same EOQ.

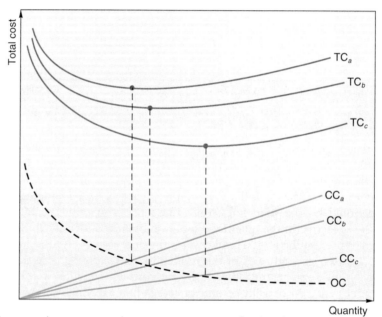

B. When carrying costs are given as a percentage of unit price, price decreases reduce carrying costs and that causes an increase in the EOQ.

2. Only one of the curves will have the EOQ in its feasible range since the ranges do not overlap. Identify that curve.
   a. If the feasible EOQ is on the lowest price curve, that is the optimal order quantity.
   b. If the feasible EOQ is on any other curve, compute the total cost for the EOQ and for the price breaks of all *lower* cost curves. Compare the total costs; the quantity (EOQ or price break) that yields the lowest total cost is the optimal order quantity.

The maintenance department of a large hospital uses about 816 cases of liquid cleanser annually. Ordering costs are $12, carrying costs are $4 per case a year, and the new price schedule indicates that orders of less than 50 cases will cost $20 per case, 50 to 79 cases will cost $18 per case, 80 to 99 cases will cost $17 per case, and larger orders will cost $16 per case. Determine the optimal order quantity and the total cost.

Example 5

Solution

See Figure 12–10.

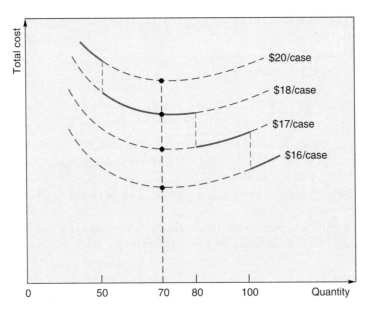

Figure 12–10

D = 816 cases per year S = $12 H = $4 per case per year

Range	Price
1 to 49	$20
50 to 79	18
80 to 99	17
100 or more	16

1. Compute the common EOQ: $\sqrt{\dfrac{2DS}{H}} = \sqrt{\dfrac{2(816)12}{4}} = 70$ cases

2. The 70 cases can be bought at $18 per case since 70 falls in the range of 50 to 79 cases. The total cost to purchase 816 cases a year, at the rate of 70 cases per order, will be

$$\begin{aligned} TC_{70} &= \text{Carrying cost} + \text{Order cost} + \text{Purchase cost} \\ &= (Q/2)H \quad\quad + (D/Q_0)S \quad + PD \\ &= (70/2)4 \quad\quad + (816/70)12 + 18(816) = \$14{,}968 \end{aligned}$$

(continued)

Example 5

(concluded)

Since lower cost curves exist, each must be checked against the minimum cost generated by 70 cases at $18 each. In order to buy at $17 per case, at least 80 cases must be purchased. (Because the TC curve is rising, 80 cases will have the lowest TC for that curve's feasible region.) The total cost at 80 cases will be

$$TC_{80} = (80/2)4 + (816/80)12 + 17(816) = \$14,154$$

To obtain a cost of $16 per case, at least 100 cases per order are required, and the total cost will be

$$TC_{100} = (100/2)4 + (816/100)12 + 16(816) = \$13,354$$

Therefore, since 100 cases per order yields the lowest total cost, 100 cases is the overall optimal order quantity.

When carrying costs are expressed as a percentage of price, the procedure for determining the best purchase quantity is:

1. Beginning with the lowest price, compute the EOQs for each price range until a feasible EOQ is found (i.e., until an EOQ is found that falls in the quantity range for its price).
2. If the EOQ for the lowest price is feasible, it is the optimal order quantity. If the EOQ is not the lowest price range, compare the total cost at the price break for all *lower* prices with the total cost of the feasible EOQ. The quantity that yields the lowest total cost is the optimum.

Example 6

Surge Electric uses 4,000 toggle switches a year. Switches are priced as follows: 1 to 499, 90 cents each; 500 to 999, 85 cents each; and 1,000 or more, 82 cents each. It costs approximately $18 to prepare an order and receive it, and carrying costs are 18 percent of purchase price per unit on an annual basis. Determine the optimal order quantity and the total annual cost.

Solution

See Figure 12–11.

$$D = 4{,}000 \text{ switches per year} \qquad S = \$18 \qquad H = 0.18P$$

Range	Unit price	H
1 to 499	$0.90	$0.18(0.90) = 0.1620$
500 to 999	$0.85	$0.18(0.85) = 0.1530$
1,000 or more	$0.82	$0.18(0.82) = 0.1476$

a. Find the EOQ for each price, starting with the lowest price, until a feasible EOQ is located.

$$EOQ_{0.82} = \sqrt{\frac{2DS}{H}} = \sqrt{\frac{2(4{,}000)18}{0.1476}} = 988 \text{ switches}$$

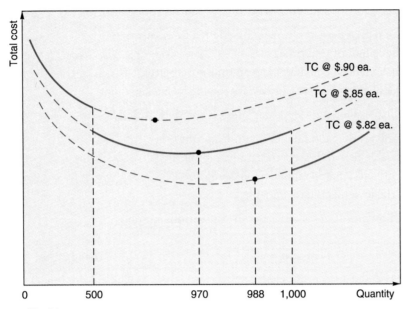

Figure 12–11

Since 988 switches will cost $0.85 each rather than $0.82 each, 988 is not a feasible EOQ. Next, try $0.85 per unit:

$$EOQ_{0.85} = \sqrt{\frac{2(4,000)18}{0.153}} = 970 \text{ switches}$$

This is feasible; 970 switches falls in the $0.85 range of 500 to 999.

b. Compute TC for 970, and compare it to the total cost of the minimum quantity necessary to obtain a price of $0.82 per switch:

$$TC = \text{Carrying costs} \quad + \text{Ordering costs} \quad + \text{Purchasing costs}$$

$$= \left(\frac{Q}{2}\right)H \quad + \quad \left(\frac{D}{Q}\right)S \quad + \quad PD$$

$$TC_{970} = (970/2)(0.153) \quad + (4,000/970)18 \quad + 0.85(4,000) = \$3,548$$
$$TC_{1,000} = (1,000/2)(0.1476) + (4,000/1,000)18 + 0.82(4,000) = \$3,426$$

Thus, the minimum-cost order size is 1,000 switches.

This completes our discussion of EOQ models.

WHEN TO REORDER

EOQ models answer the question of how much to order, but not the question of when to order. The latter is the function of models that identify the **reorder point (ROP)** in terms of a *quantity:* the reorder point occurs when the quantity on hand drops to a predetermined amount. That amount generally includes expected demand during lead time and perhaps an extra cushion of stock, which serves to reduce the probability of experiencing a stock-out during lead time.

Reorder point (ROP)

Point at which the quantity of items on hand drops to a predetermined amount.

There are four determinants of the reorder point quantity:

1. The rate of demand (usually based on a forecast).
2. The length of lead time.
3. The extent of demand and lead time variability.
4. The degree of stock-out risk acceptable to management.

We will consider reorder point models for these cases:

1. Constant demand rate, constant lead time.
2. Variable demand rate, constant lead time.
3. Constant demand rate, variable lead time.
4. Variable demand rate, variable lead time.

The following symbols are used in the various models:

Demand	Lead time
d = Constant demand rate	LT = Constant lead time
$\bar{d}$ = Average demand rate	$\overline{LT}$ = Average lead time
σ_d = Standard deviation of demand rate or forecast error	σ_{LT} = Standard deviation of lead time

The models generally assume that any variability in either demand rate or lead time can be adequately described by a normal distribution. However, this is not a strict requirement—the models provide approximate reorder points even in cases where actual distributions depart substantially from normal.

The discussion begins with the simplest case (demand and lead time both constant) and proceeds to models that can be used when either demand or lead time, or both, is variable.

CONSTANT DEMAND RATE AND CONSTANT LEAD TIME

When both the demand (usage) rate and lead time are constant, there is no risk of a stock-out created by increased demand or lead times longer than expected. In such a case, the ROP is equal to the product of usage rate and lead time; no extra cushion of stock is needed.

Example 7

Tingly takes Two-a-Day vitamins, which are delivered to his home by a routeman seven days after an order is called in. At what point should Tingly telephone his order in?

Solution

$$\text{Usage} = 2 \text{ vitamins per day}$$
$$\text{Lead time} = 7 \text{ days}$$
$$\text{ROP} = \text{Usage} \times \text{Lead time}$$
$$= 2 \text{ vitamins per day} \times 7 \text{ days} = 14 \text{ vitamins}$$

Thus, Tingly should reorder when 14 vitamin tablets are left.

VARIABLE DEMAND RATES AND/OR VARIABLE LEAD TIMES

The concept of reorder points is easy to grasp when both demand rate and lead time are constant. In fact, this is the main reason for discussing that case, since under normal circumstances, one or the other of these, or both, exhibits some variability. In order to discuss these more realistic cases, two additional concepts must be introduced: *safety stock* and *service level*.

Safety Stock   When there are variations in either the demand rate or the lead time, the possibility of stock-outs must be dealt with. Unlike the case of constant demand and lead time, it is no longer known exactly how much stock will be needed to satisfy demand during lead time. Variations in the demand rate can result in a temporary surge in demand, which will drain inventory more quickly than expected, and variations in delivery times can lengthen the time a given supply must cover. In order to compensate for uncertainties in either demand rate or lead time, additional stock must be carried to reduce the risk of a stock-out during the lead time interval. This buffer, or **safety stock,** is stock that is held in excess of expected demand. In essence, it is a form of insurance.

> **Safety stock**
>
> Stock that is held in excess of expected demand when demand rate and/or lead time is variable.

Figure 12–12 illustrates how safety stock can reduce the risk of a stock-out during lead time (LT). Note that stock-out protection is needed only during lead time. If there is a sudden surge at any point during the cycle, this will trigger another order, and once that order is received, the danger of an imminent stock-out is negligible.

In general, when variations exist in usage or lead time the ROP is

$$\text{ROP} = \frac{\text{Expected demand}}{\text{during lead time}} + \text{Safety stock} \qquad (12\text{--}10)$$

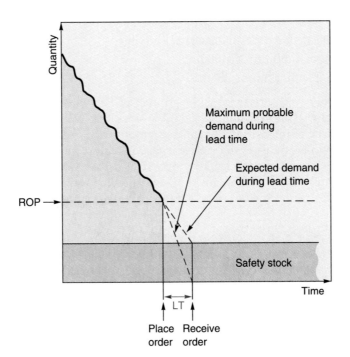

Figure 12–12

Safety stock reduces the risk of a stock-out while waiting for an order to be delivered

Example 8

∎

Paul's Plant Place uses an average of 200 plastic bags per day, and lead time averages four days. Because both usage rate and lead times are variable, Paul carries a safety stock of 100 bags to lessen the chance of a stock-out. Determine the ROP.

Solution

$$\text{ROP} = \frac{\text{Expected demand}}{\text{during lead time}} + \text{Safety stock}$$
$$= 200 \text{ bags per day} \times 4 \text{ days} + 100 \text{ bags} = 900 \text{ bags}$$

Thus, Paul should reorder when existing stock equals 900 bags.[3]

Service level

Probability that demand will not exceed supply during lead time.

Service Level   Because it costs money to hold safety stock, a manager must carefully weigh the cost of carrying safety stock against the reduction in stock-out risk it provides, since the service level increases as the risk of stock-out decreases. Order cycle **service level** can be defined as the probability that demand will not exceed supply during lead time (i.e., that the amount of stock on hand will be sufficient to meet demand). Hence, a service level of 95 percent implies a probability of 95 percent that demand will not exceed supply during lead time. An equivalent statement is that demand will be satisfied in 95 percent of such instances. It does *not* mean that 95 percent of demand will be satisfied. The risk of a stock-out is the complement of service level; a customer service level of 95 percent implies a stock-out risk of 5 percent. That is,

Service level = 100 percent − Stock-out risk

A bit later we will see how the order cycle service level relates to the *annual* service level.

The amount of safety stock that is appropriate for a given situation depends on the following factors:

1.   The average demand rate and average lead time.
2.   Demand and lead time variabilities.
3.   The desired service level.

For a given order cycle service level, the greater the variability in either demand rate or lead time, the greater the amount of safety stock that will be needed to achieve that service level. Similarly, for a given amount of variation in demand rate or lead time, achieving an increase in the service level will require increasing the amount of safety stock. Selection of a service level may reflect stock-out costs (e.g., lost sales, customer dissatisfaction), or it might simply be a policy variable (e.g., the manager wants to achieve a specified service level for a certain item).

Variable Demand Rate, Constant Lead Time

This model assumes that demand during lead time is composed of a series of *independent* daily demands that can be described by a normal distribution. In order to use

---

[3] This answer assumes that demand rates and lead times are independent. The same assumption underlies all of the ROP models described in this chapter.

the model, it is necessary to know the average daily demand rate and its standard deviation. That information is then used to determine the expected demand and standard deviation of demand for the lead time period.

Figure 12–13 illustrates daily rates that are normally distributed. In effect, each day's demand is analogous to a random draw from a normal distribution, and we want to estimate demand for the entire lead time interval.

Expected demand is nothing more than the sum of average daily demands during lead time. Thus, if average daily demand is 7 units per day, and if lead time is 10 days, then expected total demand during lead time is 7 units per day times 10 days, or 70 units. This quantity will tend to be normally distributed and have a

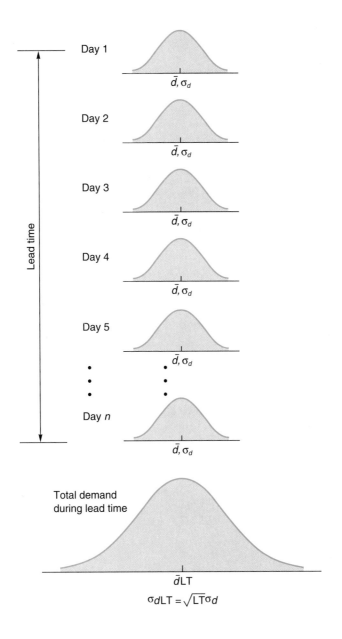

Figure 12–13

Total demand during lead time is normally distributed with a mean equal to the sum of daily means and a variance equal to the sum of daily variances

Figure 12–14

Service level is the probability that demand will not exceed the ROP amount

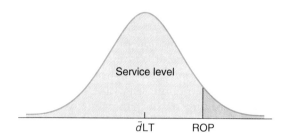

variance that is equal to the sum of the individual (daily) variances.[4] If the daily variance equals 4 (i.e., the daily standard deviation equals 2), the total variance for lead time is $4 \times 10 = 40$. Then the standard deviation of the total demand is the square root of 40, which is 6.32. (*Note:* This assumes that daily demands are independent.)

For variable demand with constant lead time, the reorder point is:

$$\text{ROP} = \frac{\text{Expected demand}}{\text{during lead time}} + \frac{\text{Safety}}{\text{stock}}$$

$$= \bar{d}\text{LT} + z\sqrt{\text{LT}}(\sigma_d) \qquad (12\text{–}11)$$

where

$$\bar{d} = \text{Average demand rate}$$
$$\text{LT} = \text{Lead time}$$
$$\sigma_d = \text{Standard deviation of demand rate}$$
$$z = \text{Number of standard deviations from the mean}$$

Note that the standard deviation of lead time demand is $\sqrt{\text{LT}}(\sigma_d)$. The service level is equal to the probability that demand will not exceed the quantity on hand at the reorder point. For a normal distribution, this amounts to the area under the curve to the left of ROP, as shown in Figure 12–14.

Example 9

A pharmacy dispenses a generic drug at an average rate of 50 milligrams per day. An examination of pharmacy records suggests that daily demand is approximately normal and has a standard deviation of 5 milligrams per day. Lead time is four days, and the pharmacist wants a stock-out risk that does not exceed 1 percent.

a.   Determine the ROP.
b.   How much safety stock should be carried?
c.   What service level would a reorder point of 215 mg provide?

Solution

$$\bar{d} = 50 \text{ mg per day}$$
$$\sigma_d = 5 \text{ mg per day}$$
$$\text{LT} = 4 \text{ days}$$

---

[4]Variance = (Standard deviation)^2.

a. Service level = 100% − Risk = 99%; $z = 2.33$ (Appendix B, Table B)

$$ROP = \bar{d}LT + z\sqrt{LT}(\sigma_d)$$
$$= 50(4) + 2.33\sqrt{4}(5) = 223.3 \text{ mg}$$

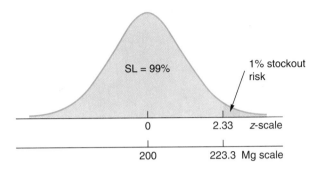

b. $SS = z\sqrt{LT}(\sigma_d) = 2.33\sqrt{4}(5) = 23.3 \text{ mg.}$

c. $z = \dfrac{ROP - \text{Expected demand during lead time}}{\sqrt{LT}(\sigma_d)} = \dfrac{215 - 200}{\sqrt{4}(5)} = 1.5$

This equates to a service level of .9332 (from Appendix B, Table B).

Example 10

Jack's Pizza Parlor uses 1,000 large cans of tomatoes a month, at an average rate of 40 per day for each of the 25 days per month the parlor is open. Usage can be approximated by a normal distribution with a standard deviation of 3 cans per day. Lead time is constant at 4 days. Monthly carrying costs are $0.02 per can, and ordering costs are $2.

a. Determine the economic order quantity.

b. For a service level of 99 percent, how many cans of tomatoes should Jack have on hand when he reorders?

Solution

a. Ordinarily, demand and carrying costs will be in annual amounts. However, the fact that they are *both* expressed here in monthly amounts is acceptable and will not affect the answer if left in those units.

$$D = 1,000 \text{ cans per month} \qquad S = \$2 \qquad H = \$0.02 \text{ per can per month}$$

$$Q_0 = \sqrt{\frac{2DS}{H}} = \sqrt{\frac{2(1,000)2}{.02}} = 447 \text{ cans}$$

b. $\bar{d} = 40 \text{ cans per day} \qquad \sigma_d = 3 \text{ cans per day} \qquad LT = 4 \text{ days}$

$$ROP = \bar{d}LT + z\sqrt{LT}(\sigma_d) = 40(4) + 2.33\sqrt{4}(3) = 174 \text{ cans}$$

Constant Demand Rate, Variable Lead Time

A variable lead time can assume any of a variety of patterns. For purposes of illustration, let's assume it can be described by a normal distribution. When lead time is normally distributed, the expected demand during lead time is normally distributed, but its variance does not encompass any summing of variances, as in the preceding

Figure 12–15

With constant demand and normally distributed lead time, total usage during lead time will be normally distributed

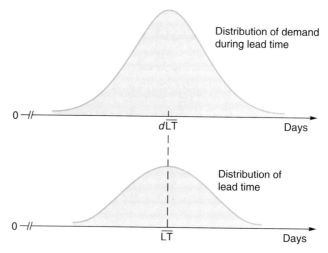

model. The reason is that the actual lead time in any given cycle will be *one* number (e.g., two weeks) rather than a series of numbers (i.e., lead time demands).

In this case, the expected demand during lead time is equal to $d\overline{LT}$, and the standard deviation of demand during lead time is equal to $d\sigma_{LT}$ (see Figure 12–15). The reorder point is

$$\text{ROP} = d\overline{LT} + zd\sigma_{LT} \qquad (12\text{–}12)$$

where

$$d = \text{Constant demand rate}$$
$$\overline{LT} = \text{Average lead time}$$
$$\sigma_{LT} = \text{Standard deviation of lead time}$$

Example 11

An automatic burner uses 2.1 gallons of oil per day. Lead time is normally distributed with a mean of six days and a standard deviation of two days. Determine the ROP to have a service level of 98 percent. How much of that quantity is safety stock?

Solution

$$d = 2.1 \text{ gallons per day} \qquad \overline{LT} = 6 \text{ days} \qquad \sigma_{LT} = 2 \text{ days}$$

$$\text{ROP} = d\overline{LT} + zd\sigma_{LT}$$

$$= 2.1(6) + 2.055(2.1)2$$
$$= 12.6 + 8.63 = 21.23 \text{ gallons} \qquad \text{Safety stock} = 8.63 \text{ gallons}$$

Variable Demand Rate and Variable Lead Time

When both the demand rate and the lead time are variable, it seems reasonable that safety stock should be larger than if one of these were constant, in order to compensate for the increased variability. In this case, expected demand during lead time is average daily demand multiplied by average lead time (in days).

If daily demand is normally distributed and if lead time is also normally distributed, then total demand during lead time will be normally distributed with a mean equal to $\overline{d}(\overline{LT})$. Its variance is actually the sum of the variances of demand and lead time, and the standard deviation is the square root of that sum:

$$\begin{array}{l}\text{Standard deviation of total} \\ \text{demand during lead time}\end{array} = \sqrt{\sigma^2_{\text{demand}} + \sigma^2_{\text{lead time}}} \qquad (12\text{–}13)$$

where

$$\sigma_{\text{demand}} = \sqrt{\overline{LT}}\ \sigma_d$$
$$\sigma_{\text{lead time}} = \overline{d}\sigma_{\text{LT}}$$

Hence,

$$\sigma_{dLT} = \sqrt{(\sqrt{\overline{LT}}\ \sigma_d)^2 + (\overline{d}\sigma_{\text{LT}})^2} = \sqrt{\overline{LT}\sigma^2_d + \overline{d}^2\sigma^2_{\text{LT}}} \qquad (12\text{–}14)$$

$$\text{ROP} = \overline{d}(\overline{LT}) + z\sqrt{\overline{LT}\sigma^2_d + \overline{d}^2\sigma^2_{\text{LT}}} \qquad (12\text{–}15)$$

(Note that every variable under the square root sign is squared except $\overline{LT}$.)

Consumption of Mug Beer at a local tavern is known to be normally distributed with a mean of 150 bottles per day and a standard deviation of 10 bottles per day. Delivery time is also normally distributed with a mean of six days and a standard deviation of one day. How many bottles of Mug should be on hand at reorder time in order to be 90 percent sure of not running out before the delivery arrives?

Example 12

∎

Solution

$$\overline{d} = 150 \text{ bottles per day} \qquad \overline{LT} = 6 \text{ days}$$
$$\sigma_d = 10 \text{ bottles per day} \qquad \sigma_{\text{LT}} = 1 \text{ day}$$
$$\begin{aligned}\text{ROP} &= \overline{d}(\overline{LT}) + z\sqrt{\overline{LT}\sigma^2_d + \overline{d}^2\sigma^2_{\text{LT}}} \\ &= 150(6) + 1.28\sqrt{6(10)^2 + 150^2(1)^2} \\ &= 900 \quad + +1.28\sqrt{23,100} = 1,095 \text{ bottles}\end{aligned}$$

SHORTAGES AND SERVICE LEVELS

The ROP computation does not reveal the expected *amount* of shortage for a given lead time service level. The expected number of units short can, however, be very useful to a manager, sometimes even more useful than the service level figure. This quantity can easily be determined from the same information that is used to compute the ROP, with one additional piece of information, which is contained in Table 12–3. Use of the table assumes that the distribution of lead time demand can

Table 12–3

Normal distribution service levels and unit normal loss function

z	Lead time service level	E(z)	z	Lead time service level	E(z)	z	Lead time service level	E(z)	z	Lead time service level	E(z)
−2.40	.0082	2.403	−0.80	.2119	0.920	0.80	.7881	0.120	2.40	.9918	0.003
−2.36	.0091	2.363	−0.76	.2236	0.889	0.84	.7995	0.112	2.44	.9927	0.002
−2.32	.0102	2.323	−0.72	.2358	0.858	0.88	.8106	0.104	2.48	.9934	0.002
−2.28	.0113	2.284	−0.68	.2483	0.828	0.92	.8212	0.097	2.52	.9941	0.002
−2.24	.0125	2.244	−0.64	.2611	0.798	0.96	.8315	0.089	2.56	.9948	0.002
−2.20	.0139	2.205	−0.60	.2743	0.769	1.00	.8413	0.083	2.60	.9953	0.001
−2.16	.0154	2.165	−0.56	.2877	0.740	1.04	.8508	0.077	2.64	.9959	0.001
−2.12	.0170	2.126	−0.52	.3015	0.712	1.08	.8599	0.071	2.68	.9963	0.001
−2.08	.0188	2.087	−0.48	.3156	0.684	1.12	.8686	0.066	2.72	.9967	0.001
−2.04	.0207	2.048	−0.44	.3300	0.657	1.16	.8770	0.061	2.76	.9971	0.001
−2.00	.0228	2.008	−0.40	.3446	0.630	1.20	.8849	0.056	2.80	.9974	0.0008
−1.96	.0250	1.969	−0.36	.3594	0.597	1.24	.8925	0.052	2.84	.9977	0.0007
−1.92	.0274	1.930	−0.32	.3745	0.576	1.28	.8997	0.048	2.88	.9980	0.0006
−1.88	.0301	1.892	−0.28	.3897	0.555	1.32	.9066	0.044	2.92	.9982	0.0005
−1.84	.0329	1.853	−0.24	.4052	0.530	1.36	.9131	0.040	2.96	.9985	0.0004
−1.80	.0359	1.814	−0.20	.4207	0.507	1.40	.9192	0.037	3.00	.9987	0.0004
−1.76	.0392	1.776	−0.16	.4364	0.484	1.44	.9251	0.034	3.04	.9988	0.0003
−1.72	.0427	1.737	−0.12	.4522	0.462	1.48	.9306	0.031	3.08	.9990	0.0003
−1.68	.0465	1.699	−0.08	.4681	0.440	1.52	.9357	0.028	3.12	.9991	0.0002
−1.64	.0505	1.661	−0.04	.4840	0.419	1.56	.9406	0.026	3.16	.9992	0.0002
−1.60	.0548	1.623	0.00	.5000	0.399	1.60	.9452	0.023	3.20	.9993	0.0002
−1.56	.0594	1.586	0.04	.5160	0.379	1.64	.9495	0.021	3.24	.9994	0.0001
−1.52	.0643	1.548	0.08	.5319	0.360	1.68	.9535	0.019	3.28	.9995	0.0001
−1.48	.0694	1.511	0.12	.5478	0.342	1.72	.9573	0.017	3.32	.9995	0.0001
−1.44	.0749	1.474	0.16	.5636	0.324	1.76	.9608	0.016	3.36	.9996	0.0001
−1.40	.0808	1.437	0.20	.5793	0.307	1.80	.9641	0.014	3.40	.9997	0.0001
−1.36	.0869	1.400	0.24	.5948	0.290	1.84	.9671	0.013			
−1.32	.0934	1.364	0.28	.6103	0.275	1.88	.9699	0.012			
−1.28	.1003	1.328	0.32	.6255	0.256	1.92	.9726	0.010			
−1.24	.1075	1.292	0.36	.6406	0.237	1.96	.9750	0.009			
−1.20	.1151	1.256	0.40	.6554	0.230	2.00	.9772	0.008			
−1.16	.1230	1.221	0.44	.6700	0.217	2.04	.9793	0.008			
−1.12	.1314	1.186	0.48	.6844	0.204	2.08	.9812	0.007			
−1.08	.1401	1.151	0.52	.6985	0.192	2.12	.9830	0.006			
−1.04	.1492	1.117	0.56	.7123	0.180	2.16	.9846	0.005			
−1.00	.1587	1.083	0.60	.7257	0.169	2.20	.9861	0.005			
−0.96	.1685	1.049	0.64	.7389	0.158	2.24	.9875	0.004			
−0.92	.1788	1.017	0.68	.7517	0.148	2.28	.9887	0.004			
−0.88	.1894	0.984	0.72	.7642	0.138	2.32	.9898	0.003			
−0.84	.2005	0.952	0.76	.7764	0.129	2.36	.9909	0.003			

be adequately represented by a normal distribution. If it can, the expected number of units short in each order cycle is given by this formula:

$$E(n) = E(z)\sigma_{dLT} \tag{12–16}$$

where

$E(n) =$ Expected number of units short per order cycle

$E(z) =$ Standardized number of units short listed in Table 12–3

$\sigma_{dLT} =$ Standard deviation of lead time demand

Example 13

■

The standard deviation of lead time demand is known to be 16 units. Lead time demand is approximately normal.

a. For a lead time service level of 90 percent, determine the expected number of units short for any order cycle.

b. What lead time service level would an expected shortage of 2 units imply?

Solution

σ_{dLT} = 16 units

a. Lead time (cycle) service level = .90. From Table 12–3, $E(z)$ = 0.048. Using Formula 12–16, $E(n)$ = 0.048(16 units) = 0.768 unit.

b. For the case where $E(n)$ = 2, we must solve for $E(z)$ and then use Table 12–3 to determine the lead time service level that implies. Thus, $E(n) = E(z)\sigma_{dLT}$, so $E(z) = E(n) / \sigma_{dLT} = 2/16 = 0.125$. From Table 12–3, this implies a service level of approximately 78 percent (interpolating).

The expected number of units short is just that—an expected or *average* amount; the exact number of units short in any given cycle will be an amount close to that. Moreover, if discrete items are involved, the number of units short in any cycle must be an integer.

Having determined the expected number of units short for an order cycle, we can now determine the expected number of units short per year. It is simply the product of the expected number of units short per cycle and the number of cycles (orders) per year. Thus,

$$E(N) = E(n)\frac{D}{Q} \tag{12–17}$$

where $E(N)$ = Expected number of units short per year.

Example 14

■

Given the following information, determine the expected number of units short per year.

$D = 1,000 \qquad Q = 250 \qquad E(n) = 2.5$

Solution

Using the formula $E(N) = E(n)\dfrac{D}{Q}$

$$E(N) = 2.5\left(\frac{1,000}{250}\right) = 10.0 \text{ units per year}$$

It is sometimes convenient to think of service level in annual terms. For instance, one definition of annual service level is the percentage of demand filled directly from inventory. Thus, if $D = 1,000$, and 990 units were filled directly from inventory (shortages totaling 10 units over the year were recorded), the annual service level would be 990/1,000 = 99 percent. Annual service level is related to, but generally more than, lead time service level. The two service levels can be related using the following formula:

$$E(N) = (1 - SL_{annual})D \tag{12–18}$$

Using Formulas 12–17 and 12–16, $E(N) = E(n)D/Q = E(z) \ \sigma_{dLT}D/Q$. Thus,

$$(1 - SL_{annual}) = \frac{E(z)\sigma_{dLT}}{Q} \tag{12–19}$$

Example 15

Given a lead time service level of .90, $D = 1,000$, $Q = 250$, and $\sigma_{dLT} = 16$, determine the annual service level.

Solution

From Table 12–3, $E(z) = 0.048$ for a 90 percent lead time service level. Using Formula 12–19, we find:

$$(1 - SL_{annual}) = \frac{0.048(16)}{250} = .003$$

Solving for the annual service level yields

$$SL_{annual} = 1 - .003 = .997$$

Note that in the preceding example, a lead time service level of 90 percent provided an annual service level of 99.7 percent. Naturally, different values of D, Q, and σ_{dLT} will tend to produce different results for a cycle service level of 90 percent. Nonetheless, in general, the annual service level will be greater than the cycle service level. In addition, since the annual service level as we have defined it relates to the percentage of units short per year, it may make sense to base cycle service levels on a specified annual service level. This would mean setting the annual level, using Formula 12–19 to solve for $E(z)$, and then using that value to obtain the service level for the order cycles.

HOW MUCH TO ORDER: FIXED-ORDER-INTERVAL MODEL

When inventory replenishment is based on EOQ/ROP models, *fixed* quantities of items are ordered at varying time intervals. Just the opposite occurs under the **fixed–order–interval (FOI)** model: orders for *varying* quantities are placed at fixed time intervals (weekly, every 20 days, etc.).

Fixed-order-interval model

Orders for varying quantities are placed at fixed time intervals.

There are a number of differences between these two approaches to reordering. Both are sensitive to demand experience just prior to reordering, but in somewhat different ways. In the fixed-quantity model, a higher-than-normal demand causes a *shorter time* between orders, whereas in the fixed-interval model, the result would be a *larger order size*. Another difference is that the fixed-quantity model requires close monitoring of inventory levels in order to know *when* the amount on hand has reached the reorder point, and the fixed-interval model requires only a periodic review (i.e., physical inspection) of inventory levels just prior to placing an order to determine *how much* is needed.

REASONS FOR USING

Under certain conditions, the use of fixed-order intervals is quite practical. In some cases, a supplier's policy might encourage orders at fixed intervals. Even if that is not the case, grouping orders for items from the same supplier can produce savings in shipping costs. Furthermore, some situations do not readily lend themselves to continuous monitoring of inventory levels. Many retail operations (e.g., drugstores, small grocery stores) fall into this category. The alternative for them is to use fixed order intervals, which require only periodic checks of inventory levels.

DETERMINING THE AMOUNT TO ORDER

If the demand rate and lead time are both constant, the fixed-interval model and the fixed quantity model function identically. The differences in the two models become apparent only when examined under conditions of variability. As in the ROP model, there can be variations in demand only, in lead time only, or in both demand and lead time. However, for the sake of simplicity, and because it is perhaps the most frequently encountered situation, the discussion here will focus on only *variable demand and constant lead time*.

Figure 12–16 provides a comparison of the fixed-quantity and fixed-interval systems. Notice that in the fixed-quantity arrangement, orders are triggered by a *quantity* (ROP), and in the fixed-interval arrangement, orders are triggered by a *time*. Because of this, the fixed-interval system must have stock-out protection for lead time plus the next order cycle, but the fixed-quantity system needs protection only during lead time since additional orders can be placed at any time and will be received shortly (lead time) thereafter. Consequently, there is a greater need for safety stock in the fixed-interval model than there is in the fixed-quantity model. Note, for example, the large dip into safety stock during the second order cycle with the fixed-interval model.

Order size in the fixed-interval model is determined by the following computation:

$$
\begin{array}{cccc}
\text{Amount} \\ \text{to order}
\end{array} =
\begin{array}{c}
\text{Expected demand} \\ \text{during protection} \\ \text{interval}
\end{array} +
\begin{array}{c}
\text{Safety} \\ \text{stock}
\end{array} -
\begin{array}{c}
\text{Amount on hand} \\ \text{at reorder time}
\end{array}
$$

$$
= \quad \bar{d}(\text{OI} + \text{LT}) \quad + z\sigma_d\sqrt{\text{OI} + \text{LT}} - \quad A \tag{12–20}
$$

where

    OI = Order interval (length of time between orders)

    A = Amount on hand at reorder time

As in previous models, it is assumed that demand during the protection interval is normally distributed.

Figure 12–16

Comparison of fixed-quantity and fixed-interval ordering

A. Reordering fixed quantities

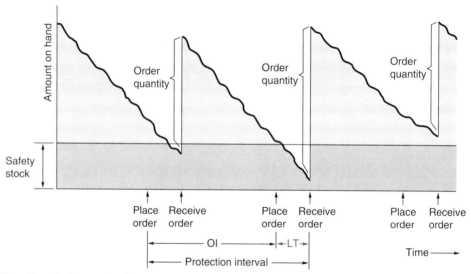

B. Reordering at fixed intervals

Example 16

■

Given the following information, determine the amount to order.

$\bar{d}$ = 30 units per day   Desired service level = 99 percent

σ_d = 3 units per day   Amount on hand at reorder time = 71 units

LT = 2 days   OI = 7 days

Solution

$$z = 2.33 \text{ for 99 percent service level}$$

$$\underset{\text{to order}}{\text{Amount}} = \bar{d}(\text{OI} + \text{LT}) + z\sigma_d\sqrt{\text{OI} + \text{LT}} - A$$

$$= 30(7 + 2) + 2.33(3)\sqrt{7 + 2} - 71 = 220 \text{ units}$$

Benefits and Disadvantages

The fixed-interval system results in the tight control needed for A items in an A-B-C classification due to the periodic reviews it requires. In addition, when two or more items come from the same supplier, grouping orders can yield savings in ordering, packing, and shipping costs. Moreover, it may be the only practical approach if inventory withdrawals cannot be closely monitored.

On the negative side, the fixed-interval system necessitates a larger amount of safety stock for a given risk of stock-out due to the need to protect against shortages during an entire order interval plus lead time (instead of lead time only), and this increases the carrying cost. Also, there are the costs of the periodic reviews.

OPERATIONS STRATEGY

Inventories are a necessary part of doing business—but having too much inventory is not good. One reason for this is that inventories tend to hide problems; they make it easier to "live with" problems rather than eliminate them. Another reason is that inventories are costly to maintain. Consequently, a wise operations strategy is to work toward reducing inventories. This can be accomplished by (1) reducing lot sizes and (2) reducing safety stocks.

Observers have noted that Japanese manufacturers seem to use smaller lot sizes than their Western counterparts. The reason for this is that the Japanese have adopted a different perspective on inventory carrying costs. In addition to the usual components (storage, handling, obsolescence, etc.), they also recognize the opportunity costs of disrupting work flow, inability to place machines and workers closer together (which encourages cooperation, socialization, and communication), and hiding problems related to product quality and equipment breakdown. When these are factored in, carrying costs become higher—perhaps much higher—than before. The impact of an EOQ with revised (higher) holding costs is illustrated in Figure 12–17. Recall that carrying costs and ordering costs are equal at the EOQ. A higher carrying cost results in a steeper carrying-cost line, and the resulting intersection with the ordering-cost line occurs at a smaller quantity—hence a smaller EOQ.

Although it can be argued that these costs are not readily quantifiable, the point is that Western manufacturers should probably reassess holding costs under this new light and revise estimated holding costs upward.

The second factor in the EOQ model that can contribute to smaller lot sizes is the setup or ordering processing cost. There are numerous examples of cases where these costs have been reduced through research efforts. Note, however, that whereas a reduction due to carrying costs stems from a reassessment of those costs, a reduction due to ordering or setup costs must come from actively pursuing improvement. Together, these cost reductions can lead to even smaller lot sizes, as illustrated in Figure 12–18.

Additional reductions in inventory can be achieved by reducing the amount of safety stock that is carried. Important factors in safety stock are lead time and lead time variability; reductions in these will result in lower safety stocks. Such reductions can often be realized by working with suppliers, by choosing suppliers that are located close to the buyer, and by shifting to smaller lot sizes. Note that if either lead time or lead time variability is zero, *no* safety stock will be needed!

In attempting to achieve the reductions discussed here, an A-B-C approach can be very beneficial. This means that all phases of operation should be examined, and

Figure 12–17

Revised (increased) carrying costs result in a smaller EOQ

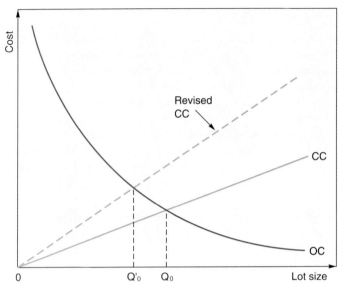

Figure 12–18

Reductions in both ordering/setup cost and carrying cost result in much smaller lot sizes

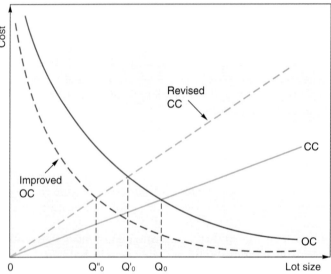

those showing the greatest potential for improvement (the A items) should be attacked first. Early results will demonstrate the benefits of this strategy to both management and workers, making both parties more willing to lend their support to additional efforts.

Last, but certainly not least, it is important to make sure that inventory records be kept *accurate* and *up to date*. Estimates of holding costs, ordering costs, setup costs, and lead times should be reviewed periodically.

SUMMARY

Good inventory management is often the mark of a well-run organization. Inventory levels must be planned carefully in order to balance the cost of holding inventory and the cost of providing reasonable levels of customer service. Successful inventory management requires a system to keep track of inventory transactions, accurate information about demand and lead times, realistic estimates of certain inventory-related costs, and a priority system for classifying the items in inventory and allocating control efforts.

The models described in this chapter are relevant for instances where demand for inventory items is *independent*. Three classes of models are described: EOQ, ROP, and fixed-interval. These are all appropriate if unused items can be carried over into subsequent periods. The single-period model is appropriate when items cannot be carried over; it is described in the supplement to this chapter. EOQ models address the question of *how much to order*. The ROP models address the question of *when to order* and are particularly helpful in dealing with situations that include variations in either demand rate or lead time. ROP models involve service level and safety stock considerations. When the time between orders is fixed, the FOI model is useful. The models presented in this chapter are summarized in Table 12–4.

Table 12–4

Summary of inventory formulas

Model	Formula	Symbols
1. Basic EOQ	$Q_0 = \sqrt{\dfrac{2DS}{H}}$ (12–2) $TC = \dfrac{Q}{2}H + \dfrac{D}{Q}S$ (12–1) Length of order cycle $= \dfrac{Q_0}{D}$ (12–3)	$Q_0 =$ Economic order quantity $D =$ Annual demand $S =$ Order cost $H =$ Annual carrying cost per unit
2. Economic run size	$Q_0 = \sqrt{\dfrac{2DS}{H}}\sqrt{\dfrac{p}{p-u}}$ (12–5) $I_{max} = \dfrac{Q_0}{p}(p-u)$ (12–6) $TC = \dfrac{I_{max}}{2}H + \dfrac{D}{Q}S$ (12–4)	$Q_0 =$ Optimal run or order size $p =$ Production or delivery rate $u =$ Usage rate $I_{max} =$ Maximum inventory level
3. Quantity discounts	$TC = \dfrac{Q}{2}H + \dfrac{D}{Q}S + PD$ (12–9)	$P =$ Unit price

4. Reorder point under:
   a. Constant demand and lead time
   b. Variable demand rate
   c. Variable lead time
   d. Variable lead time and demand
	$ROP = d(LT)$
	 $ROP = \bar{d}LT + z\sqrt{LT}\,(\sigma_d)$ (12–11)
	 $ROP = \bar{d}\overline{LT} + zd(\sigma_{LT})$ (12–12)
	 $ROP = \bar{d}\,\overline{LT} + z\sqrt{\overline{LT}\sigma_d^2 + \bar{d}^2\sigma_{LT}^2}$ (12–15)
		$ROP =$ Quantity on hand at reorder point
		 $d =$ Demand rate
		 $LT =$ Lead time
		 $\bar{d} =$ Average demand rate
		 $\sigma_d =$ Standard deviation of demand rate
		 $z =$ Standard normal deviation
		 $\overline{LT} =$ Average lead time
		 $\sigma_{LT} =$ Standard deviation of lead time

Table 12–4

Summary of inventory formulas

Model	Formula	Symbols

5. ROP shortages
  a. Units short per cycle
 	
  b. Units short per year
 	
  c. Annual service level
	$E(n) = E(z)\sigma_{dLT}$ (12–16)
	
	$E(N) = E(n)\dfrac{D}{Q}$ (12–17)
	
	$(1 - \text{SL}_{\text{annual}}) = \dfrac{E(z)\sigma_{dLT}}{Q}$ (12–19)
		$E(n) =$ Expected
		    number short
		    per cycle
		$E(z) =$ Standardized
		    number short
		$\sigma_{dLT} =$ Standard devia-
		    tion of lead
		    time demand
		$E(N) =$ Expected
		    number short
		    per year
		$\text{SL}_{\text{annual}} =$ Annual service
		    level

6. Fixed interval	$Q = \bar{d}(\text{OI} + \text{LT}) + z\sigma_d\sqrt{\text{OI} + \text{LT}} - A$ (12–20)	$\text{OI} =$ Time between
		    orders
		$A =$ Amount on
		    hand at order
		    time

KEY TERMS

A-B-C approach, 592
dependent demand, 585
economic order quantity
  (EOQ), 593
fixed-order-interval (FOI)
  model, 618
holding (carrying) costs, 590
independent demand, 585
inventory, 584

ordering costs, 591
periodic system, 588
perpetual inventory system, 588
quantity discounts, 601
reorder point (ROP), 607
safety stock, 609
service level, 610
shortage costs, 591
two-bin system, 588
universal product code, 589

SOLVED PROBLEMS

Problem

1. *Basic EOQ.* A toy manufacturer uses approximately 32,000 silicon chips annually. The chips are used at a steady rate during the 240 days the plant operates. Annual holding cost is 60 cents per chip, and ordering cost is $24. Determine:

  a. The optimal order size.
  b. The number of workdays in an order cycle.

Solution

$D = 32{,}000$ chips per year $S = \$24$
$H = \$.60$ per unit per year

a. $Q_0 = \sqrt{\dfrac{2DS}{H}} = \sqrt{\dfrac{2(32,000)\$24}{\$.60}} = 1,600$ chips.

b. $\dfrac{Q_0}{D} = \dfrac{1,600 \text{ chips}}{32,000 \text{ chips/yr.}} = \dfrac{1}{20}$ year (i.e., $\tfrac{1}{20} \times 240$ days), or 12 days.

Problem

2. *Noninstantaneous delivery.* The Dine Corporation is both a producer and a user of brass couplings. The firm operates 220 days a year and uses the couplings at a steady rate of 50 per day. Couplings can be produced at a rate of 200 per day. Annual storage costs are $1 per coupling, and machine setup costs are $35 per run.

    a. Determine the economic run size.

    b. Approximately how many runs per year will there be?

    c. Compute the maximum inventory level.

    d. Determine the length of the *pure consumption* portion of the cycle.

Solution

$D = 50$ units per day $\times$ 220 days per year $= 11,000$ units per year

$S = \$35$

$H = \$1$ per unit per year

$p = 200$ units per day

$u = 50$ units per day

a. $Q_0 = \sqrt{\dfrac{2DS}{H}} \sqrt{\dfrac{p}{p - u}} = \sqrt{\dfrac{2(11,000)35}{1}} \sqrt{\dfrac{200}{200 - 50}} = 1,013$ units.

b. Number of runs per year: $D/Q_0 = 11,000/1,013 = 10.86$, or 11.

c. $I_{max} = \dfrac{Q_0}{p}(p - u) = \dfrac{1,013}{200}(200 - 50) = 759.75$ or 760 units.

d. Length of cycle $= \dfrac{Q_0}{u} = \dfrac{1,013 \text{ units}}{50 \text{ units per day}} = 20.26$ days

    Length of run $= \dfrac{Q_0}{p} = \dfrac{1,013 \text{ units}}{200 \text{ units per day}} = 5.065$ days

    $\begin{aligned}\text{Length of pure consumption portion} &= \text{Length of cycle} - \text{Length of run} \\ &= 20.26 - 5.065 = 15.20 \text{ days.}\end{aligned}$

Problem

3. *Quantity discounts.* A small manufacturing firm uses roughly 3,400 pounds of chemical dye a year. Currently the firm purchases 300 pounds per order and pays $3 per pound. The supplier has just announced that orders of 1,000 pounds or more will be filled at a price of $2 per pound. The manufacturing firm incurs a cost of $100 each time it submits an order and assigns an annual holding cost of 17 percent of the purchase price per pound.

    a. Determine the order size that will minimize the total cost.

    b. If the supplier offered the discount at 1,500 pounds instead of at 1,000 pounds, what order size would minimize total cost?

Solution

$$D = 3,400 \text{ pounds per year} \qquad S = \$100 \qquad H = 0.17P$$

a. Compute the EOQ for $2 per pound:

$$Q_{\$2/pound} = \sqrt{\frac{2DS}{H}} = \sqrt{\frac{2(3,400)100}{0.17(2)}} = 1,414 \text{ pounds.}$$

Since this quantity is feasible at $2 per pound, it is the optimum.

b. When the discount is offered at 1,500 pounds, the EOQ for the $2 per pound curve is no longer feasible. Consequently, it becomes necessary to compute the EOQ for $3 per pound and compare the total cost for that order size with the total cost using the price break quantity (i.e., 1,500).

$$Q_{\$3/pound} = \sqrt{\frac{2DS}{H}} = \sqrt{\frac{2(3,400)100}{0.17(3)}} = 1,155 \text{ pounds}$$

$$TC = \left(\frac{Q}{2}\right)H \quad + \quad \left(\frac{D}{Q}\right)S \quad + \quad PD$$

$$TC_{1,155} = \left(\frac{1,155}{2}\right)0.17(3) + \left(\frac{3,400}{1,155}\right)100 + 3(3,400)$$

$$= \quad \$294.53 \quad + \quad \$294.37 \quad + \$10,200 = \$10,789$$

$$TC_{1,500} = \left(\frac{1,500}{2}\right)0.17(2) + \left(\frac{3,400}{1,500}\right)100 + 2(3,400)$$

$$= \quad \$255 \quad + \quad \$226.67 \quad + \$6,800 = \$7,282$$

Hence, because it would result in a lower total cost, 1,500 is the optimal order size.

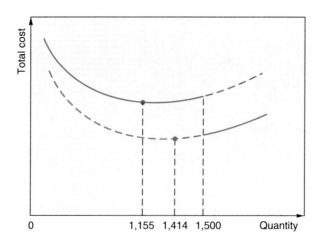

Problem

4. *ROP for variable demand and constant lead time.* The housekeeping department of a motel uses approximately 400 washcloths per day. The actual amount tends to vary with the number of customers who stay on any given night. Usage can be approximated by a normal distribution that has a mean of 400 and a standard deviation of 9 washcloths per day. A linen supply

company delivers towels and washcloths with a lead time of three days. If the motel policy is to maintain a stock-out risk of 2 percent, what is the minimum number of washcloths that must be on hand at reorder time, and how much of that amount can be considered safety stock?

Solution

$$\bar{d} = 400 \text{ washcloths per day} \qquad LT = 3 \text{ days}$$
$$\sigma_d = 9 \text{ washcloths per day} \qquad \text{Risk} = 2\%, \text{ so service level} = 98\%$$

From Appendix B, Table B, the z value that corresponds to an area under the normal curve to the left of z for 98 percent is about $+2.055$.

$$ROP = \bar{d}LT + z\sqrt{LT}\sigma_d = 400(3) + 2.055\sqrt{3}(9)$$
$$= 1,200 + 32.03, \text{ or approximately } 1,232$$

Safety stock is approximately 32 washcloths.

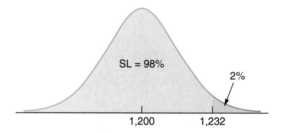

Problem

5. *ROP for constant demand and variable lead time.* The motel in the preceding example uses approximately 600 bars of soap each day, and this tends not to vary by more than a few bars either way. Lead time for soap delivery is normally distributed with a mean of six days and a standard deviation of two days. A service level of 90 percent is desired. Find the ROP.

Solution

$$d = 600 \text{ bars per day}$$
$$SL = 90\%, \text{ so } z = +1.28 \text{ (from Appendix B, Table B)}$$
$$\overline{LT} = 6 \text{ days}$$
$$\sigma_{LT} = 2 \text{ days}$$
$$ROP = d\overline{LT} + zd(\sigma_{LT})$$
$$= 600(6) + 1.28(600)2$$
$$= 5,136 \text{ bars of soap}$$

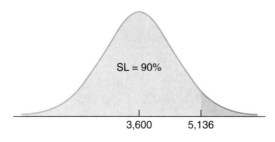

Problem

6. *ROP for variable demand rate and variable lead time.* The motel replaces broken glasses at a rate of 25 per day. In the past, this quantity has tended to vary normally and have a standard deviation of 3 glasses per day. Glasses are ordered from a Cleveland supplier. Lead time is normally distributed with an average of 10 days and a standard deviation of 2 days. What ROP should be used to achieve a service level of 95 percent?

Solution

$$\bar{d} = 25 \text{ glasses per day} \qquad \overline{LT} = 10 \text{ days}$$
$$\sigma_d = 3 \text{ glasses per day} \qquad \sigma_{LT} = 2 \text{ days}$$
$$SL = 95\%, \text{ so } z = +1.65 \text{ (Appendix B, Table B)}$$

$$ROP = \bar{d}\,\overline{LT} + z\sqrt{\overline{LT}\sigma_d^2 + \bar{d}^2\sigma_{LT}^2}$$
$$= 25(10) + 1.65\sqrt{10(3)^2 + (25)^2(2)^2}$$
$$= 334 \text{ glasses}$$

SL = 95%

250   334

Problem

7. *Shortages and service levels.* The manager of a store that sells office supplies has decided to set an annual service level of 96 percent for a certain model of telephone answering equipment. The store sells approximately 300 of this model a year. Holding cost is $5 per unit annually, ordering cost is $25, and $\sigma_{dLT} = 7$.

    a. What average number of units short per year will be consistent with the specified annual service level?

    b. What average number of units short per cycle will provide the desired annual service level?

    c. What lead time service level is necessary for the 96 percent annual service level?

Solution

$$SL_{annual} = 96\% \qquad D = 300 \text{ units} \qquad H = \$5 \qquad S = \$25 \qquad \sigma_{dLT} = 7$$

a. $E(N) = (1 - SL_{annual})D = (1 - .96)(300) = 12 \text{ units.}$

b. $E(N) = E(n)\dfrac{D}{Q}$. Solving for $E(n)$, we have

$$E(n) = E(N)/\left(\frac{D}{Q}\right) = 12/\left(\frac{300}{Q}\right)$$

$$Q = \sqrt{\frac{2DS}{H}} = \sqrt{\frac{2(300)(25)}{5}} = 54.77 \text{ (round to 55)}$$

Then $E(n) = 12/\left(\dfrac{300}{55}\right) = 2.2$.

c. In order to find the lead time service level, we need the value of $E(z)$. Since we know the value of $E(n)$ is 2.2 and that $E(n) = E(z)\sigma_{dLT}$, we have $2.2 = E(z)(7)$. Solving gives us $E(z) = 2.2/7 = 0.314$. Interpolating in Table 12–3 gives us the approximate lead time service level. Thus,

$$\frac{0.307 - 0.314}{0.307 - 0.324} = \frac{.5793 - x}{.5793 - .5636}$$

Solving, $x = .5728$.

[To interpolate, find the two values between which the computed number falls in the $E(z)$ column. Then find the difference between the computed value and one end of the range, and divide by the difference between the two ends of the range. Perform the corresponding calculation on the two service levels using x for the unknown value, and solve for x. Often, simply "eyeballing" the unknown value will suffice.]

Problem

8. *Fixed-order-interval model.* A lab orders a number of chemicals from the same supplier every 30 days. Lead time is 5 days. The assistant manager of the lab must determine how much of one of these chemicals to order. A check of stock revealed that eleven 25-ml jars are on hand. Daily usage of the chemical is approximately normal with a mean of 15.2 ml per day and a standard deviation of 1.6 ml per day. The desired service level for this chemical is 95 percent.

    a. How many bottles of the chemical should be ordered?
    b. What is the average amount of safety stock of the chemical?

Solution

$\bar{d} = 15.2$ ml per day, OI $= 30$ days, SL $= 95\%$ requires $z = 1.65$

$\sigma_d = 1.6$ ml per day, LT $= 5$ days, $A = 11$ jars $\times$ 25 ml per jar $= 275$ ml

a. $\dfrac{\text{Amount}}{\text{to order}} = \bar{d}(\text{OI} + \text{LT}) + z\sigma_d\sqrt{\text{OI} + \text{LT}} - A$

$= 15.2(30 + 5) + 1.65(1.6)\sqrt{30 + 5} - 275$

$= 272.62$ ml

Convert this to number of jars: $\dfrac{272.62 \text{ ml}}{25 \text{ ml per jar}} = 10.90$ or 11 jars.

b. *Safety stock* $= z\sigma_d\sqrt{\text{OI} + \text{LT}}$

$= 1.65(1.6)\sqrt{30 + 5} = 15.62$ ml.

DISCUSSION AND REVIEW QUESTIONS

1. What are the primary reasons for holding inventory?
2. What are the requirements for effective inventory management?
3. Briefly describe each of the costs associated with inventory.
4. Contrast independent and dependent demand with respect to inventories.
5. List the major assumptions of the EOQ model.
6. Why isn't price considered explicitly in the basic EOQ model? How is it sometimes indirectly included?
7. How would you respond to the criticism that EOQ models tend to provide misleading results because values of D, S, and H are, at best, educated guesses?
8. What are quantity discounts? What three costs enter into the order quantity decision when discounts are available?
9. What is safety stock, and why is it held?
10. Under what circumstances would the amount of safety stock held be:
    a. Large?
    b. Small?
    c. Zero?
11. What is meant by the term *service level*? Generally speaking, how is service level related to the amount of safety stock held?
12. Describe briefly the A–B–C approach to inventory control.
13. The purchasing agent for a company that assembles and sells air-conditioning equipment in a Latin American country has noted that the cost of compressors has increased significantly each time they have been reordered. The company uses an EOQ model to determine order size. What are the implications of this price escalation with respect to order size? What factors other than price must be taken into consideration?
14. Explain how a decrease in setup time can lead to a decrease in the average amount of inventory a firm holds, and why that would be beneficial.

PROBLEMS

1. A large bakery buys sugar in 100-pound bags. The bakery uses an average of 1,344 bags a year. Preparing an order and receiving a shipment of sugar involves a cost of $3 per order. Annual carrying costs are $14 per bag.
    a. Determine the economic order quantity.
    b. What is the average number of bags on hand?
    c. How many orders per year will there be?
    d. Compute the total cost of ordering and carrying sugar.
2. A gasoline pump is used to remove water from construction sites 300 days a year. The generator consumes 80 liters of fuel each day. Storage and handling costs are $4 per liter a year, and ordering and receiving the shipments of fuel involve a cost of $12 each.
    a. Find the optimal order size for fuel.
    b. Compute the annual ordering cost and the annual carrying cost.
    c. Are the annual ordering and carrying costs always equal at the EOQ?
    d. If storage and handling costs increase to $5 per liter per year, by how much will the total cost change?
3. Garden Variety Flower Shop uses 800 clay pots a month. The pots are purchased at $1 each. Annual carrying costs are estimated to be 25 percent of cost, and ordering costs are $30 per order.
    a. Determine the economic order quantity and the total annual carrying and ordering costs.

b. Suppose an analysis shows the actual carrying costs are roughly double the current estimate. What impact would this have on the total annual carrying and ordering costs?

4. A produce distributor uses 800 packing crates a month, which it purchases at a cost of $10 each. The manager has assigned an annual carrying cost of 35 percent of the purchase price per crate. Ordering costs are $28. Currently the manager orders once a month. How much could the firm save annually in ordering and carrying costs by using the EOQ?

5. A chemical firm produces sodium bisulfate in 100-pound bags. Demand for this product is 20 tons per day. The capacity for producing the product is 50 tons per day. Setup costs $100, and storage and handling costs are $5 per ton a year. The firm operates 200 days a year.
   a. How many bags per run are optimal?
   b. What would the average inventory be for this lot size?
   c. Determine the approximate length of a production run, in days.
   d. About how many runs per year would there be?
   e. How much could the company save annually if the setup cost could be reduced to $25 per run?

6. A food processor uses approximately 27,000 glass jars a month for its fruit juice product. Because of storage limitations, a lot size of 4,000 jars has been used. A safety stock of 500 jars is kept to reduce the risk of running out of jars before a new shipment arrives. Monthly holding cost is 18 cents per jar, and reordering cost is $60 per order. The company operates an average of 20 days a month.
   a. What penalty is the company incurring by its present order size?
   b. The manager would prefer ordering 10 times each month but would have to justify any change in order size. One possibility is to simplify order processing to reduce the ordering cost. What ordering cost would enable the manager to justify ordering every other day?
   c. Suppose that after investigating ordering cost, the manager is able to reduce it to $50. How else could the manager justify using an order size that would be consistent with ordering every other day?

7. The Friendly Sausage Factory (FSF) can produce hot dogs at a rate of 5,000 per day. FSF supplies hot dogs to local stores and restaurants at a steady rate of 250 per day. The cost to prepare the equipment for producing hot dogs is $22. Annual holding costs are 15 cents per hot dog. The factory operates 300 days a year. Find:
   a. The optimal run size.
   b. The number of runs per year.
   c. The length (in days) of a run.

8. A firm that trains crane operators guarantees its graduates an annual salary of at least $10,000, which it pays from the time of graduation until the student is employed. Demand for graduates is steady throughout the year and averages 100 per year. The cost per class for the firm is $4,100, regardless of class size.
   a. What is the optimal class size?
   b. How often should the course be offered?

9. A jewelry firm buys semiprecious stones that it uses in making bracelets and rings. The supplier quotes a price of $8 per stone for quantities of 600 stones or more, $9 per stone for orders of 400 to 599 stones, and $10 per stone for lesser quantities. The jewelry firm operates 200 days per year. Usage rate is 25 stones per day, and ordering costs are $48.
   a. If carrying costs are $1 per year for each stone, find the order quantity that will minimize total annual cost.
   b. If annual carrying costs are 30 percent of unit cost, what will the optimal order size be?
   c. If lead time is six working days, at what point should the company reorder?

10. A mail-order house buys gummed labels in boxes of 8,000. The firm uses 18,000 boxes a year. Carrying costs are 20 cents per box a year, and ordering costs are $32. The following price schedule applies. Determine:
    a.   The optimal order quantity.
    b.   The number of orders per year.

Number of boxes	Price per box
1,000 to 1,999..................	$1.25
2,000 to 4,999..................	1.20
5,000 to 9,999..................	1.18
10,000 or more	1.15

11. A charitable organization assembles and sells novelty items. Annual demand is 80,000 units, ordering and preparation costs run $60, and carrying costs are 30 percent of unit price per year. For quantities of 5,000 units or fewer, the cost is 12 cents per unit; for 5,001 to 9,800 units, the cost is 10 cents per unit; and for larger orders, the cost is 8 cents per unit. Find the optimal order size.

12. A manufacturer of baby strollers purchases the seat portion of the stroller from a supplier who lists these prices: less than 1,000 seats, $5 each; 1,000 to 3,999, $4.95 each; 4,000 to 5,999, $4.90 each; and 6,000 or more, $4.85 each. Ordering costs are $50, annual carrying costs are 40 percent of purchase cost, and annual usage is 4,900 seats. Determine an order quantity that will minimize total cost.

13. A newspaper publisher uses roughly 800 feet of baling wire each day to secure bundles of newspapers while they are being distributed to carriers. The paper is published Monday through Saturday. Ordering lead time is six workdays. What is the appropriate reorder point quantity, given that the company desires a service level of 95 percent, assuming that stock-out risk for various levels of safety stock are as follows: 1,500 feet, 0.10; 1,800 feet, 0.05; 2,100 feet, 0.02; and 2,400 feet, 0.01.

14. Demand for walnut fudge ice cream at the Sweet Cream Dairy can be approximated by a normal distribution with a mean of 21 gallons per week and a standard deviation of 3.5 gallons per week. The new manager desires a service level of 90 percent. Lead time is two days, and the dairy is open seven days a week. (*Hint:* Work in terms of weeks.)
    a.   If an ROP model is used, what ROP would be consistent with the desired service level?
    b.   If a fixed-interval model is used instead of an ROP model, what order size would be needed for the 90 percent service level with an order interval of 10 days and a supply of 2 gallons on hand at the order time?

15. A large accounting firm uses five 100-sheet boxes of letterhead stationery a week. Experience suggests that usage can be well approximated by a normal distribution with a mean of five boxes per week and a standard deviation of one-half box per week. Two weeks are required to fill an order for letterhead stationery. Ordering cost is $2, and annual holding cost is 20 cents per box.
    a.   Determine the economic order quantity for minimizing ordering and carrying costs, assuming a 52-week year.
    b.   If the firm reorders when the supply on hand is 12 boxes, compute the risk of a stock-out.
    c.   If, instead of an ROP, a fixed interval of seven weeks is used for reordering, what risk of stock-out does the firm incur if it orders 36 boxes when the amount on hand is 12 boxes?

16. A large automotive repair shop uses an average of 40 repair kits per week. Usage can be described by a normal distribution that has a mean of 40 and a standard deviation of 6. Lead time for ordering the repair kits is also normal, with a mean of seven days and a standard deviation of one-half day. A stock-out risk of 1 percent is being used. The workweek is seven days.
    a.   What ROP is appropriate?
    b.   How much could safety stock be cut if average lead time could be reduced to one day? How much additional reduction would a risk of 5 percent yield?
    c.   What are some possible ways that lead time might be reduced?

17. The manager of a furniture manufacturing plant hopes to achieve a better allocation of inventory control efforts by adopting an A–B–C approach to inventory control. Given the monthly usages listed in the following table, classify the items in A, B, and C categories according to dollar usage.

Item	Usage	Unit cost
4021.......	50	$1,400
9402.......	300	12
4066.......	40	700
6500.......	150	20
9280.......	10	1,020
4050.......	80	140
6850.......	2,000	15
3010.......	400	20
4400.......	7,000	5

18. Ned's Natural Foods sells unshelled peanuts by the pound. Historically, Ned has observed that daily demand is normally distributed with a mean of 80 pounds and a standard deviation of 10 pounds. Lead time also appears normally distributed with a mean of eight days and a standard deviation of one day.
    a.   What ROP would provide a 90 percent lead time service level?
    b.   What is the expected number of units (pounds) short per cycle? (*Hint:* Use Formula 12–14 for σ_{dLT}.)

19. Regional Supermarket is open 360 days per year. Daily use of cash register tape averages 10 rolls. Usage appears normally distributed with a standard deviation of 2 rolls per day. Ordering tape involves a cost of $1, and carrying costs are 40 cents per roll a year. Lead time is three days.
    a.   What is the EOQ?
    b.   What ROP will provide a lead time service level of 96 percent?
    c.   What is the expected number of units short per cycle with 96 percent? Per year?
    d.   What is the annual service level?

20. An automatic machine produces rivets from bar stock at a rate of 1,200 per day, 250 days a year. The order size is 2,000 feet. Fifteen rivets can be cut from one foot of stock. Delivery lead time on stock is known to be normally distributed with a mean of nine days and a standard deviation of two days.
    a.   How much bar stock is used per day?
    b.   How much safety stock is needed for a stock-out risk of 3 percent for each order cycle? (Use $\sigma_{dLT} = d\sigma_{LT}$.)
    c.   What is the annual service level?
    d.   By how much could safety stock be reduced if average lead time could be reduced by five days and lead time variability could be cut in half?

21. A service station uses 1,200 cases of oil a year. Ordering cost is $40, and annual carrying cost is $3 per case. The station owner has specified an *annual* service level of 98 percent. What ROP is appropriate if lead time demand is normally distributed with a mean of 80 cases and a standard deviation of 4 cases? What is the lead time service level?

22. A drugstore uses fixed order cycles for many of the items it stocks. The manager wants a service level of .98. Determine the order size that will be consistent with this service level for these items for an order interval of 14 days and a lead time of 2 days:

Item	Average daily demand	Standard deviation	Quantity on hand
K033	60	5	420
K144	50	4	375
L700	8	2	160

SELECTED BIBLIOGRAPHY

Buffa, Elwood, and James S. Dryer. *Essentials of Management Science/Operations Research.* New York: John Wiley & Sons, 1978.

Chase, Richard B., and Nicholas J. Aquilano. *Production and Operations Management.* 6th ed. Homewood, Ill.: Richard D. Irwin, 1992.

Fogarty, Donald W., and Thomas R. Hoffmann. *Production and Inventory Management.* Cincinnati, Ohio: South-Western Publishing Co., 1983.

Love, Stephen F. *Inventory Control.* New York: McGraw-Hill, 1979.

Peterson, R., and E. A. Silver. *Decision Systems for Inventory Management and Production Planning.* 2nd ed. New York: John Wiley & Sons, 1984.

Tersine, Richard J. *Principles of Inventory and Materials Management.* 3rd ed. New York: Elsevier North-Holland, 1987.

Vollman, Thomas E.; William L. Berry; and D. Clay Whybark. *Manufacturing Planning and Control Systems.* 3rd ed. Homewood, Ill.: Richard D. Irwin, 1992.

CASE HARVEY INDUSTRIES

Background

Harvey Industries, a Wisconsin company, was incorporated in 1950 and specializes in the assembly of high-pressure washer systems and in the sale of repair parts for these systems. The products range from small portable high-pressure washers to large industrial installations for snow removal from vehicles stored outdoors during the winter months. Typical uses for high-pressure water cleaning include:

Automobiles
Airplanes
Building maintenance
Barns
Engines
Ice cream plants
Lift trucks
Machinery
Swimming pools

Industrial customers include General Motors, Ford, Chrysler, Delta Airlines, United Parcel Service, and Shell Oil Company.

Although the industrial applications are a significant part of its sales, Harvey Industries is primarily an assembler of equipment for coin operated self-service car wash systems. The typical car wash is of concrete block construction with an equipment room in the center, flanked on either side by a number of bays. The cars are driven into the bays where the owner can wash and wax the car, utilizing high-pressure hot water and liquid wax. A dollar bill changer is available to provide change for the use of the equipment and the purchase of various products from dispensers. The products include towels, whitewall cleaner, and upholstery cleaner.

In recent years Harvey Industries has been in financial difficulty. The company has lost money for three of the last four years, with the last year's loss being $17,174 on sales of $1,238,674. Inventory levels have been steadily increasing to their present levels of $124,324.

The company employs 23 people with the management team consisting of the following key employees: president, sales manager, manufacturing manager, controller, and purchasing manager. The abbreviated organization chart reflects the reporting relationship of the key employees and the three individuals who report directly to the manufacturing manager.

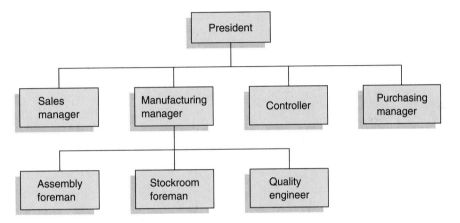

Current Inventory Control System

The current inventory control "system" consists of orders for stock replenishment being made by the stockroom foreman, the purchasing manager, or the manufacturing manager whenever one of them notices that the inventory is low. An order for replenishment of inventory is also placed whenever someone (either a customer or an employee in the assembly area) wants an item and it is not in stock.

Some inventory is needed for the assembly of the high-pressure equipment for the car wash and industrial applications. There are current and accurate bills of material for these assemblies. The material needs to support the assembly schedule are generally known well in advance of the build schedule.

The majority of inventory transactions are for repair parts and for supplies used by the car washes, such as paper towels, detergent, and wax concentrate. Because of the constant and rugged use of the car wash equipment, there is a steady demand for the various repair parts.

The stockroom is well organized, with parts stored in locations according to each vendor. The number of vendors is relatively limited, with each vendor generally supplying many different parts. For

example, the repair parts from Allen Bradley, a manufacturer of electrical motors, are stocked in the same location. These repair parts will be used to provide service for the many electrical motors that are part of the high-pressure pump and motor assembly used by all of the car washes.

Because of the heavy sales volume of repair parts, there are generally two employees working in the stockroom—a stockroom foreman who reports to the manufacturing manager and an assistant to the foreman. One of these two employees will handle customer orders. Many customers stop by and order the parts and supplies they need. Telephone orders are also received and are shipped by United Parcel Service the same day.

The assembly area has some inventory stored on the shop floor. This inventory consists of low-value items that are used every day, such as nuts, bolts, screws, and washers. These purchased items do not amount to very much dollar volume throughout the year. Unfortunately, often times the assembly area is out of one of these basic items and this causes a significant amount of downtime for the assembly lines.

Paperwork is kept to a minimum. A sales slip listing the part numbers and quantities sold to a customer is generally made out for each sale. If the assembly department needs items that are not stocked on the assembly floor, someone from that department will enter the stockroom and withdraw the necessary material. There is no paperwork made out for the items needed on the assembly floor.

There were 973 different part numbers purchased for stock last year and those purchases amounted to $314,673. Although the company does not utilize a computer, it does have some accurate records on how much money was spent on each part number last year. An analysis of the data shows that $220,684 was spent on just 179 of the part numbers.

Fortunately for Harvey Industries, most of the items they purchase are stocked by either the manufacturer or by a wholesaler. When it is discovered that the company is out of stock on an item, it generally takes only two or three days to replenish the stock.

Due to the company's recent losses, its auditing firm became concerned about the company's ability to continue in business. Recently the company sold off excess vacant land adjoining its manufacturing facility to generate cash to meet its financial obligations.

New President

Because of the recent death of the owner, the Trust Department of a Milwaukee Bank (as trustee for the estate) has taken over the company's affairs and has appointed a new company president. The new president has identified many problem areas—one of which is improper inventory control. He has retained you as a consultant to make specific recommendations concerning a revised inventory control system. What are your recommendations and their rationale?

Source: This case was prepared by Donald F. Condit of the Lawrence Technological University. Southfield, Michigan, as a basis for class discussion rather than to illustrate either effective or ineffective organizational practices. Presented at Midwest Case Writers Association Workshop, 1984, and accepted by referees of the Midwest Case Writers Association for international distribution. Reprinted by permission.

CASE   THE DEWEY STAPLER COMPANY

From: Martin Crane, Sales Manager

To: Allen Grace, President

Dear Allen:

Well, it has been a very disappointing year. We've missed our quota by 10 or 15 percent in virtually every district and this is the year I had such high hopes for. When we decided to open up four branch warehouses rather than shipping from our central location only, I was convinced that this would give us better customer service. The last of the warehouses was opened up last May, just before our peak summer season, so perhaps some of the problem is just not having enough experience with branch warehouses. But I think it goes deeper than that.

Our warehouse people are authorized to keep a one-month supply of inventory on hand. While I know you feel strongly that the substantial increase in inventory we had during the year was due to the warehouse program, I can't see why it requires any more inventory to keep a month's supply on hand in four branches and a main location than it did to keep a month's supply on hand back at the main location.

A month's supply is a month's supply no matter how you look at it.

To my way of thinking, the real problem is customer service. Our salespeople are demoralized. They simply can't get the stock shipped out of the warehouses because the warehouses don't have it on hand. Forty percent of our customer orders, of course, are still being shipped out of the main location. Our warehouse people tell me that these customer orders get preference and their stock replenishment orders are pushed aside.

Allen, we've got to solve this problem. There's no sense in having a sales force if we can't have the stock to back them up. I propose the plant location be required to ship warehouse stocking orders just the same as they ship customer orders. They should treat the warehouses like a customer. In fact, the warehouses are their *biggest* customer and should be serviced accordingly. I propose also that the one-month inventory guideline be removed. Let the warehouse people stock whatever they think they need to support the salesforce. I would volunteer to have my district managers sit with the branch warehouse people to give them some idea of what they should really be ordering.

Allen, this branch warehouse program has been as big a disappointment to me as it has to you. I know you're concerned about the fact that inventories have been going up, but I frankly attribute that to poor management back at the plant. And, quite honestly,

Allen, I don't think that people at the plant realize our problems out here in the field and are giving us the kind of support we need. Without it, we have no chance of making the sales quota. Instead of selling, I'm spending most of my time playing chaplain to a bunch of demoralized salespeople.

Sincerely,

Martin

From: Robert Ellers, Inventory Manager

To: Allen Grace, President

Dear Mr. Grace:

You asked me what my plans were to respond to Martin Crane's letter of January 5. I don't know where to start. This warehouse program has really torn us apart.

We thought that when branch warehouses were added, we would simply have to split some of the stock we had among the warehouses. Instead, we've had to build up the inventory very substantially. We don't get any plans from the warehouses at all. All we see is orders. We have no idea what their inventory position is when we get the orders and we only get them two to three weeks before we have to ship them. Then comes the moment of truth. We have a shortage on a particular item. Here's a customer order and also a warehouse stock replenishment order. Does the warehouse really need it? We know the customer does. In practice, I must admit we wind up waiting until the warehouse screams although we know we may very well be hurting customer service at the branch warehouses.

Mr. Grace, I'm more worried about *this* year than I was about last. Some of the warehouses that had been on the air since year before last showed a disturbing tendency to keep their inventories low during the off-season so that they could boast about their inventory turnover. Then during the peak season, they expect me to turn the faucet on back at the plant. We don't have enough storage space at the plant to build up the inventory required during the off-season in order to keep people working at a steady rate. We need this inventory buildup in order to give good service during the peak season. I've been told repeatedly by plant management that we must keep people working at a steady rate.

All this squabbling about inventory levels prompts me to suggest an approach. We normally would manufacture in a lot size that would be equivalent to about a three-month's supply. When we do that, why don't I just ship a three-month's supply out to each branch warehouse, and then we won't have to bother worrying about them until the next lot is manufactured. Then they can't complain that they're not getting their fair share.

One of the disturbing elements that you may not have heard about is that Frank, our traffic manager, has now suggested that we ship to the West Coast warehouses by sea. This would mean going through the Panama Canal and would substantially increase our lead time and reduce our flexibility. He says, "Flexibility is like motherhood. I'm talking a $50,000 savings in transportation costs, and if you guys have to work a little harder to make that happen, so be it."

Mr. Grace, I really am almost at my wit's end. Perhaps one of the things we ought to consider would be a computer system for tying all of the warehouses together so we could cover a shortage at one warehouse by shipping from another warehouse. Last September, I checked on items that were out of stock in the Atlanta warehouse and I found that virtually everyone of them was in adequate supply throughout the system; i.e., we either had them in Dallas, Los Angeles, Chicago, or back at the main plant. This type of computer system would be expensive, but perhaps this is the answer to our service problem.

Sincerely,

Robert Ellers

CASE   *(concluded)*

Question

The Dewey Stapler Company has some very serious problems. There are a number of misconceptions about inventory management in the company that need to be corrected. Take the position of a consultant being called in by Allen Grace, the president. You have enough information in these letters to give him some very helpful recommendations. Write a memo outlining your thoughts. Include a discussion of what will happen to service levels if total inventory investment remains constant.

Source: Reprinted by permission from Oliver W. Wright, *Production and Inventory Management in the Computer Age* (Boston: Cahners, 1974).

THE SINGLE-PERIOD MODEL

After completing this supplement, you should be able to:

1. Describe situations in which the single-period model would be appropriate.

2. Solve typical problems that involve shortage costs and excess costs.

3. Use the single-period model to estimate ranges of shortage or excess costs.

LEARNING OBJECTIVES

SUPPLEMENT OUTLINE

Single-period model

Model for ordering of perishables and other items with limited useful lives.

The **single-period model** is used to handle ordering of perishables (such things as fresh fruits and vegetables, seafood, and cut flowers) as well as items that have a limited useful life (such as newspapers and magazines.) What sets these items apart from those previously discussed is that unsold or unused items are not typically carried over from one period to the next, at least not without penalty. Day-old baked goods, for instance, are often sold at reduced prices, leftover seafood may be discarded, and out-of-date magazines may be offered to used book stores at bargain rates. At times, there may even be some cost associated with disposal of leftover goods. We can also include in the single-period category spare parts for specialized equipment. The *period* in such cases is the life of the equipment, assuming that the parts cannot be used for other equipment.

INTRODUCTION

Analysis of single-period situations generally focuses on two costs: shortage and excess. Shortage cost may include a charge for loss of customer goodwill as well as the opportunity cost of lost sales. Generally, **shortage cost** is unrealized profit per unit. That is,

Shortage cost

Unrealized profit per unit.

$$C_{\text{shortage}} = C_s = \text{Revenue per unit} - \text{Cost per unit}$$

If a shortage or stock-out relates to an item used in production or a spare part for a machine, then *shortage cost refers to the actual cost of lost production.*

Excess cost pertains to items left over at the end of the period. In effect, excess cost is the difference between purchase cost and salvage value. That is,

Excess cost

Difference between purchase cost and salvage value of items left over at the end of a period.

$$C_{\text{excess}} = C_e = \text{Original cost per unit} - \text{Salvage value per unit}$$

Note that if there is cost associated with disposing of excess items, the salvage will be negative and will therefore *increase* the excess cost per unit.

The goal of the single-period model is to identify the order quantity, or stocking level, that will minimize the long-run excess and shortage costs.

There are two general categories of problems that we will consider: those for which demand can be approximated using a continuous distribution (perhaps a theoretical one such as a uniform or normal distribution) and those for which demand can be approximated using a discrete distribution (say, historical frequencies or a theoretical distribution such as the Poisson). The kind of inventory in question can give an indication of which type of model might be appropriate. For example, demand for petroleum, liquids, and gases would tend to vary over some *continuous scale,* thus lending itself to description by a continuous distribution. Demand for houses, cars, and typewriters is expressed in terms of the *number of units* demanded and lends itself to description by a discrete distribution.

CONTINUOUS STOCKING LEVELS

The concept of identifying an optimal stocking level is perhaps easiest to visualize when demand is *uniform.* Choosing the stocking level is similar to balancing a seesaw, but instead of having a person on each end of the seesaw, we have excess cost per unit (C_e) on one end of the distribution and shortage cost per unit (C_s) on the other. The optimal stocking level is analogous to the fulcrum of the seesaw; the stocking level equalizes the cost weights, as illustrated in Figure 12S-1.

The *service level* is the *probability* that demand will not exceed the stocking level, and computation of the service level is the key to determining the optimal stocking level, S_o:

$$\text{Service level} = \frac{C_s}{C_s + C_e} \qquad\qquad \textbf{(12S–1)}$$

where

C_s = Shortage cost per unit

C_e = Excess cost per unit

If actual demand exceeds S_o, there is a shortage; hence, C_s is on the right end of the distribution. Similarly, if demand is less than S_o, there is an excess, so C_e is on the left end of the distribution. When $C_e = C_s$, the optimal stocking level is halfway between the endpoints of the distribution. If one cost is greater than the other, S_o tends to be closer to the *larger* cost.

Sweet cider is delivered weekly to Pappy's Produce Stand. Demand varies uniformly between 300 liters per week and 500 liters per week. Pappy pays 20 cents per liter for the cider and charges 80 cents per liter for it. Unsold cider has no salvage value and cannot be carried over into the next week due to spoilage. Find the optimal stocking level and its stock-out risk for that quantity.

Example 1

Solution

$$
\begin{aligned}
C_e &= \text{Cost per unit} \;-\; \text{Salvage value per unit} \\
&= \$0.20 \qquad\qquad - \$0 \\
&= \$0.20 \text{ per unit}
\end{aligned}
$$

$$
\begin{aligned}
C_s &= \text{Revenue per unit} - \text{Cost per unit} \\
&= \$0.80 \qquad\qquad - \$0.20 \\
&= \$0.60 \text{ per unit}
\end{aligned}
$$

$$\text{SL} = \frac{C_s}{C_s + C_e} = \frac{\$0.60}{\$0.60 + \$0.20} = .75$$

Thus, the optimal stocking level must satisfy demand 75 percent of the time. For the uniform distribution, this will be at a point equal to the minimum demand plus 75 percent of the difference between maximum and minimum demands:

$$S_o = 300 + 0.75(500 - 300) = 450 \text{ liters}$$

Example 1
(concluded)

The stock-out risk is $1.00 - \text{SL} = 1.00 - 0.75 = 0.25$.

A similar approach applies if demand is normally distributed.

Example 2

Pappy's Stand also sells a blend of cherry juice and apple cider. Demand for the blend is approximately normal with a mean of 200 liters per week and a standard deviation of 10 liters per week. $C_s = 60$ cents per liter, and $C_e = 20$ cents per liter. Find the optimal stocking level for the apple-cherry blend.

Solution

$$\text{SL} = \frac{C_s}{C_s + C_e} = \frac{\$0.60}{\$0.60 + \$0.20} = .75$$

This indicates that 75 percent of the area under the normal curve must be to the left of the stocking level. From Appendix B, Table B we see that a value of z between $+0.67$ and $+0.68$, say, $+0.675$, will satisfy this. Thus,

$$S_o = 200 \text{ liters} + 0.675(10 \text{ liters}) = 206.75 \text{ liters}$$

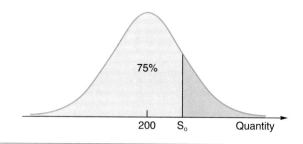

DISCRETE STOCKING LEVELS

When stocking levels are discrete rather than continuous, the service level computed using the ratio $C_s/(C_s + C_e)$ usually does not coincide with a feasible stocking level (e.g., the optimal amount may be between, say, five and six units). The solution is to stock at the next highest level (e.g., six units). In other words, choose the stocking level so that the desired service level is equaled or *exceeded*. This concept is illustrated in Figure 12S–2.

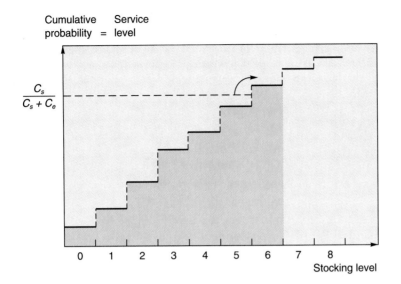

Figure 12S–2

The service level achieved must equal or exceed the ratio

$$\frac{C_s}{C_s + C_e}$$

Historical records on the usage of spare parts for several large hydraulic presses are to be used as an estimate of usage for spares of a newly installed press. Stock-out costs involve downtime expenses and special ordering costs. These average $4,200 per unit short. Spares cost $800 each, and unused parts have zero salvage. Determine the optimal stocking level.

Example 3

∎

Number of spares used	Relative frequency	Cumulative frequency
0......................	.20	.20
1......................	.40	.60
2......................	.30	.90
3......................	.10	1.00
4 or more	.00	
	1.00	

Solution

$$C_s = \$4,200 \qquad C_e = \$800$$

$$SL = \frac{C_s}{C_e + C_s} = \frac{\$4,200}{\$800 + \$4,200} = .84$$

The cumulative-frequency column indicates the percentage of time that demand did not exceed (was equal to or less than) some amount. For example, demand does not exceed one spare 60 percent of the time, or two spares 90 percent of the time. Thus, in order to achieve a service level of *at least* 84 percent, it is necessary to stock two spares (i.e., to go to the next highest stocking level).

Example 4

Demand for long-stemmed red roses at a small flower shop can be approximated using a Poisson distribution that has a mean of four dozen per day. Profit on the roses is $3 per dozen. Leftover flowers are marked down and sold the next day at a loss of $2 per dozen. Assume that all marked-down flowers are sold. What is the optimal stocking level?

Solution

$$C_s = \$3 \qquad C_e = \$2 \qquad SL = \frac{C_s}{C_s + C_e} = \frac{\$3}{\$3 + \$2} = .60$$

Obtain the cumulative frequencies from the Poisson table (Table C in Appendix B) for a mean of 4.0:

Demand (dozen per day)	Cumulative frequency
0	.018
1	.092
2	.238
3	.434
4	.629
5	.785
⋮	⋮

Compare the service level to the cumulative frequencies. Stock four dozen in order to attain a service level that exceeds .60.

One final point about discrete stocking levels: If the computed service level is *exactly* equal to the cumulative probability associated with one of the stocking levels, there are two equivalent stocking levels in terms of minimizing long-run cost: the one with equal probability and the next higher one. For instance, in the preceding example, if the ratio had been equal to .629, we would be indifferent between stocking four dozen and stocking five dozen roses each day.

SOLVED PROBLEM

Problem

A firm that installs cable TV systems has a certain piece of equipment that it carries two spare parts for. The parts cost $500 each and have no salvage value. Part failures can be modeled by a Poisson distribution with a mean of two failures during the useful life of the equipment. Holding and disposal costs are negligible. Estimate the apparent range of shortage cost.

Solution

C_s is unknown $C_e = \$500$

Using the Poisson table (Appendix B, Table C) for a mean of 2, we obtain these values:

Number of failures	Cumulative probability
0	.135
1	.406
2	.677
3	.857
4	.947
5	.983
⋮	⋮

We know that for the optimal stocking level, the service level must usually be rounded up to a feasible stocking level. Hence, we know that the service level must have been between .406 and .677 in order to make two units the optimal level. By setting the service level equal first to .406 and then to .677, we can establish bounds on the possible range of shortage costs:

$$\frac{C_s}{C_s + \$500} = .406, \text{ so } C_s = .406(\$500 + C_s)$$

Solving, we find $C_s = \$341.75$. Similarly,

$$\frac{C_s}{C_s + \$500} = .677, \text{ so } C_s = .677(\$500 + C_s)$$

Solving, we find $C_s = \$1,047.99$. Hence, the apparent range of shortage cost is \$341.75 to \$1,047.99.

DISCUSSION AND REVIEW QUESTIONS

1. What is the single-period model, and under what circumstances is it appropriate?
2. Can the optimal stocking level in the single-period model ever be less than expected demand? Explain briefly.
3. Explain what is meant by the phrase "estimate the range of shortage costs." (See the Solved Problem.)

PROBLEMS

1. Demand for jelly doughnuts on Saturdays at Don's Doughnut Shoppe is shown in the following table. Determine the optimal number of doughnuts, in dozens, to stock if labor, materials, and overhead are estimated to be 80 cents per dozen, doughnuts are sold for \$1.20 per dozen, and leftover doughnuts at the end of each day are sold the next day for one-half off. What is the resulting service level?

Demand (dozens)	Relative frequency
19	.01
20	.05
21	.12
22	.18
23	.13
24	.14
25	.10
26	.11
27	.10
28	.04
29	.02

2. A public utility intends to buy a turbine as part of an expansion plan and must now decide on the number of spare parts to order. One part, no. X135, can be purchased for $100 each. Carrying and disposal costs are estimated to be 145 percent of the purchase price over the life of the turbine. A stock-out would cost roughly $88,000 due to downtime, ordering, and "special purchase" factors. Historical records based on the performance of similar equipment operating under similar conditions suggest that demand for spares will tend to approximate a Poisson distribution with a mean of 3.2 parts for the useful life of the turbine. Find the optimal number of spares to order.

3. Skinner's Fish Market buys fresh Boston bluefish daily for $1.40 per pound and sells it for $1.90 per pound. At the end of each business day, any remaining bluefish is sold to a producer of cat food for 80 cents per pound. Daily demand can be approximated by a normal distribution with a mean of 80 pounds and a standard deviation of 10 pounds. Determine the optimal stocking level.

4. A small grocery store sells fresh produce, which it obtains from a local farmer. During the strawberry season, demand for fresh strawberries can be reasonably approximated using a normal distribution with a mean of 40 quarts per day and a standard deviation of 6 quarts per day. Excess costs run 35 cents per quart. The grocer orders 49 quarts per day. What is the implied cost of shortage per quart? Why might this be a reasonable figure?

5. Demand for devil's food whipped-cream layer cakes at a local pastry shop can be approximated using a Poisson distribution with a mean of six per day. The manager estimates it costs $3 to prepare each cake. Fresh cakes sell for $4, and day-old cakes sell for $3 each. What stocking level is appropriate if one half of the day-old cakes are sold and the rest thrown out?

6. Burger Prince buys top-grade ground beef for $1.00 per pound. A large sign over the entranceway guarantees that the meat is fresh daily. Any leftover meat is sold to the local high school cafeteria for 80 cents per pound. Four hamburgers can be prepared from each pound of meat. Burgers sell for 60 cents each. Labor, overhead, meat, buns, and condiments cost 50 cents per burger. Demand is normally distributed with a mean of 400 pounds per day and a standard deviation of 50 pounds per day. What daily order quantity is optimal? (*Hint:* Shortage cost must be in dollars per pound.)

7. Demand for rug-cleaning machines at Clyde's U-Rent-It is shown on the following page. Machines are rented by the day only. Profit on the rug cleaners is $10 per day. Clyde has four rug-cleaning machines.

Demand	Frequency
0	.30
1	.20
2	.20
3	.15
4	.10
5	.05
	1.00

a. Assuming that Clyde's stocking decision is optimal, what is the implied range of excess cost per machine?

b. Your answer from part *a* has been presented to Clyde, and he protests that the amount is *too low*. Would this suggest an increase or a decrease in the number of rug machines he stocks? Explain.

c. Suppose now that the $10 mentioned as profit is instead the excess cost per day for each machine and that the shortage cost is unknown. Based on the assumption that four machines is optimal, what is the implied range of shortage cost per machine?

8. Refer to the Solved Problem. For what range of shortage cost would carrying no spare parts be the best strategy?

CHAPTER THIRTEEN

MATERIAL REQUIREMENTS PLANNING

After completing this chapter, you should be able to:

1. Describe the conditions under which MRP is most appropriate.

2. Describe the inputs, outputs, and nature of MRP processing.

3. Contrast regenerative and net-change updating.

4. Explain how requirements in a master schedule are translated into material requirements for lower-level items.

5. Discuss possible uses of safety stock and safety time.

6. Explain how an MRP system is useful in capacity requirements planning.

7. Outline the potential benefits as well as some of the difficulties users have encountered with MRP.

8. Describe MRP II and how it relates to MRP.

Here are the views of managers in two companies that have tried material requirements planning (MRP):

"I don't know how we managed to get along without MRP for as long as we did. Our scheduling has gone from a state of turmoil to relative calm. We have achieved a substantial reduction in inventory size and cost, and yet our customer-service levels have actually improved quite a bit. We are more than satisfied with MRP; it allows us to *plan* instead of having to spend all of our time trying to *react* to one crisis after another. I would strongly recommend that all manufacturing firms adopt MRP or some similar approach."

"We had heard so many good things about MRP that we couldn't wait to get started, but so far, it seems like we've just been spinning our wheels. We're not even close to going online with it, and yet we've already exceeded our original time estimates and our costs are out of sight. Everyone is discouraged at this point, especially the brass. There is even some talk now of just scrapping the whole darn idea."

These two views reflect the range of reactions that typifies efforts of manufacturing firms to implement and use material requirements planning. This chapter examines the major issues of this current topic, including the need for this approach, the basic concepts of planning requirements, the benefits and limitations, and some reasons for the difficulties some firms have encountered. It then goes on to describe MRP II, an expanded approach to resource planning that incorporates MRP.

The preceding chapter focused on inventory management under conditions of *independent* demand. In this chapter, the focus is on managing inventories that have *dependent* or *derived* demand.

DEPENDENT VERSUS INDEPENDENT DEMAND

As noted in the previous chapter, a major distinction in the way inventories are managed results from the nature of demand for those items. When demand for items is *derived* from plans to make certain products, as it is in the case of raw materials, parts, and subassemblies used in producing a finished product, those items are said to have **dependent demand**. Hence, the parts and materials that go into the production of an automobile are examples of dependent demand since the total amount of parts and raw materials that will be needed during any time period is a function of the number of cars that will be produced. Conversely, demand for the finished cars is independent in the sense that a car is not a component of another item.

Independent demand is fairly stable, once allowances are made for seasonal variations, but dependent demand tends to be sporadic or "lumpy": large quantities are used at specific points in time with little or no usage at other times. For example, a firm that produces lawn and garden equipment might make a variety of items, such as trimmers, lawn mowers (push, self-propelled, mulching), and small tractors. Suppose that the various products are produced periodically—in one week, push mowers are produced; in the next week, mulching mowers; and in the next, tractors. Some components may be used in most of the items (nuts and bolts, screws, and similar parts). It would make sense to have a continual inventory of these parts because they are always needed. However, other parts might be used for just one item. Consequently, there is demand for those parts only when that item is being produced. That might be once every eight or nine weeks—the rest of the time, demand is zero. Hence, demand is "lumpy." Because of these tendencies, indepen-

Dependent demand

Demand for items that are subassemblies or component parts to be used in the production of finished goods.

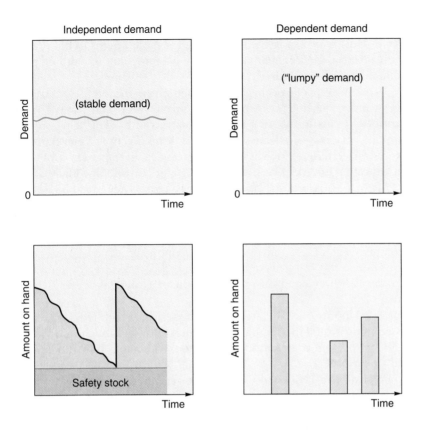

Figure 13–1

Comparison of
independent and
dependent demand

dent-demand items must be carried on a continual basis, but dependent-demand items need only be stocked just prior to the time they will be needed in the production process. Moreover, the predictability of usage of dependent-demand items means that there is little or no need for safety stock. Figure 13–1 illustrates the contrasts in independent- and dependent-demand inventories.

AN OVERVIEW OF MRP

Material requirements planning (MRP) is a computer-based information system designed to handle ordering and scheduling of dependent-demand inventories (e.g., raw materials, component parts, and subassemblies). A production plan for a specified number of finished products is translated into requirements for component parts (raw materials, etc.) working backward, using lead time information to determine when and how much to order. Hence, requirements for end items generate requirements for lower-level components, which are broken down by planning periods (e.g., weeks) so that ordering, fabrication, and assembly can be scheduled for timely completion of end items while inventory levels are kept reasonably low.

Material requirements planning is as much a philosophy as it is a technique, and as much an approach to scheduling as it is to inventory control.

Historically, ordering and scheduling of assembled products suffered from two difficulties. One was the enormous task of setting up schedules, keeping track of large numbers of parts and components, and coping with schedule and order changes. The other was the lack of differentiation between independent demand

Material requirements planning

Computer-based information system for ordering and scheduling of dependent-demand inventories.

and dependent demand; all too often, techniques that were designed for independent-demand items were being used to handle assembled items, which resulted in excessive inventories. Consequently, inventory planning and scheduling presented major problems for manufacturers.

In the 1970s, manufacturers began to recognize the importance of the distinction between independent- and dependent-demand items and to approach these two categories of items in different ways. Much of the burden of record keeping and determining material requirements in many firms has now been transferred to computers, using techniques such as MRP. A great deal of the credit for publicizing MRP and educating potential users about MRP goes to Joseph Orlicky, author of the book *Material Requirements Planning* (New York: McGraw-Hill, 1975) and George Plossl, Oliver Wight, and the American Production and Inventory Control Society (APICS).

MRP begins with a schedule for finished goods that is converted into a schedule of requirements for the subassemblies, component parts, and raw materials needed to produce the finished items in the specified time frame. Thus, MRP is designed to answer three questions: *what* is needed, *how much* is needed, and *when* is it needed.

The primary inputs of MRP are a bill of materials, which tells what a finished product is composed of; a master schedule, which tells how much finished product is desired and when; and an inventory records file, which tells how much inventory is on hand or on order.

This information is processed using various computer programs to determine the *net* requirements for each period of the planning horizon.

Outputs from the process include planned-order schedules, order releases, changes, performance-control reports, planning reports, and exception reports.

These topics are discussed in more detail in subsequent sections. An overview of an MRP system is provided in Figure 13–2.

MRP INPUTS

As illustrated in Figure 13–2, there are three major sources of information in an MRP system: a master schedule, a bill-of-materials file, and an inventory records file. Let's consider each of these inputs.

THE MASTER SCHEDULE

Master schedule

One of three primary inputs in MRP; states which end items are to be produced, when these are needed, and in what quantities.

The **master schedule** states which end items are to be produced, when these end items are needed, and what quantities are needed. Figure 13–3 illustrates a portion of a master schedule that shows planned output for end item X for the planning horizon. The schedule indicates that 100 units of X will be needed (e.g., for shipments to customers) at the *start* of week 4 and that another 150 units will be needed at the *start* of week 8.

The quantities in a master schedule can come from a number of different sources, including customer orders, forecasts, orders from warehouses to build up seasonal inventories, and external demand.

The master schedule separates the planning horizon into a series of time periods or time *buckets*. These are often in weeks. However, the time buckets need not be of equal length. In fact, the near-term portion of a master schedule may be in

MRP inputs   MRP processing   MRP outputs

Figure 13–2   Overview of MRP

Week number

Item: X	1	2	3	4	5	6	7	8
Quantity				100				150

Figure 13–3

A master schedule for end item X

weeks, but later portions may be in months or quarters. Usually, plans for those more distant time periods are more tentative than near-term requirements.

Although there is no set period of time that a master schedule must cover, most managers like to plan far enough into the future that they have some general idea of probable upcoming demands for the near future. It is important, though, that the master schedule cover the *stacked* or **cumulative lead time** necessary to produce the end items. This amounts to the sum of the lead times that sequential phases of the production or assembly process require, as illustrated in Figure 13–4, where a total of nine weeks of lead time is needed from ordering parts and raw materials until final assembly is completed.

Generally speaking, a master schedule is generated initially in terms of what is *needed* and not what is *possible,* so the initial schedule may or may not be feasible given the limits of the production system. Moreover, what appears on the surface to be a feasible master schedule may not be so when end items are translated into requirements for procurement, fabrication, and assembly. Unfortunately, the MRP system cannot distinguish between a feasible master schedule and a nonfeasible one. Consequently, it is often necessary to run a proposed master schedule through

Cumulative lead time

The sum of the lead times that sequential phases of a process require, from ordering of parts or raw materials, to completion of final assembly.

Figure 13–4

The planning horizon must cover the cumulative lead time

MRP processing in order to obtain a clearer picture of actual requirements, which can then be compared to available capacity. If it turns out that the current master schedule is not feasible, a decision may be made to increase capacity (e.g., through overtime or subcontracting) or to revise the master schedule. In the latter case, this may entail several revisions, each of which is run through the system until a feasible plan is obtained. At that point, the master schedule is *frozen*, at least for the near-term time periods, thus establishing a firm schedule from which to plan requirements.

Stability in short-term production plans is very important; without it, changes in order quantity and/or timing can render material requirements plans almost useless. To minimize such problems, many firms establish a series of time intervals, called **time fences**, during which changes can be made to orders. For example, a firm might specify time fences of 4 weeks, 8 weeks, and 12 weeks, with the nearest fence being most restrictive and the farthest fence being least restrictive: Beyond 12 weeks, changes are expected; from 8 to 12 weeks, substitutions of one end item for another may be permitted as long as the components are available and the production plan is not compromised; from 4 to 8 weeks, the plan is fixed, but small changes may be allowed; and the plan is frozen out to the four-week fence.

THE BILL-OF-MATERIALS FILE

A **bill of materials (BOM)** contains a listing of all of the assemblies, subassemblies, parts, and raw materials that are needed to produce one unit of a finished product. Thus, each finished product has its own bill of materials.

The listing in the bill-of-materials file is hierarchical; it shows the quantity of each item needed to complete one unit of the following level of assembly. The nature of this aspect of a bill of materials is perhaps most readily grasped by considering a **product structure tree**, which shows the bill of materials in chart form. A simple product structure tree is illustrated in Example 1.

Time fences

Series of time intervals during which order changes are allowed or restricted; the nearest fence is most restrictive to change, the farthest is least restrictive.

Bill of materials

One of the three primary inputs of MRP; a listing of all of the raw materials, parts, subassemblies, and assemblies needed to produce one unit of a finished product.

Product structure tree

Visual depiction of the requirements in a bill of materials, where all components are listed by levels.

Example 1

Here is a simple product tree diagram for a "popsicle." The end item (in this case, the finished product), is shown at the top of the tree. Just beneath it are the subassemblies, or major components, that must be put together to obtain the end item. Beneath each of these are the components that are needed to make those major components. At each stage going down in the tree, the components (parts, materials) needed to make one unit of the next higher item in the tree are shown. For instance, the tree indicates that two sticks, flavoring, and water are needed for the "popsicle." (See Figure 13–5.)

(continued)

Figure 13–5

Product structure tree for popsicles

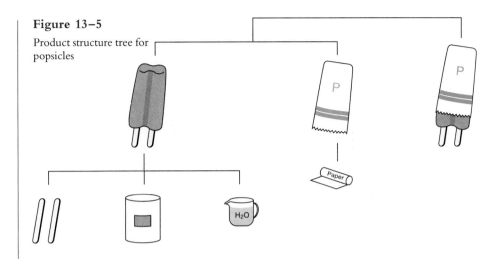

The value of this illustration is that it illustrates the *concept* of a product tree in very simple terms. As a practical matter, products that are produced using MRP are *assembled* products, such as refrigerators and lawn mowers; items such as "popsicles" are typically made in batches or even continuously, and demand is often not "lumpy," so MRP wouldn't be appropriate.

IBM CADAM software can also be used to help prepare a bill of materials. This diagram shows a bill of materials for a pump along with several different views of the complete product with the subassemblies.

A product structure tree is useful in illustrating how the bill of materials is used to determine the quantities of each of the ingredients (requirements) needed to obtain a desired number of end items.

Now let's consider the product tree shown in Figure 13–6.

We see that end item X is composed of two Bs and one C. Moreover, each B requires three Ds and one E, and each D requires four Es. Similarly, each C is made up of two Es and two Fs. These *requirements* are listed by *level,* beginning with level 0 for the end item, then level 1 for the next level, and so on. The items at each level are *components* of the next level up and are *parents* of their respective components. Note that the quantities of each item in the product structure tree refer only to the amounts needed to complete the assembly in the next level up.

Figure 13–6

A product structure tree
for end item X

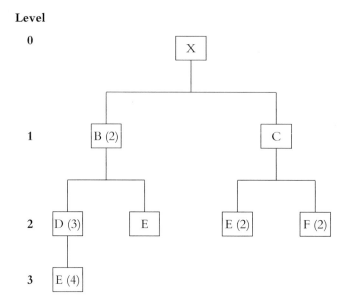

Level

0

1

2

3

Example 2

Using the information presented in Figure 13–6, do the following:

a. Determine the quantities of B, C, D, E, and F needed to assemble one X.

b. Determine the quantities of these components that will be required to assemble 200 Xs.

Solution

a.

Component		Quantity
B ....2 Bs per X		= 2
D ....3 Ds per B × 2 Bs per X		= 6
E ....4 Es per D × 3 Ds per B × 2 Bs per X		= 24
E ....1 E per B × 2 Bs per X		= 2
C ....1 C per X		= 1
E ....2 Es per C × 1 C per X		= 2
F ....2 Fs per C × 1 C per X		= 2

Note that E appears in three separate places; its total requirements can be determined by summing the separate amounts, which gives 28.

b. In order to assemble 200 units of X, the quantities of each component must be multiplied by 200. Hence, there must be 200(2) = 400 Bs, 200(6) = 1,200 Ds, 200(28) = 5,600 Es, and so on.

Determining total requirements is usually more complicated than the preceding example might suggest. For one thing, many products have considerably more components. For another, the issue of *timing* is also essential (i.e., when must the components be ordered or made) and must be included in the analysis. Finally, for a variety of reasons, some of the components/subassemblies may be on hand (i.e., currently in inventory). Consequently, in determining total requirements, the amounts on hand must be *netted out* (i.e., subtracted from the apparent requirements) in order to determine the true requirements. Fortunately, the process for doing this is not difficult. It will be demonstrated shortly.

When requirements are calculated in an MRP system, the computer, in effect, scans the product structure *level by level,* starting at the top. When a component (such as E in Figure 13–6) appears on more than one level, its total requirements cannot be determined until all levels have been scanned. From a computational standpoint, this is somewhat inefficient. A simplification sometimes used to increase efficiency is **low-level coding**, which involves restructuring the BOM so that all occurrences of an item are made to coincide with the lowest level in which the item appears. Figure 13–7 illustrates how component E, which appears in three different levels of product Y, can be rearranged so that it appears at only one level.

Low-level coding

A simplified restructuring of the BOM so that all occurrences of an item are made to coincide with the lowest level in which it appears.

Comment   When the concept of low-level coding comes up, students are often puzzled by the following question: What happens if a component that appears at different levels is "buried" at an upper level and can't be lowered, as G seems to be in Figure 13–8? The answer, in terms of Figure 13–8, has two parts. One is that low-level coding is not limited to items at the end of "branches." The parent (G) and its components (and theirs, if necessary) can all be lowered, if need be, to achieve low-level coincidence. The other part of the answer lies in the fact that parent G should have the *same* components anywhere it appears in the product structure. In other words, the components H and I would always be required to assemble one G. If, for some reason, there is an exception to this, then one of the Gs should be given a different name; each name should carry a unique set of component requirements irrespective of where it appears in the product structure.

It is extremely important that the bill of materials accurately reflect the composition of a product, particularly since errors at one level become magnified by the multiplication process used to determine quantity requirements. As obvious as this might seem, many companies find themselves with incorrect bills-of-material rec-

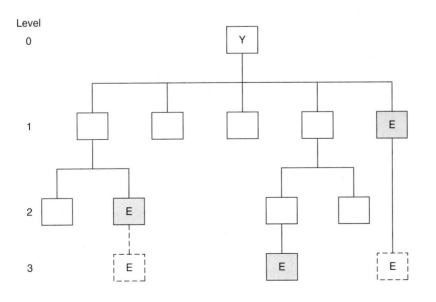

Figure 13–7

Low-level coding for Component E

Figure 13–8

One G seems to be buried, apparently preventing low-level coding

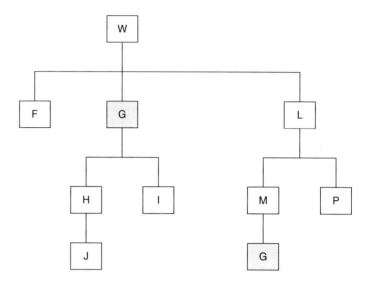

ords. These make it impossible to effectively determine material requirements; moreover, the task of correcting these records can be complex and time-consuming. Nevertheless, accurate records are a prerequisite for effective MRP.

THE INVENTORY RECORDS FILE

Inventory records file

One of the three primary inputs in MRP; includes information on the status of each item by time period.

The **inventory records file** is used to store information on the status of each item by time period. This includes gross requirements, scheduled receipts, and expected amount on hand. It also includes other details for each item, such as supplier, lead time, and lot size. In addition, changes due to stock receipts and withdrawals, canceled orders, and similar events are recorded in this file.

Like the bill of materials, the inventory records file must be accurate; erroneous information on requirements or lead times can have a detrimental impact on the MRP, and create turmoil when incorrect quantities are on hand, or expected delivery times are not met.

MRP PROCESSING

MRP processing involves taking the end-item requirements specified by the master schedule and "exploding" them into *time-phased* requirements for assemblies, parts, and raw materials using the bill of materials offset by lead times. The time-phasing of requirements can be readily seen in the assembly time chart in Figure 13–9. For example, raw materials D, F, and I must be ordered at the start of week 2, part C at the start of week 4, and part H at the start of week 5 in order to be available for delivery as planned.

The quantities that are generated by exploding the bill of materials are *gross requirements:* they do not take into account any inventory that is currently on hand or due to be received. The materials that must actually be acquired to meet the demand generated by the master schedule are the *net material requirements.*

The determination of the net requirements *(netting)* is the core of MRP processing. It is accomplished by subtracting from gross requirements the sum of inven-

Figure 13–9

Assembly time chart showing material order points needed to meet scheduled availability of the end item

tory on hand and any scheduled receipts, and then adding in safety stock requirements, if applicable:

$$
\begin{array}{c}
\text{Net} \\
\text{requirements} \\
\text{in period } t
\end{array}
=
\begin{array}{c}
\text{Gross} \\
\text{requirements} \\
\text{in period } t
\end{array}
-
\begin{array}{c}
\text{Projected} \\
\text{inventory} \\
\text{in period } t
\end{array}
+
\begin{array}{c}
\text{Safety} \\
\text{stock}
\end{array}
\qquad \textbf{(13–1)}
$$

(For simplicity, safety stock is omitted from computations in examples and problems.) Net requirements are sometimes adjusted to include an allowance for waste, although, for simplicity, this is not included in examples or problems.

The timing and sizes of orders (i.e., materials ordered from suppliers or work started within the firm) are determined by *planned-order releases*. The timing of the receipts of these quantities is indicated by *planned-order receipts*. Depending on ordering policy, the planned-order releases may be multiples of a specified quantity (e.g., multiples of 50 units), or they may be equal to the quantity needed at that time. There are other possibilities, but these two seem to be the most widely used. The following example illustrates the difference between these two ordering policies as well as the general concepts of time-phasing material requirements in MRP. As you work through the example, you may find it useful to refer to the following list of terms.

Gross requirements: The total expected demand for an item or raw material during each time period without regard to the amount on hand. For end items, these quantities are shown in the master schedule; for components, these quantities equal the planned-order releases of their immediate "parents."

Gross requirements

Total expected demand for an item or raw material during each time period.

Scheduled receipts
Open orders scheduled to arrive from vendors or elsewhere in the pipeline.

Projected on hand
Expected amount of inventory that will be on hand at the beginning of each time period.

Net requirements
The actual amount needed in each time period.

Planned-order receipts
Quantity expected to be received by the beginning of the period in which it is shown.

Planned-order releases
Planned amount to order in each time period; planned-order receipts offset by lead time.

Scheduled receipts: Open orders scheduled to arrive from vendors or elsewhere in the pipeline.

Projected on hand: The expected amount of inventory that will be on hand at the *beginning* of each time period: Scheduled receipts + available from last period.

Net requirements: The actual amount needed in each time period.

Planned-order receipts: The quantity expected to be received by the *beginning* of the period in which it is shown. Under lot-for-lot ordering, this quantity will equal net requirements. Under lot-size ordering, this quantity may exceed net requirements. Any excess is added to available inventory in the *next* time period.

Planned-order releases: Indicates a *planned* amount to order in each time period; equals planned-order receipts offset by lead time. This amount generates gross requirements at the next level in the assembly or production chain. When an order is executed, it is removed from the "planned-order receipts" and "planned-order release" rows and entered in the "scheduled receipts" row.

These quantities are used in a time-phased plan in this format:

Week number:	1	2	3	4	5	6	7	8
Item:								
Gross requirements								
Scheduled receipts								
Projected on hand								
Net requirements								
Planned-order receipts								
Planned-order releases								

Example 3

A firm that produces wood shutters and bookcases has received two orders for shutters: one for 100 shutters and one for 150 shutters. The 100-unit order is due at the start of week 4 of the current schedule, and the 150-unit order is due for delivery at the start of week 8. Each shutter consists of four slatted wood sections and two frames. The wood sections are made by the firm, and fabrication takes one week. The frames are ordered, and lead time is two weeks. Assembly of the shutters requires one week. There is a scheduled receipt of 70 wood sections in (i.e., at the beginning of) week 1. Determine the size and timing of planned-order releases necessary to meet delivery requirements under each of these conditions:

1. Lot-for-lot ordering (i.e., order size equal to net requirements).
2. Lot-size ordering with a lot size of 320 units for frames and 70 units for wood sections.

Solution

Example 3

(continued)

a. Develop a master schedule:

Week number:	1	2	3	4	5	6	7	8
Quantity:				100				150

b. Develop a product structure tree:

Shutter

Frames (2)   Wood sections (4)

c. Develop an assembly-time chart:

Week number

d. Using the master schedule, determine gross requirements for shutters. Next, compute net requirements. Assuming *lot-for-lot ordering,* determine planned-order receipt quantities and the planned-order release timing to satisfy the master schedule (see Figure 13–10).

Since the master schedule calls for 100 shutters to be ready for delivery at the start of the fourth week, and since no shutters are projected to be on hand at that time, the net requirements are also 100 shutters. Therefore, planned receipts for the fourth week equal 100 shutters. Since shutter assembly requires one week, this means a planned-order release at the start of the third week. Using the same logic, 150 shutters must be assembled during the seventh week in order to be available for delivery at the start of the eighth week.

The planned-order release of 100 shutters at the start of the third week means that 200 frames (gross requirements) must be available at that time. Since none are expected to be on hand, this generates net requirements of 200 frames and necessitates planned receipts of 200 frames by the start of the third week. With a two-week lead time, this means that 200 frames must be ordered at the start of the first week. Similarly, the planned-order release of 150 shutters at week 7 generates gross and net requirements of

Example 3

(continued)

300 frames for week 7 as well as planned receipts for that time. The two-week lead time means frames must be ordered at the start of week 5.

The planned-order release of 100 shutters at the start of the third week also generates gross requirements of 400 wood sections at that time. However, because 70 wood sections are expected to be on hand, net requirements are $400 - 70 = 330$. This means a planned receipt of 330 by the start of the third week. Since fabrication time is one week, the fabrication must start (planned-order release) at the beginning of week 2.

Similarly, the planned-order release of 150 shutters at week 7 generates gross requirements of 600 wood sections at that point. Since no on-hand inventory of wood sections is projected, net requirements are also 600, and planned-order receipt is 600 units. Again, the one-week lead time means 600 sections are scheduled for fabrication at the start of the sixth week.

Figure 13–10

MRP schedule with lot-for-lot ordering

Master schedule for shutters:

Week number	1	2	3	4	5	6	7	8
Quantity				100				150

Shutters: LT = 1 week		1	2	3	4	5	6	7	8
	Gross requirements				100				150
	Scheduled receipts								
	Projected on hand								
	Net requirements				100				150
	Planned-order receipts				100				150
	Planned-order releases			100				150	

times 2   times 2

Frames: LT = 2 weeks		1	2	3	4	5	6	7	8
	Gross requirements				200				300
	Scheduled receipts								
	Projected on hand								
	Net requirements				200				300
	Planned-order receipts				200				300
	Planned-order releases	200					300		

times 4   times 4

Wood sections: LT = 1 week		1	2	3	4	5	6	7	8
	Gross requirements				400				600
	Scheduled receipts	70							
	Projected on hand	70	70	70					
	Net requirements				330				600
	Planned-order receipts				330				600
	Planned-order releases			330				600	

e. Under *lot-size ordering,* the only difference is the possibility that planned receipts will exceed net requirements; the excess is recorded as projected inventory in the following period. For example, in Figure 13–11, the order size for frames is 320 units. Net requirements for week 3 are 200; thus, there is an excess of 320 − 200 = 120 units, which become projected inventory in the next week. Similarly, net frame requirements of 180 units are 140 less than the 320 order size; again, the excess becomes projected inventory in week 9. The same thing happens with wood sections: an excess of planned receipts in periods 3 and 7 is added to projected inventory in periods 4 and 8. Note that the order size must be in *multiples* of the lot size; for week 3 it is 5 times 70, and for week 7 it is 9 times 70.

Figure 13–11

MRP schedule with lot sizes for components

Master schedule for shutters

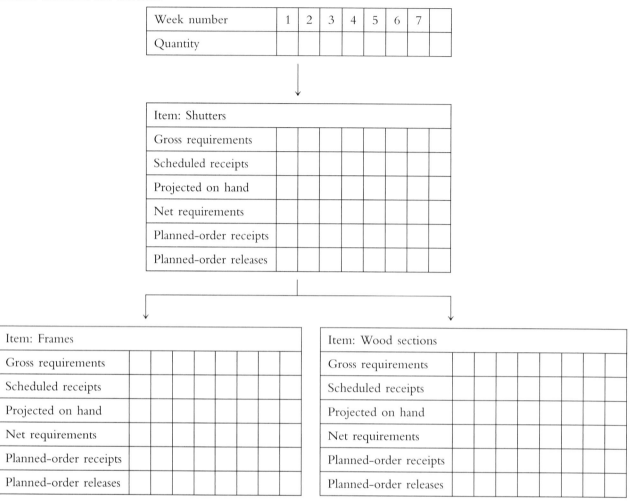

Figure 13–12

Net requirements at each level determine gross requirements at the next

Another perspective on the process of determining material requirements for subassembly components is given in Figure 13–12.

Example 3 is useful for describing some of the main features of MRP processing, but it understates the enormity of the task of keeping track of material requirements, especially in situations where the same subassemblies, parts, or raw materials are used in a number of different products. Differences in timing of demands and quantities needed, as well as revisions caused by late deliveries, high scrap rates, and canceled orders, all have an impact on processing.

Consider, for example, bracket G, which is used for end items W, X, and Y, as shown by the product trees in Figure 13–13. For the sake of simplicity, assume that all lead times are one week. Suppose that the master schedule for these products is as shown in Figure 13–14. Note that these are the *gross requirements* for these end items; *net requirements* will be less by the amount of any on-hand inventories. The

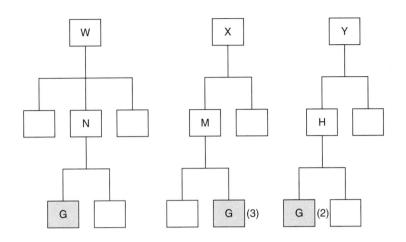

Figure 13–13

Bracket G is used in three different products

Week number

End item	1	2	3	4	5	6	7
W			50		70		60
X			200			100	
Y		30			80	90	

Figure 13–14

Master schedule for end items that use bracket G

Week number

Net requirements for G due to:	1	2	3	4	5	6	7
N	40		50		40		
M	120			240			
H				160	120		
Total	160		50	400	160		
Gross requirements	160		50	400	160		
Projected on hand	200	40	40	0	0		
Net requirements			10	400	160		

Figure 13–15

Net requirements for bracket G

same holds true for net requirements for subassemblies N, M, and H. Each of these factors must be taken into account in calculating net material requirements for G. The gross requirements for G by parent might look something like the schedule shown in Figure 13–15, with the net requirements for G equal to the sum of these amounts minus any projected on-hand inventory of G, which is also shown in Figure 13–15. (*Note:* the on-hand quantities of the end items are not given, nor are those quantities given for parents N, M, and H. However, the point here is *not* the computations, but that gross requirements for bracket G are generated by the net requirements of all of its parents. See the lower portion of Figure 13–15.)

Pegging

The process of identifying the parent items that have generated a given set of material requirements for an item.

The term **pegging** is used to denote working this process in reverse, that is, identifying the parent items that have generated a given set of material requirements for some item such as G. Although the process may appear simple enough given the product trees and schedules shown here, when this information is computerized, special efforts must be made so that requirements can be traced to specific parents.

The importance of the computer becomes quite evident when you stop to realize that a typical firm would have not one but many end items for which it needs to develop material requirements plans, each with its own set of components. Inventories on hand and on order, schedules, order releases, and so on must all be updated as changes and rescheduling occur. Without the aid of a computer, the task would be quite hopeless; with the aid of a computer, all of these things can be accomplished with a lot less difficulty.

Updating the System

There are two basic approaches to updating MRP records: *regenerative* and *net change*. A **regenerative system** is one that is updated periodically; a **net-change system** is one that is continuously updated.

Regenerative system

Approach that updates MRP records periodically.

Net-change system

Approach that updates MRP records continuously.

A regenerative system is essentially a batch-type system that compiles all changes (e.g., new orders, receipts) that occur within the time interval (e.g., week) and periodically updates the system. Using that information, a revised production plan is developed (if needed), in the same way that the original plan was developed (i.e., exploding the bill of materials, level by level, etc.).

In a net-change system, the basic production plan is modified to reflect changes as they occur. Hence, if some purchased parts had to be returned to a vendor because they were defective, this information is entered into the system as soon as it becomes known. Only the *changes* would be exploded through the system, level by level; the basic plan would not be regenerated.

The regenerative system is best suited to systems that are fairly stable, whereas the net-change system is best suited to systems that have frequent changes. The obvious disadvantage of a regenerative system is the potential amount of lag between the time information becomes available and the time it can be incorporated into the material requirements plan. On the other hand, processing costs are typically less using regenerative systems, and there is the possibility that changes that occur in a given time period will end up canceling each other, thereby avoiding the need to modify the plan and then remodify it. The disadvantages of the net-change system relate to the computer processing costs involved in continuously updating the system and the fact that many small changes can keep the system in a constant state of flux. One way around this is to enter minor changes periodically, but enter major changes immediately. The primary advantage of the net-change system is that management can have up-to-date information for planning and control purposes.

MRP OUTPUTS

MRP systems have the ability to provide management with a fairly broad range of outputs. These are often classified as *primary reports,* which are the main reports, and *secondary reports,* which are optional outputs.

Primary reports concern production and inventory planning and control. These reports normally include the following:

1. A schedule of **planned orders**, which indicates the amount and timing of future orders.
2. **Order releases**, which authorize the execution of planned orders.
3. **Changes** to planned orders, which can include revisions of due dates or order quantities as well as cancellations of orders.

Secondary reports concern such things as performance control, planning, and exceptions:

1. **Performance-control reports** are used to evaluate system operation. They aid managers by measuring deviations from plans, including missed deliveries and stock-outs, and by providing information that can be used to assess cost performance.
2. **Planning reports** are useful in forecasting future inventory requirements. They include purchase commitments and other data that can be used to assess future material requirements.
3. **Exception reports** call attention to major discrepancies such as late and overdue orders, excessive scrap rates, reporting errors, and requirements for nonexistent parts.

The wide range of outputs generally permits users to adapt MRP to their particular needs.

OTHER CONSIDERATIONS

Aside from the main details of inputs, outputs, and processing, there are a number of other aspects of MRP that the manager must be knowledgeable about. These include the question of whether to hold safety stock, lot sizing choices, and the possible use of MRP for items that are not finished products.

SAFETY STOCK

Theoretically, inventory systems with dependent demand should not require safety stock below the end-item level. In fact, this is one of the main advantages of an MRP approach. Supposedly, safety stock is not needed because usage quantities can be projected once the master schedule has been established. Practically speaking, however, there may be exceptions to this. For example, a bottleneck process or one with varying scrap rates can cause shortages in downstream operations. Furthermore, shortages can occur if orders are late or fabrication or assembly times are longer than expected. On the surface, these are the kinds of conditions that lend themselves to the use of safety stock to maintain smooth operations. The problem is somewhat complicated when dealing with multiechelon items (i.e., multiple-level items such as assembled products) by the fact that a shortage of *any* component will prevent manufacture of the final assembly. However, a major advantage of MRP would be lost by holding safety stock for all lower-level items.

MRP systems deal with these problems in several ways. The first step is for a manager to identify those activities or operations that are subject to variability and then to determine the extent of that variability. When lead times are variable, the

Planned orders
Schedule indicating the amount and timing of future orders.

Order releases
Authorization for the execution of planned orders.

Changes
Revisions of due dates or order quantities, or cancellations of orders.

Performance-control reports
Evaluation of system operation, including deviations from plans and cost information.

Planning reports
Data useful for assessing future material requirements.

Exception reports
Data on any major discrepancies encountered.

concept of safety *time* is often used instead of safety *stock*. This results in scheduling orders for arrival or completion sufficiently ahead of the time they are needed to eliminate or substantially reduce the chance of having to wait for those items. When quantities tend to vary, some safety stock may be called for, but the manager must carefully weigh the need and cost of carrying the extra stock. Frequently, managers elect to carry safety stock for end items, because these are subject to random demand, and for selected lower-level operations when safety time is not feasible, say, due to capacity limitations.

LOT SIZING

Lot sizing

Choosing a lot size for ordering or production.

An important issue in inventory management, whether for independent- or dependent-demand items, is choosing a lot size to order or for production. This is called **lot sizing**. For independent-demand items, economic order sizes and economic run sizes are widely used. However, for dependent-demand systems, there is a much wider variety of plans used for determining lot sizes, mainly because no one plan has a clear advantage over the others. Some of the most popular plans for lot sizing are described in this section.

For either independent- or dependent-demand systems, a primary goal of inventory management is to minimize the sum of ordering cost (or setup cost) and holding cost. It is often the case with independent demand that demand is uniformly distributed throughout the planning horizon (e.g., six months, year). Demand tends to be much more lumpy for dependent demand, and the planning horizon shorter (say, three months), so that economic lot sizes are usually much more difficult to identify. Consider the situation depicted in Figure 13–16. Period demands vary from 1 to 80 units, and no demand size repeats, at least over the horizon shown.

Economies can be realized by grouping order or run sizes. This would be the case if the additional cost incurred by holding the extra units until they were used led to a savings in setup or ordering cost. This determination can be very complex at times, for several reasons. One is that combining period demands into a single order, particularly for middle-level or end items, has a cascading effect down through the product tree. That is, in order to achieve this grouping, items at lower levels in the tree must also be grouped. Hence, their setup and holding costs must also be incorporated into the decision. Another reason is the uneven period demands and the relatively short planning horizon. These factors require a continual recalculation and updating of lot sizes. Not surprisingly, the methods used to handle the lot-sizing question range from complex ones, which attempt to include all relevant costs, to very simple ones, which are easy to use and understand. And in certain cases, the simple models seem to approach cost minimization, although generalizations are difficult. Let's consider some of these models.

Figure 13–16

Demand for part K

	Period				
	1	2	3	4	5
Demand	70	50	1	80	4
Cumulative demand	70	120	121	201	205

Lot-for-lot ordering is perhaps the simplest of all the approaches used. The order or run size for each period is set equal to demand for that period. This method was demonstrated in Example 3. Not only is the order size obvious, but it also virtually eliminates holding costs for parts carried over to other periods. Its two chief drawbacks are that it usually involves many different order sizes and so cannot take advantage of economies associated with a fixed order size (e.g., standard containers and other standardized procedures), and it involves a new setup for each run. If setup costs can be significantly reduced, this approach may approximate a minimum-cost lot size.

Economic order quantity models (covered in Chapter 12) are sometimes used. They can lead to minimum costs if usage is fairly uniform. This is sometimes the case for lower-level items that are common to different parents and for raw materials. However, the more lumpy demand is, the less appropriate such an approach is. Since demand tends to be most lumpy at the end-item level, EOQ models tend to be less useful for end items than for items and materials at the lowest levels.

Fixed-period ordering provides coverage for some predetermined number of periods (e.g., two or three). In some instances, the span is simply arbitrary; in other cases, a review of historical demand patterns may lead to a more rational designation of a fixed period length. A simple rule would be: Order to cover a two-period interval. The rule can be modified when common sense suggests a better way. For example, take a look at the demands shown in Figure 13–16. Using a two-period rule, an order size of 120 units would cover the first two periods. The next two periods would be covered by an order size of 81 units. However, the demands in periods 3 and 5 are so small, it would make sense to combine them both with the 80 units and order 85 units.

The *part period* model represents another attempt to balance setup and holding costs. The term *part period* refers to holding a part or parts over a number of periods. For instance, if 10 parts were held for two periods, this would be $10 \times 2 = 20$ part periods. The economic part period (EPP) can be computed as the ratio of setup costs to the cost to hold a unit for one period. Thus, the formula for computing the EPP is:

$$\text{EPP} = \frac{\text{Setup cost}}{\text{Unit holding cost per period}} \qquad (13\text{–}2)$$

In order to determine an order size that is consistent with the EPP, various order sizes are examined for a planning horizon, and each one's number of part periods is determined. The one that comes closest to the EPP is selected as the best lot size. The order sizes that are examined are based on cumulative demand. Example 4 illustrates this approach.

The *Wagner-Whitin algorithm* attempts to minimize the sum of ordering and carrying costs using dynamic programming to select the ordering strategy to cover net requirements in each period for the complete net-requirements schedule. The advantage of this approach is that the algorithm identifies a relatively few strategies, which it then compares, selecting the one that minimizes total costs. The disadvantage of the technique is that its complexity makes it highly unlikely that the average user will be able to understand it, which not only decreases the chance of having the technique selected for use in the first place, but also increases the risk of misusing it or misinterpreting the results.

The choice of a lot-sizing technique must take into account the nature of demand (degree of uniformity), the relative importance of carrying costs versus

Example 4

Use the *part period* method to determine order sizes for this demand schedule:

	Period							
	1	**2**	**3**	**4**	**5**	**6**	**7**	**8**
Demand	60	40	20	2	30	—	70	50
Cumulative demand	60	100	120	122	152	152	222	272

Setup cost is $47 per run for this item, and unit holding cost is $.56 per period.

Solution

1. First compute the EPP: EPP = $47/$.56 = 83.93, which rounds to 84 part periods.
2. Next, try the cumulative lot sizes, beginning with 60, until the part periods approximate the EPP. Continue this process for the planning horizon. This leads to the following:

Period	Lot size	Extra inventory carried	×	Periods carried	=	Part periods	Cumulative part periods
1	60	0		0		0	0
	100	40		1		40	40
	120	20		2		40	80
	122	2		3		6	86★ [closest to 84]
5	30	0		0		0	0
	100	70		2		140	140★ [closest to 84]
8	50	0		0		0	0

The computations of part periods indicate that 122 units should be ordered to be available at period 1, and 100 units should be ordered to be available at period 5. The next lot will be ordered for period 8, but we do not have enough information now to determine its size.

The lot sizes considered for period 1 correspond to cumulative demand. Once the best lot size has been identified, the cumulative demand is set equal to zero and then summed beginning with the next period. In this case, the lot size of 122 covers the first four periods, so cumulative demand is started next for period 5. That next lot size covers through period 7, and the count begins again at period 8.

The process works quite well for the first lot size since the cumulative number of part periods is quite close to the EPP, but the effect of lumpy demand is very apparent for the second lot size of 100 (140 part periods is not very close to 84 part periods).

ordering costs, and any other considerations that affect ordering. It appears that no one technique is suited to all conditions.

Regardless of the lot-sizing technique in use, there is always the possibility of adjustments in order sizes due to allowance for shrinkage or scrap, minimum and maximum order quantities established by management (e.g., do not order more than five months' supply), operating or shipping constraints (e.g., 200 pieces per run or 12 dozen per shipment) that require rounding of order sizes (usually up) to these amounts, and similar factors.

CAPACITY REQUIREMENTS PLANNING

One of the most important features of MRP is its ability to aid managers in capacity planning. As noted previously, a master schedule that appears feasible on the surface may turn out to be far from feasible in terms of resource requirements needed for fabrication and/or subassembly operations of lower-level items.

Capacity requirements planning is the process of determining short-range capacity requirements. The necessary inputs include planned-order releases for MRP, the current shop load, routing information, and job times. Outputs include load reports for each work center. When variances (underloads or overloads) are projected, remedies such as alternative routings, changing or eliminating lot sizing or safety stock requirements, and lot splitting may be considered. Moving production forward or backward can be very challenging due to precedence requirements as well as availabilities of components.

An overview of the capacity planning process is presented in Figure 13–17. The process begins with a proposed or tentative master schedule that must be tested

Capacity requirements planning
The process of determining short-range capacity requirements.

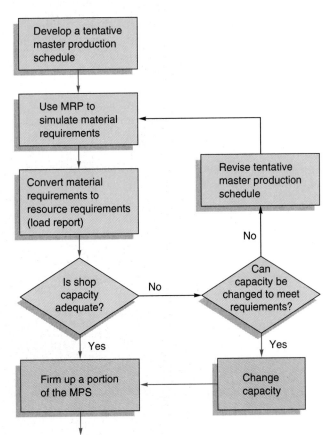

Figure 13–17

Using MRP to assist in planning capacity requirements

Source: Stephen Love, *Inventory Control* (New York: McGraw-Hill, 1979), p. 164. Reprinted by permission.

Figure 13–18

A hypothetical department
load report

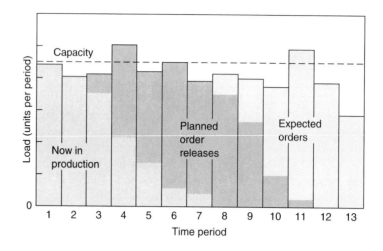

for feasibility and possibly adjusted before it becomes permanent. The proposed
schedule is processed using MRP to ascertain the material requirements the schedule would generate. These are then translated into resource (i.e., capacity) requirements, often in the form of a series of **load reports** for each department or work
center that compare known and expected future capacity requirements with projected capacity availability. The nature of a load report is illustrated in Figure 13–
18. It shows expected resource requirements (i.e., usage) for jobs currently being
worked on, for planned orders, and for expected orders for the planning horizon.
Given this sort of information, the manager can more easily determine whether
there is sufficient capacity to satisfy these requirements. If there is enough capacity,
the portion of the master schedule that generates these requirements can be frozen.
In the load report illustrated in Figure 13–18, planned-order releases in the fourth
time period will cause an overload. However, it appears possible to accommodate
demand by slightly shifting some orders to adjacent periods. Similarly, an overload
appears likely in period 11, but that too can be handled by shifting some jobs to
adjacent time periods. In cases where capacity is insufficient, a manager may be able
to increase capacity (by scheduling overtime, transferring personnel from other
areas, or subcontracting some of the work) if this is possible and economical, or else
revise the master schedule and repeat the process until an acceptable master schedule is obtained.

 If the master schedule must be revised, this generally means that the manager
must assign priorities to orders, since some orders will be finished later than originally planned.

 An important aspect of capacity requirements planning is the conversion of
quantity requirements into labor and machine requirements. This is accomplished
by multiplying each period's quantity requirements by standard labor and/or machine requirements per unit. For instance, if 100 units of product A are scheduled in
the fabrication department, and each unit has a labor standard time of 2 hours and a
machine standard time of 1.5 hours, the 100 units of A convert into these capacity
requirements:

  Labor: 100 units × 2 hours/unit = 200 labor hours
  Machine: 100 units × 1.5 hours/unit = 150 machine hours

These capacity requirements can then be compared to available department capacity
to determine the extent to which capacity will be utilized by this product. For

Load reports

Reports for a department
or work center that
compare known and
expected future capacity
requirements with
projected capacity
availability.

example, if the department has 200 labor hours and 200 machine hours available, labor utilization will be at 100 percent because all of the labor capacity will be required by this product. However, machine capacity will be underutilized:

$$\frac{\text{Required}}{\text{Available}} \times 100 = \frac{150 \text{ hours}}{200 \text{ hours}} \times 100 = 75 \text{ percent}$$

Underutilization may mean that unused capacity can be used for other jobs; overutilization indicates that available capacity is insufficient to handle requirements. To compensate, production may have to be rescheduled, or overtime may be needed.

BENEFITS AND LIMITATIONS OF MRP

MRP offers a number of benefits for the typical manufacturing or assembly type of operation. These generally include:

1. Low levels of in-process inventories.
2. The ability to keep track of material requirements.
3. The ability to evaluate capacity requirements generated by a given master schedule.
4. A means of allocating production time.

The benefits of MRP depend in large measure on the use of a computer to maintain up-to-date information on material requirements.

In order to implement and operate an effective MRP system, it is necessary to have:

1. A computer and the necessary software programs to handle computations and maintain records.
2. Accurate and up-to-date:
    a.   Master schedules.
    b.   Bills of materials.
    c.   Inventory records.
3. Integrity of file data.

Unfortunately, some firms that have attempted to install an MRP system have seriously underestimated the importance of these items. In many cases, bills of materials have been outdated because design changes were not incorporated into the records, leading to parts lists that did not correspond to actual requirements for assembly of the finished product. In addition, it is not unusual for a firm to discover that the same part is being carried under different part numbers, making it difficult to develop meaningful records. Moreover, some firms have encountered resistance from foremen and others, often along the line of: "We've managed for 30 years without this stuff, so why bother with it now?"

Because of these obstacles, it can take a year or more to implement MRP, taking into account employee education, training, and *convincing,* and correction of record-keeping deficiencies.

On the whole, the introduction of MRP has led to major improvements in scheduling and inventory management. Nonetheless, it has not proved to be the cure-all that many hoped it would be. Consequently, manufacturers are beginning to take a much broader approach to resource planning. One such approach is referred to as MRP II.

MRP II

In the early 1980s, materials requirements planning was expanded into a much broader approach for planning and scheduling the resources of manufacturing firms. This expanded approach has been dubbed MRP II, which refers to **manufacturing resources planning**. It has not replaced MRP, nor is it an improved version of MRP. Rather, it represents an effort to expand the scope of production resource planning and to involve other functional areas of the firm in the planning process. Marketing and finance are the two most notable areas that are impacted by—and have an impact on—the manufacturing plan.

In too many instances, production, marketing, and finance operate without complete knowledge or seeming regard for what the other areas of the firm are doing. Obviously, to be most effective, all areas of the firm need to focus on a common set of goals. A major purpose of MRP II is to integrate these primary functions as well as other functions such as personnel, engineering, and purchasing in the planning process.

Material requirements planning is at the heart of the process, which is illustrated in Figure 13–19. The process begins with an aggregation of demand from all sources (e.g., firm orders, forecasts, safety stock requirements). Production, marketing, and finance personnel work toward developing a master schedule. Although manufacturing people will have a major input in determining that schedule and a major responsibility for making it work, marketing and finance will also have important inputs and responsibilities. The rationale for having these functional areas work together is the increased likelihood of developing a plan that will work and that everyone can live with. Moreover, because each of these functional areas has been involved in formulating the plan, they will have reasonably good knowledge of the plan and more reason to work toward achieving it.

In addition to the obvious manufacturing resources needed to support the plan, financing resources will be needed and must be planned for, both in amount and timing. Similarly, marketing resources will also be needed in varying degrees throughout the process. In order for the plan to work, it must be determined that all of these necessary resources will be available as needed. Often, an initial plan must be revised based on an assessment of the availability of various resources. Once these have been decided, the master schedule can be firmed up.

At this point, material requirements planning comes into play, generating material and schedule requirements. Then more detailed capacity requirements planning must be done to determine if these more specific capacity requirements can be met. Again, some adjustments in the master schedule may be required.

As the schedule unfolds and actual work begins, a variety of reports help managers to keep a pulse on how well actual experience complies with plans and to make any necessary adjustments to keep operations on track.

In effect, this is a continuing process, with the master schedule being updated and revised as necessary to achieve corporate goals. The business plan that governs the entire process also usually undergoes changes, although these tend to be less frequent than the changes made at lower levels (i.e., the master schedule).

Finally, it should be noted that most MRP II systems have the capability to do simulation. This enables managers to answer a variety of "what if" questions, thereby gaining a better appreciation of available options and their consequences.

Since MRP is at the heart of MRP II, the computer is, again, an important tool in MRP II, one that is heavily relied on for information processing.

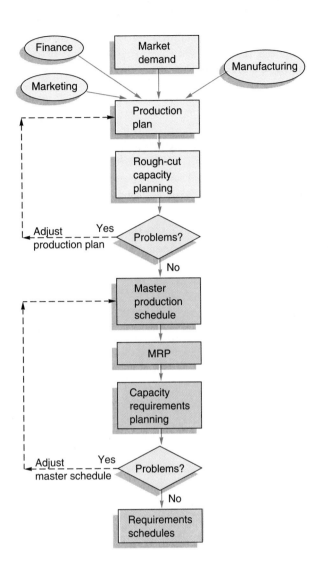

Figure 13–19

An overview of MRP II

Material requirements planning (MRP) is an information system used to handle ordering of dependent-demand items (i.e., components of assembled products). The planning process begins with customer orders, which are used along with any backorders to develop a master schedule that indicates the timing and quantity of finished items. The end items are exploded using the bill of materials, and material requirements plans are developed that show quantity and timing for ordering or producing components.

The main features of MRP are the time-phasing of requirements, calculating component requirements, and planned-order releases. In order to be successful, MRP requires a computer program and accurate master schedules, bills of materials, and inventory data. Firms that have not had reasonably accurate records or schedules have experienced major difficulties in trying to implement MRP.

SUMMARY

MRP II is a second-generation approach to planning that incorporates MRP; it has a broader scope to manufacturing resource planning in that it links business planning, production planning, and the master schedule.

KEY TERMS

bill of materials, 654
capacity requirements
  planning, 671
changes, 667
cumulative lead time, 654
dependent demand, 650
exception reports, 667
gross requirements, 659
inventory records file, 658
load reports, 672
lot sizing, 668
low-level coding, 657
manufacturing resources
  planning (MRP II), 674
master schedule, 652
material requirements planning
  (MRP), 651

net-change system, 666
net requirements, 660
order releases, 667
pegging, 666
performance-control reports, 667
planned-order receipts, 660
planned-order releases, 660
planned orders, 667
planning reports, 667
product structure tree, 654
projected on hand, 660
regenerative system, 666
scheduled receipts, 660
time fences, 654

SOLVED PROBLEMS

Problem

1. The following product structure tree indicates the components needed to assemble one unit of product W. Redraw the tree so that it conforms to low-level coding, and determine the quantities of each component that will be needed to assemble 100 units of W.

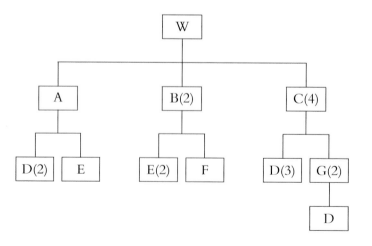

Solution

An easy way to compute and keep track of component requirements is to do it right on the tree, as illustrated below. Using low-level coding, it is then

relatively simple to group like items in order to determine overall requirements.

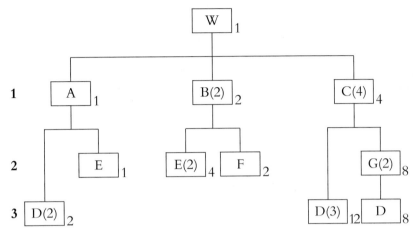

Summary:

Level	Item	(1 W) Quantity	(100 W) Quantity
0.............	W	1	100
1.............	A	1	100
	B	2	200
	C	4	400
2.............	E	5	500
	F	2	200
	G	8	800
3.............	D	22	2,200

Problem

2. The product structure tree for end item E is shown below. The manager
   wants to know the material requirements for ordered part R that will be

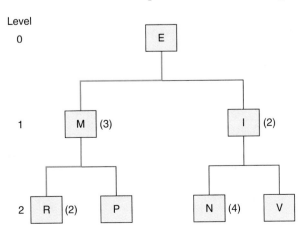

needed to complete 120 units of E by the start of week 5. Lead times for items are: one week for level 0 items, one week for level 1 items, and two weeks for level 2 items. There is a scheduled receipt of 60 units of M at the *end* of week 1 and 100 units of R at the *start* of week 1. Lot-for-lot ordering is used.

Solution

A *partial* assembly-time chart that includes R and leads to completion of E by the start of week 5 looks like this:

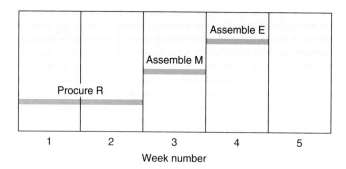

The master schedule for E and requirements plans for E, M, and R follow.

Master schedule for E

Week number	1	2	3	4	5
Quantity					(120)

Item: E LT = 1 week					
Gross requirements					(120)
Scheduled receipts					
Projected on hand					0
Net requirements					120
Planned-order receipts					(120)
Planned-order releases				(120)	

Multiplied by 3
(see product tree)

Item: M LT = 1 week					
Gross requirements				(360)	
Scheduled receipts		60			
Projected on hand		60	60	60	
Net requirements				300	
Planned-order receipts				(300)	
Planned-order releases			(300)		

Multiplied by 2
(see product tree)

Item: R LT = 2 weeks					
Gross requirements			(600)		
Scheduled receipts	100				
Projected on hand	100	100	100		
Net requirements			500		
Planned-order receipts			(500)		
Planned-order releases	(500)				

The table entries are arrived at as follows:

Master schedule: 120 units of E to be available at the start of week 5.

Item E: Gross requirements equal quantity specified in master schedule. Since there is no on-hand inventory, net requirements also equal 120 units. Using lot-for-lot ordering, 120 units must be scheduled to be available at the start of week 5. Since there is a one-week lead time for assembly of Es, an order will need to be released (i.e., work started) at the beginning of week 4.

Item M: The *gross* requirements for M are three times E's *net* requirements since each E requires three Ms. These must be available at the start of week 4. The net requirements are 60 units less due to the 60 units expected to be on hand at that time. Hence, 300 additional units of M must be available at the start of week 4. With the one week lead time, there must be an order release at the start of week 3.

Item R: Since each M requires two units of R, 600 Rs will be needed to assemble 300 units of M. However, 100 units will be on hand, so only 500 need to be ordered. Since there is a lead time of two weeks, the 500 Rs must be ordered at the start of week 1.

Problem

3. *Capacity requirements planning.* Given the following production schedule in units and the production standards for labor and machine time for this product, determine the labor and machine capacity requirements for each

week. Then compute the percent utilization of labor and machines in each week if labor capacity is 200 hours per week and machine capacity is 250 hours per week.

Production schedule:

Week	1	2	3	4
Quantity	200	300	100	150

Standard times:

Labor	.5 hours/unit
Machine	1.0 hours/unit

Solution

Convert the quantity requirements into labor and machine requirements by multiplying the quantity requirements by the respective standard times (i.e., multiply each quantity by .5 to obtain the labor hours and multiply each quantity by 1.0 to obtain the machine hours):

Week	1	2	3	4
Quantity	200	300	100	150
Labor hours	100	150	50	75
Machine hours	200	300	100	150

To compute utilization, divide the capacity requirements by the available capacity and multiply by 100. The results are:

Week	1	2	3	4
Labor	50%	75%	25%	37.5%
Machine	80%	120%	40%	60%

Note that machine capacity in week 2 is overutilized (i.e., capacity is insufficient) because the utilization exceeds 100 percent.

DISCUSSION AND REVIEW QUESTIONS

1. Contrast independent and dependent demand.
2. When is MRP appropriate?
3. Briefly define or explain each of these terms:
   a. Master schedule.
   b. Bill of materials.
   c. Inventory records file.
   d. Gross requirements.
   e. Net requirements.

  f. Time-phased plan.
  g. Low-level coding.

4. What is meant by the term *level-by-level processing?* Why does it require low-level coding?

5. What factors can create safety stock requirements in an MRP system?

6. What is meant by the term *safety time?*

7. Contrast *net-change* systems and *regenerative* systems for MRP.

8. Briefly discuss the requirements for effective MRP.

9. What are some of the main advantages and limitations of MRP?

10. How can the use of MRP contribute to productivity?

11. Briefly describe MRP II and indicate how it relates to MRP.

12. What is lot sizing, and why is it an issue with lumpy demand?

13. What is the goal of lot sizing? What are some of the methods used for lot sizing in MRP systems? At what level is an economic lot size usually most relevant? Why?

14. Contrast planned-order receipts and scheduled receipts.

---

1. Given the product structure tree below, do the following: **PROBLEMS**
  a. Redraw the tree so that it conforms to low-level coding.
  b. Determine the quantities of each of the components that will be required to assemble 60 units of P.

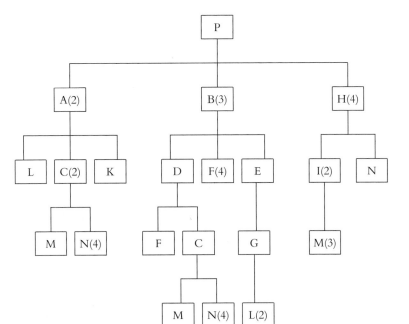

2. Given the following listing of parents and components, construct two product structure trees using low-level coding, and then determine what quantity of each item will be required to make 125 units of end item W and 50 units of end item Y.

W	A	B	D	C
A(2)	D(2)	F(2)	F(4)	H
B(4)	E		E(2)	G(2)
C(4)			G(4)	

Y	A	B	D	K	C
A	D(2)	F(2)	F(4)	L	H
B(2)	E		E(2)	C(4)	G(2)
K(3)			G(4)		

3. Determine material requirements plans for parts N and V and subassembly I as described in Solved Problem 2.

   a. Assume that there are currently 100 Ns on hand and scheduled receipts of 40 Is and 10 Vs at the beginning of week 3. No Es are on hand; 120 Es are needed at the start of week 5.

   b. Assume on-hand and scheduled receipts as in part *a*. But now suppose that 100 Es are needed at the start of week 5 and 50 at the start of week 7. Also, use multiples of these order sizes: N, 800; V, 200. Use lot-for-lot ordering for I.

   c. Using your answer to *b*, update the MRP for part V, using the additional information that follows, for each of these cases: (1) one week has elapsed (making it the start of week 2), and (2) three weeks have elapsed (making it the start of week 4). *Note:* start your revised plans so that the updated time in each case is designated as week 1.

     The updated master schedule now has an order for 100 units of E in week 8 of case 1 (i.e., week 9 under the former master schedule). Assume all orders are released and received as planned.

4. A firm that produces electric golf carts has just received an order for 200 carts, which are to be ready for delivery at the start of week 8. Information concerning the product structure, lead times, and quantities on hand is shown in the following table. Using this information, do each of the following:

   a. Construct a product tree.

   b. Construct an assembly time chart.

   c. Develop a material requirements plan that will provide 200 golf carts by week 8 assuming lot-for-lot ordering.

Parts list for electric golf cart	Lead time	Quantity on hand
Electric golf cart	1	0
Top	1	40
Base	1	20
Top		
Supports (4)	1	200
Cover	1	0
Base		
Motor	2	300
Body	3	50
Seats (2)	2	120

Parts list for electric golf cart	Lead time	Quantity on hand
Body		
Frame..................	1	35
Controls................	1	0
Wheel assemblies (4)	1	240

5. (Refer to the previous problem.) Assume there has been a change in the quantity and timing of orders for golf carts, which is apparently due to unusually mild weather. The revised plan calls for 100 golf carts at the start of week 6, 100 at the start of week 8, and 100 at the start of week 9.
   a. Develop a master schedule for this revised plan.
   b. Determine the timing and quantities for orders for tops and bases.
   c. Assume now that due to equipment problems, capacity for assembling bases is 50 units per week. Revise your material plan for bases to reflect this, but still meet delivery dates.

6. Assume that you are the manager of Assembly, Inc., and that you have just received an order for 40 units of an industrial robot, which are to be delivered at the start of week 7 of your schedule. Using the following information, determine how many units of subassembly G should be ordered and the timing of those orders, given that subassembly G must be ordered in multiples of 80 units. Assume that there is no other use for the components of this particular robot.

Item	Lead time (weeks)	On hand	Components
Robot	2	10	B,G,C(3)
B	1	5	E,F
C	1	20	G(2),H
E	2	4	—
F	3	8	—
G	2	15	—
H	1	10	—

7. A manufacturing firm buys a certain part in varying quantities throughout the year. Ordering cost is $11 per order, and carrying cost is $.14 per piece per month. Given the following demand schedule for the part for the next eight months, what order sizes would be indicated using an economic part period approach, and when should each order be received?

Month	Demand
1	—
2	80
3	10
4	30
5	—
6	30
7	—
8	30

8. A firm periodically produces a part that is a basic component of an assembled product it makes. Each time the part is run, a fixed cost of $125 is incurred. The cost to carry one unit for a week has been estimated to be $1.65. For the demand schedule shown, determine the quantity and timing of runs that would be consistent with an economic part period approach. Assume a one-week lead time for each run.

Week	Demand
1	40
2	20
3	100
4	20
5	—
6	20
7	80

9. Assume that you are the manager of a shop that assembles power tools. An order has just been received for 50 chain saws, which are to be shipped at the start of week 8. Pertinent information on the saws is:

Item	LT (weeks)	On hand	Components
Saw	2	15	A(2),B(1),C(3)
A	1	10	E(3),D(1)
B	2	5	D(2),F(3)
C	2	30	E(2),D(2)
D	1	20	
E	1	10	
F	2	30	

Develop a product structure tree, an assembly time chart, and a master schedule. Also, develop the material requirements plan for component E.

10. End item P is composed of three subassemblies: K, L, and W. K is assembled using 3 Gs and 4 Hs; L is made of 2 Ms and 2 Ns; and W is made using 3 Zs. On-hand inventories are 20 Ls, 40 Gs, and 200 Zs. Scheduled receipts are 10 Ks at the start of week 3 and 30 Ks at the start of week 6.

One hundred Ps are to be shipped at the start of week 7. Lead times are two weeks for subassemblies and one week for components G, H, and M. Final assembly of P requires two weeks. Develop each of the following:
   a. A product structure tree.
   b. An assembly time chart.
   c. A master schedule for P.
   d. A material requirements plan for K, G, and H.

11. Product P is made of two subassemblies, A and B, and part C: 2 As, 3 Bs, and 4 Cs are needed for each P. Each A requires 3 Ms and 4 Ns; each B requires 4 Cs and 5 Ds. (*Note:* this problem does not involve an MRP because times are not included; it relates only to the *quantities* needed.)
   a. If 25 Ps are needed and there are 10 units of A, B, and C on hand, how many additional Cs will be needed?
   b. Suppose now that the bill of materials incorrectly shows that each B requires 8 Cs (instead of 4). How many leftover Cs will there be?

c. Suppose that the bill of materials incorrectly shows that each B requires 2 Cs. How many Cs will be needed *in addition* to the number based on the erroneous bill of materials? What problems might this cause if it is not discovered before final assembly? What costs will be incurred if the error results in too many Cs ordered, as in part *b*?

12. The MRP Department has a problem. Their computer "died" just as it spit out the following information: Planned order release for item J27 = 640 units in week two. The firm has been able to reconstruct all the information they lost except the Master Schedule for end item 565. The firm is fortunate because J27 is used only in 565s. Given the following product structure tree and associated inventory status record information, determine what master schedule entry for 565 was exploded into the material requirements plan that killed the computer.

Part #	On hand	Lot size	Lead time
565	0	Lot-for-lot	1 week
X43	60	120	1 week
N78	0	Lot-for-lot	2 weeks
Y36	200	Lot-for-lot	1 week
J27	0	Lot-for-lot	2 weeks

13. The Bloomington Bike Co. produces two models—the Basic and the Supra. Herb Hoosier, the owner, plans to assemble 15 Basics and 10 Supras each week during periods 4–8. Product structure trees for each bike are shown below.

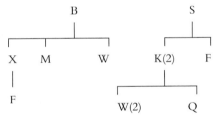

Develop the material requirements plan for component parts K and W over the next 8 weeks. Data on all lead times, current inventory, and ordering rules are given below.

Item	LT (weeks)	On hand	Lot-sizing rule
B	2	5	Lot-for-lot
S	2	2	Lot-for-lot
X	1	5	Q = 25
W	2	2	Multiples of 12
F	1	10	Q = 30
K	1	3	Lot-for-lot
Q	1	15	Q = 30

Scheduled receipts are as follows:

Period 1:   20 Bs; 18 Ws
Period 2:   20 Ss; 15 Fs

14. A company that manufactures paving material for driveways and parking lots expects the demand for its product for the next four weeks to be as follows:

Week	1	2	3	4
Material (tons)	40	80	60	70

The company's labor and machine standards and available capacities are:

	Labor	Machine
Production standard (hour/ton)	4	3
Weekly production capacity (hours)	300	200

a. Determine the capacity utilization for both labor and machine for each of the four weeks.
b. In which weeks do you foresee a problem? What options would you suggest to resolve these? What costs would be relevant in making a decision on choosing an option?

15. A company produces two very similar products that both go through a three-step sequence that involves fabrication, assembly, and packaging. Each step requires one day for a lot to be completely processed and moved to the next department. Processing requirements for the departments (hours per unit) are:

	Fabrication		Assembly		Packaging	
Product	Labor	Machine	Labor	Machine	Labor	Machine
A	2	1	1.5	1	1	.5
B	1	1	1	1	1.5	.5

Department capacities are all 700 hours of labor and 500 hours of machine time, except for Friday, when capacities are 200 hours for both labor and machine time. The production schedule for next week is:

Day	Mon	Tues	Wed	Thurs	Fri
A	200	400	100	300	100
B	300	200	200	200	200

a. Develop a production schedule for each department that shows the capacity requirements for each product and the total load for each day. Ignore changeover time.
b. Evaluate the projected loading for the first three days of the week. Is the schedule feasible? What suggestions can you make in terms of balancing the load?

Blumberg, D. F. "Factors Affecting the Design of a Successful MRP System." *Production and Inventory Management* 21, no. 4 (4th quarter 1980), pp. 50–62.

Fox, Robert E. "OPT vs. MRP: Thoughtware versus Software." *Inventories & Production Magazine* 3, no. 6 (November–December 1983).

———. "MRP, Kanban, or OPT: What's Best?" *Inventories & Production Magazine* 2, no. 4 (July–August 1982).

LaForge, R. C. "MRP and the Part-Period Algorithm." *Journal of Purchasing Management,* Winter 1982, pp. 21–26.

Love, Stephen. *Inventory Control.* New York: McGraw-Hill, 1979.

Orlicky, Joseph. *Material Requirements Planning.* New York: McGraw-Hill, 1975.

Schulz, T. "MRP to BRP: The Journey of the 80's." *Production and Inventory Management Review and APICS News* 1 (October 1981), p. 29.

Theisen, E. C., Jr. "New Game in Town—The MRP Lot Size." *Production and Inventory Management,* 2nd quarter 1974, pp. 1–13.

Vollmann, Thomas E.; William L. Berry; and D. Clay Whybark. *Manufacturing, Planning and Control Systems.* 2nd ed. Homewood, Ill.: Richard D. Irwin, 1988.

Wight, Oliver W. *The Executive's Guide to Successful MRP II.* Williston, Vt.: Oliver Wight Limited Publications, 1982.

SELECTED BIBLIOGRAPHY

CHAPTER FOURTEEN

JUST–IN–TIME SYSTEMS

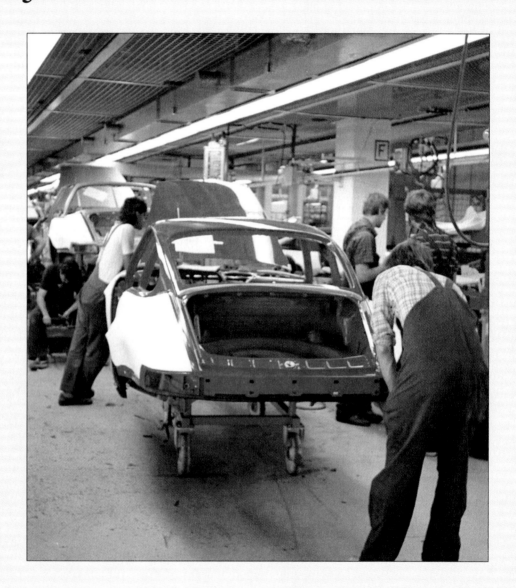

14

After completing this chapter, you should be able to:

1. Explain what is meant by the term *just-in-time (JIT) production system*.
2. List each of the key elements of a JIT system and explain its importance.
3. List the benefits of JIT systems.
4. Outline the considerations important in converting a traditional mode of production to a JIT system.
5. List some of the obstacles that might be encountered when converting to a JIT system.

Just-in-time

Repetitive production system in which processing and movement of materials and goods occur just as they are needed, usually in small batches.

he term **just-in-time (JIT)** is used to refer to a repetitive production system in which both the movement of goods during production, and deliveries from suppliers, are carefully timed so that at each step of the process the next (usually small) batch arrives for processing just as the preceding batch is completed. (Hence, the name *just-in-time*.) The result is a system in which there are neither idle items waiting to be processed, nor idle workers and equipment waiting for items to process.

The just-in-time phenomenon is characteristic of *lean production systems,* which, you may recall, operate with very little "fat" (e.g. excess inventory, extra workers, wasted space). JIT pertains to the timing of the flow of parts and material through the system, and the timing of services. Companies that employ the JIT/lean production approach typically enjoy a competitive advantage over companies that use a more traditional approach to repetitive processing: they have lower processing costs, fewer defectives, greater flexibility, and are able to bring new or improved products to the market more quickly.

This chapter describes the JIT/lean production approach, including the basic elements of these systems, and what it takes to make them work effectively. We will look at the benefits of these systems, along with a list of potential obstacles that may be encountered when companies that have been operating under a traditional system attempt to convert to a JIT/lean production system.

INTRODUCTION

The JIT approach was developed at the Toyota Motor Company of Japan by Mr. Taiichi Ohno (who eventually became vice president of manufacturing) and several of his colleagues. The development of JIT in Japan was probably influenced by the fact that Japan is a crowded country with few natural resources. Not surprisingly, the Japanese have become very sensitive to waste and inefficiency. They regard scrap and rework as waste, and they regard inventory as an evil because it takes up space and ties up resources. The following article provides a description of a JIT system.

The article on pages 691 and 692 provides a number of very important insights on the just-in-time approach to manufacturing, along with some reasons for the successes Japanese manufacturers have achieved.

In some respects, the just-in-time concept was operational a half century ago at the Rouge, Henry Ford's great industrial complex:

> Nothing in the period that followed was too good for the Rouge; it had the best blast furnaces, the best machine tools, the best metal labs, the best electrical systems, the most efficient efficiency experts. At its maturity in the mid-twenties, the Rouge dwarfed all other industrial complexes. It was a mile and a half long and three quarters of a mile wide. Its eleven hundred acres contained ninety-three buildings, twenty-three of them major. There were ninety-three miles of railroad track on it and twenty-seven miles of conveyor belts. Some seventy-five thousand men worked there, five thousand of them doing nothing but keeping it clean, using eighty-six tons of soap and wearing out five thousand mops each month. By the standards of the day the Rouge was, in fact, clean and quiet. Little was wasted. A British historian of the time, J. A. Spender, wrote of its systems: "If absolute completeness and perfect adaptation of means to end justify the word, they are in their own way works of art." Dissatisfied with the supply and quality of the steel he was getting from the steel companies, Ford asked how much it would cost to build a steel plant within the Rouge. About $35

"If American automobile king Henry Ford I were alive today, I am positive he would have done what we did with our Toyota production system."
—Taiichi Ohno in his 1978 book
The Toyota Production System

TOYOTA CITY, Japan—Groping to explain "how Japan does it," experts have made much of the close ties between business and government and of the loyalty of Japan's highly skilled workers to their employers. They've noted the fierce competitiveness of Japanese companies in their home market, the nation's high savings rate, even the relative scarcity of lawyers.

Doubtless these are among the pieces needed to solve the puzzle. But some management consultants who've studied how Japan makes such high-quality, competitively priced products say there's another piece often overlooked. The Japanese, they say, have proved themselves increasingly adroit at organizing and running manufacturing operations. Japanese managers may lack the MBAs or the ability to plot big-picture business strategy of their American counterparts. But they know how to run factories.

"There's a growing acceptance that Japanese success is based at least in part on the development of manufacturing techniques that often tend to outrun our own," says management consultant Rex Reid, head of A. T. Kearney's Toyota office.

One of the most interesting examples of Japanese production management skills is a concern quite familiar to Americans: Toyota Motor Co., the largest-selling foreign automaker in the U.S.

Believe in Their System

Toyota officials resist claiming that their way of building autos is better than anyone else's. They're somewhat embarrassed by the exuberant projections of Henry Ford's behavior essayed by their former chief production executive, Taiichi Ohno, in his 1978 book. But Toyota men clearly remain believers in what Mr. Ohno called "the Toyota production system."

For a first-hand look at the system, take a walk through the Tsutsumi plant here in Toyota City, a town of 280,000 in central Japan that's the site of 8 of Toyota's 10 factories. Over here, Muneo Nakahara, 26 years old and an 8-year Toyota veteran, is doing his job. With the help of an overhead crane that Mr. Nakahara controls from a hand-held device, he hoists auto engines onto a conveyor belt that will take them to be matched up with auto bodies.

Mr. Nakahara is lifting the engines onto the conveyor from a small flat-bed truck that has brought them from the engine plant. Only two trucks carrying just 12 engines apiece park at Mr. Nakahara's post at any given time, so every few minutes an empty truck drives back to the engine plant and a new one takes its place.

That's the first feature of the Toyota system: no inventories. Toyota's factories keep on hand only that amount of parts needed for immediate production, from a few minutes' worth up to a few hours' worth, depending on the part. When fresh parts are needed—and only when they're needed—they're delivered from other Toyota plants or from outside suppliers directly to the production line.

Outsiders who've seen Toyota in action often call this the "kanban system," *kanban* being the Japanese work for the piece of paper enclosed in clear plastic that accompanies each bin of parts. (When a worker on the line begins drawing from a new bin, he removes the kanban and routes it back to the supplier, for whom it serves as an order for a new bin of parts.) But Toyota officials say the pieces of paper are just tools. They call this inventory control aspect of their broader system the "just-in-time" system.

The same philosophy guides the meshing of operations within each plant. An assembly line that is building subcomponents makes just that number of subcomponents immediately needed at the next stage of production. When it's made enough, it's changed over to build some other kind of subcomponent for a while. Likewise, the final assembly line first builds one kind of car, then another, in small lots—only as much as called for in actual orders from Toyota's sales unit. Toyota engineers "average" and "level" production among the lines to coordinate output without building inventories. They compare auto assembly to rowing a boat: Everybody has to be pulling on the oars at the same rate.

"They concentrate very heavily on avoiding end-item and intermediate-item storage," says a Ford official in Detroit who's seen the system at work. "They throw out the whole concept of mass production."

The benefits are substantial. Toyota doesn't need space for inventory, people to handle and control inventory, or borrowed money to finance inventory. "It cuts costs in a lot of ways," says an official of Nissan Motor Co., Japan's second-largest automaker, which has adopted an inventory control system similar to its rival's in some plants.

Then there are the side benefits. Because Toyota is constantly changing over its machines to make new things, its workers have become fast at repair and changeover. In his book, Mr. Ohno cites a mold on a press that took two to three hours to change in the 1940s. Today "it takes only three minutes to change the mold," Mr. Ohno says.

Aside from its emphasis on holding down inventories, Toyota's system stresses quality controls. Throughout the Tsutsumi plant are boards with electric lights to indicate conditions on each assembly line. A red light means a line has been stopped because of a problem. Every worker has a button or cord with which he can stop the line, and he's told to use it whenever he thinks something's wrong with the operation of the line or when he spots defects in the product.

"We lose production temporarily this way," concedes Fujio Cho, manager of the production control department at Toyota's headquarters. "But in our experience stopping lines helps us detect problems early and avoid bad practices."

Another feature that becomes clear is the company's penchant for training workers to do more than one job. The man who runs one machine switches off every few moments to run another. The man who feeds rear windows to a robot also "tags" car shells with instructions telling workers farther down the line what to install in them. This versatility allows Toyota to realign its work force more efficiently when business is bad.

Indeed, "recession" thinking underlies a big part of Toyota's system. Much of the system originated in the late 1940s and early 1950s, when Toyota was producing exclusively for a domestic market that wasn't every strong. The company has been operating on the conventional assumption that it's most efficient to produce in large lots, "but that kind of thinking has pushed us close to bankruptcy, because

the large lots we were producing couldn't be sold," says Mr. Cho. Toyota couldn't lay off workers—Japan's a "life-time" employment system—so Toyota executives hit upon the simple yet radical idea that still pervades its operations: Overproduction is waste.

Special Relationship

It is, of course, open to question whether Toyota's is the best way to make cars, and Toyota officials themselves doubt whether other automakers could adopt it readily. They note among other problems that it takes a special kind of relationship with suppliers to make the system work.

Fully 50 of Toyota's 250 suppliers are headquartered in Toyota City, and almost all have plants here. They have to be close to make all those deliveries every day. It still shocks Toyota officials to be told that American automakers buy parts from suppliers all over the United States and even from suppliers in Europe and Japan. Toyota's most distant supplier is a five-hour drive away.

Then, too, suppliers must have close working relations with Toyota to adjust to Toyota's peculiar needs. It isn't surprising that many of Toyota's suppliers do all or most of their business with Toyota, and that Toyota owns large blocks of the stock of some of its most important suppliers. Many suppliers, even those Toyota doesn't own, have adopted Toyota's production system for their own operations. It improves coordination with Toyota and helps them avoid getting stuck with the inventory buildup that Toyota refuses to get stuck with.

The point isn't whether Toyota's system is best. The point is that it's very good and that Toyota is in many ways typical of Japanese manufacturers in its continual striving to improve production techniques. When experts talk about the competitiveness of Japanese products in international markets, that's something that shouldn't be forgotten.

At Ford's Rouge plant, some JIT principles were employed long ago. Here, workers put the finishing touch on 1947 models of the Mercury.

million, Sorensen told him. "What are you waiting for?" said Ford. Equally dissatisfied with both the availability and the quality of glass, he built a glass factory at the Rouge as well. The price of glass had been roughly 30 cents a square foot early in the life of the T; soon it had soared to $1.50 a foot. With the glass plant at the Rouge, the price of glass came down to 20 cents a foot. Barges carrying iron ore would steam into the inland docks, and even as they were tying up, huge cranes would be swinging out to start the unloading. The process was revolutionary. On Monday morning a barge bearing ore would arrive in a slip, and the ore would go to the blast furnace. By Tuesday it would be poured into a foundry mold and later that day would become an engine. John DeVenter, a business historian, wrote in awe: "Here is the conversion of raw material to cash in approximately thirty-three hours." Some sixty years later Toyota would be credited for its just-in-time theory of manufacturing, in which parts arrived from suppliers just in time to be part of the final assembly. But in any real sense that process began at the Rouge. Toasting Philip Caldwell, the head of Ford who in 1982 was visiting Japan, Eiji Toyoda, of the Toyota company, said, "There is no secret to how we learned to do what we do, Mr. Caldwell. We learned it at the Rouge."
—*Source: David Halberstam,* The Reckoning, *(New York: Morrow, 1986), pp. 87–88.*

A widely held view of JIT is that it is simply a system for scheduling production that results in low levels of work-in-process and inventory. But in its truest sense, JIT represents a *philosophy* that encompasses every aspect of the process, from design to after the sale of a product. Moreover, the key element of a JIT system is *quality*.

In JIT systems, quality is *ingrained* in both the product and the process. Companies that use JIT have achieved a level of quality that *enables* them to function with small batch sizes and tight schedules. JIT systems have very high reliability; major sources of inefficiency and disruption have been eliminated, and workers have been trained not only to function in the system, but also to *continuously improve* it.

In the following section, the key elements of JIT systems are described. They provide a basis for understanding how these systems function.

KEY ELEMENTS OF JIT SYSTEMS

JIT systems are designed to achieve a smooth flow of production using minimal inventories. The systems are fairly flexibly, with a high degree of worker participation in problem solving, continuous improvement, and attention to detail. However, the most important aspect of a JIT system is that *quality is built into the system.* High quality is a prerequisite for this system; no other element is as critical.

The key elements of the system are these:

1. High quality levels.
2. Production smoothing.
3. Low inventories.
4. Small lot sizes.
5. Quick, low-cost setups.
6. Layout.
7. Preventive maintenance and repair.
8. Multifunctional workers.
9. A cooperative spirit.
10. Few, reliable suppliers.
11. A *pull system* of moving goods.
12. Problem solving.
13. Continual improvement.

Let's examine each of these elements.

HIGH QUALITY LEVELS

As mentioned, JIT systems require high quality levels. The systems are geared to a smooth flow of work; the appearance of problems due to poor quality creates disruption in this flow. In fact, because small lot sizes and the absence of buffer stock result in low in-process inventories, if problems occur, production must cease until they have been resolved. Obviously, shutting down an entire process is costly and cuts into planned output levels, so it becomes imperative to try to avoid shutdowns, and to quickly resolve problems when they do appear.

JIT systems use a three-part approach to quality. One part is to design quality into the product and the production process. The fact that JIT systems produce standardized product leads to standardized job methods, workers who are very familiar with their jobs, and the use of standardized equipment, all of which contribute to high quality levels. Moreover, the cost of product design quality (i.e., building quality in at the *design* stage) can be spread over many units, yielding a low cost per unit.

The second part to the approach is to insist that vendors provide high-quality materials and parts to minimize disruptions due to problems with incoming goods. Once a high degree of confidence in vendor quality has been achieved, the time and cost of inspecting incoming goods can be practically eliminated.

The third part to the approach is to make workers responsible for producing goods of high quality. This requires providing adequate equipment and tools to do the work, providing proper training in work methods and in measuring quality and detecting errors, supporting and encouraging worker efforts to improve quality, and giving workers the authority to make changes when problems are found.

A central technique of JIT systems is to minimize defects through the use of **autonomation** (note the extra syllable *on* in the middle of the word). This refers to the automatic detection of defects during production. It can be used with machines

Autonomation

Automatic detection of defects during production.

or manual operations. It consists of a mechanism for detecting defects when they occur, and a mechanism for stopping production for purposes of correcting the cause of the defects. Thus, the halting of production forces immediate attention to the problem, after which an investigation of the problem is conducted, and corrective action is taken to resolve the problem.

PRODUCTION SMOOTHING

JIT production requires a smooth flow of goods through the system to achieve a meshing of the different operations and the movement of goods and materials from the supplier to the final output. Every activity must be carefully coordinated because there is very little slack. Therefore, aggregate production schedules are set over a time horizon (often a month) in order for production and purchasing schedules to be established. The monthly plan provides the basis for determining an *average* daily production plan. The plan may be revised slightly, perhaps weekly, as updated information such as sales orders become available. Surprisingly, these systems can handle variety by keeping final assembly schedules flexible. For example, in the final assembly of automobiles, customer orders can be filled on a *daily* basis by changing the mix for final assembly. If a customer wants air conditioning or a specific color, the system can tolerate that variety. Note, however, that companies using JIT production typically restrict the number of options available to a relatively small number. Not as extreme as Henry Ford in the 1920s ("You can have any color you want, as long as it's black"), but the selections are fairly limited so as to minimize disruptions to smooth production schedules.

LOW INVENTORIES

People readily associate the term *just-in time* with low inventories. And, in fact, one of the hallmarks of JIT systems is low inventories—of purchased parts and raw materials, work in process, and finished goods.

There are three important aspects of low inventories. Two reflect benefits, and one reflects a basic requirement of JIT systems. The first, obvious benefit of low inventories is the savings of space—warehouse space and space in work areas. Savings are also realized by not having to tie up money in idle inventory. The second benefit, more subtle, is a key aspect of the JIT philosophy. Inventories are buffers that tend to cover up recurring problems that are never resolved, partly because they aren't obvious and partly because the presence of inventory makes them seem less serious. When a machine breaks down, it won't disrupt the system if there is a sufficient inventory of the machine's output to feed into the next workstation. This use of inventory as the "solution" can lead to increasing amounts of inventory if breakdowns increase. A better solution would be to investigate the *causes* of machine breakdowns and focus on eliminating them. Similar problems with quality, unreliable vendors, and scheduling can also be "solved" by having ample inventories to fall back on. However, carrying all that extra inventory creates a tremendous burden in cost and space and allows problems to go unresolved.

The JIT approach is to pare down inventories gradually in order to uncover the problems. Once they are uncovered and solved, more inventory is removed, additional problems are found and solved, and so on. A useful analogy is a boat on a pond that has large, hidden rocks, as in Figure 14–1. The rocks represent problems that can hinder production (the boat). The water in the pond that covers the rocks

Figure 14–1

Large rocks are hidden by a high water level (A). Lower water level (B) reveals rocks. Once the rocks are removed, the water level (inventory) can be lowered (C).

is the inventory in the system. As the water level is slowly lowered, the largest rocks are the first to appear (i.e., those problems are the first to be identified). At that point, efforts are undertaken to remove these rocks from the water (i.e., resolve these problems). Once that has been accomplished, additional water is removed from the pond, revealing the next layer of rocks, which are then worked on. As more and more of the rocks are removed, the need for water to cover them diminishes. Likewise, as more and more of the major production problems are solved, there is less and less need to rely on inventory.

The third important aspect of low inventories reflects a basic requirement of JIT systems: to be able to operate with low inventories, the major problems must have already been resolved. Thus, low inventories are the result of a *process* of successful problem solving, one that has occurred over time. Furthermore, because it is unlikely that all problems will be found and resolved, it is necessary to be able to deal quickly with problems when they do occur. Hence, there is a continuing need to identify and solve problems in a short time span to prevent new problems from disrupting the smooth flow of work through the system.

SMALL LOT SIZES

Small lot sizes, both in the production process and in deliveries from suppliers, yield a number of benefits that enable JIT systems to operate effectively. One is that with small lots moving through the system, in-process inventory is considerably less than with large lots. This reduces carrying costs, space requirements, and clutter in the workplace. Another advantage is that when problems with quality occur, inspection and rework costs are less because there are fewer items in a lot to inspect and rework.

Small lots also permit greater flexibility in scheduling. Repetitive systems typically produce a variety of products. In traditional systems, this generally means long production runs of each product, one after the other. Although this spreads the setup cost for a run over many items, it also results in long cycles over the entire range of products. For instance, suppose a firm has three products, A, B, and C. In a traditional system, there would be a long run of product A (say, covering two or three days or more), then a long run of product B, and then a long run of product C before the sequence would repeat. In contrast, a JIT system, using small lots, would frequently shift from producing A to producing B and C. This flexibility enables JIT systems to respond more quickly to changing customer demands for output: JIT

JIT approach

AAA BBBBBBB **CC** AAA BBBBBBB **CC** AAA BBBBBBB **CC** AAA BBBBBBB **CC**

Time ⟶

Large-lot approach

AAAAAAAAAAAA BBBBBBBBBBBBBBBBBBBBBBBBBBBBBBBB **CCCCCCCCC** AAAAAAAAAAAA

Time ⟶

Figure 14–2

JIT versus large lot run sizes

systems can produce just what is needed, when it is needed. The contrast between small and large lot sizes is illustrated in Figure 14–2.

It is worth noting that in the JIT philosophy, the ideal lot size is one unit. Although that quantity may not always be a realistic goal because of practical considerations that require minimum lot sizes (e.g., machines that process multiple items simultaneously, heat-treating equipment that processes multiple items simultaneously, and machines with very high setup times), the goal is still to reduce the lot size as much as possible because small lot sizes have numerous benefits.

Quick, Low-Cost Setups

Small lots and changing product mixes require frequent setups. Unless these are quick and relatively inexpensive, the time and cost to accomplish them is prohibitive. Often, workers are trained to do their own setups. Moreover, programs to reduce setup time and cost are used to achieve the desired results; a deliberate effort is required, and workers are usually a valuable part of the process.

Setup tools and equipment and setup procedures must be simple and standardized. Multipurpose equipment or attachments can help to reduce setup time. For instance, a machine with multiple spindles that can easily be rotated into place for different job requirements can drastically reduce job changeover time. Moreover, *group technology* may be used to reduce setup cost and time by capitalizing on similarities in recurring operations. For instance, parts that are similar (in shape, materials, etc.) may require very similar setups. Processing them in sequence on the same equipment can reduce the need to completely change a setup; minor adjustment may be all that is necessary.

Layout

Traditional factories often use layouts based on processing requirements (i.e., work centers designed to handle a certain type of processing, such as drilling, cutting, or packaging). Consequently, in traditional manufacturing systems, a group of parts moves from one processing center to the next. Each move adds to the time in which parts are in the system, as lots wait to be moved, wait at the next center to be processed, and so on. This also adds to the amount of inventory in the system. In such systems, the time devoted to actually working on a part may constitute less than 5 percent of the time a part is in the system. For the remaining 95 percent of the time, no useful purpose is served by having the part in the system; no value is added. In a real sense, there is a considerable amount of waste and inefficiency.

JIT systems commonly use layouts based on product requirements. Equipment is arranged to handle streams of similar products with similar processing or assembly requirements. This avoids having to move large lots of parts around the work area;

parts pass in small lots from one work center to the next with little or no waiting and with substantially less need for in-process inventory. Moreover, material handling costs are greatly reduced, as is the space needed to support a given level of output. Factories tend to be smaller and more efficient, and machines can be moved closer together, which has the further benefit of enhancing communication among workers.

PREVENTIVE MAINTENANCE AND REPAIR

Preventive maintenance
Maintaining equipment in good operating condition and replacing parts with a tendency to fail before they actually do fail.

Because JIT systems have very little in-process inventory, equipment breakdowns can be very disruptive. To minimize breakdowns, companies use **preventive maintenance** programs, which emphasize maintaining equipment in good operating condition and replacing parts that have a tendency to fail before they actually fail. Workers are often responsible for maintaining their own equipment.

Even with preventive maintenance, there will be occasional equipment failures. Companies must be prepared for this, so as to quickly return equipment to working order. This may mean maintaining supplies of critical spare parts and making other provisions for emergency situations, perhaps maintaining a small force of repair people or training workers to do certain repairs themselves.

Note, too, that when breakdowns do occur, they indicate a potential area for improvement. Thus, breakdowns become opportunities to be exploited in a JIT environment.

MULTIFUNCTIONAL WORKERS

Multifunctional workers
Workers that are trained to operate machinery, handle setups, and perform maintenance and minor repairs.

In traditional production systems, it is not unusual to find that a worker is trained for a relatively narrow set of tasks. For instance, some workers are trained to operate machinery, others to handle setups, and still others to perform maintenance and repair. JIT systems feature **multifunctional workers**, trained to handle all of those tasks. That does not mean that workers are trained as master mechanics; major repairs are usually handled by repair people. However, workers are expected to be able to handle adjustments and minor repairs as well as do their own setups. Remember, though, that under JIT systems, efforts are made to simplify setups, making it more appropriate to assign them to operators.

Workers in JIT systems are often trained to handle more than one production operation. That way, if a worker falls behind, others will be able to assist him or her in maintaining the schedule.

Workers are responsible for checking the quality of their own work and monitoring the quality of work they receive as input to their stations. Workers are also expected to participate in problem solving. In spite of all this worker involvement, there is the expectation that workers will strictly adhere to schedules, and if a worker believes that he or she has discovered an improved way of doing a task, that idea is to be submitted to others and approved before it is implemented. Hence, workers are not permitted to alter established methods or routines individually.

The concept of flexible workers has much to offer, but it is not without a downside. One negative aspect is the training cost and time that may be required to cross-train highly skilled workers. Another is that workers may resist flexibility for reasons such as loss of job security and the burden of learning new skills. Older workers may be shunted off to early retirement rather than be retrained because their benefit time would be much shorter than that of younger workers. Thus, it is important for companies to carefully consider which jobs are best suited to multi-functional workers, and which are not. In all likelihood, the lowest skilled jobs are the ones that will lead to the benefits of flexible workers.

A Cooperative Spirit

JIT systems require a cooperative spirit among workers, management, and vendors. Unless that is present, it is doubtful that a truly effective JIT system can be achieved. The Japanese have been very successful in this regard, partly because in the Japanese culture, respect and cooperation are ingrained. In Western cultures, workers, managers, and vendors have historically been strongly at odds with each other. Consequently, a major consideration in operating under a JIT system is to achieve and maintain a spirit of mutual respect and cooperation. This requires an appreciation of the importance of cooperation and a tenacious effort by management to instill and maintain that spirit.

Few, Reliable Suppliers

Most JIT systems extend to suppliers, who are required to deliver high-quality parts and/or materials, in small lots, at fairly precise intervals.

Traditionally, buyers have assumed the role of monitoring the quality of purchased goods, inspecting shipments for quality and quantity, and returning poor-quality goods to the vendor for rework. In JIT systems, there is little slack, so poor-quality goods cause a disruption in the smooth flow of work. Moveover, having to inspect incoming goods is viewed as inefficient because it does not add value to the product. For these reasons, the burden of insuring quality is shifted to the vendor. Buyers work with vendors to help them achieve the desired quality levels and to impress upon them the importance of consistent, high-quality goods. The ultimate goal of the buyer is to be able to *certify* a vendor as a producer of high-quality goods. The implication of this certification is that a vendor can be relied on to deliver high-quality goods *without the need for buyer inspection.*

Suppliers must also be willing and able to ship in small lots on a regular basis. Ideally, suppliers themselves will be operating under JIT systems. Buyers can often help suppliers convert to JIT production based on their own experiences. In effect, the supplier becomes part of an extended JIT system that integrates the facilities of buyer and supplier. If a supplier is dedicated to only one or a few buyers, this will make integration easier. Practically speaking, a supplier is likely to have many different buyers, some using traditional systems and others using JIT. Consequently, compromises may have to be made to both buyers and suppliers.

Such a spirit of cooperation between buyer and seller has not traditionally been present. In fact, traditionally, buyers and vendors have had a somewhat adversarial relationship. Buyers have generally regarded price as a major determinant in sourcing. Moreover, buyers have typically used *multiple-source* purchasing, which means having a list of potential vendors and buying from several to avoid getting locked into a sole source. In this way, buyers can play vendors off against each other to get better pricing arrangements or other concessions. The downside of this is that vendors cannot rely on a long-term relationship with a buyer; therefore, vendors have not felt loyalty to a particular buyer. Furthermore, vendors have often sought to protect themselves from losing a buyer by increasing the number of buyers they supply.

Under JIT purchasing, good vendor relationships are very important. Buyers take measures to reduce their lists of suppliers, concentrating on maintaining close working relationships with a few good ones. Because of the need for frequent, small deliveries, many buyers attempt to find local vendors to shorten the lead time for deliveries as well as to reduce lead time variability. An added advantage of having vendors nearby is quick response when problems do arise.

JIT purchasing is enhanced by *long-term* relationships between buyers and vendors. Vendors are more willing to commit resources to the job of shipping according to a buyer's JIT system given a long-term relationship. Moreover, price often becomes secondary to the other aspects of the relationship (e.g., consistent high quality; flexibility; frequent, small deliveries; and quick response to problems).

A key feature of many lean production systems is the relatively small number of suppliers used. In traditional production, companies often deal with hundreds or even thousands of suppliers, in a highly centralized arrangement not unlike a giant wheel with many, many spokes. The company is at the hub of the wheel, and the spokes radiate out to suppliers, who each must deal directly with the company. Very often, one supplier does not know who the other suppliers are or what they are doing. Each supplier works to specifications provided by the buyer. Suppliers have very little basis (or motivation) for suggesting improvements. Moreover, as companies often play one supplier off against others, the sharing of information is more risky than rewarding. In contrast to this, lean production companies may employ a tiered approach for suppliers: they use relatively few first-tier suppliers who work directly with the company, and who supply major subassemblies. The first-tier suppliers are responsible for dealing with second-tier suppliers who provide components for the subassemblies, thereby relieving the final buyer from dealing with large numbers of suppliers.

We find a good example of this in the automotive industry. Suppose a certain model has an electric seat. The seat and motor together might entail about 250 separate parts. A traditional producer might use over 50 suppliers for the electric seat, but a lean producer might use a single (first-tier) supplier who has the responsibility for the entire seat unit. The company would provide specifications for the overall unit, but leave to the supplier the details of the motor, springs, and so on. The first-tier supplier, in turn, might subcontract the motor to a second-tier supplier, the track to another second-tier supplier, and the cushions and fabric to still another second-tier supplier. These second-tier suppliers might similarly subcontract some of their work to third-tier suppliers, and so on. Each tier has only to deal with those just above it or just below it. Suppliers on each level are encouraged to work with each other, and motivated to do so because that increases the probability that the resulting item (e.g., the seat) will meet or exceed the final buyer's expectations. In this "team of suppliers" approach, all suppliers benefit from a successful product, and each supplier bears full responsibility for the quality of its portion of the product.

PULL VERSUS PUSH

The terms *push* and *pull* are used to describe two different systems for moving work through a production process. In a **push system**, when work is finished at a workstation, the output is *pushed* to the next station; or, in the case of the final operation, it is pushed on to final inventory. Conversely, in a **pull system**, control of moving the work rests with the *following* operation; each workstation *pulls* the output from the preceding station as it is needed; output of the final operation is

Push system

System for moving work where output is pushed to the next station as it is completed.

Pull system

System for moving work where a workstation pulls output from the preceding station as it is needed.

pulled by customer demand or the master schedule. Thus, in a pull system, work is moved in response to demand from the next stage in the process, whereas in a push system, work is pushed on as it is completed, with no regard for whether the next station is ready for the work. Consequently, work may pile up at workstations that fall behind schedule, say, because of equipment failure or the detection of a problem with quality.

JIT systems use the pull approach to control the flow of work, with each workstation gearing its output to the demand presented by the next workstation. Traditional production systems use the push approach for moving work through the system. In JIT systems, there is communication backward through the system from station to station, so that work moves "just in time" for the next operation; the flow of work is thereby coordinated, and the accumulation of excessive inventories between operations is avoided. Of course, some inventory is usually present because operations are not instantaneous. If a workstation waited until it received a request from the next workstation before *starting* its work, the next station would have to wait for the preceding station to perform its work. Therefore, by design, each workstation produces just enough output to meet the (anticipated) demand of the next station. This can be accomplished by having the following workstation communicate its need for input sufficiently ahead of time to allow the preceding station to do the work. Or there can be a small buffer of stock between stations; when the buffer decreases to a certain level, this signals the preceding station to produce enough output to replenish the buffer supply. The size of the buffer depends on the cycle time at the preceding work station: if the cycle time is short, little or no buffer will be needed; if the cycle time is long, a considerable amount of buffer will be needed. Note, however, that production occurs only in response to *usage* of the following station; work is *pulled* by the demand generated by the next operation.

Another way to describe the pull system is that work flow is dictated by "next-step demand." There are a variety of ways in which such demand can be communicated, including a shout or a wave, but by far the most commonly used device is the **kanban** card. *Kanban* is a Japanese term that means *signal* or *visible record*. When a worker needs materials or work from the preceding station, he or she uses a kanban card to communicate this. In effect, the kanban card is the authorization to move or work on parts. In kanban systems, no part or lot can be moved or worked on without one of these cards.

Kanban

Card that communicates demand for work or materials from the preceding station.

The system works this way: A kanban card is affixed to each container. When a workstation needs to replenish its supply of parts, a worker goes to the area where these parts are stored and withdraws one container of parts. Each container holds a predetermined quantity. The worker removes the kanban card from the container and posts it in a designated spot where it will be clearly visible, and the worker then moves the lot to the workstation. The posted kanban is then picked up by a stock person who replenishes the stock with another container, and so on down the line. Demand for parts triggers a replenishment, and parts are supplied as usage dictates. Similar withdrawals and replenishments occur all the way up and down the line from vendors to finished-goods inventories, all controlled by kanbans. In fact, if supervisors decide the system is too loose because inventories are building up, they may decide to withdraw some kanbans, thereby tightening the system. Conversely, if the system seems too tight, additional kanbans may be introduced to bring the system into balance.

It is apparent that the number of kanban cards in use is an important variable. The ideal number of kanban cards can be computed using this formula:

This hardware delivery cart with dedicated, "triggered" tote pans is part of the Kanban system at John Deere's Horicon works.

$$N = \frac{DT(1 + X)}{C}$$ (14–1)

where

  N = Total number of containers

  D = Planned usage rate of using work center

  T = Average waiting time for replenishment of parts plus average production time for a container of parts

  X = Policy variable set by management that reflects possible inefficiency in the system (the closer to 0, the more efficient the system)

  C = Capacity of a standard container (should be no more than 10 percent of daily usage of the part)

Note that D and T must use the same time units (e.g., minutes, days).

PROBLEM SOLVING

Problem solving is a cornerstone of any JIT system. Of interest are problems that interrupt, or have the potential to interrupt, the smooth flow of work through the system. When such problems surface, it becomes important to resolve them quickly. This may entail *temporarily* increasing inventory levels while the problem is investigated, but the intent of problem solving is to *eliminate* the problem, or a least greatly reduce the chances of it recurring.

  Problems that occur during production must be dealt with quickly. Some companies use a light system to signal problems; in Japan, such a system is called **andon**. Each workstation is equipped with a set of three lights. A green light means no problems, an amber light means a worker is falling a little bit behind, and a red light indicates a serious problem. The purpose of the light system is to keep others in the

Andon

System of lights used at each workstation to signal problems or slowdowns.

Usage at a work center is 300 parts per day, and a standard container holds 25 parts. It takes an average of .12 day for a container to complete a circuit from the time a kanban card is received until the container is returned empty. Compute the number of kanban cards needed if $X = .20$.

Example 1

Solution

$N = ?$ $\qquad\qquad$ $C = 25$ parts per container

$D = 300$ parts per day $\qquad$ $X = .20$

$T = .12$ day

$$N = \frac{300(.12)(1 + .20)}{25} = 1.728 \text{ (round to two containers)}$$

Note that rounding up will cause the system to be looser, and rounding down will cause it to be tighter. Generally, rounding up is used.

---

system informed and to enable workers and supervisors to immediately see when and where problems are occurring.

Japanese companies have been very successful in forming teams composed of workers and managers that routinely work on problems. Moreover, workers are encouraged to report problems and potential problems to the teams. Teams may use *brainstorming* to generate possible solutions, where members meet and share thoughts and ideas on how problems might be resolved. The essence of these sessions is to encourage free thinking, so criticism is discouraged. Furthermore, a group may prefer to withhold analysis of ideas when they are presented in order to keep from stifling initiative or creating an atmosphere in which there is hesitancy in presenting potential solutions.

Groups may also use various statistical tools and quality control techniques (described in Chapter 10) such as sampling, control charts, and cause-and-effect diagrams.

It is important that management at all levels actively support and become involved in problem solving. This also includes a willingness to provide financial support and to recognize achievements. It is desirable to formulate goals with the help of workers, publicize the goals, and carefully document accomplishments. Goals give workers something tangible to strive for, and recognition can help maintain worker interest and morale.

CONTINUAL IMPROVEMENT

The central theme of a true just-in-time approach is to work toward continual improvement of the system—reducing inventories, reducing setup cost and time, improving quality, increasing the output rate, and generally cutting waste and inefficiency. Toward that end, problem solving becomes a way of life—a "culture" that must be assimilated into the thinking of management and workers alike. It becomes a never-ending quest for improving operations as all members of the organization strive to improve the system. Continuous improvement is described in Chapter 10.

JIT VERSUS TRADITIONAL MANUFACTURING

The preceding pages have described JIT systems and compared them to traditional manufacturing systems. Table 14–1 provides a brief overview of those comparisons.

Table 14–1

Comparison of JIT and typical U.S. manufacturing philosophies

Factors	JIT	American philosophy
Inventory	A liability. Every effort must be expended to do away with it.	An asset. It protects against forecast errors, machine problems, late vendor deliveries. More inventory is "safer."
Lot size	Immediate needs only. A minimum replenishment quantity is desired for both manufactured and purchased parts.	Formulas. We're always revising the optimum lot size with some formula based on the trade-off between the cost of inventories and the cost of setup.
Setups	Make them insignificant. This requires either extremely rapid changeover to minimize the impact on production or the availability of extra machines already set up. Fast changeover makes small lot sizes practical and allows a wide variety of parts to be made frequently.	Low priority issue. Maximum output is the usual goal. Rarely does similar thought and effort go into achieving quick changeover.
Queues	Eliminate them. When problems occur, identify the causes and correct them. The correction process is aided when queues are small.	Necessary investment. Queues permit succeeding operations to continue in the event of a problem with the feeding operation. Also, by providing a selection of jobs, factory management has a greater opportunity to match varying operator skills and machine capabilities, combine setups, and, thus, contribute to the efficiency of the operation.
Vendors	Coworkers; part of the team. Multiple deliveries for all active items are expected daily. The vendor takes care of the needs of the customer, and the customer treats the vendor as an extension of the factory.	Adversaries. Multiple sources are the rule, and it's typical to play them off against each other.
Quality	Zero defects. If quality is not 100%, production is in jeopardy.	Tolerate some scrap. We usually track what the actual scrap has been and develop formulas for predicting it.
Equipment maintenance	Constant and effective. Machine breakdowns must be minimal.	As required. Not critical because we have queues available.
Lead times	Keep them short. This simplifies the job of marketing, purchasing, and manufacturing, as it reduces the need for expediting.	The longer the better. Most foremen and purchasing agents want more lead time, not less.

Factors	JIT	American philosophy
Workers	Management by consensus. Changes are not made until consensus is reached, whether or not a bit of arm twisting is involved. The vital ingredient of "ownership" is achieved.	Management by edict. New systems are installed in spite of the workers, not thanks to the workers. Then we concentrate on measurements to determine whether or not they're doing their jobs.

Source: *Modern Materials Handling,* Copyright 1982 in article by Walter E. Goddard, Oliver Wight Education Associates, by Cahners Publishing Company, Division of Reed Holdings, Inc.

MRP II VERSUS KANBAN[1]

Although the goals of MRP II and kanban are essentially the same (i.e., to improve customer service, reduce inventories, and increase productivity), their approaches are quite different. Neither MRP nor kanban is a stand-alone system—each exists within a larger framework. MRP II is basically a computerized system; kanban is a manual system.

Kanban systems generally involve very small lot sizes, short lead times, and high-quality output, and they exemplify teamwork. Kanban is essentially a two-bin type of inventory: supplies are replenished semiautomatically when they reach a predetermined level. MRP II is more concerned with projecting requirements and with planning and leveling capacity via the computer.

A major benefit of the kanban system is its simplicity; a major benefit of MRP II is its ability to handle complex planning and scheduling quickly and efficiently. It also handles changes fairly easily. In addition, MRP II is capable of simulation (i.e., it enables management to answer "what if" questions) for capacity planning.

A comparison of how eight manufacturing functions are controlled by kanban and MRP II is presented in Table 14–2. Note that the two are the same in terms of employing a master schedule (products to be built) but differ in terms of every other function. Note, too, that the kanban approach is considerably less formal than MRP II.

The philosophies that underlie JIT systems are quite different from the philosophies that manufacturers have traditionally held. Hence, a major effort would be required to change from MRP II to kanban. That will not occur without the support of top management, and, even then, it will undoubtedly require much effort on all levels to overcome the ingrained resistance to such management changes. Chief among these management philosophies is that inventories of safety stocks should be maintained "just in case" something goes wrong. Realistically speaking, the focus has to shift from "who's to blame?" to "let's fix this so it won't happen again."

Whether manufacturers should adopt the kanban method is debatable. Some form of it may be useful, but kanban is merely an information system; by itself it offers little in terms of helping manufacturers become more competitive and/or productive. By the same token, MRP alone will not achieve those results either. Instead, it is the overall approach to manufacturing that is crucial; it is the commit-

---

[1]Based on an article by Walter E. Goddard, "Kanban versus MRP II—Which Is Best for You?" *Modern Materials Handling,* November 5, 1982.

Table 14–2

Comparison of kanban and MRP II

Functions	Categories	Kanban system	MRP II
Rates of output	Families of products	Leveling	Production plan
Products to be built	Finished goods for make-to-stock, customer orders for make-to-order	Master production schedule	Master production schedule
Materials required	Components—both manufactured and purchased	Kanban cards	Material requirements planning (MRP)
Capacity required	Output for key work centers and vendors	Visual	Capacity requirements planning (CRP)
Executing capacity plans	Producing enough output to satisfy plans	Visual	Input/output controls (I/O)
Executing material plans—manufactured items	Working on right priorities in factory	Kanban cards	Dispatching reports
Executing material plan—purchased items	Bringing in right items from vendors	Kanban cards and unofficial orders	Purchasing reports
Feedback information	What cannot be executed due to problems	Andon	Anticipated delay reports

Note: The same functions are performed by every manufacturing company; however, the tools used by kanban differ greatly from the MRP II tools. Under kanban, the tools are manual—kanban cards, andon lights, visual checks, and oral orders. Under MRP II, the most important tool is the computer.

Source: Reprinted from Walter E. Goddard, "Kanban versus MRP II—Which Is Best for You?" *Modern Materials Handling,* November 5, 1982.

ment and support of top management and the continuing efforts of all levels of management to find new ways to improve their manufacturing planning and control techniques, and then to adapt those techniques to fit their own particular set of circumstances, that will determine the degree of success. What can be said is that problems must be identified and eliminated in the manufacturing cycle and that improved methods of production planning and control are needed—improvements that will come about only through the effort and determination of everyone (i.e., workers and management, including top management).

BENEFITS OF JIT SYSTEMS

JIT systems have a number of important benefits that are attracting the attention of traditional companies. The main benefits are:

1. Reduced levels of in-process inventories, purchased goods, and finished goods.
2. Reduced space requirements.
3. Increased product quality and reduced scrap and rework.

4. Reduced manufacturing lead times.

5. Greater flexibility in changing the production mix.

6. Smoother production flow, with fewer disruptions caused by problems due to quality, shorter setup times, multiskilled workers who can help each other and substitute for others in case of absenteeism.

7. Increased productivity levels and utilization of equipment.

8. Worker participation in problem solving.

9. Pressure to build good relationships with vendors.

10. Reduction in the need for certain indirect labor, such as material handlers.

READING   DEVELOPING THE JIT PHILOSOPHY

Successful implementation of JIT requires involvement from all levels of management in all disciplines

"Our improvement in just-in-time has to be credited to the involvement of higher management and management across many disciplines," says Tom Jensch, Avon's director of materials management.

Every two weeks, at Avon's headquarters in New York City, senior management holds an inventory meeting to discuss progress in JIT. Included in that meeting are top-level managers from finance, marketing, merchandising, purchasing and strategic planning.

"It's a working meeting," says Jensch. "You don't just go in and listen to how the inventory numbers came in at the end of the month. We talk about specific marketing plans for items. How risky are they from an inventory standpoint? What can we do to minimize the risk? We can end up affecting designs of new products by getting away from unique containers and using stock containers if that's important to reduce the inventory risks. We talk about marketing flow and what we are going to do if a product oversells or undersells."

Management involvement doesn't begin and end with that one meeting. "We hold a monthly meeting with lower levels of management and nonmanagement people where we process ideas that have come out of the senior management meeting," says Jensch. "We are also working to come up with new ideas. In

this meeting are the appropriate people from marketing, finance, purchasing and materials control who are actually the hands-on inventory people. They are much closer to the front lines. It's a communication meeting, to share information and then follow up on various inventory projects we have initiated."

In addition, management from New York meets with inventory control people from Avon's three manufacturing facilities every six weeks. "The purpose of these meetings is to review inventory progress with the manufacturing facilities, to bring to them some of the new ideas that have been stimulated here in New York, to hear from them the new ideas and opportunities that they've identified and to see how we can work together to best process those ideas," says Jensch.

One of the ideas that went through this process and was implemented was the Vendor Proximity Program—the development of suppliers closer to Avon's manufacturing facilities. "Personnel at Avon's manufacturing plant in Suffren, N.Y., were having great success with JIT and we realized that all of the plant's suppliers were within a one-day transit time," says Jensch. After discussing this at inventory meetings, the company decided to seek vendors closer to its other two manufacturing sites in Morton Grove, Ill., and Springdale, Ohio.

Reprinted with permission from CPI Purchasing, September 1990.

CONVERTING TO A JIT SYSTEM

The success of JIT systems in Japan has attracted keen interest among U.S. manufacturers. A number of well-known firms have converted a portion of their operations to JIT systems.

To increase the probability of successful conversion, companies should adopt a carefully planned approach that includes the following elements:

1. Make sure top management is committed to the conversion and that they know what will be required. Make sure that management is *involved* in the process. And make sure that management knows what it will cost and how long it will take to complete the conversion, and what results can be expected.

2. Study the operations carefully; decide which parts will need the most effort to convert.

3. Obtain the support and cooperation of workers. Prepare training programs that include sessions in setups, maintenance of equipment, cross-training for multiple tasks, cooperation, and problem solving. Make sure workers are fully informed on what JIT is and why it is desirable. Reassure workers that their jobs are secure.

4. Begin by trying to reduce setup times while maintaining the current system. Enlist the aid of workers in identifying and eliminating existing problems (bottlenecks, poor quality, etc.).

5. Gradually convert operations, beginning at the *end* of the process and working *backward*. At each stage, make sure the conversion has been relatively successful before moving on. Do not begin to reduce inventories until major problems have been resolved.

6. Convert suppliers to JIT as one of the last steps. Be prepared to work closely with them. Start by narrowing the list of vendors, identifying those who are willing to embrace the JIT philosophy. Give preference to vendors who have long-term track records of being reliable. Try to use vendors located nearby if quick response time is important. Establish long-term commitments with vendors. Insist on high standards of quality and adherence to strict delivery schedules.

7. Be prepared to encounter obstacles to conversion.

OBSTACLES TO CONVERSION

There can be numerous obstacles to conversion. Among the most crucial are these:

1. Management may not be totally committed or may be unwilling to devote the necessary resources to conversion. This is perhaps the most serious impediment; the conversion is most likely doomed without total commitment.

2. Workers and/or management may not display a cooperative spirit. The system is predicated on cooperation. Managers may resist because JIT shifts some of the responsibility from management to workers and gives workers more control over the work. Manager resistance can be a serious obstacle to successful conversion. Workers themselves may resist because shared responsibility and cooperation are new to them; people generally resist change, preferring the known to the unknown.

3. Suppliers may resist, for several reasons:
   a. Buyers may not be willing to commit the resources necessary to help the supplier adapt to the JIT systems.
   b. They may be uneasy about long-term commitments to a buyer.
   c. Frequent, small deliveries may be difficult, especially if the supplier has other buyers that use traditional systems.

d. The burden of quality control will shift to the supplier.

e. Frequent engineering changes resulting from continuing JIT improvements by the buyer.

The Down Side of Conversion

Despite the many advantages of JIT production systems, there are a number of other considerations that must be taken into account when planning a conversion.

The key consideration is the amount of time and cost requirements for achieving conversion. These can be substantial, as it is absolutely essential that the major sources of disruption in the system be eliminated. Management must be prepared to commit the resources necessary to achieve the high level of quality and ability to function on a tight schedule. That means attention to even the smallest of details during the design phase, and substantial efforts to debug the system to the point where it runs smoothly. Beyond that, there must be the capability of responding quickly when problems arise, and a commitment on the part of management and workers to continuously improve the system. Although each case is different, a general estimate of the time required for conversion would be one to three years.

Another consideration relates to small lot sizes. While small lot sizes allow for flexibility in changing the product mix, they typically result in (1) increased transportation costs, and (2) traffic congestion due to frequent deliveries. So although inventory holding costs (and space) decrease, other costs increase, and the potential for congestion must be dealt with.

The following reading illustrates the point that converting to a JIT system can sometimes be a formidable undertaking. Firms must decide whether a JIT approach will be advantageous.

READING   JIT AND QUALITY: A PERFECT FIT

A company that plans to implement just-in-time manufacturing must have an established quality program to use as a foundation, according to several quality leaders in the chemical industry.

"Just-in-time is an integral part of the quality process," says Theodore C. Kuchler, quality manager, Chemicals and Pigments Dept., Du Pont Co. "It is a tool that can be used to accomplish continuous improvement."

From New York to Japan the words "continuous improvement" can be found in corporate literature describing quality programs. But where does just-in-time, or JIT, come into play, particularly in the chemical process industry?

Loosely defined, JIT is a manufacturing concept which eliminates anything that does not add value to the product. Successful quality programs revolve around strong supplier relationships—with purchasing playing a critical role—and top management commitment. And JIT is no different.

"There is a misconception of what just-in-time truly is," says Thomas Cummins, manager, total quality, Monsanto Chemical Co. "The heart of just-in-time is process capability, and the very first need is a stable, capable and predictable process effort."

In order to achieve a capable and predictable process, most companies feel an emphasis on quality is necessary. "Quality and just-in-time are interrelated," says David E. Winkler, vice president, manufacturing convenience meals, Campbell Soup Co.

"Companies can say they have just-in-time, but if they don't have a reliable system in place that is compatible with the just-in-time concept, then they are not going to be very successful," he says.

JIT and quality work well together because both strive to improve the way companies operate. JIT, unlike the quality process, cannot stand alone over the long haul. It is considered by many to be part of the quality process, rather than vice versa.

"Just-in-time without quality?" asks Neal Kane, quality manager, specialty chemicals, Du Pont Co. "It may be possible, but it is very risky. There would be limits as to how far a company could proceed without a quality process."

"You could say you have just-in-time without the quality process," says Gary Childers, manager of quality, planning and administration, Union Carbide Corp. "But eventually the system would break down because you would be placing too much of a demand on it. You need to have the quality process."

Changing Attitudes

Ten years ago, Union Carbide looked at suppliers as just that: companies that provide materials and supplies. "We simply said, 'This is what we want,'" says Childers. "Today, along with our expectations of them, we tell them what they can expect from us."

Childers proposes an interesting reason why companies have begun looking at suppliers differently. "Throughout industry there is a gigantic demand for good suppliers," he says. "And pretty soon, they will be more selective about their customers."

He says companies who enter into JIT looking for immediate results often are those companies which, after a brief tryout, abandon the concept. "Don't go for an answer like short leadtimes or inventory reductions," says Childers. "That's the wrong attitude. It is a step-by-step journey."

Part of that journey involves changing the attitudes of plant managers who are accustomed to having stacks of materials in inventory available whenever they want it. And removing such a security blanket takes time.

"We've been working on the subject of change for 10 years," says Campbell Soup's Winkler, former vice president of Campbell's Quality Proud program. "To try and do it overnight would be difficult, if not impossible."

Winkler says a key to successful JIT is "to keep in mind that you're trying to make money by better utilizing your assets. Inventories are just one way of reducing pressure to do things right." He says JIT forces purchasing and manufacturing to do better jobs of forecasting and to understand the value of recognizing problems.

Once this is accomplished, a series of "hidden costs"—excess warehouse space, the double handling of some materials and needless paperwork—are identified. "Then the emphasis is where it should be—on maintaining a reliable and flexible supply," Winkler says.

Intangible Benefits

The Organic Peroxides Div. of Atochem North America, Inc., has a situation which is not unique in the chemical industry. Some organic peroxides, which are used in the manufacturing of plastics, are sold as controlled-temperature products.

"Certain products, if they reach room temperature, could create serious problems," says Gerald P. Franco, Atochem's quality assurance coordinator. "As a result, deliveries to some of our customers have become smaller and more frequent."

The benefits to Atochem's customers include improved product quality, less storage space needed for the peroxides and, as a result, increased safety because less of the material is stored on the customer's plant site.

Benefits to Atochem involve the trickle-down effect to their suppliers. "We knew our shipments were becoming more frequent," says Franco. "So, in turn, we had to make sure our suppliers could get us the materials we need when we need them. It placed a greater emphasis on scheduling and production.

"In order to supply materials on a certain day at a certain time—my definition of just-in-time—one needs to have his house in order," he says. "And to achieve this Atochem has initiated its total quality performance process."

Monsanto is another company which became aware of just-in-time manufacturing needs "when our customers started asking us about it," says Cummins. "We became interested about four to five years ago, at the same time our customers did."

He says one of the biggest benefits to come from working on JIT is that it necessitates a closer relationship between customers and suppliers. "The customer has expectations, and suppliers have capabilities," he says. "We have to understand how these match, and then support each other."

Purchasing Plays a Big Role

Because both quality and JIT are company-wide efforts, there is not one area that stands out as the most critical to their success. But the purchasing function provides "the first value—the raw materials to which later value is added," writes Richard J. Schonberger in *World Class Manufacturing, The Lessons of Simplicity Applied.*

At Atochem, purchasing is in charge of the supplier rating system, which covers 13 different areas including on-time deliveries, communication and various other requirements. "Purchasing's role is paramount," says Franco. "We give them as much ownership of the supplier quality process as possible."

Franco says it is purchasing's job to find the best suppliers and keep them informed of what Atochem's requirements and specifications are. Purchasing, therefore, must understand the long-term and short-term goals of the company.

Monsanto's purchasing group also conducts in-depth quality supplier surveys, and has completed about 400 over the last two years. The goal is to make individuals more familiar with suppliers and their capabilities.

"Purchasing also needs to be conversant in what we're doing so that they can be looking for suppliers who can perform to our needs," says Cummins. "They need to be there at the very first meeting. There's no doubt purchasing plays a key role in our enterprise because we need good, high-quality materials coming in."

"Quality and just-in-time both lead to a natural reduction of suppliers, whether or not it is a stated goal," says Du Pont's Kane. "One goal—and this is mainly purchasing's responsibility—is to establish partnerships, and you come to the realization pretty quickly that you can't be partners with everybody."

Working with Suppliers

"Purchasing has the background about how reliable suppliers have been," Kane says. "They're an important part in facilitating contracts and building supplier relationships."

Carbide's Childers says it has been a purchasing practice for years to measure the performance of suppliers in areas like price and on-time deliveries. "Now with an emphasis on just-in-time and quality we measure 'soft stuff,' too," he says. "We look at how they communicate, do they try to improve relationships, how accurate are their invoices.

"Through these measurements we can differentiate suppliers, and give more business to good suppliers and less to others," he says. "But we don't want the mindset of reducing suppliers; we want the mindset of working with suppliers to improve quality."

He says measuring performances pinpoints trouble spots so that they can be addressed, then solved. And suppliers are encouraged to participate because they realize more business awaits the top performers.

"We'll work with suppliers to tighten specifications," he says. "And after awhile, we become more comfortable with them and they become more comfortable with us."

Du Pont's Kuchler says with JIT there is no room for adversarial relationships between buyers and sellers. To improve operations, companies must work together throughout the supply chain by clearly communicating needs.

"What the end customer is demanding is not something that can be accomplished by someone in the middle of the supply chain," says Kuchler. "There needs to be closer relationships throughout the process, and this leads to the interesting philosophical question of sharing information."

Kuchler says Du Pont handles this sensitive issue on a case-by-case basis, but he acknowledges that the practice will become more common in the future. "It goes back to the mindset about quality," he says. "Historically, there has been a focus on cost and short-term results and today's stock market performance. Now the focus is more on the continuous improvement process, and the understanding that these results can crank out on the bottom line, too."

He says much of any company's success depends on the abilities of its suppliers, which in turn puts a great emphasis on purchasing, or at Du Pont, on the Materials and Logistics Dept. But, more importantly, every employee needs to be involved if companies want to be profitable short term as well as in business long term.

"Everybody must be going in the same direction because you've got to have competitive results in the short term if you want to play the game," Kuchler says. "But if you want to be around long term, you've got to constantly strive to improve, which in some cases can hurt short-term results. Balancing these issues is the tough part."

Leadership Needed

Kuchler says JIT is one of the mechanisms which can lead to improving quality, but before all employees move to adopt the concepts, they must see the total commitment of top management.

"Quality and just-in-time mean a fundamental change in the way the industry does business," he says. "To accomplish meaningful results, it must be leadership driven."

"You have to have a commitment to JIT, and have patience even though at first you see no benefits," agrees Du Pont's Kane. "You have to wait for the benefits to happen." There may be some immediate improvements, but more often than not, companies must wait for the majority of benefits to happen.

After only two months of JIT manufacturing, which gave Du Pont's plant operators more involvement in a specialty chemical processing step, there has been a 30% improvement in capacity of a particular specialty chemical.

Other companies have experienced shorter lead-times and improved deliveries from suppliers, lower rejection rates and financial savings from reduced inventory levels. But perhaps the greatest value of JIT is that it forces companies to look at process quality, and not product quality.

Quality and JIT Breed Results

Monsanto's Cummins agrees that to have a successful quality process with JIT, top management involvement and support are musts. And, he says, it is just as important that "total" quality be the goal instead of quality.

"They can be the same thing," he says. "But we need to be sure everyone is focusing on process improvement. In some people's minds, quality tends to relate to what are the properties and characteristics of the products we are presenting."

To avoid the "knee-jerk reaction" to just-in-time as another term for inventory reductions, Monsanto refers to its total quality process as Optimized Operations. "It is everything rolled into one," says Cummins. "Total quality, statistical process control, JIT, vendor relationships. It helps everyone focus on process improvements."

Campbell Soup also does not want the entire focus of its process on its final product. "Quality is more than 'How's the product taste?'" says Winkler. "We want to expand the quality process, which of course includes the final product. The products, in this case, would become another part of the process, and just-in-time would be another part."

The Next Step in Quality

Although the chemical process industry usually runs on demand, "the industry, quite often, makes something, then runs around and tries to sell it," says Monsanto's Cummins, "JIT, ideally, has companies operating at the rate material is needed."

This philosophical difference prevents many companies from adopting JIT concepts. But as quality becomes more and more ingrained in daily operations, JIT appears to be the next logical step. "Just in-time," says Carbide's Childers, "is a natural outgrowth of working on the quality process."

Robert Kennedy, chairman of the board and chief executive officer of Union Carbide Corp., has an informal definition of the company's quality process. "If it ain't perfect," he has said, "it can be made better." The same definition could be applied to just-in-time, a philosophy that can constantly be improved and refined.

"What we're talking about with just-in-time is a production and manufacturing system that pulls through based on customer requirements rather than push through supplies," says Winkler of Campbell Soup. "What JIT tries to do, when successfully implemented, is cut down on the cycle time and improve quality throughout the process."

Indeed, in more ways than one, JIT and quality are more alike than different. "Like perfect quality," writes Schonberger in *Japanese Manufacturing Techniques,* his first of three books on JIT, "absolute just-in-time performance is never attained, but rather is an ideal to be pursued aggressively."

Reprinted with permission from *CPI Purchasing,* September 1990.

JIT IN SERVICES

JIT in services is a natural extension of the JIT concept. The most obvious example is just-in-time deliveries: delivering supplies of parts and materials to the production floor—or the next operation—as they are needed. In effect, delivery is "available when requested." Nonmanufacturing examples of this include Domino Pizza, Federal Express, and 911.

Another example of JIT delivery is described in the following box.

READING   BOX MAKER KEEPS THE LID ON LEADTIMES

Al Johnson of Davidson Exterior Trim in Americas, Ga., thinks Georgia Box is the best in the business.

"It's our number-one supplier as far as JIT delivery is concerned; it's never early or late," says Johnson. "Moreover, its leadtime on any size box is three or four days; other box makers want at least two weeks. And in a pinch we can call in the morning and get boxes by the afternoon."

Davidson (a division of Textron) makes bumpers and fascias for GM and Chrysler—as many as 14,000 bumpers a day when auto business is going strong. That means Davidson needs a lot of boxes, in different sizes but mostly big boxes: A two-week supply could easily fill 50,000 sq. ft. of warehouse space. But thanks to JIT delivery from Georgia Box, only half that space is utilized today, even though the daily production rate is twice what it used to be. In a good year, Davidson would spend as much as $2 million on corrugated boxes.

How is Georgia Box able to offer shorter leadtimes than other box makers? Short setup times. According to Georgia Box's president, Stanley Walker, setup times can vary from 30 seconds to 15 minutes tops. The industry norm is anywhere from a half-hour to an hour.

Setups are all computerized, says Walker. "For repeat orders, all one has to do is punch in three numbers; for new orders, box dimensions need to be keyed into the computer. With a traditional manual system, you had to go in with wrenches, adjust the scoring, and set ink registrations.

"Very few sheet plants have this type of computerized equipment," adds Walker. "We can produce 50 million sq. ft. of box board per month on one shift." Even the big-time corrugators would be impressed.

Sheet plants, corrugators—that's how the box business is divided up. The latter group comprises the large integrated paper mills that make their own linerboard as well as corrugated boxes, while the much smaller sheet plants buy their board from the corrugators. Sheet plants handle low-volume orders, while the corrugators prefer big production runs.

With short setup times, Georgia Box is able to handle both types of businesses. Since putting in the computerized equipment three years ago, its sales have doubled, from $18 million to $36 million.

Reprinted with permission from *Purchasing*, September 13, 1990.

JIT service can be a major competitive advantage for companies that can achieve it. An important key to JIT service is the ability to provide service when it is needed. That requires flexibility on the part of the provider, which generally means short setup times, and it requires clear communication on the part of the requester. If a requester can determine when it will need a particular service, a JIT server can *schedule* deliveries to correspond to those needs, eliminating the need for continual requests, and reducing the need for provider flexibility (and therefore, probably reducing the cost of the JIT service).

The JIT philosophy of production offers new perspectives on manufacturing that must be given serious consideration by managers in repetitive manufacturing who wish to be competitive.

Potential adopters should carefully study the requirements and benefits of lean production systems, as well as difficulties and strengths of their current systems, before making a decision on whether or not to convert to JIT. Careful estimates of time and cost to convert are essential, as is an assessment of how likely workers, managers, and suppliers are to cooperate in such an approach.

OPERATIONS STRATEGY

The decision to convert can be sequential, giving management an opportunity to gain firsthand experience with portions of JIT without committing themselves wholesale. For instance, improving vendor relations, reducing setup times, and improving quality are all worthwhile goals on their own. Similarly, efforts to reduce waste and inefficiency are also desirable goals. Moreover, a level production schedule is a necessary element of a JIT system, and achieving that will also be useful under a traditional system of operation.

The important thing is to not dismiss the concept of lean production without serious consideration, for it could turn out to give a formidable competitive advantage, either to one's own company or one's competitors.

SUMMARY

Just-in-time (JIT) is a system of lean production used mainly in repetitive manufacturing, in which goods move through the system and tasks are completed just in time to maintain the schedule. Such systems require very little inventory because successive operations are closely coordinated.

Lean systems require that sources of potential disruption to the even flow of work be eliminated. High quality is stressed because problems with quality can disrupt the process. Quick, low–cost setups; special layouts; allowing work to be pulled through the system rather than pushed through; and a spirit of cooperation are all important features of lean systems. So, too, are problem solving aimed at reducing disruptions and making the system more efficient, and an attitude of working toward continual improvement.

Key benefits of JIT/lean systems are reduced inventory levels, high quality, flexibility, reduced lead times, increased productivity and equipment utilization, reduced amounts of scrap and rework, and reduced space requirements.

JIT differs in many ways from traditional systems used by Western companies. The benefits of JIT systems have attracted the attention of U.S. manufacturers, causing many to consider converting their operations to JIT. In doing so, careful attention must be given to obtaining the support of top management, achieving a cooperative spirit throughout the organization, reducing setup times, and establishing good relationships with a small number of vendors.

KEY TERMS

andon, 703
autonomation, 694
just-in-time (JIT), 690
kanban, 701

multifunctional workers, 698
preventive maintenance, 697
pull system, 700
push system, 700

SOLVED PROBLEM

Problem

Determine the number of containers that would be appropriate for a workstation that uses 100 parts per hour if the time for a container to complete a cycle (move, wait, empty, return, fill) is 90 minutes and a standard container holds 84 parts. An efficiency factor of 0.10 is currently in use.

Solution

$N = ?$

$D = 100$ parts per hour

$T = 90$ minutes (1.5 hours)

$C = 84$ parts

$X = 0.10$

$$N = \frac{D(T)(1 + X)}{C} = \frac{100(1.5)(1 + .10)}{84} = 1.96 \text{ (round to 2) containers}$$

DISCUSSION AND REVIEW QUESTIONS

1. List the major elements of just-in-time systems, and briefly indicate how JIT systems differ from traditional production systems on each of those elements.
2. What are the main benefits of a JIT system?
3. Describe the philosophy that underlies JIT (i.e., what is JIT intended to accomplish?).
4. What are some of the main obstacles that must be overcome in attempting to convert from a traditional system to JIT?
5. Briefly discuss vendor relations in JIT systems in terms of the following issues:
   a. Why they are important.
   b. How they tend to differ from the more adversarial relations of the past.
   c. Possible reasons that suppliers might be hestitant about JIT purchasing.
6. It has been said by some Japanese that Henry Ford's assembly line provided some of the rationale for JIT. What features of assembly lines are common to JIT systems?
7. Explain the kanban aspect of a JIT system.
8. Contrast push and pull methods of moving goods and materials through production systems.
9. What difficulties did U.S. automobile manufacturers encounter when they tried to use a kanban approach? Why did they have these difficulties?
10. Explain this statement: A key aspect of JIT systems is problem solving.
11. Explain this statement: Excessive inventories tend to inhibit system improvement.
12. Why are small lot sizes a goal of JIT systems?

PROBLEMS

1. A manager wants to determine the number of containers to use for a kanban system that will be installed next month. The process in question will have a usage rate of 80 pieces per hour. Because the process will be new, the manager has assigned an efficiency factor of .35. Containers each hold 45 pieces and take an average of 75 minutes to complete a cycle. How many containers should be used? Also, as the system improves, will more containers or fewer be required?

2. A JIT system uses kanban cards to authorize production and movement of materials. In one portion of the system, a work center uses an average of 100 pieces per hour while running. The manager has assigned an efficiency factor of .20 to the center. Standard containers are designed to hold six dozen parts each. The cycle time for parts containers is about 105 minutes. How many containers are needed?

3. A machine cell uses 200 pounds of a certain material each day. Material is transported in vats that hold 120 pounds each. Cycle time for the vats is about two hours. The manager has assigned an efficiency factor of .08 to the cell. The plant operates on an eight-hour day. Determine the number of vats to use.

SELECTED BIBLIOGRAPHY

Alster, Norm. "What Flexible Workers Can Do." *Fortune* (February 13, 1989), pp. 62–66.

Blackburn, Joseph D. *Time-Based Competition.* Homewood, Ill.: Business One Irwin, 1991.

Burton, Terence T. "JIT/Repetitive Sourcing Strategies: 'Tying the Knot' with Your Suppliers." *Production and Inventory Management* (Fourth quarter 1988), pp. 38–41.

Connell, Gale W. "Quality at the Source: The First Step in Just-in-Time Production," *Quality Progress* (November 1984), pp. 44–45.

Crosby, Leon B. "The Just-in-Time Manufacturing Process: Control of Quality and Quantity." *Production and Inventory Management* (Fourth quarter 1984), pp. 21–33.

Goddard, Walter E. "Kanban versus MRP II—Which Is Best for You?" *Modern Materials Handling* (November 5, 1982), pp. 40–48.

Hall, Robert W. *Attaining Manufacturing Excellence.* Homewood, Ill.: Richard D. Irwin, 1987.

Hannah, Kimball H. "Just-in-Time: Meeting the Competitive Challenge." *Production and Inventory Management* (Third quarter 1987), pp. 1–3.

Monden, Yasuhiro. "What Makes the Toyota Production System Really Tick?" *Industrial Engineering* 13, no. 1 (January 1981), pp. 38–46.

Nakane, J., and Robert W. Hall. "Management Specs for Stockless Production." *Harvard Business Review* (May–June 1983), pp. 84–91.

Schonberger, Richard J. *Japanese Manufacturing Techniques: Nine Hidden Lessons in Simplicity.* New York: Free Press, 1982.

———. *World Class Manufacturing.* New York: Free Press, 1986.

Stalk, George, Jr. "Time—The Next Source of Competitive Advantage." *Harvard Business Review* (July–August 1988), pp. 41–51.

Weiss, Andrew. "Simple Truths of Japanese Manufacturing." *Harvard Business Review* (July–August 1984), pp. 119–25.

Womack, James P.; Daniel T. Jones; and Daniel Roos. *The Machine That Changed the World.* New York: Harper Perennial, 1990.

14

Materials Management and Purchasing

After completing this supplement, you should be able to:

1. Define *materials* and briefly describe the materials management function.
2. Describe how purchasing interfaces with other areas of the organization and with suppliers.
3. Outline the objectives of purchasing.
4. Describe the purchasing cycle, especially determination of price and sources of supply.
5. Discuss the issue of centralized purchasing versus decentralized purchasing.
6. Describe and discuss value analysis.
7. Discuss the importance of good vendor relations, and compare suppliers as partners versus suppliers as adversaries.
8. Discuss the logistics aspects of materials management.

Materials
All physical items used during a production process.

Materials management
The purchasing, storage, and movement of materials during production, and the distribution of finished goods.

F or our purposes, **materials** are the physical items used during the production process. They include not only the parts and raw materials that become the finished goods, but also the physical items needed to support the production process, such as fuels, lubricants, tools, machinery, forms, and anything else that is purchased, moved, stored, or shipped. **Materials management** is concerned with purchasing, storage, and movement of materials during production and with distribution of finished goods. Figure 14S–1 provides an overview of the range of materials management.

The subject matter in this supplement is organized into two major topics: purchasing and logistics.

PURCHASING

The purchasing function is responsible for obtaining material inputs for the operating system. This section describes the purchasing function as it operates in most organizations. It begins by discussing how purchasing interacts with other functional areas of the organization and with outside suppliers. We will examine the determination of sources of supply and price, along with the concept of value analysis.

PURCHASING INTERFACES

As a service function, purchasing has interfaces with a number of other functional areas, as well as with outside suppliers. Purchasing is the connecting link between the organization and its suppliers. In this capacity, it exchanges information with suppliers and functional areas. The interactions between purchasing and these other areas are briefly summarized in the following paragraphs.

Operating units constitute the main source of requests for purchased materials, and close cooperation between these units and the purchasing people is mandatory if quality, quantity, and delivery goals are to be met. Cancellations, changes in specifications, or changes in quantity or delivery times must be communicated immediately in order for purchasing to be effective.

The purchasing department may require the assistance of the *legal* department in contract negotiations as well as in drawing up bid specifications for nonroutine purchases. In addition, the legal department may be called on to help interpret legislation on pricing, product liability, and contracts with suppliers.

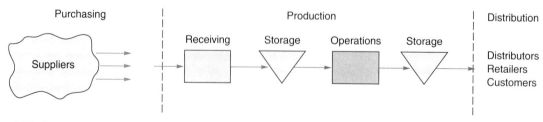

Figure 14S–1

Overview of materials management

Accounting is responsible for handling payments to suppliers and must be notified promptly when goods are received in order to take advantage of possible discounts. In many firms, *data processing* is handled by the accounting department, which involves keeping inventory records, checking invoices, and monitoring vendor performance.

Design and *engineering* usually prepare material specifications, which must be communicated to purchasing. Because of its contacts with suppliers, purchasing is often in a position to pass information about new products and materials improvements on to design personnel. Also, design and purchasing people may work closely to determine if changes in specifications, design, or materials can reduce the cost of purchased items (see the following section on value analysis).

Receiving checks incoming shipments of purchased items to determine if quality, quantity, and timing objectives have been met, and moves the goods to temporary storage. Purchasing must be notified when shipments are late; accounting must be notified when shipments are received so that payments can be made; and both purchasing and accounting must be apprised of current information on continuing vendor evaluation.

Suppliers or vendors work closely with purchasing to learn what materials will be purchased and what kinds of specifications will be required in terms of quality, quantity, and deliveries. Purchasing must rate vendors on cost, reliability, and so on (see the following section on vendor analysis). Good supplier relations can pay dividends on rush orders and changes, and vendors provide a good source of information on product and material improvements.

Figure 14S–2 summarizes the purchasing interfaces.

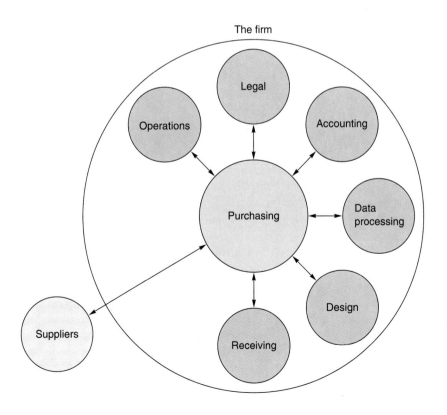

The firm

Figure 14S–2

Purchasing interfaces with functional areas of the firm and with suppliers

PURCHASING OBJECTIVES

The basic objectives of purchasing can be summarized as follows:

1. To determine the quality and quantity needed and when an item is needed.
2. To obtain a reasonable price.
3. To maintain good relations with suppliers.
4. To maintain sources of supply.
5. To be knowledgeable on prices, new products, and new services that become available.

THE PURCHASING CYCLE

Purchasing cycle

Series of steps that begin with a request for purchase, and end with notification of shipment received in satisfactory condition.

The **purchasing cycle** begins with a request from within the organization to purchase material, equipment, supplies, or other items from outside the organization, and the cycle ends when the purchasing department is notified that a shipment has been received in satisfactory condition. The main steps in the cycle are:

1. *The requisition is received by purchasing.*   The requisition includes (*a*) a description of the item or material desired, (*b*) the quantity and quality necessary, (*c*) desired delivery dates, and (*d*) who is requesting the purchase.
2. *A supplier is selected.*   The purchasing department must identify suppliers who have the capability of supplying the desired goods. If no suppliers are currently listed in the files, new ones must be sought. If one or more suppliers are available, vendor ratings may be referred to in choosing among vendors, or perhaps rating information can be relayed to the vendor with the thought of upgrading future performance.
3. *The order is placed with a vendor.*   If the order involves a large expenditure, particularly for a one-time purchase, say, of equipment, vendors will usually be asked to bid on the job, and operating and design personnel may be asked to assist in negotiations with a vendor. Large-volume, continuous-usage items may be covered by blanket purchase orders, which often involve annual negotiation of prices with deliveries subject to request throughout the year. Moderate-volume items may also have blanket purchase orders, or they may be handled on an individual basis. Small purchases may be handled directly between the operating unit requesting the item and the supplier, although care must be taken so that some control is exercised over those purchases—otherwise, they tend to get out of hand.
4. *Monitoring orders.*   Routine follow-up on orders, particularly large orders or those with lengthy delivery schedules, allows the purchasing department to foresee delays and relay this information to the appropriate operating units. Likewise, changes in quantity and delivery needs of the operating units must be relayed to suppliers so they have time to adjust their plans.
5. *Receiving orders.*   Incoming shipments from vendors must be checked for quality and quantity. Purchasing must be notified, as must accounting and the operating unit that requested the goods. If the goods are not received in satisfactory condition, they may have to be returned to the supplier for credit or replacement, or subjected to detailed inspection. Again, purchasing, accounting, and the operating unit must be notified. In either case, vendor evaluation records must be updated.

1. Select an item that has a high annual dollar-volume. This can be a purchased part or material or a service.
2. Identify the function of the item.
3. Obtain answers to questions such as these:
   a. Is the item necessary; does it add value, or can it be eliminated?
   b. Are there alternative sources for the item?
   c. Can it be provided internally?
   d. What are the advantages of the present arrangement?
   e. What are the disadvantages of the present arrangement?
   f. Could another part, material, or service be used instead?
   g. Can specifications be made less stringent to save cost or time?
   h. Can two or more items be combined?
   i. Can more (less) processing be done on the item to save on cost?
   j. Do suppliers/providers have suggestions for improvements?
   k. Do employees have suggestions for improvements?
   l. Can packaging be improved or made less costly?
4. Analyze the answers obtained plus answers to other questions that arise, and make recommendations.

Table 14S–1

Value analysis overview

VALUE ANALYSIS

Value analysis refers to an examination of the *function* of purchased parts and materials in an effort to reduce the cost and/or improve the performance of those items. Typical questions that would be asked as part of the analysis include: Could a cheaper part or material be used? Is the function necessary? Can the function of two or more parts or components be performed by a single part for a lower cost? Can a part be simplified? Could product specifications be relaxed, and would this result in a lower price? Could standard parts be substituted for nonstandard parts? Table 14S–1 provides a checklist of questions that can be used to guide a value analysis.

Value analysis
Examination of the function of purchased parts and materials in an effort to reduce cost and/or improve performance.

Naturally, such an investigation cannot be performed each time materials are ordered. However, value analysis should be conducted periodically on large dollar-volume items because of the potential savings.

Although purchasing does not ordinarily have the authority to implement changes on the basis of a value analysis, it can make suggestions to operating units, to designers, and to suppliers, which may lead to improved performance of purchased goods and/or reduction of the cost of those goods. Purchasing can offer a different perspective to the analysis, and purchasing people, because of their association with suppliers, possess information not known to others within the organization. If a fair amount of technical knowledge is required to review a part or product, a team can be formed with representatives from design and/or operations to work with purchasing in conducting the analysis.

MAKE OR BUY

There are times when an organization must consider whether to make or buy a certain item. This issue can arise in a number of ways, such as in response to unreliable suppliers, idle capacity of an organization, the desire to achieve greater control over the production process, and increasing costs.

Generally, the factors that are taken into account in deciding whether to make or buy are the following:

1. Cost to make versus cost to buy, including startup costs.
2. Stability of demand and possible seasonality.
3. Quality available from suppliers compared to a firm's own quality capabilities.
4. The desire to maintain close control over operations.
5. Idle capacity available within the organization.
6. Lead times for making versus buying.
7. Who has patents, expertise, and so on, if these are factors.
8. Stability of technology; if a technology is changing, it may be better to use a supplier.
9. The degree to which the necessary operations are consistent with, or in conflict with, current operations.

EVALUATING SOURCES OF SUPPLY (VENDOR ANALYSIS)

In many respects, choosing a vendor involves taking into account many of the same factors associated with making a major purchase (e.g., a car or a stereo system). A company considers price, quality, the supplier's reputation, past experience with the supplier, and service after the sale; this process is called **vendor analysis.** The main difference is that a company, because of the quantities it orders and because of production requirements, often provides suppliers with detailed specifications of the materials or parts it wants instead of buying items off the shelf, although even large companies buy standard items that way.

Vendor analysis
Evaluating the sources of supply in terms of price, quality, reputation, and service.

The main factors to look at when a company selects a vendor are:

1. *Price.* This is the most obvious factor, along with any discounts offered, although it may not be the most important factor.
2. *Quality.* A company may be willing to spend more money to obtain desired-quality parts.
3. *Services.* Special services can sometimes be very important in choosing a supplier. Replacement of defective items, instruction in the use of equipment, repair of equipment, and similar services can be instrumental in selecting one supplier over another.
4. *Location.* Location of a supplier can have impact on shipping time, transportation costs, and response time for rush orders or emergency service. Local buying can create goodwill in the community by helping the local economy.
5. *Inventory policy of supplier.* If a supplier maintains an inventory policy of keeping spare parts on hand, this could be helpful in case of an emergency breakdown of equipment.
6. *Flexibility.* The willingness and ability of a supplier to respond to changes in demand, as well as a willingness to accept design changes, could be important considerations.

DETERMINING PRICES

There are essentially three ways that prices are determined: published price lists, competitive bidding, and negotiation.

In many instances, organizations buy products and services that have fixed or *predetermined prices*. This is generally the case for standard items that are bought infrequently and/or in small quantities.

For large orders of standard products and services, *competitive bidding* is often used. This involves sending requests for bids to potential suppliers, which ask vendors to quote a price for a specified quantity and quality of items or for a specified service to be performed. Government purchases of standard goods or services are usually made using competitive bidding.

Negotiated purchasing is used for special purchasing situations, such as cases where specifications are vague, when one or a few customized products or services are involved (e.g., space exploration), and when few potential sources exist. There are several myths concerning negotiated purchasing that should be recognized:

1. Negotiation is a win-lose confrontation.
2. The main goal is to obtain the lowest possible price.
3. Each negotiation is an isolated transaction.[1]

Realistically speaking, no one likes to be taken advantage of. Furthermore, contractors and suppliers need a reasonable profit to survive. Therefore, a take-it-or-leave-it approach or one that capitalizes extensively on the weaknesses of the other party will serve no useful purpose and may have detrimental effects that surface at a later time. The most reasonable approach is one of give and take, with each side giving and receiving some concessions.

CENTRALIZED VERSUS DECENTRALIZED PURCHASING

Centralized purchasing means that purchasing is handled by one special department. **Decentralized purchasing** means that individual departments or separate locations handle their own purchasing requirements.

Centralized purchasing may be able to obtain lower prices than decentralized units if the higher volume created by combining orders enables it to take advantage of quantity discounts offered on large orders. Centralized purchasing may also be able to obtain better service and closer attention from suppliers. In addition, centralized purchasing often enables companies to assign certain categories of items to specialists, who tend to be more efficient because they are able to concentrate their efforts on relatively few items instead of spreading themselves across many items.

Decentralized purchasing has the advantage of awareness of differing "local" needs and being better able to respond to those needs. Decentralized purchasing usually can offer quicker response than centralized purchasing. In the case of widely scattered locations, decentralized purchasing may be able to save on transportation costs by buying locally, which has the added attraction of creating goodwill in the community.

Some organizations manage to take advantage of both centralization and decentralization by permitting individual units to handle certain items while centralizing purchases of other items. For example, small orders and rush orders may be handled locally, or by departments, while centralized purchases would be used for high-

Centralized purchasing
Purchasing is handled by one special department.

Decentralized purchasing
Individual departments or separate locations handle their own purchasing requirements.

[1] Richard J. Tersine, *Production/Operations Management: Concepts, Structure, and Analysis,* 2nd ed. (New York: Elsevier North-Holland Publishing, 1985), p. 598.

volume, high-value items for which discounts would be applicable or for which specialists could provide better service than local buyers or departments could.

SUPPLIER RELATIONS

American firms are becoming increasingly aware of the importance of building good relations with their suppliers. In the past, too many firms regarded their suppliers as adversaries and dealt with them on that basis. One lesson many have learned from the Japanese is that there are numerous benefits from having good supplier relations. Among them are supplier flexibility in terms of accepting changes in delivery schedules, quality, and quantities. Moreover, suppliers can often help identify problems and offer suggestions for solving them. Thus, simply choosing and switching suppliers on the basis of price is a very shortsighted approach for handling an ongoing need.

Many Japanese firms rely on one or a few suppliers to handle their needs. In contrast, many U.S. firms deal with numerous suppliers. Perhaps they want to remain flexible, and possibly there are some advantages in playing one off against the others. However, it would appear that in many instances, firms have too many suppliers to deal with, although reducing that number to one or a few, as the Japanese have done, may be too extreme. A realistic approach would be to move in the direction of reducing the number of suppliers used.

Keeping good relations with suppliers is increasingly recognized as an important factor in maintaining a competitive edge. Many companies are adopting a view of suppliers as partners rather than adversaries. This viewpoint stresses a stable relationship with relatively few reliable suppliers who can provide high-quality supplies, maintain precise delivery schedules, and remain flexible relative to changes in productive specifications as well as delivery schedules. A comparison of the two contrasting views of suppliers is provided in Table 14S–2.

Table 14S–2	Aspect	Partner	Adversary
The supplier as partner versus adversary	Number of suppliers	One or a few	Many; play one off against the others
	Length of relationship	Long-term	May be brief
	Low price	Moderately important	Major consideration
	Reliability	High	May not be high
	Openness	High	Low
	Quality	Insured at the source; vendor-certified	Buyer inspects; may be unreliable
	Volume of business	High	May be low due to many suppliers
	Location	Proximity may be stressed for short lead times and service	Widely dispersed
	Flexibility	Relatively high	Relatively low

LOGISTICS

Logistics refers to the movement of materials within a production facility and to incoming and outgoing shipments of goods and materials.

Logistics
Movement of materials and supplies.

MOVEMENT WITHIN A FACILITY

Figure 14S–3 provides an overview of the many instances where materials must be moved within a production facility, beginning with removing materials from incoming vehicles and placing them in a receiving area. The numerous instances of materials movement include:

1. From incoming vehicles to receiving.
2. From receiving to storage.
3. From storage to the point of use (e.g., work center, office, maintenance).
4. From one work center to the next, or to temporary storage.
5. From the last operation to final storage.
6. From storage to packaging/shipping.
7. From shipping to outgoing vehicles.

Figure 14S–3

Overview of materials movement

Note that in some instances, the goods being moved are supplies; in other instances, the goods are actual products or partially completed products; and in still other instances, the goods are raw materials or purchased parts.

Movement of materials must be coordinated to arrive at the appropriate destinations at appropriate times. Care must be taken so that items are not lost, stolen, or damaged during movement.

Incoming and Outgoing Shipments

Traffic management

Overseeing the shipment of incoming and outgoing goods.

Overseeing the shipment of incoming and outgoing goods comes under the heading of **traffic management**. This function handles schedules and decisions on shipping methods and times, taking into account costs of various alternatives, government regulations, the needs of the organization relative to quantities and timing, and such external factors as potential shipping delays or disruptions (e.g., highway construction, truckers' strikes).

Computer tracking of shipments often helps to maintain knowledge of the current status of shipments as well as provide other up-to-date information on costs and schedules.

Bar Coding

Bar codes

Patterns of black lines and white spaces that can be read by scanning devices, containing a variety of information.

Bar codes are the patterns of alternating wide and narrow black lines and white spaces, and numbers and symbols, that you see on everyday products at supermarkets and other retail stores. The bar codes (or universal product codes, as mentioned in Chapter 12) are read by scanning devices that use the information for a variety of purposes, such as recording prices and quantities, printing sales receipts, and updating inventory records.

Bar codes are also used in manufacturing and distribution. In distribution, they enable companies to keep track of items in warehouses and en route to customers; managers can instantaneously determine the location of any item in the system and its status (e.g., en route to customer, delivered to customer, etc.). In manufacturing, bar codes are used to track the progress of jobs as they move through the production process. In addition, by scanning bar codes of jobs just before each operation, specific processing instructions for the job at each operation can be provided to operators. They are also used to update inventory records, monitor quality losses, and monitor productivity. Similarly, employee attendance and location can also be tracked with employee bar codes. And bar codes can be used for automatic sorting and packing of items as they move down a conveyor line.

The scanners that are used for reading bar codes can be hand held or fixed position (supermarkets used fixed-position scanners at checkouts). The scanners use light beams to read the bar codes. These can range from low-level probes (infrared or light-emitting diodes) to laser beams. The low-level scanners must actually touch the bar code to read it; higher level intensity beams just have to be close to the bar code, they do not need to touch it. Laser scanners use either a fixed beam or a moving beam. The fixed-beam scanner requires that the bar code be moved across the scanning field, either by moving the scanner, or moving the object to be scanned. The moving-beam scanner can read bar codes while both the object and the scanner are stationary.

Bar codes provide companies with a tremendous ability to monitor and control items in manufacturing and distribution by providing accurate, up-to-date information on quantity, quality, location, and other data. This enables managers to realize significant improvements in productivity and effectiveness, and to provide outstanding levels of customer service.

DISTRIBUTION

Distribution is the shipping of goods from the company through a distribution system to warehouses, retail customers, or final customers. Often, distribution is managed by the *marketing* function rather than the production function.

Distribution
The shipping of goods from a company to warehouses, retail customers, or final customers.

SUMMARY

Materials management is the management of materials over the entire range of the production process, beginning with purchasing and ending with distribution. It covers movement of materials within the organization as well as storage.

Purchasing is responsible for obtaining material inputs for the organization. This includes the actual purchasing of materials as well as supplier selection and conducting value analyses on purchased items. The basic design question in purchasing is whether to centralize or decentralize it. Centralization provides for closer control and may produce certain economies, whereas decentralized purchasing tends to produce quick response and may better serve local needs. Value analysis may be performed periodically to assure that purchased item cost-benefit is being optimized. Vendors are evaluated for cost, service after the sale, reliability, and quality.

Logistics involves movement of materials within the organization, incoming and outgoing shipments, and distribution.

KEY TERMS

bar codes, 726
centralized purchasing, 723
decentralized purchasing, 723
distribution, 727
logistics, 725
materials, 718

materials management, 718
purchasing cycle, 720
traffic management, 726
value analysis, 721
vendor analysis, 722

DISCUSSION AND REVIEW QUESTIONS

1. Briefly describe the materials management function.
2. Briefly describe how purchasing interacts with other functional areas of the firm such as accounting and design.
3. Describe value analysis. Why is purchasing a good location for this task?
4. Should the supplier with the highest quality–lowest price combination always be selected over others? Explain.
5. Discuss the issue of centralization versus decentralization as it applies to the purchasing function.
6. Discuss the determination of prices.
7. Discuss the importance of good supplier relations. Compare the supplier-as-partner versus supplier-as-adversary viewpoints.
8. Describe the logistics aspects of materials management.

SELECTED BIBLIOGRAPHY

Ammer, Dean S. *Material Management and Purchasing*. Homewood, Ill.: Richard D. Irwin, 1980.

Hall, Robert. *Zero Inventories*. Homewood, Ill.: Dow Jones-Irwin, 1983.

Heinritz, Stuart F.; Paul V. Farrell; and Clifton Smith. *Purchasing: Principles and Applications*. Englewood Cliffs, N.J.: Prentice Hall, 1986.

Kraljic, Peter. "Purchasing Must Become Supply Management." *Harvard Business Review*, September–October 1983, p. 109.

Leenders, M. R., et al. *Purchasing and Material Management*. 8th ed. Homewood, Ill.: Richard D. Irwin, 1985.

Riggs, James L. *Production Systems: Planning, Analysis and Control*. 3rd ed. Santa Barbara, Calif.: Wiley/Hamilton, 1981.

Tersine, Richard J. *Materials Management and Inventory Systems*. 3rd ed. New York: Elsevier North-Holland Publishing, 1987.

READING Shaping Up Your Suppliers *Joel Dreyfuss*

Small manufacturing companies are in crisis. Their main customers, the big boys of U.S. industry, have been humbled by global competition and are seeking their salvation in higher standards of quality and productivity. The big companies can't find redemption alone. So, like passionate converts, they are spreading the gospel of efficiency to their suppliers. Suddenly, small companies whose greatest concern was once to simply get the product out the door are under pressure to adopt the latest technologies, use quality control methods, *and* slash prices.

The suppliers often do not understand the new processes and management techniques their customers want them to embrace. Says L. Joseph Thomas, professor of manufacturing at Cornell's Johnson School of Management: "Small companies are less likely than large companies to have made improvements for productivity. They're concerned about meeting the payroll and not about the longer term." Besides, if the suppliers do manage to come up to their customers' idea of quality, they expect to be paid more, not less. They're not the world's best experts in management.

Suppliers had better learn fast. Most large U.S. manufacturers are reducing their number of vendors in order to control quality. Says Charles E. Lucier, a Booz Allen & Hamilton vice president: "Most want two or three suppliers instead of ten or 12." They will give preference to those close to home. Russell W. Meyer, the chairman of Cessna Aircraft, the small-plane manufacturer headquartered in Wichita, says: "We spend a lot of time with subcontractors. It's a lot easier to work with someone in Wichita than with someone in Los Angeles."

To make the cut, suppliers will have to go through a rigorous survival drill. Buyers routinely send inspection teams to rate a small company's plants. They want to see Japanese-style just-in-time manufacturing and delivery techniques, statistical process controls that identify causes of defects, and the ability to handle data electronically.

Some small companies resist, either from ignorance or from fear. Says Joseph A. Bockerstette, a manufacturing specialist at consultant Coopers & Lybrand: "Many suppliers feel just-in-time is a way for FORTUNE 500 companies to dump on them." When a large company begins asking for three deliveries a day, a small supplier may end up stockpiling the goods the customer wants. Craig Skevington, president of Factory Automation & Computer Technologies, a consulting firm near Albany, New York, that specializes in manufacturing, says, "Just-in-time becomes just-in-case."

The stringent requirements could bring a wave of restructuring among little manufacturers as wrenching as the one the large companies went through. Because the small fry are great sources of innovation and new jobs, Skevington and others worry that a weakened small manufacturing sector could chill entrepreneurship and hurt the ability of the U.S. to generate new products.

Joe Keeler's message is simple. "Get costs out of the system," says Keeler, manager of Materials Purchasing for Union Carbide Chemicals and Plastics Co., Inc. (UCC&P). "That's what American industry needs to do if we are to remain competitive worldwide."

Costs, says Keeler, can be anything from inventories to double handling of materials to invoices. And one way these costs can be eliminated—something UCC&P has done to the tune of millions of dollars in savings—is through "vendor stocking," a program that incorporates just-in-time manufacturing concepts.

JIT requires that UCC&P have confidence in suppliers. "Confidence comes after years of building relationships," Keeler says. "Confidence is established with people, not just the companies, and it reaches a point where you believe that suppliers will work in your best interest."

UCC&P reached this point with several of its maintenance, repair and operating (MRO) equipment suppliers in the late 1960s when its vendor stocking program began. Although not called just-in-time at Union Carbide, vendor stocking achieves many of the same benefits.

"We are interested in optimizing our business operations by eliminating waste," says Keeler. "Working with suppliers in areas like inventory reductions is the first step toward that goal."

Many plant managers look at inventories as safety nets. When a piece of equipment breaks down, they like to know that there is an immediate and ample supply next door. It's a mindset that has developed over the years, and one that must be broken for successful just-in-time purchasing.

"It takes some selling of the concept to the [internal] user," says Brian Moughty, materials manager at UCC&P's Texas City, Texas, plant. "But without their support, it will never work."

Inventory Reductions

Union Carbide began its vendor stocking program by concentrating on the less critical items, like steel pipe, and then moving slowly from there into other areas. "It took one success, and that gave us the liberty to go to the other areas," says Keeler. "And the first thing that happens is that it enables investments to be made into the facilities."

At the Texas City plant, orders for pipe, valves and fittings are supplied within two hours from Wallace Co., a local supplier. The initial goal was not just to go to "a stockless supply," says Moughty. "The goal was to improve service."

The plant reduced the number of materials it carries in inventory by 180 items, representing an average on-hand value of about $140,000. Carrying costs—interest expenses on money invested in inventory, property taxes, and fees to operate and maintain a warehouse—have been reduced by $42,000/yr. (Union Carbide calculates carrying costs as 30% of the value of the inventory on hand.)

Increased Deliveries

For operations to succeed without inventories on site, suppliers must be willing to increase the number of deliveries they make. In the mid-1970s, UCC&P's South Charleston, W.Va., facility decided to eliminate its bearings inventory.

The supplier, Bearing Distributor, bought back South Charleston's bearings inventory—about $250,000 worth—and increased deliveries from an average of two per week to three to five per day.

"It's important to note that we did not see any increase in price due to the increased service," says Marshall Sprigg, group leader, Consolidated Purchasing. "Just as importantly, we have been working with this supplier for some time, and we have established an excellent relationship with them."

Smith Fastener, a local supplier to South Charleston for the past 12 years, makes two scheduled deliveries a day, up from two per week. The plant's inventory of fasteners has been reduced from about $200,000 in 1978 to less than $10,000 today.

Benefits to Supplier

Suppliers usually don't absorb inventories and adjust schedules around customers just because they are nice people; they do it because there is some payback. Benefits usually include more business, the most attractive carrot for suppliers. Wallace, the pipe, valve and fittings supplier to the Texas City plant, recently was awarded a contract by Union Carbide for a new line of valves, previously on contract with another supplier.

Also, with many chemical plants located relatively close to each other, MRO suppliers often need large inventories of the most common items. The cost of carrying a unique pipe or adding extra items is outweighed by new business opportunities.

READING   *(continued)*

Tangible benefits of JIT at Union Carbide:

Product: Fasteners
Inventory reduction: $400,000
Cost savings: $120,000/yr in carrying costs

Product: Bearings
Inventory reduction: $250,000
Cost savings: $75,000/yr in carrying costs

Product: Piping
Inventory reduction: $182,000
Cost savings: $55,000/yr in carrying costs, plus $45,000/yr in productivity

Product: Pipe, valves, fittings
Inventory reduction: $140,000
Cost savings: $42,000/yr in carrying costs

Product: V-belts, hoses
Inventory reduction: $50,000
Cost savings: $15,000/yr in carrying costs

Product: Gas cylinders
Inventory reduction: $10,000
Cost savings: $3,000/yr in carrying costs

(Inventory reductions are in 1990 dollars.)
Source: Union Carbide Chemicals and Plastics Co., Inc.

"To satisfy our demand, therefore, suppliers do not have to increase inventory levels drastically," says Sprigg. "They can usually just increase the rate at which they turn over their existing inventories."

A less tangible benefit is that JIT buying forces suppliers to improve their internal processes, which in turn benefits all customers, not just Union Carbide. "Suppliers must provide a high level of service on a consistent basis," says Sprigg. "They can't achieve this consistency by special handling Union Carbide's orders."

Supplier Selection Criteria

Of course, suppliers must be willing to enter into partnerships with customers, and accept the increased responsibilities that come with that. If a supplier talks about partnerships, but is unwilling to provide certain services, then it's time to rethink the relationship.

"If you start with a lousy supplier, then just-in-time is not going to work," says Sprigg. "You need good suppliers—suppliers who know your business." Proximity of the supplier to the plant also is key, because the closer its location the quicker the service. But distance alone does not determine a good supplier.

For UCC&P, good suppliers are defined by performance in areas like on-time deliveries, accurate invoices and responses to new ideas, all of which are tracked over a period of time. The goal is not to hop from one supplier to the next, but to work with one supplier who wants a stake in the success of UCC&P's business.

"It's a matter of belief today, from top management all the way through the system, that changing suppliers costs us money," says Keeler. "We want suppliers who know our requirements and suppliers who strive to meet them.

"They are the ones who can save us money," he says. "They are also the suppliers who will be more innovative and who come up with ideas to lower costs for both of us."

A case in point is Industrial Rubber Products Co., a supplier of v-belts, rubber utility hoses and chemical transfer hoses to the South Charleston plant. In the late 1970s, the plant eliminated these items from its inventory, and relied solely on Industrial Rubber. Savings: $50,000 in inventory and $15,000/yr in carrying costs.

"They also began providing additional services—things they volunteered to do," says Sprigg.

Each week, Industrial Rubber sends a truck throughout the plant to pick up damaged hoses. Once back at the shop, repairmen determine if the repair cost will be less than 40% of the cost of a new hose. If so, they repair, test, tag and deliver the hose back to where they picked it up. Industrial Rubber issues a repair report, and maintains a log book.

"They were doing some of the same record-keeping Carbide was doing," says Sprigg. "So they came to use and said, 'Why do it twice?' By eliminating the duplicate effort, our employees are free to work on other things."

Improved Services

It's difficult to place a dollar figure on some improvements created by JIT, but the very nature of it forces frequent communication and accurate forecasting by

READING   *(concluded)*

both suppliers and users. Says Sprigg, "JIT forced a closer relationship, which made these services possible." And, one of the less tangible benefits is improved safety.

Iweco, a gas cylinder supplier to the Texas City plant, began supplying the plant on an as-needed basis a few years back. UCC&P's average inventory was reduced about $10,000 and carrying costs about $3,000/yr. Iweco committed to a next-day delivery, when orders are placed by noon the day before.

Gas cylinders are not always a critical item, so the next-day delivery satisfied UCC&P's needs. More importantly, users had to forecast their needs better so they would not be caught waiting for supplies.

The best part of the deal, however, appears to be a minor issue on the surface. Iweco said it would deliver to the user and offload the heavy cylinders.

"We had been taking [the cylinders] off their truck, then putting them on our truck and driving to the [internal] user," says Moughty. "It doesn't sound like a big deal, but eliminating double handling increased our safety factor. We also designed racks near offloading sites to facilitate deliveries."

JIT Opportunities

UCC&P has expanded their vendor stocking program into areas outside of MRO, including lumber and safety supplies. Also, materials with short shelf lives like catalysts and similar chemicals, as well as batteries, have been eliminated from inventories.

Keeler says raw materials offer some possibilities for JIT purchasing. "We have so much invested in raw materials I would think we should try," he says. "But most of our raw materials suppliers are further away, which would be one problem. There are some opportunities, though."

Reduction of raw materials inventory, particularly those materials which are potentially hazardous, provides safety benefits and cost savings. Disposal costs associated with items that exceed their shelf life can exceed the original purchase price.

"By removing hazardous materials from inventory, we reduce the potential for safety or environ-

---

Intangible benefits of JIT at Union Carbide:

· Improved supplier relationships
· Improved communications
· Improved service to user
· Improved on-time deliveries
· Improved safety
· Reduced disposal costs
· Eliminated double handling

---

mental incident," says Sprigg. "There's a tangible benefit in terms of reduced carrying costs, but how can you put a dollar value on possible chemical exposure to people?"

Indeed, much of UCC&P's success with vendor stocking depends on the willingness of its people to cooperate and trust suppliers, and vice versa. "It certainly is a two-way street," says Keeler.

McJunkin Corp., a supplier of piping materials to the South Charleston facility, operates "free stores" locations within the plant, stocking inventories and handling the paperwork. Inventory has been reduced $182,000, and cost savings include $55,000/yr in carrying costs and $45,000/yr in the productivity of Union Carbide personnel.

"Instead of issuing material from a central storeroom, material is kept in the areas where it is used," says Sprigg. "Free stores works on an honor system, and we need cooperation from everyone."

Cooperation comes from allowing the employees to see for themselves the positive effects that programs like vendor stocking can have on production. "Once they see that it works, they're all for it," says Moughty. "But you have to remember it can't be done without the support of the people."

Source: *CPI Purchasing, September 1990.* Reprinted by permission.

SCHEDULING

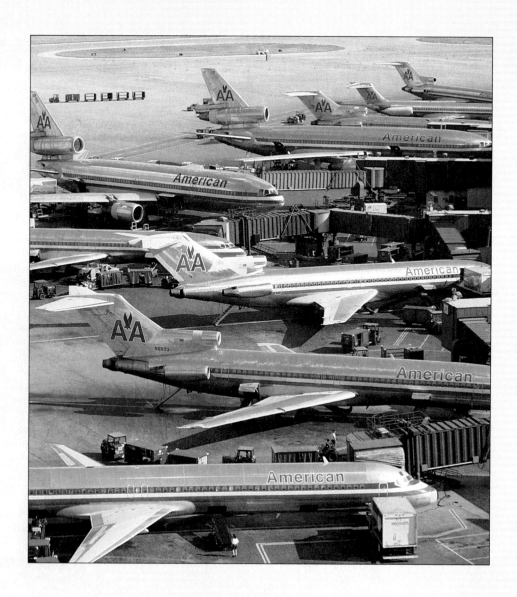

15

After completing this chapter, you should be able to:

1. Explain what scheduling involves and the importance of good scheduling.

2. Discuss scheduling needs in high-volume systems.

3. Discuss scheduling needs in job shops.

4. Use and interpret Gantt charts, and use the assignment method for loading.

5. Discuss and give examples of commonly used priority rules.

6. Describe some of the unique problems encountered in service systems, and describe some of the approaches used for scheduling service systems.

Scheduling

Establishing the timing of the use of equipment, facilities, and human activities in an organization.

Within an organization, **scheduling** pertains to establishing the timing of the use of specific resources of that organization. It relates to the use of equipment, facilities, and human activities. Scheduling occurs in every organization, regardless of the nature of its activities. For example, manufacturers must schedule production, which means developing schedules for workers, equipment, purchases, maintenance, and so on. Hospitals must schedule admissions, surgery, nursing assignments, and support services such as meal preparation, security, maintenance, and cleaning. Educational institutions must schedule classrooms, instruction, and students. And lawyers, doctors, dentists, hairdressers, and auto repair shops must schedule appointments.

In the decision-making hierarchy, scheduling decisions are the final step in the transformation process before actual output occurs. Many decisions about system design and operation have to be made long before scheduling decisions, such as capacity of the system, equipment selection, selection and training of workers, design of products and services, and so on. Consequently, scheduling decisions must be made within the constraints established by many other decisions, making them fairly narrow in scope and latitude.

Generally speaking, the objectives of scheduling are to achieve trade-offs among conflicting goals, which include efficient utilization of staff, equipment, and facilities, and minimization of customer waiting time, inventories, and process times.

Scheduling tasks are largely a function of the volume of system output. High-volume systems require approaches substantially different from those required by job shops, and project scheduling requires still different approaches. In this chapter, we will consider scheduling for high-volume systems, intermediate-volume systems, and low-volume (job shop) scheduling. We will leave until the next chapter the subject of project scheduling.

SCHEDULING IN HIGH-VOLUME SYSTEMS

Scheduling encompasses allocating workloads to specific work centers and determining the sequence in which operations are to be performed. High-volume systems are characterized by standardized equipment and activities that provide identical or highly similar operations on customers or products as they pass through the system. Consequently, the goal is to obtain a smooth rate of flow of goods or customers through the system in order to get a high utilization of labor and equipment. High-volume systems are often referred to as **flow systems**, and scheduling in these systems is referred to as **flow-shop scheduling**. Examples of high-volume products include autos, typewriters, radios and televisions, stereo equipment, toys, and appliances. In process industries, examples include petroleum refining, sugar refining, mining, waste treatment, and the manufacturing of fertilizers. Examples of services include cafeteria lines, news broadcasts, and mass inoculations. Because of the highly repetitive nature of these systems, many of the loading and sequence decisions are determined during the design of the system. The use of highly specialized tools and equipment, the arrangement of equipment, the use of specialized material-handling equipment, and the division of labor are all designed to enhance the flow of work through the system, since all items follow virtually the same sequence of operations.

Flow system

High-volume system with standardized equipment and activities.

Flow-shop scheduling

Scheduling for the high-volume flow system.

A major aspect in the design of flow systems is *line balancing,* which concerns allocating the required tasks to workstations so that they satisfy technical (sequencing) constraints and are balanced with respect to equal work times among stations. Highly balanced systems result in the maximum utilization of equipment and personnel as well as the highest possible rate of output. Line balancing is discussed in Chapter 7.

In setting up flow systems, designers must consider the potential discontent of workers related to the specialization of job tasks these systems entail: high work rates are often achieved by dividing the work into a series of relatively simple tasks that are assigned to different workers. The resulting jobs tend to be boring and monotonous and may give rise to fatigue, absenteeism, turnover, and other problems, all of which have a tendency to reduce productivity and disrupt the smooth flow of work through the system. These problems and potential solutions are elaborated on in Chapter 8, which deals with the design of work systems.

In spite of the built-in attributes of flow systems related to scheduling, there remain a number of problems with respect to scheduling. One stems from the fact that few flow systems are *completely* devoted to a single product or service; most must handle a variety of sizes and models. Thus, an automobile manufacturer will assemble many different combinations of cars—two-door and four-door models, some with air conditioning and some not, some with deluxe trim and others with standard trim, some with tape decks, some with tinted glass, and so on. The same can be said for producers of appliances, electronic equipment, toys, and so on. Each change involves slightly different inputs that must be scheduled into the line, such as different parts and materials and different processing requirements. If the line is to operate smoothly, the flow of materials and the work must be coordinated. This requires scheduling the inputs, the processing, and the outputs, as well as scheduling purchases. In addition to achieving a smooth flow, it is important to avoid excessive buildup of inventories. Again, each variation in size or model will tend to have somewhat different inventory requirements, so that additional scheduling efforts will be needed.

Another source of scheduling requirements is disruptions to the system that result in less than the desired amount of output. These can be caused by equipment failures, material shortages, accidents, and absences. Practically speaking, it is usually not possible to increase the rate of output to compensate for these factors, mainly due to the fact that flow systems are designed to operate at a given rate. Instead, strategies involving subcontracting or overtime are often required, although subcontracting on short notice is not always feasible. Sometimes work that is partly completed can be made up off the line.

The reverse situation can also impose scheduling problems, although less severe. This happens when the desired amount of output is more than the usual rate. However, instead of slowing the ensuing rate of output, it is usually necessary to operate the system at the usual rate, but for fewer hours. For instance, a production line might operate for seven hours a day instead of eight for a while.

High-volume systems usually involve automated or specialized equipment for processing and handling. Moreover, they perform best when there is a high, uniform output. Consequently, the following factors often determine the success of such a system:

1. *Process and product design.* Here, cost and manufacturability are important, as is achieving a smooth flow through the system.
2. *Preventive maintenance.* Keeping equipment in good operating order can minimize breakdowns that would disrupt the flow of work.

3. *Rapid repair when breakdowns occur.* This can require specialists as well as stocks of critical spare parts.

4. *Optimal product mixes.* Techniques such as linear programming can be used to determine optimal blends of inputs to achieve desired outputs at minimal costs. This is particularly true in the manufacture of fertilizers, animal feeds, and diet foods.

5. *Minimization of quality problems.* Quality problems can be extremely disruptive, requiring shutdowns while problems are resolved. Moreover, when output fails to meet quality standards, the labor, material, time, and other resources that went into it have been wasted, in addition to the loss of output.

6. *Reliability and timing of supplies.* Shortages of supplies is an obvious source of disruption and must be avoided. On the other hand, if the solution is to stock-pile supplies, that can lead to high carrying costs. Shortening supply lead times, developing reliable supply schedules, and carefully projecting needs are all useful in this regard.

SCHEDULING IN INTERMEDIATE-VOLUME SYSTEMS

Intermediate-volume system outputs fall between the standardized type of output of the high-volume systems and made-to-order output of job shops. Like the high-volume systems, intermediate-volume systems typically produce standard outputs. And if manufacturing is involved, the products may be made for stock rather than for special order. However, the volume of output in such cases is not large enough to justify devoting continual production. Instead, it is more economical to process these items *intermittently.* Thus, intermediate-volume work centers periodically shift from one job to another. In contrast to a job shop, though, the run sizes are relatively large. Examples of products made in these systems include canned foods, baked goods, paint, and cosmetics.

The three basic issues in these systems are the *run size* of jobs, the *timing* of jobs, and the *sequence* jobs should be processed in.

Sometimes, the issue of run size can be determined by using a model such as the economic run size model discussed in the chapter on inventory management. The run size that would minimize setup and inventory costs is

$$Q_0 = \sqrt{\frac{2DS}{H}} \sqrt{\frac{p}{p - u}} \qquad\qquad \textbf{(15–1)}$$

This approach works well in the context of a single product but must be modified somewhat when multiple products are involved. One reason is that setup costs can be dependent on the order of processing: some products will have similar setups, so it may be less expensive to process them in sequence to take advantage of that. Another difficulty arises because usage is not always as smooth as assumed in this model. Consequently, some products will tend to be used up faster than expected and have to be replenished sooner. Also, because multiple products are to be processed, it is not always possible to schedule production to correspond with optimum run intervals.

Another approach that is often used is to base production on a master schedule that is developed using customer orders and forecasts of demand. For companies that are engaged in assembly operations, an MRP approach (described in Chapter

13) would then be used to determine the quantity and projected timing of jobs for components. The manager would then compare projected requirements with projected capacity, and develop a feasible schedule from that information. For companies that are engaged in producing goods that are processed rather than assembled (e.g., food products, such as canned goods and beverages; publishing, such as magazines; paints and cleaning supplies) a somewhat different approach would be used. The lead times typically of assembly operations are usually absent or at least much shorter in mixing type operations, which means that the *time-phasing* information provided by MRP would not be an important factor.

The *timing* of jobs may evolve from customer orders and forecasts. Another common approach is based on calculation of **runout time**, which measures the length of time before current supplies will be depleted, taking into account the current demand rate:

Runout time

Length of time before current supplies will be depleted at the current demand rate.

$$\text{Runout time} = \frac{\text{Current inventory}}{\text{Demand rate}} \qquad (15\text{--}2)$$

Runout time indicates how long it will be before a given item will incur a stockout. The runout time is computed for each product, and the products are ranked according to this measure. The lower the runout time, the more crucial it is to replenish the supply of an item. Here is an example of the calculations:

Product	Inventory (units)		Demand (units/week)		Runout time (weeks)
A	400	÷	100	=	4.0
B	120	÷	100	=	1.2
C	50	÷	20	=	2.5

Product A has a runout time of 4.0 weeks, product B has a runout time of 1.2 weeks, and product C has a runout time of 2.5 weeks. Consequently, the processing order would be B-C-A.

Modifications to the economic run size formula that allow for multiple products and dependent setups, and elaboration of the runout time approach, are somewhat beyond the scope of this text. However, both topics are covered in more detail in the references found at the end of this chapter, if you are interested.

SCHEDULING IN LOW-VOLUME SYSTEMS

The characteristics of low-volume systems (job shops) are quite different from those of high- and intermediate-volume systems. Products are made to order, and orders usually differ considerably in terms of processing requirements, materials needed, processing time, and processing sequence and setups. Because of these circumstances, **job-shop scheduling** is usually fairly complex. This is compounded by the fact that it is impossible to establish firm schedules prior to receiving the actual job orders.

Job-shop scheduling

Scheduling for low-volume systems with many variations in requirements.

Job shop processing gives rise to two basic issues for schedulers: how to distribute the workload among work centers and what job processing sequence to use.

LOADING

Loading refers to the assignment of jobs to processing (work) centers. In cases where a job can only be processed by a specific center, loading presents little difficulty. However, problems arise when two or more jobs are to be processed and there are a number of work centers capable of performing the required work. In such cases, the operations manager needs some way of assigning jobs to the centers.

When making assignments, managers often seek an arrangement that will either minimize processing and setup costs, minimize idle time among work centers, or minimize job completion time, depending on the situation.

A number of approaches are used for loading, ranging from pure intuition to linear programming. We will look at two of these approaches in the following sections: the use of Gantt charts and the assignment method of linear programming.

Gantt charts are visual aids used for a variety of purposes related to loading and scheduling. They derive their name from Henry Gantt, who pioneered the use of charts for industrial scheduling in the early 1900s. Gantt charts can be used in a number of different ways, two of which are illustrated in Figure 15–1, which shows scheduling classrooms for a semester and scheduling hospital operating rooms for a day.

The purpose of Gantt charts is to organize and clarify the actual or intended use of resources in a *time framework*. In most cases, a time scale is represented horizon-

Loading

The assignment of jobs to processing centers.

Gantt charts

Charts used as visual aids for loading and scheduling purposes.

Figure 15–1

Examples of charts used for scheduling

tally, and resources to be scheduled are listed vertically. The use of the resources is reflected in the body of the chart.

Managers may use the charts for trial-and-error schedule development to get an idea of what different arrangements would involve. Thus, a tentative surgery schedule might reveal insufficient allowance for surgery that extends beyond its expected duration and can be revised accordingly. Use of the chart for classroom scheduling would help avoid assigning two different classes to the same room at the same time.

There are a number of different types of Gantt charts. Two of the most commonly used are the *load chart* and the *schedule chart*.

A **load chart** depicts the loading and idle times for a group of machines or a list of departments. A typical load chart is illustrated in Figure 15–2. This particular chart indicates that work center 3 is completely loaded for the entire week, center 4 will be available after noon on Tuesday, and the other two centers have idle time scattered throughout the week. This information can help a manager rework loading assignments to better utilize the centers. For instance, if all centers perform the same kind of work, the manager might want to free one center for a long job or a rush order. It also shows when certain jobs are scheduled to start and finish, and where idle time is expected.

A manager often uses a **schedule chart** to monitor the progress of jobs. The vertical axis on this type of Gantt chart shows the orders or jobs in progress, and the horizontal axis shows time. The chart indicates which jobs are on schedule and which are behind or ahead.

A typical schedule chart is illustrated in Figure 15–3. It shows the current status of a landscaping job along with planned and actual starting and finishing times for the five stages of the job. We can see from the chart that approval was on schedule, as was ordering of trees and shrubs. The site preparation was a bit behind schedule. The trees were received earlier than expected, and planting is ahead of schedule. However, the shrubs have not yet been received. The chart indicates some slack between scheduled receipt of shrubs and shrub planting, so if the shrubs arrive by the end of the week, it appears the schedule can still be met.

In spite of the obvious benefits of these charts, they also possess certain limitations, the chief one being the need to repeatedly update the chart to keep it current. In addition, a chart does not directly reveal costs associated with alternative loadings. Finally, a job's processing time may vary depending on the work center involved: certain stations or work centers may be capable of processing some jobs faster than other stations. Again, that situation would increase the complexity of

Load chart

A Gantt chart that shows the loading and idle times for a group of machines or list of departments.

Schedule chart

A Gantt chart that shows the orders or jobs in progress and whether they are on schedule.

Work center	Mon.	Tues.	Wed.	Thurs.	Fri.
1	Job 3			Job 4	
2		Job 3	Job 7		✕
3	Job 1	✕		Job 6	Job 7
4	Job 10				

☐ Processing

☒ Center not available (e.g., maintenance)

Figure 15–2

A Gantt load chart

Figure 15–3

Progress chart for landscaping job

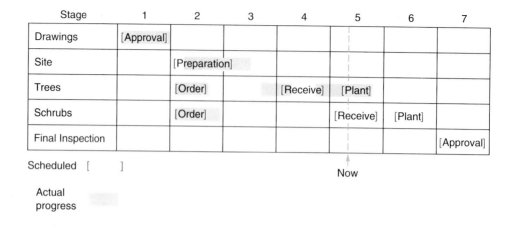

Stage	1	2	3	4	5	6	7
Drawings	[Approval]						
Site		[Preparation]					
Trees		[Order]		[Receive]	[Plant]		
Schrubs		[Order]			[Receive]	[Plant]	
Final Inspection							[Approval]

Scheduled [   ]

Actual progress

Now

evaluating alternative schedules. Nonetheless, Gantt charts are the most widely used devices for scheduling.

The **assignment model** is a special-purpose linear-programming model that is useful in situations that call for assigning tasks or other work requirements to resources. Typical examples include assigning jobs to machines or workers, territories to salespeople, and emergency calls to telephone repair crews. The idea is to obtain an optimum *matching* of tasks and resources. Commonly used criteria include costs, profits, efficiency, and performance.

A typical problem is illustrated in Table 15–1, where four jobs are to be assigned to four machines. The problem is arranged in a format that will facilitate evaluation of assignments. The numbers in the body of the table represent the value or cost associated with each job-machine combination. In this case, the numbers represent costs. Thus, it would cost $8 to do job 1 on machine A, $6 to do job 1 on machine B, and so on. If the problem involved minimizing the cost for job 1 alone, it is apparent that it would be assigned to machine C since that combination has the lowest cost. However, that assignment does not take into account the other jobs and their potential costs, which is important since the lowest-cost assignment for any one job may not be consistent with a minimum-cost assignment when all jobs are considered.

If there are to be *n* matches, there are *n*! different possibilities. In this case, there are 4! = 24 different matches. One approach would be to investigate each match and select the one with the lowest cost. However, even for a problem of this small size, considerable time and effort would be called for. Instead, a much simpler approach is to use a procedure called the **Hungarian method** to identify the lowest-cost solution.

To be able to use the Hungarian method, a one-for-one matching is required. Each job, for example, must be assigned to only one machine. It is also assumed that every machine is capable of handling every job, and that the costs or values associated with each assignment combination are known and fixed (i.e., not subject to variation).

Once the relevant cost information has been acquired and arranged in tabular form, the basic procedure of the Hungarian method is:

1. Subtract the smallest number in each row from every number in the row. Enter the results in a new table.

Assignment model

A linear-programming model for optimal assignment of tasks and resources.

Hungarian method

Method of assigning jobs by a one-for-one matching to identify the lowest-cost solution.

Table 15–1

A typical assignment problem

	Machine			
	A	**B**	**C**	**D**
1	8	6	2	4
2	6	7	11	10
Job 3	3	5	7	6
4	5	10	12	9

2. Subtract the smallest number in each column of the new table from every number in the column. Enter the results in another table.

3. Test to see if an optimum assignment can be made. This is accomplished by determining the *minimum* number of lines that are needed to cover all zeros. If the number of lines equals the number of rows, an optimum assignment is possible. In that case, go to step 6. Otherwise go on to step 4. Note that "cover" means "cross out."

4. If the number of lines is less than the number of rows, modify the table in this way:
   a. Subtract the smallest uncovered number from every uncovered number in the table.
   b. Add the smallest uncovered number to the numbers at *intersections* of covering lines.

5. Repeat steps 3 and 4 until an optimal table is obtained.

6. Make the assignments. Begin with rows or columns with only one zero. Match items that have zeros, using only one match for each row and each column. Cross out both the row and the column after the match.

Determine the optimum assignment of jobs to machines for the following data below (from Table 15–1).

Example 1

	Machine				Row
	A	**B**	**C**	**D**	**minimum**
1	8	6	2	4	2
2	6	7	11	10	6
Job 3	3	5	7	6	3
4	5	10	12	9	5

Solution

a. Subtract the smallest number in each row from every number in the row, and enter the results in a new table. The result of this *row reduction* is:

(continued)

Example 1

(continued)

Machine

	A	B	C	D
1	6	4	0	2
Job 2	0	1	5	4
3	0	2	4	3
4	0	5	7	4
Column minimum	0	1	0	2

b. Subtract the smallest number in each column from every number in the column, and enter the results in a new table. The result of this *column reduction* is:

Machine

	A	B	C	D
1	6	3	0	0
Job 2	0	0	5	2
3	0	1	4	1
4	0	4	7	2

c. Determine the minimum number of lines needed to cover (cross out) all zeros. (Try to cross out as many zeros as possible when drawing lines.)

d. Since only three lines are needed to cover all zeros, this is not the optimum.

e. Subtract the smallest uncovered value (in this case, 1) from every uncovered number, and add it to numbers that are at the intersections of covering lines. The results are:

Machine

	A	B	C	D
1	7	3	0	0
Job 2	1	0	5	2
3	0	0	3	0
4	0	3	6	1

Example 1

(concluded)

f.　Determine the minimum number of lines needed to cover all zeros (four). Since this equals the number of rows, the optimum assignment can be made.

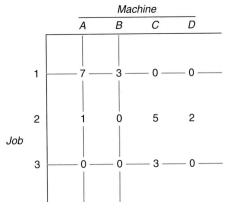

	Machine			
	A	B	C	D
1	7	3	0	0
2	1	0	5	2
3	0	0	3	0
4	0	3	6	1

g.　Make assignments: Start with rows and columns with only one zero. Match jobs with machines that have a zero cost:

		Machine			
		A	B	C	D
	1	7	3	[0]	0
Job	2	1	[0]	5	2
	3	0	0	3	[0]
	4	[0]	3	6	1

As you can see, the progress is relatively simple compared to some of the other linear-programming techniques. One extension of this technique that is worth knowing is the ability to use it to prevent undesirable assignments. For example, union rules may prohibit one person's assignment to a particular job, or a manager might wish to avoid assigning an unpleasant job to the person who did it last. Whatever the reason, specific combinations can be avoided by assigning a relatively high cost to that combination. In the previous example, if we wish to avoid combination 1–A, assigning a cost of $50 to that combination will achieve the desired effect because $50 is much greater than the other costs. In a situation involving profits instead of costs, the profits can be converted to *relative costs* by subtracting every number in the table from the largest number and then proceeding as in a minimization problem.

The simplicity of the Hungarian method belies its usefulness when the assumptions are met. Not only does it provide a rational method for making assignments, it guarantees an optimal solution, often without the use of a computer. In fact, computers are necessary only for fairly large problems.

SEQUENCING

Although loading decisions determine the machines or work centers that will be used to process specific jobs, they do not indicate the *order* in which the jobs waiting

Table 15–2

Possible priority rules

FCFS (first come, first served): Jobs are processed in the order in which they arrive at a machine or work center.

SPT (shortest processing time): Jobs are processed according to processing time at a machine or work center, shortest job first.

DD (due date): Jobs are processed according to due date, earliest due date first.

CR (critical ratio): Jobs are processed according to smallest ratio of due date to processing time.

S/O (slack per operation): Jobs are processed according to average slack time (time until due date minus remaining time to process). Compute by dividing slack time by number of remaining operations, including the current one.

Rush: Emergency or preferred customers first.

Sequencing

Determining the order in which jobs at a work center will be processed.

at a given work center are to be processed. **Sequencing** is concerned with determining job processing order.

If work centers are lightly loaded and if jobs all require the same amount of processing time, sequencing presents no particular difficulties. However, for heavily loaded work centers, especially in situations where relatively lengthy jobs are involved, the order of processing can be very important in terms of costs associated with jobs waiting for processing and in terms of idle time at the work centers. In this section, we will examine some of the ways in which jobs are sequenced.

Priority rules

Simple heuristics used to select the order in which jobs will be processed.

Typically, a number of jobs will be waiting for processing. **Priority rules** are simple heuristics used to select the order in which the jobs will be processed. Some of the most common are listed in Table 15–2. The rules generally involve the assumption that job setup cost and time are *independent* of processing sequence. In using these rules, job processing times and due dates are important pieces of information. **Job time** usually includes setup and processing times. Jobs that require

Job time

Time needed for setup and processing of a job.

similar setups can lead to reduced setup times if the sequencing rule takes this into account (the rules described here do not). Due dates may be the result of delivery times promised to customers, MRP processing, or managerial decisions. They are subject to revision and must be kept current to give meaning to sequencing choices. Also, it should be noted that due dates associated with all rules except S/O and CR are for the operation about to be performed; due dates for S/O and CR are typically final due dates for orders rather than intermediate, departmental deadlines.

The effectiveness of any given sequence is commonly judged in terms of one of three measures: average completion time, average job lateness, or average number of jobs at a work center. Two of these measures, average completion time and average number of jobs at a work center, are directly related; that is, they both produce the same results. However, a measure of average completion time can be useful in establishing future promised delivery dates, while a measure of the number of jobs in the system can be useful in determining the amount of work-in-process inventories.

Of these rules, Rush scheduling is quite simple and needs no explanation. The other rules are illustrated in the following two examples.

Example 2

∎

Processing times (including setup times) and due dates for six jobs waiting to be processed at a work center are given in the following table. Determine the sequences of processing according to each of these rules:

Example 2

(continued)

a. FCFS.

b. SPT.

c. DD.

d. CR.

Job	Processing time (days)	Due date (days)
A	2	7
B	8	16
C	4	4
D	10	17
E..............	5	15
F..............	12	18

Assume jobs arrived in the order shown.

Solution

a. The FCFS sequence is simply A–B–C–D–E–F. The measures of effectiveness are:

(1) *Average completion time:* $120/6 = 20$ days.

(2) *Average job lateness:* $54/6 = 9$ days.

(3) *Average number of jobs at the work center:* $120/41 = 2.93$.

Job sequence	(1) Processing time	(2) Flow time	(3) Due date	(2) − (3) Days late [0 if negative]
A	2	2	7	0
B	8	10	16	0
C................	4	14	4	10
D	10	24	17	7
E	5	29	15	14
F	12	41	18	23
	41	120		54

The flow time column indicates *cumulative* processing time, so summing these times and dividing by the total number of jobs processed indicates the average time each job spends at the work center. Similarly, the average number of jobs at the center is found by summing the flow times and dividing by the total processing time.

b. Using the SPT rule, the job sequence is A–C–E–B–D–F (see the following table). The resulting values for the three measures of effectiveness are:

(1) *Average completion time:* $108/6 = 18$ days.

(2) *Average job lateness:* $40/6 = 6.67$ days.

(3) *Average number of jobs at the work center:* $108/41 = 2.63$.

Sequence	(1) Processing time	(2) Flow time	(3) Due date	(2) − (3) Days late [0 if negative]
A	2	2	7	0
C	4	6	4	2
E	5	11	15	0
B	8	19	16	3
D	10	29	17	12
F	12	41	18	23
	41	108		40

Example 2

(concluded)

c. Using earliest due date as the selection criterion, the job sequence is C-A-E-B-D-F. The measures of effectiveness are (see table):
    (1) *Average completion time:* 110/6 = 18.33 days.
    (2) *Average job lateness:* 38/6 = 6.33 days.
    (3) *Average number of jobs at the work center:* 110/41 = 2.68.

Sequence	(1) Processing time	(2) Flow time	(3) Due date	(2) − (3) Days late [0 if negative]
C...............	4	4	4	0
A...............	2	6	7	0
E...............	5	11	15	0
B...............	8	19	16	3
D...............	10	29	17	12
F...............	12	41	18	23
	41	110		38

d. Using the critical ratio (Due date − Current date) ÷ Processing time, the job sequence is C-F-D-B-E-A, and the resulting values for the three measures of effectiveness are:
    (1) *Average completion time:* 160/6 = 26.67 days.
    (2) *Average job lateness:* 85/6 = 14.17 days.
    (3) *Average number of jobs at the work center:* 160/41 = 3.90.

Sequence	(1) Critical ratio	(2) Processing time	(3) Flow time	(4) Due date	(3) − (4) Days late
C...............	1.0	4	4	4	0
F...............	1.5	12	16	18	0
D...............	1.7	10	26	17	9
B...............	2.0	8	34	16	18
E...............	3.0	5	39	15	24
A...............	3.5	2	41	7	34
		41	160		85

The results of these four rules are summarized in Table 15–3.

Table 15–3

Comparison of the four rules

Rule	Average completion time (days)	Average lateness (days)	Average number of jobs at the work center
FCFS	20.00	9.00	2.93
SPT	18.00	6.67	2.63
DD	18.33	6.33	2.68
CR	26.67	14.17	3.90

In this example, the SPT rule was the best according to two of the measures of effectiveness and a little worse than the DD rule on average lateness. The CR rule was the worst in every case. For a different set of numbers, the DD rule (or perhaps another rule not mentioned here) might prove superior to SPT in terms of average job lateness or some other measure of effectiveness. However, SPT is always superior in terms of minimizing flow time and, hence, in terms of minimizing the average number of jobs at the work center and completion time. It is best for each shop or organization to consider carefully its own circumstances and the measures of effectiveness it feels are important, when selecting a rule to use.

Generally speaking, the FCFS rule and the CR rule turn out to be the least effective of the rules.

The primary limitation of the FCFS rule is that long jobs will tend to delay other jobs. If a process consists of work on a number of machines, machine idle time for downstream workstations will be increased. However, for service systems in which customers are directly involved, the FCFS rule is by far the dominant priority rule, mainly because of the inherent "fairness" but also perhaps because of the inability to obtain realistic estimates of processing times for individual jobs. The FCFS rule also has the advantage of simplicity.

Because the SPT rule always results in the lowest average completion time, it can result in lower in-process inventories. And because it often provides the lowest average lateness, it can result in better customer service levels. Finally, since it always involves a lower average number of jobs at the work center, there tends to be less congestion in the work area. SPT also minimizes downstream idle time.

The major disadvantage of the SPT rule is that it tends to make long jobs wait, perhaps for rather long times (especially if new, shorter jobs are continually added to the system). Various modifications may be used in an effort to avoid this. For example, after waiting for a given time period, any remaining jobs are automatically moved to the head of the line. This is known as the *truncated* SPT rule.

The DD rule directly addresses due dates and usually minimizes lateness. Although it has intuitive appeal, its main limitation is that it does not take processing time into account. One possible consequence is that it can result in some jobs waiting a long time, which adds both to in-process inventories and to shop congestion.

The CR rule is easy to use and has intuitive appeal. Although it had the poorest showing in Example 2 for all three measures, it usually does quite well in terms of minimizing job lateness. Therefore, if job lateness is important, the CR rule might be the best choice among the rules.

Let's take a look now at the S/O (slack per operation) rule.

Using the S/O rule, the designated job sequence may change after any given operation, so it is important to reevaluate the sequence after each operation. Note that any of the previously mentioned priority rules could be used on a station-by-station basis for this situation; the only difference is that the S/O approach incorporates downstream information in arriving at a job sequence.

In actuality, there are many priority rules available to sequence jobs, and some other rule might provide superior results for a given set of circumstances. Our purpose in examining these few rules is to provide insight into the nature of sequencing rules.

The following section describes a special-purpose algorithm that can be used to sequence a set of jobs that must all be processed at the same two machines or work centers.

Example 3

Use the S/O rule to schedule the following jobs. Note that processing time includes the time remaining for the current and subsequent operations. In addition, we will need to know the number of operations remaining, including the current one.

Job	Remaining processing time	Due date	Remaining number of operations
A 4	14	3
B 16	32	6
C 8	8	5
D 20	34	2
E 10	30	4
F 18	30	2

Solution

Determine the difference between the due date and the processing time for each operation. Divide the amount by the number of remaining operations, and rank them from low to high. This yields the sequence of jobs:

	(1) Remaining processing	(2) Due	(3) (2) − (1)	(4) Remaining number of	(5) (3) ÷ (4)	(6)
Job	time	date	Slack	operations	Ratio	Rank
A 4	14	10	3	3.33	3
B 16	32	16	6	2.67	2
C 8	8	0	5	0	1
D 20	34	14	2	7.00	6
E 10	30	20	4	5.00	4
F 18	30	12	2	6.00	5

The indicated sequence (see column 6) is C–B–A–E–F–D.

SEQUENCING JOBS THROUGH TWO WORK CENTERS

Johnson's rule

Technique for minimizing completion time for a group of jobs to be processed on two machines or at two work centers.

Johnson's rule is a technique that can be used to minimize the throughput (completion) time for a group of jobs that are to be processed on two machines or at two successive work centers.[1] It also minimizes the total idle time at the work centers. In order for the technique to be used, several conditions must be satisfied:

1. Job time (including setup and processing) must be known and constant for each job at each work center.
2. Job times must be independent of the job sequence.
3. All jobs must follow the same two-step work sequence.
4. Job priorities cannot be used.
5. All units in a job must be completed at the first work center before the job moves on to the second work center.

---

[1] S. M. Johnson, "Optimal Two- and Three-Stage Production with Setup Times Included," *Naval Research Quarterly* 1 (March 1954), pp. 61–68.

Determination of the optimum sequence involves these steps:

1. List the jobs and their times at each work center.
2. Select the job with the shortest time. If the shortest time is at the first work center, schedule that job first; if the time is at the second work center, schedule the job last. Break ties arbitrarily.
3. Eliminate the job and its time from further consideration.
4. Repeat steps 2 and 3, working toward the center of the sequence, until all jobs have been scheduled.

A group of six jobs are to be processed through a two-step operation. The first operation involves degreasing, and the second involves painting. Determine a sequence that will minimize the total completion time for this group of jobs. Processing times are as follows:

Example 4

| Job | **Processing time (hours)** | |
	Work center 1	Work center 2
A	5	5
B	4	3
C	8	9
D	2	7
E	6	8
F	12	15

Solution

a. Select the job with the shortest processing time. It is job D, with a time of two hours.

b. Since the time is at the first center, schedule job D first. Eliminate job D from further consideration.

c. Job B has the next shortest time. Since it is at the second work center, schedule it last and eliminate job B from further consideration. We now have:

1st	2d	3d	4th	5th	6th
D					B

d. The remaining jobs and their times are:

Job	1	2
A	5	5
C	8	9
E	6	8
F	12	15

Note that there is a tie for the shortest remaining time: job A has the same time at each work center. It makes no difference, then, whether we place it toward the beginning or the end of the sequence. Suppose we place it toward the end arbitrarily. We now have:

(continued)

Example 4

(concluded)

	1st	2d	3d	4th	5th	6th
	D				A	B

e. The shortest remaining time is six hours for job E at work center 1. Thus, schedule that job toward the beginning of the sequence (after job D). Thus,

	1st	2d	3d	4th	5th	6th
	D	E			A	B

f. Job C has the shortest time of the remaining two jobs. Since it is for the first work center, it is placed third in the sequence. Finally, the remaining job (F) is assigned to the fourth position and the result is:

	1st	2d	3d	4th	5th	6th
	D	E	C	F	A	B

g. The easiest way to determine the throughput time and idle times at the work centers is to construct a chart:

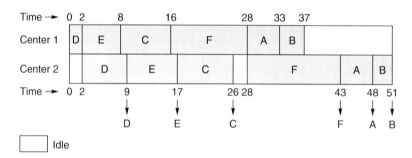

Thus, the group of jobs will take 51 hours to complete. The second work center will wait two hours for its first job and also wait two hours after finishing job C. Center 1 will be finished in 37 hours. Of course, idle periods at the beginning or end of the sequence could be used to do other jobs or for maintenance or setup/teardown activities.

When significant idle time at the second work center occurs, job splitting at the first center just prior to the occurrence of idle time may alleviate some of it and also shorten throughput time. In the preceding example, this was not a problem. The last solved problem at the end of this chapter illustrates the use of job splitting.

OPTIMIZED PRODUCTION TECHNOLOGY

Optimized Production Technology (OPT) is a proprietary software package owned by Creative Output, Inc., of Milford, Connecticut. Information on the package is somewhat limited due to the proprietary nature of the technique. However, it is said to involve the use of mathematical programming, networking, and simulation.

A basic feature of OPT is the special attention it directs to bottleneck operations. The rationale of OPT is that bottleneck operations have an impact on an entire plant, and the best way to schedule a plant is to identify the bottleneck operations and try to optimize their use. The nonbottleneck operations are not critical and can therefore be treated differently. The OPT philosophy contends that the standard costs of bottleneck operations are understated because they don't take into account the fact that these operations constrain the entire system. Hence, OPT begins its scheduling procedure with the bottleneck operations and attempts to maximize their output. In essence, OPT is a finite loading procedure.

OPT consists of four basic modules:

1. *Buildnet*. This contains data on a plant's raw materials, purchased parts, products, work center capabilities, and customer orders.
2. *Serve*. This module identifies the bottleneck operations by running load profiles for each operation or work center.
3. *Split*. This module divides the system into two categories: critical operations (i.e., bottlenecks) and noncritical operations.
4. *Brain*. This module contains a set of algorithms that actually perform the scheduling.

OPT simulates different schedules and then selects a schedule based on the simulations.

There are two lot sizes in the OPT approach, a *process batch* and a *transfer batch*. The process batch is a lot size released to the shop. To optimize the output of bottlenecks, large batches (few setups) are run. However, since nonbottleneck operations have idle time, it does not make sense to attempt to maximize their output; there is nothing to gain by increasing idle time. Consequently, smaller lot sizes and more frequent setups can be used on such operations. The small batch sizes are the transfer lots. Hence, OPT deliberately schedules a variety of lot sizes, unlike more conventional approaches that use a single lot size throughout a shop for a job. You might think of this as lot splitting with multiple split sizes. An important feature of the software is selection of the appropriate lot size for each operation.

As you might expect, OPT directs its use of both safety stock and safety time to facilitate flow through bottleneck operations. By concentrating these resources, it seeks to gain the maximum benefit from them and generally minimize inventories otherwise devoted to this purpose.

Since OPT is still relatively new, widespread experience of its use is not yet available. Nonetheless, users have reported a number of benefits. One is that OPT appears to be quicker and less costly to implement than a system such as MRP. Like MRP, OPT requires extensive preliminary effort to obtain accurate, up-to-date information in data files on work standards, machine capabilities, product structures, and so on. OPT seems to require even more detail than MRP, and many view the process of going through this effort as an important benefit because of the improved data base it produces.

SCHEDULING IN SERVICE SYSTEMS

Scheduling service systems presents certain problems not generally encountered in manufacturing systems. This is due primarily to (1) the inability to store or inventory services and (2) the random nature of customer requests for service. In some situations, the second difficulty can be moderated by using appointment or reservation systems, but the inability to store services in most cases is a fact of life that managers must contend with.

An important goal in service systems is to match the flow of customers and service capabilities. An ideal situation is one in which there is a smooth flow of customers through the system. This would occur if each new customer arrives at the precise instant that the preceding customer's service is completed, in a case such as a physician's office, or, in a case such as air travel, where the demand just equals the number of available seats. In each of these situations, customer waiting time would be minimized, and there would be full utilization of the service system staff and equipment. Unfortunately, because of the random nature of customer requests for service that generally prevails in service systems, it is nearly impossible to provide service capability that will match demand. Moreover, if service times are subject to variability—say, because of differing processing requirements—the inefficiency of the system is compounded. The inefficiencies can be reduced if arrivals can be scheduled (e.g., appointments), as in the case of doctors and dentists. However, there are many situations in which appointments are not possible (supermarkets, gas stations, theaters, hospital emergency rooms, repair of equipment breakdowns). Chapter 17, on queuing analysis, focuses on those kinds of situations. There, the emphasis is on intermediate-term decisions related to service capacity. In this section, we will concern ourselves with short-term *scheduling,* in which much of the capacity of a system is essentially fixed, and the goal is to achieve a certain degree of customer service by efficient utilization of that capacity.

APPOINTMENT SYSTEMS

Appointment systems are intended to control the timing of customer arrivals in order to minimize customer waiting while achieving a high degree of capacity utilization. A doctor can use an appointment system to schedule office patients during the afternoon, leaving the mornings free for hospital duties. Similarly, an attorney can schedule clients around court appearances. Even with appointments, however, problems can still arise due to lack of punctuality on the part of patients or clients, no-shows, and the inability to completely control the length of contact time (e.g., a dentist might run into complications in filling a tooth and have to spend additional time with a patient, thus backing up later appointments). Some of this can be avoided—say, by trying to match the time reserved for a patient or client with the specific needs of that case rather than setting appointments at regular intervals. Even with the problems of late arrivals and no-shows, the appointment system is a tremendous improvement over allowing random arrivals.

RESERVATION SYSTEMS

Reservation systems are designed to enable service systems to formulate a fairly accurate estimate of the demand on the system for a given time period and to minimize customer disappointment generated by excessive waiting or inability to obtain service. Reservation systems are widely used by resorts, hotels and motels, and restaurants as well as in some modes of transportation (airlines, car rentals). In the case of restaurants, reservations enable management to spread out or group customers so that demand matches service capabilities. As with appointment systems, late arrivals and no-shows can disrupt the system. One approach to the no-show problem would be to use decision theory. The problem can also be viewed as a single-period inventory problem, as described in the supplement to Chapter 12.

SCHEDULING MULTIPLE RESOURCES

In some situations, it is necessary to coordinate the use of more than one resource. For example, hospitals must schedule surgeons, operating rooms, operating room staffs, recovery room staffs, admissions, special equipment, nursing staffs, and so on. Similarly, educational institutions must schedule faculty, classrooms, audiovisual equipment, and students. As you might guess, the greater the number of resources that must be scheduled, the greater the complexity of the problem, and the less likely it becomes that an optimum schedule can be achieved. The problem is further complicated by the variable nature of such systems. For example, educational institutions frequently change their course offerings, student enrollments change, and students exhibit different course-selection patterns.

Some schools and hospitals are using computer programs to assist them in devising acceptable schedules, although many appear to be using intuitive approaches, with varying degrees of success.

Airlines are another example of service systems that require the scheduling of multiple resources. Flight crews, aircraft, baggage handling equipment, ticket counters, gate personnel, boarding ramps, and maintenance personnel all have to be coordinated. Furthermore, government regulations on the number of hours a pilot can spend flying place an additional restriction on the system. Another interesting variable is the fact that, unlike most systems, the flight crews and the equipment do not remain in one location. Moreover, the crew and the equipment are not usually scheduled as a single unit. Flight crews are often scheduled so that they return to their base city every two days or more often, and rest breaks must be considered. On the other hand, the aircraft may be in almost continuous use except for periodic maintenance and repairs. Consequently, flight crews commonly follow different trip patterns than that of the aircraft.

Scheduling can either help or hinder operations strategy. If scheduling is done well, products and services can be made or delivered in a timely manner. Resources can be used to best advantages, and customers will be satisfied. If scheduling is not done well, the result will be inefficient use of resources, and possibly dissatisfied customers.

The implication is clear: Management should not overlook the important role that scheduling plays in the success of an organization, giving a competitive advantage if handled well, or disadvantage if done poorly. Time-based competition depends on good scheduling. Coordination of materials, equipment use, and employee time is an important function of operations management. It is not enough to have a good design, superior quality, and the other elements of a well-run organization if scheduling is done poorly—just as it is not enough to own a well-designed and well-made car, with all the latest features for comfort and safety, if the owner doesn't know how to drive it!

OPERATIONS STRATEGY

SUMMARY

Scheduling involves the timing and coordination of operations. Such activities are fundamental to virtually every organization. Scheduling problems differ according to whether a system is designed for high volume, intermediate volume, or as a job shop. Scheduling problems are particularly complex for job shops because of the variety of jobs these systems are required to process.

The two major problems in job-shop scheduling are assigning jobs to machines or work centers, and designating the sequence of job processing at a given machine or work center. Gantt load charts are frequently employed to help managers visualize workloads, and they are useful for describing and analyzing sequencing alternatives. In addition, both heuristic and optimizing methods are used to develop loading and sequencing plans. For the most part, the optimization techniques can be used only if certain assumptions can be made.

Customer requirements in service systems generally present very different circumstances from those encountered in manufacturing systems. Appointment and reservation systems can sometimes be used for scheduling purposes, although not all systems are amenable to this. When multiple resources are involved, the task of balancing the system can be fairly complex.

KEY TERMS

assignment model, 740
flow-shop scheduling, 734
flow system, 734
Gantt chart, 738
Hungarian method, 740
job-shop scheduling, 737
job time, 744
Johnson's rule, 748
load chart, 739

loading, 738
Optimized Production
  Technology (OPT), 750
priority rules, 744
runout time, 737
schedule chart, 739
scheduling, 734
sequencing, 744

SOLVED PROBLEMS

Problem

1. *The assignment method.* The following table contains information on the cost to run three jobs on four available machines. Determine an assignment plan that will minimize opportunity costs.

		Machine			
		A	B	C	D
Job	1	12	16	14	10
	2	9	8	13	7
	3	15	12	9	11

Solution

In order for us to be able to use the assignment method, the numbers of jobs and machines must be equal. To remedy this situation, add a *dummy* job with costs of 0, and then solve as usual:

	Machine			
	A	**B**	**C**	**D**
1	12	16	14	10
2	9	8	13	7
Job 3	15	12	9	11
(dummy) 4	0	0	0	0

a. Subtract the smallest number from each row. The results are:

	Machine			
	A	**B**	**C**	**D**
1	2	6	4	0
2	2	1	6	0
Job 3	6	3	0	2
4	0	0	0	0

b. Subtract the smallest number in each column. (Because of the dummy zeros in each column, the resulting table will be unchanged.)

c. Determine the minimum number of lines needed to cover the zeros. One possible way is:

	Machine			
	A	*B*	*C*	*D*
1	2	6	4	0
2	2	1	6	0
Job 3	6	3	0	2
4	0	0	0	0

d. Since the number of lines is less than the number of rows, modify the numbers.

(1) Subtract the smallest uncovered number (1) from each uncovered number.

(2) Add the smallest uncovered number to numbers at line intersections. The result is:

	Machine			
	A	**B**	**C**	**D**
1	1	5	4	0
2	1	0	6	0
Job 3	5	2	0	2
4	0	0	1	1

e. Test for optimality:

Since the minimum number of lines equals the number of rows, an optimum assignment can be made.

f. Assign jobs to machines. Start with rows 1 and 3, since they each have one zero, and columns A and C, also with one zero each. The result is:

g. Compute total costs, referring back to the original table:

```
1-D  . . . . . . .  $10
2-B  . . . . . . .    8
3-C  . . . . . . .    9
4-A  . . . . . . .    0
                   $27
```

h. The implication of assignment 4–A is that machine A will not be assigned one of these jobs. It may remain idle or be used for another job.

Problem

2. *Priority rules.* Job times (including processing and setup) are shown in the following table for five jobs waiting to be processed at a work center:

Job	Job time (days)	Due date (days)
a	12	15
b	6	24
c	14	20
d	3	8
e	7	6

Determine the processing sequence that would result from each of these priority rules:

a. FCFS.
b. SPT.
c. DD.
d. CR.

Solution

(Assume job times are independent of processing sequence.)

a. FCFS:

Job	Order
a	1
b	2
c	3
d	4
e	5

b. SPT:

Job	Job time	Order
a	12	4
b	6	2
c	14	5
d	3	1
e	7	3

c. DD:

Job	Due date	Order
a	15	3
b	24	5
c	20	4
d	8	2
e	6	1

d. CR:

Job	CR	Order
a	1.25	2
b	4.00	5
c	1.43	3
d	2.67	4
e	0.86	1

Problem

3. *S/O rule.* Using the following information, determine an order processing sequence using the S/O priority rule.

Order	Processing time remaining (days)	Due date (days)	Number of operations remaining
A	20	30	2
B	11	18	5
C	10	6	2
D	16	23	4

Solution

(Assume times are independent of processing sequence.)

	(1) Remaining processing time	(2) Due date	(3) (2) − (1) Slack	(4) Number of operations	(5) Ratio	(6) Rank (sequence)
Order						
A	20	30	10	2	5.00	4
B	11	18	7	5	1.40	2
C	10	6	−4	2	−2.00	1
D	16	23	7	4	1.75	3

(Note that one ratio is negative. When negatives occur, assign the *lowest* rank to the *most negative* number.)

Problem

4. *Sequencing jobs through two work centers.* Use Johnson's rule to obtain the optimum sequence for processing the jobs shown through work centers A and B.

	Job times (hours)	
Job	Work center A	Work center B
a	2.50	4.20
b	3.80	1.50
c	2.20	3.00
d	5.80	4.00
e	4.50	2.00

Solution

a. Identify the smallest time: job b (1.50 hours at work center B). Since the time is for B, schedule this job last.

b. The next smallest time is for job e (2.00 hours at B). Schedule job e next to last.

c. Identify the smallest remaining job time: job c (2.20 hours at center A). Since the time is in the A column, schedule job c first. At this point, we have:

c, —, —, e, b

d. The smallest time for remaining jobs is 2.50 hours for job a at center A. Schedule this job after job c. The one remaining job (job d) fills the remaining slot. Thus, we have:

c–a–d–e–b

Problem

5. For the previous problem, determine what effect splitting jobs c, d, e, and b in work center A would have on the idle time of work center B and on the throughput time. Assume that each job can be split into two equal parts.

Solution

We assume that the processing sequence remains unchanged and proceed on that basis. The solution from the previous problem is shown in the following chart. The next chart shows job processing at center B when splitting is used.

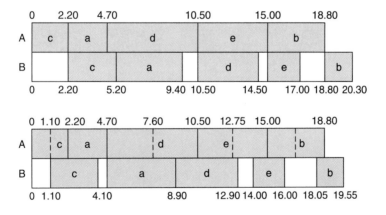

An inspection of these two figures reveals that throughput time has decreased from 20.30 hours to 19.55 hours. In addition, the original idle time was 5.6 hours, and after splitting certain jobs it was reduced to 4.85 hours. Hence, some improvement was achieved. Note, though, that for jobs toward the end of the sequence, processing times at B are generally less than at A. As a result, jobs such as e and b at B were scheduled so that they were *centered* around the finishing times of e and b, respectively, at A, in order to avoid having to break the jobs due to waiting for the remainder of the split job from A. Thus, the greatest advantage from job splitting generally comes from splitting earlier jobs when Johnson's rule is used for sequencing.

DISCUSSION AND REVIEW QUESTIONS

1. Why is scheduling fairly simple for continuous systems but fairly complex for job shops?
2. What are the main decision areas of job-shop scheduling?
3. What are Gantt charts? How are they used in scheduling? What advantages are associated with Gantt charts?
4. What are the basic assumptions of the assignment method of linear programming?
5. Briefly describe each of these priority rules:
   a. FCFS.
   b. SPT.
   c. DD.
   d. S/O.
   e. Rush.
6. Why are priority rules needed?
7. What problems do service systems present for scheduling the use of resources that are not generally found in manufacturing systems?
8. Doctors' and dentists' offices frequently schedule patients at regularly spaced intervals. What problems can this create? Can you suggest an alternative approach that might reduce these problems? Under what circumstances would regularly spaced appointments constitute a reasonable approach to patient scheduling?
9. How are scheduling and productivity related?
10. What factors would you take into account in deciding whether or not to split a job?

PROBLEMS

1. Use the assignment method to determine the best way to assign workers to jobs, given the following cost information. Compute total cost for your assignment plan.

		Job		
		A	B	C
Worker	1	5	8	6
	2	6	7	9
	3	4	5	3

2. Rework the previous problem treating the numbers in the table as profits instead of costs. Compute the total profit.
3. Assign trucks to delivery routes so that total costs are minimized, given the cost data shown. What are total costs?

		Route				
		A	B	C	D	E
	1	4	5	9	8	7
	2	6	4	8	3	5
Truck	3	7	3	10	4	6
	4	5	2	5	5	8
	5	6	5	3	4	9

4. Develop an assignment plan that will minimize processing costs, given the information shown, and interpret your answer.

	Machine		
	A	**B**	**C**
1	12	8	11
2	13	10	8
Job **3**	14	9	14
4	10	7	12

5. Use the assignment method to obtain a plan that will minimize the processing costs in the following table under these conditions:
   a. The combination 2-D is undesirable.
   b. The combinations 1–A and 2-D are undesirable.

		Machine			
	A	**B**	**C**	**D**	**E**
1	14	18	20	17	18
2	14	15	19	16	17
Job **3**	12	16	15	14	17
4	11	13	14	12	14
5	10	16	15	14	13

6. The following table contains information concerning four jobs that are awaiting processing at a work center.

Job	Job time (days)	Due date (days)
A	14	20
B	10	16
C	7	15
D	6	17

   a. Sequence the jobs using (1) FCFS, (2) SPT, (3) DD, and (4) CR. Assume the list is by order of arrival.
   b. For each of the methods in part *a,* determine (1) the average completion time, (2) the average lateness, and (3) the average number of jobs at the work center.
   c. Is one method superior to the others? Explain.

7. Using the information presented in the following table, identify the processing sequence that would result using (1) FCFS, (2) SPT, (3) DD, and (4) CR. For each method, determine (1) average job completion time, (2) average job lateness, and (3) average number of jobs in the system. Jobs are listed in order of arrival.
   Hint: First determine the total job time for each job by computing the total processing time for the job and then adding in the setup time. All times, and the due dates, are in hours.

Job	Processing time per unit	Units per job	Setup time	Due date
a	0.14	45	0.7	4
b	0.25	14	0.5	10
c	0.10	18	0.2	12
d	0.25	40	1.0	20
e	0.10	75	0.5	15

8. The following table shows orders to be processed at a machine shop as of 8 A.M. Monday. The jobs have different operations they must go through. Processing times are in days. Jobs are listed in order of arrival.

   a. Determine the processing sequence at the first work center using each of these rules: (1) FCFS, (2) S/O.

   b. Compute the effectiveness of each rule using each of these measures: (1) average completion time, (2) average number of jobs at the work center.

Job	Processing time (days)	Due date (days)	Remaining number of operations
A	8	20	2
B	10	18	4
C	5	25	5
D	11	17	3
E	9	35	4

9. A wholesale grocery distribution center uses a two-step process to fill orders. Tomorrow's work will consist of filling the seven orders shown. Determine a job sequence that will minimize the time required to fill the orders.

	Time (hours)	
Order	Step 1	Step 2
A	1.20	1.40
B	0.90	1.30
C	2.00	0.80
D	1.70	1.50
E	1.60	1.80
F	2.20	1.75
G	1.30	1.40

10. The times required to complete each of eight jobs on two machines are shown in the table that follows. Each job must follow the same sequence, beginning with machine A and moving to machine B.

   a. Determine a sequence that will minimize throughput time.

   b. Construct a chart of the resulting sequence, and find B's idle time.

   c. For the sequence determined in part a, how much would B's idle time be reduced by splitting the last two jobs in half?

Job	Time (hours) Machine A		Machine B	
a	16		5	⑦
b	3	②	13	
c	9		6	⑥
d	8		7	⑤
e	2	①	14	
f	12		4	⑧
g	18		14	③
h	20		11	④

11. Given the operation times provided:
    a. Develop a job sequence that minimizes idle time at the two work centers.
    b. Construct a chart of the activities at the two centers, and determine each one's idle time, assuming no other activities are involved.

	Job times (in minutes)					
	A	**B**	**C**	**D**	**E**	**F**
Center 1	20 ②	16 ①	43 ③	60	35	42
Center 2	27	30	51	12 ⑥	28 ④	24 ⑤

12. A shoe repair operation uses a two-step sequence that all jobs in a certain category follow. For the group of jobs listed,
    a. Find the sequence that will minimize total completion time.
    b. Determine the amount of idle time for workstation B.
    c. What jobs are candidates for splitting? Why? If they were split, how much of a reduction in idle time and throughput time would there be?

	Job times (in minutes)				
	a	**b**	**c**	**d**	**e**
Station A	27 ②	18 ①	70	26	15
Station B	45	33	30 ③	24 ④	10 ⑤

13. A foreman has determined processing times at a work center for a set of jobs and now wants to sequence them. Given the information shown, do the following:
    a. Determine the processing sequence using (1) FCFS, (2) SPT, (3) DD, and (4) CR. For each sequence, compute the average job lateness, the average completion time, and the average number of jobs at the work center. The list is in FCFS order.
    b. Using the results of your calculations in part a, show that the average completion time and the average number of jobs measures are equivalent for all four sequencing rules.

Job	Job time (days)	Due date	Operations remaining
a	4.5	10	2
b	6.0	17	4
c	5.2	12	3
d	1.6	27	5
e	2.8	18	3
f	3.3	19	1

14. Given the information in the following table, determine the processing sequence that would result using the S/O rule.

Job	Remaining processing time (days)	Due date	Remaining number of operations
a	5	8	2
b	6	5	4
c	9	10	4
d	7	12	3
e	8	10	2

15. Use the runout method to designate the order in which the following jobs are to be processed and interpret your results.

Job	Inventory (pounds)	Demand (pounds per day)
A	450	40
B	210	20
C	180	30
D	760	80

16. A department has a mixing machine that has limited capacity. Five products are mixed using this machine. The manager uses a variation of the runout formula to determine runout times. It involves dividing the sum of production capacity and inventory by the demand rate.

   Given the following information, develop a processing order for the products listed using the runout time method. Interpret your results.

Product	Production capacity (units)	Inventory (units)	Demand rate (units per week)
A	400	300	200
B	500	400	300
C	350	150	100
D	250	250	250
E	150	100	200

17. (Refer to the formula mentioned in the previous problem.) Given this information on production rates, inventory, and demand rates, determine processing order for the products listed using the runout method.

Product	Production rate (units/hour)	Inventory (units)	Demand rate (units/day)
A	40	200	70
B	50	150	80
C	30	100	80
D	20	100	90

Available production capacity is seven hours. Interpret your results.

18. Given this information on job times and due dates, determine the optimal processing sequence using (1) FCFS, (2) SPT, (3) DD, and (4) CR. For each method, find the average job completion time and the average job lateness.

Job	Job time (hours)	Due date (hours)
a	3.5	7
b	2.0	6
c	4.5	18
d	5.0	22
e	2.5	4
f	6.0	20

19. The Budd Gear Co. specializes in heat treating gears for many of the automobile companies. This morning at 8 A.M., when Budd's shop opened, there were five orders (listed in order of arrival) waiting to be processed.

Order	Order size (units)	Per unit time in heat treatment (minutes/unit)	Due date (min. from now)
A	16	4	160
B	6	12	200
C	10	3	180
D	8	10	190
E	4	1	220

a. If the due date rule is used, what sequence should be used?
b. What will be the average job lateness?
c. What will be the average number of jobs in the system?
d. Would the SPT rule produce better results in terms of lateness?

SELECTED BIBLIOGRAPHY

Baker, K. R. *Introduction to Sequencing and Scheduling*. New York: John Wiley, 1974.

Buffa, Elwood S., and Jeffery G. Miller. *Production-Inventory Systems: Planning and Control.* 3rd ed. Homewood, Ill.: Richard D. Irwin, 1979.

Chase, Richard, and Nicholas Aquilano. *Production and Operations Management*. 6th ed. Homewood, Ill.: Richard D. Irwin, 1992.

Fogarty, Donald W., and Thomas R. Hoffman. *Production and Inventory Management*. Cincinnati: South-Western Publishing, 1983.

McClain, John O., and L. Joseph Thomas. *Operations Management: Production of Goods and Services*. 2nd ed. Englewood Cliffs, N.J.: Prentice Hall, 1985.

Schonberger, Richard J. *Operations Management: Improving Customer Service*. 4th ed. Homewood, Ill.: Richard D. Irwin, 1991.

Tersine, Robert J. *Production/Operations Management: Concepts, Structure, and Analysis*. 2nd ed. New York: Elsevier-North Holland Publishing, 1985.

Vollman, Thomas E.; William L. Berry; and D. Clay Whybark. *Manufacturing Planning and Control Systems*. 2nd ed. Homewood, Ill.: Richard D. Irwin, 1988.

Maintenance

After completing this supplement, you should be able to:

1. Explain the importance of maintenance in production systems.
2. Describe the range of maintenance activities.
3. Discuss preventive maintenance and the key issues associated with it.
4. Discuss breakdown maintenance and the key issues associated with it.
5. State how the Pareto phenomenon pertains to maintenance decisions.

LEARNING OBJECTIVES

SUPPLEMENT OUTLINE

Maintaining the production capability of an organization is an important function in any production system. **Maintenance** encompasses all those activities that relate to keeping facilities and equipment in good working order, and making necessary repairs when breakdowns occur, so that the system can perform as intended.

Maintenance activities are often organized into two groups: (1) buildings and grounds, and (2) equipment maintenance. Buildings and grounds people are responsible for the appearance and functioning of buildings, parking lots, lawns, fences, and the like. Equipment maintenance people are responsible for maintaining machinery and equipment in good working condition and making all necessary repairs.

INTRODUCTION

The goal of maintenance is to keep the production system in good working order at minimal cost. Decision makers have two basic options with respect to maintenance. One option is *reactive:* It is to deal with breakdowns or other problems when they occur. This is referred to as **breakdown maintenance**. The other option is *proactive:* It is to reduce breakdowns through a program of lubrication, adjustment, cleaning, inspection, and replacement of worn parts. This is referred to as **preventive maintenance**.

Decision makers try to make a trade-off between these two basic options that will result in minimizing their combined cost. With no preventive maintenance, breakdown and repair costs would be tremendous. Furthermore, hidden costs such as the cost of wages while equipment is not in service, and lost production, must be factored in. So must the cost of injuries, or damage to other equipment or facilities, or to other units in production. However, beyond a certain point, preventive maintenance activities are wasteful.

As an example, if a person never had the oil changed in his or her car, never had it lubricated, and never had the brakes or tires inspected, but simply had repairs done when absolutely necessary, preventive costs would be negligible but repair costs could be quite high, considering the wide range of parts (engine, steering, transmission, tires, brakes, etc.) that could fail. In addition, property damage and injury costs might be incurred, plus there would be the uncertainty of when failure might occur (e.g., on the expressway during rush hour, or late at night). On the other hand, having the oil changed and the car lubricated every morning would obviously be excessive because automobiles are designed to perform for much longer periods without oil changes and lubrications. The best approach is to seek a balance between preventive maintenance and breakdown maintenance. The same concept applies to maintaining production systems: Strike a balance between prevention costs and breakdown costs. This concept is illustrated in Figure 15S–1.

The age and condition of facilities and equipment, the degree of technology involved, the type of production process, and similar factors enter into the decision of how much preventive maintenance is desirable. Thus, in the example of a new automobile, little preventive maintenance may be needed since there is little risk of breakdowns. As the car ages and becomes worn through use, the desirability of preventive maintenance increases because the risk of breakdowns increases. Thus, when tires and brakes begin to show signs of wear, they should be replaced before they fail; dents and scratches should be periodically taken care of before they begin to rust; and the car should be lubricated and have its oil changed after exposure to high levels of dust and dirt. Also, inspection and replacement of critical parts that

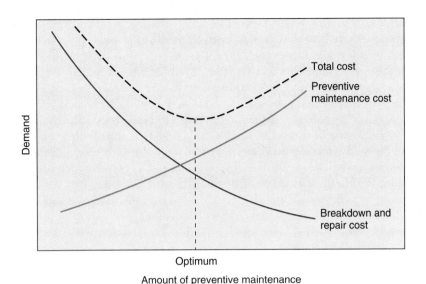

Total maintenance cost as a function of preventive maintenance effort

tend to fail suddenly should be performed before a road trip to avoid disruption of the trip and costly emergency repair bills.

PREVENTIVE MAINTENANCE

The goal of preventive maintenance (PM) is to reduce the incidence of breakdowns or failures in the plant or equipment to avoid the associated costs. Those costs can include loss of output; idle workers; schedule disruptions; injuries; damage to other equipment, products, or facilities; and repairs, which may involve maintaining inventories of spare parts, repair tools and equipment, and repair specialists.

Preventive maintenance is *periodic*. It can be scheduled according to the availability of maintenance personnel and to avoid interference with operating schedules. Preventive maintenance is generally scheduled using some combination of the following:

1. The result of planned inspections that reveal a need for maintenance.
2. According to the calendar (passage of time).
3. After a predetermined number of operating hours.

Ideally, preventive maintenance will be performed just prior to a breakdown or failure because this will result in the longest possible use of facilities or equipment without a breakdown. **Predictive maintenance** is an attempt to determine when to perform preventive maintenance activities. It is based on historical records and analysis of technical data to predict when a piece of equipment or part is about to fail. The better the predictions of failures are, the more effective preventive maintenance will be. A good preventive maintenance effort relies on complete records for each piece of equipment. Records must include such information as date of installation, operating hours, dates and types of maintenance, and dates and types of repairs.

Some Japanese companies have workers perform preventive maintenance on the machines they operate, rather than use separate maintenance personnel for that task. Called **total preventive maintenance**, this approach is consistent with JIT

Predictive maintenance
An attempt to determine when best to perform preventive maintenance activities.

Total preventive maintenance
JIT approach where workers perform preventive maintenance on the machines they operate.

systems and lean production, where employees are given greater responsibility for quality, productivity, and the general functioning of the system.

In the broadest sense, preventive maintenance extends back to the design and selection stage of equipment and facilities. Maintenance problems are sometimes *designed into* a system. For example, equipment may be designed in such a way that it needs frequent maintenance, or maintenance may be difficult to perform (e.g., the equipment has to be partially dismantled in order to perform routine maintenance). An extreme example of this was a certain car model that required the engine block to be lifted slightly in order to *change the spark plugs!* In such cases, it is very likely that maintenance will be performed less often than if its performance had been less demanding. In other instances, poor design can cause equipment to wear out at an early age, or experience a much higher than expected breakdown rate. *Consumer Reports,* for example, publishes breakdown data annually on automobiles. A check of that report indicates that some models tend to break down with a much higher frequency than other models.

One possible reason for maintenance problems being designed into a product is that other aspects of design have been accorded greater importance. Cost is one such aspect. Another is appearance; an attractive design may be chosen over a less attractive one that has higher ease of maintenance. Customers may contribute to this situation; the buying public probably has a greater tendency to select an attractive design over one that offers "ease of maintenance."

Obviously, durability and ease of maintenance can have long-term implications for preventive maintenance programs. Training of employees in proper operating procedures and in how to keep equipment in good operating order—and providing the incentive to do so—are also important. More and more, U.S. organizations are taking a cue from the Japanese, and transferring routine maintenance (cleaning, adjusting, inspecting) to the users of equipment, in an effort to give them a sense of responsibility and awareness of the equipment they use and to cut down on abuse and misuse of the equipment.

BREAKDOWN PROGRAMS

The risk of a breakdown can be greatly reduced by an effective preventive maintenance program. Nonetheless, occasional breakdowns do still occur. Consequently, even firms with good preventive practices have some need for breakdown programs. Of course, the organizations that rely less on preventive maintenance have an even greater need for effective ways of dealing with breakdowns.

Unlike preventive maintenance, breakdowns cannot be scheduled but must be dealt with on an irregular basis (i.e., as they occur). Among the major approaches used to deal with breakdowns are the following:

1. *Standby or backup equipment* that can be quickly pressed into service.
2. *Inventories of spare parts* that can be installed as needed, thereby avoiding lead times involved in ordering parts, and buffer inventories, so that other equipment will be less likely to be affected by short-term downtime of a particular piece of equipment.
3. *Operators* who are able to perform at least minor repairs on their equipment.
4. *Repair people* who are well trained and readily available to diagnose and correct problems with equipment.

The degree to which an organization pursues any or all of these approaches depends on how important a particular piece of equipment is to the overall production system. At one extreme is equipment that is the focal point of a system (printing presses for a newspaper; or vital operating parts of a car, such as brakes, steering, transmission, ignition, and engine). At the other extreme is equipment that is seldom used because it does not perform an important function in the system, and equipment for which substitutes are readily available.

The implication is clear: Breakdown programs are most effective when they take into account the degree of importance a piece of equipment has in the production system, and the ability of the system to do without it for a period of time. Note that the Pareto phenomenon exists in such situations: a relatively few pieces of equipment will be extremely important to the functioning of the system, thereby justifying considerable effort and/or expense; some will require moderate effort or expense; and some will justify little effort or expense.

REPLACEMENT

When breakdowns become frequent and/or costly, the question arises as to whether repairs should be made or the equipment replaced. Again, the manager is faced with a trade-off decision. Obviously, costs are an important consideration: What would be the cost of replacement versus what would be the cost of continued maintenance? This question can sometimes be difficult to resolve, especially if future breakdowns cannot be readily predicted. Historical records may help to project future experience. Another factor is technological change; newer equipment may have features that favor replacement over maintenance, whether it be preventive or breakdown maintenance. On the other hand, the removal of old equipment and the installation of new equipment may cause disruptions to the system, perhaps greater than the disruptions caused by breakdowns. Also, employees may have to be trained to operate the new equipment. Finally, forecasts of future demand for the use of the present or new equipment must be taken into account. Note that the demand for the replacement equipment might differ because of the different features it has. For instance, demand for output of the current equipment might be two years, while demand for output of the replacement equipment might be much longer than that.

These decisions can be fairly complex, involving a number of different factors. On the other hand, most of us are faced with a similar decision with our personal automobiles: When do I trade it in for a replacement?

Maintaining the productive capability of an organization is an important function. Maintenance includes all of the activities related to keeping facilities and equipment in good operating order and maintaining the appearance of buildings and grounds.

The goal of maintenance is to minimize the total cost of keeping the facilities and equipment in good working order. Maintenance decisions typically reflect a trade-off between preventive maintenance, which seeks to reduce the incidence of breakdowns and failures, and breakdown maintenance, which seeks to reduce the impact of breakdowns when they do occur.

SUMMARY

---

breakdown maintenance, 768	**preventive maintenance,** 768	**KEY TERMS**
maintenance, 768	**total preventive**	
predictive maintenance, 769	**maintenance,** 769	

DISCUSSION AND REVIEW QUESTIONS

1. What is the goal of a maintenance program.
2. List the costs generally associated with breakdown of equipment.
3. What are three different ways in which preventive maintenance is scheduled?
4. Explain the term *predictive maintenance* and the importance of good records.
5. List the major approaches organizations use to deal with breakdowns.
6. Explain how the Pareto phenomenon applies to:
   a. Preventive maintenance.
   b. Breakdown maintenance.
7. Discuss the key points of this supplement with respect to maintenance of an automobile.

SELECTED BIBLIOGRAPHY

Hall, Robert W. "Total Productive Maintenance—Essential to Maintain Progress." *Target* 3, no. 3 (Fall 1987), pp. 4–11.

Hora, Michael E. "The Unglamorous Game of Managing Maintenance." *Business Horizons* 30, no. 3 (May–June 1987), pp. 67–75.

Mann, Lawrence, Jr. *Maintenance Management.* Rev. ed. Lexington, Mass.: Lexington Books, 1983.

Nolden, Carol. "Predictive Maintenance: Route to Zero Unplanned Downtime." *Plant Engineering* 41, no. 4 (February 1987), pp. 38–43.

Wireman, Terry. *Preventive Maintenance.* Reston, Va.: Reston, 1984.

CHAPTER SIXTEEN

PROJECT MANAGEMENT

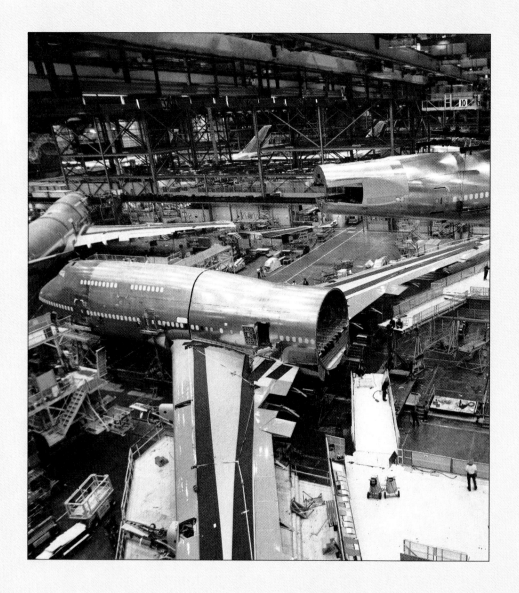

After completing this chapter, you should be able to:

1. Give a general description of PERT/CPM techniques.

2. Construct simple network diagrams.

3. List the kinds of information that a PERT or CPM analysis can provide.

4. Analyze networks with deterministic times.

5. Analyze networks with probabilistic times.

6. Describe activity "crashing" and solve typical problems.

7. Discuss the behavioral aspects of projects in terms of project personnel and the project manager.

Projects

Unique, one-time operations designed to accomplish a specific set of objectives in a limited time frame.

Managers typically oversee a variety of operations. Some of these involve routine, repetitive activities, but others involve nonroutine activities. Under the latter heading are **projects**: unique, one-time operations designed to accomplish a specific set of objectives in a limited time frame. Examples of projects include constructing a shopping complex, installing a new computer system, moving a firm to a new location, launching a space shuttle, and introducing a new product or service to the marketplace.

Most projects have certain elements in common. Often they involve considerable cost. They usually have a long time horizon, and they involve a large number of activities that must be carefully planned and coordinated in order for the project to be completed within time, cost, and performance guidelines. Goals must be established, and priorities must be set. Tasks must be identified, and time estimates must be made. Resource requirements must also be projected, and budgets must be prepared. Once underway, progress must be monitored to assure that project goals and objectives will be achieved.

The project approach enables an organization to focus attention and concentrate efforts on accomplishing a narrow set of objectives within a limited time and budget framework. This can produce significant benefits compared with other approaches that might be considered. Even so, projects present a manager with a host of problems that differ in many respects from those encountered with more routine types of activities. The problems of planning and coordinating project activities can be quite formidable for large projects, which typically have hundreds or even thousands of activities that must be carefully planned and monitored if a project is to proceed according to schedule and at a reasonable cost.

The chapter introduces the basic concept of project management. It begins with a brief discussion of some behavioral aspects of project management, along with some of the difficulties project managers are apt to encounter. The main portion of the chapter is devoted to a description of graphical and computational methods that are used for planning and scheduling projects.

BEHAVIORAL ASPECTS OF PROJECT MANAGEMENT

Project management differs from management of more traditional activities mainly because of its limited time framework, which gives rise to a host of rather unique problems. This section describes more fully the nature of projects and their behavioral implications. We will pay special attention to the role of the project manager.

THE NATURE OF PROJECTS

Projects go through a series of stages—a life cycle—which include project planning, execution of major activities, and project phaseout. During this life cycle, a variety of skill requirements are involved. An analogous set of circumstances exists in constructing a house. Initially a site must be found, and plans must be drawn up and approved by the owner and possibly a town building commission or other regulatory agency. Then a succession of personnel become involved, starting with those doing the site preparation, then laying the foundation, erecting the frame, roofing, constructing exterior walls, wiring and plumbing, installing kitchen and bathroom fixtures and appliances, interior finishing work, and painting and carpeting work. Similar sequences are found on large construction projects, in R&D work, in the aerospace industry, and in virtually every other instance where projects are being carried out.

In effect, projects bring together personnel with diverse knowledge and skills, most of whom remain associated with the project for less than its full life. Some personnel go from project to project as their contributions become needed, and others are "on loan," either on a full-time or part-time basis, from their regular jobs. The latter is usually the case when a special project exists within the framework of a more traditional organization. Certain kinds of organizations tend to be involved with projects on a regular basis; examples include consulting firms, architects, writers and publishers, and construction firms. In fact, it is not uncommon to have organizations or departments spending virtually all of their time involved with projects.

Some organizations use a *matrix organization* that allows them to integrate the activities of a variety of specialists within a functional framework. For instance, they have certain people who prepare proposals, others who concentrate exclusively on engineering, others who devote their efforts to marketing, and so on.

THE PROJECT MANAGER

The central figure in a project is the project manager. He or she bears the ultimate responsibility for the success or failure of the project. The role of the project manager is one of an organizer—a person who is capable of working through others to accomplish the objectives of the project.

The job of project manager can be both difficult and rewarding. The manager must coordinate and motivate people who sometimes owe their allegiance to other managers in their functional areas. In addition, the people who work on a project frequently possess specialized knowledge and skills that the project manager does not have. Nevertheless, the manager is expected to guide and evaluate their efforts. Project managers must often function in an environment that is beset with uncertainties. Even so, budgets and time constraints are usually imposed, which can create additional pressures on project personnel. Finally, the project manager may not have the authority he or she needs to accomplish all the objectives of the project. Instead, the manager must sometimes rely on persuasion and the cooperation of others to realize project goals.

The rewards of the job of project manager come from the challenges of the job, the benefits of being associated with a successful project as well as the personal satisfaction of seeing it through to its conclusion.

THE PROS AND CONS OF WORKING ON PROJECTS

People are selected to work on special projects because the knowledge or abilities they possess are needed. In some instances, however, their supervisors may be reluctant to allow them to interrupt their regular jobs, even on a part-time basis, because it may require training a new person to do a job that will be temporary. Moreover, managers don't want to lose the output of good workers. The workers themselves are not always eager to participate in projects because it may mean working for two bosses (which can lead to problems because it violates the unity-of-command principle), and may cause disruption of friendships and daily routines, and the risk of being replaced on the current job. Furthermore, there may be fear of being associated with an unsuccessful project for the adverse effect it might have on career advancement. In too many instances, when a project is phased out and the project team disbanded, team members tend to drift away from the organization for lack of a new project and the difficulty of returning to former jobs. This tendency is more pronounced after involvement with lengthy projects and is less likely to occur when a team member works on a part-time basis, although that approach has its own drawbacks in terms of divided loyalty and dual bosses.

In spite of the potential risks of being involved in a project, there are certain potential rewards that attract people to them. One is the dynamic environment that surrounds a project, often a marked contrast to the more staid environment in which some may feel trapped. Some individuals seem to thrive in more dynamic environments; they welcome the challenge of working under pressure and solving new problems. Then, too, projects may present opportunities to meet new people and to increase future job opportunities, especially if the project is at all successful. And being associated with a project can be a source of status among fellow workers. Finally, working on projects frequently inspires a team spirit, increasing morale and motivation to achieve successful completion of project goals.

PLANNING AND SCHEDULING WITH GANTT CHARTS

The Gantt chart is a popular tool for planning and scheduling *simple* projects. It enables a manager to initially schedule project activities and then to monitor progress over time by comparing planned progress to actual progress. A Gantt chart for a bank's plan to establish a new direct marketing department is illustrated in Figure 16–1. To prepare the chart, the vice president who was in charge of the project had to first identify the major activities that would be required. Next, time estimates for each activity were made, and the sequence of activities was determined. Once completed, the chart indicated which activities were to occur, their planned dura-

Figure 16-1

Gantt chart for bank example

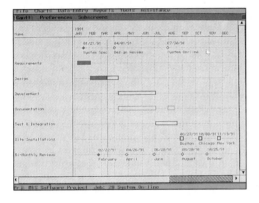

Software programs can assist in project management. Here are examples of electronic Gantt charts from Microsoft Project, SAS, and SCITOR.

tion, and when they were to occur. Then, as the project progressed, the manager was able to see which activities were ahead of schedule and which activities were delaying the project. This enabled the manager to direct attention where it was needed most to speed up the project in order to finish on schedule.

The obvious advantage of a Gantt chart is its simplicity, and this accounts for its popularity. However, Gantt charts fail to reveal certain relationships among activities that can be crucial to effective project management. For instance, if one of the early activities in a project suffers a delay, it would be important for the manager to be able to easily determine which later activities would have to be delayed as a result. Conversely, some activities may safely be delayed without affecting the overall project schedule. Again, a Gantt chart does not directly reveal this. Gantt charts are most useful for simple projects, say, where activities are simultaneous or where a string of sequential activities is involved. And on more complex projects, Gantt charts can be useful for initial project planning, which then gives way to the use of *networks,* the subject of the following sections.

PERT AND CPM

PERT (program evaluation and review technique) and **CPM** (critical path method) are two of the most widely used techniques for planning and coordinating large-scale projects. By using PERT or CPM, managers are able to obtain:

1. A graphical display of project activities.
2. An estimate of how long the project will take.

PERT

Program evaluation and review technique, for planning and coordinating large projects.

CPM

Critical path method, for planning and coordinating large projects.

3. An indication of which activities are the most critical to timely project completion.

4. An indication of how long any activity can be delayed without lengthening the project.

PERT and CPM were developed independently during the late 1950s. PERT evolved through the joint efforts of Lockheed Aircraft, the U.S. Navy Special Projects Office, and the consulting firm of Booz, Allen & Hamilton in an effort to speed up the Polaris missile project. At the time, there was considerable concern on the part of the U.S. government that the Soviet Union might be gaining nuclear superiority over the United States, and early completion of the project was given top priority by the Department of Defense. The project was a huge one, with over 3,000 contractors involved, and many thousands of activities. The use of PERT was quite successful: PERT is generally credited for shaving two years off the length of the project. Partly for that reason, PERT or some similar technique is now required on all large government projects.

CPM was developed by J. E. Kelly of the Remington Rand Corporation and M. R. Walker of Du Pont to plan and coordinate maintenance projects in chemical plants.

Although the two techniques were developed independently, they have a great deal in common. Moreover, many of the initial differences between them have disappeared as users borrowed certain features from one technique for use with the other. For example, PERT originally stressed probabilistic activity time estimates, because the environment in which it developed was typified by high uncertainty. In contrast, the tasks for which CPM was developed were much less uncertain, so CPM originally made no provision for variable time estimates. At present, either technique can be used with deterministic or probabilistic times. Other initial differences concerned the mechanical aspects of developing project networks. However, from a conceptual standpoint, most of these differences were relatively minor. To avoid confusion, we will not delve into the differences here. For practical purposes, the two techniques are the same; the comments and procedures described will apply to CPM analysis as well as to PERT analysis of projects.

THE NETWORK DIAGRAM

Network (precedence) diagram

Diagram of project activities that shows the sequential relationships by the use of arrows and nodes.

One of the main features of PERT and related techniques is their use of a **network** or **precedence diagram** to depict major project activities and their sequential relationships. Recall the bank example that used a Gantt chart (see Figure 16–1). A network diagram for that same problem is shown in Figure 16–2. The diagram is composed of a number of arrows and nodes. The arrows represent the project activities. Note how much clearer the sequential relationship of activities is with a network chart than with a Gantt chart. For instance, it is apparent that ordering the furniture and remodeling both require that a location for the office has been identified. Likewise, interviewing must precede training. However, interviewing and training can take place independently of activities associated with locating a facility, remodeling, and so on. Hence, a network diagram is generally the preferred approach for visual portrayal of project activities.

You should know that there are two slightly different conventions for constructing these network diagrams. Under one convention, the *arrows* are used to designate activities; under the other convention, the *nodes* are used to designate

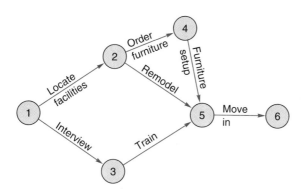

Figure 16–2

A simple project network diagram

activities. These conventions are referred to as **activity-on-arrow (A-O-A)** and **activity-on-node (A-O-N)**. To avoid confusion, the discussion here will focus primarily on the activity-on-arrow convention. Then, later in the chapter, a comparison of the two conventions will be given. For now, we shall use the arrows for activities. **Activities** consume resources and/or *time*. The nodes in the A-O-A approach represent the starting and finishing of activities, which are called **events**. Events are points in time. Unlike activities, they do not consume either resources or time.

Activities can be referred to in either of two ways. One is by their endpoints (e.g., activity 2-4) and the other is by a letter assigned to an arrow (e.g., activity c). Both methods are illustrated in this chapter.

The network diagram describes sequential relationships among major activities on a project. For instance, activity 2-4 cannot be started, according to the network, until activity 1-2 has been completed. A **path** is a sequence of activities that leads from the starting node to the finishing node. Thus, the sequence 1-2-4-5-6 is a path. There are two other paths in this network: 1-2-5-6 and 1-3-5-6. The length (of time) of any path can be determined by summing the expected times of the activities on that path. The path with the longest time is of particular interest because it governs project completion time. In other words, expected project duration equals the expected time of the longest path. Moreover, if there are any delays along the longest path, there will be corresponding delays in project completion time. Conversely, attempts to shorten project completion must focus on the longest sequence of activities. Because of its influence on project completion time, the longest path is the **critical path**, and its activities are referred to as **critical activities**.

Paths that are shorter than the critical path can experience some delays and still not affect the overall project completion time as long as the ultimate path time does not exceed the length of the critical path. The allowable slippage for any path is called the path **slack**, and it reflects the difference between the length of a given path and the length of the critical path. The critical path, then, has zero slack time.

NETWORK CONVENTIONS

Developing and interpreting network diagrams requires some familiarity with networking conventions. Although there are many that could be mentioned, the discussion here will concentrate on some of the most basic, and most common, features of network diagrams. This will provide sufficient background for understanding the basic concepts associated with precedence diagrams and allow you to solve typical problems.

One of the main features of a precedence diagram is that it reveals which activities must be performed in *sequence* (i.e., there is a precedence requirement) and which can be performed independently of each other. For example, in the following diagram, activity *a* must be completed before activity *b* can begin, and activity *b* must be completed before activity *c* can begin.

If the diagram had looked like the one following, both activities *a* and *b* would have to be completed before activity *c* could begin, but *a* and *b* could be performed at the same time; performance of *a* is independent of performance of *b*.

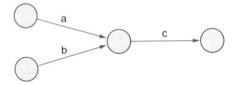

If activity *a* must precede *b* and *c*, the appropriate network would look like this:

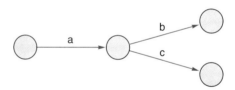

When multiple activities enter a node, this implies that all those activities must be completed before any activities that are to begin at that node can start. Hence, in this next diagram, activities *a* and *b* must both be finished before either activity *c* or activity *d* can start.

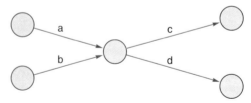

When two activities both have the same beginning and ending nodes, a *dummy* node and activity is used to preserve the separate identity of each activity. In the diagram below, activities *a* and *b* must be completed before activity *c* can be started.

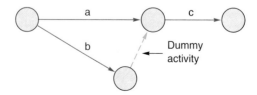

Separate identities are particularly important for computer analysis, because most computer programs identify activities by their endpoints; activities with the same endpoints could not be distinguished from each other, although they might have quite different expected times.

There are actually a number of different uses of dummy activities. Another common use is depicted below:

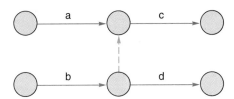

In this situation, activities *a* and *b* must both precede activity *c*. However, *d*'s start is dependent only on completion of activity *b*, and *not* on activity *a*'s completion.

The primary function of dummy activities is to clarify relationships. As far as time is concerned, a dummy activity has an activity time equal to zero.

For reference purposes, nodes are numbered typically from left to right:

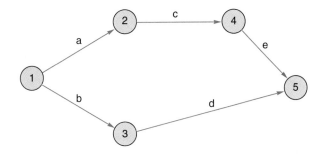

Starting and ending arrows are sometimes used during development of a network for increased clarity.

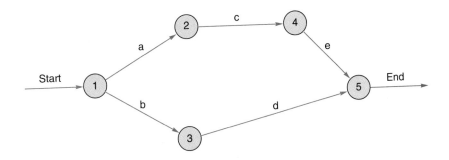

DETERMINISTIC TIME ESTIMATES

The main determinant of the way PERT and CPM networks are analyzed and interpreted is whether activity time estimates are *probabilistic* or *deterministic*. If time estimates can be made with a high degree of confidence that actual times will not differ significantly, we say the estimates are **deterministic**. On the other hand, if estimated times are subject to variation, we say the estimates are **probabilistic**.

Deterministic
Time estimates that are fairly certain.

Probabilistic
Estimates of times that are subject to variation.

Probabilistic time estimates must include an indication of the extent of probable variation.

This section describes analysis of networks with deterministic time estimates. A later section deals with probabilistic times.

One of the best ways to gain an understanding of the nature of network analysis is to consider a simple example.

Example 1

Given the information provided in the accompanying network diagram, determine each of the following:

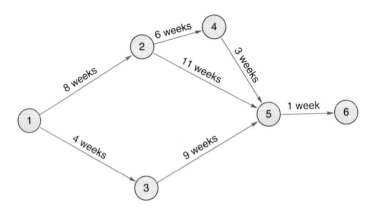

a.   The length of each path.
b.   The critical path.
c.   The expected length of the project.
d.   Amount of slack time for each path.

Solution

a.   As shown in the following table, the path lengths are 18 weeks, 20 weeks, and 14 weeks.
b.   The longest path (20 weeks) is 1–2–5–6, so it is the critical path.
c.   The expected length of the project is equal to the length of the critical path (i.e., 20 weeks).
d.   We find the slack for each path by subtracting its length from the length of the critical path, as shown in the last column of the table. (*Note:* It is sometimes desirable to know the slack time associated with activities. The next section describes a method for obtaining those slack times.)

Path	Length (weeks)	Slack
1–2–4–5–6	$8 + 6 + 3 + 1 = 18$	$20 - 18 = 2$
1–2–5–6	$8 + 11 + 1 = 20\star$	$20 - 20 = 0$
1–3–5–6	$4 + 9 + 1 = 14$	$20 - 14 = 6$

$\star$ Critical path length.

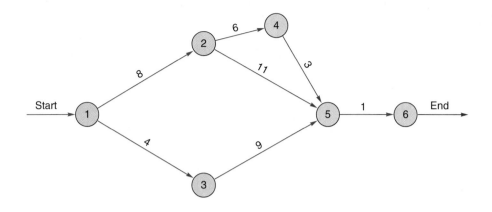

Figure 16–3

A COMPUTING ALGORITHM

Many real-life project networks are much larger than the simple network illustrated in the preceding example; they often contain hundreds or even thousands of activities. Because the necessary computations can become exceedingly complex and time-consuming, large networks are generally analyzed by computer programs rather than manually. The intuitive approach just demonstrated does not lend itself to computerization because, in many instances, path sequences are not readily apparent. Instead, an algorithm is used to develop four pieces of information about the network activities:

ES, the earliest time activity can start, assuming all preceding activities start as early as possible.

EF, the earliest time the activity can finish.

LS, the latest time the activity can start and not delay the project.

LF, the latest time the activity can finish and not delay the project.

Once these values have been determined, they can be used to find:

1. Expected project duration.
2. Slack time.
3. Which activities are on the critical path.

The three examples that follow illustrate how these values are computed using the precedence diagram of Example 1, which is repeated here for convenient reference.

COMPUTING ES AND EF TIMES

Computation of earliest starting and finishing times is aided by two simple rules:

1. The earliest finish time for any activity is equal to its earliest start time plus its expected duration, t:

   $$EF = ES + t$$

2. For nodes with one entering arrow, ES for activities at such nodes is equal to EF of the entering arrow. For nodes with multiple entering arrows, ES for activities leaving such nodes equals the largest EF of the entering arrow.

Example 2

▋

Compute the earliest starting time and earliest finishing time for each activity in the diagram shown in Figure 16–3.

Solution

Begin by placing brackets at the two ends of each starting activity:

For each activity, the earliest starting time, ES, and the earliest finishing time, EF, we determine and place in the brackets in this manner:

Do this for all activities, beginning at the left side of the precedence diagram and moving to the right side.

Once ES has been determined for an activity, EF can be found by adding the activity time, t, to ES: $ES + t = EF$.

Use an ES of 0 for all starting activities. Thus, here activities 1-2 and 1-3 are assigned ES values of 0. This permits computation of the EF for each of these activities:

$$EF_{1-2} = 0 + 8 = 8 \qquad \text{and} \qquad EF_{1-3} = 0 + 4 = 4$$

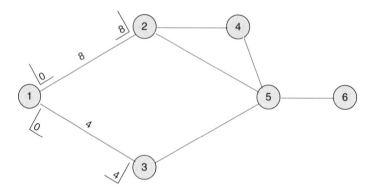

The EF time for an activity becomes the ES time for the next activity to follow it in the diagram. Hence, because activity 1-2 has an EF time of 8, both activities 2-4 and 2-5 have ES times of 8. Similarly, activity 3-5 has an ES time of 4.

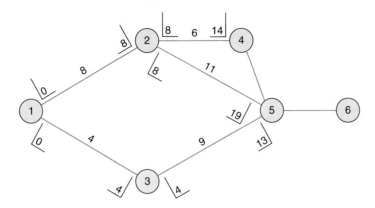

This permits calculation of the EF times for these activities: $EF_{2-4} = 8 + 6 = 14$; $EF_{2-5} = 8 + 11 = 19$; and $EF_{3-5} = 4 + 9 = 13$.

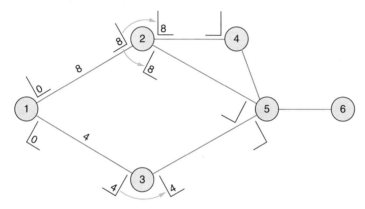

The ES for activity 4-5 is the EF time of activity 2-4, which is 14. Using this figure, we find the EF for activity 4-5 is 17: $EF_{4-5} = 14 + 3 = 17$.

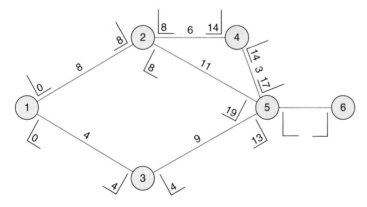

In order to determine the ES for activity 5-6, we must realize that activity 5-6 cannot start until *every* activity that precedes it is finished. Therefore, the *largest* of the EF times for the three activities that precede activity 5-6 determines ES_{5-6}. Hence, the ES for activity 5-6 is 19.

(continued)

Example 2

(concluded)

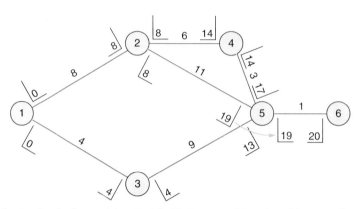

Then the EF for the last activity, 5-6, is 20: $EF_{5-6} = 19 + 1 = 20$. Note that the latest EF is the project duration. Thus, the expected length of the project is 20 weeks.

COMPUTING LS AND LF TIMES

Computation of the latest starting and finishing times is aided by the use of two rules:

1. The latest starting time for each activity is equal to its latest finishing time minus its expected duration:

$$LS = LF - t \qquad\qquad (16-2)$$

2. For nodes with one leaving arrow, LF for arrows entering that node equals the LS of the leaving arrow. For nodes with multiple leaving arrows, LF for arrows entering that node equals the smallest LS of leaving arrows.

Finding ES and EF times involves a "forward pass" through the network; finding LS and LF times involves a "backward pass" through the network. Hence, we must begin with the EF of the last activity and use that time as the LF for the last activity. Then we obtain the LS for the last activity by subtracting its expected duration from its LF.

Example 3

Compute the latest finishing and starting times for the precedence diagram developed in Example 2.

Solution

The LS and LF times must be added to the brackets on the diagram.

Begin by setting the LF time of the last activity equal to the EF of that activity. Thus,

$$LF_{5-6} = EF_{5-6} = 20 \text{ weeks}$$

Obtain the LS time for activity 5-6 by subtracting the activity time, t, from the LF time:

$$LS_{5-6} = LF_{5-6} - t = 20 - 1 = 19.$$

Mark these values on the diagram:

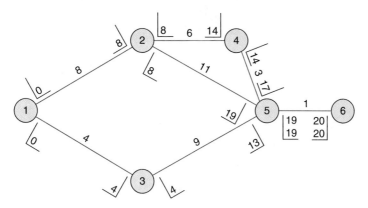

The ES time of 19 for activity 5-6 now becomes the LF time for each of the activities that precede activity 5-6. This permits determination of the LS times for each of those activities: Subtract the activity time from the LF to obtain the LS time for the activity. The LS time for activity 3-5 is $19 - 9 = 10$.

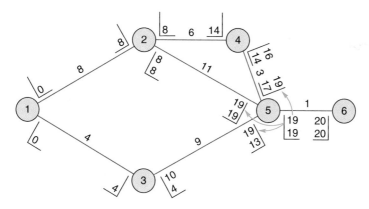

Next, the LS for activity 4-5, which is 16, becomes the LF for activity 2-4, and the LS for activity 3-5, which is 10, becomes the LF for activity 1-3. And using these values, we find the LS for each of these activities by subtracting the activity time from the LF time.

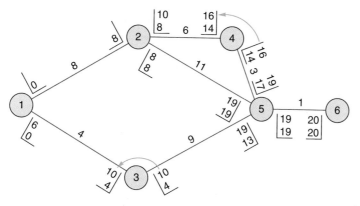

(continued)

Example 3

(concluded)

The LF for activity 1-2 is the *smallest* of the two LS times of the activities that 1-2 precedes. Hence, the LF time for activity 1-2 is 8. The reason we use the smallest time is that activity 1-2 must finish at a time that permits all following activities to start no later than their LS times.

Once the LF time of activity 1-2 has been determined, find its LS time by subtracting the activity time of 8 from the LF time of 8. Hence, the LS time is 0.

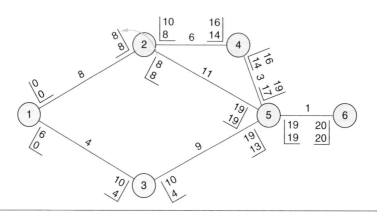

Computing Slack Times

The slack time can be computed in either of two ways:

$$\text{Slack} = \text{LS} - \text{ES} \quad \text{or} \quad \text{LF} - \text{EF} \tag{16–3}$$

Example 4

Compute slack times for the precedence diagram of Figure 16–3.

Solution

We have the opinion of using either the starting times or the finishing times. Suppose we choose the starting times. Using ES times computed in Example 2 and LS times computed in Example 3, slack times are:

Activity	LS	ES	(LS − ES) Slack
1-2............	0	0	0
1-3............	6	0	6
2-4............	10	8	2
2-5............	8	8	0
3-5............	10	4	6
4-5............	16	14	2
5-6............	19	19	0

The critical path using this computing algorithm is denoted by activities with zero slack time. Thus, the table in the preceding example indicates that activities 1-2, 2-5, and 5-6 are all critical activities, which agrees with the results of the intuitive approach demonstrated in Example 1.

		STARTING SCHEDULE				
		EARLY		LATE		
ACTIVITY	TIME	ES	EF	LS	LF	SLACK
1-2	8.00	0.00	8.00	0.00	8.00	0.00
1-3	4.00	0.00	4.00	6.00	10.00	6.00
2-4	6.00	8.00	14.00	10.00	16.00	2.00
2-5	11.00	8.00	19.00	8.00	19.00	0.00
3-5	9.00	4.00	13.00	10.00	19.00	6.00
4-5	3.00	14.00	17.00	16.00	19.00	2.00
5-6	1.00	19.00	20.00	19.00	20.00	0.00

Table 16-1

Computer printout

THE CRITICAL PATH SEQUENCE IS:

SNODE	FNODE	TIME
1	2	8.00
2	5	11.00
5	6	1.00
		20.00

Knowledge of slack times provides managers with greater detail for planning allocation of scarce resources and for directing control efforts toward those activities that might be most susceptible to delaying the project than the more simplistic intuitive approach does. In this regard, it is important to recognize that the activity slack times are based on the assumption that all of the activities on the same path will be started as early as possible and not exceed their expected times. Furthermore, if two activities are both on the same path (e.g., activities 2-4 and 4-5 in the preceding example) and have the same slack (e.g., two weeks), this will be the *total* slack *available to both*. In essence, the activities have *shared slack*. Hence, if the first activity uses all of the slack, there will be zero slack for the other activity, and that much less slack for all following activities on that same path.

As noted above, this algorithm lends itself to computerization. A computer printout for this problem would appear something like the one shown in Table 16-1.

PROBABILISTIC TIME ESTIMATES

The preceding discussion assumed that activity times were known and not subject to variation. While that assumption is appropriate in some situations, there are many others where it is not. Consequently, those situations require a probabilistic approach.

The probabilistic approach involves *three* time estimates for each activity instead of one:

1. **Optimistic time**: The length of time required under optimum conditions; represented by the letter *o*.
2. **Pessimistic time**: The length of time that will be required under the worst conditions; represented by the letter *p*.

Optimistic time

The length of time required under optimum conditions.

Pessimistic time

The length of time required under the worst conditions.

3.   **Most likely time**: The most probable amount of time that will be required; represented by the letter m.

These time estimates should be made by managers or others with knowledge about the project.

The **beta distribution** is generally used to describe the inherent variability in time estimates (see Figure 16–4). Although there is no real theoretical justification for using the beta distribution, it has certain features that make it attractive in practice: The distribution can be symmetrical or skewed to either the right or the left according to the nature of a particular activity; the mean and variance of the distribution can be readily obtained from the three time estimates listed above; and the distribution is unimodal with a high concentration of probability surrounding the most likely time estimate.

Of special interest in network analysis are the average or expected time for each activity t_e, and the variance of each activity time, σ_i^2. The expected time is computed as a weighted average of the three time estimates.

$$t_e = \frac{o + 4m + p}{6} \tag{16–4}$$

The standard deviation of each activity's time is estimated as one sixth of the difference between the pessimistic and optimistic time estimates. (Analogously, essentially all of the area under a normal distribution lies within three standard deviations of the mean, which is a range of six standard deviations.) The variance is found by squaring the standard deviation. Thus,

$$\sigma^2 = \left[\frac{(p - o)}{6} \right]^2 \quad \text{or} \quad \frac{(p - o)^2}{36} \tag{16–5}$$

The size of the variance reflects the degree of uncertainty associated with an activity's time: the larger the variance, the greater the uncertainty. Hence, an activity with a variance of 16 would have more uncertainty as to its eventual duration than one with a variance of 6.

It is also desirable to compute the standard deviation of the expected time for *each path*. This can be accomplished by summing the variances of the activities on a path and then taking the square root of that number. That is,

$$\sigma_{\text{path}} = \sqrt{\Sigma(\text{variances of activities on path})} \tag{16–6}$$

Figure 16–4

A beta distribution is used
to describe probabilistic
time estimates

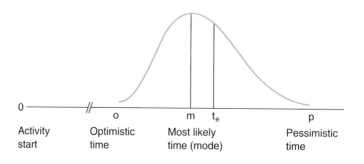

The network diagram for a project is shown in the accompanying figure, with three time estimates for each activity. Activity times are in months. Do the following:

Example 5

a. Compute the expected time for each activity and the expected duration for each path.
b. Identify the critical path.
c. Compute the variance of each activity and the variance of each path.

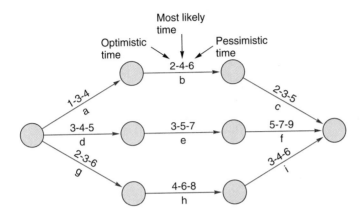

Solution

a.

Path	Activity	Times o	m	p	$t_e = \dfrac{o + 4m + p}{6}$	Path total
a–b–c	a	1	3	4	2.83 ⎫	
	b	2	4	6	4.00 ⎬	10.00
	c	2	3	5	3.17 ⎭	
d–e–f	d	3	4	5	4.00 ⎫	
	e	3	5	7	5.00 ⎬	16.00
	f	5	7	9	7.00 ⎭	
g–h–i	g	2	3	6	3.33 ⎫	
	h	4	6	8	6.00 ⎬	13.50
	i	3	4	6	4.17 ⎭	

b. The path that has the longest expected duration is the critical path. Since path d–e–f has the largest path total, it is the critical path.

Path	Activity	Times o	m	p	$\sigma^2_{act.} = \dfrac{(p - o)^2}{36}$	σ^2_{path}	σ_{path}
a–b–c	a	1	3	4	$(4 - 1)^2/36 = 9/36$ ⎫		
	b	2	4	6	$(6 - 2)^2/36 = 16/36$ ⎬	$34/36 = 0.944$	0.97
	c	2	3	5	$(5 - 2)^2/36 = 9/36$ ⎭		

(continued)

Example 5

(concluded)

Path	Activity	Times o	m	p	$\sigma^2_{act.} = \dfrac{(p-o)^2}{36}$	σ^2_{path}	σ_{path}
d-e-f	d	3	4	5	$(5-3)^2/36 = 4/36$	36/36 = 1.00	1.00
	e	3	5	7	$(7-3)^2/36 = 16/36$		
	f	5	7	9	$(9-5)^2/36 = 16/36$		
g-h-i	g	2	3	6	$(6-2)^2/36 = 16/36$	41/36 = 1.139	1.07
	h	4	6	8	$(8-4)^2/36 = 16/36$		
	i	3	4	6	$(6-3)^2/36 = 9/36$		

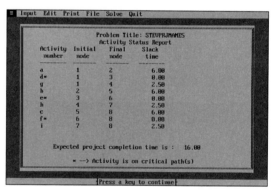

Lotfi and Pegels DSS-POM (2.1c) data entry for Example 5. The next screen is the solution for part (c). The third screen shows the earliest and latest times for each event and the slack times. The final screen shows the critical path.

Knowledge of the expected path times and their standard deviation enables a manager to compute probabilistic estimates of the project completion time, such as these:

The probability that the project will be completed within 17 months of its start is about 84 percent.

The probability that the project will take longer than 18 months is approximately 2 percent.

Statements of this sort are based on the assumption that the duration time of a path is a random variable that is normally distributed around the expected path time. The rationale for a normal distribution is that we are summing activity times (random variables), and sums of random variables tend to be normally distributed when the number of items being summed is large. However, even when the number of items is relatively small, the normal distribution provides a reasonable approximation to the actual distribution.

The next example illustrates the use of a normal distribution to determine the probabilities of various completion times. Before we look at that example, it is important to make note of two points. One relates to **independence**. It is assumed that path duration times are independent of each other. In essence, this requires two things: Activity times are independent of each other, and each activity is only on one path. For activity times to be independent, the time for one must not be a function of another's time; if two activities were always early or late together, they would not be considered independent. The assumption of independent *paths* is usually considered to be met if only a *few* activities in a large project are on multiple paths. Even then, common sense should govern the decision of whether the independence assumption is justified.

A second important point is that a project is not completed until all of its activities have been completed, not just those on the critical path. It sometimes happens that another path requires more time than the critical path, in which case the project runs longer than expected. Hence, it can be risky to focus exclusively on the critical path. Instead, one must consider the possibility that at least one other path will delay timely project completion. This requires determining the probability that *all* paths will finish by a specified time. To do that, find the probability that each path will finish by the specified time, and multiply the resulting probabilities. Note that only paths with expected times that are relatively close to that of the critical path need to be considered, since it would be highly unlikely that a path with a much shorter expected time would exceed the critical path's time. A simple rule of thumb is to treat the probability of timely completion of a path as 100 percent if its expected time plus 2.5 of *its* standard deviation is less than the specified time. These concepts are illustrated in the following example.

Independence

Assumption that path duration times are independent of each other; requiring that activity times be independent, and that each activity is on only one path.

Using the information from the preceding example, answer the following questions:

a. Can the paths be considered independent? Why?

b. What is the probability that the project can be completed within 17 months of its start?

c. What is the probability that the project will be completed within 15 months of its start?

d. What is the probability that the project will not be completed within 15 months of its start?

Solution

a. Yes, the paths can be considered independent since no activity is on more than one path and we have no information that would suggest that any activity times are interrelated.

Example 6

(continued)

Example 6

(continued)

b. To answer questions of this nature, we must take into account the degree to which the path distributions "overlap" the specified completion time. This concept is illustrated in the accompanying figure, which shows the three path distributions, each centered on that path's expected duration, and the specified completion time of 17 months.

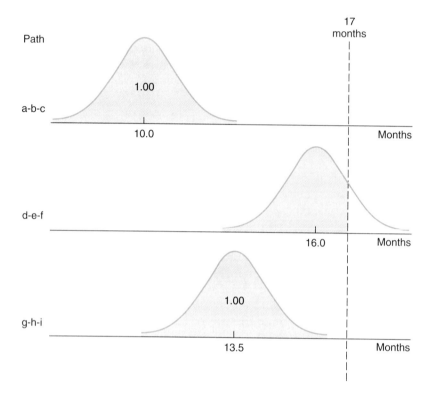

The shaded portion of each distribution corresponds to the probability that the part will be completed within the specified time. Observe that paths a-b-c and g-h-i are well enough to the left of the specified time that it is highly likely that both will be finished by month 17, but that the critical path overlaps the specified completion time. Hence, we need consider only the distribution of path d-e-f in assessing the probability of completion by month 17. To do so, we must first compute the value of z using the relationship

$$z = \frac{\text{Specified time} - \text{Expected time}}{\text{Path standard deviation}} \qquad (16\text{--}7)$$

In this instance, we find

$$z = \frac{17 - 16}{1.00} = +1.00$$

Turning to Appendix B, Table B with $z = +1.00$, we see that the area under the curve to the left of z is .8413. Hence, the probability of the project finishing within 17 months of its start is 84.13 percent.

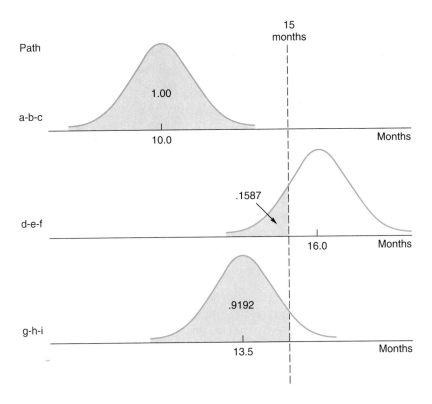

c. This question illustrates how to handle a problem in which more than one of the distributions overlap the specified time. Note in the accompanying figure that paths d-e-f and g-h-i overlap month 15. This means that both paths have the potential for delaying the project beyond the 15 months.

   Although the figure is useful in expressing the concept of overlapping paths, we need a more rigorous approach to determine which paths to consider and what each path's probability of completion is. This requires computing a value of z using Formula 16–7 for each path. Then, any path with a z of more than $+2.50$ is treated as having a completion probability of 100 percent; the others will be used to determine the *joint* probability of all finishing by the specified time. For this problem, with a specified time of 15 months, the z values are:

Path	$z = \dfrac{15 - \text{Expected path duration}}{\text{Path standard deviation}}$	Probability of completion in 15 months
a-b-c	$\dfrac{15 - 10.00}{0.97} = +5.15$	1.00
d-e-f	$\dfrac{15 - 16.00}{1.00} = -1.00$	.1587
g-h-i	$\dfrac{15 - 13.50}{1.07} = +1.40$	.9192

From Appendix B, Table B, the area to the *left* of $z = -1.00$ is .1587, and the area to the *left* of $z = +1.40$ is .9192. The joint probability of all finishing before month 15 is the product of their probabilities: $1.00(.1587)(.9192) = .1459$.

ACTIVITY-ON-NODE DIAGRAM

An alternate method for drawing network diagrams involves placing the activities on nodes (A-O-N) rather than on arrows. The result is a slightly different diagram. We can begin to get an appreciation for the differences by comparing the two approaches to a given problem. Consider this set of project activities:

Activity	Precedes
a	c
b	d,e
c	f
d	g
e	g
f	End
g	End

Figure 16–5 illustrates both types of networks.

One obvious difference in the two approaches is that there are more nodes in the A-O-N approach. Generally speaking, this will be the rule. A second difference is that the A-O-A network has a dummy arrow that is necessary to correctly show the precedence relationship that exists. A-O-N networks eliminate the need for dummy activities, which is an advantage of having activities on nodes.

In practice, both approaches are used. Most PERT/CPM computer programs

Figure 16–5

A comparison of the A-O-A and A-O-N methods of network representation

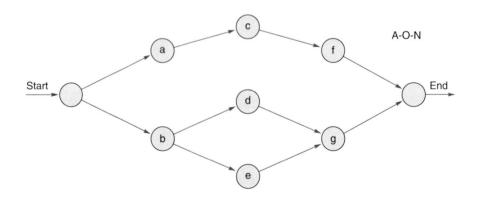

can handle either convention, but some do require one or the other. Often the choice of method depends more on personal preference or established procedures.

SIMULATION

The preceding section illustrated a method for computing the probability that a project would be completed in a specified length of time. That discussion assumed that the paths of the project were *independent;* that is, the same activities are not on more than one path. If an activity were on more than one path and it happened that the completion time for that activity far exceeded its expected time, all paths that included that activity would be affected and, hence, their times would not be independent. In situations where activities are on multiple paths, one must consider if the preceding approach can be used. For instance, if only a few activities are on multiple paths, and particularly if the paths are *much* shorter than the critical path, that approach may still be reasonable. Moreover, for purposes of illustration, as in the text problems and examples, we treat the paths as being independent when, in fact, they may not be.

In practice, when *dependent* cases occur, an approach that is often used is *simulation*. It amounts to a form of repeated sampling wherein many passes are made through the PERT network. In each pass, a randomly selected value for each activity time is made based on the characteristics of the activity's probability distribution (e.g., its mean, standard deviation, and distribution type). After each pass, the expected project duration is determined by adding the times along each path and designating the time of the longest path as the project duration. After a large number of such passes (say, several hundred), there is enough information to prepare a frequency distribution of the project duration times. This distribution can be used to make a probabilistic assessment of the actual project duration, allowing for the fact that some activities are on more than one path. The last problem in the supplement to Chapter 17 illustrates this.

TIME-COST TRADE-OFFS: CRASHING

Estimates of activity time for projects usually are made for some given level of resources. In many situations, it is possible to reduce the length of a project by injecting additional resources. The impetus to shorten projects may reflect efforts to avoid late penalties, to take advantage of monetary incentives for timely or early completion of a project, or to free resources for use on other projects. In new product development, shortening may lead to a strategic benefit: beating the competition to the market. In some cases, however, the desire to shorten the length of a project merely reflects an attempt to reduce the indirect costs associated with running the project, such as facilities and equipment costs, supervision, and labor and personnel costs. Managers often have certain options at their disposal that will allow them to shorten, or **crash**, certain activities. Among the most obvious options are the use of additional funds to support additional personnel or more efficient equipment, and the relaxing of some work specifications. Hence, a project manager may be able to shorten a project, thereby realizing savings on indirect project costs, by increasing *direct* expenses to speed up the project. The goal in evaluating time-cost trade-offs is to identify a plan that will minimize the sum of the indirect and direct project costs.

Crash

Shortening activity durations.

In order to make a rational decision on which activities (if any) to crash, and on the extent of crashing desirable, a manager needs certain information:

1. Regular time and crash time estimates for each activity.
2. Regular cost and crash cost estimates for each activity.
3. A list of activities that are on the critical path.

Activities on the critical path are potential candidates for crashing, since shortening noncritical activities would not have an impact on total project duration. From an economic standpoint, activities should be crashed according to crashing costs: crash those with the lowest costs first. Moreover, crashing should continue as long as the cost to crash is less than the benefits received from crashing. These benefits might take the form of incentive payments for early project completion as part of a government contract, or they might reflect savings in the indirect project costs, or both. Figure 16–6 illustrates the basic relationship between indirect, direct, and total project costs due to crashing.

The general procedure for crashing is:

1. Obtain estimates of regular and crash times and costs for each activity.
2. Determine the lengths of all paths and path slack times.
3. Determine which are the critical activities.
4. Crash critical activities, in order of increasing costs, as long as crashing costs do not exceed benefits. (Note that two or more paths may become critical as the original path becomes shorter, so that subsequent improvements will require simultaneous shortening of two or more paths. In some cases, it will be most economical to shorten an activity that is on two [or more] of the critical paths. This is true whenever the crashing cost of a joint activity is less than the sum of crashing one activity on each separate path.)

Figure 16–6

Crashing activities★

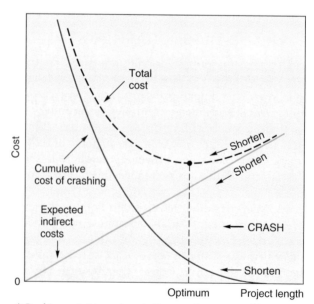

★Crashing activities reduce indirect project costs and increase direct costs; the optimum amount of crashing results in minimizing the sum of these two types of costs.

Using the following information, develop an optimum time-cost solution. Assume that indirect project costs are $1,000 per day.

Example 7

Activity	Normal time	Crash time	Cost per day to crash
a..............	6	6	—
b	10	8	$500
c..............	5	4	300
d	4	1	700
e..............	9	7	600
f.............	2	1	800

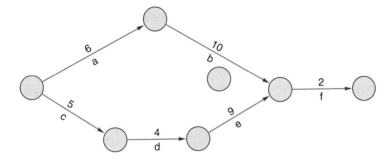

Solution

a. Determine which activities are on the critical path, its length, and the length of the other path:

Path	Length
a–b–f..............	18
c–d–e–f	20 (critical path)

b. Rank the critical path activities in order of lowest crashing cost, and determine the number of days each can be crashed.

Activity	Cost per day to crash	Available days
c.................	$300	1
e.................	600	2
d	700	3
f.................	800	1

c. Begin shortening the project, one day at a time, and check after each reduction to see which path is critical. (After a certain point, another path may equal the length of the shortened critical path.) Thus:
   (1) Shorten activity c one day at a cost of $300. The length of the critical path now becomes 19 days.
   (2) Activity c cannot be shortened any more. Shorten activity e one day at a cost of $600. The length of path c–d–e–f now becomes 18 days, which is the same as the length of path a–b–f.
   (3) Since the paths are now both critical, further improvements will necessitate shortening one activity on each.

(continued)

Example 7

(concluded)

The remaining points for crashing and their costs are:

Path	Activity	Crash cost (per day)
a–b–f	a	No reduction possible
	b	$500
	f	800
c–d–e–f	c	No further reduction possible
	d	$700
	e	600
	f	800

At first glance, it would seem that crashing f would not be advantageous, since it has the highest crashing cost. However, f is on both paths, so shortening f by one day would shorten *both* paths (and hence, the project) by one day for a cost of $800. The option of shortening the least expensive activity on each path would cost $500 for b and $600 for e, or $1,100. Thus, shorten f by one day. The project duration is now 17 days.

(4) At this point, no additional improvement is feasible. The cost to crash b is $500 and the cost to crash e is $600, for a total of $1,100, and that would exceed the project costs of $1,000 per day.

(5) The crashing sequence is summarized below:

	Length after crashing _n_ days:			
Path	_n_ = 0	1	2	3
a–b–f........	18	18	18	17
c–d–e–f......	20	19	18	17
Activity				
crashed....		c	e	f
Cost........		$300	$600	$800

ADVANTAGES AND LIMITATIONS OF PERT

PERT and similar project scheduling techniques can provide important services for the project manager. Among the most useful features are:

1. Use of these techniques forces the manager to organize and quantify available information and to recognize where additional information is needed.

2. The techniques provide a graphical display of the project and its major activities.

3. They identify (*a*) activities that should be closely watched because of the potential for delaying the project and (*b*) other activities that have slack time and so can be delayed without affecting project completion time. This raises the possibility of reallocating resources in order to shorten the project.

No analytical technique is without limitations. Among the more important limitations of PERT are the following:

1. When developing the project network, one or more important activities may be omitted.

2. Precedence relationships may not all be correct as shown.

3. Time estimates may include a fudge factor; managers feel uncomfortable about

making time estimates because they appear to commit themselves to completion within a certain time period.

4. The use of a computer is essential for large projects.

SUMMARY

Projects are composed of a unique set of activities established to realize a given set of objectives in a limited time span. The nonroutine nature of project activities places a set of demands on the project manager that are different in many respects than those required for the manager of more routine operations activities, both in planning and coordinating the work and in the human problems encountered.

PERT and CPM are two commonly used techniques for developing and monitoring projects. Although each technique was developed independently and for expressly different purposes, time and practice have erased most of the original differences, so that now little distinction can be made between the two. Either one provides the manager with a rational approach to project planning along with a graphical display of project activities. Both depict the sequential relationships that exist among activities and reveal to managers which activities must be completed on time in order to achieve timely project completion. Managers can use that information to direct their attention toward the most critical activities.

Two slightly different conventions can be used for constructing a network diagram. One designates the arrows as activities; the other designates the nodes as activities. To avoid confusion, this chapter emphasized only one approach, the activity-on-arrow model.

The task of developing and updating project networks quickly becomes complex for projects of even moderate size, so that the task is often handled by computer programs, which involve the use of some computing algorithm.

A deterministic approach is used for determining project duration estimates when activity times can be fairly well established. When activity times are subject to some uncertainty, a probabilistic approach is more realistic, and estimates of the length of such projects should be couched in probabilistic terms.

In some instances, it may be possible to shorten, or crash, the length of a project by shortening one or more of the project activities. Typically, such gains are achieved by the use of additional resources, although in some cases, it may be possible to transfer resources among project activities. Generally, projects are shortened to the point where the cost of additional reduction would exceed the benefit of additional reduction, or to the point where further improvements, although desirable, would be physically impossible.

KEY TERMS

activities, 781
activity-on-arrow, 781
activity-on-node, 781
beta distribution, 792
CPM, 779
crash, 799
critical activities, 781
critical path, 781
deterministic, 783
events, 781
independence, 795

most likely time, 792
network diagram, 780
optimistic time, 791
path, 781
PERT, 779
pessimistic time, 791
precedence diagram, 780
probabilistic, 783
projects, 776
slack, 781

Problem

1. The following table contains information related to the major activities of a research project. Use the information to do the following:
    a. Draw a precedence diagram.
    b. Find the critical path.
    c. Determine the expected length of the project.

Activity	Precedes	Expected time (days)
a . . . . c,b		5
c . . . . d		8
d i		2
b i		7
e . . . . f		3
f . . . . j		6
i . . . . j		10
j . . . . End		8
g . . . . h		1
h . . . . k		2
k . . . . End		17

Solution

a. In constructing networks, these observations can be useful:

(a) Activities with no predecessors are at the beginning (left side) of the network.

(2) Activities with multiple predecessors are located at path intersections. Start the network diagram by identifying and charting all activities with no predecessors:

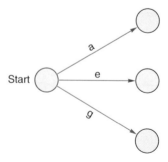

Next, complete the diagram in sections. Go down the activity list, in order when possible, to avoid overlooking any activities. The process is illustrated in the following diagram.

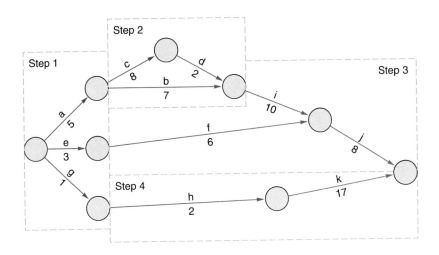

Here are some additional hints for constructing a precedence diagram:
(1) Use pencil.
(2) Start with a single node, and end with a single node.
(3) Try to avoid having paths cross each other.
(4) Number nodes from left to right.
(5) Have activities going from left to right.
(6) Use only one arrow between any pair of nodes.

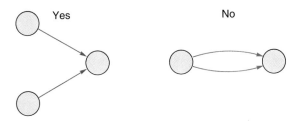

b. and *c.*

Path	Length (days)
a–c–d–i–j★	5 + 8 + 2 + 10 + 8 = 33†
a–b–i–j	5 + 7 + 10 + 8 = 30
e–f–j	3 + 6 + 8 = 17
g–h–k	1 + 2 + 17 = 20

★Critical path.
†Expected project duration.

Problem
2. Using the computing algorithm, determine the slack times for the follow-ing diagram. Identify the activities that are on the critical path.

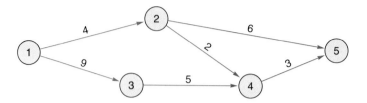

Solution

The task of determining ES, EF, LS, and LF times can be greatly simplified by setting up two brackets for each activity, as illustrated below:

The bracket at the left end of each activity will eventually be filled in with the earliest and latest *starting* times, and the bracket at the right end of each activity will be filled in with the earliest and latest *finishing* times:

This is accomplished in a two-step process. First, the earliest starting times and earliest finishing times are determined, working from left to right, as shown in the following diagram.

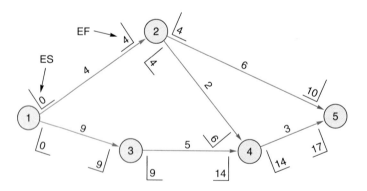

Thus, activity 1-2 can start at 0. With a time 4, it can finish at 0 + 4 = 4. This establishes the earliest start for all activities that begin at node 2. Hence, 2-5 and 2-4 can start no earlier than 4. Activity 2-5 has an early finish of 4 + 6 = 10, and activity 2-4 has an early finish of 4 + 2 = 6. At this point, it is impossible to say what the earliest start is for 4-5: that will depend on which activity, 3-4 or 2-4, has the latest EF. Consequently, it is necessary to compute ES and EF along the lower path. Assuming an ES of 0 for 1-3, its EF will be 9, so 3-4 will have an ES of 9 and an EF of 9 + 5 = 14.

Considering that the two activities entering node 4 have EF times of 6 and 14, the earliest that activity 4-5 can start is the *larger* of these, which is 14. Hence, activity 4-5 has an ES of 14 and an EF of $14 + 3 = 17$.

Now compare the EFs of the activities entering the final node. The largest of these, 17, is the expected project duration.

The LF and LS times for each activity can now be determined by working backward through the network (from right to left). The LF for the two activities entering node 5 is 17—the project duration. In other words, in order for the project to finish in 17 weeks, these last two activities must both finish by that time.

In the case of activity 4-5, the LS necessary for an LF of 17 is $17 - 3 = 14$. This means that both 2-4 and 3-4 must finish no later than 14. Hence, their LF times are 14. Activity 3 has an LS time of $14 - 5 = 9$, making the LF of activity 1-3 equal to 9, and its LS equal to $9 - 9 = 0$.

Activity 2-4, with an LF time of 14, has an LS time of $14 - 2 = 12$. Activity 2-5 has an LF of 17 and therefore an LS of $17 - 6 = 11$. Thus, the latest 2-5 can start is 11, and the latest 2-4 can start is 12 in order to finish by week 17. Since activity 1-2 precedes *both* of these activities, it can finish no later than the *smaller* of these, which is 11. Hence, 1-2 has an LF of 11 and an LS of $11 - 4 = 7$.

The ES, EF, LF, and LS times are shown on the following network.

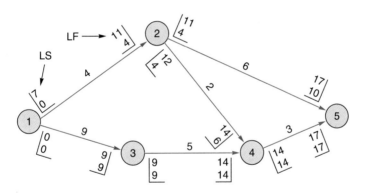

The slack time for any activity is the difference between *either* LF and EF *or* LS and ES. Thus,

Activity	LS	ES	Slack	or	LF	EF	Slack
1-2........	7	0	7		11	4	7
2-5........	11	4	7		17	10	7
2-4........	12	4	8		14	6	8
1-3........	0	0	0		9	9	0
3-4........	9	9	0		14	14	0
4-5........	14	14	0		17	17	0

The activities with zero slack times indicate the critical path. In this case the critical path is 1-3-4-5.

When working problems of this nature, keep in mind the following:

a. For nodes with multiple entering activities, the ES time for leaving activities of that node is the *largest* EF of the entering activities.

b. For nodes with multiple leaving activities, the LF for an entering activity for that node is the *smallest* LS of the leaving activities.

Problem

3. Expected times and variances for the major activities of an R&D project are depicted in the following PERT chart. Determine the probability that project completion time will be:

   a. Less than 50 weeks.

   b. More than 50 weeks.

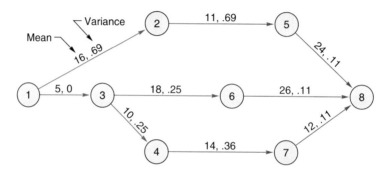

Solution

a. Compute the mean and standard deviation for each path:

Path	Expected time (weeks)	Standard deviation (weeks)
1-2-5-8	$16 + 11 + 24 = 51$	$\sqrt{.69 + .69 + .11} = 1.22$
1-3-6-8	$5 + 18 + 26 = 49$	$\sqrt{.00 + .25 + .11} = 0.60$
1-3-4-7-8...	$5 + 10 + 14 + 12 = 41$	$\sqrt{.00 + .25 + .36 + .11} = 0.85$

b. Compute the z score for each path for the length specified. For any path that has a score of more than $z = +2.50$, treat its probability of completion before the specified time as 1.00.
Use

$$z = \frac{50 - t_{path}}{\sigma_{path}}$$

The probability that each path will be completed in 50 weeks or less is shown in the corresponding diagram. (Probabilities are from Appendix B, Table B.) The probability that the project will be completed in 50 weeks or less depends on all three paths being completed in that time. Because z for path 1-3-4-7-8 is greater than $+2.50$, it is treated as having a probability of completion in 50 weeks of 100 percent. It is less certain that the other two paths will be completed in that time. The probability that *both* will not exceed 50 is the *product* of their individual probabilities of completion. Thus, .2061(.9525) = .1963.

   The probability that the project *will* exceed 50 weeks is the complement of this number, which is 1.000 − .1963 = .8037.

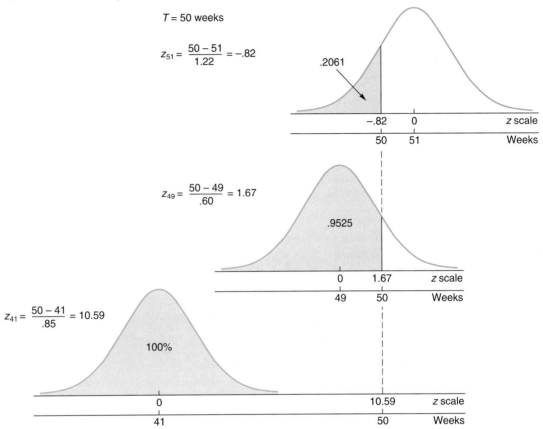

T = 50 weeks

$$z_{51} = \frac{50 - 51}{1.22} = -.82$$

$$z_{49} = \frac{50 - 49}{.60} = 1.67$$

$$z_{41} = \frac{50 - 41}{.85} = 10.59$$

(Note that it is *not* the product of the complements of the path probabilities.)

Problem

4. Indirect costs for a project are $12,000 per week for as long as the project lasts. The project manager has supplied the cost and time information shown. Use the information to:
    a. Determine an optimum crashing plan.
    b. Graph the total costs for the plan.

Activity	Crashing potential (weeks)	Cost per week to crash
a	3	$11,000
b	3	3,000 first week, $4,000 others
c	2	6,000

(continued)

Activity	Crashing potential (weeks)	Cost per week to crash
d 1		$1,000
e 3		6,000
f 1		2,000

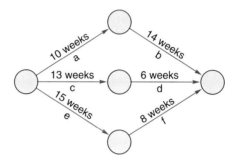

Solution

a. (1) Compute path lengths and identify the critical path:

Path	Duration (weeks)
a–b	24 (critical path)
c–d	19
e–f	23

(2) Rank critical activities according to crashing costs:

Activity	Cost per week to crash
b	$ 3,000
a	11,000

Activity b should be shortened one week since it has the lower crash-ing cost. This would reduce indirect costs by $12,000 at a cost of $3,000, for a net savings of $9,000. At this point, paths a–b and e–f would both have a length of 23 weeks, so both would be critical.

(3) Rank activities by crashing costs on the two critical paths:

Path	Activity	Cost per week to crash
a–b	b	$ 4,000
	a	11,000

(continued)

Path	Activity	Cost per week to crash
e-f. . . . . e		$2,000
	f	6,000

Choose one activity on each path to crash: b on a-b and f on e-f, for a total cost of $4,000 + $2,000 = $6,000 and a net savings of $12,000 − $6,000 = $6,000.

(4) Check to see which path(s) might be critical: a-b and e-f would be 22 weeks in length, and c-d would still be 19 weeks.

(5) Rank activities on the critical paths:

Path	Activity	Cost per week to crash
a-b . . . . b		$ 4,000
	a	11,000
e-f. . . . . e		6,000
	f	(no further crashing possible)

Crash b on path a-b and e on e-f for a cost of $4,000 + $6,000 = $10,000, for a net savings of $12,000 − $10,000 = $2,000.

(6) At this point, no further improvement is possible: paths a-b and e-f would be 21 weeks in length, and one activity from each path would have to be shortened. This would mean a at $11,000 and e at $6,000 for a total of $17,000, which exceeds the $12,000 potential savings in indirect costs.

b. The following table summarizes the results, showing the length of the project after crashing n weeks:

Path	$n = 0$	1	2	3
a-b	24	23	22	21
c-d	19	19	19	19
e-f	23	23	22	21
Activity crashed		b	b,f	b,e
Crashing costs ($000)		3	6	10

A summary of costs for the preceding schedule would look like this:

Project length	Cumulative weeks shortened	Cumulative crashing costs ($000)	Indirect costs ($000)	Total costs ($000)
24 0		0	24(12) = 288	288
23 1		3	23(12) = 276	279
22 2		3 + 6 = 9	22(12) = 264	273
21 3		9 + 10 = 19	21(12) = 252	271
20 4		19 + 17 = 36	20(12) = 240	276

The graph of total costs is as follows.

1. What are some of the basic differences between project planning and scheduling and production planning and scheduling?

2. "A probabilistic approach to estimating project duration is generally preferred." Comment.

3. Identify the term being described for each of the following:
   a. A sequence of activities in a project.
   b. The longest time sequence of activities in a project.
   c. Used when two activities have the same starting and finishing points.
   d. The difference in time length of any path and the critical path.
   e. Used to denote the beginning or end of an activity.
   f. The statistical distribution used to describe variability of an activity time.
   g. The statistical distribution used to describe project variability.
   h. Shortening an activity by allocating additional resources.

4. Explain the concept of shared slack.

5. Can you envision a situation in which resources might be *subtracted* from a project, in a kind of reverse time-cost trade-off? Explain briefly.

6. List the main advantages of PERT. List the main limitations.

7. What are dummy activities, and why are they used?

8. Why might a probabilistic estimate of a project's completion time based solely on the variance of the critical path be misleading? Under what circumstances would it be acceptable?

9. Define each of these terms, and indicate how each is determined.
   a. Optimistic time estimate.
   b. Most likely time estimate.
   c. Pessimistic time estimate.
   d. Expected activity time.
   e. Variance of an activity time.
   f. Standard deviation of a path's time.

10. Could PERT or CPM be used to schedule nonproject activities? Explain your reasoning briefly.
11. Why might a person wish to be associated with a critical path activity? What are some of the reasons one might have for not wanting such an association?
12. What are some of the potential benefits of working on a special project in one's firm? What are some of the risks?
13. What are some of the aspects of the project manager's job that make it more demanding than that of a manager working in a more routine organizational framework?
14. What is the main benefit of a project organization over more traditional forms of operations management for project work?

---

1. For each of the following network diagrams, determine both the critical path and the expected project duration. The quantities on the arrows represent expected activity times.

PROBLEMS

a.

b.

c.

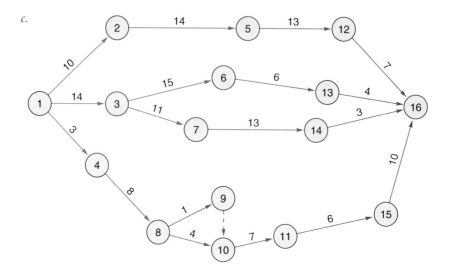

2. Using the information provided in the accompanying table, do the following:
   a.   Construct a network diagram.
   b.   Determine the critical activities.
   c.   Compute the length of the critical path.

Activity	Estimated time (days)
1-2	5
2-3	6
2-4	4
3-6	9
6-7	2
4-5	4
4-7	18
5-7	10

3. The information shown pertains to a project that is about to commence. As the project manager, which activities would you be concerned with in terms of timely project completion? Explain.

Activity	Precedes	Estimated time (days)
a	b	15
b	c,d	12
c	e	6
d	End	5
e	End	3
f	g,h	8
g	i	8
h	j	9
i	End	7
j	k	14
k	End	6

4. Construct a precedence diagram for each of the following cases. Note that each case requires the use of a dummy activity.

a.	Activity	Precedes activity	b.	Activity	Precedes activity
	a	d		j	l,n
	b	e,f		k	r
	c	g		l	m
	d	k		m	end
	e	k		n	p
	f	h,i		p	end
	g	i		q	s,t
	h	end		r	v
	i	end		s	v
	k	end		v	end
				t	v,w
				w	end

5. For each of the problems listed, determine the following quantities for each activity: earliest start time, latest start time, earliest finish time, latest finish time, and slack. List the critical activities, and determine the expected duration of the project.
    a. Problem 1a.
    b. Problem 1b.
    c. Problem 2.
    d. Problem 3.

6. Reconsider the network diagram of Problem 1a. Suppose that after 12 weeks, activities 1–2, 1–3, and 2–4 have been finished; 2–5 is 75 percent finished; and 3–6 is half finished. How many weeks after the original start time should the project be finished?

7. Three recent college graduates have formed a partnership and have opened an advertising firm. Their first project consists of activities listed in the following table.
    a. Draw the precedence diagram.
    b. What is the probability that the project can be completed in 24 days or less? In 21 days or less?
    c. Suppose it is now the end of the seventh day and that activities a and b have been completed while d is 50 percent completed. Time estimates for the completion of d are 5, 6, and 7. Activities c and h are ready to begin. Determine the probability of finishing the project in 24 days and the probability of finishing in 21 days.

		Time in days		
Activity	Pre-cedes	Opti-mistic	Most likely	Pessi-mistic
a......... c	c	5	6	7
b .... h	h	8	8	11
c......... e	e	6	8	11
d .... f	f	9	12	15
e......... End	End	5	6	9
f......... g	g	5	6	7
g......... End	End	2	3	7
h i	i	4	4	5
i......... End	End	5	7	8

8. The new director of special events at a large university has decided to completely re-vamp graduation ceremonies. Toward that end, a PERT chart of the major activities has been developed. The chart has five paths with expected completion times and variances as shown in the table. Graduation day is 17 weeks from now. Assuming the project begins now, what is the probability that the project will be completed before:
   a. Graduation time?
   b. The end of week 16?
   c. The end of week 13?

Path	Expected duration (weeks)	Variance
A 10		1.21
B 8		2.00
C 12		1.00
D 15		2.89
E 14		1.44

9. The following precedence diagram reflects three time estimates for each activity. Determine:
   a. The expected completion time for each path and its variance.
   b. The probability that the project will require more than 49 weeks.
   c. The probability that the project can be completed in 46 weeks or less.

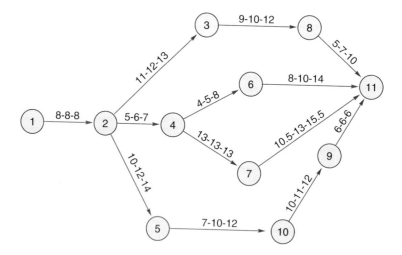

10. A project manager has compiled a list of major activities that will be required to install a computer information system in her firm. The list includes estimated completion times for activities and precedence relationships:

Activity	Precedes	Estimated times (weeks)
a . . . . d,f		2-4-6
d . . . . e		6-8-10
e . . . . h		7-9-12

Activity	Precedes	Estimated times (weeks)
h . . . . End		2-3-5
f . . . . g		3-4-8
g . . . . End		5-7-9
b i		2-2-3
i . . . . j		2-3-6
j . . . . k		3-4-5
k . . . . End		4-5-8
c . . . . m		5-8-12
m . . . . n		1-1-1
n . . . . o		6-7-11
o . . . . End		8-9-13

If the project is finished within 27 weeks of its start, the project manager will receive a bonus of $1,000; and if the project is finished within 28 weeks of its start, the bonus will be $500. Find the probability of each bonus.

11. Construct an activity-on-node diagram for the set of activities listed in Problem 3.

12. Construct an activity-on-node diagram for the set of activities listed in Problem 2. To facilitate this, replace the activity designations (1-2, 2-3, etc.) with letters (a, b, c, etc.).

13. The project manager of a task force planning the construction of a domed stadium had hoped to be able to complete construction prior to the start of the next college football season. After reviewing construction time estimates, it now appears that a certain amount of crashing will be needed to insure project completion before the season opener. Given the following time and cost estimates, determine a minimum-cost crashing schedule that will shave five weeks off the project length.

Activity	Pre-cedes	Normal time (weeks)	Crashing costs First week	Crashing costs Second week
a . . . . b		12	$15,000	$20,000
b . . . . k		14	10,000	10,000
c . . . . d,e,f		10	5,000	5,000
d . . . . g		17	20,000	21,000
e . . . . h		18	16,000	18,000
f i		12	12,000	15,000
g . . . . m		15	24,000	24,000
h . . . . n,p		8	—	—
i . . . . j		7	30,000	—
j . . . . p		12	25,000	25,000
k . . . . End		9	10,000	10,000
m . . . . End		3	—	—
n . . . . End		11	40,000	—
p . . . . End		8	20,000	20,000

14. A construction project has indirect costs totalling $40,000 per week. Major activities in the project and their expected times are shown in this precedence diagram:

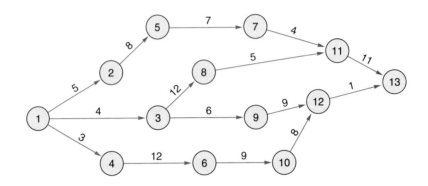

Crashing costs for each activity are:

	Crashing costs ($000)		
Activity	First week	Second week	Third week
1-2.........	$18	$22	$—
2-5.........	24	25	25
5-7.........	30	30	35
7-11.........	15	20	—
11-13.........	30	33	36
1-3.........	12	24	26
3-8.........	—	—	—
8-11.........	40	40	40
3-9.........	3	10	12
9-12.........	2	7	10
12-13.........	26	—	—
1-4.........	10	15	25
4-6.........	8	13	—
6-10.........	5	12	—
10-12.........	14	15	—

a. Determine the optimum time-cost crashing plan.
b. Plot the total-cost curve that describes the least expensive crashing schedule that will reduce the project length by six weeks.

15. Chuck's Custom Boats (CCB) builds luxury yachts to customer order. CCB has just landed a contract with a mysterious New York banker (Mr. T). Relevant data are shown below. The complication is that Mr. T wants delivery in 32 weeks or he will impose a penalty of $375 for each week his yacht is late.

Activity	Precedes	Normal time (weeks)	Crashing costs	
			1st week	2nd week
K	L,N	9	$410	$415
L	M	7	125	—
N	J	5	45	45
M	Q	4	300	350
J	Q	6	50	—
Q	P,Y	5	200	225
P	Z	8	—	—
Y	End	7	85	90
Z	End	6	90	—

Develop a crashing schedule.

SELECTED BIBLIOGRAPHY

Bierman, Harold, Jr.; Charles P. Bonini; and Warren H. Hausman. *Quantitative Analysis for Business Decisions.* 8th ed. Homewood, Ill.: Richard D. Irwin, 1991.

Buffa, Elwood, and James S. Dyer. *Essentials of Management Science/Operations Research.* New York: John Wiley & Sons, 1978.

Burman, P. J. *Precedence Networks for Project Planning and Control.* New York: McGraw-Hill, 1972.

Hoare, H. R. *Project Management Using Networks.* New York: McGraw-Hill, 1973.

Kerzner, Harold. *Project Management for Executives.* New York: Van Nostrand Reinhold, 1984.

Levin, Richard I.; Charles A. Kirkpatrick; and David S. Rubin. *Quantitative Approaches to Management.* 5th ed. New York: McGraw-Hill, 1982.

Moder, J.; E. W. Davis; and C. Phillips. *Project Management with CPM and PERT.* New York: Van Nostrand Reinhold, 1983.

Reeser, Clayton. *Management: Functions and Modern Concepts.* Glenview, Ill.: Scott, Foresman, 1973.

Wiest, J. D., and F. K. Levy. *A Management Guide to PERT/CPM.* 2nd ed. Englewood Cliffs, N.J.: Prentice Hall, 1977.

CASE   THE CASE OF THE MEXICAN CRAZY QUILT

"The mission of the project which you will head is to get our new Mexican subsidiary company ready for take-over by Mexican managers. My hope is that you will be able to do this in about two years," explained Robert Linderman, president of Linderman Industries, Inc., to Carl Conway, newly appointed project manager for "Operation Mexicano." Conway had been hired specifically for this assignment because of his experience in managing large defense projects in the aerospace industry.

"The first thing that I will have to do is put a project team together," said Conway. "I imagine that you have in mind my drawing people from the functional divisions."

"Yes, I have already sent memoranda to the division managers informing them that you will be asking for some of their key people to work under you for about two years," said Linderman. "In addition, I have advised them to be prepared to process work orders from Operation Mexicano with the personnel and equipment of their organizations. Later on in the project's life, you will begin to get Mexican personnel, both managers and technicians, into your organization. These people will have Mexican supervisors, but until the the mission is accomplished, they also will report to you. I will have to admit that you are going to have some complex authority relationships, especially as you personally will be responsible to the president of the subsidiary, Felix Delgado, as well as to me."

Conway began to make his plans for the project team. The plant building was available and empty in Mexico City, and it was important to get equipment purchased and installed as soon as possible. A plant layout would have to be prepared, but before that could be done there would have to be a manufacturing plan. Therefore, he needed to recruit an industrial engineer, a production planner, and an equipment buyer. They, in turn, would have to build their own staffs.

He made an appointment with Sam Sargis, corporate manager of industrial engineering. "I have had a preliminary talk with Bob Cates about his joining Operation Mexicano, and he is quite interested," Carl said. "Will you release him to me?"

"Why, I'm grooming Cates to take over my job when I retire," replied Sargis. "He is my best man. Let me pick someone else for you, or better still, you just tell me what industrial engineering work you want done, and I will have it done for you."

"Sorry, I want Cates," said Carl firmly. "And besides, you are not due to retire for five years. This will be good experience for him."

For production planning, Carl had in mind Bert Mill, an older man with extensive experience in managing production operations, but Mill rejected his offer. "I talked it over with my wife," he said, "and we feel that at my age I shouldn't take a chance on not having a job to come back to when Operation Mexicano is finished."

Carl next talked to Emil Banowetz, who was assistant to Jim Burke, the vice president for manufacturing, and Banowetz decided that he would like to join the project team. However, Burke told Conway that if Banowetz were forcibly taken away from him, he would give Mr. Linderman his resignation, so Carl decided to back down. He finally accepted a man that Burke recommended.

Filling the equipment buyer's slot was easy. The director of procurement phoned Carl and said that a senior buyer, Humberto Guzman, had requested permission to ask for the assignment, and that he strongly recommended him. Guzman had been purchasing

agent for a large mining company in Mexico for about 10 years.

Carl had about the same experiences in getting the people he wanted for the functions of engineering, quality control, cost, marketing, and advertising as he did for the first three positions; in other words, he won some confrontations with the division managers and lost some. For personnel, he got Dr. Juan Perez, who was slated to be personnel director of the subsidiary company, to affiliate temporarily with the project team.

The first brush that Project Mexicano had in getting a functional division to do work for it came when Carl's engineering man, Frank Fong, reported to him that the engineering vice president, who was formerly Fong's boss, refused to authorize top priority to the changing of dimensions in the production drawings to the metric system. Carl had to take this issue to Linderman, who ruled in his favor. The defeated vice president, of course, did not take kindly to the decision.

The next incident revolved about Carl's desire to have a pilot run of products made with metric measurements for shipment to Mexico. The purpose was to test the market acceptance of the Linderman articles. Jim Burke stated flatly that there was no way that his production workers could be trained to work with metric drawings. Carl quickly saw that this was an issue that he was not going to win, so he had his buyer, Guzman, work with the newly appointed manufacturing manager for the subsidiary in getting a run of the products subcontracted in Mexico City.

Bob Cates made a special trip from Mexico City to present Carl with an interesting problem. The Mexican industrial engineer, whom Bob was supposed to be training, had his own ideas about plant layout. When they differed from Bob's, as they usually did, he would take his complaint directly to Felix Delgado, the president of the Mexican subsidiary. Because Delgado's competence was primarily in finance, he would not know how to decide the argument and would simply table it. Carl took examples of some of the disagreements to Bob's former boss, Sam Sargis, who quite unexpectedly ruled against Bob's proposed methods. Carl saw that there was bad feeling by Sargis against Bob for leaving his department, which boded ill for Bob's return. To solve the immediate problem, however, Carl asked Dr. Perez to try to reconcile the situation in Mexico City.

CASE   *(concluded)*

Despite these problems, and many more of a similar nature, Project Mexicano was successful, and the transition to Mexican management was made in just a little over two years. By a curious twist, through Dr. Perez's intercession Felix Delgado became very impressed by Bob Cates and convinced him to accept the job of director of industrial engineering for the Mexican company. Humberto Guzman also stayed on to head the procurement operation.

Other members of the project team were not so fortunate. Linderman Industries was laying off personnel when the project ended in 1990, and only the project production man was able to get a job in the company at as high a level as the one he had when he joined the team. The cost expert elected to leave Linderman because he said the glamour of Project Mexicano had spoiled him for any routine job.

Carl Conway had a difficult decision of his own to make. Robert Linderman said that he was extremely pleased with his performance and that something good would open up in the company for him soon. In the meantime, there was a staff assignment available for him. Carl had seen enough project managers in the aerospace industry who had figuratively rotted on staff assignments when their projects were completed to be somewhat wary.

Questions

1. Was Linderman Industries' adoption of project organization an appropriate one for getting the Mexican subsidiary started?

2. In consideration of Robert Linderman's letting the division manager know that the project manager would be asking for some of their key people, why would Conway have any difficulty in getting the ones he wanted?

3. Would you expect that many people would turn down a chance to join a project organization, as Bert Mill did?

4. Why would Conway take his problem with the engineering vice president to Linderman and have it resolved in his favor, yet back down in two disputes with the manufacturing vice president?

5. What could Linderman Industries have done to assure good jobs for the people coming off Project Mexicano, including Carl Conway, the project manager?

Source: *Management: The Key to Organizational Effectiveness,* rev. ed. by Clayton Reeser and Marvin Loper. Copyright © 1978, Scott, Foresman and Company. Reprinted by permission.

CASE   FANTASY PRODUCTS

Company Background

The Fantasy Products Company is a manufacturer of high-quality small appliances intended for home use. Their current product line includes irons, a small hand-held vacuum, and a number of kitchen appliances such as toasters, blenders, waffle irons, and coffeemakers. Fantasy Products has a strong research and development department that continually searches for ways to improve existing products as well as developing new products.

Currently, the research and development department is working on the development of a new kitchen appliance that will chill foods quickly much as a microwave oven heats them quickly, although the technology involved is quite different. Tenta-

tively named The Big Chill, the product will initially carry a price tag of around $125 and therefore the target market consists of upper income groups. At this price, it is expected to be a very profitable item. R&D engineers now have a working prototype and are satisfied that, with cooperation from the production and marketing people, the product can be ready in time for the all important Christmas buying season. A target date has been set for product introduction that is 24 weeks away.

Current Problem

Fantasy Products Marketing Vice President Vera Sloan has recently learned from reliable sources that a competitor is also in the process of developing a simi-

---

CASE *(continued)*

---

lar product that it intends to bring out at almost exactly the same time. In addition, her source indicated that the competitor plans to sell its product, which will be smaller than The Big Chill, for $99 in the hope of appealing to upper-middle as well as upper income groups. Vera, with the help of several of her key people who are to be involved in marketing The Big Chill, has decided that in order to compete, the selling price for The Big Chill will have to be lowered to within $10 of the competitor's price. At this price level, it will still be profitable, although not nearly as profitable as originally anticipated.

However, Vera is wondering whether it would be possible to expedite the usual product introduction process in order to beat the competition to the market. If possible, she would like to get a six-week jump on the competition; this would put the product introduction date only 18 weeks away. During this initial period, Fantasy Products could sell The Big Chill for $125, reducing the selling price to $109 when the competitor's product actually enters the market. Since forecasts based on market research show that sales during the first six weeks will be about 2,000 per week, there is an opportunity for considerable extra profit if the early introduction can be accomplished. In addition, there is a certain amount of prestige involved in being first to the market. This should help enhance The Big Chill's image during the anticipated battle for market share.

Data Collection

Since Fantasy Products has been through the product introduction process a number of times, the R&D department has developed a list of the tasks that must be accomplished and the order in which they must be

completed. Although the times and costs vary depending on the particular product, the basic process does not. The list of activities involved and their precedence relationships are presented in Table 1. Time and cost estimates for the introduction of The Big Chill are presented in Table 2. Note that some of the activities can be completed on a crash basis, with an associated increase in cost.

Questions

Fantasy Products needs to decide whether to bring The Big Chill to market 18 weeks from now as Vera Sloan is recommending. As the project management specialist in the R&D department, you have been asked to answer the following questions:

1. When would the project be completed using normal times?

2. Is it possible to complete the project in 18 weeks? What would the associated additional cost be? Which activities would need to be completed on a crash basis?

3. Is the additional cost justified in terms of the increased profits expected?

4. The estimated demand is very uncertain; how much can this number vary without changing the recommendations you are making?

5. Is there some time frame other than the 18 weeks Vera has recommended that would make more sense in terms of profits?

Source: Used with permission from Robert J. Thieraus, Margaret Cunningham, and Melanie Blackwell, Xavier University, Cincinnati, Ohio.

Table 1

List of activities and precedence relationships

Activity	Description	Immediate predecessor
A	Select and order equipment	—
B	Receive equipment from supplier	A
C	Install and set up equipment	A
D	Finalize bill of materials	B
E	Order component parts	C
F	Receive component parts	E
G	First production run	D,F
H	Finalize marketing plan	—
I	Produce magazine ads	H
J	Script for TV ads	H
K	Produce TV ads	J
L	Begin ad campaign	I,K
M	Ship product to customers	G,L

Table 2

Time and cost estimates

Activity	Normal time	Normal cost	Crash time	Crash cost
A	3	$ 2,000	2	$ 4,500
B	8	9,000	6	12,000
C	4	2,000	2	7,000
D	2	1,000	1	2,000
E	2	2,000	1	3,000
F	5	0	5	0
G	6	12,000	3	24,000
H	4	3,500	2	8,000
I	4	5,000	3	8,000
J	3	8,000	2	15,000
K	4	50,000	3	70,000
L	6	10,000	6	10,000
M	1	5,000	1	5,000

CHAPTER SEVENTEEN

WAITING LINES

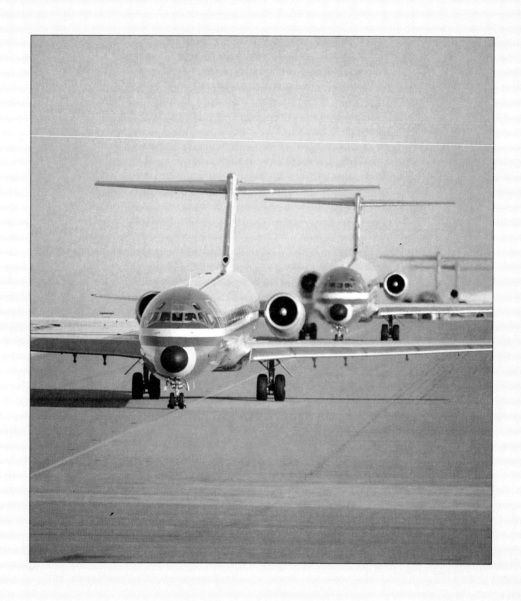

17

After completing this chapter, you should be able to:

1. Explain why waiting lines form in underloaded systems.

2. Identify the goal of queuing (waiting-line) analysis.

3. List the measures of system performance that are used in queuing.

4. Discuss the assumptions of the basic queuing models presented.

5. Solve typical problems.

T he preceding article pokes fun at one of life's realities: having to wait in line. No doubt those waiting in line would all agree that the solution to the problem is obvious: simply add more servers or else do something to speed up service. Although both ideas may be potential solutions, there are certain subtleties that must be dealt with. For one thing, most service systems have the capacity to process more customers over the long run than they are called on to process. Hence, the problem of customers waiting is a short-term phenomenon. The other side of the coin is that at certain times the system is empty, and *servers* are idle, waiting for customers. Thus, by increasing the service capacity, the server idle time would increase even more. Consequently, in designing service systems, the designer must weigh the cost of providing a given level of service capacity against the potential (implicit) cost of having customers wait for service. This planning and analysis of service capacity frequently lends itself to **queuing theory**, which is a mathematical approach to the analysis of waiting lines.

Queuing theory

Mathematical approach to the analysis of waiting lines.

WAITING—A NEW POPULAR PASTIME MISS MANNERS *Judith Martin*

Many things in life are worth waiting for, but not all that long. Miss Manners would put a time limit on how long one should wait for salespeople to finish their conversations with each other before writing up one's order, or for a spouse who has departed with someone else to realize what a terrible mistake that was.

Nevertheless, waiting is now in a class with working as a popular pastime. A *waitologist* has estimated that the average adult spends one tenth of his or her waking moments waiting, at a minimum. There are waits for buses, banks, stores, theaters, gas stations, court cases, elevators, driver's licenses, and dentist appointments.

One could easily pass one's life enduring just such basic waits. But there are also intermediary waits, such as waiting for the rain to stop, and advanced waits, such as waiting for your ship to come in. Some of these go in fashions. There was a time when all of America was waiting to be discovered by a movie talent scout in a drug store, and now everyone is waiting for a television camera to come along and ask her to tell the world what she thinks.

It is the elementary, and comparatively short-term wait with which Miss Manners is concerned. If you want to hear about the others, you will just have to wait.

It is perfectly correct, although not many people realize it, to refuse to wait on the telephone. When Miss Manners is asked "Can you hold on for a minute?" she often replies, "No," and it is too bad that the person on the other end ties up his own line by putting her on hold anyway, because that person has not waited for Miss Manners' reply.

One should also refuse to wait for inefficient or indefinite service. A restaurant should be able to tell you how long the wait will be, and a service person should not keep you waiting except to attend a previous customer.

It is rude to refuse to wait by announcing that one's needs take precedence over those of other waiting people. Miss Manners can think of no circumstances in which a person transacting the ordinary business of life can plead with legitimacy that it is more outrageous to expect him to wait than to expect it of others. "Let me go through, please—I'm in labor," perhaps, but then what are you doing at the stockings sale, anyway?

The only polite way to wait, if one must do so, is to bring one's own portable work or amusement. An unoccupied person waiting in line is by definition a potential raving maniac. A nice Jane Austen novel ready-to-go has preserved even the naturally tranquil spirits of Miss Manners. Even using conversations as a means to pass the time is dangerous, in Miss Manners' opinion. Two people quietly discussing what a shame it is to have to wait are, by the same definition, a potential mob.

Waiting lines are commonly found wherever customers arrive *randomly* for services. Some examples of waiting lines we encounter in our daily lives include the lines at supermarket checkouts, fast-food restaurants, airport ticket counters, theaters, post offices, and toll booths. In many business situations, the "customers" are not people but orders waiting to be filled, trucks waiting to be unloaded, jobs waiting to be processed, or equipment awaiting repairs. Still other examples include ships waiting to dock, planes waiting to land, hospital patients waiting for a nurse, and cars waiting at a stop sign.

The foundation of modern queuing theory is based on studies made in the early part of this century by Danish telephone engineer A. K. Erlang involving automatic dialing equipment. Prior to World War II, there were very few attempts to apply queuing theory to business problems. However, since that time, queuing theory has been applied to a wide range of problems.

The mathematics of queuing can be quite complex; for that reason, the emphasis here will not be on the mathematics but on the concepts that underlie the use of queuing in analyzing waiting-line problems. We shall rely on the use of formulas and tables for analysis.

We shall begin our discussion of queuing with an examination of what is perhaps the most fundamental issue in waiting line theory: Why is there waiting?

WHY IS THERE WAITING?

Many people are surprised to learn that waiting lines tend to form *even though a system is basically underloaded*. For example, a fast-food restaurant may have the capacity to handle an average of 200 orders per hour and yet experience waiting lines even though the average number of orders is only 150 per hour. The key word here is *average*. In reality, customers arrive at random intervals rather than at evenly spaced intervals, and some orders take longer to fill than others. In other words, both arrivals and service times exhibit a high degree of variability. As a result, there are times when the system becomes temporarily overloaded, and that gives rise to waiting lines; at other times, the system is idle because there are no customers. Thus, although a system may be *underloaded* from a *macro* standpoint, because of variabilities in arrivals and service there will be times when the system is *overloaded* from a *micro* standpoint. It follows, then, that in systems where variability is minimal or nonexistent (say, because arrivals can be scheduled and service time is constant), waiting lines do not ordinarily form.

GOAL OF QUEUING ANALYSIS

The goal of queuing is essentially to minimize total costs. There are two basic categories of cost in a queuing situation: those associated with customers waiting for service and those associated with capacity. Capacity costs are the costs of maintaining the ability to provide service. Examples include the number of bays in a car wash, the number of checkouts in a supermarket, the number of repairmen to handle equipment breakdowns, and the number of lanes on a highway. When a service facility is idle, there is a loss of capacity since it cannot be stored. The costs of customer waiting include the salaries paid to employees while they wait for service (mechanics waiting for tools, the drivers of trucks waiting to unload), the cost of the space for waiting (size of doctor's waiting room, length of driveway at a car wash,

Figure 17–1

The goal of queuing analysis is to minimize the sum of two costs: customer waiting costs and service capacity costs

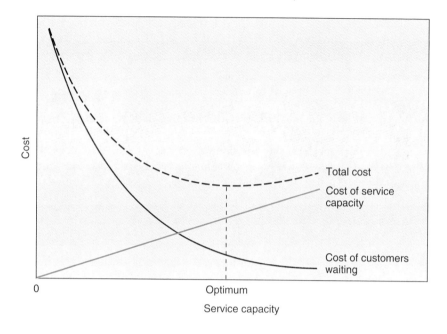

fuel consumed by planes waiting to land), and any loss of business due to customers refusing to wait and possibly going elsewhere in the future.

A practical difficulty that is frequently encountered is pinning down the cost of customer waiting time, especially since major portions of that cost are not a part of accounting data. One approach often used is to treat waiting times or line lengths as a policy variable: a manager simply specifies an acceptable level of waiting and directs that capacity be established to achieve that level.

The goal of queuing analysis is to balance the cost of providing a level of service capacity with the cost of customers waiting for service. This concept is illustrated in Figure 17–1. Note that as capacity increases, its cost increases. For simplicity, the increase is shown as a linear relationship. Although a step function is often more appropriate, use of a straight line does not significantly distort the picture. As capacity increases, the number of customers waiting, and the time they wait, tends to decrease, thereby decreasing waiting costs. As is the case with trade-off cost relationships, total costs can be represented as a U-shaped curve. The goal of analysis is to identify a level of service capacity that will minimize total cost. (Unlike the situation in the inventory EOQ model, the minimum point on the total cost curve is *not* usually where the two cost lines intersect.)

SYSTEM CHARACTERISTICS

There are numerous queuing models from which an analyst can choose. Naturally, much of the success of the analysis will depend on choosing an appropriate model. Model choice is dependent on the characteristics of the system under investigation. The main characteristics are:

1.   The population source.
2.   The number of servers (channels).
3.   Arrival and service patterns.
4.   The queue discipline (order of service).

POPULATION SOURCE

The approach to use to analyze a queuing problem depends on whether there is a limit to the potential number of customers. There are two possibilities: *infinite-source* and *finite-source* populations. In an **infinite-source** situation, the potential number of customers greatly exceeds system capacity. Infinite-source situations exist whenever service is *unrestricted*. Examples are supermarkets, drugstores, banks, restaurants, theaters, amusement centers, and toll bridges. Theoretically, large numbers of customers from the "calling population" can request service at any time. When the potential number of customers is limited, a **finite-source** situation exists. An example is a repairer responsible for a certain number of machines (the potential number of machines that might need repairs at any one time cannot exceed the number of machines assigned to the repairer). Similarly, an operator may be responsible for loading and unloading a bank of four machines, a nurse may be responsible for answering patient calls for a 10-bed ward, a secretary may be responsible for taking dictation from three executives, and a company shop may perform repairs as needed on the firm's 20 trucks.

Infinite source
Customer arrivals are unrestricted.

Finite source
Customer population where potential number of customers is limited.

NUMBER OF SERVERS (CHANNELS)

The capacity of a queuing system is a function of the capacity of each server and the number of servers being used. The terms *server* and **channel** are synonomous, and it is generally assumed that each channel can handle one customer at a time. Systems can be either *single-* or *multiple-channel*. (If a group of servers work together as a team, such as a surgical team, that is treated as a single-channel system.) Examples of single-channel systems are small grocery stores with one checkout counter, some theaters, single-bay car washes, and drive-in banks with one teller. Figure 17–2 illustrates a single-channel queuing system. Multiple-channel systems (those with more than one server) are commonly found in banks, at airline ticket counters, at auto service centers, and at gas stations.

Channel
A server in a service system.

A related distinction is the number of steps or *phases* in a queuing system. For example, at some college registrations, students go from desk to desk to have courses assigned and then move to final checkers and the bursar's table. Each location constitutes a separate phase where queues can (and usually do) form.

Figure 17–3 illustrates some of the most common queuing systems found in practice. Because it would not be possible to cover all of these cases in sufficient detail in the limited amount of space available here, our discussion will focus on *single-phase* systems.

ARRIVAL AND SERVICE PATTERNS

Waiting lines are a direct result of arrival and service variability. They occur because random, highly variable arrival and service patterns cause systems to be temporarily

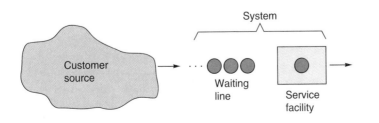

Figure 17–2

A single-channel queuing system

Figure 17–3

Four common variations of queuing systems

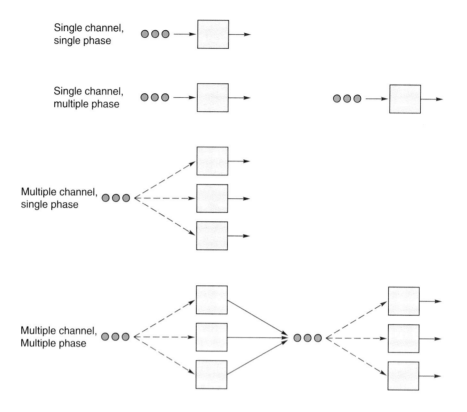

Figure 17–4

Poisson and negative exponential distributions

overloaded. In many instances, the variabilities can be described by theoretical distributions. In fact, the most commonly used models assume that the customer arrival *rate* can be described by a Poisson distribution and that the service *time* can be described by a negative exponential distribution. These distributions are illustrated in Figure 17–4.

The Poisson distribution often provides a reasonably good description of customer arrivals per unit of time (e.g., per hour). Figure 17–5A illustrates how

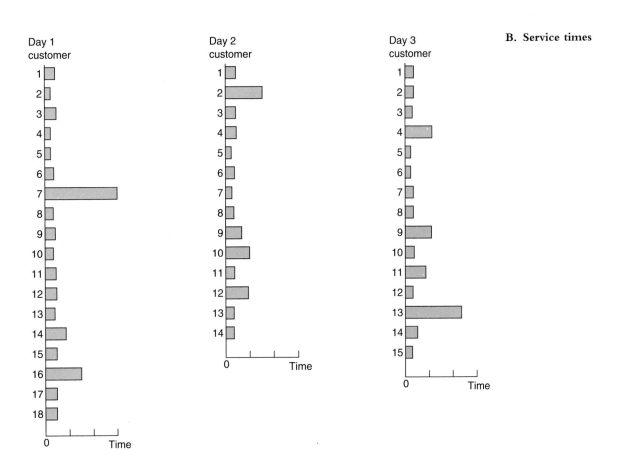

Figure 17–5

Poisson arrivals and exponential service times

A. Customer arrivals

B. Service times

Poisson-distributed arrivals (say, accidents) might occur during a three-day period. Note that in some hours, there are three or four arrivals, in other hours there are one or two arrivals, and in some hours, there are no arrivals.

The negative exponential distribution often provides a reasonably good description of customer service times (e.g., first aid care for accident victims). Figure 17–5B illustrates how exponential service times might appear for the customers whose arrivals are illustrated in Figure 17–5A. Note that most service times are very short—some are close to zero—but a few require a relatively long service time. That is typical of a negative exponential distribution.

Waiting lines are most likely to occur when arrivals are bunched or when service times are particularly lengthy, and they are very likely to occur when both factors are present. For instance, note the long service time of customer 7 on day 1, as shown in Figure 17–5B. Note in Figure 17–5A that the seventh customer arrived just after 10 o'clock, and that the next two customers arrived shortly after that, making it very likely that a waiting line formed. A similar situation occurred on day 3 with the last 3 customers: The relatively long service time for customer 13 (Figure 17–5B), and the short time before the next two arrivals (Figure 17A, day 3) would create (or increase the length of) a waiting line.

It is interesting to note that the Poisson and negative exponential distributions are alternate ways of presenting the same basic information. That is, if service time is exponential, then the service rate is Poisson. Similarly, if the customer arrival rate is Poisson, then the interarrival time (i.e., the time between arrivals) is exponential. For example, if a service facility can process 12 customers per hour (rate), average service time is five minutes. Similarly, if the arrival rate is 10 per hour, then the average time between arrivals is six minutes. Hence, the models described here generally require that arrival and service rates lend themselves to description using a Poisson distribution, or equivalently, that interarrival and service times lend themselves to description using a negative exponential distribution. In practice, it is necessary to verify that these assumptions are met. Sometimes this is done by collecting data and plotting them, although the preferred approach is to use a chi-square goodness-of-fit test for that purpose. A discussion of the chi-square test is beyond the scope of this text. However, most basic statistics textbooks cover the topic.

Research has shown that these assumptions are often appropriate for customer arrivals but less likely to be appropriate for service. In situations where the assumptions are not reasonably satisfied, the alternatives would be to (1) develop a more suitable model, (2) search for a better (and usually more complex) existing model, or (3) resort to computer simulation. Each of these alternatives requires more effort or cost than the ones presented here.

QUEUE DISCIPLINE

Queue discipline

The order in which customers are processed.

Queue discipline refers to the order in which customers are processed. All but one of the models to be described here assume that service is provided on a *first-come, first-served* basis. This is perhaps the most commonly encountered rule. We find first-come service at banks, stores, theaters, restaurants, four-way stop signs, registration lines, and so on. Examples of systems that do not serve on a first-come basis include hospital emergency rooms, rush orders in a factory, and computer processing of programs. In these and similar situations, customers do not all represent the same waiting costs; those with the highest costs (e.g., most seriously ill) are processed first, even though other customers may have arrived earlier.

MEASURES OF SYSTEM PERFORMANCE

The operations manager typically looks at five measures when evaluating existing or proposed service systems. Those measures are:

1. The average number of customers waiting, either in line or in the system.
2. The average time customers wait, either in line or in the system.
3. System utilization, which refers to the percentage of capacity utilized.
4. The implied cost of a given level of capacity and its related waiting line.
5. The probability that an arrival will have to wait for service.

Of these measures, system utilization bears some elaboration. It reflects the extent to which the servers are busy rather than idle. On the surface, it might seem that the operations manager would want to seek 100 percent utilization. However, as illustrated in Figure 17–6, increases in system utilization are achieved at the expense of increases in both the length of the waiting line and the average waiting time. In fact, these values become exceedingly large as utilization approaches 100 percent. The implication is that under normal circumstances, 100 percent utilization is not a realistic goal. Instead, the operations manager should try to achieve a system that minimizes the sum of waiting costs and capacity costs.

QUEUING MODELS: INFINITE-SOURCE

There are many queuing models available for a manager or analyst to choose from. The discussion here will include four of the most basic and most widely used models. The purpose is to provide an exposure to a range of models rather than an extensive coverage of the field. The four models described here are listed below. All assume a Poisson arrival rate. Moreover, the models pertain to a system operating under *steady state* conditions; that is, they assume the average arrival and service rates are stable. The models are:

1. Single channel, exponential service time.
2. Single channel, constant service time.
3. Multiple channel, exponential service time.
4. Multiple priority service.

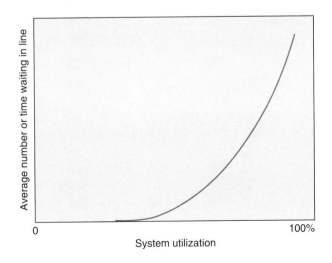

Figure 17–6

The average number waiting in line and the average time customers wait in line increase exponentially as the system utilization increases

Table 17–1	Symbol	Represents
Infinite-source symbols	λ	Customer arrival rate
	μ	Service rate
	L_q	The average number of customers waiting for service
	L_s	The average number of customers in the system (waiting or being served)
	ρ	The system utilization
	W_q	The average time customers wait in line
	W_s	The average time customers spend in the system (waiting in line and service time)
	$1/\mu$	Service time
	P_0	The probability of zero units in the system
	P_n	The probability of n units in the system
	M	The number of servers (channels)
	L_{max}	The maximum expected number waiting in line

To facilitate your use of queuing models, Table 17–1 provides a list of the symbols used for the infinite-source models.

BASIC RELATIONSHIPS

There are certain basic relationships that hold for all infinite-source models. Knowledge of these can be very helpful in deriving desired performance measures, given a few key values. These basic relationships are:

1. The average number being served is the ratio of arrival rate to service rate:

$$r = \frac{\lambda}{\mu} \tag{17–1}$$

[*Note:* λ and μ must be in the same units (e.g., customers per hour, customers per minute)]

2. The average number in the system is the average number in line plus the average number being served:

$$L_s = L_q + r \tag{17–2}$$

3. The average time in line is the average number in line divided by the arrival rate:

$$W_q = \frac{L_q}{\lambda} \tag{17–3}$$

4. The average time in the system is the sum of the time in line plus service time:

$$W_s = W_q + \frac{1}{\mu} \tag{17–4}$$

5. System utilization is the ratio of arrival rate to service capacity:

$$\rho = \frac{\lambda}{M\mu} \tag{17–5}$$

All infinite-source models require that system utilization be less than 1.0; the models apply only to underloaded systems.

The average number waiting in line, L_q, is a key value because it is a determinant of some of the other measures of system performance, such as the average number in the system, the average time in line, and the average time in the system. Hence, L_q will usually be one of the first values you will want to determine in problem solving.

Example 1

∎

Customers arrive at a bakery at an average rate of 18 per hour on weekday mornings. The arrival distribution can be described by a Poisson distribution with a mean of 18. Each clerk can serve a customer in an average of four minutes; this time can be described by an exponential distribution with a mean of 4.0 minutes.

   a.   What are the arrival and service *rates?*

   b.   Compute the average number of customers being served at any time.

   c.   Suppose it has been determined that the average number of customers waiting in line is 3.6. Compute the average number of customers in the system (i.e., waiting in line or being served), the average time customers wait in line, and the average time in the system.

   d.   Determine the system utilization for $M = 2, 3,$ and 4 servers.

Solution

   a.   The arrival rate is given in the problem: $\lambda = 18$ customers per hour. The service time can be changed to a comparable *hourly* rate by first restating the time in hours and then taking its reciprocal. Thus, (4 minutes per customer)/(60 minutes per hour) $= 1/15 = 1/\mu$. Its reciprocal is $\mu = 15$ customers per hour.

   b. $r = \dfrac{\lambda}{\mu} = \dfrac{18}{15} = 1.2$ customers.

   c.   Given: $L_q = 3.6$ customers.

$$L_s = L_q + r = 3.6 + 1.2 = 4.8 \text{ customers}$$

$$W_q = \frac{L_q}{\lambda} = \frac{3.6}{18} = 0.20 \text{ hours per customer, or } 0.20 \text{ hours}$$

$$\times\ 60 \text{ minutes/hour} = 12 \text{ minutes}$$

$W_s = $ Waiting in line plus service

$$= W_q + \frac{1}{\mu} = 0.20 + \frac{1}{15} = 0.267 \text{ hours, or approximately 16 minutes}$$

   d.   System utilization is $\rho = \dfrac{\lambda}{M\mu}$

$$\text{For } M = 2, \rho = \frac{18}{2(15)} = .60$$

$$\text{For } M = 3, \rho = \frac{18}{3(15)} = .40$$

$$\text{For } M = 4, \rho = \frac{18}{4(15)} = .30$$

Hence, as the system capacity as measured by $M\mu$ increases, the system utilization for a given arrival rate decreases.

Table 17–2	Performance measure	Equation	
Formulas for basic single-server model	Average number in line	$L_q = \dfrac{\lambda^2}{\mu(\mu - \lambda)}$	**(17–6)**
	Probability of zero units in the system	$P_0 = 1 - \left(\dfrac{\lambda}{\mu}\right)$	**(17–7)**
	Probability of n units in the system	$P_n = P_0\left(\dfrac{\lambda}{\mu}\right)^n$	**(17–8)**

MODEL 1: SINGLE CHANNEL, EXPONENTIAL SERVICE TIME

The simplest model involves a system that has one server (or a single crew). The queue discipline is first-come, first-served, and it is assumed that the customer arrival rate can be approximated by a Poisson distribution and service time by a negative exonential distribution. There is no limit on length of queue.

Table 17–2 lists the formulas for the single-channel model, which should be used in conjunction with formulas 17–1 through 17–5.

Example 2

An airline is planning to open a satellite ticket desk in a new shopping plaza, staffed by one ticket agent. It is estimated that requests for tickets and information will average 15 per hour, and requests will have a Poisson distribution. Service time is assumed to be exponentially distributed. Previous experience with similar satellite operations suggests that mean service time should average about three minutes per request. Determine each of the following.

a. System utilization.
b. Percent of time the server (agent) will be idle.
c. The expected number of customers waiting to be served.
d. The average time customers will spend in the system.
e. The probability of zero customers in the system and the probability of four customers in the system.

Solution

$\lambda = 15$ per hour

$\mu = \dfrac{1}{\text{Service time}} = \dfrac{1 \text{ customer}}{3 \text{ minutes}} \times 60 \text{ minutes per hour}$
$= 20$ customers per hour

a. $\rho = \dfrac{\lambda}{M\mu} = \dfrac{15}{1(20)} = .75$

b. Percentage idle time $= 1 - \rho = 1 - .75 = .25$, or 25 percent

c. $L_q = \dfrac{\lambda^2}{\mu(\mu - \lambda)} = \dfrac{15^2}{20(20 - 15)} = 2.25$ customers

$$d. \quad W_s = \frac{L_q}{\lambda} + \frac{1}{\mu} = \frac{2.25}{15} + \frac{1}{20} = 0.20 \text{ hours, or 12 minutes}$$

$$e. \quad P_0 = 1 - \frac{\lambda}{\mu} = 1 - \frac{15}{20} = .25; \quad P_4 = P_0\left(\frac{\lambda}{\mu}\right)^4 = .25\left(\frac{15}{20}\right)^4 = .079$$

MODEL 2: SINGLE CHANNEL, CONSTANT SERVICE TIME

As noted previously, waiting lines are a consequence of random, highly variable arrival and service rates. If the variability of either or both can be reduced or eliminated, waiting lines can be shortened noticeably. A case in point is a system with constant service time. The effect of a constant service time is to cut in half both the average number of customers waiting in line and the average time customers spend waiting in line. Similar improvements can be realized by smoothing arrival times (e.g., by use of appointments). In effect, the formulas 17–1 through 17–6 can be used for problems with constant service time as long as the computed value of L_q is divided by 2.

Wanda's Car Wash & Dry is an automatic, five-minute operation with a single bay. On a typical Saturday morning, cars arrive at a mean rate of eight per hour, with arrivals tending to follow a Poisson distribution. Find:

a. The average number of cars in line.
b. The average time cars spend in line and service.

Example 3

Solution

$\lambda = 8$ cars per hour
$\mu = 1$ per 5 minutes, or 12 per hour

$$a. \quad L_q = \frac{\lambda^2}{2\mu(\mu - \lambda)} = \frac{8^2}{2(12)(12 - 8)} = 0.667 \text{ cars}$$

$$b. \quad W_s = \frac{L_q}{\lambda} + \frac{1}{\mu} = \frac{0.667}{8} + \frac{1}{12} = 0.167 \text{ hours, or 10 minutes}$$

MODEL 3: MULTIPLE CHANNEL

A multiple-channel system exists whenever there are two or more servers working *independently* to provide service to customer arrivals. Use of the model involves the following assumptions:

1. A Poisson arrival rate and exponential service time.
2. Servers all work at the same average rate.
3. Customers form a single waiting line (in order to maintain first-come, first-served processing).

Formulas for the multiple-channel model are listed in Table 17–3. Obviously, the multiple-channel formulas are more complex than the single-channel formulas, especially the formulas for L_q and P_0. These formulas are shown primarily for completeness; actual determination of their values can be made using Table 17–4, which gives values of L_q and P_0 for selected values of λ/μ and M.

To use Table 17–4, compute the value of λ/μ and round according to the number of decimal places given for that ratio in the table. Then simply read the values of L_q and P_0 for the appropriate number of channels, M. For instance, if $\lambda/\mu = 0.50$ and $M = 2$, the table provides a value of 0.033 for L_q and a value of .600 for P_0. These values can then be used to compute other measures of system performance. Note that the formulas in Table 17–3 and the values in Table 17–4 yield *average* amounts (i.e., expected values). Note also that Table 17–4 can also be used for single-channel problems (i.e., $M = 1$).

Table 17–3	Performance measure	Equation	
Multiple-channel queuing formulas	Average number in line	$$L_q = \dfrac{\lambda\mu\left(\dfrac{\lambda}{\mu}\right)^M}{(M-1)!(M\mu-\lambda)^2}P_0$$	(17–9)
	Probability of zero units in the system	$$P_0 = \left[\sum_{n=0}^{M-1}\dfrac{\left(\dfrac{\lambda}{\mu}\right)^n}{n!} + \dfrac{\left(\dfrac{\lambda}{\mu}\right)^M}{M!\left(1-\dfrac{\lambda}{M\mu}\right)}\right]^{-1}$$	(17–10)
	Average waiting time for an arrival not immediately served	$$W_a = \dfrac{1}{M\mu-\lambda}$$	(17–11)
	Probability that an arrival will have to wait for service	$$P_w = \left(\dfrac{\lambda}{\mu}\right)^M\dfrac{P_0}{M!\left(1-\dfrac{\lambda}{M\mu}\right)}$$	(17–12)

Table 17–4

Infinite-source values for L_q and P_0 given λ/μ and M

λ/μ	M	L_q	P_0	λ/μ	M	L_q	P_0	λ/μ	M	L_q	P_0
0.15	1	0.026	.850	0.45	1	0.368	.550	0.65	1	1.207	.350
	2	0.001	.860		2	0.024	.633		2	0.077	.509
0.20	1	0.050	.800		3	0.002	.637		3	0.008	.521
	2	0.002	.818	0.50	1	0.500	.500	0.70	1	1.633	.300
0.25	1	0.083	.750		2	0.033	.600		2	0.098	.481
	2	0.004	.778		3	0.003	.606		3	0.011	.495
0.30	1	0.129	.700	0.55	1	0.672	.450	0.75	1	2.250	.250
	2	0.007	.739		2	0.045	.569		2	0.123	.455
0.35	1	0.188	.650		3	0.004	.576		3	0.015	.471
	2	0.011	.702	0.60	1	0.900	.400	0.80	1	3.200	.200
0.40	1	0.267	.600		2	0.059	.538		2	1.152	.429
	2	0.017	.667		3	0.006	.548		3	0.019	.447

Table 17-4

(continued)

λ/μ	M	L_q	P_0	λ/μ	M	L_q	P_0	λ/μ	M	L_q	P_0
0.85	1	4.817	.150	1.9	3	0.688	.128	2.9	5	0.293	.052
	2	0.187	.404		4	0.136	.145		6	0.081	.054
	3	0.024	.425		5	0.030	.149		7	0.023	.055
	4	0.003	.427		6	0.007	.149	3.0	4	1.528	.038
0.90	1	8.100	.100	2.0	3	0.889	.111		5	0.354	.047
	2	0.229	.379		4	0.174	.130		6	0.099	.049
	3	0.030	.403		5	0.040	.134		7	0.028	.050
	4	0.004	.406		6	0.009	..135		8	0.008	.050
0.95	1	18.050	.050	2.1	3	1.149	.096	3.1	4	1.902	.032
	2	0.277	.356		4	0.220	.117		5	0.427	.042
	3	0.037	.383		5	0.052	.121		6	0.120	.044
	4	0.005	.386		6	0.012	.122		7	0.035	.045
1.0	2	0.333	.333	2.2	3	1.491	.081		8	0.010	.045
	3	0.045	.364		4	0.277	.105	3.2	4	2.386	.027
	4	0.007	.367		5	0.066	.109		5	0.513	.037
1.1	2	0.477	.290		6	0.016	.111		6	0.145	.040
	3	0.066	.327	2.3	3	1.951	.068		7	0.043	.040
	4	0.011	.367		4	0.346	.093		8	0.012	.041
1.2	2	0.675	.250		5	0.084	.099	3.3	4	3.027	.023
	3	0.094	.294		6	0.021	.100		5	0.615	.033
	4	0.016	.300	2.4	3	2.589	.056		6	0.174	.036
	5	0.003	.301		4	0.431	.083		7	0.052	.037
1.3	2	0.951	.212		5	0.105	.089		8	0.015	.037
	3	0.130	.264		6	0.027	.090	3.4	4	3.906	.019
	4	0.023	.271		7	0.007	.091		5	0.737	.029
	5	0.004	.272	2.5	3	3.511	.045		6	0.209	.032
1.4	2	1.345	.176		4	0.533	.074		7	0.063	.033
	3	0.177	.236		5	0.130	.080		8	0.019	.033
	4	0.032	.245		6	0.034	.082	3.5	4	5.165	.015
	5	0.006	.246		7	0.009	.082		5	0.882	.026
1.5	2	1.929	.143	2.6	3	4.933	.035		6	0.248	.029
	3	0.237	.211		4	0.658	.065		7	0.076	.030
	4	0.045	.221		5	0.161	.072		8	0.023	.030
	5	0.009	.223		6	0.043	.074		9	0.007	.030
1.6	2	2.844	.111		7	0.011	.074	3.6	4	7.090	.011
	3	0.313	.187	2.7	3	7.354	.025		5	1.055	.023
	4	0.060	.199		4	0.811	.057		6	0.295	.026
	5	0.012	.201		5	0.198	.065		7	0.089	.027
1.7	2	4.426	.081		6	0.053	.067		8	0.028	.027
	3	0.409	.166		7	0.014	.067		9	0.008	.027
	4	0.080	.180	2.8	3	12.273	.016	3.7	4	10.347	.008
	5	0.017	.182		4	1.000	.050		5	1.265	.020
1.8	2	7.674	.053		5	0.241	.058		6	0.349	.023
	3	0.532	.146		6	0.066	.060		7	0.109	.024
	4	0.105	.162		7	0.018	.061		8	0.034	.025
	5	0.023	.165	2.9	3	27.193	.008		9	0.010	.025
1.9	2	17.587	.026		4	1.234	.044	3.8	4	16.937	.005

Table 17–4

(continued)

λ/μ	M	L_q	P_0	λ/μ	M	L_q	P_0	λ/μ	M	L_q	P_0
3.8	5	1.519	.017	4.6	7	0.453	.009	5.3	12	0.007	.005
	6	0.412	.021		8	0.156	.010	5.4	6	6.661	.002
	7	0.129	.022		9	0.054	.010		7	1.444	.004
	8	0.041	.022		10	0.018	.010		8	0.483	.004
	9	0.013	.022	4.7	5	13.382	.003		9	0.178	.004
3.9	4	36.859	.002		6	1.752	.007		10	0.066	.004
	5	1.830	.015		7	0.525	.008		11	0.024	.005
	6	0.485	.019		8	0.181	.008		12	0.009	.005
	7	0.153	.020		9	0.064	.009	5.5	6	8.590	.002
	8	0.050	.020		10	0.022	.009		7	1.674	.003
	9	0.016	.020	4.8	5	21.641	.002		8	0.553	.004
4.0	5	2.216	.013		6	2.071	.006		9	0.204	.004
	6	0.570	.017		7	0.607	.008		10	0.077	.004
	7	0.180	.018		8	0.209	.008		11	0.028	.004
	8	0.059	.018		9	0.074	.008		12	0.010	.004
	9	0.019	.018		10	0.026	.008	5.6	6	11.519	.001
4.1	5	2.703	.011	4.9	5	46.566	.001		7	1.944	.003
	6	0.668	.015		6	2.459	.005		8	0.631	.003
	7	0.212	.016		7	0.702	.007		9	0.233	.004
	8	0.070	.016		8	0.242	.007		10	0.088	.004
	9	0.023	.017		9	0.087	.007		11	0.033	.004
4.2	5	3.327	.009		10	0.031	.007		12	0.012	.004
	6	0.784	.013		11	0.011	.077	5.7	6	16.446	.001
	7	0.248	.014	5.0	6	2.938	.005		7	2.264	.002
	8	0.083	.015		7	0.810	.006		8	0.721	.003
	9	0.027	.015		8	0.279	.006		9	0.266	.003
	10	0.009	.015		9	0.101	.007		10	0.102	.003
4.3	5	4.149	.008		10	0.036	.007		11	0.038	.003
	6	0.919	.012		11	0.013	.007		12	0.014	.003
	7	0.289	.130	5.1	6	3.536	.004	5.8	6	26.373	.001
	8	0.097	.013		7	0.936	.005		7	2.648	.002
	9	0.033	.014		8	0.321	.006		8	0.823	.003
	10	0.011	.014		9	0.117	.006		9	0.303	.003
4.4	5	5.268	.006		10	0.042	.006		10	0.116	.003
	6	1.078	.010		11	0.015	.006		11	0.044	.003
	7	0.337	.012	5.2	6	4.301	.003		12	0.017	.003
	8	0.114	.012		7	1.081	.005	5.9	6	56.300	.000
	9	0.039	.012		8	0.368	.005		7	3.113	.002
	10	0.013	.012		9	0.135	.005		8	0.939	.002
4.5	5	6.862	.005		10	0.049	.005		9	0.345	.003
	6	1.265	.009		11	0.017	.006		10	0.133	.003
	7	0.391	.010	5.3	6	5.303	.003		11	0.051	.003
	8	0.133	.011		7	1.249	.004		12	0.019	.003
	9	0.046	.011		8	0.422	.005	6.0	7	3.683	.001
	10	0.015	.011		9	0.155	.005		8	1.071	.002
4.6	5	9.289	.004		10	0.057	.005		9	0.392	.002
	6	1.487	.008		11	0.021	.005		10	0.152	.002

Table 17–4

(concluded)

λ/μ	M	L_q	P_0	λ/μ	M	L_q	P_0	λ/μ	M	L_q	P_0
6.0	11	0.059	.002	6.8	7	31.127	.000	7.6	10	1.031	.0004
	12	0.022	.002		8	3.245	.001		11	0.421	.0005
6.1	7	4.394	.001		9	1.054	.001		12	0.179	.0005
	8	1.222	.002		10	0.409	.001	7.7	8	22.636	.0001
	9	0.445	.002		11	0.167	.001		9	3.343	.0003
	10	0.173	.002		12	0.068	.001		10	1.157	.0004
	11	0.068	.002	6.9	7	66.055	.000		11	0.471	.0004
	12	0.026	.002		8	3.786	.001		12	0.201	.0004
6.2	7	5.298	.001		9	1.191	.001	7.8	8	35.898	.0001
	8	1.397	.002		10	0.460	.001		9	3.856	.0002
	9	0.504	.002		11	0.188	.001		10	1.298	.0004
	10	0.197	.002		12	0.077	.001		11	0.525	.0004
	11	0.078	.002	7.0	8	4.447	.001		12	0.244	.0004
	12	0.030	.002		9	1.347	.001	7.9	8	75.827	.00003
6.3	7	6.480	.001		10	0.517	.001		9	4.474	.00023
	8	1.598	.001		11	0.212	.001		10	1.457	.00031
	9	0.571	.002		12	0.088	.001		11	0.586	.00035
	10	0.233	.002	7.1	8	5.270	.000		12	0.251	.00036
	11	0.089	.002		9	1.525	.001	8.0	9	5.227	.00020
	12	0.035	.002		10	0.581	.001		10	1.637	.00028
6.4	7	8.077	.001		11	0.238	.001		11	0.653	.00031
	8	1.831	.001		12	0.009	.001		12	0.280	.00033
	9	0.645	.002	7.2	8	6.314	.000	8.1	9	6.161	.00017
	10	0.253	.002		9	1.729	.001		10	1.841	.00025
	11	0.101	.002		10	0.652	.001		11	0.728	.00028
	12	0.040	.002		11	0.268	.001		12	0.312	.00029
6.5	7	10.341	.001		12	0.112	.001	8.2	9	7.344	.00014
	8	2.102	.001	7.3	8	7.675	.0003		10	2.074	.00022
	9	0.730	.001		9	1.963	.0005		11	0.811	.00025
	10	0.285	.001		10	0.732	.0006		12	0.347	.00026
	11	0.115	.001		11	0.300	.0007	8.3	9	8.884	.00011
	12	0.046	.001		12	0.126	.0007		10	2.341	.00019
6.6	7	13.770	.000	7.4	8	9.511	.0003		11	0.903	.00022
	8	2.420	.001		9	2.233	.0005		12	0.386	.00024
	9	0.825	.001		10	0.820	.0006	8.4	9	10.960	.00009
	10	0.285	.001		11	0.337	.0006		10	2.647	.00017
	11	0.130	.001		12	0.142	.0006		11	1.006	.00020
	12	0.052	.001	7.5	8	12.109	.0002		12	0.429	.00021
6.7	7	19.532	.000		9	2.546	.0004	8.5	9	13.891	.00007
	8	2.796	.001		10	0.920	.0005		10	3.003	.00015
	9	0.932	.001		11	0.377	.0005		11	1.121	.00018
	10	0.363	.001		12	0.160	.0005		12	0.476	.00019
	11	0.147	.001	7.6	8	16.039	.0002				
	12	0.060	.001		9	2.912	.0004				

Example 4

Alpha Taxi and Hauling Company has 10 cabs stationed at the airport. The company has determined that during the late-evening hours on weeknights, customers request cabs at a rate that follows the Poisson distribution with a mean of 9.6 per hour. Service time is exponential with a mean of 50 minutes per customer. Assume that there is one customer per cab. Find each of the performance measures listed in Table 17–3, and the system utilization.

Solution

$$\lambda = 9.6 \text{ per hour} \qquad M = 10 \text{ cabs (servers)}$$

$$\mu = \frac{1 \text{ customer per trip}}{50 \text{ minutes per trip} \div 60 \text{ minutes per hour}}$$
$$= 1.2 \text{ customers per hour per cab}$$

$\lambda/\mu = 8.0$. From Table 17–4, with $M = 10$; $L_q = 1.637$ and $P_0 = .00028$

a. $L_q = 1.637$ customers

b. $P_0 = .00028$ (from Table 17–4)

c. $W_a = \dfrac{1}{M\mu - \lambda} = \dfrac{1}{10(1.2) - 9.6} = 0.4167 \text{ hours}$

d. $P_w = \left(\dfrac{\lambda}{\mu}\right)^M \dfrac{P_0}{M!\left(1 - \dfrac{\lambda}{M\mu}\right)} = (8)^{10} \dfrac{.00028}{10!\left(1 - \dfrac{9.6}{10(1.2)}\right)} = .414$

e. $\rho = \dfrac{\lambda}{M\mu} = \dfrac{9.6}{10(1.2)} = .80$

The process can also be worked in reverse; that is, an analyst can determine the capacity needed to achieve specified levels of various performance measures. This approach is illustrated in the following example.

Example 5

Alpha Taxi and Hauling also plans to have cabs at a new rail station. The expected arrival rate is 4.8 customers per hour, and the service rate (including return time to the rail station) is expected to be 1.5 per hour. How many cabs will be needed to achieve an average time in line of 20 minutes or less?

Solution

$$\lambda = 4.8 \text{ customers per hour}$$
$$\mu = 1.5 \text{ customers per hour}$$
$$M = ?$$

$$r = \frac{\lambda}{\mu} = \frac{4.8}{1.5} = 3.2$$

W_q (desired) $= 20$ minutes, or 0.333 hour

Using $L_q = \lambda W_q$, we can solve for L_q: 4.8/hour(0.333 hour) = 1.6 units. Thus, the average number waiting should not exceed 1.6 customers. Referring to Table 17–4, with $r = 3.2$, we find $L_q = 2.386$ for $M = 4$ and 0.513 for $M = 5$. Hence, five cabs will be needed.

Another question that often comes up in capacity planning is the amount of space to allocate for waiting lines. Theoretically, with an infinite population source, the waiting line can become infinitely long. This implies that no matter how much space is allocated for a waiting line, one can never be completely sure that the space requirements won't exceed that amount. Nonetheless, as a practical matter, one can determine a line that will not be exceeded a specified proportion of the time. For instance, an analyst may wish to know the length of line that will probably not be exceeded 98 percent of the time, or perhaps 99 percent of the time, and use that number as a planning value.

The approximate line length that will satisfy a specified percentage can be determined by solving the following equation for n:

$$n = \frac{\log K}{\log \rho} \text{ or } \frac{\ln K}{\ln \rho} \qquad \text{where } K = \frac{1 - \dfrac{\text{Specified}}{\text{percentage}}}{L_q(1 - \rho)} \qquad (17-13)$$

The resulting value of n will not usually be an integer. Generally, round *up* to the next integer and treat the value as n. However, as a practical matter, if the computed value of n is less than 0.10 above the next lower integer, round down. Thus, 15.2 would be rounded to 16, but 15.06 would be rounded to 15.

Determine the maximum length of a waiting line for specified probabilities of 95 percent and 98 percent, for a system in which $M = 2$, $\lambda = 8$ per hour, and $\mu = 5$ per hour.

Example 6

∎

Solution

$$r = \frac{8}{5} = 1.6 \qquad \text{and} \qquad \rho = \frac{8}{2(5)} = .80$$

From Table 17–4, $L_q = 2.844$ customers. For 95 percent, using Formula 17–13,

$$K = \frac{1 - .95}{2.844(1 - .80)} = .088$$

$$n = \frac{\ln .088}{\ln .80} = \frac{-2.4304}{-.2231} = 10.89, \text{ which rounds to 11.}$$

For 98 percent

$$K = \frac{1 - .98}{2.844(1 - .80)} = .035$$

$$n = \frac{\ln .035}{\ln .80} = \frac{-3.352}{-.2231} = 15.02, \text{ which rounds to 15.}$$

MODEL 4: MULTIPLE PRIORITIES

In many queuing systems, processing occurs on a first-come, first-served basis. However, there are situations in which that rule is not appropriate. The reason is that the cost or penalty incurred is not the same for all customers. For example, in a hospital emergency waiting room, a wide variety of injuries and illnesses need treatment. Some may be minor (sliver in finger), and others may be much more serious, even life-threatening. It is more reasonable to treat the most serious cases first, letting the non-serious cases wait until all serious cases have been treated. Similarly, computer processing of jobs often follows rules other than first-come, first-served (e.g., shortest job first). In such cases, a **multiple-priority model** is useful for describing system behavior.

In these systems, arriving customers are assigned to one of several *priority classes,* or categories, according to a predetermined assignment method (e.g., heart attacks, serious injuries, and unconscious persons are assigned to the highest priority class; sprains, minor cuts, bruises, rashes, etc. are assigned to the lowest class; and other problems are assigned to one or more intermediate classes). Customers are then processed by class, highest class first. Within each class, processing is first-come, first-served. Thus, all customers in the highest class would be processed before those in the next lower class, then processing would move to that class, and then to the next lower class. Exceptions would occur only if a higher priority customer arrived; that customer would be processed *after* the customer currently being processed (i.e., service would not be *preemptive*).

This model incorporates all of the assumptions of the basic multiple-server model except that priority serving is used rather than first-come, first-served. Arrivals to the system are assigned a priority as they arrive (e.g., highest priority = 1, next priority class = 2, next priority class = 3, and so on). An existing queue might look something like this:

Within each class, waiting units are processed in the order they arrived (i.e., first-come, first-served). Thus, in this sequence, the first #1 would be processed as soon as a server was available. The second #1 would be processed when that server, or another one, became available. If, in the interim, another #1 arrived, it would be next in line *ahead of the first #2.* If there were no new arrivals, the only #2 would be processed by the next available server. At that point, if a new #1 arrived, it would be processed ahead of the #3s and the #4. Similarly, a new #2 would be processed ahead of the #3s and the #4. Conversely, if a new #4 arrived, it would take its place at the end of the line.

Obviously, a unit with a low priority could conceivably wait a rather long time for processing. In some cases, units that have waited more than some specified time are reassigned a higher priority.

The appropriate formulas for this multiple-channel priority service model are given in Table 17–5.

Performance measure	Formula	Formula number	Table 17–5
System utilization Intermediate values (L_q from Table 17–4)	$\rho = \dfrac{\lambda}{M\mu}$	(17–14)	Multiple-server priority service model
	$A = \dfrac{\lambda}{(1 - \rho)L_q}$	(17–15)	
	$B_k = 1 - \displaystyle\sum_{c=1}^{k} \dfrac{\lambda_c}{M\mu}$	(17–16)	
	$(B_0 = 1)$		
Average waiting time in line for units in kth priority class	$W_k = \dfrac{1}{A \cdot B_{k-1} \cdot B_k}$	(17–17)	
Average time in the system for units in the kth priority class	$W = W_k + \dfrac{1}{\mu}$	(17–18)	
Average number waiting in line for units in the kth priority class	$L_k = \lambda_k \cdot W_k$	(17–19)	

A machine shop handles tool repairs in a large company. As each job arrives in the shop, it is assigned a priority based on urgency of the need for that tool. Requests for repair can be described by a Poisson distribution. Arrival rates are: $\lambda_1 = 2$ per hour, $\lambda_2 = 2$ per hour, and $\lambda_3 = 1$ per hour. The service rate is one tool per hour for each server, and there are six servers in the shop. Determine the following information.

Example 7

a. The system utilization.
b. The average time a tool in each of the priority classes will wait for service.
c. The average time a tool spends in the system for each priority class.
d. The average number of tools waiting for repair in each class.

Solution

$\lambda = \Sigma\lambda_k = 2 + 2 + 1 = 5$ per hour
$M = 6$ servers
$\mu = 1$ customer per hour

a. $\rho = \dfrac{\lambda}{M\mu} = \dfrac{5}{6(1)} = .833$

b. Intermediate values ($\lambda/\mu = 5/1 = 5$; from Table 17–4, $L_q = 2.938$)

$A = \dfrac{5}{(1 - .833)2.938} = 10.19$

$B_0 = 1$

(continued)

Example 7

(concluded)

$$B_1 = 1 - \frac{2}{6(1)} = \frac{2}{3} = .667$$

$$B_2 = 1 - \frac{2 + 2}{6(1)} = \frac{1}{3} = .333$$

$$B_3 = 1 - \frac{2 + 2 + 1}{6(1)} = \frac{1}{6} = .167$$

$$W_1 = \frac{1}{A \cdot B_0 \cdot B_1} = \frac{1}{10.19(1)(.667)} = 0.147 \text{ hours}$$

$$W_2 = \frac{1}{A \cdot B_1 \cdot B_2} = \frac{1}{10.19(.667)(.333)} = 0.442 \text{ hours}$$

$$W_3 = \frac{1}{A \cdot B_2 \cdot B_3} = \frac{1}{10.19(.333)(.167)} = 1.765 \text{ hours}$$

c.   Average time in system $= W_k + 1/\mu$. In this case, $1/\mu = 1/1 = 1$. Thus, we have:

Class	$W_k + 1 = W$ (hours)
1	0.147 + 1 = 1.147
2	0.442 + 1 = 1.442
3	1.765 + 1 = 2.765

d.   The average number of units waiting in each class is $L_k = \lambda_k \cdot W_k$. Thus, we have:

Class	$\lambda_k \cdot W_k = L_k$ (units)
1	2(0.147) = 0.294
2	2(0.442) = 0.884
3	1(1.765) = 1.765

Revising Priorities

If any of the waiting times computed in the preceding example are deemed too long by management (e.g, a waiting time of 0.147 hours for tools in the first class might be too long), there are several options. One is to increase the number of servers. Another is to attempt to increase the service rate, say, by introducing new methods. If such options are not feasible, another approach would be to reexamine the membership of each of the priority classifications. The reason for this is that if some repair requests, say, in the first priority class can be reassigned to the second priority class, this will tend to decrease the average waiting times for repair jobs in the highest priority classification, simply because the arrival rate of those items will be lower.

Example 8

∎

The manager of the repair shop, after consulting with the managers of the departments that use the shop's services, has been able to revise the list of tools that are given the highest priorities. This is reflected by revised arrival rates. Suppose that the revised rates are: $\lambda_1 = 1.5$, $\lambda_2 = 2.5$, and λ_3 remains unchanged at 1.0. Determine the following information:

a.   The system utilization.

b.   The average waiting time for units in each priority class.

Solution

$$\lambda = \Sigma\lambda_k = 1.5 + 2.5 + 1.0 = 5.0$$
$$M = 6$$
$$\mu = 1$$

Note that these values are the same as in the previous example.

a. $\rho = 5.0/6(1) = .833$, the same as in the previous example.

b. The value of A, since it is a function of M, μ, and λ, is the same as in the preceding example because these values are the same. Therefore, $A = 10.19$ and

$$B_0 = 1 \text{ (always)}$$

$$B_1 = 1 - \frac{1.5}{6(1)} = .75$$

$$B_2 = 1 - \frac{1.5 + 2.5}{6(1)} = .333$$

$$B_3 = 1 - \frac{1.5 + 2.5 + 1.0}{6(1)} = .167$$

Then

$$W_1 = \frac{1}{10.19(1)(.75)} = 0.131 \text{ hours}$$

$$W_2 = \frac{1}{10.19(.75)(.333)} = 0.393 \text{ hours}$$

$$W_3 = \frac{1}{10.19(.333)(.167)} = 1.765 \text{ hours}$$

In the preceding example, we find several interesting results. One is that through reduction of the arrival rate of the highest priority class, the average waiting time for units in that class has decreased. In other words, removing some members of the highest class and placing them into the next lower class reduced the average waiting time for units that remained in the highest class. Note, though, the average waiting time for the second priority class also was reduced, even though units were added to that class. Although this may appear counterintuitive, it is necessary to recognize that the *total* waiting time (when all arrivals are taken into account) will remain unchanged. We can see this by noticing that the average *number* waiting (see Example 7, part *d*) is $.294 + .884 + 1.765 = 2.943$. In Example 8, using the average waiting times just computed, the average number waiting in all three classes is

$$\sum_{k=1}^{3} \lambda_k W_k = 1.5(.131) + 2.5(.393) + 1.0(1.765) = 2.944$$

Aside from a slight difference due to rounding, the totals are the same.

Another interesting observation is that the average waiting time for customers in the third priority class did not change from the preceding example. The reason for this is that the *total* arrival rate for the two higher-priority classes did not change, and the average arrival rate for this class did not change. Hence, units assigned to the lowest class must still contend with a combined arrival rate of 4 for the two higher-priority classes.

QUEUING MODEL: FINITE-SOURCE

The finite-source model is appropriate for cases in which the calling population is limited to a relatively small number of potential calls. For instance, one person may be responsible for handling breakdowns on 15 machines; thus, the size of the calling population is 15. There may be more than one server or channel, though. For instance, due to a backlog of machines awaiting repairs, the manager might authorize an additional person to work on repairs.

Table 17–6

Finite-source queuing formulas and notation

Formulas			Notation[†]
Service factor	$X = \dfrac{T}{T + U}$	(17–20)	$D =$ Probability that a customer will have to wait in line
Average number waiting	$L = N(1 - F)$	(17–21)	$F =$ Efficiency factor: $1 -$ percentage waiting in line
Average waiting time	$W = \dfrac{L(T + U)}{N - L} = \dfrac{T(1 - F)}{XF}$	(17–22)	$H =$ Average number of customers being served
			$J =$ Average number of customers not in line or in service
Average number running	$J = NF(1 - X)$	(17–23)	$L =$ Average number of customers waiting for service
Average number being serviced	$H = FNX$	(17–24)	$M =$ Number of service channels
			$N =$ Number of potential customers
Number in population	$N = J + L + H$	(17–25)	$T =$ Average service time
			$U =$ Average time between customer service requirements per customer
			$W =$ Average time customers wait in line
			$X =$ Service factor

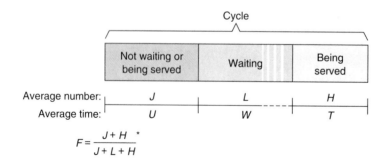

$$F = \frac{J + H}{J + L + H} \text{ }^{\star}$$

★ The purpose of this formula is to provide an understanding of F. Because the value of F is needed to compute J, L, and H, the formulas cannot be used to actually compute F. The finite queuing tables must be used for that purpose.

[†]Adapted from L. G. Peck and R. N. Hazelwood, *Finite Queuing Tables* (New York: John Wiley & Sons, 1958). Reprinted by permission.

As in the infinite-source models, arrival rates are required to be Poisson and service times exponential. A major difference between the finite- and infinite-source models is that the arrival rate of customers in a finite situation is *dependent* on the length of the waiting line: the arrival rate decreases as the length of the line increases simply because there is a decreasing proportion of the population left to generate calls for service. The limit occurs when *all* of the population are waiting in line; at that point the arrival rate is zero since no additional units can arrive.

Because the mathematics of the finite-source model can be quite complex, analysts often use finite-queuing tables in conjunction with simple formulas to analyze these systems. Table 17–6 contains a list of the key formulas and definitions. You will find it helpful to study the diagram of a cycle that is presented in the table.

Table 17–7 is an abbreviated finite-queuing table that is used to obtain values of *D* and *F*. (Most of the formulas require a value for *F*.) In order to use the finite-queuing table, follow this procedure:

1. List the values for:
   - a. *N*, population size.
   - b. *M*, number of servers/channels.
   - c. *T*, service time.
   - d. *U*, time between calls for service, per customer.
2. Compute the service factor, $X = T/(T + U)$.
3. Locate the section of the finite-queuing tables for *N*.
4. Using the value of *X* as the point of entry, find the values of *D* and *F* that correspond to *M*.
5. Use the values of *N*, *M*, *X*, *D*, and *F* as needed to compute the desired measures of system performance.

Table 17–7

Finite-queuing tables

X	M	D	F	X	M	D	F	X	M	D	F	X	M	D	F
POPULATION 5				.058	2	.019	.999	.080	2	.035	.998	.120	2	.076	.995
.012	1	.048	.999		1	.229	.984		1	.313	.969		1	.456	.927
.019	1	.076	.998	.060	2	.020	.999	.085	2	.040	.998	.125	2	.082	.994
.025	1	.100	.997		1	.237	.983		1	.332	.965		1	.473	.920
.030	1	.120	.996	.062	2	.022	.999	.090	2	.044	.998	.130	2	.089	.933
.034	1	.135	.995		1	.245	.982		1	.350	.960		1	.489	.914
.036	1	.143	.994	.064	2	.023	.999	.095	2	.049	.997	.135	2	.095	.933
.040	1	.159	.993		1	.253	.981		1	.368	.955		1	.505	.907
.042	1	.167	.992	.066	2	.024	.999	.100	2	.054	.997	.140	2	.102	.992
.044	1	.175	.991		1	.260	.979		1	.386	.950		1	.521	.900
.046	1	.183	.990	.068	2	.026	.999	.105	2	.059	.997	.145	3	.011	.999
.050	1	.198	.989		1	.268	.978		1	.404	.945		2	.109	.991
.052	1	.206	.988	.070	2	.027	.999	.110	2	.065	.996		1	.537	.892
.054	1	.214	.987		1	.275	.977		1	.421	.939	.150	3	.012	.999
.056	2	.018	.999	.075	2	.031	.999	.115	2	.017	.995		2	.115	.990
	1	.222	.985		1	.294	.973		1	.439	.933		1	.553	.885

Table 17–7

(continued)

X	M	D	F	X	M	D	F	X	M	D	F	X	M	D	F
.155	3	.013	.999	.290	2	.362	.932	.480	3	.296	.945	.950	4	.815	.838
	2	.123	.989		1	.856	.644		2	.719	.767		3	.989	.631
	1	.568	.877	.300	4	.008	.999		1	.980	.415	POPULATION 10			
.160	3	.015	.999		3	.086	.990	.500	4	.063	.992	.016	1	.144	.997
	2	.130	.988		2	.382	.926		3	.327	.936	.019	1	.170	.996
	1	.582	.869		1	.869	.628		2	.750	.748	.021	1	.188	.995
.165	3	.016	.999	.310	4	.009	.999		1	.985	.399	.023	1	.206	.994
	2	.137	.987		3	.094	.989	.520	4	.073	.991	.025	1	.224	.993
	1	.597	.861		2	.402	.919		3	.359	.927	.026	1	.232	.992
.170	3	.017	.999		1	.881	.613		2	.779	.728	.028	1	.250	.991
	2	.145	.985	.320	4	.010	.999		1	.988	.384	.030	1	.268	.990
	1	.611	.853		3	.103	.988	.540	4	.085	.989	.032	2	.033	.999
.180	3	.021	.999		2	.422	.912		3	.392	.917		1	.285	.988
	2	.161	.983		1	.892	.597		2	.806	.708	.034	2	.037	.999
	1	.683	.836	.330	4	.012	.999		1	.991	.370		1	.301	.986
.190	3	.024	.998		3	.112	.986	.560	4	.098	.986	.036	2	.041	.999
	2	.117	.980		2	.442	.904		3	.426	.906		1	.320	.984
	1	.665	.819		1	.902	.583		2	.831	.689	.038	2	.046	.999
.200	3	.028	.998	.340	4	.013	.999		1	.993	.357		1	.337	.982
	2	.194	.976		3	.121	.985	.580	4	.113	.984	.040	2	.050	.999
	1	.689	.801		2	.462	.896		3	.461	.895		1	.354	.980
.210	3	.032	.998		1	.911	.569		2	.854	.670	.042	2	.055	.999
	2	.211	.973	.360	4	.017	.998		1	.994	.345		1	.371	.978
	1	.713	.783		3	.141	.981	.600	4	.130	.981	.044	2	.060	.998
.220	3	.036	.997		2	.501	.880		3	.497	.883		1	.388	.975
	2	.229	.969		1	.927	.542		2	.875	.652	.046	2	.065	.998
	1	.735	.765	.380	4	.021	.998		1	.996	.333		1	.404	.973
.230	3	.041	.997		3	.163	.976	.650	4	.179	.972	.048	2	.071	.998
	2	.247	.965		2	.540	.863		3	.588	.850		1	.421	.970
	1	.756	.747		1	.941	.516		2	.918	.608	.050	2	.076	.998
.240	3	.046	.996	.400	4	.026	.997		1	.998	.308		1	.437	.967
	2	.265	.960		3	.186	.972	.700	4	.240	.960	.052	2	.082	.997
	1	.775	.730		2	.579	.845		3	.678	.815		1	.454	.963
.250	3	.052	.995		1	.952	.493		2	.950	.568	.054	2	.088	.997
	2	.284	.955	.420	4	.031	.997		1	.999	.286		1	.470	.960
	1	.794	.712		3	.211	.966	.750	4	.316	.944	.056	2	.094	.997
.260	3	.058	.994		2	.616	.826		3	.763	.777		1	.486	.956
	2	.303	.950		1	.961	.471		2	.972	.532	.058	2	.100	.996
	1	.811	.695	.440	4	.037	.996	.800	4	.410	.924		1	.501	.953
.270	3	.064	.994		3	.238	.960		3	.841	.739	.060	2	.106	.996
	2	.323	.944		2	.652	.807		2	.987	.500		1	.517	.949
	1	.827	.677		1	.969	.451	.850	4	.522	.900	.062	2	.113	.996
.280	3	.071	.993	.460	4	.045	.995		3	.907	.702		1	.532	.945
	2	.342	.938		3	.266	.953		2	.995	.470	.064	2	.119	.995
	1	.842	.661		2	.686	.787	.900	4	.656	.871		1	.547	.940
.290	4	.007	.999		1	.975	.432		3	.957	.666	.066	2	.126	.995
	3	.079	.992	.480	.4	.053	.994		2	.998	.444		1	.562	.936

Table 17–7

(continued)

X	M	D	F	X	M	D	F	X	M	D	F	X	M	D	F
.068	3	.020	.999	.135	2	.415	.952	.210	3	.333	.961	.290	1	.999	.345
	2	.133	.994		1	.907	.699		2	.728	.835	.300	6	.026	.998
	1	.577	.931	.140	4	.028	.999		1	.990	.474		5	.106	.991
.070	3	.022	.999		3	.132	.991	.220	5	.030	.998		4	.304	.963
	2	.140	.994		2	.437	.947		4	.124	.990		3	.635	.872
	1	.591	.926		1	.919	.680		3	.366	.954		2	.932	.653
.075	3	.026	.999	.145	4	.032	.999		2	.761	.815		1	.999	.333
	2	.158	.992		3	.144	.990		1	.993	.453	.310	6	.031	.998
	1	.627	.913		2	.460	.941	.230	5	.037	.998		5	.120	.990
.080	3	.031	.999		1	.929	.662		4	.142	.988		4	.331	.957
	2	.177	.990	.150	4	.036	.998		3	.400	.947		3	.666	.858
	1	.660	.899		3	.156	.989		2	.791	.794		2	.943	.635
.085	3	.037	.999		2	.483	.935		1	.995	.434	.320	6	.036	.998
	2	.196	.988		1	.939	.644	.240	5	.044	.997		5	.135	.988
	1	.692	.883	.155	4	.040	.998		4	.162	.986		4	.359	.952
.090	3	.043	.998		3	.169	.987		3	.434	.938		3	.695	.845
	2	.216	.986		2	.505	.928		2	.819	.774		2	.952	.617
	1	.722	.867		1	.947	.627		1	.996	.416	.330	6	.042	.997
.095	3	.049	.998	.160	4	.044	.998	.250	6	.010	.999		5	.151	.986
	2	.237	.984		3	.182	.986		5	.052	.997		4	.387	.945
	1	.750	.850		2	.528	.921		4	.183	.983		3	.723	.831
.100	3	.056	.998		1	.954	.610		3	.469	.929		2	.961	.600
	2	.258	.981	.165	4	.049	.997		2	.844	.753	.340	7	.010	.999
	1	.776	.832		3	.195	.984		1	.997	.400		6	.049	.997
.105	3	.064	.997		2	.550	.914	.260	6	.013	.999		5	.168	.983
	2	.279	.978		1	.961	.594		5	.060	.996		4	.416	.938
	1	.800	.814	.170	4	.054	.997		4	.205	.980		3	.750	.816
.110	3	.072	.997		3	.209	.982		3	.503	.919		2	.968	.584
	2	.301	.974		2	.571	.906		2	.866	.732	.360	7	.014	.999
	1	.822	.795		1	.966	.579		1	.998	.384		6	.064	.995
.115	3	.081	.996	.180	5	.013	.999	.270	6	.015	.999		5	.205	.978
	2	.324	.971		4	.066	.996		5	.070	.995		4	.474	.923
	1	.843	.776		3	.238	.978		4	.228	.976		3	.798	.787
.120	4	.016	.999		2	.614	.890		3	.537	.908		2	.978	.553
	3	.090	.995		1	.975	.890		2	.886	.712	.380	7	.019	.999
	2	.346	.967	.190	5	.016	.999		1	.999	.370		6	.083	.993
	1	.861	.756		4	.078	.995	.280	6	.018	.999		5	.247	.971
.125	4	.019	.999		3	.269	.973		5	.081	.994		4	.533	.906
	3	.100	.994		2	.654	.873		4	.252	.972		3	.840	.758
	2	.369	.962		1	.982	.522		3	.571	.896		2	.986	.525
	1	.878	.737	.200	5	.020	.999		2	.903	.692	.400	7	.026	.998
.130	4	.022	.999		4	.092	.994		1	.999	.357		6	.105	.991
	3	.110	.994		3	.300	.968	.290	6	.022	.999		5	.292	.963
	2	.392	.958		2	.692	.854		5	.093	.993		4	.591	.887
	1	.893	.718		1	.987	.497		4	.278	.968		3	.875	.728
.135	4	.025	.999	.210	5	.025	.999		3	.603	.884		2	.991	.499
	3	.121	.993		4	.108	.992		2	.918	.672	.420	7	.034	.993

Table 17–7

(concluded)

X	M	D	F	X	M	D	F	X	M	D	F	X	M	D	F
.420	6	.130	.987	.500	7	.093	.992	.580	7	.204	.977	.750	8	.307	.965
	5	.341	.954		6	.271	.966		6	.465	.927		7	.626	.897
	4	.646	.866		5	.553	.901		5	.753	.829		6	.870	.792
	3	.905	.700		4	.830	.775		4	.937	.684		5	.975	.666
	2	.994	.476		3	.972	.598		3	.994	.517		4	.998	.533
.440	7	.045	.997		2	.999	.400	.600	9	.010	.999	.800	9	.134	.988
	6	.160	.984	.520	8	.026	.998		8	.072	.994		8	.446	.944
	5	.392	.943		7	.115	.989		7	.242	.972		7	.763	.859
	4	.698	.845		6	.316	.958		6	.518	.915		6	.939	.747
	3	.928	.672		5	.606	.884		5	.795	.809		5	.991	.625
	2	.996	.454		4	.864	.752		4	.953	.663		4	.999	.500
.460	8	.011	.999		3	.980	.575		3	.996	.500	.850	9	.232	.979
	7	.058	.995		2	.999	.385	.650	9	.021	.999		8	.611	.916
	6	.193	.979	.540	8	.034	.997		8	.123	.988		7	.879	.818
	5	.445	.930		7	.141	.986		7	.353	.954		6	.978	.705
	4	.747	.822		6	.363	.949		6	.651	.878		5	.998	.588
	3	.947	.646		5	.658	.867		5	.882	.759	.900	9	.387	.963
	2	.998	.435		4	.893	.729		4	.980	.614		8	.785	.881
.480	8	.015	.999		3	.986	.555		3	.999	.461		7	.957	.777
	7	.074	.994	.560	8	.044	.996	.700	9	.040	.997		6	.995	.667
	6	.230	.973		7	.171	.982		8	.200	.979	.950	9	.630	.938
	5	.499	.916		6	.413	.939		7	.484	.929		8	.934	.841
	4	.791	.799		5	.707	.848		6	.772	.836		7	.994	.737
	3	.961	.621		4	.917	.706		5	.940	.711				
	2	.998	.417		3	.991	.535		4	.992	.571				
.500	8	.020	.999	.580	8	.057	.995	.750	9	.075	.994				

Source: L. G. Peck and R. N. Hazelwood, *Finite Queuing Tables* (New York: John Wiley & Sons, 1958). Reprinted by permission.

Example 9

■

One operator loads and unloads a bank of five machines. Service time is exponentially distributed with a mean of 10 minutes per cycle. Machines run for an average of 70 minutes between loading and unloading, and this time is also exponential. Find:

a. The average number of machines waiting for the operator.
b. The expected number of machines running.
c. Average downtime.
d. The probability that a machine will not have to wait for service.

Solution

$$N = 5 \qquad M = 1$$
$$T = 10 \text{ minutes} \qquad U = 70 \text{ minutes}$$

$$X = \frac{T}{T + U} = \frac{10}{10 + 70} = .125$$

From Table 17–7, with $N = 5$, $M = 1$, and $X = .125$, $D = .473$ and $F = .920$.

a. Average number waiting, $L = N(1 - F) = 5(1 - .92) = 0.40$ machines.

b. Expected number running, $J = NF(1 - X) = 5(.92)(1 - .125) = 4.025$ machines.

c. Downtime = Waiting time + Service time:

$$\text{Waiting time, } W = \frac{L(T + U)}{N - L} = \frac{.40(10 + 70)}{5 - .40} = 6.957 \text{ minutes}$$

Downtime = 6.957 minutes + 10 minutes = 16.957 minutes.

d. Probability of not waiting = 1 − Probability of waiting
$$= 1 - D$$
$$= 1 - .473 = .527$$

Example 10

Suppose that in the previous example, operators are paid $10 per hour, and machine downtime costs $16 per hour. Should the department add another operator if the goal is cost minimization?

Solution

Compare the total cost of the present system with the expected total cost of the proposed system:

M	Average number down, $N - J$	Average down cost (per hour), $(N - J)\$16$	Operator cost (per hour)	Total cost (per hour)
1	.975	$15.60	$10	$25.60
2	.651	10.42	20	30.42

Hence, the present system is superior because its total cost is less than the expected total cost using two operators.

OTHER APPROACHES

The discussion in this chapter has focused on designing service systems that achieve a balance between service capacity and customer waiting time. The implication is that an appropriate level of service capacity can be determined. In certain instances, such an approach may not be practical, for a variety of reasons. One is that the system may be currently in operation and indicated design changes may be too costly, or there may be space restrictions such that changes cannot reasonably be made. One alternative that is particularly suited for queuing systems in which the customers are people rather than inanimate objects is to provide some form of diversion so that the waiting time becomes more tolerable. For example, magazines and newspapers can be placed in waiting rooms, as is usually the case in doctors' and dentists' offices. Auto repair shops sometimes use radio or television, and airlines may provide in-flight movies to help occupy the time. Airlines also serve meals and snacks, which helps to make the time spent waiting (flying) more pleasant. Some other measures include placing mirrors where people wait for elevators and asking people to fill out forms, which makes waiting somewhat constructive.

Carrying this concept one step further, it is sometimes possible to derive some benefit from customer waiting. For instance, supermarkets position impulse items near checkout counters and gain additional sales, banks advertise current rates and place brochures describing bank services within easy reach of waiting customers, and restaurants have bars where customers can relax and spend money while waiting for their tables.

The implication in these ideas is that imagination and creativity can often play an important role in system design and that mathematical approaches are not the only ones worth considering.

SUMMARY

Analysis of waiting lines can be an important aspect of the design of service systems. Waiting lines have a tendency to form in such systems even though, in a macro sense, the system is underloaded. The arrival of customers at random times and variability of service times combine to create temporary overloads. When this happens, waiting lines appear. By the same token, at other times, the servers are idle.

A major consideration in the analysis of queuing systems relates to whether the number of potential customers is limited (finite-source) or whether entry to the system is unrestricted (infinite-source). Five basic queuing models are described in the chapter, four dealing with infinite-source populations and one dealing with finite-source populations. In general, the models assume that customer arrival rates can be described by a Poission distribution and that service time can be described by a negative exponential distribution.

KEY TERMS

channel, 829
finite source, 829
infinite source, 829

multiple-priority model, 844
queue discipline, 832
queuing theory, 826

SOLVED PROBLEMS

Problem

1. *Infinite source.* One of the features of a new machine shop will be a well-stocked tool crib. The manager of the shop must decide on the number of attendants needed to staff the crib. Attendants will receive $9 per hour in salary and fringe benefits. Mechanics' time will be worth $30 per hour, which includes salary and fringe benefits plus lost work time caused by waiting for parts. Based on previous experience, the manager estimates requests for parts will average 18 per hour with a service capacity of 20 requests per hour per attendant. How many attendants should be on duty if the manager is willing to assume that arrival and service rates will be Poisson-distributed? (Assume the number of mechanics is very large, so an infinite-source model is appropriate.)

Solution

$\lambda = 18$ *per hour*
$\mu = 20$ *per hour*

The solution requires a trial-and-error approach that reveals the total cost of feasible alternatives (i.e., a utilization less than 100 percent) and selection of the lowest-cost alternative. Note that the total-cost curve will always be U-shaped; increase the number of servers until the total cost shows an increase over the previous value. The optimum will be the number of servers that produced the previous total cost value. Thus,

Number of servers, M	$L_q^\star$	$L_q + \dfrac{\lambda}{\mu} = L_s$	$M(\$9)$: Server cost (per hour)	$L_s(\$30)$: Mechanic cost (per hour)	Total cost (per hour)
1	8.1	$8.1 + 0.9 = 9.0$	$\$ 9$	$\$270$	$\$279$
2	0.299	$0.299 + 0.9 = 1.129$	$\$18$	$\$ 33.87$	$\$ 52^\dagger$
3	0.03	$0.03 + 0.9 = 0.93$	$\$27$	$\$ 27.9$	$\$ 55^\dagger$

$\star L_q$: from Table 17–4, with $r = \lambda/\mu = 18/20 = 0.9$.
$\dagger$ Rounded.

Hence, two servers will produce the lowest total cost.

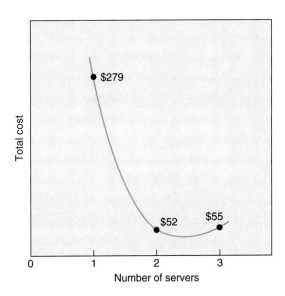

Problem

2. *Infinite source.* The following is a list of service times for three different operations:

Operation	Service time
A	8 minutes
B	1.2 hours
C	2 days

a. Determine the service rate for each operation.
b. Would the calculated rates be different if these were interarrival times rather than service times?

Solution

a. The service rate is the reciprocal of service time. Thus, the rates are:
A: 1/8 per minute = .125 per minute,
  or .125/min. × 60 min./hr. = 7.5 per hour
B: 1/1.2 per hour = .833 per hour
C: 1/2 per day = .50 per day
b. No. In either case, the rate is simply the reciprocal of the time.

Problem

3. *Finite source.* A group of 10 machines is loaded and unloaded by one of three servers. The machines run for an average of six minutes per cycle, and average time to unload and reload is nine minutes. Each time can be described by an exponential distribution. While running, the machines produce at a rate that would yield 16 units per hour if they did not have to pause to wait for a server and be loaded and unloaded. What is the average hourly output of each machine when waiting and serving are taken into account?

Solution

$T = 9$ minutes

$$U = 6 \text{ minutes; } X = \frac{T}{T + U} = \frac{9}{9 + 6} = .60$$

$M = 3$ servers; from Table 17–7, $F = .500$
$N = 10$ machines

a. Compute the average number of machines running:

$$J = NF(1 - X) = 10(.500)(.40) = 2$$

b. Determine the percentage of machines running, and multiply by output while running:

$$\frac{J}{N} \times (16 \text{ per hour}) = \frac{2}{10} \times (16 \text{ per hour}) = 3.2 \text{ per hour}$$

DISCUSSION AND REVIEW QUESTIONS

1. In what kinds of situations is queuing analysis most appropriate?
2. Why do waiting lines form even though a service system is underloaded?
3. What are the most common measures of system performance in a queuing analysis?
4. What effect would decreasing arrival and service variability have on the effective capacity of a system?
5. What approaches do supermarkets use to offset variations in customer traffic intensity?
6. Contrast *finite* and *infinite* population sources.

7. Will doubling the service rate of a single-channel system reduce the average waiting time in line by a factor of one half? Explain briefly.

8. In a multiple-channel system, what is the rationale for having customers wait in a single line, as is now being done in many banks and post offices, rather than multiple lines? (*Hint:* The average waiting time is unaffected.)

9. What happens to the length of a waiting line in a highly variable (queuing) setting if a manager attempts to achieve a high percentage of capacity utilization?

1. Repair calls are handled by one repairman at a photocopy shop. Repair time, including travel time, is exponentially distributed with a mean of two hours per call. Requests for copier repairs come in at a mean rate of three per eight-hour day (assume Poisson). Determine the following:
   a. The average number of customers awaiting repairs.
   b. System utilization.
   c. The amount of time during an eight-hour day that the repairman is not out on a call.
   d. The probability of two or more customers in the system.

2. A vending machine dispenses hot chocolate or coffee. Service time is 30 seconds per cup and is constant. Customers arrive at a mean rate of 80 per hour, and this rate is Poisson-distributed. Determine:
   a. The average number of customers waiting in line.
   b. The average time customers spend in the system.
   c. The average number in the system.

3. A small town with one hospital is supplied ambulance service via the hospital's two ambulances. Requests for ambulances during nonholiday weekends average 0.8 per hour and tend to be Poisson-distributed. Travel and assistance time averages one hour per call and follows an exponential distribution. Find:
   a. System utilization.
   b. The average number of customers waiting.
   c. Average customer waiting time.
   d. The probability that *both* ambulances will be busy when a call comes in.

4. The following information pertains to telephone calls to a motel switchboard on a typical Tuesday. Determine the average time callers wait to have their calls answered for each period and the probability that a caller will have to wait for each period.

Period	Incoming rate (calls per minute)	Service rate (calls per minute per operator)	Number of operators
Morning 1.8		1.5	2
Afternoon 2.2		1.0	3
Evening 1.4		0.7	3

5. For each case in the previous problem, determine the maximum line length for a probability of 96 percent.

6. The manager of a regional warehouse must decide on the number of loading docks to request for a new facility in order to minimize the sum of dock costs and driver-truck costs. The manager has learned that each driver-truck combination represents a cost of $300 per day and that each dock plus loading crew represents a cost of $1,100 per day.

How many docks should be requested if trucks arrive at the rate of four per day, each dock can handle five trucks per day, and both rates are Poisson?

7. A branch location of a large savings bank is open on Saturdays from 10 A.M. until 2 P.M. During that time, four tellers are on duty. Tellers can handle customer deposits and withdrawals at the rate of 28 customers per hour each. Customers arrive to do their banking at the rate of 84 per hour during this period. Determine each of the following, assuming arrival and service rates are Poisson:

   a. The average number of customers waiting in line for a teller.
   b. The expected length of time customers wait in the system.
   c. The average waiting time for customers who are not served immediately.
   d. The maximum number waiting, for a confidence (probability) of 97 percent.

8. During slow hours, a certain post office branch uses three clerks, each of whom can process customers at a rate of 1.26 per minute (Poisson). The average time between customer arrivals is 25 seconds (exponential). Determine each of the following:

   a. System utilization.
   b. The percentage of time clerks are idle.
   c. The average number of customers in line and the average waiting time for those who must wait.
   d. The maximum number waiting, for a probability of 98 percent.
   e. The manager is contemplating using only two clerks. What impact would this have on the average number waiting in line, the average waiting time, and the maximum number waiting (98 percent probability)?

9. One field representative services five customers for a computer manufacturer. Customers request assistance at an average (Poisson-distributed) rate of once every four working days. The field representative can handle an average (Poisson-distributed) of one call per day. Determine:

   a. The expected number of customers waiting.
   b. How long customers must wait, on the average, from the time a request for service is made until the service has been completed.
   c. The percentage of time the service rep will be idle.
   d. By how much would your answer to part *a* be reduced if a second field rep were added?

10. Two operators handle adjustments for a group of 10 machines. Adjustment time is exponentially distributed and has a mean of 14 minutes per machine. The machines operate for an average of 86 minutes between adjustments. While running, each machine can turn out 50 pieces per hour. Find:

   a. The probability that a machine will have to wait for an adjustment.
   b. The average number of machines waiting for adjustment.
   c. The average number of machines being serviced.
   d. The expected hourly output of each machine, taking adjustments into account.
   e. Machine downtime represents a cost of $70 per hour; operator cost (including salary and fringe benefits) is $15 per hour. What is the optimum number of operators?

11. One operator services a bank of five machines. Machine running time and service time are both exponential. Machines run for an average of 90 minutes between service requirements, and service time averages 35 minutes. The operator receives $10 per hour in salary and fringe benefits, and machine downtime costs $35 per hour per machine.

   a. If each machine produces 60 pieces per hour while running, find the average hourly output of each machine, when waiting and service times are taken into account.
   b. Determine the optimum number of operators.

12. Trucks arrive at the loading dock of a wholesale grocer at the rate of 1.2 per hour. A single crew consisting of two workers can load a truck in about 30 minutes. Crew members receive $10 per hour in wages and fringe benefits, and trucks and drivers

reflect an hourly cost of $60. The manager is thinking of adding another member to the crew. The service rate would then be 2.4 trucks per hour. Assume rates are Poisson. Would the third crew member be economical? Would a fourth member be justifiable if the resulting service capacity were 2.6 trucks per hour?

13. (Refer to Problem 6.) If the cost for waiting space is $100 per day, how many docks would be optimum if a probability of .95 is used for the maximum line length?

14. Customers arriving at a service center are assigned to one of three categories (1, 2, or 3, with category 1 given the highest priority) for servicing. Records indicate that an average of nine customers arrive per hour and that one third are assigned to each category. There are two servers, and each can process customers at the rate of five per hour. Arrival and service rates can be described by Poisson distributions.
   a. What is the utilization rate for this system?
   b. Determine the average waiting time for units in each class.
   c. Find the average number of customers in each class that are waiting for service.

15. A manager must determine requirements for waiting space for customers. A priority system is used to process customers, who are assigned to one of two classes when they enter the processing center. The highest-priority class has an arrival rate of four per hour; the other class has an arrival rate of two per hour. Both can be described as Poisson-distributed. There are two servers, and each can process customers in an average of six minutes.
   a. What is the system utilization?
   b. Determine the number of customers of each class that are waiting for service.
   c. Determine the average waiting time for each class.
   d. If the manager could alter the assignment rules so that arrival rates of the two classes were equal, what would be the revised average waiting time for each priority class?

16. A priority waiting system assigns arriving customers to one of four classes. Arrival rates (Poisson) of the classes are shown in the following table:

Class	Arrivals per hour
1	2
2	4
3	3
4	2

Five servers process the customers, and each can handle three customers per hour.
   a. What is the system utilization?
   b. On the average, how long do customers in the various classes wait for service? How many are waiting in each class, on the average?
   c. If the arrival rate of the second priority class could be reduced to three units per hour by shifting some arrivals into the third priority class, how would your answers to part b change?
   d. What observations can you make based on your answers to part c?

17. Referring to the preceding problem, suppose that each server could handle four customers per hour. Answer the questions posed in the preceding problem. Explain why the impact of reassigning customers is much less than in the preceding problem.

SELECTED BIBLIOGRAPHY

Buffa, Elwood. *Operations Management*. 3rd ed. New York: John Wiley & Sons, 1972.

Chase, Richard, and Nicholas Aquilano. *Production and Operations Management*. 6th ed. Homewood, Ill.: Richard D. Irwin, 1992.

Griffin, W. *Queuing: Basic Theory and Applications*. Columbus, Ohio: Grid Publishing, 1978.

Hillier, Frederick S., and Gerald J. Lieberman. *Introduction to Operations Research,* 3rd ed. San Francisco: Holden-Day, 1980.

Peck, L. G., and R. N. Hazelwood. *Finite Queuing Tables*. New York: John Wiley & Sons, 1958.

Stevenson, William J. *Introduction to Management Science*. 2nd ed. Homewood, Ill.: Richard D. Irwin, 1992.

17

SIMULATION

After completing this supplement, you should be able to:

1. Explain what is meant by the term *simulation*.

2. List some of the reasons for simulation's popularity.

3. Explain how and why random numbers are used in simulation.

4. Outline the advantages and limitations of simulation as a tool for decision making.

5. Describe the alternatives that a manager would reject before choosing simulation as a decision-making tool.

6. Solve typical problems that require the use of simulation.

Simulation is a descriptive technique that involves developing a model of a process and then conducting experiments on the model to evaluate its behavior under certain conditions. Unlike many of the other models that have been described in this text, simulation is not an optimizing technique. In fact, simulation does not produce a solution per se. Instead, it enables decision makers to test *their* solutions on a model that reasonably duplicates a real process; simulation models enable decision makers to experiment with decision alternatives using a *what if* approach.

The use of simulation as a decision-making tool is fairly widespread, and you are undoubtedly familiar with some of the ways it is used. For instance, space engineers simulate space flight in laboratories to permit future astronauts to become accustomed to working in a weightless environment. Similarly, airline pilots often undergo extensive training with simulated landings and takeoffs before being allowed to try the real thing. Many universities use management games as a means of simulating business environments. Tire designers evaluate alternative tread designs using machines that simulate conditions that produce tire wear and handling problems. There are many other examples of applications of simulation techniques; these few are mentioned to illustrate the nature and diversity of their use.

There are a number of reasons for the popularity of simulation. Among the most important are:

1. Many situations are too complex to permit development of a mathematical solution; the degree of simplification needed would seriously affect the results. In contrast, simulation models are often able to capture the richness of a situation without sacrificing simplicity, thereby enhancing the decision process.
2. Simulation models are fairly simple to use and to understand.
3. Simulation enables the decision maker to conduct experiments on a model that will help in understanding process behavior, while avoiding the risks of conducting tests on the model's real-life counterpart.
4. Extensive computer software packages are available, making it easy to use fairly sophisticated models.
5. Simulation can be used for a wide range of situations.
6. There have been numerous successful applications of these techniques.

STEPS IN THE SIMULATION PROCESS

Regardless of the type of simulation involved, there are certain basic steps used for all simulation models:

1. Identify the problem and set objectives.
2. Develop the simulation model.
3. Test the model to be sure that it reflects the system being studied.
4. Develop one or more experiments (conditions under which the model's behavior will be examined).
5. Run the simulation and evaluate the results.
6. Repeat steps 4 and 5 until you are satisfied with the results.

The first step in problem solving of any sort is to clearly *define the problem and set objectives* that the solution is intended to achieve; simulation is no exception. A clear statement of the objectives can provide not only guidance for model development but also the basis for evaluation of the success or failure of a simulation. In general, the goal of a simulation study is to determine how a system will behave under certain conditions. The more specific a manager is about what he or she is looking for, the better the chances that the simulation model will be designed to accomplish that. Toward that end, the *scope* and *level of detail* of the simulation must be decided on. This indicates the required degree of complexity of the model as well as the information requirements of the study.

The next step in simulations is *model development*. Typically, this involves deciding on the structure of the model and then writing a computer program to carry out the simulations. (Although for instructional purposes, the examples and problems in this chapter are primarily *manual,* in most real-life applications, computers are used to conduct the simulations. This stems from the need for large numbers of runs, the complexity of simulations, and the need for record keeping of results.) Data gathering is an important part of model development. The amount and type of data needed are a direct function of the scope and level of detail of the simulation. The data are needed for both model development and evaluation. Naturally, the model must be designed to enable evaluation of key decision alternatives.

The *validation* phase is closely related to model development. Its main purpose is to determine if the model adequately depicts real system performance. This is usually accomplished by comparing the results of simulation runs with known performance of the system under the same circumstances. If such a comparison cannot be made, say, because real-life data are difficult or impossible to obtain, an alternative is to employ a test of reasonableness, in which the judgments and opinions of individuals familiar with the system or similar systems are relied on for confirmation that the results are plausible and acceptable. Still another aspect of validation is careful consideration of the assumptions of the model and the values of parameters used in testing the model. Again, the judgments and opinions of those familiar with the real-life system and those who must use the results are essential. Finally, note that model development and model validation go hand in hand: model deficiencies uncovered during validation prompt model revisions, which lead to the need for further validation efforts and perhaps further revisions.

The fourth step in simulation is *designing experiments*. Experiments are the essence of a simulation; they help answer the *what if* questions posed in simulation studies. By going through the process, the manager or analyst is able to learn about system behavior.

The fifth step in simulation is to *run the simulation model*. If a simulation model is deterministic and all parameters are known and constant, only a single run will be needed for each *what if* question. If the simulation is probabilistic, with parameters subject to random variability, multiple runs will be needed to obtain a clear picture of the results. In this text, probabilistic simulations are the focal point of the discussion, and we shall limit comments to that sort of simulation. Probabilistic simulation is essentially a form of random sampling, with each run representing one observation. Consequently, statistical theory can be used to determine appropriate sample sizes. In effect, the larger the degree of variability inherent in simulation results, the greater the number of simulation runs needed to achieve a reasonable level of confidence in the results as true indicators of model behavior.

The last step in the simulation process is to *analyze and interpret the results*. Interpretation of the results depends to a large extent on the degree to which the simulation model approximates reality; the closer the approximation, the less need there is to "adjust" the results. Moreover, the closer the approximation of the model to reality, the less the risk inherent in applying the results.

MONTE CARLO SIMULATION

There are many different kinds of simulation techniques. Our discussion will focus on probabilistic simulation using the **Monte Carlo method**. The technique gets its name from the famous Mediterranean resort often associated with games of chance. In fact, the chance element is an important aspect of Monte Carlo simulation; this approach can be used only when a process has a **random**, or chance, component.

In the Monte Carlo method, a manager develops a probability distribution that reflects the random component of the system under study. Random samples taken from this probability distribution are analogous to observations made on the system itself. As the number of observations increases, the results of the simulation will more closely approximate the random behavior of the real system, provided an appropriate model has been developed. Sampling is accomplished by the use of random numbers.

The basic steps in the process are as follows:

1. Identify a probability distribution for each random component of the system.
2. Work out an assignment so that intervals of random numbers will correspond to the probability distribution.
3. Obtain the random numbers needed for the study.
4. Interpret the results.

The random numbers used in Monte Carlo simulation can come from any source that exhibits the necessary randomness. Typically, they come from one of two sources: Large studies depend on computer-generated random numbers, and small studies commonly make use of numbers from a table of random digits like the one shown in Table 17S–1. The digits are listed in pairs for convenience, but they can be used singly, in pairs, or in whatever grouping is called for in a given problem.

There are two important features of the sets of random numbers that are essential to simulation. One is that the numbers are uniformly distributed. This means that for any size grouping of digits (e.g., two-digit numbers), every possible out-

Monte Carlo method

Probabilistic simulation technique used when a process has a random component.

Random

Chance.

Table 17S–1

Random digits

	1	2	3	4	5	6	7	8	9	10	11	12
1	18	20	84	29	91	73	64	33	15	67	54	07
2	25	19	05	64	26	41	20	09	88	40	73	34
3	73	57	80	35	04	52	81	48	57	61	29	35
4	12	48	37	09	17	63	94	08	28	78	51	23
5	54	92	27	61	58	39	25	16	10	46	87	17
6	96	40	65	75	16	49	03	82	38	33	51	20
7	23	55	93	83	02	19	67	89	80	44	99	72
8	31	96	81	65	60	93	75	64	26	90	18	59
9	45	49	70	10	13	79	32	17	98	63	30	05
10	01	78	32	17	24	54	52	44	28	50	27	68
11	41	62	57	31	90	18	24	15	43	85	31	97
12	22	07	38	72	69	66	14	85	36	71	41	58

come (e.g., 34, 89, 00) has the same probability of appearing. The second feature is that there are no discernible patterns in sequences of numbers to enable one to predict numbers further in the sequence (hence the name *random* digits). This feature holds for any sequence of numbers; the numbers can be read across rows as well as up or down columns.

When using the table it is important to avoid always starting in the same spot; that would result in the same sequence of numbers each time. Various methods exist for choosing a random starting point. One can use the serial number of a dollar bill to select the row, column, and direction of number selection. Another approach is to use rolls of a die. For our purposes, the starting point will be specified in each example or problem so that we may all obtain the same results.

The process of simulation will become clearer as we work through some simple problems.

Example S–1

The manager of a machine shop is concerned about machine breakdowns. A decision has been made to simulate breakdowns for a 10-day period. Historical data on breakdowns over the last 100 days are given in the following table:

Number of breakdowns	Frequency
0	10
1	30
2	25
3	20
4	10
5	5
	100

Simulate breakdowns for a 10-day period. Read two-digit random numbers from Table 17S–1, starting at the top of column 1 and reading down.

Solution

a. Develop a cumulative probability distribution for breakdowns:
   (1) Convert frequencies into probabilities by dividing each frequency by the sum of the frequencies. Thus, 10 becomes $10/100 = .10$, 30 becomes $30/100 = .30$, and so on.
   (2) Develop cumulative probabilities by successive summing. The results are shown in the following table:

Number of breakdowns	Frequency	Probability	Cumulative probability
0	10	.10	.10
1	30	.30	.40
2	25	.25	.65
3	20	.20	.85
4	10	.10	.95
5	5	.05	1.00
	100	1.00	

(continued)

Example S–1

(concluded)

b. Assign random-number intervals so that they correspond to the cumulative probabilities for breakdowns. (*Note:* Two-digit numbers are used because the probabilities are given to two decimal places.) We want there to be a 10 percent probability of obtaining the event "0 breakdowns" in our simulation. Therefore, we must designate 10 percent of the possible random numbers as corresponding to that event. Since the numbers are evenly distributed between 00 and 99 (i.e., there are 100 two-digit numbers), we assign the 10 numbers 00 to 09 to that event.

Similarly, we assigns the numbers 10 to 39 to "one breakdown," 40 to 64 to "two breakdowns," 65 to 84 to "three breakdowns," 85 to 94 to "4 breakdowns" and 95 to 99 to five breakdowns." (Note that the ending digit of each random-number interval is 1 less than the cumulative probability, and the interval begins at the cumulative probability for the last event, except for the first one, which begins at 00.) The results are as follows:

Number of breakdowns	Frequency	Probability	Cumulative probability	Corresponding random numbers
0	10	.10	.10	00 to 09
1	30	.30	.40	10 to 39
2	25	.25	.65	40 to 64
3	20	.20	.85	65 to 84
4	10	.10	.95	85 to 94
5	5	.05	1.00	95 to 99
	100	1.00		

c. Obtain the random numbers from Table 17S–1, column 1, as specified in the problem:

18   25   73   12   54   96   23   31   45   01

d. Convert the random numbers into numbers of breakdowns:

18 falls in the interval 10 to 39 and corresponds, therefore, to one breakdown on day 1.

25 falls in the interval 10 to 39, which corresponds to one breakdown on day 2.

73 corresponds to three breakdowns on day 3.

12 corresponds to one breakdown on day 4.

54 corresponds to two breakdowns on day 5.

96 corresponds to five breakdowns on day 6.

23 corresponds to one breakdown on day 7.

31 corresponds to one breakdown on day 8.

45 corresponds to two breakdowns on day 9.

01 corresponds to no breakdowns on day 10.

These results are summarized in the following table:

Day	Random number	Simulated number of breakdowns
1	18	1
2	25	1
3	73	3
4	12	1
5	54	2
6	96	5

Day	Random number	Simulated number of breakdowns
7................ 23		1
8................ 31		1
9................ 45		2
10................ 01		0
		17

The mean number of breakdowns for this 10-period simulation is $17/10 = 1.7$ breakdowns per day. Compare this to the *expected* number of breakdowns based on the historical data:

$$0(.10) + 1(.30) + 2(.25) + 3(.20) + 4(.10) + 5(.05) = 2.05 \text{ per day}$$

Several points are worth noting:

1. This simple example is intended to illustrate the basic concept of Monte Carlo simulation. If our only goal were to estimate the average number of breakdowns, we would not have to simulate; we could base the estimate on the historical data alone.
2. The simulation should be viewed as a *sample;* it is quite likely that additional runs of 10 numbers would produce different means.
3. Because of the variability inherent in the results of small samples, it would be unwise to attempt to draw any firm conclusions from them; in an actual study, much larger sample sizes would be used.

In some cases, it is helpful to construct a flowchart that describes a simulation, especially if the simulation will involve periodic updating of system values (e.g., amount of inventory on hand), as illustrated in the following example.

The manager of a small truck dealership wants to acquire some insight into how a proposed policy for reordering trucks might affect order frequency. Under the new policy, two trucks are to be ordered whenever the number of trucks on hand is five or fewer. Due to the nearness of the dealer to the home office, orders can be filled overnight. According to the dealer's records, the probability distribution for daily demand is:

Example S–2

Demand, x	$P(x)$
0....................	.50
1....................	.40
2....................	.10

a. Construct a flowchart that describes a 10-day simulation.
b. Use two-digit random numbers from Table 17S–1, column 11, reading down. Assume a beginning inventory of seven trucks.

(continued)

Example S–2

(concluded)

Solution

a.

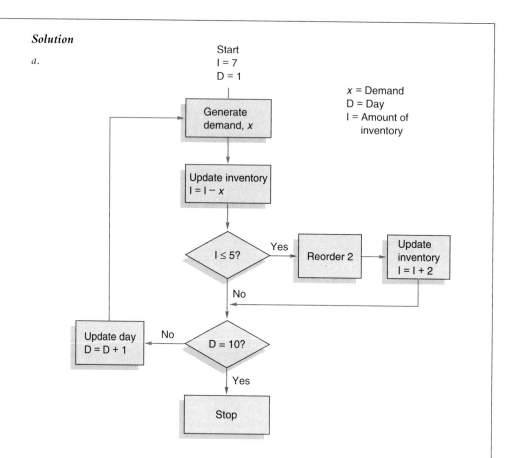

b. (1) Specify random number ranges for demand:

x	P(x)	Cumulative P(x)	Ranges
0........	.50	.50	00–49
1........	.40	.90	50–89
2........	.10	1.00	90–99

(2) Obtain random numbers, convert to demand, update inventory accordingly, and reorder when necessary:

Day	Random number	Demand, x	Beginning inventory	Ending inventory
1 54		1	7	6
2 73		1	6	5 (reorder 2; new beginning inventory = 5 + 2)
3 29		0	7	7
4 51		1	7	6
5 87		1	6	5 (reorder 2; new beginning inventory = 5 + 2)
6 51		1	7	6

Day	Random number	Demand, x	Beginning inventory	Ending inventory
7 99		2	6	4 (reorder 2; new beginning inventory = 4 + 2)
8 18		0	6	6
9 30		0	6	6
10 27		0	6	6

SIMULATING THEORETICAL DISTRIBUTIONS

In many instances, a simulation will involve the use of theoretical distributions. Among the most frequently encountered theoretical distributions are the Poisson, normal, and exponential distributions. Being able to simulate these distributions will greatly enhance your knowledge and appreciation of simulation.

For simulation of a Poisson distribution, the mean of the distribution is required. Knowledge of the mean enables one to obtain cumulative probabilities for the distribution from Appendix B, Table C; these, in turn, provide the basis for random-number assignments. Table 17S–1 can be used to obtain random numbers; three-digit random numbers must be read from Table 17S–1 to achieve correspondence. The following example illustrates these concepts.

Example S–3

The number of lost-time accidents at a large plant has been determined from historical records to be two per day. Moreover, it has been determined that this accident rate can be well approximated by a Poisson distribution that has a mean of 2.0. Simulate five days of accident experience for the plant. Read random numbers from columns 1 and 2 of Table 17S–1.

Solution

First obtain the cumulative distribution from Appendix B, Table C for a mean of 2.0, and make the range assignments:

x	Cumulative probability	Random number ranges
0	.135	000 to 134
1	.406	135 to 405
2	.677	406 to 676
3	.857	677 to 856
4	.947	857 to 946
5	.983	947 to 982
6	.995	983 to 994
7	.999	995 to 998
8	1.000	999

Next obtain three-digit numbers from Table 17S–1. Reading from columns 1 and 2 as instructed, we find 182, 251, 735, 124, and 549.

(continued)

Example S–3

(concluded)

Finally, convert the random numbers into number of lost-time accidents using the established set of ranges. Since 182 falls in the second range, it corresponds to one accident on day 1. The second random number, 251, falls in the same range, indicating one accident on day 2. The number 735 falls between 677 and 856, which corresponds to three accidents on day 3; 124 corresponds to 0 accidents on day 4; and 549 corresponds to two accidents on day 5.

Table 17S–2

Normally distributed random numbers

	1	2	3	4	5	6	7	8	9	10
1	1.46	0.09	−0.59	0.19	−0.52	−1.82	0.53	−1.12	1.36	−0.44
2	−1.05	0.56	−0.67	−0.16	1.39	−1.21	0.45	−0.62	−0.95	0.27
3	0.15	−0.02	0.41	−0.09	−0.61	−0.18	−0.63	−1.20	0.27	−0.50
4	0.81	1.87	0.51	0.33	−0.32	1.19	2.18	−2.17	1.10	0.70
5	0.74	−0.44	1.53	−1.76	0.01	0.47	0.07	0.22	−0.59	−1.03
6	−0.39	0.35	−0.37	−0.52	−1.14	0.27	−1.78	0.43	1.15	−0.31
7	0.45	0.23	0.26	−0.31	−0.19	−0.03	−0.92	0.38	−0.04	0.16
8	2.40	0.38	−0.15	−1.04	−0.76	1.12	−0.37	−0.71	−1.11	0.25
9	0.59	−0.70	−0.04	0.12	1.60	0.34	−0.05	−0.26	0.41	0.80
10	−0.06	0.83	−1.60	−0.28	0.28	−0.15	0.73	−0.13	−0.75	−1.49

The normal distribution can be important in many problems. There are a number of ways to simulate a normal distribution, but perhaps the simplest is to use a table of normally distributed random numbers, such as Table 17S–2. The basis of the table is a normal distribution with a mean of 0 and a standard deviation of 1.00. Like all such tables, the numbers are arranged randomly, so that when they are read in any sequence they exhibit "randomness." In order to use the table, we must have the parameters of a normal distribution (i.e., its mean and standard deviation) in mind. Numbers obtained from the random number table can then be converted to "actual" values by multiplying the standard deviation by the random number and adding this amount to the mean. That is:

$$\text{Simulated value} = \text{Mean} + \text{Random number} \times \text{Standard deviation} \quad \textbf{(17S–1)}$$

In effect, the random number equates to a normal z value, which indicates how far a particular value is above or below the distribution mean.

Example S–4

It has been determined that the time required to perform a certain task can be described by a normal distribution that has a mean of 30 minutes and a standard deviation of 4 minutes. Simulate times for three jobs using the first three values in column 1 of Table 17S–2.

Solution

The first three values are: 1.46, −1.05, and 0.15. The simulated values are:

For   1.46, 30 + 1.46(4) = 35.84 minutes.
For −1.05, 30 − 1.05(4) = 25.80 minutes.
For   0.15, 30 + 0.15(4) = 30.60 minutes.

It is important to recognize that the last example involves a continuous variable, whereas the previous examples have involved discrete variables. (Remember that discrete variables typically take on only integer values, whereas continuous variables can take on integer and noninteger values.) Whenever possible, a model of a continuous variable should be able to simulate noninteger values as well as integer values.

Another continuous type of distribution we can consider is the uniform distribution, in which values may occur anywhere over a continuous range between two extremes, a and b, as illustrated in Figure 17S–1.

$$\text{Simulated value} = a + (b - a)(\text{Random number as a percentage}) \qquad \textbf{(17S–2)}$$

Converting the random number to a percentage simply involves placing a decimal point to the left of the number. For example, 77 becomes .77.

Job times vary uniformly between 10 and 15 minutes. Use Table 17S–1 to simulate job times for four jobs. Read numbers from column 9, going down.

Example S–5

∎

Solution

$a = 10$ minutes, $b = 15$ minutes, $a - b = 5$ minutes

a. Obtain the random numbers: 15, 88, 57, and 28.

b. Convert to simulated values:

Random number	Computation	Simulated value (minutes)
15	$10 + 5(.15)$ =	10.75
88	$10 + 5(.88)$ =	14.40
57	$10 + 5(.57)$ =	12.85
28	$10 + 5(.28)$ =	11.40

A third continuous distribution is the exponential distribution. We will concern ourselves with simulating values of negative exponential distributions, as portrayed in Figure 17S–2.

With a negative exponential distribution, the probability is fairly high that the random variable will assume a value close to zero. Moreover, the probability decreases as the specified value of the random variable increases. The probability that a random variable will take on a value greater than some specified value T, given that the variable can be described by an exponential distribution with a mean equal to $1/\lambda$, is given by the equation.

$$P(t \geq T) = e^{-\lambda t} \qquad \textbf{(17S–3)}$$

Figure 17S–2

A negative exponential distribution

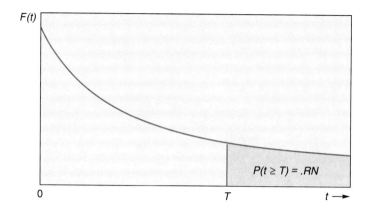

To simulate exponential values, we select a random number, place a decimal point to the left of it, set this equal to the probability $P(T)$, and solve Formula 17S–3 for t. The result is a simulated value from an exponential distribution with a mean of λ.

We can obtain an expression for t by taking the natural logarithm of both sides of the equation. Thus, with $P(T) = .RN$ (for *random number*), we have

$$\ln(.RN) = \ln(e^{-\lambda t})$$

The natural logarithm of a power of e is equal to the power itself, so

$$\ln(.RN) = \ln(e^{-\lambda t}) = -\lambda t$$

Then

$$t = -\frac{1}{\lambda}\ln(.RN) \tag{17S–4}$$

This concept is illustrated in Figure 17S–2.

Values of random numbers can be obtained using Table 17S–1, as demonstrated in the following example.

| Example S–6 | Times between breakdowns of a certain type of equipment can be described by an exponential distribution with a mean of five hours. Simulate the time between two breakdowns. Read two-digit random numbers from column 3 of Table 17S–1. |

Solution

The mean, $1/\lambda$, is 5 hours. The random numbers are 84 and 05. Using Formula 17S–4, the simulated times are:

For 84, $t = -5[\ln(.84)] = -5[-0.1744] = 0.872$ hours.
For 05, $t = -5[\ln(.05)] = -5[-2.9957] = 14.979$ hours.

Note that the smaller the value of the random number, the larger the simulated value of t.

SIMULATION APPLICATIONS

Simulation has applications across a broad spectrum of operations management problems. In some instances, the simulations are quite modest, and in others, they are rather involved. Their usefulness, in all cases, depends on the degree to which decision makers are able to answer their *what if* questions.

Generally speaking, the simulation approach is used either because optimization techniques are unavailable or because the assumptions required by an optimizing technique are not reasonably satisfied in a given situation. Queuing problems are a good example of the latter reason. Although waiting-line problems are pervasive, the rather restrictive assumptions of arrival and service distributions in many cases are simply not met. Very often, analysts will then turn to simulation as a reasonable alternative for obtaining descriptive information about the system in question.

If you were to go down the list of operations management topics, you would find that most have simulation applications. For instance, simulation is often helpful in product design and testing, facilities layout, line balancing, job design, aggregate planning, testing alternative inventory policies, scheduling, and project management. Actually, the list is quite long. The books and articles noted in the bibliography of this chapter give an indication of the richness and breadth of those applications and offer the interested reader an opportunity to explore this fascinating and useful subject in more detail.

COMPUTER SIMULATION

Although the emphasis in this supplement has been on manual simulation in order to convey the main concepts, most real-life simulations involve the use of a computer. Computers offer relatively quick and easy means of obtaining results. Many real-life applications involve fairly complex simulation models that have substantial record-keeping requirements, and computers offer a practical solution.

Over the years, a number of simulation languages have been developed that make the task of writing simulation programs much simpler compared to the use of such standard programming languages as FORTRAN and BASIC. Some of the more widely used specialty languages are SIMSCRIPT, GPSS, GASP, and DYNAMO. In addition, there are a number of other simulation packages, some of which have very narrow focuses that relate to queuing or network problems. Most of the simulation packages have certain features in common. For example, they generally provide for random number generation from a variety of statistical distributions, as well as collection and tabulation of simulation results and time keeping.

It should be noted that some managers prefer to write their own simulations, or have a member of their staff do so, using a standard programming language rather than a simulation language. In cases where simulation is used infrequently, it can be more practical to use that approach rather than go through the time and effort required to use a specialty language. For simple problems, the slight inefficiency related to the use of a standard language is not usually an important consideration.

ADVANTAGES AND LIMITATIONS OF USING SIMULATIONS

Among the main advantages of simulation are these:

1. It lends itself to problems that are difficult or impossible to solve mathematically.
2. It permits an analyst to experiment with system behavior while avoiding possible risks inherent in experimenting with the actual system.

Figure 17S–3

Choosing a solution
technique

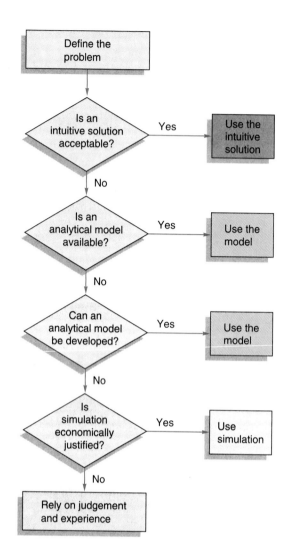

3. It compresses time so that managers can quickly discern long-term effects.
4. It can serve as a valuable tool for training decision makers by building up their experience and understanding of system behavior under a wide range of conditions.

There are also certain limitations associated with simulation. Some of the chief limitations are:

1. Simulation does not produce an optimum solution; it merely indicates an *approximate* behavior for a given set of inputs. There are two reasons for this:
    a. By design, there is inherent randomness (i.e., random numbers) in simulation.
    b. Simulations are based on models, and models are only approximations of reality.
2. For large-scale simulation, it can require considerable effort to develop a suitable model as well as considerable computer time to obtain simulations.

3. Monte Carlo simulation is applicable only in situations with elements that can be described by random variables.

Because simulation produces an approximate answer rather than an exact solution, and because of the cost of running a simulation study, simulation is not generally the first choice of a decision maker. Instead, depending on the complexity of the situation, intuitive or analytical methods should first be investigated. Very often in simple cases, an intuitive solution will be acceptable. In more complex cases, an analytical solution would be preferable, assuming an appropriate technique is available. If not, it may be possible to develop an analytical model that could be used to generate a solution. If these measures are rejected, simulation becomes the next logical possibility. However, its use may not be economically justifiable, in which case the decision maker will have to rely on judgment and experience; in effect, after reevaluating all the alternatives, the decision maker must revert to an intuitive solution, even though initially that approach did not appear acceptable. This process is outlined in Figure 17S–3.

KEY TERMS

Monte Carlo method, 864
random, 864

simulation, 862

SOLVED PROBLEMS

Problem

1. The number of customers who arrive at a transmission repair shop can be described by a Poisson distribution that has a mean of three per hour. Assuming the distribution holds for an entire eight-hour day, simulate customer arrivals for the first four hours of a day. Read random numbers from Table 17S–1, columns 4 and 5, going down.

Solution

a. Obtain cumulative probabilities of the Poisson distribution from Appendix B, Table C for the mean specified. (Those values are given below for convenience.) Determine the random number ranges.

x	Cumulative probability
0.........	.050
1.........	.199
2.........	.423
3.........	.647
4.........	.815
5.........	.916
6.........	.966
7.........	.988
8.........	.996
9.........	.999
10.........	1.000

b. Obtain the random numbers: 299, 642, 350, and .091 (*Note:* Three-digit numbers are needed because the probabilities are given to three decimal places.)

c. Convert the random numbers to numbers of arrivals. Note where each number falls in the random number range list. For instance, 299 falls between 199 and 423. Interpret this to mean two customers arrive in the first hour. Similarly, 642 is interpreted to mean three customers arrive in the second hour, 350 implies two customers in the third hour, and 091 implies one customer in the fourth hour.

In sum, the number of customers per hour for the four-hour simulation is:

Hour	Number of arrivals
1..............	2
2..............	3
3..............	2
4..............	1

Problem

2. Jobs arrive at a workstation at fixed intervals of one hour. Processing time is approximately normal and has a mean of 56 minutes per job and a standard deviation of 4 minutes per job. Using the fifth row of the table of normally distributed random numbers (Table 17S–2), simulate the processing times for four jobs, and determine the amount of operator idle time and job waiting time. Assume the first job arrives at time = 0.

Solution

a. Obtain the random numbers from the table: 0.74, −0.44, 1.53, and −1.76.

b. Convert the random numbers to simulated processing times:

Random number	Computation	Simulated time
0.74	56 + 4(0.74) =	58.96
−0.44	56 + 4(−0.44) =	54.24
1.53	56 + 4(1.53) =	62.12
−1.76	56 + 4(−1.76) =	48.96

Note that three of the times are less than the interarrival times for the jobs, meaning the operator may be idle after those three jobs. One time exceeds the one-hour interval, so the next job must wait, and possibly the job following it if the waiting plus processing time exceeds 60 minutes.

c.   Compute waiting and idle times:

Job number	Arrives at	Processing time, t (minutes)	$60 - t$ Operator idle (minutes)	$t - 60$ Next job waits (minutes)
1.............	0	58.96	1.04	—
2.............	60	54.24	5.76	—
3.............	120	62.12	—	2.12
4.............	180	48.96	8.92★	—
			15.72	2.12

★$60 - 2.12 - 48.96 = 8.92$

Problem

3.   The time between mechanics' requests for tools in a large plant is normally distributed with a mean of 10 minutes and a standard deviation of 1 minute. The time to fill requests is also normal with a mean of 9 minutes per request and a standard deviation of 1 minute. Mechanics' waiting time represents a cost of $2 per minute, and servers represent a cost of $1 per minute. Simulate arrivals for the first nine mechanic requests and their service times, and determine the mechanics' waiting time, assuming one server. Would it be economical to add another server? Explain. Use Table 17S–2, column 8 for requests and column 9 for service.

Solution

a.   Obtain random numbers and convert to times [see columns (a) and (b) in the following table for requests and columns (f) and (g) for service].

Customer arrivals				Service			
(a)	(b)	(c)	(d) $(e - c)$	(e)	(f)	(g)	(h) $(e + g)$
Random → number	Time between arrivals	Cumulative arrival time	Customer waiting time	Service begins	Random → number	Service time	Service ends
−1.12	8.88	8.88	0.00	8.88	1.36	10.36	19.24
−0.62	9.38	18.26	0.98	19.24	−0.95	8.05	27.29
−1.20	8.80	27.06	0.23	27.29	0.27	9.27	36.56
−2.17	7.83	34.89	1.67	36.56	1.10	10.10	46.66
0.22	10.22	45.11	1.55	46.66	−0.59	8.41	55.07
0.43	10.43	55.54	0.00	55.54	1.15	10.15	65.69
0.38	10.38	65.92	0.00	65.92	−0.04	8.96	74.88
−0.71	9.29	75.21	0.00	75.21	−1.11	7.89	83.10
−0.26	9.74	84.95	0.00	84.95	0.41	9.41	94.36
			4.43				

b.   Determine arrival times [column (c)] by successive adding to times between arrivals in column (b).

c.   Use arrival times for service start *unless service is still in progress on a previous request.* In that case, determine how long the arrival must wait

$(e - c)$. Column (e) values are the sum of starting time and service time [column (g)], which is the time service ends [column (h)]. Thus, service on each new request begins [column (e)] at the same time that service on the previous request ends [column (h)].

d. The simulation and resulting waiting times for the first nine arrivals are shown in the table. Total waiting time is 4.43 minutes.

e. The total cost for the 94.36 minutes (end of service on the ninth request) of the simulation is:

Waiting cost . . . .   4.43 minutes at $2 per minute = $ 8.86
Server cost . . . .   94.36 minutes at $1 per minute =   94.36
                                                                 $103.22

f. Usually, a second simulation with two servers would be needed (but with the same arrival times so that the results would be comparable). However, in this case it is apparent that a second server would increase server cost by about $94 but could not eliminate more than $8.86 of waiting cost. Hence, the second server would not be justified.

DISCUSSION AND REVIEW QUESTIONS

1. What is a simulation?
2. What are some of the primary reasons for the widespread use of simulation techniques in practice?
3. What are some of the ways simulation can be used?
4. What role do random numbers play in Monte Carlo simulations?
5. How would you respond to the following comment?
    "I ran the simulation several times, and each run gave me a different result. Therefore, the technique does not seem to be useful. I need answers!"
6. Briefly discuss the main advantage of simulation.
7. What are some of the limitations of simulation as a tool for decision making?

PROBLEMS

1. The number of jobs received by a small shop is to be simulated for an eight-day period. The shop manager has collected the following data:

Number of jobs	Frequency
2 or less	0
3	10
4	50
5	80
6	40
7	16
8	4
9 or more	0
	200

Use the third column of Table 17S–1 and read two-digit numbers, going down. Determine the average number of jobs per day for the eight-day simulation period.

2. Jack M. sells insurance on a part-time basis. His records on the number of policies sold per week over a 50-week period are:

Number sold	Frequency
0	8
1	15
2	17
3	7
4	3
	50

Simulate three five-day periods. Use Table 17S–1, column 6 for the first simulation, column 7 for the second, and column 8 for the third. In each case, read two-digit numbers, beginning at the *bottom* of the column and going *up*. For each simulation, determine the percentage of days on which two or more policies are sold.

3. After a careful study of requests for a special tool at a large tool crib, an analyst has concluded that demand for the tool can be adequately described by a Poisson distribution with a mean of two requests per day. Simulate demand for a 12-working-day period for this tool using Table 17S–1. Read three-digit numbers from columns 5 and 6 combined, starting at the *top* and reading *down* (e.g., 917, 264, 045).

4. The number of lost-time accidents at a logging firm can be described using a Poisson distribution that has a mean of four accidents per month. Using the last two columns of Table 17S–1 (e.g., 540, 733, 293), simulate accidents for a 12-month period.

5. The time a physician spends with patients can be modeled using a normal distribution that has a mean of 20 minutes and a standard deviation of 2 minutes. Using the table of normally distributed random numbers (Table 17S–2), simulate the times the doctor might spend with the next seven patients. Use column 4 of the table; start at the bottom of the column and read up.

6. Jobs are delivered to a workstation at random intervals. The time between job arrivals tends to be normally distributed with a mean of 15 minutes and a standard deviation of 1 minute. Job processing time is also normally distributed with a mean of 14 minutes per job and a standard deviation of 2 minutes.

   a. Using Table 17S–2, simulate the arrival and processing of five jobs. Use column 4 of the table for job arrival times and column 3 for processing times. *Start each column at row 4.* Find the total times jobs wait for processing.

   b. The company is considering the use of new equipment that would result in processing time that is normal with a mean of 13 minutes and a standard deviation of 1 minute. Job waiting represents a cost of $3 per minute, and the new equipment would represent an additional cost of $.50 per minute. Would the equipment be cost justified? (*Note:* Use the same arrival times and the same random numbers for processing times.)

7. Daily usage of sugar in a small bakery can be described by a uniform distribution with endpoints of 30 pounds and 50 pounds. Assuming usage is independent of the day of the week, simulate daily usage for a 10-day period. Read four-digit numbers from Table 17S–1, columns 5 and 6, going up from the bottom.

8. Weekly usage of spare parts for a specialized machine can be described by a Poisson distribution with a mean of 2.8 parts per week. Lead time to replenish the supply of spare parts is two weeks (constant). Simulate the total usage of parts during lead time 10 times, and then determine the frequency of lead time demands (i.e., what percentage of times was the demand equal to 2, 3, 4, etc.?). Read four-digit numbers from Table 17S–1, columns 8 and 9, going down.

9. (Computer exercise.) Repeat the previous problem for 100 lead time periods.

10. A repair shop breaks an average of 0.6 tool per day. The average number of days required to obtain replacements is six. (Parts are delivered by mail once each day.) Both breakages and delivery times can be described by Poisson distributions. Tools are reordered whenever three or more must be replaced.

    a. Draw a flowchart to describe this process.
    b. Simulate breakage and ordering for a 12-day period. Read three-digit numbers from Table 17S–1, columns 5 and 6, going down (e.g., 917, 264), for tool breakage, and columns 7 and 8, going down (e.g., 643, 200), for delivery time. Assume zero tools in inventory to start.

11. (Computer exercise.) Repeat the previous problem for 150 days.

12. Customers arrive randomly at a catalog department of a large store. The time between arrivals varies uniformly between 10 and 20 minutes. Service time is normal with a mean of 15 minutes and a standard deviation of 2 minutes.

    a. Simulate processing and waiting times for nine customers. Read three-digit numbers going down columns 9 and 10 of Table 17S–1 for arrivals (e.g., 156, 884, 576). Use column 8, Table 17S–2, for processing time.
    b. If management can reduce the range of arrival times to between 13 and 17 minutes, what would the impact be on customer waiting times? (Use the same service times and the same random numbers for arrival times from part a.) Round arrival times to two decimal places.

13. Probabilities have been determined for the movements of the ball in a pinball game. These are shown in the accompanying table, along with the points awarded if the ball strikes a given position. Simulate the paths of three balls, and compute the number of points awarded for each ball. Use column 1 of Table 17S–1 for the first ball, column 2 for the second ball, and column 3 for the third ball, reading down the columns.

Position	Points
A	400
B	300
C	200
D	100
E	50
F	20

Path	Proba-bility	Path	Proba-bility	Path	Proba-bility
S to A	.30	B to A	.30	D to A	.10
B	.30	B	.20	B	.05
C	.25	C	.20	C	.25
D	.10	D	.15	D	.20
E	.04	E	.10	E	.25
F	.01	F	.05	F	.15
A to A	.25	C to A	.10	E to A	.05
B	.25	B	.15	B	.10
C	.25	C	.20	C	.15
D	.10	D	.15	D	.15
E	.10	E	.25	E	.20
F	.05	F	.15	F	.35

(*Hint:* Construct a cumulative probability distribution for each of the six cases. Each new random number indicates the next position to move on. Each ball must start at S.)

14. Repeat the previous problem using columns 1, 2, and 3 for the next three balls, reading *up* from the bottom.

15. An analyst found that the length of telephone conversations in an office could be described by an exponential distribution with a mean of four minutes. Reading two-digit random numbers from Table 17S–1, column 6, simulate the length of five calls and compute the simulated average time. Why is the simulated average different from the mean of four minutes?

16. The length of time between calls for service of a certain piece of equipment can be described by an exponential distribution with a mean of 40 minutes. Service time can be described by a normal distribution with a mean of 8 minutes and a standard deviation of 2 minutes. Simulate the time until the first breakdown and the times between three breakdowns, as well as the four service times. For breakdowns, read two-digit numbers from Table 17S–1, row 7; for service times, read numbers from Table 17S–2, column 8.

17. The number of jobs per day that a repair shop gets can be described by a Poisson distribution with a mean of 3.0. Repair time per job can be described by an exponential distribution with a mean of six hours. Simulate the number of jobs received for a four-day period and the repair time for each job. What is the simulated total repair time per day? For number of jobs received, read three-digit numbers from Table 17S–1, row 1; for repair times, read three-digit numbers from row 2 of the same table.

18. A service operation consists of three steps. The first step can be described by a uniform distribution that ranges between five and nine minutes. The second step can be described by a normal distribution with a mean of seven minutes and a standard deviation of one minute, and the third step can be described by an exponential distribution with a mean of five minutes. Simulate three cycles using two-digit numbers from Table 17S–1, row 4 for step 1; Table 17S–2, row 6 for step 2; and two-digit numbers from column 4 of Table 17S–1 for step 3. Determine the simulated time for each of the three cycles.

19. A project consists of eight major activities, as illustrated in the accompanying diagram. Activity times are normally distributed with means and standard deviations as shown in the following table. Note that there are two paths through the project: 1-2-3-5 and 1-2-4-5. Project duration is defined as the largest sum of times along a path. Simulate 12 times for each activity. Use columns 1 and 2 of Table 17S–2 for activity 1-2, columns 3 and 4 for activity 2-3, columns 5 and 6 for activity 2-4, columns 7 and 8 for activity 3-5, and columns 9 and 10 for activity 4-5. Determine the project duration for each of the 12 sets, and then prepare a frequency distribution of project duration. Use categories of 25 to less than 30, 30 to less than 35, 35 to less than 40, 40 to less than 45, and 45 or more. Determine the proportion of time that a simulated duration of less than 40 days occurred. How might this information be used?

Activity	Mean (days)	Standard deviation (days)
1-2	10	2
2-3	12	2
2-4	15	3
3-5	14	2
4-5	8	1

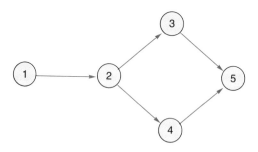

SELECTED BIBLIOGRAPHY

Barton, R. *A Primer on Simulation and Gaming.* Englewood Cliffs, N.J.: Prentice Hall, 1970.

Buffa, Elwood. *Operations Management.* 3rd ed. New York: John Wiley & Sons, 1972.

Chase, Richard, and Nicholas Aquilano. *Production and Operations Management.* 6th ed. Homewood, Ill.: Richard D. Irwin, 1992.

Graybeal, W., and U. Pooch. *Simulation: Principles and Methods.* Cambridge: Winthrop Publishers, 1980.

Law, A. M., and W. D. Kelton. *Simulation Modeling and Analysis.* New York: McGraw-Hill, 1982.

Meier, R. C.; W. T. Newell; and H. L. Pazer. *Simulation in Business and Economics.* Englewood Cliffs, N.J.: Prentice Hall, 1969.

Schmidt, J. W., and R. E. Taylor. *Simulation and Analysis of Industrial Systems.* Homewood, Ill.: Richard D. Irwin, 1970.

Shannon, Robert E. *Systems Simulation: The Art and Science.* Englewood Cliffs, N.J.: Prentice Hall, 1975.

Smith, David E. *Quantitative Business Analysis.* New York: John Wiley & Sons, 1977.

Watson, Hugh J. *Computer Simulation in Business.* New York: John Wiley & Sons, 1981.

CASE   COQUILLE REFINERY CORPORATION

The Coquille Refinery Corporation is contemplating building a crude-oil storage and docking facility on the southern coast of France. They plan to import crude oil by ship from the Middle East and distribute this crude oil by pipeline to refineries in the area.

The construction of this facility represents a substantial capital investment. Furthermore, the cost of such a facility is principally determined by its crude-oil storage capacity. You have been asked to study the problem and recommend an appropriate storage capacity; bear in mind that too large a capacity represents an unnecessary expense, but too small a capacity will result in costly later additions to the facility.

A long-term contract has been made with the Middle East supplier to furnish an average daily supply of 300,000 barrels of crude oil. Because its fleet of ships consists of 200,000-barrel tankers, the supplier expects that the arrival of its tankers will follow the distribution below:

Tanker arrivals per day	Probability
0	0.1
1	0.5
2	0.2
3	0.2

A review of past production records of refineries in the area suggests the following distribution of crude-oil demand per day:

Barrels per day	Probability
100,000	0.1
200,000	0.2
300,000	0.3
400,000	0.4

Questions

1. Consider the following issues before you simulate:
   a. What is the expected daily demand for crude oil? Why must this be so?
   b. What assumptions concerning the timing of crude-oil receipts and deliveries would require the greatest oil storage capacity?
   c. What assumption concerning receipts and deliveries would require the least oil storage capacity?
   d. Give a reason based on systems-analysis considerations why back orders should be filled from the next day's receipts rather than considered as lost sales.

2. Develop a Monte Carlo simulation model for Coquille that will generate information useful for resolving the storage capacity problem and simulate 10 days of capacity.

3. Assume a computer program was written to simulate 10,000 days of activity under the assumptions listed in question 1b. From the results of such a simulation the following distribution of

oil in storage, after a day's receipts, is determined. (Note: Negative figures represent back orders.)

Oil in storage, in thousands	Probability
−300	0.01
−200	0.04
−100	0.06
0	0.07
⋮	⋮
1,000	0.09
1,100	0.08
1,200	0.07
1,300	0.05
1,400	0.03
1,500	0.02
	1.00

a. What level of crude-oil safety stock should be carried to ensure 95 percent protection against stock-outs (1 stock-out in 20 days)?
b. If Coquille decides to use the above safety stock, what should be the oil storage capacity to ensure 90 percent protection against overruns (i.e., sufficient capacity to accommodate completely receipts 9 days out of 10)?

4. Note two ways one might determine if the simulation run length of 10,000 days is adequate.

5. Make a list of cost factors that would influence the final selection of oil storage capacity.

Source: James A. Fitzsimmons and Robert S. Sullivan, *Service Operations Management* (New York: McGraw-Hill, 1982), pp. 78–80. Reprinted by permission.

ANSWERS TO SELECTED PROBLEMS

CHAPTER 2: PRODUCTIVITY, COMPETITIVENESS, AND STRATEGY

1. Last week: Labor productivity = 37.5 book-cases per worker.
   Week before: Labor productivity = 40 book-cases per worker.

2. A crew size of two had the highest productivity (250 yards installed).

4. *a.* Before: Labor productivity = 16 carts per worker per hour.
   After: Labor productivity = 21 carts per worker per hour.

   b. Before: Multifactor productivity = .89 carts per dollar.

   After: Multifactor productivity = .93 carts per dollar.

CHAPTER 2 SUPPLEMENT: DECISION MAKING

1. *a.* Expand (80).
   b. Do nothing (50).
   c. Indifferent between do nothing and sub-contract (55).
   d. Subcontract (10).

2. *a.* Expand (62).
   c. $9.

3. Do nothing: $P(\text{high}) < .50$.
   Subcontract: $.50 < P(\text{high}) < .67$.
   Expand: $P(\text{high}) > .67$.

4. *a.*

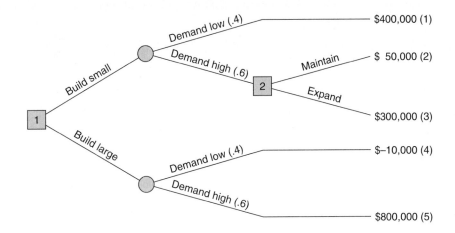

b. $164,000.

5. Large for $P(\text{low}) < .55$.
   Small for $P(\text{low}) > .55$.

6. *a.* Relocate.
   b. Renew.
   c. Relocate.

7. *a.* Renew.
   c. Yes.

9. *a.* Build large.
   b. Build small.
   c. $12.4.
   d. Build small for $P(\text{high}) < .721$.
       Build large for $P(\text{high}) > .721$.

10. Buy two ($113.5).

11. Expand ($1.57).

12. $4.

13. *a.* New staff.
    b. Redesign.
    c. New staff.
    d. New staff or redesign.

16. *b.* Alternative *c.*
    c. $P(2) > .625$.
    d. $P(1) < .375$.

CHAPTER 4: FORECASTING

2. *b.* (1) 20.86, (2) 19, (3) 19.26, (4) 20, (5) 20.4.
   d. Demand did not exceed supply.

4. *a.* 88.16 percent.
   b. 88.54 percent.

5. *a.* Starting forecast is $(800 + 810 + 808 + 812)/4 = 807.5$; $F_9 = 809.7$ cases.
   b. 804 cases.

7. *a.* 700,000 sq. ft.   *b.* 760,000 sq. ft.

8. *a.* Increasing by 15,000 bottles per year.
   b. 275 (i.e., 275,000 bottles).

9. *b.* 1,320 trees.

10. $500 - 20t$.

11. *a.* $Y_t = 204.09 + 19.76t$.   *c.* 500.49.

12. Q_1: 158; Q_2: 175; Q_3: 126; Q_4: 325.

13. Y_{11}: 267.63; Y_{12}: 274.13; Y_{13}: 280.63; Y_{14}: 287.13

14. Use periods 1 through 4 for model development.
    Starting TAF = 224
    T = 8

Period	Forecast
5	232
6	240.9
7	246.41
8	254.54
9	261.23
10	266.30
11	273.56

17. Fri. = 0.79, Sat. = 1.34, Sun. = 0.87.

22.

Day	Relative
1	.902
2	.836
3	.919
4	1.034
5	1.416
6	1.487
7	.427

24. *b.*

Jan.	800
Feb.	810
Mar.	750
Apr.	810
May	826
Jun.	850
Jul.	850
Aug.	855
Sep.	865

Oct. ... 900
Nov. ... 806
Dec. ... 900

27. *b.* $29,000.

28. *b.* $17.90.

29. *a.* $Y = 12.35 + .543x.$ *b.* $r = .539.$
    c.   Yes, yes.

30. *a.* $Y = 334.57 - 22.286x.$
    b. 178.57 ± 10.28
    c. $r = -.974.$

31. *b.* $Y = 66.33 + .584x.$ *c.*   Yes.
    d.   90.27.   *e.* $90.27 \pm 10.04.$

32. *a.* $r = +.94.$ *b.* $Y = .955 + 5.276x.$
    c.   11.51 mowers.

35. *a.* $MAD_5 = 5$ *b.* $TS_5 =$ 1.40
         $MAD_6 = 5.9$ $TS_6 = -0.17$
         $MAD_7 = 4.73$ $TS_7 = -0.63$
         $MAD_8 = 3.911$ $TS_8 = -0.26$
         $MAD_9 = 4.238$ $TS_9 = -1.42$
              etc.   etc.

36. *a.*

	MSE	MAD
Forecast 1	10.44	2.8
Forecast 2	42.44	3.6
Naive	156	10.7

37. *a.*   Initial MAD = 4.727. The tracking signal
         for month 15 is 4.087, so at that point, the
         forecast would be suspect.
    b. Σ errors = -1, Σ errors^2 = 345. Control
         limits: 0 ± 12.38 (in control). Plot reveals
         cycles in errors.

CHAPTER 5: PRODUCT AND SERVICE DESIGN

1. *a.*   .81.   *b.*   .9801.   *c.*   .9783.

2.   .9033.

3.   .9726.

4.   .93.

5. *a.*   .9315.   *b.*   .9953.   *c.*   .994.

6. *a.*   .7876.

7. *a.*   Plan 2 (.9934).

8.   .996.

9.   .995.

10.   .006.

11. *a.*   (1) .2725.   *b.*   (1) .6671.
         (2) .2019.   (2) .3935.
         (3) .1353.   (3) .1813.
    c.   (1) 21 months.   (3) 90 months.
         (2) 57 months.   (4) 138 months.

12. *a.*   .6321.   *b.*   Three months or 90 days.

13. *a.*   .3012.   *b.*   .1813.   *c.*   .5175.

14. *a.*   .2231.   *b.*   .8647.
    c.   .0878.   *d.*   .0302.

15. *a.*   .2266.   *b.*   .4400.   *c.*   .3830.

16. *a.*   (1) .9772.   *b.*   Approximately zero.
         (2) .5000.
         (3) .0013.

CHAPTER 6: PROCESS SELECTION AND CAPACITY PLANNING

1. *a.*   46,000 units.   *b.*   (1) $3,000.
                              (2) $8,200.
    c.   126,000 units.   *d.*   25,556 units.

2. *a.*   A: 8,000 units.   *b.*   10,000 units.
         B: 7,500 units.
    c.   A: $20,000.
         B: $18,000.

3. *a.*   39,683 units.   *b.* $1.71 (rounded up).

4. *a.*   A: $82.
         B: $92.
         C: $100.
    c.   A: 0 to less than 178.
         B: Never.
         C: 178+.

5.   ⅓ day, ⅔ evening.

6.   Vendor best for $Q < 63,333$. For larger quan-
     tities, produce in-house at $4 per unit.

7. *a.*   Vendor B best for 10,000 and 20,000.

8.   3 cells

CHAPTER 6 SUPPLEMENT: LINEAR PROGRAMMING

1. *a.* $x = 0$, $y = 12$, Profit = $240.
    b. $A = 25.45$, $B = 18.18$, $Z = $207.25.

2. *a.* $T = 20$, $S = 8$, $Z = $58.40.
    b. $C = 4.6$, $D = 14.4$, $Z = $24.18.

3. $H = 132$ units, $W = 36$ units, Profit =
     $6,360.

4. Deluxe = 90 bags, Standard = 60 bags,
   Profit = $243.
5. $x = 327.27$, $y = 163.64$, $Z = \$1,636.36$.
6. 500 apple, 200 grape, Revenue = $990. Fifty
   cups of sugar will be unused.
7. Final tableau:

C		10	20	0	0	
	Variables in solution	x_1	x_2	s_1	s_2	Solution quantity
0	s_1	3.0	0.0	1.0	−0.5	16.0
20	x_2	1.0	1.0	0.0	0.3	12.0
	Z	20.0	20.0	0.0	5.0	240.0
	C − Z	−10.0	0.0	0.0	−5.0	

8. *a.* (1) 485.72 to 800.
   (2) 750 to 1,080.
   (3) 145.45 to infinity.
   b. (optimality).
   C_A: $3.75 to $12.
   C_B: $1.50 to $4.80.

9. Final tableau:

C		40	30	0	0	
	Variables in solution	H	W	s_1	s_2	Solution quantity
40	H	1.0	0.0	0.3	−0.1	132
30	W	0.0	1.0	−0.1	0.2	36
	Z	40.0	30.0	9.0	2.0	6,360
	C − Z	0.0	0.0	−9.0	−2.0	

a. Fabrication: 160 to 960.
    Assembly: 300 to 1,800.
b. (optimality).
    H: $10 to $60.
    W: $20 to $120.

10. Final tableau:

C	Var	x_1	x_2	S_1	S_2	Solution quantity
18	x_1	0	1	−0.1333	0.333	10
21	x_2	1	0	+0.0667	−0.667	0
	Z	21	18	−0.99999	−8.000	180
	C − Z	0	0	0.99999	8.000	

a. Casting: 32,000 to 41,016.
   Grinding: 1,555 to infinity.
   Drilling: 2,871 to 4,050.
b. (optimality).
   C_x: \$2.67 to \$4.50.
   C_y: \$1.78 to \$3.00.

11. a. Final tableau:

C		10.5	11.75	10.8	0	0	0	
	Variables in solution	x	y	z	s_1	s_2	s_3	Solution quantity
0.00	s_1	0.0	5.6	1.6	1.0	−0.7	0.0	507.14
10.50	x	1.0	1.3	1.3	0.0	0.1	0.0	178.57
0.00	s_3	0.0	−2.1	0.9	0.0	−0.6	1.0	5.71
	Z	10.5	13.5	13.5	0.0	1.5	0.0	1875.00
	C − Z	0.0	−1.8	−2.7	0.0	−1.5	0.0	

b. Stapling, since the optimum solution exhausts that resource.

12. Final tableau:

C		2.40	2.50	3.00	0	0	0	
	Variables in solution	a	b	c	s_1	s_2	s_3	Solution quantity
2.50	b	1.17	1.0	0.0	0.17	0.0	−0.08	80
0.00	s_2	0.17	0.0	0.0	−0.33	1.0	−0.08	380
3.00	c	0.04	0.0	1.0	−0.08	0.0	0.1	50
	Z	3.04	2.5	3.0	0.17	0.0	0.1	350
	C − Z	−0.64	0.0	0.0	−0.17	0.0	−0.1	

C_a (insignificance): \$0 to \$3.00.
C_b (optimality): \$2.00 to \$3.50.
C_c (optimality): \$2.00 to \$5.00.

13. Final tableau:

C		21	18	999	0.0	999	0.0	
	Variables in solution	x_1	x_2	a_1	s_1	a_2	s_2	Solution quantity
18	x_2	0.0	1.0	0.1	−0.1	−0.3	0.3	6.7
21	x_1	1.0	0.0	−0.1	0.1	0.7	−0.7	6.7
	Z	21.0	18.0	1.0	−1.0	8.0	−8.0	260.0
	C − Z	0.0	0.0	998.0	1.0	991.0	8.0	

b.   Final tableau:

C	Var	1	2	z	s_1	s_2	s_3	b_i
3	z	.4	1.2	1	0	0	−0.200	24
0	s_1	−8.8	11.6	0	1	0	−3.6	92
0	s_2	−5.8	3.6	0	0	1	−2.6	23
	Z	1.2	3.6	3	0	0	−0.6	72
	C − Z	.8	1.4	0	0	0	.6	

16. *a.*   board = 0, holder = 50.
    b.   Cutting = 16 minutes, gluing = 0 min-
         utes, finishing = 210 minutes.

17. *a.*   A = .7143, B = 7.7143, Cost = $.91.
    b.   Carbohydrates by 20 grams.

19. Radio = 24, TV = 12, Newspaper = 8.

20. Bookcases = 31.11, food carts = 3.33, Z =
    $1,413.

21. Z = $433.

22. *a.* $.12; 1,000 pounds to 2,000 pounds.
    b. $.48.
    c.   No.
    d.   Optimal quantities would not change; Z
         would increase by $40.

23. *a.* $1.50; range is 450 to 750.
    b. $1.50/pound.
    c. $0; range 375 to infinity.
    d.   None.
    e.   150 pounds of pine bark.
    f.   Optimal quantities would not change; Z
         would increase by $75.

CHAPTER 7: FACILITIES LAYOUT

1. *a.*   Minimum is 2.4 minutes, maximum is 18
        minutes.
   b.   25 units to 187.5 units.   *c.*   Eight.
   d.   3.6 minutes.   *e.*   (1) 50 units.
                                 (2) 30 units.

2. *c.*   11.54%.   *d.*   323 units per day.

3. *a.*   2.3 minutes   *c.*   182.6 units per day.
   d.   91.3 units per day.

4. *b.*   1 minute.   *c.*   Three stations.

5. *c.*   (1) 11.1%. (2) 11.1%. (3) 33.33%.

7.

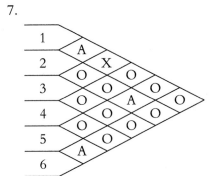

8.

1	5	4
3	8	7
6	2	

10.

3	1	8
9	7	4
5	2	6

11.

6	2	5
3	1	4

TC = $50,800.

13. A: 3; B: 5; C: 1; D: 4; E: 6; F: 2.

14. A: 1; B: 2; C: 5; D: 4; E: 9; F: 8; G: 6; H: 10;
    I: 7; J: 3.

CHAPTER 8: DESIGN OF WORK SYSTEMS

1. 15.08 minutes.

2. *a.*   1.2 minutes.
   b.   1.14 minutes.
   c.   1.27 minutes.

3.

Element	OT	NT	ST
1	0.46	0.414	0.476
2	1.505	1.280	1.472
3	0.83	0.913	1.050
4	1.16	1.160	1.334

4. 5.85 minutes.

5. 7.125 minutes.

7. 57 observations.

8. 37 cycles.

9. *a.* 12%. *b.* 163 observations.

10. 377 observations.

11.

Hour	Minute
1	0
1	47
1	56
3	38
4	24
4	27
6	26
7	15

CHAPTER 8 SUPPLEMENT: LEARNING CURVES

1. *a.* 178.8 hours.
   b. 1,121.4 hours.
   c. 2,914.8 hours.

2. *a.* 41.47 hours.
   b. 60.55 hours.
   c. 72.20 hours.

3. *a.* 56.928 days.
   b. 42.288 days.
   c. 37.512 days.

4. *a.* $P = 85$ percent.
   b. 24.64 minutes.

5. 87.9 minutes.

6. 201.26 hr.

7. *a.* 10.57 hours.
   b. 13.05 hours.
   c. 12.29 hours.

8. *a.* $80.31.
   b. 10 units.

9. 31.63 days.

10. B and C.

CHAPTER 9: LOCATION PLANNING

1. Kansas City: $256,000.

2. *a.* A: 16,854; B: 17,416; C: 17,753.
   b. C: $14,670.

3. *a.* 120 units. *b.* A: 0 to 119; B: 121+.

4. *a.* B: 0 to 33; C: 34 to 400; A: 400+.

5. C($270,000).

6. Biloxi ($160,000).

7. *a.* (1) outside; (2) city. *b.* 230 cars.

9. A.

10. *a.* B = C > A.
    b. B > C > A.

11. (5,4) is optimal.

12. (6,7).

13. (6,6).

14. (3,2.21).

CHAPTER 9 SUPPLEMENT: THE TRANSPORTATION MODEL

1.

	A	B	C
1	15		25
2	15	45	
3			50

2.

	A	B	C
1			40
2		25	35
3	30	20	

3.

	A	B	C	D
1	10	30		
2	80			
3		50	30	50

4.

	A	B	C	D	Dummy
1	13		35		
2	28	2		20	6
3		32			

5.

	A	B	C	D
1		40		
2	80	10		
3		30	30	50
Dummy	10	10		

6.

	A	B	C	D	Dummy
1	41		7		
2				56	
3		32			
Balt.		2	28	4	16

	A	B	C	D	Dummy
1	41		7		
2		2		54	
3		32			
Ph.			28	6	16

8.

	A	B	C	Dummy
1		500		
2	400			
N1		100	350	50

	A	B	C	Dummy
1		500		
2	400			
N2		100	350	50

9.

	A	B	C
1			210
2	140		
3	80	60	10
Tol.		160	

	A	B	C
1			210
2	60	80	
3		140	10
Cin.	160		

CHAPTER 10: QUALITY CONTROL AND CONTINUOUS IMPROVEMENT

1. *a.* .0124.   *b.*   24.35 pounds and 24.65 pounds.

2. *a.*   LCL: 0.996 liters.   *b.*   Not in control.
   UCL: 1.004 liters.

3. *a.*   Mean: LCL is 3.019, UCL is 3.181.
   Range: LCL is 0.1845, UCL is 0.7155.
   b.   Yes.

5. Mean: LCL is 78.88 cm.
          UCL is 81.04 cm.
   Range: LCL is 0 cm.
          UCL is 3.946 cm.
   Process is in control.

6. LCL: 0
   UCL: .0234
   Revised limits based on 12 samples:
   LCL: 0
   UCL: .0197

7. Yes, UCL = 16.266, LCL = 0.

8. Yes, UCL = 5.17, LCL = 0.

9. Yes, UCL = .098, LCL = .010.

10. 490 pieces.

11. One in 30 is "out." Tolerances seem to be met. Approximately 97% will be acceptable.

12. *a.*   LCL: 3.73
          UCL: 3.97
          Out of control.
    b.   Random variations.

13.

	Test	Number of runs Observed	Expected	Standard deviation	z	Conclude
a.	Med 18		14	2.50	1.6	Okay
	U/D 17		17	2.07	0	Okay
b.	Med 8		14	2.50	−2.40	Nonrandom
	U/D 22		17	2.07	2.41	Nonrandom

14. *a.* Med: $z = -0.52$
     U/D: $z = -1.47$
  b. Med: $z = -1.11$
     U/D: $z = -1.36$

15. Med: $z = -2.34$
  U/D: $z = -1.45$

16. 440 pieces.

18. *a.* 566 units.
  b. 62 units.
  c. $1,160.

19. Med: $z = +0.9177$
  U/D: $z = +0.5561$

20. *b.* 4.5, .192.
  c. 4.5, .086.
  d. 4.242 to 4.758.
  f. None.

CHAPTER 10 SUPPLEMENT: INSPECTION AND ACCEPTANCE SAMPLING

1. *a.* (1) Yes. (2) Yes.   *b.* .0067.
2. *b.* .0390.
3. *c.* .0024.
5. *a.* 0.16
  b. 2
  c. (1) .9638.
     (2) .0362
     (3) Accept.
     (4) Both are zero.

CHAPTER 11: AGGREGATE PLANNING

1. *b.* $6,350.
2. *a.* $4,670.
  b. $4,800.
3. *b.* $4,680.
4. $4,970.
7. B: $18,870.
  C: $18,860.

8. $18,525.
9. $18,492.50.
10. $18,190.
12. $124,960.
13. $126,650.
14. $127,000.

CHAPTER 12: INVENTORY MANAGEMENT

1. *a.* 24 bags.
  b. 12 bags.
  c. 56.
  d. $336.
2. *a.* 380 liters.
  d. Increase by $177.
3. *a.* 1,518 pots.
4. $364.
5. *a.* 10,328 bags.
  b. 3,098 bags.
  c. 10.33 days.
  d. 8.
7. *a.* 4,812.
  b. 16.
  c. 0.96 days.
8. *a.* 9.
  b. 11 times per year.
9. *a.* 693 stones.
  b. 600 stones.
10. *a.* 10,000 boxes.
  b. 1.8 orders.
11. 20,000 units.
12. Indifferent between 495 and 1,000 seats.
13. 6,600 feet.
14. *a.* 8.39 gallons.
  b. 40 gallons.
15. *a.* 72 boxes.
  b. .0023.
  c. .0228.

16. *a.* 56 kits.
18. *a.* 749 pounds; *b.* 4.078 pounds.
19. *a.* 134 rolls.
  b. 36 rolls.
  c. .055 per cycle $[\sigma_{dLT} = \sqrt{LT}\sigma_d]$.
  d. .9996.
20. *a.* 80 feet per day.
  b. 301 feet.
  c. .999.
21. ROP = 77 cases.
22. KO33: 581.
  K144: 458.
  L700: 0.

CHAPTER 12 SUPPLEMENT: THE SINGLE-PERIOD MODEL

1. 25 dozen.
2. Nine spares.
3. 78.9 pounds.
4. $4.89 per quart.
5. Five cakes.
6. 421.5 pounds.
7. *a.* $0.53 to $1.76.
  c. $56.67 to $190.00.
8. $0 to $78.03.

CHAPTER 13: MATERIAL REQUIREMENTS PLANNING

1. *b.*

Level	Item	Quantity
0	P	60
1	A	120
	B	180
	H	240
2	K	120
	D	180
	E	180
	I	480
3	C	420
	F	900
	G	180
4	L	480
	M	1,860
	N	1,920

2.

Level	Item	Quantity
0	W	125
	Y	50
1	A	300
	B	600
	K	150
2	D	600
	C	1,100
	L	150
3	F	3,600
	E	1,500
	G	4,600
	H	1,100

3. *a.*

Master Schedule for E

Week number	1	2	3	4	5	6	7	8
Quantity					120			

Item: E LT = 1 week								
Gross requirements					120			
Scheduled receipts								
Projected on hand								
Net requirements					120			
Planned order receipt					120			
Planned order release				120				

Item: I(2) LT = 1 week								
Gross requirements				240				
Scheduled receipts			40					
Projected on hand			40	40				
Net requirements				200				
Planned order receipt				200				
Planned order release			200					

Item: N(4) LT = 2 weeks								
Gross requirements			800					
Scheduled receipts								
Projected on hand	100	100	100	100				
Net requirements			700					
Planned order receipt			700					
Planned order release	700							

Item: V LT = 2 weeks								
Gross requirements			200					
Scheduled receipts			10					
Projected on hand			0					
Net requirements			190					
Planned order receipt			190					
Planned order release	190							

5. *c.*

Master Schedule for golf carts

Week number	1	2	3	4	5	6	7	8	9
Quantity						100		100	100

Item: Golf cart LT = 1 week

	1	2	3	4	5	6	7	8	9
Gross requirements						100		100	100
Scheduled receipts									
Projected on hand									
Net requirements						100		100	100
Planned order receipt						100		100	100
Planned order release					100		100	100	

Item: Bases LT = 1 week

	20	1	2	3	4	5	6	7	8	9
Gross requirements							100		100	100	
Scheduled receipts											
Projected on hand	20	20	20	20	50	100	50	100	50		
Net requirements						0		0	50		
Planned order receipt				30	50	50	50	50	50		
Planned order release			30	50	50	50	50	50			

6. Order 160 units in week 2.
7. Order 120 units in period 2 and 60 units in period 6.
8. EPP = 75.76.

CHAPTER 14: JUST-IN-TIME SYSTEMS

1. 3.
2. 3.

CHAPTER 15: SCHEDULING

1. 1-A, 2-B, 3-C.
2. 1-B, 2-C, 3-A.
3. 1-A, 2-E, 3-D, 4-B, 5-C; or 1-A, 2-D, 3-E, 4-B, 5-C.
4. 1-B, 2-C, 3-D, 4-A.
5. *a.* 1-A, 2-B, 3-C, 4-D, 5-E.
   b. 1-E, 2-B, 3-C, 4-D, 5-A.

6. *b.*

	FCFS	SPT	DD	CR
Av. compl. time	26.5	19.75	21	26.50
Av. job lateness	11	6	6	11
Av. no. of jobs	2.86	2.14	2.27	2.86

7. FCFS: a–b–c–d–e.
   SPT: c–b–a–e–d.
   DD: a–b–c–e–d.
   CR: a–d–e–b–c.

	FCFS	SPT	DD	CR
Av. compl. time	17.40	14.80	16.80	22.60
Av. job lateness	5.20	5.40	4.60	9.00
Av. no. of jobs	2.72	2.31	2.63	3.53

9. B–A–G–E–F–D–C.
10. *a.* e–b–g–h–d–c–a–f.
    c. 3 hours.
11. *a.* B–A–C–E–F–D.
12. *a.* b–a–c–d–e.
    b. 37 minutes.
    c. 15 minutes.
13. *a.*

	FCFS	SPT	DD	CR
Av. compl. time	15.25	11.12	15.60	15.68
Av. job lateness	1.7	2.33	0.55	0.30
Av. no. of jobs	3.91	2.85	4.00	4.02

14. b–c–e–a–d.

CHAPTER 16: PROJECT MANAGEMENT

1. *a.* 1–3–6–9–11–12: 31.
   b. 1–2–4–6–8–9: 37.
   c. 1–2–5–12–16: 44.
2. *b.* 1–2–4–7.
   c. 27.

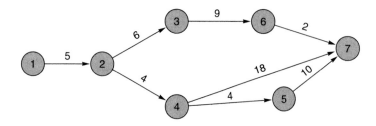

4. *a.* Summary:

Activity	ES	EF	LF	LS	Slack
1- 2	0	4	11	7	7
2- 4	4	13	21	12	8
4- 7	13	18	26	21	8
7-10	18	20	28	26	8
10-12	21	24	31	28	7
2- 5	4	12	19	11	7
5- 8	12	19	26	19	7
8-10	19	21	28	26	7
1- 3	0	10	10	0	0
3- 6	10	16	16	10	0
6- 9	16	20	20	16	0
9-11	20	25	25	20	0
11-12	25	31	31	25	0

b. Summary:

Activity	ES	EF	LF	LS	Slack
1-2	0	5	5	0	0
2-4	5	23	23	5	0
4-6	23	26	26	23	0
6-8	26	35	35	26	0
8-9	35	37	37	35	0
2-5	5	15	17	7	2
5-6	15	19	26	22	7
5-7	15	26	28	17	2
7-8	26	33	35	28	2
1-3	0	8	15	7	7
3-7	8	21	28	15	7

7. *b.* 24 days: .9686; 21 days: .2350.

8. *a.* .8755.
   b. .6881.
   c. .0204.

9. *b.* .0262.
   c. .2296.

10.

Path	Mean	Standard deviation
a-d-e-h	24.34	1.354
a-f-g	15.50	1.258
b-i-j-k	14.83	1.014
c-m-n-o	26.17	1.658

27 weeks: .6742; 28 weeks: .8698.

13. Crash schedule (1 week each): c, c, f, f, e, p.

14. *a.* Crash four weeks:
    (1) 7-11, (2) 1-2, (3) 7-11 and 6-10,
    (4) 11-13 and 4-6.

CHAPTER 17: WAITING LINES

1. *a.* 2.25 customers.
   b. 75 percent.
   c. Two hours.
   d. .5625.

2. *a.* 0.67 customers.
   b. One minute.
   c. 1.33 customers.

3. *a.* 40 percent.   *d.* .2288.
   b. 0.1523.
   c. 0.19 hour.

4. Morning: 0.3749 minute; .450.
   Afternoon: 0.6776 minute; .539.
   Evening: 0.6349 minute; .444.

5. M: 4; A: 8; E: 5.

6. One dock.

7. *a.* 1.5282 customers.
   b. 0.054 hour.
   c. 0.0357 hour.

8. *a.* 63.5 percent.
   b. 36.5 percent.
   c. 0.688 customer; 0.725 minute.
   d. Six customers.
   e. 17.587 customers, 7.32 minutes, 76 customers.
9. *a.* 0.995 customer.
   b. 2.24 days.
   c. 31.1 percent.
   d. 0.875 customer.
10. *a.* .437.
    b. 0.53 machine.
    c. 1.33 machines.
    d. 40.72 pieces.
    e. Three.
11. *a.* 28.56 pieces.
    b. Two.
12. Three.
13. Two docks.
14. *a.* .90.
    b. $W_1 = .12$ hour.
       $W_2 = .3045$ hour.
       $W_3 = 2.13$ hours.
    c. $L_1 = .36.$
       $L_2 = .91.$
       $L_3 = 6.39.$
15. *a.* 30.
    b. $L_1 = .034.$
       $L_2 = .025.$

CHAPTER 17 SUPPLEMENT: SIMULATION

1. 5.375 jobs.
2. 1: 80 percent, 2: 40 percent, 3: 40 percent.
5.

Patient	Time
1	19.44
2	20.24
3	17.92
4	19.38
5	18.96
6	16.48
7	20.66

7.

Day	Usage
1	43.932
2	48.036
3	34.908
4	32.758
5	42.186
6	30.438
7	33.298
8	41.678
9	33.526
10	30.904

8.

Period	Usage
1	2
2	1
3	3
4	1
5	1
6	4
7	5
8	3
9	1
10	2

10. *b.*

Day	Order size
1	—
2	—
3	—
4	—
5	3
6	—
7	—
8	1
9	—
10	—
11	3
12	—

13. Ball 1: 1,320 points; ball 2; 1,120 points; ball 3: 1,170 points.
14. Ball 1: 3,320 points; ball 2: 720 points; ball 3: 970 points.

TABLES

Table A

Areas under the normal
curve, 0 to z

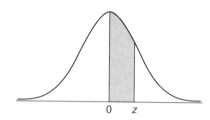

z		.00	.01	.02	.03	.04	.05	.06	.07	.08	.09
0.0	. . . . .	.0000	.0040	.0080	.0120	.0160	.0199	.0239	.0279	.0319	.0359
0.1	. . . . .	.0398	.0438	.0478	.0517	.0557	.0596	.0636	.0675	.0714	.0753
0.2	. . . . .	.0793	.0832	.0871	.0910	.0948	.0987	.1026	.1064	.1103	.1141
0.3	. . . . .	.1179	.1217	.1255	.1293	.1331	.1368	.1406	.1443	.1480	.1517
0.4	. . . . .	.1554	.1591	.1628	.1664	.1700	.1736	.1772	.1808	.1844	.1879
0.5	. . . . .	.1915	.1950	.1985	.2019	.2054	.2088	.2123	.2157	.2190	.2224
0.6	. . . . .	.2257	.2291	.2324	.2357	.2389	.2422	.2454	.2486	.2517	.2549
0.7	. . . . .	.2580	.2611	.2642	.2673	.2703	.2734	.2764	.2794	.2823	.2852
0.8	. . . . .	.2881	.2910	.2939	.2967	.2995	.3023	.3051	.3078	.3106	.3133
0.9	. . . . .	.3159	.3186	.3212	.3238	.3264	.3289	.3315	.3340	.3365	.3389
1.0	. . . . .	.3413	.3438	.3461	.3485	.3508	.3531	.3554	.3577	.3599	.3621
1.1	. . . . .	.3643	.3665	.3686	.3708	.3729	.3749	.3770	.3790	.3810	.3830
1.2	. . . . .	.3849	.3869	.3888	.3907	.3925	.3944	.3962	.3980	.3997	.4015
1.3	. . . . .	.4032	.4049	.4066	.4082	.4099	.4115	.4131	.4147	.4162	.4177
1.4	. . . . .	.4192	.4207	.4222	.4236	.4251	.4265	.4279	.4292	.4306	.4319
1.5	. . . . .	.4332	.4345	.4357	.4370	.4382	.4394	.4406	.4418	.4429	.4441
1.6	. . . . .	.4452	.4463	.4474	.4484	.4495	.4505	.4515	.4525	.4535	.4545
1.7	. . . . .	.4554	.4564	.4573	.4582	.4591	.4599	.4608	.4616	.4625	.4633
1.8	. . . . .	.4641	.4649	.4656	.4664	.4671	.4678	.4686	.4693	.4699	.4706
1.9	. . . . .	.4713	.4719	.4726	.4732	.4738	.4744	.4750	.4756	.4761	.4767
2.0	. . . . .	.4772	.4778	.4783	.4788	.4793	.4798	.4803	.4808	.4812	.4817
2.1	. . . . .	.4821	.4826	.4830	.4834	.4838	.4842	.4846	.4850	.4854	.4857
2.2	. . . . .	.4861	.4864	.4868	.4871	.4875	.4878	.4881	.4884	.4887	.4890
2.3	. . . . .	.4893	.4896	.4898	.4901	.4904	.4906	.4909	.4911	.4913	.4916
2.4	. . . . .	.4918	.4920	.4922	.4925	.4927	.4929	.4931	.4932	.4934	.4936
2.5	. . . . .	.4938	.4940	.4941	.4943	.4945	.4946	.4948	.4949	.4951	.4952
2.6	. . . . .	.4953	.4955	.4956	.4957	.4959	.4960	.4961	.4962	.4963	.4964
2.7	. . . . .	.4965	.4966	.4967	.4968	.4969	.4970	.4971	.4972	.4973	.4974
2.8	. . . . .	.4974	.4975	.4976	.4977	.4977	.4978	.4979	.4979	.4980	.4981
2.9	. . . . .	.4981	.4982	.4982	.4983	.4984	.4984	.4985	.4985	.4986	.4986
3.0	. . . . .	.4987	.4987	.4987	.4988	.4988	.4989	.4989	.4989	.4990	.4990

1. Areas under the standardized normal curve from $-\infty$ to $-z$

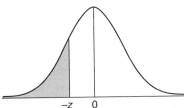

.09	.08	.07	.06	.05	.04	.03	.02	.01	.00	z
.0002	.0003	.0003	.0003	.0003	.0003	.0003	.0003	.0003	.0003	−3.4
.0003	.0004	.0004	.0004	.0004	.0004	.0004	.0005	.0005	.0005	−3.3
.0005	.0005	.0005	.0006	.0006	.0006	.0006	.0006	.0007	.0007	−3.2
.0007	.0007	.0008	.0008	.0008	.0008	.0009	.0009	.0009	.0010	−3.1
.0010	.0010	.0011	.0011	.0011	.0012	.0012	.0013	.0013	.0013	−3.0
.0014	.0014	.0015	.0015	.0016	.0016	.0017	.0018	.0018	.0019	−2.9
.0019	.0020	.0021	.0021	.0022	.0023	.0023	.0024	.0025	.0026	−2.8
.0026	.0027	.0028	.0029	.0030	.0031	.0032	.0033	.0034	.0035	−2.7
.0036	.0037	.0038	.0039	.0040	.0041	.0043	.0044	.0045	.0047	−2.6
.0048	.0049	.0051	.0052	.0054	.0055	.0057	.0059	.0060	.0062	−2.5
.0064	.0066	.0068	.0069	.0071	.0073	.0075	.0078	.0080	.0082	−2.4
.0084	.0087	.0089	.0091	.0094	.0096	.0099	.0102	.0104	.0107	−2.3
.0110	.0113	.0116	.0119	.0122	.0125	.0129	.0132	.0136	.0139	−2.2
.0143	.0146	.0150	.0154	.0158	.0162	.0166	.0170	.0174	.0179	−2.1
.0183	.0188	.0192	.0197	.0202	.0207	.0212	.0217	.0222	.0228	−2.0
.0233	.0239	.0244	.0250	.0256	.0262	.0268	.0274	.0281	.0287	−1.9
.0294	.0301	.0307	.0314	.0322	.0329	.0336	.0344	.0351	.0359	−1.8
.0367	.0375	.0384	.0392	.0401	.0409	.0418	.0427	.0436	.0446	−1.7
.0455	.0465	.0475	.0485	.0495	.0505	.0516	.0526	.0537	.0548	−1.6
.0559	.0571	.0582	.0594	.0606	.0618	.0630	.0643	.0655	.0668	−1.5
.0681	.0694	.0708	.0721	.0735	.0749	.0764	.0778	.0793	.0808	−1.4
.0823	.0838	.0853	.0869	.0885	.0901	.0918	.0934	.0951	.0968	−1.3
.0985	.1003	.1020	.1038	.1056	.1075	.1093	.1112	.1131	.1151	−1.2
.1170	.1190	.1210	.1230	.1251	.1271	.1292	.1314	.1335	.1357	−1.1
.1379	.1401	.1423	.1446	.1469	.1492	.1515	.1539	.1562	.1587	−1.0
.1611	.1635	.1660	.1685	.1711	.1736	.1762	.1788	.1814	.1841	−0.9
.1867	.1894	.1922	.1949	.1977	.2005	.2033	.2061	.2090	.2119	−0.8
.2148	.2177	.2206	.2236	.2266	.2296	.2327	.2358	.2389	.2420	−0.7
.2451	.2483	.2514	.2546	.2578	.2611	.2643	.2676	.2709	.2743	−0.6
.2776	.2810	.2843	.2877	.2912	.2946	.2981	.3015	.3050	.3085	−0.5
.3121	.3156	.3192	.3228	.3264	.3300	.3336	.3372	.3409	.3446	−0.4
.3483	.3520	.3557	.3594	.3632	.3669	.3707	.3745	.3783	.3821	−0.3
.3859	.3897	.3936	.3974	.4013	.4052	.4090	.4129	.4168	.4207	−0.2
.4247	.4286	.4325	.4364	.4404	.4443	.4483	.4522	.4562	.4602	−0.1
.4641	.4681	.4721	.4761	.4801	.4840	.4880	.4920	.4960	.5000	−0.0

Table B

(concluded)

2. Areas under the standardized normal curve from $-\infty$ to $+z$

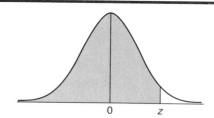

z	.00	.01	.02	.03	.04	.05	.06	.07	.08	.09
.0	.5000	.5040	.5080	.5120	.5160	.5199	.5239	.5279	.5319	.5359
.1	.5398	.5438	.5478	.5517	.5557	.5596	.5636	.5675	.5714	.5753
.2	.5793	.5832	.5871	.5910	.5948	.5987	.6026	.6064	.6103	.6141
.3	.6179	.6217	.6255	.6293	.6331	.6368	.6406	.6443	.6480	.6517
.4	.6554	.6591	.6628	.6664	.6700	.6736	.6772	.6808	.6844	.6879
.5	.6915	.6950	.6985	.7019	.7054	.7088	.7123	.7157	.7190	.7224
.6	.7257	.7291	.7324	.7357	.7389	.7422	.7454	.7486	.7517	.7549
.7	.7580	.7611	.7642	.7673	.7703	.7734	.7764	.7794	.7823	.7852
.8	.7881	.7910	.7939	.7967	.7995	.8023	.8051	.8078	.8106	.8133
.9	.8159	.8186	.8212	.8238	.8264	.8289	.8315	.8340	.8365	.8389
1.0	.8413	.8438	.8461	.8485	.8508	.8531	.8554	.8577	.8599	.8621
1.1	.8643	.8665	.8686	.8708	.8729	.8749	.8770	.8790	.8810	.8830
1.2	.8849	.8869	.8888	.8907	.8925	.8944	.8962	.8980	.8997	.9015
1.3	.9032	.9049	.9066	.9082	.9099	.9115	.9131	.9147	.9162	.9177
1.4	.9192	.9207	.9222	.9236	.9251	.9265	.9279	.9292	.9306	.9319
1.5	.9332	.9345	.9357	.9370	.9382	.9394	.9406	.9418	.9429	.9441
1.6	.9452	.9463	.9474	.9484	.9495	.9505	.9515	.9525	.9535	.9545
1.7	.9554	.9564	.9573	.9582	.9591	.9599	.9608	.9616	.9625	.9633
1.8	.9641	.9649	.9656	.9664	.9671	.9678	.9686	.9693	.9699	.9706
1.9	.9713	.9719	.9726	.9732	.9738	.9744	.9750	.9756	.9761	.9767
2.0	.9772	.9778	.9783	.9788	.9793	.9798	.9803	.9808	.9812	.9817
2.1	.9821	.9826	.9830	.9834	.9838	.9842	.9846	.9850	.9854	.9857
2.2	.9861	.9864	.9868	.9871	.9875	.9878	.9881	.9884	.9887	.9890
2.3	.9893	.9896	.9898	.9901	.9904	.9906	.9909	.9911	.9913	.9916
2.4	.9918	.9920	.9922	.9925	.9927	.9929	.9931	.9932	.9934	.9936
2.5	.9938	.9940	.9941	.9943	.9945	.9946	.9948	.9949	.9951	.9952
2.6	.9953	.9955	.9956	.9957	.9959	.9960	.9961	.9962	.9963	.9964
2.7	.9965	.9966	.9967	.9968	.9969	.9970	.9971	.9972	.9973	.9974
2.8	.9974	.9975	.9976	.9977	.9977	.9978	.9979	.9979	.9980	.9981
2.9	.9981	.9982	.9982	.9983	.9984	.9984	.9985	.9985	.9986	.9986
3.0	.9987	.9987	.9987	.9988	.9988	.9989	.9989	.9989	.9990	.9990
3.1	.9990	.9991	.9991	.9991	.9991	.9992	.9992	.9992	.9993	.9993
3.2	.9993	.9993	.9994	.9994	.9994	.9994	.9994	.9995	.9995	.9995
3.3	.9995	.9995	.9995	.9996	.9996	.9996	.9996	.9996	.9996	.9997
3.4	.9997	.9997	.9997	.9997	.9997	.9997	.9997	.9997	.9997	.9998

$$P(x \leq c) = \sum_{x=0}^{x=c} \frac{\mu^x \cdot e^{-\mu}}{x!}$$

Table C

Cumulative Poisson probabilities

$\mu \setminus x$	0	1	2	3	4	5	6	7	8	9
0.05	.951	.999	1.000							
0.10	.905	.995	1.000							
0.15	.861	.990	.999	1.000						
0.20	.819	.982	.999	1.000						
0.25	.779	.974	.998	1.000						
0.30	.741	.963	.996	1.000						
0.35	.705	.951	.994	1.000						
0.40	.670	.938	.992	.999	1.000					
0.45	.638	.925	.989	.999	1.000					
0.50	.607	.910	.986	.998	1.000					
0.55	.577	.894	.982	.998	1.000					
0.60	.549	.878	.977	.997	1.000					
0.65	.522	.861	.972	.996	.999	1.000				
0.70	.497	.844	.966	.994	.999	1.000				
0.75	.472	.827	.960	.993	.999	1.000				
0.80	.449	.809	.953	.991	.999	1.000				
0.85	.427	.791	.945	.989	.998	1.000				
0.90	.407	.772	.937	.987	.998	1.000				
0.95	.387	.754	.929	.984	.997	1.000				
1.0	.368	.736	.920	.981	.996	.999	1.000			
1.1	.333	.699	.900	.974	.995	.999	1.000			
1.2	.301	.663	.880	.966	.992	.998	1.000			
1.3	.273	.627	.857	.957	.989	.998	1.000			
1.4	.247	.592	.833	.946	.986	.997	.999	1.000		
1.5	.223	.558	.809	.934	.981	.996	.999	1.000		
1.6	.202	.525	.783	.921	.976	.994	.999	1.000		
1.7	.183	.493	.757	.907	.970	.992	.998	1.000		
1.8	.165	.463	.731	.891	.964	.990	.997	.999	1.000	
1.9	.150	.434	.704	.875	.956	.987	.997	.999	1.000	
2.0	.135	.406	.677	.857	.947	.983	.995	.999	1.000	
2.2	.111	.355	.623	.819	.928	.975	.993	.998	1.000	
2.4	.091	.308	.570	.779	.904	.964	.988	.997	.999	1.000
2.6	.074	.267	.518	.736	.877	.951	.983	.995	.999	1.000
2.8	.061	.231	.470	.692	.848	.935	.976	.992	.998	.999

Table C *(concluded)*

μ\x	0	1	2	3	4	5	6	7	8	9	10	11	12	13	14	15	16	17	18	19	20
3.0	.050	.199	.423	.647	.815	.916	.966	.988	.996	.999	1.000										
3.2	.041	.171	.380	.603	.781	.895	.955	.983	.994	.998	1.000										
3.4	.033	.147	.340	.558	.744	.871	.942	.977	.992	.997	.999	1.000									
3.6	.027	.126	.303	.515	.706	.844	.927	.969	.988	.996	.999	1.000									
3.8	.022	.107	.269	.473	.668	.816	.909	.960	.984	.994	.998	.999	1.000								
4.0	.018	.092	.238	.433	.629	.785	.889	.949	.979	.992	.997	.999	1.000								
4.2	.015	.078	.210	.395	.590	.753	.868	.936	.972	.989	.996	.999	1.000								
4.4	.012	.066	.185	.359	.551	.720	.844	.921	.964	.985	.994	.998	.999	1.000							
4.6	.010	.056	.163	.326	.513	.686	.818	.905	.955	.980	.992	.997	.999	1.000							
4.8	.008	.048	.143	.294	.476	.651	.791	.887	.944	.975	.990	.996	.999	1.000							
5.0	.007	.040	.125	.265	.440	.616	.762	.867	.932	.968	.986	.995	.998	.999	1.000						
5.2	.006	.034	.109	.238	.406	.581	.732	.845	.918	.960	.982	.993	.997	.999	1.000						
5.4	.005	.029	.095	.213	.373	.546	.702	.822	.903	.951	.978	.990	.996	.999	1.000						
5.6	.004	.024	.082	.191	.342	.512	.670	.797	.886	.941	.972	.988	.995	.998	.999	1.000					
5.8	.003	.021	.072	.170	.313	.478	.638	.771	.867	.929	.965	.984	.993	.997	.999	1.000					
6.0	.002	.017	.062	.151	.285	.446	.606	.744	.847	.916	.957	.980	.991	.996	.999	.999	1.000				
6.2	.002	.015	.054	.134	.259	.414	.574	.716	.826	.902	.949	.975	.989	.995	.998	.999	1.000				
6.4	.002	.012	.046	.119	.235	.384	.542	.687	.803	.886	.939	.969	.986	.994	.997	.999	1.000				
6.6	.001	.010	.040	.105	.213	.355	.511	.658	.780	.869	.927	.963	.982	.992	.997	.999	1.000				
6.8	.001	.009	.034	.093	.192	.327	.480	.628	.755	.850	.915	.955	.978	.990	.996	.998	.999	1.000			
7.0	.001	.007	.030	.082	.173	.301	.450	.599	.729	.830	.901	.947	.973	.987	.994	.998	.999	1.000			
7.2	.001	.006	.025	.072	.156	.276	.420	.569	.703	.810	.887	.937	.967	.984	.993	.997	.999	.999	1.000		
7.4	.001	.005	.022	.063	.140	.253	.392	.539	.676	.788	.871	.926	.961	.980	.991	.996	.998	.999	1.000		
7.6	.001	.004	.019	.055	.125	.231	.365	.510	.648	.765	.854	.915	.954	.976	.989	.995	.998	.999	1.000		
7.8	.000	.004	.016	.048	.111	.210	.338	.480	.619	.741	.835	.902	.945	.971	.986	.993	.997	.999	1.000		
8.0	.000	.003	.014	.042	.100	.191	.313	.453	.593	.717	.816	.888	.936	.966	.983	.992	.996	.998	.999	1.000	
8.2	.000	.003	.012	.037	.089	.174	.290	.425	.565	.692	.796	.873	.926	.960	.979	.990	.995	.998	.999	1.000	
8.4	.000	.002	.010	.032	.079	.157	.267	.399	.537	.666	.774	.857	.915	.952	.975	.988	.994	.997	.999	1.000	
8.6	.000	.002	.009	.028	.070	.142	.246	.373	.509	.640	.752	.840	.903	.945	.970	.985	.993	.997	.999	.999	1.000
8.8	.000	.001	.007	.024	.062	.128	.226	.348	.482	.614	.730	.822	.890	.936	.965	.982	.991	.996	.998	.999	1.000
9.0	.000	.001	.006	.021	.055	.116	.207	.324	.456	.587	.706	.803	.876	.926	.959	.978	.989	.995	.998	.999	1.000
9.5	.000	.001	.004	.015	.040	.089	.165	.269	.392	.522	.645	.752	.836	.898	.940	.967	.982	.991	.996	.998	.999

Table D Cumulative binomial probabilities

$$P(x \le c) = \sum_{x=0}^{c} \binom{n}{x} p^x (1-p)^{n-x}$$

n	x	.05	.10	.15	.20	.25	.30	.35	.40	.45	.50	.55	.60	.65	.70	.75	.80	.85	.90
1	0	.9500	.9000	.8500	.8000	.7500	.7000	.6500	.6000	.5500	.5000	.4500	.4000	.3500	.3000	.2500	.2000	.1500	.1000
	1	1.0000	1.0000	1.0000	1.0000	1.0000	1.0000	1.0000	1.0000	1.0000	1.0000	1.0000	1.0000	1.0000	1.0000	1.0000	1.0000	1.0000	1.0000
2	0	.9025	.8100	.7225	.6400	.5625	.4900	.4225	.3600	.3025	.2500	.2025	.1600	.1225	.0900	.0625	.0400	.0225	.0100
	1	.9975	.9900	.9775	.9600	.9375	.9100	.8775	.8400	.7975	.7500	.6975	.6400	.5775	.5100	.4375	.3600	.2775	.1900
	2	1.0000	1.0000	1.0000	1.0000	1.0000	1.0000	1.0000	1.0000	1.0000	1.0000	1.0000	1.0000	1.0000	1.0000	1.0000	1.0000	1.0000	1.0000
3	0	.8574	.7290	.6141	.5120	.4219	.3430	.2746	.2160	.1664	.1250	.0911	.0640	.0429	.0270	.0156	.0080	.0034	.0010
	1	.9928	.9720	.9393	.8960	.8438	.7840	.7183	.6480	.5748	.5000	.4253	.3520	.2818	.2160	.1563	.1040	.0608	.0280
	2	.9999	.9990	.9966	.9920	.9844	.9730	.9571	.9360	.9089	.8750	.8336	.7840	.7254	.6570	.5781	.4880	.3859	.2710
	3	1.0000	1.0000	1.0000	1.0000	1.0000	1.0000	1.0000	1.0000	1.0000	1.0000	1.0000	1.0000	1.0000	1.0000	1.0000	1.0000	1.0000	1.0000
4	0	.8145	.6561	.5220	.4096	.3164	.2401	.1785	.1296	.0915	.0625	.0410	.0256	.0150	.0081	.0039	.0016	.0005	.0001
	1	.9860	.9477	.8905	.8192	.7383	.6517	.5630	.4752	.3910	.3125	.2415	.1792	.1265	.0837	.0508	.0272	.0120	.0037
	2	.9995	.9963	.9880	.9728	.9492	.9163	.8735	.8208	.7585	.6875	.6090	.5248	.4370	.3483	.2617	.1808	.1095	.0523
	3	1.0000	.9999	.9995	.9984	.9961	.9919	.9850	.9744	.9590	.9375	.9085	.8704	.8215	.7599	.6836	.5904	.4780	.3439
	4	1.0000	1.0000	1.0000	1.0000	1.0000	1.0000	1.0000	1.0000	1.0000	1.0000	1.0000	1.0000	1.0000	1.0000	1.0000	1.0000	1.0000	1.0000
5	0	.7738	.5905	.4437	.3277	.2373	.1681	.1160	.0778	.0503	.0313	.0185	.0102	.0053	.0024	.0010	.0003	.0001	.0000
	1	.9974	.9185	.8352	.7373	.6328	.5282	.4284	.3370	.2562	.1875	.1312	.0870	.0540	.0308	.0156	.0067	.0022	.0005
	2	.9988	.9914	.9734	.9421	.8965	.8369	.7648	.6826	.5931	.5000	.4069	.3174	.2352	.1631	.1035	.0579	.0266	.0086
	3	1.0000	.9995	.9978	.9933	.9844	.9692	.9460	.9130	.8688	.8125	.7438	.6630	.5716	.4718	.3672	.2627	.1648	.0815
	4	1.0000	1.0000	.9999	.9997	.9990	.9976	.9947	.9898	.9815	.9688	.9497	.9222	.8840	.8319	.7627	.6723	.5563	.4095
	5	1.0000	1.0000	1.0000	1.0000	1.0000	1.0000	1.0000	1.0000	1.0000	1.0000	1.0000	1.0000	1.0000	1.0000	1.0000	1.0000	1.0000	1.0000
6	0	.7351	.5314	.3771	.2621	.1780	.1176	.0754	.0467	.0277	.0156	.0083	.0041	.0018	.0007	.0002	.0001	.0000	.0000
	1	.9672	.8857	.7765	.6554	.5339	.4202	.3191	.2333	.1636	.1094	.0692	.0410	.0223	.0109	.0046	.0016	.0004	.0001
	2	.9978	.9842	.9527	.9011	.8306	.7443	.6471	.5443	.4415	.3438	.2553	.1792	.1174	.0705	.0376	.0170	.0059	.0013
	3	.9999	.9987	.9941	.9830	.9624	.9295	.8826	.8208	.7447	.6563	.5585	.4557	.3529	.2557	.1694	.0989	.0473	.0159
	4	1.0000	.9999	.9996	.9984	.9954	.9891	.9777	.9590	.9308	.8906	.8364	.7667	.6809	.5798	.4661	.3446	.2235	.1143
	5	1.0000	1.0000	1.0000	.9999	.9998	.9993	.9982	.9959	.9917	.9844	.9723	.9533	.9246	.8824	.8220	.7379	.6229	.4686
	6	1.0000	1.0000	1.0000	1.0000	1.0000	1.0000	1.0000	1.0000	1.0000	1.0000	1.0000	1.0000	1.0000	1.0000	1.0000	1.0000	1.0000	1.0000
7	0	.6983	.4783	.3206	.2097	.1335	.0824	.0490	.0280	.0152	.0078	.0037	.0016	.0006	.0002	.0001	.0000	.0000	.0000
	1	.9556	.8503	.7166	.5767	.4449	.3294	.2338	.1586	.1024	.0625	.0357	.0188	.0090	.0038	.0013	.0004	.0001	.0000
	2	.9962	.9743	.9262	.8520	.7564	.6471	.5323	.4199	.3164	.2266	.1529	.0963	.0556	.0288	.0129	.0047	.0012	.0002
	3	.9998	.9973	.9879	.9667	.9294	.8740	.8002	.7102	.6083	.5000	.3917	.2898	.1998	.1260	.0706	.0333	.0121	.0027
	4	1.0000	.9998	.9988	.9953	.9871	.9712	.9444	.9037	.8471	.7734	.6836	.5801	.4677	.3529	.2436	.1480	.0738	.0257
	5	1.0000	1.0000	.9999	.9996	.9987	.9962	.9910	.9812	.9643	.9375	.8976	.8414	.7662	.6706	.5551	.4233	.2834	.1497
	6	1.0000	1.0000	1.0000	1.0000	.9999	.9998	.9994	.9984	.9963	.9922	.9848	.9720	.9510	.9176	.8665	.7903	.6794	.5217
	7	1.0000	1.0000	1.0000	1.0000	1.0000	1.0000	1.0000	1.0000	1.0000	1.0000	1.0000	1.0000	1.0000	1.0000	1.0000	1.0000	1.0000	1.0000

Table D *(continued)*   Cumulative binomial probabilities

n	x	.05	.10	.15	.20	.25	.30	.35	.40	.45	.50	.55	.60	.65	.70	.75	.80	.85	.90
8	0	.6634	.4305	.2725	.1678	.1001	.0576	.0319	.0168	.0084	.0039	.0017	.0007	.0002	.0001	.0000	.0000	.0000	.0000
	1	.9428	.8131	.6572	.5033	.3671	.2553	.1691	.1064	.0632	.0352	.0181	.0085	.0036	.0013	.0004	.0001	.0000	.0000
	2	.9942	.9619	.8948	.7969	.6785	.5518	.4278	.3154	.2201	.1445	.0885	.0498	.0253	.0113	.0042	.0012	.0002	.0000
	3	.9996	.9950	.9786	.9437	.8862	.8059	.7064	.5941	.4470	.3633	.2604	.1737	.1061	.0580	.0273	.0104	.0029	.0004
	4	1.0000	.9996	.9971	.9896	.9727	.9420	.8939	.8263	.7396	.6367	.5230	.4059	.2936	.1941	.1138	.0563	.0214	.0050
	5	1.0000	1.0000	.9998	.9988	.9958	.9887	.9747	.9502	.9115	.8555	.7799	.6846	.5722	.4482	.3215	.2031	.1052	.0381
	6	1.0000	1.0000	1.0000	.9999	.9996	.9987	.9964	.9915	.9819	.9648	.9368	.8936	.8309	.7447	.6329	.4967	.3428	.1869
	7	1.0000	1.0000	1.0000	1.0000	1.0000	.9999	.9998	.9993	.9983	.9961	.9916	.9832	.9681	.9424	.8999	.8322	.7275	.5695
	8	1.0000	1.0000	1.0000	1.0000	1.0000	1.0000	1.0000	1.0000	1.0000	1.0000	1.0000	1.0000	1.0000	1.0000	1.0000	1.0000	1.0000	1.0000
9	0	.6302	.3874	.2316	.1342	.0751	.0404	.0207	.0101	.0046	.0020	.0008	.0003	.0001	.0000	.0000	.0000	.0000	.0000
	1	.9288	.7748	.5995	.4362	.3003	.1960	.1211	.0705	.0385	.0195	.0091	.0038	.0014	.0004	.0001	.0000	.0000	.0000
	2	.9916	.9470	.8591	.7382	.6007	.4628	.3373	.2318	.1495	.0898	.0498	.0250	.0112	.0043	.0013	.0003	.0000	.0000
	3	.9994	.9917	.9661	.9144	.8343	.7297	.6089	.4826	.3614	.2539	.1658	.0994	.0536	.0253	.0100	.0031	.0006	.0001
	4	1.0000	.9991	.9944	.9804	.9511	.9012	.8283	.7334	.6214	.5000	.3786	.2666	.1717	.0988	.0489	.0196	.0056	.0009
	5	1.0000	.9999	.9994	.9969	.9900	.9747	.9496	.9006	.8342	.7461	.6386	.5174	.3911	.2703	.1657	.0856	.0339	.0083
	6	1.0000	1.0000	1.0000	.9997	.9987	.9957	.9888	.9750	.9502	.9102	.8505	.7682	.6627	.5372	.3993	.2618	.1409	.0530
	7	1.0000	1.0000	1.0000	1.0000	.9999	.9996	.9986	.9962	.9909	.9805	.9615	.9295	.8789	.8040	.6997	.5638	.4005	.2252
	8	1.0000	1.0000	1.0000	1.0000	1.0000	1.0000	.9999	.9997	.9992	.9980	.9954	.9899	.9793	.9596	.9249	.8658	.7684	.6126
	9	1.0000	1.0000	1.0000	1.0000	1.0000	1.0000	1.0000	1.0000	1.0000	1.0000	1.0000	1.0000	1.0000	1.0000	1.0000	1.0000	1.0000	1.0000
10	0	.5987	.3487	.1969	.1074	.0563	.0282	.0135	.0060	.0025	.0010	.0003	.0001	.0000	.0000	.0000	.0000	.0000	.0000
	1	.9139	.7361	.5443	.3758	.2440	.1493	.0860	.0464	.0233	.0107	.0045	.0017	.0005	.0001	.0000	.0000	.0000	.0000
	2	.9885	.9298	.8202	.6778	.5256	.3828	.2616	.1673	.0996	.0547	.0274	.0123	.0048	.0016	.0004	.0001	.0000	.0000
	3	.9990	.9872	.9500	.8791	.7759	.6496	.5138	.3823	.2660	.1719	.1020	.0548	.0260	.0106	.0035	.0009	.0001	.0000
	4	.9999	.9984	.9901	.9672	.9219	.8497	.7515	.6331	.5044	.3770	.2616	.1662	.0949	.0473	.0197	.0064	.0014	.0001
	5	1.0000	.9999	.9986	.9936	.9803	.9527	.9051	.8338	.7384	.6230	.4956	.3669	.2485	.1503	.0781	.0328	.0099	.0016
	6	1.0000	1.0000	.9999	.9991	.9965	.9894	.9740	.9452	.8980	.8281	.7340	.6177	.4862	.3504	.2241	.1209	.0500	.0128
	7	1.0000	1.0000	1.0000	.9999	.9996	.9984	.9952	.9877	.9726	.9453	.9004	.8327	.7384	.6172	.4744	.3222	.1798	.0702
	8	1.0000	1.0000	1.0000	1.0000	1.0000	.9999	.9995	.9983	.9955	.9893	.9767	.9536	.9140	.8507	.7560	.6242	.4557	.2639
	9	1.0000	1.0000	1.0000	1.0000	1.0000	1.0000	1.0000	.9999	.9997	.9990	.9975	.9940	.9865	.9718	.9437	.8926	.8031	.6513
	10	1.0000	1.0000	1.0000	1.0000	1.0000	1.0000	1.0000	1.0000	1.0000	1.0000	1.0000	1.0000	1.0000	1.0000	1.0000	1.0000	1.0000	1.0000

P

Table D *(concluded)* Cumulative binomial probabilities

n	x	.05	.10	.15	.20	.25	.30	.35	.40	.45	.50	.55	.60	.65	.70	.75	.80	.85	.90
15	0	.4633	.2059	.0874	.0352	.0134	.0047	.0016	.0005	.0001	.0000	.0000	.0000	.0000	.0000	.0000	.0000	.0000	.0000
	1	.8290	.5490	.3186	.1671	.0802	.0353	.0142	.0052	.0017	.0005	.0001	.0000	.0000	.0000	.0000	.0000	.0000	.0000
	2	.9638	.8159	.6042	.3980	.2361	.1268	.0617	.0271	.0107	.0037	.0011	.0003	.0001	.0000	.0000	.0000	.0000	.0000
	3	.9945	.9444	.8227	.6482	.4613	.2969	.1727	.0905	.0424	.0176	.0063	.0019	.0005	.0001	.0000	.0000	.0000	.0000
	4	.9994	.9873	.9383	.8358	.6865	.5155	.3519	.2173	.1204	.0592	.0255	.0093	.0028	.0007	.0001	.0000	.0000	.0000
	5	.9999	.9978	.9832	.9389	.8516	.7216	.5643	.4032	.2608	.1509	.0769	.0338	.0124	.0037	.0008	.0001	.0001	.0000
	6	1.0000	.9997	.9964	.9819	.9434	.8689	.7548	.6098	.4522	.3036	.1818	.0950	.0422	.0152	.0042	.0008	.0006	.0000
	7	1.0000	1.0000	.9994	.9958	.9827	.9500	.8868	.7869	.6535	.5000	.3465	.2131	.1132	.0500	.0173	.0042	.0036	.0003
	8	1.0000	1.0000	.9999	.9992	.9958	.9848	.9578	.9050	.8182	.6964	.5478	.3902	.2452	.1311	.0566	.0181	.0168	.0022
	9	1.0000	1.0000	1.0000	.9999	.9992	.9963	.9876	.9662	.9231	.8491	.7392	.5968	.4357	.2784	.1484	.0611	.0617	.0127
	10	1.0000	1.0000	1.0000	1.0000	.9999	.9993	.9972	.9907	.9745	.9408	.8796	.7827	.6481	.4845	.3135	.1642	.1773	.0556
	11	1.0000	1.0000	1.0000	1.0000	1.0000	.9999	.9995	.9981	.9937	.9824	.9576	.9095	.8273	.7031	.5387	.3518	.3958	.1841
	12	1.0000	1.0000	1.0000	1.0000	1.0000	1.0000	.9999	.9997	.9989	.9963	.9893	.9729	.9383	.8732	.7639	.6020	.6814	.4510
	13	1.0000	1.0000	1.0000	1.0000	1.0000	1.0000	1.0000	1.0000	.9999	.9995	.9983	.9948	.9858	.9647	.9198	.8329	.9126	.7941
	14	1.0000	1.0000	1.0000	1.0000	1.0000	1.0000	1.0000	1.0000	1.0000	1.0000	.9999	.9995	.9984	.9953	.9866	.9648	1.0000	1.0000
	15	1.0000	1.0000	1.0000	1.0000	1.0000	1.0000	1.0000	1.0000	1.0000	1.0000	1.0000	1.0000	1.0000	1.0000	1.0000	1.0000	1.0000	1.0000
20	0	.3585	.1216	.0388	.0115	.0032	.0008	.0002	.0000	.0000	.0000	.0000	.0000	.0000	.0000	.0000	.0000	.0000	.0000
	1	.7358	.3917	.1756	.0692	.0243	.0076	.0021	.0005	.0001	.0000	.0000	.0000	.0000	.0000	.0000	.0000	.0000	.0000
	2	.9245	.6769	.4049	.2061	.0913	.0355	.0121	.0036	.0009	.0002	.0000	.0000	.0000	.0000	.0000	.0000	.0000	.0000
	3	.9841	.8670	.6477	.4114	.2252	.1071	.0444	.0160	.0049	.0013	.0003	.0000	.0000	.0000	.0000	.0000	.0000	.0000
	4	.9974	.9568	.8298	.6296	.4148	.2375	.1182	.0510	.0189	.0059	.0015	.0003	.0000	.0000	.0000	.0000	.0000	.0000
	5	.9997	.9887	.9327	.8042	.6172	.4164	.2454	.1256	.0553	.0207	.0064	.0016	.0003	.0000	.0000	.0000	.0000	.0000
	6	1.0000	.9976	.9781	.9133	.7858	.6080	.4166	.2500	.1299	.0577	.0214	.0065	.0015	.0003	.0000	.0000	.0000	.0000
	7	1.0000	.9996	.9941	.9679	.8982	.7723	.6010	.4159	.2520	.1316	.0580	.0210	.0060	.0013	.0002	.0000	.0000	.0000
	8	1.0000	.9999	.9987	.9900	.9591	.8867	.7624	.5956	.4143	.2517	.1308	.0565	.0196	.0051	.0009	.0001	.0000	.0000
	9	1.0000	1.0000	.9998	.9974	.9861	.9520	.8782	.7553	.5914	.4119	.2493	.1275	.0532	.0171	.0039	.0006	.0000	.0000
	10	1.0000	1.0000	1.0000	.9994	.9961	.9829	.9468	.8725	.7507	.5881	.4086	.2447	.1218	.0480	.0139	.0026	.0002	.0000
	11	1.0000	1.0000	1.0000	.9999	.9991	.9949	.9804	.9435	.8692	.7483	.5857	.4044	.2376	.1133	.0409	.0100	.0013	.0001
	12	1.0000	1.0000	1.0000	1.0000	.9998	.9987	.9940	.9790	.9420	.8684	.7480	.5841	.3990	.2277	.1018	.0321	.0059	.0004
	13	1.0000	1.0000	1.0000	1.0000	1.0000	.9997	.9985	.9935	.9786	.9423	.8701	.7500	.5834	.3920	.2142	.0867	.0219	.0024
	14	1.0000	1.0000	1.0000	1.0000	1.0000	1.0000	.9997	.9984	.9936	.9793	.9447	.8744	.7546	.5836	.3828	.1958	.0673	.0113
	15	1.0000	1.0000	1.0000	1.0000	1.0000	1.0000	1.0000	.9997	.9985	.9941	.9811	.9490	.8818	.7625	.5852	.3704	.1702	.0432
	16	1.0000	1.0000	1.0000	1.0000	1.0000	1.0000	1.0000	1.0000	.9997	.9987	.9951	.9840	.9556	.8929	.7748	.5886	.3523	.1330
	17	1.0000	1.0000	1.0000	1.0000	1.0000	1.0000	1.0000	1.0000	1.0000	.9998	.9991	.9964	.9879	.9645	.9087	.7939	.5951	.3231
	18	1.0000	1.0000	1.0000	1.0000	1.0000	1.0000	1.0000	1.0000	1.0000	1.0000	.9999	.9995	.9979	.9924	.9757	.9308	.8244	.6083
	19	1.0000	1.0000	1.0000	1.0000	1.0000	1.0000	1.0000	1.0000	1.0000	1.0000	1.0000	1.0000	.9998	.9992	.9968	.9885	.9612	.8784
	20	1.0000	1.0000	1.0000	1.0000	1.0000	1.0000	1.0000	1.0000	1.0000	1.0000	1.0000	1.0000	1.0000	1.0000	1.0000	1.0000	1.0000	1.0000

PHOTO CREDITS

Chapter 1

Page 2: Courtesy of Toyota USA; **page 5:** Courtesy of Cunard; **page 14:** Courtesy of the Mead Corporation; **page 15:** Courtesy of Bank One; **page 28:** Courtesy of Toyota USA; **page 30:** Courtesy of International Business Machines Corporation; **page 31:** Courtesy of Cilcorp.

Chapter 2

Page 34: Courtesy of Highland Superstores, Inc.; **page 42;** Courtesy of Sony Corporation; **page 43:** Courtesy of Saab-Scania Division; **page 47:** Courtesy of Cadillac; **page 47:** Courtesy Federal Express Corporation. All rights reserved; **page 47:** © Dave Bartruff/FPG International.

Chapter 3

Page 94: Courtesy of Ford Motor Company; **page 102:** © Aldo Mauro; **page 102:** © Blaine Harrington; **page 102:** Courtesy of Career IV; **page 106:** © Jamie Tanaka; **page 108:** Courtesy of Cadillac; **page 115:** © Damian Strohmeyer.

Chapter 4

Page 122: © Jon Feingersh/The Stock Market; **page 129:** Courtesy of The Toro Company.

Chapter 5

Page 190: Courtesy of International Business Machines Corporation; **page 193:** Courtesy of International Business Machines Corporation; **page 202:** Courtesy of International Business Machines Corporation; **page 207:** By Caroline Parsons; **page 203:** Courtesy of Sanyo Electric Co.; **page 209:** Courtesy of International Business Machines Corporation.

Chapter 6

Page 228: © Michael L. Abramson; **page 231:** Courtesy of CACI Products Company; **page 235:** Courtesy of Republic Engineered Steels Inc.; **page 237:** Courtesy of ABB Robotics Inc.; **page 238:** Courtesy of ABB Robotics Inc.; **page 239:** Courtesy of International Business Machines Corporation; **page 236:** Courtesy International Business Machines Corporation.

Chapter 7

Page 308: © Michael L. Abramson; **page 313:** Courtesy of CACI Products Company; **page 319:** © Michael L. Abramson.

Chapter 8

page 352: By Kevin Horan; **page 356:** Courtesy of Ford Motor Company; **page 360:** Courtesy of SAS Institute, Inc.; **page 362:** Courtesy of Ford Motor Company; **page 367:** Courtesy of Ford Motor Company.

Chapter 9

Page 418: Courtesy of Ameranda Hess; **page 423:** Courtesy of Ameranda Hess; **page 424:** © Carolyn Cole; **page 426:** Courtesy Saturn Corporation; **page 428:** Courtesy of Toyota USA.

Chapter 10

Page 482: © Jeff Zoruba/The Stock Market; **page 484:** © Michael L. Abramson; **page 487:** Courtesy of Geo. J. Meyer Manufacturing; **page 503:** Courtesy of Ford Motor Company; **page 505:** © Michael L. Abramson.

Chapter 11

Page 548: By Rob Kinmouth; **page 553:** By Rob Kinmouth; **page 558:** Courtesy of International Business Machines Corporation.

Chapter 12

Page 582: Courtesy of USX Corporation; **page 586:** © Matthew McVay/SABA; **page 591:** © Matthew McVay/SABA; **page 590:** © George Disario/The Stock Market.

Chapter 13

Page 648: Courtesy of Digital Equipment Corporation **page 655:** Courtesy of International Business Machines Corporation.

Chapter 14

Page 688: Courtesy of Porsche North America, Inc.; **page 701:** Courtesy of John Deere Horicon Works; **page 693:** FPG International.

Chapter 15

page 732: Courtesy of American Airlines.

Chapter 16

Page 774: Courtesy of Boeing; **page 779:** Courtesy of Microsoft, The SAS Institute, and SCITOR.

Chapter 17

Page 824: Courtesy of American Airlines.

INDEX